McGraw-Hill Series in Forest Resources

Avery and Burkhart: Forest Measurements
Daniel, Helms, and Baker: Principles of Silviculture
Davis, Johnson, Howard, and Bettinger: Forest Management
Edmonds: Forest Health and Protection
Hardin, Leopold, and White: Harlow and Harrar's Textbook of Dendrology
Heathcote: Environmental Problem Solving
Klemperer: Forest Resource Economics and Finance
Nyland: Silviculture: Concept and Applications
Sharpe, Hendee, and Sharpe: Introduction to Forestry and Renewable Resources
Shaw: Introduction to Wildlife Management
Sigler: Wildlife Law Enforcement

Walter Mulford was Consulting Editor of this series from its inception in 1931 until January 1, 1952.

Henry J. Vaux was Consulting Editor of this series from January 1, 1952, until July 1, 1976.

Paul V. Ellefson, University of Minnesota, is currently our Consulting Editor.

Accurate measurements are essential for scientifically managing forest resources. (Photograph by Tom Stewart.)

FOREST MEASUREMENTS

FIFTH EDITION

Thomas Eugene Avery

Forestry Consultant (Retired)

Harold E. Burkhart

Virginia Polytechnic Institute and State University

Boston   Burr Ridge, IL   Dubuque, IA   Madison, WI   New York
San Francisco   St. Louis   Bangkok   Bogotá   Caracas   Kuala Lumpur
Lisbon   London   Madrid   Mexico City   Milan   Montreal   New Delhi
Santiago   Seoul   Singapore   Sydney   Taipei   Toronto

McGraw-Hill Higher Education

A Division of The **McGraw-Hill** *Companies*

FOREST MEASUREMENTS, FIFTH EDITION

Published by Mcgraw-Hill, a business unit of The McGraw-Hill Companies, Inc., 1221 Avenue of the Americas, New York, NY 10020. Copyright © 2002, 1994, 1983, 1967 by The McGraw-Hill Companies, Inc. All rights reserved. Previously published under the title of *Natural Resources Measurements,* copyright © 1975 by McGraw-Hill, Inc. All rights reserved. No part of this publication may be reproduced of distributed in any form or by any means, or stored in a database or retrieval system, without the prior written consent of The McGraw-Hill Companies, Inc., including, but not limited to, in any network or other electronic storage or transmission, or broadcast for distance learning.

Some ancillaries, including electronic and print components, may be available to customers outside the United States.

 This book is printed on recycled, acid-free paper containing 10% postconsumer waste.

1 2 3 4 5 6 7 8 9 0 QPF/QPF 0 9 8 7 6 5 4 3 2 1

ISBN 0–07–366176–7

Publisher: *Edward E. Bartell*
Developmental editor: *Kassi Radomski*
Marketing manager: *Heather K. Wagner*
Project manager: *Richard H. Hecker*
Production supervisor: *Sherry L. Kane*
Coordinator of freelance design: *Michelle M. Meerdink*
Photo research coordinator: *John C. Leland*
Senior supplement producer: *Audrey A. Reiter*
Media technology producer: *Judi David*
Compositor: *Carlisle Communications, Ltd.*
Typeface: *11/12 Times Roman*
Printer: *Quebecor World Fairfield, PA*

Library of Congress Cataloging-in-Publication Data

Avery, Thomas Eugene.
    Forest measurements / Thomas Eugene Avery, Harold E. Burkhart.—5th ed.
      p.   cm.
    Includes bibliographical references and index.
    ISBN 0–07–366176–7
    1. Forests and forestry–Mensuration. I. Burkhart, Harold E. II. Title.

SD555 .A93   2002
634.9′285—dc21

00–069940
CIP

www.mhhe.com

ABOUT THE AUTHORS

THOMAS EUGENE AVERY (B.S. University of Georgia, M.F. Duke University, Ph.D. University of Minnesota) is the author of three university textbooks in current use and has published more than 60 technical articles in professional journals. He has worked for the private forest industry, the U.S. Forest Service, and several major universities, and was formerly Head of the Department of Forestry at the University of Illinois. Dr. Avery has had professional forestry experience in West Germany, New Zealand, and Australia; he has held national office in the Society of American Foresters and the American Society of Photogrammetry. In 1987 he received the Alan Gordon Memorial Award from the American Society of Photogrammetry, and he has been listed in *American Men of Science* and *Who's Who in America.* Dr. Avery is retired and lives in Texas.

HAROLD E. BURKHART holds a B.S. degree in forestry from Oklahoma State University and M.S. and Ph.D. degrees in forest biometrics from the University of Georgia. He has been a faculty member in the Department of Forestry, Virginia Polytechnic Institute and State University, since 1969. From 1976–1977, Dr. Burkhart was Senior Research Fellow at the Forest Research Institute in Rotorua, New Zealand. He has published extensively in professional journals on the subjects of forest growth and yield prediction and on forest inventory and sampling. His contributions to forestry education have been recognized through awards from several organizations, including the International Union of Forestry Research Organizations Scientific Achievement Award, the Virginia Academy of Science J. Shelton Horsley Research Award, the Virginia Tech Alumni Award for Research Excellence, the State Council of Higher Education for Virginia Outstanding Faculty Award, and the Society of American Foresters Barrington Moore Memorial Award. A former editor of the journal *Forest Science,* he is a Fellow in the American Association for the Advancement of Science and the Society of American Foresters.

CONTENTS IN BRIEF

CONTENTS

PREFACE

This fifth edition of *Forest Measurements,* prepared by the coauthor, is intended for introductory courses in forest measurements. Emphasis is on the measurement of timber, with detailed coverage on measuring products cut from tree boles, measuring attributes of standing trees, inventorying volumes of forest stands, and predicting growth of individual trees and stands of trees. Background information on statistical methods, sampling designs, land measurements and use of aerial photographs is also provided. An introduction to assessing range, wildlife, water, and recreation resources associated with forested lands comprises the last chapter. The measurement principles and techniques discussed apply to any inventory that includes assessment of the tree overstory, regardless of whether the inventory is conducted for timber, range, wildlife, watershed, recreation, or other management objectives.

With an introductory text of this nature, the final arbiters of what should and should not be included are the course instructors who adopt and use the book for their classes. Thus, the contents of this fifth edition were determined largely through a detailed questionnaire sent to forestry instructors in the United States and Canada. Most of the respondents were pleased with the fourth edition format, but several requested expansion or addition of specific topics. We have accommodated requests for expanded coverage where possible.

The recent rapid advances in electronic and computing technologies have had a profound impact on how forest resources are assessed. New topics in this edition include use of electronic devices for measuring distances, electronic equipment for recording field data, global positioning systems (GPS) for determining locations, and geographic information systems (GIS) for storing, retrieving, summarizing, and analyzing forest inventory data. Information on use of extendable poles for measuring tree heights and on measurement of tree crowns has also been added. The chapter on point sampling has been revised to encompass a more formal presentation of the estimating formulas and expanded to include an introduction to use of permanent points for estimating forest growth. A glossary of terms commonly used, but specific to forest resource measurements, has been added, and answers to selected problems have been provided, thus enabling students to readily evaluate their comprehension of the material. All principal topics covered in the fourth edition have been retained, with appropriate revision and updating incorporated to account for recent advances.

As with previous editions, we have attempted to present the text in a straightforward fashion that is easily grasped by students. It is presumed that readers will have some background in algebra and plane trigonometry; a prior knowledge of basic statistics and sampling methods will also be helpful, although basic concepts are presented herein. A knowledge of calculus, while not essential, will be useful for some of the material. Explanations that assume a background in calculus are placed in separate sections which can be omitted without loss of continuity.

English units of measurement are used, although metric equivalents or examples are also given in some instances. It is virtually impossible to give *both* systems equal treatment because many basic tree measurements are not directly comparable in English and metric units.

We extend sincere thanks to those instructors who have offered helpful suggestions for improvements in this text. Special thanks go to all instructors in the United States and Canada who responded to our questionnaire. Various individuals provided assistance with specific sections; in that regard we thank V. Clark Baldwin and Gregory A. Reams of the U.S. Forest Service for their help in updating the section of Forest Inventory and Analysis (FIA) and Karen Launchbaugh of the University of Idaho for reviewing the material on assessing rangelands. In addition, the following reviewers, selected by McGraw-Hill, provided comments:

John Duff Bailey, Northern Arizona University
Eddie Bevilacqua, SUNY, College of Environmental Science & Forestry
Thomas B. Brann, University of Maine
Quang V. Cao, Louisiana State University
Roger C. Chapman, Washington State University
Richard F. Daniels, University of Georgia
Lawrence R. Gering, Clemson University
George Gertner, University of Illinois
Samantha Gill, California Polytechnic State University
John A. Kershaw, Jr., University of New Brunswick
David R. Larsen, University of Missouri
Valerie LeMay, University of British Columbia
Carl Newton, University of Vermont
Carl W. Ramm, Michigan State University
David D. Reed, Michigan Technological University
Andrew Robinson, University of Idaho
Robert Rogers, University of Wisconsin-Stevens Point
Charles M. Ruffner, Southern Illinois University
Charles M. Strauss, The Pennsylvania State University
Hans Zuuring, University of Montana

The insightful and helpful suggestions of reviewers resulted in numerous improvements to the final manuscript.

Colleagues at Virginia Polytechnic Institute and State University were very helpful during the preparation of the fifth edition of *Forest Measurements*. Our thanks are extended to Richard G. Oderwald, Philip J. Radtke, and Ralph L. Amateis for their advice and assistance with preparation of the fifth edition manuscript. Stephen P. Prisley and Randolph H. Wynne provided valuable guidance on the sections dealing with land measurements, aerial photography, and geographic information systems. In addition, Dean F. Stauffer reviewed the section on measuring wildlife resources, W. Michael Aust evaluated the material on measuring water resources, and Gregory J. Buhyoff and Jeffrey L. Marion commented on the treatment of measuring recreational resources. Bronson P. Bullock, Mahadev Sharma, Gudaye Tasissa, and James A. Westfall provided valuable support by obtaining reference materials and checking numeric solutions. Finally, for capable aid with numerous details of manuscript preparation, we thank Connie N. Linkous.

Visit the McGraw-Hill Agriculture and Forestry Website at *http://www.mhhe.com/catalogs/sem/agriculture/*. For student and instructor supplemental materials, click on the link Forest Measurements.

Thomas Eugene Avery
Harold E. Burkhart

1

INTRODUCTION

1-1 Purpose of Book   This book is intended for introductory courses in forest measurements. Although a "how-to-do-it" approach is employed, there are still many measurement problems for which no completely satisfactory solutions exist. Furthermore, there is room for considerable improvement in currently employed techniques and instruments. During recent years, new technologies have been employed to electronically measure distances, determine locations, capture field measurement data, and summarize and analyze forest inventory information in a spatially explicit manner. To a large degree, however, we are still measuring timber volumes, tree form, growth, cull factors, and mortality much as foresters have done for decades. The continued need for personnel with imagination and inventiveness is clearly apparent.

1-2 Need for Measurements   Management of forested land requires knowledge of the location and current volume of timber resources. Because forests are dynamic, biological systems, estimates of growth for various management strategies are also required. Forest measurements can be considered a part of forest management; the role of measurements is to supply the numerical data required to make prudent management decisions.

The field of forest measurements is concerned with direct measurements, sampling, and prediction. Direct measurements require appropriate use of instruments to obtain the desired data. Examples of direct measurements are measuring tree diameter at breast height using calipers and measuring tree height using hypsometers. Because forested lands are typically extensive in area and the property of interest is likely to contain tens of thousands of trees, foresters commonly measure only a sample of the trees and then expand the sample values appropriately to obtain estimates for the population of interest. Prediction also is an important aspect of forest measurements. For instance, the weight of a standing tree cannot be measured directly, but it can be predicted using easily measured tree attributes such as diameter at breast height and total tree height. The science of statistics, in particular sampling techniques and regression analysis (quantifying associations between variables), plays a central role in forest measurements. Mathematics is fundamental to statistics and forest measurements, and with the vast amounts of data and complexity of the analyses involved, computer science has become an integral component.

This book is concerned with the measurement of the tree overstory on forested land. The coverage includes measuring products cut from tree boles, measuring attributes (diameter, height, age, etc.) of standing trees, quantifying stand characteristics (volumes, weights, etc.), and measuring past growth and predicting future growth of individual trees and stands of trees. Regardless of the land management objectives—timber, wildlife, recreation, watershed, or a combination of these resources—the timber overstory must be quantified for informed decision making. Forest cover is an important part of wildlife habitat, and the understory component can often be successfully related (using regression analysis) to the overstory characteristics. The recreation potential of wildland is a function of many variables, including the timber overstory. Water yields are related to the composition and density of the tree canopy. The sampling methods and measurement principles discussed in this book are applicable to all natural resource management situations that require quantitative information about the tree component of the land base. While an in-depth treatment of specialized techniques for sampling and measuring wildlife populations, recreation resources, water yields, and other resources associated with forested land is outside the scope of a text primarily concerned with tree measurements, an introduction to these topics is provided (Chap. 18). Additional information on measurement of nontimber resources associated with forests can be obtained from the *Forestry Handbook* (Wenger, 1984), *Research and Management Techniques for Wildlife and Habitats* (Bookhout, 1996), and textbooks and references on subjects such as wildlife, recreation, range, and watershed management.

1-3 Measurement Cost Considerations   In almost all resource inventories, cost factors are of primary importance; the forester must continually seek out more efficient methods for counting, measuring, and appraisal. The basic objective of most inventories is to obtain an estimate of acceptable statistical precision for the lowest possible expenditure. To achieve this objective requires a sound knowledge of sampling methods because once the specific needs of management have been determined, the resource inventory becomes essentially a sampling problem.

The measurement of various resource parameters adds no real value to the materials or benefits being assessed; therefore, such measurements are regarded as service functions rather than control functions. Measuring techniques must be subordinate to the productive or beneficial phases of an operation, for the operation itself cannot be modified just to accommodate an inventory requirement. For example, every visitor to a crowded public campground cannot be delayed and required to complete a detailed questionnaire on recreational preferences—nor can a sawmill be shut down in order to measure or weigh a recent delivery of logs. Instead, an appropriate sampling scheme must be designed and employed to obtain the essential resource measurements without disrupting normal activities.

It is an obvious though commonly overlooked fact that the amount expended for a given inventory task should be geared to the value of the products or services being measured. Also, the nearer one approaches the finished product or ultimate benefit, the greater can be the allowable cost of measurement. Thus the measurement of high-quality black walnut trees, which may be worth several thousand dollars each, justifies a much greater unit expense than the assessment of small pine trees for pulpwood. Similarly, the value of finished lumber warrants a greater inventory cost than the scaling of logs. Forest managers who become "cost conscious" early in their careers have an attribute that will be highly respected by their employers.

1-4 Abbreviations and Symbols   In many scientific disciplines, there are periodic attempts to standardize the nomenclature, symbols, and abbreviations associated with various quantities. Unfortunately, symbols adopted for one discipline may have entirely different connotations in another scientific field. In this book, we have attempted to employ abbreviations and symbols commonly found in forestry literature in the United States.

In accordance with the publisher's standards, abbreviations and symbols for measurement units are used without periods, except when they spell a word (e.g., in. for inch). With this provision in mind, the more common symbols and abbreviations used herein are as follows:

Abbreviation or symbol	Meaning
B, b	cross-sectional areas of logs or bolts
BA, ba	basal area
BAF, baf	basal-area factor (point sampling)
bd ft	board feet
cd	cord
CFI	continuous forest inventory
cu ft	cubic feet

continued

Abbreviation or symbol	Meaning	*continued*
D, d	tree or log diameter (at any specified point)	
dbh	diameter breast height	
dib	diameter inside bark	
dob	diameter outside bark	
f	frequency (statistical notation)	
GIS	geographic information system	
GPS	global positioning system	
H, h	height	
L, l	log or bolt length	
M	thousand	
MBF	thousand board feet	
N, n	number of (statistical notation)	
RF	representative fraction	
sp gr	specific gravity	
V, v	volume	

NUMERICAL CONSIDERATIONS

1-5 Scales of Measurement   In the broadest sense, measurement is the assignment of numerals to objects or events according to rules. The fact that numerals can be assigned under different rules leads to different kinds of scales and different kinds of measurement (Stevens, 1946).

Four scales of measurement—nominal, ordinal, interval, and ratio—are recognized. The *nominal scale* is used to number objects for identification. For instance, one might develop numerical codes for species identification in a forest inventory. Because the numbers are assigned only for identification purposes, no meaningful analyses (except perhaps frequency of occurrence) can be performed on the numerical data.

The *ordinal scale* is used to express rank or position in a series. Numerical codes of 1, 2, 3, and 4 could be used to designate the tree-crown classes dominant, codominant, intermediate, and suppressed, respectively. When applying ordinal scales, the successive intervals on the scale are not necessarily equal, nor can one necessarily infer that an equal difference on the scale (e.g., a difference of one unit) means the same thing at all positions along the scale. However, the rank ordering does have meaning when an ordinal scale is used to quantify phenomena such as tree-crown classes, lumber grades, or site-quality classes.

The *interval scale* involves a series of graduations marked off at uniform intervals from an arbitrary origin. The zero point on an interval scale is a matter of convention or convenience. An example of an interval scale is temperature as measured on the Celsius or Fahrenheit scale. Equal intervals of temperature are scaled off from an arbitrary zero agreed upon for each scale.

Ratio scales are the ones most commonly applied in forest measurements. For ratio scales, as with interval scales, there is equality of intervals between successive points on the scale; however, an absolute zero is always implied. Quantities such as the height of trees, the volume per unit area of stands, and the weight of truckloads of logs are measured on a ratio scale.

Foresters routinely take measurements with different scales. For instance, on a forest inventory plot a forester might record the timber type using a nominal scale, the site productivity using an ordinal scale, the date of stand origin using an interval scale, and the height of a tree using a ratio scale. One cannot legitimately perform all mathematical operations on measurements from the various scales. The analysis and interpretation of data must take into account the measurement scale. From the standpoint of arithmetic operations, only counting is appropriate for nominal- or ordinal-scale measurements. Counting, addition, subtraction, multiplication, and division are all appropriate for data obtained on interval and ratio scales. Percentage changes are also permissible for ratio-scale measurement data because there is a true zero point.

1-6 Significant Digits and Rounding Off When recording, summarizing, and presenting numeric information, an appropriate number of significant digits should be used, and rules for rounding off numbers should be applied consistently. The significant digits in a number may be determined by reading from left to right, beginning with the first nonzero digit and ending with the last digit written. If the last digit is zero, it must result from observation rather than rounding off to be counted as significant. The numbers 51, 5.1, and 0.51 all have two significant figures, the 5 and the 1. The number 500 has one, two, or three significant digits, depending on whether one or both of the zeros denote an actual observation or have resulted from rounding off.

One should not record more significant digits than were observed. For instance, a length measurement of 45 feet taken to the nearest foot should not be recorded as 45.0, since this implies that the measurement is more precise than it actually is. Conversely, one should not omit significant zeros in decimals. For example, a measurement should be recorded as 45.0, rather than 45, if the zero is significant.

To minimize personal bias and assure a degree of consistency in computations, it is desirable to adopt a systematic technique for rounding off numbers. The necessity for such a method arises when a calculated value apparently falls exactly halfway between the units being used, that is, when the number 5 immediately follows the digit positions to be retained.

As an example, suppose the values of 27.65 and 104.15 are to be rounded off to 1 decimal place. A commonly used rule is to ignore the 5 when the digit preceding it is an even number; thus 27.65 becomes 27.6. Conversely, if the digit preceding the 5 is an odd number its value is raised by one unit. Therefore, in the example here, 104.15 would be recorded as 104.2.

Rounding off should be done after all intermediate calculations have been completed. Intermediate calculations should be carried at least two places beyond that of the final rounded figures.

1-7 English versus Metric Systems   In spite of its obvious complexities and disadvantages, the English system persists as the primary basis for measurements in the United States. The more logical metric system, devised and adopted in France around 1790, has gained acceptance in scientific research, but foresters are still surveying by feet and acres rather than meters and hectares. Bills requiring universal adoption of the metric system have been introduced several times in the Congress of the United States, but none have yet been enacted into law.

Admittedly, an abrupt changeover to the metric system would result in considerable confusion for an extended period of time. For example, the conversion of real estate records alone would require years of revising deeds and property descriptions, highway markers and automobile speedometers would require changes from miles to kilometers, and so on. The myriad of problems that would be generated seems to assure that adoption of the metric system in this country will proceed gradually.

Although the English system appears to be grounded in concepts of human anatomy, the metric system was formulated from geodetic measurements. The fundamental metric unit, the meter, was originally defined as being equal to one ten-millionth of the meridional distance from the equator to the Earth's poles. In terms of English units, the meter is approximately 39.37 in. in length, or slightly longer than 1 yd. Several common equivalents for converting English to metric units and vice versa are as follows:

Converting English units to metric system		
1 in. or 1000 mils	=	2.5400 cm
1 ft or 12 in.	=	30.4800 cm
1 yd or 3 ft	=	0.9144 m
1 U.S. statute mile or 5,280 ft	=	1.6093 km
1 acre or 43,560 sq ft	=	0.4047 ha
1 cu ft or 1,728 cu in.	=	0.0283 m^3

Converting metric units to English system		
1 cm or 10 mm	=	0.3937 in.
1 dm or 10 cm	=	3.9370 in.
1 m or 10 dm	=	39.3700 in.
1 km or 1,000 m	=	0.6214 U.S. statute mile
1 ha or 10,000 m^2	=	2.4710 acres
1 m^3 or 1,000,000 cm^3	=	35.3147 cu ft

PRESENTING INFORMATION

1-8 Preparation of Graphs   The presence of a meaningful relationship between two variables can be quickly and clearly depicted by plotting paired values. Ordinary numerical tabulations can be immediately visualized and interpreted, and trends can be established. Furthermore, errors and abnormal values are easily detected, and minor irregularities in a relationship may often be eliminated by establishing a curve through a series of plotted points.

In the plotting of graphical data, independent variables are placed on the horizontal, or *X,* axis, and dependent variables are plotted along the vertical, or *Y,* axis. Measurements along the *X* axis are known as *abscissas;* those on the *Y* axis are termed *ordinates.* Graduations for the *X* and *Y* axes need not be identical; instead, each scale may be expanded to the maximum degree in keeping with the ranges of data that must be accommodated. Though not absolutely essential, it is often desirable to arrange each scale to show the graph origin, or the *zero-zero* coordinate point. Other general rules of graphical presentation are as follows:

1. Scale units and complete identifications of variables should be clearly lettered on each axis. All labels should be oriented for easy reading, as illustrated in Figure 1-1.

2. Plotted points should be denoted by dots, small circles, or other appropriate symbols, and weights (frequency) should be indicated for each point.

3. Each graph should carry a figure number and a complete descriptive title.

Many software packages are now available for performing interactive graphics. These programs allow the user to quickly and easily produce a variety of graphics that clearly display the important characteristics of the data.

FIGURE 1-1
Tree volume-dbh relationship for 32 red pines in Chippewa County, Michigan.

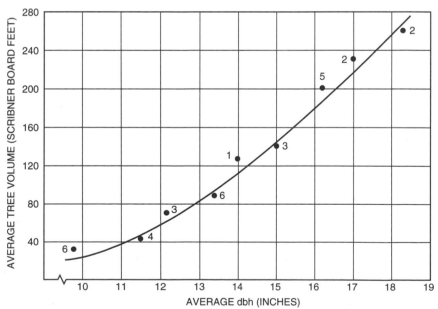

1-9 Preparation of Technical Reports   As a professional group, foresters are sometimes inclined to minimize the value of neat, concise, and well-written technical reports. Yet in many instances, such reports may provide the only concrete evidence of work accomplished and thus may constitute the prime basis for judgment of field proficiency by supervisors.

It goes without saying that one must be more than an accomplished grammarian; no amount of flowing penmanship can compensate for deficiencies in fieldwork and data collection. Nevertheless, the importance of producing technically accurate and grammatically correct reports can hardly be overemphasized.

The text of the report should be neatly presented, with figures and tables preferably placed on separate pages and numbered consecutively. Drawings, graphs, and charts should be shown at an appropriate size and scale. Although a single format cannot be expected to meet the requirements for all reports, the following outline may prove useful for student term papers or technical reports on assigned experiments:

Title page   Title in capital letters and centered on page, followed by author's name. Lower part of page should show location of study (e.g., Cripple Creek National Forest) and the date (month and year completed).

Table of contents   Listing of chapter headings and major subdivisions, along with corresponding page numbers.

Introduction   Statement of the problem, justification and importance of the study, specific objectives, and practical considerations.

Review of previous work   A concise, critical review of published literature bearing on the problem, including a statement on the relationship of the present study to previous research.

The study area   Location of the study and a description of the area involved (e.g., physiography, forest types, site conditions, climatic factors, legal description, size of area, ownership, management or silvicultural history).

Collection of field data or laboratory procedure   For some studies "Design of the experiment" may be a more appropriate heading. List all data collected, arrangement of field samples, special instruments or techniques employed, illustration of field forms, size of crews, time or expense involved, and special problems encountered.

Analysis of results   Compilation of field data, statistical procedures, and presentation and discussion of results.

Summary and conclusions   A brief synopsis of the study undertaken, results obtained, and implications of the findings. For some types of reports, a brief summary or abstract may be required at the beginning of the discussion (i.e., preceding the introduction).

Literature cited   Arranged in standard form according to an acceptable style manual or in conformance with requirements of a specific technical publication.

Appendix   Copies of field forms and/or original raw data are often included here. Detailed statistical formulas or computations may also be shown. The various sections of the appendix should be designated by alphabetical divisions or by use of Roman numerals.

1-10 Reviews of Technical Literature   Among principal sources of forest inventory literature are research papers issued by state and federal experiment stations, the *Journal of Forestry, Forest Science, Forestry Chronicle,* and the *Canadian Journal of Forest Research.* The forester who expects to comprehend and evaluate such articles must adopt a disciplined attitude to the reading of scientific literature. If an abstract precedes the main report, this should be read first, followed by a rapid scanning of the entire article. Then, if the study appears to be of special interest or utility, the article should be carefully reread.

Although an abstract may obviate the necessity of making notes on each article, it is well to look for salient points. After noting the locale of the study and the author's affiliation, the reader should identify the primary objectives of this study. Next, it may be appropriate to note the laboratory procedure or statistical design employed, along with the number and type of samples measured. Finally, any tables or graphical presentations should be studied to see whether they fully substantiate the author's principal findings or conclusions. Only by taking such an analytical approach can the reader expect to gain any significant benefit from reports of specialized research.

PROBLEMS

1-1 Convert the following measurements as specified:
  a 51.3 miles to kilometers
  b 50 m^3 per ha to cu ft per acre
  c 2,000 cu ft per acre to m^3 per ha
  d 500 trees per ha to trees per acre
1-2 Be able to write equations for.
  a determining the radius for a circular plot when the area is known.
  b determining the length of the hypotenuse of a right triangle.
  c determining the length of one side of a square plot when the area is known.
1-3 For each of the following, indicate if the measurement would be made on a nominal, ordinal, interval, or ratio scale:
  a Number of trees per acre
  b Cubic volume in a log
  c Log grade
  d Designation for forest types on a map
1-4 Without using instruments or scales, explain how you might determine the height of a tree from its shadow length.
1-5 Round off the following numbers to 4, 3, and 2 significant figures:
  a 7.6495
  b 95.75002
  c 495,461
  d 0.89687
1-6 Prepare an abstract of not more than 250 words for a published technical article dealing with some phase of forest inventory.

REFERENCES

Bookhout, T. A. (ed.). 1996. *Research and management techniques for wildlife and habitats,* 5th ed. The Wildlife Society, Bethesda, Md. 740 pp.

Cleveland, W. S. 1985. *The elements of graphing data.* Wadsworth Advanced Book Program, Monterey, Cal. 323 pp.

Ffolliott, P. F., Robinson, D. W., and Space, J. C. 1982. Proposed metric units in forestry. *J. Forestry* **80:**108–109.

Helms, J. A. (ed.). 1998. *The dictionary of forestry.* The Society of American Foresters, Bethesda, Md. 210 pp.

Rains, M. T., and Larson, D. E. 1978. *Graphics in forestry: A guide to effective display of data.* U.S. Forest Service, Atlanta, Ga. 12 pp.

Reed, D. D., and Mroz, G. D. 1997. *Resource assessment in forested landscapes.* John Wiley & Sons, New York, 386 pp.

Schuster, E. G., and Zuuring, H. R. 1986. Quantifying the unquantifiable. *J. Forestry* **84:**25–30.

Stevens, S. S. 1946. On the theory of scales of measurement. *Science* **103:**677–680.

———. 1968. Measurement, statistics, and the schemapiric view. *Science* **161:**849–856.

Tufte, E. R. 1983. *The visual display of quantitative information.* Graphics Press, Cheshire, Conn. 197 pp.

U.S. Department of Commerce. 1972. *The International System of Units (SI).* National Bureau of Standards, Special pub. 330, Government Printing Office, Washington, D.C. 42 pp.

Wenger, K. F. (ed.). 1984. *Forestry handbook,* 2d ed. John Wiley & Sons, New York. 1,335 pp.

CHAPTER 2

STATISTICAL METHODS

2-1 Introduction   To the practicing forester, an understanding of statistical techniques and sampling methods has become as important as a knowledge of dendrology or type mapping. Whether designing a timber inventory or reading a scientific article, a background in statistics is essential. Because forestry students usually complete one or more statistics courses prior to work in forest mensuration, this chapter is intended only as a brief review of applied techniques. Emphasis is placed on how to handle routine computations and (to a lesser degree) how to interpret the meaning of certain statistical quantities. Derivations and theory are purposely avoided, because they are best treated in textbooks devoted strictly to these subjects.

The reader is reminded that the procedures discussed in this chapter were not designed specifically for the solution of forestry problems. Rather, they are standard statistical methods that have been found useful in forest-oriented situations.

2-2 Bias, Accuracy, and Precision   Although most persons have a general idea of the distinction among these three terms, it is appropriate here to define the terms from the statistical viewpoint. *Bias* is a systematic distortion arising from such sources as a flaw in measurement or an incorrect method of sampling. Measurements of 100-ft units with a tape only 99 ft long will be biased; similarly, biases may occur when timber cruisers consistently underestimate tree heights or arbitrarily shift field plot locations to obtain what they regard as more typical samples.

Accuracy refers to the success of estimating the true value of a quantity, and *precision* refers to the clustering of sample values about their own average. A biased estimate may be precise, but it cannot be accurate; thus it is evident that accuracy and precision are not synonymous or interchangeable terms. As an example, a forester might make a series of careful measurements of a single tree with an instrument that is improperly calibrated or out of adjustment. If the measurements closely cluster about their average value, they are precise. However, as the instrument is out of adjustment, the measured values will be biased and considerably off the true value, and the resulting estimate is not accurate. The failure to attain an accurate result may be due to the presence of bias, the lack of precision, or both.

Target shooting serves as a helpful analogy for understanding bias, precision, and accuracy (Fig. 2-1). If shots are closely clustered near the bull's-eye, the shooter is precise, unbiased, and accurate. Shots that are tightly clustered but off the center of the target are precise but biased, and thus they are not accurate. A pattern of shots that is widely scattered about the bull's-eye is imprecise, unbiased, and inaccurate. Shots widely scattered and far from the target center are both imprecise and biased and, hence, are not accurate.

FIGURE 2–1
To be termed accurate, results must be both unbiased and precise (a). Inaccurate results stem from bias (b and d), imprecision (c and d), or both.

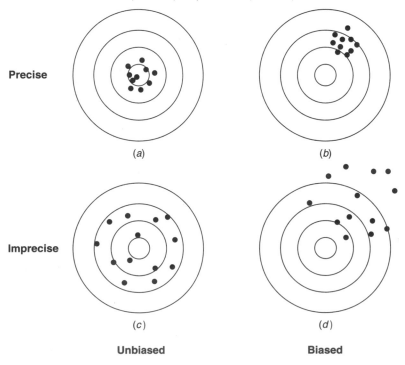

Precise

(a)   (b)

Imprecise

(c)   (d)

Unbiased   Biased

2-3 Calculating Probabilities   For purposes of discussion, probability may be defined as the relative frequency with which an event takes place "in the long run." If an observed event A occurs x times in n trials, the probability or relative frequency is

$$P(\text{A}) = \frac{x}{n}$$

For example, if a balanced coin is tossed in an unbiased fashion, one would expect to obtain "heads" about 50 percent of the time; that is, the probability is 0.50. If the same coin is tossed 100 times and heads occur only 41 times, the observed relative frequency of heads is $\frac{41}{100}$, or 0.41. Still, the likelihood of getting heads on any given toss is 0.50, and "over the long run" (thousands of unbiased tosses) one would expect the observed relative frequency to closely approximate 0.50.

Coin flipping is an example of *independent* events; the occurrence of heads or tails on one toss has no predictable effect on the outcomes of subsequent tosses. As the expected probability of obtaining heads on a single toss is $\frac{1}{2}$, the probability of obtaining two heads (or two tails) in a row is $\frac{1}{2} \times \frac{1}{2} = \frac{1}{4}$, or one chance in four. Thus, *for two independent events, the probability that both will occur is the product of their individual probabilities.*

As another example of events that are apparently independent, assume that the probability of owning a bicycle is 0.17, the probability of having red hair is 0.04, and the probability of being a college student is 0.21. If the assumption of independence is correct, the probability that a randomly selected individual will be a red-headed college student with a bicycle is $0.17 \times 0.04 \times 0.21$, or 0.001428 (roughly 14 chances in 10,000). These events have been referred to as *apparently* independent, because truly independent happenings are difficult to establish, except by statistical design and randomization.

If the occurrence of one event A precludes the occurrence of some other event B and vice versa, A and B are said to be *mutually exclusive*. In a single appearance at bat, a baseball player may walk or hit safely but cannot do both. If the probability of drawing a walk is 0.104 and the probability of a safe hit is 0.310, the probability that the player will *either* draw a walk *or* hit safely is $0.310 + 0.104 = 0.414$ (roughly 41 chances in 100). Thus, *for mutually exclusive events, the probability that at least one or the other will occur is the sum of their individual probabilities.*

Probabilities are always positive numbers, and they range between 0 and 1. The probability that the Earth will continue to revolve on its axis for another year is unknown but assumed to be 1. If this is true, the probability that it will not do so is 0. Nevertheless, there are few events that can be described in such absolute terms. When the probability of an event happening is 0.75 (three times in four), the probability that it will *not* occur is $1 - 0.75$, or 0.25 (one chance in four).

2-4 Factorial Notation, Permutations, and Combinations   When very few events are involved, various outcomes can be simply counted; in other instances, special mathematical formulas are helpful. Assume, for example, that a four-volume set of books is placed upright on a shelf in a completely random order. The number of possible arrangements (permutations) of n things is n factorial (designated as $n!$), or $(n)(n - 1)(n - 2) \ldots (2)(1)$. For our four books, this is $4! = (4)(3)(2)(1) = 24$. Because the books can be shelved in 24 possible ways, the probability of their being put in correct order is 1 out of 24.

A useful formula for calculating the number of possible different events (combinations) involving a things, b things, $\ldots$, z things is $n = (a)(b)(c) \ldots (z)$. As an illustration, suppose a forest cover-type map is to be prepared to depict six species composition classes, five tree-height classes, three stand-density classes, and three soil-site conditions. The total number of possible cover types is $n = (6)(5)(3)(3) = 270$ combinations.

The term *combination* implies that two groups are composed of different items; for example, the sets *ABC, ABD,* and *ACD* are all different combinations. By contrast, the term *permutation* denotes the arrangement of a set of items. The sets *ABC, ACB,* and *BAC* are all the same combination, but they are different permutations. It is therefore obvious that a given population will have many more permutations than combinations. To illustrate this point, it may be presumed that one wishes to determine how many slates of officers (permutations) and how many different committees (combinations) of four individuals each can be selected from a group of 10 persons.

The number of permutations, or arrangements, of r items that can be formed from a total of n items is computed as $n! \div (n - r)!$. For our example, this is $10! \div 6! = 5,040$ slates of officers. In most inventory situations, the forester is concerned more with combinations of sampling units than with permutations.

The number of different combinations of r items that can be formed from a total of n items is computed as $n! \div r!(n - r)!$. In this example, $r = 4$ and $n = 10$; therefore,

$$\text{Combinations} = \frac{10!}{4!6!} = \frac{10 \cdot 9 \cdot 8 \cdot 7 \cdot 6 \cdot 5 \cdot 4 \cdot 3 \cdot 2 \cdot 1}{(4 \cdot 3 \cdot 2 \cdot 1)(6 \cdot 5 \cdot 4 \cdot 3 \cdot 2 \cdot 1)}$$
$$= 210 \text{ committees}$$

STATISTICAL CONCEPTS

2-5 Analysis of Data   Statistical data can be obtained by means of a sample survey (Chap. 3) or an experiment. The raw data usually consist of an unorganized set of numerical values. Before these data can be used as a basis for inference about a population or phenomenon of interest, or as a basis for decision, they must be summarized and the pertinent information must be extracted.

Tabular and graphical forms (Sec. 1-8) of presentation may be used to summarize and describe quantitative data. While these techniques are valuable for showing important features of the data, statistical methods for the most part require concise numerical descriptions. Measures of central tendency or location and measures of dispersion or scatter, as well as measures of association between variables, are important tools for analyzing and interpreting forestry data. These statistical concepts, along with the methods of computation, are discussed in the sections that follow.

2-6 Populations, Parameters, and Variables   A *population* may be defined as the aggregate of all arbitrarily defined, nonoverlapping *sample units*. If individual trees are the sample unit, then all trees on a given area of land could be considered a population.

Constants that describe the population as a whole are termed *parameters*. A *statistic* is a quantitative characteristic that describes a sample obtained from a population. Statistics are used to estimate population parameters. The *sample* itself is merely the aggregate of sample units from which measurements or observations are taken.

Populations are generally classed as being *finite* or *infinite*. A finite population is one for which the total number of sample units can be expressed as a finite number. The number of trees in a tract of land and the number of sawmills in a geographic region are both examples of finite populations.

Infinite populations are those in which the number of sample units is not finite. Also, populations from which samples are selected and replaced after each drawing may be regarded as equivalent to infinite populations. From a practical viewpoint, all the gray squirrels in North America or all the ponderosa pines in the southwestern United States may be treated as infinite populations. As described in later sections of this chapter, the distinction between these two classes of populations becomes important when a relatively large number of sample units is drawn from a finite population. In statistical notation, finite population size is denoted by N, and the number of sample units observed is indicated by n.

Without variation in forest characteristics such as tree volumes, there would be few sampling problems. Any characteristic that may vary from one sample unit to another is referred to as a *variable*. Variables that may occupy any position along a scale are termed *continuous variables*. Tree weights and heights are conceptually continuous variables, as are air temperature, wind velocity, and atmospheric pressure.

Qualitative variables and variables that are commonly described by simple counts (integers) are termed *discrete variables*. Most of the statistical procedures described in this chapter are applicable to continuous, rather than discrete, variables.

2-7 Frequency Distributions   The *frequency distribution* defines the relative frequency with which different values of a variable occur in a population. Each population has its own distinct type of distribution. If the form of the distribution is known, it is possible to predict the proportion of individuals that are within any specified limits.

The most common distribution forms are the normal, binomial, and Poisson. The *normal distribution* is associated with continuous variables, and it is the form most used by foresters. The arithmetic techniques for handling data from normally distributed populations are relatively simple in comparison with methods developed for other distributions. Regardless of the distribution followed by a given variable, the means of large samples from the distribution are expected to have a distribution that approaches normality. Consequently, estimates and inferences may be based on this assumption.

STATISTICAL COMPUTATIONS

2-8 Mode, Median, and Mean   These values are referred to as measures of central tendency. The *mode* is defined as the most frequently appearing value or class of values in a set of observations. The *median* is the middle value of the series of observations when they have been arranged in order of magnitude, and the arithmetic *mean* is simply the arithmetic average of the set of observations. For a majority of statistical analyses, the mean is the most useful value of the three. In populations that are truly normally distributed, values for the mode, median, and mean are identical.

Following are observations of diameters at breast height (dbh, measured in inches) taken on a sample of 26 trees. These values, listed haphazardly (as tallied), are

dbh, as tallied		
8	9	10
8	9	9
5	7	7
10	5	8
9	8	9
10	7	8
8	7	7
5	8	8
7	8	
$n = 26$		

The measurements can be arranged in a frequency table, where the indicated dbh is the midpoint of the diameter class, as follows:

Frequency table	
dbh	No. of trees
5	3
6	0
7	6
8	9
9	5
10	3
	26

For this set of observations, 8 in. is the modal diameter class. This class is easily detected in the frequency table but is less discernible in the unorganized listing. If there had been nine trees in any other class as well as nine in the 8-in. class, the distribution would have been termed *bimodal.* When three or more values have the same frequency or when each value appears only once, no apparent mode can be specified.

The median position is found by adding 1 to the number in the sample and dividing by 2, that is $(n + 1) \div 2$. With an odd number of observations, the median is merely picked out as the middle ranking value. Thus in a sample of seven observations ranked as 2, 4, 9, 12, 17, 24, and 50, the 12 is the median value. Had there been only six observations (eliminating the 50), the median position would have fallen between the 9 and 12. Its value would be recorded as the arithmetic average of these two numbers, or $(9 + 12) \div 2 = 10.5$. For the 26 tree diameters previously noted, the median position is $(26 + 1) \div 2$, or 13.5. As both the thirteenth and fourteenth values fall within the 8-in.-dbh class, the median value is recorded as 8 in.

Both the median and the mode are unaffected by extreme values. Thus as measures of central tendency, the median and mode may be more informative than the arithmetic mean when a few extreme values are observed.

The sample *mean,* or arithmetic average, is commonly designated as $\bar{x}$ and computed from

$$\bar{x} = \frac{\Sigma x}{n}$$

where Σ = sum of (over entire sample)
$\quad x$ = value of an individual observation
$\quad n$ = number of observations in sample

For the 26 tree diameters under consideration, the sample mean is $204 \div 26 = 7.85$ in.

2-9 The Range and Average Deviation   In a series of sample values, the *range* is merely the difference between the highest and the lowest value recorded. For the 26 tree diameters listed previously, the range is therefore $10 - 5$, or 5 in. Although based solely on extreme values, the range is a useful indicator of the dispersion or variability of a set of observations, and it also has some utility in providing estimates of the standard deviation. A rough estimate of the standard deviation (Sec. 2-10) can be computed as

$$s = \frac{R}{4}$$

where s = standard deviation
$\quad R$ = range (largest minus smallest value)

The *average deviation* (AD), though largely supplanted by the standard deviation, provides an easily computed measure of the dispersion of individual variables about their sample mean. It is computed as the arithmetic average of deviations from the mean (ignoring algebraic signs). Using the same symbols as in Section 2-8, the formula is

$$AD = \frac{\Sigma\,|x - \bar{x}|}{n}$$

The average deviation for the 26 tree diameters is calculated as

$$AD = \frac{27.20}{26} = 1.05 \text{ in.}$$

The calculated value indicates that the average deviation of the individual dbh measurements from their mean of 7.85 in. is 1.05 in. Although this measure of dispersion about the arithmetic mean is not widely used for making statistical inferences, it is sometimes used as a measure of the reliability of prediction equations or tables (e.g., tree volume equations).

2-10 Variance and Standard Deviation   The variance and the standard deviation are measures of the dispersion of individual observations about their arithmetic mean. In a normally distributed population, approximately two-thirds (68 percent) of the observations will be within ± 1 standard deviation of the mean. About 95 percent will be within 1.96 standard deviations, and roughly 99 percent within 2.58 standard deviations. In succeeding sections, the standard deviation will be used to evaluate the reliability of sample estimates.

The *standard deviation* of a population is a parameter, and it is commonly denoted by the Greek letter sigma (σ). The sample standard deviation is a statistic that is an estimate of the population parameter σ, and it is symbolized by s. For sample data, the *variance,* which is defined as the sum of squared deviations from the mean divided by $n - 1$, is denoted by s^2 and is computed first; then the standard deviation is derived by taking the square root of the variance. The estimated standard deviation is calculated from

$$s = \sqrt{\frac{\Sigma x^2 - (\Sigma x)^2/n}{n - 1}}$$

This is equivalent to the formula

$$s = \sqrt{\frac{\Sigma(x - \bar{x})^2}{n - 1}}$$

where $\bar{x}$ is the arithmetic mean and $(x - \bar{x})^2$ is the squared deviation of an individual observation from the arithmetic mean.

The first formula is easier to use for calculations. For the 26 measurements of tree diameters, the standard deviation is

$$s = \sqrt{\frac{1650 - (204)^2/26}{25}} = \sqrt{1.98} = 1.41 \text{ in.}$$

If the population sampled is normally distributed, it is expected that about two-thirds of the individual tree diameters will fall within ± 1.41 in. of the population mean.

2-11 Coefficient of Variation   The ratio of the standard deviation to the mean is known as the *coefficient of variation* (CV). It is usually expressed as a percentage value. Because populations with large means tend to have larger standard deviations than those with small means, the coefficient of variation permits a comparison of relative variability about different-sized means. The magnitude of the variance and standard deviation also depends on the measurement units used, but the coefficient of variation will be the same for a given set of observations regardless of the unit of measure. A standard deviation of 5 for a population with a mean of 15 indicates the same relative variability as a standard deviation of 30 with a mean of 90. The coefficient of variation in each instance would be 0.33, or 33 percent.

For the 26 tree diameters, the mean is 7.85 and the standard deviation is 1.41. The coefficient of variation CV from the sample is

$$\text{CV} = \frac{s}{\bar{x}}(100) = \frac{1.41}{7.85}(100) = 18\%$$

2-12 Standard Error of the Mean   The standard deviation is a measure of the variation of individual sample observations about their mean. Inasmuch as individuals vary, there will also be variation among means computed from different samples of these individuals. A measure of the variation among sample means is the *standard error of the mean*. It may be regarded as a standard deviation among the means of samples of a fixed size n. The standard error of the mean can be used to compute confidence limits for a population mean (Sec. 2-13) or to determine the sample size required to achieve a specified sampling precision (Sec. 3-5).

Calculation of the standard error of the mean depends on the manner in which the sample was selected. For simple random sampling from an infinite population, the formula for the estimated standard error of the mean $s_{\bar{x}}$ is

$$s_{\bar{x}} = \sqrt{\frac{s^2}{n}}$$

When sampling without replacement from a finite population, the formula becomes

$$s_{\bar{x}} = \sqrt{\frac{s^2}{n}\left(\frac{N-n}{N}\right)}$$

The term $(N - n) \div N$ is referred to as the finite population correction; in this term, N denotes the population size and n is the actual sample size. The finite population correction serves to reduce the standard error of the mean when relatively large samples are drawn without replacement from finite populations.

If it is assumed that the 26 tree diameters were drawn without replacement from a population of only 200 stems, the standard error of the mean would be computed as

$$s_{\bar{x}} = \sqrt{\frac{1.98}{26}\left(\frac{200-26}{200}\right)} = 0.26 \text{ in.}$$

This value indicates that if several samples of 26 units each were randomly drawn from the same population, the standard deviation among the sample means might be expected to be approximately 0.26 in. The value of the finite population correction is always less than one, but it approaches unity when the sampling intensity is very low. If less than 5 percent of the population appears in the sample, the finite population correction is sometimes omitted.

If the 26 tree diameters had been drawn from an infinite population or from one that was quite large in relation to the sample size, the standard error of the mean would have been computed simply as

$$s_{\bar{x}} = \sqrt{\frac{1.98}{26}} = 0.28 \text{ in.}$$

2-13 Confidence Limits   It is recognized that sample means vary about the true mean of the population. Thus an estimate of the mean, by itself, is not very informative. To make an estimate more meaningful, confidence limits can be computed to establish an interval which, at some specified probability level, would be expected to include the true mean. The standard error of the mean and t values (Appendix Table 6) are used for establishing confidence limits. For simple random samples from normally distributed populations, the confidence limits for the population mean are computed by

$$\text{Mean} \pm t \text{ (standard error)} \quad \text{or} \quad \bar{x} - ts_{\bar{x}} \text{ to } \bar{x} + ts_{\bar{x}}$$

Under ordinary circumstances, one does not know the underlying distribution of the population being sampled. However, the distribution of *means* from reasonably large samples, almost regardless of the distribution of the underlying parent population, will approach normality, and the confidence interval, as shown, is appropriate.

In using Appendix Table 6 for the distribution of t, the column labeled df refers to *degrees of freedom,* which in the case of a simple random sample will be equal to one less than the sample size (that is, $n - 1$). The columns labeled *probability* refer to the level of odds demanded. If one wishes to state that the confidence interval will include the true mean unless a 1-in-20 chance occurs (95 percent probability level), the t values in the 0.05 column are used. If one wishes to establish confidence limits at the 99 percent probability level, the 0.01 column in the t table is used, and so forth.

For the sample of 26 tree diameters, the estimated mean was 7.85 in., and the standard error of the mean (for sampling without replacement) was ± 0.26 in. Because only 26 observations were taken, there are $26 - 1$, or 25, df. The 95 and 99 percent t values are read from Appendix Table 6 as 2.060 and 2.787, respectively. Confidence limits for these probability (P) levels are

$P = 0.95;\ 7.85 - (2.060)(0.26)$ to $7.85 + (2.060)(0.26) = 7.31$ to 8.39 in.
$P = 0.99;\ 7.85 - (2.787)(0.26)$ to $7.85 + (2.787)(0.26) = 7.13$ to 8.57 in.

Therefore, if the 26 units were randomly selected from a normally distributed population, the interval between 7.31 and 8.39 in. includes the true population mean, unless a 1-in-20 chance has occurred in sampling. In other words, the population mean will be included in the interval unless this random sample is one of those which, by chance, yields a sample mean and standard error such that the interval constructed from it will not include the mean. Such would happen, on the average, once in every 20 samples. Similarly, unless a 1-in-100 chance has occurred, the true mean is included in the interval of 7.13 to 8.57 in. It can be seen from these examples that the higher the probability level, the wider the confidence limits must be expanded.

The forester must remember that confidence limits and accompanying statements of probability account for *sampling variation only.* It is assumed that sampling procedures are unbiased, field measurements are without error, and no computational mistakes are included. If these assumptions are incorrect, confidence statements may be misleading.

2-14 Covariance The *covariance* is a measure of how two variables vary in relation to each other. If there is little or no association between two variables, the covariance will be close to zero. In cases where large values of one variable tend to be associated with small values of another variable, the covariance will be negative. When large values of one variable tend to be associated with large values of another variable, the covariance will be positive.

The sample covariance of two variables, x and y, is symbolized by s_{xy} and is defined as

$$s_{xy} = \frac{\Sigma(x - \bar{x})(y - \bar{y})}{n - 1}$$

The computing formula is

$$s_{xy} = \frac{\Sigma xy - \dfrac{(\Sigma x)(\Sigma y)}{n}}{n - 1}$$

2-15 Simple Correlation Coefficient   The magnitude of the covariance is related to the units of measure used for x and y. A measure of the degree of linear association between two variables that is independent of the units of measure is the *simple correlation coefficient (r)*

$$r = \frac{s_{xy}}{\sqrt{s_x^2 s_y^2}}$$

where s_x^2 and s_y^2 represent the sample variances of x and y, respectively.

The correlation coefficient can range from -1 to $+1$, with values near -1 or $+1$ indicating very strong association. Negative correlation coefficients indicate that large values of one variable are associated with small values of the other variable. When the correlation coefficient is positive, large values of one variable tend to be associated with large values of the other variable. If two variables are independent, the correlation coefficient will tend to be near zero. The converse is not necessarily true, however. A correlation near zero does *not* mean that two variables are independent, but that there is no apparent *linear* association between the variables—they could be strongly related in a curvilinear manner.

2-16 Expansion of Means and Standard Errors   In most instances, estimates of means per sample plot are multiplied by a constant to scale the estimates to a more useful basis. If a forest inventory utilizes ¼-acre plots, for example, the mean volume per plot is multiplied by 4 to put the estimated mean on a per acre basis. Or for a tract of 500 acres, the mean volume per plot would be multiplied by 2,000 (the number of possible ¼ acres in the tract) to estimate the total volume.

The rule to remember is that expansion of sample means must be accompanied by a similar expansion of standard errors. Thus if the mean volume per ¼-acre plot is 1,500 bd ft with a standard error of 60, the mean volume per acre is 4(1,500) $\pm$

4(60), or 6,000 ± 240 bd ft. Variances are expanded by multiplying by the constant squared. In this example, the variance of the estimate of the mean volume per ¼ acre is $60^2 = 3,600$; on an acre basis, the estimate would be $(4^2)(3,600) = 57,600$. Taking the square root of 57,600 gives 240 bd ft for the estimate of the standard error of the mean on an acre basis.

When area is known, estimates on a tract basis are expanded similarly—that is, the mean is multiplied by the area, the standard error by the area, and the variance by the area squared. Continuing with the preceding example, for a tract of 500 acres, the total volume would be expressed as 2,000(1,500) ± 2,000(60), or 3,000,000 ± 120,000 bd ft.

The foregoing examples presume the use of expansion factors having no error. However, sample-based estimates of area are (or should be) also accompanied by standard errors. Thus the expansion of per acre volume to total tract volume becomes one of deriving the product of volume times area and computing a standard error applicable to this product (Meyer, 1963). The computation may be illustrated by assuming *independent* inventories that produced the following estimates and standard errors for volume $\overline{V}$ and area A:

Mean volume: 18 ± 2 cd per acre
Tract acreage: 52 ± 1.5 acres

If (and only if) these two estimates are independent, their product and its standard error may be computed by

$$\overline{V}A \pm \sqrt{\overline{V}^2(s_A)^2 + A^2(s_{\overline{V}})^2}$$

where $\overline{V}$ = estimated mean volume per acre
  A = estimated number of acres
  $s_{\overline{V}}$ = standard error of mean volume per acre
  s_A = standard error of area estimate

Substituting the sample problem data yields the total volume and its standard error:

$$(18)(52) \pm \sqrt{(18)^2(1.5)^2 + (52)^2(2)^2} = 936 \pm 107.45 \text{ cd (tract total)}$$

2-17 Mean and Variance of Linear Functions   Quite often the variable of interest is a linear function of two or more other variables. In general terms, if the variable of interest Z is a linear function of k variables, that is,

$$Z = c_1x_1 + c_2x_2 + \ldots + c_kx_k$$

where $c_1, c_2 \ldots c_k$ are constants, then the mean of Z would be estimated as

$$\bar{Z} = c_1\bar{x}_1 + c_2\bar{x}_2 + \cdots + c_k\bar{x}_k$$

or

$$= \Sigma c_i\bar{x}_i$$

When variables are independent, the variance of the sum is the sum of the variances. Thus the estimated variance of Z would be

$$s_Z^2 = c_1^2 s_1^2 + c_2^2 s_2^2 + \cdots + c_k^2 s_k^2$$

or

$$= \Sigma c_i^2 s_i^2$$

where s_1^2 denotes the variance of x_1, etc. If the x's are not independent, the variance of Z is estimated as

$$s_Z^2 = c_1^2 s_1^2 + c_2^2 s_2^2 + \cdots + c_k^2 s_k^2$$

$$+ 2c_1 c_2 s_{12} + \cdots + 2c_{k-1} c_k s_{k-1,k}$$

or

$$= \Sigma c_i^2 s_i^2 + 2\underset{i \neq j}{\Sigma\Sigma} c_i c_j s_{ij}$$

where s_{12} denotes the covariance of x_1 and x_2, etc.

These general relationships are very important and are commonly employed in forestry. If, for example, the mean volume per acre on a timbered tract was estimated to be $\bar{x}_1$ by a simple random sample and 5 years later another completely independent simple random sample was taken for which the mean volume per acre was $\bar{x}_2$ (note that n_2 need not equal n_1), growth per acre (G) could be estimated as

$$G = \bar{x}_2 - \bar{x}_1$$

If the relationships just specified for linear functions of variables are applied, the variance of G would be

$$s_G^2 = (1)^2\left(\frac{s_2^2}{n_2}\right) + (-1)^2\left(\frac{s_1^2}{n_1}\right)$$

$$= s_{\bar{x}_2}^2 + s_{\bar{x}_1}^2$$

because $\bar{x}_1$ and $\bar{x}_2$ are independent. If, on the other hand, the second inventory was conducted by returning to the *same plot centers* as those used on the first occasion (thus, $n_2 = n_1 = n$), the two estimates $\bar{x}_1$ and $\bar{x}_2$ would not be independent but would be expected to have a positive covariance term (s_{12}). The mean growth per acre would be estimated as with independent samples, but the variance for the estimate of growth would now be

$$s_G^2 = \frac{(1)^2 s_2^2 + (-1)^2 s_1^2 + (2)(1)(-1)s_{12}}{n}$$

$$= s_{\bar{x}_2}^2 + s_{\bar{x}_1}^2 - \frac{2S_{12}}{n}$$

Since s_{12} is expected to be a relatively large positive quantity, the variance of estimated growth is expected to be much smaller with repeated measurements on the same plots than with independent sample plots. This relationship is the basis for the use of permanent sample plots when the primary objective is to estimate growth (Chap. 10).

SIMPLE LINEAR REGRESSION

2-18 Definitions   In analyzing various resource measurements, it may be important to quantify the degree of association between two or more variables. Such associations can often be examined by regression analysis. The simplest type of relationship that can exist between two quantities is one that can be represented by a straight line. Thus a *simple linear regression* describes a straight-line relationship that exists between two quantities: one dependent variable Y and one independent variable X.

The quantity that is being estimated by the regression line is termed the *dependent variable,* and the quantity measured in order to predict the associated value is called the *independent variable.* When these paired quantities are shown graphically, it is conventional to plot Y values along the vertical axis (*ordinate*) of the graph and X values along the horizontal axis (*abscissa*). This would be termed a *relationship* of Y on X.

When each Y value is graphically plotted against its corresponding X value, the resulting representation is termed a *scatter diagram.* Since the purpose of such a diagram is to determine whether or not a relationship exists between the two variables, this should be the first analytical step following data collection. Careful inspection of the scatter diagram will also provide an indication of the strength of the relationship and its probable form, that is, whether or not the association can be logically represented by a straight line (Fig. 2-2).

For those rare situations where all the plotted points fall exactly on a line, a perfect linear relationship exists. Such will rarely (if ever) be the case with biological data, but the smaller the deviations from a line, the stronger the linear relationship between the two variables. Where Y values increase with X values this

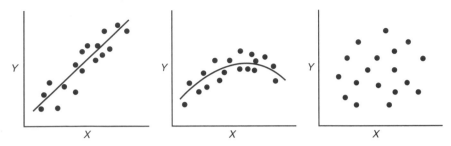

FIGURE 2-2
Scatter diagrams that suggest a linear relationship (left), a curvilinear relationship (middle), and no relationship (right).

is termed a *positive, or direct, correlation;* if Y values decrease as X values become larger, a *negative, or inverse, correlation* is said to exist. If the plotted points are not indicative of a straight-line relationship, it is sometimes possible to make a simple *transformation* of one or both of the variables so that the relationship becomes linear in form. (See Appendix Table 10 for some common transformations.) Squaring a variable or expressing it in logarithmic terms are examples of transformations.

2-19 A Linear Equation   When a linear trend exists between two variables, a regression equation of the form $\hat{Y} = b_0 + b_1 X$ may be fitted to the plotted points. In this equation, $\hat{Y}$ refers to the estimated value of the dependent variable, X is the value of the independent variable, and b_0 and b_1 are regression coefficients established from analysis of the data. After these coefficients have been determined, b_0 denotes the value of the Y intercept, which is the value of Y when X equals zero; the coefficient b_1 is the value that establishes the slope of the straight line. Therefore, a line represented by the equation $\hat{Y} = -3 + 2X$ would intercept the Y axis at an ordinal value of -3, that is, three units below the origin of the graph. The slope coefficient of 2 means that the line would rise two units vertically along the Y axis for each unit horizontally along the X axis.

When the regression line is fitted to the plotted points by the method of "least squares," the line will pass through the point defined by the means of X and Y. The principle of *least squares* is that the sum of the squared deviations of the observed values of Y from the regression line will be a minimum. The least squares method gives the best unbiased estimates of the slope and intercept if the following assumptions are satisfied:

1 The X values are measured without error.
2 The variance of Y is the same at all levels of X (i.e., a homogeneous variance is assumed).
3 For each value of X, Y is normally and independently distributed.

TABLE 2-1
PAIRED VALUES OF TREE-CROWN VOLUME AND BASAL-AREA GROWTH

Crown volume X	Basal-area growth Y	Crown volume X	Basal-area growth Y	Crown volume X	Basal-area growth Y
22	0.36	7	0.25	81	0.66
6	0.09	2	0.06	93	0.69
93	0.67	53	0.47	99	0.71
62	0.44	70	0.55	14	0.14
84	0.72	5	0.07	51	0.41
14	0.24	90	0.69	75	0.66
52	0.33	46	0.42	6	0.18
69	0.61	36	0.39	20	0.21
104	0.66	14	0.09	36	0.29
100	0.80	60	0.54	50	0.56
41	0.47	103	0.74	9	0.13
85	0.60	43	0.64	2	0.10
90	0.51	22	0.50	21	0.18
27	0.14	75	0.39	17	0.17
18	0.32	29	0.30	87	0.63
48	0.21	76	0.61	97	0.66
37	0.54	20	0.29	33	0.18
67	0.70	29	0.38	20	0.06
56	0.67	50	0.53	96	0.58
31	0.42	59	0.58	61	0.42
17	0.39	70	0.62		
			Total	3,050	26.62
			Mean ($n = 62$)	49.1935	0.42935

2-20 A Sample Problem   Suppose we observe that pine trees with large crowns appear to grow faster than trees with small crowns. Since we would like to be able to predict the growth of trees from their relative crown sizes, we decide to use regression analysis to determine whether a strong relationship exists between the two variables. A sample from the area of interest results in 62 paired measurements of tree-crown volumes X and basal-area growth Y. In Table 2-1, crown volume is in 100 cu ft, and basal-area growth is in square feet.

First, the paired measurements are plotted to determine whether there is any visual evidence of a relationship between the two variables. The resulting scatter diagram (Fig. 2-3) does indicate a general linear trend of direct correlation, and so it was decided to fit an equation of the form $\hat{Y} = b_0 + b_1 X$ to the plotted points by the method of least squares (Freese, 1967).

After selecting the model to be fitted, the next step is to calculate the corrected sums of squares (SS) and cross products (SP) by applying the following equations.

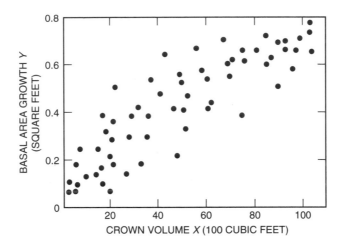

FIGURE 2-3
Scatter diagram of basal-area growth Y on crown volume X for 62
trees. *(From Freese, 1967.)*

The corrected sum of squares for Y:

$$SS_y = \sum^n Y^2 - \frac{\left(\sum^n Y\right)^2}{n}$$

$$= (0.36^2 + 0.09^2 + \cdots + 0.42^2) - \frac{26.62^2}{62}$$

$$= 2.7826$$

The corrected sum of squares for X:

$$SS_x = \sum^n X^2 - \frac{\left(\sum^n X\right)^2}{n}$$

$$= (22^2 + 6^2 + \cdots + 61^2) - \frac{3,050^2}{62}$$

$$= 59,397.6775$$

The corrected sum of cross products:

$$SP_{xy} = \sum^n (XY) - \frac{\left(\sum^n X\right)\left(\sum^n Y\right)}{n}$$

$$= [(22)(0.36) + (6)(0.09) + \cdots + (61)(0.42)] - \frac{(3,050)(26.62)}{62}$$

$$= 354.1477$$

According to the principle of least squares, the best estimates of the regression coefficients (b_0 and b_1) are obtained as follows:

$$b_1 = \frac{SP_{xy}}{SS_x} = \frac{354.1477}{59{,}397.6775} = 0.005962$$

$$b_0 = \overline{Y} - b_1\overline{X} = 0.42935 - (0.005962)(49.1935) = 0.13606$$

Substituting these estimates in the general equation gives

$$\hat{Y} = 0.13606 + 0.005962X$$

where $\hat{Y}$ is used to indicate that we are dealing with an estimated value of Y.

With this equation, we can estimate the annual basal-area growth $\hat{Y}$ from measurements of crown volume X.

2-21 Indicators of Fit   There are several methods of determining how well the regression line fits the sample data. One method is to compute the proportion of the total variation in Y that is associated with the regression on X. This ratio is sometimes called the *coefficient of determination,* or the *squared correlation coefficient* (r^2).

First, we must calculate the sum of squares due to the regression (also called the *reduction sum of squares*). Referring to the determination of b_1, we have

$$\text{Regression } SS = \frac{(SP_{xy})^2}{SS_x} = \frac{(354.1477)^2}{59{,}397.6775} = 2.1115$$

Next, the total variation in Y is estimated by $SS_y = 2.7826$ (as previously calculated), and

$$\text{Coefficient of determination } (r^2) = \frac{\text{regression } SS}{\text{total } SS} = \frac{2.1115}{2.7826} = 0.76$$

A common means of interpreting the r^2 value is that "76 percent of the variation in Y is associated with X." Or, in this particular example, 76 percent of the variation in basal-area growth can be "explained" by measurements of crown volume.

In addition to the coefficient of determination, the standard error of estimate $S_{y \cdot x}$ is customarily reported as an indicator of fit to the data. The standard error of estimate is defined as

$$S_{y \cdot x} = \sqrt{\frac{\sum\limits_{}^{n}(Y - \hat{Y})^2}{n - 2}}$$

and is easily computed as

$$S_{y \cdot x} = \sqrt{\frac{SS_y - (SP_{xy})^2/SS_x}{n - 2}}$$

For the present example,

$$S_{y \cdot x} = \sqrt{\frac{2.7826 - (354.1477)^2/59,397.6775}{60}}$$

$$= 0.106 \text{ sq ft}$$

2-22 Regression through the Origin   In many situations with biological data, theory calls for a straight line that passes through the origin. That is, when the independent variable X is zero, the value of the dependent variable Y must also be zero. Such a straight-line relationship can be written as

$$\hat{Y} = b_1 X$$

When no intercept term is estimated (i.e., the equation is conditioned to pass through the origin), the estimate of the slope coefficient is computed as

$$b_1 = \frac{\sum\limits_{}^{n} XY}{\sum\limits_{}^{n} X^2}$$

where $\sum\limits_{}^{n} XY$ is the *uncorrected* sum of cross products and $\sum\limits_{}^{n} X^2$ is the *uncorrected* sum of squares for X.

2-23 Hazards of Interpretation   A strong correlation between two variables (e.g., an r of 0.90 or greater) implies only that the variables are closely associated. Such correlations are *not* evidence of a cause-and-effect relationship; in many instances, both quantities may be directly affected by a third element that has not been taken into consideration. For example, if prices for both pork and eggs rise at similar rates, one might find a high correlation between these two values over a period of time. However, instead of one price *causing* the other to rise, both prices are probably being pushed upward by a third factor, such as general increases in the cost of producing farm products.

Since many completely unrelated variables can be associated by "nonsense correlations," the necessity for rational thinking in data collection is of paramount importance. Before attempting to employ regression analysis, the forest manager should have sound biological reasons for associating changes in one quantity with those in another quantity. Unless reliable and representative data are collected through use of an unbiased sampling plan, regression analysis may prove to be a futile exercise.

2-24 Multiple Regression   Finally, it should be again stressed that the preceding discussion has dealt only with simple linear regression (i.e., the treatment of one dependent and one independent variable). Frequently, however, the dependent variable is related to more than one independent variable. If this relationship can be estimated by using *multiple regression* analysis, it may allow more precise predictions of the dependent variable than is possible by a simple regression. The general model for a multiple regression is

$$\hat{Y} = b_0 + b_1 X_1 + b_2 X_2 + \cdots + b_k X_k$$

where $b_0, b_1, b_2, \ldots, b_k$ are regression coefficients that are estimated from analysis of the data. Details for handling multiple regression analysis are not treated in this chapter but may be found in most textbooks on statistical methods.

PROBLEMS

2-1 For the sample data presented below

1	7	17	16
5	14	7	7
10	15	18	

    a Compute the following measures of central tendency:
       1 Mean
       2 Median
       3 Mode
    b Compute the following measures of dispersion:
       1 Variance
       2 Standard deviation
       3 Range
       4 Average deviation
    c Calculate the coefficient of variation.
    d Place 95 percent confidence limits on the mean.
2-2 Draw a random sample of at least 30 observations from a population in your field of interest. Then, compute the mean and standard error of the mean, and place 95 percent confidence limits on the sample mean. (*Note:* Remember to apply the finite population correction, if applicable.)

2-3 Given the following pairs of values

X	Y	X	Y
2	3	4	3
4	2	7	7
6	7	6	5
8	5	11	9
10	9		

  a Find the regression equation, $\hat{Y} = b_0 + b_1 X$

  b Compute the following indicators of fit:

    1 Coefficient of determination (r^2)

    2 Standard error of estimate $(s_{y \cdot x})$

  c What is the predicted value of Y, given $X = 7$?

2-4 By simple random sampling, obtain paired measurements of two variables that you believe to be linearly correlated. If a scatter diagram indicates that a straight-line relationship exists, then **(a)** fit a simple linear regression to the plotted points by the method of least squares, and **(b)** compute the coefficient of determination for the association. (*Note:* If a linear relationship is not indicated by the scatter diagram, attempt to transform one or both variables so that the trend of plotted points becomes a linear one.)

2-5 Given the following sample data on X, Y pairs

X	Y	X	Y
0	0	−1	1
1	1	3	9
−3	9	−4	16
4	16	2	4
−2	4		

  a Compute the simple correlation coefficient (r) between X and Y.

  b Plot the values of Y versus X. Is there a relationship between X and Y? Interpret the computed value of r in view of the relationship exhibited in the data plot.

2-6 Theory indicates that the relationship between two variables of interest, X and Y, should be linear and should pass through the origin. The following sample data on X, Y pairs were collected:

X	Y	X	Y
20	24	1	1
15	17	27	28
6	7	12	12
11	10	3	5

a Plot Y versus X. Does the assumption of a straight-line relationship that passes through the origin seem reasonable?

b Fit the regression line

$$\hat{Y} = b_1 X$$

2-7 The following are the average heights of dominant trees, age in years, and measures of available water for 16 stands of a commercially important tree species.

Height (ft)	Age	Available water	Height (ft)	Age	Available water
33	13	0.90	20	9	0.98
34	12	0.92	23	10	1.65
21	9	0.89	38	17	0.88
30	13	0.59	47	18	0.77
35	12	1.24	21	8	0.78
25	10	0.57	39	15	0.94
21	8	0.77	38	14	0.70
48	16	0.91	40	15	1.00

a Find the equation for the regression of height on age.
b Find the equation for the regression of height on available water.
c Which variable, age or available water, is the better predictor of height?

REFERENCES

Draper, N. R., and Smith, H. 1998. *Applied regression analysis,* 3d ed. John Wilcy & Sons, New York. 706 pp.

Freese, F. 1962. Elementary forest sampling, *U.S. Dept. Agr. Handbook* 232, Government Printing Office, Washington, D.C. 91 pp.

———. 1967. Elementary statistical methods for foresters. *U.S. Dept. Agr. Handbook* 317, Government Printing Office, Washington, D.C. 87 pp.

Huntsberger, D. V., and Billingley, P. 1973. *Elements of statistical inference,* 3d ed. Allyn and Bacon, Inc., Boston. 349 pp.

Kitchens, L. J. 1998. *Exploring statistics: A modern introduction to data analysis and inference,* 2d ed. Duxbury Press, Pacific Grove, Cal. 940 pp.

Meyer, W. H. 1963. Some comments on the error of the total volume estimate. *J. Forestry* **61:**503–507.

Myers, R. H. 1990. *Classical and modern regression with applications,* 2d ed. PWS-Kent Publishing Co., Boston. 488 pp.

Rao, P. V. 1998. *Statistical research methods in the life sciences.* Duxbury Press, Pacific Grove, Cal. 889 pp.

CHAPTER 3

SAMPLING DESIGNS

3-1 Introduction   Chapter 2 provides an overview of basic statistical methods. Most statistical methods are based on the assumption that a simple random sample has been drawn. However, samples can be drawn in many possible ways. When the sampling procedure varies, the analysis of the sample data must be varied accordingly. The most appropriate method of selecting the samples and, by extension, of analyzing the sample data, depends on the objectives of the survey, the nature of the population to be sampled, and the prior or auxiliary information available about the target population.

The purpose of this chapter is to discuss sampling designs that have been widely applied for inventorying forests. Background information is given on the various sampling procedures, along with the formulas for estimating the population parameters and the reliability of those estimates.

3-2 Sampling versus Complete Enumeration   The objective of sample surveys is to gain information about a population. Sometimes the population is relatively small, and so sampling may not be necessary because every unit of the population can be observed. When all individual units of the population are observed, the survey is termed a *complete enumeration.*

Complete enumerations are generally prohibitively expensive and time-consuming to perform. However, there are situations in which a complete enumeration is required (that is, the data of interest must be recorded, analyzed, or presented on an individual-unit basis) or is a feasible alternative. For example, a woodlot owner may offer for sale a number of black walnut trees of large size and value. If the owner wishes to sell the trees on an individual-standing-tree basis, then the size and value of each tree must be determined. Alternatively, the owner may sell the trees on a lump-sum basis. The total value of the population of black walnut trees could then be estimated by a complete enumeration or by an appropriately drawn sample.

On small tracts, it is sometimes feasible to measure all trees of interest. The method has the advantage of determining the mean rather than estimating it. However, a combination of high costs and the need for timely information greatly limits application of complete enumerations. For most inventories of forest resources, it is not economically feasible to measure or count 100 percent of the population about which inferences must be made. Furthermore, the time required for complete enumerations of large populations would render the data obsolete by the time they could be amassed, collated, and summarized. Furthermore, foresters confronted with many trees to measure sometimes tend to use imprecise measurement techniques. Sample surveys, with fewer but more precise measurements, are often more accurate than complete enumerations.

Aside from time and cost factors, sampling is also necessary when testing procedures are destructive. All seeds cannot be evaluated in germination tests because there would be none left for sowing. Similarly, all fishes cannot be dissected to study concentrations of chemical elements if there are to be any left for anglers or for human consumption. In business and industry, as well as in forest management, sampling is an accepted means of obtaining information about populations that cannot be subjected to complete census.

The ultimate objective of all sampling is to obtain reliable data from the population sampled and to make certain inferences about that population. How well this objective is met depends on items such as the rule by which the sample is drawn, the care exercised in measurement, and the degree to which bias can be avoided. Of all the techniques described in this book, the concept of sampling is perhaps the most important.

3-3 The Sampling Frame   As stated previously, the objective of all sampling is to make some inference about a population from the observations composing the sample. The method of selecting the nonoverlapping sampling units to be included in a sample is referred to as the *sampling design,* and a listing of all possible sampling units that might be drawn is termed the *sampling frame.*

Establishment of a reliable sampling frame can be a difficult task. For example, if an individual campground visitor is specified as the sampling unit, a registration list that includes the occupants of all entering motor vehicles may or may not compose a satisfactory sampling frame. Those persons who enter the campground on foot or horseback would probably be excluded from such a sampling frame; other visitors might arrive at such a time that they somehow avoid the necessity of

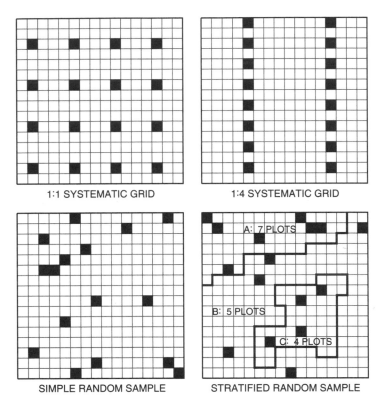

FIGURE 3-1
Four possible arrangements of 16 samples in a population composed of 256 square plots.

registration. Fortunately, in most field circumstances, differences between the sampling frame and the population are inconsequential. Otherwise, inferences based on a sample drawn from the frame may be questionable.

After the individual sampling unit and the sampling frame have been defined, it is then necessary to decide on the sampling design to be employed. Figure 3-1 illustrates three of the basic designs often used by forest managers: simple random sampling, systematic sampling, and stratified sampling.

SIMPLE RANDOM AND SYSTEMATIC SAMPLING

3-4 Simple Random Sampling   Many statistical procedures assume simple random sampling. By this approach, *every possible combination of sampling units* has an equal and independent chance of being selected. This is *not* the same as simply requiring that every sampling unit in the population have an equal chance of being selected. This latter requirement is met by many forms of restricted randomization and even by some systematic designs.

Allowing every possible combination of n sampling units an equal chance of being selected is easily accomplished. It is only necessary that, at any state of the sampling, the selection of a particular unit be in no way influenced by the other units that have been selected or will be selected. To state it another way, the selection of any given unit should be completely independent of the selection of all other units. One way to do this is to assign every unit in the population a number and to draw n numbers from a table of random digits. A modification of this technique consists of drawing random intersection points in a coordinate system based on column and row numbers designating each plot.

Sampling units may be selected with or without replacement. If selection is with replacement, each unit is allowed to appear in the sample as often as it is selected. In sampling without replacement, a particular unit is allowed to appear in the sample only once. Most forest resource sampling is without replacement.

Regardless of whether the selection is with or without replacement, the population mean is estimated by the arithmetic average of the sample observations, that is,

$$\bar{y} = \frac{\Sigma y}{n}$$

A first step in computing an estimate of the standard error of the mean is to estimate the variance of individual values of x:

$$s^2 = \frac{\Sigma y^2 - (\Sigma y)^2/n}{n - 1}$$

In sampling with replacement (or from infinite populations), the standard error is

$$s_{\bar{y}} = \sqrt{\frac{s^2}{n}}$$

The finite population correction should be included if sampling is without replacement from a finite population:

$$s_{\bar{y}} = \sqrt{\frac{s^2}{n}\left(\frac{N - n}{N}\right)}$$

Confidence intervals are established as

$$\bar{y} \pm ts_{\bar{y}}$$

where t (2-tailed) has $n - 1$ degrees of freedom.

3-5 Sampling Intensity   To plan a timber inventory that is statistically and practically efficient, enough sampling units should be measured to obtain the desired standard of precision—no more and no less. As an example, one might wish to estimate the mean volume per acre of a timber stand and have a 95 percent probability of being within $\pm$ 500 bd ft per acre of the true mean. A formula for computing the required sampling intensity for simple random samples may be derived by transforming the relationship for the confidence limits on the mean (Sec. 2-13). Excluding the finite population correction, the formula may be expressed as

$$n = \left(\frac{ts}{E}\right)^2$$

where E is the desired half-width of the confidence interval and other symbols are as described in Chapter 2.

Solving this formula requires an estimate of the standard deviation expressed *in the same units* as the desired precision E. This estimate may be obtained by measuring a small preliminary sample of the population or by using the standard deviation obtained from previous sampling of the same or a similar population. The first method is likely to be most reliable, if the expense of a preliminary survey can be accepted. In the example proposed earlier, assume that preliminary measurement of 25 field plots provided the following data:

$$\bar{y} = 4{,}400 \text{ bd ft per acre}$$

$$s = 2{,}000 \text{ bd ft per acre}$$

The original objective was to be within $\pm$ 500 bd ft per acre, with a confidence level of 95 percent. For the 95 percent level, t is generally set equal to 2, although initial guesses of the sample size (and thus df and t) can be used in an iterative solution for a more refined estimate of sample size. In most cases, however, the precision of the other required information in the sample-size formula does not justify use of the iterative solution for t. In this example, the *desired* half-width of the confidence interval, $E = 500$, is substituted in the formula, along with the estimated standard deviation and a value of 2 for t:

$$n = \left[\frac{(2)(2{,}000)}{500}\right]^2 = 64 \text{ sample units}$$

When sampling without replacement from finite populations, the sample-size formula is

$$n = \frac{1}{\left(\dfrac{E}{ts}\right)^2 + \dfrac{1}{N}}$$

where N represents the number of sampling units in the population.

Formulas for calculating the required sample size for simple random sampling can be written in several ways. If the allowable error is expressed as a percent of the mean and an estimate of the coefficient of variation (CV) in percent is available, the required sample size (for infinite populations) can be calculated from

$$n = \left[\frac{(t)(\text{CV})}{A} \right]^2$$

where A is allowable error, expressed as a percent of the mean, and the other symbols are as previously described.

With an estimated coefficient of variation of 50 percent, for example, one might wish to determine the number of observations needed to estimate a population mean within $\pm$ 5 percent at a probability level of 0.80. In other words, the desired half-width of the confidence interval is specified as 5 percent of the mean. From Appendix Table 6, the t value (infinite df and probability column of 0.2) is read as 1.282. Therefore, the total number of sampling units required to achieve the specified precision is approximately

$$n = \left[\frac{(1.282)(50)}{5} \right]^2 = 164.4, \text{ or } 165, \text{ sample units}$$

Trial substitutions in this formula will demonstrate the fact that the number of samples required is increased *4 times* when (1) the coefficient of variation is doubled, as from 25 to 50 percent, or (2) the specified allowable error is reduced by one-half. These are important facts for consideration in balancing costs and desired precision in resource inventories.

The sample-size formula for sampling without replacement from finite populations (with allowable error expressed as a percent of the mean) is

$$n = \frac{1}{\left[\dfrac{A}{(t)(\text{CV})} \right]^2 + \dfrac{1}{N}}$$

As the population size N becomes large, results from this formula approach those from the formula for infinite populations.

3-6 Effect of Plot Size on Variability   At a given scale of measurement, small sample plots usually exhibit more relative variability (i.e., have a larger coefficient of variation) than large plots. The variance in volume per acre on ¼-acre plots is usually larger than the variance in volume per acre on ½-acre plots but slightly smaller than that for ⅕-acre plots. The relation of plot size to variance changes from one population to another. In general, large plots tend to have less relative variability because they average out the effect of tree clumps and stand openings. In uniform populations (e.g., plantations), changes in plot size have little effect on variance. In nonuniform populations, the relation of plot size to variance depends on how clumps of trees and open areas compare with the sizes of plots.

Although plot sizes have often been chosen on the basis of experience, the objective should be the selection of the most efficient size. Usually, this is the smallest size commensurate with the variability produced. Where the coefficient of variation has been determined for plots of a given size, the coefficient of variation for different-sized plots may be approximated by a formula suggested by Freese (1962):

$$(CV_2)^2 = (CV_1)^2 \sqrt{\frac{P_1}{P_2}}$$

where CV_2 = estimated coefficient of variation for new plot size
CV_1 = known coefficient of variation for plots of previous size
P_1 = previous plot size
P_2 = new plot size

Note that the same relationship can be applied with variances in lieu of coefficients of variation squared. If the coefficient of variation for ⅕-acre plots is 30 percent, the estimated coefficient of variation for ⅒-acre plots would be computed as

$$(CV_2)^2 = (30)^2 \sqrt{\frac{0.2}{0.1}} = 900(1.414) = 1,272.6$$
$$CV_2 = \sqrt{1,272.6} = 36 \text{ percent}$$

The coefficients of variation of 36 percent for ⅒-acre plots versus 30 percent for ⅕-acre sampling units may now be compared as to relative *numbers* of plots needed. Assume, for example, that the ⅕-acre plots produced a sample mean of 4 cd per plot, which is equivalent to 20 cd per acre. The sample standard deviation is 30 percent of this value, or ± 6 cd per acre. The total number of ⅕-acre plots needed to estimate the mean volume per acre within ± 2 cd at a probability level of 95 percent (approximating t as 2) is estimated as

$$n = \left[\frac{(2)(6)}{2} \right]^2 = 36 \text{ plots}$$

The reader should note that it is necessary to have the standard deviation and the allowable error in the same units before substitution in the formula. In this instance, these values are ± 6 and ± 2 cd per acre, respectively. For comparison with the preceding results, the standard deviation for ⅒-acre plots, expressed on a per acre basis, would be $0.36(20) = \pm 7.2$ cd per acre. The number of $\frac{1}{10}$-acre plots required to meet the previous standards of precision would be

$$n = \left[\frac{(2)(7.2)}{2}\right]^2 = 51.84, \text{ or } 52, \text{ plots}$$

The choice between thirty-six $\frac{1}{5}$-acre plots versus fifty-two $\frac{1}{10}$-acre plots is a decision that now rests on the relative time or costs involved. Some aspects of sampling "efficiency" are discussed in Section 3-21.

3-7 Systematic Sampling   Under this system, the initial sampling unit is randomly selected or arbitrarily established on the ground; thereafter, plots are mechanically spaced at uniform intervals throughout the tract of land. For example, if a 5 percent sample is desired, every twentieth sampling unit would be selected.

Systematic sampling has been popular for assessing timber and range conditions because (1) sampling units are easy to locate on the ground and (2) they appear to be more "representative" since they are uniformly spaced over the entire population. Although these arguments *may* be true, the drawback is that it is usually difficult—if not impossible—to estimate the variance (or standard error) for one systematic sample.

Rectangular spacings or square grid layouts may yield efficient estimates under certain conditions, but the accuracy can also be poor if there is a periodic or cyclic variation inherent in the population (Fig. 3-2). Furthermore, assessment of the precision presents a formidable problem, since simple random sampling techniques cannot be logically applied to systematic designs. An exception occurs where the elements of the population are in random order. In those rare cases in which this situation exists (and can be recognized), a systematic sample may be analyzed as a simple random sample. Nevertheless, it would be inaccurate to presume that most

FIGURE 3-2
Systematic sampling can be badly biased when applied to populations with periodic variation. *(Adapted from Philip, 1994.)*

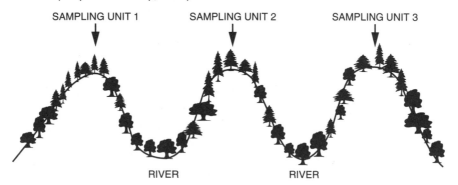

SAMPLING UNIT 1   SAMPLING UNIT 2   SAMPLING UNIT 3

RIVER   RIVER

populations of plant communities are in random order. Unfortunately, there is no practical alternative to assuming the population is in random order and using the formulas for simple random sampling when computing estimates from systematic samples. (Note that the standard error would be computed for sampling *without* replacement.) Although estimates of the mean are generally satisfactory, estimates of sampling precision based on such manipulations must be regarded, at best, as approximations.

In summary, experience has shown that systematic sampling is generally satisfactory for estimating means in typical forest conditions. When an objective numerical statement of precision need not be appended to inventory estimates, systematic sampling may provide more information for the time (or money) expended than simple random sampling. In cases in which estimates of variance are important or little is known about the basic characteristics of the population being sampled (e.g., the extent to which it falls into patterns), it is safer to select a random rather than a systematic sample.

STRATIFIED RANDOM SAMPLING

3-8 Stratifying the Population   In typical applications of stratified random sampling, a population is divided into subpopulations of known size, and a simple random sample of at least two units is selected in each subpopulation. This approach has several advantages. If the strata are constructed so that their averages are different and their variances are small in relation to the total population variance, the estimate of the population mean will be considerably more precise than that given by a simple random sample of the same size. Also, it may be desirable to have separate estimates for each subpopulation (e.g., for different vegetative types or administrative subunits), and it may be administratively more efficient to sample by subpopulations.

The first step in estimating the overall population mean from a stratified sample is to compute the sample mean $\bar{y}_h$ for each stratum. Stratum means are computed exactly the same as for simple random samples—that is, they are the arithmetic averages of the sample observations from an individual stratum. These stratum means are then combined into a weighted overall mean in which the weights are equal to the strata sizes. Thus the estimate of the overall population mean $\bar{y}_{st}$ would be

$$\bar{y}_{st} = \frac{\sum_{h=1}^{L} N_h \bar{y}_h}{N}$$

where L = number of strata

N_h = total number of units in stratum h $(h = 1, \ldots, L)$

N = total number of units in all strata $\left(N = \sum_{h=1}^{L} N_h \right)$

To determine the standard error of $\bar{y}_{st}$, it is first necessary to compute the variance among individuals within each stratum, s_h^2. These variances are computed in the same manner as for simple random sampling. Thus the variance for stratum I would be

$$s_I^2 = \frac{\sum y_I^2 - (\sum y_I)^2/n_I}{n_I - 1}$$

where n_I represents the number of sample units observed in stratum I.

From the stratum variances, the standard error of the mean is estimated as

$$s_{\bar{y}_{st}} = \sqrt{\frac{1}{N^2} \sum_{h=1}^{L} \frac{N_h^2 s_h^2}{n_h}}$$

when sampling is with replacement, and

$$s_{\bar{y}_{st}} = \sqrt{\frac{1}{N^2} \sum_{h=1}^{L} \left[\frac{N_h^2 s_h^2}{n_h} \left(\frac{N_h - n_h}{N_h} \right) \right]}$$

when sampling is without replacement. In the standard error formulas, $n_h =$ the number of units observed in stratum h.

Confidence intervals for the mean are computed as

$$\bar{y}_{st} \pm t s_{\bar{y}_{st}}$$

where the number of degrees of freedom for t can be approximated by

$$(n_1 - 1) + (n_2 - 1) + \cdots + (n_L - 1)$$

that is as

$$\sum_{h=1}^{L} (n_h - 1)$$

for moderate to large sample sizes within each stratum.

A stratified random sample may combine the features of aerial and ground estimating, offering a means of obtaining timber volumes with high efficiency. Photographs are used for area determination, for allocation of field samples by volume classes, and for designing the pattern of fieldwork. For each stratum, tree volumes or other data are obtained on the ground by conventional methods. In the example that follows, emphasis is on methods of allocating a fixed number of inventory plots among the various strata recognized.

Assume, for example, that a tract of land containing 300 acres has been subdivided into five distinct timber-volume classes (strata) by interpretation of aerial photographs. Using data from inventories in similar timber, it is possible to compute a preliminary approximation of the standard deviation for each stratum:

Volume class	Stratum area (acres)	Std. dev. (cords/acre)	Area × std. dev.
I	15	20	300
II	45	70	3,150
III	110	35	3,850
IV	60	45	2,700
V	70	25	1,750
Total	300	...	11,750

Assuming that a total of 150 sampling units will be measured on the ground, there are two common procedures for distributing the field plots among the five volume classes. These methods are known as *proportional allocation* and *optimum allocation*.

3-9 Proportional Allocation of Field Plots This approach calls for distribution of the 150 field plots in proportion to the *area* of each type. The general formula is

$$n_h = \left(\frac{N_h}{N}\right)n$$

For the five volume classes, the number of plots in each stratum would be computed as follows:

$$\text{Class I:} \frac{15}{300}(150) = 7 \text{ plots}$$

$$\text{Class II:} \frac{45}{300}(150) = 23 \text{ plots}$$

$$\text{Class III:} \frac{110}{300}(150) = 55 \text{ plots}$$

$$\text{Class IV:} \frac{60}{300}(150) = 30 \text{ plots}$$

$$\text{Class V:} \frac{70}{300}(150) = \frac{35 \text{ plots}}{150 \text{ plots}}$$

One disadvantage of proportional allocation is that large areas receive more sample plots than small ones, irrespective of variation in volume per acre. Of course, the same limitation applies to simple random and systematic sampling.

Nevertheless, when the various strata can be reliably recognized and their areas determined, proportional allocation will generally be superior to a nonstratified sample of the same intensity.

3-10 Optimum Allocation of Field Plots   With this procedure, which is sometimes called *Neyman allocation,* the 150 sample plots are allocated to the various strata by a plan that results in the smallest standard error possible with a fixed number of observations. Determining the number of plots to be assigned to each stratum requires first a product of the area and standard deviation for each type (Sec. 3-8). In general terms, for a sample of size n, the number of observations n_h to be made in stratum h is

$$n_h = \left[\frac{N_h s_h}{\displaystyle\sum_{h=1}^{L} N_h s_h} \right] n$$

The number of plots to be allocated to each stratum is computed by expressing each product of "area times standard deviation" as a proportion of the product sum (11,750 in this example). Thus the 150 field plots would be distributed in the following manner:

$$\text{Class I: } \frac{300}{11,750} (150) = \quad 4 \text{ plots}$$

$$\text{Class II: } \frac{3,150}{11,750} (150) = \quad 40 \text{ plots}$$

$$\text{Class III: } \frac{3,850}{11,750} (150) = \quad 49 \text{ plots}$$

$$\text{Class IV: } \frac{2,700}{11,750} (150) = \quad 35 \text{ plots}$$

$$\text{Class V: } \frac{1,750}{11,750} (150) = \frac{22 \text{ plots}}{150 \text{ plots}}$$

No matter which method of allocation is used, according to the general theory of stratified random sampling, field plots are located within each stratum by simple random sampling. In practice, systematic sampling is sometimes employed in lieu of simple random sampling. When systematic samples are taken within each stratum, it is commonly assumed that the within-stratum populations are randomly distributed and the standard formulas for estimating the mean, standard error, and confidence intervals are applied.

It will be noted that optimum allocation results in a different distribution of the field plots among the various strata. By comparison with proportional allocation, fewer plots are assigned to classes I, III, and V (i.e., those strata with relatively small standard deviations) and more plots are allotted to classes II and IV (those strata with relatively large standard deviations). Thus the relative variations within the volume classes more than offset the factor of stratum area in this particular example. When stratum areas and standard deviations can be determined reliably, optimum allocation is usually the preferred method for distributing a fixed number of inventory plots.

3-11 Sample Size for Stratified Sampling   Overall sample size needed to achieve a desired degree of precision at a specified probability level can be computed for stratified random sampling in a similar fashion as was shown for simple random sampling in Section 3-5. The exact form of the sample-size formula varies somewhat depending on the method of allocating the sample to the strata. When the sample is to be taken with proportional allocation, the sample-size formula is

$$n = \left(\frac{t}{E}\right)^2 \frac{\sum\limits_{h=1}^{L} N_h s_h^2}{N}$$

if the sampling is with replacement, and

$$n = \frac{N \sum\limits_{h=1}^{L} N_h s_h^2}{\dfrac{N^2 E^2}{t^2} + \sum\limits_{h=1}^{L} N_h s_h^2}$$

if the sampling is without replacement. In these equations, n is the total sample size, E is the desired half-width of the confidence interval, and other symbols remain as defined previously for stratified random sampling.

When optimum allocation is applied, the equations for overall sample size are

$$n = \left(\frac{t}{(N)(E)}\right)^2 \left(\sum\limits_{h=1}^{L} N_h s_h\right)^2$$

when sampling is with replacement, and

$$n = \frac{\left(\sum\limits_{h=1}^{L} N_h s_h\right)^2}{\dfrac{N^2 E^2}{t^2} + \sum\limits_{h=1}^{L} N_h s_h^2}$$

when sampling is without replacement.

REGRESSION AND RATIO ESTIMATION

3-12 Regression Estimation   Regression estimators, like stratification, were developed to increase the precision or efficiency of sampling by making use of supplementary information about the population being studied (Freese, 1962). In the case of regression estimators, the mean or total of a second variable that is related to the primary variable of interest is known. The mean or total of the supplementary variable for the population as a whole can be used to improve the precision with which one estimates the population average of the primary variable. In practice, the supplementary variable may be available through a population census (complete enumeration) completed at some time before the sample.

When regression estimation procedures are applied, two related variables (x and y) are measured on each sample unit. Although one is interested in the y variable, because the x variable is chosen such that it is more easily measured and is strongly correlated with the y variable, one can increase overall precision by devoting part of the sampling resources to observing the x variable. To use regression estimation one might measure x_i on all N units in a population to determine the population mean, μ_x. Then one measures x_i and y_i on a simple random sample of n observations and uses a regression model to combine these data for a precise estimate of the mean of y.

Use of the regression estimator will be illustrated by using data from the *Forestry Handbook* (Wenger, 1984). In this example, a forester wants to estimate the sawtimber volume on a 5-acre tract. The dbh of all 1,273 trees on the tract is carefully measured, and the population mean basal area per tree is computed as 1.40 sq ft. A simple random sample of 20 trees is then drawn, and both the basal area (x_i) and the volume (y_i) are determined. The data from the sample, along with summary statistics, are shown below:

Tree number	dbh (in.)	x = basal area (ft^2)	y = volume (ft^3)	r = ratio (y_i/x_i)
1	11.0	0.67	17.5	26.12
2	22.8	2.84	85.7	30.18
3	15.0	1.22	31.8	26.07
4	15.6	1.16	33.9	29.22
5	13.0	0.92	25.0	27.17
6	21.3	2.46	66.8	27.15
7	15.7	1.35	46.4	34.37
8	12.6	0.86	18.6	21.63
9	14.1	1.09	27.1	24.86
10	13.4	0.98	28.2	28.78
11	14.1	1.09	30.0	27.52
12	14.6	1.16	29.3	25.26
13	16.5	1.49	48.2	32.35
14	13.0	0.92	26.8	29.13

continued

continued

Tree number	dbh (in.)	x = basal area (ft²)	y = volume (ft³)	r = ratio (yᵢ/xᵢ)
15	13.4	0.98	22.9	23.37
16	11.8	0.76	24.3	31.97
17	14.1	1.09	25.0	22.94
18	15.4	1.28	32.1	25.08
19	17.7	1.71	49.6	29.01
20	15.4	1.28	32.9	25.70
Means		$\bar{x} = 1.27$	$\bar{y} = 35.1$	$\bar{r} = 27.39$
Variances		$s_x^2 = 0.287$	$s_y^2 = 284$	$s_r^2 = 10.78$

The linear regression estimate of the population mean of y $(\bar{y}_R)$ is

$$\bar{y}_R = \bar{y} + b(\mu_x - \bar{x})$$

where $\bar{y}$ is the mean of y and $\bar{x}$ is the mean of x from the simple random sample, μ_x is the population mean of x, and b is the linear regression slope coefficient (Chap. 2). To apply the linear regression estimator, one must assume a straight-line relationship between x and y, where the scatter of the y observations is roughly the same throughout the range of the x observations. Plotting y versus x (Fig. 3-3) shows that the required assumptions are reasonable for these data.

By carrying through with the required computations, the linear regression slope coefficient is estimated as

$$b = \frac{SP_{xy}}{SS_x} = \frac{167.2}{5.455} = 30.65$$

where SP_{xy} is the corrected sum of cross products of x and y and SS_x is the corrected sum of squares of x. Substituting the computed slope value and the sample means of y and x into the estimating equation for the population mean of y gives

$$\bar{y}_R = 35.1 + 30.65(1.40 - 1.27)$$
$$= 39.1$$

Note that if there is a positive relationship between x and y; and if $\bar{x}$ is below the true mean of x, μ_x, one would expect $\bar{y}$ to be below the true mean of y by an amount $b(\mu_x - \bar{x})$ where b, the slope coefficient, is the number of unit changes in y per unit change in x. Thus, in this example, $\bar{y}$ is adjusted upward; a downward adjustment in $\bar{y}$ would have resulted had the sample mean of x been greater than the population mean.

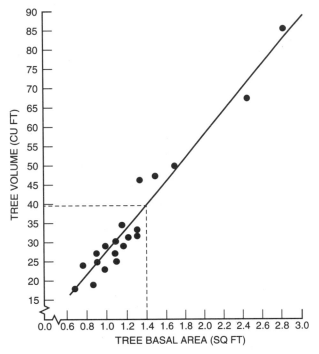

FIGURE 3-3
Relationship between basal area and volume from a simple
random sample of 20 trees. *(Adapted from Wenger, 1984.)*

The standard error of $\bar{y}_R$ can be estimated as

$$S_{\bar{y}_R} = \sqrt{S_{y \cdot x}^2 \left[\frac{1}{n} + \frac{(\mu_x - \bar{x})^2}{SS_x} \right] \left(1 - \frac{n}{N} \right)}$$

In the standard error formula, $s_{y \cdot x}^2$ is the estimate of variability of the individual
y values about the regression of y on x (Sec. 2-21); the computing formula is

$$S_{y \cdot x}^2 = \frac{SS_y - (SP_{xy})^2/SS_x}{n - 2}$$

where SS_y is the corrected sum of squares of y. For this example the estimated variance about regression is

$$S_{y \cdot x}^2 = \frac{5,393 - (167.2)^2/5.455}{18}$$

$$= 14.90$$

$$S_{\bar{y}_R} = \sqrt{14.90\left[\frac{1}{20} + \frac{(1.40 - 1.27)^2}{5.455}\right]\left(1 - \frac{20}{1{,}273}\right)}$$
$$= 0.8825 \text{ cu ft}$$

Note that for this small sampling fraction, the finite population correction factor $(1 - n/N)$ could be omitted with no significant impact on the result.

Confidence intervals on the mean can be computed as

$$\bar{y}_R \pm tS_{\bar{y}_R}$$

where t has $n - 2$ degrees of freedom. The 95 percent confidence interval for this example would be

$$39.1 \pm (2.101)(0.8825)$$
$$39.1 \pm 1.854$$
or
$$37.246 \text{ to } 40.954$$

3-13 Comparison of Regression Estimation to Simple Random Sampling
Suppose that a simple random sample of size 20 were taken in which the y values (cubic volumes) only were measured and that the samples were the same as that shown in Section 3-12. How would the estimates compare with those from the regression estimation procedure?

The mean of y would be estimated as

$$\bar{y} = \frac{\sum\limits_{i=1}^{n} y_i}{n} = \frac{702.1}{20} = 35.1$$

as compared with 39.1 for the regression estimate. The estimate of the standard error of the mean for this simple random sample would be

$$S_{\bar{y}} = \sqrt{\frac{S_y^2}{n}\left(1 - \frac{n}{N}\right)}$$
$$= \sqrt{\frac{284}{20}\left(1 - \frac{20}{1{,}273}\right)}$$
$$= 3.7386 \text{ cu ft}$$

as compared with 0.8825 for the regression estimate. Confidence intervals for a simple random sample are computed as

$$\bar{y} \pm tS_{\bar{y}}$$

where t has $n - 1$ degrees of freedom. Substituting in the appropriate values gives

$$35.1 \pm 2.093(3.7386)$$
$$35.1 \pm 7.825$$
or $\qquad 27.275 \text{ to } 42.925$

The standard error is much bigger and the confidence interval much wider for the simple random sample. In an actual application, the sample size for the simple random sample should be made somewhat larger if part of the sampling resources had not been devoted to measuring x, a supplementary variable. However, impressive gains in precision are possible with regression estimation when the correlation between x and y is near 1, as it is in this case ($r = 0.975$).

3-14 Ratio Estimation The regression estimation procedure presented in Section 3-12 is one of a family of related procedures that enables one to increase sampling efficiency by making use of information about a supplementary variable. Two other members of this family of related procedures will be presented: the ratio-of-means estimator and the mean-of-ratios estimator.

The *ratio-of-means estimator* is appropriate when the relationship of y to x is in the form of a straight line passing through the origin and when the variance of y at any given level of x is proportional to the value of x (i.e., the variance of y is not assumed constant, as in the regression estimation procedure). The ratio estimate of the mean of y is

$$\bar{y}_{RM} = R\mu_x$$

where $\quad R = \dfrac{\bar{y}}{\bar{x}}$ or $\dfrac{\Sigma y_i}{\Sigma x_i}$

μ_x = known population mean of x

For large samples (generally taken as $n > 30$), the standard error of the ratio-of-means estimator can be approximated by

$$S_{\bar{y}_{RM}} = \sqrt{\left(\frac{S_y^2 + R^2 S_x^2 - 2RS_{xy}}{n} \right)\left(1 - \frac{n}{N} \right)}$$

In practice, the most appropriate estimator should be chosen and applied in any given situation. For purposes of illustration, however, the ratio-of-means estimator will be applied to the same data as were used in the regression estimation example. First, the estimate of R is computed as

$$R = \frac{\bar{y}}{\bar{x}} = \frac{35.1}{1.27} = 27.64$$

and then the population mean of y is estimated as

$$\bar{y}_{RM} = R\mu_x = (27.64)(1.40) = 38.7$$

which is reasonably close to the estimate of 39.1 obtained with the linear regression estimator.

Although the sample size is small ($n = 20$), the formula for large sample sizes will be used to approximate the standard error of the estimate of the mean of y:

$$
\begin{aligned}
S_{\bar{y}_{RM}} &= \sqrt{\left(\frac{S_y^2 + R^2 S_x^2 - 2RS_{xy}}{n}\right)\left(1 - \frac{n}{N}\right)} \\
&= \sqrt{\frac{284 + (27.64)^2(0.287) - 2(27.64)(8.80)}{20}\left(1 - \frac{20}{1{,}273}\right)} \\
&= 0.9092 \text{ cu ft}
\end{aligned}
$$

Note that, despite having a sample of only 20 trees, this approximation is quite close to the estimate of 0.8825 computed for the linear regression estimator.

The second ratio estimator that is commonly used is called the *mean-of-ratios estimator*. This estimator is appropriate when the relation of y to x is in the form of a straight line passing through the origin and the variance of y at any given level of x is proportional to x^2 (rather than proportional to x as for the ratio-of-means estimator). As the name mean-of-ratios implies, the ratio (r_i) of y_i to x_i is computed for each pair of observations. Then the estimate of the mean of y for the population is computed as

$$\bar{y}_{MR} = R\mu_x$$

where $R = \dfrac{\sum\limits_{i=1}^{n} r_i}{n}$

To compute the standard error of this estimate, one must first estimate the variability of the individual ratios (r_i) as

$$S_r^2 = \frac{\sum\limits_{i=1}^{n} r_i^2 - \dfrac{\left(\sum\limits_{i=1}^{n} r_i\right)^2}{n}}{n - 1}$$

The standard error of the mean-of-ratios estimator $(\bar{y}_{MR})$ is then

$$S_{\bar{y}_{MR}} = \mu_x \sqrt{\frac{S_r^2}{n}\left(1 - \frac{n}{N}\right)}$$

Again, one can use the same data on tree basal area and volume to illustrate the computations with the mean-of-ratios procedure. The individual ratio values are computed from the data as $r_1 = 17.5/0.67 = 26.12$, $r_2 = 85.7/2.84 = 30.18$, ... $r_{20} = 32.9/1.28 = 25.70$. The mean of these r_i values is 27.39. Thus the estimate of the population mean of y would be

$$\bar{y}_{MR} = R\mu_x$$
$$= (27.39)(1.40) = 38.3$$

which is close to the ratio-of-means estimator value of 38.7.

The standard error of the mean for the mean-of-ratios procedure is computed as

$$S_{\bar{y}_{MR}} = \mu_x \sqrt{\frac{S_r^2}{n}\left(1 - \frac{n}{N}\right)}$$
$$= 1.4\sqrt{\frac{10.78}{20}\left(1 - \frac{20}{1,273}\right)}$$
$$= 1.0197 \text{ cu ft}$$

In this example, the standard error for the mean-of-ratios procedure is also near the comparable statistic for the ratio-of-means estimator (0.9092).

DOUBLE SAMPLING

3-15 Double Sampling with Regression and Ratio Estimators   Regression and ratio estimators require that the population mean of the supplementary variable x be known. When the population mean is not known, it is sometimes efficient to take a large sample in which x alone is measured. The purpose of this large sample is to develop a good estimate of μ_x, the population mean of x. In a survey designed to make estimates for some other variable y, it may pay to devote part of the resources to this preliminary sample, although this means that the size of the sample in the main survey on y may be reduced. This technique is known as *double sampling* or *two-phase sampling*. Double sampling is applied in cases where the gain in precision from using ratio or regression estimators (or other methods where supplementary information is required) more than offsets the loss in precision due to reduction in the size of the main sample.

Suppose that a large sample is taken in order to obtain a reliable estimate of the mean of x. On a subsample of the units in this large sample, the y values are also measured to provide an estimate of the relationship between y and x. The large sample mean for x is then applied to the fitted relationship to obtain an estimate of the population mean of y. If the relationship between y and x is linear and there appears to be a homogeneous variance of y at all levels of x, then the regression estimator would be appropriate. The computing formula for estimating the mean of y (denoted $\bar{y}_{Rd}$) when the linear regression estimator is applied in a double sample is

$$\bar{y}_{Rd} = \bar{y}_2 + b(\bar{x}_1 - \bar{x}_2)$$

where $\bar{y}_{Rd}$ = estimate of the population mean of y
  $\bar{x}_1$ = mean of x from the large sample
  $\bar{x}_2$ = mean of x from the small sample
  $\bar{y}_2$ = mean of y from the small sample
  b = linear regression slope coefficient computed as SP_{xy}/SS_x from the small sample

The standard error of $\bar{y}_{Rd}$ (denoted $S_{\bar{y}_{Rd}}$) can be estimated as

$$S_{\bar{y}_{Rd}} = \sqrt{S_{y\cdot x}^2\left(\frac{1}{n_2} + \frac{(\bar{x}_1 - \bar{x}_2)^2}{SS_x}\right)\left(1 - \frac{n_2}{n_1}\right) + \frac{S_y^2}{n_1}\left(1 - \frac{n_1}{N}\right)}$$

where $S_{y\cdot x}^2$ = variance about the fitted regression of y on x from the small sample
  S_y^2 = variance of the y values in the small sample
  SS_x = corrected sum of squares for x from the small sample
  n_1 = number in the large sample
  n_2 = number in the small sample
  N = number in the population

For sampling with replacement or for very small sampling fractions, the term $(1 - n_1/N)$ is omitted.

Confidence intervals at the 95 percent level can be approximated as

$$\bar{y}_{Rd} \pm 2S_{\bar{y}_{Rd}}$$

Ratio estimators can also be applied in a double-sampling context. The computing formulas for the ratio-of-means estimator are

$$\bar{y}_{\text{RM}d} = R\bar{x}_1$$

where $R = \bar{y}_2 / \bar{x}_2$

$$S_{\bar{y}_{\text{RM}d}} = \sqrt{\left(1 - \frac{n_2}{n_1}\right)\left(\frac{S_y^2 + R^2 S_x^2 - 2RS_{xy}}{n_2}\right) + \frac{S_y^2}{n_1}\left(1 - \frac{n_1}{N}\right)}$$

where S_{xy} is the estimated covariance of x and y, S_x^2 is the variance of the x values, and all other symbols remain as defined in this section.

In the case of the mean-of-ratios estimator, the estimating formulas for the mean of y and the standard error of the mean are

$$\bar{y}_{\text{MR}d} = R\bar{x}_1$$

where $R = \dfrac{\displaystyle\sum_{i=1}^{n_2} r_i}{n_2}$

$$S_{\bar{y}_{\text{MR}d}} = \sqrt{\bar{x}_1^2 \frac{S_r^2}{n_2}\left(1 - \frac{n_2}{n_1}\right) + \frac{S_y^2}{n_1}\left(1 - \frac{n_1}{N}\right)}$$

As before, the symbols remain as defined in this section and Section 3-14.

The total cost (C) of a double sample can be written as

$$C = n_1 C_1 + n_2 C_2$$

where C_1 is the cost per observation in the large sample, n_1 is the large sample size, C_2 is the cost per sample in the small sample, and n_2 is the small sample size. Part of the sampling resources are used to obtain the large sample, but C_1 is generally quite small compared with C_2; thus n_2 is not substantially less than if a simple random sample on y alone had been taken. However, it is worth emphasizing that a double-sampling design is feasible only if the gains due to using regression or ratio estimators (or other procedures that utilize supplementary information about the population) more than offset the smaller sample size for y.

3-16 Double Sampling for Stratification   Recall that stratified random sampling requires that the strata sizes be known in advance of sampling. If large gains due to stratification are expected, it may be efficient to use part of the sampling resources to estimate the strata sizes and then to draw a sample and compute population estimates based on the estimated strata sizes. This procedure is another example of double sampling.

In stratified random sampling the N_h values are assumed to be known. The N_h values can be estimated in a double-sampling design when they are not known in advance of sampling. Consider a case in which two timber types are represented on a tract for which an estimate of the overall volume is desired. Past experience indicates that large gains in sampling efficiency will be realized by stratifying by timber type. The area by timber type is not known, but aerial photos of the tract are available. A dot grid (Sec. 4-12) is placed over the tract, which, from a boundary-line survey, has a known total area of 40 acres. The sample size of the random dots is 1,000 (that is, $n_1 = 1,000$). Of the 1,000 dots, 600 fall in the pine type and 400 in the hardwood type. Thus the sizes of the two strata can be estimated as

$$\hat{N}_h = N\left(\frac{n_{1h}}{n_1}\right)$$

where $\hat{N}_h$ indicates the estimated value for N_h. For this example, the strata sizes are estimated as

$$\text{Pine: } \hat{N}_1 = 40\left(\frac{600}{1,000}\right) = 24$$

$$\text{Hardwood: } \hat{N}_2 = 40\left(\frac{400}{1,000}\right) = 16$$

Next a small sample ($n_2 = 20$) of ground plots is taken. This is to be a stratified sample with proportional allocation. The estimated strata sizes can be used to allocate the sample as follows:

$$\text{Number in pine type} = n_{21} = \left(\frac{24}{40}\right)20 = 12$$

$$\text{Number in hardwood type} = n_{22} = \left(\frac{16}{40}\right)20 = 8$$

That is,

$$n_{2h} = \left(\frac{\hat{N}_h}{N}\right)n_2$$

After the fieldwork is complete, the estimate of the overall population mean is computed as before, except that estimated weights rather than known weights are applied. Suppose the following strata statistics were computed from the field plots:

$$\text{Pine: } \bar{y}_1 = 5,400 \text{ bd ft/acre}$$

$$\text{Hardwood: } \bar{y}_2 = 3,800 \text{ bd ft/acre}$$

The estimated overall population mean would be

$$\bar{y}_{std} = \frac{\sum_{h=1}^{L} \hat{N}_h \bar{y}_h}{N}$$

$$= \frac{24(5,400) + 16(3,800)}{40}$$

$$= 4,760 \text{ bd ft/acre}$$

While the computations thus far are analogous to those in which the strata weights are known, the computation of the standard error of the mean is complicated by the fact that the strata sizes are now estimated rather than known. Provided the strata sizes are precisely estimated, the formula for the standard error of the mean given in Section 3-8 can be applied. The $\hat{N}_h$ values must be used in place of N_h, but the formula provides a reasonably good approximation of the standard error of the mean for double samples with reliable estimates of the strata sizes. Confidence intervals at the 95 percent level can then be approximated by setting the t value equal to 2. For additional information about double sampling for stratification and methods for estimating the associated sampling error, readers are referred to the more advanced books (such as Cochran, 1977) cited at the end of this chapter.

CLUSTER AND TWO-STAGE SAMPLING

3-17 Cluster Sampling   The objective of sample survey design is to obtain a specified amount of information about a population parameter at minimum cost. In some circumstances, cluster sampling gives more information per unit cost than do simple random or other alternative sampling methods. A *cluster sample* is a sample in which each sampling unit is a collection, or cluster, of elements (Scheaffer, Mendenhall, and Ott, 1996). There are two primary reasons for applying cluster sampling:

1 A list of the elements of the population may not be available from which to select a random sample, but it may be feasible to develop a list of all clusters. A forester may wish to estimate the mean height of all seedlings in a nursery. No list of seedlings exists, so it is not feasible to select individual seedlings at random. However, a sampling frame of all possible rows in the seedling beds can be constructed, a random sample of rows can be drawn, and heights of seedlings in the rows can be measured. The seedlings are the elements, and the rows are the clusters.

2 Even when a list of elements is available, it may be more economical to randomly select clusters rather than individual elements. In the case of estimating mean seedling height, even if a list of all seedlings were available, it may be more efficient to measure seedlings in rows rather than individual seedlings scattered over all nursery beds.

In summary, cluster sampling is attractive if the cost of obtaining a frame that lists all population elements is high or if the cost of obtaining observations increases as the distance separating the elements increases.

The first task in cluster sampling is to specify appropriate clusters. For maximum precision in cluster sampling, clusters should be formed so that the individuals within a cluster vary as much as possible. In practice, elements within a cluster are generally physically close together and, hence, tend to have similar characteristics. Consequently, the amount of information about the population parameters may not be increased substantially as the cluster sizes increase. As a general rule, the number of elements within a cluster should be small relative to the population size, and the number of clusters in the sample should be reasonably large.

The following notation, from Scheaffer, Mendenhall, and Ott (1996), will be used for cluster sampling:

N = number of *clusters* in the population

n = number of clusters selected by simple random sampling

m_i = number of elements in cluster i $(i = 1, \ldots, N)$

$$\overline{m} = \frac{\sum\limits_{i=1}^{n} m_i}{n} = \text{average cluster size for the sample}$$

$$M = \sum\limits_{i=1}^{N} m_i = \text{number of elements in the population}$$

$$\overline{M} = \frac{M}{N} = \text{average cluster size for the population}$$

y_i = total of all oberservations in the ith cluster

The estimator for the population mean of y is the sample mean $\overline{y}_c$, which is computed as

$$\overline{y}_c = \frac{\sum\limits_{i=1}^{n} y_i}{\sum\limits_{i=1}^{n} m_i}$$

The standard error of $\overline{y}_c$ can be estimated as

$$S_{\overline{y}_c} = \sqrt{\left(\frac{N-n}{Nn\overline{M}^2}\right) \frac{\sum\limits_{i=1}^{n} (y_i - \overline{y}_c m_i)^2}{n-1}}$$

where $\overline{M}$ can be estimated by $\overline{m}$ if M is unknown and where the 95 percent confidence interval can be approximated as

$$\overline{y}_c \pm 2S_{\overline{y}_c}$$

To illustrate cluster sampling, suppose that a forester wishes to estimate the average height of trees in a plantation. The plantation is divided into 400 row-segments, each containing an equal number of original planting spaces (but not an equal number of surviving trees due to differential mortality rates). A simple random sample of 20 row-segments is selected from the 400 segments that compose the plantation. All trees in the sampled segments are measured, and the following results obtained:

Number of trees (m_i)	Sum of tree heights (y_i)	Average height (ft)	Number of trees (m_i)	Sum of tree heights (y_i)	Average height (ft)
4	144	36	5	210	42
3	120	40	3	111	37
5	175	35	4	132	33
2	82	41	7	294	42
4	156	39	4	176	44
6	264	44	2	78	39
3	120	40	6	276	46
3	117	39	4	164	41
5	230	46	5	165	33
4	164	41	5	185	37
$\sum_{i=1}^{20} m_i = 84$			$\sum_{i=1}^{20} y_i = 3{,}363$		

The estimate of the population mean is

$$\overline{y}_c = \frac{\displaystyle\sum_{i=1}^{n} y_i}{\displaystyle\sum_{i=1}^{n} m_i} = \frac{3{,}363}{84} = 40.04 \text{ ft}$$

Since $\overline{M}$ is unknown, it must be estimated with $\overline{m}$ when computing the standard error of the mean; for this example

$$\overline{m} = \frac{\displaystyle\sum_{i=1}^{n} m_i}{n} = \frac{84}{20} = 4.2$$

Thus, the estimate of the standard error of the mean is

$$
S_{\bar{y}_c} = \sqrt{\left(\frac{400 - 20}{(400)(20)(4.2)^2} \right) \left(\frac{[144 - (40.04)(4)]^2 + \cdots + [185 - (40.04)(5)]^2}{19} \right)}
$$
$$
= 1.678 \text{ ft}
$$

While worthwhile gains in precision are theoretically possible with appropriate clustering, in practice this is generally not the case since clustering is typically based on physical proximity, which tends to ensure that the elements of a cluster are similar rather than dissimilar. Cluster sampling is applied for reasons of convenience and in an effort to achieve a given precision at a lower cost than is possible with alternative sampling designs. A cluster sample will be more precise than a simple random sample of the same size if the elements within clusters vary more on the average than do the elements in the population as a whole.

3-18 Two-Stage Sampling Clusters often contain too many elements to obtain a measurement on each, or the elements are similar and measurement of only a few elements provides information on the entire cluster (Scheaffer, Mendenhall, and Ott, 1996). When either situation occurs, one can select a simple random sample of clusters and then take a simple random sample of elements within each cluster. This procedure is called a *two-stage sample.*

To illustrate two-stage sampling, one might consider the problem of estimating the mean volume per acre on 640 acres of timberland that is divided into square blocks of 40 acres each. Assume that the 40-acre blocks are plantations of various ages and that the 40-acre plantations can in turn be subdivided into squares of 100 original planting spaces (the number of trees now present in each 100-space square will vary). Sampling units will be the square plots consisting of 100 original planting spaces. Since the 40-acre blocks are scattered, the travel time between blocks is large; however, it is obviously not possible to measure all elements (plots) in the blocks selected for sampling. Conversely, once a block is located, it would not be efficient to measure only one plot. Hence the designer of the inventory decides to select six blocks by simple random sampling and then to select three sample plots at random from each block selected in the first stage. In the sampling literature, the 40-acre blocks would be termed *primary sampling units* (primaries) and the plots *secondary sampling units* (secondaries). There will be n blocks (in our case, $n = 6$) selected with m plots (in this example, $m = 3$) selected within each of the selected blocks.

If y_{ij} designates the volume of the jth sample plot ($j = 1 \ldots m$) on the ith sample block ($i = 1 \ldots n$), the estimated mean volume per plot is

$$
\bar{y}_{ts} = \frac{\displaystyle\sum_{i=1}^{n} \sum_{j=1}^{m} y_{ij}}{mn}
$$

The standard error of the estimated mean for this case (in which the primaries are equal in size and the number of elements per cluster is equal) is given by (Freese, 1962):

$$S_{\bar{y}_{ts}} = \sqrt{\frac{1}{mn}\left[S_B^2 \left(1 - \frac{n}{N} \right) + \frac{nS_W^2}{N}\left(1 - \frac{m}{M} \right) \right]}$$

where n = number of primaries sampled

N = total number of primaries in the population

m = number of secondaries sampled in each of the primaries selected for sampling

M = total number of secondaries in each primary

S_B^2 = sample variance between primaries when sampled by m secondaries per primary

S_W^2 = sample variance among secondaries within primaries

The variances S_B^2 and S_W^2 are computed from the equations

$$S_B^2 = \frac{\dfrac{\displaystyle\sum_{i=1}^{n}\left(\displaystyle\sum_{j=1}^{m} y_{ij}\right)^2}{m} - \dfrac{\left(\displaystyle\sum_{i=1}^{n}\displaystyle\sum_{j=1}^{m} y_{ij}\right)^2}{mn}}{n-1}$$

$$S_W^2 = \frac{\displaystyle\sum_{i=1}^{n}\displaystyle\sum_{j=1}^{m} y_{ij}^2 - \dfrac{\displaystyle\sum_{i=1}^{n}\left(\displaystyle\sum_{j=1}^{m} y_{ij}\right)^2}{m}}{n(m-1)}$$

If the number of primary units sampled (n) is a small fraction of the total number of primary units (N), the standard error formula simplifies to

$$S_{\bar{y}_{ts}} = \sqrt{\frac{S_B^2}{mn}}$$

When n/N is fairly large but the number of secondaries (m) sampled in each selected primary is only a small fraction of the total number of secondaries (M) in each primary, the standard error formula can be expressed as

$$S_{\bar{y}_{ts}} = \sqrt{\frac{1}{mn}\left[S_B^2 \left(1 - \frac{n}{N} \right) + \frac{nS_W^2}{N} \right]}$$

The timber-volume estimation example will be carried through to illustrate the application of these formulas. Suppose the six primaries with three secondaries within each primary were selected with the following result:

Block (primary)	Plot (secondary)	Volume (ft^3)	Block (primary)	Plot (secondary)	Volume (ft^3)
1	1	500	4	1	210
	2	650		2	185
	3	610		3	170
2	1	490	5	1	450
	2	475		2	300
	3	505		3	500
3	1	940	6	1	960
	2	825		2	975
	3	915		3	890

Substituting into the computing formula for the estimated mean plot gives

$$\bar{y}_{ts} = \frac{\sum\limits_{i=1}^{n}\sum\limits_{j=1}^{m} y_{ij}}{mn} = \frac{(500 + 650 + \cdots + 890)}{3(6)} = \frac{10,550}{18} = 586.1 \text{ ft}^3 \text{ per plot}$$

In order to compute the standard error of the mean, the quantities S_B^2 and S_W^2 are first computed as

$$S_B^2 = \frac{\dfrac{(1,760^2 + \cdots + 2,825^2)}{3} - \dfrac{(10,550)^2}{(3)(6)}}{6 - 1}$$

$$= 250,188.9$$

$$S_W^2 = \frac{(500^2 + \cdots + 890^2) - \left(\dfrac{1,760^2 + \cdots + 2,825^2}{3}\right)}{6(3 - 1)}$$

$$= 3,869.4$$

Since the total number of 40-acre blocks in the 640-acre tract is $N = 16$ and the total number of plots in each 40-acre block is $M = 160$, the standard error of the mean, on a plot basis, is

$$S_{\bar{y}_{ts}} = \sqrt{\frac{1}{(3)(6)}\left[250,188.9\left(1 - \frac{6}{16}\right) + \frac{(6)(3,869.4)}{16}\left(1 - \frac{3}{160}\right)\right]}$$

$$= 93.628 \text{ ft}^3 \text{ per plot}$$

The 95 percent confidence interval, on a per plot basis, is approximated as

$$586.1 \pm (2)(93.628)$$
or
$$398.844 \text{ to } 773.356 \text{ ft}^3$$

For a fixed number of sample observations, two-stage sampling is usually less precise than simple random sampling. Two-stage sampling may, however, permit us to obtain the desired precision at a lower cost by reducing the cost per observation. Usually the precision and cost both increase as the number of primaries is increased and the number of secondaries per sampled primary is decreased. The total cost of the survey can generally be reduced by taking fewer primaries and more secondaries per primary, but precision usually suffers. References listed at the end of this chapter (Freese, 1962; Cochran, 1977) contain formulas for estimating the optimum number of secondaries per primary from the standpoint of giving the greatest precision for a given expenditure.

In the preceding examples, equal weight was given to all primaries. While equal weight is logical for the illustration in which the tract was divided into equal-sized blocks of 40 acres each, it may not be the most efficient selection scheme if the primaries vary greatly in size. If, for example, stands are used as the primary and the forest population of interest is composed of stands that vary widely in size, a two-stage sampling scheme that takes primary size into account may be desired. Extensions of two-stage sampling, including selecting primaries with probability proportional to size, are contained in numerous textbooks on sample survey techniques (such as Schreuder, Gregoire, and Wood, 1993; Shiver and Borders, 1996).

SAMPLING FOR DISCRETE VARIABLES

3-19 Simple Random Sampling for Attributes The formulas for estimates, standard deviations, confidence limits, etc., that were discussed in the previous sections apply to data that are on a continuous or nearly continuous quantitative scale of measurement. These methods may not be applicable if each unit observed is classified according to a qualitative attribute, such as alive or dead, deciduous or evergreen, forest or nonforest. Data such as counts in two mutually exclusive classes follow what is known as the *binomial distribution,* and slightly different statistical formulas are required.

Assume that a forester wishes to estimate the proportion of surviving seedlings in a young plantation. Because the plantation was planted at exact regular spacing, it is possible to choose individual seedlings for observation by randomly selecting pairs of random numbers and letting the first number stand for a row and the second number designate the seedling within the row. The forester can go to each randomly chosen spot and observe the seedling, recording its status as live or dead. A survey in which 50 seedlings were randomly chosen showed that 40 of these were alive. The estimate of the proportion alive ($\overline{P}$) is

$$\overline{P}_S = \frac{\text{number alive}}{\text{total number observed}} = \frac{40}{50} = 0.80$$

The standard error of $\overline{P}_S$ (Freese, 1962) is

$$S_{\overline{P}_S} = \sqrt{\frac{\overline{P}_S(1 - \overline{P}_S)}{n - 1}\left(1 - \frac{n}{N}\right)}$$

where n = number of units (seedlings in this example) observed. Given that the total number of trees in the plantation, N, is 5,000, one can substitute into the formula for the standard error of $\overline{P}_S$ to obtain

$$S_{\overline{P}_S} = \sqrt{\frac{(0.80)(1 - 0.80)}{50 - 1}\left(1 - \frac{50}{5,000}\right)}$$
$$= 0.05686$$

For large samples, the 95 percent confidence interval can be computed as

$$\overline{P}_S \pm \left[2S_{\overline{P}_S} + \frac{1}{2n}\right]$$

In this example the confidence interval, approximated with the formula for large samples, is

$$0.80 \pm \left[(2)(0.05686) + \frac{1}{2(50)}\right]$$

$$0.80 \pm 0.12372$$
or $\qquad$ 0.67628 to 0.92372

3-20 Cluster Sampling for Attributes   In attribute sampling, the cost of selecting and locating an individual is usually very high relative to the cost of determining whether or not the individual has a certain characteristic (Freese, 1962). Hence, some form of cluster sampling is usually preferred over simple random sampling. In cluster sampling, a group of individuals becomes the unit of observation, and the unit value is the proportion of the individuals in the group having the specified attribute. When clusters are reasonably large and all of the same size, the procedures for computing estimates of means and standard errors are similar to those for data measured on a continuous scale.

Returning to the example of estimating the proportion of surviving seedlings in a plantation, it would likely be more efficient to select plots of a given size and to determine the proportion of surviving trees in each plot. The plots, in this example, can be constructed such that there is an equal number of seedlings in each. Suppose that plots with 20 seedlings each are constructed; thus there are 250 possible plots in the population (i.e., $N = 250$). A simple random sample of size 10 gives the following results:

Plot no.	1	2	3	4	5	6	7	8	9	10
Proportion alive	0.75	0.80	0.80	0.85	0.70	0.90	0.70	0.75	0.80	0.65

If P_i is the proportion alive in the ith plot, the mean proportion alive would be estimated by

$$\overline{P}_c = \frac{\sum_{i=1}^{n} P_i}{n} = \frac{(0.75 + \cdots + 0.65)}{10} = \frac{7.7}{10} = 0.77$$

The variance of P can be computed as

$$S_{P_c}^2 = \frac{\sum_{i=1}^{n} P_i^2 - \frac{\left(\sum_{i=1}^{n} P_i\right)^2}{n}}{n-1}$$

$$= \frac{(0.75^2 + \cdots + 0.65^2) - \frac{(7.7)^2}{10}}{9}$$

$$= 0.005667$$

Substituting into the formula for the standard error of the mean gives

$$S_{\overline{P}_c} = \sqrt{\frac{S_{P_c}^2}{n}\left(1 - \frac{n}{N}\right)} = \sqrt{\frac{0.005667}{10}\left(1 - \frac{10}{250}\right)} = 0.02332$$

As in simple random sampling with data measured on a continuous scale, a confidence interval for the mean can be computed as

$$\overline{P}_c \pm t(S_{\overline{P}_c})$$

where t = the value of t with $n - 1$ degrees of freedom. For this example, the 95 percent confidence interval would be

$$0.77 \pm 2.262 \,(0.02332)$$
$$0.77 \pm 0.05275$$
or
$$0.71725 \text{ to } 0.82275$$

3-21 Relative Efficiencies of Sampling Plans   In controlling the intensity of various sampling plans, one must fix (1) the sample size, (2) the sampling variance, or (3) the cost. The best sampling design for a given estimation problem is one that provides the desired precision (in terms of confidence limits on the estimate) for the lowest cost or, if the cost itself is fixed in advance of sampling, the one that obtains an estimate of the greatest precision for the funds available.

The relative efficiency of alternative procedures or various sampling plans may, therefore, be calculated from the elements of cost and precision. If the costs required to achieve the *same* level of precision (sample variance) are known for plans A and B, then the relative efficiency of the two plans may be computed as a ratio of the two expenditures. For example, if plan A cost $800 and plan B achieved the same level of precision for $600, then the relative efficiency would be calculated as $800 \div 600 = 1.33$; that is, plan B is 1.33 times as efficient as plan A.

For those situations in which alternative plans do not result in the same level of precision, an index of efficiency may be computed as the product of the squared standard error and the cruising time (or expenditure) required. To illustrate, the following results of five inventories of the same tract may be considered:

Inventory plan	Standard error of mean (bd ft)	Time (hr)	(Standard error)^2 × time	Efficiency (rank)
A	215.6	10	464,834	3
B	192.5	11	407,619	2
C	224.0	8	401,408	1
D	316.8	6	602,173	5
E	267.8	8	573,735	4

In this example, inventory plan C proved most efficient (rank 1) because of the lowest product of squared standard error and time. Although plan B was more precise, it ranked second in overall efficiency because of the larger time factor. If this method of ranking timber inventory plans appears to penalize estimates with large standard errors, it should be remembered that halving a standard error requires not merely twice as many sampling units but *4 times as many.* On the other hand, time is regarded as a linear variable because reducing time by one-half is expected to lower cruising costs proportionately.

PROBLEMS

3-1 Using 1-acre plots and measuring volume in cords, a simple random sample (without replacement) of size 12 was executed on a 100-acre tract. Following are the plot observations:

Volume per acre (cords)		
34	42	31
27	48	38
29	35	41
29	42	19

a Estimate the mean volume per acre.
b Estimate the standard error of the mean.
c Compute 95 percent confidence limits for the mean.

3-2 Draw a simple random sample of at least 50 observations from a population in your field of interest. Then, **(a)** place 90 percent confidence limits on the sample mean, and **(b)** compute the total number of sample units that would be required to estimate the population mean within $\pm$ 10 percent at a confidence probability of 95 percent. (*Note:* Remember to apply the finite population correction, if applicable.)

3-3 Given the following sample data

x	y
5	20
6	18
8	21
9	30
10	38
12	45

and given μ_x (true mean of x) = 8.5,
a Estimate the population mean of y using the ratio-of-means approach.
b Estimate the population mean of y using the mean-of-ratios approach.

3-4 Select a local tract of land that can be subdivided into three or more strata according to vegetation, soil types, or timber volumes. Then design ground inventories to estimate some population parameter by **(a)** systematic sampling, **(b)** simple random sampling, and **(c)** an optimum allocation of field plots based on stratified random sampling. Use the *same number and size* of field plots for all three sampling designs. Compare results and relative efficiencies of the three systems.

3-5 An estimate of the mean volume (with associated measures of precision) is desired for a large timbered tract. Aerial photographs of the area are available. It is inexpensive to measure volume per acre on aerial photo plots but expensive to measure volume per acre by locating field plots on the ground. Because we expect a high correlation between volume measured on aerial photo plots and volume measured at the same point on the ground, a double sample is suggested. A large sample of aerial photo volume plots is established. The large-sample data are as follows:

n_1 = number of observations in large sample = 250
N = number of sample units in the population = 2,000
$\bar{x}_1$ = large sample mean of x = 1,800 ft³/acre

From the large sample photo points, 12 points are selected at random. Each of these 12 points is visited on the ground, and the ground volume per acre is observed. The small-sample data are shown below:

x, photo estimate (ft³/acre)	y, ground measured (ft³/acre)
700	900
1,700	2,400
1,000	1,450
3,400	3,700
1,300	1,900
1,400	1,500
3,000	3,700
3,000	3,200
2,200	2,300
1,700	1,900
2,500	2,800
2,700	3,300

a Plot the 12 pairs of observations. Does the variability of y appear to be approximately the same at all values of x? Does the relationship of y to x appear to be linear?

b Apply the linear regression estimate in a double-sampling context to estimate the mean volume per acre.

c Estimate the standard error of the mean from part b. Place 95 percent confidence limits on the mean.

d Assume that the values for y were obtained in a simple random sample of size 12. Estimate the mean volume per acre, estimate the standard error of the mean, and compute 95 percent confidence limits for the mean. Compare these estimates (realizing that if part of the sampling resources were not devoted to the aerial photo plot measurements, the simple random sample size could be increased slightly) with those from the double sample.

3-6 A forest scientist wishes to estimate the average leaf area on a plant. The relation between leaf area and leaf weight can be used to increase precision of the area estimate. Since the weight of individual leaves and the total weight and number of leaves on the plant can be determined quickly and inexpensively, this suggests use of regression estimates. On a plant the *true mean* (μ_x) weight per leaf was determined to be 2.5 g. Following is a sample of leaves that were weighed and for which leaf area was determined:

x, weight (g)	y, area (cm²)
2.0	161
2.5	193
1.7	129
2.1	174
3.0	232

    a Use a linear regression estimator to obtain an estimate of the mean area per leaf.

    b Calculate the standard error of the estimated mean area per leaf. (Total number of leaves on the plant $= 50$; i.e., $N = 50$.)

3-7 A nursery manager wants to estimate the average height of seedlings in the nursery beds. Because the beds were sowed at uniform spacing and because the germination percentage of seeds was high, it is possible to divide the beds into 500 equal-sized plots of 50 seedlings each. From these 500 plots (primaries), 10 are selected at random, and the height is measured on 5 randomly selected seedlings (secondaries) in each plot. The data are as follows:

Plot	Height of seedlings (in.)
1	12, 11, 12, 10, 13
2	10, 9, 7, 9, 8
3	6, 5, 7, 5, 6
4	7, 8, 7, 7, 6
5	10, 11, 13, 12, 11
6	14, 15, 13, 12, 13
7	8, 6, 7, 8, 7
8	9, 10, 8, 9, 9
9	7, 10, 8, 9, 9
10	12, 11, 12, 13, 12

    a Estimate the average height of seedlings in the nursery beds.

    b Compute the standard error of the mean from part **a**, and place 95 percent confidence limits on the mean.

3-8 In addition to proportional and optimum allocation (Secs. 3-9 and 3-10), sampling units in a stratified random sample can be allocated equally to strata. Under what circumstances would equal allocation be appropriate? Would equal allocation be appropriate for the example presented in Sections 3-8 through 3-10?

REFERENCES

Chojnacky, D. C. 1998. Double sampling for stratification: A forest inventory application in the Interior West. *U.S. Forest Serv., Rocky Mountain Research Sta., Res. Paper RMRS-RP*-7. 15 pp.

Cochran, W. G. 1977. *Sampling techniques,* 3d ed. John Wiley & Sons, New York. 428 pp.

Freese, F. 1962. Elementary forest sampling, *U.S. Dept. Agr. Handbook* 232, Government Printing Office, Washington, D.C. 91 pp.

Hamilton, D. A., Jr. 1979. Setting precision for resource inventories: The manager and the mensurationist. *J. Forestry* **77:**667–670.

Johnson, E. W. 2000. *Forest sampling desk reference.* CRC Press, Boca Raton, Fla. 985 pp.

MacLean, C. D. 1972. Improving inventory volume estimates by double sampling on aerial photographs. *J. Forestry* **70:**748–749.

Mesavage, C., and Grosenbaugh, L. R. 1956. Efficiency of several cruising designs on small tracts in north Arkansas. *J. Forestry* **54:**569–576.

Philip, M. S. 1994. *Measuring trees and forests,* 2d ed. CAB International, Wallingford, United Kingdom. 310 pp.

Reich, R. M., and Arvanitis, L. G. 1992. Sampling unit, spatial distribution of trees, and precision. *No. J. Appl. For.* **9:**3–6.

Scheaffer, R. L., Mendenhall, W. III, and Ott, L. 1996. *Elementary survey sampling,* 5th ed. Duxbury Press, Belmont, Cal. 501 pp.

Schreuder, H. T., Gregoire, T. G., and Wood, G. B. 1993. *Sampling methods for multiresource forest inventory.* John Wiley & Sons, New York. 446 pp.

Shiver, B. D., and Borders, B. E. 1996. *Sampling techniques for forest resource inventory.* John Wiley & Sons, New York. 356 pp.

Stuart, A. 1984. *The ideas of sampling.* Statistical Monograph No. 4. Charles Griffin and Company, Ltd., High Wycombe, England. 91 pp.

Vries, P. G. de. 1986. *Sampling theory for forest inventory.* Springer-Verlag, New York. 399 pp.

Wenger, K. F. (ed.). 1984. *Forestry handbook,* 2d ed. John Wiley & Sons, New York. 1,335 pp.

CHAPTER 4

LAND MEASUREMENTS

4-1 Applications of Surveying A knowledge of the elements of land surveying is essential to the inventory forester. Although foresters may rarely be responsible for original property surveys, they are often called upon to retrace old lines, locate property boundaries, and measure land areas. To adequately perform these tasks, foresters should be adept in pacing, chaining, running compass traverses, and various methods of area estimating. They should also be familiar with the principal systems of land subdivision found in a particular region of the country.

Surveying is the art of making field measurements that are used to determine the lengths and directions of lines on the Earth's surface. If a survey covers such a small area that the Earth's curvature may be disregarded, it is termed *plane surveying*. For larger regions, where the curvature of the Earth must be considered, *geodetic surveys* are required. Under most circumstances, the forester is concerned with plane surveying, namely, the measurement of distances and angles, the location of boundaries, and the estimation of areas.

The fundamental unit of horizontal distance employed by foresters is the *surveyor's, or Gunter's, chain* of 66 ft. The chain is divided into 100 equal parts that are known as links; each link is thus 0.66 ft, or 7.92 in., in length. Distances on all U.S. Government Land Surveys are measured in chains and links. The simple conversion from chained dimensions to acres is one reason for the continued popularity of this measurement standard. Areas expressed in square chains can be immediately converted to acres by dividing by 10. Thus a tract 1-mile square (80 chains on a side) contains 6,400 square chains, or 640 acres.

MEASURING DISTANCES

4-2 Pacing Horizontal Distances Pacing is perhaps the most rudimentary of all techniques for determining distances in the field; nonetheless, accurate pacing is an obvious asset to the timber cruiser or land appraiser who must determine distances without the aid of an assistant. With practice and frequently measured checks, an experienced pacer can expect to attain an accuracy of 1 part in 80 when traversing fairly level terrain.

The pace is commonly defined as the average length of two natural steps; that is, a count is made each time the same foot touches the ground.[1] A natural walking gait is recommended, because this pace can be most easily maintained under difficult terrain conditions. One should never attempt to use an artificial pace based on a fixed step length such as exactly 3 ft. Experienced pacers have demonstrated that the natural step is much more reliable.

In learning to pace, a horizontal distance of 10 to 40 chains should be staked on level or typical terrain. This course should be paced over and over until a consistent gait has been established. The average number of paces required, divided by the measured course distance, gives the number of paces per chain. Most foresters of average height and stride have a natural pace of 12 to 13 paces (double steps) per chain. It is also helpful to compute the exact number of feet per pace, for pacing is often relied upon in locating boundaries of sample plots during a timber cruise.

Uniform pacing is difficult in mountainous terrain, because measurement of horizontal rather than slope distance is the prime objective. Steps are necessarily shortened in walking up and down steep hillsides, and special problems are created when obstructions such as deep stream channels are encountered. Thus some individual technique must be devised to compensate for such difficulties.

The inevitable shortening of the pace on sloping ground can be handled by repeating the count at certain intervals, as 1, *2, 2,* 3, 4, 5, *6, 6,* and so on. Or if pace lengths are cut in half, counts may be restricted to every other pace. For obstructions that cannot be traversed at all (such as streams and rivers), the distance to some well-defined point ahead can be ocularly estimated; then a nonpaced detour can be made around the obstacle.

Paced distances should always be field-recorded as horizontal distances in chains or feet—not in terms of actual paces. When accurate mental counts become tedious, a reliable pacing record can be kept by a written tally or by using a hand-

---

[1]Some foresters prefer to count *every step* as a pace. Advantages claimed for this technique are (1) less chance of losing count, (2) fewer problems with fractional paces, and (3) easier adjustments for slope.

tally meter. The importance of regular pacing practice cannot be overstressed; without periodic checks, neither accuracy nor consistency can be expected.

4-3 Chaining Horizontal Distances   Foresters often find it necessary to measure horizontal distances using steel, cloth, or plastic tapes. Thus, a short description of chaining horizontal distances is provided. Two persons, traditionally called the head chainman and the rear chainman, are needed for accurate measurement with a tape. On level terrain, the chain can be stretched directly on the ground. If 11 chaining pins are used, one is placed at the point of origin, and the head chainman moves ahead with 10 pins and the "zero end" of the chain. The head chainman may carry the compass, keeping the party and the chain on the correct bearing line at all times; alternatively, the rear chainman can assume the duties of using a compass to maintain a straight and proper course.

A good head chainman paces the length of the tape in order to anticipate approximately when the chaining interval will be reached. When the end of the tape approaches the rear chainman, that person calls, "Chain!" The head chainman pulls the tape taut until the rear chainman yells, "Stick!" Upon sticking the pin, the head chainman replies, "Stuck!" The rear chainman picks up the first pin, and the procedure is repeated until the desired length has been measured. When the head chainman "sticks" the last pin, 10 chain intervals will have been covered. The rear chainman then passes the 10 pins that have been collected to the head chainman for continuing the measurement. A distance of 12 chains and 82 links is recorded as 12.82 chains.

In rough terrain, where the chain is held high off the ground, plumb bobs may be used at each end to aid in proper pin placement and accurate measurement of each interval. On steep slopes, it may be necessary to "break chain," that is, to use only short sections of the tape for holding a level line. In mountainous country where horizontal distance cannot be chained directly, slope distances can be measured and converted to horizontal measurements by use of a trailer tape. Experienced foresters can expect an accuracy of 1 part in 1,000 to 1 in 2,500 by careful chaining of horizontal distances.

The principal sources of error in chaining are (1) allowing the chain to sag instead of keeping it taut at the moment of measurement, (2) aligning incorrectly (i.e., not keeping on the proper compass bearing), (3) making mistakes in counting pins, and (4) reading or recording the wrong numbers.

Precautions must be observed in chaining to avoid loops or tangles that will result in a broken or permanently "kinked" tape. The ends of the tape should be equipped with leather thongs, and the loss of chaining pins can be minimized by tying colored plastic flagging to each. Steel chains should be lightly oiled occasionally to prevent rust and properly coiled, or "thrown," when not in use.

4-4 Methods of Tape Graduation   Tapes used in forest surveying are commonly 1 or 2 chains in length. They are usually graduated in link intervals, with

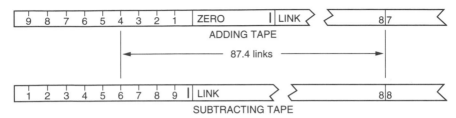

FIGURE 4-1
Reading fractional distances with adding and subtracting tapes.

the first (and often the last) link graduated in tenths to measure fractional distances. Two commonly used methods of graduating the fractional length at the zero end are shown in Figure 4-1. Before using an unfamiliar tape, one should carefully observe where zero is located and the method used to graduate the fractional link.

Tapes with an additional link beyond the zero end, graduated from zero to 1 link in tenths, are called *adding tapes*. With the rear chainman holding a full-link graduation, the head chainman reads the additional length beyond the zero mark and *adds* this reading to the full-link reading to obtain the distance between the two points. For example, if the rear chainman is holding 87 links and the head chainman 0.4, the distance between the two points is 87.4 links, or 0.874 chain.

The other type of tape commonly found in practice is graduated from zero to the last link by full-link intervals and with the first link (and often the last) further graduated in tenths; these are called *subtracting tapes*. With a full-link graduation held by the rear chainman, the head chainman reads the tenths from the graduated link at the zero end and *subtracts* the reading from the full-link value to obtain the distance between the two points. Thus if the rear chainman were holding 88 links and the head chainman were holding 0.6 link, the distance between two points would be 88.0 − 0.6, or 87.4 links. The adding tape is generally preferred, since errors in measurement and recording are less likely to occur.

4-5 Electronic Distance Measurement   Electronic distance measurement (EDM) instruments have been used for surveying since the late 1960s. With the advent of hand-held electronic laser-based instruments, EDM technology is now being applied to many forestry purposes. Liu (1995) evaluated an EDM device for conducting traverse surveys of forest stands. He found a mean closure precision of around $\frac{1}{500}$. This closure precision exceeds the accuracy generally specified for forest traverse work ($\frac{1}{100}$ or $\frac{1}{50}$) and surpasses the accuracy typically attained in forest conditions with traditional surveying equipment ($\frac{1}{65}$). In another evaluation of a possible application of EDM technology, Peet, Morrison, and Pellow (1997) used a hand-held electronic laser-based surveying instrument for stem mapping trees in forest plantations and found the practical working distance for such measurements to be approximately 20 m (66 ft).

Hand-held instruments provide the same basic information as a surveyor's standard total station, albeit at lower accuracy. A surveyor's total station measures, in a single instrument, the slant distance, azimuth, and vertical angle of a target object. From these three basic measurements, the (*x, y, z*) coordinates of a target object can be computed (Peet, Morrison, and Pellow, 1997). A surveyor's standard total station requires the use of a tripod (which is optional with hand-held devices) and is inherently more accurate, but hand-held devices provide sufficient accuracy for many purposes.

Hand-held instruments like the Criterion (Carr, 1992) determine distance by measuring the time of flight of short pulses of infrared light. Since the speed of light is constant, the time it takes the laser pulse to travel to the target and back is directly proportional to the distance to the target. When determining distance with a laser device, the accuracy is affected by the surface of the object. Hence, for the most precise results, a reflector is attached to the object of interest when distances are measured. Currently available hand-held instruments are highly efficient for measuring distances when 10 cm (4 in.) accuracy is sufficient.

Laser EDM devices are simple and easy to use. The digital display feature eliminates the need to interpret analog scales on conventional surveying instruments, thus speeding instrument reading time and reducing recording errors. In addition to surveying functions, tree measurement (height, diameter at any height) features are often incorporated into a single unit. A microprocessor is built into these sophisticated instruments to provide basic calculations and a serial interface to other devices is provided for further computations (e.g., area determination or tree volumes).

USING MAGNETIC COMPASSES

4-6 Nomenclature of the Compass   In elemental form, a compass consists of a magnetized needle on a pivot point, enclosed in a circular housing that has been graduated in degrees. Because the Earth acts as a huge magnet, compass needles in the northern hemisphere point in the direction of the horizontal component of the magnetic field, commonly termed *magnetic north.* If a sighting base is attached to the compass housing, it is then possible to measure the angle between the line of sight and the position of the needle. Such angles are referred to as magnetic *bearings,* or *azimuths.*

Bearings are horizontal angles that are referenced to one of the quadrants of the compass, namely, NE, SE, SW, or NW. Azimuths are comparable angles measured clockwise from due north, thus reading from 0 to 360°. Relationships between bearings and azimuths are illustrated in Figure 4-2. It will be seen that a bearing of N60°E corresponds to an azimuth of 60°, while a bearing of S60°W is the same as an azimuth of 240°. The angle formed between magnetic north and true north is called *magnetic declination,* and allowance must be made for this factor in converting magnetic bearings and azimuths to true angular readings.

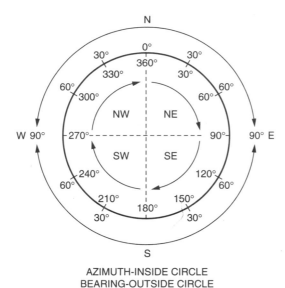

AZIMUTH-INSIDE CIRCLE
BEARING-OUTSIDE CIRCLE

FIGURE 4-2
Relationship of compass
bearings and azimuths.

4-7 Magnetic Declination In North America, corrections may be required for either *east* or *west* declination, the former when the north magnetic pole is east of true north and the latter when it is west of true north. Isogonic charts illustrating magnetic declination are issued periodically by government agencies (Fig. 4-3); recent, as well as past, information on magnetic declination can also be obtained from the Internet. On isogonic charts, points having equal declination are connected by lines known as *isogons*. The line of zero declination (no corrections required) passing through the eastern section of the country is called the *agonic line*. It will be noted that areas east of the agonic line have west declination, while areas west of the agonic line have east declination.

The agonic line has been shifting westward at a rate of approximately 1 min per year. In some parts of the conterminous United States, however, the change in declination is as high as 4 to 5 min annually. Because the position of the north magnetic pole is constantly shifting, it is important that current declination values be used in correcting magnetic bearings. Where reliable data cannot be obtained from isogonic charts, the amount of declination can be determined by establishing a true north-south line through observations on the sun or Polaris, the North Star. The magnetic bearing of this true line provides the declination for that locality. As an alternative to this approach, any existing survey line whose true bearing is known can be substituted.

4-8 Allowance for Declination In establishing or retracing property lines, angles should preferably be recorded as *true* bearings or azimuths. The simplest and most reliable technique for handling declination is to set the allowance directly on

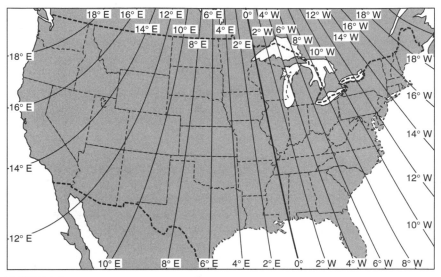

FIGURE 4-3
Magnetic declination chart of the conterminous United States, epoch 2000. *(Figure produced by L. R. Newitt, Geological Survey of Canada, Natural Resources Canada, using data from Geomagnetic Reference Field 2000.)*

the compass itself. Thus the graduated degree circle must be rotated until the north end of the compass needle reads true north when the line of sight points in that direction. For most compasses, this requires that the graduated degree circle be turned counterclockwise for east declination and clockwise for west declination.

When there is no provision for setting the declination directly on the compass, the proper allowance can be made mentally in the field, or magnetic bearings may be recorded and corrected later in the office. For changing magnetic azimuths to true readings, east declinations are added and west declinations are subtracted. Thus if a magnetic azimuth of 105° is recorded where the declination is 15° east, the true azimuth would be 120°.

Changing magnetic bearings to true bearings is slightly more confusing than handling azimuths because declinations must be added in two quadrants and subtracted in the other two. The proper algebraic signs to be used in making such additions or subtractions are illustrated in Figure 4-4.

Accordingly, if a magnetic bearing of S40°E is recorded where the declination is 5° west, the true bearing (obtained by addition) would be S45°E. In those occasional situations in which true bearings and azimuths must be converted back to magnetic readings, all algebraic signs in Figure 4-4 should be reversed.

4-9 Use of the Compass   Whether hand or staff compasses are used, care must be exercised to avoid local magnetic attractions such as wire fences, overhead

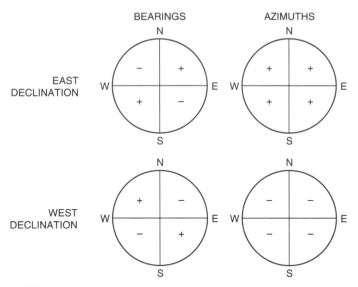

FIGURE 4-4
Algebraic signs for changing magnetic bearings and azimuths to true
angles.

cables, and iron deposits. In running a traverse, "backsights" of 180° should be taken
to check all compass bearings. When such backsights fail to agree with foresights
and no instrument errors can be detected, it is likely that some form of local attraction is present. Here it may be necessary to shorten or prolong the bearing line in
question so that a new turning point outside the attraction area can be used for the
compass setup. Compasses having needles immersed in liquid are generally less
susceptible to local attractions than nondampened types.

   Most good compasses are provided with a means of clamping the needle in a
fixed position while the instrument is being transported. After each bearing is read,
the needle should be tightened before moving to a new compass position; adherence to this practice will save considerable wear on the sensitive needle pivot
point. To ensure accurate compass readings, novices must be cautious to see that
(1) the compass is perfectly level, (2) the sights are properly aligned, (3) the needle swings freely before settling, and (4) all readings are taken from the *north end*
of the needle. Hand compass shots should not normally exceed 5 chains, and staff
compass sights should be limited to about 10 chains per setup.

AREA DETERMINATION

   4-10 Simple Closed Traverse   For purposes of this discussion, it is assumed
that the primary objectives of a field survey are to locate the approximate boundaries

of a tract and determine the area enclosed. Where there are no ownership disputes involved, a simple closed traverse made with staff compass and chain will often suffice for the purposes stated. For most surveys, three persons constitute a minimum crew, and a fourth may be used to advantage. The party chief establishes compass lines and records field notes, two individuals chain horizontal distances, and the fourth member handles a range pole at each compass station.

The most reliable property corner available is selected as a starting point; the traverse may be run clockwise or counterclockwise around the tract from this origin. Backsights and frontsights should be taken on each line and numbered stakes driven at all compass stations. Immediately upon completion of the traverse, *interior angles* should be computed. If bearings have been properly read and recorded, the sum of all the interior angles should be equal to $(n - 2)$ $180°$, where n is the number of sides in the traverse.

After interior angles have been checked, the traverse should be plotted at a convenient scale (e.g., 10 chains per in.). If horizontal distances between stations have been correctly chained, the plotted traverse should appear to "close." At this point, the tract area included may be accurately computed by the double meridian distance (DMD) method, or the area can be closely approximated by other techniques. DMD procedures are detailed in all surveying textbooks and computer software is readily available to implement these procedures; hence this approach will not be presented here. Graphical techniques, dot grids, planimeters, and transects are often used by foresters in estimating areas.

4-11 Graphical Area Determination   It may be presumed that a closed compass traverse is plotted at a scale of 10 chains per in. on cross-section paper having 100 subdivisions per sq in. All 1-in. squares thus represent 10 acres, and small squares are 0.1 acre. The total acreage can be quickly determined by counting all small squares enclosed. Where less than one-half of a square is inside the tract boundary, it is ignored; squares bisected by an exterior line are alternately counted and disregarded. The method is fast and reasonably accurate when traverses are correctly plotted and when finely subdivided cross-section paper is employed.

4-12 Dot Grids   If a piece of clear tracing material were placed over a sheet of cross-section paper and pin holes punched at all grid intersections, the result would be a dot grid. Thus dot grid and graphical methods of area determination are based on the same principle; dots *representing* squares or rectangular areas are merely counted in lieu of the squares themselves. The principal gain enjoyed is that fractional squares along tract boundaries are less troublesome, for the dot determines whether or not the square is to be tallied. If an area is mapped at a scale of 10 chains per in., as in the previous example, and a grid having 25 dots per sq in. is used, each dot will represent $^{10}\!/_{25}$, or 0.4, acre.

Dot grids are commonly used to approximate areas on aerial photographs as well as maps. If the terrain is essentially level and photo scales can be accurately

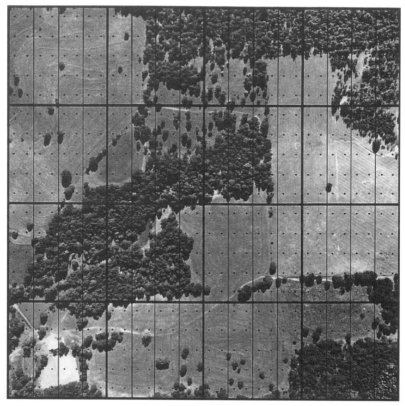

FIGURE 4-5
Dot grid positioned over part of an aerial photograph. Photo scale is 566 ft/in., or about 7.35 acres/sq in. As there are 40 dots per sq in., each dot has a conversion value of approximately 0.18 acre. *(Courtesy Tobin Surveys, Inc.)*

determined, this technique provides a quick and easy method of area estimation (Fig. 4-5). In regions of rough topography where photographic scales fluctuate widely, area measurements should be made on maps of controlled scale rather than directly on contact prints. Additional uses of aerial photographs are given in Chapter 13.

The optimum number of dots to be counted per square inch depends on the map scale employed, size of area involved, and precision desired. Grids commonly used by foresters may have from 4 to more than 100 dots per sq in. Denser grids are used when the size of the region is small or when more precision is needed. Grids with low dot densities are used for larger tracts or when less precision is needed. In all cases, however, it is recommended that an *average* dot count be obtained by several random orientations of a grid over the same area.

In summary, dot grids are a relatively simple and inexpensive tool for estimating areas on maps or photographs. However, care must be taken because dot grids are considered to be a less precise method than planimeters for area determination.

4-13 Planimeters   A planimeter is a device designed to estimate map or photo area; it is composed of three basic parts: a weighted polar arm of fixed length, a tracer arm hinged on the unweighted end of the polar arm, and a rolling wheel that rests on the map and to which is attached a vernier scale.

There are two basic types of planimeter, polar compensating and linear rolling. A *polar compensating planimeter* rotates around a fixed point and is limited in the sizes of the areas it can measure. A *linear rolling planimeter* has no fixed point and thus is not limited by a fixed point. Both types of planimeter are available in electronic form, in which the results can be read directly from a display on the device.

In use, the pointer of the instrument is run around the boundaries of an area in a *clockwise* direction; usually the perimeter is traced two or three times for an average reading. From the vernier scale, the area in square inches (or other units) is read directly and converted to desired area units on the basis of the map or photo scale. Prolonged use of the planimeter is somewhat tedious, and a steady hand is essential for tracing irregular tract boundaries.

It is often useful to check planimeter estimates of area by use of dot grids, and vice versa. Relative accuracy of the two methods can be approximated by measuring a few tracts of known area. Since individual preferences vary, it may also be informative to compare the *time* required for each estimation technique.

4-14 Transects   The transect method is basically a technique for proportioning a known area among various types of land classifications, such as forests, cultivated fields, and urban uses. An engineer's scale is aligned on a photograph or map so as to cross topography and drainage at right angles. The length of each type along the scale is typically recorded to the nearest 0.1 in. Proportions are developed by relating the total measure of a given classification to the total linear distance. For example, if 10 equally spaced, parallel lines 15 in. long are established on a given map, the total transect length is 150 in. If forest land is intercepted for a total measure of 30 in., this particular classification would be assigned an acreage equivalent to $^{30}/_{150}$, or 20 percent, of the total area. The transect method is simple and requires no special equipment when lines are established with an engineer's scale. Common area conversions for the English and metric systems are given in Table 4-1.

TABLE 4-1
CONVERSIONS FOR SEVERAL UNITS OF AREA MEASUREMENT

Square feet	Square chains	Acres	Square miles	Square meters	Hectares	Square kilometers
4,356	1	0.1	0.000156	404.687	0.040469	0.000405
43,560	10	1	0.0015625	4,046.87	0.404687	0.004047
27,878,400	6,400	640	1	2,589,998	258.9998	2.589998
107,638.7	24.7104	2.47104	0.003861	10,000	1	0.01
10,763,867	2,471.04	247.104	0.386101	1,000,000	100	1

4-15 Topographic Maps   Topographic quadrangle maps (Fig. 4-6) have been prepared for sizable areas of the United States by various governmental agencies. Persons concerned with land surveying often find such maps useful in retracing ownership lines and estimating areas. Topographic maps contain information important to foresters. *Contours,* or lines connecting points of equal elevation, help forest managers visualize the terrain. Roads are numbered and named, and the names of larger streams are also present. Features such as buildings and cemeteries are shown on such maps and are often helpful when locating the property of interest. Current indexes showing map coverage available in each of the 50 states may be obtained free by contacting the U.S. Geological Survey (USGS).

FIGURE 4-6
Portion of a U.S. Geological Survey 7 1/2-min topographic quadrangle map showing the Hayters Gap, Virginia, area. *(Photograph by Rick Griffiths.)*

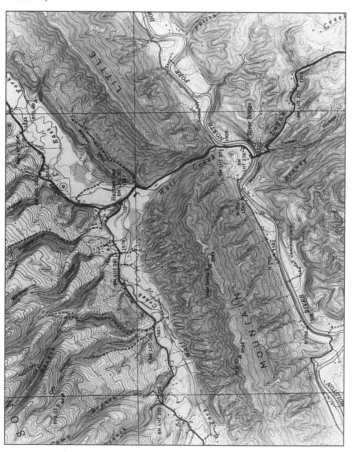

The national topographic map series includes quadrangles and other map series published by the USGS. A map series is a family of maps conforming to the same specifications or having some common unifying characteristic (such as scale). Adjacent maps of the same quadrangle series can generally be combined to form a single large map. The principal map series and their essential characteristics are tabulated below:

Map series	Scale	Standard quadrangle size (latitude-longitude)
7 ½ min	1:24,000	7 ½ × 7 ½ min
Puerto Rico 7 ½ min	1:20,000	7 ½ × 7 ½ min
15 min	1:62,500	15 × 15 min
Alaska 1:63,360	1:63,360	16 × 20 to 36 min
U.S. 1:250,000	1:250,000	1 × 2°
U.S. 1:1,000,000	1:1,000,000	4 × 6°

Maps of Alaska and Hawaii may vary from these standards. The first all-metric topographic maps published by the USGS cover portions of Alaska. Map scale has been set at 1:25,000, and contour intervals are 5, 10, or 20 m. Distances, spot elevations, and similar data are shown in both metric and English units.

COLONIAL LAND SUBDIVISION

4-16 Metes and Bounds Surveys   A sizable segment of the United States, notably in the original 13 colonies, was subdivided and passed into private ownerships prior to the inauguration of a system for disposal of public lands in 1785. Many of these early land holdings were marked off and described by "metes and bounds," a procedure sometimes facetiously referred to as "leaps and bounds."

The term *mete* implies an act of metering, measuring, and assigning by measure, and *bounds* refers to property boundaries or the limiting extent of an ownership. In some instances, older metes and bounds surveys may consist entirely of descriptions rather than actual measurements, e.g., "starting at a pine tree blazed on the east side, thence along a hedgerow to a granite boulder on the bank of the Wampum River, thence along the river to the intersection of Cherokee Creek . . . ," etc. Fortunately, most metes and bounds descriptions are today referenced by bearings, distances, and permanent monuments. Even so, parcels of land are shaped in unusual and seemingly haphazard patterns, and a multitude of legal complexities can be encountered in attempting to establish the location of a disputed boundary along an old stone fence that disintegrated 50 years ago. Descriptions of metes and bounds surveys can ordinarily be obtained from plat books at various county court houses.

THE U.S. PUBLIC LAND SURVEY

4-17 History   Most of the United States west of the Mississippi River and north of the Ohio River, plus Alabama, Mississippi, and portions of Florida, has been subdivided in accordance with the U.S. Public Land Survey (Fig. 4-7). The first law governing public land surveys was enacted by Congress in 1785. That part of the Northwest Territory which later became the state of Ohio was the experimental area for the development of the rectangular system. The original intent was to establish *townships* exactly 6 miles square, followed by subdivision into 36 sections of exactly 1 mile square each. At first, no allowance was made for curvature of the Earth, and numerous problems resulted. However, survey rules were revised by later acts of Congress, and the present system evolved as a culmination of these changes.

Adoption of a rectangular system marked the transition from metes and bounds surveys that prevailed in most of the colonial states to a systematic method for describing the public lands. Surveyors responsible for the earliest public land surveys were faced with such obstacles as crude instruments, unfavorable or dangerous field conditions, and changing survey rules. Consequently, survey lines and corners in the field were not always located with the desired precision. To eliminate litigation and costly resurveys, the original corners as established on the ground legally stand as the true corners, regardless of irregularities or inconsistencies.

4-18 The Method of Subdivision   The origin of a system begins with an *initial point,* usually established by astronomical observation. Passing through and extending outward from the initial point is a true north-south line known as a *principal meridian* and a true east-west *base line* that corresponds to a parallel of latitude. These two lines constitute the main axes of a system, and there are more than 30 such systems in existence (Fig. 4-7). Each principal meridian is referenced by a name or number, and the meridian is marked on the ground as a straight line. The base line is curved, being coincident with a geographic parallel. Starting at the initial point, the area to be surveyed is first divided into *tracts* approximately 24 miles square, followed by subdivision into 16 *townships* approximately 6 miles square, and then into 36 sections approximately 1 mile square. An idealized system is shown in Figure 4-8.

4-19 The 24-Mile Tracts   At intervals of 24 miles north and south of the base line, *standard parallels* are extended east and west of the principal meridian. These parallels are numbered north and south from the base line, as "first standard parallel north," and so on. At 24-mile intervals along the base line and along all standard parallels, *guide meridians* are run on *true north* bearings; these lines thus correspond to geographic meridians of longitude. Each guide meridian starts from a standard corner on the base line or on a standard parallel and ends at a closing corner on the next standard parallel to the north. Standard parallels are never

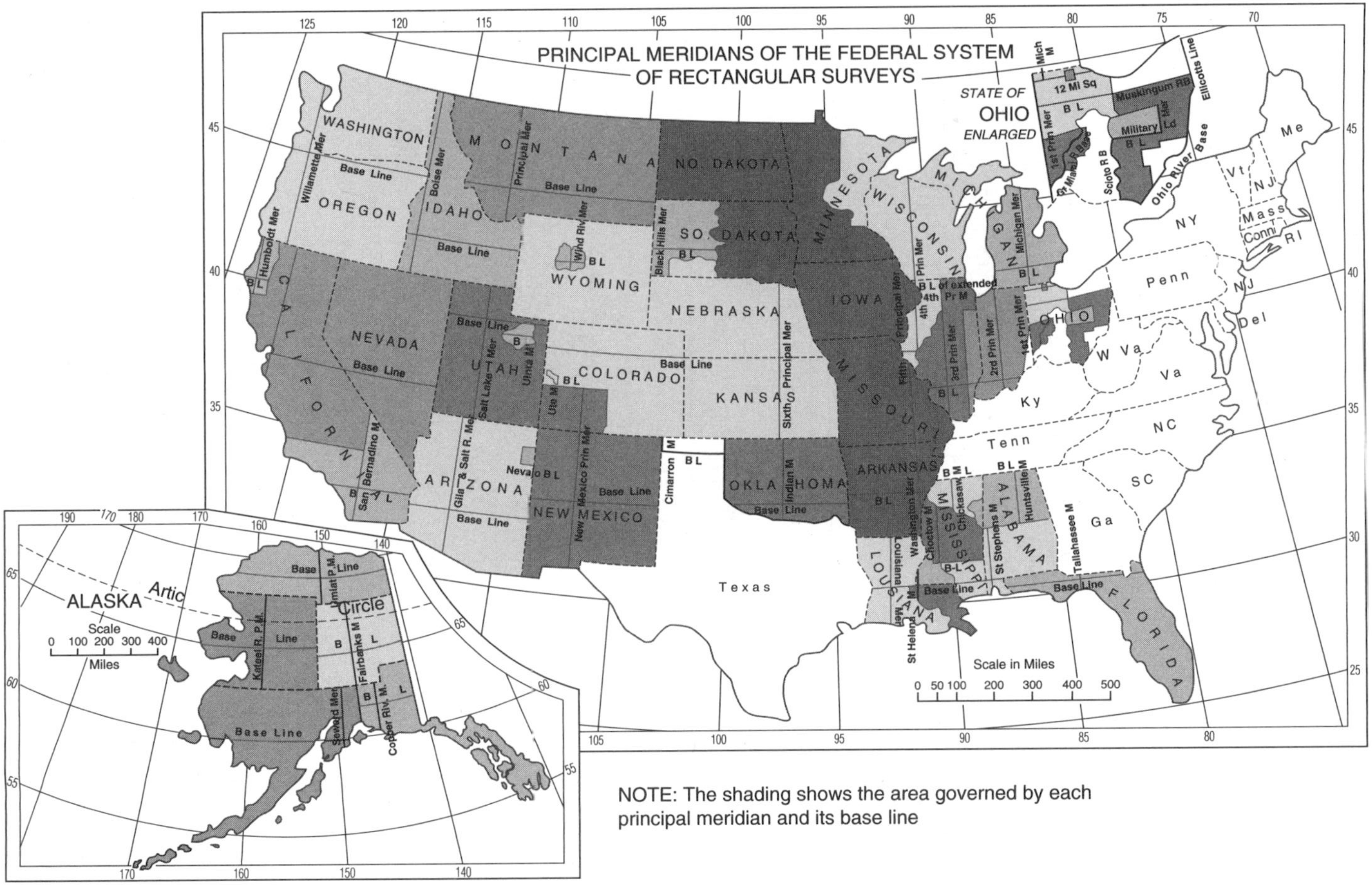

PRINCIPAL MERIDIANS OF THE FEDERAL SYSTEM OF RECTANGULAR SURVEYS

STATE OF OHIO ENLARGED

NOTE: The shading shows the area governed by each principal meridian and its base line

Scale in Miles

0 50 100 200 300 400 500

ALASKA

Scale
0 100 200 300 400
Miles

FIGURE 4-7
States subdivided under the U.S. Public Land Survey. *(Courtesy U.S. Department of the Interior.)*

85

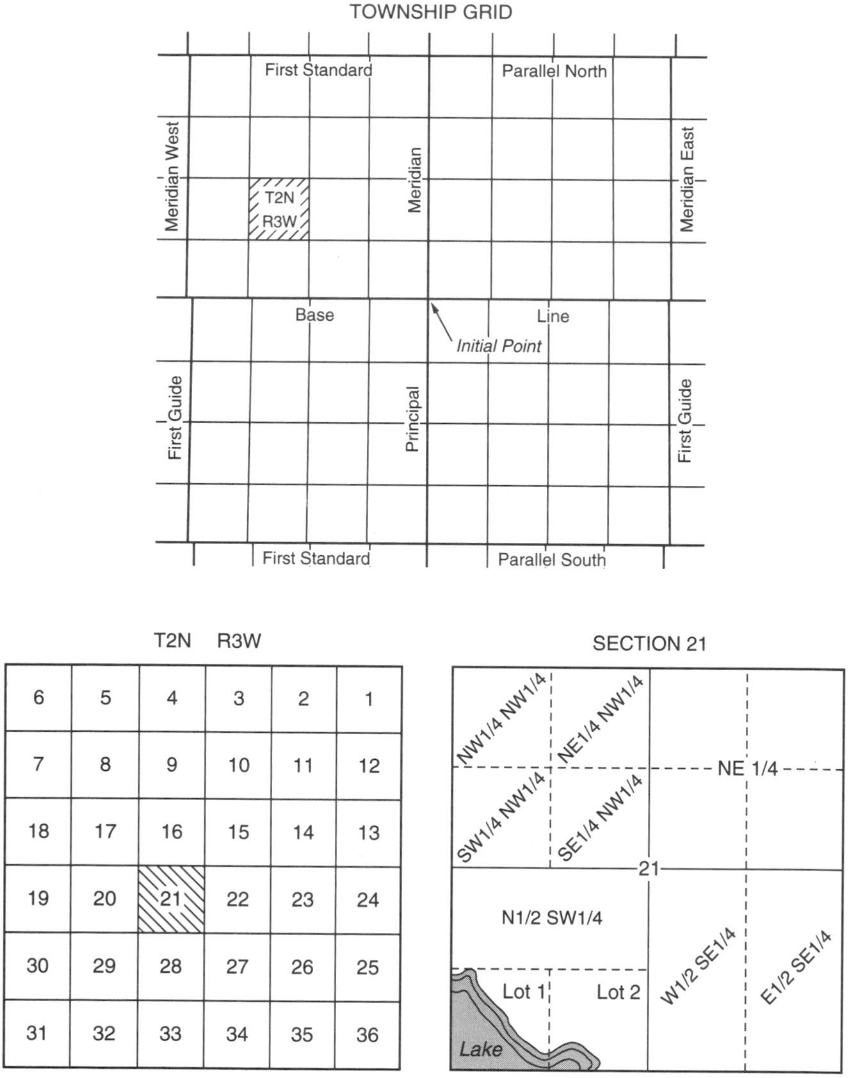

TOWNSHIP GRID

T2N   R3W

6	5	4	3	2	1
7	8	9	10	11	12
18	17	16	15	14	13
19	20	21	22	23	24
30	29	28	27	26	25
31	32	33	34	35	36

SECTION 21

FIGURE 4-8
Idealized subdivision of townships and sections.

crossed by guide meridians. Guide meridians are numbered east and west from the principal meridian as "first guide meridian east" and so forth.

The tracts are 24 miles wide at their southern boundaries, but because guide meridians converge, they are less than 24 miles wide at their northern boundaries. As a result, there are two sets of corners along each standard parallel. *Standard corners* refer to guide meridians north of the parallel, while *closing corners* are those less than 24 miles apart which were established by the guide meridians from the south closing on that parallel. Convergence of meridians is proportional to the distance from the principal meridian; the offset of the second guide meridian is double that of the first, and that of the third guide meridian is 3 times as great. Of course, actual offsets on the ground may differ from theoretical distances because of inaccuracies in surveying.

4-20 Townships   The 24-mile tracts are divided into 16 townships, each roughly 6 miles square, by north-south *range lines* and east-west *township lines.* Range lines are established as true meridians at 6-mile intervals along each standard parallel and are run due north to the next standard parallel. Township lines are parallels of latitude that join township corners at intervals of 6 miles on the principal meridian, guide meridians, and range lines. Since range lines converge northward just as guide meridians do, the width of a township decreases from south to north, the shape is trapezoidal rather than square, and the area is always less than the theoretical 36 square miles.

The survey of townships within the 24-mile tract begins with the southwest township and continues northward until the entire west range is completed; then it moves to the next range eastward and again proceeds from south to north. Townships are numbered consecutively northward and southward from the base line and eastward and westward of the principal meridian. As illustrated in Figure 4-8, T2N, R3W denotes a township that is 6 miles north of the base line and 12 miles west of the principal meridian.

4-21 Establishment of Sections and Lots   Beginning in the southeast corner of a township, sections of approximately 640 acres are formed by running lines 1 mile apart parallel to eastern range lines and 1 mile apart parallel to southern township lines. By starting in the southeastern part of the township, irregularities are thrown into the northern and western tiers of sections in each township. Survey lines are first run around section 36, then 25, 24, 13, 12, and 1. The township subdivision thus starts at the eastern boundary and proceeds from south to north, establishing one tier of sections at a time. Sections are numbered as in Figure 4-8.

Survey corners actually established on the ground include section corners and quarter corners, the latter being set at intervals of 40 chains for subdividing the sections into 160-acre tracts. These quarter sections may later be further divided into 40-acre parcels known as "forties." A complete land description begins with the smallest land parcel and covers each division in order on a size basis; the specific principal meridian involved is also part of the description. Thus the forty composing the most northwesterly portion of section 21 (Fig. 4-8) would be described as NW¼ NW¼ S.21, T2N, R3W, 5th P. M. To derive the approximate number of acres in a subdivision, the area of the section is multiplied by the product of the fractions in the legal description. From the previous example, ¼ × ¼ × 640 = 40 acres.

Accumulation of irregularities in northern and western tiers of sections often results in parcels of land that have an area considerably less than the 40 or 160 acres intended. Such subdivisions may be individually numbered as *lots.* Also, navigable streams and large bodies of water encountered on survey lines are meandered by running traverses along their edges. *Meander corners* set during such surveys may result in the recognition of additional irregularly shaped lots that commonly range from 20 to 60 acres in size.

4-22 Survey Field Notes   Complete sets of field notes describing public land surveys can be obtained from the U.S. General Land Office in Washington, D.C., and from most state capitals. Field notes are public records, and only a nominal charge is made for copying them. They include bearings and distances of all survey lines; descriptions of corners, monuments, and bearings objects; and notes on topography, soil quality, and forest cover types.

Field notes are essential for locating lost or obliterated survey corners from bearings objects or "witness trees." On original surveys, such objects were identified and located by recording a bearing and distance from the corner to the object. As a result, lost corners may be reestablished by reversing all bearings and chaining the specified distances from witnesses or bearings objects. Specific procedures for relocating original survey lines and corners are detailed in the U.S. Department of Interior's *Manual of Instructions for the Survey of the Public Lands of the United States* (1973).

4-23 Marking Land Survey Lines   In forested regions where land has been subdivided in accordance with the U.S. Public Land Survey, specific rules are sometimes formulated for marking trees so that different classes of land lines can be easily identified. Trees along township, range, and section lines may be marked with three bark blazes, preferably placed vertically on the tree stem near eye level. Quarter-section lines are referenced by two blazes, and finer subdivisions (such as forty lines) are indicated by a single blaze.

To avoid injury to trees, bark blazes 4 to 6 in. in diameter should be made with a drawknife and then painted with an appropriate color. When feasible, it is desirable to have blazing techniques and paint colors standardized in a given forest region, especially where numerous ownerships are represented. The following marking paint colors have been recommended by foresters in the Great Lake States:

Type of marking	Paint color
Property boundaries	Blue
Sale boundaries	Red
Cut trees	Yellow or orange
Leave trees	Light green
Research and inventory plots	White
Trails	Aluminum

GLOBAL POSITIONING SYSTEMS

4-24 Purpose of GPS   Global positioning systems (GPS) can be used to accurately determine locations on the Earth's surface. GPS technology permits both navigation (getting from one point to another) and mapping (determining perimeters of areas and location of features). Based on signals from satellites, GPS provides a convenient, inexpensive, and accurate means of determining location under many circumstances.

The global positioning system consists of 24 satellites spaced in six orbital planes to provide complete coverage of the Earth's surface (Fig. 4-9). Positioned at an altitude of approximately 11,000 mi (17,600 km), each satellite completely circles the Earth at 12-hour intervals. These satellites transmit signals; GPS receivers read the signals. The signal indicates which satellite is transmitting, where it is, and when it sent the message. By collecting information from several satellites and using triangulation principles, a GPS receiver determines its position. Information on speed and direction of travel is provided by updating GPS-determined positions.

Originally developed for use by the United States military services, GPS is now available for general use worldwide. Police and emergency services workers, as well as motorists, backpackers, canoeists, and many others, increasingly rely on GPS for navigational information. While GPS technology has not yet fully supplanted conventional surveying applications for forestry purposes, it is now commonly used for determining tract boundaries, locating field plots, delineating wetlands, laying out roads and trails, and identifying areas of insect, disease, or fire damage.

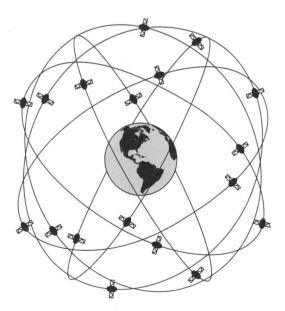

FIGURE 4-9
GPS satellites orbiting the Earth provide a basis for accurately determining locations.

4-25 How GPS Works   It is necessary to have a basic understanding of how GPS works in order to use the technology effectively and to recognize the conditions under which it might not perform well. To apply the principles of triangulation to determine location, distances from fixed objects must be known. As shown in Figure 4-10, if the distances from three fixed objects are known, the location is determined exactly. Because the location of the GPS satellites orbiting the Earth can be determined very accurately, these space vehicles can serve as "fixed" objects for determining locations on the planet. Typically at least five or six satellites are overhead and "visible" (in that their radiowaves can be received) at any spot on the Earth at any given time. Obstructions—such as mountains, buildings, tree trunks, and other large objects—can block signals from one or more of these satellites, and all satellites may not be functioning perfectly. Consequently, the number of useful satellites may be reduced below the minimum of four that are needed to determine horizontal and vertical locations, but this condition is relatively rare.

Five tracking stations spaced around the equator constantly monitor the location of each GPS satellite, thus allowing the satellites to be treated as fixed objects. Due to gravity, solar wind, and other factors, the orbits are not quite constant. If a satellite moves out of its assigned orbit, the tracking stations inform the satellite where it actually is in relation to where it is supposed to be, and the satellite broad-

FIGURE 4-10
Knowing the distance from three fixed objects and applying triangulation allows the determination of location.

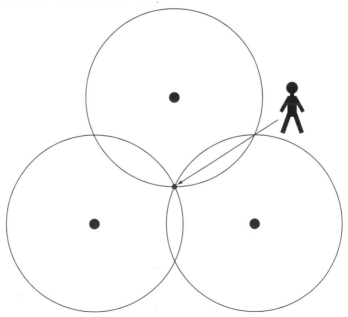

casts the necessary correction as part of its signal. If a satellite gets too far out of orbit, small jets controlled from a remote ground station may be used to move it back into position (Oderwald and Boucher, 1997).

The GPS satellites continuously broadcast one-way signals at two frequencies within the L-band region of the microwave spectrum. These signals travel at the speed of light (186,000 mi per sec). Hence one means of getting distance from the satellites to a point on Earth is to multiply the rate of signal travel by the amount of time required to reach a receiver at a selected location (i.e., distance = rate × time). To determine the location of a point in terms of longitude, latitude, and elevation (X, Y, Z), signals from four satellites are required—three for the X, Y, Z coordinates and a fourth for time. GPS receivers accept data from the satellites and then, provided enough usable signals are available, solve mathematical equations to estimate location.

Each satellite broadcasts an *ephemeris* (its own location) and an *almanac* (the location of all other satellites). Thus, after a GPS receiver has located one satellite, the almanac can be read to locate the others that should be visible. Locational data are stored in the receiver, eliminating the need to gather ephemeris and almanac information every time a position is reported. New almanac data must be collected and stored in the receiver periodically (at least once per month) in order to keep the almanac current.

Determining location by triangulation requires the distance from a given location to the visible satellites be determined very precisely. Distances can be determined in a number of ways from the several types of signals that are constantly broadcast. Two types of signals, coarse acquisition code and carrier phase code, are commonly used for civilian GPS applications. A third type of signal, P code, is generally reserved for military use. While distances are determined very differently with coarse acquisition code and carrier code signals, the end result is the same.

Coarse acquisition code, or C/A code, is currently the most widely used GPS signal. GPS satellites are equipped with very accurate clocks, and GPS receivers generate codes that match codes generated by GPS satellites at the same time. The difference in time between the satellite emitting a signal and the receiver intercepting that signal is used to estimate distance (Fig. 4-11). This distance to the satellite is termed a "pseudorange" because it is only an estimate of the distance. The clocks in the satellite and the receiver do not have exactly the same time, and only ⅟₂₀ of a second is required for the signal to reach the receiver from a satellite. Hence, small errors in time determination can cause large errors of distance estimation. Although C/A code or pseudoranging is less accurate than other methods, it is a simple and cost-effective means for determining positions of fixed points.

Carrier phase measurement is based on a more detailed analysis of satellite signals. The *carrier phase code* is a continuous signal; distance from the satellite to the receiver is determined by counting the number of complete and fractional wavelengths between the two points. Carrier phase is much more accurate than the

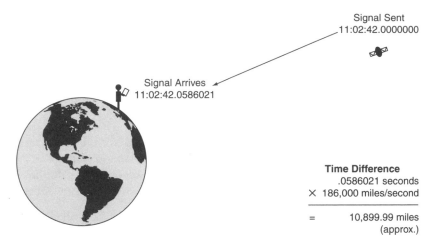

FIGURE 4-11
Time difference (the basis of C/A code or pseudoranging) can be used to estimate the distance to a satellite. *(Adapted from Oderwald and Boucher, 1997.)*

C/A code approach to distance estimation. GPS receivers that utilize carrier phase signals can be used for surveying, installing bench marks, and other applications requiring very precise locations. While carrier phase distance measurement is very accurate, it is time consuming and expensive to obtain. For most forestry applications, the accuracy afforded by C/A code equipment and techniques is adequate.

4-26 GPS Accuracy   A number of factors influence the accuracy of GPS location estimates so that no given determination is exact. However, by knowing the sources of GPS location errors and appropriately correcting for them, locational estimates with sufficient accuracy can be obtained. Because of the uncertainty, or "fuzz," in GPS distance estimates, triangulation by satellite establishes a region, or box, in which the location is likely (Fig. 4-12) rather than an exact location as illustrated in Figure 4-10. By careful use of GPS equipment and procedures, the size of the locational "box" can be made acceptably small.

All of the GPS signals are in the L-band (between the microwave and radio regions) of the frequency spectrum. L-band waves penetrate clouds, fog, rain, and a certain amount of vegetation, including forest canopies. Signals from satellites low on the horizon are more susceptible to blockage from tree trunks, but signals from satellites that are overhead can send signals through the leaves. When under a forest canopy, reception may be improved by raising the receiver antenna.

There are several sources of error due to the characteristics of measuring distance from GPS satellites. While these errors cannot be controlled, they can largely be corrected after the fact. The principal sources of error are:

• **Satellite Location**—no one satellite at any given time is precisely in its assigned orbit, leading to "ephemeris errors."

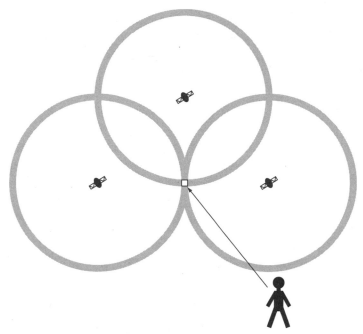

FIGURE 4-12
Due to uncertainty in distance measurements, triangulation from satellites results in location estimates that are not exact. *(Adapted from Oderwald and Boucher, 1997.)*

- **Satellite Clocks**—although the atomic clocks carried by satellites are highly precise and frequently adjusted from remote ground stations (making the time error less than one millisecond), there are slight deviations in time. Each satellite broadcasts its clock error as part of its signal, making correction of satellite time possible.
- **Receiver Clock**—the clock in the GPS receiver must be exactly synchronized with the satellite clocks to avoid error in distance estimation. Fortunately, consistency of time is sufficient, but receiver clock error is relatively large as compared to error in the satellite clocks.
- **Atmosphere**—various layers of the atmosphere can deflect satellite signals. The ionosphere and troposphere also cause atmospheric interference. When satellites are directly overhead, and the signal passes perpendicularly through the atmosphere, the amount of deflection is minimal.
- **Multipath**—delays in signal receipt resulting from the signal bouncing off objects between the satellite and receiver are termed "multipath errors." Multipath errors can be created by trees in a forest, but the greatest multipath problem occurs in cities due to interference from large buildings.

Prior to May 2, 2000, for security reasons the U.S. government introduced deliberate error into the satellite signals. This signal degradation was called selective

TABLE 4-2
GPS RANGE ERRORS UNDER "NORMAL" CONDITIONS

Error source	Expected Range Error (Uncorrected)*
Clock and ephemeris	5 to 10 feet
Atmospheric and ionospheric	10 to 15 feet
Group transmission delays	3 feet
Receiver noise	5 feet
Multipath signal	7 feet
Total	30 to 40 feet

*Selective availability, when activated, resulted in an expected range error of 0 to 100 feet.
Source: Adapted from Bolstad, 1993.

availability and abbreviated SA. Selective availability created a sizable error in GPS locational information. SA, which globally degraded the civilian GPS signal below the degree of locational precision available for military purposes, has been replaced by procedures that can degrade GPS signals on a regional basis during periods of military conflict or crisis. A summary of GPS range errors is shown in Table 4-2. The imprecision in raw GPS locational information can be greatly reduced by applying correction methods.

4-27 Differential Correction   The impact of range errors in GPS information can be reduced by collecting data over a period of time and averaging the results. Whether one or several readings are taken at chosen points, differential correction may be applied to greatly improve accuracy. *Differential correction* involves simultaneous data collection using two receivers. One receiver, called the base station, is situated over a point of known location. Another receiver, often called the rover, is used to collect data at unknown field points. If both receivers are tracking the same satellites, the ephemeris, clock, atmospheric, and other errors should be similar for both sets of readings. Because the base location is known, the difference can be calculated between true and GPS observed positions. An offset based on this difference can be applied to the field data collected by the roving receiver, thereby improving positioning accuracy. Under typical conditions, the base station must be within 200 mi (320 km) of the rover for acceptable results. Ideally, base stations occupy surveyed locations that are free from obstructions, have large antennas, and are connected to a computer for data storage. If such a permanent base station is not available, a rover can be set up as a temporary base station. Maps based on corrections from a temporary base will be correct in relative location, but they may be in error with regard to absolute location. The amount of error in absolute location depends on how accurately the base receiver for the temporary station is located.

Differential correction is often done as a post-processing correction. Field data are collected with roving receivers and then data from base stations are downloaded using vendor-supplied software to make the necessary corrections. Real-time corrections are also possible. The corrections are computed exactly the same as for postprocessing applications, but the values are then broadcast immediately to the rovers. The roving receiver applies the correction to its current measurements and adjusts location measurements accordingly. While convenient, real-time correction is less accurate than postprocessing corrections due to inherent errors in broadcasting from the base station to the rovers in the field.

Differential correction was mandatory for many GPS applications when SA was involved, and it may still be required when highly accurate results are needed. Differential correction procedures remove or greatly reduce all errors except multipath, which is entirely a receiver error.

4-28 GPS Data   GPS information can be used to prepare maps, build databases, and supply information to Geographic Information Systems (GIS) software for mapping and storage (Chap. 14). Locational information from GPS receivers is useful for determining points, lines, and areas. A point is simply the location of one spot. The receiver checks all available satellites and estimates its location at a particular instant in time. Points can be based on single or multiple readings (Fig. 4-13). A single-reading point generally has more error than a point that is based on an average of multiple readings. The more single points that are averaged, the better the accuracy will be, but this improved accuracy comes at the cost of increased field time for collecting the readings. The number of readings needed depends on the anticipated use of the data and satellite reception.

Lines are connected points that are typically used on maps to represent roads, streams, boundaries, and other lineal features. The receiver collects single-point locations at selected intervals and collectively stores the points as part of a line.

FIGURE 4-13
GPS data can be gathered in the form of points or lines. *(Adapted from Oderwald and Boucher, 1997.)*

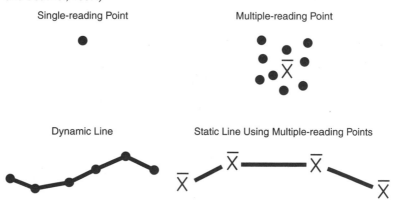

Accuracy of the line is quite good even when single-reading points are taken because many points are gathered and error in any given point will distort the line only at that point. The intervals between the single-point locations that define a line are set to suit the field situation. For example, one might take readings at one- or two-second intervals when walking a winding creek or boundary but use five-second intervals for walking a relatively straight boundary segment (Oderwald and Boucher, 1997). The best interval to use depends on the field conditions and the intended application of the information. Lines can also be based on multiple readings at each point (Fig. 4-13). By taking multiple readings at each interval and then connecting the averages, a more accurate determination of the line is possible. Lines composed of single points are termed *dynamic* because the observer is moving along the line collecting single readings at a selected time interval. Conversely, lines composed of multiple-reading points are called *static* because the observer stops at intervals to collect data before moving to the next data collection point.

Areas can be computed from GPS data. The GPS software will insure closure between the beginning and ending points. Like lines, areas can be based on single-reading or multiple-reading points. The ability to compute areas by connecting points and lines after the fact using GPS mapping software is a highly attractive feature of GPS technology.

4-29 GPS Receivers   Many different types of GPS receivers are available. The principal difference in receivers is the number of satellites that can be tracked at one time. Each satellite that is tracked requires one channel. Receivers commonly have 6, 8, or 12 channels.

Receivers for use in the field are typically hand-held. The basic components of hand-held units are an antenna, the GPS engine, the computer to process and store readings, and a battery (Fig. 4-14). Fixed or stationary receivers commonly have 8 or 12 channels, are powered by electricity, and are interfaced with computers to process and store signal information. The antenna of a fixed receiver is typically mounted on a roof or pole. These fixed receivers, or base stations, supply differential correction information. Although fixed receivers are relatively expensive, each base station can supply correction information to as many roving hand-held units as desired.

Roving GPS receivers may also be roughly categorized as *navigating* or *mapping receivers*. For navigating applications, portability and extended battery life are overriding considerations. While these are the least accurate of the GPS receivers, they provide sufficient accuracy for their intended use. Mapping receivers, on the other hand, have more options available for storing locational information, including multiple-reading points and static and dynamic lines. Many mapping receivers also permit the recording of attribute data with the geographic coordinates of features. This capacity enables users to store descriptive information such as plot identifier numbers, road or stream classes, or forest stand

FIGURE 4-14
Hand-held GPS receivers are an efficient and effective means of determining field locations.

descriptors when the GPS coordinates are collected. These data can then be transferred to geographic information systems (Chap. 14). Because of their relatively sophisticated capabilities, mapping receivers must have larger computer capacity (which requires more power and a larger battery) than navigating receivers. One should select the GPS receiver that has the capabilities required for the intended applications.

PROBLEMS

4-1 What should be the sum of the interior angles for closed traverses having **(a)** 3 sides, **(b)** 8 sides, and **(c)** 12 sides?

4-2 Establish a pacing course and determine your **(a)** number of paces per chain, **(b)** number of paces required to measure the radii of ⅒-, ⅕-, and ¼-acre circular plots, and **(c)** number of feet per pace.

4-3 Convert the following bearings to azimuths: **(a)** N45°W, **(b)** S32°W, **(c)** N15°E, **(d)** S61°E.

4-4 Change these magnetic bearings to true bearings, utilizing the declination specified for your locality: **(a)** N35°E, **(b)** S88°E, **(c)** S10°W, **(d)** N61°W. Convert the true bearings to backsights.

4-5 Assume you have a dot grid with 36 dots per sq in. What acreage will be represented by each dot at map scales of **(a)** 330 ft per in., **(b)** 25 chains per in., **(c)** 1 mile per in.?

4-6 Measure a given map area by means of the graphical method, dot grid, transects, and planimeter. Which technique is fastest? Which do you feel is most precise?

4-7 Determine the acreage in the following parcels of land that were surveyed in accordance with the U.S. Public Land Survey system: **(a)** NW¼, SW¼, S. 27; **(b)** NW¼, S. 28; **(c)** S½, SW¼, S. 14; **(d)** NW¼, SW¼, SE¼, S. 31.

4-8 On standard USGS topographic quandrangles, how are contours and bench marks designated? What technique is used to denote woodland cover? What map symbols are used for **(a)** railroads, **(b)** power transmission lines, **(c)** churches, **(d)** schools, and **(e)** airfields?

REFERENCES

Bolstad, P. V. 1993. GPS basics: Forestry applications. *The Compiler* **11(3)**:4–8.

Bondesson, L., Ståhl, G., and Holm, S. 1998. Standard errors of area estimates obtained by traversing and GPS. *Forest Sci.* **44**:405–413.

Boucher, B. A., and Oderwald, R. G. 1994. Global positioning and forest inventory. *The Compiler* **12(2)**:23–26.

Brown, C. M. 1962. *Boundary control and legal principles.* John Wiley & Sons, New York. 275 pp.

Carr, B. 1992. Using laser technology for forestry and engineering applications. *The Compiler* **10(4)**:5–16.

Campbell, J. B. 1996. *Introduction to remote sensing,* 2d ed. The Guilford Press, New York. 622 pp.

Davis, R. E., Foote, F. S., and Kelly, J. W. 1966. *Surveying: Theory and practice,* 5th ed. McGraw-Hill Book Company, New York. 1,096 pp.

Decker, C. J., and Bolstad, P. V. 1996. Global positioning system (GPS) accuracies in eastern U.S. deciduous and coniferous forests. *So. J. Appl. For.* **20:**81–84.

Evans, D. L., Carraway, R. W., and Simmons, G. T. 1992. Use of global positioning system (GPS) for forest plot location. *So. J. Appl. For.* **16:**67–70.

Gerlach, F. L. 1991. GPS in forestry. *The Compiler* **9(2):**3–6.

Leick, A. 1995. *GPS satellite surveying,* 2d ed. John Wiley & Sons, New York. 560 pp.

———. 1993. GPS accuracy: Can GPS fill the need for GIS? *The Compiler* **11(3):**18–27.

Liu, C. J. 1995. Using portable laser EDM for forest traverse surveys. *Can. J. For. Res.* **25:**753–766.

———, and Brantigan, R. 1995. Using differential GPS for forest traverse surveys. *Can. J. For. Res.* **25:**1,795–1,805.

Naesset, E. 1999. Point accuracy of combined pseudorange and carrier phase differential GPS under forest canopy. *Can. J. For. Res.* **29:**547–553.

Oderwald, R. G., and Boucher, B. A. 1997. *Where in the world and what? An introduction to global positioning systems.* Kendall/Hunt Publishing Company, Dubuque, Iowa. 64 pp.

Peet, F. G., Morrison, D. J., and Pellow, K. W. 1997. Using a hand-held electronic laser-based survey instrument for stem mapping. *Can. J. For. Res.* **27:**2,104–2,108.

U.S. Department of the Army. 1964. *Elements of surveying.* Tech. Manual TM 56-232, Government Printing Office, Washington, D.C. 247 pp.

U.S. Department of Commerce. 1962. *Magnetic poles and the compass.* Serial 726, Coast and Geodetic Survey, Government Printing Office, Washington, D.C. 9 pp.

U.S. Department of the Interior. 1973. *Manual of instructions for the survey of the public lands of the United States.* Government Printing Office, Washington, D.C. 333 pp.

Warren, B. J., and Cook, W. L. 1984. Surveying. Pp. 1,089–1,116 in *Forestry handbook,* K. F. Wenger (ed.), John Wiley & Sons, New York.

Wilson, R. L. 1989. *Elementary forest surveying and mapping.* O.S.U. Bookstores, Inc., Corvallis, Oreg. 181 pp.

Wolf, P. R., and Brinker, R. C. 1994. *Elementary surveying,* 9th ed. HarperCollins College Publishers, New York. 760 pp.

CHAPTER 5

CUBIC VOLUME, CORD MEASURE, AND WEIGHT SCALING

5-1 Logs, Bolts, and Scaling Units   When trees are cut into lengths of 8 ft or more, the sections are generally referred to as *logs*. By contrast, shorter pieces are called *sticks,* or *bolts*. The process of measuring volumes of individual logs is termed *scaling*. Logs may be scaled in terms of cubic feet, cubic meters, board feet, weight, and other units. The *cubic foot* is an amount of wood equivalent to a solid cube that measures $12 \times 12 \times 12$ in. and contains 1,728 cu in. The *cubic meter,* used in countries that have adopted the metric system, contains 35.3 cu ft. The *board foot* is a plank 1 in. thick and 12 in. square; it contains 144 cu in. of wood. The present discussion is concerned with log scales expressed in cubic volumes; board-foot volumes and scaling of sawlogs are described in Chapter 6.

5-2 Computing Cross-Sectional Areas   Although tree cross sections rarely form true circles, they are normally presumed to be circular for purposes of computing cross-sectional areas. In measuring cubic-foot contents of logs, it is desirable to derive cross-sectional areas in square feet rather than in square inches; cubic volumes are then derived by multiplying average cross-sectional area times log length in feet. As diameters instead of radii of logs are measured, area in square inches may be derived by

$$\text{Area in square inches} = \frac{\pi D^2}{4}$$

where D is the log diameter in inches.

For this relationship, it is then necessary to divide the result by 144 to convert the area to square feet. This is most easily accomplished in one step by reducing the formula as follows:

$$\text{Area} = \frac{\pi D^2}{4(144)} = \frac{3.1416D^2}{576} = 0.005454D^2$$

By this simple conversion, cross-sectional areas are derived in square feet when diameters are measured in inches.

5-3 Log Volumes and Geometric Solids   If logs were perfectly cylindrical, cubic volumes would be derived by merely multiplying cross-sectional area in square units of length times log length. However, as logs taper from one end to another, only short sections of perhaps a few inches can logically be treated as cylinders. Still, there are several common geometric solids from which truncated sections can be extracted to approximate log forms (Fig. 5-1). Volumes of these solids of revolution are computed as follows:

Name of solid	Volume computation
Paraboloid	Area/2 × length
Conoid	Area/3 × length
Neiloid	Area/4 × length

As a rule, trees approximate the shape of truncated neiloids when the effects of butt swell are apparent. Logs from middle sections of tree stems are similar to truncated paraboloids, while upper logs approach the form of conoids.

Cubic volumes for all solids of revolution are computed from the product of their *average* cross-sectional area and length. Thus in computing log volumes, the principal problem encountered is that of accurately determining the elusive average cross section. Three common formulas applied to this end are

$$\text{Huber's: Cubic volume} = (B_{1/2})L$$
$$\text{Smalian's: Cubic volume} = \frac{(B + b)}{2}L$$
$$\text{Newton's: Cubic volume} = \frac{(B + 4B_{1/2} + b)}{6}L$$

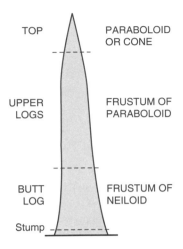

TOP   PARABOLOID
                       OR CONE

UPPER   FRUSTUM OF
LOGS   PARABOLOID

BUTT   FRUSTUM OF
LOG   NEILOID   **FIGURE 5-1**
                                        Geometric shapes assumed by different
Stump   portions of tree boles.

where $B_{1/2}$ = cross-sectional area at log midpoint
      B = cross-sectional area at large end of log
      b = cross-sectional area at small end of log
      L = log length

Areas and volumes are computed inside bark and may be expressed in either English or metric units. Huber's formula assumes that the average cross-sectional area is found at the midpoint of the log; unfortunately, this is not always true. The formula is regarded as intermediate in accuracy, but its use is limited because (1) bark measurements or empirical bark deductions are required to obtain mid-diameters inside bark and (2) the midpoints of logs in piles are often inaccessible and cannot be measured.

Smalian's formula, though requiring measurements at both ends of the log, is the easiest and least expensive to apply. It also happens to be the least accurate of the three methods, especially for butt logs having flared ends. Allowances must be made for excessive butt swell by ocularly projecting a normal taper line through-out the log or by cutting flared logs into short lengths to minimize the effect of un-usual taper. Otherwise, log volumes may be overestimated by application of an average cross-sectional area that is too large. Because it has neither of the disad-vantages cited for Huber's formula, Smalian's method of volume computation holds the greatest promise of the three for production log scaling.

Newton's formula necessitates the measurement of logs at the midpoint and at both ends. Although it is more accurate than the other two methods, the expense incurred in application limits its use to research, experimental techniques, and checks against other cubic volume determinations. It will be noted that for perfect cylinders, all three formulas provide identical results.

5-4 Scaling by the Cubic Foot   For species having a limited degree of natural taper, logs may be simply scaled as cylinders based on small-end diameters or cross sections. Such an approach has an obvious time and cost advantage over Smalian's method which requires measuring both ends of the log; furthermore, volume outside the scaling cylinder may be safely ignored for short log sections. Disregarding taper would be quite logical for items such as rotary-cut veneer logs because little or no commercial veneer is produced until these logs have been reduced to cylindrical form.

Where log lengths are variable, taper cannot be completely disregarded. An allowance for volume outside the scaling cylinder may be made by applying a *fixed rate of taper* to all logs of a given species-group. For example, a taper rate of ½ in. per 4 ft of length might be established for a certain species. The volume of a 16-ft log with a small-end diameter of 20 in. would be computed by 4-ft sections as follows:

Diameter (in.)	Area (sq ft)		Length (ft)		Volume (cu ft)
20.0	2.1817	×	4	=	8.7268
20.5	2.2921	×	4	=	9.1684
21.0	2.4053	×	4	=	9.6212
21.5	2.5212	×	4	=	10.0848
					37.6012 or 38

This computational procedure would not be followed by scalers themselves, of course. Instead, they would read the appropriate value from a special table showing volumes for many combinations of log diameters and lengths. Such tables are called *log rules*.

There have been numerous attempts to promote the cubic foot as the national log-scaling unit in the United States. However, the obvious advantages of a clearly defined measure that is independent of utilization standards, manufacturing efficiencies, and final product form have not completely prevailed. The U.S. Forest Service has adopted cubic-foot scaling of logs and timber for sales on national forests (U.S. Department of Agriculture [USDA] , 1991), but board-foot scaling is still commonly used in many sectors of the forest products industry. Weight scaling of sawlogs also has possibilities for providing an objective standard of measurement.

5-5 Inscribed Square Timbers   It is sometimes necessary to determine quickly the dimensions of square timbers that can be cut from logs of various scaling diameters. Such information may be useful in measuring hewed products such as railroad ties or timbers when the outer portions of logs are wasted or ignored. The problem is basically one of fitting the largest possible square inside a circle of a specified size. A formula that will provide the length of this side S of an inscribed square from log diameter D is

$$\text{Side } S = \sqrt{\frac{D^2}{2}}$$

Cubic volumes of inscribed square timbers may be determined by merely squaring the length of the side and multiplying by log length. When the side is measured in inches and length is expressed in feet, the product must be divided by 144 for conversion to cubic feet.

MEASURING STACKED WOOD

5-6 The Cord   A standard cord of wood is a rick that measures $4 \times 4 \times 8$ ft and contains 128 cu ft. Inasmuch as this space includes wood, bark, and sizable voids, the cord is more of an indication of space occupied than actual wood measured. Of course, cordwood is not necessarily cut into 4-ft lengths, and it is rarely stacked in rectangular ricks having 32 sq ft of surface area. Any stacked rick of roundwood may be converted to standard cords using

$$\text{cords} = \frac{\text{Width (ft)} \times \text{height (ft)} \times \text{stick length (ft)}}{128}$$

When cordwood is cut into lengths shorter than 4 ft (e.g., firewood), a rick having 32 sq ft of surface area may be referred to as a *short cord*. If a similar rick is made up of bolts longer than 4 ft, it may be termed a *long cord,* or *unit.* In the United States, pulpwood is commonly cut into lengths of 5, 5.25, and 8.33 ft. When these stick lengths are multiplied by a cord surface area of 32 sq ft, the resulting units occupy 160, 168, and 266.6 cu ft of space, respectively. The *cunit* refers to 100 cu ft of *solid wood* rather than to stacked volume. Typical specifications for pulpwood purchased in the United States are as follows:

1 Bolts must be at least 4 in. in diameter inside bark at the small end and cut to the specified length.
2 Bolts must not exceed (18 to 24) inches in diameter outside bark at the large end.
3 Wood must be sound and straight.
4 Ends must be cut square and limbs trimmed flush.
5 No burned or rotten wood will be accepted.
6 All nails and other metals must be removed from bolts.
7 Mixed loads of pines and hardwoods are not acceptable.

Where the metric system is employed, stacked wood is measured in cubic meters; 1 m^3 is equivalent to 35.3 cu ft. A stacked rick of wood is converted to cubic meters by simply measuring all three dimensions of the rick in meters and obtaining the product of these dimensions:

$$m^3 = \text{width (m)} \times \text{height (m)} \times \text{bolt length (m)}$$

5-7 Solid Contents of Stacked Wood   Purchasers of cordwood and pulpwood are primarily interested in the amount of solid-wood volume contained in various ricks rather than in the total space occupied. The tabulation that follows provides a rough approximation of the volume of wood and bark for ricks with 32 sq ft of surface area and varying bolt lengths:

Size of rick (ft)	Space occupied (cu ft)	Solid wood and bark (cu ft)
4 × 8 × 4	128	90
4 × 8 × 5	160	113
4 × 8 × 5.25	168	119
4 × 8 × 6	192	136
4 × 8 × 8.33	266.6	181

It should be borne in mind that the foregoing values are merely estimates that can vary greatly in individual situations. The species, method of piling, diameter and length of sticks, straightness, and freedom from knots can exert a significant influence on these average values, as illustrated in Figures 5-2 to 5-4. Thus the cord method of measurement has been used in the past primarily because of simplicity and convenience rather than because of its accuracy.

When cubic-foot conversions are desired for solid wood alone, the volume of bark present must also be considered in establishing pulpwood values. For many

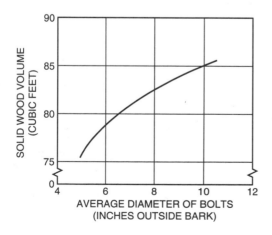

FIGURE 5-2
Influence of average bolt diameter on solid-wood volume of stacked cordwood. *(From Taras, 1956.)*

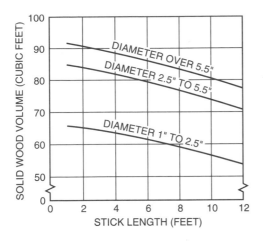

FIGURE 5-3
Influence of length of stick on solid-wood volume of a cord for conifers. *(From Taras, 1956.)*

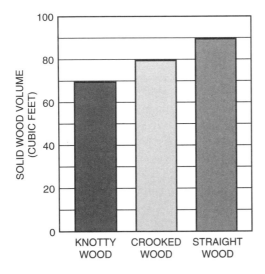

FIGURE 5-4
Effect of stick quality on solid-wood volume of 5-ft cordwood. *(From Taras, 1956.)*

coniferous species, bark may compose 10 to 30 percent of the total stick volume; in the Great Lake States, for example, the average is about 14 percent. Depending on bark volume and other factors outlined, the solid-wood content of a stacked cord may range from about 60 to 95 cu ft. A value of 79 has been widely used in the Great Lake States, and U.S. Forest Service studies in the South produced averages of 72 cu ft per cord for southern pines and 79 for pulping hardwoods. Mills purchasing pulpwood have traditionally developed their own cubic-foot conversions based on the size and quality of wood being purchased; there is no single value that can be considered reliable in any given forest region.

Estimates of solid-wood content can be made with a steel tape graduated into 100 equal parts. The tape is stretched diagonally across the ends of the stacked bolts, and the number of graduations falling on wood (as opposed to bark and voids) provides the desired proportion. Several observations should be made for each rick to obtain reliable estimates.

5-8 An Ideal Measure   The perfect unit of measurement would be one that is absolute, unambiguous, accurate, simple, and inexpensive to apply (Ker, 1962). If only peeled or debarked wood were purchased and sticks could be individually measured, the cubic foot might be a logical unit for adoption. However, since low-value pulpwood bolts cannot be economically handled as separate items, this technique could be accurate but certainly not simple or inexpensive. The *xylometer,* or water-immersion method, has also been considered for determining cubic volumes, but few equipment models have progressed beyond the experimental stage. By this technique, volume of wood is derived through application of Archimedes' principle; the measured volume of water displaced is equivalent to the cubic volume of wood immersed.

WEIGHT SCALING OF PULPWOOD

5-9 The Appeal of Weight Scaling   The use of weight as a measure for purchasing wood is not a new idea; mine timbers and pine stumps utilized in the wood naval-stores industry have been purchased on a weight basis for many years. The appeal of weight scaling in the pulpwood industry may be largely attributed to changes in the locale of measurement and purchases. Whereas wood was formerly scaled in the forest, measurements are now made at concentration yards or at the mill. Since 1955, a large segment of the pulp and paper industry has adopted weight scaling in lieu of linear measurements for stacked pulpwood.

Weight/price equivalents are usually based on studies of freshly cut wood. It is thus implicit that mills favor green wood with a high moisture content. As green wood is preferred in most instances, there is some incentive for producers to deliver their wood immediately after cutting. While there are indications that many species lose very little moisture during the first 4 to 8 weeks in storage, the widespread belief that pulpwood seasons and loses weight rapidly works in favor of mills that desire freshly cut material. From the mill inventory viewpoint, the greener the wood delivered, the longer it can be stored at the yard without deterioration—an important consideration in warm and humid regions.

In many regions, and for many species, moisture content is relatively stable throughout the year and an average weight/volume factor is applied through all seasons. There are, however, some notable exceptions to this relative stability. For instance, Marden, Lothner, and Kallio (1975) found that moisture content of wood and bark of aspen in northern Minnesota varied from a low of less than 80 percent in the summer to a high of over 100 percent in the winter (Fig. 5-5). When seasonal variation in moisture content is significant, weight/volume factors must be adjusted accordingly in order to derive payments that are fair for both buyer and seller.

5-10 Variations in Weight Most mills now utilizing weight scaling have developed their own local conversions by making paired weighings and cordwood measurements of thousands of purchases. Weight equivalents may vary by species, mill localities, and points of wood origin. The influence of former measures in cords is reflected in the newer weight units; instead of wood being purchased by the ton or hundredweight, prices are usually based on average weights per standard cord.

The principal factors contributing to weight variations for a given species are wood volume, moisture content, and specific gravity. Variations in wood volume, or the actual amount of solid wood in a cord, are caused by differences in bolt diameter, length, quality, and bark thickness. Moisture content varies within species

FIGURE 5-5
Seasonal variation in moisture content of aspen in northern Minnesota. *(From Marden, Lothner, and Kallio, 1975.)*

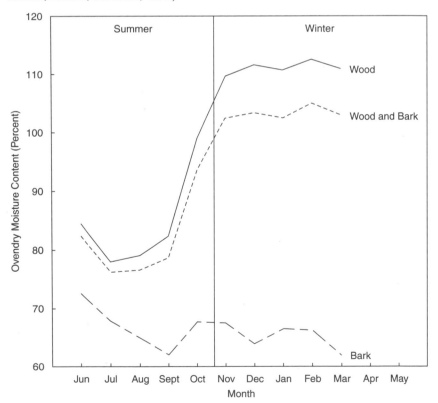

for heartwood versus sapwood. Specific gravity is affected by percent of summerwood and position in the tree; density tends to decrease from the lower to the upper portion of the stem.

5-11 Wood Density and Weight Ratios   From a knowledge of moisture content and specific gravity (based on ovendry weight and green volume), the weight (lb) per cubic foot of any species may be computed by

$$\text{Density} = \text{sp gr} \times 62.4\left(1 + \frac{\%\,\text{moisture content}}{100}\right)$$

The utility of this formula is illustrated by this example: assume that a weight/cord equivalent is required for loblolly pine, a species having a specific gravity of 0.46, moisture content of 110 percent, solid-wood volume per cord of 72 cu ft, and an estimated bark weight of 700 lb per cd. Substituting in the formula, we have

$$\text{Density} = 0.46 \times 62.4\left(1 + \frac{110}{100}\right) = 60.3 \text{ lb per cu ft}$$

As there are 72 cu ft of wood per cord, the green weight of solid wood per cord is 72×60.3, or 4,342 lb. By adding the bark weight of 700 lb, the total weight is found to be 5,042 lb per cd. Weight equivalents in Table 5-1 were derived by this procedure.

The foregoing technique of computing weight/cord ratios is valid only when both specific gravity and moisture content are accurately determined because small variations in these factors can result in large weight changes. For each 0.02 change in specific gravity at a level of 100 percent moisture content, the weight of wood will change about 2.5 lb per cu ft. At the 100 percent level, a moisture content difference of 5 percent can cause a weight change of 1 to 2 lb per cu ft. In a cord

TABLE 5-1
COMPUTATION OF PULPWOOD WEIGHTS FOR SOUTHERN PINES

Species	Specific gravity	Moisture content (%)	Density (lb per cu ft)	Solid volume per cord (cu ft)	Weight of solid wood (lb)	Estimated bark weight (lb)	Total weight of wood and bark (lb)
Loblolly pine	0.46	110	60.3	72	4,342	700	5,042
Longleaf pine	0.53	105	67.8	72	4,882	650	5,532
Shortleaf pine	0.44	120	60.4	72	4,349	500	4,849
Slash pine	0.52	120	71.4	72	5,141	500	5,641

Source: Taras, 1956.

having 72 cu ft of solid wood, the 0.02 change in specific gravity alone could mean a loss or gain of 180 lb of wood, while the stated moisture difference might involve 72 to more than 100 lb (Taras, 1956).

Table 5-2 was derived by solving the wood-density formula for a wide range of specific gravities and wood moisture contents. It may therefore be applied in developing approximate weight factors for a variety of tree species. The reader should remember, however, that most mills develop their price ratios by actual scaling of delivered wood rather than by this theoretical approach.

For those who wish to compute wood densities directly in metric units, the preceding relationship is modified to

$$\text{Density} = \text{sp gr} \times 1{,}000 \left(1 + \frac{\% \text{ moisture content}}{100} \right)$$

The validity of this relationship can be verified from the earlier example. The previous result of 60.3 lb per cu ft multiplied by a conversion factor of 16.0185 is equivalent to 965.92 kg/m^3. From the modified formula, we have

$$\text{Density} = 0.46 \times 1{,}000 \left(1 + \frac{110}{100} \right) = 966 \text{ kg/m}^3$$

TABLE 5-2
WEIGHT IN POUNDS PER CUBIC FOOT OF GREEN WOOD AT VARIOUS VALUES OF SPECIFIC GRAVITY AND MOISTURE CONTENT

Moisture content of wood (%)	Weight in pounds per cubic foot for specific gravities* of:										
	0.30	0.34	0.38	0.42	0.46	0.50	0.54	0.58	0.62	0.66	0.70
30	24.3	27.6	30.8	34.1	37.3	40.6	43.8	47.0	50.3	53.5	56.8
40	26.2	29.7	33.2	36.7	40.2	43.7	47.2	50.7	54.2	57.7	61.2
50	28.1	31.8	35.6	39.3	43.1	46.8	50.5	54.3	58.0	61.8	65.5
60	30.0	33.9	37.9	41.9	45.9	49.9	53.9	57.9	61.9	65.9	69.9
70	31.8	36.1	40.3	44.6	48.8	53.0	57.3	61.5	65.8	70.0	74.3
80	33.7	38.2	42.7	47.2	51.7	56.2	60.7	65.1	69.6	74.1	78.6
90	35.6	40.3	45.1	49.8	54.5	59.3	64.0	68.8	73.5	78.2	83.0
100	37.4	42.4	47.4	52.4	57.4	62.4	67.4	72.4	77.4	82.4	87.4
110	39.3	44.6	49.8	55.0	60.3	65.5	70.8	76.0	81.2	86.5	91.7
120	41.2	46.7	52.2	57.7	63.1	68.6	74.1	79.6	85.1	90.6	96.1
130	43.1	48.8	54.5	60.3	66.0	71.8	77.5	83.2	89.0	94.7	100.5
140	44.9	50.9	56.9	62.9	68.9	74.9	80.9	86.9	92.9	98.8	104.8
150	46.8	53.0	59.3	65.5	71.8	78.0	84.2	90.5	96.7	103.0	109.2

*Based on weight when ovendry and volume when green. Values may be converted to kilograms per cubic meter by multiplying by 16.0185.
Source: U.S. Department of Agriculture, 1999.

5-12 Advantages of Weight Scaling   The technique of weight scaling round-wood materials continues to be widely applied because of these and other reasons:

1 It encourages delivery of freshly cut wood to the mill.

2 The method is fast, requires no special handling, and saves time for both buyer and seller. A greater volume of wood can be measured in a shorter time period and with fewer personnel.

3 Weight scaling is more objective than manual scaling, and positive records of all transactions are provided by automatically stamped weight tickets.

4 Incentive is provided for better piling of wood on trucks; this tends to increase the volume handled by the supplier.

5 Woodyard inventories are more easily maintained because of greater uniformity in recordkeeping.

PROBLEMS

5-1 Compute the volume (in cubic feet) for the following logs according to Huber's, Smalian's, and Newton's formulas (ib = inside bark):

a small-end diameter (ib) = 6.1 in.
midpoint diameter (ib) = 7.5 in.
large-end diameter (ib) = 9.0 in.
length = 16 ft

b small-end diameter (ib) = 24.0 in.
midpoint diameter (ib) = 26.4 in.
large-end diameter (ib) = 28.7 in.
length = 32 ft

c small-end diameter (ib) = 10.4 in.
midpoint diameter (ib) = 10.9 in.
large-end diameter (ib) = 11.5 in.
length = 8 ft

d small-end diameter (ib) = 32.0 in.
midpoint diameter (ib) = 32.8 in.
large-end diameter (ib) = 33.7 in.
length = 18 ft

5-2 From your instructor or a logging operation, obtain dimensions of three merchantable logs cut from the same tree. Determine cubic volumes of each by Huber's, Smalian's, and Newton's formulas. Tabulate results and explain reasons for any differences noted.

5-3 Compute the volume, in standard cords, of the following stacks of wood:

a 16 ft × 80 ft × 8 ft

b 12 ft × 31 ft × 5 ft

c 15 ft × 32 ft × 8.33 ft

d 40 ft × 80 ft × 16 ft

5-4 Determine the gross volume of pulpwood (in standard cords) on a railroad car or truck in your locality. Make notes on stick quality, length, range of diameters, and method of piling. Compute the total *value* of the wood at the locale of measurement by application of current pulpwood prices in your vicinity.

5-5 For a given species, the average specific gravity is 0.48, the moisture content is 105 percent, the solid wood content per cord is 75 cubic feet, and the weight of bark is 800 pounds per cord. Compute the weight, in pounds, of an average cord.

5-6 Construct a working model of a xylometer. Use the model to determine the cubic volumes of 10 small pieces of roundwood. Compare these volumes with volumes computed by Smalian's and Huber's formulas for the same pieces. Explain reasons for the differences.

5-7 Given the following data from paired scaling and weighing of seven truckloads of pulpwood, compute the weight per cord for each load and the average weight per cord.

Load	Cord scale	Total weight (lbs)
1	3.5	17,600
2	4.1	20,400
3	3.7	18,000
4	4.0	20,700
5	3.9	19,900
6	4.2	21,100
7	3.6	18,800

5-8 Construct a display board of tree cross sections illustrating changes in wood specific gravity from stump to tree top. Use cross sections extracted at intervals of 4 ft for an important timber species in your locality.

REFERENCES

Anonymous. 1953. Weights of various woods grown in the United States. *U.S. Dept. Agr., Forest Serv., Forest Prod. Lab. Tech. Note* 218. 8 pp.

Figueiredo Filho, A., Amaral Machado, S., and Araujo Carneiro, M. R. 2000. Testing accuracy of log volume calculation procedures against water displacement techniques (xylometer). *Can. J. For. Res.* **30:** 990–997.

Hallock, H., Steele, P., and Selin, R. 1979. Comparing lumber yields from board-foot and cubically scaled logs. *U.S. Dept. Agr., Forest Serv., Forest Prod. Lab. Res. Paper FPL* 324. 16 pp.

Ker, J. W. 1962. The theory and practice of estimating the cubic content of logs. *Forestry Chron.* **38:**168–172.

Marden, R. M., Lothner, D. C., and Kallio, E. 1975. Wood and bark percentages and moisture contents of Minnesota pulpwood species. *U.S. Forest Serv., North Central Forest Expt. Sta., Research Paper* NC-114. 9pp.

Taras, M. A. 1956. Buying pulpwood by weight as compared with volume measure. *U.S. Forest Serv., Southeast. Forest Expt. Sta., Sta. Paper* 74. 11 pp.

U.S. Department of Agriculture. 1991. *National forest cubic scaling handbook.* U.S. Forest Serv. FSH 2409.11a, Washington, D.C. (no page numbers).

U.S. Department of Agriculture. 1999. *Wood handbook: Wood as an engineering material.* U.S. Forest Service. Forest Prod. Soc., Madison, Wis. (various paging).

Zon, R. 1903. Factors influencing the volume of solid wood in the cord. *Forestry Quart.* **1:**125–133.

CHAPTER 6

LOG RULES, SCALING PRACTICES, AND SPECIALTY WOOD PRODUCTS

6-1 Log Rules A *log rule* is a table or formula showing estimated volumes, usually in board feet, for various log diameters and lengths. The process of applying log rules, termed *log scaling,* involves determining log dimensions and, if necessary, making allowances for defects. During the past century, at least 100 board-foot log rules have been devised, and several have been widely adopted. However, none of these rules can accurately predict the mill output of boards, except when near-cylindrical logs are sawed according to rigid assumptions on which the rules are based. Although the scaler might employ any of several rules that indicate different log volumes, the *board-feet log scale* and *board feet of lumber* are rarely equal.

The board foot is equivalent to a plank 1 in. thick and 12 in. (1 ft) square; it contains 144 cu in. of wood. Although the board foot has been a useful and fairly definitive standard for the measure of sawed lumber, it is an ambiguous and inconsistent unit for log scaling. The formula commonly used for determining the board-foot content of sawed lumber is

$$\text{bd ft} = \frac{\text{thickness (in.)} \times \text{width (in.)} \times \text{length (ft)}}{12}$$

Accordingly, a 1-in. × 12-in. × 12-ft plank contains 12 bd ft, and a 2-in. × 8-in. × 24-ft plank includes 32 bd ft. This method of computation is not entirely correct even for sawed lumber because of accepted dimensional differences between rough green boards versus finished (seasoned and planed) lumber. A green "two-by-four" may be originally cut to the nominal size of 2 × 4 in., but it can be acceptable in finished form and sold as a two-by-four if it measures only 1½ × 3½ in. The purchaser of 1,000 bd ft of finished lumber is therefore likely to receive considerably less than the volume implied by rigid adherence to the formula cited.

6-2 General Features of Board-Foot Log Rules   To be considered equitable to both buyer and seller, a log rule must be *consistent;* volumes should be directly correlated with log sizes over the entire range of dimensions encountered. Few log rules currently in use can meet this simple requirement. Most of the differences between board-foot log scale and the sawed lumber tally can be attributed to the inflexible assumptions that necessarily underlie such rules:

1 Logs are considered to be cylinders, and volumes are derived from the small ends of logs. Volume outside the scaling cylinder, resulting from log taper, is generally ignored. In a few instances, a fixed rate of taper is presumed to somewhat compensate for this volume loss.

2 It is assumed that all logs will be sawed into boards of a certain thickness (usually 1 in.) with a saw of a specified thickness, or *kerf.*

3 A fixed procedure for sawing the log and allowing for slabs is postulated (Fig. 6-1).

4 There is a tacit implication that all sawmills operate at a uniform level of efficiency that provides equal lumber yields from similar logs. The fact that some mills may be able to cut and market shorter or narrower boards than others is disregarded.

As a corollary to these assumptions, the terms *minimum board width* and *maximum scaling length* are worthy of definition. Minimum board width refers to the narrowest board for which volume would be computed by a given log rule. For most rules, the minimum board width is not smaller than 4 in. or larger than 8 in. Maximum scaling length indicates the longest tree section that may be scaled as a single log. Such a limitation is essential where log rules include no taper allowance; otherwise an entire tree might be scaled from the top end as a 6-in. log. In the United States, local scaling practices usually limit the maximum scaling length to 16 ft in the east and 20 to 40 ft in the west.

Log rules have been constructed from empirical rules of thumb, sawmill lumber tallies, ratios of board feet to cubic feet, diagrams, mathematical formulas, and combinations of these techniques. The three most commonly used log rules in the United States are the Scribner, Doyle, and International ¼-in. All three are included in the Appendix (Appendixes 3, 4, and 5).

FIGURE 6-1
One method of sawing a ponderosa pine log. Losses due to saw kerf, slabs, and shrinkage are apparent. Log diameter is about 15 in.

DERIVATION OF LOG RULES

6-3 Mill-Tally Log Rules   Any sawmill may construct its own empirical log rule by keeping careful lumber tallies of boards cut from various-sized logs. Such rules may provide excellent indicators of log volume at the particular sawmills where they are compiled. However, as they represent only one example of manufacturing efficiency and utilization practice, they are rarely reliable for general use in other localities. The utility of mill-tally log rules is generally limited to mills performing *custom sawing,* which is the production and sale of boards from logs supplied by customers.

6-4 Board Foot-Cubic Foot Ratios   From a purely theoretical viewpoint, 1 cu ft of solid wood contains 12 bd ft of lumber. This mathematical conversion, however, presumes that the cubic foot is rectangular in shape and that twelve 1-in. boards can somehow be extracted without loss of saw kerf. When 1-in. boards must be sawed from round logs, with attendant losses in squaring the log and allowing for kerf, the conversion factor is more likely to range between 4 and 8 bd ft per cu ft. Adding to the difficulty of adopting a uniform conversion is the fact that the board foot-cubic foot ratio changes with log diameter, method of slabbing the log, saw thickness, and sizes of boards produced.

Other factors being constant, the board foot-cubic foot ratio increases with log diameter, because a smaller percentage of cubic volume is wasted in squaring up larger logs. Board foot-cubic foot relationships of 5:1 or 6:1 are sometimes recommended for rough conversions, but there is no single factor that is worthy of complete endorsement. Although the cubic foot alone might constitute an ideal scaling unit, its conversion to the less reliable board foot is unrealistic at best. (See Sec. 6-9.)

6-5 Scribner Log Rule   Developed by J. M. Scribner around 1846, this rule was derived from diagrams of 1-in. boards drawn to scale within cylinders of various sizes. A saw kerf of ¼ in. is presumed. The exact minimum board width allowed is not definitely known, although it appears to have been 4 in. for at least some log diameters. No taper allowance was included, so the rule ignores all volume outside scaling cylinders projected from small ends of logs. Therefore, this rule will normally underestimate the mill output of lumber. The underestimate generally increases as the scaling length increases. When volumes of 16-ft logs are desired, the rule-of-thumb formula $0.8 (D - 1)^2 - D/2$ provides a close approximation of the Scribner log rule (Grosenbaugh, 1952).

In general, the Scribner rule is considered to be intermediate in accuracy, although it does not provide board-foot volumes that are entirely consistent with changing log diameters. A slight modification of the rule is the Scribner Decimal C log rule. Here, the original Scribner volumes are rounded off to the nearest 10 bd ft, and the last zero is dropped. This innovation is presumably an aid to the scaler who must record and total volumes for large numbers of logs. The Scribner Decimal C has been applied extensively in western United States. For eastern forests, the International ¼-in. rule is often used.

Those interested in constructing their own diagram log rules may do so by carefully drafting a series of circles representing the desired range of log diameters. It is then necessary to decide upon the minimum acceptable board width and the saw kerf to be employed. End views of boards are drawn to scale within each circle (Fig. 6-2). When all diagrams have been completed, the number of board feet in each log may be computed by

$$\text{bd ft} = \frac{\text{total number of sq in. of diagram boards}}{12} \times \text{log length (ft)}$$

6-6 Doyle Log Rule   This rule, devised by Edward Doyle around 1825, is based on the mathematical formula

$$\text{bd ft} = \left(\frac{D - 4}{4} \right)^2 L$$

where D is the log diameter in inches and L is the log length in feet.

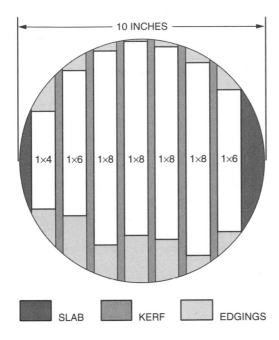

FIGURE 6-2
One method of constructing a diagram log rule; end views of boards are drawn to scale within circles that represent the range of log sizes to be scaled.

For 16-ft logs, the formula may be reduced to merely $(D - 4)^2$. Despite the fact that the formula is algebraically incorrect, use of the rule has persisted in southern and eastern United States. It was originally intended that the rule provide a slabbing allowance of 4 in. and a saw kerf of $\frac{5}{16}$ in., or 25 percent. The 4-in. slab deduction is more than twice the amount ordinarily needed, and the kerf deduction is actually only about 4.5 percent. The net result is a highly inaccurate and inconsistent log rule that greatly underscales small logs because of the excessive slab deduction. Conversely, large logs are overscaled, for the insufficient kerf deduction is no longer absorbed by the heavy slab deduction.

The biggest fault of the Doyle rule lies in its inconsistency rather than its basic inaccuracy. The fact that volumes increase erratically with changing log diameters prohibits uniform adjustments in log prices to compensate for the abortive scale values. The rule can thus be considered a fair basis for transactions only when both buyers and sellers of logs are fully aware of its deficiencies. To provide a slight concession to the seller of small logs, some purchasers may either allow the inclusion of one bark thickness in measuring log diameters or record a scale equal to the log length when Doyle values are less than that amount. However, such local rules of thumb do little to alleviate the inherent inequalities of this anomalous rule.

In a few localities, the more erratic attributes of the Doyle and Scribner log rules are combined to form a diabolical yardstick called the *Doyle-Scribner log rule.* Doyle volumes are employed to underscale logs to about 24 to 28 in.; then the rule changes over to Scribner values to maintain the lowest possible board-foot values. If log prices are adjusted accordingly, the rule may be used without argument. All too often, however, it is the occasional seller of logs who may be unfamiliar with local scaling practices, and the buyer gains an undue advantage in the transaction.

6-7 International Log Rule   This rule, based on a reasonably accurate mathematical formula, is the only one in common use that makes an allowance for log taper. Devised in 1906 by Judson Clark, the International rule includes a fixed taper allowance of ½ in. per 4 ft of log length. Thus scale values for a 16-ft log are derived by totaling board-foot volumes of four 4-ft cylinders, each ½ in. larger in diameter than the previous one. In addition to the allowance for taper, the rule also provides rational deductions for slabbing and saw kerf. The original International ⅛-in. rule assumed a ⅛-in. saw kerf, plus ¹⁄₁₆-in. allowance for board shrinkage, giving a total deduction of ³⁄₁₆ in. The International ¼-in. rule, devised from the original, provides a ¼-in. saw kerf plus ¹⁄₁₆ in. for shrinkage, or a total kerf deduction of ⁵⁄₁₆ in. Slabs are deducted in the form of an imaginary plank 2.12 in. thick and having a width equal to log diameter. It is assumed that all logs are cut into boards 1 in. thick.

Construction of the International ⅛-in. rule begins with the simple cross-sectional area formula

$$\text{Area} = \frac{\pi D^2}{4} = 0.7854\, D^2$$

When log diameter D is substituted in inches, area is determined in square inches. Since 1 bd ft has a cross-sectional area of 12 sq in., the number of solid board feet in a cylinder is thus

$$\text{Solid bd ft} = \frac{0.7854\, D^2}{12}\, L, \text{ or } 0.06545\, D^2 L$$

where L is the log length in feet.

If the full cross-sectional area of a log could be cut into boards without loss of saw kerf, the foregoing formula would constitute a mathematically correct method of computing board-foot contents. As this is not the case, deductions must be made for kerf (sawing out the boards) and for slabs (squaring the log). The percentage p of log volume lost in saw kerf is derived by

$$p = \frac{k}{t + k}$$

where k is the saw kerf in inches and t is the board thickness in inches.

For the International ⅛-in. rule (³⁄₁₆-in. total deduction for kerf and board shrinkage), the kerf percentage for sawing 1-in. boards is

$$p = \frac{^{3}/_{16}}{1 + {^{3}/_{16}}} = {^{3}/_{19}} = 0.158 \text{ or about } 15.8 \text{ percent}$$

With a fixed maximum scaling length of 4 ft, the International ⅛-in. rule now becomes

$$\text{bd ft} = (1 - p)0.06545\ D^2L, \text{ or } (1 - 0.158)0.06545\ D^2(4)$$

and $\quad$ $\text{bd ft} = (0.842)0.06545\ D^2(4) = 0.22\ D^2$

The expression $0.22\ D^2$ includes the correct saw kerf allowance, but no deduction has been made for loss of log volume due to slabbing. Whereas kerf deductions are related to total log volume, slab allowances are closely associated with log diameter or circumference. Thus a correct slab deduction can be made by (1) decreasing log diameter or (2) extracting a plank with a width equal to log diameter. For the International rule, the latter method is used by removal of an imaginary plank 2.12 in. thick. The board-foot volume of the plank is computed for a 4-ft log section by

$$\text{Deduction for slabs and edgings} = \frac{2.12\ D}{12} \times 4 = 0.71\ D$$

When this final deduction is appended to the previously derived portion of the formula, the complete International ⅛-in. rule for a 4-ft log section is

$$\text{bd ft} = 0.22\ D^2 - 0.71\ D$$

Some years after the International ⅛-in. rule was published, it was modified to make it applicable for sawmills employing a ¼-in. kerf (total kerf and shrinkage allowance of ⁵/₁₆ in.). Instead of all scale values being recomputed by the process described here, the ⅛-in. rule was reduced by the converting factor of 0.905. Thus, for 4-ft sections, the formula for the ¼-in. rule may be expressed as $0.905\ (0.22\ D^2 - 0.71\ D)$. For 16-ft log lengths, a simpler formula, $0.8\ (D - 1)^2$, will provide approximate volumes for the International ¼-in. rule (Grosenbaugh, 1952).

If the slab deduction for a formula log rule were made by reducing log diameter rather than by the International "plank method," a mathematically sound rule might be expressed as

$$\text{bd ft} = (1 - p)0.06545\ (D - s)^2\ L$$

where p = proportion of log volume lost as kerf
$\quad D$ = log diameter, in.
$\quad s$ = slab deduction, in.
$\quad L$ = log length, ft

As no log taper allowance is automatically included in the rule, this factor must be controlled by placing limitations on the maximum scaling length.

Of the three principal log rules described here, the International is undoubtedly the most consistent, and it becomes quite accurate for mills producing mainly 1-in. boards with a ¼-in. saw thickness. The International ¼-in. rule has been officially adopted by several states and is widely used in various localities. In spite of its relative virtues, however, it has never gained the favor accorded such rules as the Scribner and even the Doyle for scaling work. Unrealistic as it may seem, many foresters are required to derive forest inventory data with the International rule and then handle log sales based on Scribner or Doyle volumes. As outlined in subsequent sections, conversions from one log rule to another are erratic and troublesome at best.

6-8 Overrun and Underrun   Comparisons of log rule values by various scaling diameters are presented in Table 6-1. The contrast in board-foot volumes for logs of identical sizes is even more strikingly illustrated by Figure 6-3, in which the International rule is used as a standard of comparison. For logs 10 in. in diameter, the Doyle value constitutes less than 60 percent of the International scale, and the Scribner volume amounts to less than 85 percent. For 25- to 30-in. logs, all three log rules show a reasonable agreement. Beyond this point, the Scribner rule underscales logs, and the Doyle rule gives values much too large. The trends graphically shown here explain the reason for the devious combination log rule that utilizes Doyle volumes to about 24 in. and then abruptly switches to the Scribner scale.

The preceding comparison is not intended to convey the impression that the International log rule is faultless; nevertheless, it is a consistent rule that often

TABLE 6-1
COMPARISON OF BOARD-FOOT LOG RULES FOR 16-FT LOGS

Log diameter (in.)	Log rule				
	International ¼-in. (bd ft)	Scribner (bd ft)	Scribner Decimal C (bd ft)	Doyle (bd ft)	Doyle-Scribner (bd ft)
8	40	32	30	16	16
12	95	79	80	64	64
16	180	159	160	144	144
20	290	280	280	256	256
24	425	404	400	400	400
28	585	582	580	576	582
32	770	736	740	784	736
36	980	923	920	1,024	923
40	1,220	1,204	1,200	1,296	1,204

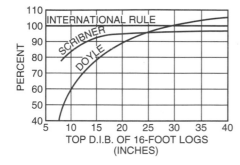

FIGURE 6-3
Relationships between three log rules for board-foot volumes of 16-ft logs. The International ¼-in. rule is used as the standard of comparison. *(Adapted from Schnur and Lane, 1948.)*

closely approximates sawmill tallies. There is always some disparity between log scale and lumber yield. If the lumber output is greater, the excess difference is called *overrun*. When log scale values are larger than sawed output, an *underrun* occurs. Overrun and underrun are expressed as a percent of log scale by

$$\text{percent of overrun or underrun} = \frac{\text{mill tally} - \text{log scale}}{\text{log scale}} \times 100$$

For a given set of log sizes and sawmilling practices, the amount of overrun or underrun is primarily dependent on the log rule used for scaling. This fact can be verified at any mill by checking a random selection of logs, as shown in Table 6-2. Here, scale values and lumber tallies were recorded for 15 logs at a hardwood mill in Arkansas. All logs were cut into 1-in. boards with a saw kerf loss of ¼ in. Overrun averaged 3.3 percent for the International ¼-in. rule and nearly 37 percent for the Doyle rule. Discrepancies of this magnitude are acceptable only when prices paid for logs are adjusted according to the scaling rule locally applied.

6-9 Board-Foot Volume Conversions   In spite of the difficulties of equating various log rules and volume units such as board feet versus cords, conversions are occasionally desirable. Graphs similar to Figure 6-3 may be used to change board-foot scales from one log rule to another, or individuals may develop their own factors that reflect local sizes of logs handled. In western Oregon, Washington, and Alaska, for example, the U.S. Forest Service considers that 1,000 bd ft scaled by the Scribner Decimal C rule is roughly equal to 1,400 bd ft by the International ¼ -in. rule.

In most regions of the United States, factors have been developed for converting stacked cordwood to board feet and vice versa. A sample tabulation of such factors for the Great Lake States is shown in Table 6-3. Although it is theoretically possible to convert cordwood of any size to board-foot units, results are questionable unless bolts are large enough to have been scaled as *bona fide* logs.

TABLE 6-2
SCALE AND OVERRUN COMPARISON OF DOYLE AND INTERNATIONAL ¼-IN. LOG
RULES*

Log no.	Scaling diameter (in.)	Log length (ft)	Doyle scale (bd ft)	International scale (bd ft)	Lumber tally (bd ft)
1	13	10	50	70	83
2	11	14	43	70	70
3	16	12	108	130	127
4	11	16	49	80	107
5	11	16	49	80	70
6	15	12	91	115	112
7	18	12	147	170	174
8	11	12	37	55	55
9	10	12	27	45	45
10	13	12	61	85	82
11	10	14	32	55	55
12	16	12	108	130	124
13	11	12	37	55	65
14	19	12	169	190	190
15	12	12	48	70	87
Totals (bd ft)			1,056	1,400	1,446
Overrun (percent)			+36.9	+3.3	

*Based on data collected by the senior author at a circular sawmill in southeast Arkansas.

TABLE 6-3
NUMBER OF ROUGH CORDS PER THOUSAND BOARD FEET,
LAKE STATES*

Bolt top dib (in.)	Cords per MBF			No. of 8-ft bolts per cord
	Doyle	Scribner Decimal C	International ¼-in.	
6	11.1	4.4	2.2	45
7	6.7	3.0	3.0	33
8	5.0	4.0	2.7	25
9	4.2	2.5	2.5	20
10	3.5	2.1	2.1	16
11	3.2	2.5	2.2	13
12	2.8	2.3	2.0	11
13	2.5	2.0	1.8	10
14	2.5	2.1	1.9	8
15	2.4	2.0	1.9	7

*Conversions assume an average of 79 cu ft of solid wood per standard cord.
Source: Adapted from Ralston, 1956.

BOARD-FOOT LOG SCALING

6-10 Scaling Straight, Sound Logs   The scaling of a straight and sound log is simply a matter of determining its length and average diameter inside bark (dib) at the small end. Lengths may be estimated or measured with a tape. Diameters are commonly determined with a *scale stick,* i.e., a rule graduated in inches and imprinted with log rule volumes for varying lengths. The "average" log diameter to be scaled is ocularly selected in most cases. However, on unusually elliptical logs the two extreme diameters may be measured for computing an average value.

Depending on local scaling practices, the minimum scaling diameter is ordinarily set at 6 to 8 in. Smaller logs are given zero scale or *culled,* (i.e., disregarded and eliminated from the scale record). When log diameters fall exactly halfway between scale-stick graduations (such as 12.5 in.), it is customary to drop back to the lower value—12 in. in this instance. Scaling diameters definitely above the halfway mark are raised to the next largest graduation; thus a 12.6-in. log would be scaled as 13 in.

Log lengths are usually taken at 2-ft intervals, although 1-ft intervals are used for certain species. All logs should have a trim allowance of 2 to 6 in. When logs are cut "scant" (without sufficient trim allowance) or in odd lengths, the scale is ordinarily based on the next shortest acceptable length. When long logs or tree-length sections are being scaled, the locally adopted maximum scaling length should be observed to avoid loss of volume due to excessive taper.

6-11 Log Defects   If a log is straight and free from defects, the gross scale (as read from the scale stick) is also the *net,* or *sound, scale.* From the standpoint of log scaling, defects include only those imperfections that will result in losses of wood *volume* in sawing the log. By contrast, those imperfections affecting log *quality,* or *grade,* only are not regarded as scaling defects. Thus scale deductions are made for such items as rot, wormholes, ring shake, checks, splits, and crook but not for sound knots, coarse grain, light sap stain, or small pitch pockets.

Making scale deductions for log defects is basically a matter of (1) determining the type and extent of the defect and (2) computing the board-foot volume that will be lost as a result. When the defect volume is subtracted from gross log scale, the usable volume remaining is the net, or sound, scale. Although certain guides or rules can be developed to somewhat standardize deduction techniques, the extent of many interior log defects can be learned only by working with experienced scalers and seeing defective logs sawed into boards on the mill carriage.

A point worthy of mention is that no deductions are made for defects outside the scaling cylinder or for those that penetrate 1 in. or less into the scaling cylinder. Defects outside the scaling cylinder are disregarded because this volume is ordinarily excluded from the original log scale (except for the International rule). Defects that penetrate the scaling cylinder 1 in. or less may be ignored because this portion of the log is normally lost in slabbing anyhow. If, for example, an exterior defect penetrates 3 in. into the cylinder of a log scaled by the Scribner rule, only the last 2 in. of penetration would be considered in making a scale deduction.

The principal forms of quantitative log defects encountered are

1 Interior defects, such as heartrot or decay, hollow logs, and ring shake (mechanical separation of annual rings)

2 Exterior, or peripheral, defects, such as sap rot, seasoning checks, wormholes, catface, and fire or lightning scars

3 Crook defects, such as excessive sweep, crook, and forked or "crotched" logs

4 Operating defects, such as breakage, splits, and end brooming

6-12 Board-Foot Deduction Methods   Defect deductions can be accomplished by at least three approaches: by reducing log diameters, by reducing log lengths, or by diagramming defects for mathematical computations. Exterior, or peripheral, defects (checks, sap rot) are best handled by diameter reductions. Butt rot and many crook defects are accommodated by reducing log lengths. For internal and partially hidden defects, the diagram-formula method is suitable. By this method, interior defects are enclosed by an imaginary solid and the board-foot contents computed for subtraction from gross log scale. Deductions are made as 1-in. boards, and that part of the defective section that would normally be lost as saw kerf is not deductible. For the Scribner and other cylinder log rules assuming 1-in. boards and a ¼-in. kerf, the standard deduction formula is

$$\text{bd ft loss} = \frac{w \times t \times l}{15}$$

where w = width of defect enclosure, in.

$\quad\quad t$ = thickness of defect enclosure, in.

$\quad\quad l$ = length of defect enclosure, ft

One inch is usually added to both the width and the thickness of the defect in calculating the deduction. For defects that run from one end of a log to the other, measurements are taken at the larger defect exposure. It will be recognized that this is the basic board-foot formula for lumber (Sec. 6-1), except that the denominator has been changed from 12 to 15. This reduction to 80 percent of the solid board-foot content effectively removes the 20 percent deduction due to a ¼-in. saw kerf, because this portion would be lost anyway. For the International ¼-in. rule, where the kerf-shrinkage allowance is actually ⁵⁄₁₆ in., a denominator of 16 rather than 15 has been suggested for the formula. Several common log defects are illustrated in Figure 6-4. In three instances, the standard deduction formula has been used for determining net log scales.

All nine logs illustrated have scaling diameters of 24 in. and lengths of 16 ft; gross scale by the Scribner Decimal C log rule is 40 (400 bd ft). For purposes of illustration here, it is assumed that log and board lengths are acceptable only in

SCRIBNER DECIMAL C LOG RULE

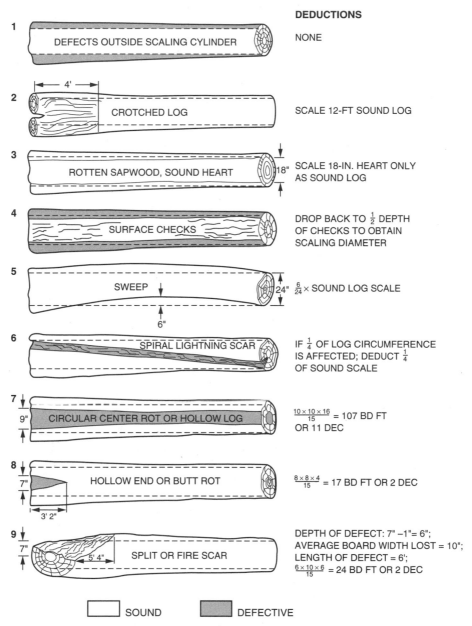

DEDUCTIONS

1 DEFECTS OUTSIDE SCALING CYLINDER — NONE

2 CROTCHED LOG — SCALE 12-FT SOUND LOG

3 ROTTEN SAPWOOD, SOUND HEART — 18" SCALE 18-IN. HEART ONLY AS SOUND LOG

4 SURFACE CHECKS — DROP BACK TO $\frac{1}{2}$ DEPTH OF CHECKS TO OBTAIN SCALING DIAMETER

5 SWEEP — 24" $\frac{6}{24} \times$ SOUND LOG SCALE

6 SPIRAL LIGHTNING SCAR — IF $\frac{1}{4}$ OF LOG CIRCUMFERENCE IS AFFECTED; DEDUCT $\frac{1}{4}$ OF SOUND SCALE

7 CIRCULAR CENTER ROT OR HOLLOW LOG — $\frac{10 \times 10 \times 16}{15} = 107$ BD FT OR 11 DEC

8 HOLLOW END OR BUTT ROT — $\frac{8 \times 8 \times 4}{15} = 17$ BD FT OR 2 DEC

9 SPLIT OR FIRE SCAR — DEPTH OF DEFECT: 7" −1"= 6"; AVERAGE BOARD WIDTH LOST = 10"; LENGTH OF DEFECT = 6'; $\frac{6 \times 10 \times 6}{15} = 24$ BD FT OR 2 DEC

☐ SOUND   ▨ DEFECTIVE

FIGURE 6-4
Typical log defects and methods of computing deductions by the Scribner Decimal C log rule.

2-ft multiples, with a minimum length of 8 ft. Minimum board width is 4 in. Where deductions have been computed, they are rounded off to the nearest 10 bd ft and converted to decimal scale. In most cases, deductions are made in accordance with the *National Forest Log Scaling Handbook* (USDA, 1985).

Log 1 As all defective material is outside the scaling cylinder, no deduction is necessary.

Log 2 The 4-ft crotched portion is deemed unusable; thus the length is reduced, and the scale for a sound 12-ft log is recorded.

Log 3 Because of rotten sapwood, only the heartwood portion of this log is scaled. The deduction is automatically made in scaling by diameter reduction.

Log 4 For surface or sun checks that penetrate along the radii of the log, it is common practice to drop back to one-half the depth of the checks to obtain the scaling diameter. If the checks here were 4 in. deep on all sides, the scaling diameter would be $24 - (2 + 2) = 20$ in. The reason for not scaling entirely inside the checks is that the loss due to checks is not usually as great in the interior of a log as it is at the ends.

Log 5 Sweep results in a deduction only when it causes a deviation that exceeds the top taper. For the log illustrated, a sweep of 6 in. was established by projecting the scaling cylinder straight through the log. As losses due to sweep are related to log size, the deduction may be approximated by expressing the sweep measurement as a percent of scaling diameter. In this example, the deduction is $\frac{6}{24} \times 400 = 100$, or 10 decimal scale. Both sweep and crook can be minimized by careful log bucking. When logs are excessively crooked, deductions are made by merely reducing the length as in log 2.

Log 6 Sector or V-shaped defects bear the same relationship to log volume as the sector bears to a circle. For the spiral lightning scar affecting one-fourth of the log circumference, the deduction is one-fourth of the gross scale. Wormholes and frost cracks may also be handled by this method of deduction.

Log 7 The standard deduction formula is applied for hollow logs and those with center rot; such defects are usually larger at the butt end of a log, because they tend to follow the configuration of annual rings. In this example, the defect encompasses a 9-in. circle at its larger end. One inch must be added in boxing the defect to allow for sawing around it. The deduction is thus (10 in. $\times$ 10 in. $\times$ 16 ft)/15, or 11 decimal scale.

Log 8 When logs are hollow or decayed at one end only, considerable judgment and experience is required to determine the depth of the defect. In this example, the defect is 7 in. in diameter and slightly more than 3 ft deep. Again, 1 in. is added to allow for sawing around the defect and the depth of the hollow is increased to 4 ft, because boards are acceptable only in 2-ft multiples. The deduction is thus (8 in. $\times$ 8 in. $\times$ 4 ft)/15, or 2 decimal scale. It should be noted that if the defect had penetrated more than 8 ft into the length of the log, it would have been deducted for the full 16 ft—just as if the log had been hollow. This would be necessary because boards opposite the defect would be less than the minimum acceptable length of 8 ft.

Log 9   Splits, fire scars, or catfaces may be handled by merely reducing log length or by applying the deduction formula. In the latter case, it is necessary to determine (1) the length of the defect with respect to the projected scaling cylinder, (2) the depth of the defect into the scaling cylinder, and (3) the average board width lost because of the defect. As shown here, the length is 5 ft 4 in., or 6 ft. The depth of 7 in. is reduced by 1 in. because of slabbing loss, and the average board width lost is estimated as 10 in. The deduction is therefore (6 in. × 10 in. × 6 ft)/15, or 2 decimal scale.

6-13 Cull Percent Deduction Methods   When log defects are computed in terms of board feet as in Section 6-12, a different deduction formula is required for each log rule used. A simpler and more logical approach is to estimate the defect volume as a *percent* of total log volume, thereby avoiding deduction methods that are tied to the inconsistencies of a particular log rule. When defects are computed as cull percents, the volume to be deducted can be easily translated into board feet, cubic feet, or other desired units. L. R. Grosenbaugh (1952) has devised five basic cull percent formulas for handling common log defects.[1] In all cases, d refers to the average diameter of the log at the small end in inches, and L is the length in feet.

Rule 1   Proportion lost when defect affects entire section:

$$\text{Cull percent} = \frac{\text{length of defective section}}{L}$$

Rule 2   Proportion lost when defect affects wedge-shaped sector:

$$\text{Cull percent} = \frac{\text{length of defective section}}{L} \times \frac{\text{central angle of defect}}{360°}$$

Rule 3   Proportion lost when log sweeps (or when its curved central axis departs more than 2 in. from an imaginary chord connecting the centers of its end-areas; ignore sweep less than 2 in.):

$$\text{Cull percent} = \frac{\text{maximum departure minus 2 in.}}{d}$$

---

[1]In reality, Grosenbaugh's formulas provide cull proportions rather than cull percents; they may be regarded as percents if multiplied by 100.

Rule 4   Proportion lost when log crooks (or when a relatively short section deflects abruptly from straight axis of longer portion of log):

$$\text{Cull percent} = \frac{\text{length of deflecting section}}{L} \times \frac{\text{maximum deflection}}{d}$$

Rule 5   Proportion lost when average cross section of interior defect is enclosed in ellipse (or circle) with major and minor diameters measurable in inches:

$$\text{Cull percent} = \frac{(\text{major})(\text{minor})}{(d - 1)^2} \times \frac{\text{length of defect}}{L}$$

When rule 5 is applied, a defect in the peripheral inch of log (slab collar) can be ignored, but the ellipse should enclose a band of sound wood at least ½ in. thick. When it is necessary to use a rectangle instead of an ellipse to enclose the defect, the cull percent will be five-fourths as much as for an ellipse with the same diameters as the rectangle. An obvious modification when a ring of rot surrounds a sound heart with average diameter H (in inches) is to estimate the sound proportion as $(H - 1)^2/(d - 1)^2$ and the defective proportion as $1 - [(H - 1)^2/(d - 1)^2]$.

In the rare case when cubic scale for products other than sawlogs is being used, sweep ordinarily is not considered to cause loss and $(d + 1)^2$ is used instead of $(d - 1)^2$ as a divisor for interior defect deduction.

Applications of the preceding formulas are illustrated in Figure 6-5. Cull percents are multiplied by gross log volume to derive the defect volume in terms of desired units. These values are then subtracted from gross log volumes to arrive at net, or sound, scales.

6-14 Merchantable versus Cull Logs   Logs are considered merchantable (valuable enough for utilization) if they can be profitably converted into a salable product such as lumber. Nonmerchantable logs are referred to as *culls*. If minimum dimensional requirements are met, the distinction between merchantable and cull logs is usually determined by the amount of defect encountered. In many localities, logs are considered merchantable only if they are at least 50 percent sound. The exact percentage applied, of course, is dependent on log size and species. A high-value, black walnut veneer log might be acceptable if only 30 percent sound, but a yellow pine log having a comparable defect would probably be culled. Thus merchantability limits vary with locality, kind of log, and changing economic conditions.

6-15 Scaling Records   Log-scaling data are recorded on specially printed forms, in scale books, or with electronic data recorders (Sec. 9-6). A complete scaling record includes the individual log number, species, diameter, length, gross scale, type and amount of defect, and net scale. When few log defects are encountered, the

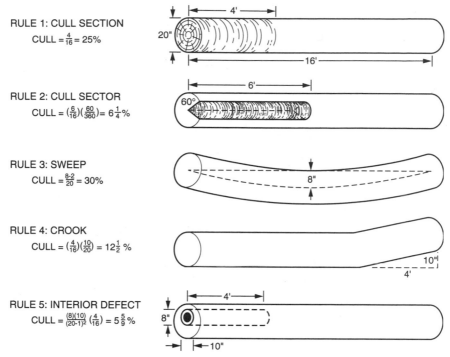

RULE 1: CULL SECTION
$$CULL = \tfrac{4}{16} = 25\%$$

RULE 2: CULL SECTOR
$$CULL = (\tfrac{6}{16})(\tfrac{60}{360}) = 6\tfrac{1}{4}\%$$

RULE 3: SWEEP
$$CULL = \tfrac{8-2}{20} = 30\%$$

RULE 4: CROOK
$$CULL = (\tfrac{4}{16})(\tfrac{10}{20}) = 12\tfrac{1}{2}\%$$

RULE 5: INTERIOR DEFECT
$$CULL = \tfrac{(8)(10)}{(20-1)^2}(\tfrac{4}{16}) = 5\tfrac{5}{9}\%$$

FIGURE 6-5
Application of cull percent deductions for log defects. *(Adapted from Grosenbaugh, 1952.)*

essential tally may occasionally be limited to species, log length, and gross scale. Log diameters are normally needed only for calculating defect deductions.

To conserve writing space and time, the type of defect can be indicated by locally accepted letter codes. Suggested designations are rot, R; sweep, S; wormholes, W; crack, C; catface or fire scar, F; and so on. The completed scaling record should additionally show the location or name of purchaser, scaler's initials, date, and log rule used. When gross scales are in terms of a decimal scale, defect deductions should be computed accordingly.

Standardized scaling records are essential when such tallies are the basis for log sales and purchases. When complete records of log dimensions and defects are required, scalers are more likely to make all measurements carefully. Furthermore, "check scaling" by supervisory personnel is most effective when specific data for each log are clearly noted.

6-16 Log Scanning   Logs are typically purchased on the basis of stick or weight scaling at mills or concentration areas. Prior to sawing, it is now common practice at large conversion facilities to scan logs. Laser scanning devices (Fig. 6-6) are used to

FIGURE 6-6
Laser scanning devices can be used to develop detailed log profiles.
*(Adapted from information provided by Laser Measurement
International, Inc.)*

generate detailed profiles of logs. By combining multiple sensors, a full 3D (three dimensional) image can be produced. If logs are moving along a chain or conveyor at
a speed of 300 feet per minute, scanners currently available provide a reading every
inch. The detailed profiles developed are fed into computer programs which supply
information on optimal bucking and sawing of the logs. At present, scanning devices
in operation provide detailed information on log diameter, sweep, taper, nodal
swelling, and other external characteristics. Current developments indicate that information on internal defects, as well as external characteristics of logs, will also be
obtainable via scanning technology.

LOG GRADING

6-17 Need for Log Grading   In addition to being scaled, which involves estimating the board-foot content, logs may also be graded. Grading entails placing
logs in quality classes. Since logs of different quality (i.e., different grades) vary

in value per unit volume, both scale and grade are needed for determining the value of a given assortment of logs.

Defects in logs fall into two main categories: (1) those that result in losses of wood volume and (2) those that reduce strength or appearance or otherwise limit utility of the sawn products. The first are scaling defects, and the second are grading defects.

Log grades, and by extension grading rules, are related to the quality of the products to be produced from logs. Even with the product specified, the problem of developing meaningful grades remains elusive. For instance, a given log may produce lumber of several grades. Furthermore, since the objective is to maximize the value of each log, the proportion of grades will vary with manufacturing technology and market conditions. Hence, it is not surprising that grading practices have not been widely standardized. However, there are general principles and procedures of grading that have been found useful and that should be kept in mind.

6-18 Hardwood Log Grading   Four log-use classes have been designated to cover current hardwood utilization practices. These classes are (Rast, Sonderman, and Gammon, 1973)

1 *Veneer class.* Includes high-value logs as well as some relatively low value logs that can be utilized as veneer logs.

2 *Factory class.* Includes logs adapted to the production of boards that later can be remanufactured so as to remove most defects and obtain the best yields of clear face and sound cuttings.

3 *Construction class.* Includes logs suitable for sawing into ties, timbers, and other items to be used for structural purposes.

4 *Local-use class.* Includes logs suitable for products not usually covered by standard specifications: crating, pallet parts, mine timbers, industrial blocking, secondary farm buildings, etc.

After logs are designated in one of the four log-use categories, they can then be graded according to their size, abnormalities, and surface characteristics. In most lumber mills, veneer logs (which are typically the most valuable class) are withdrawn and shipped to a hardwood veneer plant. Two grades of hardwood veneer logs—*prime veneer* and *veneer*—are recognized. Logs in the factory class are then placed into log grades (designated F1, F2, F3). The specifications for these grades are closely related to the specifications for standard hardwood lumber grades. The quality range of construction-class logs is often limited, and the class may be considered a grade; however, in some instances this class is further divided into grades. Requirements for classification into the local-use category are limited. In general, if the log meets minimum size requirements (8 in. scaling diameter, 8 ft scaling length) and is one-third or more sound, it can be classified in the local-use category. Grades are usually not recognized within the local-use class.

To summarize, the typically applied log-use classes and the grades recognized within each class of hardwood logs are

	Log-use class			
	Veneer	Factory	Construction	Local-use
Grades:	Prime veneer, Veneer	F1, F2, F3	No grades	No grades

6-19 Softwood Log Grading   There are numerous grade specifications for softwood logs. However, two log-use classes cover most softwood utilization practices:

1 *Veneer class.* Includes high-value logs as well as some relatively low-value logs that can be utilized as veneer logs.

2 *Sawlog class.* Includes logs adapted to the production of yard and structural lumber.

Grading factors used for softwood logs are log diameter, log length, sweep, and cull. At a typical sawmill, veneer logs are removed and sold separately, if markets are available. Grading specifications for veneer logs vary by species and region and are generally complex.

A variety of grading systems have been developed for softwood sawlogs. While some of the grading rules are rather detailed and involved, a relatively simple system developed by the U.S. Forest Service for southern pine sawlogs that will be sawed into standard yard and structural lumber has been found to be quite effective. The clear-face log grading rules for southern pine logs (Schroeder, Campbell, and Rodenback, 1968) serve as an example of a softwood log grading system.

Logs are graded in three steps. First, one must determine the number of clear faces of the log. (A *face* is one-fourth the circumference of the log surface and extends the full length of the log.) One attempts to include as many defects as possible in one face so that the maximum number of clear faces are obtained. On the basis of the number of clear faces, the log is tentatively classified into one of three grades:

Grade 1   Logs with three or four clear faces
Grade 2   Logs with one or two clear faces
Grade 3   Logs with no clear faces

After a tentative log grade is established from the face examination, the log is reduced one grade for each of the following:

1 *Sweep.* Degrade any tentative grade 1 or 2 log one grade if sweep is 3 in. or more *and* equals or exceeds one-third the scaling diameter of the log.

2 *Heartrot.* Degrade any tentative grade 1 or 2 log one grade if evidence of advanced heartrot is found.

Note: No log is degraded below grade 3 if its net scale is at least one-third the gross log scale after deductions have been made for sweep and/or rot. Logs with total scaling deductions for sweep and rot exceeding two-thirds the gross scale of the log are classified cull.

The clear-face grading system for southern pine logs is easy and quick to use, and it has been found to be as accurate for predicting lumber-grade yields as more complex log grading methods.

WEIGHT SCALING OF SAWLOGS

6-20 Advantages and Limitations   In general, the advantages of weight scaling pulpwood as cited in Chapter 5 apply equally well to transactions involving sawlogs. The chief difference is that price adjustments must be made in weight scaling sawlogs to take care of variations in log quality and size. Without such adjustments, crooked or defective logs might command the same price as straight, clear logs, and small-diameter logs (yielding less lumber per ton) could bring as much as larger logs (Page and Bois, 1961).

Circumstances most favorable to weight scaling of sawlogs exist when truckloads are made up of a single species and when there is a relatively narrow range of log diameters present on any given load. It is therefore not surprising that numerous experiments in sawlog weight scaling have been conducted with southern pine logs. Such logs are fairly uniform in size and quality, with few defect deductions being required. On the other hand, mixed hardwood logs of varying quality, degree of soundness, and log size present severe obstacles to effective weight scaling.

Changing from stick scaling to weight scaling raises many questions, the primary one being, What log weight provides an equivalent for 1,000 bd ft of lumber? There is no single or ready answer to this query, of course. Approximations for several species are presented in Table 6-4, but it must be recognized that these values are affected not only by log size and quality but also by such items as moisture content, wood density, and proportion of heartwood versus sapwood. As in measuring pulpwood, volume-weight conversions are preferably based on local measurements by purchasers of logs.

6-21 Volume-Weight Relationships for Sawlogs   Because of the ingrained custom of using board-foot log rules, volume-weight conversions are likely to be initially based on predicted log scales rather than on expected lumber yields. A series of 50 to 100 paired weighings and stick-scaled truckloads will provide a basis for determining the number of pounds or tons per thousand board feet (MBF), according to a particular log rule (Fig. 6-7). Recoverable volume varies by log size; consequently, both the total weight and the number of logs must be known

TABLE 6-4
AVERAGE GREEN WEIGHTS OF LOGS PER THOUSAND BOARD FEET OF LUMBER

Species	Weight (lb)	Species	Weight (lb)
Ash, white	11,100	Maple, red	11,900
Aspen (Popple)	10,800	Maple, sugar	12,900
Basswood	9,500	Oak, red	14,800
Beech	12,700	Oak, white	14,400
Birch, yellow	13,200	Pine, jack	11,500
Cedar, western red	6,200	Pine, loblolly	12,400
Cherry, black	10,500	Pine, longleaf	11,100
Chestnut	12,600	Pine, Norway (red)	9,700
Cottonwood	10,700	Pine, pitch	12,400
Cypress, southern	11,800	Pine, shortleaf	10,400
Elm, slippery	12,600	Pine, slash	12,200
Elm, white	11,300	Pine, sugar	11,500
Fir, balsam	10,400	Pine, white	9,000
Fir, Douglas	8,700	Pine, yellow (western)	11,300
Gum, black	10,400	Poplar, yellow (tulip)	8,800
Gum, red (sweet)	10,600	Redwood	8,900
Hackberry	11,300	Spruce, black	7,700
Hemlock, eastern	11,200	Sycamore	12,000
Hickory	14,700	Walnut, black	11,900
Locust, black	13,400	Willow, black	11,800

Note: The presumed range of log diameter is 10 to 16 in.
Source: U.S. Forest Service.

FIGURE 6-7
Truckloads of sawlogs are weighed and then the logs are scaled to develop volume-weight relationships. *(Courtesy U.S. Forest Service.)*

when log sizes encompass a wide diameter range. Equations based on truckload weights and the number of logs on the load have been successfully employed to predict sawlog volumes.

As an example, Markstrom and King (1993) derived the following equation for ponderosa pine and white spruce cut from relatively young, small timber in a commercial thinning operation on the Black Hills National Forest:

$$Y = 0.0840W - 11.2617N$$

where Y = net board-foot volume, Scribner scale, for a truckload of logs
  W = total weight (pounds) of logs on truck
  N = number of logs on the truck

Because diameter is a fair indication of log quality, the log count per ton is also useful as a rough grading index or as a basis for premium payments.

Ideally, weight-volume relationships for sawlogs would either be derived on the basis of an expected mill tally of lumber or be computed independently of *any* presumed product. Except for custom and apathy, there is no reason why round-wood materials cannot be purchased and sold strictly on the basis of weight—without an implied conversion back to cords or board feet. Such a changeover might well be initiated if the United States were to adopt the metric system for measuring primary wood products.

SPECIALTY WOOD PRODUCTS

6-22 Specialty Products Defined   As arbitrarily applied in this book, specialty wood products encompass an agglomeration of logs, bolts, roundwood, timbers, and stumps that are distinctive because of their shapes, sizes, quality, measurement standards, or intended use. Aside from veneer logs, the items included here may be additionally classified as products purchased in individual units (i.e., piece products such as poles or railroad ties) or products purchased in bulk form (e.g., mine timbers and fuel wood).

6-23 Veneer Logs   Illogical as it may appear, veneer logs are ordinarily measured and purchased in terms of board-feet log scale. To compensate for the fact that size and quality standards are more stringent than for most sawlogs, a premium price is paid for logs of veneer quality (Fig. 6-8). This price may sometimes amount to two or three times the price paid for logs that are sawed into yard lumber. Although grading specifications for veneer logs vary widely, quality requirements are based largely on species, log diameter, and freedom from defects such as crook, knots, bird peck, wormholes, ring shake, stains, and center rot.

Instead of scaling veneer logs in terms of board feet, it would be more realistic to compute their contents in cubic feet or calculate expected yield in terms of veneer sheets of a given thickness. For rotary-cut veneers obtained from sound logs, output can be closely estimated from the difference between two cylinders—one based on the dib of the veneer bolt at the small end and the other based on a presumed core diameter. Thus the maximum surface area of rotary-cut veneer to be expected from a sound wood cylinder may be computed by

$$\text{Veneer yield in square feet} = \frac{B - b}{t} w$$

FIGURE 6-8
Eastern hardwood logs purchased for the manufacture of rotary-cut veneers. *(Courtesy U.S. Forest Service.)*

where B = cross-sectional area of log at small end (sq ft)
    b = cross-sectional area of residual core (sq ft)
    t = veneer thickness (thousandths of a foot)
    w = sheet width (log length) (ft)

For excessively tapered logs, actual yields may be greater than that indicated, because some veneer is obtained from material outside the presumed cylinder. On the other hand, yields may be less for logs having interior defects. Nevertheless, for sound logs the formula will provide predictions that are much more reliable and realistic than scale methods based on board feet. The relationship can also be easily adapted to metric units.

6-24 Poles and Piling   These are roundwood products selected primarily for strength, durability (or capability for preservative treatment), and resistance to exposure and mechanical stresses. Along with several other piece products, they are grouped according to distinct classes and price grades on the basis of species, dimensions, straightness, and freedom from defects (Fig. 6-9).

The principal species utilized for poles are southern pines, western red-cedar, western hemlock, northern white cedar, lodgepole pine, and Douglas-fir. As a rule, poles are marketed under specifications compiled by the American Standards Association (Williston, 1957). Poles are grouped into one of 10 size classes, de-

FIGURE 6-9
Peeled pine poles awaiting preservative treatment at a mill in
Mississippi. *(Courtesy U.S. Forest Service.)*

pending on length, minimum top circumference, and minimum circumference 6 ft
from the butt end.

Wood piling may be of any species that will withstand driving impact and support the loads imposed. Specifications are based on intended use, straightness, uniformity of taper, soundness, and dimensions (length, minimum top diameter, and
both minimum and maximum diameters at 3 ft from the butt end). Most piling, especially if used in salt water, is pressure-treated with creosote as protection against
shipworms.

Piling is purchased at a stated price per linear foot for specified dimensions, and
value accrues rapidly with increasing length and desired taper characteristics.
Standard specifications for round timber piling are available from the American
Society for Testing and Materials (Williston, 1957). In general, poles and piling
must be peeled at the time of cutting. Therefore, the woodland owner anticipating
the sale of such roundwood should carefully study the purchaser's requirements
before trees are severed from the stump.

6-25 Fence Posts   Posts are round, split, or sawed piece products ranging
from about 3 to 8 in. in diameter. Lengths are usually 7 to 8 ft, though some posts

are as long as 20 ft. If posts are split and untreated, they are preferably made from durable species such as various cedars, redwood, white oak, or catalpa. Those that are peeled, seasoned, and treated with preservatives are commonly made from red oak, southern pines, western pines, and Douglas-fir.

Posts may be cut from trees too small for efficient utilization as pulpwood or from the top sections of pulpwood and sawlog trees. If preservative treatment is required, posts are peeled either when cut or at concentration yards. The worth of posts as stumpage (standing trees) may be minimal, but this value (and retail price) is increased considerably by seasoning and preservative treatment. Nondurable species are commonly pressure-treated with a wood preservative.

6-26 Railroad Ties   The principal species used for railroad crossties are red and white oaks, Douglas-fir, gums, and southern pines. Today, most ties utilized by leading railroads are sawed (rather than hand-hewn) and pressure-treated with preservatives to prolong service life. Red oak is a preferred species, because it is dense, strong, and easily treated, and possesses superior resistance to mechanical wear. There are seven standard classes of crossties, based on width. Ties for standard gauge railroads are 8, 8½, or 9 ft long.

Before felling trees intended for conversion into railroad ties, the forester should check with local buyers or railroad agents about acceptable timber species and quantities that can be marketed. Trees of hardwood species are preferably cut in fall or winter when seasoning progresses slowly and there is less chance for end-checking of logs, sap stains, and incipient decay. Ties must be straight-grained, with ends cut square and all bark removed. Defects such as bark seams, decay, splits, shakes, holes, and unsound knots are not permitted in high-grade ties.

Expected yields of crossties from standing trees or logs can be computed by diagramming various tie dimensions within circles representing cross-sectional areas of logs. The technique is analogous to that of determining the size of inscribed square timbers (Sec. 5-5) or constructing a diagram log rule (Sec. 6-5). Tabulations of predicted yields by tie class and log size are referred to as *tie log rules*. Such rules are of considerable aid in evaluating alternative product uses for standing timber.

6-27 Mine Timbers   More than three-fourths of the mine timbers used in the United States and Canada are cut from assorted hardwoods such as beech, maple, hickory, ash, poplar, gum, and oak. Depending on local custom and requirements, mine timbers may be round, split, hand-hewn, or sawed. Because dimensions vary from place to place, the following specifications are merely indicative of size ranges encountered.

Mine props are round timbers used as supports for roofs and sides of tunnels; they range from 4 to 14 in. in diameter and 3 to 12 ft long. *Lagging* is round timber about 3 in. in diameter and 7 ft long; it is used behind props and caps to form the sides and roofs of tunnels. *Caps* are hewn or sawed timbers of various sizes that are placed across the tops of paired props as a support for roof lagging. *Sills* are hewn or sawed foundations for props, ranging from 8 to 12 in. across the widest face and of varied lengths. *Mine ties* are ordinary track ties 4 to 5 in. wide on the face and 3 to 5 ft long.

Mine timbers are commonly purchased on a green-weight basis, though certain sawed items (e.g., mine ties) may be handled as piece products or measured in terms of board feet. Round and untreated mine props may be sold without removal of bark. Mine timbers are used primarily in areas where coal, iron ore, copper, lead, zinc, and silver are extracted. Thus the principal markets are found in regions producing large quantities of these minerals.

6-28 Stumps for the Wood Naval-Stores Industry   In southeastern United States, residual stumps of old-growth longleaf and slash pines are utilized for the extraction of turpentine, rosin, and various pine oils. Only heartwood (sometimes referred to as *lightwood*) is valuable; hence wood producers prefer older stumps from which all sapwood has been removed by weathering and decay. Stumps and taproots are "pushed" out of the ground with large bulldozers equipped with coarsely toothed blades. Then they are loaded onto trucks or railroad cars for transport to one of more than a dozen steam-and-solvent extraction plants in Alabama, Florida, Georgia, Louisiana, or Mississippi.

Pine stumpwood is purchased by the ton, and, where stumps are readily accessible, profitable removal operations may be conducted for yields as low as 1 ton (five to eight average stumps) per acre. In general, stump lands are classed as "operable" if the area will support harvesting equipment during average seasons, if the area can be worked without undue damage to live trees, and if the stumpwood tract size is 25 acres or larger.

Inventories, or cruises, of pine stumps are accomplished by use of sample strips or plots similar to those designed for tallies of live timber (Chap. 10). Tracts are designated as operable, timber-locked, inaccessible, or nonproductive, and stumps are tallied by three to five groundline diameter categories. Foresters concerned with inventories or leases of stumpwood may obtain prices and additional specifications from wood naval-stores extraction plants.

6-29 Bolts and Billets   *Bolts* are short sections of logs, usually less than 8 ft long (e.g., veneer bolts). When bolts are split or sawed lengthwise, they are called *billets.* Collectively, bolts and billets are used for such products as cooperage, excelsior, handles, vehicle parts, shingles, baseball bats, pencils, and matches. A variety of hardwood and coniferous species are utilized. For example, white oak is used for tight cooperage, hickory for handles, western red-cedar for shingles, ash for baseball bats, and white pine for matches.

In general, bolts and billets are shorter than 8 ft in length, are less than 12 in. in diameter, and must be composed of high-quality materials. However, exact size and grade requirements are so diversified that accurate specifications must be obtained locally. Bolts under 12 in. in diameter are usually measured and sold in terms of stacked cords; those 12 in. and larger may be scaled in board feet. Billets may be sold by piece counts, short cords, or standard cords.

6-30 Fuel Wood With increased emphasis on energy conservation, firewood has once again become an important forest product in the United States and Canada. Firewood is commonly measured and sold in terms of stacked *short cords* or *face cords,* for example, a 4-ft × 8-ft stack of wood with stick lengths that range from about 16 in. to 2 ft or more. Thus a face cord of 16-in.-long firewood is actually one-third of a standard cord. As with pulpwood, the amount of *solid* wood contained depends on stick diameters, straightness, and care in stacking.

In some parts of Anglo-America, firewood is sold by the ton. Persons who purchase wood by weight instead of volume should seek out the driest wood available; the weight of unseasoned firewood is greatly influenced by its moisture content. And although bark is rarely removed from firewood, sticks over 8 in. in diameter should be split to facilitate seasoning.

Firewood is usually cut and marketed locally. As a result, a wide variety of species are utilized, with preference given to dense hardwoods such as oak, hickory, beech, birch, maple, ash, and elm. The heavier species weigh about 2 tons per cord and in a dry condition will provide about as much heat as a short ton of coal, 175 gal of domestic fuel oil, or 24,000 cu ft of natural gas (USDA, 1978).

PROBLEMS

6-1 Compute the total volume and total value for these items of lumber:
   a 139 pieces 3 in. × 6 in. × 16 ft @ $228.50 per MBF
   b 254 pieces 2 in. × 4 in. × 18 ft @ $232.45 per MBF
   c 346 pieces 2 in. × 8 in. × 20 ft @ $336.00 per MBF
6-2 Devise a diagram log rule for scaling diameters of 10 through 20 in., by 2-in. classes. Assume a saw kerf of ¼ in., board thickness of 1 in., minimum board width of 6 in., and a uniform log length of 16 ft. Compare diagram volumes with those listed for the Scribner log rule.
6-3 Assume that the log shown in Figure 6-2 is 16 feet in length.
   a Compute the total board-foot volume for the boards shown in the diagram.
   b Calculate the total cubic-foot volume of the log, assuming it is a perfect cylinder.
   c Compute the board foot-cubic foot ratio for this log.
6-4 Visit a sawmill in your own locality, and conduct a simple study of mill overrun based on two different log rules. Tabulate results as shown in Table 6-2.
6-5 The following tabulation of mill overrun or underrun for southern pine logs was compiled by the U.S. Forest Service (Campbell, 1962):

		Percent of overrun or underrun		
Log dib (in.)	Doyle	Scribner Decimal C	International ¼-in.	No. of logs
6	+400	+28	−2	89
7	200	26	−2	102
8	130	23	−3	134
9	90	21	−3	162
10	70	19	−4	155
11	50	17	−4	132
12	42	14	−5	167
13	32	12	−5	119
14	26	10	−6	128
15	20	8	−6	85
16	16	5	−7	74
17	12	3	−8	43
18	8	1	−8	42
19	4	−2	−9	22
20	0	−4	−9	16
21	−2	−6	−10	8
22	−4	−8	−11	8
23	−6	−10	−11	3
24	−8	−13	−12	2
Total				1,491

Plot percent of overrun (+) or underrun (−) over log diameter for each of the three log rules, then

a Compute the mean and standard deviation of the overrun/underrun values for the Doyle, Scribner, and International log rules.

b Which of the three log rules is the most consistent? The least consistent?

6-6 Select 10 to 20 defective sawlogs for a sample scaling project. Tally by log number, species, diameter, length, gross scale, type and amount of defect, and net scale. Record gross volumes in terms of the Scribner Decimal C log rule. Compute defect deductions by using (a) board-foot deduction methods described in Section 6-12 and (b) Grosenbaugh's cull percent formulas outlined in Section 6-13.

6-7 Use the data in Table 6-2 on log-scaling diameter, log length, and lumber tally to develop a mill-tally log rule.

a Plot lumber tally (Y) versus log diameter (D), log length (L), and log diameter squared times length (D^2L). Which variable (D, L, or D^2L) is more closely related to lumber tally?

b Develop a mill-tally log rule by fitting the simple linear regression

$$Y = b_0 + b_1 X$$

where Y = lumber tally (bd ft)
$X = D^2L$

6-8 Investigate sawlog weight-scaling practices in your own locality. Determine which species are involved, average green log weights per MBF, and average number of logs per ton. Prepare a written report on your findings.

6-9 Determine minimum log diameters that are required to produce crossties of the following dimensions: (a) 6 × 6 in., (b) 8 × 8 in., (c) 10 × 10 in.

6-10 Compile a veneer log rule by use of the formula presented in Section 6-23. Assume a bolt length of 4, 6, or 8 ft, and compute veneer yields for logs 14 to 36 in. in diameter, by 2-in. classes. Base your table on a standard veneer thickness of $\frac{1}{16}$ in.

REFERENCES

Amateis, R. L., Burkhart, H. E., Greber, B. J., and Watson, E. E. 1984. A comparison of approaches for predicting multiple-product yields from weight-scaling data. *Forest Sci.* **30:**991–998.

Anonymous. 1972. System scales logs automatically; uses infrared scan, digital control. *Forest Industries* (Sept.). 4 pp.

Bower, D. R. 1962. Volume-weight relationships for loblolly pine sawlogs. *J. Forestry* **60:**411–412.

Campbell, R. A. 1962. Overrun—southern pine logs. *U.S. Forest Serv., Southeast. Forest Expt. Sta., Res. Note* 183. 2 pp.

————. 1964. Forest Service log grades for southern pine. *U.S. Forest Serv., Southeast. Forest Expt. Sta., Res. Paper SE*-11. 17 pp.

Freese, F. 1973. A collection of log rules. *U.S. Dept. Agr., Forest Serv., Forest Prod. Lab. Gen. Tech. Rep. FPL* 1. 65 pp.

Grosenbaugh, L. R. 1952. Shortcuts for cruisers and scalers. *U.S. Forest Serv., Southern Forest Expt. Sta., Occas. Paper* 126. 24 pp.

Haygreen, J. G., and Bowyer, J. L. 1996. *Forest products and wood science,* 3d ed. Iowa State University Press, Ames, Iowa. 484 pp.

Ker, J. W. 1966. The measurement of forest products in Canada: Past, present and future historical and legislative background. *Forestry Chron.* **42:**29–38.

Markstrom, D. C., and King, R. M. 1993. Cubic foot/weight scaling of Rocky Mountain sawtimber. *U.S. Forest Serv., Rocky Mountain Forest and Range Expt. Sta., Res. Paper RM*-311. 9 pp.

McKinley, T. W. 1953. Veneer tables: Surface feet tabulations for rotary cut and special veneers. *J. Forestry* **51:**826–827.

Page, R. H., and Bois, P. J. 1961. Buying and selling southern yellow pine saw logs by weight. *Georgia Forest Res. Council Rept.* 7. 9 pp.

Ralston, R. A. 1956. The break-even point for rough 8-foot bolts merchantable as sawlogs or cordwood. *U.S. Forest Serv., Lake States Forest Expt. Sta., Tech. Note* 469. 2 pp.

Rast, E. D., Sonderman, D. L., and Gammon, G. L. 1973. A guide to hardwood log grading. *U.S. Forest Serv., Northeast. Forest Expt. Sta., Gen. Tech. Rep. NE*-1. 31 pp.

Schnur, G. L., and Lane, R. D. 1948. Log rule comparison: International ¼-inch, Doyle, and Scribner. *U.S. Forest Serv., Central States Forest Expt. Sta., Note* 47. 6 pp.

Schroeder, J. G., Campbell, R. A., and Rodenback, R. C. 1968. Southern pine log grades for yard and structural timber. *U.S. Forest Serv., Southeast. Forest Expt. Sta., Res. Paper SE*-39. 9 pp.

U.S. Department of Agriculture. 1978. *Firewood for your fireplace.* Government Printing Office, Washington, D.C. Leaflet 559. 2 pp.

————. 1985. *National Forest Log Scaling Handbook.* U.S. Forest Service, Government Printing Office, Washington, D.C. 247 pp.

————. 1999. *Wood handbook: Wood as an engineering material.* U.S. Forest Service. Forest Prod. Soc., Madison, Wis. (various paging).

Williston, H. L. 1957. Pole grower's guide. *U.S. Forest Serv., Southern Forest Expt. Sta., Occas. Paper* 153. 34 pp.

CHAPTER 7

MEASURING STANDING TREES

7-1 Tree Diameters The most frequent tree measurement made by foresters is diameter at breast height. In the United States, diameter at breast height (dbh) is defined as the average stem diameter, outside of the bark, at a point 4.5 ft above ground as measured from the uphill side of the stem. In countries that use the metric system, dbh is usually taken 1.3 m above ground. Direct measurements are usually made with a diameter tape, tree caliper, or Biltmore stick. Collectively, instruments employed in determining tree diameters are referred to as *dendrometers*.

With a diameter tape, tree circumference is the variable actually measured (Fig. 7-1). The tape graduations, based on the relationship between the diameter and circumference of a circle, permit direct readings of tree diameter, usually to the nearest 0.1 in. If a steel diameter tape is level and pulled taut, it is the most *consistent* method of measuring dbh. However, as tree cross sections are rarely circular, taped readings of irregular trees are likely to be positively biased.

Wooden or steel tree calipers provide a quick and simple method of directly measuring dbh. For ordinary cruising work, a single caliper measurement will usually suffice (Fig. 7-2). Directional bias can be minimized by measuring all diameters from the tree face closest to a cruise plot center. If stem cross sections are decidedly elliptical, two caliper readings at right angles should be made and the average diameter recorded. When caliper arms are truly parallel and in correct ad-

FIGURE 7-1
Using a steel diameter tape, the dbh of this pine tree is measured as 11.8 in.

justment, the instrument gives reliable measures of dbh to the nearest 0.1 in. Calipers are ideal for trees up to about 18 in. in diameter. The diameter tape is often preferred for bigger stems because large calipers are bulky and awkward to handle in thick underbrush.

A modification of the conventional caliper is the diameter "fork," a two-pronged instrument that can be held in one hand while measuring small trees. One prong of the fork is movable and spring-loaded, resulting in an automatic adjustment to the sides of the stem. Diameters are read from a built-in-arc type scale on the fork.

The Biltmore stick is a straight wooden stick specially graduated for direct readings of dbh. Based on a principle of similar triangles, the stick must be held horizontally against the tree dbh at a predetermined distance from the observer's eye (Fig. 7-3). The cruiser's perspective view is compensated for by the dbh graduations; i.e., the inch units get progressively shorter as tree diameters increase. Thus it is possible to measure a 40-in.-diameter tree with a stick about 25 in. long.

Scale graduations for the Biltmore stick may be computed by

$$\text{dbh graduation} = \sqrt{\frac{AD^2}{A + D}}$$

FIGURE 7-2
Measuring tree dbh with wooden calipers. *(Photograph by Rick Griffiths.)*

where *A* is the fixed distance from the eye to the stick in inches, and *D* is any selected tree diameter in inches.

On commercially manufactured Biltmore sticks, diameter graduations are usually based on a fixed distance of 25 in. from the observer's eye to dbh. However, foresters may construct sticks based on a different arm reach by use of the preceding formula (Avery, 1959). Because of the difficulty of maintaining the proper distance from eye to tree, the Biltmore stick must be regarded as a rather crude measuring device. With care, diameters of small trees can be read to the nearest full inch, but accuracy tends to decrease for larger trees because of the shortened intervals between inch graduations. The Biltmore stick is handy for occasional cruising work, but tree calipers or the diameter tape should be used for more reliable measurements of individual trees.

7-2 Diameter at Breast Height for Irregular Trees   Whatever the type of dendrometer used, constant care must be exercised to measure trees exactly at dbh—or at a rational deviation from this point when irregular stems are encountered. For trees growing on slopes, for example, it is recommended that dbh be measured 4.5 ft above ground from the *uphill* side of the tree. Figure 7-4 il-

FIGURE 7-3
Measuring tree dbh with a Biltmore stick. *(Photograph by Rick Griffiths.)*

lustrates suggested methods of maintaining consistency in obtaining diameter measurements.

When swellings, bumps, depressions, or branches occur 4.5 ft above ground, tree diameters are usually taken just above the irregularity at a point where it ceases to affect normal stem form. If a tree forks immediately above dbh, it is measured below the swell resulting from the double stem. Stems that fork below dbh are considered as two separate trees, and diameters are measured (or estimated) approximately 3.5 ft above the fork. Cypress, tupelo gum, and other swell-butted species are measured 1.5 ft above the pronounced swell, or "bottleneck," if the swell is more than 3 ft high. Such measurements are usually referred to as *normal diameters* and are abbreviated dn.

When there is heavy snow cover on the ground or when diameters are measured under floodwater conditions, a pole should be used as a probe to locate true ground level; otherwise, the point of diameter measurement may be made too high up on the tree stem.

If successive diameter measurements are taken on the same trees (as on permanent sample plots), relative accuracy can be improved by marking the exact

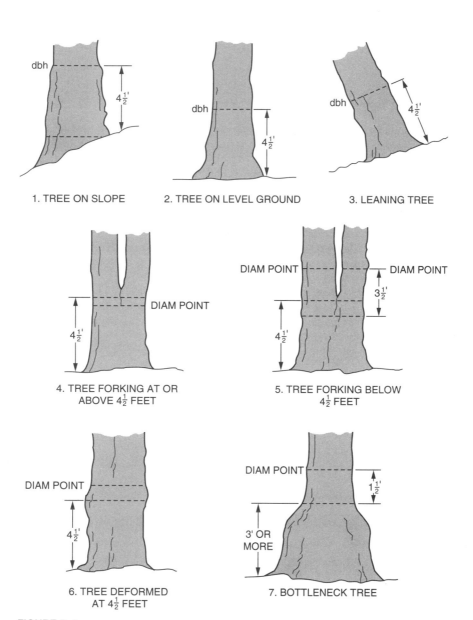

1. TREE ON SLOPE   2. TREE ON LEVEL GROUND   3. LEANING TREE

4. TREE FORKING AT OR ABOVE $4\frac{1}{2}$ FEET

5. TREE FORKING BELOW $4\frac{1}{2}$ FEET

6. TREE DEFORMED AT $4\frac{1}{2}$ FEET

7. BOTTLENECK TREE

FIGURE 7-4
Points of dbh measurement for sloping ground or irregular tree stems. *(Courtesy: U.S. Forest Service.)*

dbh point on each tree. And when calipers are used, measurements should be made *in the same direction* each time.

7-3 Measuring Bark Thickness   Although dbh measurements are made outside bark, a common objective for computing tree volume is the diameter inside bark (dib). Reliable measures of bark thickness are essential because the breast-height ratio of dib/dob is often applied to estimate inside-bark diameters for inaccessible points on the tree stem.

The standard measurement tool employed is called a *bark gauge* (Fig. 7-5). Since bark thickness tends to vary from one side of a tree to another, a minimum of two readings should be taken. When dob is obtained with calipers, the two bark measurements should be made exactly where the caliper arms make contact with the tree stem. The two readings are added together and subtracted from dob to obtain dib.

Where dbh is determined with a diameter tape, bark thickness should be measured radially from the wood surface to the contour of the tape. Two or more thicknesses should be measured, depending on the eccentricity of the cross section. By this technique, bark thickness is regarded as the difference in diameters of two

FIGURE 7-5
Measuring bark thickness at breast height.

concentric circles, one defined by the bark surface, the other by the interior wood surface (Mesavage, 1969b).

When commercially manufactured bark gauges are not available, a fair substitute can be improvised by filing graduations on the steel bit of a sharpened screwdriver, or by using a carpenter's brace and auger bit.

7-4 Tree Diameter Classes   Although tree diameters are commonly measured to the nearest 0.1 in., it is often expedient to group such measurements into diameter classes. If 1-in. classes are used, it is customary to drop back to the lower value when diameters fall exactly halfway between inch graduations—just as in log scaling (Sec. 6-10). Thus the class boundaries or true class limits for 8-in. trees are 7.6 to 8.5 in.; the 9-in. class ranges from 8.6 to 9.5 in., and so on. Two-inch class boundaries are commonly defined for 8-in. trees as 7.1 to 9.0 in., for 10-in. trees as 9.1 to 11.0 in., and so on.

7-5 Basal Area and Mean Diameter   Tree-stem diameter measurements are often converted to cross-sectional areas. The cross-sectional area at breast height is called *basal area*. To compute tree basal area, one commonly assumes that the tree stem is circular in cross section at breast height. Thus the formula for calculating basal area is (Sec. 5-2)

$$BA(ft^2) = \frac{\pi dbh^2}{4(144)} = 0.005454 \ dbh^2$$

when basal area is desired in square feet and dbh is measured in inches. If metric units are used, basal area is desired in m^2, and dbh is measured in cm, then the formula for basal area is

$$BA(m^2) = \frac{\pi dbh^2}{4(10,000)} = 0.00007854 \ dbh^2$$

Average dbh of a stand of trees is a highly informative statistic for forest managers. Two average dbh values are in common use. The arithmetic mean dbh ($\overline{dbh}$) is simply the sum of the tree dbh values divided by the number of trees; that is,

$$\overline{dbh} = \frac{\sum_{i=1}^{n} dbh_i}{n}$$

Alternatively, the *quadratic mean diameter* (also termed the diameter of the tree of mean basal area) may be computed. If basal area (BA) is in square feet and dbh is in inches, one notes from the first expression in Section 7-5 for basal area that

$$dbh^2 = \frac{BA}{0.005454}$$

The quadratic mean dbh ($\overline{\mathrm{dbh}_q}$) in inches is computed by determining the mean basal area in square feet per tree ($\overline{\mathrm{BA}}$) and substituting into the following formula:

$$\overline{\mathrm{dbh}_q} = \sqrt{\frac{\overline{\mathrm{BA}}}{0.005454}}$$

Computation of quadratic mean dbh in metric units follows by analogy. It should be noted that, for typical tree-diameter data, the two mean dbh values will not be equal, but rather the quadratic mean dbh will be slightly larger than the arithmetic mean dbh.

7-6 Upper-Stem Diameters   Out-of-reach diameters are frequently required in studies of tree form, taper, and volume. Although such diameters are best obtained by direct measurement, the use of ladders and climbing irons is time-consuming, awkward, and often hazardous. As a result, a number of diverse upper-stem dendrometers have been proposed. These include such items as calipers attached to a pole, binoculars with a mil scale in one eyepiece, telescopic stadia devices, and split-image rangefinders. A comprehensive investigation of optical dendrometers has been conducted by Grosenbaugh (1963).

Most upper-stem dendrometers are limited in usefulness because either they do not provide sufficient accuracy or they are prohibitively expensive. Some are also quite complex in operation. An ideal upper-stem dendrometer would be simple to use, portable, relatively inexpensive, accurate at all tree heights, and operable independently of distance from point of measurement. Although it may be unrealistic to expect all these attributes in a single instrument, several are incorporated in the pentaprism tree caliper (Wheeler, 1962).

In effect, the penta prism caliper may be compared to an imaginary giant caliper that can be clamped on a tree stem at any point and from any distance without special calibration. Two pentaprisms, one fixed and the other movable, are mounted so that extended parallel lines of sight may be viewed simultaneously (Fig. 7-6). Prisms are oriented so that the right side of the tree stem is brought into coincidence with the left side, which is viewed directly. A scale is provided so that dob may be read through the fixed (left-hand) prism at the point of coincidence.

Tests of the Wheeler pentaprism caliper indicate that upper-stem diameters as high as 50 ft above ground may be read to an accuracy of 0.2 to 0.5 in. Greater accuracy may be feasible if an optical-lens system is used to replace the sighting tube on original models of the instrument.

The Barr and Stroud optical dendrometer has been used extensively for measuring upper-stem diameters. Mounted on a tripod, this instrument is a split-image, coincident-type magnifying rangefinder for estimating inaccessible diameters, heights, and distances. The last model manufactured, model FP 15, is designed to the following accuracy specifications:

FIGURE 7-6
Measuring an upper-stem diameter with the Wheeler pentaprism tree caliper.
(Courtesy U.S. Forest Service.)

Diameter   0.1 in. for tree diameters from 1.5 to 10 in., and 1 percent for diameters from 10 to 200 in.

Height   1.5 percent at all heights above 10° elevation.

Distance   0.2 percent at 45 ft, 0.6 percent at 90 ft, 1.2 percent at 300 ft, 2.2 percent at 600 ft, and 6.8 percent at 2,000 ft.

The instrument readings are nonlinear for both distance and diameter; scale readings must therefore be transformed by using tables supplied by the manufacturer or by using special computer programs. Such conversions can be tedious when a large number of readings are involved.

Field tests of this instrument have shown that the manufacturer's claims for accuracy can be substantiated under good sighting conditions. With reliable dendrometer readings, volume growth for the upper stem may be determined on standing trees by repeated measurements at specified time intervals.

Where reliable instruments are available for measuring upper-stem diameters of standing trees, log volumes may be determined by *height accumulation,* a concept of tree measurement developed by Grosenbaugh (1954). In essence, this technique consists of selecting tree diameters above dbh in a specified progression; then tree height to each diameter is estimated, recorded, and accumulated. In contrast to usual tree measurement procedures, outside bark diameter at selected intervals is treated as the independent variable, and heights are recorded at irregular intervals. This technique permits individual trees to be broken down into various product uses and recombined with similar sections from other trees.

TREE HEIGHTS

7-7 Height Poles For smaller trees, height can be measured directly with height poles (Fig. 7-7). *Height poles* (sometimes called height sticks) consist of sections of light-weight material (usually fiberglass) that can be extended to form a measuring stick of length equal to the height of the tree being measured. The base section of the pole is scaled (e.g., feet and tenths of feet, or meters and decimeters) such that total height can be read directly from the last extended section. Poles can be used quite efficiently for trees up to 40 feet (12 m) or so in total height; for trees taller than 40 feet, poles tend to be cumbersome and slow to use.

Two people are required to measure trees efficiently with height poles. One person stands at the base of the tree and extends the pole by adding sections at the bottom of the pole (or by pulling interior sections out of the base section of the pole) while guiding the tip of the pole along the tree bole until the tip is even with the top of the tree. The second person in the crew serves as an observer to help align the pole tip with the top of the tree and as a recorder of the measurements.

Although efficient and accurate for smaller trees, poles are not a practical means of determining heights for larger timber. Hence, a wide variety of hypsometers for indirect measurement of height have been developed.

FIGURE 7-7
With the tip of the extendable pole aligned with the tip of the tree (left), total height of this eastern white pine tree is read (to nearest decimeter) as 11.1 m (right).

7-8 Height Measurement Principles Instruments used for measuring tree heights are collectively referred to as *hypsometers*. Many types of height-measuring devices and instruments have been evolved, but only a few have gained wide acceptance by practicing foresters. Thus only two of the more common designs are discussed here. The basic trigonometric principle most frequently embodied in hypsometers is illustrated in Figure 7-8. The observer stands at a fixed horizontal distance from the base of the tree, usually 50, 66, or 100 ft. Tangents of angles to the top and base of the tree are multiplied by horizontal distance to derive the height of each measured section of the stem. The Abney level and several *clinometers* or *altimeters* (Fig. 7-9) operate on this principle, yielding height readings directly in feet or meters at fixed horizontal distances from the tree.

For accurate results, trees must not lean more than 5° from the vertical, and the fixed horizontal distance must be determined by taped measurement or careful pacing. Instruments equal in caliber to the Abney level will provide readings within 2 to 5 percent of true heights, provided both points of tree measurement are clearly discernible. Leaning trees should be measured at right angles to the direction of lean to minimize height errors.

When using an instrument such as the Abney level on gentle terrain, a level line of sight from the observer's eye will usually intercept the tree stem somewhere between stump height and the tree top. As a result, angular readings to the base and the top of the tree will appear on *opposite sides* of the zero point on the graduated instrument scale. In such instances, the two readings must be *added* together to obtain the desired height value.

In mountainous terrain, the observer's hypsometer position may be below the base of the tree or occasionally above the desired upper point of measurement. If a level line of sight from the observer fails to intercept the tree stem, both angular

FIGURE 7-8
Principle of height measurement with the Abney level and similar hypsometers.

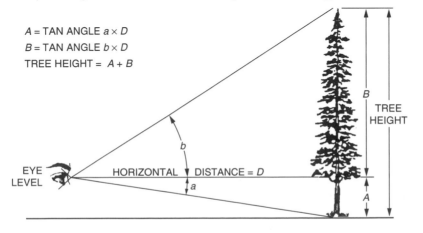

A = TAN ANGLE $a \times D$
B = TAN ANGLE $b \times D$
TREE HEIGHT = $A + B$

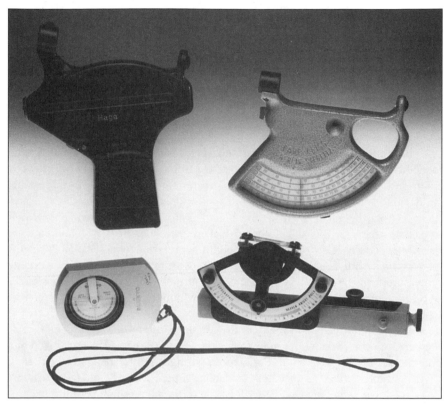

FIGURE 7-9
Examples of hypsometers (upper left, Haga altimeter; upper right, Blume-Leiss; lower left, Suunto clinometer; lower right, Abney level). *(Photograph by Rick Griffiths.)*

readings will then appear on the *same side* of the instrument zero point. Tree height is derived by taking the *difference* between the two readings.

7-9 Merritt Hypsometer   This linear scale, often imprinted on one face of a standard Biltmore stick, is based on a principle of similar triangles. It is normally used for determining merchantable log heights rather than total heights, and graduations are placed at 16-ft log intervals or 8-ft half-log intervals. As with the Biltmore stick, the hypsometer must be positioned at a fixed distance from the eye and the observer must stand a specified distance from the tree. In use, the Merritt hypsometer is held vertically with the lower end of the stick on a line of sight to tree-stump height. With the stick held plumb, the observer then glances up to note the log height at the desired point on the upper stem. Improvised rules may be calibrated for any desired arm reach and specified distance by

$$\frac{\text{Arm reach (in.)}}{\text{Distance from tree (ft)}} = \frac{\text{scale interval (in.)}}{\text{log height (ft)}}$$

The ratio is solved to determine the scale interval, and this distance is uniformly marked off on a straight rule to define the desired log-height spacings. The Merritt hypsometer is a useful aid for estimating tree heights by log intervals, but it is not reliable for precise work.

7-10 Total versus Merchantable Heights   *Total tree height* is the linear distance from ground level to the upper tip of the tree crown. The tip of the crown is easily defined when trees have conical shapes, but it may not be readily discernible for deciduous trees having irregular or round-topped crowns. Thus the measurement of total height is more applicable to coniferous trees having *excurrent* branching characteristics than to broad-leaved deciduous trees with *deliquescent* branching patterns. Recording of total heights is preferred to merchantable lengths on permanent sample plots when tree-growth measurements are based on periodic remeasurements of the same trees. Here, measurement of the entire stem is likely to be more objective and less subject to errors of judgment than heights measured to an ocularly selected merchantable top.

Merchantable tree height refers to the usable portion of the tree stem, that is, the part for which volume is computed or the section expected to be utilized in a commercial logging operation. For smooth, straight stems, merchantable height may be simply defined as the length from an assumed stump height to an arbitrarily fixed upper-stem diameter. Exact location of the upper-diameter limit may require considerable proficiency in ocular estimation, perhaps including occasional checks with an upper-stem dendrometer.

When upper limits of stem merchantability are not dictated by branches, crook, or defect, minimum top diameters may be chosen as a percentage of dbh. With sawtimber-sized trees, for example, minimum top diameters may be set at approximately 60 percent of dbh for small trees, 50 percent of dbh for medium-sized trees, and 40 percent of dbh for large trees. This procedure, more often applied to conifers than to hardwoods, rationally presumes that the larger the dbh, the rougher the upper stem of a tree. Thus top-log-scaling diameters will be larger for mature or old-growth trees than for smaller, second-growth stems. When merchantable heights are tallied for inventory purposes, minimum top diameters must be selected in accordance with the particular volume equation to be used. Failure to observe this precaution will result in highly inaccurate estimates of individual tree volume.

7-11 Sawlog Merchantability for Irregular Stems   For many hardwood species, minimum top diameters and sawlog merchantability are regulated by tree form, branches, stem roughness, or defect (rotten cull material). Some typical stem forms that may be encountered in sawlog height determination are illustrated in Figure 7-10. Bole sections designated as *upper stem* refer to sound portions un-

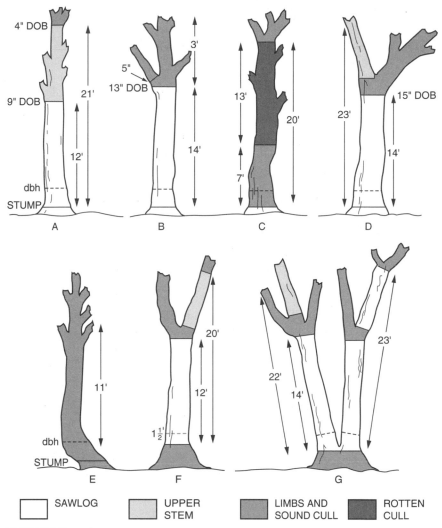

FIGURE 7-10
Merchantable height limits for irregular bole forms. *(Courtesy U.S. Forest Service.)*

suitable for sawlogs but usable for lower-grade products such as fence posts or pulpwood. Limbs and sound cull material are considered unmerchantable because of roughness, form, or size. Following is a brief description prepared by the U.S. Forest Service for each tree pictured:

A: Sawtimber tree   Sawlog length terminates at 9-in. top dob. Meets minimum qualifications of a 12-ft sawlog. Upper stem portion contains no cull and terminates at 4 in. dob. Sawlog length is recorded as 12 ft; bole length as 21 ft.

B: Sawtimber tree Sawlog portion terminated by limbs at 13 in. dob. Contains no cull and meets minimum grade specifications. Both bole length and sawlog length are 14 ft. Portion between whorls of limbs is large enough in diameter but not in length to qualify as upper stem (i.e., it is less than 4 ft long).

C: Rotten cull tree Although sawlog portion is 20 ft long, a 13-ft section of rotten cull prevents utilization of a log meeting minimum grade specifications; thus the entire sawlog portion is culled. Because more than half the volume in that portion is rotten, the tree is classed as a rotten cull.

D: Sawtimber tree Sawlog portion terminates because of branching at 15-in. or top dob. Right-hand fork is too limby to qualify as upper stem, but 7 ft of left-hand fork qualifies as upper stem.

E: Rough tree Sawlog top terminates by branches 11 ft above crooked butt. No sawlog meeting minimum requirements present.

F: Sawtimber tree Despite sound cull in the sawlog portion due to butt swell, a 12-ft sawlog is present. Seven feet of right-hand fork qualifies as upper stem. Left-hand fork does not qualify because of crook.

G: Two sawtimber trees Because lowest fork is below dbh, each fork is appraised and recorded as a separate tree. The lower 14-ft section in the left-hand fork meets requirements for a sawtimber tree. A 6-ft portion of the largest stem in upper fork qualifies as upper stem material. In the main right-hand fork, a 13 ½-ft sawlog plus a 9-ft sawlog (with an intervening 1-ft section of sound cull) is recorded as 23 ft of sawlog length.

TREE FORM EXPRESSIONS

7-12 Form Factors and Quotients The comparison of tree bole forms with various solids of revolution (cylinders, paraboloids, etc.) may be expressed in numerical terms as *form factors*. Such ratios are derived by dividing stem volume by the volume of a chosen solid. However, as form factors cannot be computed until essential stem diameters are obtained, it has become customary to express stem configuration in terms of form quotients derived directly from the diameter ratios themselves.

A *form quotient* is the ratio of some upper-stem diameter to dbh. The value is always less than unity and is usually expressed as a percentage. Higher form quotients indicate lower rates of stem taper and correspondingly greater tree volumes. For a given species, form quotients are lowest for open-grown trees with long live crowns and highest for forest-grown trees with relatively short crowns. Thus for given soil and site conditions, stand density has an indirect effect on tree-taper rates. The primary expression of form that has been used in the United States is known as *Girard form class*.

7-13 Girard Form Class This form quotient is computed as the ratio between stem diameter *inside* of the bark at the top of the first 16-ft log and dbh *outside* of the bark. With a log trimming allowance of 0.3 ft and a 1-ft stump, the

FIGURE 7-11
The points of diameter measurement for determining Girard form class are shown by tree bands at breast height and at the top of the first 16-ft log. This ponderosa pine has a form class of 82 and a total height of 69 ft.

upper-stem measurement is taken 17.3 ft above ground. As an example, a tree with a first-log-scaling diameter of 16 in. and a dbh of 20 in. has a Girard form class of $16 \div 20 = 0.80$, or 80 percent (Fig. 7-11).

Sawtimber volume tables based on Girard form class assume that trees having the same diameter and merchantable height will have similar, though not necessarily identical, rates of taper in the sawlog portion *above the first log*. It is thereby implied that all volume differences in trees of the same diameter and merchantable height may be attributed largely to taper variations occurring *in the first log.* Girard form-class tables are *composite* volume tables; they are compiled independently of tree species and are applicable to both coniferous and broad-leaved trees.

For swell-butted species such as cypress and tupelo gum, diameter measured 1.5 ft above the pronounced swell should be substituted for dbh in computing Girard form class. Measurement of the scaling diameter remains at 17.3 ft above ground; thus the two diameters may be only 6 to 10 ft apart in some cases. For trees deformed by chipped turpentine faces at breast height, the normal diameter should be measured just above the highest face. Although the diameter here will be smaller, form class will be higher, resulting in a compensating volume increase.

7-14 Form Measurements   Most foresters prefer form expressions based on relatively accessible measurements, a factor that has probably contributed to the popularity of Girard form class. Even here, the diameter measurement at 17.3 ft can rarely be ocularly estimated with precision and consistency; thus it is usually better to have a carefully measured sample of a few stems rather than rough estimates of form class for each tree tallied. Obtaining reliable inside-bark measurements at the top of the first 16-ft log implies the use of ladders or climbing irons—an expensive and time-consuming task. As an alternative, however, dob at the top of the first log can be determined with an optical dendrometer, and the corresponding dib computed from a breast-height ratio of dib/dob. Or the form class can be ocularly estimated by using a simple sighting device such as that suggested by Wiant (1972). When applying Girard form-class values, the difference between one class and another (e.g., 79 versus 80) amounts to approximately 3 percent in terms of merchantable tree volume.

TREE CROWNS

7-15 Importance of Crown Measures   Larger crown sizes generally produce higher growth rates for trees of a given species and age. Crown characteristics are useful for predicting responses to silvicultural treatments, such as thinning and fertilizer applications. Consequently, crown measures are often incorporated in growth and yield models (Chap. 17) as part of the information used to estimate tree growth. Crown size, which is a surrogate for the amount of photosynthetically active foliage, is typically quantified via measures of crown width and length (Fig. 7-12).

7-16 Crown Width   Crown profiles are irregular and the branches of neighboring trees are often interlocked. Although the determination of crown width (or crown diameter) is not simple, a number of workable definitions have been applied. As with tree boles, the area of a tree's crown is typically determined by calculating an average diameter and then assuming a circular shape. Average

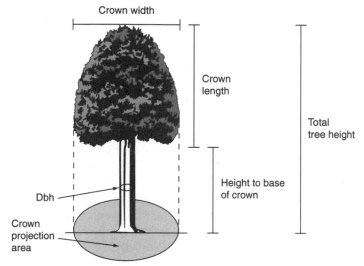

FIGURE 7-12
Crown width and length are commonly measured on standing trees.

diameter for crowns may be defined in a variety of ways, but some of the more commonly employed definitions are

- the average of the maximum and minimum diameter
- the average of maximum diameter and the diameter measured at right angles to the axis of the maximum
- the average of a diameter chosen either at random or in some prespecified direction and a second diameter taken at right angles to the first

For highly irregular crowns, more than two diameter measurements may be taken and averaged. For very small trees, where the crown is within the reach of the observer, crown width can be measured directly. When crowns are above the reach of observers but low enough that the edges can be easily discerned, widths may be determined by looking up and positioning the zero end of a tape or measuring stick at the edge of the crown with another person making an ocular estimate of the far edges of the crown and reading the measurement. For larger trees, there is too much error involved in ocularly estimating the crown edges. In such cases, the edges of two opposite sides of the crown are projected vertically to the ground using a plumb line, optical prism, or other instrument capable of projecting a vertical line of sight. The crown edges are marked on the ground and the horizontal distance between the marks is measured with a tape. Diameters of tree crowns can also be measured on aerial photographs (Chap. 13), but these measurements are generally not as reliable as ground measurements because only parts of the crown are visible, and hence measurable, on the photograph.

7-17 Crown Length   The length of green crown may be defined as the vertical distance from the tip (highest growing point) to the lowest live foliage. While the upper limit can generally be objectively defined, the base of tree crowns is often very difficult to ascertain. Epicormic shoots and occasional branches with a small amount of foliage are usually ignored. If the crown base extends lower on one side of the bole, a point midway between the two sides might be used to define the lower limit. For conifers, the lower margin of the crown might be defined as the lowest live branch that is part of the main green crown or as the lowest whorl of branches (where the minimum number of branches that constitute a whorl might be defined differently for different species) that make up the crown.

Height to the base of the live crown is measured with a hypsometer, typically at the same time tree height is measured. Hence, it is a convenient measurement to take. Crown length is computed as total tree height minus height to the base of the live crown. The variables of crown length and total height are often converted to crown ratio—defined as green crown length divided by total tree height—which is a measure of tree vigor that is useful for predicting future tree growth and response to silvicultural treatments.

7-18 Crown Surface Area and Volume   After acceptable measurements of average crown diameter and crown length are obtained, crown surface area and crown volume can be approximated by assuming the crown is some regular geometric solid. It is common to assume that tree crowns are cones or paraboloids. If one assumes that a cone is a reasonable approximation for the crown, the surface area and volume can be computed as

$$\text{Surface area (ft}^2, \text{m}^2) = \frac{\pi d_b}{2} \sqrt{L^2 + \left(\frac{d_b}{2}\right)^2}$$

$$\text{Volume (ft}^3, \text{m}^3) = \frac{\pi d_b^2 L}{12}$$

where

d_b = diameter (ft, m) at the crown base,
L = crown length (ft, m)

Crown surface area and crown volume have been found to be meaningful surrogates for foliage amounts and, hence, useful for predicting tree growth. In lieu of assuming that tree crowns assume the shape of cones or paraboloids, one can use equations for predicting crown profiles (e.g. , the equations of Baldwin and Peterson, 1997, for loblolly pine, or the equations of Hann, 1999, for Douglas-fir trees) to determine crown surface areas and volumes.

TREE AGE

7-19 Definitions   The age of a tree is defined as the elapsed time since germination of the seed or the time since the budding of the sprout or cutting from which the tree developed. The age of a plantation is commonly taken from the year it was formed (i.e., exclusive of the age of the nursery stock that may have been planted).

The terms "even-aged" and "uneven-aged" are often applied to forest stands; therefore, it is appropriate to define these expressions. *Even-aged stands* are composed of a single age class in which the range of tree ages usually does not exceed 20 percent of the rotation age (Helms, 1998). *Uneven-aged stands* consists of three or more distinct age classes, either intimately mixed or in small groups. *All-aged stands* are rarities that are virtually nonexistent. In theory, they include trees of all ages from minute seedlings to the harvest, or rotation, age.

The selection of sample trees for age and site index determinations in even-aged stands requires an evaluation of relative dominance or crown levels for various trees. Four crown classes are recognized:

1 *Dominant.* Trees with crowns extending above the general level of the crown cover and receiving full light from above and partly from the side; larger than the average trees in the stand, with crowns well developed but possibly somewhat crowded on the sides.

2 *Codominant.* Trees with crowns forming the general level of the crown cover and receiving full light from above but comparatively little from the sides; usually with medium-sized crowns more or less crowded on the sides.

3 *Intermediate.* Trees shorter than those in the two preceding classes but with crowns either below or extending into the crown cover formed by codominant and dominant trees and receiving little direct light from above and none from the sides; usually with small crowns considerably crowded on the sides.

4 *Suppressed.* Trees with crowns entirely below the general level of the crown cover and receiving no direct light either from above or from the sides.

7-20 Age from Annual Rings   Many tree species found in northern temperate zones grow in diameter by adding a single and distinctive layer of wood each year. The formation of this layer starts at the beginning of the growing season and continues well through it. Springwood (or earlywood) is more porous and lighter in color than summerwood (or latewood). The combination of one springwood and one summerwood band comprises a year's growth. On a stem cross section, these bands appear as a series of concentric rings. A count of the number of rings at any height gives the number of years' growth that the tree has undergone since attaining that height; thus, a ring count made on the cross section at ground level provides the total age of the tree.

If the annual ring count is made on a stump cross section or higher up on the stem, the count provides the age of the tree from that point upward. It is therefore necessary to add the number of years required for the tree to attain the height of measurement to derive total tree age.

Although the most reliable ring counts are made on complete cross sections, it is obvious that, except on logging operations, this method involves destructive sampling. Ages of standing trees are therefore determined by extracting a radial core of wood with an instrument called an *increment borer.* The hollow auger of the increment borer is pressed against the standing tree (usually at breast height) and turned until the screw bit reaches the center of the tree. A core of wood is forced into the hollow auger; the borer is then given a reverse turn to snap the core loose and permit its removal with an extractor. The number of annual rings on the core gives the age of the tree from the point of the boring upward (Fig. 7-13).

The reliability of annual ring counts depends on the species and the environmental conditions under which a particular tree may be growing. Fast-growing coniferous species in northern temperate zones usually provide the easiest counts. Difficulties are encountered when there is little contrast between springwood and summerwood, as in the case of some diffuse-porous, deciduous broad-leaved species.

Trees growing under adverse environmental conditions may produce extremely narrow or almost nonexistent rings that are difficult to count except on sanded cores or cross sections. A catastrophe such as an extended drought or tree defoli-

FIGURE 7-13
Extraction of a core of wood with an increment borer (left) and measurement of the core (right). Annual rings are discernible in the right-hand view. *(Courtesy U.S. Forest Service.)*

ation by insects, followed by favorable growth conditions, can lead to the formation of *false rings*. Such rings, which often display an incomplete circumference, may be distinguishable only when cross sections are available for analysis.

7-21 Age without Annual Rings   In many forest regions of the world (e.g., Australia, New Zealand, and numerous other countries in tropical or southern temperate zones), tree growth is generally *not* characterized by annual rings. Annual rings are usually absent in tropical conifers and in diffuse-porous, evergreen broad-leaved species unless they are growing in subalpine or alpine conditions. Therefore, except where plantations are established, it may only be possible to approximate individual tree ages.

For a limited number of species around the world (e.g., *Pinus strobus*), the age of young trees may be estimated from branch whorls. The seasonal height growth of the tree begins with the bursting of the terminal bud, which lengthens to form the leader. At the base of the leader, a circle of branchlets grows out at the same time, thus marking the height of the tree as it was before the season's growth started. The following year, the process is repeated, and so on. A count of these branch whorls will give the approximate age of the tree. For some species, 2 to 4 years must be added to account for the early growth years when no whorls were produced.

When neither annual rings nor branch whorls can be relied upon, age determination for trees in natural stands is extremely difficult. *Relative tree age* can be roughly gauged by the relative size of the tree, shape and vigor of the crown, and texture or color of the bark. Occasionally, the age of trees in naturally regenerated even-aged stands can be closely approximated from the year of the logging operation that resulted in the establishment of the stand. In similar fashion, trees whose germination followed a catastrophic event such as a fire or hurricane can also be dated. And in a few instances, counting the annual rings of *indicator species* may help to ascertain the ages of nearby trees that do not exhibit annual rings. For example, ring counts on certain scrub species have been used to assist in determining the age of associated eucalyptus trees in Tasmania (Carron, 1968).

PROBLEMS

7-1 Determine the arithmetic mean and the quadratic mean diameter for the following set of dbh values (in inches):

6, 11, 9, 15, 19, 7, 8, 12

Convert the two means from inches to centimeters.

7-2 Number 20 standing trees of varying diameters. Ocularly estimate each dbh to the nearest inch. Then, in order, remeasure diameters with (a) a Biltmore stick, (b) a diameter tape, and (c) calipers. Tabulate all measurements on a single tally sheet according to tree number. Using the average of two caliper readings as a standard, obtain plus or minus deviations for the other three diameter estimates. Discuss your findings and preferences in a brief written report.

7-3 Determine total tree height (to nearest 0.1 ft or m) from each of the following sets of measurements:

  a horizontal distance 100 ft; sighting at base −5 degrees; sighting at top +45 degrees

  b horizontal distance 50 ft; sighting at base +5 degrees; sighting at top +45 degrees

  c horizontal distance 80 ft; sighting at base −60 degrees; sighting at top −2 degrees

  d horizontal distance 30 m; sighting at base −3 degrees; sighting at top +58 degrees

7-4 Number 20 standing trees of varying total or merchantable heights. In order, obtain heights by (a) ocular estimation, (b) Merritt hypsometer, (c) Abney level, and (d) any other available clinometer. Tabulate and analyze findings in a brief written report.

7-5 For a white pine tree with dbh of 10.0 in., total height of 70 ft, diameter inside bark at 17.3 ft above ground equals 7.8 in., and bole volume equals 15.4 cu ft:

  a Compute the form quotient commonly called Girard form class.

  b Determine the form factor by using a cylinder (with diameter equal to the dbh and length equal to the total height of the subject tree) as the basis for comparison.

7-6 Construct a Biltmore stick and Merritt hypsometer for your own arm reach. Graduate the rule by 1-in.-diameter classes and for height intervals most commonly used in your locality.

7-7 A tree crown was measured as 6 ft in diameter at the base and 18 ft in length. Assume that the crown shape can be approximated as a cone, and compute the crown surface area (ft^2) and volume (ft^3).

7-8 Number 5 to 10 standing trees (preferably mature conifers), and determine for each (a) Girard form class and (b) another expression of tree form suggested by your instructor. Use an upper-stem dendrometer for obtaining out-of-reach diameters. Which form expression is most easily derived in the field, and which is most commonly used in your region?

REFERENCES

Avery, T. E. 1959. An all-purpose cruiser stick. *J. Forestry* **57:**924–925.

Baldwin, V. C., Jr., and Peterson, K. D. 1997. Predicting the crown shape of loblolly pine trees. *Can. J. For. Res.* **27:**102–107.

Bechtold, W. A., Zarnoch, S. J., and Burkman, W. G. 1998. Comparisons of modeled height predictions to ocular height estimates. *So. J. Appl. For.* **22:**216–221.

Biging, G. S., and Wensel, L. C. 1988. The effect of eccentricity on the estimation of basal area and basal area growth. *Forest Sci.* **34:**338–342.

Binot, J.-M., Pothier, D., and Lebel, J. 1995. Comparison of relative accuracy and time requirement between the caliper, the diameter tape and an electronic tree measuring fork. *Forestry Chron.* **71:**197–200.

Brickell, J. E. 1970. More on diameter tapes and calipers. *J. Forestry* **68:**169–170.

Bruce, D. 1975. Evaluating accuracy of tree measurements made with optical instruments. *Forest Sci.* **21:**421–426.

Carron, L. T. 1968. *An outline of forest mensuration.* Australian National University Press, Canberra, A. C. T. 224 pp.

Clark, N. A., Wynne, R. H., and Schmoldt, D. L. 2000. A review of past research on dendrometers. *Forest Sci.* **46:**570–576.

Cole, W. G. 1995. Hardwood tree crown measurement guide. Ontario Forest Research Institute, Sault Ste. Marie, Ontario, Canada. 18 pp.

Gregoire, T. G., Zedaker, S. M., and Nicholas, N. S. 1990. Modeling relative error in stem basal area estimates. *Can. J. For. Res.* **20**:496–502.

Grosenbaugh, L. R. 1954. New tree-measurement concepts: Height accumulation, giant tree, taper, and shape. *U.S. Forest Serv., Southern Forest Expt. Sta., Occas. Paper* 134. 32 pp.

———. 1963. Optical dendrometers for out-of-reach diameters: A conspectus and some new theory. *Forest Sci. Monograph* 4. 47 pp.

———. 1981. Measuring trees that lean, fork, crook, or sweep. *J. Forestry* **79**:89–92.

Hann, D. W. 1999. An adjustable predictor of crown profile for stand-grown Douglas-fir trees. *Forest Sci.* **45**:217–225.

Helms, J. A. (ed.) 1998. *The dictionary of forestry.* The Society of American Foresters, Bethesda, Md. 210 pp.

Howe, G. T., and Adams, W. T. 1988. Clinometer versus pole measurement of tree heights in young Douglas-fir progeny tests. *West. J. Appl. For.* **3**:86–88.

Jackson, M. T., and Petty, R. O. 1973. A simple optical device for measuring vertical projection of tree crowns. *Forest Sci.* **19**:60–62.

Jonsson, B. 1981. An electronic caliper with automatic data storage. *Forest Sci.* **27**:765–770.

Matern, B. 1990. On the shape of the cross-section of a tree stem. An empirical study of the geometry of mensurational methods. *Swedish Univ. of Agr. Sci. Report* 28. 46 pp.

Mesavage, C. 1965. Definition of merchantable sawtimber height. *J. Forestry* **63**:30–32.

———. 1969a. New Barr and Stroud dendrometer, model FP 15. *J. Forestry* **67**:40–41.

———. 1969b. Measuring bark thickness. *J. Forestry* **67**:753–754.

———, and Girard, J. W. 1946. Tables for estimating board-foot content of timber. U.S. Forest Service, Government Printing Office, Washington, D.C. 94 pp.

Rennie, J. C. 1979. Comparison of height measurement techniques in a dense loblolly pine plantation. *So. J. Appl. For.* **3**:146–148.

Skovsgaard, J. P., Johannsen, V. K., and Vanclay, J. K. 1998. Accuracy and precision of two laser dendrometers. *Forestry* **71**:131–139.

Wheeler, P. R. 1962. Penta prism caliper for upper-stem diameter measurements. *J. Forestry* **60**:877–878.

Wiant, H. V. 1972. Form class estimates—A simple guide. *J. Forestry* **70**:421–422.

Williams, M. S., Bechtold, W. A., and La Bau, V. J. 1994. Five instruments for measuring tree height: An evaluation. *So. J. Appl. For.* **18**: 76–82.

CHAPTER 8

VOLUMES AND WEIGHTS OF STANDING TREES

8-1 Purpose of Volume and Weight Equations   Volume equations are used to estimate the average contents for standing trees of various sizes and species. Volume units most commonly employed are board feet, cubic feet, cords, or cubic meters. Volumes may be estimated for some specific merchantable portion of the stem only or for the total stem. In some instances volumes are predicted for both the sawlog material and the pulpwood top sections.

Board-foot volume equations are usually based on existing log rules; thus they can never be more reliable than the log rule selected as a basis for their construction. The principal objective in compiling such equations is to obtain a board-foot estimate for standing trees that would correspond with the volume obtained if the same trees were felled, bucked, and scaled as logs. Thus such equations are used in timber estimating as a means of ascertaining the volume and value of standing trees in a forested tract.

In the past, tree volumes were read from tables, but in modern practice, equations are generally used to predict tree volumes. However, the term *volume table* has persisted in forestry usage as a generic term meaning tabulations *or* equations that show the contents of standing trees. Tree weight equations are analogous to volume equations except that weights (green or dry) rather than volumes of standing trees are predicted. Weight equations are generally expressed in terms of pounds or kilograms.

8-2 Types of Tree Volume and Weight Equations The principal variables ordinarily associated with standing tree volume or weight are diameter at breast height (dbh), tree height, and, in some cases, tree form. Height may be expressed as total tree height or length of the merchantable stem. Although merchantable stem length is more highly correlated with merchantable volume than is total tree height, it is a difficult variable to define precisely and to measure consistently in the field. Consequently, for species that are typically single-stemmed, total height is generally used when predicting both total and merchantable volumes.

Tree volume equations that are based on the single variable of dbh are commonly referred to as *local volume equations;* those that require the user to also obtain tree height and possibly form or taper are referred to as *standard volume equations.* These labels are often misleading, for they tend to imply that local volume equations are somehow inferior to standard volume equations. Such an assumption is not necessarily true, particularly when the local equation in question is derived from a standard volume equation. More appropriate labels for these two types of volume or weight equations would be *single-entry* and *multiple-entry equations.*

Volume equations, whether of the single-entry or multiple-entry variety, may also be classified as *species equations* or *composite equations.* In the first instance, separate equations are constructed for each important timber species or groups of species that are similar in terms of tree form. On the other hand, composite equations are intended for application to diverse species, often including both conifers and hardwoods. To compensate for inherent differences in stem taper and volume between various species groups, provision is usually made for additionally measuring tree form, or correction factors are developed for various species. Otherwise, composite equations will overestimate volumes of some trees while underestimating volumes of others.

The main disadvantage of species equations is the large number of species encountered in most regions. When it is not feasible to construct separate equations for each species, those of similar taper and shape may be grouped together. To avoid such difficulties, composite equations utilizing some measurement of tree form in lieu of species differentiation have been adopted in several regions.

MULTIPLE-ENTRY VOLUME EQUATIONS

8-3 Form-Class versus Non-Form-Class Equations Multiple-entry volume equations provide an estimate of individual tree volume based on dbh, height, and, sometimes, a measure of tree form. Tree form is a difficult variable to describe, and there is often a high degree of variability in form, both within and between species. Nevertheless, many form-class volume equations have been prepared, and those based on Girard form class are typical of the equations still in use.

The measurement of Girard form class was discussed in the previous chapter (Sec. 7-13). Form-class volume tables based on this concept of butt-log taper are among the most widely accepted standard tables in eastern United States.

Although a number of equations to approximate the values in the Mesavage-Girard tables have been published (e.g. Wiant, 1986; Mawson and Conners, 1987), the tabular entries are often used. The biggest disadvantages in using these tables are (1) the general tendency toward rough estimates of form class rather than actual measurements and (2) the wide variations in upper-stem form that cannot be adequately accommodated by measuring butt-log taper only. The fact that each change in form class (as from 77 to 78) accounts for about 3 percent of merchantable tree volume should serve as a precaution against purely ocular estimates of this independent variable.

Multiple-entry board-foot volume tables have been compiled from International, Scribner, and Doyle log rules for form classes of 65 to 90 (Mesavage and Girard, 1946). Table 8-1, based on form class 80 and the International rule, provides an abridged example of the format employed. The user must first determine the form class of the tree; then only dbh and sawlog length in 16-ft logs and half logs are needed to derive merchantable board-foot volumes. In most published versions, these tables cover a dbh range of 10 to 40 in. (by 1-in. classes) and a height range of one to six logs.

8-4 Compilation of Mesavage-Girard Form-Class Tables   In the original tabulations of the Mesavage-Girard form-class tables, the scaling diameter of the

TABLE 8-1
STANDARD VOLUME TABLE, INTERNATIONAL
¼-IN. RULE, FORM CLASS 80

dbh (in.)	Volume by 16-ft logs (bd ft)			
	1	2	3	4
10	39	63	80	
12	59	98	127	146
14	83	141	186	216
16	112	190	256	305
18	144	248	336	402
20	181	314	427	512
22	221	387	528	638
24	266	469	644	773
26	315	558	767	931
28	367	654	904	1,096
30	424	758	1,050	1,272
32	485	870	1,213	1,480
34	550	989	1,383	1,691
36	620	1,121	1,571	1,922
38	693	1,256	1,772	2,167
40	770	1,403	1,977	2,432

Source: Mesavage and Girard, 1946.

butt log is derived from the estimated or measured form class. Thus for a 20-in.-dbh three-log tree of form class 80, the scaling diameter of the first log is 0.80 × 20, or 16 in. Scaling diameters for all upper logs are derived from a single taper table, an abridged version of which appears as Table 8-2. For the tree in question, a taper rate of 1.7 in. is assigned to the second log and 1.9 in. to the third log.

Reference to the International ¼-in. rule for 16-ft logs indicates a scale volume of 181 bd ft for the 16-in. butt log. For the second log, the scaling diameter is 16 minus 1.7, or 14.3 in., and the log scale is 142 bd ft. For the third log, the scaling diameter is 14.3 minus 1.9, or 12.4 in., and the log scale is 104 bd ft. By totaling the scale values for the three logs (181 + 142 + 104), the standing tree volume of 427 bd ft is derived (Fig. 8-1). This calculated tree volume may be verified by reference to Table 8-1.

The Mesavage-Girard form-class tables have enjoyed a long and useful life, but sizable volume errors can occur when the upper-stem taper for a particular species differs appreciably from rigidly assumed taper rates or when form class is not accurately determined in the field. There is a general trend away from the use of tabulations of tree volumes and toward the direct computation of volumes from mathematical formulas. Before proceeding ahead to the next section, interested readers may obtain a review of regression analysis, the statistical technique commonly used to estimate coefficients in tree volume and weight equations, in Chapter 2.

TABLE 8-2
UPPER-LOG TAPER (INCHES) BY 16-FT LOGS

dbh (in.)	2-log tree 2d log	3-log tree 2d log	3d log	4-log tree 2d log	3d log	4th log
10	1.4	1.2	1.4			
12	1.6	1.3	1.5	1.1	1.4	1.9
14	1.7	1.4	1.6	1.2	1.5	2.0
16	1.9	1.5	1.7	1.2	1.6	2.1
18	2.0	1.6	1.8	1.3	1.7	2.2
20	2.1	1.7	1.9	1.4	1.8	2.4
22	2.2	1.8	2.0	1.4	2.0	2.5
24	2.3	1.8	2.2	1.5	2.2	2.6
26	2.4	1.9	2.3	1.5	2.3	2.7
28	2.5	1.9	2.5	1.6	2.4	2.8
30	2.6	2.0	2.6	1.7	2.5	3.0
32	2.7	2.0	2.7	1.7	2.5	3.1
34	2.8	2.1	2.7	1.8	2.5	3.3
36	2.8	2.1	2.8	1.8	2.6	3.4
38	2.9	2.1	2.8	1.9	2.6	3.4
40	2.9	2.2	2.8	1.9	2.7	3.4

Source: Mesavage and Girard, 1946. (Table abridged.)

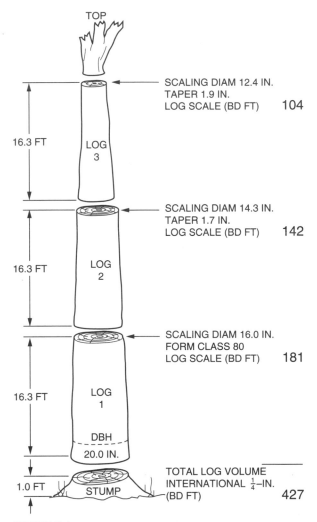

FIGURE 8-1
Derivation of merchantable tree volume for Mesavage-Girard form-class tables.

8-5 Constructing Multiple-Entry Volume Equations The preferred method for constructing tree volume equations is by regression analysis. By this approach, a number of independent variables can be analyzed to determine their relative value in predicting the dependent variable of tree volume. And regression equations involving several independent variables and hundreds of sample observations can be efficiently solved using computers.

Although many independent variables have been incorporated into regression equations for predicting tree volume, measurements of stem diameter and height tend to account for the greatest proportion of the variability in volume. Thus tree volumes for a given species may be predicted from the "combined variable" method described by Spurr (1952):

$$V = b_0 + b_1 \text{ dbh}^2 H$$

This formula is, of course, identical to the equation $Y = b_0 + b_1 X$. One merely substitutes the combined variable of "diameter squared times height" for the quantity X in the basic equation for a straight-line relationship. Solution of the equation is by simple linear regression techniques.

The diameters, heights, and volumes required to develop the volume function are ideally obtained by direct stem measurements of felled trees. It is important that a representative sample of trees spanning the full range of sizes (dbh and heights) of interest be obtained. If felled trees are not available, volumes may be computed from optical dendrometer measurements of standing trees. By this approach, diameter readings are made at intervals along the stem, and sectional volumes are computed by Smalian's or another suitable formula. These sectional volumes are then summed to produce an estimate of the portion of stem volume of interest.

Although form is not explicitly included as an independent variable in this volume function, differences in tree taper tend to be accounted for by the employment of separate prediction equations for each species or species group. Also, form is implicitly considered through the fitting of the intercept term b_0. Assuming that total height is employed to estimate merchantable volume, the intercept for a straight line would typically be negative. This is because there is zero merchantable volume Y for positive values of diameter squared times height X. Thus when the straight-line relationship is extended to $X = 0$, it crosses the Y axis below the origin (i.e., at a negative value). This negative constant b_0, which is subtracted regardless of tree size, is a large portion of the $b_1 \text{ dbh}^2 H$ value for a small tree but a small portion for a large tree, thus implying poorer form for small trees than for large trees.

The volume table shown in Table 8-3 was derived by fitting the combined-variable equation to data from ponderosa pine in the Front Range of Colorado. The resultant equation (from Edminster, Beeson, and Metcalf, 1980) is

$$V = -0.44670 + 0.00216 \text{ dbh}^2 H$$

where V = cubic feet, inside bark, from stump height of 1 ft to 4-in. top
diameter (inside bark)
dbh = diameter at breast height, in.
H = total tree height, ft

TABLE 8-3
MERCHANTABLE CUBIC-FOOT VOLUME TABLE FOR PONDEROSA PINE*

dbh (in.)	Total height above ground (ft)								
	20	30	40	50	60	70	80	90	100
5	0.9	1.5	2.2	2.8					
6	1.4	2.3	3.2	4.1					
7	2.0	3.2	4.4	5.6	6.8				
8	2.7	4.2	5.8	7.4	8.9	10.5			
9	3.5	5.4	7.4	9.3	11.2	13.2			
10	4.3	6.7	9.1	11.5	13.8	16.2			
11	5.3	8.1	11.0	13.8	16.7	19.5	22.4		
12	6.3	9.7	13.1	16.4	19.8	23.2	26.6		
13	7.4	11.4	15.3	19.2	23.2	27.1	31.0		
14		13.2	17.7	22.3	26.8	31.3	35.9		
15		15.1	20.3	25.5	30.7	35.9	41.1		
16		17.2	23.1	29.0	34.8	40.7	46.6	52.5	
17		19.4	26.0	32.6	39.2	45.9	52.5	59.1	
18		21.7	29.1	36.5	43.9	51.3	58.7	66.1	
19		24.2	32.4	40.6	48.8	57.0	65.3	73.5	
20		26.8	35.9	44.9	54.0	63.1	72.2	81.2	
21			39.5	49.5	59.5	69.4	79.4	89.4	
22			43.3	54.2	65.2	76.1	87.0	98.0	108.9
23			47.3	59.2	71.1	83.1	95.0	106.9	118.8
24				64.4	77.3	90.3	103.3	116.2	129.2
25				69.8	83.8	97.9	111.9	126.0	140.0
26				75.4	90.6	105.7	120.9	136.1	151.2
27				81.2	97.6	113.9	130.2	146.6	162.9
28					104.8	122.4	139.9	157.5	175.0
29					112.3	131.1	149.9	168.7	187.5
30					120.1	140.2	160.3	180.4	200.5

*Cubic-foot volume, inside bark, from a stump height of 1 ft to a 4-in. top diameter (inside bark). Computed from $V = -0.44670 + 0.00216\ dbh^2 H$; coefficient of determination = 0.9744; standard error of estimate ±3.0 cu ft (14.29% of mean). Dbh classes represent full inches (e.g., 5-in. class includes 5.0 to 5.9), and midpoints were used when generating the table (e.g., 5.5 in. was used for the 5-in. class, etc.).
Source: Edminster, Beeson, and Metcalf, 1980.

In the construction of equations for total tree volume, the combined-variable function, as shown at the beginning of Section 8-5, may be used, or the equation may be conditioned to pass through the origin, giving

$$V = b_1\ dbh^2 H$$

Conditioning through the origin may be desirable for *total* tree volume prediction when predicted values for very small trees are desired. Such conditioning is not recommended for *merchantable* volume prediction, however, because merchantable volume equations should logically have negative intercepts. The equation $V = b_1$ dbh^2H is called the "constant form factor" equation because form is not explicitly or implicitly included. All trees, regardless of size, are assumed to be of similar form.

In addition to the merchantable cubic-foot volume equation shown previously, Edminster, Beeson, and Metcalf (1980) also developed an equation for total cubic-foot volume from ponderosa pine data. To predict total volume, the constant form factor model was employed:

$$V = 0.00226 \text{ dbh}^2H$$

where V is cubic feet, inside bark, of the entire stem, including stump and top, and dbh and H are as previously defined.

Another equation form that has been widely applied in past studies for predicting tree volumes is the model originally suggested by Schumacher and Hall (1933):

$$V = a \text{ dbh}^bH^c$$

The Schumacher and Hall equation, shown in its nonlinear form, can be transformed to a linear equation:

$$Y = b_0 + b_1 X_1 + b_2 X_2$$

and the coefficients can be estimated by standard linear regression methods by applying a logarithmic transformation, that is,

$$\ln V = b_0 + b_1 \ln \text{ dbh} + b_2 \ln H$$

where $Y = \ln V$
  $X_1 = \ln$ dbh
  $X_2 = \ln H$

The Schumacher and Hall equation, as shown here, passes through the origin and is appropriate for predicting *total* volume. When predicting *merchantable* volume, however, the equation should be conditioned to pass through an appropriate point by translating the axes.

Logarithmic volume equations have the advantage of more nearly satisfying the homogeneity-of-variance assumption of ordinary regression, but suffer from the disadvantage that a transformation bias is introduced. The transformation bias results from the fact that the transformed regression equation passes through the arithmetic means of the logarithms of the X and Y variables—which are the geometric means of the original variables. Geometric means are always less than arithmetic means, unless all values in a set of numbers are identical, and hence an underprediction bias is introduced. This bias is generally not large, however, and various bias correction factors have been proposed (Flewelling and Pienaar, 1981). Past experience has shown that the logarithmic tree volume expression proposed by Schumacher and Hall generally provides results similar to those from arithmetic tree volume expressions such as the combined-variable equation.

Equations that involve form class in addition to dbh and height have been fitted to tree data by regression techniques. One model that has been used, the "combined-variable form-class formula," is

$$V = b_0 + b_1 F + b_2 \, \text{dbh}^2 H + b_3 F \, \text{dbh}^2 \, H$$

where F is a measure of form, generally Girard form class. This formula is sometimes simplified to the "short-cut form-class formula" (Spurr, 1952):

$$V = b_0 + b_1 F \, \text{dbh}^2 H$$

8-6 Selecting a Multiple-Entry Volume Equation   For most timber inventories and forest management plans, the forester has a wide selection of multiple-entry volume equations available for possible use. The choice of a reliable equation requires careful scrutiny and an objective evaluation. To determine whether a particular equation is suitable for a given inventory project, these and other questions might be appropriately asked:

1 For what species and locality was the equation developed?
2 How many sample trees formed the basis for the fitted equation?
3 Who is the author or publisher of the equation?
4 What type of height and form measurements are required?
5 Are merchantability limits and units of volume suitable for the project at hand?
6 How were tree volumes originally obtained in deriving the equation?
7 What method of equation fitting was used?
8 What evidence of equation accuracy and reliability is available?

If feasible, it is desirable to visit a harvesting operation on timberlands similar to that where the volume equation will be applied. Then one can measure the dbh, height (according to the definition used in the volume equation construction), and form (if needed) for the range of sizes of trees that are being cut. Felled-tree volumes should be obtained according to the utilization standards used to construct the volume equation being evaluated. Volumes for each of the sample trees can then be predicted from the independent variables (dbh, height) and compared with the measured volumes. Although individual trees will vary considerably from predicted averages in volume equations, the mean difference between actual and predicted volumes for samples of 50 to 100 trees should be near zero. If the mean difference is not near zero, bias is indicated. One might also examine the trend of differences across dbh and height classes to determine whether the equation provides acceptable accuracy for the desired range of tree sizes.

For a given species or species group, foresters often have an array of multiple-entry volume equations from which to choose. These equations are commonly constructed from sample data obtained from a restricted portion of the region where the species occurs. Consequently, there has been much interest in "locality effects" on tree volume equations. How much variation might one expect due to the location from which the sample data were obtained? Can a volume equation, based on tree data from one locality, be safely applied in another area? After a thorough study of factors affecting the total volume, Spurr (1952) concluded that "the locality, type of growth, and site where a tree grows apparently do not affect total cubic-foot volume sufficiently to justify the development of more than one volume table for a given species." Since that time, there has been additional evidence to support Spurr's conclusion. For example, in a study involving four data sets for plantation-grown loblolly pine that were similar in age but widely separated geographically, Van Deusen, Sullivan, and Matney (1981) concluded that a single volume-prediction equation can be used through much of the range of a given species.

8-7 Making Allowances for Various Utilization Standards Multiple-entry volume equations commonly provide estimates of the contents of tree boles from stump height to a fixed top diameter. With multiple products being cut from tree boles and rapidly changing utilization standards, it is important to have the option of obtaining volume estimates to various top diameters and between given top diameters. These volume estimates should be consistently and logically related so that they sum to the total stem volume. Furthermore, for given combinations of dbh and total height, the volume to a 4-in. top, for example, should always be less than the volume to a 3-in. top.

One approach to providing flexibility in volume equations, while maintaining logical relationships, is to apply volume-ratio equations. In this approach, the ratio of merchantable volume to total volume is predicted; multiplying the ratio times the total volume gives the desired merchantable volume. Volume equations have been developed for several species by using this general approach (e.g., Honer, 1967).

Equations developed by Burkhart (1977) will be used to illustrate the volume-ratios procedure. First, total stem volume is predicted by using the combined-variable model. The equation for total cubic-foot volume, outside bark, of plantation-grown loblolly pine is

$$V = 0.34864 + 0.00232 \, \text{dbh}^2 H$$

where dbh is in inches and H is total tree height in feet. Next, the ratio of merchantable stem volume divided by total stem volume is predicted from dbh and top diameter. The equation for outside-bark volume ratios with outside bark top diameters is

$$R = 1 - 0.32354 \, (d_t^{3.1579}/\text{dbh}^{2.7115})$$

where R = merchantable cubic-foot volume to top diameter d_t/total stem
      volume, cu ft
   d_t = top dob, in.

The reader should note that this equation is conditioned so that when $d_t = 0$ (i.e., when one is at the tip of the tree), the ratio R equals 1, and multiplying R times total volume thus gives total volume.

To demonstrate the application of these prediction equations, it may be assumed that merchantable volumes to 4- and 6-in. tops are desired for a tree that measures 10 in. dbh and 75 ft total height. One first substitutes the tree dimensions into the total-volume equation

$$V = 0.34864 + 0.00232(10^2)(75)$$
$$= 17.75 \text{ cu ft}$$

Cubic-foot volume to a 4-in. top diameter is computed by substituting in the ratio equation and then by multiplying the estimated ratio times the total volume. Substituting the selected top limit and measured dbh gives

$$R = 1 - 0.32354(4^{3.1579}/10^{2.7115})$$
$$= 0.950$$

which is multiplied times the total volume to compute cubic-foot volume to a 4-in. top. Therefore,

$$V_4 = (17.75)(0.950)$$
$$= 16.86 \text{ cu ft}$$

Similarly, cubic-foot volume to a 6-in. top is computed as

$$R = 1 - 0.32354(6^{3.1579}/10^{2.7115})$$
$$= 0.820$$
$$V_6 = (17.75)(0.820)$$
$$= 14.56 \text{ cu ft}$$

Cubic-foot volume between top limits of 4 and 6 in. can be computed by subtraction ($16.86 - 14.56 = 2.30$ cu ft).

8-8 Tree Volumes from Taper Equations   Taper curves allow for changing utilization standards; if tree profiles can be accurately described, then volume for any merchantability limit or segment can be computed. Much work has been done on developing taper equations, and some of the results are quite complex. The relatively simple parabolic function presented by Kozak, Munro, and Smith (1969) will be used to illustrate the use of taper equations. This function has been found to fit well over about 85 percent of a tree bole, with lack of fit occurring primarily near the butt and top sections of the tree:

$$d^2/\text{dbh}^2 = b_0 + b_1(h/H) + b_2(h^2/H^2)$$

where d = diameter at any given height h above ground
$\qquad H$ = total tree height
b_0, b_1, b_2 = regression coefficients

Estimated upper-stem diameters are obtained by rearranging the function as

$$d = \text{dbh}\sqrt{b_0 + b_1(h/H) + b_2(h^2/H^2)}$$

To obtain volumes for any desired portion of the tree bole, diameters for short segments can be predicted. The predicted diameters can be used to compute volumes of the segments, and the segment volumes can be summed to obtain volume for the desired portion of the tree bole. More precise estimates of volume can be obtained, however, through mathematical integration of the taper equation (Sec. 8-9).

Taper curves can also be used to estimate the height at a specified diameter. By applying the quadratic formula to the parabolic taper equation used for illustrative purposes here, one can obtain an expression for height h above ground to any specified diameter d for trees of given dbh and total height values:

$$h = \frac{-b_1 H - \sqrt{(b_1 H)^2 - 4b_2\left(b_0 H^2 - \dfrac{d^2 H^2}{\text{dbh}^2}\right)}}{2b_2}$$

Such equations allow estimation of merchantable heights to specified top diameters and computation of lineal footage for specific products.

Taper curves provide maximum flexibility for computing volumes of any specified portions of tree boles. Tree boles are highly variable, however, and it is difficult to describe their shapes over entire lengths without resorting to rather complex functions. Solutions for volume and height to specified diameters naturally become more difficult computationally when complex taper equations are used. However, modern computers have largely eliminated the computational difficulties associated with taper equations.

Estimated volumes from taper equations are biased, because the sum of squared deviations about diameter (or some function of diameter) is minimized in the regression fitting process rather than the sum of squared deviations about volume. This bias is generally not large, however, and techniques have been developed for fitting "compatible" taper equations (Demaerschalk, 1972; Reed and Green, 1984). A compatible taper equation, when integrated, produces an identical estimate of total volume to that given by an existing total-volume equation.

8-9 Integrating Taper Functions For those readers with a background in calculus, this section describes how to obtain tree volumes through mathematical integration of taper equations. The expression for stem cross-sectional area is integrated over the length desired. If one assumes that tree cross sections are circular in shape, then the area in square feet when diameter d is measured in inches would be

$$\text{Area} = \frac{\pi d^2}{4(144)} = 0.005454 d^2$$

Integrating the expression for area in square feet over the length desired in feet will give the volume in cubic feet for that segment. That is,

$$V \text{ (cu ft)} = 0.005454 \int_{h_1}^{h_2} d^2 \, dh$$

where h_1 and h_2 denote the limits of integration.

Assuming that the Kozak, Munro, and Smith (1969) taper model is employed,

$$d^2/\text{dbh}^2 = b_0 + b_1(h/H) + b_2(h^2/H^2)$$

and

$$d^2 = \text{dbh}^2[b_0 + b_1(h/H) + b_2(h^2/H^2)]$$

Substituting the expression for d^2 into the integral for volume results in

$$V = 0.005454\text{dbh}^2 \int_{h_1}^{h_2} [b_0 + b_1(h/H) + b_2(h^2/H^2)] dh$$

Solving the integral results in

$$V = 0.005454\text{dbh}^2[b_0(h) + (b_1/2)(h^2/H) + (b_2/3)(h^3/H^2)]\Big|_{h_1}^{h_2}$$

Coefficients for coastal Douglas-fir from Kozak, Munro, and Smith (1969) are

$$b_0 = 0.85458$$
$$b_1 = -1.29771$$
$$b_2 = 0.44313$$

Suppose that the volume of the 32-ft segment from 32 to 64 ft above ground is desired for a Douglas-fir tree measuring 30 in. dbh and 150 ft in total height. Substituting into the expression for volume results in

$$
\begin{aligned}
V = {} & \{0.005454(30)^2[0.85458(64) - (1.29771/2)(64^2/150) \\
& + (0.44313/3)(64^3/150^2)]\} - \{0.005454(30)^2[0.85458(32) \\
& - (1.29771/2)(32^2/150) + (0.44313/3)(32^3/150^2)]\} \\
= {} & 76.4 \text{ cu ft (inside bark)}
\end{aligned}
$$

If the taper equation is integrated over the total bole length (i.e., from 0 to H, where H denotes total tree height), an expression for total tree volume will result. Following through with the same parabolic taper function, we have

$$
0.005454 \text{dbh}^2 [b_0(h) + (b_1/2)(h^2/H) + (b_2/3)(h^3/H^2)] \Big|_0^H
$$

$$
= \{0.005454 \text{dbh}^2 [b_0(H) + (b_1/2)(H^2/H) + (b_2/3)(H^3/H^2)]\} - 0
$$

Noting that the above expression can be written as

$$
0.005454[b_0 + (b_1/2) + (b_2/3)]\text{dbh}^2 H
$$

and setting $0.005454[b_0 + (b_1/2) + (b_2/3)]$ equal to b, we note that the implied volume equation is

$$
V = b(\text{dbh}^2 H)
$$

which is a logical model for total tree volume, that is, the constant form factor equation.

SINGLE-ENTRY VOLUME EQUATIONS

8-10 Advantages and Limitations   Volume equations based on the single variable of dbh may be constructed from existing multiple-entry volume equations or from the scaled measure of felled trees. Such equations are particularly useful for quick timber inventories, because height and form estimates are not required and trees can be tallied by species and dbh only. Elimination of height and form determinations also tends to assure greater uniformity in volume estimates, particularly when two or more field parties are cruising within the same project area.

Construction of volume equations based on dbh alone presumes that a definitive height-diameter relationship exists for the species under consideration, in other words, that trees of a given diameter class tend to be of similar height and form. If this is true, all trees in a given dbh class can be logically assigned the same average volume. Height-diameter or volume-diameter relationships can often be established for hardwood or coniferous species growing under relatively uniform site and stand density conditions. When soils and topography are notably varied, it is usually nec-essary to derive single-entry equations for each broad site class encountered.

Volume equations based on dbh alone are sometimes compiled for inventories of relatively small areas, but this is not an essential condition; in some instances, "local" equations may be as widely applicable as "standard" volume equations. Thousands of sample trees may be represented by some so-called local equations. The exact number of sample measurements required depends upon characteristics of the tree species involved, variability of soil-site conditions, and the desired ge-ographic area of application. From 30 to 100 samples are usually considered a minimum number for small tracts, depending on the range of diameter classes to be included in the final compilation.

8-11 Constructing a Single-Entry Equation from Measurements of Felled Trees   To obtain tree volumes essential for this procedure, measurements may be obtained from felled trees on logging operations or by "scaling" standing trees with a reliable upper-stem dendrometer (Sec. 7-6). Sample trees should be se-lected in an unbiased manner and a sufficient number of measurements made to span the desired range of dbh classes for each species involved.

For each sample tree, measurements should be obtained of (1) dbh to the near-est 0.1 in., (2) tree volume in desired units, and (3) total tree height. The last item, though not actually needed for fitting the equation, serves as a useful indication of the sites or geographic areas to which the result may be applied. To illustrate the procedure of equation derivation, the data for yellow-poplar in Table 8-4 were sup-plied by the Southern Research Station, U.S. Forest Service. Cubic-foot volumes are outside bark for the main stem to a 4-in. top dob.

The felled-tree volumes are related to dbh through regression analysis. Tree volumes have a curvilinear relationship with dbh but are approximately linearly related to dbh squared (Fig. 8-2). In general form, the local volume equation rela-tionship can be expressed as

$$V = b_0 + b_1 \, \mathrm{dbh}^c$$

The cubic-foot volume data for this example follow an approximately straight-line pattern when plotted over dbh squared, indicating that c can be set equal to 2 and simplifying the model to

$$V = b_0 + b_1 \, \mathrm{dbh}^2$$

Applying simple linear regression techniques to the yellow-poplar data results in

$$V = -8.4166 + 0.2679 \, \mathrm{dbh}^2$$

Table 8-5, a single-entry, or local, volume table, was compiled by substituting diameter class midpoint values into the regression equation to obtain predicted

TABLE 8-4
YELLOW-POPLAR DATA USED IN CONSTRUCTING A SINGLE-ENTRY
VOLUME TABLE

dbh (in.)	Volume (cu ft)	Total ht. (ft)	dbh (in.)	Volume (cu ft)	Total ht. (ft)
6.0	4.7	65	16.1	59.5	98
6.3	5.3	63	16.2	48.3	86
7.2	7.0	69	16.8	76.2	105
7.4	7.4	63	17.2	58.7	98
8.0	12.5	78	17.6	75.7	106
8.5	10.5	66	18.4	78.9	101
9.3	14.4	74	19.3	89.1	111
8.6	13.4	80	18.7	85.4	102
10.2	21.7	83	20.4	104.3	109
9.8	17.5	77	19.8	92.5	103
11.5	23.0	74	20.7	102.9	108
11.4	24.6	84	21.3	113.1	101
12.2	30.1	98	22.4	115.1	106
12.0	31.8	98	22.2	135.3	120
13.4	41.6	96	23.0	125.6	108
12.8	35.0	90	23.4	152.4	128
14.0	43.1	95	24.3	167.9	115
14.1	41.5	91	23.8	153.6	124
14.9	45.8	87	25.3	138.5	107
15.4	55.0	98	25.8	177.3	118

FIGURE 8-2
(a) Curvilinear relationship of tree volume to dbh and (b) the same relationship transformed
to a straight line. Based on measurements of 40 felled yellow-poplar trees in the southern
Appalachians.

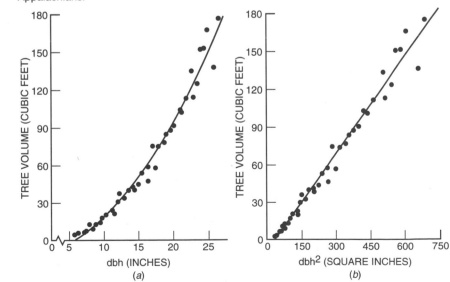

average tree volumes by dbh class. Average total heights, by dbh classes, in the sample data are shown to aid users in determining whether the table is appropriate for a given inventory situation. The average total heights were determined by substituting diameter class midpoint values in a height-dbh regression fitted to the yellow-poplar data.

This method of constructing a single-entry volume equation works reasonably well when felled trees of representative sizes are available for measurement. However, felled trees from harvesting operations rarely make up a typical sample of standing trees, because they may represent a different population or have distinctive characteristics that influenced their volume and, thus, caused them to be cut. When this is the case and felled trees are nonrepresentative samples, single-entry volume equations derived from such data would be biased and unreliable. As an alternative, tree volumes might be obtained from random samples of standing trees, or equations might be constructed from height-diameter relationships as described in the next section.

TABLE 8-5
SINGLE-ENTRY VOLUME TABLE FOR
YELLOW-POPLAR*

dbh (in.)	Volume (cu ft)	Average total height (ft)
6	1.2	58
7	4.7	66
8	8.7	72
9	13.3	77
10	18.4	82
11	24.0	86
12	30.2	89
13	36.9	92
14	44.1	95
15	51.9	97
16	60.2	99
17	69.0	101
18	78.4	103
19	88.3	105
20	98.8	106
21	109.7	107
22	121.3	109
23	133.3	110
24	145.9	111

*Based on measurements of 40 felled trees. Tree volumes are in cubic feet (outside bark) to a 4-in. top dob. Equation: $V = -8.4166 + 0.2679\ dbh^2$; coefficient of determination $= 0.978$.

8-12 Derivation from a Multiple-Entry Equation   This method of deriving
a single-entry volume equation is dependent on a well-established height-diameter
relationship and the existence of a reliable "standard" equation from which volumes
may be calculated. Field measurements of 50 to 100 merchantable or total heights,
spanning the desired range of tree dbh classes, should be obtained from the selected
project area. If the multiple-entry volume equation to be used is based on merchantable heights, field measurements must be carefully taken to identical top diameters or merchantability limits. An example of height-diameter data for 54 Sierra
redwood trees is shown in Table 8-6.

Numerous height-diameter regression models have been proposed and used in
the past. Because the basic height-diameter relationship is not linear, but is sigmoid in shape over the full range of diameters (Fig. 8-3a), a transformation must
be made to apply linear regression methods for estimating coefficients in the relationship. One model that has been found satisfactory for a wide range of species
and for both total and merchantable tree heights is

$$\ln H = b_0 + b_1 \, \text{dbh}^{-1}$$

When height values are transformed to logarithms and dbh measurements to re-
ciprocals of the original values, a straight-line relationship exists between the

TABLE 8-6
HEIGHT-DIAMETER DATA FOR 54 YOUNG-GROWTH SIERRA
REDWOOD TREES

dbh (in.)	Total ht. (ft)	dbh (in.)	Total ht. (ft)	dbh (in.)	Total ht. (ft)
12.5	62	12.0	60	45.0	148
13.0	65	30.6	115	52.4	153
46.8	135	22.4	95	30.7	110
30.7	120	38.0	128	38.4	132
56.5	145	56.5	145	25.3	100
14.0	61	44.1	133	18.0	90
44.0	133	60.0	130	35.1	122
59.9	160	60.0	160	24.0	111
16.5	75	30.3	107	43.5	140
45.0	121	15.2	76	24.9	89
56.0	140	36.0	137	42.0	137
26.2	103	51.4	144	51.9	131
36.4	116	21.1	95	59.6	145
58.7	160	34.2	129	17.5	72
36.8	120	20.7	81	54.0	135
45.7	133	48.6	143	40.0	130
18.4	82	57.3	153	23.5	91
27.5	108	13.5	71	45.0	127

transformed values (Fig. 8-3b); thus simple linear regression techniques can be used to solve for b_0 and b_1 in the transformed model. The application of linear regression analysis to the data in this example results in

$$\ln H = 5.21909 - 14.32872 \text{ dbh}^{-1}$$

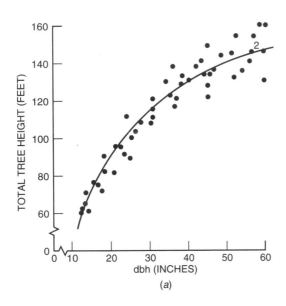

(a)

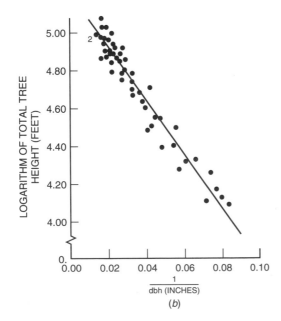

$\frac{1}{\text{dbh (INCHES)}}$

(b)

FIGURE 8-3
(a) Curvilinear relationship of tree height to dbh for second-growth Sierra redwood trees and (b) the same relationship transformed to a straight line.

where ln H is the natural logarithm of total tree height in feet and dbh is in inches. Figure 8-3 shows the height-diameter data and the fitted regression line on a transformed and an arithmetic scale.

Average heights were predicted for 2-in. dbh classes by substituting into the height-diameter equation. The midpoint of each dbh class and the predicted height were then substituted into the multiple-entry volume equation derived by Wensel and Schoenheide (1971):

$$\ln V = -6.66790 + 1.54423 \ln \text{dbh} + 1.29808 \ln H$$

to obtain average predicted gross cubic-foot volumes by dbh class. These average values were tabulated into a single-entry volume table (Table 8-7). The completed

TABLE 8-7
SINGLE-ENTRY VOLUME TABLE FOR YOUNG-GROWTH
SIERRA REDWOOD*

dbh class (in.)	Tree volume (cu ft)	Average total height (ft)
12	11.0	56
14	17.4	66
16	25.2	75
18	34.4	83
20	44.8	90
22	56.5	96
24	69.4	102
26	83.3	106
28	98.3	111
30	114.3	115
32	131.3	118
34	149.2	121
36	168.0	124
38	187.7	127
40	208.2	129
42	229.5	131
44	251.6	133
46	274.5	135
48	298.1	137
50	322.5	139
52	347.5	140
54	373.3	142
56	399.7	143
58	426.9	144
60	454.6	146

*Height-diameter equation: ln $H = 5.21909 - 14.32872 \text{ dbh}^{-1}$.
Volume is gross cubic feet; multiple-entry volume equation: ln $V = -6.66790 + 1.54423 \ln \text{dbh} + 1.29808 \ln H$. Volume equation from Wensel and Schoenheide, 1971.

table includes average predicted heights from the height-diameter regression as an indication of the conditions to which the table may be safely applied.

8-13 Tarif Tables   The term *tarif* is of Arabic origin and simply means tabulated information. In the context of tree volume estimation, *tarif tables* are collections of local volume tables (Table 8-8). Tarif tables are based on the assumption that volume has a linear relationship to diameter squared or to basal area. When English units are used and cubic volume to a 4-in. top limit is the dependent variable, the straight-line relationship intercepts at a basal area of 0.087 sq ft, the basal area of a 4-in. tree (Fig. 8-4). The volume of the tree with a basal area of 1.0 sq ft is called the *tarif number.* With two points fixed (basal area = 0.087 sq ft, volume = 0 cu ft; and basal area = 1.0 sq ft, volume = tarif number in cu ft) on a straight line, the entire local volume table for a given tarif number is specified. The tarif numbers, which represent different tree forms, are used to specify which local volume or tarif table to use.

Users must select an appropriate tarif, or local volume, table for the area of interest. One means of determining a tarif number is to use felled-tree measurements. The method proceeds as follows:

1 Select representative trees in the area of interest (typically 20 to 30 trees are selected).

2 Fell the trees, measure the volume of each tree, and, for each tree, find the table giving the closest match to the measured volume for a tree of the measured dbh.

3 Average the tarif numbers from the felled trees, and use the mean tarif number when selecting the volume table to use for inventory purposes in that stand.

Felled-tree information is time-consuming and expensive to obtain. As an alternative, volume can be computed from diameter and height data obtained with

TABLE 8-8
EXAMPLE OF A TARIF TABLE

dbh (in.)	Volume in cubic feet (ib, to 4-in. top dib) for tarif numbers of				
	20	25	30	35	40
6	2.4	3.0	3.6	4.2	4.8
7	3.9	4.9	5.9	6.9	7.9
8	5.7	7.2	8.6	10.0	11.5
9	7.8	9.7	11.7	13.6	15.5
10	10.0	12.5	15.1	17.6	20.1
11	12.5	15.7	18.8	22.0	25.1
12	15.3	19.1	22.9	26.8	30.6
13	18.3	22.9	27.4	32.0	36.6
14	21.5	26.9	32.3	37.6	43.0
15	25.0	31.2	37.5	43.7	50.0

Source: Abridged from Turnbull, Little, and Hoyer, 1980.

optical dendrometer measurements (Sec. 7-6) on standing sample trees. Although some loss in information is inevitable when using standing-tree rather than felled-tree data, it can be an attractive alternative when time and cost constraints prohibit tree felling.

Another alternative to felled-tree data is to use tarif *access tables*. For a species, these tables list the tarif numbers estimated for a tree of measured dbh and height. When the access table approach is taken, the procedure is

1 Select representative trees in the area of interest (in practice, 20 to 30 trees are usually chosen).

2 Measure the dbh and height of the sample trees. For each dbh-height sample tree, use the species-specific access tables to obtain a tarif number.

3 Average the tarif numbers from the sample trees, and use the mean tarif number to determine the local volume (tarif) table to use for estimating volume in that stand.

Tabulations termed *comprehensive tarif tables* have been developed that provide tree volumes in several units of measure and utilization limits, as well as volume/basal-area ratios and growth multipliers, all within a related system. In addition to the tabular approach, equations have been developed to estimate tarif numbers and volumes for various top limits and units of measure. Equations are more readily implemented in computing systems than are tables.

FIGURE 8-4
Volume/basal-area relationship used to construct tarif tables.

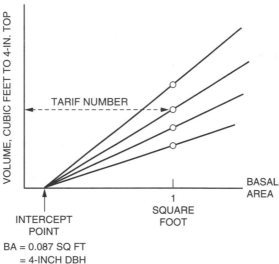

TREE WEIGHT EQUATIONS

8-14 Field Tallies by Weight   The continued emphasis on weight scaling as a basis of payment for pulpwood and sawlogs has spurred interest in field tallies based on tree weights rather than on various units of volume. It is logical that standing trees should be measured in the same units as those on which log purchases and sales are transacted.

Any ordinary volume table can be converted to a weight basis if weight-volume equivalents can be reliably established. For example, if it has been determined that a given species has a mean specific gravity of 0.47 and a mean moisture content of 110 percent, the weight per cubic foot would be (see Sec. 5-11)

$$\text{lb per cu ft (green)} = 0.47 \times 62.4 \left(1 + \frac{110}{100} \right)$$

$$= 61.6$$

$$\text{lb per cu ft (dry)} = 0.47 \times 62.4 \left(1 + \frac{0}{100} \right)$$

$$= 29.3$$

A standing tree having a volume of 20 cu ft inside bark would then be assigned a green weight (without bark) of

$$(20)(61.6) = 1{,}232 \text{ lb}$$

or a dry weight of

$$(20)(29.3) = 586 \text{ lb}$$

The same technique can be used to convert volume tables expressed in board feet or cords, provided that acceptable weight equivalents are derived. As previously outlined, Tables 5-1 and 6-4 provide pulpwood and sawlog weight approximations for a number of commercial timber species.

8-15 Weight Equations for Tree Boles   In lieu of converting volume tables to weight tables, it is preferable to weigh a series of sample trees and to relate tree weight to tree dimensions (dbh and height) via regression models similar to those used for volume prediction. Green weight of sycamore trees from an 11-year-old plantation in Georgia was predicted by employing the combined-variable model (Belanger, 1973). The resulting equation is

$$\text{Green bole weight (3-in. top dob)} = -32.35109 + 0.15544 \text{ dbh}^2 H$$

where dbh is in inches and H is total tree height in feet. Table 8-9 was compiled from this equation.

TABLE 8-9
GREEN-WEIGHT TABLE FOR PLANTATION-GROWN SYCAMORE, IN POUNDS*

dbh (in.)	Total height (ft)							
	45	50	55	60	65	70	75	80
4	80	92	104	117	129			
5	143	162	181	201	220	239		
6		247	275	303	331	359	387	
7			387	425	463	501	539	
8			515	565	614	664	714	764
9				723	786	849	912	975
10					978	1,056	1,133	1,211

*Equation: $W = -32.35109 + 0.15544 \, dbh^2H$, where W is green weight (including bark) to a 3-in. top dob; coefficient of determination = 0.99.
Source: Belanger, 1973.

TABLE 8-10
DRY-WEIGHT TABLE FOR PLANTATION-GROWN SYCAMORE, IN POUNDS*

dbh (in.)	Total height (ft)							
	45	50	55	60	65	70	75	80
4	30	36	41	46	52			
5	58	66	74	83	91	99		
6		103	115	127	139	151	163	
7			162	179	195	212	228	
8			218	239	260	282	303	325
9				307	334	361	388	415
10					417	450	484	517

*Equation: $W = -17.67910 + 0.06684 \, dbh^2H$, where W = dry weight (including bark) to a 3-in. top dob; coefficient of determination = 0.99.
Source: Belanger, 1973.

Although most transactions are in terms of green weight, dry weight is more appropriate when the wood will be utilized for pulped products. Dry weight is more highly correlated with the final yield of pulped products than is green weight, which is influenced by variations in moisture content. Dry weight, as green weight, can be assessed in standing trees through use of appropriate tables or equations. Belanger (1973) also developed a combined-variable equation to predict the dry weight of sycamore trees:

$$\text{Dry bole weight (3-in. top dob)} = -17.67910 + 0.06684 \, dbh^2H$$

Table 8-10 contains dry-weight values from this equation. When appropriate tree weight equations are available, standing timber can be assessed in pounds or kilograms as readily as in volume units.

8-16 Biomass Equations With increasing emphasis on complete tree utilization and use of wood as a source of energy, tables and equations have been developed to show the weights of total trees and of their components (bolewood, branches, foliage). These equations, commonly referred to as "biomass equations," are generally expressed in terms of dry weight and may include only the aboveground portion or the entire tree, including roots.

Equations for estimating biomass of individual Engelmann spruce trees were developed by Landis and Mogren (1975). Employing the following model:

$$Y = b_0 + b_1 \, \text{dbh}^2$$

where Y is tree component dry weight in kilograms and dbh is tree diameter at breast height in centimeters, they computed the equations shown in Table 8-11. Thus by measuring dbh on standing Engelmann spruce trees, the total aboveground biomass or the dry weight of various tree components can be estimated.

Similar sets of equations have been developed for other species. A commonly employed regression model in several studies of biomass equation construction (such as Clark and Schroeder, 1977; Taras and Phillips, 1978; Edwards and McNab, 1979) is

$$\ln Y = b_0 + b_1 \ln \text{dbh}^2 H$$

where Y = total tree or component weight
 dbh = diameter at breast height (or diameter at ground line for saplings)
 H = total tree height

This model is sometimes referred to as the "logarithmic combined-variable formula."

TABLE 8-11
EQUATIONS FOR ESTIMATING BIOMASS OF INDIVIDUAL ENGELMANN SPRUCE TREES*

Tree component (Y), dry wt (kg)	Equation	Coefficient of determination
Total aboveground biomass	$Y = -36.94 + 0.42 \, \text{dbh}^2$	0.97
Stem wood	$Y = -25.26 + 0.25 \, \text{dbh}^2$	0.96
Stem bark	$Y = -2.55 + 0.06 \, \text{dbh}^2$	0.98
Branch wood and bark	$Y = -7.78 + 0.07 \, \text{dbh}^2$	0.90
Foliage	$Y = -0.56 + 0.03 \, \text{dbh}^2$	0.88

*Dbh is in cm.
Source: Landis and Mogren, 1975.

PROBLEMS

8-1 Use the procedures described in Section 8-4 for the compilation of the Mesavage-Girard form-class volume tables and the upper-log taper shown in Table 8-2 to compute the volume table entry, according to Doyle scale, for a tree with dbh 14 inches, merchantable height 2 logs, and form class 75 percent.

8-2 Construct a single-entry tree volume table based on the direct measurement of felled trees.

8-3 The following data are from 20 loblolly pine trees:

dbh (in.)	Total height (ft)	Volume (cu ft to 4-in. top dob)	dbh (in.)	Total height (ft)	Volume (cu ft to 4-in. top dob)
12	65	20.5	7	50	5.2
8	59	8.4	12	56	20.2
5	42	1.8	9	60	11.8
10	64	13.9	5	35	1.6
11	58	15.5	12	62	21.4
8	64	9.8	11	67	18.8
7	57	6.4	7	71	7.5
5	44	3.3	7	51	5.6
12	64	21.5	11	57	15.6
5	42	2.2	7	61	6.3

   a Plot cubic-foot volume versus dbh, dbh^2, total height, and dbh^2 times total height. Do the relationships conform to expected trends?

   b Use the given data and the combined-variable formula to compute a cubic-foot volume equation.

   c Calculate the coefficient of determination and standard error of estimate for the resulting equation.

   d Use your regression equation to predict the cubic-foot volume for a loblolly pine measuring 8 in. dbh and 60 ft total height.

8-4 Construct a single-entry tree volume table based on a height-dbh relationship for a local species.

8-5 Use the taper equation for Douglas-fir shown in Section 8-9 to solve for the diameter (inside bark) at 8 ft and 24 ft above ground level for a tree 20 in. dbh and 120 ft total height. Compute the cubic-foot volume of this 16-ft segment using the predicted diameters and Smalian's formula. Apply mathematical integration techniques to solve for the cubic-foot volume of the same segment, and compare the result with that obtained using Smalian's formula.

8-6 Convert an existing tree volume table into a tree weight table.

8-7 Given the following taper function

$$d^2/dbh^2 = 0.9(h/H)$$

where d = upper-stem diameter at any given height h above ground, and H = total tree height.

    a In what units is upper-stem diameter (d) predicted?

    b Integrate the taper function to solve for volume (cu ft) between 16 and 32 feet above ground for a tree 16 in. dbh and 80 ft total height.

    c Integrate the taper function from 0 to H (ground level to tree tip) to develop an expression for total tree volume in cubic feet.

8-8 Conduct a thorough search of literature reporting on standard volume equations, and tabulate the frequency of different equation forms used. What is the most common form of equation fitted? Summarize your findings in a brief written report.

REFERENCES

Amateis, R. L., and Burkhart, H. E. 1987. Cubic-foot volume equations for loblolly pine trees in cutover, site-prepared plantations. *So. J. Appl. For.* **11**:190–192.

Amidon, E. L. 1984. A general taper functional form to predict bole volume for five mixed-conifer species in California. *Forest Sci.* **30**:166–171.

Belanger, R. P. 1973. Volume and weight tables for plantation-grown sycamore. *U.S. Forest Serv., Southeast. Forest Expt. Sta., Res. Paper SE*-107. 8 pp.

Bell, J. F., Marshall, D. D., and Johnson, G. P. 1981. Tarif tables for mountain hemlock developed from an equation of total stem cubic-foot volume. *Oregon State Univ. Res. Bull.* 35. 46 pp.

Brister, G. H., and Lauer, D. K. 1985. A tarif system for loblolly pine. *Forest Sci.* **31**:95–108.

———, Clutter, J. L., and Skinner, T. M. 1980. Tree volume and taper functions for site-prepared plantations of slash pine. *So. J. Appl. For.* **4**:139–142.

Burkhart, H. E. 1977. Cubic-foot volume of loblolly pine to any merchantable top limit. *So. J. Appl. For.* **1**(2):7–9.

Cao, Q. V., Burkhart, H. E., and Max, T. A. 1980. Evaluation of two methods for cubic-volume prediction of loblolly pine to any merchantable limit. *Forest Sci.* **26**:71–80.

Clark, A., III, and Schroeder, J. G. 1977. Biomass of yellow-poplar in natural stands in western North Carolina. *U.S. Forest Serv., Southeast. Forest Expt. Sta., Res. Paper SE*-165. 41 pp.

Clark, A., III, and Souter, R. A. 1994. Stem cubic-foot volume tables for tree species in the South. *U.S. Forest Serv., Southeast. Forest Expt. Sta., Res. Paper SE*-290. 241 pp.

Clutter, J. L. 1980. Development of taper functions from variable-top merchantable volume equations. *Forest Sci.* **26**:117–120.

Cunia, T. 1964. Weighted least squares method and construction of volume tables. *Forest Sci.* **10**:180–191.

Demaerschalk, J. P. 1972. Converting volume equations to compatible taper equations. *Forest Sci.* **18**:241–245.

Edminster, C. B., Beeson, R. T., and Metcalf, G. E. 1980. Volume tables and point-sampling factors for ponderosa pine in the Front Range of Colorado. *U.S. Forest Serv., Rocky Mt. Forest and Range Expt. Sta. Res. Paper RM*-218. 14 pp.

Edwards, M. B., and McNab, W. H. 1979. Biomass prediction for young southern pines. *J. Forestry* **77**:291–292.

Flewelling, J. W., and Pienaar, L. V. 1981. Multiplicative regression with lognormal errors. *Forest Sci.* **27**:281–289.

Honer, T. G. 1967. Standard volume tables and merchantable conversion factors for the commercial tree species of central and eastern Canada. *Forest Mgt. Res. and Services Inst., Ottawa, Ontario, Inf. Rep.* FMR-X-5. 21 pp. plus appendices.

Kozak, A. 1988. A variable-exponent taper equation. *Can. J. For. Res.* **18:**1363–1368.

———, Munro, D. D., and Smith, J. H. G. 1969. Taper functions and their application in forest inventory. *Forestry Chron.* **45:**278–283.

Landis, T. D., and Mogren, E. W. 1975. Tree strata biomass of subalpine spruce-fir stands in southwestern Colorado. *Forest Sci.* **21:**9–12.

Madgwick, H. A. I., Olah, F. D., and Burkhart, H. E. 1977. Biomass of open-grown Virginia pine. *Forest Sci.* **23:**89–91.

Martin, A. J. 1984. Testing volume equation accuracy with water displacement techniques. *Forest Sci.* **30:**41–50.

Mawson, J. C., and Conners, M. E. 1987. Girard form-class volume equations. *No. J. Appl. For.* **4:**58.

Max, T. A., and Burkhart, H. E. 1976. Segmented polynomial regression applied to taper equations. *Forest Sci.* **22:**283–289.

Mesavage, C., and Girard, J. W. 1946. *Tables for estimating board-foot content of timber.* U.S. Forest Service, Washington, D.C. 94 pp.

Perez, D. N., Burkhart, H. E., and Stiff, C. T. 1990. A variable-form taper function for *Pinus oocarpa* Schiede in Central Honduras. *Forest Sci.* **36:**186–191.

Reed, D. D., and Green, E. J. 1984. Compatible stem taper and volume ratio equations. *Forest Sci.* **30:**977–990.

Schumacher, F. X., and Hall, F. 1933. Logarithmic expression of timber-tree volume. *J. Agr. Res.* **47:**719–734.

Scrivani, J. A. 1989. An algorithm for generating "exact" Girard form class volume table values. *No. J. Appl. For.* **6:**140–142.

Solomon, D. S., Droessler, T. D., and Lemin, R. C. 1989. Segmented quadratic taper equations for spruce and fir in the Northeast. *No. J. Appl. For.* **6:**123–126.

Spurr, S. H. 1952. *Forest inventory.* The Ronald Press Company, New York. 476 pp.

Taras, M. A., and Phillips, D. R. 1978. Aboveground biomass of slash pine in a natural sawtimber stand in southern Alabama. *U.S. Forest Serv., Southeast. Forest Expt. Sta., Res. Paper SE*-188. 31 pp.

Ter-Mikaelian, M. T., and Korzukhin, M. D. 1997. Biomass equations for sixty-five North American tree species. *For. Ecol. and Manage.* **97:**1–24.

Turnbull, K. J., Little, G. R., and Hoyer, G. E. 1980. *Comprehensive tree volume tarif tables,* 3d ed. Department of Natural Resources, Olympia, Wash. 132 pp.

Van Deusen, P. C., Sullivan, A. D., and Matney, T. G. 1981. A prediction system for cubic foot volume of loblolly pine applicable through much of its range. *So. J. Appl. For.* **5:**186–189.

Wensel, L. C. 1971. I. Tree volume equations from measurements taken with a Barr and Stroud optical dendrometer. *Hilgardia* **41:**55–64.

———, and Schoenheide, R. L. 1971. II. Young growth gross volume tables for Sierra redwood [*Sequoia gigantea* (Lindl.) Decne]. *Hilgardia* **41:**65–76.

Wiant, H. V., Jr. 1986. Formulas for Mesavage and Girard's volume tables. *No. J. Appl. For.* **3:**124.

Williams, M. S., and Schreuder, H. T. 2000. Guidelines for choosing volume equations in the presence of measurement error in height. *Can. J. For. Res.* **30:**306–310.

CHAPTER 9

FOREST INVENTORY

9-1 Introduction   The usual purpose of a timber inventory is to determine, as precisely as available time and money will permit, the volume (or value) of standing trees in a given area. To attain this objective requires (1) a reliable estimate of the forest area and (2) measurement of all or an unbiased sample of trees within this area. No reliable timber inventory can be planned until the forester knows the location of all tract corners and boundary lines; recent aerial photographs and maps are therefore genuine assets for working in unfamiliar terrain.

The choice of a particular inventory system, often made at the forester's discretion, is governed by relative costs, size and density of timber, area to be covered, precision desired, number of people available for fieldwork, and length of time allowed for the estimate. Other things being equal, the intensity of sampling tends to increase as the size of the tract decreases and as the value of the timber increases.

9-2 Classes of Timber Surveys   The organization, intensity, and precision required in a timber inventory are logically based on the planned use of information collected. Therefore, no work should be initiated until inventory objectives have been clearly outlined and the exact format of summary forms to be compiled is known.

Depending on primary objectives, timber surveys may be conveniently classi-fied as (1) land acquisition inventories, (2) inventories for logging or timber sales, (3) management plan inventories or continuous forest inventory systems, and (4) special surveys designed for evaluating conditions such as stand improvement needs, plantable areas, insect and disease infestations, or timber trespass.

For land acquisition or timber sales, the principal information desired is net volume and value of merchantable trees growing in operable areas. In simple terms, a stand is usually classed as "operable" when merchantable trees can be logged at a profit. Notations on timber quality, by species, are commonly required. For land acquisition surveys, additional information is needed on soil or site qual-ity, presence of nonmerchantable growing stock, and proximity of the tract to mills or primary markets. Where timber values are relatively high, acquisition or sale inventories should be of an intensity that will produce estimates of mean volume within ±10 percent or less.

Management plan cruises, designed for providing information on timber growth, yield, and allowable cut, are no longer considered essential in all regions. In many instances, such cruises have been replaced by systems that make use of permanent sample plots. As a rule, either type of cruise is of low intensity, and the information collected is primarily intended for broad-based management deci-sions and long-range planning. As a result, inventory data are summarized by large administrative units rather than by cutting compartments or logging units.

Special surveys are so diversified that few general rules can be stipulated. For lo-cating spot insect or disease infestations, a survey might merely consist of an accu-rate forest type map with "trouble areas" located visually from aerial observations. Similarly, understocked stands in need of planting might be mapped from existing aerial photographs. In other instances, a 100 percent tree tally might be made for de-termining the number and volume of trees suitable for poles, piling, or veneer logs. Special surveys are also required in timber trespass cases. The estimation of timber volumes removed from cutover areas is discussed in a later section of this chapter.

9-3 Inventory Planning   Regardless of the kind of inventory being under-taken, a carefully developed plan is needed to execute the inventory efficiently. Inventory planning may be informally developed and executed by the forester (in the case of many timber cruises) or thoroughly documented in a formal plan (in the case of regional or national assessments).

The following checklist includes the major items that should be considered in planning a forest inventory. All items do not apply to all types of inventories, and the checklist is applicable to inventory of timber. If other resources are to be as-sessed at the same time as the timber assessment, the checklist should be expanded appropriately.

   1 Purpose of the inventory
      a Why the inventory is required
      b How the resulting information will be used

2 Background information
  a Past surveys, reports, maps, photographs
  b Personnel, funding, or time constraints
3 Description of area to be inventoried
  a Location
  b Size
  c Terrain, accessibility, and transportation factors
4 Information required from inventory
  a Tables and graphs
  b Maps
  c Outline of narrative report
5 Inventory design
  a Identification of the sampling unit
  b Construction of the sampling frame
  c Selection of a sampling technique
  d Determination of the sample size
6 Measurement procedures
  a Location of sampling units
  b Establishment of sampling units
  c Measurements of sampling units
    i Instruments and instructions for use
    ii Tree and other plot measurements
  d Recording of field data
  e Supervision and quality control
7 Compilation and calculation procedures
  a Data editing
  b Relationships to convert observed or measured attributes to quantities of interest (e.g., tree-volume tables)
  c Formulas for estimating means, totals, and corresponding standard errors
  d Description of calculation methods
8 Reporting of results, maintenance and storage of records
  a Number and distribution of copies
  b Storage and retrieval of data
  c Plans for updating inventory

9-4 Forest Inventory and Analysis   Forest Inventory and Analysis (FIA), formerly called the U.S. Forest Survey, is making the transition from a periodic to an annual assessment of the nation's forest and range resources. Historically state-by-state inventories, originally authorized by the McSweeney-McNary Forest Research Act of 1928, provided the basis for periodic assessments. The initial forest inventories were begun around 1930. Reinventories, normally planned at intervals of 8 to 15 years, have been completed on much of the 747 million acres (302 million ha) of forest land in the United States. The Renewable Resources

Planning Act of 1974, the National Forest Management Act of 1976, and the Forest and Rangeland Renewable Resources Act of 1978 amended and broadened the assessment provision of the original act to include 820 million acres (332 million ha) of range lands. The Pollution Research Act of 1988 resulted in the Forest Health Monitoring (FHM) program, which is charged with monitoring the health and productivity of forest ecosystems in relation to atmospheric pollution. The Agricultural Research, Extension, and Education Reform Act of 1998 (Farm Bill) directs FIA to change from a periodic to an annual inventory system by 2003 for most states. Interior Alaska, Hawaii, and territorial islands (e.g., Puerto Rico and the Virgin Islands) will continue to be assessed with periodic inventories. In order to meet reporting requirements of the 1998 Farm Bill and to increase program efficiency, the FIA and FHM field sampling programs have been merged. All FHM plots are a subset of the FIA plots.

FIA is essentially a continuous inventory system based on permanent sample units that are sometimes supplemented by temporary sample elements. Historically, FIA work units that are located at regional research stations of the USDA Forest Service have had primary responsibility for the fieldwork, data analysis, and published results. This paradigm has changed in recent years: in some regions of the country, state forestry organizations are collaborating in the collection of field data, and the USDA Forest Service is responsible for quality assurance of all data. The western United States is scheduled to measure 10 percent of all sample plots per year, and the eastern United States is scheduled to measure 15 percent per year, with the option to measure 20 percent per year if resources are available. After initiation of an annual survey in a state, the data collected in a year will be available in electronic format within 90 days of the end of that year. At the conclusion of each five year period, FIA will publish a report that contains a description of the state inventory of forests and their resources and incorporates all sample data collected over the five years. Statistical and analytical reports of the FIA data for the various states are available from U.S. Forest Service research stations.

The primary objectives of FIA are to provide the resource data needed for national assessments of this nation's forest and range resources. Every five years, FIA information from the individual states is summarized and incorporated into a national assessment. Each assessment includes a determination of the present and potential productivity of the land and of such other facts as may be necessary and useful in the determination of ways and means to balance the demand for and supply of these renewable resources. Assessments encompass all ownerships of forest and range lands and all benefits derived from uses of these lands. In turn, each assessment serves as the basis for development of a program for the nation's renewable resources. Each program is intended to implement those actions deemed necessary to assure an adequate supply of forest and range resources in the future while maintaining the integrity and quality of the environment.

SPECIAL INVENTORY CONSIDERATIONS

9-5 Tree Tallies   In accordance with the tree volume or tree weight tables to be used, standing trees may be tallied by simple counts, by diameter at breast height (dbh) and species only, or by various combinations of dbh, species, merchantable height, total height, form, individual tree-quality classes, and so on. Merchantable height limitations and tree form expressions have been described in Chapter 7.

Inventory foresters should be particularly careful in estimating tree heights; upper limits of stem merchantability often change from one species or locality to another. When ocular estimates of tree heights are permitted, timber cruisers will nevertheless make periodic checks by *measuring* every tenth or twentieth tree. Proficiency and consistency in inventory work are dependent on constant checks of estimation techniques.

It is essential that neat, concise, and accurate records be maintained when trees are measured and tallied in the field. When paper forms are used, foresters generally adopt the dot-dash system for indicating the number of trees tallied. The first four tallies are made by forming a small square with four pencil dots; the next four tallies are indicated by drawing successive lines between the dots to make a completed square; and the ninth and tenth tallies are denoted by diagonals placed within the square. A simplified tally form illustrating this technique is shown in Figure 9-1.

FIGURE 9-1
Sample tally of standing trees by dbh and height classes.

dbh (INCHES)	TREE HEIGHT CLASSES (FEET)					TREE TOTALS
	20	40	60	80	100	
10	• • •					3
12	• • • •	• • • •				6
14	•	• • • •	⊓	• •		13
16		• •	⊠ • • •	⊠	• •	27
18	•	• • •	⊓ • •	⊓		17
20		•	⊓ • •	⊠		16
TREE TOTALS	6	10	24	23	19	82

DOT-DASH TALLY METHOD

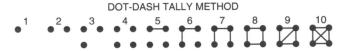

   Portable electronic data recorders are now commonly used. However, when paper tally sheets are used, data should be recorded in pencil because inked recordings tend to smear and become illegible when record sheets get wet. Erasures can be avoided by circling erroneous tallies; partial erasures often result in confusion and lead to later errors in office computations, particularly when several different persons are required to decipher field tabulations. Tally sheets, including pertinent locational headings, should be filled out completely *in the field.* Organization is just as important in field recordkeeping as it is in office bookkeeping.

9-6 Electronic Data Recorders   Small, lightweight, hand-held computers designed for field use are readily available and commonly used for collecting forestry data. These rugged devices are watertight and operable in a wide range of temperature conditions. Electronic data recorders allow measurements to be entered into memory at the time of observation, viewed on a small screen, and transferred later for further computerized processing and analysis (Fig. 9-2). By capturing data electronically in the field and downloading it directly into a computer, the data entry step required for computer-processing of the information is eliminated.

   Electronic devices for collecting data in the field are described as field computers, portable data recorders, data loggers, electronic data recorders, and so on.

FIGURE 9-2
Electronic data recorders (EDR) are an efficient means of capturing, checking, and transferring measurement data.

Although no single label has gained universal acceptance, the term electronic data recorder (EDR) is fairly commonly used and reasonably descriptive, so it will be applied for this discussion.

Electronic data recorders have found their widest use with large organizations and large projects. It may not be economically attractive to those who collect a limited amount of field data to invest in EDRs because of the relatively large initial cost of computer hardware, software, and personnel training. However, when large amounts of field data are collected, the time and money saved by eliminating the computer data entry step alone quickly surpasses the investment in EDR hardware and software. Furthermore, after crews are proficient with the equipment, electronic data recorders are generally faster than paper forms for recording measurements.

Recording data is only one of the functions of EDR, however. The devices can also be programmed to monitor data input, detect measurement and recording errors, and process results in the field so that certain decisions can be made on the spot. Thus these machines can improve data quality as well as data collection efficiency. For example, an EDR can be programmed to check for illogical diameter, height, species, or other entries by having a message come up on the screen advising that the questionable data be verified. Such field checks save significant amounts of time in later editing of data and possibly returning to field locations to verify or correct suspicious observations. As another example, an EDR can be programmed to compute plot volumes and variability in the field as the timber inventory is being conducted. This information can be used to adjust the sample size needed to achieve a desired precision level. With a sample size determined using observations from the population of interest, a minimum number of samples can be taken to achieve the desired precision level. Data processing in the field as the inventory is conducted—rather than in the office after fieldwork is completed—greatly reduces the risk of having to return to the area to acquire more samples.

A large variety of EDRs are available commercially, so the selection of the most appropriate equipment potentially can be a daunting and challenging undertaking. However, assuming that the investment in hardware, software, and training can be justified, there are several key points that should be evaluated when selecting EDRs for specific applications:

- Ease of data entry
- Ease of reading screen under differing light conditions (dense canopy, bright sunlight)
- Range of weather conditions under which the unit is expected to operate
- Availability of desired applications software
- Ease of updating software for changing needs
- Data storage capacity of unit
- Operating life of batteries under field use
- Weight of unit and ease of carrying in the field

• Ease of interfacing EDR unit with other electronic measurement devices (such as global positioning systems [GPS], electronic distance measurement [EDM] devices, and electronic calipers)

While this basic list provides a start on the search for an appropriate EDR, adapters of this technology may elect to consult comprehensive published reviews such as Gilluly, Hubbard, and White (1995), buyer's guides (e.g., in the June, 1999, issue of the *Journal of Forestry*), trade magazines, and manufacturers' brochures for additional information in order to make a highly informed choice.

9-7 Tree-Defect Estimation   The ability to make proper allowance for defective trees encountered on timber inventories requires experience that can be gained only by (1) getting repeated practice in estimating standing tree defects and (2) observing the sawing and utilization of defective logs at various mills.

When entire trees are classed as culls, they are either omitted from the field tally or recorded by species and dbh in a separate column of the tally sheet. For merchantable trees with evidence of interior defects, deductions for unsound portions of the stem may be handled by one of the following techniques:

1 For *visible defects,* dimensions of tallied trees are reduced in proportion to the estimated amount of defect. Thus a 22-in.-dbh three-log tree might be recorded as an 18-in.-dbh tree with three logs or possibly as a 22-in.-dbh tree with 2½ logs. Refinements may be made in this technique by applying the defect-deduction formulas for log volumes as suggested by Grosenbaugh (Sec. 6-13).

2 For *hidden defects,* all trees are tallied in the field as sound. After gross volumes have been computed, a percentage is deducted in proportion to the total amount of timber presumed to be defective. Although this method will usually produce more consistent results than individual tree allowances, the drawback is the difficulty of deciding on the amount of the deduction to be applied to various species.

9-8 The Complete Tree Tally   Under limited circumstances when scattered, high-value trees occur on small tracts, a complete or 100 percent tree tally may be feasible. Every tree of the desired species and size class may be measured, or the tally may consist of a 100 percent *count* of all stems plus a subsample (every *n*th tree) of actual measurements. The choice of methods depends on the stumpage value of trees inventoried, allowable costs, and desired precision.

Advantages of the complete tree tally are as follows:

1 More accurate estimates of total volume are possible because every tree can be tallied by species, dbh, height, and quality class.

2 Deductions for defect can be accurately assessed, because cull percentages can be applied to individual trees as they are tallied.

3 It is not necessary to determine the exact area of the tract. Once boundaries have been located, the total estimate can be made without regard to area.

Disadvantages of the complete tree tally are

1 High costs. Because of expense and time required, the 100 percent inventory is usually limited to small tracts or to individual trees of extra-high stumpage value.

2 Trees must often be marked as they are recorded to avoid omissions or duplications in the field tally. This requires additional time and/or added personnel.

9-9 Organizing the Complete Tree Tally   For dense stands of timber with large numbers of trees, it is desirable to have three persons in the field party. Two carry tree calipers for quick dbh measurements, while the third serves as recorder. If the area exceeds 10 acres (4 ha) in size, it is helpful to first lay out rectangles of about 4×10 chains by using stout cord or twine. Then, depending on topography and underbrush, parallel strips 1 to 2 chains wide can be traversed through each rectangle.

Fieldwork in dense stands proceeds most efficiently when it is feasible to merely count merchantable trees and restrict actual measurements to every tenth or twentieth stem. For pure stands that require little or no cull deductions, an alternative procedure might employ only caliper measurements of dbh for all stems, with volumes derived from single-entry volume equations. To ensure that no trees are overlooked or tallied twice, each stem should be marked at eye level on the side facing the unmeasured portion of the stand. In deciduous forests, complete stem tallies are preferably made during the dormant season when trees are leafless.

9-10 Timber Inventory as a Sampling Process   Except for those circumstances in which a complete tree tally is justified, the conduct of a timber inventory, or "cruise," is a sampling process. Among the considerations involved in developing an efficient sampling scheme are sample size, plot size and shape, and the sampling design (e.g., whether systematic, simple random, stratified random, etc.). Many of these considerations were discussed in Chapter 3.

Regardless of inventory objectives, the method of selecting sample trees for measurement is based on the concept of sampling probability. The methods of concern are (1) probability proportional to frequency (Chap. 10), (2) probability proportional to size, or point sampling (Chap. 11), and (3) probability proportional to prediction, or 3P sampling (Chap. 12).

SUMMARIES OF CRUISE DATA

9-11 Stand and Stock Tables   Although estimating total stand volume is a major objective of most forest inventories, such information is most useful when it is summarized by tree sizes and species groups. It is important to know that a given stand contains 1 million bd ft of timber, but it is more valuable to know how this volume is distributed among various species groups and diameter classes. Thus the compilation of stand and stock tables is often a prime requisite in summarizing cruising results.

TABLE 9-1
COMBINED STAND AND STOCK TABLE FOR MIXED HARDWOODS
ON A TRACT OF 107.2 ACRES IN GREENE COUNTY, GEORGIA

dbh (in.)	No. of trees		Cubic-foot volumes*	
	Tract total	Per acre average	Tract total	Per acre average
5	1,195.5	11.2	1,730.4	16.1
6	1,432.6	13.4	3,767.6	35.1
7	1,455.1	13.6	5,667.8	52.9
8	1,150.6	10.7	6,294.4	58.7
9	1,128.0	10.5	8,379.0	78.2
10	1,082.9	10.1	10,622.4	99.1
11	823.4	7.7	11,142.7	103.9
Total	8,268.1	77.2	47,604.3	444.0

*Cubic-foot volumes are inside bark of the merchantable stem to a variable top
diameter not smaller than 3 in.

A *stand table* is a tabulation of the total *number* of stems (or average number of stems per acre or ha) in a stand or compartment, by dbh classes and species. A *stock table* lists the total *volume* of stems (or average volume per acre or ha) in a stand, by dbh classes and species. As stock tables are derived from stand tables, they are sometimes combined into the same tabulation as shown by Table 9-1. This summary for mixed hardwood species includes oaks, gums, yellow-poplar, ash, and sycamore on a tract of 107.2 acres. Total numbers of trees and volumes are shown, as well as per acre averages.

9-12 Timber Volumes from Stump Diameters   In timber trespass cases, it may be necessary to determine the volume of trees illegally removed during a clandestine logging operation. Since stem diameters cannot be measured at breast height, they must be estimated by species or species groups from available stump diameters. The conversion may be estimated by use of regression equations, or ratios may be derived "on location" from sample measurements of trees left standing.

As an example, relationships between stump diameter (outside bark, taken at 4 inches above the ground) and dbh (outside bark) have been established for lodgepole pine in Montana from measurements of trees in stands of varying characteristics (Schlieter, 1986). The linear regression for the Ballard North stand on the Deerlodge National Forest is

$$\text{dbh} = 0.428 + 0.728(\text{stump dob})$$

The coefficient of determination (Sec. 2-21) is 0.96 for this fitted equation, and the standard error of estimate is $\pm$ 0.247 in.

Once each dbh has been ascertained, volumes may be determined from single-entry volume equations. Or, if tree tops have not been scattered, lengths of removed merchantable stems may be obtained by measuring distances between paired stumps and tops. With this additional information, volumes can be derived from multiple-entry equations. When the cutover area is too large for a 100 percent stump tally, partial estimates based on sample plots may be used as in conventional inventories. The final volume summary should be accompanied by an appraisal of the stumpage value of timber removed, along with notes and photographs documenting damage to real property or to residual standing trees.

SALES OF STANDING TIMBER

9-13 Stumpage Value   The sale value of standing timber is known as its *stumpage value.* For a given species, size (volume), and quality of timber, stumpage prices are highest when trees are accessible (easily logged) and located near concentration yards or primary markets. If a forest owner participates in harvesting, his income from the enterprise is increased in accordance with the value added by cutting, loading, and hauling to wood dealers or directly to mills. To determine *which* trees to sell and when to sell them, foresters must be intimately acquainted with local markets and prevailing prices, and they should learn to anticipate seasonal or periodic fluctuations in demands for various types of stumpage. Only by becoming thoroughly familiar with specifications for various wood products can the forest manager expect to realize consistently high returns from timber sales.

9-14 Methods of Selling Standing Timber   For handling sales of stumpage, trees to be cut (or those to be left standing) should be marked, or a cruise should be made by species and product designations. High-value trees, such as those to be utilized for veneer logs or poles, should be logged first. This cutting may be followed by removal of sawlogs, specialty bolts and billets, and tie logs. Finally, residual tops and smaller trees may then be converted into pulpwood, round mine timbers, fence posts, or fuel wood. Relative values of these products are dictated by local markets, and failure to observe rational priorities in cutting operations may severely penalize the seller of standing timber.

If the forest owner has made a reliable inventory or if timber is to be removed by clearcutting, sales may be made on a lump-sum basis. As with all business transactions, this is a reasonable approach provided both buyer and seller are well-informed as to market values and volume of wood involved. In other instances, sale prices may be based on marked trees, on minimum diameter or merchantability limits, or on log scale as determined after trees are cut and skidded to a landing.

9-15 Timber-Sale Contracts   For most sales of standing timber, even for small tracts of low-value species, it is desirable to draw up a simple written agreement to protect both buyer and seller and to avoid unnecessary misunderstandings in the transaction. A timber-sale contract contains sections on (1) location and description of timber, (2) prices and terms of payment, (3) utilization standards and related conditions of timber removal, and (4) procedures for settling disputes. The sample contract that follows, intended primarily for farmers and small woodlot owners, is reproduced from a bulletin of the USDA.

SAMPLE TIMBER-SALE AGREEMENT

_____ , of _____ , _____ ,
   (I or we) (Name of Purchaser)   (Post Office)   (State)
hereinafter called the purchaser, agree to purchase from _____ of
                                         (Seller's Name)
_____ , _____ , hereinafter called the seller, the designated
  (Post Office)   (State)
trees from the area described below.

  I DESCRIPTION OF SALE AREA:
    (Describe by legal subdivisions, if surveyed)

  II TREES DESIGNATED FOR CUTTING: (Cross out A or B—use only one clause.)
    A All _____ trees marked by the seller, or his agent, with paint spots
          (species)
    below stump height; also dead trees of the same species which are merchantable for _____.
               (Kind of forest products)
    B All _____ trees merchantable for _____
        (species)   (Kind of forest products)
    which measure _____ inches or more outside the bark at a point not less than 6 inches above the ground; also other _____ trees
                             (species)
    marked with paint spots below stump height by the seller or his agent.

  III CONDITIONS OF SALE:
    A The purchaser agrees to the following:
      1 To pay the seller the sum of $_____ for the above-described trees and to make payments in advance of cutting in amounts of at least $_____ each.
      2 To waive all claim to the above-described trees unless they are cut and removed on or before _____.
                      (Date)
      3 To do all in his power to prevent and suppress forest fires on or threatening the Sale Area.
      4 To protect from unnecessary injury young growth and other trees not designated for cutting.

5 To pay the seller for undesignated trees cut or injured through carelessness at the rate of $_____ each for trees measuring 10 to
_____ inches in diameter at stump height and $_____ each for
trees _____ inches or over in diameter.

6 To repair damage caused by logging to ditches, fences, bridges, roads,
trails, or other improvements damaged beyond ordinary wear and tear.

7 Not to assign this agreement in whole or in part without the written
consent of the seller.

B The seller agrees to the following:

1 To guarantee title to the forest products covered by this agreement
and to defend it against all claims at his expense.

2 To allow the purchaser to use unmerchantable material from tops of
trees cut or from trees of _____ species for necessary logging
improvements free of charge, provided such improvements are left in
place by the purchaser.

3 To grant the freedom of entry and right-of-way to the purchaser and
his employees on and across the area covered by this agreement and
also other privileges usually extended to purchasers of stumpage
which are not specifically covered, provided they do not conflict with
specific provisions of this agreement.

C In case of dispute over the terms of this agreement we agree to accept
the decision of an arbitration board of three selected persons as final.
Each of the contracting parties will select one person and the two selected will select a third to form this board.

Signed in duplicate this _____ day of _____ 20__

_____	_____
(Witness)	(Purchaser)
_____	_____
(Witness)	(Seller)

PROBLEMS

9-1 The following data were collected by measuring dbh and stump diameter (inside bark)
on 10 red oak trees:

dbh (in.)	Stump, dib (in.)	dbh (in.)	Stump, dib (in.)
14.1	17.2	7.9	9.1
10.5	11.3	10.4	12.3
9.0	10.0	12.8	14.2
16.4	18.6	17.0	20.0
7.1	7.5	13.2	16.0

a Compute a simple linear regression, $Y = b_0 + b_1 X$, where Y = dbh in inches and X = stump dib in inches for estimating tree dbh from measured stump diameter.

b Compute the coefficient of determination (r^2) and the standard error of estimate for the regression equation fitted in part **a.**

c Do the measures of goodness of fit computed in part **b** indicate that dbh can be reliably estimated from measured stump diameter?

9-2 Prepare a written report on the inventory system (or systems) used by a local forest industry or a local forestry consultant.

9-3 The following tree tally was recorded on 20 ⅕-acre plots established in a 50-acre stand of yellow-poplar:

dbh (in.)	Number of trees on 20 plots	dbh (in.)	Number of trees on 20 plots
8	50	12	130
9	95	13	100
10	105	14	70
11	110	15	40

Using the local volume equation values for yellow-poplar shown in Table 8-5, compile a combined stand and stock table in the same format as that of Table 9-1.

9-4 Review the most recent U.S. Forest Service report that deals with the forest resources of your state and prepare a 250-word abstract of the report.

REFERENCES

Aho, P. E. 1974. Defect estimation for grand fir in the Blue Mountains of Oregon and Washington. *U.S. Forest Serv., Pacific Northwest Forest and Range Expt. Sta., Res. Paper PNW*-175. 12 pp.

Bylin, C. V. 1982. Estimating dbh from stump diameter for 15 southern species. *U.S. Forest Serv., Southern Forest Expt. Sta., Res. Note SO*-286. 3 pp.

Frayer, W. E., and Furnival, G. M. 1999. Forest survey sampling designs: A history. *J. Forestry* **97(12):**4–10.

Gillespie, A. J. R. 1999. Rationale for a national annual forest inventory program. *J. Forestry* **97(12):**16–20.

Gilluly, D., Hubbard, K., and White, J. 1995. Electronic data recorders for forestry: A comprehensive buyer's guide II. *The Compiler* **13(4):**5–28.

Hair, D. 1973. The nature and use of comprehensive timber appraisals. *J. Forestry* **71:**565–567.

Hamilton, R. 1977. *Timber sale contracts.* Cooperative Extension Serv., Univ. of Nebraska, Lincoln, Neb. 4 pp.

Hansen, M. H. 1996. Portable technologies improving forestry field work. *J. Forestry* **94(6):** 29–30.

Husch, B. 1971. *Planning a forest inventory.* F.A.O., Rome, Italy. 120 pp.

Johnson, E. W. 1976. Information needed and the design of an inventory. *U.S. Forest Serv., N.E. Area, State and Private Forestry, Res. Inventory Note* 6. 4 pp.

Kozak, A., and Omule, S. A. Y. 1992. Estimating stump volume, stump inside bark diameter and diameter at breast height from stump measurements. *Forestry Chron.* **68:**623–627.

Ojasvi, P. R., Ramm, C. W., Lantagne, D. O., and Bruggink, J. 1991. Stump diameter and DBH relationships for white oak and black oak in the Lower Peninsula of Michigan. *Can. J. For. Res.* **21:**1596–1600.

McClure, J. P., Cost, N. D., and Knight, H. A. 1979. Multiresource inventories—A new concept for forest survey. *U.S. Forest Serv., Southeast. Forest Expt. Sta., Res. Paper SE*-191. 68 pp.

Reams, G. A., and Van Deusen, P. C. 1999. The southern annual forest inventory system. *J. Agric., Biol., and Env. Stat.* **4:**346–360.

Reams, G. A., Roesch, F. A., and Cost, N. D. 1999. Annual forest inventory: Cornerstone of sustainability in the South. *J. Forestry* **97(12):**21–26.

Roesch, F. A., and Reams, G. A. 1999. Analytical alternatives for an annual inventory system. *J. Forestry* **97(12):**33–37.

Scott, C. T., Köhl, M., and Schnellbächer, H. J. 1999. A comparison of periodic and annual forest surveys. *Forest Sci.* **45:**433–451.

Schlieter, J. A. 1986. Estimation of diameter at breast height from stump diameter for lodgepole pine. *U.S. Forest Serv., Intermountain Research Sta., Res. Note INT*-359. 4 pp.

Stage, A. R., and Alley, J. R. 1972. An inventory design using stand examinations for planning and programming timber management. *U.S. Forest Serv., Intermountain Forest Expt. Sta., Res. Paper INT*-126. 17 pp.

U.S. Department of Agriculture. 1958. Measuring and marketing farm timber. *Farmers' Bull.* 1210, U.S. Forest Service, Washington, D.C. 33 pp.

———. 1982. Forest Service resource inventory: An overview. *U.S. Forest Serv., Forest Resources Economics Research Staff*, Washington, D.C. 22 pp.

Van Deusen, J. L. 1975. Estimating breast height diameters from stump diameters for Black Hills ponderosa pine. *U.S. Forest Serv., Rocky Mt. Forest and Range Expt. Sta., Res. Note RM*-283. 3 pp.

Warton, E. H. 1984. Predicting diameter at breast height from stump diameters for northeastern tree species. *U.S. Forest Serv., Northeast. Forest Expt. Sta., Res. Note NE*-322. 4 pp.

Wildman, W. D., Oderwald, R. G., Boucher, B. A., and Helm, A. C. 1997. Hand-held field computers and inventory software—Weighing costs and benefits. *The Compiler* **15(1):**28–30.

CHAPTER 10

INVENTORIES WITH SAMPLE STRIPS OR PLOTS

10-1 Fixed-Area Sampling Units Many forest inventories are carried out using fixed-area sampling units. These fixed-area sampling units are called *strips* or *plots,* depending on their dimensions. Sample plots can be any shape (e.g., square, rectangular, circular, or triangular); however, square- and circular-plot shapes are most commonly employed. A strip can be thought of as a rectangular plot whose length is many times its width.

When employing sample plots or strips, the likelihood of selecting trees of a given size for measurement is dependent on the *frequency* with which that tree size occurs in the stand. That is, strip and plot inventories are methods of selecting sample trees with *probability proportional to frequency.* Within the sample area defined by the strips or plots, individual trees are tallied in terms of the characteristics to be assessed, such as species, dbh, and height. Then the sample-area tallies are expanded to a per-unit-area basis by applying an appropriate expansion factor.

STRIP SYSTEM OF CRUISING

10-2 Strip-Cruise Layout With this system, sample areas take the form of continuous strips of uniform width that are established through the forest at equally spaced intervals, such as 5, 10, or 20 chains. The sample strip itself is usually

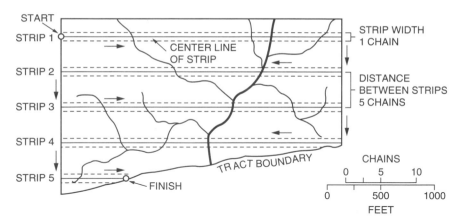

FIGURE 10-1
Diagrammatic plan for a 20 percent systematic strip cruise. Sample strips 1 chain wide are spaced at regular intervals of 5 chains.

TABLE 10-1
EXAMPLE OF CRUISING INTENSITIES FOR
1-CHAIN SAMPLE STRIP WIDTHS

Distance between strip centerlines			
ft	chains	No. of strips per "forty"	Nominal cruise percent
1,320	20	1	5
660	10	2	10
330	5	4	20
165	2½	8	40

1 chain wide, although it may be narrowed to ½ chain in dense stands of young timber or increased to 2 chains and wider in scattered, old-growth sawtimber. Strips are commonly run straight through the tract in a north-south or east-west direction, preferably oriented to cross topography and drainage at right angles (Fig. 10-1). By this technique, all soil types and timber conditions from ridge top to valley floor are theoretically intersected to provide a representative sample tally.

Strip cruises are usually organized to sample a predetermined percentage of the forest area. One-chain sample strips spaced 10 chains apart provide a nominal 10 percent estimate, and ½-chain strips at 20-chain intervals produce a nominal 2½ percent cruise (Table 10-1). The conversion factor to expand sample volume to total volume may be derived by (1) dividing the cruising percentage into 100 or (2) dividing the total tract acreage by the number of acres sampled.

The computation of cruise intensity and expansion factor can be expressed in formula form. If W = strip width, D = distance between strip centerlines, and W and D are in the same units, then nominal cruise intensity (I) in percent equals

$$I = \frac{W}{D}(100)$$

It is important to remember that nominal cruise percent and actual cruise percent are seldom equal because timbered tracts generally are not perfectly rectangular in shape. The actual cruise percentage can be calculated as

$$\left(\frac{\text{Area in sample}}{\text{Total tract area}}\right)100$$

In this calculation, area in sample and total tract area must be in the same units.

To convert sample volume to total tract volume, one computes the expansion, or blow-up, factor (EF) as

$$\text{EF} = \frac{100}{\text{cruise percent}}$$

In the computation of the expansion factor, the cruise percent should be the actual, not the nominal, percent. Alternatively, the expansion factor can be computed as total tract area/area in sample. The estimate of total volume for the entire tract is obtained by multiplying volume tallied in all the sample strips times the expansion factor.

10-3 Computing Tract Acreage from Sample Strips   If the boundaries of a tract are well-established, but the total area is unknown, a fixed cruising percentage may be decided upon, and the tract area can be estimated from the total chainage of strips composing the sample. A 5 percent cruise utilizing strips 1 chain wide spaced at 20-chain intervals provides a good example. The centerline of the first sample strip is offset 10 chains from one corner of the tract (i.e., one-half the planned interval between lines), and parallel strips are alternately run 20 chains apart until the entire area has been traversed by a pattern similar to that shown in Figure 10-1. If 132 lineal chains of sample strips are required, the area sampled is $(132 \times 1)/10 = 13.2$ acres. Because the strips were spaced for a 5 percent estimate, the total tract area is approximately 20×13.2, or 264 acres. The expansion factor of 20 is also used to convert the sampled timber volume to total tract volume.

When trees are tallied according to forest types and acreages are desired for each type encountered, the preceding technique may also be used to develop these breakdowns. If the 132 lineal chains of strip were made up of 90 chains intersecting a coniferous type and 42 chains intersecting a hardwood type, sampled areas would be 9 and 4.2 acres, respectively. Applying the expansion factor of 20 would result in estimated areas of 180 acres for conifers and 84 acres for hardwoods. Although this procedure does not necessarily provide exact values, it generally gives a reasonably good indication of the relative proportions by types.

10-4 Field Procedure for Strip Cruising Accurate determination of strip lengths and centerlines on the ground requires that distances be chained rather than paced; thus a two-person crew is needed for reliable fieldwork. One person locates the centerline with a hand or staff compass and also serves as head chainman; the other cruises the timber on the sample strip and acts as rear chainman. Either person may handle the tree tally, depending on underbrush and density of the timber. The width of the sample strip is ordinarily checked by occasional pacing from the 2-chain tape being dragged along as a moving centerline. Trailer tapes may be used where slope corrections are necessary. When offsetting between strip centerlines, it is important that the distance be carefully measured *perpendicularly* to the orientation of the strips. Because many timbered tracts have irregular borders, it is also important to "square off" the ends of strips so that the strip area can be computed easily as a rectangle.

In an efficient cruising party, the compassman is always 1 to 1½ chains ahead of the cruiser, and the sampling progresses in a smooth, continuous fashion. Experienced cruisers learn to "size up" tree heights well ahead, because there is a tendency toward underestimation when standing directly under a tree. At the end of each cruise line, the strip chainage should be recorded to the nearest link. Strip cruising can be speeded up appreciably by tallying tree diameters only and determining timber volumes from single-entry volume equations.

When timber type maps are prepared as cruising progresses, strips are preferably spaced no more than 10 chains apart. There are few forest stands where the cruiser can map more than 5 chains to either side of the centerline without having to make frequent side checks to verify the trends of type boundaries, streams, trails, or fence lines. The preferred technique for mapping is to sketch cruise lines directly on a recent aerial photograph; approximate type lines and drainage can also be interpreted in advance of fieldwork. Then, during the conduct of fieldwork, type lines can be verified and cover types correctly identified with the photographs in hand.

10-5 Pros and Cons of Strip Cruising The strip system of cruising is not as popular as in previous years. Its loss of favor is probably because two-person crews are needed and volume estimates are difficult to analyze statistically unless the tally is separated every few chains (resulting in a series of contiguous rectangular plots). In addition to items cited previously, the principal advantages claimed for strip cruising are

1 Sampling is continuous, and less time is wasted in traveling between strips than would be the case for a plot cruise of equal intensity.

2 In comparison with a plot cruise of the same intensity, strips have fewer borderline trees, because the total perimeter of the sample is usually smaller.

3 With two persons working together, there is less risk to personnel in remote or hazardous regions.

Disadvantages of strip cruising are as follows:

1 Errors are easily incurred through inaccurate estimation of strip width. Since the cruiser is constantly walking while tallying, there is little incentive to leave the centerline of the strip to check borderline trees.

2 Unless tree heights are checked at a considerable distance from the bases of trees, they may be easily underestimated.

3 Brush and windfalls are more of a hindrance to the strip cruiser than to the plot cruiser.

4 It is difficult to make spot checks of the cruise results because the strip centerline is rarely marked on the ground.

LINE-PLOT SYSTEM OF CRUISING

10-6 The Traditional Approach   As the name implies, line-plot cruising consists of a systematic tally of timber on a series of plots that are arranged in a rectangular or square grid pattern. Compass lines are established at uniform spacings, and plots of equal area are located at predetermined intervals along these lines. Plots are usually circular in shape, but they may also take the form of squares, rectangles, or triangles. In the United States, ¼- and ⅕-acre circular plots are most commonly employed for sawtimber tallies; smaller plots are preferred for cruising poletimber or sapling stands. For inventories where a wide variety of timber sizes will be encountered, it is often efficient to use concentric circular plots with each centered at the same point. As an example, ⅕-acre plots might be used to tally sawtimber trees, ⅒-acre plots for pulpwood trees, and ¹⁄₁₀₀₀-acre plots for regeneration counts. Radii for circular plots frequently used in timber inventory are given in Table 10-2.

As with the strip method, systematic line-plot inventories are often planned on a percent cruise basis. In Figure 10-2, for example, ⅕-acre plots are spaced at intervals of 4 chains on cruise lines that are 5 chains apart. As each plot "represents" an area of 20 square chains, the nominal cruising percentage is computed as

$$\frac{\text{Plot size in acres}}{\text{Acres represented}} \times 100 = \frac{0.2 \text{ acres}}{2 \text{ acres}} \times 100 = 10 \text{ percent}$$

By the same token, 10 percent estimates may also be accomplished by spacing the same ⅕-acre plots at intervals of 2½ × 8 chains, 2 × 10 chains, and so on. If a 1:1 square grid arrangement is desired, the intervals between both plot centers and

TABLE 10-2
RADII FOR SEVERAL SIZES OF CIRCULAR SAMPLE PLOTS

Plot size (acre)	Plot radius (ft)	Plot size (ha)	Plot radius (m)
1	117.8	1	56.42
1/2	83.3	1/2	39.89
1/4	58.9	1/4	28.21
1/5	52.7	1/5	25.23
1/10	37.2	1/10	17.84
1/20	26.3	1/20	12.62
1/25	23.5	1/25	11.28
1/40	18.6	1/40	8.92
1/50	16.7	1/50	7.98
1/100	11.8	1/100	5.64
1/300	6.8	1/300	3.26
1/500	5.3	1/500	2.52
1/1000	3.7	1/1000	1.78

FIGURE 10-2
Diagrammatic plan for a 10 percent systematic line-plot cruise utilizing 1/5-acre circular sampling units.

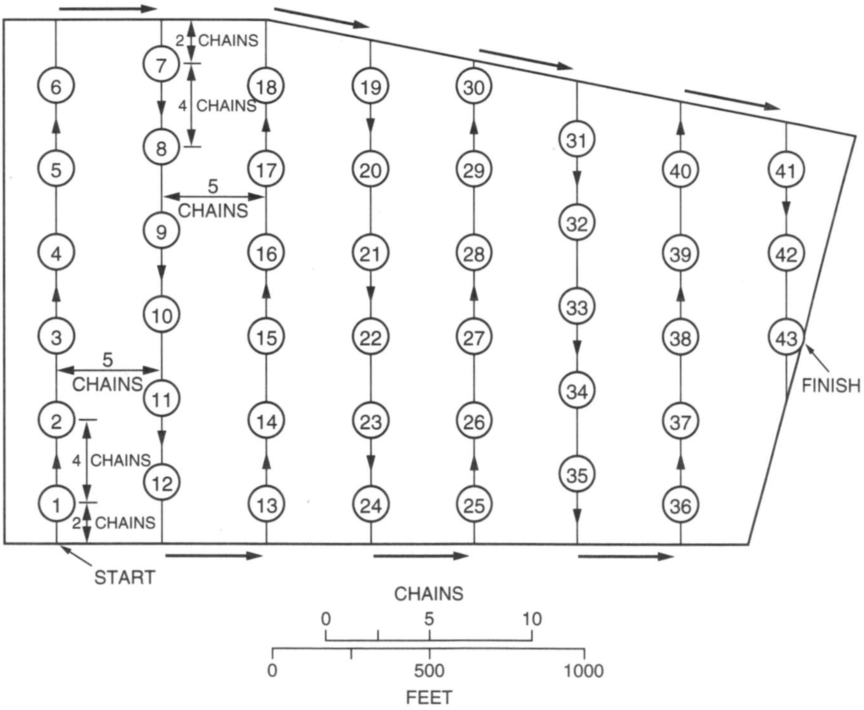

compass lines would be calculated as $\sqrt{20}$ square chains, or 4.47×4.47 chains. Similar computations can be made for other plot sizes and cruising intensities. Cruise expansion factors are calculated by the same methods described for strip cruises.

The number and spacing of plots for line-plot cruises can be expressed in formula form; in order to express the desired relationships algebraically, the following symbols (after Burkhart, Barrett, and Lund, 1984) are defined:

A = total tract area,
A_p = area of all plots,
$P = A_p/A$ = intensity of cruise as a decimal,
a = area of one plot,
n = number of plots,
L = distance between lines,
B = distance between plots on a line,

where A, A_p, and a are all in square units of L and B. When line plot cruises are designed on a percentage basis, P is specified. Assuming that the total area of the tract being inventoried is known, the area of the sample is

$$A_p = AP$$

The plot size (a) is specified in advance, thus the number of plots (n) needed is

$$n = \frac{A_p}{a}$$

Next, one must determine how to space the plots. If B and L are in chains and A, A_p, and a are in acres, then

$$P = \frac{\dfrac{a}{BL}}{10} = \frac{a(10)}{BL}$$

That is, each sample plot of "a" acres represents an area $BL / 10$ acres (there are 10 square chains per acre). The expression for P can be algebraically rearranged as

$$B = \frac{a(10)}{LP}$$

or

$$L = \frac{a(10)}{BP}$$

Thus, if either B or L (as well as P) is specified, the other can be computed readily. For square spacing (that is, $B = L$), we have

$$P = \frac{a(10)}{B^2}$$

and

$$B = \sqrt{\frac{a(10)}{P}}$$

To design a 10 percent line-plot cruise for an 86-acre tract using ⅕-acre sample plots, the sample area is computed as

$$A_p = AP = 86(0.1) = 8.6 \text{ acres}$$

Next, the number of plots needed is computed as

$$n = \frac{A_p}{a} = \frac{8.6}{0.2} = 43$$

If the distance between lines (L) is specified to be 5 chains, then the distance between plots on lines will be

$$B = \frac{a(10)}{LP} = \frac{0.2(10)}{5(0.1)} = 4 \text{ chains}$$

Figure 10-2 shows a line-plot cruise utilizing ⅕-acre plots spaced 5 by 4 chains.

10-7 Plot Cruise Example   For purposes of illustration, it may be assumed that a line-plot cruise was performed using ⅕-acre plots on a 34-acre tract. Fifteen plots were established, and the volume per plot was computed for each with the following result:

Plot	Volume (ft³/0.2 acre)	Plot	Volume (ft³/0.2 acre)	Plot	Volume (ft³/0.2 acre)
1	500	6	415	11	470
2	710	7	310	12	545
3	425	8	200	13	450
4	900	9	490	14	605
5	610	10	600	15	510

The estimated mean volume per plot is

$$\bar{y} = \frac{\Sigma y_i}{n} = \frac{7,740}{15} = 516 \text{ ft}^3/0.2 \text{ acre}$$

and the estimated volume per acre is

$$(516)(5) = 2,580 \text{ ft}^3/\text{acre}$$

The reliability of the estimated mean is indicated by the magnitude of the standard error of the mean and the width of the computed confidence interval. Although line-plot cruises are systematic samples, and thus precision can only be approximated, the standard error of the mean is generally estimated using the formula for simple random sampling (Sec. 3-4), namely

$$S_{\bar{y}} = \sqrt{\frac{s^2}{n}\left(\frac{N-n}{N}\right)}$$

where s^2 = variance among individual sampling units
$\quad n$ = sample size (15 in this case)
$\quad N$ = population size (expressed in number of sampling units or
$\qquad (34)(5) = 170$ in this illustration)

For this example, the variance, s^2, is computed as

$$s^2 = \frac{\sum y_i^2 - \dfrac{(\sum y_i)^2}{n}}{n-1} = \frac{4,371,800 - \dfrac{(7,740)^2}{15}}{14}$$
$$= 26,997$$

and the standard error of the mean is

$$S_{\bar{y}} = \sqrt{\frac{26,997}{15}\left(\frac{170-15}{170}\right)} = 40.5 \text{ ft}^3/0.2 \text{ acre or } 202.5 \text{ ft}^3/\text{acre}$$

The 95 percent confidence interval for the mean on a per acre basis is established as

$$\bar{y} \pm t_{(n-1 \text{ d.f.})} S_{\bar{y}}$$
$$2,580 \pm (2.145)(202.5)$$
$$2,580 \pm 434.36$$
or $\quad 2,145.64$ to $3,014.36$ ft^3/acre

10-8 Sampling Intensity and Design The intensity of plot sampling is governed by the variability of the stand, allowable inventory costs, and desired standards of precision. The coefficient of variation in volume per unit area should first be estimated, either on the basis of existing stand records or by measuring a preliminary field sample of, perhaps, 10 to 30 plots. Then the proper sampling intensity can be calculated by the procedures outlined in Chapter 3.

The trend is away from the concept of fixed cruising percentages, for it is not the sampling fraction that is important; it is the number of sampling units (of a specified kind) needed to produce estimates with a specified precision. In the final analysis, the best endorsement for a given plot size and sampling intensity is an unbiased estimate of stand volume that is bracketed by acceptable confidence limits.

In addition to determining the sampling intensity, it is necessary to decide on the *sampling design,* that is, the method of selecting the nonoverlapping plots for field measurement. When sample plots are employed, the *sampling frame* is defined as a listing of all possible plots that may be drawn from the specified (finite) population or tract of land. The sample plots to be visited on the ground can be selected randomly from such a listing.

In spite of the statistical difficulties associated with systematic sampling designs, such cruises are still employed frequently. Where estimates of sampling precision are regarded as unnecessary, systematic sampling may provide a useful alternative to random sampling methods.

10-9 Cruising Techniques   Circular-plot inventories are often handled by one person, but two or three persons can be used efficiently when square or rectangular plots are employed. Field directions are established with a hand or staff compass, and intervals between sample plots may be either taped or paced. The exact location of plot centers is unimportant, provided the centers are established in an unbiased manner. When "check cruises" are to be made, plot centers or corners should be marked with stakes, with cairns, or by reference to scribed trees.

With square or rectangular plots, the four corner stakes make it a simple matter to determine which trees are inside the plot boundaries. However, with circular plots, inaccurate estimation of the plot radii is a common source of error. As a minimum, four radii should be measured to establish the sample perimeter. If an ordinary chaining pin is carried to denote plot centers, a tape can be tied to the pin for one-person checks of plot radii. When trees appear to be borderline, the center of the stem (pith) determines whether they are "in" or "out." For plots on sloping ground, one must be careful to measure horizontal (not slope) distances when checking plot boundaries.

Inaccurate estimation of plot radii is one of the greatest sources of error in using circular samples. The gravity of such errors is exemplified by a 2½ percent cruise; every stem erroneously tallied or ignored has its volume expanded 40 times. Thus the failure to include one tree having a volume of 300 bd ft will result in a final estimate that is 12,000 bd ft too low.

Separate tally sheets are recommended for each plot location and species; descriptive plot data can be handwritten or designated by special numerical codes. It is usually most efficient to begin the tally at a natural stand opening (or due north) and record trees in a clockwise sweep around the plot. When the tally is completed, a quick stem count made from the opposite direction provides a valuable check on the number of trees sampled.

10-10 Boundary Overlap   A problem arises when a plot does not lie wholly within the area being sampled. This problem, commonly referred to as *edge-effect bias* or *boundary overlap,* can introduce a bias in the plot cruise statistics if it is not treated properly. When large areas are cruised with small circular plots, the bias due to boundary overlap is usually negligible. However, for small areas, especially long, narrow tracts with a high proportion of edge trees, appropriate precautions should be taken to guard against bias caused by boundary overlap.

One method of dealing with the boundary-overlap problem is to move plot centers (back on the line of travel in the case of line-plot cruises) until the entire plot lies in the area being sampled. This method is generally satisfactory if the timber along the edge is similar to that in the remainder of the tract, but it is not likely to be suitable for small woodlots that have edges strikingly different from the tract interior. Adjustment of the plot-center location may introduce bias because the trees in the edge zone may be undersampled.

In a cruise of small tracts with a high proportion of "edge," a procedure for dealing with boundary overlap should be adopted. The *mirage method* developed by Schmid in 1969 and described by Beers (1977) and others in the American forestry literature is a simple and, for most situations, easily applied technique. When the plot center falls near the stand boundary so that the plot is not completely within the tract being sampled, the cruiser measures the distance D from plot center to the boundary. A correction-plot center is then established by going this distance D beyond the boundary. All trees in the overlap of the original plot and the correction plot are tallied twice (Fig. 10-3).

Similar boundary-overlap problems arise when volume estimates are being summarized by different types and a sample plot happens to fall at a transition line that divides two types. If the cruise estimate is to be summarized by types and

FIGURE 10-3
The mirage method for correction of boundary-overlap bias when circular plots are used. Trees in the shaded area are tallied twice.

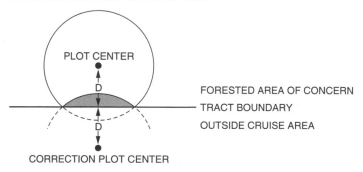

expansion factors for each type (including nonforest areas) are determined, the plot should be moved until it falls *entirely* within the type indicated by its original center location, or a boundary-overlap correction, such as the mirage method, should be applied.

In contrast to the foregoing, plots should not be shifted if a single area expansion factor is to be used for deriving total tract volumes. Under these conditions, edge effects, type transition zones, and stand openings are typically part of the population; therefore, a representative sample would be *expected* to result in occasional plots that are part sawtimber and part seedlings—or half-timbered and half-cutover land. To arbitrarily move these plot locations would result in a biased sample.

10-11 Merits of the Plot System   The principal advantages claimed for line-plot cruising over the strip system are as follows:

1 The system is suitable for one-person cruising.

2 Cruisers are not hindered by brush and windfalls as in strip cruising, for they do not have to tally trees while following a compass line.

3 A pause at each plot center allows the cruiser more time for checking stem dimensions, borderline trees, and defective timber.

4 The tree tally is separated for each plot, thus permitting quick summaries of data by timber types, stand sizes, or area condition classes.

USE OF PERMANENT SAMPLE PLOTS

10-12 Criteria for Inventory Plots   The periodic remeasurement of permanent sample plots is statistically superior to successive independent inventories for evaluating *changes* in forest conditions. When independent surveys are repeated, the sampling errors of both inventories must be considered in assessing stand differences or changes over time. But when identical sample plots are remeasured, sampling errors relating to such differences are apt to be lower; that is, the precision of "change estimates" is improved. In addition, trees initially sampled but absent at a later remeasurement can be classified as to the cause of removal (e.g., harvested yield, natural mortality, and so on).

Regardless of whether temporary or permanent sampling units are employed for an inventory, two basic criteria must be met: the field plots must be *representative* of the forest area for which inferences are made, and they must be *subjected to the same treatments* as the nonsampled portion of the forest. If these conditions are not fully achieved, inferences drawn from such sampling units will be of questionable utility.

One attempt to ensure that sampling units are representative of equal forest areas is illustrated by some rigid continuous forest inventory (CFI) procedures whereby field plots are systematically arranged on a square grid basis; thus each plot represents a fixed and equal proportion of the total forest area. However, such sampling designs tend to be inflexible in meeting the changing requirements of management and therefore are not recommended for most forest inventories. Even though systematic samples are sometimes quite efficient, especially from the viewpoint of reducing field travel time, it is generally better to use other methods of sampling that will permit calculation of the reliability of sample estimates.

10-13 Sampling Units: Size, Shape, and Number   Circular sample plots of ⅕ acre have been widely used for CFI systems in the past. Nevertheless, square or rectangular plots may be more efficient because the establishment of four corner stakes, however inconspicuously, improves the chances for plot relocation at a later date. Depending on the size and variability of timber stands, an ideal plot size for second-growth forests will generally fall in the range of ½ to ¼ acre.

As outlined previously, the *number* of permanent sample plots to be established and measured is dependent on the variability of the quantity being assessed and the desired sampling precision. For tracts of 50,000 to 100,000 acres, sampling errors of ±10 to 20 percent might be desired for current volume, with ±20 to 30 percent being accepted for growth (probability level of 0.95). If this precision is maintained on parcels of 50,000 to 100,000 acres, the overall precision for an entire forest holding of 1 to 3 million acres should be approximately ±2 to 3 percent for current volume and ±5 percent for growth.

10-14 Field-Plot Establishment   Increasingly, global positioning systems (Chap. 4) are being used to establish the locations of permanent field plots. If global positioning systems are not available, recent aerial photographs and topographic maps are invaluable aids for the initial location, establishment, and relocation of permanent sample plots. All pertinent data relative to bearings of approach lines, distances, and reference points or monuments should be recorded on a plot-location sheet *and* on the back of the appropriate aerial photograph. It is essential that such information be complete and coherent because subsequent plot relocations are often made by entirely different field crews.

Plot centers or corner stakes are preferably inconspicuous and are referenced by using a permanent landmark at least 100 to 300 ft distant and by recording bearings and distances to two or more scribed or tagged "witness trees" that are nearer (but not within) the plot. There is some disagreement as to whether permanent plots should be marked (1) conspicuously, so that they can be easily relocated, or (2) inconspicuously, to ensure that they are accorded the same treatment as non-sampled portions of the forest. The trend is toward essentially "hidden plots," for it is mandatory that they be subjected to *exactly* the same conditions or treatments as the surrounding forest, whether this be stand improvement, harvesting, fires, floods, or insect and disease infestations. Only under these conditions can it be assumed that the sample plots are representative.

Small sections of welding rods, projecting perhaps 6 to 12 in. above ground level, are useful for plot corner stakes. Where it becomes feasible to use more massive iron stakes, it may be possible to find them again with a "dip needle" or other magnetic detection devices. If individual trees on the plot are marked at all, the preferable method is to nail numbered metal tags into the stumps near ground level so that they will not be noticeable to timber markers and other forest workers. As an alternative to tagging the sample trees, individual stem locations may be numbered and mapped by coordinate positions on a plot-diagram sheet.

10-15 Field-Plot Measurements   The inventory forester in charge of the permanent plot system should assume the responsibility for training field crews and for deciding how measurements should be taken on each sample plot. Standardized field procedures are emphasized because *consistency in measurement techniques* is as important as precision for evaluating changes over time.

To avoid problems arising from periodic variations in tree merchantability standards, field measurements should be planned so that tree volumes are expressed in terms of cubic measure (inside bark) for the entire stem, including stump and top. It may also be necessary to estimate the volume of branch wood on some operations. Techniques for predicting merchantable volumes for various portions of trees are given in Chapter 8.

The field information collected for each sampling unit is recorded under one of two categories: plot description data and individual tree data. The exact measurements required will differ for each inventory system; thus the following listings merely include *examples* of the data that may be required:

Plot data	Individual tree data
Plot number and location	Tree number
Date of measurement	Species
Forest cover type	dbh
Stand size and condition	Total height
Stand age	Merchantable stem lengths
Stocking or density class	Form or upper-stem diameters
Site index	Crown class
Slope or topography	Tree-quality class
Soil classification	Vigor
Understory vegetation	Diameter growth
Treatments needed	Mortality (and cause)

All field measurement data are numerically coded and recorded on tally forms or directly onto a machine-readable medium for computer processing. Plot inventories are preferably made immediately after a growing season and prior to heavy snowfall. For tracts smaller than 100,000 acres, it may be possible to establish all plots in a single season and remeasure them within similar time limitations. On larger areas, fieldwork may be conducted each fall on a rotation system that reinventories about one-fifth of the forest each year.

10-16 Periodic Reinventories Permanent sample plots are commonly remeasured at intervals of 3 to 10 years, depending on timber growth rates, expected changes in stand conditions, and the intensity of management. The interval must be long enough to permit a measurable degree of change, but short enough so that a fair proportion of the trees originally measured will be present for remeasurement. At each reinventory, trees that have attained the minimum diameter during the measurement interval are tallied as ingrowth. Also, felling records are kept to correct yields for those plots cut during the measurement interval. This information, along with mortality estimates, is essential for the prediction of future stand yields.

The data needed to calculate volume growth include stand tables prepared from two consecutive inventories, felling records, mortality estimates, and a volume-prediction equation that is applicable to the previous and present stands. First, the stand tables for the two inventories are converted to corresponding stock tables; then, the difference in volume, after accounting for harvested yields and mortality, represents the growth of the plot.

One of the problems facing field crews who must remeasure permanent sampling units is that of *finding the plots.* Difficulties with relocating plots can be greatly reduced with global positioning systems technology, but there are still many permanent plot installations without GPS coordinates. When plots are inconspicuously marked, relocation time can make up a sizable proportion of the total time allotted for reinventories. A study conducted by Nyssonen (1967) in Norway revealed that, after a 7-year interval, 4 to 8 percent of the permanent sample plots could not be found again. Where plots *could* be relocated, the time required for transportation, relocation (which was done without the aid of GPS), and measurement was distributed as follows:

Activity	Percent of total time
Transport by a vehicle	20.6
Walking to, between, and from the plots	22.6
Searching for the plots	12.9
Sample plot measurement	35.7
Pauses	8.2
Total	100.0

Even though time factors will obviously differ for every inventory system, the foregoing tabulation serves to illustrate some of the nonproductive aspects that should be recognized in the application of permanent plot-inventory systems.

REGENERATION SURVEYS WITH SAMPLE PLOTS

10-17 Need for Regeneration Surveys Evaluations of forest regeneration efforts are of critical importance in on-the-ground forest management.

Regeneration may be evaluated at different times in the forest production cycle, and various methods may be used. To devise the most suitable regeneration evaluation system, one must first identify survey objectives.

The primary needs for regeneration information are (1) to determine regeneration status or potential, (2) to demonstrate compliance with conservation laws, (3) to determine the effectiveness of the regeneration method employed, (4) to identify the needs for additional cultural treatments (e.g., thinning, release from competing vegetation), and (5) to collect data for predicting future yields (Stein, 1984a).

The two main methods used to conduct regeneration surveys are distance sampling methods and fixed-area sample-plot methods. Distance sampling methods will not be discussed here. Rather, attention will be focused on sampling techniques based on sample plots. Fixed-area plots can serve three distinctive regeneration evaluation objectives (Stein, 1984b): (1) determine the presence or absence of trees, (2) obtain a quantitative estimate of the number of trees per unit area, and (3) measure changes in numbers, size, or composition of trees that occur with the passage of time. The methodology that serves each objective is known, respectively, as the stocked-quadrat method, plot-count method, and staked-point method.

10-18 Stocked-Quadrat Method   The *stocked-quadrat method* is based on the presence or absence of a tree on the plot. It was developed to place evaluation emphasis on tree distribution. The basic concept of the stock-quadrat method is that if a given area is divided into squares of such a size that one established seedling per square will fully stock the square at maturity, then the percentage of units stocked, regardless of the total number of seedlings per acre, indicates the proportion of land being utilized for tree growth. Developers of the stocked-quadrat method have identified its two key features as (1) it automatically compares actual stocking against a defined fully stocked stand and (2) the size of the sample plot used must have a logical relation to full stocking.

If, for example, 250 well-distributed stems per acre at maturity were defined as "full stocking," then the appropriate plot size for applying the stocked-quadrat method would be 1/250 acre. One would proceed by locating 1/250-acre plots (randomly or perhaps systematically) through the area of interest. Field application of the stocked-quadrat method is simple and fast. Each sample plot is classified as stocked if at least one acceptable tree (to be acceptable the tree must meet the species, size, and competitive position criteria set for the survey) is found and as nonstocked if no acceptable tree is found. The tally obtained by locating a sufficient number of plots of the correct size provides a direct estimate of stocking— that is, the percentage of the area occupied by trees. Stocking percent is computed by dividing the number of plots stocked by the total number established. The stocking percent so obtained provides an estimate of the area occupied by well-spaced trees; however, it does not reveal the pattern of stocking on the area.

Stocking pattern can be ascertained by plotting the location of stocked and non-stocked plots on a map of the surveyed area. While a single plot at each sample location is recommended (Stein, 1984b), cluster samples—large quadrats divided into four quadrants—are sometimes used to increase data collected relative to the time spent in travel between plots.

10-19 Plot-Count Method   This method is applied when the objective of the regeneration survey is to estimate the number of trees per acre. The plot-count method is simple in concept and straightforward in application. Plots are located, randomly or systematically, throughout the area of interest. Sample plots of uniform size and shape are searched for acceptable trees. The average number of trees per plot is determined, and this average is expanded to a per-acre basis. No specific stocking goal need be specified prior to sampling to apply the plot-count method.

Circular plots are often used for regeneration plot counts. The most appropriate plot size will vary depending on the density (numbers per unit area) of the regeneration and the amount of competing vegetation. When adopting a plot size, several practical matters must be taken into consideration. Because the entire area of each plot must be searched for trees, search time increases with increasing plot size. Furthermore, large plots are more difficult to search thoroughly than small plots, and some trees may be missed on large plots.

Computing the average number of trees per acre from plot-count data is a straightforward procedure. However, the average number of acceptable seedlings does not provide useful information on the pattern of tree distribution in the area. Plotting tree-count data by sample-plot location can provide useful information on distribution. Plot-count data can also be analyzed statistically to aid in interpreting the uniformity of distribution (for example, a small coefficient of variation would indicate relatively uniform distribution, whereas a large coefficient of variation would indicate nonuniform distribution of trees per acre).

10-20 Staked-Point Method   This method is used when the survey objective is to estimate changes in tree survival or growth over time. Permanent plots are required for the staked-point method, whereas temporary plots are usually used in the stocked-quadrat and plot-count methods.

Extra costs are associated with the staked-point method, because the plots and trees must be marked so that they can be relocated. However, repeated examination of a representative sample is required for obtaining reliable data for certain objectives.

As with other regeneration survey methods, different plot sizes and shapes can be employed in the staked-plot method. The most appropriate approach to analyzing the data will depend on the sample design used and the measurement data obtained.

PROBLEMS

10-1 Compute the nominal cruising percents and expansion factors for the following systematic samples:

  a Strips ½ chain wide spaced 10 chains apart
  b Four 1-chain strips run through a quarter section of land
  c Plots of ⅒ acre spaced at 2½ × 5 chains
  d Plots of ⅕ acre spaced at 5 × 15 chains

10-2 For the same plot sizes shown in Table 10-2, compile a similar tabulation for *square* sample plots. In lieu of plot radii, show the length of one side of the squares in feet and in meters.

10-3 a If you space 1-chain strips at 10-chain intervals through a square section of land and tally 350 MBF on the sample, what would be the total-volume estimate for the entire tract?

  b If you space ¼-acre circular plots at 5 × 10 chains through a 240-acre tract, and the volume tallied on the sample is 68.4 MBF, what would be the total-volume estimate for the entire tract?

  c How many lineal chains of sample strips 1 chain wide would be run through a township to obtain a 2 percent cruising intensity?

  d If you made a 0.05 percent inventory of the total land area in a state consisting of 30 million acres, how many ¼-acre circular plots would be required? For a square grid arrangement of samples, what would be the distance (in chains) between plots?

10-4 Design and conduct a field study to compare the relative efficiencies of circular, square, and rectangular sample plots in your locality.

10-5 The coefficient of variation for ⅒-acre circular plots was estimated to be 90 percent for a timbered tract of 50 acres. If one wishes to estimate the mean volume per acre of this tract within ±20 percent unless a 1-in-20 chance occurs,

  a Compute the number of plots to be measured assuming simple random sampling without replacement.

  b Calculate the distance between plot centers in chains assuming the plots will be systematically established on a square grid.

10-6 Assume that desirable stocking for mature timber of species of interest is 150 trees per acre.

  a When conducting a stocked-quadrat survey of regeneration for this species, what plot size should be used?

  b Suppose that 50 plots were established. Acceptable trees were found on 42 plots. What is the stocking percent?

10-7 Using the data in the line-plot cruise example in Section 10-7:

  a Compute the coefficient of variation on a per plot and a per acre basis.

  b Estimate the total volume on the tract and establish the 95 percent confidence interval for the estimated total.

10-8 A plot-count regeneration survey was conducted using ⅟₁₀₀-acre plots located randomly over the tract of interest. The tree count per plot follows:

Plot	Count	Plot	Count
1	5	6	1
2	2	7	2
3	4	8	2
4	0	9	6
5	3	10	3

a Estimate the mean number of trees per acre.

b Compute the coefficient of variation for numbers of trees per acre.

c Compute the 90 percent confidence interval for the mean.

REFERENCES

Avery, T. E., and Newton, R. 1965. Plot sizes for timber cruising in Georgia. *J. Forestry* **63**:930–932.

Beers, T. W. 1977. Practical correction of boundary overlap. *So. J. Appl. For.* **1**:16–18.

Brand, D. G. 1988. A systematic approach to assess forest regeneration. *Forestry Chron.* **64**:414–420.

Burkhart, H. E., Barrett, J. P., and Lund, H. G. 1984. Timber inventory. Pp. 361–411 in *Forestry handbook,* K. F. Wenger (ed.), John Wiley & Sons, New York.

Fowler, G. W., and Arvanitis, L. G. 1979. Aspects of statistical bias due to the forest edge: Fixed-area circular plots. *Can. J. For. Res.* **9**:383–389.

Johnson, F. A., and Hixon, H. J. 1952. The most efficient size and shape of plot to use for cruising in old-growth Douglas-fir timber. *J. Forestry* **50**:17–20.

Kendall, R. H., and Sayn-Wittgenstein, L. 1960. A rapid method of laying out circular plots. *Forestry Chron.* **36**:230–233.

Nyssonen, A. 1967. *Remeasured sample plots in forest inventory.* Norwegian Forest Research Inst., Vollebekk, Norway, 25 pp.

Schmid, P. 1969. Sichproben am Waldrand. *Mitt. Schweiz. Anst. Forstl. Versuchswes* **45**:234–303.

Stein, W. I. 1984a. Regeneration surveys: An overview. Pp. 111–116 in *New forests for a changing world,* Proceedings of the 1983 Society of American Foresters National Convention, Portland, Oreg.

———. 1984b. Fixed-plot methods for evaluating forest regeneration. Pp. 129–135 in *New forests for a changing world,* Proceedings of the 1983 Society of American Foresters National Convention, Portland, Oreg.

Wiant, H. V., and Yandle, D. O. 1980. Optimum plot size for cruising sawtimber in Eastern forests. *J. Forestry* **78**:642–643.

Zeide, B. 1980. Plot size optimization. *Forest Sci.* **26**:251–257.

CHAPTER 11

INVENTORIES WITH POINT SAMPLES

11-1 The Concept of Point Sampling *Point sampling* is a method of selecting trees to be tallied on the basis of their *sizes* rather than by their frequency of occurrence. Sample points, somewhat analogous to plot centers, are located within a forested tract, and a simple prism or angle gauge that subtends a fixed angle of view is used to "sight in" each tree diameter at breast height (dbh). Tree boles close enough to the observation point to completely fill the fixed sighting angle are tallied; stems too small or too far away are ignored (Fig. 11-1). The resulting tree tally may be used to compute basal areas, volumes, or numbers of trees per unit area.

The probability of tallying a given tree depends on its cross-sectional area and the sighting angle used. The smaller the angle, the more stems will be included in the sample.

In the case of plot sampling (Chap. 10), the per-acre expansion factor for all trees, regardless of size, is the reciprocal of the plot area in acres. If, for example, ⅕-acre plots are used, the tree frequencies, basal areas, volumes, etc., can be expanded from a plot to a per-acre basis by multiplying by 5. In point sampling, the expansion factor varies by tree size. Point sampling is a highly efficient method for selecting sample trees because larger, higher-valued trees are more likely to be included than smaller stems. By selecting sample trees with probability proportional to size, a specified precision for volume or value per acre can usually be

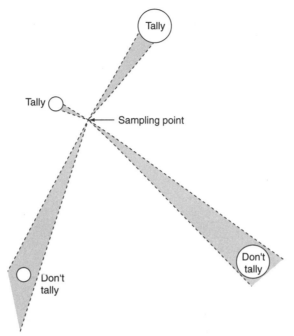

FIGURE 11-1
Trees with diameters at breast height (represented by
circles) that appear as large as or larger than a fixed
sighting angle are included in the tally of point samples.

achieved with a smaller number of individual trees included than with methods
that select trees with equal probability regardless of size.

Point sampling does not require direct measurements of either plot areas or tree
diameters. A predetermined basal-area factor (BAF) is established in advance of
sampling, and resulting tree tallies can be easily converted to basal area per unit
area. The relationship between basal area and tree volume makes it feasible to use
point sampling for obtaining conventional timber inventory data when "counted"
trees are recorded by merchantable or total height classes. Point sampling was developed in 1948 by Walter Bitterlich, a forester of Salzburg, Austria. The introduction and adoption of the method in North America were largely due to the
efforts of Lewis R. Grosenbaugh.

11-2 Nomenclature and Variants   The method of including trees in a forest
inventory when their boles at dbh appear larger than a fixed angle is known by
many different names, including "angle-count sampling," "Bitterlich method,"
"plotless cruising," "prism cruising," "variable-plot sampling," "variable-radius
plot sampling," and "point sampling." Although Bitterlich's original expression in

German, "Winkelzählprobe" (which translates into English as "angle-count sampling"), is descriptive of the method, the term "point sampling" is widely used. In addition to sighting trees at dbh, which is sometimes called "horizontal point sampling," methods have been developed to project vertical angles and select sample trees based on their height ("vertical point sampling"). The principles and methods of horizontal point sampling are developed in detail here; after mastering the basics of this commonly-applied form of angle-count sampling, other variants can be quickly learned and applied. For simplicity, the term "point sampling" will be used unless some form of selection other than sighting tree boles at dbh is intended.

11-3 Selecting a Sighting Angle Basal area (BA) conversion factors are dependent on the sighting angle (or "critical angle") arbitrarily selected. The sighting angle chosen, in turn, is largely based on the average size and distribution of trees to be sampled. Furthermore, from the standpoint of subsequent volume computations, it is desirable to select a sighting angle having a BAF that can be expressed as a whole number rather than as a fractional number.

In eastern United States, a predetermined sighting angle of 104.18 min (BAF of 10 sq ft per acre, or 10) is commonly used in second-growth sawtimber or dense poletimber stands. Critical angles of 73.66 min (BAF 5) and 147.34 min (BAF 20) are often employed for light-density pole stands and for large, old-growth sawtimber, respectively. With small, scattered stems, the sighting angle is narrowed so that it will extend farther out for trees of minimum diameter; conversely, where large tree diameters are common, the angle is enlarged to reduce excessively heavy field tallies.

Depending on the region, average tree size, and amount of underbrush restricting line-of-sight visibility, the BAF is usually chosen to provide an average tally of 5 to 12 trees per sample point. In western United States, where larger timber predominates, a BAF of 20 to 60 is in common use. For "West Side" Douglas-fir, a BAF of 40 might be regarded as typical, but an instrument with a BAF of 20 would be more frequently encountered in sampling stands of "East Side" ponderosa pine.

11-4 Plot Radius Factor To illustrate the meaning of BA conversions listed in Table 11-1, a sighting angle of 104.18 min (BAF 10) may be presumed. As this angle can also be defined by placing a 1-in. horizontal intercept on a sighting base of 33 in. (column 4 of Table 11-1), it follows that all trees located no farther than 33 times their diameter from the sample point will be tallied. Accordingly, a 1-in.-dbh tree must be within 33 in. of the point, a 12-in.-dbh tree will be tallied up to 396 in. (33 ft) away, and a 24-in.- or 2-ft-dbh tree will be recorded up to a distance of 66 ft (Fig. 11-2). This 1:33 ratio of tree diameter to plot radius, a constant for the specified angle of 104.18 min, has a value of 2.75 ft (33 ÷ 12) when expressed as a *plot radius factor*. Thus for each full inch added to stem diameter, a tree can be 2.75 ft farther from the sample point and still be tallied.

TABLE 11-1
COMMON BASAL-AREA FACTORS AND ANGLE SIZES USED IN POINT SAMPLING

English units				
Basal-area factor (ft^2/acre)	Angle size (min)	Angle size (diopters)	Ratio (tree diameter to plot radius)	Plot radius factor[a]
5	73.66	2.14	1/46.7	3.889
10	104.18	3.03	1/33.0	2.750
15	127.59	3.71	1/26.9	2.245
20	147.34	4.29	1/23.3	1.944
25	164.73	4.79	1/20.9	1.739
30	180.46	5.25	1/19.0	1.588
35	194.92	5.67	1/17.6	1.470
40	208.38	6.07	1/16.5	1.375
50	232.99	6.79	1/14.8	1.230
60	255.23	7.44	1/13.5	1.123

Metric units				
Basal-area factor (m^2/ha)	Angle size (min)	Angle size (diopters)	Ratio (tree diameter to plot radius)	Plot radius factor[b]
1	68.76	2.00	1/50.0	0.500
2	97.11	2.82	1/35.4	0.354
3	118.96	3.46	1/28.9	0.289
4	137.52	4.00	1/25.0	0.250
5	153.48	4.46	1/22.4	0.224
6	168.53	4.90	1/20.4	0.204
7	181.91	5.29	1/18.9	0.189
8	194.25	5.65	1/17.7	0.177
9	205.88	5.99	1/16.7	0.167
10	217.61	6.33	1/15.8	0.158

[a]Plot radius factor times tree dbh in in. gives limiting distance in ft.
[b]Plot radius factor times tree dbh in cm gives limiting distance in m.

HOW POINT SAMPLING WORKS

11-5 Imaginary Tree Zones   As the plot radius factor for BAF 10 has been developed in the preceding section, all subsequent explanations of point-sampling theory and tree volume conversions in this chapter will presume a sighting angle of 104.18 min and a BAF of 10 sq ft per acre. Nevertheless, the underlying principles discussed may be applied to any other angle or BAF.

Because each tree "sighted in" must be within 33 times its diameter of the sample point to be tallied, it is convenient to presume that all trees are encircled with imaginary zones whose radii are exactly 33 times the diameter of each tree stem. All these imaginary circles that encompass a given sampling point on the ground represent trees to be tallied (Fig. 11-3). Thus the probability of tallying any given

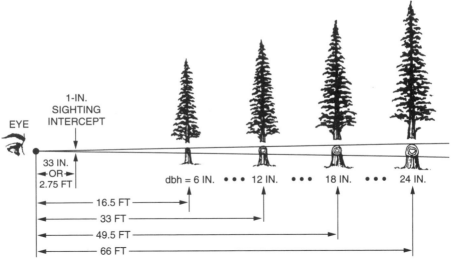

FIGURE 11-2
Tree sizes and limiting distances for a 1:33 angle gauge.

FIGURE 11-3
Imaginary zones proportional to stem basal area and encircling each tree determine which trees will be tallied at a given point. *(Adapted from Hovind and Rieck, 1970.)*

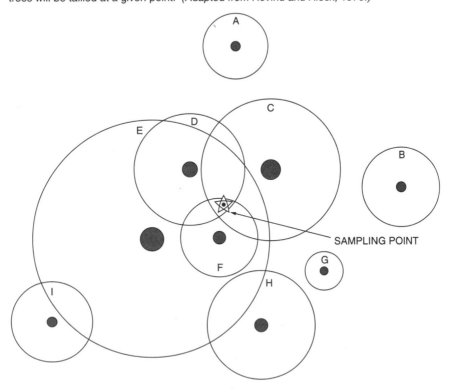

tree is proportional to its stem BA. A 12-in.-dbh stem has 4 times the probability of being counted as a 6-in.-dbh stem.

11-6 Equality of Tree Basal Area on a Per-Acre Basis For the sighting angle of 104.18 min, each tallied tree (regardless of its size or relative position to the sampling point) represents 10 sq ft of BA on a *per-acre basis*. The reason for this is that each stem and its imaginary zone represent a definite part of an acre and a specific number of trees per acre, depending on its size. The derivation of values for 6-in.- and 12-in.-dbh trees in Table 11-2 provides an explanation, or "proof," of this theory.

Considering the 6-in. dbh first, its imaginary "plot" radius is read from Table 11-2 (column 2) as 16.50 ft. This hypothetical zone represents an imaginary plot of 0.0196 acre around each 6-in.-dbh stem (column 3 of Table 11-2). By dividing 0.0196 into 1 acre, it can be seen from column 4 that there can be 51.02 such areas fitted into a single acre. Thus when one 6-in.-dbh tree is tallied,

TABLE 11-2
DERIVATION OF THE BASAL-AREA FACTOR OF 10 SQ FT PER ACRE FOR POINT SAMPLING

Tree dbh (in.) (1)	Imaginary plot radius (ft) (2)	Imaginary plot size (acres) (3)	Trees per acre* (no. of stems) (4)	Basal area per tree (sq ft) (5)	Basal area per acre (sq ft) (6)
4	11.00	0.0087	114.94	0.087	10
6	16.50	0.0196	51.02	0.196	10
8	22.00	0.0349	28.65	0.349	10
10	27.50	0.0545	18.35	0.545	10
12	33.00	0.0785	12.74	0.785	10
14	38.50	0.1069	9.35	1.069	10
16	44.00	0.1396	7.16	1.396	10
18	49.50	0.1767	5.66	1.767	10
20	55.00	0.2182	4.58	2.182	10
22	60.50	0.2640	3.79	2.640	10
24	66.00	0.3142	3.18	3.142	10
26	71.50	0.3687	2.71	3.687	10
28	77.00	0.4276	2.34	4.276	10
30	82.50	0.4909	2.04	4.909	10
32	88.00	0.5585	1.79	5.585	10
34	93.50	0.6305	1.59	6.305	10
36	99.00	0.7069	1.41	7.069	10
Method of calculation:	dbh $\times$ 2.75	$\dfrac{\pi r^2}{43{,}560}$	$\dfrac{1}{\text{plot size}}$	$0.005454 \times \text{dbh}^2$	(4) $\times$ (5)

*Exact value for number of trees per acre may vary slightly, depending upon number of decimal places expressed for imaginary plot size.

it is tacitly assumed that there are 51.02 such stems per acre. Accordingly, the BA of a 6-in.-dbh tree (0.196 sq ft from column 5), multiplied by 51.02 trees per acre, yields the "constant" BAF of 10 sq ft *per acre* (column 6).

For 12-in.-dbh stems, the imaginary plot radius is 33 ft, and the implied plot size is 0.0785 acre. Only 12.74 trees per acre are assumed—one-fourth the number of 6-in.-dbh trees expected. However, 12-in.-dbh trees have 4 times the BA of 6-in.-dbh stems, and this value (0.785 sq ft) from column 5, multiplied by 12.74 trees per acre, again produces a BA of 10 sq ft per acre. The same result applies to all other tree sizes encountered when sampling with a BAF 10 angle gauge.

IMPLEMENTING POINT SAMPLING

11-7 The Stick-Type Angle Gauge   This simple, horizontal angle gauge often consists of a wooden rod with a peep sight at one end and a metal intercept at the other. To establish a sighting angle of 104.18 min (BAF 10), an intercept 1 in. wide on a 33-in. sighting base can be easily improvised. Gauges for other factors can be constructed according to ratios provided in Table 11-1. Regardless of the ratio desired, the sighting base should be at least 24 in. long; otherwise, it is difficult to keep both the intercept and the tree in focus simultaneously.

When the stick gauge is used, all tree diameters larger than the defined angle are counted; those smaller are ignored. Trees that appear to be exactly the same size as the intercept should be checked by measuring their exact dbh and the distance from the sampling point to the tree center. The product of dbh and the appropriate plot radius factor (2.75 for BAF 10) determines whether the tree is "in" or "out."

With a stick gauge, the observer's eye represents the vertex of the sighting angle; hence the stick must be pivoted or revolved about this exact point for a correct tree tally. When properly calibrated for use by a particular individual, the stick gauge may be just as accurate as other more expensive point-sampling devices. In dense sapling or pole stands and where heavy underbrush is encountered, the stick gauge is often easier to use than more sophisticated relascopes or prisms.

11-8 The Spiegel Relascope   This is a versatile, hand-held instrument developed for point sampling by Walter Bitterlich (Fig. 11-4). It is a compact and rugged device that may be used for determining BA per unit area, upper-stem diameters, and tree heights. Both metric and American scale versions are sold. The American scale relascope provides for direct readings at horizontal distances of 66 and 99 ft with correction for slope, and measurement of slope on percent, degree, and topographic scales. Sighting angles are provided for factors of 5, 10, 20, or 40 sq ft per acre, and the instrument automatically corrects each angle for slope. The base has a tripod socket for use when especially precise measurements are desired.

Establishment of sighting angles with the Spiegel relascope is somewhat analogous to measuring distances with transit and stadia rod; the principal difference is that the relascope subtends a horizontal angle, and the transit and stadia system is

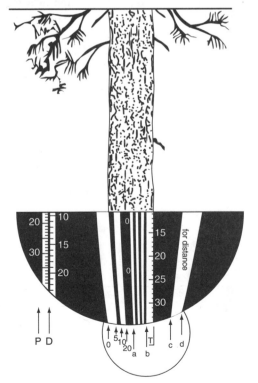

FIGURE 11-4
The Spiegel relascope (top) can be used for doing point sampling and for determining upper-stem diameters and tree heights (photograph courtesy *U.S. Forest Service*); graduations of the relascope with American Scale are shown on the bottom.

based on a vertically projected angle. The Spiegel relascope is complex in design but relatively simple to use. Its principal disadvantages are that it is relatively expensive and lacks the optical qualities for good sighting visibility on dark and rainy days.

11-9 The Wedge Prism A properly ground and calibrated prism is merely a tapered wedge of glass that bends or deflects light rays at a specific offset angle. When a tree stem is viewed through such a wedge, the bole appears to be displaced, as if seen through a camera rangefinder. The amount of offset, or displacement, is controlled by the prism strength, measured in diopters. As one prism diopter is equal to a right angle displacement of one unit per 100 units of distance, a 3.03-diopter prism will produce a displacement of one unit per 33 units of distance (i.e., a critical angle of 104.18 min). Other prism-strength relationships are given in Table 11-1.

Field use of the prism requires that it be held precisely over the sampling point at all times, for this point and *not the observer's eye* is the pivot from which the stand is "swept" by a 360° circle. Any tree stems that are only partially offset when viewed through the wedge are counted; all others are not tallied (Fig. 11-5). Trees that appear to be borderline should be measured and checked with the appropriate plot radius factor.

The prism may be held at any convenient distance from the eye, provided it is always positioned directly over the sampling point. Proper orientation also requires that the prism be held in a vertical position and at right angles to the line of sight; otherwise, large errors in the tree tally may result (Fig. 11-6).

The wedge prism is simple, relatively inexpensive, portable, and as accurate as other angle gauges when properly calibrated and used. Some sighting difficulties

FIGURE 11-5
Use of the wedge prism for point sampling.

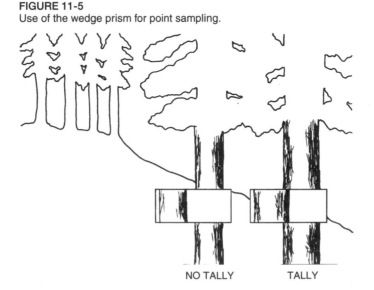

NO TALLY   TALLY

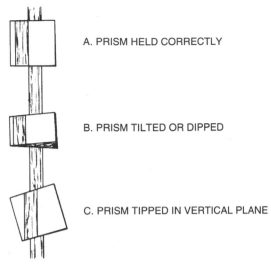

A. PRISM HELD CORRECTLY

B. PRISM TILTED OR DIPPED

C. PRISM TIPPED IN VERTICAL PLANE

FIGURE 11-6
Correct and incorrect methods of holding the wedge
prism. *(Adapted from Hovind and Rieck, 1970.)*

are found in dense stands where displaced bole sections are offset into one another, and special corrections must be applied when slopes of 15 percent and greater are encountered. However, the latter disadvantage may be cited for all point-sampling devices except the Spiegel relascope.

Many different instruments have been devised for use in point sampling, but the purpose of all of them is the same—to project a fixed angle for use in determining which trees to include in the tally.

11-10 Calibration of Prisms or Angle Gauges If unknown, the basal area factor of an instrument can be determined by setting up a target of known width (for example, 1 ft) against a contrasting background. With the angle gauge or prism in proper orientation, the observer backs away from the target until the target exactly fills the sighting angle. The exact distance from target to instrument is then measured and the BAF (in sq ft per acre) computed by

$$\text{BAF} = 10{,}980\left(\frac{W}{D}\right)^2$$

where W is the target width in feet and D is the distance to target in feet.

The foregoing formula is not exact when a flat target is used in calibration but only when the target is a circular cross section with diameter W. With small critical angles, however, this simple approximation is usually satisfactory because of the near equality of sine and tangent functions for narrow angles.

11-11 Corrections for Slope Unless the Spiegel relascope is used to establish sighting angles, corrections must be made in point sampling when slope is 15 percent or greater, i.e., a 15-ft rise or drop in elevation per 100 horizontal feet (Stage, 1959). In general, the sighting angle must be reduced so that, when sighting along the slope, trees will appear appropriately "in" or "out" for a corresponding horizontal distance from the sampling point. The reduction in sighting angle is usually accomplished through instrument adjustments.

When the wedge prism is used, an approximate on-the-ground compensation for slope can be made by tilting the top edge of the prism through the estimated slope angle—at right angles to the line of slope. If a flat-based prism is used and an Abney level or Suunto clinometer is employed to determine slope, an efficient means of accomplishing the prism rotation is

1 Measure the slope with the Abney level or Suunto clinometer.
2 Set the prism on the clinometer and rotate the combined unit through an angle equivalent to the slope.
3 Sight the tree in question at breast height.

For stick-type angle gauges, the sighting angle can be reduced by making the intercept narrower or the sighting base longer. One practical solution is to construct an angle gauge with a sliding intercept so that the sighting base can be made longer for slope correction. If the sighting base for zero slope is denoted by L, then the appropriate sighting base for any given amount of slope is

$$L_S = \frac{L}{\cos S}$$

where S is the slope angle in degrees. Note that $\cos S$ will be less than 1 and, thus, L_s will be greater than L. A stick of sufficient length can be used as the base and a sliding intercept mounted on the stick. Slope percents are marked directly on the stick, thus enabling the observer to make a rapid adjustment of the target setting. In the field, slope percent from the observer's eye at the sampling point to the dbh of trees that appear just "out" is determined. The intercept is appropriately adjusted on the stick, and the tree is sighted again. Trees that appear "in" or "borderline" on moderate to steep slopes are tallied, and no additional checking is needed. Most trees that are "out" will be obviously so, and the checking procedure just described will not be needed.

In lieu of making instrument adjustments, one can compensate for slope by checking all doubtful trees by measuring dbh and horizontal distance from the sampling point to the tree center at dbh. Doubtful trees are those that appear slightly "out" along the slope distance. This procedure of measuring doubtful trees is satisfactory in situations where slope corrections are infrequently needed.

11-12 Doubtful Trees, Limiting Distances, and Bias Most cruisers possess some degree of observer bias when "sighting in" doubtful trees. In a strict sense, questionable trees occur only when the distance from the sampling point to the stem center is precisely equal to tree dbh times plot radius factor. Therefore, if doubtful trees are regularly checked by careful measurement, the "borderline" tree is effectively eliminated.

When a tree appears borderline, the dbh should be measured to the nearest 0.1 inch and the horizontal distance from the sampling point to the center of the tree measured to the nearest 0.1 foot. If the tree dbh times the plot radius factor is equal to or greater than the measured distance from the sample point to tree center, the tree is counted; otherwise it is ignored. As an example, a tree that appeared borderline with a BAF 10 instrument was measured as 12.4 inches dbh. The horizontal distance from the sample point to the center of the tree was determined as 34.0 feet. Multiplying tree dbh times plot radius factor (12.4×2.75) gives a limiting distance of 34.1 feet. Since the computed limiting distance exceeds the measured horizontal distance, the tree is counted. The careful handling of doubtful trees in point sampling is essential to obtain unbiased results.

For trees that lean to the left or right of the observer, the angle gauge should be rotated so that the vertical axis of the gauge parallels the axis of the leaning tree.

Trees that lean severely toward or away from the observer and appear questionable should be checked by measuring the tree dbh and horizontal distance to the tree center. When checking the status of such leaning trees, the tree center is commonly assumed to be a point vertically above the center of the tree cross section at the groundline.

Precautions are necessary to avoid missing or double-counting trees. After each obvious tree is tallied, the cruiser can sway from side to side to detect trees behind others. When brush or other obstructions make it necessary to move from the sampling point to view certain stems, special care must be exercised to maintain the correct distances from obscured trees. Failure to maintain proper distance relationships can result in sizable errors in the tally, especially when using a large BAF.

When dbh is obscured by limbs or underbrush, the cruiser can sight the tree at a visible point higher on the stem. Trees that qualify for inclusion at some point above dbh also qualify at dbh unless the tree leans toward the sampling point, and the distance is critical.

If points are relatively close together and some large individual trees are in the population, it is possible for the same tree to appear "in" from two or more points. When this situation occurs, all trees that are large enough to tally on more than one point should be counted each time they appear "in." Failure to include all trees that appear "in" at all points will result in a biased estimate of overall volume per acre (or ha).

11-13 Boundary Overlap When part of a tree's imaginary "plot" extends beyond the boundary of the forest tract being sampled, boundary overlap occurs. In these situations, the probability of the sample point falling within the tree's imaginary plot zone is less than that for a tree of the same size that is not near the boundary. The bias created by boundary overlap is negligible on large forest areas having a small proportion of edge or where the forest outside the boundary is similar to that within the boundary. However, the bias can be considerable on small areas where the proportion of edge is great. If compensation is not made, especially on long, narrow tracts where the proportion of edge is large, sizable bias can result.

The mirage method of boundary-overlap correction (described for fixed-area plots in Sec. 10-10) is recommended when point-sample cruising is employed. If a point falls sufficiently close to the boundary such that boundary overlap *might* occur, one determines the distance D from the sampling point to the forest boundary. The cruiser then proceeds the distance D out from the boundary to establish a correction point, sights back toward the forested area with the angle gauge, and tallies all trees that appear "in" from the correction point. If overlap is present, certain trees will appear "in"; thus they are tallied twice—at the original point and again at the correction point. If there is no overlap, no trees will appear "in" from the correction point.

11-14 Choice of Instruments In summary, the selection of a point-sampling sighting gauge is largely a matter of balancing such factors as costs, efficiency, and personal preferences. All the devices described here will provide a reliable tree tally if they are properly calibrated and carefully used. Accordingly, the following generalizations will be primarily useful to the newer advocates of point sampling:

1 When steep slopes are regularly encountered, the Spiegel relascope is preferred.

2 For relatively flat topography, either the wedge prism or the stick gauge may be used. The prism is particularly desirable for persons who wear eyeglasses, because the vertex of the sighting angle occurs at the prism rather than at the observer's eye. However, the prism is difficult to use in dense stands due to displacement of stem sections into one another.

3 The simple stick gauge, though largely supplanted by the prism, is preferable in dense stands—especially if the cruiser does not wear eyeglasses. Cruisers who use point sampling only occasionally will find the stick gauge more reliable because there are fewer ways for errors to result with this device than with the wedge prism.

VOLUME CALCULATIONS

11-15 Example of Computational Procedures It may be assumed that a point-sample cruise was performed using a BAF 10 instrument at 12 points on a 40-acre tract. The objective of the inventory was to estimate the BA, number of trees, and board-foot volume for trees 10-in. dbh and larger. A summary of the tree tally is given in Table 11-3.

TABLE 11-3
FREQUENCY OF STEMS TALLIED BY DBH AND
HEIGHT CLASSES

dbh (in.)	Height (no. of logs)			Total
	1	2	3	
10	20	7	...	27
12	8	25	7	40
14	...	10	5	15
16	...	4	7	11
Total	28	46	19	93

11-16 Basal Area per Acre   As previously described, each tree tallied in point sampling, *regardless of its size,* represents the same amount of BA on a per-acre basis. Thus an estimate of average BA per acre for any tract may be computed by

$$\text{BA per acre} = \frac{\text{total trees tallied}}{\text{no. of points}} \times \text{BAF}$$

With a BAF 10 and 93 trees tallied at 12 points, the estimated BA per acre of trees 10-in. dbh and larger is $(93/12) \times 10 = 77.5$ sq ft per acre.

11-17 Trees per Acre   Because each diameter class has a different imaginary plot zone, the per-acre conversion factor varies from class to class. Consequently, it is necessary to compute the per-acre conversion factor for each dbh class, convert the tree tally in each class to a per-acre basis, and then summarize for an overall estimate of trees per acre. In formula form, the average number of trees per acre for any given diameter class is

$$\text{Trees per acre} = \frac{(\text{no. trees tallied})(\text{per-acre conversion factor})}{\text{total no. of points}}$$

where the per-acre conversion factor for BAF 10 (Table 11-2) is

$$\frac{43{,}560}{\pi(\text{dbh} \times 2.75)^2} \quad \text{or} \quad \frac{\text{BAF}}{\text{BA per tree}}$$

The BAF divided by BA per tree is often called the *tree factor* (symbolized here as TF_i). A separate tree factor is computed for each dbh class. Thus, in formula form, the trees per acre for all dbh classes of interest can be computed as

$$\text{Trees per acre} = \frac{\Sigma (n_i)(\text{TF}_i)}{n_p}$$

where n_i = number of trees in size class i, TF_i = tree factor for size class i, and n_p = number of sample points.

Computing values for the cruise data given in Table 11-3, one obtains

$$\text{10-in. class} = \frac{27(18.35)}{12} = 41 \text{ trees per acre}$$

$$\text{12-in. class} = \frac{40(12.74)}{12} = 42 \text{ trees per acre}$$

$$\text{14-in. class} = \frac{15(9.35)}{12} = 12 \text{ trees per acre}$$

$$\text{16-in. class} = \frac{11(7.16)}{12} = 7 \text{ trees per acre}$$

$$\text{Total} = 102 \text{ trees per acre in the 10-in.-dbh class and larger}$$

11-18 Volume per Acre by the Volume-Factor Approach   Prior to conducting a timber inventory, one must select an appropriate volume table. The Mesavage-Girard form-class volume table shown in Chapter 8 was selected for this cruise example. The relevant volume-table entries for the cruise data are

dbh (in.)	Board-foot volume by 16-ft logs, International ¼-in., form class 80		
	1	2	3
10	39	63	...
12	59	98	127
14	...	141	186
16	...	190	256

Volume factors, which show the volume per acre represented by trees of given dbh-height combinations, can be readily computed by multiplying the tree factor times the volume per tree. That is

$$\text{Volume per acre} = (\text{trees/acre})(\text{volume/tree})$$

which can be expressed in formula form as

$$VF_i = (TF_i)(v_i)$$

where VF_i is used to represent the "volume factor," and "v_i" the volume per tree for size class i. For the present example, the tree factor for a 10-inch, 1-log tree is 18.35, and the volume table being employed shows a tree of these dimensions as having 39 board feet. Thus, each 10-inch, 1-log tree tallied represents

$$(18.35)(39) = 716 \text{ board feet per acre}$$

A complete volume factors table with relevant entries for the present timber inventory example can be derived as follows:

| | Board-foot volume per acre | | |
| | Height (no. of logs) | | |
dbh (in.)	1	2	3
10	716	1,156	...
12	752	1,248	1,618
14	...	1,318	1,739
16	...	1,360	1,833

An estimate of volume per acre can be computed as the sum of the volume factors divided by the number of points; that is

$$\text{Volume per acre} = \frac{\sum (n_i)(VF_i)}{n_p}$$

Following through with the numeric example developed here gives

$$\begin{aligned}
\text{Volume per acre} = &[(20)(716) + (7)(1,156) + (8)(752) + \\
&(25)(1,248) + (7)(1,618) + (10)(1,318) \\
&+ (5)(1,739) + (4)(1,360) + (7)(1,833)]/12 \\
= &9,258 \text{ board feet per acre}
\end{aligned}$$

11-19 Volume per Acre by the Volume/Basal-Area Ratios Approach   An alternative approach to using the per-acre conversion factors for computing volume-per-acre estimates (as shown in the previous section) involves the use of volume/BA ratios. As an initial step, one calculates the volume per square foot of BA for the volume table or equation being applied. For example, a 10-in., 1-log tree for the Mesavage-Girard International ¼-in., form class 80 table has 39 bd ft, and the BA is $0.005454(10)^2 = 0.545$ sq ft. Thus the volume/BA ratio is $39/0.545 = 72$ bd ft per sq ft of BA. Dividing all entries of the form-class volume table by the corresponding BA gives the following ratios:

dbh (in.)	Board-foot volume per sq ft of basal area by 16-ft logs		
	1	2	3
10	72	116	. . .
12	75	125	162
14	. . .	132	174
16	. . .	136	183

The volume per acre can then be estimated as the average volume/BA ratio times the BA per acre; that is

$$\text{Volume per acre} = \frac{\text{sum of ratios}}{\text{no. of trees}} \times \text{BA per acre}$$

$$= \frac{\Sigma r_i}{n} \times \text{BA per acre}$$

In this example, the sum of the volume/BA ratios would be

$$20(72) + 7(116) + 8(75) + 25(125) + 7(162) + 10(132)$$
$$+ 5(174) + 4(136) + 7(183) = 11,126$$

It will be recalled that 93 trees were tallied on 12 points, thus giving an estimated BA per acre of 77.5 sq ft. Substituting this information into the volume-per-acre formula gives

$$\frac{11,126}{93} \times 77.5 = 9,272 \text{ bd ft per acre}$$

The discrepancy between this volume-per-acre estimate and that obtained through the stand-table approach (9,258 bd ft per acre) is due solely to rounding off errors.
An alternative formula to volume computation when the ratios approach is used is

$$\text{Volume per acre} = \frac{\text{sum of ratios}}{\text{no. of points}} \times \text{BAF}$$

$$= \frac{\Sigma r_i}{n_p} \times \text{BAF}$$

where r_i = volume/BA ratios for size class i
n_p = number of sample points

Substituting values for this example gives

$$\frac{11{,}126}{12} \times 10 = 9{,}272 \text{ bd ft per acre}$$

Table 11-4 provides a summary of relevant formulas for computing inventory statistics from point sampling data.

11-20 Estimating Precision   If an overall estimate of basal area, trees, and volume per acre (ha) is all that is required, only a cumulative tally is needed. If,

TABLE 11-4
SUMMARY OF FORMULAS FOR COMPUTING FOREST INVENTORY STATISTICS FROM POINT SAMPLING DATA*

Variable	Formula	Units English	Metric
BAF	$c\left(\dfrac{W}{D}\right)^2$	ft²/acre for $c = 10{,}890$	m²/ha for $c = 2{,}500$
PRF	$\dfrac{D}{(k)(W)}$	ft for $k = 12$	m for $k = 100$
TF_i	BAF/BA_i	trees/acre	trees/ha
VF_i	$(TF_i)(v_i)$	volume/acre	volume/ha
BA/unit area	$\left(\dfrac{n}{n_p}\right)BAF$	ft²/acre	m²/ha
Trees/unit area	$\dfrac{\Sigma\,(n_i)(TF_i)}{n_p}$	trees/acre	trees/ha
Volume/unit area			
Volume factor approach	$\dfrac{\Sigma\,(n_i)(VF_i)}{n_p}$	volume/acre	volume/ha
Volume/BA ratios approach	$\left(\dfrac{\Sigma\, r_i}{n}\right)BA/\text{unit area}$	volume/acre	volume/ha
OR	$\left(\dfrac{\Sigma\, r_i}{n_p}\right)BAF$	volume/acre	volume/ha

*In this table, BAF = basal area factor in ft²/acre or m²/ha; W = tree diameter when the tree is in the borderline condition; D = the distance from the vertex of the sighting angle to the center of the tree (W and D must be in the same units); PRF = plot radius factor, the limiting distance in ft (when multiplied times tree dbh in inches) or in m (when multiplied times tree dbh in cm); TF_i = trees per acre represented by a tree of BA_i in ft², or trees per ha represented by a tree of BA_i in m²; VF_i = volume per acre (ha) for a tree of volume v_i; n = number of trees in sample; n_i = number of trees in sample of size i ($\Sigma n_i = n$); n_p = number of points in sample; r_i = ratio of tree volume to tree basal area for a tree in size class i.

however, one desires to estimate the standard error as well as the mean and to place confidence intervals on the mean, then at each point the tally must be kept separate. Suppose that the tree tally shown in Table 11-3 was distributed as follows for the 12 sample points:

Point no.	Tree tally	Point no.	Tree tally
1	5 10-in., 1-log 4 12-in., 2-log	7	1 14-in., 3-log 2 16-in., 2-log 2 16-in., 3-log
2	1 12-in., 1-log 4 14-in., 2-log	8	4 12-in., 2-log
3	7 10-in., 1-log 1 10-in., 2-log 4 12-in., 2-log	9	8 10-in., 1-log 3 10-in., 2-log
4	No trees tallied	10	7 12-in., 1-log 3 14-in., 2-log
5	5 12-in., 2-log	11	3 10-in., 2-log 8 12-in., 2-log 4 12-in., 3-log
6	3 12-in., 3-log 3 14-in., 2-log 1 14-in., 3-log 3 16-in., 3-log	12	3 14-in., 3-log 2 16-in., 2-log 2 16-in., 3-log

Using the volume factors derived in Section 11-18, the volume on each point can be computed. For point 1

$$\text{Volume per acre} = \frac{\Sigma\,(n_i)(\text{VF}_i)}{n_p}$$

$$= \frac{(5)(716) + (4)(1{,}248)}{1} = 8{,}572 \text{ bd ft/acre}$$

Note that n_p (number of points in sample) $= 1$ when computations are performed for individual points.

Following through for the 12 points gives the following results:

Point	Bd ft/acre	Point	Bd ft/acre	Point	Bd ft/acre
1	8,572	5	6,240	9	9,196
2	6,024	6	16,046	10	9,218
3	11,160	7	8,125	11	19,924
4	0	8	4,992	12	11,603

The estimated mean volume per acre is

$$\bar{y} = \frac{\Sigma y_i}{n_p} = \frac{8,572 + 6,024 + \cdots + 11,603}{12} = 9,258 \text{ bd ft/acre}$$

The variance among individual points is

$$S^2 = \frac{\Sigma y_i^2 - \dfrac{(\Sigma y_i)^2}{n_p}}{n_p - 1} = \frac{1,322,794,090 - \dfrac{(111,100)^2}{12}}{11}$$

$$= 26,744,842$$

and the standard error of the mean for this simple random sample is

$$S_{\bar{y}} = \sqrt{\frac{S^2}{n_p}} = \sqrt{\frac{26,744,842}{12}}$$

$$= 1,493 \text{ bd ft/acre}$$

Placing 95 percent confidence intervals on the mean results is

$$\bar{y} \pm (t)(S_{\bar{y}})$$
$$9,258 \pm (2.201)(1,493)$$
$$9,258 \pm 3,286$$
or
$$5,972 \text{ to } 12,544 \text{ bd ft/acre}$$

where t has $n_p - 1$ (11 in this example) degrees of freedom.

11-21 Field Tally by Height Class   Examination of the volume/basal-area ratios computed in Section 11-19 shows that they do not vary greatly within height classes (indeed, the ratios are constant within height classes for some volume tables). Thus, dbh tallies can be omitted and trees can be recorded by height classes alone without much loss of accuracy when estimating overall volume by point-sampling techniques.

Tree volume can be expressed by the constant form factor equation:

$$V = b_1(\text{dbh})^2 H$$

where H represents some measure of tree height. Since BA is equal to a constant times dbh squared, volume per square foot of BA can be expressed as

$$\frac{V}{\text{BA}} = \frac{b_1(\text{dbh})^2 H}{c(\text{dbh})^2} = kH$$

and the variable of dbh is eliminated. In the foregoing expression, k represents the volume per square foot of BA per unit of height. Hence $k \times$ BAF is equal to the volume per acre represented by each unit of height, and a cumulative height tally of "in" trees is all that is needed to get a quick estimate of volume. The average number of height units per point times the volume per acre represented by each height unit equals average volume per acre.

One might, for example, use the following board-foot volume equation:

$$V = 0.30624(\text{dbh})^2 H$$

where dbh is in inches and H is the number of 16-ft sawlogs. The volume per square foot of basal area is

$$\frac{V}{\text{BA}} = \frac{0.30624(\text{dbh})^2 H}{0.005454(\text{dbh})^2} = 56.1H$$

Assuming a BAF of 10, each 16-ft sawlog represents 561 (56.1×10) bd ft per acre.

If a cruiser tallied eighty-six 16-ft sawlogs on 20 points by using a BAF 10 instrument, then the estimated volume per acre is

$$\frac{86}{20} \times 561 = 2{,}412 \text{ bd ft per acre}$$

To obtain an estimate of BA per acre, it would be necessary to know how many trees were tallied on the 20 points. Further, per-acre conversion factors, and thus number of trees per acre, cannot be computed unless "in" trees are tallied by dbh.

11-22 Point Sampling in a Double-Sampling Context   Point sampling can be efficiently applied in a double-sampling design (Sec. 3-15). Basal area per acre is easily and quickly determined with point-sampling methodology, because only a tree count is needed. Determining volume per acre, however, requires that the "in" trees be tallied by dbh and/or height classes. Thus the volume points are more time-consuming and expensive to establish. Consequently part of the sampling resources might be devoted to establishing a large number of points in which basal area per acre only is determined. Basal area per acre is highly correlated with volume per acre, the variable of ultimate interest. Hence, double sampling with a regression or ratio estimator is suggested.

As an example, suppose that 20 BAF 10 points were randomly located on a forested tract. On 10 of the points, called *basal-area points,* only a tree count was taken. Trees were tallied by dbh and total height on the other 10 points, called *volume points.* A summary of the 20 points follows:

	Basal-area points	Volume points	
	Basal area (sq ft per acre)	Basal area (sq ft per acre)	Volume (cu ft per acre)
	30	20	378
	40	10	284
	10	60	1,239
	60	90	2,132
	80	10	257
	70	70	1,484
	40	50	1,070
	20	80	1,762
	90	30	690
	50	100	2,173
Total	490	520	11,469

Plotting the volume per acre versus basal area per acre shows a strong linear relationship with a homogeneous variance. Thus, the linear regression estimator was chosen.

The estimate of the mean for a linear regression estimator in a double sample is computed as

$$\bar{y}_{Rd} = \bar{y}_2 + b(\bar{x}_1 - \bar{x}_2)$$

where $\bar{y}_{Rd}$ = estimate of the population mean volume per acre
   $\bar{y}_2$ = mean volume per acre for the small sample
   b = linear regression slope coefficient (computed from the small sample)
   $\bar{x}_1$ = mean basal area per acre from the large sample
   $\bar{x}_2$ = mean basal area from the small sample

For the data in this example, with a large sample of size 20 ($n_1 = 20$) and a small sample of size 10 ($n_2 = 10$), the numerical values are

$$\bar{x}_1 = \frac{490 + 520}{20} = 50.5 \text{ sq ft per acre}$$

$$\bar{x}_2 = \frac{520}{10} = 52.0 \text{ sq ft per acre}$$

$$\bar{y}_2 = \frac{11,469}{10} = 1,146.9 \text{ cu ft per acre}$$

$$b = \frac{SP_{xy}}{SS_x} = \frac{219,142}{9,960} = 22.0$$

$$\bar{y}_{Rd} = 1,146.9 + 22.0 (50.5 - 52.0)$$

$$= 1,113.9 \text{ cu ft per acre}$$

The standard error of the mean can be estimated as

$$S_{\bar{y}_{Rd}} = \sqrt{S_{y \cdot x}^2 \left[\frac{1}{n_2} + \frac{(\bar{x}_1 - \bar{x}_2)^2}{SS_x} \right] \left(1 - \frac{n_2}{n_1} \right) + \frac{S_y^2}{n_1}}$$

where

$$S_{y \cdot x}^2 = \frac{SS_y - (SP_{xy})^2 / SS_x}{n_2 - 2}$$

$$S_y^2 = \frac{SS_y}{n_2 - 1}$$

Following through with this numerical example gives

$$S_{\bar{y}_{Rd}} = \sqrt{5{,}569.6 \left[\frac{1}{10} + \frac{(50.5 - 52.0)^2}{9{,}960} \right] \left(1 - \frac{10}{20} \right) + \frac{540{,}685}{20}}$$

$$= 165.3 \text{ cu ft per acre}$$

The 95 percent confidence limits for the mean can be approximated as

$$\bar{y}_{Rd} \pm 2S_{\bar{y}_{Rd}}$$

Using numerical values from this example gives

$$1{,}113.9 \pm 2(165.3)$$
$$1{,}113.9 \pm 330.6$$

or   783.3 to 1,444.5 cu ft per acre

In practice, foresters generally establish four or five basal-area points for each volume point, and the ratio-of-means estimator (Sec. 3-15) is often applied. However, this numerical example illustrates the general concept and utility of applying point sampling in a double-sampling design.

11-23 Estimating Growth from Permanent Points   Point sample inventories can be taken at two different times to provide an estimate of growth. If the sample points are independently established at the two times, the resultant growth estimate will be unbiased, but it will not be precise (i.e., it will have a large standard error). By establishing permanent points, much as permanent plots might be established (Chap. 10), and remeasuring the same points at periodic intervals, reliable estimates of growth can be obtained. Although, if properly executed, permanent points will provide unbiased and relatively precise estimates of growth, the use of remeasured points presents some special problems not encountered with the employment of permanent plots. Special care must be taken in assessing ingrowth and handling trees that were "out" at the first measurement but "in" and larger-than-the-threshold dbh (the minimum dbh for inclusion in volume computations) at the second measurement. Permanent sampling systems are installed to estimate forest growth and its components. The fundamental components of forest growth are survivor growth, ingrowth, mortality, and cut (Beers, 1962). *Survivor growth, S,* is the increase in volume of trees that survived the growth period and were of measurable size at the beginning of the period. *Ingrowth, I,* is the end-of-period volume of trees growing into measurable size during the growth period. *Mortality, M,* and *cut, C,* are the beginning-of-period volumes of trees which died or were cut during the growth period. The difference between the average volume per acre (ha) at the end of a growth period, V_2, and the volume at the beginning of the growth period, V_1, is called the net increase and is defined as

$$V_2 - V_1 = S + I - M - C$$

where *S, I, M,* and *C* are expressed on a per acre (or ha) basis.

The application of estimating equations for the components of growth and for the net increase is reasonably straightforward when permanent, fixed-area plots are established. When permanent points are utilized, some special definitions and field measurement procedures are required in order to obtain satisfactory estimates of growth and its components. With permanent points there are six distinct situations (Fig. 11-7) that may occur with trees observed on the sample point at the second measurement (Martin, 1982). Four of these categories include trees that were "in" at the first measurement, namely

1 *survivor* trees, which are above the threshold dbh and "in" at both measurements;

2 *ingrowth* trees, which were below the threshold dbh and "in" at the first measurement but grew sufficiently to exceed the threshold dbh at the second measurement;

3 *mortality* trees, which were above the threshold dbh and "in" at the first measurement but died prior to the second measurement; and

4 *cut* trees, which were above the threshold dbh and "in" at the first measurement but were cut prior to the second measurement.

The two additional groups, which include trees that were "out" at the first measurement, have been named and defined as:

5 *ongrowth* trees were below the threshold dbh and "out" at the first measurement but above the minimum dbh and "in" at the second measurement;

6 *nongrowth* trees were above the threshold dbh and "out" at the first measurement but "in" at the second measurement.

With appropriate field measurements of the trees in each category, estimates of growth components and net increase can be computed from measurements of permanent points (details of estimating equations are contained in the references cited at the end of this chapter). When permanent points are used, a cluster of points,

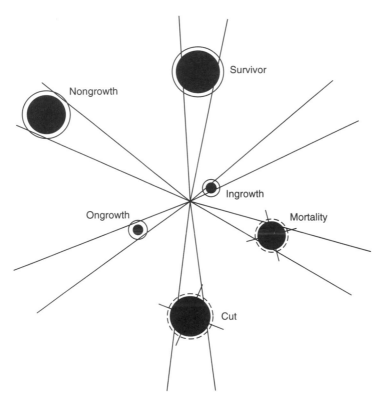

FIGURE 11-7
Possible situations for trees observed on the second occasion of measurement of a permanent point sample. *(Adapted from Bitterlich, 1984.)*

rather than a single point, may be established at each location. The locations are permanently marked just as with permanent plots, and individual sample trees are typically tagged and numbered. In addition, it is common practice to record the distance to and bearing of each sample tree from the sample point. While the efficiency of point sampling for estimating current volume with temporary sampling locations is undisputed, the complications of a continuously changing expansion factor due to tree growth has often discouraged the use of permanent points for estimating growth and change.

POINT-SAMPLE CRUISING INTENSITY

11-24 Comparisons with Conventional Plots   There is no fixed plot size when using point sampling; hence it is not possible to compute cruise intensity on a conventional area-sample basis. Each tree has its own imaginary plot radius (depending on the BAF used), and the exact plot size cannot be easily determined, even after the tally has been made. However, approximations can be made on the basis of the *average* stem diameter encountered at a given point.

Assuming an even-aged plantation with a single dbh class of 6 in. and a critical angle of 104.18 min, the area sampled would have a radius of 6 × 2.75, or 16.5 ft—equivalent to about 1/50 acre. If the dbh class were doubled to 12 in., the effective sample area would quadruple to about 1/12 acre. To sample a full 1/5 acre, average dbh would have to be about 19 in.

It follows, then, that use of BAF 10 sample points in lieu of the same number of 1/5- or 1/4-acre plots will usually result in a tally of fewer trees. From a statistical standpoint, however, the selection of trees according to size rather than frequency may more than offset this reduction of sample size—and with an additional saving in time. Conversely, it must be remembered that smaller samples of any kind require larger expansion, or blow-up, factors. Thus when point sampling is adopted, the so-called borderline trees must always be closely checked, for the erroneous addition or omission of a single stem can greatly reduce accuracy.

11-25 Number of Sampling Points Needed The only accurate method of determining how many sample points should be measured is to determine the standard deviation (or coefficient of variation) of BA or volume per acre from a preliminary field sample. When this has been done, sampling intensity may be derived by formulas described in Chapter 3. If the statistical approach is not feasible, the following rules of thumb will often provide acceptable results:

1 If the BAF is selected according to tree size so that an average of 5 to 12 trees are counted at each point, use the same number of points as 1/5-acre plots.

2 With a BAF 10 angle gauge and timber that averages 12 to 15 in. in diameter, use the same number of points as 1/10-acre plots.

3 For reliable estimates, never use fewer than 30 points in natural timber stands or less than 20 points in even-aged plantations.

11-26 Point Samples versus Plots Of the numerous field comparisons of point sampling and plot cruising, one of the more extensive evaluations was made by the U.S. Forest Survey in southeast Texas (Grosenbaugh and Stover, 1957). In this test, BAF 10 point samples were measured from the centers of 655 circular 1/4-acre plots that were distributed throughout 12 counties. Per-acre comparisons were made for BA, cubic-foot volumes, and board-foot volumes.

Differences in mean volumes by the two sampling methods were not significant at the 5 percent level. Coefficients of variation for point sampling were only 7 to 12 percent larger than for the 1/4-acre plots, and standard errors were within 0.5 percent of each other. It was estimated that 20 percent more point samples would be needed to provide the same precision in cubic volume as derived from the plots; however, even with these additional samples, the points could be measured in considerably less field time.

11-27 Attributes and Limitations   In summary, the principal advantages of point sampling over plot cruising are

1 It is not necessary to establish a fixed plot boundary; thus greater cruising speed is possible.

2 Large high-value trees are sampled in greater proportions than smaller stems.

3 BA and volume per acre may be derived without direct measurement of stem diameters.

4 When volume-per-acre conversions are developed in advance of fieldwork, efficient volume determinations can be made in a minimum of time. Thus the method is particularly suited to quick, reconnaissance-type cruises.

The main drawbacks to point sampling are

1 Heavy underbrush reduces sighting visibility and cruising efficiency.

2 Because of the relatively small size of sampling units, carelessness and errors in the tally (when expanded to tract totals) are likely to be more serious than in plot cruising.

3 Slope compensation causes difficulties that may result in large errors unless special care is exercised. Similar difficulties are encountered in strip and line-plot cruising, of course.

4 Unless taken into account, problems can arise in edge-effect bias when sampling very small tracts or long, narrow tracts.

PROBLEMS

11-1 A randomly-located point in a forest stand was used as the center of a 1/20-acre fixed-area plot. All trees in the plot were measured for dbh (in inches) with the following results:

6.1	5.9	8.6
7.2	12.4	9.2
4.0	9.0	6.5

At the same point, a BAF 20 (ft^2/acre) instrument was used to select tally trees. All trees were measured for dbh with the following result:

6.5	12.4	16.0

a Estimate the number of trees and the basal area per acre for the plot sample.

b Estimate the number of trees and the basal area per acre for the point sample.

c Are tree dbh measurements required to estimate trees per acre in plot samples? Can one estimate basal area per acre from plot samples without acquiring dbh measurements on the trees included?

d Are tree dbh measurements necessary to estimate basal area per acre when point samples are employed? Can one estimate numbers of trees per acre using point sampling without measuring dbh of the tally trees?

11-2 Establish 10 or more sample points in a forested tract to compare relative efficiencies of the stick-type angle gauge, the Spiegel relascope, and the wedge prism for determining basal area per acre (or ha).

11-3 Using the tree tally by point shown in the example in Section 11-20:

    a Estimate the total basal area per acre at each point, and compute the mean basal area per acre.

    b Compute the standard error of the mean for basal area per acre.

    c Establish a 90 percent confidence interval for the mean.

    d Compute the coefficient of variation for volume per acre and for basal area per acre. Which is more variable? Why?

11-4 Prepare a compilation similar to Table 11-2 for dbh values 4 through 10 inches and BAF 20 square feet per acre.

11-5 By using a BAF 20 instrument, 180 trees were tallied at 25 points. The sum of the volume (cu ft) / basal-area ratios for all tallied trees is 5,340.

    a Estimate the average BA per acre.

    b Estimate the average cubic-foot volume per acre.

11-6 Investigate and report on point sampling practices in your area. Include information on BAFs in common use, types of instruments employed, and methods for locating sample points (random, systematic, etc.).

11-7 The following constant form factor volume equation predicts volume, V, in cords from dbh in inches and the number of 5-ft pulpwood sticks, H, in loblolly pine trees:

$$V = 0.00022(\text{dbh})^2 H$$

By using a BAF 5 instrument, a total of 980 pulpwood sticks was tallied at 20 points. Estimate the mean cordwood volume per acre.

11-8 Establish 30 to 50 randomly selected points in a forest area. Make independent point-sample and circular-plot inventories based on the same center points. Compare results as to mean volumes, confidence limits on the sample means, average number of trees tallied per sample unit, and inventory time per sample unit.

11-9 Apply the ratio-of-means technique (Sec. 3-15) to the data in Section 11-22 to estimate the population mean volume per acre and the standard error of the mean. Compute approximate 95 percent confidence limits for the mean.

11-10 Assume that the 10 volume-per-acre observations shown in Section 11-22 were obtained using simple random sampling. Estimate the mean volume per acre and the standard error of the mean, and place 95 percent confidence limits on the mean. Compare the results with those shown in Section 11-22 for the linear regression estimator.

REFERENCES

Beers, T. W. 1962. Components of forest growth. *J. Forestry* **60**:245–248.

———— and Miller, C. I. 1964. Point sampling: Research results, theory, and applications. *Purdue Univ. Agr. Expt. Sta., Res. Bull.* 786. 56 pp.

Bell, J. F., and Dilworth, J. R. 1997. *Log scaling and timber cruising.* O.S.U. Bookstores, Inc., Corvallis, Oreg. 444 pp.

Bitterlich, W. 1948. Die Winkelzählprobe. *Allgem. Forest-u, Holzw. Ztg.* **59**(1/2):4–5.

————. 1984. *The relascope idea.* Commonwealth Agricultural Bureau, Slough, England. 242 pp.

Bruce, D. 1955. A new way to look at trees. *J. Forestry* **53**:163–167.

Burkhart, H. E., Barrett, J. P., and Lund, H. G. 1984. Timber inventory. Pp. 361–411 in *Forestry handbook,* K. F. Wenger (ed.), John Wiley & Sons, New York.

Ducey, M. J. 1999. What expansion factor should be used in binned probability proportional to size sampling? *Can. J. For. Res.* **29**:1290–1294.

Eriksson, M. 1995. Compatible and time-additive change component estimators for horizontal-point-sampled data. *Forest Sci.* **41**:796–822.

Gregoire, T. G. 1982. The unbiasedness of the mirage correction procedure for boundary overlap. *Forest Sci.* **28**:504–508.

————. Estimation of forest growth from successive surveys. *Forest Ecol. and Manage.* **56**:267–278.

Grosenbaugh, L. R. 1952. Plotless timber estimates—New, fast, easy. *J. Forestry* **50**:32–37.

————, and Stover, W. S. 1957. Point-sampling compared with plot-sampling in southeast Texas. *Forest Sci.* **3**:2–14.

Hovind, H. J., and Rieck, C. E. 1970. Basal area and point-sampling: Interpretation and application. *Wisconsin Conservation Dept. Tech. Bull.* 23. 52 pp. (Revised.)

Hradetzky, J. 1995. Concerning the precision of growth estimation using permanent horizontal point samples. *Forest Ecol. and Manage.* **71**:203–210.

Husch, B., Miller, C. I., and Beers, T. W. 1982. *Forest mensuration,* 3d ed. John Wiley & Sons, New York. 402 pp.

Lynch, T. B., and Huebschmann, M. M. 1992. Estimating diameter increment by DBH class with horizontal point sampling data. *Forest Ecol. and Manage.* **51**:285–299.

Martin, G. L. 1982. A method for estimating ingrowth on permanent horizontal sample points. *Forest Sci.* **28**:110–114.

Merten, P. R., Wiant, H. V., Jr., and Rennie, J. C. 1996. Double sampling saves time when cruising Appalachian hardwoods. *No. J. Appl. For.* **13**:116–118.

Oderwald, R. G. 1981. Point and plot sampling—The relationship. *J. Forestry* **79**:377–378.

————, and Gregoire, T. G. 1995. Overstated volumes from "pushing" the point. *So. J. Appl. For.* **19**:162–165.

Oderwald, R. G., and Jones, E. 1992. Sample sizes for point, double sampling. *Can. J. For. Res.* **22**:980–983.

Ritchie, M. W. 1997. Minimizing the rounding error from point sample estimates of tree frequencies. *West. J. Appl. For.* **12**:108–114.

Robinson, D. W. 1969. The Oklahoma State angle gauge. *J. Forestry* **67**:234–236.

Roesch, F. A., Jr., Green, E. J., and Scott, C. T. 1989. New compatible estimators for survivor growth and ingrowth from remeasured horizontal point samples. *Forest Sci.* **35**:281–293.

Stage, A. R. 1959. A cruising computer for variable plots, tree heights, and slope correction. *J. Forestry* **57**:835–836.

Van Deusen, P. C., Dell, T. R., and Thomas, C. E. 1986. Volume growth estimation from permanent horizontal points. *Forest Sci.* **32**:415–422.

Wensel, L. C., Levitan, J., and Barber, K. 1980. Selection of basal area factor in point sampling. *J. Forestry* **78**:83–84.

CHAPTER 12

INVENTORIES WITH 3P SAMPLING

12-1 Introduction The 3P (probability proportional to prediction) system of timber inventory was designed for situations in which a highly precise estimate of the volume or value of standing trees is required. Although 3P sampling is not a feasible alternative to conventional fixed-area and point-sampling methods (Chaps. 10 and 11) for many operational cruises, it has found use in special circumstances. An example is a lump-sum timber sale made on the basis of cruising standing timber. If a list of individual trees in the timber sale were available prior to sampling, sample trees could be selected from the list to estimate the overall sale volume. In most forest inventory work, a list is not available, nor is it feasible to compile a list of the population prior to sampling. The 3P system is a variation of list sampling that does not require a list of the population prior to performing the inventory.

The 3P scheme exploits the ability of timber cruisers to estimate volume or some related numerical value in trees. By visiting every tree in a timber sale and estimating its volume, for example, the cruiser would have an estimate of total volume in the sale. This estimate will be either higher or lower than the actual volume. To correct the total estimated volume, a few sample trees are selected and measured. The average ratio of the measured volume to the estimated volume in the sample trees is computed and used to adjust the total estimated volume.

12-2 Components of 3P Inventory The 3P method of timber inventory, as conceived and developed by L. R. Grosenbaugh, consists of three components: (1) a rule (3P) for selecting sample trees, (2) a method for observing the variables of interest (such as volume determined by using an optical dendrometer or scaled volume from felled trees) on the sample trees selected, and (3) use of computer programs to transform the sample observations to estimates for the whole forest (e.g., to compute the volume of sample trees from dimensions observed with an optical dendrometer). These three components—selection, measurement, and computation—are interrelated in any forest inventory, and all must be considered. The purpose of this chapter is to present the basic concepts and principles involved in the design and execution of a 3P timber inventory. Details on the use of various instruments for measurement of standing trees and on the use of computer programs developed by Grosenbaugh to convert these measurements to whole tract estimates can be found in the references listed at the end of the chapter.

The 3P procedure involves measurement of volume or a related numerical value for a sample of trees in the population of interest. Because direct measurement of tree volumes (and similar values) is time-consuming and expensive, only a small number can be chosen. Thus an efficient, unequal-probability selection rule (the 3P selection rule) is needed to determine which trees to measure. In 3P sampling, the predicted tree attribute (e.g., volume) is paired with a random number from a specially constructed list. Trees with predicted values greater than or equal to the matched random number are measured—thus the probability of selection is proportional to prediction. With this selection scheme, the larger the tree's numerical value, the more chance it has of being selected for measurement.

To illustrate how this unequal-probability selection rule works, suppose that a numerical value is predicted for each tree in a specific population, and the predicted number will always be an integer from 1 through 10. After the value is estimated, it is compared with a random number drawn from the integers 1 through 10; each integer is equally likely to occur. If the predicted value for the tree is greater than or equal to the random number drawn, the tree is selected as a part of the sample. Thus if the tree's predicted value is 2, it has 2 chances in 10 of being selected as part of the sample (i.e., it will be selected only if the random integer is 1 or 2; the probability of drawing a 1 or a 2 is 0.1 plus 0.1, or 0.2). If the tree's predicted value is 8, for example, the chances of its being selected as part of the sample are 8 in 10. Hence, with this selection rule, the probability of inclusion in the sample is proportional to the predicted numerical value of the tree.

Tree volume equations (Chap. 8) are appropriate and highly useful in many timber inventory situations. However, the sample trees used to construct the volume equation may have been selected from a population of trees that is different from the one being inventoried. Consequently, some bias is likely when volume equations are applied. In cases where accurate and precise estimates of volume are needed, and when this volume must be determined in standing trees (i.e., there is no opportunity to measure the cut products directly), measurements can be made on a sample of trees in the population being inventoried. This approach thus avoids the application of volume equations and the bias that is likely to result. Direct measurement of tree volume or some related value constitutes the measurement aspect of a 3P inventory.

Measurement of sample trees creates large quantities of data that are best handled through computer programs to produce estimates of total tract volume and associated sampling errors.

HOW 3P IS APPLIED

12-3 Timber-Sale Example   Inventories with 3P sampling were originally applied to timber sales where each tree in the population (all of the marked trees) was visited and a volume, value, or related attribute predicted. A sample of this marked-tree population was selected for detailed measurement. The steps in conducting a 3P sample for the purpose of estimating the total volume of timber marked for sale will serve to illustrate the application of 3P sampling. For this example, the "3P variable" is volume—that is, the predicted variable for each tree is its volume.

12-4 Preliminary Steps   Before the actual 3P sample is conducted, some preliminary information is needed. The steps involved in obtaining this preliminary data are

1 Determine the number of trees n_e to be precisely measured for volume (this is termed the *expected sample size* in 3P inventories) with the following formula, previously described in Chapter 3:

$$n_e = \left[\frac{(t)(CV)}{A} \right]^2$$

where n_e = number of sample trees needed to achieve precision of A, with probability level determined by t

t = quantity from t distribution (generally taken as 1 for 67 percent and 2 for 95 percent probability levels, respectively)

CV = coefficient of variation, percent, of y_i = measured-volume/ estimated-volume values

A = allowable error, percent

The variation in 3P sampling is related to the ratio of measured to estimated volume, and most cruisers obtain a coefficient of variation (CV) of 15 to 20 percent. In typical 3P sampling situations, the allowable sampling error is set at 1.5 to 2 percent, which might then require that around 100 to 200 trees be measured (67 percent probability level). The CV for the ratio of measured to estimated volume depends greatly on the skill and experience of the cruiser, of course. As a general guide, with trained personnel, 100 or so sample trees are usually sufficient for an allowable error of 1.5 percent; beginners require about 200 sample trees for this precision.

In addition to the computation of the expected number of sample trees, some preliminary information about the area to be inventoried is required. This information can be obtained from previous cruises of similar forest types or from a reconnaissance cruise through the area of interest. Specifically, the cruiser must obtain the following information.

2 Estimate the sum of the volumes, $\hat{T}_x$, of the N trees in the population of interest:

$$\hat{T}_x = \sum_{i=1}^{N} X_i$$

where X_i is the cruiser's estimate of individual-tree volume. Note that the actual sum of estimated volumes is known only after the inventory is completed.

3 Estimate the maximum individual-tree volume expected, K. That is:

$$K = \text{maximum } X_i$$

The maximum tree volume expected is obtained at the time the total volume $\hat{T}_x$ is estimated.

Besides obtaining an estimated total volume and maximum tree volume, it is also necessary to obtain the following information.

4 Estimate the number, N, of trees in the population of interest.

With information on the total volume and maximum tree volume expected, it is now possible to perform step 5.

5 Generate a population-specific set of random numbers from 1 to $K + Z$. The variable Z is used to control the expected number of sample trees in the actual 3P cruise. An equal number of each integer from 1 to K is generated; numbers greater than K are assigned a rejection symbol to facilitate the use of the selection rule in the field (-0 will be used for the rejection symbol). In 3P sampling, the probability P of a given tree's being selected for measurement is

$$P = \frac{X_i}{K + Z}$$

where X_i represents the tree's estimated volume. This implies that the number of sample trees that will be measured in any given 3P cruise will be approximately $\hat{T}_x/(K + Z)$. We want the actual number to approximate the expected number as computed by the formula shown in step 1. Thus we can set n_e equal to $\hat{T}_x/(K + Z)$ and compute the value for Z as

$$Z = \frac{\hat{T}_x}{n_e} - K$$

Computer programs are available for generation of these tailor-made random numbers, the quantity of which must equal or exceed the number N of trees in the population of interest.

12-5 Field Procedure   The preliminary work outlined in steps 1 to 5 (of Sec. 12-4) can commonly be achieved in about one day. After completing these initial steps, the cruiser is ready to proceed with the 3P cruise. In the field, the cruiser visits each of the N trees in the population. The area being cruised is often divided into strips 1 to 2 chains wide to ensure that each tree is visited but that the same tree is not tallied twice. The edges of these strips can be marked with kite string, paint, or ribbons. At each tree the cruiser must

1 Estimate tree volume.
2 Record the estimate.
3 Draw a random number from the set of integers from 1 through K.
   a If the random number is less than or equal to the volume estimate X_i, precisely measure the tree volume.
   b If a rejection symbol ("-0") is drawn or if the integer is greater than the estimated volume, move on to the next tree.

In field practice, two-person field crews are commonly used. The cruiser estimates the volume and calls this estimate to the assistant who carries the random number list and makes the comparison. This practice avoids the possibility of bias, since the cruiser has no notion of what the next random number might be.

Because ocular volume estimates are difficult for inexperienced cruisers, they sometimes measure diameter at breast height (dbh) with a Biltmore stick and enter a single-entry volume equation to obtain the "estimated" volume. This "local" volume equation value is compared with the appropriate random integer to determine whether the tree should be precisely measured for volume.

In some cases, trees are found that are larger than K, the estimated largest tree. When this happens, the tree is cruised, and its volume is kept separate and later added to the 3P estimated volume. (Trees with volumes larger than K are commonly termed *sure-to-be-measured.*) It is sometimes desirable to set K slightly less than the largest tree value expected, thus ensuring that all the largest, most valuable trees in the population will be measured.

The sample trees can be measured immediately, or they can be marked and located on a map so that the cruiser can return to obtain the measurements after all volume estimates are completed.

12-6 Sample-Tree Measurement Various methods of sample-tree measurement, including conventional tree measurements, have been used with 3P selection. A description of the two primary methods that have been applied for obtaining detailed sample-tree measurements in 3P inventories follows:

1 Optical dendrometers have been used to measure upper-stem diameters, which are then converted to volumes of standing trees. A number of instruments for measuring upper-stem diameters without resorting to climbing or felling trees are available commercially. One instrument that has been widely applied for dendrometry of sample trees in 3P samples is the Barr and Stroud dendrometer. This sophisticated dendrometer, which is a short-base rangefinder with magnifying optics, permits the measurement of diameter and the height to that diameter for points on the visible portion of tree boles. These measurements are converted to "measured volume" for the 3P sample trees.

Although the Barr and Stroud instrument provides excellent measurement data, it is an expensive instrument that requires skilled operators to use it effectively. Also, computer programs are needed to efficiently convert the instrument readings to tree volumes. Studies have shown (e.g., Yocom and Bower, 1975) that, for many purposes, satisfactory tree volume determinations can be made with less sophisticated instruments, such as the Spiegel relascope.

2 Falling, bucking, and scaling of sample trees has been applied. For situations in which timber is defective and breakage is likely for felled trees (as with mature timber in the western United States), measurement of net volume in standing trees is subject to considerable error. In these circumstances, the 3P sample trees may be felled, bucked, and scaled according to local utilization standards for their volume, defect, and grade. Sample trees felled as part of the inventory are sent to the mill when the area is logged. This system is sometimes referred to as *fall, buck, and scale cruising* (Johnson and Hartman, 1972).

12-7 3P Computations After the cruise has been completed and the sample trees measured, one can compute an estimate of the total volume of the N trees in the population, $\hat{T}_y$, as

$$\hat{T}_y = T_x \left(\frac{\sum_{i=1}^{n} \dfrac{Y_i}{X_i}}{n} \right)$$

where $T_x = \displaystyle\sum_{i=1}^{N} X_i$ is now the sum of the observed X_i values.

Note that this estimate of total volume is simply the sum of the predicted volumes for all trees adjusted by the mean ratio of observed over predicted volumes of the sample trees. If any sure-to-be-measured trees are encountered, their volume must be added to $\hat{T}_y$ to obtain an estimate of the overall population total. The symbol n denotes the actual number of sample trees measured. For large samples, the number measured should be close to the number desired (denoted previously as n_e). However, minor differences will occur because of vagaries associated with random numbers in the sample-tree selection process.

If trees with an estimated volume greater than K are encountered, their volume is added to $\hat{T}_y$ when estimating total volume. These sure-to-be-measured trees are not included in the computation of variance, however.

The variance of $\hat{T}_y$ can be estimated by one of several different approaches. One approximating formula that should give satisfactory results is

$$S_{\hat{T}_y}^2 = \frac{\sum_{i=1}^{n}\left(\dfrac{Y_i T_x}{X_i} - \hat{T}_y\right)^2}{n(n-1)}$$

Additional formulas for approximating the variance of 3P estimates have been presented by Schreuder, Sedransk, and Ware (1968), Grosenbaugh (1976), and others.

12-8 Numerical Example   In practice, 3P sampling is applied in reasonably large populations. For small populations, a complete enumeration would likely be more economical than a 3P sample. However, a greatly simplified example with a small artificial population can be effectively used to illustrate the application of the 3P concepts and computations just described.

Suppose that we have a forest of 10 trees that we wish to inventory by 3P sampling. In this example, the 3P variable is board-foot volume. The actual volumes of the trees, although unknown to us, are given in Table 12-1.

One conducts the preliminary steps for the 3P inventory as follows:

1 Determine the number of trees, n_e, to be precisely measured for volume. For this computation, assume a CV of the ratios of measured to estimated volume of 20 percent, an allowable error A of 10 percent, and a probability level of 67 percent (i.e., $t = 1$), which gives

$$n_e = \frac{(1)^2 (20)^2}{(10)^2} = 4$$

2 Conduct a reconnaissance cruise to estimate the volume of the total population $\hat{T}_x$, the maximum individual-tree volume expected K, and the number

TABLE 12-1
BOARD-FOOT VOLUMES IN EXAMPLE
FOREST OF 10 TREES

Tree no.	Actual volume (bd ft)
1	200
2	80
3	300
4	50
5	400
6	160
7	110
8	40
9	60
10	250
Total	1,650

N of trees in the population. Assume that the precruise resulted in the following values:

$$\hat{T}_x = 1{,}700 \text{ bd ft}$$
$$K = 350 \text{ bd ft}$$
$$N = 12$$

3 Using the precruise information, generate a population-specific set of random numbers from 1 to $K + Z$. The value of Z is computed as

$$Z = \frac{1{,}700}{4} - 350 = 75$$

Since we estimated N to be equal to 12, we will generate 12 random numbers from 1 to $K + Z$ (425), with numbers greater than K (350) being assigned a rejection symbol (-0). Note that this set of random numbers will result in the selection of one 3P sample tree for about every 425 bd ft of volume.

4 Proceed to the field and visit each of the N trees in the population. Suppose that the 3P cruise gave the results shown in Table 12-2. Tree number 5 must be measured because its estimated volume exceeds K. Trees 1, 7, and 10 are 3P sample trees because their estimated volumes are greater than or equal to the corresponding random integer.

A summary of this 3P cruise is given in Table 12-3.

5 Compute an estimate of the total volume and variance of this estimate by using the formulas given in Section 12-7.

TABLE 12-2
ESTIMATED VOLUMES AND RANDOM NUMBERS
GENERATED BY 3P CRUISE

Tree no.	Estimated volume (bd ft)	Random number
1	180	112
2	90	327
3	300	311
4	60	−0
5	380	−0
6	150	266
7	100	100
8	50	287
9	80	261
10	300	81
. . .	. . .	−0
. . .	. . .	74

TABLE 12-3
SUMMARY OF 3P CRUISE

Tree no.	Measured volume		Estimated volume	Meas./est.
	3P	Sure-to-measure		
1	200	. . .	180	1.111
2	. . .	. . .	90	. . .
3	. . .	. . .	300	. . .
4	. . .	. . .	60	. . .
5	. . .	400	. . .	. . .
6	. . .	. . .	150	. . .
7	110	. . .	100	1.100
8	. . .	. . .	50	. . .
9	. . .	. . .	80	. . .
10	250	. . .	300	0.833
Total	. . .	400	1,310	3.044

$$\text{Total volume} = \hat{T}_y + (\text{sure-to-be-measured})$$

$$= T_x \left(\frac{\sum\limits_{i=1}^{n} \dfrac{Y_i}{X_i}}{n} \right) + (\text{sure-to-be-measured})$$

$$= 1{,}310(1.015) + 400$$
$$= 1{,}330 + 400$$
$$= 1{,}730 \text{ bd ft}$$

$$\text{Variance} = S_{\hat{T}_y}^2 = \frac{\sum\limits_{i=1}^{n}\left(\dfrac{Y_i T_x}{X_i} - \hat{T}_y\right)^2}{n(n-1)}$$

$$= \left[\left(\frac{200}{180}(1{,}310) - 1{,}330\right)^2 + \left(\frac{110}{100}(1{,}310) - 1{,}330\right)^2\right.$$

$$\left. + \left(\frac{250}{300}(1{,}310) - 1{,}330\right)^2\right] \times \frac{1}{3(2)}$$

$$= 14{,}148$$

One will recall that only the 3P sample trees enter into the computation of variance; thus n equals 3 in this example.

EXTENSIONS, ATTRIBUTES, AND LIMITATIONS OF BASIC 3P SAMPLING

12-9 Extensions of Basic 3P Sampling   There are many extensions of 3P sampling for situations in which it is not feasible to visit every tree in the population. These extensions have generally consisted of multistage sampling designs. For example, work has been done on combining point sampling (first stage) with 3P sampling (second stage) in a two-stage design.

In such a two-stage design, point-sampling techniques are used to select a subset of trees from the total population. Trees selected by the point sample are then assessed for some 3P variable. One might recall that trees are selected with probability proportional to their basal area (dbh^2) in point sampling. Thus if we make the 3P variable height, measurement trees would be selected with probability proportional to dbh^2 times height, which is highly correlated with volume.

Those interested in extensions of the basic 3P methods described here should consult the literature. References cited at the end of this chapter provide an introduction to this literature.

12-10 Attributes and Limitations of 3P Sampling   It should be noted that 3P sampling is not limited to timber inventory alone, that 3P variables other than volume have been used successfully, and that many different techniques and instruments can be applied for obtaining the "measured" value of the 3P variable. The 3P selection rule (probability proportional to prediction) has many potential applications in forest sampling other than just selecting trees for volume measurement, and optical dendrometers are useful in a host of measurement applications besides 3P timber volume estimation. For any inventory, the forester must select the sample design, field measurement methods, and instruments that will provide the required information at an acceptable cost.

In summary, 3P sampling has found its greatest application in timber inventory situations in which

1 There are relatively few stems per unit area, and each individual tree is of relatively high value.

2 Each stem is utilized for several different products.

3 There is no convenient place or time in the harvesting and utilization process where the products can be scaled by conventional methods.

Under the circumstances listed, a 3P sample design similar to the basic example given here may be feasible. For cases involving numerous stems per unit area, each being of relatively low value, the basic 3P scheme will likely not be efficient.

PROBLEMS

12-1 The following values were determined for a timbered tract that is to be inventoried with 3P sampling:

Number of trees n_e to be measured   140
Estimate of sum of volumes $\hat{T}_x$ of N trees in population   1,800,000 bd ft
Estimate of maximum individual-tree volume expected K 620 bd ft

Compute the value for Z that should be used when generating the random numbers list for this tract.

12-2 Prepare a written report on possible applications for 3P sampling procedures (other than the timber sale example discussed in this chapter).

12-3 Given the following data from a 3P cruise of a population of 15 trees, estimate the total cubic-foot volume and its associated variance for this 3P cruise.

	Measured volume (cu ft)		Estimated
Tree no.	3P	Sure-to-measure	volume (cu ft)
1	. . .	. . .	20
2	14	. . .	16
3	. . .	. . .	31
4	25	. . .	22
5	. . .	. . .	14
6	. . .	. . .	7
7	. . .	41	. . .
8	. . .	. . .	16
9	30	. . .	27
10	. . .	. . .	17
11	. . .	. . .	38
12	. . .	46	. . .
13	. . .	. . .	5
14	8	. . .	10
15	. . .	. . .	16

12-4 For a given timber tract in your area, conduct a reconnaissance cruise to determine $\hat{T}_x$, K, and N. Submit a written report describing the procedures used and the time required to develop this information.

REFERENCES

Bell, J. F., and Dilworth, J. R. 1997. *Log scaling and timber cruising.* O.S.U. Bookstores, Inc., Corvallis, Oreg. 444 pp.

Furnival, G. M., Gregoire, T. G., and Grosenbaugh, L. R. 1987. Adjusted inclusion probabilities with 3P sampling. *Forest Sci.* **33:**617–631.

Gregoire, T. G., and Valentine, H. T. 1999. Composite and calibration estimation following 3P sampling. *Forest Sci.* **45:**179–185.

Grosenbaugh, L. R. 1964. Some suggestions for better sample-tree-measurement. *Soc. Amer. Foresters (1963, Boston, Mass.) Proc.:*36–42.

———. 1965. Three-pee sampling theory and program "THRP" for computer generation of selection criteria. *U.S. Forest Serv., Pacific Southwest Forest and Range Expt. Sta., Res. Paper PSW-*21. 53 pp.

———. 1967a. The gains from sample-tree selection with unequal probabilities. *J. Forestry* **65:**203–206.

———. 1967b. STX—Fortran-4 program for estimates of tree populations from 3P sample-tree-measurements. *U.S. Forest Serv., Pacific Southwest Forest and Range Expt. Sta., Res. Paper PSW-*13, 2d ed., rev. 76 pp.

———. 1974. STX-3-3-73: Tree content and value estimation using various sample designs, dendrometry methods, and V-S-L conversion coefficients. *U.S. Forest Serv., Southeast. Forest Expt. Sta., Res. Paper SE-*117. 112 pp.

———. 1976. Approximate sampling variance of adjusted 3P sampling estimates. *Forest Sci.* **22:**173–176.

Hartman, G. B. 1967. Some practical experience with 3-P sampling and the Barr and Stroud dendrometer in timber sales. *Soc. Amer. Foresters (1966, Seattle, Wash.) Proc.:*126–130.

Johnson, F. A., and Hartman, G. B., Jr. 1972. Fall, buck, and scale cruising. *J. Forestry* **70:**566–568.

———, Dahms, W. G., and Hightree, P. E. 1967. A field test of 3P cruising. *J. Forestry* **65:**722–726.

Mesavage, C. 1971. STX timber estimating with 3P sampling and dendrometry. *U.S. Dept. Agr. Handbook* 415, Government Printing Office, Washington, D.C. 135 pp.

Schreuder, H. T., Brink, G. E., and Wilson, R. L. 1984. Alternative estimators for point-Poisson sampling. *Forest Sci.* **30:**803–812.

———, Sedransk, J., and Ware, K. D. 1968. 3-P sampling and some alternatives, I. *Forest Sci.* **14:**429–453.

Wiant, H. V., Jr. 1976. Elementary 3P sampling. *West Va. Univ. Agr. and Forestry Expt. Sta. Bull.* 650T. 31 pp.

Williams, M. S., Schreuder, H. T., and Terrazas, G. H. 1998. Poisson sampling—The adjusted and unadjusted estimator revisited. *U.S. Forest Serv., Rocky Mountain Res. Sta., Res. Note RMRS-RN-*4. 10 pp.

Yocom, H. A., and Bower, D. R. 1975. Estimating individual tree volumes with Spiegel Relaskop and Barr and Stroud dendrometers. *J. Forestry* **73:**581–582, 605.

CHAPTER 13

USING AERIAL PHOTGRAPHS

13-1 Purpose of Chapter   Aerial photographs are useful tools of the forest manager. A basic knowledge of the location and extent of the forest is critical to the management of forest resources. Aerial photographs are used to develop maps, but these maps have somewhat different properties than those described in Chapter 4. Aerial photographs are also useful in designing and conducting field inventories (Chaps. 9 through 12) and can actually be used to estimate tree and stand characteristics directly in ways analogous to field methods.

This chapter includes information on how aerial photographs can be used to identify basic forest-cover types and how various stand parameters can be estimated from aerial photographs. Only the most elementary techniques are described here. Readers interested in nonphotographic imagery (e.g., satellites, thermal scanners, radar, and aerial videography) and detailed photogrammetric procedures should consult the references cited at the end of the chapter.

13-2 Types of Aerial Photographs   As a general rule, foresters are primarily concerned with *vertical photographs,* that is, those taken with an aerial camera pointed straight down toward the Earth's surface. Consecutive exposures in each flight line are overlapped to allow three-dimensional study with a stereoscope. Although few (if any) aerial photographs are truly vertical views, they are usually presumed to be vertical when exposures are tilted no more than 3°. Unless otherwise specified, the terms *photo* and *photograph* as used in this chapter will denote vertical aerial photographs.

Oblique photographs are exposures made with the camera axis pointed at an angle between the vertical and the horizon. Although obliques are useful for panoramic views, they are not easily adapted to stereoscopic study or to photo measurement; hence they are seldom used for forest inventory purposes.

Mosaics are assembled by cutting, matching, and pasting together portions of individual vertical exposures; the result is a large photograph that appears to be a single print. *Controlled mosaics* (those compiled at a uniform scale from ground reference points) provide good map approximations. However, controlled mosaics are quite expensive and cannot be viewed three dimensionally. Except for pictorial displays, their use by foresters is limited.

13-3 Black-and-White Aerial Films   Selection of the proper film is an important factor in distinguishing vegetation classes on aerial photos. Foresters usually rely on two types of black-and-white films, panchromatic and infrared, and two kinds of color films, normal color and infrared color.

Images on *panchromatic film* are rendered in varying shades of gray, with each tone comparable to the density of an object's color as seen by the human eye. Panchromatic is a superior black-and-white film for distinguishing objects of truly different colors; it is recommended for such projects as highway route surveys, urban planning, mapping, and the locating of property ownership boundaries (Fig. 13-1). Since old roads and trails are easily seen, panchromatic prints are also useful as field maps for the land manager who must find routes over unfamiliar terrain.

Because panchromatic film is only moderately sensitive to the green portion of the spectrum, most healthy vegetation appears in similar gray tones on the prints. Where only coniferous (needleleaf) trees are present, panchromatic film may be preferred for the classification of forest vegetation. On the other hand, if deciduous (broadleaf) vegetation is interspersed with coniferous trees, separation of the different types can be more easily accomplished by using black-and-white infrared film.

Gray tones on *infrared film* apparently result from the degree of infrared reflection of objects rather than from their true colors. For example, broadleaf vegetation is highly reflective and, therefore, photographs in light tones of gray; coniferous, or needleleaf, vegetation tends to be less reflective in the near-infrared portion of the spectrum and, consequently, registers in much darker tones. This characteristic makes infrared film the preferred black-and-white emulsion for delineating timber types in mixed forests.

Bodies of water absorb infrared light to a high degree and, thus, register as quite dark on the film unless heavily silt-laden. This rendition is useful for determining the extent of river tributaries, canals, tidal marshes, swamps, and shorelines. Infrared films are superior to panchromatic materials for penetration of haze.

FIGURE 13-1
Panchromatic stereogram of a forested area in eastern Texas being developed for housing (above). Scale is about 1:12,000. Below is a large-scale photograph covering the block outlined on the stereogram. *(Courtesy United Aerial Mapping.)*

13-4 Color Aerial Films   *Normal color film* is sensitized to all visible colors; it provides imagery with natural color rendition when properly exposed and processed. The emulsion has proved especially valuable for identifying soil types, rock outcrops, and forest vegetation. Normal color can also penetrate water, and it is therefore useful for subsurface exploration, hydrographic control, and the delineation of shoreline features. As is the case with most color films, correct exposures require conditions of bright sunlight.

Color films are usually processed to produce positive color transparencies rather than ordinary paper prints. In most instances, conventional color photographs are superior to black-and-white pictures for studies of natural vegetation, because the human eye can distinguish many more color variations than gray tones.

Infrared color film has proved especially valuable for carrying out a variety of forest-survey projects, such as the early detection of disease and insect outbreaks in timber stands, and for detecting soil and vegetation patterns disturbed by human activity. Basic to such application is the identification of tree species or forest-cover types, a task that requires information on the infrared reflectivity of various types of foliage. Since healthy broadleaf trees have a higher infrared reflectivity than healthy needleleaf trees, their photographic images can usually be separated on these kinds of exposures.

Obviously, no single film emulsion serves all purposes. Instead, the varied tones and patterns produced by differing ranges of film sensitivity complement each other, and the maximum amount of information can be extracted only when several types of imagery covering the same area are studied simultaneously.

13-5 Seasons for Aerial Photography   The best season for obtaining aerial photographs depends on the nature of the features to be identified or mapped, the film to be used, and the number of days suitable for photographic flights during a given time of the year. Other factors being equal, aerial surveys are likely to be less expensive in areas where sunny, clear days predominate during the desired photographic season.

Foresters interested in vegetation studies will usually specify that aerial photographs be taken during the growing season, particularly when deciduous plants constitute an important component of the vegetative cover. When it is essential that deciduous trees, evergreens, and mixtures of the two groups be delineated, either black-and-white infrared or color infrared film is frequently specified. In regions where evergreen plants predominate, however, panchromatic film or normal color film may be used with equal success.

Several research projects involving black-and-white photography of forest areas have indicated that the best timing for infrared coverage is from mid-spring to early summer—after all trees have produced some foliage but prior to maximum leaf pigmentation. Successful panchromatic photographs of timberlands can be made throughout the year; but, in northern United States and Canada, best results have been obtained in late fall—just before deciduous tree species, such as aspen or tamarack, shed their leaves. For a brief period of perhaps 2 weeks' duration, foliage color differences will provide good photographic contrasts between most of the important timber species in this region.

13-6 Determining Photographic Scales   The vertical aerial photograph presents a true record of angles, but measures of horizontal distances vary widely with changes in ground elevations and flight altitudes. The nominal scale (as 1:20,000) is representative only of the *datum,* an imaginary plane passing through a specified ground elevation above sea level. Calculation of the average photo scale will increase the accuracy of subsequent photo measurements.

Aerial cameras in common use have focal lengths of 6, 8.25, or 12 in. (0.5, 0.6875, or 1 ft). This information, coupled with the altitude of the aircraft above ground datum, makes it possible to determine the *representative fraction* (RF), or natural scale:

$$RF = \frac{\text{focal length (ft)}}{\text{flying height above ground (ft)}}$$

The exact altitude of the aircraft is rarely known to the interpreter, however, and photo scale is more often calculated by

$$RF = \frac{\text{photographic distance between two points (ft)}}{\text{ground or map distance between same points (ft)}}$$

As an example, the distance between two road intersections might be measured on a vertical photograph as 3.6 in. (0.3 ft). If the corresponding ground distance is measured as 3,960 ft, the representative fraction would be computed as

$$RF = \frac{0.3}{3,960} = \frac{1}{13,200} \quad \text{or } 1:13,200$$

It is not essential to calculate the scale of every photograph in a flight strip. In hilly terrain, every third or fifth print may be used; in flat topography, every tenth or twentieth may be used. Scales of intervening photos can be obtained by interpolation.

13-7 Photogeometry   It is important to note here that although aerial photographs are used for mapping purposes, they are not maps in the true sense of the word. Maps have a single known scale, and if no drafting error is made, objects on maps are shown in their correct locations relative to one another. Aerial photographs, however, have image displacements, and distortions created by tilt of the aircraft, varying elevations, and imperfect camera lenses, in addition to the scale changes discussed in Section 13-6. While the effects of these displacements and other factors on maps are usually small, they can create significant problems if the terrain is rugged, if flying heights are very low, or if the aerial camera is excessively tilted.

Orthophotographs are, however, very similar to maps. An *orthophotograph* is a reproduction, prepared from ordinary perspective photographs, in which image displacements caused by tilt and relief have been entirely removed. When these unique photographs are assembled into an *orthophotomosaic,* the result is a picture map with both scale and planimetric detail of high reliability. When such mosaics are overprinted onto standard mapping quadrangles, they are referred to as *orthophotoquads.*

13-8 Aligning Prints for Stereoscopic Study   Photographic flights are planned so that prints will overlap about 60 percent of their width in the line of flight and about 30 percent between flight strips. For effective stereoviewing, prints must be trimmed to a nominal 9-in. × 9-in. size, preserving the four fiducial marks in the photo corners or at the midpoint of each of the edges. The *principal point* (PP) is at the center of the photo and is located by the intersection of lines drawn from opposite sets of fiducial marks. The *conjugate principal points* (CPPs, or points that correspond to PPs of adjacent photos) are located by stereoscopic transfer from overlapping prints. Each photo, thus, has one PP and two CPPs, except prints at the ends of flight lines, which have only one CPP.

To align the photographs for stereoscopic study, a print is selected and fastened down with shadows toward the viewer. The adjacent photo is placed with its CPP about 2.2 in. (average interpupillary distance) from the corresponding PP on the first photo. The second photo is positioned with flight lines superimposed. A lens stereoscope is placed with its long axis parallel to the flight line and with the lenses over corresponding photo images. In this way an overlapping strip 2.2 in. wide and nearly 9 in. long can be viewed by moving the stereoscope up and down the overlap area (Fig. 13-2).

COVER-TYPE IDENTIFICATION AND MAPPING

13-9 Forest Type Recognition   Interpreters of forest vegetation should be well versed in plant ecology and the various factors that influence the distribution of native trees and shrubs. Field experience in the region of interest is also a prime requisite because many cover types must be deduced or inferred from associated factors instead of being recognized directly from their photographic images.

An inferential approach to cover-type identification becomes more and more important as image scales and resolution qualities are reduced. Range managers may rely exclusively on this technique where they must evaluate the grazing potential for lands obscured by dense forest canopies.

The degree to which cover types and plant species can be recognized depends on the quality, scale, and season of photography; the type of film used; and the in-

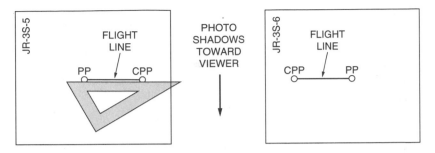

A. PRELIMINARY PHOTO ORIENTATION

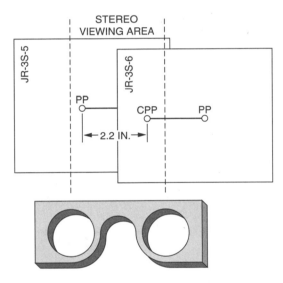

B. FINAL PHOTO ALIGNMENT

FIGURE 13-2
Alignment of 9-in. by 9-in. vertical photographs for viewing with a lens stereoscope.

terpreter's background and ability. The shape, texture, and tone (color) of plant foliage as seen on vertical photographs can also be influenced by stand age or topographic site. Furthermore, such images may be affected by time of day, sun angle,
atmospheric haze, clouds, or inconsistent processing of negatives and prints. In
spite of insistence on rigid specifications, it is often impossible to obtain uniform
imagery of extensive land holdings. Nevertheless, experienced interpreters can reliably distinguish cover types in diverse vegetation regions when photographic
flights are carefully planned to minimize such limitations.

The first step in cover-type recognition is to determine which types should and
should not be expected in a given locality. It will also be helpful for the interpreter
to become familiar with the most common plant and environmental associations

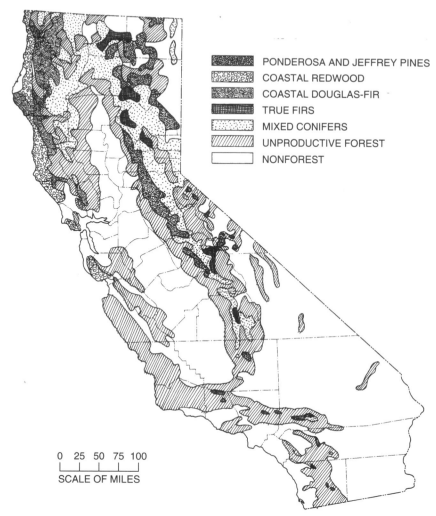

FIGURE 13-3
Generalized forest type map of California. *(Courtesy U.S. Forest Service.)*

of those types most likely to be found. Much of this kind of information can be derived from generalized cover-type maps (Fig. 13-3) and by ground or aircraft
checks of the project area in advance of photo interpretation.

In some regions, photo-interpretation keys are available as aids in the recognition of forest cover types; such keys can be especially useful when they are illustrated with high-quality stereograms. Vegetation keys for Anglo-American types
are most easily constructed for northern and western forests where conifers predominate. In these regions, there are relatively few species to be considered, and

crown patterns are fairly distinctive for each important group. It should also be noted that forest type recognition can often be improved by using color photographs (especially color infrared) instead of black-and-white imagery.

13-10 Identifying Individual Species   The identification of an individual species through aerial photography is most easily accomplished when that species occurs naturally in pure, even-aged stands. Under such circumstances, the cover type and the plant species are synonymous. Therefore, reliable delineations *may* be made from medium-scale aerial photography. As a rule, however, individual plants can be identified only from large-scale photography (Fig, 13-4). Table 13-1, based on a synopsis of several research reports, illustrates the relationship between photo scale and expected levels of plant recognition.

FIGURE 13-4
Stereogram showing live white pines (large, dark crowns) and dead balsam firs killed by the spruce budworm (smaller, whitish crowns). Scale is about 132 ft per in. *(Courtesy U.S. Forest Service.)*

TABLE 13-1
RELATIONSHIP BETWEEN PHOTOGRAPHIC SCALE AND EXPECTED LEVELS OF PLANT RECOGNITION

Photographic scale	General level of plant discrimination
1:30,000–1:100,000	Recognition of broad vegetative types, largely by inferential processes
1:10,000–1:30,000	Direct identification of major cover types and species occurring in pure stands
1:2,500–1:10,000	Identification of individual trees and large shrubs
1:500–1:2,500	Identification of individual range plants and grassland types

Photographic identification of individual plants requires that interpreters become familiar with a large number of species *on the ground*. For example, there are more than a thousand species of woody plants that occur naturally in the United States; foresters and range managers can rarely identify more than one-fourth of this number.

13-11 Timber Type Maps   Type maps are no longer considered essential by all foresters, but at times their cost may be justified. A general ownership map showing principal roads, streams, and forest types may be desired for management planning and illustrative purposes. When making a photo-controlled ground cruise where precise forest-area estimates are required, it may be necessary to measure stand areas on controlled maps of known scale rather than directly on contact prints; this is particularly important when topography causes wide variation in photo scales.

The wise interpreter will delineate only those forest types that can be consistently recognized. For maximum accuracy, type lines should be drawn under the stereoscope. Wherever feasible, it is recommended that forest-cover types be coded according to the system devised by the Society of American Foresters (Eyre, 1980). In the past, timber type maps have assumed a wide variety of forms from one locale to another, but it is advantageous to employ uniform symbols for designating tree species and stand-size classes.

13-12 Using Photos for Field Travel   Although photographic flights are planned to run either north-south or east-west, few prints will be oriented precisely with the cardinal directions. If one wishes to travel cross-country with the aid of a vertical photograph, it is usually necessary to first establish a line of known compass direction on the print. This reference line may be transferred to the photo from existing maps or located directly on the ground by taking the compass bearing of any straight-line feature (e.g., a road or field edge).

Once the reference line is drawn on the photograph, it should be extended so that it intersects the proposed line of cross-country travel. The angle between the two lines is then measured with a protractor to establish the bearing of the travel route. If one wishes to travel to a specific point or field plot along the proposed line, the photo scale should be determined as precisely as possible; then the travel distance can be determined directly on the print with an engineer's scale.

BASIC FOREST MEASUREMENTS

13-13 Measuring Area and Distance   Areas, distances, and direction are measured on photographs just as they are on maps (Chap. 4). Area is estimated with a dot grid or planimeter. Ground distances are calculated by measuring a photo distance and converting it to ground units using photo scale. Compass bearings and azimuths can be determined on photographs if a base line of known direction can be established on the photo. It should be remembered, however, that photographs are not maps, and the displacements and variation present on photos occasionally degrade these measurements. Area measurements are typically affected most and thus warrant extra care.

13-14 Measuring Heights by Parallax To determine heights of objects on stereopairs of photographs, it is necessary to measure or estimate (1) absolute stereoscopic parallax and (2) differential parallax. *Absolute stereoscopic parallax,* measured parallel to the line of flight, is the algebraic difference of the distances of the two images from their respective PPs. Except in mountainous terrain, the average photo base length is ordinarily used as an approximation of absolute stereoscopic parallax. It is measured as the mean distance between the PP and CPP for an overlapping pair of photographs.

Differential parallax is the difference in the absolute stereoscopic parallax at the top and the base of the object, measured parallel to the flight line. The basic formula for conversion of parallax measurements on aerial photographs is

$$h = (H)\frac{dP}{P + dP}$$

where h = height of measured object
 H = height of aircraft above ground datum
 dP = differential parallax
 P = absolute stereoscopic parallax at base of object being measured

If object heights are to be determined in feet, the altitude of the aircraft must also be in feet. Absolute stereoscopic parallax and differential parallax must be expressed in the same units; ordinarily, these units will be in thousandths of inches or hundredths of millimeters.

13-15 Parallax-Measuring Devices Differential parallax, dP, is usually measured stereoscopically with a parallax wedge or with a stereometer employing the "floating-mark" principle; use of the stereometer is detailed here.

The typical stereometer (or parallax bar) has two lenses attached to a metal frame that houses a vernier and a graduated metric scale. The left lens contains a fixed reference dot; the dot on the right lens can be moved laterally by means of the vernier. The stereometer is placed over the stereoscopic image parallel to the line of flight (Fig. 13-5). The right-hand dot is moved until it fuses with the reference dot and appears as a single dot resting on the ground, and the vernier reading is recorded to the nearest 0.01 mm. Then the vernier is turned until the fused dot appears to "float" at the elevation of the top of the object. A second vernier reading is taken, and the difference between the two readings is the differential parallax, dP. This value can be substituted in the parallax formula without conversion if the absolute parallax, P, is also expressed in millimeters.

FIGURE 13-5
Lens stereoscope with attached stereometer. This "floating-dot" instrument can be used to measure the heights of objects on vertical stereopairs of photographs. *(Courtesy Carl Zeiss, Inc.)*

As an example, assume that the two stereometer readings for a building were 10.75 mm (ground) and 9.63 mm (top). The differential parallax is therefore 1.12 mm. If we have an average photo base P of 91.44 mm and an aircraft flying height (H) of 3,600 ft, the height of the building (h) would be computed as

$$h = (3,600)\frac{1.12}{91.44 + 1.12} = 43.56 \text{ ft}$$

Once the photographic specifications are fixed, the expected precision of height measurement is largely dependent on the stereoscopic perception of the individual interpreter. At photo scales of 1:10,000 to 1:15,000, skilled interpreters can determine the heights of clearly defined objects within ± 5 to 10 ft. Measurement precision tends to improve as photo scales become larger, that is, as aircraft heights above the ground datum decrease.

13-16 Tree-Crown Diameters Measurements of tree-crown diameters are of interest because, for many species, these measurements may be closely correlated with stem diameters. Such relationships have been verified for a number of

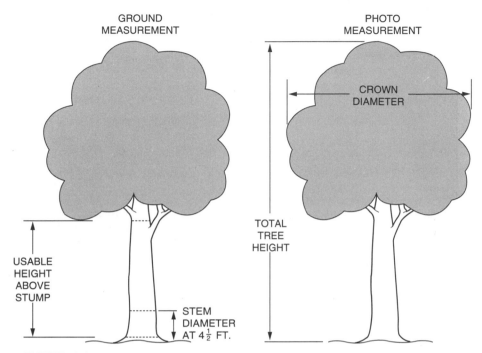

FIGURE 13-6
Comparison of ground and photographic measurements in the determination of individual tree volumes.

conifers, notably those occurring in open-grown, even-aged stands. As a result, tree volume tables based on crown diameter (in lieu of dbh) can be constructed for use with aerial photographs.

Crown diameters may be measured either on the ground or on aerial photographs (Fig. 13-6). The difference in perspective afforded by the two measurement techniques can lead to varying results, even for the same trees. If the crowns are imaged on small-scale photographs, for example, only that part of the diameter visible from above is measured; narrow, single branches and irregular crown perimeters may not be resolved by the photographic system. Therefore, photo-measured crown diameters are sometimes smaller than crown measurements made on the ground.

If an aerial volume table is based on *photo measurements* of tree crowns, the biases and/or errors of the interpreter are incorporated into the table. This will be acceptable, provided other interpreters with different biases do not have to use the same table. If *ground measurements* of crown diameters are used instead, each interpreter first measures a group of "test trees" to establish an individual photo/ground adjustment ratio. Such tables can then be utilized by large numbers of interpreters.

CROWN DIAMETER SCALE

CENTRAL STATES FOREST EXPERIMENT STATION

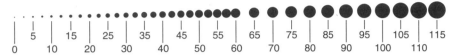

NUMBERS INDICATE DOT SIZE IN THOUSANDTHS OF AN INCH

FIGURE 13-7
A simple dot-type scale for measuring crown diameters on vertical photographs. Such
scales are usually printed on transparent film. *(Courtesy U.S. Forest Service.)*

The assessment of crown diameter is a simple linear measure (Sec.7-16). On
the ground, two persons with steel tape and plumb bobs align themselves at opposite edges of the tree crown by using a vertical sighting device such as a
periscope. Two or more diameter measurements are taken for each tree. Very small
individual branches and minor crown irregularities are usually ignored. The nearer
the widest part of the crown is to ground level, the more accurate the resulting
measurement.

Various scales, tube magnifiers, and "wedges" are available for measuring
crown diameters on aerial photographs (Fig. 3-7). Careful observers can mea-sure
within ± 0.1 mm, and so accuracy is dependent on image scale, film resolution,
and individual ability. Care must be exercised to avoid the inclusion of crown
shadows as part of the measurement. It has been observed that most aerial-photo
measurements tend to improve as one changes from paper prints to black-and-
white film diapositives to color transparencies. Improvements are partially due to
higher resolution and, with color transparencies, better contrast between tree images and backgrounds.

13-17 Tree Counts   One of the easiest and most common forest measurements
made on aerial photographs is number of trees per unit area, or tree count. Number
of trees per unit area is a commonly used measure of stand density (Chap. 15). Tree
counts are used to expand individual-tree volume estimates to a unit-area basis, and,
in some instances, as an input variable for growth and yield models. If tree count can
be reliably estimated from aerial photographs, the time savings may be significant
since it may take 25 to 50 times longer to measure a plot in the field than on an aerial photograph.

The procedure for estimating the number of trees per unit area on aerial photographs is simple. Since it is generally not feasible to count every tree in the area
of interest, a sampling process analogous to field procedures is used. A plot of
known dimension is constructed on clear material and placed over the photo in a
random (or systematic) fashion within the boundaries of the tract of interest. Next,
the number of crowns within the plot is tallied and then expanded to a per-unit-

area basis using the scale of the photographs. The process is repeated until an adequate sample size is attained, then averages are computed. Some confusion often occurs in the counting process because individual crowns may be difficult to identify and because the variable of interest is stems per unit area, not crowns per unit area. In many forest stands, there is not a one-to-one correspondence between the total number of stems per unit area and the number of visible crowns per unit area.

The accuracy of aerial-photo-based tree counts varies considerably and is highly dependent upon stand age, stand structure, and the characteristics of the aerial photographs used. Photo-based tree counts typically decrease in number and accuracy on smaller-scale photos because smaller crowns merge and become difficult to discern. Thus, scale of the photographs must be carefully selected. Season of acquisition and film type can also affect the accuracy of tree counts. The most successful applications of photo-based tree counts have been in relatively young, even-aged stands of intolerant species, such as southern pines or Douglas-fir. For instance, the number of surviving stems in 3-, 4-, and 5-year-old loblolly pine plantations in Virginia was estimated within about 10 percent using large-scale, 35-mm aerial photographs. The least successful situations involve tolerant species where significant numbers of smaller stems are obscured by taller, upper-canopy-level trees. Even in the best of situations, it is virtually impossible to locate and tally every tree in photo plots. Adjustment factors or equations have been successfully used to correct for these inherent omissions.

13-18 Individual-Tree Volumes   Multiple-entry tree volume tables based on dbh and total height can be converted to aerial volume tables when correlations can be established between crown diameters and stem diameters. Photo determinations of crown diameter are substituted for the usual ground measures of dbh, and total heights are measured on stereoscopic pairs of photographs by the parallax method (Table 13-2).

Volume estimates based on this approach or on prediction equations will generally have a lower precision (i.e., greater standard error) than those estimates based on dbh and height because tree volumes are more closely correlated with dbh than with crown diameter. And, of course, dbh can be measured with greater precision. Nevertheless, aerial tree volume tables have proved to be cost-efficient for many inventories, particularly for coniferous species growing in relatively inaccessible regions.

As an example, the Forest Management Institute of Ottawa, Canada, has successfully used large-scale aerial photography to inventory a forest of approximately 2,700 km^2 in the Mackenzie River Delta, Northwest Territories. An equation was developed to estimate tree volumes (largely white spruce) on the delta; it was applied to all trees on selected photo sample plots to provide plot-volume estimates. An inventory objective was to estimate total timber volume within ± 20 percent at a probability level of 0.95. The aerial-photo approach proved to be the most cost-efficient means of achieving this objective.

TABLE 13-2
INDIVIDUAL-TREE AERIAL VOLUME TABLE FOR SECOND-GROWTH SOUTHERN
PINES, CU FT*

Crown diameter class (ft)	Total tree height (ft)						
	50	60	70	80	90	100	110
10	9.5	11.5	12.5	15.0	17.5	19.5	....
12	12.5	14.5	16.5	18.0	20.5	22.5	....
14	15.0	17.0	19.0	23.5	25.0	27.5	30.5
16	17.5	20.5	24.0	27.5	30.5	33.0	36.0
18	....	23.5	27.0	30.5	34.5	38.0	42.5
20	....	28.0	33.5	36.0	40.0	45.5	49.0
22	....	32.5	37.0	42.5	46.5	52.0	57.5
24	....	37.0	42.5	48.5	54.5	60.0	66.0
26	....	42.5	47.5	54.0	61.0	67.5	75.5
28	....	....	53.0	60.5	70.5	76.0	83.0
30	....	....	60.5	68.0	78.0	85.5	94.5

*Based on 324 trees in Arkansas, Louisiana, and Mississippi. Gross volumes are inside bark and include the merchantable stem to a variable top averaging 6 in. ib.

Large-scale, high-quality aerial photography is essential for obtaining reliable crown-diameter and height measurements of individual trees. Furthermore, image resolution must be sufficient to permit reliable *stem counts* so that tree volumes can be expanded to an area basis. Black-and-white film diapositives or color transparencies at a scale of 1:5,000 or larger are recommended for consistent photographic interpretation results.

13-19 Aerial Stand-Volume Tables   Where only small-scale aerial photographs are available to interpreters, emphasis is on measurement of *stand variables* rather than individual-tree variables. Aerial stand-volume tables are multiple-entry tables that are usually based on assessments of two or three photographic characteristics of the dominant-codominant crown canopy: average stand height, average crown diameter, and percent of crown closure. These tables are usually derived by multiple regression analysis; photographic measurements of the independent variables are made by several skilled interpreters when developing the volume-prediction equation.

13-20 Crown Closure   Photographic and ground measurements of tree heights and crown diameters have been described in Chapter 7 and previous sections of Chapter 13. Crown closure, also referred to as *crown cover* and *canopy closure,* is defined by photo interpreters as the percent of a forest area occupied by the vertical projections of tree crowns. The concept is primarily applied to even-aged stands or to the dominant-codominant canopy level of uneven-aged stands. When used in this context, the maximum value possible is 100 percent.

FIGURE 13-8
An indication of tree-crown closure
as seen from a ground-level camera.
(Courtesy Ben Jackson.)

In theory, crown closure is associated with stand volume because such estimates are approximate indicators of stand density, e.g., number of stems per acre.
Since basal areas and numbers of trees cannot be determined directly from small-
scale photography, crown closure is sometimes substituted for these variables in
stand-volume-prediction equations. Photographic estimates of crown closure are
normally used because reliable ground evaluations are much more difficult to obtain (Fig. 13-8).

At photo scales of 1:15,000 and smaller, crown-closure estimates are usually
made by ocular judgment, and stands are grouped into 10 percent classes. Ocular
estimates are easiest in stands of low density, but they become progressively more
difficult as closure percentages increase. Minor stand openings are difficult to see
on small-scale photographs, and they are often shrouded by tree shadows. These
factors can lead to overestimates of crown closure, particularly in dense stands.
And if ocular estimates are erratic, the variable of crown closure may contribute
very little to the prediction of stand volume.

With high-resolution photographs at scales of 1:5,000 to 1:15,000, it may be
feasible to derive crown-closure estimates with the aid of finely subdivided dot
grids. Here, the proportion of the total number of dots that falls on tree crowns provides the estimate of crown closure. This estimation technique has the virtue of

TABLE 13-3
AERIAL-PHOTO STAND-VOLUME TABLE FOR EVEN-AGED DOUGLAS-FIR IN THE
PACIFIC NORTHWEST, IN 100 CU FT PER ACRE*

Stand height (ft)[†]	Crown closure (%)[‡]								
	15	25	35	45	55	65	75	85	95
40	5	8	11	13	14	15	15	14	13
50	7	11	15	18	20	21	22	21	20
60	9	15	20	24	27	29	30	29	28
70	12	19	25	31	34	37	39	39	38
80	14	24	31	38	43	46	48	49	49
90	17	28	38	45	52	56	59	61	61
100	21	33	45	54	61	67	72	74	75
110	24	39	52	63	72	79	85	88	90
120	28	45	60	73	83	92	99	103	106
130	31	51	68	83	95	106	114	120	124
140	35	57	77	94	108	121	130	138	143
150	40	64	86	105	122	136	148	157	163
160	44	71	96	118	136	153	166	177	185
170	49	79	106	130	152	170	185	198	208
180	54	87	117	144	168	188	206	220	232
190	59	95	128	158	184	208	227	244	257
200	64	104	140	173	202	228	250	269	284
210	70	113	152	188	220	249	274	295	313
220	75	122	165	204	239	271	298	322	342
230	81	132	178	220	259	293	324	351	373
240	87	142	192	238	280	317	351	380	406
250	94	152	206	256	301	342	379	411	439
260	100	163	221	274	323	367	408	443	474

*Gross volume, in trees 5 in. and larger, from stump to top limit of 4 in. dib.
†Average height of dominants and codominants, as measured in the field.
‡Includes all trees in the major canopy; average photo estimate of several experienced interpreters.
Table based on 282 one-fifth-acre plots, largely in western Oregon.

Source: Pope, 1962.

producing a reasonable degree of consistency among various photo interpreters; it
is therefore recommended wherever applicable.

Table 13-3, compiled for Douglas-fir stands, is based on the variables of total
stand height and crown-closure percent.

13-21 Stand-Volume Estimates   Once an appropriate aerial stand-volume
table has been selected (or constructed), there are several procedures that can be
employed to derive stand volumes. One approach is as follows:

1 Outline tract boundaries on the photographs, utilizing the effective area of
every other print in each flight line. This assures stereoscopic coverage of the area
on a minimum number of photographs and avoids duplication of measurements by
the interpreter.

2 Delineate important forest types. Except where type lines define stands of relatively uniform density and total height, they should be further broken down into homogeneous units so that measures of height, crown closure, and crown diameter will apply to the entire unit. Generally, it is unnecessary to recognize stands smaller than 5 to 10 acres.

3 Determine the area of each condition class with dot grids or a planimeter. This determination can sometimes be made on contact prints.

4 By stereoscopic examination, measure the variables for entering in the aerial stand-volume table. From the table, obtain the average volume per acre for each condition class.

5 Multiply volumes per acre from the table by condition-class areas to determine gross volume for each class.

6 Add class volumes for the total gross volume on the tract.

13-22 Adjusting Photo Volumes by Field Checks   Aerial volume tables are not generally reliable enough for purely photographic estimates, and some allowance must be made for differences between gross-volume estimates and actual net volumes on the ground. Therefore, a portion of the stands (or condition classes) that are interpreted should be checked in the field. If field volumes average 600 cu ft per acre as compared with 800 cu ft per acre for the photo estimates, the adjustment ratio would be 600/800, or 0.75. When the field checks are representative of the total area interpreted, the ratio can be applied to photo volume estimates to determine adjusted net volume. It is desirable to compute such ratios by forest types, because deciduous, broad-leaved trees are likely to require larger adjustments than conifers.

The accuracy of aerial volume estimates depends not only upon the volume tables used but also on the ability of interpreters who make the essential photographic assessments. Since subjective photo estimates often vary widely among individuals, it is advisable to have two or more interpreters assess each of the essential variables.

OBTAINING AERIAL PHOTOGRAPHS

13-23 The Options   Aerial photographs can be obtained by purchasing existing imagery, by taking the necessary pictures yourself, or by contracting for new coverage through a private aerial-survey company. Each solution has its own advantages and limitations. For example, existing photography has the advantage of low cost, but it may be outdated or available only as black-and-white prints. Do-it-yourself photography is often sufficient for small areas of spot coverage, but the amateur rarely has the equipment and professional expertise to photograph large land areas with required standards of precision. And contracting for a special aerial survey, the choice most likely to result in superior pictures, may be rather costly for small or irregularly shaped land areas.

13-24 Photography from Commercial Firms   A wide selection of photographic negatives are held by private aerial-survey companies in the United States and Canada. In many instances, prints can be ordered directly from these companies after permission is obtained from the original purchaser. A large share of the available coverage has been obtained on panchromatic film with aerial cameras having distortion-free lenses. As a result, photographs are ideally suited for stereoscopic study because of fine image resolution and a high degree of three-dimensional exaggeration. Scales are usually 1:25,000 or larger for recent photography. In addition to contact prints and photo index sheets, most aerial-mapping organizations will also sell reproductions of special atlas sheets or controlled mosaics. These items can be useful for pictorial displays and administrative planning.

Prints purchased from private companies may cost more than those from public agencies, but they are often of higher quality and at larger scale—factors that may offset any price differential. Quotations and photo indexes can be obtained by direct inquiry to the appropriate company. Names and addresses of leading photogrammetric concerns are available in current issues of *Photogrammetric Engineering and Remote Sensing.*

13-25 Photography from the U.S. Government   Most of the United States has been photographed in recent years for various federal agencies. Although there is no central repository that can supply prints of all government imagery, a large portion can be purchased at reasonable prices through the U.S. Departments of Agriculture or Interior. The U.S. Geological Survey maintains a data base of existing aerial photography called the Aerial Photography Summary Record System. Search requests are free and available to the public through the USGS. As a rule, most photographs purchased through federal agencies range in scale from about 1:12,000 to 1:40,000. Panchromatic film is commonly used, although infrared and color films are increasing in popularity. Also, there is an increasing amount of high-altitude color photography (scale 1:60,000 to 1:125,000) available from some agencies.

The age of existing photography usually varies from about 2 to 8 years, with agricultural regions, urban areas, and large reservoirs being rephotographed at the most frequent intervals. Photo index sheets of existing photography (Fig. 13-9) can be viewed at local or regional offices of the Agricultural Stabilization and Conservation Service, the U.S. Forest Service, or the U.S. Geological Survey.

13-26 Photography from the Canadian Government   The National Air Photo Library is the central storehouse for the Canadian government's aerial photography, including the Yukon, the Northwest Territories, and the Provinces of Newfoundland, Labrador, Nova Scotia, Prince Edward Island, Manitoba, and Saskatchewan. Photography obtained specifically for other provinces may be available through various agencies within those provinces. Written inquiries should include a map of the area involved, a statement regarding the proposed use of the photography, and specifications as to whether stereoscopic coverage is desired.

FIGURE 13-9
Portion of an aerial-photo index sheet for Montgomery County, Texas. *(Courtesy U.S.
Department of Agriculture.)*

13-27 Taking Your Own Pictures   If oblique or near-vertical photographs taken with small-format cameras are sufficient for supplementary coverage of project areas, the do-it-yourself approach provides an alternative for limited types of aerial surveys. High-wing monoplanes offer good side visibility and low stalling speeds; such aircraft can be rented (with pilot) at reasonable hourly rates. Under certain circumstances, it may be permissible to remove the aircraft door on the passenger's side to obtain even better visibility during flights.

For oblique exposures taken through aircraft windows, standard press cameras work quite well. When cameras must be exposed to the aircraft slipstream, however, rigidly designed lens systems should be used instead of those with folding bellows. Surplus military-reconnaissance cameras can sometimes be rented or purchased, but most scientists seem to prefer conventional 35-mm or 70-mm formats because films are readily available and inexpensive and cameras can be equipped with interchangeable lenses and motorized film drives. Furthermore, imagery in these two formats can be optically enlarged (e.g., for map revision and updating) by use of ordinary slide projectors.

The negative scales of do-it-yourself aerial photography will generally range from about 1:2,500 to 1:25,000. Additional suggestions on techniques are provided in references listed at the end of the chapter.

13-28 Contracting for New Photography   This is the preferred method of obtaining photographic coverage since specifications such as film, filter, scale, and season can be placed under the control of the buyer. As a rule, the cost per square mile for special coverage decreases as photo scales become smaller and as land areas become larger. For coverage at a scale of 1:15,840 (4 in. per mile), a good camera crew can photograph 750 to 900 square miles in 5 to 8 hours of flying time. Thus photography of small land areas is dictated more by the cost of relocating the photographic aircraft and crew than by the actual flying time required.

When there is a choice to be made between two or more aerial-survey companies, the purchaser is advised to request photographic samples from each company. Such print samples provide useful guidelines to the quality of work that may be expected. Foresters who feel unqualified to evaluate sample photography should retain the services of a consultant to assist in drawing up photographic specifications, defining areas to be covered, and inspecting the finished product. When special flights are justified, contract specifications should be thoroughly discussed by buyer and contractor prior to actual flights. A few extra days of advance planning will sometimes alleviate the need for reflights and will help prevent possible disputes arising from definitions of stereoscopic coverage, exposure quality, or film-processing deficiencies.

13-29 Other Remote-Sensing Tools   Aerial photographs have been used successfully by natural resource managers for decades. Aerial photography is only one of the many products of the field called *remote sensing*. In the past 30 years, the remote-sensing discipline has produced other tools that may be helpful to foresters in certain situations. Satellite imagery has been applied in British Columbia to update cutting records and maps. Aerial infrared video has been used to monitor the spread of insects and disease. Thermal scanners have been used to locate hot spots and fire position in the western United States. While each of these tools is specialized in its application and has limitations, resource managers should consider all available tools when gathering data and gaining information needed to make informed decisions.

PROBLEMS

13-1 Determine the representative fraction (RF) for each of the following sets of data:
  a camera focal length = 6 in.; flying height above ground = 3,000 ft.
  b camera focal length = 8.25 in.; flying height above ground = 4,200 ft.
  c photographic distance between two points = 7.62 cm; ground distance between the same points = 4,152 ft.
  d photographic distance between two points = 2.4 in.; ground distance between the same points = 600 ft.
13-2 Using a set of aerial photographs from your own locality, determine the average scale (a) as a representative fraction, (b) in feet or chains per inch, and (c) in acres per square inch. Then establish a line of known compass bearing on the photographs.
13-3 For the following representative fractions (RFs), determine the feet per inch, chains per inch, and acres per square inch that would be represented on vertical aerial photographs: 1:7,920, 1:10,000, 1:15,840, and 1:20,000.
13-4 Determine the heights of 10 trees, buildings, or other objects from parallax measurements. After completion of photographic estimates, obtain ground measurements of the same objects with an Abney level or other hypsometer. Compare results, and explain reasons for differences noted.
13-5 Using the measurement data that follow, determine the height of each tree by applying the parallax formula from Section 13-14.

$$H = \text{height of airplane above ground datum}$$
$$P = \text{absolute stereoscopic parallax at base of tree}$$
$$dP = \text{differential parallax}$$

Determine the height of each tree in the units used for H.
  a $H = 5,000$ ft; $P = 90.00$ mm; $dP = 1.05$ mm.
  b $H = 4,200$ ft; $P = 84.62$ mm; $dP = 1.10$ mm.
  c $H = 1,000$ m; $P = 92.01$ mm; $dP = 1.17$ mm.
  d $H = 7,000$ ft; $P = 3.602$ in.; $dP = 0.041$ in.
  e $H = 1,800$ m; $P = 4.116$ in.; $dP = 0.052$ in.
13-6 Using local photographs, stratify a forest area by three to five volume or type categories. Design ground cruises based on (a) stratified random sampling and (b) simple random sampling. Use the same number of field plots for both cruises. Compare results and relative efficiencies of the two systems.

REFERENCES

Aldred, A. H., and Hall, J. K. 1975. Application of large-scale photography to a forest inventory. *Forestry Chron.* **51:**1–7.

——, and Sayn-Wittgenstein, L. 1972. Tree diameters and volume from large-scale aerial photographs. *Can. Forest Serv., Ottawa, Ontario, Information Report FMR-X*-40. 39 pp.

Avery, T. E. 1978. Forester's guide to aerial photo interpretation (revised). *U.S. Dept. Agr. Handbook* 308, Government Printing Office, Washington, D.C. 41 pp.

——, and Berlin, G. L. 1992. *Fundamentals of remote sensing and airphoto interpretation.* Macmillan Publishing Co., Riverside, N.J. 472 pp.

——, and Canning, J. 1973. Tree measurements on large-scale aerial photographs. *New Zealand J. Forestry* **18:**252–264.

Bonner, G. M. 1968. A comparison of photo and ground measurements of canopy density. *Forestry Chron.* **44:**12–16.

Ciesla, W. M. 1974. Forest insect damage from high-altitude color-IR photos. *Photogram. Eng.* **40:**683–689.

Croft, F., and Kessler, B. 1996. Remote sensing, image processing, and GIS: Trends and forecasts. *J. Forestry* **94(6):**31–35.

Eyre, F. H. (ed.). 1980. *Forest cover types of the United States and Canada.* Society of American Foresters, Washington, D.C. 148 pp.

Holmgren, P., and Thuresson, T. 1998. Satellite remote sensing for forestry planning— A review. *Scandinavian J. For. Res.* **13:**90–110.

Kippen, F. W., and Sayn-Wittgenstein, L. 1964. Tree measurements on large-scale, vertical 70-mm air photographs. *Forest Res. Br., Can. Dep. For. Pub.* 1053. 16 pp.

Kirby, C. L. 1980. A camera and interpretation system for assessment of forest regeneration. *Environ. Can., Can. Forest Serv., North. Forest Res. Cent., Edmonton, Alberta, Information Report NOR-X*-221. 8 pp.

Lillesand, T. M., and Kiefer, R. W. 2000. *Remote sensing and image interpretation,* 4th ed. John Wiley & Sons, New York. 724 pp.

Madill, R. J., and Aldred, A. H. 1977. Forest resource mapping in Canada. *The Can. Surv.* (March), pp. 9–20.

Paine, D. P. 1981. *Aerial photography and image interpretation for resource management.* John Wiley & Sons, New York. 571 pp.

Philipson, W. R. (ed.). 1997. *Manual of photographic interpretation,* 2d ed. American Society for Photogrammetry and Remote Sensing, Bethesda, Md. 689 pp.

Pope, R. B. 1962. Constructing aerial photo volume tables. *U.S. Forest Serv., Pacific Northwest Forest and Range Expt. Sta., Res. Paper* 49. 25 pp.

Smith, J. L., and Mead, R. A. 1981. A comparison of two aerial photo volume tables for pine stands in Mississippi. *So. J. Appl. For.* **5:**92–96.

——, Zedaker, S. M., and Heer, R. C. 1989. Estimating pine density and competition conditions in young pine plantations using 35 mm aerial photography. *So. J. Appl. For.* **13:**107–112.

Woodcock, W. E. 1976. Aerial reconnaissance and photogrammetry with small cameras. *Photogram. Eng. Remote Sens.* **42:**503–511.

Wynne, R. H., and Carter, D. B. 1997. Will remote sensing live up to its promise for forest management? *J. Forestry* **95(10):**23–26.

Wynne, R. H., Oderwald, R. G., Reams, G. A., and Scrivani, J. A. 2000. Optical remote sensing for forest area estimation. *J. Forestry* **98(5):**23–26.

14

GEOGRAPHIC
INFORMATION SYSTEMS

14-1 What Is a GIS? Geographic Information Systems (GISs) are automated systems for the capture, storage, retrieval, analysis, and display of spatial data. The need for spatial information, such as maps, in planning and management has long been recognized. Likewise, the added information that can be gained from overlaying maps has been put to use in many different fields of urban and land-use planning. While maps can be manually drawn on transparencies to a common scale and overlain, this is a slow, tedious, and expensive process. Geographic information systems provide an efficient way to overlay layers of map data, but their capabilities are by no means limited to formulating and producing maps. Although geographic information systems have their roots in cartography, they have evolved into powerful data management, analysis, and display tools. GIS involves aspects of the academic disciplines of geography, cartography, computer science, and mathematics, coupled with the technologies of remote sensing, global positioning systems (Chap. 4), and computer hardware and software. This confluence of multiple disciplines and technologies has spawned the interdisciplinary field of geographic information science (sometimes called "geomatics").

The capabilities of GISs are ideally suited for forest resource management, which involves many different kinds of information that must be spatially referenced. For instance, GISs can make forest inventory information more powerful by integrating it with other data commonly needed to make management decisions. Managers may need to know the location of roads, streams, threatened or endangered species, or sensitive soils when developing management plans. Combining forest inventory data with other land-resource information allows managers to make more informed decisions.

A GIS consists of procedures to store and manipulate geographically referenced data. Geographically referenced (spatial) data that pertain to a location on the Earth's surface are any data that can be represented on a map as a point, line, or area (Fig. 14-1). Storing and quickly manipulating geographically referenced data requires high-capacity, high-speed computing systems. According to Aronoff's (1989:39) definition, "A GIS is a computer-based system that provides the following four sets of capabilities to handle georeferenced data: 1. input; 2. data management (data storage and retrieval); 3. manipulation and analysis; and 4. output." In a book on forest measurements, it is not possible to cover all of the various aspects of GIS in detail. However, this technology is now widely applied in resource management, and a basic understanding of the elements and potential of GISs is essential. References cited at the end of the chapter provide additional detail on the structure and use of GIS.

FIGURE 14-1
Geographically referenced data (spatial data) can be represented as a point (A), line (B), or area (C). An example of features that can be represented by each respective data type is an elevation bench mark, a river, and a lake.

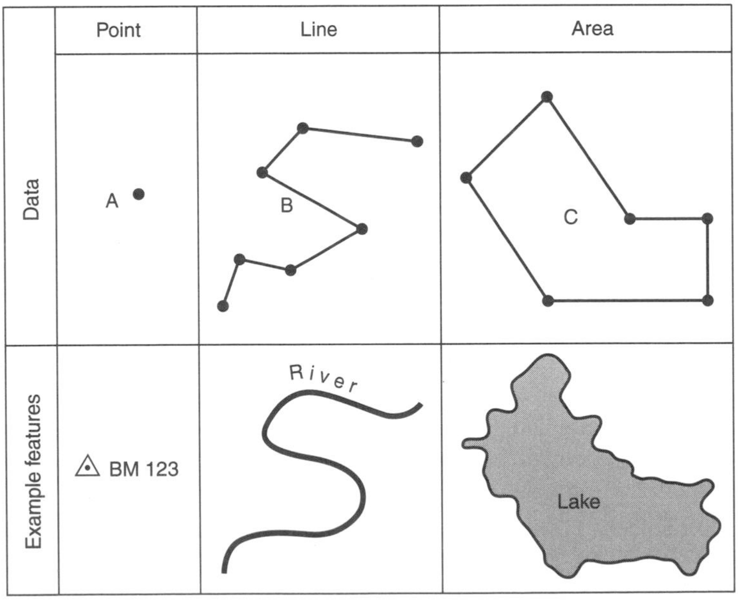

GIS DATA STRUCTURES

14-2 Data Formats   Spatial data are represented in GISs in two different ways: the raster format and the vector format (Fig. 14-2). In raster format, a grid is used to represent the area of interest. The location of features is indicated by a designated code in each grid cell containing that feature. Vector data represent geographic features by coordinates of points, lines, and polygons. Points designate small features or individuals, such as a den tree, a surveying bench mark, and the like. Lines are used to represent linear features such as roads and streams, whereas polygons are employed to designate areas such as lakes or forest stands. Polygons are bounded on all sides by a series of straight-line segments.

14-3 Raster Data   Raster data are stored in the computer as a matrix with the cells referenced by rows and columns. In the land-cover map shown in Figure 14-3, cells designated "1" are forests, cells with a value of "2" are croplands, and cells coded with a value of "3" are rangelands. The cell labels can be linked to records of

FIGURE 14-2
Comparison of the Raster and Vector Data Models. The landscape in (A) is shown in a raster representation (B) and in a vector representation (C). The pine forest stand (P) and spruce forest stand (S) are area features. The river (R) is a line feature, and the house (H) is a point feature. *(Adapted from Aronoff, 1989.)*

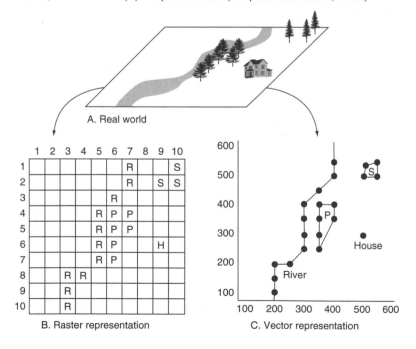

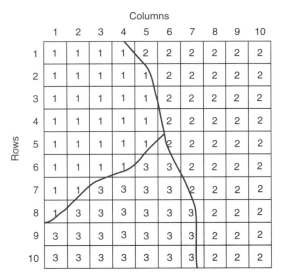

FIGURE 14-3
Land cover as represented in a simple raster system.
Cells with a "1" are forests, cells with a "2" are
croplands, and cells with a "3" are rangelands. *(Adapted
from Koeln, Cowardin, and Strong, 1996.)*

an attribute file. For instance, if cells labeled "1" in Figure 14-3 represent a forest stand for which an inventory has been conducted, one could link to the attributes (e.g., species, number of trees, basal area, and volume per acre or ha) determined in the inventory and associate those attributes with the land-cover map. The ability to associate attributes with spatial location is a powerful feature of GISs.

Because the raster system is a two-dimensional matrix, various types of geographical data are stored as different layers in the GIS. These individual maps or layers are often referred to as "themes." The locations of each feature in each theme are stored in the computer data base, and the characteristics associated with that feature are linked to it. Figure 14-4 shows how forest type, soil type, and topography maps can be converted to raster format for ease in performing overlay analyses.

When using raster systems, a grid cell size must be selected (the cells are usually square). The dimensions of the cells determine the spatial resolution possible. Because positions are defined by the cell row and column numbers, the position of features is only recorded to the nearest cell. The cell size used can vary tremendously, depending on the size of the area being studied and analyzed and on the objectives for the GIS analyses. Cell sizes of several acres (or ha) may be adequate for state or regional planning, whereas a cell size of 0.1 acre (0.04 ha) or smaller may be required for many forest resource management applications. Data storage requirements increase dramatically as the cell size is reduced. Reducing the cell

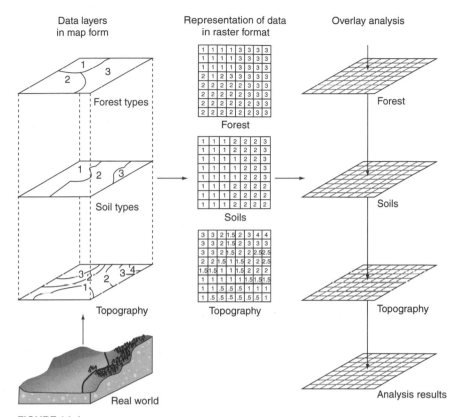

FIGURE 14-4
An overlay analysis, with three data layers, using raster data files. *(Adapted from Aronoff, 1989.)*

size by one-half increases the data storage required by a factor of four. Conversely, as cell size increases, the precision with which features can be represented decreases. Choosing an appropriate cell size for a particular GIS application is a compromise between the cost of data storage and computer time and the resolution of the representation of the geographic features of interest (Koeln, Cowardin, and Strong, 1996).

14-4 Vector Data   The vector format provides high precision in representing the location of features (Fig. 14-2). In vector format, points may be represented by a pair of coordinates (x, y), lines by an ordered list of pairs of coordinates, and areas by polygons with ordered pairs of coordinates that close the polygon (the first and last pair being the same) (Fig. 14-5).

The coordinates of vector data can be any arbitrary units but usually are recorded using a common geographic reference, such as UTM (Universal

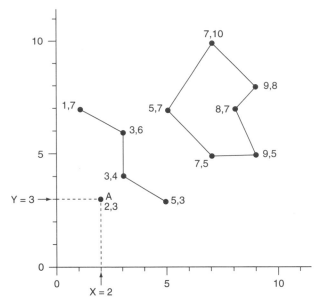

FIGURE 14-5
Points, lines, and polygons are represented as XY coordinate
strings in the vector data format. *(Adapted from Aronoff, 1989.)*

Transverse Mercator), state plane, or latitude and longitude coordinates. A number of systems have been devised to organize and store vector data such that the adjacency of features can be represented and mapped and the features can be linked to an attribute data base. Most vector systems now represent and store georeferenced data using topological models, which provide information on the adjacency and connectivity of geographical features (Aronoff, 1989). A topological structure facilitates spatial analyses, such as contiguity and connectivity studies, which are essential to informed forest landscape management. Additional detail about storage and manipulation of vector data can be found in references on GIS cited at the end of the chapter.

14-5 Raster versus Vector Systems Early GISs were either raster- or vector-based. Neither system is ideal for all purposes, so most modern GISs handle both raster and vector data, but many were designed primarily for one data format. When the geographic information of primary interest is spatial variability of a landscape characteristic, the raster representation is generally better. On the other hand, if the principal information of interest is the distribution of features in space or the conditions that apply to area features (such as forest stands), then the vector representation tends to be better. Table 14-1 contains a comparison of raster and vector data models. GISs that quickly and efficiently convert among rasters,

TABLE 14-1
COMPARISON OF RASTER AND VECTOR DATA MODELS

	Raster model	Vector model
Advantages	1. The raster format is a simple data structure. 2. Overlay operations are easily and efficiently implemented. 3. High spatial variability is efficiently represented. 4. It is well-suited for efficient manipulation and enhancement of digital images.	1. The vector format provides a more compact data structure and hence requires less storage space than the raster model. 2. It provides efficient encoding of topology and, as a result, more efficient implementation of operations that require topological (adjacency and connectivity of features) information. 3. The vector model is better suited to supporting graphics that closely approximate hand-drawn maps.
Disadvantages	1. The raster data structure is less compact. 2. Topological (adjacency and connectivity of features) relationships are more difficult to represent. 3. The output of graphics is less aesthetically pleasing because boundaries tend to have a blocky appearance rather than the smooth lines of hand-drawn maps.	1. The vector data structure is more complex than a simple raster. 2. Overlap operations are more difficult to implement. 3. The representation of high spatial variability is inefficient. 4. Manipulation and enhancement of digital images cannot be effectively done in the vector domain.

Source: Adapted from Aronoff, 1989.

vectors, and other data structures that are appropriate for the application being performed (or can perform analyses using a combination of data formats) are now becoming available.

GEOGRAPHIC COORDINATE SYSTEMS

14-6 Types of Coordinate Systems   Descriptions of location are often given with reference to somewhere else (such as "On Elm Street, two blocks south of Main Street"). Locations that are identified with respect to some other place are called *relative locations.* In a GIS, locations are typically specified with respect to the Earth as a whole. These are termed *absolute locations* because they are fixed with respect to an origin (a "zero point"). Converting maps and other spatial data into numbers requires a standard way to encode locations on the Earth. Maps are drawn by hand or by computer on a flat surface such as a piece of paper or a computer screen. Locations are usually given in (x, y) format; that is, an east-west distance or an easting followed by a north-south distance or a northing. The pair of numbers is referred to as a *coordinate pair* or, more simply, a *coordinate.* Coordinate systems are standard ways of listing coordinates. Maps on a common coordinate system will automatically be aligned with each other (Clarke, 1999).

While map dimensions are simple and the (x, y) axes are at right angles to each other, locations on the Earth's surface are not so simply derived. To make a flat map of the Earth's curved surface requires that something—scale, shape, area, or direction—be distorted. The extent to which the Earth's curvature can be removed depends on which of the various coordinate systems is used, how big of an area is mapped, and what projection system is applied. There are numerous coordinate systems, but the three most commonly used for forestry applications in the United States are latitude and longitude, Universal Transverse Mercator (UTM), and the state plane system.

14-7 The Latitude and Longitude System   The Earth's *equator* and the *prime meridian* are used as the origin for the latitude and longitude (or geographic coordinates) system (Fig. 14-6). The fact that the origin (zero point) is in the ocean

FIGURE 14-6
The latitude and longitude system is a commonly used geographic coordinate system. *(Adapted from Clarke, 1999.)*

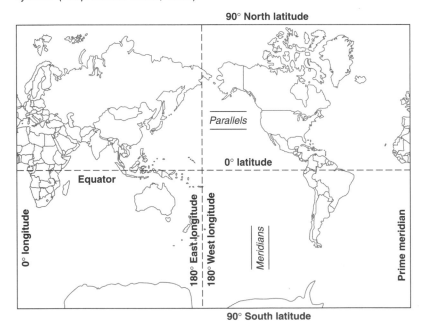

off West Africa is not critical; locations can be fixed using any arbitrarily chosen origin. Latitudes go from 90 degrees south (-90) to 90 degrees north ($+90$). Degrees are divided into minutes and minutes into seconds. Analogous to time, there are 60 minutes per degree, and 60 seconds per minute. Longitudes are the same, except that the range is -180 to $+180$ degrees.

14-8 The Universal Transverse Mercator Coordinate System The Universal Transverse Mercator (UTM) system is commonly used in GISs. Coordinates of vector-based features and cells of raster-based GISs can be aligned along the UTM grid. UTM divides the Earth into north-south strips by establishing zones running from pole to pole. The UTM system consists of 60 east-west zones, with each zone being 6 degrees of longitude wide. Each of these zones is numbered consecutively, starting with zone 1. The first zone starts at 180 degrees west at the international date line and runs east from 180 to 174 degrees west longitude. The final zone, zone 60, starts at 174 degrees east longitude and extends east for 6 degrees to the date line. UTM zones 10 through 19 contain the 48 contiguous states of the U.S. (Fig. 14-7).

Because the equator intersects the central meridian of the system at right angles, this point is used to orient the UTM grid system. Each zone has its own numbering system. To establish a coordinate system origin for a zone, separate numbering is used for the two hemispheres. For the southern hemisphere, the zero northing is the South Pole, and northings are given in meters north of this reference point. The numbering of northings starts again at the equator, which is set to 0 meters north in northern hemisphere coordinates. Northings are

FIGURE 14-7
The Universal Transverse Mercator (UTM) geographic coordinate system divides the Earth into 60 zones. Shown here are the UTM zones for the 48 contiguous states of the U.S. *(Adapted from Clarke, 1999.)*

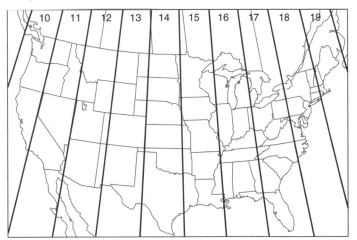

recorded in meters north of the equator for the northern hemisphere. The UTM divides the Earth north-south into 20 zones of latitude, starting at the equator. These zones encompass 8 degrees each except for the most northerly and southerly which are 12 degrees in height. Because of severe distortion near the poles, the UTM projection is intended for mapping only between 84 degrees north and 80 degrees south.

14-9 The State Plane Coordinate System   Much geographic information in the United States is referenced under the state plane coordinate system (SPCS). The SPCS is used for legal descriptions of property and for engineering applications where highly accurate surveying is required. Based on both the transverse Mercator and the Lambert projections, the SPCS typically uses units of feet (although metric versions are now available). SPCS consists of a different map projection for each state. States are divided into a varying number of zones (typically 1 to 5), depending on size, with each zone having an arbitrarily determined origin. Because relatively small zones are projected, the distortion is minimal and can be determined accurately. A disadvantage, however, is a lack of universality and difficulty in matching data across state lines.

GIS DATA SOURCES, ENTRY, AND QUALITY

14-10 Deriving Digital Maps   To use a GIS, all data must be converted to digital form. Map information is typically in analog form, that is, it exists as drawings on paper. Such map information is converted to a set of numbers for use in a computerized GIS through a process called *digitizing,* which can be defined as the conversion of spatial information into computer-readable form. Studies have shown that between 60 and 90 percent of the time and money spent on a typical GIS project involves finding the right maps and converting them into computer readable form via digitizing. Fortunately this is a one-time cost for initial entry. To remain usable, the information must be kept up-to-date, but updating costs are relatively small compared to establishing the original data base. Furthermore, maps in digital form can be used repeatedly in a GIS for many different projects. Fundamental information like road networks, river and stream patterns, soils, landforms, etc. are required for a host of resource analysis objectives.

Digital data for use in GISs can be acquired in a variety of ways. The data may exist in digital form, and it is a matter of finding or buying it. Often the data exist, but only in analog form, and it must be converted to digital format by digitizing. In some cases, maps of interest do not exist so one must use remote sensing data, aerial photography (Chap. 13), or field data collection by surveyors or GPS (Global Positioning Systems, Chap. 4) to derive the initial map. Even when the maps of interest are in digital form, they may not be current or may not have all of the features needed. Consequently, most GIS projects involve digitizing at least a portion of the spatial information required.

14-11 Existing Map Data   There are many sources for paper maps, including map libraries, federal, state, and local government agencies, and commercial companies. Books, such as *The Map Catalog* (Makower, 1986), *Maps for America* (Thompson, 1987), and *Inventory of World Topographic Mapping* (Böhme, 1989, 1991, 1993), are another place to locate map information. The U.S. federal government is a major source of digital map data. While many U.S. federal agencies create and distribute digital maps, there are three primary sources for GIS applications, namely, the U.S. Geological Survey (USGS), which is part of the Department of the Interior, the U.S. Bureau of the Census, and the National Oceanic and Atmospheric Administration (NOAA), both of which are part of the Department of Commerce.

In addition to library sources, computer network services can be used to search for map information. Many major providers of map information make their data available through the World Wide Web, a network of file servers available over the Internet.[1] These data can often be acquired over the Internet at little or no cost. In cases for which information is not yet available for retrieval over computer networks, it is available on CD-ROM or other storage media. In obtaining public data from government sources, it is important to note the "metadata" (documentation about the data) that agencies are required to supply with digital spatial data. The U.S. government established a "national spatial data infrastructure" (NSDI) to serve as a clearinghouse for federally-produced spatial data, and it serves as a rich source of material for GIS applications.

There are obvious cost and time advantages to obtaining existing digital data when possible. However, existing data sources are seldom adequate for all aspects of typical GIS applications. Hence, geocoding information from nondigital sources, formulating needed map information from remotely sensed data, and obtaining spatial information in the field remain important aspects of GIS activities.

14-12 Digitizing and Scanning   In the early GIS packages, maps were encoded and entered by hand (manual entry by keyboard is still done on occasion). With the advent of special-purpose digitizing hardware, most geocoding is now done by computer. The two most commonly used technologies for getting maps into the computer are semiautomated digitizing (or, *digitizing*) and *scanning*.

Digitizing is somewhat like tracing. It involves a digitizing tablet (rather like a drafting table) to which the map is fixed, and a stylus or cursor is used by a human operator to select coordinates of features to be extracted from the map (Fig. 14-8). The digitizing table electronically encodes the position of the cursor. The efficiency and accuracy of digitizing depends on the quality of the digitizing software, the skill of the operator, and the complexity of the map being digitized. Feature

---

[1]World Wide Web addresses: USGS http://www.usgs.gov; Bureau of the Census http://www. census.gov; and NOAA http://www.noaa.gov.

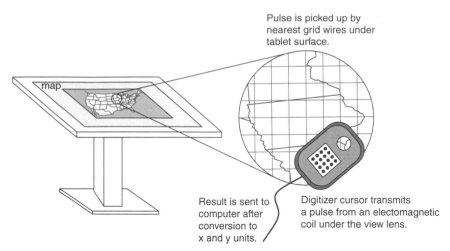

Pulse is picked up by nearest grid wires under tablet surface.

Result is sent to computer after conversion to x and y units.

Digitizer cursor transmits a pulse from an electomagnetic coil under the view lens.

FIGURE 14-8
Digitizing is a common method for converting maps to digital format for use in GIS. *(Adaped from Clarke, 1999.)*

labels or other attributes of the feature must be assigned, and the digitized data must be thoroughly edited to insure good quality information.

Automated digitizing is usually referred to as *scanning.* Optical scanners, which are somewhat analogous to copying machines, and specialized software are used to convert information from paper maps (or film negatives, Mylar separations, or other materials that were used in the map production) to digital computer files. Large, high-quality scanners, called *drum scanners,* are most commonly used for maps. Drum scanners can receive an entire sheet map and scan it at a fine resolution. As resolution technology improves, desktop scanners are becoming more widely used as geocoding devices. Typically, desktop scanners can only process a section of a map at a time. Although desktop scanners may lack the resolution or, more commonly, the format size required for most GIS applications, the technology is certain to advance, making them feasible for a wide range of digitizing uses. Following scanning, visual inspection and editing is required to ensure that errors have not been introduced due to the resolution or color separation limitations of the optical scanner.

14-13 Field and Image Data An increasing amount of data for GIS projects comes from a combination of field data, global positioning data, and imagery (Clarke, 1999). Field data are collected using standard surveying methods, recorded in notebooks, and then entered into a computer program to convert the measurements into eastings, northings, and elevations. The first stage in the surveying process, that of setting the control, is usually done by locating a USGS bench mark or by using GPS equipment. Many mapping-grade GPS receivers can make conversions into any of several coordinate systems, and most can download data directly to a computer.

Imagery data, such as aerial photographs or satellite images, are now commonly used for input layers to a GIS. Remotely sensed data have several obvious advantages for use in GIS. Satellite systems, such as U.S. LANDSAT and French SPOT, acquire data for large areas in a short time span, thus providing essentially uniform coverage with respect to time and level of detail. Satellite-acquired data are in digital form and provided in standard formats. Further, these data are available for most of the Earth's land areas and are relatively inexpensive.

There remain problems and difficulties with imagery data, however. Images may not be available for the desired dates or seasons, classifications needed to enter the data into a GIS may not be completely reliable, and the level of detail in the satellite data may not match that from other sources. Nevertheless, remote sensing is a vital and important data source for GIS activities.

Campbell (1996) outlined the following procedures for incorporating remotely sensed data into a GIS:

1 Manual interpretation of aerial photographs or satellite images produces a map, or set of maps, that depicts boundaries between a set of categories (e.g., soil or land-use classes). Then these boundaries are digitized to provide the digital files suitable for entry into the GIS.

2 Digital remote sensing data are analyzed or classified using automated methods to produce conventional (paper) maps and images, which are then digitized for entry into the GIS.

3 Digital remote sensing data are analyzed or classified using automated methods and then retained in digital format for entry into the GIS, using reformatting or geometric corrections as required.

4 Digital remote sensing data are entered directly in their raw form as data for the GIS (usually used only as a last resort, after other measures have proved impractical).

The most satisfactory approach to take will depend on the specific requirements of a particular project, the time allowed, and the kinds of equipment and amount of financial resources available.

14-14 Errors and Accuracy   Information in GIS is subject to error. The term "error" is used here to mean both "mistakes" in terms of measurements and data recording and "variation" in a statistical sense. Accuracy of position means that features are plotted on the map close to their correct location in the real world. It is important to understand the nature of errors in spatial data and the effect they may have on the quality of maps and analyses made with GIS.

Error is introduced into the layers of geographic information systems in a variety of ways. A brief description of some of the more important sources of error follows:

- Positional errors occur when the coordinates of a map feature differ from the true geographic coordinates of that feature. Additional positional errors can be introduced into GIS maps when paper maps are digitized.
- Boundary errors may be introduced when a line is drawn between polygons. Even when the boundary is sharp, there can be considerable uncertainty in its location when it is transferred to a digital map. Error problems are exacerbated when boundaries are not sharply delineated (such as the transition between forest types).
- Classification errors result when a point or polygon is not identified correctly. Remotely sensed data are especially prone to problems of incorrect classification.

Another aspect of data accuracy is the attribute information. A map could be perfectly acceptable as far as spatial relationships and appearance are concerned, but the attributes of the features could be in error. In some instances, it may be possible to treat this type of error as a misclassification. Attributes may be derived from published sources, in which case it may not be possible to estimate the error. In other cases, attributes are estimated by standard sampling procedures, and the error for individual polygons, say, can be estimated.

In order to use GIS intelligently, one must know and understand the amount and distribution of error in the GIS database. The quality of the base data, along with the method and process of geocoding the data for entry into the GIS, are the primary sources of error. Errors generally accumulate through the stages of data acquisition, storage, retrieval, overlays, and analysis. An appreciation for and understanding of error is essential for appropriate use of GIS information.

GIS ANALYSIS FUNCTIONS

14-15 Analysis—The Power of GIS   Geographic information systems provide an efficient and flexible means of generating maps, but the power of GIS lies in its analysis capabilities. Much of the initial time and expense in developing a GIS involves developing the various data layers. Once these data layers are in the system, maps can be readily produced, but the unique capability of GIS is in the analyses that can be performed to provide useful information for resource management decisions. A GIS provides information on what is present and where it is located; but, more importantly, it can be used to determine what is where. Maps provide information on where features are located, and a powerful analysis tool is created by linking spatial locations to information on the attributes of features.

To handle the data in a GIS, a model must be adopted. A data model is a logical construct for the storage and retrieval of information. A GIS must have two data models, a map data model and an attribute data model, and a link between them to tie the attributes and geography together. Database Management Systems (DBMS) have been developed for the sorting, reordering, subsetting, and searching functions required to manage large files. All GISs contain an internal DBMS,

TABLE 14-2
A CLASSIFICATION OF GIS ANALYSIS FUNCTIONS

1. **Maintenance and Analysis of the Spatial Data**
   A. Format Transformations
   B. Geometric Transformations
   C. Transformations Between Map Projections
   D. Conflation
   E. Edge Matching
   F. Editing of Graphic Elements
   G. Line Coordinate Thinning
2. **Maintenance and Analysis of the Attribute Data**
   A. Attribute Editing Functions
   B. Attribute Query Functions
3. **Integrated Analysis of Spatial and Attribute Data**
   A. Retrieval/Classification/Measurement
      i. Retrieval
      ii. Classification
      iii. Measurement
   B. Overlay Operations
   C. Neighborhood Operations
      i. Search
      ii. Line-in-Polygon and Point-in-Polygon
      iii. Topographic Functions
      iv. Thiessen Polygons
      v. Interpolation
      vi. Contour Generation
   D. Connectivity Functions
      i. Contiguity Measures
      ii. Proximity
      iii. Network
      iv. Spread
      v. Seek
      vi. Intervisibility
      vii. Illumination
      viii. Perspective View
4. **Output Formatting**
   A. Map Annotation
   B. Text Labels
   C. Texture Patterns and Line Styles
   D. Graphic Symbols

Source: Adapted from Aronoff, 1989.

or they can be linked to a DBMS. At present, most GIS packages employ what is called a relational DBMS, which allows multiple files with dissimilar attribute structures to be connected by a common key attribute.

14-16 Spatial Analysis Functions GIS techniques provide a host of sophisticated analysis functions. Aronoff (1989) classified these analysis functions into four groups: (1) maintenance and analysis of the spatial data, (2) maintenance and analysis of the attribute data, (3) integrated analysis of spatial attribute data, and (4) output formatting. These major groups were further subdivided into types of functions (Table 14-2). The first two primary functions deal with maintaining the GIS data, and the fourth pertains to producing output from the system. The real power of GIS lies in the ability to integrate the analysis of spatial and attribute data.

14-17 Cartographic Modeling   The functions of a GIS can be brought together to perform "cartographic modeling." Cartographic modeling is a term coined to describe the use of basic GIS processes in a logical sequence to solve complex spatial problems. First developed to model land-use planning alternatives, cartographic modeling can be applied to any decision situation that requires integrated analysis of multiple geographically distributed factors. An example of a problem amenable to cartographic modeling would be the siting of a roadway through a national park.

Cartographic models are capable of dynamic simulations and provide spatial "what if" scenarios. Maps, not only of current conditions, but of possible future conditions, can be formulated by incorporating a means of projecting resource characteristics into the future. Forest growth models (Chap. 17), for example, might be linked with forest inventory information to project forest characteristics through time. Landscape-level impacts of implementing different management alternatives can be estimated through dynamic cartographic modeling.

The combination of GIS capabilities with timely and efficient resource inventories will play an increasingly important role in resource management decision making.

PROBLEMS

14-1 Suppose you are delineating soil series on maps of scale 1:20,000 by using an instrument with line width 0.05 inches. Calculate the ground distance to which the line width corresponds in (a) inches, (b) feet, and (c) meters.

14-2 Using the Internet, search for information about digital map data that are available online for your local area. Make an inventory of the data you were successful in locating, noting the source and cost of the data.

14-3 Assume that each cell in Figure 14-3 is 0.1 acres in size. Determine in acres and ha the (a) total represented, (b) area in forests, (c) area in croplands, and (d) area in rangelands.

14-4 How would you select a cell size for creating a raster-based data base for your state? List all of the factors that should be considered and recommend a cell size.

14-5 The likelihood that the information from combined, independent data layers is all correct can be calculated as the product of the probabilities of correct classification for each layer. Assume that the data classification in each layer is independent and that each layer can be classified with 90 percent accuracy. Estimate the proportion of maps that would be correctly classified if (a) two layers, (b) four layers, or (c) six layers of mapped data were used.

14-6 Investigate the different types of data base management systems (DBMS) that are available, and contrast and compare the different structures for GIS application purposes.

REFERENCES

Aronoff, S. 1989. *Geographic information systems: A management perspective.* WDL Publications, Ottawa, Ontario. 294 pp.

Berry, J. K. 1987. Fundamental operations in computer-assisted map analysis. *Int. J. Geogr. Inf. Syst.* **1:**119–136.

Böhme, R. 1989. *Inventory of world topographic mapping.* Vol. 1: Western Europe, North America and Australasia. International Cartographic Association/Elsevier Science Publishing Co., New York. 196 pp.

———. 1991. *Inventory of world topographic mapping.* Vol. 2: South America, Central America and Africa. International Cartographic Association/Elsevier Science Publishing Co., New York. 520 pp.

———. 1993. *Inventory of world topographic mapping.* Vol. 3: Eastern Europe, Asia, Oceania and Antarctia. International Cartographic Association/Elsevier Science Publishing Co., New York. 447 pp.

Bolstad, P. V., and Smith, J. L. 1992. Errors in GIS. *J. Forestry* **90:**21–26, 29.

Burrough, P. A., and McDonnel, R. A. 1998. *Principles of geographical information systems.* Oxford University Press, New York. 333 pp.

Campbell, J. 1993. *Map use and analysis,* 2d ed. Wm. C. Brown, Dubuque, IA. 429 pp.

Campbell, J. B. 1996. *Introduction to remote sensing,* 2d ed. The Guilford Press, New York. 622 pp.

Clarke, K. C. 1999. *Getting started with geographic information systems,* 2d ed. Prentice Hall, Upper Saddle River, N.J. 338 pp.

Congalton, R. G., and Green, K. 1992. The ABCs of GIS. *J. Forestry* **90:**13–20.

Faust, N. L., Anderson, W. H., and Starr, J. L. 1991. Geographic information systems and remote sensing future computing environment. *Photogram. Eng. Remote Sens.* **57:** 655–668.

Koeln, G. T., Cowardin, L. M., and Strong, L. L. 1996. Geographic information systems. Pp. 540–566 in *Research and management techniques for wildlife and habitats,* 5th ed., rev., T. A. Bookhout (ed.), The Wildlife Society, Bethesda, Md.

Makower, J. (ed.). 1986. *The map catalog.* Vintage Books, New York. 252 pp.

Reed, D. D., and Mroz, G. D. 1997. *Resource assessment in forested landscapes.* John Wiley & Sons, New York. 386 pp.

Thompson, M. M. 1987. *Maps for America,* 3d ed. U.S. Government Printing Office, U.S. Geological Survey, Washington, D.C. 265 pp.

Vitek, J. D., Walsh, S. J., and Gregory, M. S. 1984. Accuracy in geographic information systems: An assessment of inherent and operational errors. *Pecora* **9:**296–302.

Walsh, S. J., Lightfoot, D. R., and Butler, D. R. 1987. Recognition and assessment of error in geographic information systems. *Photogram. Eng. Remote Sens.* **53:**1,423–1,430.

CHAPTER 15

SITE, STOCKING, AND STAND DENSITY

15-1 The Concept of Site   In forestry terminology, *site* refers to the area in which a tree or a stand grows; the environment of a site determines the type and quality of the vegetation the area can carry. If required, site may be classified qualitatively into site *types,* by their climate, soil, and vegetation, or quantitatively into site *classes,* by their potential to produce primary wood products (Helms, 1998).

Insofar as foresters are concerned, the primary purposes of site measurement are (1) to identify the potential productivity of forest stands, both present and future, and (2) to provide a frame of reference for land management diagnosis and prescription. In the United States, most attention has been given to the first purpose, while little attention has specifically been directed toward the second (Jones, 1969).

Theoretically, it should be possible to measure site directly by analyzing the many factors affecting the productivity of forests, such as soil nutrients and moisture, temperature regimes, available light, topography, and so on. Although attempts at direct measurement of site have been made, such an approach may not be of immediate value to the practicing forester; consequently, indirect estimates of site are frequently employed.

15-2 Direct Measurement of Forest Productivity   When available, historical yield records of forest productivity provide a direct measure of site quality. Averaging productivity from multiple rotations of fully stocked stands of the desired species provides excellent information on given sites. Unfortunately, productivity data like these do not exist for most forest sites, and the actual yield can be affected by such factors as genetic composition, stand density, competing vegetation, pests, and the climate experienced during the period over which the growth was measured. Consequently, indirect methods of evaluating site quality are generally used. The most common indirect method for assessing site quality for wood-producing purposes involves measurement of tree heights on the site.

15-3 Tree Height as a Measure of Site Quality   Of all the commonly applied indirect measures of site, tree height in relation to tree age has been found the most practical, consistent, and useful indicator. Theoretically, height growth is sensitive to differences in site quality, little affected by varying density levels and species compositions, relatively stable under varying thinning intensities, and strongly correlated with volume. This measure of site is termed *site index.* Site index is the most widely accepted quantitative measure of site in the United States.

As generally applied, site index is estimated by determining the average total height and age of dominant and codominant trees in well-stocked, even-aged stands. When these two variables (total height and age) have been ascertained for a given species, they are used as coordinates for interpolating site index (height at a specified index age, such as 25, 50, or 100 years) from a specially prepared set of curves (Fig. 15-1) or for substitution into a site-index equation. Referring to Figure 15-1, if one measured a stand at age 20 with a height of 45 feet, the site index (height at age 50) is estimated to be 70 feet.

In preparing site-index curves for various species, either age at breast height or total age may be used as the independent variable. Site-index curves for plantations are generally based on number of years since planting as the age variable. Thus age can be obtained from planting records, eliminating the need for increment borings. For trees growing in natural stands, age at breast height is often preferable, because this is a standard point of tree-diameter measurement and a convenient height for making increment borings. When total age is used, it is necessary to estimate the number of years required for the tree to grow from seed to the height where an increment boring is made; this number, which is especially variable for more tolerant species, is then added to the annual ring count to obtain total age. Use of age at breast height in lieu of total age eliminates the need for such arbitrary correction factors.

15-4 Field Measurement of Site Index   To determine the site index of a forest stand, average total height and age are determined from measurements obtained from *site trees.* Site trees should meet certain specifications, such as being dominant or codominant and even-aged, showing no evidence of crown damage, disease, sweep, crook, forking, or prolonged suppression.

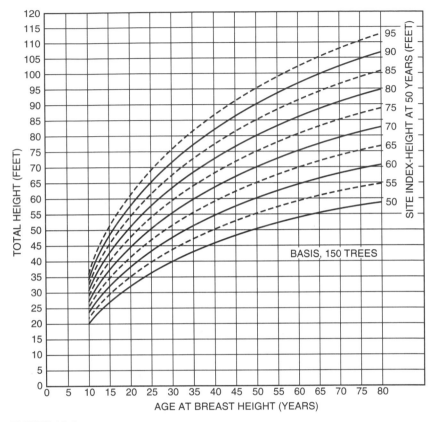

FIGURE 15-1
Site-index relationships for East Texas longleaf pine. The index age is 50 years. *(From Larson and Moehring, 1972.)*

Measurements of total height are commonly made with a hypsometer, while age may be determined by extracting an increment core. The number of trees measured depends upon the variability of total heights and ages in the stand being evaluated. The number of sampling units required to estimate total height and age for a given confidence interval and probability level can be determined by application of the formula for computing sampling intensity (Chap. 3). As an example, if the average total height is to be measured within ± 5 ft at a confidence probability of 95 percent (*t* value of 2) and a preliminary sample of five total-height measurements indicates a standard deviation of ± 7.5 ft, the required number of height measurements may be calculated as

$$n = \left[\frac{(2)(7.5)}{5} \right]^2 = 9 \text{ measurements}$$

For the site index to be expressed on a standard basis, an index age must be presumed. For most regions, the period in the life of the stand that approximates the culmination of mean annual growth (Chap. 16) in well-stocked stands has been selected as the index age. Accordingly, 100 years has been used for most western species and 50 years for eastern species. Site-index curves based on an index age of 25 years are available for plantations that are managed on rotations shorter than 50 years.

15-5 Construction of Site-Index Curves If one measures a stand that is at an index age, the average height of dominants and codominants is the site index. In most instances, however, stands measured are less than or greater than the index age. Consequently, a set of curves (Fig. 15-1) or an equation is needed to project the dominant stand height to the standard reference age.

Early site-index curves were constructed by graphical techniques. Data on heights and ages were collected from a variety of stands on different site-quality land and of varying ages. These paired height-age values were then plotted on graph paper, and a "guide" curve was drawn to depict the general trend in the data. All other site-index curves were then proportional to the guide curve. For example, if the guide curve passed through height 100 ft at index age (the "site-index-100 curve"), then the site-index-90 curve was drawn by multiplying values on the guide curve by 0.9, the site-index-110 curve by multiplying the guide curve by 1.1, etc. When such curves for different site-index classes are proportional, they are termed *anamorphic* (i.e., all curves have the same shape).

Anamorphic site-index curves are now constructed by regression techniques (Chap. 2). Plotting height over age for pure, even-aged stands results in a generally sigmoid shape; thus some transformation of the variables is needed if linear regression methods are applied. The most common transformation is

$$\ln H_d = b_0 + b_1 A^{-1}$$

This is a special case of the simple linear regression model

$$Y = b_0 + b_1 X$$

where Y is the logarithm of the height of dominants and codominants, H_d, and X is the reciprocal of stand age, A.

The guide curve for a set of anamorphic site-index curves can be established by fitting the model of the logarithm of the height and the reciprocal of age to data from stands of varying site qualities and ages. To avoid bias in the guide curve, it is important that, insofar as possible, all site-index classes of interest be represented approximately equally at all ages. If only poor-quality sites are sampled for the older ages, for example, the guide curve will tend to "flatten" too quickly and bias the entire family of site-index curves.

After the guide curve is estimated, an equation for site index as a function of measured age and height can be constructed by noting that when age is equal to index age A_i, height is equal to site index S; that is,

$$\ln S = b_0 + b_1 A_i^{-1}$$

This implies that

$$b_0 = \ln S - b_1 A_i^{-1}$$

Substituting the implied definition for b_0 into the original guide-curve equation results in

$$\begin{aligned} \ln H_d &= \ln S - b_1 A_i^{-1} + b_1 A^{-1} \\ &= \ln S + b_1 (A^{-1} - A_i^{-1}) \end{aligned}$$

This can be used to generate site-index curves, and the equation can be algebraically rearranged as

$$\ln S = \ln H_d - b_1 (A^{-1} - A_i^{-1})$$

This is the form used to estimate site index (height at index age) when age and height measurements are given.

Site-index curves constructed by the anamorphic method just described may not provide fully satisfactory results. The guide-curve technique is sound only if the average site quality in the sample data is approximately the same for all age classes. If the average site quality varies systematically with age, the guide curve will be biased. In many timber types, younger stands are associated with generally better sites, whereas older stands are concentrated on the poorer sites left to harvest last. When a negative age–site quality correlation exists in the data, the height-age guide curve will be biased—showing excessive growth at younger ages and insufficient growth at older ages. Because all site-index curves are proportional to the guide curve, if it is biased the entire family of anamorphic curves will be biased. Consequently the estimation of an unbiased guide curve is of primary importance when the anamorphic technique is applied to develop site-index curves.

Another weakness of anamorphic site-index curves is the assumption of a common shape for all site classes. For many species, the height-curve shape varies with site quality—higher-quality lands generally exhibit more pronounced sigmoid shapes and lower-quality lands produce height-growth patterns that are "flatter." Families of site-index curves that display differing shapes for different site-index classes are termed *polymorphic*. In recent years, polymorphic site-index curves have been constructed for many different species. When available, polymorphic curves generally reflect height-growth trends across a wide range of site qualities more accurately than anamorphic curves and, thus, are generally preferred.

When constructing polymorphic site-index equations, height is expressed as a function of age and some other variable(s) such as site index. For example, the following function, which describes height H_d as a function of stand age A and site index S, base age 50 years, was used to develop polymorphic site-index curves for eastern white pine (Beck, 1971b):

$$H_d = [63.36 + 0.68208S][1 - e^{(-0.01007 + 0.00030S)A}]^{1.9094}$$

It should be noted that, in application, most polymorphic curves require that one measure only the stand height and age in order to estimate site index.

15-6 Interspecies Site-Index Relationships   Direct application of the site-index method requires that suitable site trees of the species of interest be present. For situations in which this requirement is not met but there are suitable site trees of another species available for measurement, interspecies site-index relationships have been developed. An equation relating the site index of two species can be developed by measuring the site index on areas where site trees for both species occur together and then computing a regression to predict the site index of one species from that of the other.

Olson and Della-Bianca (1959) investigated site-index relationships among several species and species groups occurring in the Piedmont region of Virginia, North Carolina, and South Carolina. They related the site index of several species to that of yellow-poplar, which is a site-sensitive species. For example, Olson and Della-Bianca's regression equation to relate site index of black oak to that of yellow-poplar is

$$Y = 39.7 + 0.45X$$

where Y = site index of black oak (feet at base age 50 years)
    X = site index of yellow-poplar (feet at base age 50 years)

While equations relating site index between species have been useful in forest management, these predictions must be used with care. In order to develop equations relating the site index of two species, the species must be found together. Some species will occur together on certain site types but not on others. Data sets used to derive species site-index conversion equations, by necessity, only contain the types of sites where the two species naturally occur in mixture. Thus the regression equation computed from the data may not be applicable to sites where the species of interest is not present but the predictor species is.

15-7 Periodic Height Growth   An alternative to basing site-quality evaluation on current stand height is to use information on periodic height growth. The use of height growth for some relatively short period during the life of the stand to assess site quality is commonly referred to as the *growth-intercept method*. Growth-intercept values can be used directly as measures of site quality, but they are usually used to calculate site-index estimates. This approach was developed primarily for use in young stands because site-index curves have been found unreliable for juvenile stands. The growth-intercept method is most feasible for species that put on a single well-defined whorl of lateral branches each growing season.

The best indication of current growing conditions is current height increment, which may be discerned from measurement of the terminal leader (Spurr and Barnes, 1980). For taller trees, however, this can be a difficult and time-consuming task. Very early height growth can be greatly affected by herbaceous competition, and thus it would not be a useful indicator of site potential. For the middle part of the height-age curve, height growth is relatively constant; thus, it is this middle portion that is used when applying the growth-intercept approach. Although the details vary in the past applications, all growth-intercept methods involve the measurement of length of a specified number of successive annual internodes, beginning at some defined point on the stem. A growth-intercept definition applied in several instances "is the height growth for the 5-year period that begins when breast height is reached." However, Alban (1972) found that the precision of estimating site index for red pine was much improved by measuring the 5-year growth intercept beginning at 8 feet above ground rather than at breast height. Alban's growth-intercept equation, developed from natural stands of red pine in Minnesota, follows:

$$SI = 32.54 + 3.434X$$

where SI = site index (feet at base age 50 years)
  X = 5-year growth intercept in feet (height growth for the 5-year period that begins from the first whorl above 8 ft from ground level)

In application, a sample of trees is selected and growth intercept is measured on the sample trees; then the average growth intercept is computed and substituted into the site-index prediction equation.

In addition to having been found more useful than total height for estimating site index in young stands of certain species, growth intercept has the advantage of eliminating the need to measure age. Age measurements can be costly to obtain and are subject to error. The growth-intercept method also eliminates the need to measure total tree heights, which in dense stands can be a difficult and time-consuming measurement. The method suffers from the disadvantages that short-term climatic fluctuations may render the results inaccurate and that sometimes the early growth of a stand does not accurately reflect later growth.

15-8 Physical-Factors Approach   Foresters often need an estimate of site quality on areas where forest stands do not presently exist or where the extant stands do not contain suitable site trees. In these situations an alternative to measuring tree heights and ages is necessary. One alternative that has received widespread attention involves using environmental factors (e.g., topographic and/or soils variables) to predict site quality (generally expressed as the site index for a particular species of interest). A productivity-estimation method based on the relatively permanent features of soil and topography can be used on any site, regardless of the presence, absence, or condition of the vegetation.

The environmental-factors approach typically involves measuring site index and topographic and soils variables in a sample of stands throughout some defined physiographic region and climatic zone. (Climatic variables are sometimes included as well.) The measured site index is then related to the topographic and soils variables by means of linear regression analysis. The prediction equation developed from data from sites where suitable stands for site-index determination are found is then applied to sites where site index cannot be measured because of a lack of suitable site trees. While this approach has a strong intuitive appeal, validation of the resultant equations has often shown that the site-index predictions are not reliable—especially if the equation is applied outside the geographic region in which it was developed.

An example of the physical-factors approach is the equation developed by Sprackling (1973) to estimate the site index of Engelmann spruce growing on granitic soils in southern Wyoming and northern Colorado. The following soil and topographic factors were selected for possible inclusion in the regression equation to estimate site index: (1) aspect, (2) slope percent, (3) slope position, (4) elevation, (5) soil depth to the C horizon, and (6) texture of the B horizon. Analysis indicated that two variables can be used to estimate the site index of Engelmann spruce (Fig. 15-2):

$$Y = -106.63509 + 62.46021X_1 + 809{,}396.2X_2$$
$$R^2 = 0.646; \ S_{y \cdot x} = 9.00 \text{ ft}$$

where Y = site index (feet at base age 100 years)

X_1 = logarithm base 10 of soil depth in inches to the top of the C horizon

X_2 = 1/elevation in ft

R^2 = coefficient of determination

$S_{y \cdot x}$ = standard error of estimate

15-9 Indicator-Plant Approach   The presence, abundance, and size of understory plants can serve as useful indicators of forest site quality. While understory plants are often more affected by overstory density and composition, site history, and localized disturbance than overstory trees, they also tend to recover from disturbance more quickly. In cases where the understory plants have a relatively narrow ecological tolerance, they can serve as useful indicators of growing conditions for trees.

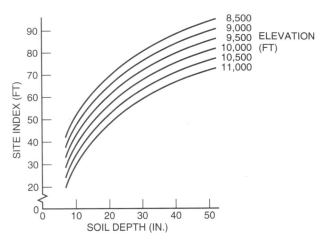

FIGURE 15-2
Site index for Engelmann spruce on granitic soils in northern
Colorado and southern Wyoming in relation to soil depth and
elevation. *(From Sprackling, 1973.)*

Understory plant communities of northern coniferous forests are relatively simple; only a few plant species occur in the understory, and communities are distinct and easily recognized (Carmean, 1975). Consequently, the indicator-plant approach has been found more applicable in the forests of northern Europe and in Canada than in other areas. Although attempts have been made to develop indicator-plant methods in more southerly latitudes of North America, the results have not been very successful because the sites have often been repeatedly disturbed and there is a complex variety of understory plant communities.

In some instances the indicator-plant approach has been combined with the height-age concept, and site-index curves have been developed for distinct understory vegetal types. Thus, despite the limitations and complexities of applying the technique, indicator plants can supplement other site-quality evaluation methods.

Practicing foresters should be aware of indicator-plant/site-quality relationships, since this information can provide a quick appraisal or useful supplementary information for assessing site quality. However, the following limitations must be kept in mind: (1) the method permits site evaluation only in relative or qualitative terms, (2) the understory characteristics are generally quite sensitive to disturbances such as fire or grazing, (3) understory vegetation generally reflects only the fertility of the topmost horizons of the soil profile—deeper horizons may have little impact on understory vegetation but greatly influence site quality for tree growth—and (4) a sound background in plant ecology is a prerequisite for reliable classifications.

15-10 Limitations of Site Index The main drawbacks that have been cited regarding the use of site index as a measure of forest productivity are as follows:

1 Exact stand age is often difficult to determine, and small errors can cause relatively large changes in the site-index estimate.

2 The concept of site index is not well-suited for uneven-aged stands, areas of mixed-species composition, or open lands.

3 Effects of stand density are not considered except by arbitrary selection of site trees in well-stocked stands that have been unaffected by past suppression. Other variables associated with stand volume (i.e., dbh and stem form) are not directly taken into account. As a result, an index based on total height and age alone may not provide a valid estimate of the growing capacity for a particular site.

4 Site index is not a constant; instead, it may change periodically due to environmental and climatic variations or management activities.

5 Except in limited instances, the site-index value for one species cannot be translated into a usable index for a different species on the same site (Doolittle, 1958).

In spite of these limitations, site index is a useful tool because it provides a simple numerical value that is easily measured and understood by the practicing forester. Its use will apparently be continued until the day when the varied factors affecting the productivity of forests can be reduced to an equally simple and quantitative measurement.

STOCKING AND STAND DENSITY

15-11 Definitions   Although stocking and stand density are terms that are often applied interchangeably, the two terms are not synonymous. *Stand density* denotes a quantitative measurement of the stand, whereas *stocking* refers to the adequacy of a given stand density to meet some management objective. Accordingly, stands may be referred to as understocked, fully stocked, or overstocked. A stand that is "overstocked" for one management objective could be "understocked" for another.

Stand density is a quantitative term describing the degree of stem crowding within a stocked area; it can be expressed in absolute or relative terms. Absolute measures of density are determined directly from a given stand without reference to any other stand. For example, number of trees per acre is an absolute measure that expresses the density of trees on an area basis. Relative density is based on a selected standard density. If, for instance, "fully stocked" is defined on a basal-area basis, the ratio of the measured basal area in a stand to that of the fully stocked ideal is a relative measure of stand density. The problem of what constitutes full stocking makes application of relative density measures difficult.

15-12 Measures of Stocking   The main difficulty arising from the application of stocking concepts is that of deciding just what should constitute full stocking for a particular species on a given site. As outlined by Bickford et al. (1957), the stocking that results in maximum yield is the ideal that forest managers often strive to attain. Although stocking can also be specified in terms of the capacity of an area to support trees, most foresters think of stocking in terms of "best growth" rather than as a measure of site occupation.

As a holdover from European forestry practices, stands that are fully stocked have also been referred to as *normal* stands. The theory was developed that maximum volume increment would be obtained with full or normal stocking. Thus an ideal and regulated normal forest would be composed of a normal distribution of age classes, normal growing stock, and, consequently, a normal increment. In such a hypothetical forest, tree crowns are fitted together so that no sunlight is wasted, and each crown is matched with a root system that fully utilizes the soil (Bickford et al., 1957).

As a follow-up to the foregoing concept, normal yield tables were compiled to describe the expected production of normal forests (Chap. 17). Such tables were based on the "average best," pure, even-aged stands that could be located for various species and site conditions. In brief, the normal forest represented a paradox— a goal to be sought by forest managers, but one that was both unrealistic and unattainable, if not undesirable.

Fortunately, the elusive concept of normality has largely been erased from American forest management. Even under the hazardous assumption that a normal forest can be attained (and recognized when existent), it has become increasingly apparent that so-called full stocking does not necessarily imply maximum volume growth. Furthermore, the utility of normal yield tables is severely handicapped by the fact that no reliable methods are available for predicting yields of nonnormal or understocked stands.

Stocking levels are of prime concern to the forest manager because controlled changes in these levels may allow the forester to shorten or lengthen the rotation, favor desired species, and maximize the yield of selected timber products. Although the extremes of stocking can be easily recognized, full stocking can only be defined as a closed canopy stand that represents the "average best" to be found. Understocked stands are characterized by trees of rough form, excessive taper, and a high live-crown ratio. Overstocked stands may represent a stagnated condition, with trees exhibiting a low live-crown ratio and numerous dead stems. In both instances, the result is a reduction in net volume increment of wood products of interest from the "fully stocked" ideal.

Because of difficulties with defining stocking in a forest management context, quantitative measures of stand density are generally used to derive silvicultural prescriptions and to predict growth and yield.

15-13 Basal Area per Acre   Because it is objective, easily understood, and simple to measure by point-sampling techniques, basal area (BA) per acre provides a logical expression of stand density. Stand BA is the cross-sectional area (in square feet at dbh) of all stems, or of some specified portion of the stand, expressed on a per-acre basis. In countries that employ the metric system, BA is stated in square meters per ha.

Stand BA is highly correlated with the volume and growth of forest stands. Numerous variable-density yield tables have been derived by regression analysis by using the variables of BA per acre, site index, and stand age for a given species. In addition, many silvicultural considerations, such as thinning intensity, are commonly based on B-A measurements.

15-14 Trees per Acre As an expression of stand density, number of trees per acre has limited value in natural stands, but it has been extensively used in planted stands. Many of the variable-density yield tables for planted stands are based on number of trees per unit area, and silvicultural prescriptions for plantations are often made in terms of tree numbers rather than BA per acre.

15-15 Stand-Density Index Measures of density based on the two component parts of BA—number of trees per unit area and diameter of the tree of average BA—have been called *stand-density indices* (Spurr, 1952). In 1933 Reineke pointed out that plotting the logarithm of number of trees per acre against the logarithm of average diameter of fully stocked stands generally resulted in a straight-line relationship. He also found that the same slope could, in most cases, be used to define the limits of maximum stocking. This negatively sloping line, termed the *reference curve,* was expressed by

$$\log N = -1.605 \log D + k$$

where N = number of trees per acre
D = diameter of tree of average BA
k = a constant varying with species

In this section, all logarithms are base 10 and are denoted as log.
By definition, when D equals 10 in., log N equals log SDI (where SDI is the stand-density index); that is,

$$\log \text{SDI} = -1.605(1) + k$$

which implies that

$$k = \log \text{SDI} + 1.605$$

Substituting the implied definition for k into the reference-curve formula gives

$$\log N = \log \text{SDI} + 1.605 - 1.605 \log D$$

which can be rearranged as

$$\log \text{SDI} = \log N + 1.605 \log D - 1.605$$

to provide an expression for computing stand-density index from number of trees per acre and diameter of the tree of average BA.

One might assume that a stand with BA 120 sq ft and 480 trees per acre is measured. The diameter of the tree of average basal area D is

$$\sqrt{\frac{120/480}{0.005454}} = 6.77 \text{ in.}$$

Substituting into the stand-density index formula gives

$$\begin{aligned} \log \text{SDI} &= \log (480) + 1.605 \log (6.77) - 1.605 \\ &= 2.4093 \\ \text{SDI} &= 257 \end{aligned}$$

Stand-density index is reasonably well-correlated with stand volume and growth, and several variable-density yield tables have been constructed using it. However, in most cases BA is fully as satisfactory as stand-density index, and because it is more simply obtained, it is preferred as a measure of density.

15-16 3/2 Law of Self-Thinning   The so-called 3/2 law of self-thinning, like Reineke's stand-density index, is based on the concept of a maximum size-density relationship. In the case of the 3/2 law of self-thinning, the logarithm of mean tree volume or weight is plotted against the logarithm of the number of trees per unit area. For pure, even-aged stands that are sufficiently crowded such that competition-induced mortality ("self-thinning") is occurring, the slope of the line of logarithm of mean volume versus logarithm of trees per unit area has been found to be approximately $-3/2$, but the intercept varies by species. That is,

$$\log \overline{V} = - 3/2 \log N + a$$

where $\overline{V}$ = mean tree volume
   N = number of trees per unit area (acre or ha)
   a = a constant varying with species

Obviously, the 3/2 law of self-thinning is closely related to the stand-density index—in fact, the two can be shown to be mathematically equivalent. Reineke's stand-density index was developed with log N on the left-hand side of the equation. Rearranging the 3/2 relationship with log N on the left-hand side gives

$$-3/2 \log N = \log \overline{V} - a$$

Assuming that mean tree volume is proportional to the diameter of the tree of average BA raised to the power of 2.4 (Bredenkamp and Burkhart, 1990), that is,

$$\overline{V} = c\overline{D}^{2.4}$$

where c is a constant, and substituting the definition for $\overline{V}$ into the rearranged equation for the 3/2 relationship, one obtains

$$-3/2 \log N = \log c + 2.4 \log \overline{D} - a$$

Multiplying the preceding equation by $-2/3$ and combining the constants into a single term, designated k, results in

$$\log N = -1.6 \log \overline{D} + k$$

which is the stand-density index reference line.

Although the two concepts are mathematically equivalent, due to measurement considerations and historical precedent the stand-density index has been applied widely in forestry, whereas the 3/2 law of self-thinning has been utilized prevalently by plant ecologists. There are examples of applications of the 3/2 relationship in forestry, such as the stand-density management diagrams for plantations of coastal Douglas-fir developed by Drew and Flewelling (1979).

15-17 Relative Spacing   The average distance between trees divided by the average height of the dominant canopy has been termed *relative spacing*. Assuming square spacing, the average distance between trees can be computed as the square root of the number of square feet per acre (43,560) divided by the number of trees per acre. This average distance between trees in feet is then divided by the average height of the dominant canopy in feet to compute relative spacing. In formula form, relative spacing (RS) is computed as

$$RS = \frac{\sqrt{43,560/N}}{H_d}$$

where N = number of trees per acre
$\quad H_d$ = average height of the dominant canopy, ft

The comparable formula in metric units is

$$RS = \frac{\sqrt{10,000/N}}{H_d}$$

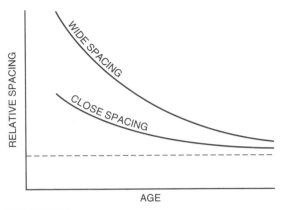

FIGURE 15-3
Time trends of relative spacing in stands of different
density. *(Adapted from Clutter et al., 1983.)*

where N = number of trees per ha
H_d = average height of the dominant canopy, m

The constant 10,000 is the number of square meters per ha. Because RS is a unit-less number, its value will be the same for any given stand regardless of whether English or metric units are used.

For even-aged stands, relative spacing initially drops rapidly; then it levels off at a lower limit (Fig. 15-3). After reaching the lower limit, RS will increase some-what if the stand is carried to an advanced age. The lower limit of relative spacing is fairly constant for a given species regardless of the site quality and the initial density. Loblolly pine, for example, achieves a minimum relative spacing of ap-proximately 0.15 (Lemin and Burkhart, 1983), whereas *Eucalyptus grandis* reaches a much lower value of around 0.05 (Bredenkamp and Burkhart, 1990).

Although it may not be immediately obvious, relative spacing is closely related to stand-density index. Height has been found to be proportional to diameter raised to the power of 0.8 (Curtis, 1970); that is,

$$H = aD^{0.8}$$

Assuming that the height of the dominant canopy (H_d) can be related to the quad-ratic mean diameter (D) by the preceding relationship, then H_d in the relative spac-ing formula can be replaced by $aD^{0.8}$, giving

$$RS = \frac{\sqrt{b/N}}{aD^{0.8}}$$

where b is an appropriate constant (43,560 or 10,000). After combining the constants b and a into a single constant (denoted c), the RS formula can be rewritten as

$$RS = \sqrt{cN^{-1}} D^{-0.8}$$

Squaring both sides gives

$$RS^2 = cN^{-1}D^{-1.6}$$

Taking the logarithm of both sides yields

$$2 \log RS = \log c - \log N - 1.6 \log D$$

Rearranging the above equation gives

$$\log N = \log c - 2 \log RS - 1.6 \log D$$

If RS is at or near its lower limit, it can be assumed constant, and the terms $\log c - 2 \log RS$ can be set equal to a constant called k, giving

$$\log N = -1.6 \log D + k$$

which is, of course, the stand-density index reference line.

Relative spacing has been found useful for predicting mortality and for deriving thinning schedules (Wilson, 1979).

15-18 Crown Competition Factor   Developed by Krajicek, Brinkman, and Gingrich (1961), crown competition factor (CCF) is a measure of stand density rather than of crown cover. CCF reflects the area available to the average tree in a stand in relation to the maximum area it could use if it were open-grown.

To compute CCF values, the crown-width/dbh relationship for open-grown trees of the species of interest must be established. Generally, a simple linear regression of the form

$$CW = b_0 + b_1 \, dbh$$

suffices to establish this relationship. Alexander (1971) computed the following equation for open-grown Engelmann spruce trees in Colorado and southern Wyoming:

$$CW = 4.344 + 1.029 \, dbh$$

where CW is in feet and dbh is in inches.

Assuming that the crowns of open-grown trees are circular in shape, the maximum crown area (MCA), expressed as percent of an acre, that can be occupied by the crown of a tree with a specified bole diameter is computed as

$$\text{MCA} = \frac{\pi(\text{CW})^2(100)}{(4)(43,560)} = 0.0018(\text{CW})^2$$

Inserting the equation for Engelmann spruce results in

$$\text{MCA} = 0.0018(4.344 + 1.029 \text{ dbh})^2$$
$$= 0.0340 + 0.0161 \text{ dbh} + 0.0019 \text{ dbh}^2$$

CCF for a stand is computed from a stand table by summing the MCA values for each diameter class and dividing by the area in acres. In formula form, the expression for CCF for this example is

$$\text{CCF} = \frac{1}{a}(0.0340 \, \Sigma \, n_i + 0.0161 \, \Sigma \, \text{dbh}_i n_i + 0.0019 \, \Sigma \, \text{dbh}_i^2 n_i)$$

where a = plot or stand size, acres
$\quad n_i$ = number of trees in ith dbh class
dbh_i = midpoint of ith dbh class, in.

As an example, the following stand table resulted from the measurement of three $\frac{1}{10}$-acre plots (i.e., $a = 0.3$ acre):

dbh	n_i	$\text{dbh}_i n_i$	$\text{dbh}_i^2 n_i$
4	50	200	800
5	45	225	1,125
6	43	258	1,548
7	20	140	980
8	17	136	1,088
9	11	99	891
10	5	50	500
Total	191	1,108	6,932

CCF would be computed as

$$\text{CCF} = \frac{1}{0.3}[0.0340(191) + 0.0161(1,108) + 0.0019(6,932)]$$
$$= 125$$

Although not as widely used as BA, CCF has proved useful in comparing different measures of stand density, and it has been found to be highly correlated with growth and yield for various species.

15-19 Stocking Guides   Measures of stand density have been used to derive stocking charts. These charts, or guides, are based on the precept that gross increment varies little over a fairly wide range of stand density. The U.S. Forest Service, and many other organizations, has adopted the basic approach of Gingrich (1967) when developing stocking guides for timber management purposes.

As an example, a stocking guide for eastern white pine is presented in Figure 15-4. This stocking guide, like many others, is a nomogram depicting the relationship between basal area, trees per acre, and the quadratic mean diameter at breast height. On this chart, the A curve is considered the upper limit in stocking for practical management. The B curve represents minimum stocking for full utilization of the site. Stands above the A curve are considered overstocked, stands between the A and B curves are deemed adequately stocked, and stands below the B curve are regarded understocked (Philbrook, Barrett, and Leak, 1973).

Stocking charts can be used to guide thinning schedules. For instance, stands might be considered for thinning when stocking approaches the A curve. Stocking after thinning should be near the B curve. For stands at or above the A curve, it may be best to reduce the growing stock down near the B curve in several successive

FIGURE 15-4
Stocking guide for nearly pure even-aged white pine stands in the northeastern United States. *(Adapted from Philbrook, Barrett, and Leak, 1973.)*

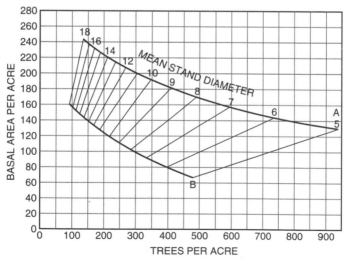

thinnings. While stocking charts do not define thinning schedules, they have been found useful for focusing attention on relationships between stand density and tree size. Also, there are no time dimensions on stocking charts of the type described here. However, if growth relationships are available (such as by application of growth models, Chap. 17), one can inscribe lines on stocking charts that describe the development and thinning of a stand over time.

15-20 Measures of Point Density   The stand-density measures discussed thus far are aimed at providing an estimate of the "average" competition level in stands. Point-density measures attempt to quantify the competition level at a given point or tree in the stand. These competition indices provide an estimate of the degree to which growth resources (e.g., light, water, nutrients, and physical growing space) may be limited by the number, size, and proximity of neighbors. The actual competition processes among trees are much more complex than can be described by a reasonably simple mathematical index. However, these indices have been found useful for predicting tree mortality and growth.

A large number of competition indices have been developed. Three classes or types of competition indices described here are (1) area-overlap measurement, (2) distance-weighted size ratio indices, and (3) area-available (or polygon) indices.

Area-overlap measures are based on the concept that there is a competition-influence zone around each tree. Typically, this area over which the tree is assumed to compete for site resources is represented by a circle whose radius is a function of tree size. The competitive stress experienced by a given tree is assumed to be a function of the extent to which its competition circle overlaps those of neighboring trees (Fig. 15-5). Various definitions of the area of influence, the measure of overlap, and the use of weights when summing areas of overlap have led to a large number of point-density expressions, although all are conceptually

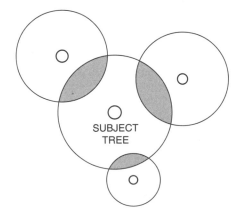

FIGURE 15-5
An illustration of the competition zone overlap used in the definition of point-density measures. *(Adapted from Clutter et al., 1983.)*

similar. An example of the area overlap type of point-density measure is the competition index proposed by Gerrard (1969):

$$CI_i = \frac{1}{A_i} \sum_{j=1}^{n} a_j$$

where CI_i = competition index for subject tree i
   A_i = area of competition circle for subject tree i
   n = number of competitors
   a_j = area of overlap of the jth competitor

The basic premise of Gerrard's index is that the competitive stress sustained by a tree is directly proportional to the area of overlap of its competition circle with those of its neighbors and inversely proportional to the area of its own competition circle.

   Competition measures based on distance-weighted size ratios involve the sum of the ratios between the size of each competitor to the subject tree, weighted by a function of the distance between the competing trees. The most common measure of tree size is dbh, but other measures (e.g., height, crown size) have also been employed. The index developed by Hegyi (1974), and modified by Daniels (1976) to use point-sampling concepts in the definition of competitors, provides an example of this type of point-density measure:

$$CI_i = \sum_{j=1}^{n} \frac{D_j/D_i}{DIST_{ij}}$$

where CI_i = competition index of the ith subject tree
   n = number of competitors (defined by a fixed-radius circle centered at the subject tree or by the number of trees "in" with a fixed BAF sweep with the vertex of the angle centered at the ith tree)
   D_j = dbh of the jth competitor
   D_i = dbh of the ith subject tree
   $DIST_{ij}$ = distance between subject tree i and the jth competitor

From the formulation of this index, it is clear that relatively large trees close to the subject tree are assumed to exert more competitive influence than smaller trees that are farther away.

   The third general type of point-density measure that will be presented is based on area available to the subject tree. This approach involves constructing polygons around the subject tree by connecting the perpendicular bisectors of the distance between the subject tree and its competitors (Fig. 15-6). The polygon area for each tree has been termed *area potentially available* (APA). A basic premise underlying APA is that, within limits, larger APA values should result in a higher survival rate and

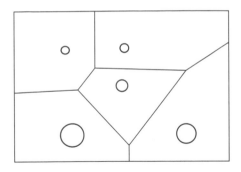

FIGURE 15-6
Polygons constructed by bisecting
intertree distances. *(Adapted from
Daniels, Burkhart, and Clason, 1986.)*

more tree growth (at least in certain dimensions, for example, dbh). If the perpendicular bisectors are placed equidistant between the subject tree and its competitors, the polygons are mutually exclusive and collectively exhaustive of the total area (that is, the individual polygon areas sum to the total area). Various weighting factors, based on tree size, have been used to determine the placement of the bisecting lines between the subject and competitor trees. The asymmetric division of the intertree distances resulting from weighting by tree size (for example, dbh, basal area, total height) may result in open areas. While weighted-distance polygon areas are mutually exclusive, they may not be collectively exhaustive of the stand area.

A number of studies have compared the efficacy of various point-density measures for predicting tree growth (Opie, 1968; Gerrard, 1969; Johnson, 1973; Daniels, 1976; Alemdag, 1978; Noone and Bell, 1980; Martin and Ek, 1984; Daniels, Burkhart, and Clason, 1986; Tomé and Burkhart, 1989; Biging and Dobbertin, 1995). The results of these comparisons have been variable, with no index being shown to be universally superior. Some indices seem to be better suited to certain species than others, and within species the performance of a particular index may vary with the stage of stand development and with the management practices followed.

PROBLEMS

15-1 Given the following data on stand ages A and average height of dominants and codominants H_d:

Age (yr)	Height (ft)	Age (yr)	Height (ft)	Age (yr)	Height (ft)
90	161	27	75	50	89
68	124	24	60	40	82
56	138	23	72	30	69
47	90	20	60	25	61
36	100	100	137	82	111
33	88	82	108	44	72
30	81	60	96	. . .	. . .

a Fit the following simple linear regression to the data:

$$\ln H_d = b_0 + b_1 A^{-1}$$

b Following procedures described in Section 15-5, use the fitted relationship from part **a** to estimate site index, base age 50 years, for a stand 25 years of age and 60 feet in height.

15-2 Assess the site quality of a forest stand in your locality by determining the site index and using an appropriate site-index relationship.

15-3 The following data were obtained on *one* ⅕-acre plot in a loblolly pine plantation:

dbh (in.)	No. trees tallied	dbh (in.)	No. trees tallied
5	7	9	9
6	10	10	5
7	12	11	3
8	24	12	2

a Compute the BA per acre and the number of trees per acre.
Previous research established the following relationships for loblolly pines in the area of interest:

$$\log N = -1.605 \log D + 4.1$$

where N = number of trees per acre
D = diameter of tree of average BA, in.

and

$$CW = 3.56 + 1.61 \, dbh$$

where CW = crown width, ft, for open-grown trees
dbh = diameter at breast height, in., for open-grown trees

b Using the data and previously derived relationships given, compute the stand-density index and the CCF.

15-4 Prepare a brief report on (a) the use of soil characteristics to measure site quality in your locality or (b) the possibilities of using indicator plants of lesser vegetation as a measure of site in your locality.

15-5 An even-aged stand has an average dominant height of 45 ft and 400 trees per acre. Assuming square spacing:
a Compute the relative spacing.
b Given that the stand as described is to be thinned to a relative spacing of 0.30, compute the number of stems per acre that would remain following thinning.

15-6 On recent aerial photographs of your locality, locate 10 to 30 circular sample plots that represent a wide density range in terms of crown closure. Then, visit each plot and obtain ground estimates of BA per unit area for the dominant-codominant stems that were visible on the photographs. Plot B-A values over crown closure. If a definite trend is evident, fit a regression equation to the plotted points. Explain possible reasons for the pattern of plotted points obtained.

REFERENCES

Alban, D. H. 1972. An improved growth intercept method for estimating site index of red pine. *U.S. Forest Serv., North Central Forest Expt. Sta., Res. Paper NC*-80. 7 pp.

Alemdag, I. S. 1978. Evaluation of some competition indexes for the prediction of diameter increment in planted white spruce. *Can. For. Serv., For. Manage. Inst., Inf. Rep. FMR-X*-108. 39 pp.

Alexander, R. R. 1971. Crown competition factor (CCF) for Engelmann spruce in the central Rocky Mountains. *U.S. Forest Serv., Rocky Mt. Forest and Range Expt. Sta., Res. Note RM*-188. 4 pp.

Bailey, R. L., and Clutter, J. L. 1974. Base-age invariant polymorphic site curves. *Forest Sci.* **20:**155–159.

Beck, D. E. 1971a. Growth intercept as an indicator of site index in natural stands of white pine in the Southern Appalachians. *U.S. Forest Serv., Southeast. Forest Expt. Sta., Res. Note SE*-154. 6 pp.

———. 1971b. Height-growth patterns and site index of white pine in the Southern Appalachians. *Forest Sci.* **17:**252–260.

Bickford, C. A., et al. 1957. Stocking, normality, and measurement of stand density. *J. Forestry* **55:**99–104.

Biging, G. S., and Dobbertin, M. 1995. Evaluation of competition indices in individual tree growth models. *Forest Sci.* **41:**360–377.

Bredenkamp, B. V., and Burkhart, H. E. 1990. An examination of spacing indices for *Eucalyptus grandis. Can. J. For. Res.* **20:**1909–1916.

Burkhart, H. E., and Tennent, R. B. 1977. Site index equations for radiata pine in New Zealand. *N. Z. J. Forestry Sci.* **7:**408–416.

Cao, Q. V., Baldwin, V. C., Jr., and Lohrey, R. E. 1997. Site index curves for direct-seeded loblolly and longleaf pines in Louisiana. *So. J. Appl. For.* **21:**134–138.

Carmean, W. H. 1972. Site index curves for upland oaks in the Central States. *Forest Sci.* **18:**109–120.

———. 1975. Forest site quality evaluation in the United States. *Adv. Agronomy* **27:**209–258.

Clutter, J. L., Fortson, J. C., Pienaar, L. V., Brister, G. H., and Bailey, R. L. 1983. *Timber management: A quantitative approach.* John Wiley & Sons, New York. 333 pp.

Curtis, R. O. 1970. Stand density measures: An interpretation. *Forest Sci.* **16:**403–414.

———. 1982. A simple index of stand density for Douglas-fir. *Forest Sci.* **28:**92–94.

Daniels, R. F. 1976. Simple competition indices and their correlation with annual loblolly pine tree growth. *Forest Sci.* **22:**454–456.

———, Burkhart, H. E., and Clason, T. R. 1986. A comparison of competition measures for predicting growth of loblolly pine trees. *Can J. For. Res.* **16:**1230–1237.

Doolittle, W. T. 1958. Forest soil-site relationships and species comparisons in the Southern Appalachians. *Soil Sci. Soc. Am. Proc.* **22:**455–458.

Doruska, P. F., and Nolen, W. R., Jr. 1999. Use of stand density index to schedule thinnings in loblolly pine plantations: A spreadsheet approach. *So. J. Appl. For.* **23:**21–29.

Drew, T. J., and Flewelling, J. W. 1977. Some recent Japanese theories of yield-density relationships and their application to Monterey pine plantations. *Forest Sci.* **23:**517–534.

———. 1979. Stand density management: An alternative approach and its application to Douglas-fir plantations. *Forest Sci.* **25:**518–532.

Elfving, B., and Kiviste, A. 1997. Construction of site index equations for *Pinus sylvestris* L. using permanent plot data in Sweden. *For. Ecol. and Manage.* **98:**125–134.

Gerrard, D. J. 1969. Competition quotient: A new measure of the competition affecting individual forest trees. *Mich. Agr. Expt. Sta., Res. Bull.* 20. 30 pp.

Gingrich, S. F. 1967. Measuring and evaluating stocking and stand density in upland hardwood forests in the Central States. *Forest Sci.* **13:**38–53.

Hegyi, F. 1974. A simulation model for managing jack-pine stands. Pp. 74–90 in *Growth models for tree and stand simulation,* J. Fries (ed.), Royal College of Forestry, Stockholm, Sweden.

Helms, J. A. (ed.) 1998. *The dictionary of forestry.* The Society of American Foresters, Bethesda, Md. 210 pp.

Johnson, E. W. 1973. Relationship between point density measurements and subsequent growth of southern pines. *Auburn Univ., Ala. Agr. Expt. Sta., Bull.* 447. 109 pp.

Johnson, J. E., Haag, C. L., Bockheim, J. G., and Erdmann, G. G. 1987. Soil-site relationships and soil characteristics associated with even-aged red maple (*Acer rubrum*) stands in Wisconsin and Michigan. *Forest Ecol. and Manage.* **21:**75–89.

Jones, J. R. 1969. Review and comparison of site evaluation methods. *U.S. Forest Serv., Rocky Mt. Forest and Range Expt. Sta., Res. Paper RM*-51. 27 pp.

Krajicek, J. E., Brinkman, K. A., and Gingrich, S. F. 1961. Crown competition—A measure of density. *Forest Sci.* **7:**35–42.

Larson, E. H., and Moehring, D. M. 1972. Site index curves for longleaf pine in East Texas. *Texas A & M Univ., Dept. Forest Sci., Res. Note* No. 1. 3 pp.

Lemin, R. C., Jr., and Burkhart, H. E. 1983. Predicting mortality after thinning in old-field loblolly pine plantations. *So. J. Appl. For.* **7:**20–23.

Martin, G. L., and Ek, A. R. 1984. A comparison of competition measures and growth models for predicting plantation red pine diameter and height growth. *Forest Sci.* **30:**731–743.

Milner, K. S. 1992. Site index and height growth curves for ponderosa pine, western larch, lodgepole pine, and Douglas-fir in western Montana. *West. J. Appl. For.* **7:**9–14.

Monserud, R. A. 1985. Comparison of Douglas-fir site index and height growth curves in the Pacific Northwest. *Can. J. For. Res.* **15:**673–679.

Nelson, T. C., and Bennett, F. A. 1965. A critical look at the normality concept. *J. Forestry* **63:**107–109.

Nigh, G. D., and Love, B. A. 1999. How well can we select undamaged site trees for estimating site index? *Can. J. For. Res.* **29:**1989–1992.

Noone, C. S., and Bell, J. F. 1980. An evaluation of eight intertree competition indices. *Oregon State Univ., For. Res. Lab., Res. Note* 66. 6 pp.

Oliver, W. W. 1972. Height intercept for estimating site index in young ponderosa pine plantations and natural stands. *U.S. Forest Serv., Pacific Southwest Forest and Range Expt. Sta., Res. Note PSW*-276. 4 pp.

Olson, D. F., Jr., and Della-Bianca, L. 1959. Site index comparisons for several tree species in the Virginia-Carolina Piedmont. *U.S. Forest Serv., Southeast. Forest Expt. Sta., Sta. Paper* 104. 9 pp.

Opie, J. E. 1968. Predictability of individual tree growth using various definitions of competing basal area. *Forest Sci.* **14:**314–323.

Philbrook, J. S., Barrett, J. P., and Leak, W. B. 1973. A stocking guide for eastern white pine. *U.S. Forest Serv., Northeast. Forest Expt. Sta., Res. Note NE*-168. 3 pp.

Reineke, L. H. 1933. Perfecting a stand-density index for even-aged forests. *J. Agr. Res.* **46:**627–638.

Richardson, B., Kimberley, M. O., Ray, J. W., and Coker, G. W. 1999. Indices of interspecific plant competition for *Pinus radiata* in the central north island of New Zealand. *Can. J. For. Res.* **29:**898–905.

Schröder, J., and Gadow, K., von. 1999. Testing a new competition index for Maritime pine in northwestern Spain. *Can. J. For. Res.* **29:**280–283.

Sprackling, J. A. 1973. Soil-topographic site index for Engelmann spruce on granitic soils in northern Colorado and southern Wyoming. *U.S. Forest Serv., Rocky Mt. Forest and Range Expt. Sta., Res. Note RM*-239. 4 pp.

Spurr, S. H. 1952. *Forest inventory.* The Ronald Press Company, New York. 476 pp.

———, and Barnes, B. V. 1980. *Forest ecology,* 3d ed. John Wiley & Sons, New York. 687 pp.

Strub, M. R., Vasey, R. B., and Burkhart, H. E. 1975. Comparison of diameter growth and crown competition factor in loblolly pine plantations. *Forest Sci.* **21:**427–431.

Tomé, M., and Burkhart, H. E. 1989. Distance-dependent competition measures for predicting growth of individual trees. *Forest Sci.* **35:**816–831.

Wang, G. G. 1995. White spruce site index in relation to soil, understory vegetation, and foliar nutrients. *Can. J. For. Res.* **25:**29–38.

West, P. W. 1983. Comparison of stand density measures in even-aged regrowth eucalypt forest of southern Tasmania. *Can. J. For. Res.* **13:**22–31.

Wilson, F. G. 1946. Numerical expression of stocking in terms of height. *J. Forestry* **44:**758–761.

———. 1979. Thinning as an orderly discipline: A graphic spacing schedule for red pine. *J. Forestry* **77:**483–486.

Zeide, B. 1987. Analysis of the 3/2 power law of self-thinning. *Forest Sci.* **33:**517–537.

CHAPTER 16

TREE-GROWTH AND
STAND-TABLE PROJECTION

16-1 Increases in Tree Diameter Tree growth is an intermittent process characterized by changes in stem form and dimension over a period of time. In temperate forests, a growing tree adds a yearly layer of wood just under the bark, from ground level to tip and all around the stem. In cross section, these layers appear as annual rings (Fig. 16-1). Accordingly, tree age can be determined by counting the rings, and the volume of each ring is a measure of the wood added to the central stem that particular year.

Annual rings tend to be wider during the early life of a tree; as age increases, the ring width gradually decreases, resulting in a reduction of annual diameter increment. Even though the *width* of each ring normally decreases as the tree becomes older, this thinner wood layer is added over a larger stem diameter, or bole surface. Therefore, the *volume* of wood added annually may be equal to or greater than that of previous years. In addition to age, the rate of diameter growth is dependent on the soil moisture availability and the amount of leaf surface functioning in the photosynthetic process. Wider spacing among trees results in more root-growing space and larger crowns, which, in turn, lead to faster diameter growth.

16-2 Increases in Tree Height Changes in tree height are of prime concern for predicting future stand composition and for selecting the ideal crop trees in pure stands. The typical course of height growth is illustrated by the sigmoid curve in

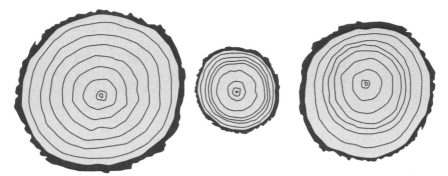

FIGURE 16-1
Typical pattern of diameter increment for trees that are free to grow (left); grown in relatively dense, unthinned stands (center); and grown in relatively dense stands but released by thinning (right). *(Adapted from Gadow and Bredenkamp, 1992.)*

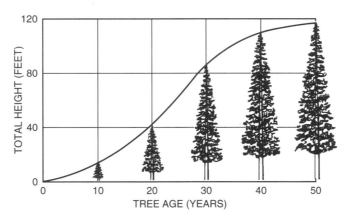

FIGURE 16-2
Cumulative height-growth pattern followed by many coniferous species.

Figure 16-2. Height growth proceeds slowly until the seedling is well-established; this is followed by a period of rapid growth during the next 20 to 30 years, depending on the species and site involved. As a tree begins to attain maturity, height growth gradually tapers off but never completely ceases as long as the tree is living and healthy.

The cumulative growth curve in Figure 16-2 follows the same general configuration for most functions of tree growth—whether height, diameter, basal area (BA), or cubic volume. Although the exact form of the cumulative growth curve will differ with the variable used and climatic fluctuations, the elongated S-shaped pattern is a characteristic that can be invariably expected. From this, it can be seen that wood production in the central stem of a tree can be predicted by measuring

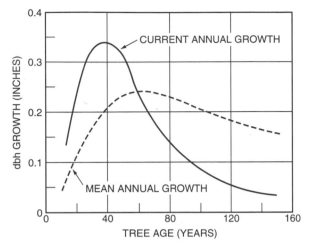

FIGURE 16-3
Graphic comparison of the current annual and mean annual
growth of a tree.

past rates of diameter and height growth. Indeed, the primary objective of most
tree-growth studies is the reliable prediction of future wood yields.

16-3 Periodic and Mean Annual Growth   The increase in tree size for one
year is referred to as the *current annual growth* (or *current annual increment*).
Because current growth is difficult to measure for a single year, the average annual
growth over a period of 5 to 10 years is commonly substituted instead. The difference
in tree size between the start and the end of a growth period, divided by the number
of years involved, is properly termed *periodic annual growth* (or *periodic annual increment*). By contrast, the *mean,* or *average, annual growth* (also called *mean annual
increment*) is derived by dividing total tree size at any point in time by total age.

Current or periodic annual growth, whether based on volume or other tree size
characteristics, increases rapidly, reaches a crest, and then drops off rapidly. In comparison, mean annual growth increases more slowly, attains a maximum at a later
age, and falls more gradually. When curves of current and mean annual growth are
plotted over tree age, they intersect at the peak of the latter (Fig. 16-3). Similar relationships are exhibited on a stand basis, as well as on a tree basis (Sec. 17-2).

16-4 Past Growth from Complete Stem Analysis   The most accurate
method of gauging accumulated tree volume growth is by complete stem analysis.
Although it is possible to obtain needed measurements and annual ring counts by
climbing and boring standing trees, the usual technique requires that sample trees
be felled and cut into sections at the end of a designated growth period. Diameter
inside bark (dib) at the beginning of the growth period is derived by counting

annual rings back to the desired year. The total starting volume of all tree sections is subtracted from current volume to obtain cubic-foot growth.

The exact method followed in making a complete stem analysis, including points of stem measurement and intervals between sections, varies according to tree form and desired precision. Therefore, the procedures outlined in Table 16-1 and illustrated in Figure 16-4 are intended merely to serve as an illustration of the

TABLE 16-1
SIMPLIFIED STEM-ANALYSIS COMPUTATIONS FOR A TREE-GROWTH PERIOD
OF 8 YEARS

Section height above ground (ft)	Average diameter (in.)	Cross-sectional area (sq ft)	Average cross-sectional area (sq ft)		Section length (ft)	Section volume (cu ft)
			(Stump)	1.163	1	1.163
1	14.6	1.163				
			(Section 1)	1.028	10	10.280
11	12.8	0.894				
			(Section 2)	0.748	10	7.480
21	10.5	0.601				
			(Section 3)	0.507	10	5.070
31	8.7	0.413				
			(Section 4)	0.280	10	2.800
41	5.2	0.147				
			(Top)	0.049	9	0.441
50	0.0	(Conoid)				

Present total height: 50 ft   Present cubic volume: 27.234

Section height above ground (ft)	Average diameter (in.)	Cross-sectional area (sq ft)	Average cross-sectional area (sq ft)		Section length (ft)	Section volume (cu ft)
			(Stump)	0.799	1	0.799
1	12.1	0.799				
			(Section 1)	0.712	10	7.120
11	10.7	0.624				
			(Section 2)	0.533	10	5.330
21	9.0	0.442				
			(Section 3)	0.374	10	3.740
31	7.5	0.307				
			(Section 4)	0.204	10	2.040
41	4.3	0.101				
			(Top)	0.034	2	0.068
43	0.0	(Conoid)				

Previous total height: 43 ft   Previous cubic volume: 19.097
Gross volume increase: 8.137 cu ft
Periodic annual growth: 8.137/8 = 1.017 cu ft per year

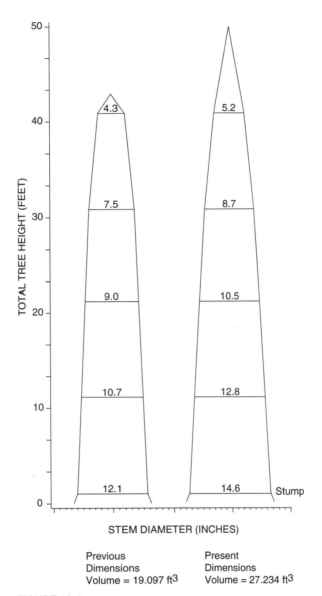

FIGURE 16-4
Tree volume growth can be determined by stem analysis. The
tree shown here grew 8.137 cu ft over an eight-year period.

computations involved. In this example, an 8-year growth period is presumed for a coniferous tree having a total height of 50 ft at the time of felling.

The tree is severed 1 ft above ground to minimize effects of butt swell; it is cut into uniform 10-ft lengths, excepting the final 9-ft top section. Present dib is obtained at each cutting point; for elliptical cross sections, this is derived by averaging minimum and maximum diameters. Next, average cross-section diameters are converted to cross-sectional area in square feet, followed by computations of present cubic volume for each section.

In Table 16-1, stump content is computed as the volume of a cylinder; that is, taper in the first 1-ft section is ignored. *Present* volumes of the four 10-ft sections are derived from Smalian's formula, and content of the top 9-ft section is computed as the volume of a conoid.

To obtain *previous* stem volume, diameters are measured by counting back eight annual rings from the present. Cubic volumes for stump and lower stem sections are calculated as before. For the top section, however, previous length must be determined by making several trial-and-error cuts from the tip downward—until the first ring preceding the growth period is located. Once the previous top length has been measured, its cubic content is again computed as the volume of a conoid (or other suitable geometric solid).

The difference in stem volume between the beginning and end of the specified time period represents gross growth. When this value is divided by the number of years in the period (8 in this example), the result is a measure of periodic annual growth.

Some stem analyses require that sectional cuts be made at both stump and diameter at breast height (dbh) levels, depending on the objectives. In such cases, the stem section below dbh is usually regarded as a cylinder for purposes of deriving cubic volume. Cutting intervals above dbh may also be shortened to 4 ft or less when greater precision is desired. During inclement weather, stem sections about 1 in. thick can be extracted at desired intervals and the actual analysis performed indoors.

16-5 Tree Growth as a Percentage Value   The calculation of tree growth in percentage terms is an expression of the average rate of change in size or volume over a given time period (Belyea, 1959). Because each year's annual ring is added over the cumulative size of the tree stem, tree growth has been most frequently regarded as a compound interest relationship. Despite the apparent logic of the compound interest theory, however, observations of actual volumes in uncut timber stands at three or more points in time indicate that tree growth is sometimes best described by *simple interest rates* (Grosenbaugh, 1958).

Actually, the argument of compound versus simple interest is largely an academic question, because growth percent alone has little practical value in management decision making. A large number of growth percent formulas have been proposed in previous years, but many are misleading because of the inherent nature of tree growth itself. Because the base dimensions of a tree are constantly increasing, a uniform annual increment results in a progressively lower and lower annual interest rate as the tree gets larger. Thus when the absolute increment remains constant, interest rates can appear astounding for small trees but strictly mediocre for larger ones.

Compound interest formulas are readily available in standard texts on forest finance and valuation. In terms of simple interest, the growth percentage in volume at any age is the current (periodic) annual growth divided by the "base volume" at the beginning of the growth period. Expressed as a formula, annual simple interest rates may be computed by

$$\text{Growth percent} = \frac{V_2 - V_1}{n \times V_1}(100)$$

where V_2 = volume or tree size at end of growth period
   V_1 = volume or tree size at start of growth period
   n = number of years in growth period

Substituting growth values from Table 16-1, the annual simple interest rate would be

$$\text{Growth percent} = \frac{27.234 - 19.097}{8(19.097)}(100) = 5.3 \text{ percent}$$

16-6 Predictions of Tree Growth   As stated earlier, the principal reason for analyzing the past growth of trees is to establish a pattern for predicting future growth. From the standpoint of practical forest management, growth prediction is usually approached from a *stand* basis rather than in terms of individual trees. However, because tree growth is the integral component of stand growth, the trends of tree size increases are appropriately considered first. Stand-growth prediction is discussed in subsequent sections.

Because the rate of tree growth in diameter, height, form, or volume is heavily dependent on relative age, prediction of future yields from past growth should be limited to short periods of time—usually not more than 5 to 10 years. Otherwise, large errors will result from the assumption that future growth will be equivalent or similar to past growth. As a rule, growth predictions are most reliable during the midlife of a tree, which is when size increases can be characterized by the central (near-linear) portion of the cumulative growth curve. When cumulative growth curves are available for the desired species, future growth for short time periods can be approximated by extrapolation of such trends. Curves of periodic or mean annual growth can be utilized in like fashion, but this procedure is not reliable for extended time periods.

16-7 Future Yields from Growth Percentage   This approach is analogous to the foregoing technique, for it presumes that future growth will proceed at the same *rate* as past growth. Even though this may be a reasonable postulation for a 3- to 5-year span, it is not recommended for longer periods. The annual growth rate of 5.3 percent derived in Section 16-5 may be used as a simple example. Projecting the present tree volume of 27.234 cu ft ahead by 3 years would result in a theoretical increase of 15.9 percent. Thus future tree volume would be computed as (1.159)(27.234), or 31.564 cu ft.

16-8 Growth Prediction from Diameter and Height Increases   Assume that a tree 14 in. in diameter and 65 ft tall had a dbh of 12 in. and a height of 55 ft 10 years ago. An obvious conclusion is that trees *now* 12 in. in diameter and 55 ft tall (on the same site and in the same relative position in the canopy) will grow 2 in. in diameter and 10 ft in height during the next 10 years. Actual rates of diameter and height increases may be obtained from complete stem analyses, from increment borings of standing trees, or from periodic remeasurement of permanent sample plots.

One simple method of short-term growth prediction for individual trees accommodates changes in height growth by use of a "local" volume equation or height/dbh curve for the desired species.[1] Rates of diameter increase are obtained from increment borings at dbh. In the example that follows, the annual cubic-volume growth per tree (outside bark) is based on the number of annual rings in the last ½ in. of tree radius.

Assume that a tree with a dbh of 12.8 in. has a present merchantable volume of 20.4 cu ft, outside bark, as computed from a local volume equation. An increment boring at dbh shows four annual rings in the last ½ in. of tree radius; that is, the tree required 4 years to produce the last full inch of diameter growth. When this tree was exactly 1 in. smaller in diameter, or 11.8-in. dbh, its merchantable volume was 17.2 cu ft—as computed from the same "local" volume equation. The difference in volume of 3.2 cu ft was thus produced in 4 years, for a periodic annual growth of 3.2/4, or 0.8 cu ft.

For the next 3 to 5 years, it is reasonably safe to assume that cubic volume will continue to increase at the rate of past growth, yielding a merchantable tree volume of 22.8 cu ft within 3 years or 24.4 cu ft after 5 years. As emphasized in Section 16-6, tree growth is a near-linear function of age during the middle years of stem development, particularly if the stand is relatively undisturbed by fire, heavy cutting, or unusual changes in density and competition.

Because the relationship of bark thickness to diameter outside bark (dob) changes as a tree grows, predictions more than 5 years ahead should properly be based on wood growth alone (i.e., inside bark measurements). In such instances, future dbh values are developed by computing inside-outside bark ratios for each diameter class involved.

Where continuous forest inventory (CFI) systems are established, the most reliable method of obtaining growth information is by repeated measurements of the

[1]This procedure may not be suited to long-term growth prediction. Over long periods of time, significant changes may occur in the height/dbh relationship for even-aged stands.

FIGURE 16-5
Increment borings from stems with eccentric cross sections will
display wide differences in growth, depending on the radii
selected. Note the acceleration of diameter increment following
release from competition.   *(Courtesy U.S. Forest Service.)*

same trees on permanent sample plots. The technique of complete stem analysis
is also recommended, especially for research studies dealing with patterns and
fluctuations in growth cycles. Although the increment borer is a useful inventory
tool, this method of growth determination probably ranks below the other two in
terms of reliability. Some species exhibit widely divergent patterns of radial
growth from one side of the tree to another as viewed on an increment core, depending on live-crown configuration (Fig. 16-5). Many ring-porous hardwoods
are extremely difficult to bore with conventional equipment, and certain diffuse-
porous species have inconspicuous annual ring delineations. Even though these
factors are often beyond the control of the inventory forester, they can nevertheless contribute to erroneous growth estimates.

STAND-TABLE PROJECTION

16-9 Components of Stand Growth   The basic elements of stand growth are
accretion, mortality, and ingrowth (Gilbert, 1954). *Accretion* is the growth on all
trees that were measured at the beginning of the growth period. It includes the
growth on trees that were cut during the period plus those trees that died and were

utilized. *Mortality* is the volume of trees initially measured that died during a growth period and were not utilized. The volume of those trees that grew into the lowest inventoried diameter class during the growth period is termed *ingrowth.*

Gross growth is a measure of the change in total volume for a given stand. In any given diameter class, it is the change in volume, plus mortality, during the growth period.

Net growth represents the stand-volume increment based on the initial trees after mortality has been deducted. When ingrowth is added to net growth, the result is volume increase, or *production* (a measure of the net change in volume during a specified growth period). If certain trees were harvested during a growth period, yield volume must also be considered in computing production values.

16-10 Characteristics of Stand-Table Projection   This method of growth prediction recognizes the structure of a stand, and growth projections are made according to dbh classes. The method is best suited to uneven-aged, low-density, and immature timber stands. In dense or overmature forests where mortality rates are high, stand-table projection may be of questionable value for providing reliable information on net stand growth.

The procedure ordinarily followed in the stand-table projection method of growth prediction may be briefly summarized as follows:

1 A present stand table showing the number of trees in each dbh class is developed from a conventional inventory.

2 Past periodic growth, by dbh classes, is determined from increment borings or from remeasurements of permanent sample plots. When increment borings are used, growth values must be converted from an inside-bark basis to outside-bark readings.

3 Past diameter growth rates are applied to the present stand table to derive a future stand table showing the predicted number of trees in each dbh class at the end of the growth period. Numbers of trees in each class must then be corrected for expected mortality and predicted ingrowth.

4 Both present and future stand tables are converted to stock tables by use of an appropriate local volume equation. Thus for short growth periods, the expected changes in tree height during the growth period are inherently accommodated by diameter increases.

5 Periodic stand growth is obtained as the difference between the total volume of the present stand and that of the future stand.

16-11 Diameter Growth   Rates of diameter growth outside bark are best obtained from repeated measurements of permanent sample plots. Consecutive inventories of the same trees provide a direct evaluation of combined wood and bark increment at dbh. As a result, many of the problems encountered in estimating stem growth from increment borings can be avoided.

TABLE 16-2
ANNUAL DIAMETER GROWTH BY DIAMETER CLASS IN ALABAMA*

dbh class (in.)	Pine species			Hardwood species		
	No. of sample trees	Mean growth (in.)	Standard deviation (in.)	No. of sample trees	Mean growth (in.)	Standard deviation (in.)
6	522	0.22	0.13	733	0.13	0.10
8	352	0.23	0.13	416	0.13	0.11
10	179	0.24	0.12	255	0.13	0.10
12	88	0.22	0.12	122	0.14	0.10
14	40	0.24	0.14	66	0.14	0.10
16	11	0.26	0.19	40	0.13	0.09
18	10	0.21	0.09	18	0.16	0.10
20+	8	0.18	0.09	12	0.15	0.13
All diameters	1,210	0.22	0.13	1,662	0.13	0.10

*Diameter growth (outside bark) based on remeasurements of 2,872 trees by the U.S. Forest Service.
Source: Judson, 1965.

As an example, Table 16-2 was compiled from remeasurements of dbh outside bark for southern pines and hardwoods distributed throughout the state of Alabama. Tree species and diameters were sampled in proportion to occurrence. All the major southern pines were represented; the principal hardwoods sampled were red and white oaks, hickories, yellow-poplar, sweetgum, and tupelos. The lack of a definite differentiation in growth by diameter classes was attributed to the moderate stand-density levels common in that state (Judson, 1965). Tabulations of this nature, however, are ideally suited to efficient stand-table projections.

When diameter growth is not available in the foregoing form, it is customary to rely on increment borings at dbh instead. Assuming we wish to estimate diameter growth (outside bark) for the last 10 years, estimates for each dbh class might be handled according to the following step-by-step procedure:

1 Measure present dbh to the nearest 0.1 in. and subtract diameter bark thickness to obtain present dib at breast height.

2 From an increment boring, obtain the 10-year wood growth in diameter and subtract from present dib to derive dib at breast height 10 years ago.

3 For each diameter class recognized, plot present diameter bark thickness over present dib at breast height. Draw a smooth, balanced curve (or fit a regression equation) through the plotted points. Read off appropriate bark thicknesses for each dib 10 years ago (step 2), and add these values together to arrive at an estimate of dbh (outside bark) 10 years ago.

4 Subtract dbh (outside bark) 10 years ago from present dob to derive the estimated growth in diameter during the stated time period. If future growth is presumed to equal past growth, this information may be applied directly in a stand-table projection.

16-12 Stand Mortality and Ingrowth   The reliability of stand-table projections leans heavily on the derivation of realistic estimates of mortality and ingrowth. As with diameter increment, such information is preferably obtained from consecutive reinventories of permanent sample plots; in reality, there is no other sound procedure for making these predictions. Mortality rates are desired for each dbh recognized in the stand table because the natural demise of smaller stems is usually much greater than for larger diameters. Only when growth predictions are made for very short time periods (perhaps 3 years or less) can mortality be regarded as a negligible factor.

For growth predictions of 5 to 10 years, ingrowth is usually accounted for by having the present stand table include several diameter classes below the minimum dbh desired in the future stand table. As an illustration, if 10-year growth predictions are planned for trees 10-in. dbh and larger, the initial stand table might include all stems that might logically grow into the 10-in.-dbh class during the interim (e.g., those stems presently 6 in. or more in diameter).

16-13 A Sample Stand Projection   For purposes of illustration, it will be assumed that the information on pine species in Table 16-2 represents a 20-acre stand for which a 10-year volume-growth prediction is desired for stems in the 10-in.-dbh class and larger. Present and future board-foot volumes are to be derived from a local volume table based on the Scribner log rule. The present stand table, including adjustments for mortality and applicable decadal growth rates, appears as shown in Table 16-3. The 6-in. and 8-in. trees are included in the present stand table to accommodate ingrowth into larger-diameter classes.

TABLE 16-3
PRESENT STAND TABLE, MORTALITY, AND EXPECTED 10-YEAR DIAMETER
GROWTH FOR A 20-ACRE PINE STAND IN ALABAMA

dbh class (in.)	Present stand (no. of stems)	Expected mortality (percent)	Expected survival (no. of stems)	10-year dbh growth (in.)
6	522	40	313	2.2
8	352	35	229	2.3
10	179	25	134	2.4
12	88	20	70	2.2
14	40	15	34	2.4
16	11	10	10	2.6
18	10	10	9	2.1
20+	8	20	6	1.8
Total	1,210		805	

Because mortality has been deducted from the present stand in Table 16-3, the next step is the application of diameter growth rates in deriving a future stand table. The upward movement of trees into larger-dbh classes is proportional to the ratio of growth to the chosen diameter-class interval:

$$\text{Growth-index ratio} = \frac{g}{i}$$

where g is the diameter growth in inches and i is the diameter-class interval in inches. Using the 6-in.-dbh class from Table 16-3 as an example,

$$\text{Growth-index ratio} = \frac{2.2}{2.0} = 1.10$$

The interpretation of a growth-index ratio of 1.10 is that 100 percent of the trees move up one dbh class, and 0.10, or 10 percent, of these advance two classes. Thus, of the 313 trees expected to survive in the 6 in. class, 90 percent (282 trees) move up to the 8-in. class, and 10 percent (31 trees) move all the way to the 10-in. class. None will remain in the 6-in. class in this instance. If the growth-index ratio had been less than unity, for example, 0.80, 80 percent of the trees would move up one class interval, and 20 percent would remain in the present dbh class. For the dbh classes in Table 16-3, growth-index ratios and the future stand table are shown in Table 16-4.

Once the future stand table has been derived, present and future volumes (stock tables) can be obtained from an appropriate local volume equation

TABLE 16-4
APPLICATION OF GROWTH-INDEX RATIOS IN DERIVING A FUTURE STAND TABLE
FOR A 20-ACRE PINE STAND IN ALABAMA

dbh class (in.)	Present stand surviving (no. of stems)	Growth-index ratio (g/i)	No change	1 class	2 classes	Future stand table (no. of stems)
6	313	1.10	0	282	31	0
8	229	1.15	0	195	34	282
10	134	1.20	0	107	27	226
12	70	1.10	0	63	7	141
14	34	1.20	0	27	7	90
16	10	1.30	0	7	3	34
18	9	1.05	0	8	1	14
20	6	0.90	1	5	0	12
22	0	...	0	0	0	6
Total	805	...	1	694	110	805

Column group header: No. of stems moving up (by dbh classes) spans the "No change", "1 class", and "2 classes" columns.

TABLE 16-5
PREDICTED 10-YEAR VOLUME PRODUCTION OF A 20-ACRE PINE
STAND IN ALABAMA

dbh class (in.)	Present stand table (no. of stems)	Future stand table (no. of stems)	Scribner volume per tree (bd ft)	Present stock table (bd ft)	Future stock table (bd ft)	Volume production (bd ft)
6	313	0				
8	229	282				
10	134	226	42	5,628	9,492	3,864
12	70	141	86	6,020	12,126	6,106
14	34	90	136	4,624	12,240	7,616
16	10	34	201	2,010	6,834	4,824
18	9	14	280	2,520	3,920	1,400
20	6	12	369	2,214	4,428	2,214
22	0	6	481	0	2,886	2,886
Total	805	805	...	23,016	51,926	28,910

(Table 16-5). Volume production is computed for each dbh class as the differ-ence between present and future volumes. For this hypothetical stand, the pre-dicted net volume growth for the 10-year period is 28,910 bd ft, or 1,445 bd ft per acre. On an *annual* basis, the predicted growth per acre is estimated as 144.5 bd ft.

PROBLEMS

16-1 Express growth for each of the following trees as an annual simple interest rate (Sec. 16-5):
  a $V_1 = 16.0 \text{ ft}^3$, $V_2 = 19.6 \text{ ft}^3$, $n = 3$ years
  b $V_1 = 1.7 \text{ m}^3$, $V_2 = 2.0 \text{ m}^3$, $n = 5$ years
  c $V_1 = 500 \text{ bd ft}$, $V_2 = 680 \text{ bd ft}$, $n = 4$ years
  d $V_1 = 7.7 \text{ ft}^3$, $V_2 = 10.5 \text{ ft}^3$, $n = 10$ years
16-2 Prepare curves of periodic and mean annual growth for an important timber species growing in your locality. Does the culmination of mean annual growth roughly co-incide with the accepted rotation age for that species? Give reasons for differences, if any.
16-3 Suppose a tree with dbh equal to 8.00 in. grows with a constant basal-area incre-ment of 0.0345 sq ft per year over the next 5 years. (a) Compute the diameter in-crement for the tree just described for each year of the 5-year period. (b) With a constant basal-area increment, is the diameter increment constant, increasing, or decreasing?
16-4 Make a complete stem analysis of a tree that is 20 to 40 years old. Using a growth pe-riod of 5 to 10 years, compute (a) present cubic volume, (b) periodic annual growth, and (c) predicted future volume 5 to 10 years hence.
16-5 Following are growth-index ratios by dbh class:

dbh class (in.)	Growth-index ratio (g/i)	dbh class (in.)	Growth-index ratio (g/i)
6	1.45	14	1.00
8	1.30	16	0.90
10	1.20	18	0.85
12	1.10	20	0.80

    a Apply the growth-index ratio values given to the present stand table shown in Table 16-4 to develop a future stand table.

    b Use the future stand table developed in part **a** in conjunction with the local volume table given in Table 16-5 to derive a future stock table and volume-production values by dbh class.

16-6 Predict periodic annual growth of an uneven-aged stand in your locality by applying the stand-table projection method.

REFERENCES

Belyea, H. C. 1959. Two new formulae for predicting growth percent. *J. Forestry* **57**:104–107.

Cameron, R. J., and Lea, R. 1980. Band dendrometers or diameter tapes? *J. Forestry* **78**:277–278.

Cao, Q. V., and Baldwin, V. C., Jr. 1999. A new algorithm for stand table projection models. *Forest Sci.* **45**:506–511.

Ffolliott, P. F. 1965. Determining growth of ponderosa pine in Arizona by stand projection. *U.S. Forest Serv., Rocky Mt. Forest and Range Expt. Sta., Res. Note RM*-52. 4 pp.

Gadow, K., von, and Bredenkamp, B. 1992. *Forest Management.* Academica, Pretoria, South Africa. 151 pp.

Gilbert, A. M. 1954. What is this thing called growth? *U.S. Forest Serv., Northeast. Forest Expt. Sta. Paper* 71. 5 pp.

Grosenbaugh, L. R. 1958. Allowable cut as a new function of growth and diagnostic tallies. *J. Forestry* **56**:727–730.

Herman, F. R., DeMars, D. J., and Woollard, R. F. 1975. Field and computer techniques for stem analysis of coniferous forest trees. *U.S. Forest Serv., Pacific Northwest Forest and Range Expt. Sta., Res. Paper PNW*-194. 51 pp.

Judson, G. M. 1965. Tree diameter growth in Alabama. *U.S. Forest Serv., Southern Forest Expt. Sta., Res. Note SO*-17. 3 pp.

Liming, F. G. 1957. Homemade dendrometers. *J. Forestry* **55**:575–577.

Meyer, H. A. 1952. Structure, growth, and drain in balanced, uneven-aged forests. *J. Forestry* **50**:85–92.

Nepal, S. K., and Somers, G. L. 1992. A generalized approach to stand table projection. *Forest Sci.* **38**:120–133.

Pienaar, L. V., and Harrison, W. M. 1988. A stand table projection approach to yield prediction in unthinned even-aged stands. *Forest Sci.* **34**:804–808.

Smith, R. B., Hornbeck, J. W., Federer, C. A., and Krusic, P. J., Jr. 1990. Regionally averaged diameter growth in New England forests. *U.S. Forest Serv., Northeast. Forest Expt. Sta., Res. Paper NE*-637. 26 pp.

Zedaker, S. M., Burkhart, H. E., and Stage, A. R. 1987. General principles and patterns of conifer growth and yield. Pp. 203–241 in *Forest vegetation management for conifer production*, J. D. Walstad and P. J. Kuch (eds.), John Wiley & Sons, New York.

CHAPTER 17

GROWTH AND YIELD MODELS

17-1 Introduction Forest management decisions are predicated on information about both current and future resource conditions. Inventories taken at one instant in time provide information on current volumes and related statistics. Forests are dynamic biological systems that are continuously changing, and it is necessary to project these changes to obtain relevant information for prudent decision making.

Stand dynamics (i.e., the growth, mortality, reproduction, and associated changes in the stand) can be predicted through direct or indirect methods. Direct methods, such as the stand-table projection technique discussed in Chapter 16, involve field observations in existing stands. Past growth and mortality trends are used to infer future trends in the stands observed.

There are many situations in which direct observation of forest growth and mortality are not feasible, however. Diameter growth, mortality, and ingrowth relationships developed through stand-table projection techniques are not reliable for long periods of time. Furthermore, managers often wish to evaluate a broad range of treatment alternatives. Inferences from past growth are limited to the conditions under which that growth occurred. Also, the costs of direct observation are sometimes prohibitive. Consequently, foresters often rely on indirect methods of predicting stand dynamics—i.e., growth, mortality, and related quantities of a stand are inferred from the study of other stands. These inferences are made through the use of tables, equations, or computer simulation models. Techniques for forecasting stand dynamics are collectively referred to as growth and yield models.

Growth and yield forecasts may be required for a short-term or long-term basis, for the overall stand volume, or for volume by product and size classes. With the wide variety of existing stand conditions and the diverse objectives and needs of users of growth and yield models, it is not surprising that numerous approaches have been proposed. These approaches range from models that provide only a specified aggregate stand volume to models with information about individual trees. Regardless of the structural complexity and amount of output detail provided, all growth and yield models have a common purpose: to produce estimates of stand characteristics [such as the volume, basal area (BA), and number of trees per unit area] at specified points in time. Representative examples of growth and yield models are discussed in this chapter. These examples are indicative of points along a continuum of modeling complexity. Many of the growth and yield models that are used operationally in forestry are mixtures of the model types described here. Descriptions of growth and yield models for even- and uneven-aged stands are provided.

17-2 Growth and Yield Relationships   Before proceeding further, it is important to define the terms growth and yield. *Growth* is the increase (increment) over a given period of time. *Yield* is the total amount available for harvest at a given time. Thus yield can be regarded as the summation of the annual increments. To be meaningful, growth and yield values must be qualified with regard to the part of the tree and the portion of the stand being considered. Further, one must be certain of the unit of measure being used and, for growth, of the time period involved.

The factors most closely related to growth and yield of forest stands are (1) the point in time in stand development, (2) the site quality, and (3) the degree to which the site is occupied. For even-aged stands, these factors can be expressed quantitatively through the variables of stand age, site index, and stand density, respectively. The measure of stand density most commonly used in growth and yield models for natural stands has been BA per unit area, whereas most models for planted stands have employed number of trees per unit area. For a given site index and initial stand-density level, volume per unit area (yield) plotted over stand age results in a sigmoid curve (Fig. 17-1). The growth curve (often referred to as current annual growth or current annual increment) increases up to the inflection point of the yield curve and decreases thereafter. Another important quantity is the mean annual growth or increment, defined as the yield at any given age divided by the total number of years (age) required to achieve that yield. Rotation age is sometimes set as the age of maximum mean annual increment because, for a given parcel of land, that is the harvest age which will maximize total wood production from a perpetual series of rotations. The rotation age actually selected, however, is also dependent on trends in stumpage values, tree size specifications for various products, and other management considerations. One will note that, in Figure 17-1,

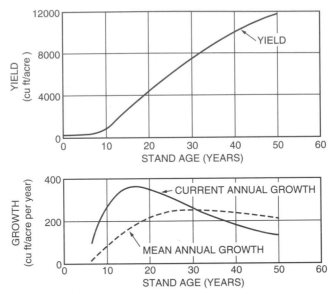

FIGURE 17-1
Relationship between yield, current annual growth, and mean
annual growth for even-aged stands with a specified site index
and initial stand density.

the current annual growth curve crosses the mean annual growth curve at the latter's highest value. Section 17-3 contains a description of the equations used to
construct Figure 17-1 and the mathematical relationships between these curves.

17-3 Mathematical Relationships between Growth and Yield   The yield
curve in Figure 17-1 was generated from the equation

$$Y = e^{10 - 32A^{-1}}$$

where Y is the yield in cubic feet per acre and A is the stand age in years. Equations
of this type are often fitted by linear regression techniques after performing logarithmic transformations. That is, the equation $\ln Y = b_0 + b_1 A^{-1}$ can be fitted as
a simple linear regression, where $\ln Y$ denotes the natural logarithm of Y. Because
yield is the summation of the annual increments, or, to state it another way, growth
is the rate of change in the yield function, the growth curve (current annual
growth) can be derived through methods of differential calculus. Taking the first
derivative of yield with respect to age (dY/dA) gives the current annual growth G
equation

$$G = (e^{10 - 32A^{-1}})(32A^{-2})$$

To compute the age at which growth is maximized, one takes the derivative of growth with respect to age (dG/dA) or the second derivative of yield with respect to age (d^2Y/dA^2), sets the quantity equal to zero, and solves for A:

$$dG/dA = (e^{10-32A^{-1}})[-2(32)A^{-3}] + (32A^{-2})(e^{10-32A^{-1}})(32A^{-2}) = 0$$

Simplifying and solving results in

$$A = 16 \text{ years}$$

To obtain the age of maximum mean annual growth or increment (denoted by MAI here), one divides the yield function by age (this gives the MAI function by definition), takes the first derivative with respect to age, sets the result equal to zero, and solves for age:

$$\text{MAI} = (e^{10-32A^{-1}})(A^{-1})$$
$$d\text{MAI}/dA = (e^{10-32A^{-1}})(-A^{-2}) + (A^{-1})(e^{10-32A^{-1}})(32A^{-2}) = 0$$

The solution for A is

$$A = 32 \text{ years}$$

GROWTH AND YIELD MODELS FOR EVEN-AGED STANDS

17-4 Normal Yield Tables   Yield prediction began in the United States with the development of normal yield tables for natural stands. Temporary plots were deliberately located in fully stocked or "normal" density portions of a series of stands of varying ages representing various site qualities. These plot observations of volume per unit area were then sorted into site-quality classes, and volume values were plotted over age. A volume-age curve was then drawn through the points for each site-quality class by using graphical techniques. Values were read from the curve for selected site-quality classes and ages to compile a normal yield table. Table 17-1 is an example of a normal yield table for Douglas-fir in the Pacific Northwest. It should be noted that many normal yield tables contain auxiliary information, such as BA, number of trees per unit area, and diameter distributions, as well as volume per unit area.

Normal yield tables were constructed in an era when only two variables could be included readily by graphical techniques. Thus analysts eliminated the variable of density by holding it constant at fully stocked or "normal" levels. With modern computing technology and analytical techniques, there is no longer any need to restrict the number of variables considered in growth and yield analyses.

TABLE 17-1
NORMAL YIELD TABLE FOR DOUGLAS-FIR IN THE PACIFIC
NORTHWEST, BOARD FEET PER ACRE, SCRIBNER RULE*

Age (years)	Site index (ft; base age 100)				
	80	110	140	170	200
30	0	0	300	2,600	8,000
40	0	200	4,500	11,900	24,400
50	30	3,300	12,400	27,400	44,100
60	1,100	8,100	23,800	42,800	62,000
70	2,400	14,000	35,200	57,200	78,200
80	4,400	20,100	45,700	70,000	92,500
90	6,900	26,000	55,000	81,000	104,800
100	9,600	31,400	62,800	90,400	115,100
110	12,200	36,300	69,400	98,300	123,700
120	14,700	40,700	75,000	105,100	131,100
130	17,000	44,700	80,000	111,000	137,700
140	19,200	48,300	84,500	116,300	143,500
150	21,300	51,600	88,600	121,200	148,700
160	23,300	54,600	92,400	125,700	153,500

*Volume of all trees 11.6-in. dbh and larger. Assumed stump height is 2 ft; minimum top diameter is 8 in.; trimming allowance is 0.3 ft for each 16-ft log.
Source: McArdle, Meyer, and Bruce, 1961.

Normal yield tables were generally regarded as a model of an ideal, fully stocked forest to be striven for in management. Today, few foresters believe that the stands shown in normal yield tables constitute a rational management goal. However, for some timber types, the only yield tables available are normal yield tables, and it is important for foresters to be acquainted with the methods used to construct these tables in order to apply them when necessary.

When constructing normal yield tables, one assumes that the temporary plots used have always been fully stocked. A series of fully stocked stands of various ages in a given site-quality class is taken to represent stages in a single growth curve. These assumptions and procedures are questionable because most stands that are fully stocked at a given time have been overstocked or understocked at some previous time in their development. Consequently, the stand progressions implied in normal yield tables are not likely to be found in nature.

In addition, the definition of normal, or fully stocked, is subjective, and it is not likely that a normal stand would be recognized if it existed. The utility of normal yield tables is severely limited because no reliable methods are available for predicting yields of nonnormal or understocked stands. The usual procedure has been to compute the ratio of the BA of the stand of interest to the BA shown for the normal yield table and to apply this ratio to the volume. This procedure has not, however, proved to be very satisfactory, because of difficulties in attempting to project changes in this ratio through time.

17-5 Empirical Yield Tables   An empirical yield table is similar to a normal yield table except that it supposedly applies to "average" rather than full, or normal, stocking. Thus the problem of defining normal stocking is eliminated, but an empirical yield table applies only to the average density levels found on the sample plots used. Consequently, difficulties in the application of these tables are similar to those for normal yield tables—adjustments must be made for deviations from the "average" density of the yield-table plots when applying empirical tables to other stands. Empirical yield tables provide few advantages over normal yield tables; the principal idea behind their construction was that the resultant tables should more closely approximate realizable yields under operational forest management than would the values from normal yield tables.

The term *empirical yield table* is somewhat of a misnomer because all yield tables are ultimately empirical, for they are based on plot observations from a specified forest population. However, the term is fairly well-established in forestry terminology as a means of identifying yield tables that apply to "average" stand density. Modern growth and yield modeling techniques do not rely on either "normal" or "average" density concepts but, instead, include density as a dynamic part of the stand-projection system. Such growth and yield models are commonly termed *variable-density* tables (or equations).

17-6 Variable-Density Growth and Yield Equations   A multiple regression approach to yield estimation, which takes stand density into account, was first applied by MacKinney and Chaiken (1939). Their prediction model for natural stands of loblolly pine was

$$\log Y = b_0 + b_1 A^{-1} + b_2 S + b_3 \log \text{SDI} + b_4 C$$

where $\log Y$ = logarithm of yield (total cu ft per acre of loblolly pine)
A^{-1} = reciprocal of stand age
S = site index
$\log \text{SDI}$ = logarithm of stand-density index
C = composition index (BA per acre of loblolly pine divided by total stand BA)

The measure of density used was Reineke's stand-density index (Sec. 15-15), and a "composition index" was included because not all of the sample plots were pure loblolly pine. This milestone study in quantitative analysis for growth and yield estimation is akin to methods still being used. Since MacKinney and Chaiken's work, many investigators have used multiple regression techniques to predict growth and/or yield for total stands or for some merchantable portion of stands. Stand-level variables, such as age, site index, BA, or number of trees per acre, are used to predict some specified aggregate stand volume. No information on volume distribution by size class is provided; thus resultant equations from this approach are sometimes referred to as *whole-stand models.*

The variable forms used in subsequent analyses have generally been similar to those employed by MacKinney and Chaiken. Logarithmic transformation of yield is generally made prior to equation fitting to conform to the assumptions customarily made in linear regression analysis. Furthermore, the use of the logarithm of yield as the dependent variable is a convenient way to mathematically express the interaction of the independent variables in their effect on yield. In other words, a unit change in site index, for example, has a differential effect on yield, depending on the level of the other independent variables (age and stand density). This differential effect—sometimes called *interaction*—would not be the case if the dependent variable were yield and interaction terms were not explicitly included.

In most yield analyses, stand age has been expressed as a reciprocal to make allowances for the "leveling off" (asymptotic) effect of yield with increasing age. Site index is not often transformed prior to fitting, but sometimes logarithmic or reciprocal transformations are employed. In some models, height of the dominant stand has been used in conjunction with age and the variable site index has been eliminated. (Note that if any two of the three variables—age, site index, height of the dominant stand—are known, the third can be determined.) Use of height rather than site index has the advantage that it is a measured rather than a predicted variable and, thus, more nearly satisfies the assumptions of regression analysis. The measure of stand density is commonly subjected to logarithmic transformation—particularly in models employing BA—but the exact form in which density is included is quite variable, especially for plantation models that utilize number of trees per unit area as a predictor variable.

Early work did not attempt to relate growth analyses to yield analyses, although the biological relationships can be readily expressed mathematically. Buckman (1962) and Clutter (1963) were the first researchers in the United States to explicitly recognize the mathematical relationships between growth and yield in their analyses. Clutter derived compatible growth and yield models for loblolly pine by ensuring that the algebraic form of the yield model could be obtained by mathematical integration of the growth model. Subsequently, Sullivan and Clutter (1972) extended Clutter's models by estimating yield and cumulative growth as a function of initial stand age, initial BA, site index, and future age. When the future age equals the current age (i.e., when the projection period is zero years), the projection model is reduced to a conventional yield model. Thus it is simultaneously a yield model for current conditions and a projection, or growth, model for future conditions.

As an example of compatible growth and yield models, the following equations (adapted from Sullivan and Clutter, 1972) were published by Knoebel, Burkhart, and Beck (1986) for thinned stands of yellow-poplar:

$$\ln Y_2 = 5.35740 - 102.45728(S^{-1}) - 21.95901(A_2^{-1}) \tag{1}$$
$$+ 0.97473(A_1/A_2)(\ln BA_1) + 4.11893(1 - A_1/A_2)$$
$$+ 0.01293(S)(1 - A_1/A_2)$$

where Y_i = stand volume per acre at age A_i
  S = site index, ft (base age 50)
  BA_i = basal area, sq ft per acre, at age A_i
  A_i = stand age at time i (A_1 = present stand age, A_2 = projected stand age)
  $\ln$ = natural logarithm

Note that when $A_2 = A_1 = A$ (i.e., the projection period is zero years) and $BA_1 = BA_2 = BA$, then equation 1 reduces to the conventional yield model

$$\ln Y = 5.35740 - 102.45728(S^{-1}) - 21.95901(A^{-1})$$
$$+ 0.97473(\ln BA) \tag{2}$$

Projected BA per acre is computed by

$$\ln BA_2 = (A_1/A_2)(\ln BA_1) + 4.22571(1 - A_1/A_2) \tag{3}$$
$$+ 0.013265(S)(1 - A_1/A_2)$$

Table 17-2, a variable-density yield table, was prepared by substituting appropriate values for current age, site index, and BA into equation 2. Equations 1 through 3 can also be used to project stand growth. For example, one might assume that a stand growing on site-index-110 land is 40 years old and has 90 sq ft of BA per acre. From equation 2, the current volume is estimated as

$\ln Y = 5.35740 - 102.45728(110^{-1}) - 21.95901(40^{-1}) + 0.97473(\ln 90)$
$\ln Y = 8.2631$
  $Y = 3,878$ cu ft per acre

To estimate the yield 10 years hence (i.e., at age 50), one substitutes $A_1 = 40$, $A_2 = 50$, $S = 110$, and $BA_1 = 90$ into equation 1 and solves for Y, resulting in

$$\ln Y_2 = 5.35740 - 102.45728(110^{-1}) - 21.95901(50^{-1})$$
$$+ 0.97473(40/50)(\ln 90) + 4.11893(1 - 40/50)$$
$$+ 0.01293(110)(1 - 40/50)$$
$$\ln Y_2 = 8.6039$$
$$Y_2 = 5,453 \text{ cu ft per acre}$$

TABLE 17-2
VARIABLE-DENSITY YIELD TABLE FOR THINNED STANDS OF YELLOW-POPLAR
TOTAL CUBIC-FOOT VOLUME PER ACRE*

Age (years)	Site index (ft; base age 50)	Basal area (sq ft per acre)					
		50	70	90	110	130	150
20	90	1027	1425				
	100	1151	1597				
	110	1263	1753				
	120	1365	1895	2421			
	130	1458	2023	2585			
30	90	1481	2055	2626			
	100	1659	2303	2942	3578		
	110	1821	2528	3230	3927	4622	
	120	1968	2732	3490	4244	4995	
	130	2102	2917	3727	4532	5334	6132
40	90	1778	2468	3153	3834	4512	5188
	100	1992	2766	3533	4296	5056	5813
	110	2187	3035	3878	4716	5550	6381
	120	2363	3280	4191	5097	5998	6896
	130	2524	3503	4476	5442	6405	7364
50	90	1984	2754	3519	4279	5036	5790
	100	2223	3086	3943	4795	5643	6488
	110	2440	3388	4328	5263	6194	7121
	120	2637	3661	4677	5688	6694	7696
	130	2817	3910	4995	6074	7148	8218
60	90	2135	2964	3786	4604	5418	6229
	100	2392	3321	4243	5159	6072	6980
	110	2626	3645	4657	5663	6664	7662
	120	2838	3939	5033	6120	7202	8280
	130	3030	4207	5374	6535	7691	8842
70	90	2249	3123	3989	4851	5709	6564
	100	2521	3499	4470	5436	6397	7355
	110	2767	3841	4907	5967	7022	8073
	120	2990	4151	5303	6448	7589	8725
	130	3193	4432	5663	6886	8104	9317
80	90	2339	3247	4149	5045	5937	6826
	100	2622	3639	4649	5654	6653	7649
	110	2877	3994	5103	6205	7303	8396
	120	3110	4317	5515	6706	7892	9074
	130	3321	4610	5889	7162	8428	9689

*Yields are for wood and bark of the total stem for all trees 4.5-in. dbh and larger.
Source: Knoebel, Burkhart, and Beck, 1986.

Alternatively, one can project the BA to age 50 by using equation 3. Here, one would substitute the projected basal area (BA_2) for BA, the projected age A_2 for A, and the site index S (note that site index does not change over time) into equation 2 and solve for yield:

$$\ln BA_2 = (40/50)(\ln 90) + 4.22571(1 - 40/50)$$
$$+ 0.013265(110)(1 - 40/50)$$
$$\ln BA_2 = 4.7368$$
$$BA_2 = 114.07 \text{ sq ft per acre}$$
$$\ln Y = 5.35740 - 102.45728(110^{-1}) - 21.95901(50^{-1})$$
$$+ 0.97473(\ln 114.07)$$
$$\ln Y = 8.6039$$
$$Y = 5{,}453 \text{ cu ft per acre}$$

Identical results are obtained by both options for projecting growth and yield because numerical consistency was ensured in the process used to estimate the coefficients in a set of analytically compatible models.

17-7 Size-Class Distribution Models The distribution of volume by size classes, as well as the overall volume, is needed as input to many forest management decisions. A variety of approaches providing the distribution of volume by size classes (generally dbh classes) have been taken in the development of growth and yield models. One widely applied technique for even-aged stands is a diameter-distribution modeling procedure. In this approach, the number of trees per unit area in each diameter class is estimated through the use of a mathematical function that provides the relative frequency of trees by diameters. Mean total tree heights are predicted for trees of given diameters in stands of specified characteristics (i.e., of specified age, site index, and stand density). Volume per diameter class is calculated by substituting the predicted mean tree heights and the diameter-class midpoints into tree volume or taper equations. Yield estimates are obtained by summing the volumes in the diameter classes of interest. Although only total stand values (e.g., age, site index, and number of trees per unit area) are needed as input, detailed stand distributional information is obtainable as output.

A typical dbh distribution for pure, even-aged stands is shown by the histogram in Figure 17-2. As a rule, these distributions have a single peak (i.e., they are unimodal) and are slightly skewed. Curves can be fitted to such diameter distributions by a variety of mathematical functions, but the two most popular functions used in past forest yield studies are the beta and the Weibull functions. Both of these functions are unimodal but highly flexible in the shapes that they can assume. Consequently, they have been found satisfactory for describing the relative frequencies by dbh class in unthinned stands where the underlying dbh distribution is generally within the range of shapes that the mathematical function can approximate.

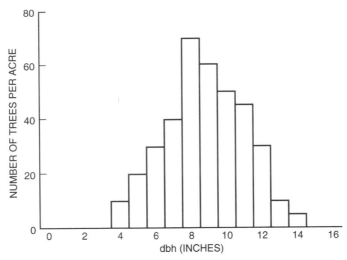

FIGURE 17-2
A typical dbh distribution for pure, even-aged stands.

Table 17-3 is a variable-density yield table for unthinned slash pine plantations that is based on the diameter-distribution analysis technique just described. It will serve as an example of how this technique is applied to forest yield prediction.

Diameter distributions shown in Table 17-3 were generated with the Weibull function. This function has three parameters, commonly denoted as *a, b,* and *c.* The *a* parameter is the "location" parameter; it indicates the lower end of the diameter distribution. "Spread" in the diameter distribution is controlled by the *b* parameter, while the "shape" of the distribution is determined by *c.* Regression equations are used to relate the parameters in the Weibull function to the stand attributes. For a given set of stand attributes, the Weibull function completely characterizes the diameter distribution.

To further illustrate this diameter-distribution modeling technique, one might consider these Table 17-3 entries: 500 trees per acre planted, age 15, site index 40. These stand characteristics are used to estimate the parameters *a, b,* and *c* in the Weibull function, which is then applied to generate the number of trees by dbh class. Under these stand conditions, the relative frequency for the 5-in.-dbh class, for example, is 0.2697. Multiplying 0.2697 times the number of surviving trees at age 15 (356) gives 96 trees per acre in the 5-in. class. Substituting a dbh value of 5 and the stand attributes (age 15, site index 40, trees surviving 356) into a height-diameter relationship results in a predicted total tree height of 25 ft. The dbh and total-height values are substituted into a tree volume equation to estimate the average volume per tree in the 5-in. class. For this illustration, each tree in the 5-in.-dbh class has a volume of

$$V = -1.045389 + 0.002706 \text{ dbh}^2 H$$
$$= -1.045389 + 0.002706(5)^2(25)$$
$$= 0.646 \text{ cu ft}$$

This volume per tree times the number of trees per acre (0.646×96) results in an estimated volume per acre of 62 cu ft. All other values in Table 17-3 are computed similarly. The volumes per acre are summed for the appropriate dbh classes to obtain an estimate of the yield per acre of the desired portion of the stand. With the entire stand table (numbers of trees per unit area) available, this technique is obviously flexible for generating stock tables (volume or weight per unit area) in any desired units and for any portion of the stand. Section 17-8 gives the equations used to develop Table 17-3 and shows, in detail, their use.

Other types of size-class distribution models have been developed for even-aged stands. The diameter-distribution analysis procedure illustrated here has been more widely applied than other alternatives, however, and it typifies the size-class distribution approach.

17-8 Example of Computations for Size-Class Distribution Model Equations and procedures used to generate Table 17-3, a variable-density yield table based on a diameter-distribution analysis technique, are demonstrated here for the age 15 entries with 500 trees per acre planted on site-index-40 land.

1 Estimate the number of trees per acre surviving at age 15 (equation from Coile and Schumacher, 1964).

$$\log T_s = \log T_p + (0.023949 - 0.012505 \log T_p) A$$

where T_s = number of trees per acre surviving
T_p = number of trees per acre planted
A = age (number of years since planting)
$\log$ = logarithm to base 10

For our example,

$$\log T_s = \log 500 + (0.023949 - 0.012505 \log 500)15$$
$$= 2.5519$$
$$T_s = 356$$

2 Compute the height of dominants and codominants at age 15 for site index 40 from a selected site-index equation (from Farrar, 1973).

$$\log H_d = \log S - 8.80405(A^{-1} - A_i^{-1}) + 22.7952(A^{-2} - A_i^{-2})$$

TABLE 17-3
VARIABLE-DENSITY YIELD TABLE, SHOWING INFORMATION BY DBH CLASSES, FOR UNTHINNED SLASH PINE PLANTATIONS*

Site index 40 (base age 25)

Age (years)	dbh (in.)	Trees planted per acre: 500			Trees planted per acre: 750			Trees planted per acre: 1,000		
		Trees per acre	Ave. ht. (ft)	Cu ft per acre	Trees per acre	Ave. ht. (ft)	Cu ft per acre	Trees per acre	Ave. ht. (ft)	Cu ft per acre
15	1	2	5	...	10	5	...	28	6	...
	2	21	13	...	58	15	...	105	16	...
	3	62	19	...	119	20	...	172	21	...
	4	98	23	...	142	24	...	167	24	...
	5	96	25	62	105	26	74	103	27	80
	6	56	28	94	47	28	79	40	28	67
	7	18	29	50	12	29	33	10	29	27
	8	3	30	12	2	30	8	1	30	4
		356		218	495		194	626		178
25	1	1	5	...	3	5	...	7	5	...
	2	8	11	...	19	13	...	33	14	...
	3	22	19	...	43	21	...	63	22	...
	4	41	26	...	64	28	...	84	28	...
	5	55	31	57	73	32	81	88	32	98
	6	56	35	132	69	36	169	75	36	184
	7	48	38	191	51	38	203	53	38	211
	8	31	40	182	31	40	182	31	40	182
	9	15	42	122	15	42	122	15	42	122
	10	6	44	65	6	44	65	6	43	63
	11	1	45	13	2	45	27	2	44	26
	12	0	...	...	0	...	...	1	45	16
		284		762	376		849	458		902

35

1	1	5	…	2	5	…	4	5	…
2	6	9	…	12	10	…	19	11	…
3	15	18	…	25	19	…	35	20	…
4	25	26	…	37	27	…	46	28	…
5	33	32	36	44	33	52	52	34	65
6	37	37	94	42	37	107	50	38	132
7	36	41	158	40	41	175	43	42	194
8	29	44	190	32	44	210	33	45	222
9	21	47	194	22	46	198	23	47	212
10	13	49	158	14	49	170	15	49	183
11	7	51	109	8	50	122	8	51	125
12	3	53	58	4	52	76	. 4	52	76
13	1	54	23	2	53	46	2	53	46
14	0	…	…	1	54	27	1	54	27
	227		1,020	285		1,183	335		1,282

Site index 60 (base age 25)

15

2	1	14	…	3	17	…	9	18	…
3	7	23	…	22	26	…	45	27	…
4	29	29	…	66	32	…	112	33	…
5	67	34	84	123	36	170	175	37	255
6	101	38	268	144	40	410	167	40	476
7	94	40	400	98	42	443	91	42	411
8	46	42	286	34	44	223	24	44	157
9	10	44	85	5	46	45	3	46	27
10	1	46	11	0	…		0	…	
	356		1,134	495		1,291	626		1,326

TABLE 17-3 (Continued)
VARIABLE-DENSITY YIELD TABLE, SHOWING INFORMATION BY DBH CLASSES, FOR UNTHINNED SLASH PINE PLANTATIONS*

Age (years)	dbh (in.)	Trees planted per acre: 500			Trees planted per acre: 750			Trees planted per acre: 1,000		
		Trees per acre	Ave. ht. (ft)	Cu ft per acre	Trees per acre	Ave. ht. (ft)	Cu ft per acre	Trees per acre	Ave. ht. (ft)	Cu ft per acre
					Site index 60 (base age 25)					
25	2	0	...	...	1	15	...	2	17	...
	3	2	25	...	6	27	...	12	29	...
	4	9	34	...	19	37	...	32	38	...
	5	23	42	41	41	44	79	61	46	126
	6	41	48	148	66	50	252	88	51	345
	7	59	53	352	83	54	507	99	55	618
	8	62	57	547	76	58	683	83	59	761
	9	50	60	605	52	61	640	52	61	640
	10	27	63	432	24	63	384	22	64	358
	11	9	65	182	7	66	143	6	66	123
	12	2	67	50	1	67	25	1	67	25
		284		2,357	376		2,713	458		2,996
35	2	0	...	...	...	...	...	1	13	...
	3	2	23	...	3	25	...	6	26	...
	4	6	34	...	11	36	...	16	38	...
	5	13	43	24	22	45	43	30	47	64
	6	24	51	94	35	53	144	46	54	193
	7	35	57	227	47	59	318	57	60	393
	8	40	63	394	52	64	521	59	65	602
	9	41	67	559	47	68	651	51	69	718
	10	33	71	599	35	72	645	36	72	663

11	20	74	463	20	75	470	20	75	470
12	9	77	260	9	77	260	9	77	260
13	3	79	105	3	80	106	3	80	106
14	1	82	42	1	82	42	1	82	42
	227		2,767	285		3,200	335		3,511

Site index 80 (base age 25)

15									
2	0	…	…	0	…	…	1	20	…
3	1	27	…	3	31	…	7	32	…
4	6	36	…	16	39	101	33	40	183
5	21	42	37	51	45	405	89	46	627
6	54	47	190	106	50	898	160	51	1,106
7	94	51	537	147	54	1,021	181	54	1,023
8	103	54	855	118	56	558	116	57	416
9	61	57	698	47	59	108	35	59	61
10	15	59	223	7	61	…	4	61	…
11	1	61	18	0	…	…	0	…	…
	356		2,558	495		3,091	626		3,416
25									
3	0	…	…	1	32	…	2	34	…
4	2	42	…	4	45	37	8	47	63
5	6	52	14	14	55	162	23	56	254
6	17	60	81	32	63	470	49	64	667
7	34	67	266	58	69	953	81	70	1,230
8	55	73	637	81	74	1,380	103	75	1,561
9	66	77	1,044	86	78	1,310	96	79	1,332
10	58	81	1,210	62	82	776	63	82	696
11	33	84	873	29	85	265	26	85	199
12	11	87	361	8	88	40	6	88	40
13	2	90	80	1	90	…	1	90	…
	284		4,566	376		5,393	458		6,042

TABLE 17-3 (Continued)
VARIABLE-DENSITY YIELD TABLE, SHOWING INFORMATION BY DBH CLASSES, FOR UNTHINNED SLASH PINE PLANTATIONS*

Age (years)	dbh (in.)	Trees planted per acre: 500			Trees planted per acre: 750			Trees planted per acre: 1,000		
		Trees per acre	Ave. ht. (ft)	Cu ft per acre	Trees per acre	Ave. ht. (ft)	Cu ft per acre	Trees per acre	Ave. ht. (ft)	Cu ft per acre
		Site index 80 (base age 25)								
35	3	0	...	...	0	...	...	1	32	...
	4	1	42	...	2	45	...	4	47	...
	5	4	55	10	7	58	20	11	59	32
	6	10	66	53	16	68	89	23	69	130
	7	19	74	166	30	76	270	40	78	371
	8	31	82	407	44	83	586	56	84	756
	9	42	88	766	57	89	1,052	65	90	1,214
	10	45	93	1,085	54	94	1,317	60	95	1,479
	11	38	98	1,179	41	99	1,286	43	99	1,348
	12	24	102	928	23	102	890	22	103	859
	13	10	106	474	9	106	426	8	106	379
	14	3	109	170	2	109	113	2	109	113
		227		5,238	285		6,049	335		6,681

*Age is number of years since planting; cubic-foot volumes are outside bark for a 4-in. top limit (ob) for all trees in the 5-in.-dbh class and larger.
Source: Diameter- and height-distribution equations from Dell et al., 1979; tree volume equation from Bennett, McGee, and Clutter, 1959.

where H_d = average height of dominants and codominants, ft
S = site index, ft (base age 25)
A_i = base age for site index

In this illustration,

$$\log H_d = \log 40 - 8.80405(15^{-1} - 25^{-1}) + 22.7952(15^{-2} - 25^{-2})$$
$$= 1.4321$$
$$H_d = 27 \text{ ft}$$

3 Using stand characteristics specified and computed in steps 1 and 2, estimate the Weibull distribution parameters and apply this estimated distribution for computing the numbers of trees in each dbh class (equations from Dell et al., 1979).

$$a = 1.3986 + 2.9217 \log H_d - 1.8477 \log A - 1.1126 \log T_s$$
$$= 1.3986 + 2.9217 \log 27 - 1.8477 \log 15 - 1.1126 \log 356$$
$$a = 0.56881$$
$$b = 2.5800 + 10.138 \log H_d - 2.5005 \log A - 3.6275 \log T_s - a$$
$$= 2.5800 + 10.138 \log 27 - 2.5005 \log 15 - 3.6275 \log 356 - 0.56881$$
$$b = 4.32615$$
$$c = 9.1471 + 6.5959 \log H_d - 7.6706 \log A - 2.4479 \log T_s$$
$$= 9.1471 + 6.5959 \log 27 - 7.6706 \log 15 - 2.4479 \log 356$$
$$c = 3.32121$$

The parameters a, b, and c completely specify a Weibull distribution, which is used to generate the relative frequencies of trees by dbh class for the given overall stand characteristics. To compute relative proportions of trees by dbh class, substitute the upper and lower limits of the class into the cumulative-distribution function. Subtracting the cumulative distribution up to the lower limit of the class from the upper limit gives the proportion of trees in that class. The Weibull cumulative-distribution function is

$$F(x) = 1 - e^{-[(x-a)/b]^c}$$

where $a \leq x \leq \infty$.

Continuing the present example and demonstrating for the 5-in.-dbh class:

$$F(5.5) = 1 - e^{-[(5.5-0.56881)/4.32615]^{3.32121}}$$
$$= 0.7866$$
$$F(4.5) = 1 - e^{-[(4.5-0.56881)/4.32615]^{3.32121}}$$
$$= 0.5169$$

Proportion in 5-in. class = 0.7866 − 0.5169 = 0.2697

Multiplying the proportion in the 5-in. class times the number of trees surviving gives the number of trees in that class:

$$(0.2697)(356) = 96$$

Analogous procedures are followed for all other dbh classes. The process is continued until a predicted frequency of less than one tree per unit area results. Note that the sum of the proportions for all dbh classes must equal 1, and thus the sum of the number of trees in all dbh classes will equal the total number surviving.

4 Use the midpoint of each dbh class and the stand attributes to predict the mean total tree height for each class (from Dell et al., 1979).

$$\log (H_d/H_i) = -0.050341 + (D_i^{-1} - D_{\max}^{-1})[3.1868$$
$$+ 0.000015708(A)(T_s) + 0.0114942(T_s)A^{-1}$$
$$- 2.0981 \log (T_s/A) + 1.4034 \log (H_d/A)]$$

where H_i = total height (ft) for trees D_i in. in dbh
$D_{\max}$ = midpoint of largest-diameter class containing at least one tree per acre, as defined by Weibull distribution and number of trees surviving

Following through for the 5-in. class (*note: $D_{\max}$ = 8 in. from Table 17-3*):

$$\log (27/H_i) = -0.050341 + (5^{-1} - 8^{-1})[3.1868$$
$$+ 0.000015708(15)(356) + 0.0114942(356)(15^{-1})$$
$$- 2.0981 \log (356/15) + 1.4034 \log (27/15)]$$
$$= 0.0259$$
$$H_i = 25 \text{ ft}$$

5 Substitute the midpoint diameter and the predicted total tree height into a tree volume or taper equation to estimate the average volume per tree in each dbh class. Using a tree volume equation from Bennett, McGee, and Clutter (1959) and the values for the 5-in. class in our example results in

$$V = -1.045389 + 0.002706 \text{ dbh}^2 H$$
$$= -1.045389 + 0.002706(5)^2(25)$$
$$= 0.646 \text{ cu ft}$$

Analogous procedures are used to compute volume per tree for the other diameter classes of interest.

6 Multiply the volume per tree times the number of trees per acre in the dbh classes of interest to obtain volume per acre for each dbh class. For the 5-in.-dbh class,

$$(0.646 \text{ cu ft per tree})(96 \text{ trees per acre}) = 62 \text{ cu ft per acre}$$

7 Sum the diameter-class values of interest to obtain an estimate of stand volume per acre.

Using equations shown in this illustration and values from Table 17-3 where appropriate (for age 15, trees per acre planted 500, and site index 40), the cubic-foot volumes per acre by dbh classes and the overall merchantable volumes are:

dbh	Volume per tree	Trees per acre	Volume per acre (cu ft)
5	0.646	96	62
6	1.682	56	94
7	2.800	18	50
8	4.150	3	12
Total			218

17-9 Individual-Tree Models for Even-Aged Stands   Approaches to predicting stand growth and yield which use individual trees as the basic unit are referred to as *individual-tree models*. The components of tree growth in these models are commonly linked together through a computer program that simulates the growth of each tree and then aggregates these to provide estimates of stand growth and yield. Models based on individual-tree growth provide detailed information about stand dynamics and structure, including the distribution of stand volume by size classes.

Individual-tree models may be divided into two classes, distance independent and distance dependent, depending on whether or not individual tree locations are required tree attributes. Distance-independent models project tree growth either individually or by size classes, usually as a function of present size and stand-level variables (e.g., age, site index, and BA per unit area). It is not necessary to know individual-tree locations when applying these models. Typically, distance-independent models consist of three basic components: (1) a diameter-growth component, (2) a height-growth component (or a height-diameter relationship to predict heights from dbh values), and (3) a mortality component. Mortality may be stochastically generated (i.e., determined through a random process), or it may be predicted as a function of growth rate.

Distance-dependent models vary in detail but are quite similar in overall concept and structure. Initial stand conditions are input or generated, and each tree is assigned a coordinate location. The growth of each tree is simulated as a function of its attributes, the site quality, and a measure of competition from neighbors. The competition index varies from model to model but in general is a function of the size of the subject tree and the size of and distance to competitors. Tree growth is commonly adjusted by a random component representing genetic and/or microsite variability. Survival is controlled either stochastically or deterministically as a function of competition and/or individual-tree attributes. Yield estimates are obtained by summing the individual-tree volumes (computed from tree volume or taper equations) and multiplying by appropriate expansion factors.

A stand simulator for loblolly pine plantations, PTAEDA2, is, in many aspects, typical of distance-dependent, individual-tree models. The PTAEDA2 model (Burkhart et al., 1987) consists of two main subsystems—one dealing with the generation of an initial precompetitive stand and another with the growth and dynamics of that stand. Management subroutines have been added to this framework to simulate varying hardwood competition levels, fertilization, and thinning. Input/output routines make the model operable and also add flexibility.

A number of options are available for creating rectangular spatial patterns in PTAEDA2. Users may specify the distance between trees and between rows in a conventional manner (e.g., 6 × 8 ft, 6 × 12 ft), allowing the program to compute the planted number of trees. Alternatively, the number of trees may be specified along with the ratio of planting distance to row width (e.g., 3:4, 1:2). If this ratio is omitted, square spacing is assumed. From this information, a simulation plot is generated and coordinate values are assigned to each of the planting locations. The juvenile stand is then advanced to an age of 8 years, when intraspecific competition is assumed to begin. At this point, predicted juvenile mortality is assigned at random. Individual-tree dimensions are then generated for the residual stand. Dbh is generated from a two-parameter Weibull distribution; the parameters of the Weibull distribution are estimated as functions of stand age, number of trees surviving, and average height of dominants and codominants at that age. Height is predicted for each tree from an equation involving dbh, average height of dominants and codominants, trees surviving, and age. Crown ratio for each tree is then calculated as a function of its total height, dbh, and age.

After assigning dimensions to each tree, the competition effect of neighboring trees is calculated for each individual tree as

$$CI_i = \sum_{j=1}^{n} \frac{dbh_j/dbh_i}{DIST_{ij}}$$

where CI_i = competition index of ith subject tree

      n = number of competitors "in" with BAF 10 sq ft per acre sweep centered at ith tree

    dbh_j = dbh of jth competitor

    dbh_i = dbh of ith subject tree

  $DIST_{ij}$ = distance between subject tree i and jth competitor

After generation of the precompetitive stand, competition is evaluated and simulated trees are grown individually on an annual basis. In general, growth in height and diameter is assumed to follow some theoretical growth potential. An adjustment or reduction factor is applied to this potential increment based on a tree's competitive status and vigor, and a random component is then added to represent microsite and/or genetic variability.

The potential height increment for each tree is the change in average height of the dominant and codominant trees, obtained as the first difference with respect to age of a site-index equation. A tree may grow more or less than this potential, depending on its individual attributes.

Crown ratio is considered to be an expression of a tree's photosynthetic potential. It is used in conjunction with competition index to compute an adjustment factor for height growth. The adjustment factor times the potential height growth (determined from a site-index equation) gives the estimated actual height growth for an individual tree with a given crown ratio and competition index.

The maximum dbh attainable for an individual tree of given height and age is considered to be equal to that of loblolly pines grown in the open. An equation describing this relationship, developed from open-grown tree data, is

$$\text{dbh}_0 = b_0 + b_1 H + b_2 A$$

where dbh_0 = dbh of open-grown trees
H = total tree height
A = age

The first difference of this equation with respect to age represents maximum potential diameter increment:

$$\text{PDIN} = b_1 \text{HIN} + b_2$$

where PDIN is the potential diameter increment and HIN is the observed height increment. This potential diameter increment is adjusted by a reduction factor that is a function of the tree's competition index and crown ratio, a measure of photosynthetic potential. A normally distributed random component is added to diameter-growth determinations.

The probability that a tree remains alive in a given year is assumed to be a function of its competitive stress (CI) and individual vigor as measured by photosynthetic potential (expressed by crown ratio, CR, in this equation). The "probability of survival" equation is

$$\text{PLIVE} = b_1 \text{CR}^{b_2} e^{-b_3 \text{CI}^{b_4}}$$

where PLIVE is the probability that a tree remains alive. In PTAEDA2, survival probability is calculated for each live tree each year and used to determine annual mortality. The calculated PLIVE is compared with a uniform random variate between zero and one. If PLIVE is less than this generated number, the tree is considered to have died.

These components, along with subroutines to simulate the effects of various levels of hardwood competition, thinning, and fertilization, were linked together in a computer program to simulate individual-tree growth and stand development. Figure 17-3 is a schematic diagram showing relationships between tree and stand components in this growth and yield model for loblolly pine plantations.

Amateis, Burkhart, and Walsh (1989) developed individual-tree diameter increment and survival equations for loblolly pine plantations by substituting a distance-independent measure of competition into the basic functional forms used in the PTAEDA2 model. The measure of competition used involves the ratio of quadratic mean dbh of the stand (computed from basal area and numbers of trees

FIGURE 17-3
Relationships between tree and stand components for an individual-tree, distance-dependent model of loblolly pine plantations. *(From Burkhart et al., 1987.)*

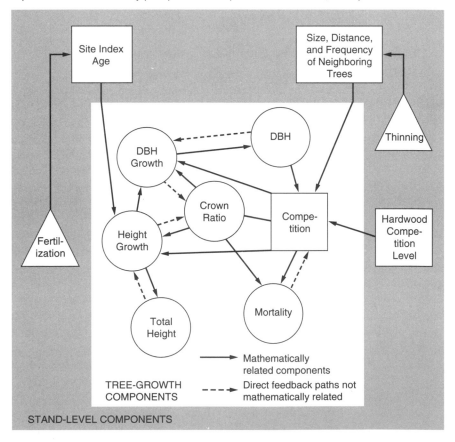

per unit area) and individual-tree dbh. Hence, the relative competitive position of each tree in the stand is expressed, but knowledge of tree locations is not required.

GROWTH AND YIELD MODELS FOR UNEVEN-AGED STANDS

17-10 Special Considerations in Modeling Uneven-Aged Stands   Uneven-aged stands are composed of trees that differ markedly in age. Consequently, age is not a usable variable for growth- and yield-prediction purposes. Also, site-quality assessment by site-index methods is questionable because of initial suppression of advance reproduction, especially for tolerant species. Furthermore, site index is an age-dependent variable. Growth and yield models without age as a variable, and without site index for assessing site quality, have been developed for uneven-aged stands. Modeling techniques for uneven-aged stands may also, in theory, be applied to even-aged conditions. However, in most situations, models involving age (such as those described in Secs. 17-4 through 17-9) have been applied to even-aged stands. Sections 17-11 through 17-13 describe approaches and provide examples of growth and yield models that have been developed specifically for uneven-aged conditions—that is, conditions for which age is not a usable variable.

17-11 Growth and Yield Equations Based on Elapsed Time   Moser and Hall (1969) developed a volume growth-rate equation for uneven-aged stands of mixed northern hardwoods. Solution of their growth-rate equation provides a yield function expressed in terms of elapsed time from a given initial condition. The variable time (in lieu of stand age) was introduced into the yield function by assigning a relative time t_0 at some identified point in the stand's development with initial condition Y_0. The resulting yield equation, expressed as a function of time and initial volume and BA, is

$$Y = [(Y_0)(8.3348\text{BA}_0^{-1.3175})]$$
$$\times [0.9348 - (0.9348 - 1.0203\text{BA}_0^{-0.0125})e^{-0.0062t}]^{-105.4}$$

where Y_0 = initial volume, cu ft per acre
$\quad$ BA_0 = initial basal area, sq ft per acre
$\quad$ t = elapsed time interval, years from initial conditions
$\quad$ Y = predicted volume, cu ft, t years after observation of initial
$\quad\quad$ conditions Y_0 and BA_0 at time t_0

If one assumes that a stand with a volume of 1,500 cu ft per acre and BA of 60 sq ft per acre is observed, then the predicted yield 10 years hence would be

$$Y = [(1,500)(8.3348\,(60)^{-1.3175})]$$
$$\times [0.9348 - (0.9348 - 1.0203\,(60)^{-0.0125})e^{-0.0062(10)}]^{-105.4}$$
$$Y = 1,885 \text{ cu ft per acre}$$

TABLE 17-4
YIELD TABLE SHOWING FINAL VOLUME (CU FT PER
ACRE) AS A FUNCTION OF INITIAL CONDITIONS AND
ELAPSED TIME FOR UNEVEN-AGED STANDS OF MIXED
NORTHERN HARDWOODS

Initial volume (cu ft per acre)	Elapsed time (years)	Initial basal area (sq ft per acre)		
		60	80	100
1,500	10	1,885	1,844	1,813
	15	2,101	2,033	1,982
	20	2,333	2,235	2,162
1,750	10	2,200	2,152	2,115
	15	2,451	2,372	2,313
	20	2,722	2,608	2,522
2,000	10	2,514	2,459	2,417
	15	2,801	2,711	2,643
	20	3,111	2,981	2,883

Source: Moser and Hall, 1969.

Table 17-4 is a yield table constructed from solution of Moser and Hall's equation for selected initial conditions and elapsed time intervals. It provides an example of an approach to yield prediction for uneven-aged stands.

17-12 Size-Class Distribution Models Using Stand-Table Projection Diameter distributions in regular, uneven-aged stands are inverse J-shapes (Fig. 17-4). Relative frequency curves, such as the Weibull function, described in Section 17-7, can assume this inverse J-shape and can, thus, be used to model diameter distributions in uneven-aged stands. Modifications are necessary, however, to express the parameters of the diameter distribution in terms of variables other than stand age. One alternative, for example, would be to express the parameters as functions of some initial value and the elapsed time from that initial value. Such a procedure would be somewhat analogous to the methods outlined in Section 17-11 for overall stand volume.

Another approach to size-class distribution modeling in uneven-aged stands is the use of the stand-table projection models developed by Ek (1974). He presented equations to predict periodic ingrowth, mortality, and survivor growth (by 2-in.-diameter classes) in northern hardwood stands. Net 5-year change (i.e., the change from t_0, the time of initial measurement, to t_1, the time of final measurement, where t_1 is 5 years after t_0) in the number of trees in a diameter class Δn was defined as

$$\Delta n = \text{stand ingrowth} - \text{mortality} - \text{upgrowth} + \text{ingrowth}$$

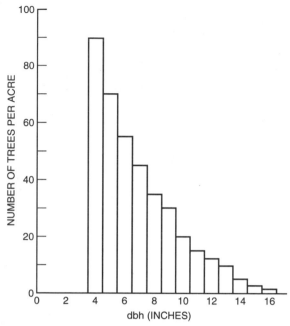

FIGURE 17-4
Typical dbh distribution for regular, uneven-aged stands.

The component equations of this generalized stand-table projection model are

$$n_{is} = 15.123N^{0.38753}e^{(-0.32908\text{BA}^{1.58011}N^{-1})} \tag{1}$$

$$n_m = 0.03443n[(\text{BA}/N)/(\text{ba}/n)]^{0.54748} \tag{2}$$

$$n_u = 0.01070n^{0.81433}S[(\text{ba}/n)/(\text{BA}/N)]^{0.14611}e^{-0.00160\text{BA}} \tag{3}$$

where n_{is} = stand ingrowth = merchantable trees at t_1 that were nonmerchantable at t_0
n_m = mortality = trees present in a diameter class at t_0 but dead at t_1
n_u = upgrowth = trees present in a diameter class at t_0 but growing into next larger diameter class at t_1
n_i = ingrowth = upgrowth from next lower measured diameter class
N = number of trees per acre in stand
BA = stand basal area, sq ft per acre
n = number of trees in specified diameter class
ba = basal area of trees in specified diameter class
S = site index (height, ft, at age 50 years)

Equations 1 through 3 can be used to project observed or hypothetical stand tables, which can then be converted to stock tables. Because of the growth rates involved for the northern hardwoods example, stand ingrowth n_{is} would be added only to the smallest merchantable class (6-in.-dbh class) when 2-in. groupings are used. Diameter-class ingrowth n_i is equal to the upgrowth n_u computed from the next lower diameter class (e.g., upgrowth computed for the 8-in. class is ingrowth to the 10-in. class). For projections longer than 5 years, a new stand table must be constructed at 5-year intervals. The new stand table is prepared by adding ingrowth trees from smaller size classes to the number of survivors in a class that did not move to the next larger class. Basal areas can be computed by using the class midpoint diameters. The new stand table then serves as the initial conditions for the next 5-year projection. Volumes can be computed by applying an appropriate size-class volume equation, such as

$$v = b_1 \mathrm{ba}^{b_2} S^{b_3} \mathrm{BA}^{b_4}$$

where v is merchantable volume in a specified diameter class, the b_i's are constants to be estimated from data, and the other variables remain as previously defined.

17-13 Individual-Tree Models That Include Uneven-Aged Stands Both distance-dependent and distance-independent individual-tree growth and yield models have been developed for mixed-species, uneven-aged and for single-species, even-aged stands. An example of the distance-dependent type is FOREST, a model published by Ek and Monserud (1974) for simulating the growth and reproduction of even- or uneven-aged mixed-species stands.

Usual input for FOREST is a set of tree coordinates and associated tree characteristics (e.g., height, diameter, age, clear bole length, and species). Tree coordinates and tree characteristics may also be generated by the program. Each tree is then "grown" for a number of projection periods based on potential growth functions, modified by an index of competition. The competition index is based on the assessment of relative tree size, crowding, and shade tolerance. Mortality is obtained when the probability of survival for a stem falls below a threshold value, which is dependent on the competitive status of a tree. In any "year" of the simulation, optional reproduction routines may be called to account for regeneration by seed and sprout production of the overstory. Silvicultural treatments, including site alteration, cutting, or pruning operations, may also be specified for implementation as the stand develops. Output of the model is in the form of periodic stand tables with yield and mortality for various products.

The Forest Vegetation Simulator (FVS) is a distance-independent, individual-tree model that can be applied to a variety of stand structures, including mixed-species, multi-aged stands. Since it was originally calibrated for northern Idaho and western Montana (Stage, 1973; Wykoff, Crookston, and Stage, 1982), numerous variants of the FVS model have been developed for different timber types throughout the United States, with the majority being for the western part of the country (Ritchie, 1999).[1]

All FVS variants have a separate set of routines for juvenile stand development. Small trees (typically those less than 3 in. dbh) are described with a different set of functions than those used for large trees. Typically the primary growth function for larger trees is the diameter increment for trees greater than 3 in. dbh, whereas height growth is the primary increment function for small-tree growth. Default growth intervals are either 5 or 10 years, depending on the FVS variant being applied, but the interval can be changed by the user.

The FVS system offers numerous extensions that allow users to integrate such factors as pest outbreaks into forecasts. Not all extensions are available for all FVS variants; users need to check periodically for current information on the availability of extensions for specific versions of FVS.

The nine FVS variants applicable to the Pacific Coast states are all very similar in execution. The primary difference among variants is the parameterization of the growth and mortality functions. Other functions, such as height-diameter relationships and tree volume equations, also vary among simulators. In most versions, site productivity is expressed as a function of some combination of slope, aspect, elevation, site index, and location. The site index function varies, depending on the variant selected and species prevalent in the region of interest. User's guides and background publications are available for most versions of FVS (Ritchie, 1999).

APPLYING GROWTH AND YIELD MODELS

17-14 Enhancing Output from Growth and Yield Models   Most growth and yield models produce information on stand density (numbers of trees, basal area, or both), stand volumes in specified units, and stand structure (diameter and height distributions). Information on stand structure is essential when evaluating wood production goals, forage quantity in the understory, suitability of forests for wildlife, potential water yields from forested areas, and aesthetic quality of forest stands in different stages of development. In addition to estimates of wood quantity (volume), when evaluating wood-products objectives, information on wood quality may be provided by incorporating functions to describe certain wood characteristics (such as knots, ring widths, and density). Armed with information on both wood quantity and quality, managers can prescribe silvicultural treatments that produce desired volumes of wood suitable for specific products.

In addition to quantitative data, such as stand and stock tables, a visual representation of stands generated by forest simulators can be produced using computer graphics technology (Fig. 17-5). With a visual image of forest stands at various

---

[1]An overview of FVS and current information on FVS variants may be found on the World Wide Web at: http://www.fs.fed.us/fmsc/fvs

FIGURE 17-5
Computer graphic capabilities can be linked to forest stand simulators to produce visual representations of stand development. This image of a mature stand was created by linking the forest vegetation simulator (FVS) to the stand visualization system (SVS). *(From Crookston and Stage, 1999.)*

stages of development, decision makers can more readily evaluate the need for, and results of, management actions such as thinning. To the extent possible, all outcomes of different silvicultural prescriptions—including the visual impacts—need to be integrated into decision processes. Models that visually represent forest development have proven valuable for presenting management options to private landowners, industrial boards, government officials, and the general public. High-quality visual display can provide helpful insights into the dynamics of forest stand development and the effects of proposed management actions. Vast amounts of abstract data can be summarized as visual imagery that allows essential information to be conveyed in a concise and easily grasped form.

17-15 Choosing an Appropriate Growth and Yield Model   Growth and yield models provide input to forest management decisions regarding individual stands, forests, and broad regions. The projection period and the level of stand detail required may vary in each case. In choosing appropriate growth and yield models, foresters must be concerned with the reliability of estimates, the flexibility to reproduce desired management alternatives, the ability to provide sufficient detail for decision making, and the efficiency for providing this information.

Although advantages and disadvantages cannot be ascribed to different modeling approaches except in the context of specific uses, general characteristics of the various alternatives can be briefly described. Equations for predicting overall stand values can generally be applied with existing inventory data and are computationally efficient. However, such equations do not provide size-class information needed to evaluate various utilization options and usually cannot be used to analyze a wide range of stand treatments.

Size-class distribution models, such as the diameter-distribution models described in Section 17-7, require only overall stand values as input but provide detailed size-class information as output. Thus alternative utilization options can be evaluated. Computationally, these models are somewhat more expensive to apply than equations for overall stand values, and they are generally not flexible enough to evaluate a broad range of stand treatments because of the required assumptions about the shape of the underlying diameter distribution.

Individual-tree models provide maximum detail and flexibility for evaluating alternative utilization options and stand treatments. They are, however, more expensive to develop, require a more detailed data base to implement, and are much more expensive to apply, requiring sophisticated computing equipment and greater execution time for comparable stand estimates than the overall stand or size-class distribution models.

17-16 A Word of Caution   When applying growth and yield models, one assumes a relatively homogeneous stand with regard to independent variables (e.g., age, site index, BA) used to predict stand values. If there is significant variation in variables such as site or stand density for a given area, the area must be stratified into reasonably homogeneous stands and predictions made separately for each of these stands to ensure accurate results.

Growth and yield predictions apply to net area; all nonproductive areas must be deducted when making estimates on an area basis.

In most growth and yield models, no allowance is made for logging breakage or other losses during harvest, and it is implicitly assumed that all material meeting minimum merchantability standards will be utilized. Adjustments must often be made in predicted values from growth and yield models to approximate volumes that are likely to be realized under local harvesting and utilization conditions.

PROBLEMS

17-1 Using the yield values shown in Table 17-1, determine the age of culmination of mean annual growth for site indexes 110, 140, 170, and 200. Are the ages of culmination consistent from a biological standpoint?

17-2 Apply linear regression techniques to fit the following model to yield values for site index 140 shown in Table 17-1:

$$\ln Y = b_0 + b_1 A^{-1}$$

where $\ln Y$ is the natural logarithm of yield and A is the stand age. Using the fitted relationships for yield, derive equations for current annual growth and mean annual growth. Solve for the age of maximum current annual and maximum mean annual growth. Are the growth relationships consistent with expectations from a biological standpoint?

17-3 Using the growth and yield equations for yellow-poplar in Section 17-6:

   a Estimate the current volume for a stand of age 30, BA per acre of 60 sq ft, and site index of 105 feet.

   b Compute the periodic (10-year) growth of the stand described in part **a** from age 30 to 40 years.

   c Calculate the mean annual increment at age 40.

   d Convert answers in parts **a**, **b**, and **c** to metric units.

17-4 For a commercially important species in your area, conduct a literature search to determine the extent and nature of growth and yield information that is available. Prepare a report on the kinds of growth and yield models developed and the relationships shown by these models for the species chosen for study.

17-5 Apply the equation for uneven-aged stands shown in Section 17-11 to develop a yield tabulation similar to Table 17-4 for the following conditions:

Initial volumes: 2,400; 2,600 cu ft per acre
Elapsed times: 5, 10 years
Initial basal areas: 90, 110 sq ft per acre

17-6 Plot histograms of the dbh distributions given in Table 17-3 for site indexes 40, 60, and 80 at age 25 with 750 trees per acre planted; for ages 15, 25, and 35 at site index 60 with 750 trees per acre planted; and for 500, 750, and 1,000 trees per acre planted with site index 60 and age 25. Are changes in the dbh distribution logically related, from a biological standpoint, to plantation age, site index, and number of trees planted?

17-7 Given the following initial stand conditions:

Site index $S = 65$ ft (base age 50)
Basal area BA $= 69$ sq ft per acre
Number of trees per acre $N = 200$

and the following initial stand table:

dbh class (in.)	Number of trees per acre
6	100
8	50
10	30
12	20

Use the stand-table projection equations from Section 17-12 to estimate a stand table 5 years hence and 10 years hence.

17-8 Compute entries similar to those shown in Table 17-3 for the 5-, 6-, and 7-in.-dbh classes in a stand of age 25, site index 70, and 900 trees per acre planted by applying the equations given in Section 17-8.

REFERENCES

Amateis, R. L., Burkhart, H. E., and Walsh, T. A. 1989. Diameter increment and survival equations for loblolly pine trees growing in thinned and unthinned plantations on cut-over, site-prepared lands. *So. J. Appl. For.* **13:**170–174.

Amateis, R. L., Radtke, P. J., and Burkhart, H. E. 1996. Growth and yield of thinned and unthinned plantations. *J. Forestry* **94(12):**19–23.

Atta-Boateng, J., and Moser, J. W., Jr. 2000. A compatible growth and yield model for the management of mixed tropical rain forest. *Can. J. For. Res.* **30:**311–323.

Bailey, R. L., and Dell, T. R. 1973. Quantifying diameter distributions with the Weibull function. *Forest Sci.* **19**:97–104.

Belcher, D. W., Holdaway, M. R., and Brand, G. J. 1982. A description of STEMS—The stand and tree evaluation and modeling system. *U.S. Forest Serv., North Central Forest Expt. Sta., Gen. Tech. Report NC*-79. 18 pp.

Bennett, F. A., and Clutter, J. L. 1968. Multiple-product yield estimates for unthinned slash pine plantations—pulpwood, sawtimber, gum. *U.S. Forest Serv., Southeast. Forest Expt. Sta., Res. Paper SE*-35. 21 pp.

———, McGee, C. E., and Clutter, J. L. 1959. Yield of old-field slash pine plantations. *U.S. Forest Serv., Southeast. Forest Expt. Sta., Paper* 107. 19 pp.

Bowling, E. H., Burkhart, H. E., Burk, T. E., and Beck, D. E. 1989. A stand-level, multi-species growth model for Appalachian hardwoods. *Can. J. For. Res.* **19**:405–412.

Buckman, R. E. 1962. Growth and yield of red pine in Minnesota. *U.S. Dept. of Agr., Forest Serv. Tech. Bull.* 1272. 50 pp.

Burk, T. E., and Nguyen, M. V. 1992. Visualizing the operation of a distance-dependent tree growth model. *The Compiler* **10(2):**10–19.

Burkhart, H. E. 1992. Scientific visualization for the study and use of forest stand simulators. *Landscape and Urban Planning* **21:**317–318.

———, Farrar, K. D., Amateis, R. L., and Daniels, R. F. 1987. Simulation of individual tree growth and stand development in loblolly pine plantations on cutover, site-prepared areas. *Virginia Poly. Inst. and State Univ., Pub. FWS*-1-87. 47 pp.

———, and Sprinz, P. T. 1984. Compatible cubic volume and basal area projection equations for thinned old-field loblolly pine plantations. *Forest Sci.* **30:**86–93.

Clutter, J. L. 1963. Compatible growth and yield models for loblolly pine. *Forest Sci.* **9:**354–371.

———, Fortson, J. C., Pienaar, L. V., Brister, G. H., and Bailey, R. L. 1983. *Timber management: A quantitative approach.* John Wiley & Sons, New York. 333 pp.

Coile, T. S., and Schumacher, F. X. 1964. *Soil-site relations, stand structure, and yields of slash and loblolly pine plantations in the Southern United States.* T. S. Coile, Inc., Durham, N.C. 296 pp.

Crookston, N. L., and Stage, A. R. 1999. Percent canopy cover and stand structure statistics from the forest vegetation simulator. *U.S. Forest Serv., Rocky Mountain Res. Sta., Gen. Tech. Report RMRS-GTR*-24. 11 pp.

Curtis, R. O., Clendenen, G. W., and DeMars, D. J. 1981. A new stand simulator for coast Douglas-fir: DFSIM user's guide. *U.S. Forest Serv., Pacific Northwest Forest and Range Expt. Sta., Gen. Tech. Report PNW*-128. 79 pp.

Daniels, R. F., and Burkhart, H. E. 1975. Simulation of individual tree growth and stand development in managed loblolly pine plantations. *Virginia Poly. Inst. and State Univ., Pub. FWS*-5-75. 69 pp.

———, and Burkhart, H. E. 1988. An integrated system of forest stand models. *For. Ecol. and Manage.* **23:**159–177.

Dell, T. R., Feduccia, D. P., Campbell, T. E., Mann, W. F., Jr., and Polmer, B. H. 1979. Yields of unthinned slash pine plantations on cutover sites in the West Gulf region. *U.S. Forest Serv., Southern Forest Expt. Sta., Res. Paper SO*-147. 84 pp.

Ek, A. R. 1974. Nonlinear models for stand table projection in northern hardwood stands. *Can. J. For. Res.* **4:**23–27.

———, and Monserud, R. A. 1974. FOREST: A computer model for simulating the growth and reproduction of mixed species forest stands. *Univ. of Wisconsin, Res. Paper* R2635. 13 pp. plus appendices.

Farrar, R. M., Jr. 1973. Southern pine site index equations. *J. Forestry* **71:**696–697.

Gadow, K., von, and Hui, G. 1999. *Modelling forest development.* Kluwer Academic Publishers, Dordrecht, The Netherlands. 213 pp.

Hilt, D. E. 1985. OAKSIM: An individual-tree growth and yield simulator for managed, even-aged, upland oak stands. *U.S. Forest Serv., Northeast. Forest Expt. Sta., Res. Paper NE*-562. 21 pp.

Huebschmann, M. M., Gering, L. R., Lynch, T. B., Bitoki, O., and Murphy, P. A. 2000. An individual-tree growth and yield prediction system for uneven-aged shortleaf pine stands. *So. J. Appl. For.* **24:**112–120.

Hyink, D. M., and Moser, J. W., Jr. 1983. A generalized framework for projecting forest yield and stand structure using diameter distributions. *Forest Sci.* **29:**85–95.

Knoebel, B. R., Burkhart, H. E., and Beck, D. E. 1986. A growth and yield model for thinned stands of yellow-poplar. *Forest Sci. Monograph* 27. 62 pp.

Lenhart, J. D. 1988. Diameter-distribution yield-prediction system for unthinned loblolly and slash pine plantations on non-old-fields in East Texas. *So. J. Appl. For.* **12:**239–242.

Lynch, T. B., and Moser, J. W., Jr. 1986. A growth model for mixed species stands. *Forest Sci.* **32:**697–706.

MacKinney, A. L., and Chaiken, L. E. 1939. Volume, yield, and growth of loblolly pine in the mid-Atlantic coastal region. *U.S. Forest Serv., Appalachian Forest Expt. Sta., Tech. Note* 33. 30 pp.

Matney, T. G., and Sullivan, A. D. 1982. Compatible stand and stock tables for thinned and unthinned loblolly pine stands. *Forest Sci.* **28:**161–171.

McArdle, R. E., Meyer, W. H., and Bruce, D. 1961. The yield of Douglas-fir in the Pacific Northwest. *U.S. Dept. of Agr., Forest Serv. Tech. Bull.* 201 (rev.). 74 pp.

McGaughey, R. J. 1997. Visualizing forest stand dynamics using the stand visualization system. Pp. 248–257 in *Proceedings of the 1997 ACSM/ASPRS Annual Convention and Exposition;* April 7–10, 1997, Seattle, Wash. Vol. 4. American Society for Photogrammetry and Remote Sensing, Bethesda, Md.

———. 1998. Techniques for visualizing the appearance of forestry operations. *J. Forestry* **96(6):**9–14.

Mitchell, K. J. 1975. Dynamics and simulated yield of Douglas-fir. *Forest Sci. Monograph* 17. 39 pp.

Moser, J. W., Jr., and Hall, O. F. 1969. Deriving growth and yield functions for uneven-aged forest stands. *Forest Sci.* **15:**183–188.

Pienaar, L. V., and Turnbull, K. J. 1973. The Chapman-Richards generalization of von Bertalanffy's growth model for basal area growth and yield in even-aged stands. *Forest Sci.* **19:**2–22.

Ritchie, M. W. 1999. A compendium of forest growth and yield simulators for the Pacific Coast states. *U.S. Forest Serv., Pacific Southwest Res. Sta., Gen. Tech. Report PSW-GTR*-174. 59 pp.

Shortt, J. S., and Burkhart, H. E. 1996. A comparison of loblolly pine plantation growth and yield models for inventory updating. *So. J. Appl. For.* **20:**15–22.

Smalley, G. W., and Bailey, R. L. 1974. Yield tables and stand structure for loblolly pine plantations in Tennessee, Alabama, and Georgia highlands. *U.S. Forest Serv., Southern Forest Expt. Sta., Res. Paper SO*-96. 81 pp.

Stage, A. R. 1973. Prognosis model for stand development. *U.S. Forest Serv., Intermountain Forest and Range Expt. Sta., Res. Paper INT*-137. 32 pp.

Sullivan, A. D., and Clutter, J. L. 1972. A simultaneous growth and yield model for loblolly pine. *Forest Sci.* **18:**76–86.

Vanclay, J. K. 1994. *Modelling forest growth and yield: Applications to mixed tropical forests.* CAB International, Wallingford, United Kingdom. 312 pp.

————, and Skovsgaard, J. P. 1997. Evaluating forest growth models. *Ecol. Modelling* **98:**1–12.

Wycoff, W. R., Crookston, N. L., and Stage, A. R. 1982. User's guide to the Stand Prognosis Model. *U.S. Forest Serv., Intermountain Forest and Range Expt. Sta., Gen. Tech. Report INT*-133. 112 pp.

Zedaker, S. M., Burkhart, H. E., and Stage, A. R. 1987. General principles and patterns of conifer growth and yield. Pp. 203–241 in *Forest vegetation management for conifer production,* J. D. Walstad and P. J. Kuch (eds.), John Wiley & Sons, New York.

CHAPTER 18

ASSESSING RANGELAND, WILDLIFE, WATER, AND RECREATIONAL RESOURCES

18-1 Purpose of Chapter   A detailed treatment of measurement and inventory of forage, wildlife, water, and recreational resources is beyond the scope of an introductory book on forest measurements. Typically, measurement of these resources is discussed in detail in textbooks that focus on management of a specific forest land resource. Nevertheless, an introduction to assessment of these resources is sometimes provided in measurements courses aimed primarily at quantifying the tree overstory. Integrated inventories that consider measurement of several resources are sometimes conducted, and many of the sampling, measurement, and prediction principles discussed in this volume apply to resources other than timber. This chapter provides a brief introduction and overview of assessing rangeland, wildlife, water, and recreational resources. Additional detail can be obtained from the references cited at the end of the chapter.

MEASURING RANGELAND RESOURCES

18-2 Forage Resources   *Rangelands* may be defined as those lands supporting vegetation suitable for grazing. The use of these lands is not limited to livestock and wildlife; rangelands may have concurrent utility for watershed protection, recreation, timber-growing, mining, or other activities. The range manager's objective is to obtain maximum coordinated use of these lands on a sustained yield basis.

Included in this section are range-measurement techniques utilized by resource managers to measure characteristics of grass, grasslike, forb, and shrub vegetation. Such information is used in developing range management plans and in evaluating the results of implemented management practices.

For estimating livestock and wildlife grazing capacity, information may be needed on forage production, patterns of forage utilization, or changes in vegetative communities resulting from grazing use or specific management practices. Measurements of vegetative cover may be desired for relating management influences on water infiltration and runoff. It may also be necessary to document changes in understory vegetation that result from timber-cutting practices because different cutting systems influence fire danger, timber regeneration, wildlife habitat, and soil erosion. And finally, vegetative measurements might be needed to determine the suitability of an area for outdoor recreational use—or to determine the effect of recreational use on changes in plant cover and composition. Thus at certain points in time, all resource managers are likely to be interested in measurements of the herbaceous and shrubby plants that are characteristic of rangelands.

18-3 Planning Range Measurements   Marking the boundaries of the planning unit or study area on maps and aerial photographs is the first step in deciding on the sampling procedures and measurements to be made. The size of the planning unit and the variability within the unit determine, to a great extent, the procedures and techniques that should be used. The specific data required, time available for measurements, accuracy desired, financing available, and abilities of resource personnel should also be considered before the collection of field data.

The range manager seldom encounters a planning unit that is sufficiently homogeneous for sampling without some degree of stratification. As a rule, this stratification is accomplished by ground surveillance, by visual reconnaissance from low-flying aircraft, or by detailed study of aerial photographs and soil survey maps. The recognition and delineation of various strata make it feasible to employ more efficient sampling procedures (e.g., stratified random sampling, Sec. 3-8).

Range sites sometimes occur in such variable patterns that it is not practical to map each site separately. The mapping unit then becomes a complex of sites. The proportion of each site within the mapping unit may be determined by applying geographic information systems (Chap. 14). Sampling in the field may be accomplished by sites, with data interpreted and applied to the mapping unit on the basis of the percentage of the sites within the complex mapping unit.

18-4 Sampling Considerations   The *time of sampling* range vegetation is important because range plant communities are composed of plants that reach their peak development at different seasons, or at different periods within a season.

There are "cool-season plants" that tend to exhibit maximum growth in early spring and fall and "warm-season plants" that grow mainly in the summer, provided moisture conditions are favorable during these periods.

Near the end of the major growing season is often the best time for many vegetation surveys because species are best recognized at this time, and total herbage and browse production are near maximum. The resource manager should realize, however, that biases may exist from sampling at this time because an important species that reached peak development earlier may have largely passed from the scene. Utilization studies may be made during the grazing period to determine seasonal patterns of use; but, if only a single utilization check is planned, it is best done toward the end of a grazing period and prior to a new plant growth period.

With respect to the *sampling design,* most of the techniques described earlier in this book (Chap. 3) apply equally to range inventories. The resource manager must decide on the technique that will provide the needed information and measure a sufficient number of sampling units to achieve the desired level of sampling precision. Stratified random sampling will often provide a cost-effective inventory system for extensive surveys when good-quality aerial photographs are available. Where systematic designs are specified, the resource manager should be aware of the pitfalls of treating such samples as if they were randomly selected (Sec. 3-7).

Sampling units for range measurements may be circular, square, or rectangular plots. As with most forms of sampling, the plot size selected should be the smallest possible for convenience and efficiency of sampling, yet large enough so that the sampling variation between plots is not extreme. The most frequently used plot sizes for range survey span from 0.1 to 1.0 m^2.

The plot size may be chosen for the attribute being measured on the basis of previous data from the same or a similar range site, or by a preliminary study accomplished to determine the best plot size and number to achieve a specified level of sampling precision. For the latter approach, data will be needed on the *time* required to measure different-sized plots and on the influence of plot *sizes* on the coefficient of variation. These relationships, along with formulas for calculating sampling intensity, are discussed in Chapter 3.

18-5 Determining Grazing Capacity   Livestock grazing capacity is usually expressed in terms of animal-unit-months (AUM). An animal unit is the equivalent of 1,000 lb of animal live weight, which has traditionally been defined as a cow and her calf. The dry-weight forage required to provide for one animal-unit-month on rangeland is approximately 600 to 900 lb.

Animal unit conversion factors may be used to convert the amount of forage required per AUM to forage requirements for a particular class of livestock or species of wildlife. Using mature cattle as a baseline of 1.00, some conversion factors are mule deer, 0.15; white-tailed deer, 0.10; pronghorn (American antelope), 0.12; sheep, 0.15; horses, 1.80 (Holechek, Pieper, and Herbel, 1995).

Grazing capacity is the number of grazing animals that can be maintained on a range without depleting the range resource. The basic calculations to determine grazing capacity from herbage- and browse-weight measurements may be summarized by the following relationship:

Grazing capacity per unit area =

$$\frac{\sum \left[\left(\begin{array}{c} \text{dry wt. per unit area} \\ \text{for each plant species} \end{array} \right) \times \left(\text{species use factor} \right) \right]}{\text{animal unit requirement}}$$

As an example, the following herbage and browse weights, along with corresponding use factors, may be assumed:

Range plant species	Weight per acre (lb)	Use factor (percent)
Blue grama	370	60
Burroweed	56	0
Poverty threeawn	224	20

If we further assume that the animal unit requirement will be approximately 750 lb/AUM, then the grazing capacity would be estimated as

$$\frac{(370 \times 0.60 + 56 \times 0.0 + 224 \times 0.20)}{750} = \frac{267}{750} = 0.36 \text{ AUM per acre}$$

Therefore, one animal unit could graze on 1 acre for 0.36 month; in other words, 2.8 acres would be required to yield forage for 1 AUM. Thirty-four acres would be needed to carry one animal unit for a year.

18-6 Clipped-Plot Technique Clipped plots may be used to determine weight of herbage and browse on range sites. The procedure is to locate plots of known area and clip herbaceous plants as near to ground level as practical, and to clip the current year's production on browse plants. Individual plant species may be clipped separately and weighed in the field, or herbage can be grouped into functional classes such as perennial grass, forbs, or browse. Then, samples of clipped species may be collected and dried to determine percentages of dry weights.

In the past, square plots that are 3.1 ft on a side (9.6 sq ft) have been popular for herbage clipping, because the plot yield in grams is converted to pounds per acre when multiplied by 10. When using the metric system, 1-m^2 plots (i.e., 1 m on a side) are popular. With this plot size, the herbage weight in grams, multiplied by 10, will be converted to yield in kilograms per ha. Various plot sizes may be used for different kinds of vegetation, of course.

Plots used to determine *total* herbage and browse weight may be clipped on range sites prior to grazing or on plots protected from grazing by wire cages. There are a number of sources of error that may be associated with clipped plots unless precautions are taken during clipping. Care must be taken to clip accurately at the plot boundary; otherwise data will be biased upward or downward. The inclusion of previous-year dry-matter production along with current growth will result in an overestimation of annual production. And carelessness in the height of clipping can introduce bias because a high proportion of the weight of some plants (e.g., bunch grasses) is near the base.

Since clipped-plot samples are expensive and time-consuming, they are largely employed in conjunction with other estimation techniques. Ocular estimates of vegetation weight, in combination with clipping and weighing, are sometimes used in range analysis. The estimator is trained to recognize plant-weight units of 5 or 10 g, or some other convenient unit, and then proceeds to estimate the number of these units for each plant species on sample plots. Ocular estimates have proved most successful when few species are present on the plots.

Clipped plots and ocular estimates can be combined in a system of double sampling (Chap. 3). By this technique, ocular estimates are made for all sample plots, then a subsample (perhaps 1 plot in 10) is clipped and weighed. The relationship between estimated and clipped plots is established by regression analysis, and all estimated data are then adjusted by using the fitted regression. The application of regression techniques to relate an easily measured attribute to herbage or browse weight is a common approach for determining plant-weight production on a range site.

18-7 Range-Utilization Estimates   The utilization of forage plants is commonly expressed as the percentage of the current year's herbage or browse weight that is removed by grazing animals. There are many different techniques for determining utilization, but the simplest method is to select a *key species* (a palatable and abundant plant) and estimate the percentage use of this species along transect lines through the range sites.

One use of the utilization percentage is for calculating a grazing capacity. If a range is stocked for 60 days with 40 animal units (80 AUM), the proper use factor for a key species is 60 percent, and the current use is estimated at 20 percent, then grazing capacity may be calculated by this relationship:

$$\frac{80 \text{ AUM}}{0.20 \text{ current use}} = \frac{x \text{ AUM}}{0.60 \text{ proper use}}$$

The grazing capacity is thus calculated as 240 AUM. One-third of this amount (80 AUM) is currently being used; therefore, there are 160 AUM remaining to be utilized.

Utilization studies are also needed to determine *where* a range is being grazed. The key species selected for this type of evaluation should be widely distributed and palatable and should be a species for which use can be easily estimated. The pattern of usage should be mapped, with notations on areas that are overgrazed or undergrazed. Armed with this information, the range manager can plan such management improvements as water development, fencing, herding, or trails in order to obtain more uniform use on a range.

Another benefit derived from utilization studies is that of learning which plants are used during different seasons of the year. This information is useful in evaluating the effects of grazing on plant vigor and in planning grazing levels and systems that will maintain the vigor of preferred herbage species.

Ocular estimates of utilization are often employed. Resource managers make such estimates by clipping plants to various levels, estimating the weights removed, and then verifying the actual utilization by clipping and weighing remaining plant parts. Such estimates may be made over general areas, on sample plots of fixed area, or on individual plants along transect lines.

Another technique employs *paired* sample plots, plants, or plant parts to estimate utilization. One of the pair is clipped *before* grazing and the other *after* grazing; the difference, expressed as a percentage of the ungrazed weight, is the utilization. For pasture studies, the forage weight differences may be obtained from caged versus open (grazed) plots, but such techniques are too expensive and require too many sampling units to be cost-effective for most range inventories.

Measurement of *twig length* before and after grazing is a technique used in some browse-utilization studies. In this case, use is not a percentage of total plant weight, but the method does provide an estimate of the *relative* degree of plant utilization. The greatest difficulties with this approach are those associated with twig growth between measurements and the problem of obtaining an unbiased and adequate sample.

The *number of grazed twigs* on browse plants may also be used to estimate relative plant utilization. With this method, individual plants and branches from each plant should be selected at random. Ten twigs (or some other convenient number), beginning at the tip of the branch, are then observed. The percentage of total twigs that are grazed provides an estimate of relative utilization for the plant species sampled. Averages for large numbers of plants may be required to obtain a reliable estimate for an entire site.

Regression techniques are useful for relating relatively "easy-to-measure" characteristics to plant utilization. Relationships between percent of utilization and average height of grazed plants or number of plants grazed can be developed for specific range sites; then, for future studies, use estimates are greatly simplified (Fig. 18-1).

One of the major problems encountered on utilization surveys is that of evaluating use during a period when regrowth may occur; this is the main reason for planning field observations near the end of the growing season for key species.

18-8 Range Condition and Trend   It has long been recognized that overgrazing of certain plant communities can be documented by changes in the species composition of those communities (Sampson, 1917). It has also been shown that

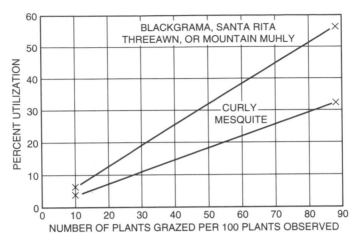

FIGURE 18-1
Relationship of percentage utilization to number of plants grazed.
(Courtesy Arizona Inter-Agency Range Committee.)

grazing capacity is influenced by the stage of plant succession on a range area, with higher grazing capacities usually associated with stages of succession closest to herbaceous climax vegetation.

Range condition is the status or stage of succession that a plant community expresses as compared with the potential or climax vegetation possible for the site. Thus the condition may be classed as excellent, good, fair, or poor, depending on present characteristics of the range site. Impacts of grazing and other influences on a range site are reflected by changes in species composition, plant cover, numbers of plants, relative vigor of plants, and soil erosion.

Trend is the direction of change—whether stable, toward the potential for the site, or away from the potential for the site. A trend toward poorer range conditions might be caused by such factors as excessive grazing, drought, fire, plant diseases, or mechanical disturbances of the soil. The range manager must be able to determine the causes of site deterioration. A poor range condition is usually an indication that improvements in management are needed to restore the site to its maximum productivity and use. Although range condition and trend evaluations tend to emphasize grazing influences, these concepts may also be extended to measure impacts of any origin on the range vegetation.

Plant cover, density, and frequency are the attributes of vegetation that are most frequently measured to determine condition and trend on range sites in response to grazing or other impacts.

Plant canopy cover is the proportion (or percentage) of the ground surface under live aerial parts of plants. *Plant basal cover* is the percentage of the ground covered by plant bases, and *total cover* may include the combined aerial parts of

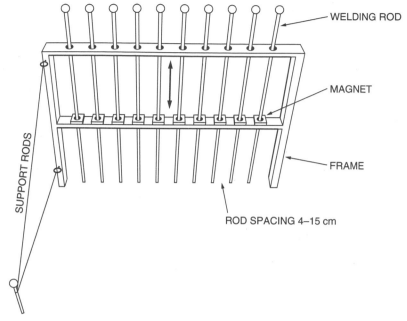

WELDING ROD

MAGNET

FRAME

ROD SPACING 4–15 cm

SUPPORT RODS

FIGURE 18-2
A point frame for sampling range vegetation.

plants, mulch, and rocks. Cover may be determined from ocular estimates of sample plots, by charting or mapping vegetation on plots, or it may be estimated from low-altitude aerial photographs.

The proportion of cover may also be estimated along taped transects, or "point frames" may be employed (Fig. 18-2). A frame holding 10 vertical or inclined pins is a standard measuring device; the pins are lowered through the vegetation, and the percentage of "hits" provides an estimate of cover.

Density is defined as the number of plants or specific plant parts per unit area of ground surface (e.g., number of mesquite plants per ha). The counting of individual plants on sample plots of known area is a simple means of deriving density estimates. For sod-forming plants, however, it is difficult to decide on which plant units to count. And in some vegetation areas, the number of plants per unit area is so large that counting is not practical. Density does not give an indication of the size of individuals unless counts are made and recorded by size classes.

Frequency is the number of plots on which a species occurs divided by the total number of plots sampled. Frequency data are used to detect changes in plant abundance and distribution on a range site over time or to identify differences in species responses to varying management practices. Estimates of frequency are simple and objective; the resource manager must merely identify the species and record its presence if it is found on the sample plot.

Selection of the proper plot size is extremely important for estimating frequency, and more than one plot size may be needed for varying plant species and plant distributions. Frequency data are easily obtained, but numerous sample plots must often be evaluated before reliable estimates can be derived.

The relative proportion of each plant species on a given range site is termed the *species composition.* It may be expressed in terms of weight, cover, or density (Society for Range Management, 1998).

A three-step method of condition and trend measurements (U.S. Forest Service, 1965) has been utilized for range analyses on lands managed by the U.S. Forest Service and Bureau of Land Management. The first step is to establish a cluster of two or three permanent transects. At regular intervals along each transect, a 2-cm- (¾-in.-) diameter loop is lowered vertically from the tape marking the transect. A tally of plant "hits," rock, litter, and bare soil within the loops is made. Then, plant cover, total ground cover (including rocks and litter), and plant composition can be estimated from the data.

The second step is to use ocular appraisals and a summary of transect data to classify current condition and trend of the site. Vegetation condition is determined by "scores" based on plant composition, cover, and plant vigor. A soil condition rating is also determined.

The third step is to take a close-up photo and a photo of the general view of the transect for future reference. These are permanent study transects; and, when data are collected for the same site at a future date, a new estimate of condition is attained, trend is indicated, and adjustments in management can be made accordingly.

MEASURING WILDLIFE RESOURCES

18-9 Animal Populations and Habitat Management of the wildlife resource implies an effort to attain a degree of balance between the food and cover available and the animal populations that are favored. Thus the inventory problems are twofold:

1 Estimating, through periodic sampling techniques, numbers of animals, composition, trend, and the natural range of various wildlife populations.

2 Determining the food and cover requirements of different species, and evaluating the adequacy of various habitat units for supporting wildlife populations.

In many respects, the problems associated with wildlife measurements are similar to those described in evaluating rangeland resources for domesticated livestock. This is particularly true with respect to wildlife habitat assessments, that is, the determination of carrying capacity, forage production, forage utilization, or condition and trend. With wild animals, however, the exact population size is rarely, if ever, known. Therefore census techniques, along with estimates of animal productivity and population trend, are also of special importance.

18-10 Population Estimates   The various techniques for measuring populations of vertebrates may be grouped into three classes: *direct* census, *indirect* census, and mark-recapture techniques. A direct census implies the counting of the animals or birds themselves; such counts may be made on drives, by visual surveillance from aircraft, from aerial photographs or thermal imagery, and by ground observations on flushing strips.

For an indirect census, observations other than animal counts are recorded, and the population estimate is derived from this indirect evidence of animal presence. Included here are bird-call counts, track counts, and pellet-group counts.

Mark-recapture methods are used to estimate population size. For example, a known number of game birds may be captured, banded, and returned to the population. When these birds are seen, recaptured, or taken by hunters at some later point in time, the ratio of the total banded birds to those recaptured can be used for estimating the population size.

The drive-census method requires a line of observers, or "beaters," moving steadily through an area to flush out the desired species. Recorders are stationed at the opposite boundaries and along the edges of the tract to count the animals pushed out. If vegetation is sparse and the line of beaters is widely spaced, each person records all birds or animals that go back through the line on their right side. A fair amount of noise is often desirable, and regular calling back and forth among beaters (to be sure that all observations are recorded) will aid in obtaining a reliable count.

The drive census is one of the oldest methods in use; and, where sufficient personnel are available, it will provide reliable population estimates. The fact that 25 to 50 persons may be needed to cover an area of 1 mi^2 tends to limit the application of the method to level terrain that is already surrounded by clearings such as firebreaks or logging roads. Under the limited circumstances in which drives are economically feasible, the data derived serve as a useful control or base for evaluating alternative census procedures.

Visual observation of wildlife from low-flying aircraft is an effective census technique in areas where animals tend to congregate and where overstory cover is relatively sparse. The method is mainly applicable to large-mammal counts in open plains country and for migratory waterfowl wintering on open coastal waters.

A common procedure involves low-level flights in a grid pattern with a pilot and observer. Helicopters, though more expensive, may be effectively used to count desert bighorn sheep in rough, low mountains or to enumerate elk that are concentrated on winter ranges with sparse tree cover. In some states, visual surveys are also used to census moose and to count breeding waterfowl on systematically spaced aerial transects.

Helicopter counts are apt to be more reliable than surveys from fixed-wing aircraft, and the slower flights may enable observers to obtain a listing of species sighted by sex and age classes. The basic census procedures are simple for good observers and pilots, especially where the exact flight paths and areas to be covered are carefully mapped out in advance.

Wildlife species that can be counted on visual surveys are also susceptible to enumeration on aerial photographs. Large-scale photography has been successfully used to count waterfowl along the Pacific Coast flyway and to determine trends in gull populations by combining visual estimates of numbers with photography of nesting areas and associated flocks. Such trend estimates do not provide a complete picture of the population, but they may be useful in detecting large annual changes (i.e., variations of 25 percent or more). For inventories of waterfowl and large mammals, photographic scales of 1:3,000 and larger are recommended; color or infrared color films should be specified to provide maximum contrast between the wildlife species and associated backgrounds or native habitats.

The *strip-flushing census method* may be used for species that will hold to cover until an observer approaches and then fly or run away when flushed. Ruffed grouse, woodcock, and even white-tailed deer may be enumerated by this technique.

The procedure is similar to a strip system of timber cruising sometimes used by foresters. The observer walks along parallel lines or transects through a tract and records the perpendicular *flushing distance* each time an animal is sighted. In practice, the technique tends to be limited to fairly level and open terrain where walking is very easy and where good visibility conditions prevail.

Indirect census methods are commonly used for smaller, short-lived animals and for big game that is relatively inaccessible because of weather, terrain, or cover. Such surveys may be less precise than a direct census, but they can provide valuable information on population trends.

Call counts are used to assess population trends for game birds such as the mourning dove. When doves migrate northward in spring, the males establish territories and attempt to attract a female by calling (cooing). In many states, a series of 20-mile routes have been established in dove habitats for checking during the calling season. Observers begin their routes just before daylight, stopping at specified intervals to count all dove calls heard during a 3-min interval. Doves seen perched or flying across the road between stops are recorded separately.

Most male birds that proclaim territories by calling can be counted by various modifications of this method. Male call counts alone do not constitute a complete census, but they may be used in conjunction with sex-ratio data to provide population estimates and trends.

Track counts is a census method that is best adapted to land areas that are crisscrossed with a grid pattern of nonsurfaced (i.e., easily imprinted) roads and trails. Checking these roads a few hours after heavy rains appears to give the best results. The technique has received limited endorsement, because counts are often highly variable, especially for low population densities.

The behavioral pattern and activity cycle of the species should be well-known to observers before this census procedure is attempted. Track counts are most useful for assessing populations when a species is migrating or when herds are moving from one seasonal range to another.

The *pellet-group-count method* is based on the assumption that periodic accumulations of animal defecations are related to population density. Assuming, for example, that mule deer and elk leave about 13 clusters of fecal pellets on the ground every 24 hours, the number of pellet groups on a range unit may be converted to one deer or elk day for each 13 groups found. To convert deer-days to numbers of animals, it is necessary to know how long the deer has been on the area (which can be determined for migratory herds), or the survey must be cleared of pellet groups and then counted *after* a known time interval (e.g., 1 month). Population density estimates from pellet-group counts are not very reliable, but they are sometimes used as a general index of habitat use or of relative abundance.

The *Lincoln-Petersen index* is a commonly used ratio method of population estimation based on the banding or marking of animals. A number of animals are captured, marked or banded, and then released back into the population. When animals from the population are later recaptured, the ratio of total banded animals to the banded individuals caught can be used to estimate the size of the population (N):

$$N = \frac{\text{total no. banded}}{\text{no. of banded caught}} \times \text{total no. caught}$$

The accuracy of the method depends upon an adequate sample size, and the banded or unbanded individuals must have an equal chance of being recaptured. Recapturing animals with food bait may result in a biased sample if "trap-happy" animals return for the bait more frequently than individuals who have not previously found it.

18-11 Habitat Measurement   Populations of wildlife tend to differ in numbers because of variations in hunting pressures, species characteristics, adaptability, and the quality of available habitats. The essential habitat components are water, food, and cover (i.e., protection from inclement weather and predators, including man).

Different types of plant cover used for nest sites, resting, bed grounds, and other purposes will also vary with the wildlife species, its size, and mobility. It is necessary to evaluate the cover requirements for each species, since adequate cover for the cottontail will be inadequate for deer. Of equal importance to the elements of water, food, and cover is the *spatial arrangement* of these components. Without the proper arrangement of the essential habitat elements, there will be a poor population or none at all. Most wildlife need *all* these elements within their normal daily range of movement; if the basic elements periodically reoccur in several locales over a landscape, a highly productive population is much more likely to develop.

Procedures previously described for estimating forage yields, use, condition, and trend of rangelands will apply equally to wildlife habitats. Measurements of the edible herbage utilized from shrubs or trees are based on twig lengths before and after browsing. Carrying capacities for various habitats are computed by the same procedure used for determining livestock grazing capacity. In fact, in some instances, a given range may be utilized by either domestic or semiwild animals. Animal unit requirements will differ for each species, of course.

An important source of wildlife food that is of minimal concern to domestic livestock is plant fruit, including acorns, nuts, and seeds. Measurements of fruit production are difficult because of variations in time of ripening and the length of time they are held on the producing plant.

Efforts to estimate fruit yields have been generally confined to acorns, nuts, or large fleshy fruits. Sampling may be based on fixed-area plots by setting funnel-type traps to collect dropped fruits or by counting fruit on sample branches of the woody plant. With trap samples, the number of fruits per trap is expanded to the number for the total crown area; four to six traps per tree are often used for estimating acorn yields.

When numbers of fruits on sample branches are used for estimation purposes, tree totals may then be expanded by determining yields from various classes of tree size, form, and species in stands of known composition and density. Area sampling consists of collecting data from small plots distributed over the entire stand. Open, unprotected plots on the ground may be useful if samples can be taken frequently during the fruiting season. Otherwise, traps must be used to protect against losses due to deterioration and animal consumption.

One measurable quantity that is related to the *arrangement* of the basic habitat elements is the amount of *edge* present on a given range. Edge may be defined as the total linear measure of the borderline between two distinct vegetation types; that is, it must be distinct in the eyes of the wildlife species under consideration. Some animals find these borders between classes of vegetation attractive because they often provide food supplies near nesting grounds, cover for travel, or a clear escape route near a bed ground.

The amount of edge is subject to periodic change because of natural succession and events such as forest fires and timber harvesting. A square opening of 20 acres surrounded by forest has less than one-third of the border or edge provided by ten scattered 2-acre openings. This fact can be an important consideration in planning clearcut logging in conjunction with wildlife habitat requirements.

There are many techniques for measuring edge on a selected range (e.g., on type maps or aerial photographs or by employing geographic information systems), but the land manager must exercise keen judgment in deciding *which edges* will be of interest and importance to a given species of wildlife. For example, a deer might not consider a difference between two grass types to be significant, whereas a grass-bush border would probably constitute an important edge.

The concept of edge is particularly important for species that are characterized by a limited home range and a small radius of daily mobility. While edge is beneficial to many wildlife species, it should be noted that it is not advantageous to all species. Each species has unique requirements for food, water, and cover. The U.S.

Fish and Wildlife Service has developed indices, called *habitat suitability indices,* which indicate the degree to which habitat requirements of selected species are met within a given area. These indices provide a numerical score, ranging from 0 to 1, that describes the relative suitability of a given area as habitat for a selected species (Reed and Mroz, 1997).

MEASURING WATER RESOURCES

18-12 Importance of Water   Water is important to resource managers in its liquid, solid, and vapor forms. It is one of our most dynamic natural resources, and at times it may completely dominate or limit the use and management of other resources on the land. During periods of heavy rainfall, runoff, or snow cover, for example, water may limit access to the land, timber harvesting, grazing, and other operational functions.

In both liquid and solid forms, water influences the production rates of timber, forage, and wildlife. In the form of snow, water provides winter recreational opportunities, and liquid water on and from wildlands affects fishing, swimming, boating, and other water-based recreational activities. In many localities, streamflow runoff derived from liquid and solid precipitation constitutes an important water-supply source for municipal, industrial, and agricultural applications downstream. Runoff may also provide significant sources of power to aid in satisfying energy needs. Excessive runoff may cause upstream and downstream damage as a result of erosion, flooding, or sedimentation. Thus, the quantity, timing, and quality of water produced from wildlands are of critical importance; either too much or too little water can be as limiting as water of impaired quality.

In vapor form, water is a factor in determining evaporation and transpiration rates from wildlands. And its contribution to atmospheric humidity may exert a significant influence on the forest-fire hazard because of the effect on fuel moisture contents.

Interactions between water and the utilization of other resources on the land can also be important. As an illustration, the harvesting of trees may increase streamflow yields, at least temporarily. At the same time, poor access-road engineering on watersheds may increase rates of erosion and sedimentation. It is therefore apparent that not only does water affect other resources, but the use and management of those resources affects water quantity and quality. To assess the significance of water both on and off the land, the resource manager should be able to inventory water in its various forms, just as is done for timber, rangelands, and wildlife resources.

18-13 Factors Affecting Runoff   The flow of a stream is essentially controlled by two factors, one depending on the physical characteristics of the watershed and the other upon weather and climatic characteristics (e.g., precipitation) that directly affect the watershed. Land managers concerned with water resources must have an appreciation of the mensurational aspects of both sets of factors to achieve desired water resource objectives and to properly evaluate available management opportunities.

A watershed is an area of internal drainage, the size and shape of which is determined by surface topography. A watershed is completely encircled by a divide or ridge line. Precipitation falling on one side of the divide drains toward the outlet or mouth of the watershed on that side of the divide; precipitation falling on the other side of the divide drains toward outlets of other watersheds. The resource manager uses the watershed as his basic land unit for planning and management purposes; in this sense, it is roughly comparable to the forester's working circle or the range manager's grazing allotment.

In essence, the watershed is a limited unit of the Earth's surface within which climatic conditions can be assessed; it also represents a system where a balance can be struck in terms of the inflow and outflow of moisture. Various sizes of watersheds may be recognized and delineated, depending on the objectives of users. Small, experimental watersheds may encompass only a few ha in area, while large watersheds may be composed of entire river basins.

18-14 Physical Characteristics of a Watershed Perhaps the easiest characteristic of a watershed to measure is its areal extent. Such evaluations are commonly made by using a planimeter or dot grids to measure the delineated area on planimetric maps, topographic maps, or aerial photographs. Area is an important consideration because the total volume of water carried by a stream is directly re lated to watershed area.

Another important consideration is the effect of watershed area on peak flows. As with total water yields, higher peak flows are usually associated with larger areas. However, when such outputs are expressed in terms of *flow per unit of watershed area,* it is the smaller watersheds that characteristically have the greater rates of flow.

The outline form or shape of a watershed can sometimes have a marked effect on streamflow patterns. For example, a long, narrow basin would be expected to have attenuated flood-discharge periods, whereas basins with round or oval shapes are expected to produce sharply peaked flood discharges. Although watershed shape is a difficult parameter to quantify, various indices have been developed for comparing the configurations of different basins. One such index, based on the degree of roundness or circularity of a watershed, may be computed by

$$\text{Shape index} = \frac{0.28 \times \text{watershed perimeter (units)}}{\sqrt{\text{watershed area (units}^2)}}$$

When a watershed is circular in shape, the index value will be approximately 1. The closer a shape-index value is to unity, the greater the likelihood that precipitation will be quickly concentrated in the main stream channel, possibly resulting in high peak flows. Watersheds that are noncircular in shape will have index values greater than unity.

The slopes of various land surfaces within a watershed, usually expressed in percentage terms, can greatly influence the velocity and associated erosive power of overland flow. In addition, slope is related to infiltration, evapotranspiration, soil moisture, and the groundwater contribution to streamflow.

For small areas, watershed slope can be estimated by computing the average slope from several on-the-ground measurements obtained with an Abney level or clinometer. For larger areas, or for evaluating a number of different watersheds, slope estimates can be computed from topographic maps issued by the U.S. Geological Survey or by use of digital terrain models. One procedure consists of randomly selecting locations within each watershed and measuring slopes directly on the contour maps; the slope for the entire watershed can then be approximated by computing an arithmetic average of these values. Watershed slope can also be estimated by the following relationship, based on determining the area between contour lines within a watershed:

$$\text{Slope (\%)} = \frac{c \times l}{a}(100)$$

where c = contour interval (ft or m)
  l = total length of contours (ft or m)
  a = area of watershed (ft^2 or m^2)

For those occasional situations in which slopes are relatively uniform over an entire watershed, an estimate of average slope may be derived by the relationship

$$\text{Slope (\%)} = \frac{e}{d}(100)$$

where e = elevational difference between the highest and lowest points on the
  watershed (ft or m)
  d = horizontal distance between high and low elevations (ft or m)

The mean elevation and the variations in elevation of a watershed are important factors with respect to temperature and precipitation patterns, especially in mountainous topography. Temperature patterns, in turn, are associated with evaporative losses and with the timing of periods of snowpack accumulation and melt. Precipitation patterns, such as annual amounts or the proportion of annual precipitation that falls as snow, may also be related to elevation and are important in assessing the total water flow from a watershed.

Transpiration and evaporation losses on a watershed, factors that affect the amount of water available for streamflow, are influenced by the general orientation or aspect of the basin. Also, the accumulation and melting of snow is related to the orientation of a watershed. For example, if the orientation is southerly, successive snowfalls may soon melt and infiltrate into the ground or produce runoff. For those watersheds with a northerly orientation, individual snowfalls may accumulate throughout the winter and melt late in the spring, producing high flow rates.

The orientation of a watershed is normally expressed in degrees azimuth or in terms of the major compass headings (i.e., N, NE, E, etc.); the designation indicates the direction that the watershed "faces." The direction of flow for the main stream channel can also be used to indicate the general orientation of a watershed.

The pattern or arrangement of natural streams on a watershed is an important physical characteristic of any drainage basin for two primary reasons. First of all, it affects the efficiency of the drainage system and thus its hydrographic characteristics. Secondly, the drainage provides the land manager with a knowledge of soil and surface conditions existing on the watershed; more specifically, the erosive forces of stream channels are related to and restricted by the type of materials from which the channels are carved. Most drainage patterns can be classed as dendritic (i.e., an irregular branching of tributaries, often with no predominant direction or orientation).

A quantitative approach to classifying streams in a basin can consist in systematically *ordering* the network of branches and tributary streams. Each nonbranching tributary, regardless of whether it enters the main stream channel or its branches, is designated a first-order stream. Streams receiving only nonbranching tributaries are termed second order; third-order streams are formed by the junction of two second-order streams, and so on (Fig. 18-3). The order number of the main stream at the bottom of the watershed indicates the extent of branching and is an indication of the size and extent of the drainage network.

Another method of quantifying the drainage network of a watershed consists of determining drainage density by the following relationship:

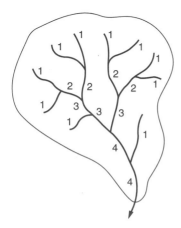

FIGURE 18-3
Horton's system of designating stream orders.

$$\text{Drainage density} = \frac{l}{a}$$

where l = total length of perennial and intermittent streams on a watershed (units)
 a = watershed area (units^2)

Drainage density is an expression of the closeness of spacing of stream channels on a watershed. In general, low drainage densities are favored in regions of highly permeable subsoils, dense vegetative cover, and low relief.

18-15 Measurement of Water Quantity   Of the various types of hydrologic information, one of the most important to a watershed manager is streamflow data. Such data can provide the manager with information on daily, seasonal, and annual runoff volumes, as well as peak and low flows. Streamflow from natural watersheds is basically a result of precipitation. This relationship is greatly modified, however, by factors such as weather, soils, vegetation, and topography. For some portions of the United States, where watershed characteristics do not differ greatly from one area to another, the streamflow measured on one watershed may be used to index flows from nearby or adjacent watersheds. Regression methods can be used for establishing these relationships. In other areas, however, the diverse nature of natural watersheds and the large number of factors affecting streamflow will often prohibit such extrapolations. Because of this situation, direct measurements of streamflow may represent the only method of accurately determining runoff from a particular watershed.

To obtain an estimate of the quantity of streamflow from a watershed, a measurement of discharge is necessary. Discharge Q, or rate of flow, is the volume of water that passes a particular location per unit of time. Two types of information are required for discharge estimates: the cross-sectional area a of the channel and the mean velocity v for this cross-sectional area. Discharge can then be computed by

$$Q = a \times v$$

Since the discharge of a stream is the product of its cross-sectional area and mean velocity, accurate measurements of both quantities are necessary. Units of discharge are cubic meters per second or liters per second.

Perhaps the simplest way of estimating discharge (and one of the least accurate) is to observe how far a floating object, tossed into the stream, travels in a given length of time. Dividing this distance by the time interval provides a rough estimate of the velocity of the water. Because the velocity at the surface is greater than the mean velocity of the stream, a reduction factor is necessary to obtain an estimate of mean velocity. This factor is commonly assumed to be about 85 percent. Using this corrected velocity and a measurement of the cross-sectional area of the stream, the discharge can be computed from the preceding formula.

Another method of measuring streamflow is based on the following relationship:

$$Q = \frac{1.49a \times r^{2/3} \times s^{1/2}}{b}$$

where Q = discharge (ft³/sec)
a = cross-sectional area (ft²)
r = hydraulic radius (ft)
s = slope of channel (ft/ft)
b = roughness coefficient

(If m and sec are used, the constant 1.49 is omitted.)

The hydraulic radius is computed by dividing the cross-sectional area a of the stream by the wetted perimeter. The roughness coefficient b must be estimated from conditions of the channel and may vary from approximately 0.030 to 0.060 for natural channels; an average value for natural streams is about 0.035. The main source of error in applying this formula (often referred to as *Manning's equation*) to natural channels results from estimating the roughness coefficient. An error of 0.001 represents about a 3 percent error in discharge. This method, also called the *slope area method,* can perhaps best be used for estimating the discharge of peak flows in natural channels where sufficient high-water marks can be determined.

A more common and accurate method of estimating stream discharge than either of the foregoing procedures is to use a stream-current meter. A current meter is an instrument used to measure the velocity of flowing water by means of a rotating element. When placed in a flowing stream, the number of revolutions per unit of time is related to the velocity of the water. To make these velocity determinations, the current meter is either mounted on a hand-held rod or suspended from a cable. Pressure-sensing devices which give a direct reading of stream velocity are also available.

The velocity of a stream varies from point to point in a given cross section, and a number of velocity measurements with a current meter are necessary to obtain a reliable estimate of discharge. Because of streambed roughness, channel configuration, and turbulence, velocity profiles of natural streams are subject to considerable variation. To properly weight the various velocities found in a given stream, the stream is divided into several vertical sections, and the mean velocity and area are determined separately for each section. The discharge Q for the entire stream can then be obtained by summing the product of area a and velocity v for each section:

$$Q = a_1 v_1 + a_2 v_2 + \cdots + a_n v_n$$

where n is the number of sections. The greater the number of sections, the closer the approximation to the true discharge. Under ideal conditions, 10 may be adequate, but an evaluation of 15 to 20 sections is desirable. The actual number taken depends primarily on the size of the stream channel and the amount of turbulence.

The velocity and depth of each vertical section can be measured from cable cars, boats, and bridges, or simply by wading. For depths greater than 0.5 m, two measurements are made for each section: at 0.2 and 0.8 of the depth of the water. These two velocities are averaged to obtain the mean velocity for that section. For depths less than 0.5 m, the current meter is set at 0.6 of the depth as measured from the water surface. For deep streams, velocity measurements are made at relatively close intervals, and the actual velocity profile is estimated; however, this method is both costly and time-consuming.

Once the discharge rate has been determined, the volume of flow can be calculated for any specified time period by

$$\text{Volume of runoff} = \text{discharge} \times \text{time}$$

A measurement of discharge is applicable only to those stream conditions and flow levels existing at the time of measurement. Yet, flow levels in natural streams usually change with time, and a relationship of discharge to some other variable is desirable. In practice, the "stage" or depth of water above a given datum at a specified stream cross section is used. When a sufficient number of stages and their associated discharges have been measured, a stream-rating curve can be constructed. This relationship, along with a record of the stage of a stream, can be used to estimate discharge for those periods when the stage is not constant (Fig. 18-4).

FIGURE 18-4
Rating curve for a natural stream channel (above) and a streamflow hydrograph developed from a rating curve and record of stage (below).

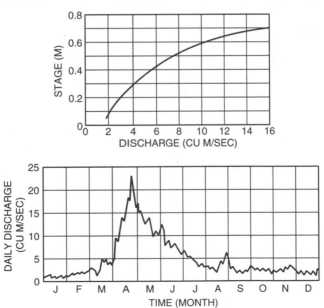

Rating curves are affected mainly by channel characteristics and thus must be developed individually for all gauging stations utilizing natural channels. Stage measurements may be obtained from systematic readings of the water-level surface on a gauge or graduated rod or from automatic water-stage recorders.

On smaller streams, the channel configuration may be modified to alter the flow characteristics along a particular stretch of channel. This is done to obtain more accurate measurements of streamflow. Two general categories of structures, weirs and flumes, may be utilized, depending upon the characteristics of the stream channel.

Weirs are among the oldest and most reliable types of structures that can be used to measure the flow of water in small streams (Fig. 18-5). A weir is usually a simple overflow structure built across an open channel to create an upstream pool. The discharge over the crest of the weir is determined by the vertical distance between the crest of the weir and the water surface in the upstream pool; this height is usually referred to as the *head*. Depending upon the shape of the opening, weirs may be identified as V notch, rectangular, or trapezoidal.

FIGURE 18-5
This trapezoidal weir at the Coweeta Hydrologic Laboratory in North Carolina is used to measure streamflow continuously. *(Courtesy U.S. Forest Service.)*

Weirs can be used most effectively whenever there is a fall of 1 ft or more over the crest. An advantage of standard weirs is that equations exist to estimate stream-flow directly without the necessity of special calibration. Weirs should not be used on streams that have considerable bedload or suspended sediment load.

Flumes are somewhat similar to weirs, and numerous types are employed, depending upon channel and stream characteristics. In contrast to weirs, flumes do not create an upstream ponding effect but instead provide a smooth length of channel that allows the stream to pass through freely. In addition, the velocity of flow is usually sufficiently high so that any suspended sediment or bedload will not be deposited. The more common types of flumes have been precalibrated, although some field measurements may be necessary to check the calibration.

Streamflow measuring devices such as weirs and flumes are usually selected to meet the specific needs for each location. Flow occurs on some watersheds only as the result of an occasional large storm. Other watersheds may have streams that flow continuously. In most cases, it is necessary to measure streamflow at low, medium, and high rates as accurately as possible. Whenever possible, equipment with a precalibrated stage-discharge relationship should be used to gauge the entire flow.

18-16 Measurement of Water Quality   Water-quality samples are obtained so that the various kinds and amounts of substances present in water can be evaluated. A sampling program is often necessary because of the difficulties in attempting to continuously monitor the water quality of a lake or stream. Knowing when, why, and where to collect samples is basic to obtaining good water-quality measurements. This requires a knowledge of not only the system being sampled but also the expected time and space distribution patterns of the variables being sampled and their behavior in solution. Nonrepresentative sampling is perhaps the major source of error in obtaining water-quality information.

One of the goals of a water-quality investigation may be to provide information from which the general composition of water can be precisely determined. Other investigations may concentrate only on specific water-quality problems. The distribution of materials in an aquatic environment is influenced by the source of the material, mobility, phase (solid, dissolved, or gaseous), and type of system (stream, lake, reservoir). Sampling sites should be both accessible and representative of major sections of a stream or lake system.

For some streams, a "grab sample" obtained with a clean glass or plastic container may provide a satisfactory sample for preliminary analysis. This method of sample collection usually assumes that stream turbulence causes adequate mixing and that the sample is representative of the entire stream cross section. A single grab sample, however, should be regarded as representative of the discharge only at the time of sampling.

Grab samples collected periodically or continuous water sampling instrumentation (e.g., coshoton wheel) can provide a reasonable indication of water quality for many streams. Systematically sampling a number of locations about the same time is of value for reconnaissance purposes. If at all possible, flow measurements should also be available at sampling sites. If streamflow and water quality are closely related, a record of stream discharge provides a convenient means for attempting an extrapolation of the chemical record.

Once obtained, the water samples may have to be treated immediately to protect against degradation of the contents. For example, provisions for freezing or otherwise preserving the sample must be available, if water samples are to be used later for organic analysis. A possible alternative is to measure certain variables in the field.

If a water sample is to be retained for later analysis in the laboratory, the sample container should be marked or tagged so that its identity is not lost. Information such as time, date, water temperature, place where the sample was obtained (e.g., middle of lake, edge of stream, etc.), and streamflow may be necessary to correctly interpret the results of a water-quality analysis.

MEASURING RECREATIONAL RESOURCES

18-17 The Problem   The last three decades have seen a heightened interest in forest-based recreational activities in the United States. Many public lands (e.g., national and state parks and some national forests, are managed *primarily* for recreational benefits, and the public increasingly looks to forest lands for recreational opportunities). During the same period, environmental legislation has mandated that recreation (and related aesthetic and ecological) values be considered more fully in forest management decisions. For these reasons, recreational resources can be as important to the land manager as the more tangible values of wood, water, and forage. Consequently, managers need some objective means of describing, comparing, assessing, or measuring recreational resources and the benefits or user satisfactions derived therefrom.

While the timber productivity of a forest can be described in terms of volume per unit of land and grazing productivity can be expressed in animal unit months, it is more difficult to define and quantify the direct productivity of recreational-aesthetic resources. It is not sufficient to simply enumerate recreational visits, overnight campground stays, or fishing boats launched over a given period of time. These measures may reflect the popularity of a resource and, therefore, may be important for guiding management activities; however, they do not measure the capacity or potential for recreation, as sites are often crowded beyond some level of ecological or social capacity.

Rather, resource managers and recreational specialists recognize that the products of recreational-aesthetic resources are the *satisfactions or benefits derived* from the recreational experience; in other words, the nature and quality of the experience better reflects what is produced than the total number of persons utilizing a resource. However, recreational experiences are only partially determined by resource conditions and facilities; what the recreation participant brings to the site in the way of equipment, knowledge, skills, companions, and so forth also plays a large role. The challenge for resource managers has been to devise methods to operationally inventory forest lands in a way that will provide valid measurements of those resource conditions that substantially shape the quality of recreational experiences.

Although much work remains to be done, considerable progress has been made in inventorying recreational resources and relating resource conditions to recreational experiences. From these efforts, workable techniques have been devised for estimating visitor use on existing recreational sites and for assessing the potential of particular areas to support various recreational pursuits. It is with these procedures that the ensuing discussions are primarily concerned.

18-18 Visitor Use of Recreational Facilities   The output of recreational management is commonly measured in terms of visitor use (i.e., visitor-days).[1] This information is valuable for scheduling visitor information programs and maintenance operations and for planning additional recreational sites or facilities. Use data are also of assistance in the prediction of the rates at which facilities depreciate. When the intensity of use on a site is compared with its capacity, patterns of use or activity changes over time can be ascertained.

Recreational use is the result of the interaction of the *supply* of opportunities provided and the *demand* of the public for such opportunities. Thus, in economic terms, use may be regarded as the *quantity* of recreation that is consumed.

An obvious means of measuring use at a recreational site is to obtain a *complete registration* of visitors entering or leaving an area. To employ this method effectively requires absolute control over access to the site, and a registration station must be staffed around the clock. This approach is usually limited to facilities where fees or permits are needed for entry. Many parks maintain entry checkpoints or registration stations during peak-use seasons, but they are rarely operated on a 24-hour basis because of the expense involved. Where such systems are feasible, they do provide an opportunity to gain detailed visitor information, including number of persons per vehicle or family unit, length of visit, types of activities pursued by different age groups, and so on.

For estimating visitor use on dispersed or undeveloped recreational sites such as wilderness areas, various systems of *self-registration* have been employed. One major problem is that many people do not voluntarily register their presence; thus this method has not worked well in areas where there are numerous routes for ingress and egress. It is sometimes feasible to designate a "calibration period" whereby the proportion of visitors who do register can be estimated to determine whether nonregistrants differ from registrants in terms of their activity and use characteristics.

---

[1]A visitor-day is usually defined as 12 visitor-hours (i.e., 2 visitor-days equal 1 calendar day).

For both estimating and regulating visitor use on dispersed sites, there appears to be considerable merit in a permit or license-fee system. By this approach, registration data can be obtained in the same manner as currently supplied by applicants for hunting and fishing licenses.

Because of the problem of counting or registering *all* visitors at recreational sites, some form of sampling may be employed to estimate visitor use. This approach, of course, creates a new problem—which persons and what proportion of the total number of visitors should be counted, registered, or interviewed? As with any public opinion poll, a *representative sample* is the objective, but this is not easily achieved with mobile populations of varying age groups, differing activity patterns, and divergent recreational preferences.

If the only information desired is the total visitor use during a particular season, a number of sample days might be selected, followed by tallies of visitors present on those dates. To account for weekly cycles of visitor use, a sampling design must be developed to select "measuring dates" having a representative proportion of weekdays, holidays, and weekends; otherwise any extrapolations from such estimates may be severely biased. Because one cannot identify or list the population in advance of sampling, true random sampling cannot be accomplished. However, statistical sampling theory can be used to devise sampling plans that employ random components when estimating recreation use, thus guarding against biased results. Essentially, these sampling plans apply stratified random sampling methods in which days and times are used as the randomly selected components to estimate total recreation use of a site (Gregoire and Buhyoff, 1999).

A variation of this technique is to stop all persons leaving the site on certain dates to determine how long they have been at the recreational facility; this approach permits an estimate of use in terms of visitor-days. One difficulty of applying such estimates is that they are valid only for the current season; the sampling must be repeated during subsequent years to update or revise use evaluations.

One method of minimizing the annual problem of sampling use is to find an indicator that is more cost-effective for predicting use than direct counts of people themselves. This approach is analogous to the indirect census techniques previously outlined for wildlife populations. Indicator measurements that have been employed include a diversity of inventory data such as vehicle counts, water consumption, number of boat launchings per unit of time, weight of garbage collected, and quantity of sewage effluent.

The essential characteristic of an indicator variable is that it should be highly correlated with the kind or pattern of recreational use to be predicted. The basic procedural steps that have been followed on many surveys are

1 Select the season of year for which predictions of visitor use are desired.

2 Choose an indicator (e.g., vehicle counts) that presumably rises and falls in the same pattern as the recreational use to be predicted. Obtain indicator data continuously throughout the season.

3 Randomly select several sample days (perhaps 10 to 30 days during the selected season) with equal representation of weekdays, holidays, and weekends. On the sample days, measure the recreational use of interest (e.g., by interviews, camper registration, turnstile counts, etc.).

4 By regression analysis, attempt to establish a relationship between the indicator data and recreational use, based on paired measurements for the sample days. Calculate the precision of the prediction equation.

5 For future seasons (assuming that use patterns are similar), continue to obtain indicator data only. Use the regression equation to predict recreational use.

The indicator most frequently used at developed, unsupervised recreational sites is an axle count obtained from an automatic traffic counter. Not only is this technique much used, but it is also much abused. The popularity of such devices may be attributed to two characteristics: they are relatively cheap, requiring little maintenance, and they produce numbers. Unless they are intelligently located, however, the data that result can be quite misleading.

In a study of recreational sites in the Appalachian Mountains, James and Ripley (1963) found strong correlations between visitor use and axle counts. In one instance, a linear equation of the form $Y = b_0 + b_1X$ was fitted to the relationship with this result:

$$Y \text{ (total visits)} = 110 + 0.3X \text{ (axle count)}$$

For some variables, of course, the relationship between an indicator variable and visitor use may be curvilinear. The sampling precision for this type of use-prediction equation may be less than that obtained in predicting other products of resource management. For example, many use surveys (based on 10 to 12 sampling days per site) produce sampling errors of $\pm$ 25 percent of the estimated variable at a probability level of 0.68.

Where water is supplied to developed recreational sites through a metered system, consumption may be closely related to hours of recreational use. In a study of a recreational site in Arizona, for example, it was found that water consumption was more highly correlated with the number of visitor-days than were axle counts. A comparison of the two indicator estimates is given in Table 18-1.

Where water meters are pretested to ensure that they accurately record low-water flow, they may have several advantages over such indicators as automatic traffic counters. Even though they may be more expensive to install, a single meter may suffice for certain sites where two or more traffic counters might be needed. Also, water meters require little maintenance, they are less susceptible to vandalism, and they are unaffected by snow and ice. And finally, meters provide added information on site water requirements, including the need for pumps or sewage disposal facilities.

TABLE 18-1
ESTIMATES OF RECREATIONAL USE ON AN ARIZONA CAMPGROUND

Activity	Based on water meter		Based on axle count	
	Estimate (visitor-days)	Sampling error* (percent)	Estimate (visitor-days)	Sampling error* (percent)
Camping	27,420	5.7	27,276	7.5
Spectator	485	21.3	408	24.2
Viewing scenery	303	18.7	266	19.9
Misc. activities	272	. . .	171	. . .
Total use	28,480	5.3	28,121	7.3

*Probability level of 0.68.
Source: James and Tyre (1967).

18-19 Assessing Potential Recreational Sites   The preceding section was concerned with measurements of visitor use, namely, the *output* of recreational planning and management. Here we are concerned with the inventory of natural resources with respect to their potential as *inputs* in the production of recreational use on developed or undeveloped areas.

Many of the measurement techniques discussed in other parts of this book are applicable to inventories of potential recreational sites. For example, the recreational planner will often require information on vegetative types, tree size and stand density, water resources, and wildlife populations. Although the assessment of these values as recreational input factors will differ from the assessment from other standpoints, the physical inventory requirements may be quite similar. Existing techniques are readily available for the physical inventory of recreational sites; the real problem is that of establishing inventory criteria, that is, standards based on what potential visitors consider a recreational resource.

As a rule, inventory criteria employed in the past have been based on a combination of physical characteristics and administrative considerations. For example, the criteria for locating potential campgrounds would include some *physical* requirements regarding the amount of slope, the kind of vegetation, and the availability of water supplies. There would also be *administrative* criteria concerning the minimum site area and the maximum distance from population centers.

The inventory itself may be conducted in a manner similar to that of preparing a land-use or a vegetation type map. Standards are established to (1) discover potential sites, (2) designate selected areas for development, and (3) rank the proposed sites by desirability classes or assign them to various management categories. The sites that meet the original standards may then be shown on a map—a presentation that makes up the finished product of the inventory. Except for statistical summaries of site areas, carrying capacities, and demographic information, few calculations are involved.

Much of the work on systems for inventorying recreational resources has focused on the concept of a spectrum of recreational opportunities. Recreational opportunities can be expressed in terms of three principal components: the activities, the setting, and the experience (U.S. Forest Service, 1982). Mixes or combinations of activities, settings, and probable experience opportunities have been arranged along a spectrum, or continuum, called the *recreation opportunity spectrum* (ROS). The ROS approach is commonly applied by agencies responsible for management of public lands.

PROBLEMS

18-1 Compute the number of animal-unit-months (AUM) represented by each of the following situations (see Sec. 18-5 for animal unit conversion factors):
  a 600 cattle for 120 days
  b 400 sheep for 60 days
  c 200 pronghorn for 90 days

18-2 Using aerial photographs of a local range area, locate the boundaries of a pasture and delineate the range sites. Then determine the area of each site with dot grids or by using a geographic information system.

18-3 In a particular wildlife population, 50 animals were banded. During a period of trapping, 10 banded and 30 unbanded individuals were captured. Use the Lincoln-Petersen index method to estimate the size of the population.

18-4 Design and conduct some form of indirect census (e.g., bird-call counts, track counts, or pellet-group counts) for a wildlife species. Prepare a written report on your findings.

18-5 A particular watershed has a perimeter of 2,950 m and an area of 64 ha. Compute the shape index for this watershed. What can you conclude about the shape of this watershed?

18-6 Obtain topographic maps of two watersheds in different portions of the United States. Delineate the watershed boundaries and classify streams on each watershed by stream order. Plot the number of streams versus stream order for each watershed on the same graph. Compute the drainage density for each watershed.

18-7 Two possible indicators of recreational use, axle count and water consumption, were measured at a recreational site. Actual recreational use was also determined for seven periods in order to explore relationships between actual use and the indicator variables. The data follow:

Recreational use (visitor days)	Axle count (number)	Water use (gal.)
485	100	2,225
600	148	4,440
710	202	5,050
390	78	2,150
514	114	3,124
595	140	3,150
410	90	2,556

    a Fit a simple linear regression to predict recreational use as a function of axle count.

    b Fit a simple linear regression to predict recreational use as a function of water use.

    c For this particular case, which variable (axle count or water use) is the better predictor of recreational use?

18-8 Assume that you have selected several sample days for interviewing families at a local campground or trailer park. If you wish to interview six family groups per day, *how* should these groups be selected? List several criteria to be observed that might improve the chances for an unbiased and representative sample.

REFERENCES

Arizona Inter-Agency Range Committee. 1972. *Proper use and management of grazing land.* 48 pp.

Bookhout, T. A. (ed.) 1996. *Research and management techniques for wildlife and habitats,* 5th ed. The Wildlife Society, Bethesda, Md. 740 pp.

Brooks, K. N., Ffolliott, P. F., Gregersen, H. M., and DeBano, L. F. 1997. *Hydrology and the management of watersheds,* 2d ed. Iowa State University Press, Ames, Iowa. 502 pp.

Brown, G. W. 1989. *Forestry and water quality,* 2d ed. O.S.U. Bookstores, Inc., Corvallis, Oreg. 142 pp.

Buckland, S. T., Anderson, D. R., Burnham, K. P., and Laake, J. L. 1993. *Distance sampling: Estimating abundance of biological populations.* Chapman & Hall, London. 446 pp.

Cook, C. W., and Stubbendieck, J. (eds.). 1986. *Range research: Basic problems and techniques.* Society for Range Management, Denver, Colo. 317 pp.

Cooperrider, A. Y., Boyd, R. J., and Stuart, H. R. (eds.). 1986. *Inventory and monitoring of wildlife habitat.* U.S.D.I. Bur. Land Management Service Center, Denver, Colo. 858 pp.

Dissmeyer, G. E., and Foster, G. R. 1984. A guide for predicting sheet and rill erosion on forest land. *U.S. Forest Serv., Southern Region, Tech. Pub. R8-TP* 6. 40 pp.

Driver, B. L., Brown, P. J., Stankey, G. H., and Gregoire, T. G. 1987. The ROS planning systems: Evaluation, basic concepts, and research needed. *Leisure Sci.* **9:**201–212.

Forest-Range Task Force. 1972. The nation's range resources—A forest-range environmental study. *Forest Resource Report* No. 19, U.S. Forest Service, Washington, D.C. 147 pp.

Golden, M. S., Tuttle, C. L., Kush, J. S., and Bradley, J. M., III. 1984. Forestry activities and water quality in Alabama: Effects, recommended practices, and an erosion-classification system. *Auburn Univ., Ala. Agr. Expt. Sta., Bull.* 555. 87 pp.

Gregoire, T. G., and Buhyoff, G. J. 1999. Sampling and estimating recreational use. *U.S. Forest Serv., Pacific Northwest Res. Sta., Gen. Tech. Report PNW-GTR-*456. 39 pp.

Holechek, J. L., Pieper, R. D., and Herbel, C. H. 1995. *Range management: Principles and practices,* 2d ed. Prentice Hall, Englewood Cliffs, N.J. 526 pp.

Hollenhorst, S. J., Whisman, S. A., and Ewert, A. W. 1992. Monitoring visitor use in backcountry and wilderness: A review of methods. *U.S. Forest Serv., Pacific Southwest Res. Sta., Gen. Tech. Report. PSW-GTR-*134. 10 pp.

James, G. A., and Henley, R. K. 1968. Sampling procedures for estimating mass and dispersed types of recreation use on large areas. *U.S. Forest Serv., Southeast. Forest Expt. Sta., Res. Paper SE-*31. 15 pp.

———, and Ripley, T. H. 1963. Instructions for using traffic counters to estimate recreation visits and use. *U.S. Forest Serv., Southeast. Forest Expt. Sta., Res. Paper SE-*3. 12 pp.

————, and Tyre, G. L. 1967. Use of water-meter records to estimate recreation visits and use on developed sites. *U.S. Forest Serv., Southeast. Forest Expt. Sta., Res. Note SE*-73. 3 pp.

O'Rourke, D. 1994. Trail traffic counters for Forest Service trail monitoring. *U.S. Forest Serv., Technology & Development Program,* Missoula, Mont. 9 pp.

Pollock, K. H., Nichols, J. D., Brownie, C., and Hines, J. E. 1990. Statistical inference for capture-recapture experiments. *Wildlife Monograph* No. 107. 97 pp.

Reed, D. D., and Mroz, G. D. 1997. *Resource assessment in forested landscapes.* John Wiley & Sons, New York. 386 pp.

Sampson, A. W. 1917. Succession as a factor in range management. *J. Forestry* **15:**593–596.

Schroeder, H. W. 1983. Measuring visual features of recreational landscapes. Pp. 189–202 in *Recreation planning and management,* S. R. Lieber and D. R. Fesenmaier (eds.), Venture Publications, State College, Pa.

Seber, G. A. F. 1982. *The estimation of animal abundance and related parameters,* 2d ed. Charles Griffin & Co. Ltd., London. 653 pp.

Society for Range Management. 1998. *Glossary of terms used in range management,* 4th ed. Society for Range Management, Denver, Colo. 32 pp.

Stoddart, L. A., Smith, A. D., and Box, T. W. 1975. *Range management,* 3d ed. McGraw-Hill Book Company, New York. 532 pp.

U.S. Forest Service. 1965. Range analysis field guide—Southwestern region. (mimeo. paper.) 153 pp.

————. 1982. *ROS user's guide.* Washington, D.C. 38 pp.

Wenger, K. F. (ed.). 1984. *Forestry handbook,* 2d ed. John Wiley & Sons, New York. 1,335 pp.

Yoho, N. S. 1980. Forest management and sediment production in the South— A review. *So. J. Appl. For.* **4:**27–36.

Yuan, S., Maiorano, B., Yuan, M., Kocis, S. M., and Hoshide, G. T. 1995. Techniques and equipment for gathering visitor use data on recreation sites. *U.S. Forest Serv., Technology & Development Program,* Missoula, Mont. 78 pp.

APPENDIX

APPENDIX TABLE 1
SELECTED CONVERSIONS: ENGLISH TO METRIC UNITS

Length		
Multiply	by	to obtain
Inches	25.40	millimeters (mm)
Inches	2.54	centimeters (cm)
Feet	30.480	centimeters (cm)
Feet	0.3048	meters (m)
Yards	0.9144	meters (m)
Chains (Gunter's)	20.1168	meters (m)
U.S. statute miles	1.6093	kilometers (km)
Nautical miles	1.852	kilometers (km)
Area		
Square inches	645.16	square millimeters (mm^2)
Square inches	6.4516	square centimeters (cm^2)
Square feet	929.03	square centimeters (cm^2)
Square feet	0.0929	square meters (m^2)
Square yards	0.8361	square meters (m^2)
Square chains	404.6856	square meters (m^2)
Acres	0.4047	hectares (ha)
Square miles	2.5899	square kilometers (km^2)
Volume		
Cubic inches	16.387	cubic centimeters (cm^3)
Cubic feet	0.02832	cubic meters (m^3)
Cubic yards	0.7646	cubic meters (m^3)
Special conversions		
Square feet per acre	0.2296	square meters per hectare (m^2/ha)
Cubic feet per acre	0.06997	cubic meters per hectare (m^3/ha)
Cubic feet per second	101.941	cubic meters per hour (m^3/h)
Feet per second	1.097	kilometers per hour (km/h)
Gallons per acre	11.2336	liters per hectare (l/ha)
Gallons per minute	0.0757	liters per second (l/s)
Pounds per acre	1.1208	kilograms per hectare (kg/ha)
Pounds per cubic foot	16.0185	kilograms per cubic meter (kg/m^3)
Number (e.g., stems) per acre	2.471	number per hectare (no./ha)

APPENDIX TABLE 2
SCALE CONVERSIONS FOR MAPS AND VERTICAL PHOTOGRAPHS

Ratio scale	Feet per inch	Inches per 1,000 feet	Inches per mile	Miles per inch	Meters per inch	Acres per square inch	Square inches per acre	Square miles per square inch
1: 500	41.667	24.00	126.72	0.008	12.700	0.0399	25.091	0.00006
1: 600	50.00	20.00	105.60	.009	15.240	.0574	17.424	.00009
1: 1,000	83.333	12.00	63.36	.016	25.400	.1594	6.273	.00025
1: 1,200	100.00	10.00	52.80	.019	30.480	.2296	4.356	.00036
1: 1,500	125.00	8.00	42.24	.024	38.100	.3587	2.788	.00056
1: 2,000	166.667	6.00	31.68	.032	50.800	.6377	1.568	.00100
1: 2,400	200.00	5.00	26.40	.038	60.960	.9183	1.089	.0014
1: 2,500	208.333	4.80	25.344	.039	63.500	.9964	1.004	.0016
1: 3,000	250.00	4.00	21.12	.047	76.200	1.4348	.697	.0022
1: 3,600	300.00	3.333	17.60	.057	91.440	2.0661	.484	.0032
1: 4,000	333.333	3.00	15.84	.063	101.600	2.5508	.392	.0040
1: 4,800	400.00	2.50	13.20	.076	121.920	3.6731	.272	.0057
1: 5,000	416.667	2.40	12.672	.079	127.000	3.9856	.251	.0062
1: 6,000	500.00	2.00	10.56	.095	152.400	5.7392	.174	.0090
1: 7,000	583.333	1.714	9.051	.110	177.800	7.8117	.128	.0122
1: 7,200	600.00	1.667	8.80	.114	182.880	8.2645	.121	.0129
1: 7,920	660.00	1.515	8.00	.125	201.168	10.00	.100	.0156
1: 8,000	666.667	1.500	7.92	.126	203.200	10.203	.098	.0159
1: 8,400	700.00	1.429	7.543	.133	213.360	11.249	.089	.0176
1: 9,000	750.00	1.333	7.041	.142	228.600	12.913	.077	.0202
1: 9,600	800.00	1.250	6.60	.152	243.840	14.692	.068	.0230
1: 10,000	833.333	1.200	6.336	.158	254.000	15.942	.063	.0249
1: 10,800	900.00	1.111	5.867	.170	274.321	18.595	.054	.0291
1: 12,000	1,000.00	1.0	5.280	.189	304.801	22.957	.044	.0359
1: 13,200	1,100.00	.909	4.800	.208	335.281	27.778	.036	.0434
1: 14,400	1,200.00	.833	4.400	.227	365.761	33.058	.030	.0517

1:							
15,000	1,250.00	.80	4.224	381.001	35.870	.028	.0560
15,600	1,300.00	.769	4.062	396.241	38.797	.026	.0606
15,840	1,320.00	.758	4.00	402.337	40.000	.025	.0625
16,000	1,333.333	.750	3.96	406.400	40.812	.024	.0638
16,800	1,400.00	.714	3.771	426.721	44.995	.022	.0703
18,000	1,500.00	.667	3.52	457.201	51.653	.019	.0807
19,200	1,600.00	.625	3.30	487.681	58.770	.017	.0918
20,000	1,666.667	.60	3.168	508.002	63.769	.016	.0996
20,400	1,700.00	.588	3.106	518.161	66.345	.015	.1037
21,120	1,760.00	.568	3.00	536.449	71.111	.014	.1111
21,600	1,800.00	.556	2.933	548.641	74.380	.013	.1162
22,800	1,900.00	.526	2.779	579.121	82.874	.012	.1295
24,000	2,000.00	.50	2.640	609.601	91.827	.011	.1435
25,000	2,083.333	.480	2.534	635.001	99.639	.010	.1557
31,680	2,640.00	.379	2.000	804.674	160.000	.006	.2500
48,000	4,000.00	.250	1.320	1,219.202	367.309	.003	.5739
62,500	5,208.333	.192	1.014	1,587.503	622.744	.0016	.9730
63,360	5,280.00	.189	1.000	1,609.347	640.00	.0016	1.0000
96,000	8,000.00	.125	.660	2,438.405	1,469.24	.0007	2.2957
125,000	10,416.667	.096	.507	3,175.006	2,490.98	.0004	3.8922
126,720	10,560.00	.095	.500	3,218.694	2,560.00	.0004	4.00
250,000	20,833.333	.048	.253	6,350.012	9,963.907	.0001	15.5686
253,440	21,120.00	.047	.250	6,437.389	10,244.202	.0001	16.00
500,000	41,666.667	.024	.127	12,700.025	39,855.627	.000025	62.2744
1,000,000	83,333.333	.012	.063	25,400.050	159,422.507	.0000062	249.0977

Source: Aerial-Photo Interpretation in Classifying and Mapping Soils, Agriculture Handbook 294, Soil Conservation Service, U.S. Department of Agriculture, Washington, D.C., 1966.

APPENDIX TABLE 3
SCRIBNER DECIMAL C LOG RULE FOR LOGS 6 TO 32 FT IN LENGTH

Diameter (in.)	Length (ft)													
	6	8	10	12	14	16	18	20	22	24	26	28	30	32
	Contents (bd ft in tens)													
6	0.5	0.5	1	1	1	2	2	2	3	3	3	4	4	5
7	0.5	1	1	2	2	3	3	3	4	4	4	5	5	6
8	1	1	2	2	2	3	3	3	4	4	5	6	6	7
9	1	2	3	3	3	4	4	4	5	6	6	7	8	9
10	2	3	3	3	4	6	6	7	8	9	9	10	11	12
11	2	3	4	4	5	7	8	8	9	10	11	12	13	14
12	3	4	5	6	7	8	9	10	11	12	13	14	15	16
13	4	5	6	7	8	10	11	12	13	15	16	17	18	19
14	4	6	7	9	10	11	13	14	16	17	19	20	21	23
15	5	7	9	11	12	14	16	18	20	21	23	25	27	28
16	6	8	10	12	14	16	18	20	22	24	26	28	30	32
17	7	9	12	14	16	18	21	23	25	28	30	32	35	37
18	8	11	13	16	19	21	24	27	29	32	35	37	40	43
19	9	12	15	18	21	24	27	30	33	36	39	42	45	48
20	11	14	17	21	24	28	31	35	38	42	45	49	52	56
21	12	15	19	23	27	30	34	38	42	46	49	53	57	61
22	13	17	21	25	29	33	38	42	46	50	54	58	63	67
23	14	19	23	28	33	38	42	47	52	57	61	66	71	75
24	15	21	25	30	35	40	45	50	55	61	66	71	76	81
25	17	23	29	34	40	46	52	57	63	69	75	80	86	92
26	19	25	31	37	44	50	56	62	69	75	82	88	94	100
27	21	27	34	41	48	55	62	68	75	82	89	96	103	110
28	22	29	36	44	51	58	65	73	80	87	95	102	109	116
29	23	31	38	46	53	61	68	76	84	91	99	107	114	122
30	25	33	41	49	57	66	74	82	90	99	107	115	123	131
31	27	36	44	53	62	71	80	89	98	106	115	124	133	142
32	28	37	46	55	64	74	83	92	101	110	120	129	138	147
33	29	39	49	59	69	78	88	98	108	118	127	137	147	157
34	30	40	50	60	70	80	90	100	110	120	130	140	150	160
35	33	44	55	66	77	88	98	109	120	131	142	153	164	175
36	35	46	58	69	81	92	104	115	127	138	150	161	173	185
37	39	51	64	77	90	103	116	129	142	154	167	180	193	206
38	40	54	67	80	93	107	120	133	147	160	174	187	200	214
39	42	56	70	84	98	112	126	140	154	168	182	196	210	224
40	45	60	75	90	105	120	135	150	166	181	196	211	226	241
41	48	64	79	95	111	127	143	159	175	191	207	223	238	254
42	50	67	84	101	117	134	151	168	185	201	218	235	252	269
43	52	70	87	105	122	140	157	174	192	209	227	244	262	279
44	56	74	93	111	129	148	166	185	204	222	241	259	278	296
45	57	76	95	114	133	152	171	190	209	228	247	266	286	304
46	59	79	99	119	139	159	178	198	218	238	258	278	297	317
47	62	83	104	124	145	166	186	207	228	248	269	290	310	331
48	65	86	108	130	151	173	194	216	238	260	281	302	324	346

APPENDIX TABLE 3 *(Continued)*

Diameter (in.)	6	8	10	12	14	16	18	20	22	24	26	28	30	32
							Contents (bd ft in tens)							
49	67	90	112	135	157	180	202	225	247	270	292	314	337	359
50	70	94	117	140	164	187	211	234	257	281	304	328	351	374
51	73	97	122	146	170	195	219	243	268	292	315	341	365	389
52	76	101	127	152	177	202	228	253	278	304	329	354	380	405
53	79	105	132	158	184	210	237	263	289	316	341	368	395	421
54	82	109	137	164	191	218	246	273	300	328	355	382	410	437
55	85	113	142	170	198	227	255	283	312	340	368	397	425	453
56	88	118	147	176	206	235	264	294	323	353	382	411	441	470
57	91	122	152	183	213	244	274	304	335	365	396	426	457	487
58	95	126	158	189	221	252	284	315	347	379	410	442	473	505
59	98	131	163	196	229	261	294	327	359	392	425	457	490	523
60	101	135	169	203	237	270	304	338	372	406	439	473	507	541
61	105	140	175	210	245	280	315	350	385	420	455	490	525	560
62	108	145	181	217	253	289	325	362	398	434	470	506	542	579
63	112	149	187	224	261	299	336	373	411	448	485	523	560	597
64	116	154	193	232	270	309	348	387	425	464	503	541	580	619
65	119	159	199	239	279	319	358	398	438	478	518	558	597	637
66	123	164	206	247	288	329	370	412	453	494	535	576	617	659
67	127	170	212	254	297	339	381	423	466	508	550	593	635	677
68	131	175	219	262	306	350	393	437	480	524	568	611	655	699
69	135	180	226	271	316	361	406	452	497	542	587	632	677	723
70	139	186	232	279	325	372	419	465	512	558	605	651	698	744
71	144	192	240	287	335	383	430	478	526	574	622	670	717	765
72	148	197	247	296	345	395	444	493	543	592	641	691	740	789
73	152	203	254	305	356	406	457	508	559	610	661	712	762	813
74	157	209	261	314	366	418	471	523	576	628	680	733	785	837
75	161	215	269	323	377	430	484	538	592	646	700	754	807	861
76	166	221	277	332	387	443	498	553	609	664	719	775	830	885
77	171	228	285	341	398	455	511	568	625	682	739	796	852	909
78	176	234	293	351	410	468	527	585	644	702	761	819	878	936
79	180	240	301	361	421	481	541	602	662	722	782	842	902	963
80	185	247	309	371	432	494	556	618	680	742	804	866	927	989
81	190	254	317	381	444	508	572	635	699	762	826	889	953	1016
82	196	261	326	391	456	521	586	652	717	782	847	912	977	1043
83	201	268	335	401	468	535	601	668	735	802	869	936	1002	1069
84	206	275	343	412	481	549	618	687	755	824	893	961	1030	1099
85	210	281	351	421	491	561	631	702	772	842	912	982	1052	1123
86	215	287	359	431	503	575	646	718	790	862	934	1006	1077	1149
87	221	295	368	442	516	589	663	737	810	884	958	1031	1105	1179
88	226	301	377	452	527	603	678	753	829	904	979	1055	1130	1205
89	231	308	385	462	539	616	693	770	847	924	1001	1078	1155	1232
90	236	315	393	472	551	629	708	787	865	944	1023	1101	1180	1259
91	241	322	402	483	563	644	725	805	886	966	1047	1127	1208	1288

APPENDIX TABLE 3 *(Continued)*

	Length (ft)													
	6	8	10	12	14	16	18	20	22	24	26	28	30	32
Diameter (in.)	Contents (bd ft in tens)													
92	246	329	411	493	575	657	739	822	904	986	1068	1150	1232	1315
93	251	335	419	503	587	671	754	838	922	1006	1090	1174	1257	1341
94	257	343	428	514	600	685	771	857	942	1028	1114	1199	1285	1371
95	262	350	437	525	612	700	788	875	963	1050	1138	1225	1313	1400
96	268	357	446	536	625	715	804	893	983	1072	1161	1251	1340	1429
97	273	364	455	546	637	728	819	910	1001	1092	1183	1274	1365	1456
98	278	371	464	557	650	743	835	928	1021	1114	1207	1300	1392	1485
99	284	379	473	568	663	757	852	947	1041	1136	1231	1325	1420	1515
100	289	386	482	579	675	772	869	965	1062	1158	1255	1351	1448	1544
101	295	393	492	590	688	787	885	983	1082	1180	1278	1377	1475	1573
102	301	401	502	602	702	803	903	1003	1104	1204	1304	1405	1505	1605
103	307	409	512	614	716	819	921	1023	1126	1228	1330	1433	1535	1637
104	313	417	522	626	730	835	939	1043	1148	1252	1356	1461	1565	1669
105	319	425	532	638	744	851	957	1063	1170	1276	1382	1489	1595	1701
106	325	433	542	650	758	867	975	1083	1192	1300	1408	1517	1625	1733
107	331	442	553	663	773	884	995	1105	1216	1326	1437	1547	1658	1768
108	337	450	563	675	788	900	1013	1125	1238	1350	1463	1575	1688	1800
109	344	459	573	688	803	917	1032	1147	1261	1376	1491	1605	1720	1835
110	350	467	583	700	817	933	1050	1167	1283	1400	1517	1633	1750	1867
111	356	475	594	710	832	951	1069	1188	1307	1426	1545	1664	1782	1901
112	362	483	604	725	846	967	1087	1208	1329	1450	1571	1692	1812	1933
113	369	492	615	738	861	984	1107	1230	1353	1476	1599	1722	1845	1968
114	375	501	626	751	876	1001	1126	1252	1377	1502	1627	1752	1877	2003
115	382	509	637	764	891	1019	1146	1273	1401	1528	1655	1783	1910	2037
116	389	519	648	778	908	1037	1167	1297	1426	1556	1686	1815	1945	2075
117	396	528	660	792	924	1056	1188	1320	1452	1584	1716	1848	1980	2112
118	403	537	672	806	940	1075	1209	1343	1478	1612	1746	1881	2015	2149
119	410	547	683	820	957	1093	1230	1367	1503	1640	1777	1913	2050	2187
120	417	556	695	834	973	1112	1251	1390	1529	1668	1807	1946	2085	2224

Source: U.S. Forest Service.

APPENDIX TABLE 4

INTERNATIONAL LOG RULE, ¼-IN. SAW KERF, FOR LOGS 8 TO 20 FT IN LENGTH

Diameter (small end of log inside bark) (in.)	Length of log (ft)							Diameter (in.)
	8	10	12	14	16	18	20	
	Volume (bd ft)							
4	....	5	5	5	5	5	10	4
5	5	5	10	10	10	15	15	5
6	10	10	15	15	20	25	25	6
7	10	15	20	25	30	35	40	7
8	15	20	25	35	40	45	50	8
9	20	30	35	45	50	60	70	9
10	30	35	45	55	65	75	85	10
11	35	45	55	70	80	95	105	11
12	45	55	70	85	95	110	125	12
13	55	70	85	100	115	135	150	13
14	65	80	100	115	135	155	175	14
15	75	95	115	135	160	180	205	15
16	85	110	130	155	180	205	235	16
17	95	125	150	180	205	235	265	17
18	110	140	170	200	230	265	300	18
19	125	155	190	225	260	300	335	19
20	135	175	210	250	290	330	370	20
21	155	195	235	280	320	365	410	21
22	170	215	260	305	355	405	455	22
23	185	235	285	335	390	445	495	23
24	205	255	310	370	425	485	545	24
25	220	280	340	400	460	525	590	25
26	240	305	370	435	500	570	640	26
27	260	330	400	470	540	615	690	27
28	280	355	430	510	585	665	745	28
29	305	385	465	545	630	715	800	29
30	325	410	495	585	675	765	860	30
31	350	440	530	625	720	820	915	31
32	375	470	570	670	770	875	980	32
33	400	500	605	715	820	930	1,045	33
34	425	535	645	760	875	990	1,110	34
35	450	565	685	805	925	1,050	1,175	35
36	475	600	725	855	980	1,115	1,245	36
37	505	635	770	905	1,040	1,175	1,315	37
38	535	670	810	955	1,095	1,245	1,390	38
39	565	710	855	1,005	1,155	1,310	1,465	39
40	595	750	900	1,060	1,220	1,380	1,540	40

APPENDIX TABLE 4 *(Continued)*

Diameter (small end of log inside bark) (in.)	Length of log (ft)							Diameter (in.)
	8	10	12	14	16	18	20	
	Volume (bd ft)							
41	625	785	950	1,115	1,280	1,450	1,620	41
42	655	825	995	1,170	1,345	1,525	1,705	42
43	690	870	1,045	1,230	1,410	1,600	1,785	43
44	725	910	1,095	1,290	1,480	1,675	1,870	44
45	755	955	1,150	1,350	1,550	1,755	1,960	45
46	795	995	1,200	1,410	1,620	1,835	2,050	46
47	830	1,040	1,255	1,475	1,695	1,915	2,140	47
48	865	1,090	1,310	1,540	1,770	2,000	2,235	48
49	905	1,135	1,370	1,605	1,845	2,085	2,330	49
50	940	1,185	1,425	1,675	1,920	2,175	2,425	50
51	980	1,235	1,485	1,745	2,000	2,265	2,525	51
52	1,020	1,285	1,545	1,815	2,080	2,355	2,625	52
53	1,060	1,335	1,605	1,885	2,165	2,445	2,730	53
54	1,100	1,385	1,670	1,960	2,245	2,540	2,835	54
55	1,145	1,440	1,735	2,035	2,330	2,640	2,945	55
56	1,190	1,495	1,800	2,110	2,420	2,735	3,050	56
57	1,230	1,550	1,865	2,185	2,510	2,835	3,165	57
58	1,275	1,605	1,930	2,265	2,600	2,935	3,275	58
59	1,320	1,660	2,000	2,345	2,690	3,040	3,390	59
60	1,370	1,720	2,070	2,425	2,785	3,145	3,510	60

Source: U.S. Forest Service

APPENDIX TABLE 5
DOYLE LOG RULE FOR LOGS 6 TO 20 FT IN LENGTH

Diameter (small end of log inside bark) (in.)	Length of log (ft)							
	6	8	10	12	14	16	18	20
	Volume (bd ft)							
8	6	8	10	12	14	16	18	20
9	9	13	16	19	22	25	28	31
10	14	18	23	27	32	36	41	45
11	18	25	31	37	43	49	55	61
12	24	32	40	48	56	64	72	80
13	30	41	51	61	71	81	91	101
14	38	50	63	75	88	100	113	125
15	45	61	76	91	106	121	136	151
16	54	72	90	108	126	144	162	180
17	63	85	106	127	148	169	190	211
18	74	98	123	147	172	196	221	245
19	84	113	141	169	197	225	253	281
20	96	128	160	192	224	256	288	320
21	108	145	181	217	253	289	325	361
22	122	162	203	243	284	324	365	405
23	135	181	226	271	316	361	406	451
24	150	200	250	300	350	400	450	500
25	165	221	276	331	386	441	496	551
26	182	242	303	363	424	484	545	605
27	198	265	331	397	463	529	595	661
28	216	288	360	432	504	576	648	720
29	234	313	391	469	547	625	703	781
30	254	338	423	507	592	676	761	845
31	273	365	456	547	638	729	820	911
32	294	392	490	588	686	784	882	980
33	315	421	526	631	736	841	946	1,051
34	338	450	563	675	788	900	1,013	1,125
35	360	481	601	721	841	961	1,081	1,201
36	384	512	640	768	896	1,024	1,152	1,280
37	408	545	681	817	953	1,089	1,225	1,361
38	434	578	723	867	1,012	1,156	1,301	1,445
39	459	613	766	919	1,072	1,225	1,378	1,531
40	486	648	810	972	1,134	1,296	1,458	1,620

Source: U.S. Forest Service.

APPENDIX TABLE 6
THE DISTRIBUTION OF t

df	Probability								
	0.5	0.4	0.3	0.2	0.1	0.05	0.02	0.01	0.001
1	1.000	1.376	1.963	3.078	6.314	12.706	31.821	63.657	636.619
2	0.816	1.061	1.386	1.886	2.920	4.303	6.965	9.925	31.599
3	0.765	0.978	1.250	1.638	2.353	3.182	4.541	5.841	12.924
4	0.741	0.941	1.190	1.533	2.132	2.776	3.747	4.604	8.610
5	0.727	0.920	1.156	1.476	2.015	2.571	3.365	4.032	6.859
6	0.718	0.906	1.134	1.440	1.943	2.447	3.143	3.707	5.959
7	0.711	0.896	1.119	1.415	1.895	2.365	2.998	3.499	5.408
8	0.706	0.889	1.108	1.397	1.860	2.306	2.896	3.355	5.041
9	0.703	0.883	1.100	1.383	1.833	2.262	2.821	3.250	4.781
10	0.700	0.879	1.093	1.372	1.812	2.228	2.764	3.169	4.587
11	0.697	0.876	1.088	1.363	1.796	2.201	2.718	3.106	4.437
12	0.695	0.873	1.083	1.356	1.782	2.179	2.681	3.055	4.318
13	0.694	0.870	1.079	1.350	1.771	2.160	2.650	3.012	4.221
14	0.692	0.868	1.076	1.345	1.761	2.145	2.624	2.977	4.140
15	0.691	0.866	1.074	1.341	1.753	2.131	2.602	2.947	4.073
16	0.690	0.865	1.071	1.337	1.746	2.120	2.583	2.921	4.015
17	0.689	0.863	1.069	1.333	1.740	2.110	2.567	2.898	3.965
18	0.688	0.862	1.067	1.330	1.734	2.101	2.552	2.878	3.922
19	0.688	0.861	1.066	1.328	1.729	2.093	2.539	2.861	3.883
20	0.687	0.860	1.064	1.325	1.725	2.086	2.528	2.845	3.850
21	0.686	0.859	1.063	1.323	1.721	2.080	2.510	2.801	3.819
22	0.686	0.858	1.061	1.321	1.717	2.074	2.508	2.819	3.792
23	0.685	0.858	1.060	1.319	1.714	2.069	2.500	2.807	3.768
24	0.685	0.857	1.059	1.318	1.711	2.064	2.492	2.797	3.745
25	0.684	0.856	1.058	1.316	1.708	2.060	2.485	2.787	3.725
26	0.684	0.856	1.058	1.315	1.706	2.056	2.479	2.779	3.707
27	0.684	0.855	1.057	1.314	1.703	2.052	2.473	2.771	3.690
28	0.683	0.855	1.056	1.313	1.701	2.048	2.467	2.763	3.674
29	0.683	0.854	1.055	1.311	1.699	2.045	2.462	2.756	3.659
30	0.683	0.854	1.055	1.310	1.697	2.042	2.457	2.750	3.646
40	0.681	0.851	1.050	1.303	1.684	2.021	2.423	2.704	3.551
60	0.679	0.848	1.045	1.296	1.671	2.000	2.390	2.660	3.460
120	0.677	0.845	1.041	1.289	1.658	1.980	2.358	2.617	3.373
∞	0.674	0.842	1.036	1.282	1.645	1.960	2.326	2.576	3.291

Source: Generated using algorithm in Minitab statistical software.

APPENDIX TABLE 7
RANDOM NUMBERS

5106	6521	7330	0064	0342	8376	3794	5226	5630	4639
5109	4365	1175	8043	0552	0109	1963	8058	4664	1046
6605	5140	6162	5301	2878	6123	9808	3114	8167	9569
7954	3300	0736	0116	7223	9616	0479	2600	0808	4399
0635	0975	6244	3885	3885	7600	4476	1079	4487	2894
7693	8898	5379	6291	9871	0856	9494	8963	1920	8409
0697	5711	8789	4862	2490	5880	8299	0900	7134	1145
3812	0447	0228	9987	3252	1178	3490	2145	7901	8146
3835	9073	1416	0746	0381	5707	7991	5730	1208	5624
6744	6923	8911	1915	8923	3686	6807	7062	8758	0445
9847	2209	8957	2180	2718	7975	2672	5854	7507	9686
7565	6940	2656	9836	1520	4019	8151	8997	5940	9373
2831	6736	3660	2894	8267	3581	3897	6492	0377	5172
2138	6670	3029	0203	4730	5756	2737	2678	1904	1243
3537	7843	2669	2790	9140	6871	4266	8227	7108	3481
2358	8095	1590	7508	8018	5833	7145	8927	1030	2419
0248	4620	9040	4894	5296	3774	6663	6856	9592	0205
6477	7864	6718	1057	7731	4015	2935	9428	8053	8680
3842	6597	4525	9405	5806	4568	7407	0158	3074	3564
7831	6156	4111	1943	4702	2627	3781	8013	2083	3608
8603	8276	4601	9016	3751	9715	0181	7216	6340	3096
9491	0826	2511	5656	7989	8832	9087	5137	8365	6479
2485	5821	0730	6042	8405	4543	5735	6409	4080	2659
7391	2742	7400	4011	1905	4348	3884	7257	7438	0911
9787	6104	5818	3266	3826	6367	0050	4895	1854	6814
7914	7925	1675	1327	6146	8498	0549	0758	9357	4528
4545	1012	1026	1568	2402	3238	6898	9141	1507	3283
6902	9340	8873	5173	1635	2207	1076	5048	8249	1615
9436	5049	1951	3116	7285	8381	2588	0932	5852	4177
3277	1524	0864	3500	8687	5594	0018	3146	4709	1853
4349	3943	3022	0011	9748	7430	6379	5381	4619	1021
8083	9890	7431	8239	8627	8572	7524	3313	5375	7964
1834	4041	2626	6707	9167	4754	6494	2060	9768	1187
3139	7084	9539	4824	5398	1345	0192	8587	5342	8815
8036	9923	8882	3870	5180	3796	3530	1500	7001	2732
1028	8813	5914	7967	5022	5706	8064	2971	2086	9686
5871	4857	9326	3953	4678	3468	0238	8851	7463	5951
6162	9300	1876	8044	5966	0054	8002	5159	4900	7532
5156	2167	8966	9018	4612	0267	8986	4829	3992	2683
3662	3661	4856	8588	0879	7279	5184	6173	3172	9959
7952	5863	5069	4285	9248	2924	4044	7962	3596	2736
9447	5086	8388	1739	2617	6069	4357	0458	8825	1598
3253	3208	5951	0534	4223	0799	2219	5173	8497	2379
2430	0986	7198	5921	0651	0879	9852	0971	3345	1923
7291	1147	2490	1461	1027	4246	0482	8286	3458	3061
2961	3230	3474	0266	6274	7704	2401	7898	2764	5172
2916	5584	4621	8444	4599	3566	7259	4792	8947	9416
0489	9446	8317	9611	3348	1207	3781	0837	0899	9107
7415	6205	7831	6455	0987	1066	2939	2702	5900	7205
7835	2788	2060	5129	5165	0851	4486	4097	3381	3342

APPENDIX TABLE 7 *(Continued)*

4232	2291	6096	9588	4909	3970	0321	2927	0976	9060
0232	0553	6118	8473	5382	5604	5122	7643	2131	6916
0060	1455	6104	7205	2618	6538	9682	9839	7524	4804
2012	9153	6880	9953	1439	2034	3422	1883	2930	6426
0809	1349	7582	8816	2065	6693	8315	1879	1144	5355
0939	3409	1378	5741	1204	0691	6088	0756	1892	4240
0893	4650	4487	2871	5422	2293	6481	9696	6889	3049
4331	5921	6071	0083	9452	7508	1201	0653	4931	8162
2760	4919	7046	8364	6239	7545	3807	3338	5417	6593
7222	4156	4160	4492	9264	1872	8476	8749	8563	8986
0609	6968	2035	7842	6911	3410	2152	4860	0054	8954
2669	4013	6498	9935	9993	8010	0262	3276	1311	0665
5312	9279	2201	6086	8965	1938	4853	2685	2354	3812
5195	6222	3291	8079	4361	8608	6138	9132	3200	7390
7044	5124	7929	7821	9769	7732	3009	0068	0787	2245
1367	1081	4195	8323	3339	6349	7596	1300	4683	2621
3472	5020	2675	8024	1094	5783	6727	5717	3942	3376
9227	1518	8581	9474	7239	2016	9191	5839	7873	0756
4104	8180	0154	1917	8294	9445	8945	1465	9493	1125
8163	9217	0352	1693	7553	3710	0409	3327	5754	5501
4871	2763	8332	4654	0194	6332	8900	7126	2884	0646
7745	6673	8951	1201	4221	8890	5219	8764	4459	9852
0076	8803	1824	9954	8313	7131	6228	7901	9944	1502
9750	4687	6246	3601	5254	3336	0192	5318	8450	9542
5577	9502	0134	4160	0549	5028	1977	8012	1489	3709
7479	6841	8844	9864	2183	9192	5083	1082	7210	6825
2048	4657	4266	1286	6675	3410	7183	5954	4005	0931
3219	4613	5579	9916	3549	2634	5405	8978	8932	8100
4323	0080	3236	9041	9137	0527	6341	6228	7662	9647
6859	9073	9002	0971	6580	1906	0469	9730	2678	6857
1332	0411	1886	9938	8290	6498	3200	6607	2931	8453
1415	5595	9341	7806	1248	5860	0663	0401	0048	6774
2890	8534	1642	1993	4465	5194	4142	2188	6066	8750
7117	3646	6312	1277	7501	1846	3170	8378	6926	3597
6675	0991	7946	6696	5952	9717	7035	0640	8542	4826
2681	8167	5877	4173	7010	9985	6735	6535	3451	0230
0866	7119	8042	4648	6555	0938	9883	8758	5617	2163
9846	9723	5827	2812	3943	8811	7505	5101	7907	2998
0303	0491	9592	6618	5220	6793	2373	1488	2222	1513
0937	2662	9498	2127	1770	4264	9379	4904	4232	6071
1232	3295	1451	3715	6115	1625	6827	7782	2481	1409
9492	8024	3546	4445	6299	9946	7470	9994	3159	3091
7577	5748	3109	6903	1271	0302	5822	2033	1206	0514
8086	1336	9462	0062	6208	0972	4760	3750	4197	1526
9317	4149	9900	4568	4501	3389	2101	4461	9836	1014
7868	2035	9977	7349	9396	7563	1526	9165	6607	3374
0743	4378	0856	1042	5419	9104	3688	8834	9280	6515
1191	7844	2435	1522	5861	8829	9896	4540	3638	6301
8938	8655	1729	6938	4972	2946	3008	3770	7861	5844
1544	6587	1031	4704	4950	3438	5901	6820	7031	3800

APPENDIX TABLE 8
BASIC MATHEMATICAL OPERATIONS

Some constants

$\pi = 3.14159\ 26536$
$e = 2.71828\ 18285$

Common notation

$x = y$	x is equal to y	$Pr\{z\} = r$	the probability of the event
$x \neq y$	x is not equal to y		z is r
$x \doteq y$	x is approximately equal to y	$E[X]$	the expected value of the random variable X
$x \approx y$	x is approximately equal to y	$C(n,r)$	the number of combinations of n objects taken r at a time
$x \simeq y$	x is approximately equal to y	$P(n,r)$	the number of permutations of n objects taken r at a time
$x < y$	x is less than y	$A\|B$	A given B
$x \leq y$	x is less than or equal to y	$+\infty$	positive infinity
		$-\infty$	negative infinity
$x > y$	x is greater than y	$\lim_{x \to a^+} f(x)$	limit of $f(x)$ as x approaches a from the right
$x \geq y$	x is greater than or equal to y		
$y = f(x_1, x_2)$	y is a function of the variables x_1 and x_2	$\lim_{x \to a^-} f(x)$	limit of $f(x)$ as x approaches a from the left
$\|-3\| = 3$	the absolute value of -3 is 3	$\int_a^b f(x)\, dx$	the integral of $f(x)$ from a to b

$$\sqrt[n]{x} = x^{1/n} \qquad e^x = \exp\{x\}$$

$$\log_e x = \ln x \qquad f'(x) = \frac{df(x)}{dx}$$

$$\log_{10} x = \log x \qquad x^{-1} = 1/x$$

Powers and roots

$$a^x \times a^y = a^{(x+y)} \qquad a^0 = 1\ [\text{if } a \neq 0] \qquad (ab)^x = a^x b^x$$

$$\frac{a^x}{a^y} = a^{(x-y)} \qquad a^{-x} = \frac{1}{a^x} \qquad \left(\frac{a}{b}\right)^x = \frac{a^x}{b^x}$$

$$(a^x)^y = a^{xy} \qquad a^{1/x} = \sqrt[x]{a} \qquad \sqrt[x]{ab} = \sqrt[x]{a}\,\sqrt[x]{b}$$

$$\sqrt[x]{\sqrt[y]{a}} = \sqrt[xy]{a} \qquad a^{x/y} = \sqrt[y]{a^x} \qquad \sqrt[x]{\frac{a}{b}} = \frac{\sqrt[x]{a}}{\sqrt[x]{b}}$$

APPENDIX TABLE 8 (*Continued*)

Logarithms

$\log_a a^x = x,\ a^x > 0$

$\log_a xy = \log_a x + \log_a y$

$\log_a b^x = x \log_a b$

$\log_a(x/y) = \log_a x - \log_a y$

$\log_a 1 = 0$

$\log_a a = 1$

Note that logarithms are not defined for negative quantities.

$\log_{10} \pi = 0.497\ 149\ 873$

$\log_e \pi = 1.144\ 729\ 886$

Change of base

$\log_a x = \log_b x / \log_b a$

$\log_{10} x = \log_e x / \log_e 10$

$\log_e x = \log_{10} x / \log_{10} e$

$\log_e x = 2.302\ 585\ 093 \log_{10} x$

$\log_{10} x = 0.434\ 294\ 482 \log_e x$

Summation relationships

$$\sum_{i=1}^{n} Y_i = Y_1 + Y_2 + \cdots + Y_n$$

$$\sum_{i=1}^{n} Y_i = \sum_{i=1}^{k} Y_i + \sum_{i=k+1}^{n} Y_i$$

$$\sum_{i=1}^{n} cY_i = c \sum_{i=1}^{n} Y_i \quad \text{where } c \text{ is a constant}$$

$$\sum_{i=1}^{n} c = nc$$

$$\sum_{i=1}^{n} (X_i + Y_i) = \sum_{i=1}^{n} X_i + \sum_{i=1}^{n} Y_i$$

Solution of polynomial equations

Linear or first degree.

$$ax + b = 0$$

$$x = -\frac{b}{a}$$

Quadratic or second degree.   Any quadratic equation may be reduced to the form,

$$ax^2 + bx + c = 0$$

$$x = \frac{-b \pm \sqrt{b^2 - 4ac}}{2a}$$

If a, b, and c are real then:

If $b^2 - 4ac$ is positive, the roots are real and unequal.

If $b^2 - 4ac$ is zero, the roots are real and equal.

If $b^2 - 4ac$ is negative, the roots are imaginary and unequal.

APPENDIX TABLE 8 *(Continued)*

Calculus

Derivatives.   In the following formulas, u and v represent functions of x, while a, c, and n represent fixed real constants and $f(u)$ is a function of x.

$$\frac{d}{dx}(a) = 0$$

$$\frac{d}{dx}(x) = 1$$

$$\frac{d}{dx}(au) = a\frac{du}{dx}$$

$$\frac{d}{dx}(u + v) = \frac{du}{dx} + \frac{dv}{dx}$$

$$\frac{d}{dx}(uv) = u\frac{dv}{dx} + v\frac{du}{dx}$$

$$\frac{d}{dx}\left(\frac{u}{v}\right) = \frac{v\frac{du}{dx} - u\frac{dv}{dx}}{v^2} = \frac{1}{v}\frac{du}{dx} - \frac{u}{v^2}\frac{dv}{dx}$$

$$\frac{d}{dx}(u^n) = nu^{n-1}\frac{du}{dx}$$

$$\frac{d}{dx}[f(u)] = \frac{d}{du}[f(u)] \cdot \frac{du}{dx}$$

$$\frac{d}{dx}(\log_a u) = (\log_a e)\frac{1}{u}\frac{du}{dx}$$

$$\frac{d}{dx}(\log_e u) = \frac{1}{u}\frac{du}{dx}$$

$$\frac{d}{dx}(a^u) = a^u(\log_e a)\frac{du}{dx}$$

$$\frac{d}{dx}(e^u) = e^u\frac{du}{dx}$$

$$\frac{d}{dx}(u^v) = vu^{v-1}\frac{du}{dx} + (\log_e u)u^v\frac{dv}{dx}$$

Integrals.   In the following expressions ln x is the logarithm to the base e; u and v are variables that depend on x; a and n are constants; and the arbitrary integration constants are omitted for simplicity.

$$\int a\,dx = ax$$

$$\int au\,dx = a\int u\,dx$$
$$\int (u + v)\,dx = \int u\,dx + \int v\,dx$$

$$\int x^n\,dx = \frac{x^{n+1}}{n + 1} \quad n \neq -1$$

$$\int \frac{dx}{x} = \ln x$$

$$\int e^x\,dx = e^x$$
$$\int e^{ax}\,dx = e^{ax}/a$$

$$\int b^{ax}\,dx = \frac{b^{ax}}{a\ln b}$$

$$\int \ln x\,dx = x\ln x - x$$

Source: Abridged and adapted from Section 25, "Mathematics and Statistics," of the *Forestry Handbook,* 2d ed. (K. F. Wenger, ed.), 1984, published by John Wiley & Sons, New York.

APPENDIX TABLE 9
TRIGONOMETRIC AND AREA FORMULAS

Solution of right triangles

$$\text{Sine } A = \frac{a}{c} = \frac{\text{opposite side}}{\text{hypotenuse}}$$

$$\text{Cosine } A = \frac{b}{c} = \frac{\text{adjacent side}}{\text{hypotenuse}}$$

$$\text{Tangent } A = \frac{a}{b} = \frac{\text{opposite side}}{\text{adjacent side}}$$

$$\text{Cotangent } A = \frac{b}{a} = \frac{\text{adjacent side}}{\text{opposite side}}$$

$$\text{Secant } A = \frac{c}{b} = \frac{\text{hypotenuse}}{\text{adjacent side}}$$

$$\text{Cosecant } A = \frac{c}{a} = \frac{\text{hypotenuse}}{\text{opposite side}}$$

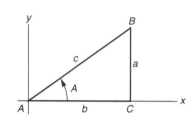

Areas of some plane figures		
Figure	Formula for Area (*A*)	Diagram
Rectangle	$A = a\,b$	
Parallelogram	$A = a\,h$	
Triangle	$A = \dfrac{a\,h}{2}$	
Trapezoid	$A = \frac{1}{2}(a + b)\,h$	
Circle	$A = \pi\,r^2$	
Ellipse	$A = \pi\,a\,b$	
Parabola	$A = \left(\frac{2}{3}\right) a\,b$	

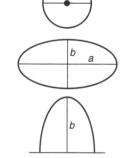

APPENDIX TABLE 10
EQUATIONS, LINEAR MODELS, AND GRAPHICAL REPRESENTATIONS OF SELECTED
FUNCTIONS AND CURVE FORMS

I. $Y = a + bX$ —— Straight line
    Linear model: $Y = b_0 + b_1 X$

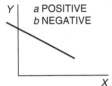
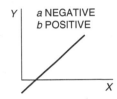

II. $(Y - a) = k(X - b)^2$ —— Second-degree parabola
    Linear model: $Y = b_0 + b_1 X + b_2 X^2$

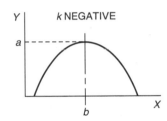
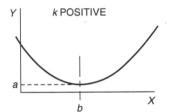

III. $(Y - a) = k/X$ —— Hyperbola

    Linear model: $Y = b_0 + b_1 \left(\dfrac{1}{X}\right)$

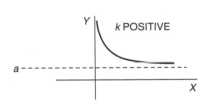
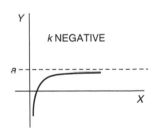

IV. $(Y - a) = k/X + bX$
    Linear model: $Y = b_0 + b_1\, 1/X + b_2 X$

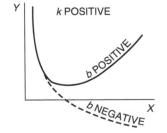
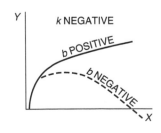

APPENDIX TABLE 10 (*Continued*)

V. $(Y - a) = k(X - b)(X - c)[X - (b + c)/2]$ —— Cubic
  Linear model: $Y = b_0 + b_1X + b_2X^2 + b_3X^3$

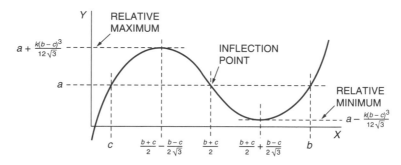

VI. $Y = aX^b c^x$
  Linear model: Log $Y = b_0 + b_1 \log X + b_2X$

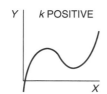

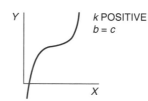

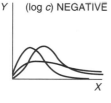

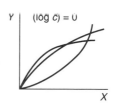

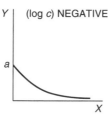
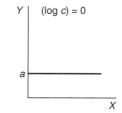

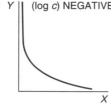
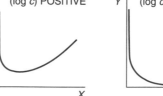

APPENDIX TABLE 10 (*Continued*)

VII. $Y = ab^{(x-c)^2}$
  Linear model: $\log Y = b_0 + b_1 X + b_2 X^2$

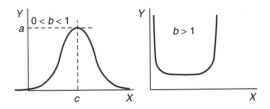

VIII. $10^Y = aX^b$
  Linear model: $Y = b_0 + b_1 \log X$

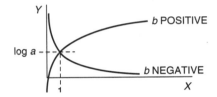

Source: Freese, Frank. 1964. Linear regression methods for forest research. *U.S. Forest Serv., Forest Products Lab., Res. Paper FPL* 17. 136 pp.

ANSWERS TO SELECTED PROBLEMS

CHAPTER 1

1-1 (a) 82.6 km; (b) 715 ft^3 per acre; (c) 139.9 m^3 per ha; (d) 202 trees per acre

1-3 (a) Ratio; (b) Ratio; (c) Ordinal; (d) Nominal

1-5 (a) 7.650, 7.65, 7.6; (b) 95.75, 95.8, 96; (c) 495,500; 496,000; 500,000; (d) 0.8969, 0.897, 0.90

CHAPTER 2

2-1 (a) (1) 10.64; (2) 10; (3) 7

(b) (1) 31.8; (2) 5.64; (3) 17; (4) 4.88

(c) 53 percent

(d) Confidence interval: $10.64 \pm (2.228)(1.7)$ or 6.85 to 14.43

2-3 (a) $Y = 0.476 + 0.788 X$

(b) (1) $r^2 = 0.78$; (2) $s_{y \cdot x} = 1.3$

(c) 5.99

2-5 (a) $r = 0$

(b) Yes; r is a measure of linear association, and the relationship between X and Y in this example is nonlinear.

2-7 (a) Ht $= -2.12 + 2.75$ (Age)

(b) Ht $= 34.7 - 2.93$ (Avail. Water)

(c) Age

CHAPTER 3

3-1 (a) Mean volume $= 34.6$ cords/acre

(b) Standard error of mean $= 2.19$ cords/acre

(c) Confidence interval: $34.6 \pm (2.201)(2.19)$ or 29.78 to 39.42

3-3 (a) 29.24

(b) 29.05

3-5 (a) Yes; Yes

(b) $Y = 2,420.83 + 1.026987 (1,800 - 2,050) = 2,164.1$

(c) $S_{\bar{y}_{Rd}} = 88.88$

Confidence interval: $2,164.1 \pm (2) (88.88)$ or $1,986.34$ to $2,341.86$

(d) $\bar{y} = 2,420.8$; $S_{\bar{y}} = 267.7$ (without f.p.c.); Confidence interval: $2,420.8 \pm (2.201)$ (267.7) or $1,831.6$ to $3,010.0$

3-7 (a) 9.46 in.

(b) $S_{\bar{y}_{ts}} = 0.785$; Approximate confidence interval: $9.46 \pm (2) (0.785)$ or 7.89 to 11.03

CHAPTER 4

4-1 (a) 180°; (b) 1,080°; (c) 1,800°

4-3 (a) 315°; (b) 212°; (c) 15°; (d) 119°

4-5 (a) 0.0694 acres per dot

(b) 1.736 acres per dot

(c) 17.78 acres per dot

4-7 (a) 40 acres; (b) 160 acres; (c) 80 acres; (d) 10 acres

CHAPTER 5

5-1

	Huber's (cu ft)	Smalian's (cu ft)	Newton's (cu ft)
(a)	4.91	5.16	4.99
(b)	121.6	122.1	121.8
(c)	5.18	5.24	5.20
(d)	105.6	106.0	105.7

5-3 (a) 80 cords

(b) 14.5 cords

(c) 31.2 cords

(d) 400 cords

5-5 5,405 lbs/cord

5-7 Load 1 = 5,029; 2 = 4,976; 3 = 4,865; 4 = 5,175; 5 = 5,103; 6 = 5,024; 7 = 5,222; Mean = 5,056 lbs/cord

CHAPTER 6

6-1 (a) 3,336 bd ft; $762.28

(b) 3,048 bd ft; $708.51

(c) 9,227 bd ft; $3,100.27

6-3 (a) 64 bd ft

(b) 8.726 cu ft

(c) 7.33 bd ft/cu ft

6-5 (a)

	Overrun/Underrun	
Log rule	Mean	Standard deviation
Doyle	56.8	98.7
Scribner	7.6	12.7
International	−6.6	3.2

(b) International; Doyle

6-7 (a) D^2L

(b) $Y = -1.35 + 0.0437 X$

6-9 (a) 8.48 in.

(b) 11.31 in.

(c) 14.14 in.

CHAPTER 7

7-1 Arithmetic mean = 10.9 in.; 27.7 cm

Quadratic mean = 11.6 in.; 29.5 cm

7-3 (a) 108.7 ft; (b) 45.6 ft; (c) 135.8 ft; (d) 49.6 m

7-5 (a) Girard form class = 0.78 or 78 percent

(b) Form factor = 0.40

7-7 Surface area = 172 ft^2; Volume = 170 ft^3

CHAPTER 8

8-1 65 bd ft

8-3 (a) yes

(b) $V = -0.281 + 0.00235$ dbh^2H

(c) $r^2 = 0.992$; $S_{y \cdot x} = 0.665$ cu ft

(d) 8.74 cu ft

8-5 Diameters = 17.55 and 15.66 in.; Cubic-foot volume by Smalian's formula = 24.14; Cubic-foot volume by integrating taper function = 24.09

8-7 (a) In the same units as dbh

(b) 6.03 cu ft

(c) $V = 0.00245$ dbh^2H

CHAPTER 9

9-1 (a) $Y = 0.971 + 0.798 X$

(b) $r^2 = 0.983$; $S_{y \cdot x} = 0.473$ in.

(c) yes

9-3

	No. of trees		Cubic-foot volume	
dbh (in.)	Tract total	Per acre average	Tract total	Per acre average
8	625.0	12.5	5,437.5	108.8
9	1,187.5	23.8	15,793.8	315.9
10	1,312.5	26.2	24,150.0	483.0
11	1,375.0	27.5	33,000.0	660.0
12	1,625.0	32.5	49,075.0	981.5
13	1,250.0	25.0	46,125.0	922.5
14	875.0	17.5	38,587.5	771.8
15	500.0	10.0	25,950.0	519.0
Total	8,750.0	175.0	238,118.8	4,762.5

CHAPTER 10

10-1 (a) 5 percent; EF = 20

(b) 10 percent; EF = 10

(c) 8 percent; EF = 12.5

(d) 2.67 percent; EF = 37.5

10-3 (a) 3,500 MBF

(b) 1,368 MBF

(c) 4,608 chains

(d) 60,000 plots; 70.71 chains

10-5 (a) 84 plots

(b) 2.44 chains

10-7 (a) CV = 31.84 percent on both a per-plot and a per-acre basis

(b) Total volume = 87,720 ft^3; Confidence interval: 72,952 to 102,488 ft^3.

CHAPTER 11

11-1 (a) Trees per acre = 180; BA per acre = 62.8 ft^2

(b) Trees per acre = 124.9; BA per acre = 60 ft^2

(c) No; No

(d) No; No

11-3 (a) BA by point: 1 = 90, 2 = 50, 3 = 120, 4 = 0, 5 = 50, 6 = 100, 7 = 50, 8 = 40, 9 = 110, 10 = 100, 11 = 150, 12 = 70; Mean BA per acre = 77.5 ft^2.

(b) $S_{\bar{y}}$ = 12.0 ft^2 per acre

(c) 56 to 99 ft^2/acre

(d) CV for volume = 55.7 percent, CV for BA = 53.7 percent; volume is more variable because it includes variation in height as well as diameter.

11-5 (a) BA = 144 ft^2/acre

(b) Volume = 4,272 ft^3/acre

11-7 Volume = 9.88 cords/acre

11-9 Mean volume = 1,113.8 ft^3/acre; Standard error of mean = 169.2 ft^3/acre; Confidence interval: 1,113.8 ± (2) (169.2) or 775.4 to 1,452.2 ft^3/acre.

CHAPTER 12

12-1 Z = 12,237

12-3 Total volume = 321 ft^3; Variance = 404.9

CHAPTER 13

13-1 (a) 1:6,000

(b) 1:6,109

(c) 1:16,608

(d) 1:3,000

13-3

RF	Feet per inch	Chains per inch	Acres per square inch
1:7,920	660.00	10.00	10.00
1:10,000	833.33	12.63	15.94
1:15,840	1,320.00	20.00	40.00
1:20,000	1,666.67	25.25	63.77

13-5 (a) 57.7 ft

(b) 53.9 ft

(c) 12.6 m

(d) 78.8 ft

(e) 22.5 m

CHAPTER 14

14-1 (a) 1,000 in.

(b) 83.33 ft

(c) 25.4 m

14-3 (a) Total = 10 acres, 4.04 ha

(b) Area in forests = 3.1 acres, 1.25 ha

(c) Area in croplands = 4.3 acres, 1.74 ha

(d) Area in rangelands = 2.6 acres, 1.05 ha

14-5 (a) 81 percent

(b) 66 percent

(c) 53 percent

CHAPTER 15

15-1 (a) $\ln H_d = 5.04 - 20.7\,A^{-1}$

(b) Site index = 91 ft

15-3 (a) BA/acre = 123.8 ft^2; Trees/acre = 360

(b) Stand density index = 248.6; CCF = 171.8

15-5 (a) Relative spacing = 0.23

(b) Trees/acre = 239

CHAPTER 16

16-1 (a) 7.50 percent

(b) 3.53 percent

(c) 9.00 percent

(d) 3.64 percent

16-3 (a) year 1 = 0.3860 in.; year 2 = 0.3690 in.; year 3 = 0.3541 in.; year 4 = 0.3408 in.; year 5 = 0.3290 in.

(b) Decreasing

16-5 (a)

dbh class (in.)	Present stand surviving (no. of stems)	Growth-index ratio (g/i)	No. of stems moving up (by dbh classes)			Future stand table (no. of stems)
			No Change	1 class	2 classes	
6	313	1.45	0	172	141	0
8	229	1.30	0	160	69	172
10	134	1.20	0	107	27	301
12	70	1.10	0	63	7	176
14	34	1.00	0	34	0	90
16	10	0.90	1	9	0	42
18	9	0.85	1	8	0	10
20	6	0.80	1	5	0	9
22	0		0	0	0	5
Total	805					805

(b)

dbh class (in.)	Present stand table (no. of stems)	Future stand table (no. of stems)	Scribner volume per tree (bd ft)	Present stock table (bd ft)	Future stock table (bd ft)	Volume production (bd ft)
6	313	0				
8	229	172				
10	134	301	42	5,628	12,642	7,014
12	70	176	86	6,020	15,136	9,116
14	34	90	136	4,624	12,240	7,616
16	10	42	201	2,010	8,442	6,432
18	9	10	280	2,520	2,800	280
20	6	9	369	2,214	3,321	1,107
22	0	5	481	0	2,405	2,405
Total	805	805		23,016	56,986	33,970

CHAPTER 17

17-1 Age of culmination of mean annual increment: site index 110 = 140; site index 140 = 110; site index 170 = 100; site index 200 = 90 years. Yes.

17-3 (a) Current volume = 2,080.8 cu ft/acre
(b) Periodic growth = 1,541.8 cu ft/acre/10 years
(c) Mean annual increment = 90.6 cu ft/acre/year
(d) 145.6 m³/ha; 107.9 m³/ha/10 years; 6.3 m³/ha/year

17-5

Initial volume (cu ft per acre)	Elapsed time (years)	Initial basal area (sq ft per acre) 90	110
2,400	5	2,656	2,635
	10	2,924	2,879
2,600	5	2,877	2,855
	10	3,168	3,119

17-7

dbh class (in.)	Trees per acre	Basal area per acre	Trees per acre 5 yrs hence	Trees per acre 10 yrs hence
6	100	19.63	102.3	97.5
8	50	17.45	57.6	63.1
10	30	16.36	33.7	37.8
12	20	15.71	22.1	24.4
14	...	...	8.0	12.4
16	...	...	...	3.9

CHAPTER 18

18-1 (a) 2,400 AUM
 (b) 120 AUM
 (c) 72 AUM
18-3 200 individuals
18-5 Shape index $= 1.0325$. Shape is circular.
18-7 (a) $Y = 202.0 + 2.63$ (axle count) with $r^2 = 0.963$
 (b) $Y = 229.5 + 0.0924$ (water use) with $r^2 = 0.815$
 (c) Axle count

accretion The growth on all surviving trees plus the growth on trees that were cut or died and were utilized between two measurements.

accuracy The closeness of a measurement or estimate to the true value.

aerial photograph A photograph of the Earth's surface taken from airborne equipment.

anamorphic curves A series of curves or equations scaled so that each is a constant times the base curve.

animal-unit-month The amount of ovendry forage required by one animal unit for a standardized period of 30 animal-unit-days. Abbr. AUM.

aspect The predominant direction of slope of the land.

azimuth A horizontal angle, measured clockwise from true north.

basal area The cross-sectional area of a single tree stem, including bark, measured at breast height, or the sum of the cross-sectional areas of all stems in a stand measured at breast height and expressed per unit of land area.

bearing A horizontal angle referenced to a quadrant, namely NE, SE, SW, or NW, measured from north or south to east or west.

bench mark A surveyed point of known position and elevation.

bias A systematic distortion that is introduced through sampling, measurement, or estimation processes.

biomass The total amount of living plant (or animal) material.

board foot The amount of wood contained in a board 1 in. thick, 12 in. long, and 12 in. wide.

breast height Standardized point for measuring tree diameters; defined as 4.5 ft above ground in the U.S., 1.3 m above ground in most countries utilizing metric units.

browse The part of shrubs, woody vines, and trees suitable for animal consumption.

brush Shrubby vegetation that is not suitable for commercial timber.

canopy The foliar cover in a forest stand (may consist of one or several layers).

cant A piece of lumber made from a log by removing two or more sides by sawing.

chain A unit of length equal to 66 ft and composed of 100 links.

cord A stack of wood that measures $4 \times 4 \times 8$ ft (128 ft^3) including wood, bark, and air space within the stack.

crown ratio The ratio of the length of live crown to total tree height.

cruise A forest inventory conducted to estimate the quantity of timber on a given area according to species, size, quality, and other characteristics.

cunit A unit of volume, generally applied to pulpwood, consisting of 100 ft^3 of solid wood.

current annual increment The growth observed in a tree or stand in a specific one-year period. Abbr. CAI.

cutting cycle The interval between partial harvests in uneven-aged stands.

443

declination, magnetic The angle between true north and magnetic north.

dendrometer A device for measuring the diameter of tree stems.

diameter at breast height Tree diameter measured outside bark at 4.5 ft (1.3 m in countries using the metric system) above ground level. Abbr. dbh.

digitizing The process of converting or encoding map data that are represented in analog form into digital information of x and y coordinates.

eastings The x-coordinates in a plane-coordinate system.

ecology The study of the interrelationships of organisms with their environment.

edge effect The modified environmental conditions or habitat along the margins or edges of forest stands or patches.

ephemeris Predictions of the current position of a GPS satellite that are transmitted in the GPS data message.

even-aged Forest stand composed of trees of the same, or approximately the same, age.

forage Browse and herbage that is available and may provide food for grazing animals or may be harvested for feeding.

forest An ecosystem characterized by tree cover.

geographic information system An information management system that accommodates the entry, storage, manipulation, retrieval, and display of spatial data. Abbr. GIS.

global positioning system A satellite-based positioning system that gives a user's position anywhere on Earth. Abbr. GPS.

graze The consumption of standing forage by livestock or wildlife.

ground datum A point on the Earth's surface used as reference for measuring the height of aerial photography and for calculating photo scale.

ground truth Measurements or observations made on the ground for the purpose of verifying interpretations made from aerial photography or remote sensing.

growth The change in size of an individual or a stand of trees over a specified time period.

habitat The place (including climate, food, water, and cover) where an animal, plant, or population lives and develops.

herb Any flowering plant except those developing persistent woody stems.

home range The area over which an animal normally travels.

hypsometer An instrument, based on geometric or trigonometric principles, for measuring tree heights.

indicator species Any plant that by its presence, frequency, or vigor, indicates any particular property of the site.

ingrowth The volume of those trees that grew into the lowest inventoried size class between two measurements.

ionosphere The outer part of the Earth's atmosphere, consisting of heavily ionized molecules.

latitude   The angular distance measured north or south of the Earth's equator. The equator has latitude 0 degrees, the south pole − 90 degrees, and the north pole + 90 degrees. (Latitudes are also called parallels.)

log rule   A formula or table for estimating the volume (usually in board feet) of lumber that may be sawed from logs of different sizes.

longitude   The angular distance measured east or west from a reference meridian (Greenwich, England) which is 0 degrees on the Earth's surface. Longitudes range from − 180 (180 degrees west) to + 180 degrees (180 degrees east). (Longitudes are also called meridians.)

map projection   A mathematical model for converting locations on the Earth's surface from spherical to planar coordinates.

mean   (1) *Arithmetic mean:* the average value of a set of observations, obtained by dividing the algebraic sum of all observations in the set by the total number of observations. (2) *Geometric mean:* calculated as the nth root of the product of n values. (3) *Quadratic mean:* the square root of the arithmetic average of the squared values of a set of observations.

mean annual increment   The total growth of a tree or stand up to a given age divided by that age. Abbr. MAI.

median   The middle observation in a set of ranked data; if the set consists of an even number of observations, the median is the average of the two middle observations.

mode   The value occurring most frequently in a set of data.

mortality   (1) In general terms: trees dying from natural causes. (2) When referring to sequential inventories: the volume of trees initially measured that died during a growth period and were not utilized.

multi-aged   Forest stand that has more than one distinct age class arising from specific disturbance and regeneration events at various times.

multipath error   The error caused by the interference of a signal that has reached a GPS receiver antenna by two or more different paths (usually caused by one path being bounced or reflected).

northings   The y-coordinates in a plane-coordinate system.

ovendry weight   The weight of a substance after it has been dried in an oven at a specific temperature to equilibrium.

overrun   Results when the mill tally is greater than the log scale.

parallax   The apparent displacement of an object, caused by a change in the point of observation.

parameter   A characteristic (generally in numeric form) that describes a specific aspect of a population.

periodic annual increment   The growth of a tree or stand observed over a specific time period divided by the length of the period. Abbr. PAI.

photogrammetry   Measurements made from aerial photographs, including area measurements, distance, direction, height, or differences in elevation or slope.

photo interpretation The art and science of identifying objects and conditions from photographs.

photo scale Photo scale, or representative fraction (RF), is the ratio of the distance measured on the photograph to the distance measured at the ground datum (measurements must be in the same units).

polymorphic curves A series of curves of different shapes.

population The aggregate of all units (may be finite or infinite) forming the subject of study.

precision The closeness of a series of measurements or estimates to their own average.

pseudorange The distance between a GPS satellite and receiver based on the correlation of a satellite-transmitted code and the local receiver's reference code, which has not been corrected for synchronization between the transmitter's clock and the receiver's clock.

range The difference between the largest and smallest value in a set of observations.

rangeland Land on which the indigenous vegetation is predominately grasses, forbs, or shrubs.

recreational area A developed or undeveloped land area reserved and managed for recreational purposes.

remote sensing The measurement of an object or phenomenon by a recording device that is not in physical contact with the object or phenomenon under study. (Often involves aerial photography or satellite imagery.)

rotation The period between regeneration and final cutting in even-aged stands.

sample A part of a population assessed to estimate characteristics of the whole population.

section A land survey subdivision of one square mile (640 acres or 259 ha).

site index The average height of the dominant stand at a specified reference age.

stand A contiguous group of trees sufficiently uniform in age-class distribution, composition, and structure, and growing on a site of sufficiently uniform quality to be a distinguishable unit.

stand density A quantitative measure of stem crowding within a stocked area.

stand table A tabulation of the total number of stems (or average number of stems per acre or ha) in a stand or compartment by dbh classes and species.

standard deviation A measure of the dispersion about the mean of a population or a sample; computed as the square root of the variance.

state plane A coordinate system commonly used in surveying applications in the lower 48 United States and based on zones drawn state-by-state on transverse Mercator and Lambert projections.

stocking Refers to the adequacy of a given stand density to meet some management objective.

stock table A tabulation of the total volume of stems (or average volume per acre or ha) in a stand or compartment by dbh classes and species.

stumpage value The sale value of standing timber.

taper The decrease in diameter of a tree stem or log from the base upwards or from the larger diameter end to the smaller end in logs.

tarif table   A series of harmonized single-entry volume tables.

township   A land survey subdivision of 6 × 6 mi, consisting of 36 sections (23,040 acres, or 9,238 ha).

tree   A woody perennial plant that has a definite crown shape and reaches a mature height of at least 16 ft (5 m).

trend   The direction of change in an attribute as observed over time.

type mapping   The process of delineating soil, vegetation, or site quality types on an aerial photograph or on a base map.

underrun   Results when the mill tally is less than the log scale.

uneven-aged   Forest stand composed of an intermingling of trees that differ markedly in age.

universal transverse mercator   A planar coordinate system, extending from 84° north to 80° south latitude and based on a specialized application of the transverse Mercator projection. Abbr. UTM.

upgrowth   Trees that grow into the next larger diameter class between two measurements.

variance   A statistical measure of the dispersion of individual observations about their arithmetic mean.

volume equation   A mathematical expression used to estimate the volume of trees from measures of diameter and height (and occasionally form).

watershed   A land area drained by a single stream, river, or drainage network.

weir   A notch in a levee, dam, or other barrier across or bordering a stream, through which the flow of water is measured or regulated.

yield   The volume of an individual or a stand of trees at various ages.

Sources: Adapted from *The Dictionary of Forestry* (J.A. Helms, ed.), 1998, published by the Society of American Foresters; *Glossary of Terms Used in Range Management,* 1998, published by the Society for Range Management; and *Dictionary of Natural Resource Management,* (J. and K. Dunster), 1996, published by UBC Press.

INDEX

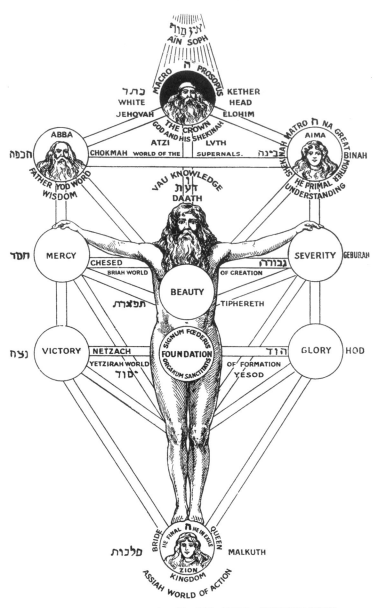

THE SACRED TREE OF THE SEPHIROTH

THE
HOLY
KABBALAH

A. E. Waite

With an Introduction by
Kenneth Rexroth

Dover Publications, Inc.
Mineola, New York

Bibliographical Note

This Dover edition, first published in 2003, is an unabridged republication of the text of the work originally published in 1929 by Williams & Norgate, London. It also includes Kenneth Rexroth's Introduction to the University Books edition (New Hyde Park, New York, 1960) of the work.

Library of Congress Cataloging-in-Publication Data

Waite, Arthur Edward, 1857–1942.
    The Holy Kabbalah / A. E. Waite ; with an introduction by Kenneth Rexroth.
        p. cm.
    Includes bibliographical references and index.
    ISBN 0-486-43222-X (pbk.)
        1. Cabala. I. Rexroth, Kenneth, 1905– II. Title.

BM525.W3 2003
296.1'6—dc22

2003055601

Manufactured in the United States of America
Dover Publications, Inc., 31 East 2nd Street, Mineola, N.Y. 11501

THE
HOLY
KABBALAH

INTRODUCTION

by Kenneth Rexroth

There is singularly little on Jewish mysticism of any sort to be found in English. Furthermore, most of it is not very rewarding. Much of it is definitely antagonistic. However Routledge published long ago, 1910 in fact, a book, *Aspects of the Hebrew Genius,* edited by Leon Simon, a collection of essays once given as lectures in the North London Jewish Literary Union. There is a chapter on Jewish mysticism by H. Sperling, and in the very first paragraph he says these tremendous words: "They (the vague mystical yearnings of man) can, however, fitly be compared to that invisible chain that binds husband to wife, parents to children, relation to relation, friend to friend, social unit to social unit. Without these lesser mysticisms society would dissolve into its first atoms; without the larger mysticism man would break away from his Maker and be flung into nothingness." On these words hang all the Law and the Prophets. This is the essence of Judaism. It is also the essence of Jewish mysticism, whether the speculations of Hellenistic Neo-Platonists. Medieval Kabbalists, Polish or Levantine Hasidim, or the sophisticated and fashionable philosophy of Martin Buber.

Kabbalism and Hasidism seem, to a Christian taught in his own religion to view Gnostic and theosophic tendencies as the source of all heresy, to be a kind of Jewish heterodoxy. They are not. Jewish orthodoxy is not defined by the correctness of the answers it gives to metaphysical and cosmological questions. The Torah, the Rites of Passage, the Ceremonies of the Holidays, the poetic and narrative books of the Bible, philosophy and fantasy, from Maimonides to Isaak Singer — the consensus of faith is never broken. Kabbalism is nothing but a transcendental way of looking at the "purely formal" rites of Circumcision, Marriage, Confirmation. There is no

VII

"Kabbalistic Mystery," however profound, that cannot be found, clearly and simply exemplified in the ceremonies of Succoth, the Feast of Tabernacles.

Under the influence of millenia of legalistic interpretation of the Law, and guided by the extreme rationalism of Maimonides and other Jewish scholastics, Judaism has come to seem, at least to the outsider, a "religion of the Book" in the most extreme sense, a code, rather than living faith. This is illusory. All the Talmuds in the world cannot make a religion. Religion is what people do — act and contemplation. Whitehead said it was what man does with his aloneness — a very Protestant, in fact, Lutheran statement, and the expression of a theory rather than of actuality. Even the most extreme neo-Lutheran, Kierkegaard, spent much of his time and energy struggling with the community of the Church of Denmark. The casuistry of rabbis, the exhortations of prophets — we must never forget that these take place in the context of a people, held together in a rite. That, after all is their only significance — to insure the integrity of the people and the continuity of the rite.

Someone back in the nineteenth century said that religion is what humanity uses to fill in the gap between technology and the physical environment. Historically this was certainly true. But it is a kind of inverse and diminishing definition. Ideally, religion is what would be left after man *knew* everything. Kabbalism, like all other Gnosticisms, does concern itself very much with knowing, with cosmology and cosmogony, the nature and process of the Universe. "You shall know and the knowledge shall make you free." Free for what? Today we are inclined to forget how trapped man was by the recalcitrance of his environment, by puzzling vagaries of the universe. Before the universe could be given significance — "valued" as we say nowadays — it had to be given coherence. Gnosticism has been accused by its opponents, from Plotinus to the present, of equating coherence and significance, structure and value. This may be true where Gnostic movements have been heretical — split off and isolated from the main body of religious development. Kabbalism is not heterodox. It is a symbolic and aesthetic elaboration of the actual cult of Israel, with which it never loses contact. The Jewish *Prayerbook* as we have it today is essentially a Kabbalistic document.* *"Credere est orare, orare est cognoscere,"* said the great Roman Catholic modernist, Father Tyrell, "To believe is to pray, to pray is to know."

When man cannot understand nature, and insofar as he cannot understand it at any point, he is confronted with an actual vacuum, and into this he projects himself. What is sought in Alchemy or the Hermetic Books or the Memphite Theology, or irrational fads like flying saucers, is the basic pattern of the human mind in symbolic garb, as it presents itself in the individual believer, and behind that, in the enduring structures of the human organism itself. As the speculative constructions of religion fall away as explanations of "reality" they assume the character of symbolic masks of states of the soul. If they persist in the practices of a cult, we say they have been etherealized. It is precisely their irrationality which keeps dogma and ritual alive. If they can be reduced to "common sense" explanations or denials they die away. Only the mysteries survive, because they correspond to the processes of man's internal life, outward visible signs of inner spiritual realities.

To go back to the beginning, Kabbalism dates back into the most obscure past of Judaism. What are the distinguishing ideas of Kabbalism? It is first of all a theory of emanations ("degenerative monism" it is called philosophically). The inscrutable Godhead fills and contains the universe. To become active and creative God emanated ten *sephiroth* or intelligences. A special prominence is given to one of these emanations, who functions as a female principle in the Deity, a demiurge and a term to creation. This is the final emanation, Malkuth the Queen, the physical manifestation of Deity in the universe. She is thought of as a Divine Woman, the Bride of God (like the Shakti of Shiva). Finally, the "innermost secrets" of the Kabbalah are what are "occult" in all occultism, erotic mysticism and a group of practices of the sort we call yoga—autonomic nervous system gymnastics. For the Kabbalist the ultimate sacrament is the sexual act, carefully organized and sustained as the most perfect mystical trance. Over the marriage bed hovers the Shekinah. Kabbalism

---

*This Prayerbook—*Siddur*—is not something relegated to Sabbath service in the Synagogue. Both man and woman use it day and night. What the Bible was to the Protestant in the great days of Dissent, this grimoire of Kabbalah is to the orthodox Jew and his wife.

also includes, of course, a group of divinatory and magical practices, manipulations of the alphabet and the text of the Pentateuch, magic spells and rites. All of these elements go back to very early days—to the beginnings of Israel in Palestine, and it is these beginnings which shed most light on both scholarly Kabbalism and popular Hasidism, and, in addition, go far to illuminate the real—the abiding spiritual meaning—of Judaism in all times and places.

By and large the special details of Kabbalism which distinguish it from the mainstreams of Jewish thought are what is "occult" in occultism everywhere, and most of the world's religions can be reinterpreted in these terms. They give Kabbalism its fascination but they do not give it its substance. As A. E. Waite so well points out—beneath the glittering and mysterious superstructure of the Kabbalah, which purports to be occult Judaism, lies—Judaism.

Kabbalism is probably the only religious movement of the Gnostic type to come full circle in this fashion, to create mysteries and explain them, to hide secrets and discover them, and come at last back to the greater mystery from which it started, but with deeper insights and wider knowledge. Insight and knowledge of what? In the last analysis of the human soul, of man within himself, united with another in marriage, united with his fellows in love. I suppose certain tendencies and individuals in Catholicism have done the same thing. Bonaventura is a sort of enraptured, orthodox Gnostic. There is the Protestant, Jacob Boehme. In modern times there have been all sorts of rationalizing, philosophizing, psychologizing movements which have in fact accomplished similar ends, from the Theosophists and A. E. Waite himself to Martin Buber and Carl Jung. These are different—either eccentric individuals or modern sophisticated cults. Whoever wrote or gathered and edited the tracts of the *Zohar,* Kabbalism shows all the signs of being a perfectly natural, Near Eastern Gnostic movement, evolved directly from the local soil, the "clerkly lore" of an "anthropological religion."

It might be wise to note some of these sources. Emanationism is found in the socalled "Memphite Theology," a text dating back to the beginnings of Egyptian civilization. Four pairs of gods emanate from Ptah in a hierarchy of power, and the creative process is described in language which still echoes in the Gospel of John. The very word "Isis" means "throne" and many of her attributes survive in the terms applied to the Shekinah, to Malkuth, to the personified Wisdom of Proverbs and finally, in the titles of the Litany of the Blessed Virgin. Pre-Hebraic Palestine is full of Els (Elohim) and Ba'als (Adonai, the Lord) and they all have consorts, at once wives, daughters and mothers — Asherah, Anat, Astarte, Ashtaroth. In Egypt they were identified with Isis, with Hathor, and with Sekmet, wife and daughter of Ptah, the ultimate creator. In the fifth century we discover Anat in an Aramaic Elephantine papyrus specifically described as the consort of Yahweh.

Asherah survives in the Scriptures as a term for the phallic pillars, *mazzeboth,* which stood beside the altars and in the holy places until the fall of the Temple. But she also survives in person and the story of Elijah is the tale of a bitter struggle with Jezebel, a regal priestess of Ba'al-Asherah. Temples of Asherah and Yahweh stood side by side in ninth century Mizpah. In the seventh century Jeremiah found children in the streets of Jerusalem gathering wood and the fathers kindling the fire and the women kneading the dough to make cakes for the Queen of Heaven. The sacred prostitutes and sodomites of the Goddess appear again and again in the Scriptures. The First Isaiah begets a son with a *zonah* — called a "prophetess" in the King James Version, Jephthah is the son of a *zonah,* Hosea's description of his relations with a sacred prostitute are amongst the most cryptic in the Bible and as late as the mid seventh century, under Manasseh, the cult was flourishing. With the Assyrian and later Babylonian and then Persian conquests, Ishtar was substituted for Ashteroth, and, as has been pointed out time and again, the *Book of Esther* (simply another English transliteration of Ishtar) is an elaborate euhemerization of the Spring New Year fertility rites and the *heirosgamos,* the sacred marriage — as the folk rites of Purim are paralleled all over the world at the season.

The most likely interpretation of the *Song of Songs* is that it is a collection of songs for group marriage rites, focused in the *heirosgamos* of priestking and priestess, which accompanied the opening of the irrigation channels from the main ditches into the dry fields. In fact, a book which casts great light on the Song of Songs is Granet's *Festivals and Songs of*

Ancient China, an interpretation of the erotic songs of the ancient Chinese collection, the *Shi Ching*. Do not misunderstand, this parallelism does not "prove" diffusion from some imagined prehistoric religious center. It shows the fundamental identity of man's response to the great rhythms of life. Nothing is more illuminating than to look up "Shekinah" or "Succoth" or "Wisdom" or "Power" or for that matter any of the other epithets of the *Sephiroth* in a good Biblical Concordance, and ponder on the mysterious sentences. Do they just seem mysterious because our attention, with minds full of presuppositions, has been directed to them? I think not. These words are keys which unlock some of the oldest material in the Scriptures, and they survive because of their traditional sanctity. The post-Esdras editors, working over the old documents, might disguise them, but they did not dare omit them, any more than they dared wipe out the memory of the sacred groves and the pillar circles and the high places. At last the Samaritan Gnostic, Simon Magus, with his consort, the Mystic Helen, a temple prostitute out of Ephesus of the great Mother, comes to meet and struggle with the earliest Christians.

Now, we must understand that we have come to view "orthodoxy" after millenia of narrowing definition. To some extent the prophets, some of them, were "orthodox" in this way, or at least they were so represented after the Persian period. But the people knew nothing about these questions. Religion for them was the whole body of cult *acts*, it was what they *did*. We think of such conflicts in terms of Athanasius vs. Arrius, Dominicans vs. Albigensians, Calvin vs. Servetus, Massachusetts vs. the Quakers and witches, and the deliberations of Senator McCarthy's Committee. They were nothing of the sort. True, the prophetic movement in Judaism and later the Rabbinical schools, represent the slow evolution of such sharpening distinctions and the purging of old practices. But the average inhabitant of Palestine went right on practicing religion as he found it in place — there — in the cult of his ancestors, and even the evolution of Yahvistic monotheism was an enormously drawn out process. The ancient folk ways have never vanished from Judaism, even at its most reformed, and today — the day I am actually writing this — Purim, C. E. 1960 — customs whose broken relics we find at the very bottom of mounds of ruins in the Holy Land linger on in the parlors of the thoroughly assimilated and Americanized "High Society" of San Francisco where I live.

Last night I went to a celebration of the hundredth anniversary of one of the city's most fashionable Congregations — an oratorio — a *Purimspiel* — *Queen Esther*, given to a packed Opera House, with a very Nordic looking Esther. At the reception afterwards the President of the Congregation said, opening his speech, "This is the happiest day of my life," and the Rabbi interrupted, "How about your marriage?" This was a joke, a wisecrack as American as anything on television — and it brought as much laughter from the audience. But it was something more, and it somehow elicited a slightly different kind of stir — an undercurrent that wouldn't have been there with a Gentile audience. That spontaneous joke had touched one of the great nerve centers of Jewry, the Sacrament of Israel, watched over and nourished under the wings of the Shekinah, that gesture, the physical embodiment of the turn in the creative process, the moment at which all being, having reached its last term, begins its long return to the inscrutable and holy center from which it came. On the buffet, along with champagne and caviar were *hamanohren*.

A. E. Waite was an odd fish out of an odder barrel. He was not only one of the few persons in modern times, Jew or Gentile, to write a sensible and sound book on Kabbalah. He was a genuine scholar of occultism who himself came out of the welter of occult sects and movements of the end of the last century. He lived in the world of Eliphas Levi, Stanislas de Guaita, "Papus," Sar Peladan, Mme. Blavatsky, A. P. Sinnett, Macgregor Mathers, Wynn Westcott, Annie Besant, and "Archbishop" Leadbeater, and more American oddities and rascals than you could shake a stick at. Some of these people are genuine literary curiosities and still make fascinating reading. Others are unbelievably fraudulent and silly. But, to a man, they are mines of misinformation, rash hypotheses and unsupportable conclusions. They are as far from being scholars as could well be imagined. It is a pity that they all, the whole movement, have never become the subjects of scholarship on a large and really serious scale, because they certainly do represent, like the Marxists or the Neo-Catholics, a significant mass movement of the human mind in its long march out of folly. The subjects they were all interested in are amongst the most interesting subjects for scholarship that exist, but they produced only two scholars, A. E. Waite and G. R. S. Mead. Mead was a Theosophist, and hence suspect in the halls of scholarship, but his is still the only readable translation of the Hermetic literature in English, he edited a Gnostic tractate, the *Pistis Sophia,* and he wrote an estimable book on Gnosticism, *Fragments of a Faith Forgotten.* There is nothing specially odd or cultish about any of these books. In contrast, the acceptably academic translation of the Hermetica, by Scott, is the work of a Higher Critic, and is a violent, shameless, distortion of the text.

Waite *was* odd, cultish and eccentric. He wrote the most dreadful prose conceivable, an awful mixture of Walter Pater, Cardinal Newman, Arthur Machen and plain vulgar pretentiousness. It is the last survival of the last spasms of literary PreRaphaelitism. Fortunately, though it was common in its day there is nothing left around to compare it with except Sebastian Evan's *High History of the Holy Grail* still to be found on shelves of out of print Everyman's Library, and William Morris' slightly lunatic translation of the Icelandic Sagas into a kind of PreRaphaelite studio code, today utterly unreadable. Waite, however, is not unreadable. You have to read between the balderdash, but it is easy to get used to. Soon you no longer notice it, and he does have, almost always, something very interesting to say. At last the absurd rituals he uses to say the simplest things come to endear him to you, like the wen on grandma's nose.

In his autobiography, Waite gives the impression that his books all came more or less by accident, as assignments from publishers. I rather doubt that, because throughout his life he seems to have followed a definite program. Eventually, and it certainly seems, systematically, he came to cover all the main aspects or traditions or myths of occultism. His works include: *The Secret Tradition in Alchemy, The Brotherhood of the Rosy Cross, The Secret Tradition in Freemasonry, The Hidden Church of the Holy Grail, The Pictorial Key to the Tarot, Raymund Lull, Louis Saint Martin,* and careful editions of the works of Eliphas Levi and the greatest of the English mystical alchemists, Thomas Vaughan, whose works are mysteriously missing from the bibliographies of Dr. Jung's many books on this subject. Besides all this he wrote a lot of dreadful poetry full of Mystic Veils and Clinking Thuribles, and a couple of general statements of his own philosophy — as well as a rather cobwebby autobiography. Self-evidently this is a program, a carefully planned work of a lifetime. The remarkable thing about it is that, coming although it does from an era of windy nonsense and smoky pretence, there is nothing seriously wrong with it. They are all books of wide, painstaking scholarship. Waite went to all the sources he could find, in itself a Herculean labor, and he exposed all the errors of quotation and interpretation in the secondary sources that he could uncover. He is almost always right. Not only is he right, but he never loses, however dear to his heart may be the misty mid-regions of Weir in which he wanders, the true scientific scholar's scepticism. In fact, since he was himself the leader of a "Mystic Circle of Seekers for Illumination," who took his somewhat absurd vows very seriously, he uses this very scholars' scepticism as a mask and a refuge. On the question of the very existence of "Spiritual Alchemy," let alone on the sexual yoga, so plainly illustrated in Chinese works on the subject, for which most alchemy is just a kind of double talk, Waite is non-committal. He leads you to the sources, quotes and analyzes them for you, and leaves you to draw your own conclusions. So likewise with the Grail legend, so with Rosicrucianism, so with occult Free-masonry, so with that *I Ching* of the Western World, the Tarot cards — he strips away the nonsense, exposes the facts, and leaves you to draw your own conclusions. With charla-tans he is merciless. Although he is in a sense a product of the school of Eliphas Levi, he never misses a chance to expose the pretensions of that most fascinating of mountebanks. With St. Martin or Lull he is careful, even reverent, although he does an excellent job of taking apart the complicated Lull legend.

The Holy Kabbalah is his greatest work. Although he was a kind of Christian, even a sort of Liberal Catholic, Kabbalah is, out of all the past, the closest thing to his own philosophy. He wrote three books on the subject, each later one incorpo-rating and correcting its predecessors. He seems to have read everything he could find on the subject in every language he knew, and meditated on it deeply and long. It has been said

BOOK II

SOURCE AND AUTHORITY OF THE KABBALAH AND THE AGE OF THE CHIEF TEXTS

ARGUMENT

The two chief cycles of Kabbalistic literature, in spite of destructive criticism, are referable to Talmudic or early post-Talmudic times, as regards sources and inspiration. There seems indeed no reason why the BOOK OF FORMATION should not derive from R. Akiba, as tradition affirms. There is no real evidence in support of the theory that R. Moses de Leon wrote the ZOHAR or BOOK OF SPLENDOUR towards the end of the thirteenth century. At the same time the opinion of a few students, not too well accredited and not adequately equipped, that these works are of great antiquity or at least pre-Christian must be set aside decisively. The attempts which refer the Kabbalah in any direct manner to some prior theosophical system must be rejected also : it has antecedents everywhere, but its analogies with other systems are explained mainly by natural likeness between independent views on fundamental problems of being. Antecedent Jewish influence through Aristobulus and Philo must not be overlooked, but also it must not be exaggerated. The Kabbalah is *sui generis*. It has many accidental connections, but fundamentally it is of and from within a school of thought in Jewry. If there be any preponderance in a given direction, the records suggest that its wider sphere of influence has been on Christian rather than on Jewish minds.

BOOK III

THE WRITTEN WORD OF KABBALISM : FIRST PERIOD

ARGUMENT

The subject-matters of Kabbalistic literature outside the SEPHER YETZIRAH, and prior to the appearance of the ZOHAR, are surveyed briefly, to indicate that there was a growth of the Tradition and to correct exaggerated notions concerning it. There are various old tracts which connect with Kabbalism but are not regarded by some modern scholarship as Kabbalistic in the technical sense. This is the case with the SEPHER YETZIRAH itself ; but there is no doubt that all such works laid claim upon oral knowledge transmitted from the past, or that it was the elements of such Oral Tradition which received developments subsequently from the commentators on SEPHER YETZIRAH, as well as from the ZOHAR, and, at a much later period, from expositors of Zoharic teaching. The attention of early Kabbalists was concentrated on the BOOK OF FORMA-

TION, and several elucidations of that work appeared between the eleventh and thirteenth centuries, under notable names.

BOOK IV

THE WRITTEN WORD OF KABBALISM: SECOND PERIOD

ARGUMENT

The text-proper of the ZOHAR and its numerous connections are examined in successive sections, in order to furnish a comprehensive notion of the materials incorporated by this composite work, prior to the study of its Doctrines at a later stage in detail. A certain prominence is given to their intimations from a mystical or theosophical point of view.

BOOK V

THE DOCTRINAL CONTENT OF THE KABBALAH IN RESPECT OF GOD AND THE UNIVERSE

ARGUMENT

The Fundamental Doctrines of the Kabbalah are shewn to be (1) A Philosophy of the Absolute ; (2) The evolution of the universe in part by way of emanation and in part by creative acts ; (3) The distinction of the evolution into four worlds, the last of which was brought into being by a process of making. The subsidiary Theosophies connected with these subjects are (1) The contrast between God in Himself and God as revealed to His people, that is, to finite intelligence ; (2) The sacramental nature of the conventional symbols in which the human Logos is formulated ; (3) The way of attainment in respect of human knowledge and wisdom in Divine Things.

BOOK VI

HIERARCHIES OF SPIRITUAL BEING

ARGUMENT

The Doctrine concerning the soul of man is of great importance in Kabbalism, for man in reality is the centre about which the whole Tradition revolves. We must have recourse to the great text of the ZOHAR for all vital intimations on the parts, divisions or states of the human soul, its pre-existence and its destiny. The developments thereof and the commentaries arising therefrom may be useful for occasional tabulations, but they add nothing of living consequence. It is otherwise concerning the Choirs of Angels and Kabbalistic Demonology : in the main they are of and belonging to that Third Period of the Written Word which will be dealt with in Book IX. The ZOHAR is casual and inchoate on these subjects, except regarding the Fall of the Angels, which will be considered in a section apart. The later Kabbalists drew materials from the TALMUDS to build up their formulated scheme of Celestial and Infernal Hierarchies.

BOOK VII

WAYS OF GOD WITH MAN

ARGUMENT

It is shewn that the Biblical Mythos concerning the Earthly Paradise is a Mystery of Sex in the mind of the Secret Tradition. The Fall of the Angels connects indirectly enough with this obscure subject, but it was responsible, *ex hypothesi*, for all uncleanness subsequently on earth and in man. It comes about in this manner that the Fall of Man belongs to the same Mystery, is developed as such at great length and with numerous variations. The wickedness which was " great upon the earth," which broke up " the fountains of the great deep " and opened " the windows of heaven " in the Deluge Legend was an iniquity of sex aberration ; and even the subsequent sacrifice of Noah, " a sweet savour " to the Lord, was sanctified and acceptable because of its high intent respecting the Supreme Mystery. There is little need to dwell upon the Covenant with Abraham in this connection ; but the foundation of the whole subject is said to abide therein. It is obvious also that the Law promulgated on Sinai was not apart therefrom ; but the history of Moses is itself a history of spiritual espousals. When the time came for a House of the Lord to be built in Zion the Great Mystery in its transcendence was illustrated by the presence of Shekinah in the Holy of Holies, as a Bride in the abode of her Spouse. Finally, the Advent of Messiah, the Divine Son of the Secret Tradition, the letter VAU in the Sacred Name of Four Letters, is to raise up her who is His Bride in exile and to prepare for the Sabbath of creation, which is a period of true bridals.

BOOK VIII

THE HIGHER SECRET DOCTRINE

ARGUMENT

The Secret Doctrine of the ZOHAR concerning the Holy Shekinah is the Mystery of Sex at its highest and she herself is the Mystery of the Oral Law. It is intimated that behind this Mystery there appears to be an authentic doctrine of Knowledge, based on experience. We are led on in this manner to a more particular study of the Mystery of Sex in the light of the Secret Tradition, and there is a sense in which it is still a study of Shekinah. It is suggested that there is or may be a Mystery of Human Nuptials behind it which has not been conceived by the heart of man in ordinary ways of life.

BOOK IX

THE WRITTEN WORD OF KABBALISM:
THIRD PERIOD

ARGUMENT

The growth of Kabbalistic literature is sketched in certain expository works or commentaries on the ZOHAR and in some independent tracts which connect with the general Tradition. Two other works are chosen for separate consideration, being one on the Mysteries of Love, because of its general diffusion, and one on the application of Kabbalistic Apparatus to Alchemy, because of the credit which it has obtained in the modern school of Hermetic students.

BOOK X

SOME CHRISTIAN STUDENTS OF THE KABBALAH

Argument

The opinion of certain modern writers—chiefly of Victorian days—that the Kabbalah is a vehicle of a Secret Doctrine concerning Absolute Religion was never held in the past, more especially as it proves on examination not only to be utterly distinct from the claim of Israel in respect of its Secret Tradition but a spurious Liberal Religion or qualified Natural Theology. Even those who ascribed the Kabbalah of old to a Divine Source were actuated chiefly by the notion that it was a disguised Christianity, and in several cases their real concern was the conversion of Jewry by its presentation from this standpoint. The chief Christian students of the subjects are reviewed in succession to establish these facts. Some minor misconceptions are corrected and some extrinsic points of interest are developed in the course of the sketches.

BOOK XI

THE KABBALAH AND OTHER CHANNELS OF SECRET TRADITION

ARGUMENT

Modern speculations on the part of believers have represented the alleged Secret Sciences as vehicles of a Great Occult Tradition ; but the question lies beyond the limits of the present inquiry, which can estimate only the quality and extent of the influence exercised by Kabbalism on other departments of " esoteric thought " in the West.   It is found that this influence has been magnified.   In the case of Ceremonial Magic it has been unquestionably large, but very small in that of Alchemy and Astrology. Freemasonry has been regarded also as a channel of Secret Tradition, but its connection with Kabbalism is at once adventitious and slight.   Among arts of divination, the claims of certain picture-symbols, known as Tarot cards, have been presented as a Key to Kabbalistic Doctrine and Tradition ; but they are dismissed for specific reasons. As a conclusion to the subject of other Channels of Secret Tradition, the Doctrine of Pure Mysticism is contrasted with that of Kabbalism, and the points reached by the investigation are brought into a single focus.

BOOK XII

FINAL CONSIDERATIONS

ARGUMENT

A brief recurrence to developments of later Kabbalism introduces a study of recent contributions to the scholarship of the whole subject and a word on its chief findings. The question of Christian elements imbedded in the ZOHAR as in a doctrinal system is considered at some length and dismissed.   There arises in fine the living question whether and in what manner the Secret Doctrine of Israel can be held to affect mystics at the present day.   It is surveyed in respect of that branch which deals with the Mystery of Sex, but afterwards in that of the Doctrine that the soul comes forth from God and that to God the soul returns.   The conclusion is that Zoharic Kabbalism, under the veils of its proper symbolism, offers a living message to those whom it concerns.

APPENDIX I

PREFACE

FEW educated persons, and certainly none belonging to the class of students for which this work is designed more especially, will require to be told that the Kabbalah is a form of Esoteric Philosophy, that it makes for itself a high claim, or that this claim has been admitted, from time to time, by persons who are entitled to our consideration. Nor will it be needful to state that the literature called Kabbalistic rose up among the Jews during the Christian centuries which succeeded their dispersal and the destruction of their Holy City. It offers a strong contrast to the sacred scriptures of Israel, which are direct, beautiful and simple, while Kabbalism is involved, obscure and even repellent occasionally, as regards its outward form. The Bible is in focus with humanity; the Kabbalah is distorted out of all correspondence with the simple senses, and we must grind our intellectual lenses with exceeding care if we would bring it into perspective.

From whatever point of view it may be approached, the Kabbalah is, however, of importance : it connects with other literatures which are included like itself under the general denomination of mystical, and there is a sense in which it has been thought, in its highest development, to stand at the head of all. It is part of the history of philosophy, and as such it entered once into the thought of Europe. It is responsible in its degeneration for all that strange tissue of symbolism and procedure which made up the Ceremonial and Philosophical Magic of the fourteenth to the seventeenth centuries ; at a comparatively late period it entered into the story of Alchemy ; it tinctured many of those conventional practices and beliefs which are called superstitious in our loose fashion of words, and the guise in which we know them is very often a Kabbalistic guise. Were it possible to suppose for a moment that behind Magic, behind Alchemy and Astrology there were any mystery of real knowledge, then it would be entitled to peculiar respect, at least by the hypothesis of some of its defenders, because it is through this seemingly impassable literature that—in their view—the road to the secret lies. It is, however, on the theosophical side and as a contribution to the thought of the past on problems of life and mind that its appeal—if any—will be found at the present day.

A comprehensive account of the Kabbalah, on the surface expository and historical, but seeking to establish its connections with other forms of alleged Secret Tradition, to determine its influence and importance from more than one standpoint, and to shew forth its contribution to the sacred science of the soul, are the design of the present work, in which regard has been paid also to the limitations and requirements of English readers—in other words, of those unacquainted with the languages, dead and living, in which Kabbalistic literature has been, with few exceptions, available heretofore. The subject has been classed as abstruse and was presented by early expositors after a highly technical fashion : in this case there is no antecedent knowledge assumed in the reader. It is to be understood otherwise that this work has been written by a Christian Mystic and chiefly for the use of mystics ; in offering materials for their judgment, it indicates also the lines of those conclusions to which the writer leans, and seeks to enforce some of them. It has been preceded in England by only two books dealing directly with the subject ; one is the slight but not inconsiderable essay of Dr. Ginsburg,[1] which is critical rather than descriptive, and is, on the whole, hostile in its tendency. The second is by S. L. MacGregor Mathers,[2] but is mainly translation and commentary from Latin sources, and, in addition to other limitations, embraces only a minute portion of an extensive literature. The present comprehensive account fulfils a distinct purpose and, it is hoped, may be held to occupy a vacant place from which there is a wide prospect, by no means deficient in consequence for those even who are not mystics, for the student of philosophy and history, and for the curious in paths of literature which the elder D'Israeli, despite the bias of his birthright, forebore to enter.

---

[1] THE KABBALAH. By C. D. Ginsburg. London, 1865.

[2] THE KABBALAH UNVEILED, containing the following books of the Zohar : 1. THE BOOK OF CONCEALED MYSTERY ; 2. THE GREATER HOLY ASSEMBLY ; 3. THE LESSER HOLY ASSEMBLY, Translated into English from the Latin version of Knorr von Rosenroth, and collated with the original Chaldee and Hebrew Text. By S. L. MacGregor Mathers, London, 1887. The Commentary is partly that of Rosenroth, and partly the work of the translator. A new impression was published in 1926. I believe also that the essay of Dr. Ginsburg has been reissued in America.

The rumour of a great literature which had subsisted—
ex hypothesi—from time immemorial in Jewry may not have
been heard of first through a signal piece of good fortune
which befell Picus de Mirandula in the fifteenth century, when
he purchased, from an unknown Israelite, certain strange
codices in manuscript; but nothing which came into his
hands and proved to be a treasure of the past was likely to lie
unnoticed on his own part; while this artist of the schools
was a trumpet of fame for anything announced by his voice
during the brilliant, too few years that he carried the quest of
learning and the proof of his attainments from place to place
in Europe. He was himself the pupil in Jewish Theosophy
of Elias del Medigo, who filled a chair at Padua and wrote
two treatises at the instance of Picus, one being on the Intellect and on Prophecy, in 1481–82, which seems to have
remained unprinted and was written in Hebrew, like its companion DE SUBSTANTIA ORBIS, the work of 1485; but this
appeared at Basle in 1629. It was edited also with a commentary by Isaac Reggio and so republished at Vienna in
1833.

Picus de Mirandula was in some sense a critic of his day,
for he wrote upon the vanity of Astrology; but it was by no
means a period which debated the authenticity of works
referred to antiquity either by repute or by the simple audacity
of claim, while it was still less concerned with polemics on
questions of authorship. I believe that I have mentioned
elsewhere how perilous it would have seemed then to have
entered such a field of research. To deny in the particular
case that, e.g., the ZOHAR—which is pre-eminently the chief
text of Kabbalism—embodies the actual discourses of Rabbi
Simeon ben Yohai might have been a prologue to impeaching
the authorship of the Pentateuch—by which I mean that it
would have opened such a vast speculative horizon that one
might have suggested the other.

There came a time, and it was not far away, when the
treasure of Picus was questioned, when people began to
distinguish between a false and a true ZOHAR, the first as the
work of one Moses de Leon, belonging to the late 13th century, and the second as something undemonstrable in respect
of age and value. The distinction remains at a high point in
the world of speculation, because no one has met with the
second; and it might not be worth while to mention it in the

present place, but it gives an opportunity of stating that the manuscripts purchased by Picus represented the identical work which has been known for six centuries and over under the name of SEPHER HA ZOHAR. An index of the codices acquired by him was published in 1651 by the French bibliographer Gaffarel,[1] and in the only full translation of the ZOHAR into a living language [2] its instalments are appended to the various sections. There are innumerable mistaken references, but the index reflects the text ; what is missing in items referred to one section may be found sometimes in another ; and though the pains of Gaffarel can in no wise be called representative as an attempted summary—it is not even the shadow—there is no question that the treasures of Picus are those which we know under the distinctive name of ZOHAR. There is no alternative text, and the differentiation given above is a supposition which can deceive no one.[3]

The contribution of Picus de Mirandula to the knowledge of the ZOHAR in Europe does not exceed to any considerable extent the simple fact of its existence. His Latin thesis on the subject cannot be termed representative, nor can anything else from his pen. It remains that he was the first Christian into whose hands the work came in any guise whatsoever, and it seems to have been that authoritative form which was represented later on by the Cremona and Mantua editions.[4] We may never know under what circumstances these were produced at their several dates,[5] and so far as I and others have been able to trace the bibliography of Kabbalism, it does

---

[1] Jacobus Gaffarel : CODICUM CABBALISTA EORUM MANUSCRIPTORUM QUIBUS EST USUS Joannes Picus, Comes Mirandulanus, INDEX, 1651.

[2] SEPHER HA ZOHAR (Le Livre de la Splendeur) Doctrine Ésotérique des Israélites. Traduit pour la première fois sur le texte chaldaique. . . . par Jean de Pauly, 6 vols., 1906–1911.

[3] Curiously enough, the report has reached us through Richard Simon, the well-known author of HIST. CRITIQUE DU VIEUX TESTAMENT. See G. C. Sommer : SPECIMEN THÉOLOGIÆ SOHARICÆ. It is of course within possibility that the statement mentioned above does not question the claims of the work published long after at Mantua and Cremona, but indicates that there was a false ZOHAR circulated by Moses de Leon and presumably now unknown.

[4] The edition of Mantua appeared in 1558 and that of Cremona almost coincidentally —1558–60. The latter is called bibliographically the GREAT ZOHAR because it contains certain tracts and fragments which are not found in the Mantua edition, whence the latter has been named the LITTLE ZOHAR. Other editions are those of Dublin, 1623 ; Amsterdam, 1714 and 1805 ; Constantinople, 1736 ; and Venice, with the date of which I am unacquainted.

[5] The Mantua edition appeared under the auspices of R. Meir ben Ephraim de Patavio and R. Jacob ben Napthali de Gazulo. See Julius Bartolocci : MAGNA BIBLIOTHECA RABBINICA, vol. iv, p. 416, col. 2, published at Rome in 1693. They were, however, the printers merely. See Ib., p. 15, col. 2.

not appear that there is any earlier codex in manuscript. As he was the first to see the volumes, so Picus was the first to discern in the ZOHAR that it incorporated various elements which have been held capable of a Christian construction—whatever its value.[1] I shall deal with them at the close of the present study, when there will be something to say on the fact that the Christian predisposition of which Mirandula may be called the prototype became—almost without exception—the predisposition, the dedication indeed, of the *literati* who followed him, up to and including those who have translated and edited the French text. Picus passed away in his youth [2] or there are indications which lend colour to the possible realisation of his great dream that the Latin Pontificate itself, in the person of Pope Julius, might have lent an ear to his eloquence and done something to approach Israel from the standpoint of Christianity in Kabbalism.[3]

Well, it was after this manner that the work began to be known in Europe, and there passed something like a century away, after which the next name to our purpose is that of William Postel. It was he who translated the SEPHER YETZIRAH—or BOOK OF FORMATION—for the first time into Latin, and thus introduced to the curious and learned of Europe the root of all Kabbalism concerning the doctrine of the SEPHIROTH, the powers and virtues of the twenty-two Hebrew letters and the mystery which resides in numbers. I must not say that THE BOOK OF FORMATION is like that legendary grain of mustard which grows into a vast tree, because the ZOHAR is in no sense its development, except in so far as letters and numerations are concerned ; but it ranks as the primitive text of accepted Kabbalistic doctrine in Israel, and the contribution of Postel to our knowledge—minute as it is—seems much more to our purpose than the detached and almost sporadic CONCLUSIONES KABBALISTICÆ of

---

[1] See his HEPTAPLUM, a sevenfold exposition concerning the six days of Genesis.—OPERA, 1572.

[2] He died at Florence in 1492.

[3] The points of correspondence observed by Picus de Mirandula led him to infer that the ZOHAR contains : (1) The Doctrine of the Holy Trinity, (2) The Fall of the Angels, (3) Original sin, understood as the Fall of Man, (4) The necessity of redemption, (5) The Incarnation of the Divine Word. With certain reserves in respect of the Trinity, and what is to be understood by redemption, these doctrines are not only to be found in the text, but are of continued recurrence therein, and yet the most surprising thing about the work, having regard to its period of origin, is the comparatively slight tincture that it has received from the Christianity in the midst of which it originated and developed.

Picus. Postel is credited by tradition with a translation of the SEPHER HA ZOHAR which would be a rare treasure, had it ever come into existence or been maintained therein.[1] I do not know how or with whom the attractive story arose, but twenty years since it took a very strong hold on the mind of French students and there was a great research after it, terminating as might have been expected. There is, however, rather more basis for the quest than mere legend, as it is impossible to read Postel's most memorable work, called CLAVIS ABSCONDITORUM, without inferring that he must have been acquainted with the text, and might therefore, by bare possibility, have undertaken such a task.[2] It speaks of the Soul of the Mediator as the first creature of God and the Law, the Reconciler of the universe, referred to the SEPHIRA BINAH, which titles and which local habitation are those of Shekinah, according to the ZOHAR.[3] This is by no means the only direction in which Postel connects with the chief text of the Secret Tradition in Israel, but it is sufficient at this point to have established the fact without enlarging thereon.

Between the period of Mirandula and that of William Postel there are, as we shall see, the names of Cornelius Agrippa and Paracelsus ; but the first connects more especially with the practical Kabbalah so called, with powers of Divine Names, mysteries of numbers, doctrines of angels and demons, drawn for the most part from sources other than the ZOHAR ; while in respect of the second his use of the word Kabbalah has no connection with any monopoly of Jewry.

Contemporary with Postel there was John Reuchlin or Cadmion, who dedicated his three books entitled DE ARTE CABALISTICA to Leo X. His work may be best described as a study of Messianic doctrine, the object of which was to shew that He who was expected by Israel had already come. I am not actually certain, but I believe that he was the first to affirm that the Hebrew name of Jesus was formed of the

---

[1] Picus de Mirandula also is said to have caused the ZOHAR to be translated into Latin, or alternatively a Latin version was one of the manuscripts which came into his possession by purchase from the unknown Jew.

[2] The legend of a Latin version is recurrent. A French gentleman of Lyons is supposed to have purchased a copy in 1890, paying many thousands of francs, and a translation is also ascribed to Gui de Viterbi. There is nothing improbable in the notion that the text may have been so rendered, and may be in hiding somewhere, though I do not set much value on the Lyons story.

[3] Later Kabbalism regarded ADAM KADMON, the Lesser Countenance of Zoharic symbolism, as the pre-existent soul of Messiah. It was also the Word in CHOKMAH.

consonants of Jehovah = יהוה with the addition of the
sacred letter SHIN = יהשׁוה—*i.e.* Jeheshuah.[1]   He quotes a
large number of Zoharic writers on Kabbalism, but does not
mention the ZOHAR, at least by name.[2]   Reuchlin wrote also
DE VERBO MIRIFICO.   Belonging to the same period as
Reuchlin there was Petrus Galatinus, an Italian convert from
Jewry, the author of DE ARCANIS CATHOLICÆ VERITATIS,[3]
drawn from the texts of Kabbalism into twelve great books
in the form of a debate between himself, a certain Hogostratin
—of whom I know nothing otherwise—and Reuchlin.   It
is a work of much greater extent and more considerable
learning than the books of the last writer and it does mention
the ZOHAR, but without shewing much first-hand acquaintance.   This also is a study of Messianic doctrine and is
masterly after its own kind.

A third name of importance is Paulus Riccius who was
another Jewish convert to Christianity, but his work on
CELESTIAL AGRICULTURE [4] did not exercise any considerable
influence.   He wrote also STATERA PRUDENTUM on the Law
of Moses, Christ and the Gospel, but the work was condemned, and a number of other treatises, including one on
the doings of the Kabbalists, which appeared at Nuremberg
in 1523.

The purpose so far of these prefatory words has been to
indicate briefly the circumstances under which the chief text
of Kabbalism came to be known in Europe, and at a later

---

[1] It should be observed that the Hebrew spelling is יֵשׁוּ.

[2] There are several editions of both these works, and they are included in the
collection of Pistorius entitled, ARTIS CABALISTICÆ SCRIPTORES, *Tomus Primus*, but
the second volume—if that was the limit intended—never appeared.   This publication
belongs to the year 1587.

[3] Petri Galatini : DE ARCANIS CATHOLICÆ VERITATIS, LIBRI XII, 1672.   The
text in this edition is followed by Reuchlin : DE ARTE CABALISTICA.   It is of course
a reprint, the work itself having been completed in 1516, according to its colophon.
An intermediate edition appeared in 1602.   Those who can suffer its prolixity will not
be unrepaid by its reading, even at this day.   The analysis of contents in respect of
the twelve books is worth giving : (1) Treats of the TALMUD ; (2) The Trinity of
Divine Persons ; (3) The Incarnation of the Son of God ; (4) The First Advent of
Messiah ; (5) The Jewish Argument that the Messiah has not come is confuted ;
(6) The Redemption of Mankind ; (7) The Blessed Virgin ; (8) Mysteries concerning
the Messiah ; (9) Rejection of the Jews and Call of the Gentiles ; (10) The Institution
of the New Law ; (11) The Passing of the Old Law ; (12) The Second Advent.
Galatinus is supposed to have possessed a copy of the lost TARGUM of Jonathan Ben
Uzziel on the hagiographical books of the Old Testament—*i.e.* prophets, *op. cit.*,
Book I., c. 3.

[4] This is the first text given in the collection of Pistorius : ARTIS CABALISTICÆ,
hoc est, Reconditæ Theologiæ et Philosophiæ Scriptorum TOMUS I.   Basle, 1587.
It is known usually as ARTIS CABALISTICÆ SCRIPTORES.

stage the Christian students and exponents of the subject will be considered in particular monographs. It is sufficient at the moment to have established the fact that there was a succession of Kabbalistic scholarship from the beginning, outside Jewry, and that its early concern was to unfold the Christian elements which it discovered in the Secret Doctrine of Israel, above all in the ZOHAR and in the Jewish literature which arose therefrom.

To those who may approach the present work from a philosophical and historical standpoint the presence of its leading motive and its more especial appeal to a single class of students will require some explanation. It was once, I believe, suggested that since the first appearance of Dr. Ginsburg's destructive criticism there has been no attention paid among English scholars to the subject of the Kabbalah. Within the region of research which has only a scholastic horizon—whether metaphysical or historical—there was no interest that calls for special mention at the period which preceded that work immediately, and it is quite true that there has been as little subsequently to its publication, but not on account of Dr. Ginsburg's criticism. There has been always or, speaking exactly, since the days of Robert Fludd and Thomas Vaughan, of Cudworth and the Cambridge Platonists, a certain class of students for whom the claims made by and on behalf of the Kabbalah have possessed importance, and this class is possibly larger now than at any date prior to 1865. It forms also intellectually a more considerable body than the academical reader might be disposed to imagine in the absence of particular acquaintance with the literature by which it is represented. One is obliged to speak of these students and thinkers under the designation of theosophical or esoteric groups, though the phrase is inexact and has been used to describe persons who have little title to consideration. A proscribed mode of thought is here, as in other cases, identified with the lesser capacities that follow it, and what was once an unpopular subject has been classed according to the waste and drift which has collected about it. But the class to which I have adverted does not in itself deserve either ridicule or contempt : it is that which believes in the perpetuation of a secret religious or more correctly mystical Tradition from an early period of human history, and this is not manifestly an absurd or unwarrantable consequence

to draw from the study of religions undertaken in a comparative sense. It is a question of evidence and should be left to
establish its values.   Now, the Kabbalah is not only, as I have
said, the Secret Theosophy of Jewry, but it has been represented further to be the channel of such a Tradition as I have
just mentioned. It is therefore not merely reasonable to
suppose, but it is true as a fact, that to theosophists and
mystics, more than all, if not unto these exclusively, an
inquiry like the present must appeal.   Other interests are
accidental ; their interest is vital.   To determine the claims
of the Kabbalah as a department and perhaps inspiring centre
of Secret Doctrine is to determine that which is of most real
moment regarding it.

It is for this reason that I have been led to consider the
Kabbalah, not only as a mystic in the accepted sense, but from
the mystical standpoint, and to recur with a certain frequency
to the belief in a Secret Doctrine of Religion, as well as to
some other connected questions which need reconsideration
at the hands of those who hold them.   If I have had in the
course of the inquiry to reduce various illusions to their
proper place in the realm of the fantastic, and have contracted
the sphere of what is called Mysticism within its proper
dimensions, I shall be justified, so far as regards my intention,
by those whom I have sought to disabuse.   It remains to say
that from its nature the foundation of Mysticism cannot be
in so-called occult science or in occult philosophy, while it is
on the historical side alone that it connects with any traditions
of the past, popular or acroamatic.[1]

Now, it is to be understood above all that these volumes
are not addressed to members of the Religion of Israel and—
at least in any primary sense—that they are not planned as a
contribution to scholarship, though it happens in the accident
of things that they are the first extended memorial of Kabbalistic literature which has appeared in this country.   They
are part of a scheme proposed long since to myself for an
exploration of the Secret Tradition in Christian Times and the
determination of that one question which matters about
Secret Tradition, as indeed about all other subjects of human

---

[1] The reason is indicated by Schopenhauer, when he remarks on the astonishing
unanimity of mystics in all ages, unlike in everything except those principles which
constitute Mysticism, and yet not holding such principles as a sect clings to its tenets,
for they are not and can never be a sect.

thought and inquiry. The question is whether on its surface
or somewhere down in its deeps, and even below the deeps,
there is any vestige of that great spiritual experiment which—
awaiting a more adequate or exact mode of definition—must
be called the Science of the Soul in God. Within historical
times it has been always in the world ; it is in the West as well
as in the East ; but it has been overlaid everywhere by heavy
veils of doctrine and practice which are particular to places
and times, to the psychological characteristics of different
races and peoples. It is of all things simple and single, which
notwithstanding it emerges everywhere in the mode of a
particular complex on account of these accretions. Thus an
universal subject which does not belong to learning, in the
formal sense of this term, has become a matter of expert
research on the one hand, while on the other it has been
represented as impossible of examination in a living and
plenary sense, except by ascetics, and, among these, usually by
those who are leading some kind of monastic or conventual
life, isolated from the world and its activities. That which
has been planned and attempted in my several studies of
Mysticism is a liberation of the subject from these old trammels,
while the variations of its outward forms have been considered in volumes devoted to the Secret Tradition, that
which is offered here to students of THEOSOPHIA MAGNA
being a final revision and digest of my old books and monographs on MYSTERIUM RECEPTIONIS in the mind of Jewry.

It is delivered to the keeping of that scattered and
unincorporated brotherhood which is of my kindred in the
spirit, as a memorial of its understanding according to the
light of an individual Christian mystic and not that of Israel,
supposing that at this day of the world there were any real
concern of Israel in these its records of the past, unless it be
in a few synagogues or ghettos of Croatia and Dalmatia. The
doctrine of TSURE and the Mystery of Shekinah are the root
of my concern in Kabbalism. They are not of my concern solely for that which they signified in a Theosophical
School of Jewry but for whatever may belong therein to the
life of Catholic Mysticism here and now. It is shewn that at
their best and highest the old Sons of the Doctrine were on a
quest which is also ours and that the experience which at
rare moments is felt in our deep of heart is no other than is
shadowed forth—sometimes a little dimly—in their obscure

records. The part of us which abides in God and communicates the sense of the Eternal is that which in their own veridic dream belongs to ATZILUTH, the Supernal World, and never leaves the Supernals. I think also that as some of us, within our own measures, do now " know in part," awaiting " that which is perfect," so also they—or some of them—were not without an inward realisation of a great reality which they expressed outwardly as the " Bond of Union."

It remains to say that while the age of the records is of large consequence on the historical side and so has been considered at length, the antiquity of Kabbalistic Tradition cannot be an essence of the consideration, having regard to the purpose set forth in these prefatory words. The implications of one's own standpoint must be acknowledged in the logic of things, and the message of the texts at their highest is all in all for me and not their date or authorship. The plays passing under the name of Shakespeare would be no less immortal plays and greatness of greatness in the world of literature, were it proved beyond challenge to-morrow that they were written by Bacon or a stableman of the Globe Tavern. So also if SEPHER HA ZOHAR is not of time immemorial but belongs to the 13th century, which almost certainly it does not in the root-matter, my investigation is not stultified. There remains the question of values, the question of life and essence. If the Tradition has warrants herein, seven hundred years will suffice for its age at need. But if it has none, it can be a matter of curious research only, supposing that it is seven thousand years old. The myths of Babylon remain Babylonian myths even if they are older than Genesis; and if the strange Tale of a Garden, with which Genesis opens, holds something within it which belongs to the spiritual deep, to the authentic legends of the soul, it signifies little enough if the figurative myth concerning the Fall of Man is a century or an age later than the BOOK OF THE DEAD.

A. E. WAITE.

BOOK I

POST-CHRISTIAN LITERATURE OF THE JEWS, INCLUDING THE TALMUD

BOOK I

POST-CHRISTIAN LITERATURE OF THE JEWS

I.—THE HIDDEN CHURCH OF ISRAEL

THE construction of the Exile placed by the " Princes of the Exile " upon the Sacred Oracles of ancient Israel cannot be dismissed as unimportant. From the period of the dispersal of the Jews after the destruction of Jerusalem by Vespasian down to our own times—the productive activities of which lie far beyond the scope of this reference—Hebrew literature has developed in many of the chief centres of Europe ; but outside the scattered remnant of the Children 'of the Covenant it has remained largely unknown. Many persons, not otherwise ill-informed, might be astonished to discover that so far back as the end of the seventeenth century there were nearly four thousand works [1] written in the Hebrew tongue which were known individually and quoted by one authority on rabbinical bibliography, namely, Julius Bartolocci, of the Reformed Order of St. Bernard.[2] Almost every conceivable department of human learning and intellectual activity is represented in this literature,[3] which, in things secular as in things sacred, has the seal of the sanctity of Israel upon all its leaves. On the purely religious side, it is otherwise an extremely curious and in some respects a profound literature, which translation has done little to make known, which is represented incompletely enough even in

---

[1] It is perhaps unnecessary to say that they were for the most part in manuscript.

[2] BIBLIOTHECA MAGNA RABBINICA : *De scriptoribus et scriptis rabbinicis, ordine alphabetico Hebraice et Latine digestis, auctore* D. Julio Bartoloccio de Cellerio, folio, 4 vols. Roma, 1678–1692. The work is paged from left to right, after the Hebrew manner.

[3] For one of the accessible collections which give some idea of its variety, see the CATALOGUE OF HEBRAICA AND JUDAICA in the Library of the Corporation of the City of London. With a Subject-Index by the Rev. A. Löwy. London, 1891.

the great and authoritative text-books of Jewish history. There is no need to add that its extent and its difficulties make it a formidable subject of approach. It is, indeed, an undiscovered country, still awaiting its Columbus,[1] a land full of wealth and mystery, of strange shrines and sanctuaries shining weirdly far away, through the darkness of our ignorance, with a light which might recall the traditional radiance of Shekinah, so foreign does it seem to that which enlightens most men who are born into the modern world.

Within this literature there is, so to speak, another and stranger literature included, the report of which has been amongst us for several centuries, and in a certain way and measure it must be admitted that it is known to some, but chiefly because it has been made available by the fathers of bibliographical erudition, the Latin-writing scholars of the past. This storehouse of Hebrew Theosophy, for such it is, has exercised a peculiar fascination on many great minds of Christendom, and its Gentile students were at one time as keen, if not as numerous as its Jewish disciples. It is called the Kabbalah, of which term there has been more than one explanation suggested in the credulous past by the makers of ridiculous romance in etymology, and it seems worth while to mention two of them in passing, as examples of the follies which have encompassed the subject of research. The word has been derived from the name of the Hindoo teacher Kapila,[2] to whom a Philosophy of Numbers is ascribed, seemingly on the slender ground that one branch of Kabbalistic literature is connected with this subject. Another fantastic suggestion makes the term an analogue of Cybele,[3]

---

[1] The work of Dr. Moritz Steinschneider, the German bibliographer of rabbinical literature, is the most important contribution to our knowledge which has been made during comparatively recent years.

[2] C. W. Heckethorn made himself responsible for this view in an enlarged edition of his very unequal and indeed negligible work on SECRET SOCIETIES OF ALL AGES. See vol. i. p. 83.

[3] The responsibility in this case rests with the late Edward Vaughan Kenealy, whose anonymous BOOK OF GOD and its sequels were quoted once upon a time by a certain class of writers as if they carried seals of authority. Its philology is of the period of Godfrey Higgins, of the author of NIMROD and of Bryant's ANCIENT MYTHOLOGY. See Kenealy's INTRODUCTION TO THE APOCALYPSE OF ADAM-OANNES, p. 613. If writers of this calibre, so-called occult " authorities " and old works belonging to the field of research are mentioned here and there in these notes, the explanation is that I know those whom I address. The student at large of things which are called mystical may have sound titles to consideration in respect of sincerity and zeal, but he is like the Victorian student of secret arts and sciences, with a fatal tendency to accept bad evidence and rely on exploded writers. It is desirable therefore to indicate, as occasion

the mythological Queen of Heaven, who is thus connected with the Jewish personification of Wisdom under a female aspect. As to the true derivation there is no room for uncertainty, and it possesses that simplicity which is so often a warrant of truth in things of language as it has been said to be in those of Nature and Art. The word comes from a Hebrew root which signifies to receive. Kabbalah equals reception.[1] The knowledge embodied in the literature which passes under this title purports to have been transmitted orally from generation to generation. The literature as it exists is the Tradition put into writing, and in this form it has been supposed by some other dreamers to be veiled—that is to say, the meaning which appears on the surface is not the true sense.[2]

The Kabbalah in any case claims to be the light of a Secret Traditional Knowledge[3] preserved among the " chosen people,"[4] and the subjects with which it is concerned, as might be expected, are Sacred and Divine Subjects : they include the most profound Mysteries of God and the Emanations of Deity ; the celestial economy ; the process of creation ; the scheme of Providence in regard to man ; the communications of God in revelation and to the just in his Church ; the offices and ministries of good and evil angels ; the nature and pre-existence of the soul, its union with matter and its metempsychosis ; the mystery of sin and its penalties ; the Messiah, His kingdom and His glory to be revealed ; the state of the soul after death and the resurrection of the dead, with occasional, too rare but pregnant intimations on the union of the soul and God. Hereof is the aspect and this the part which was conceived and unfolded *sub specie æternitatis.* Here also,

---

arises, that such sources are wrong. Were my work addressed only to scholarship, it is obvious that a different procedure would be followed herein.

[1] In Hebrew it is קבלה. The Encyclopædia Perthensis observes that the word is written also as Gabella, which is, of course, a nonsensical corruption, and would not be worth noting if it were not true in fact that it occurs in this form among a few old writers on Magic. See Encyc. Perth. iv. 543, 544.

[2] We shall see afterwards that this view is not so much to be received with caution as to be rejected utterly.

[3] One of the titles ascribed to it was חכמה נסתרה = Secret Wisdom ; the initials of these words gave another title, signifying Grace = חן. See Kitto : Cyclopædia of Biblical Literature, *s.v.* Kabbalah. (Third edition, London, 1864.)

[4] The recipients of this knowledge were termed Mekkubalim, a name which will be familiar to the readers of the astrologer Gaffarel. On this point see the worthless article, *s.v.* Kabbalah, in T. H. Blunt's Dictionary of Doctrinal and Historical Theology. London, 1872.

if anywhere, is the abiding part, rooted in everlasting values, and the one voice among many voices of old Tradition which bears a message from the past to the modern world.

It is needless to say that by a literature so considerable in its capacity there are many other subjects embraced, but these are the heads of an instruction, as I find them set forth in an excerpt from a Latin epistle in the collection of Baron von Rosenroth.[1] The Kabbalah, in a word, is the hidden thought of Israel upon doctrines of Jewish Religion, which are in many cases Christian doctrines, and upon the proper understanding of that Written Word which is referred to a Divine Origin both in Christendom and Jewry. It is obvious therefore that in a general sense it might be expected to cast light of a certain kind upon the problems of Christian faith ; but some of its expounders have held that it does this also in a more special way ; that the New Testament and the writings of the early Fathers of the Church did not only derive from the inspired memorials of the First Covenant, but from the construction placed on those memorials by this Esoteric Tradition.[2]

It may be said at once, and possibly for the relief of some for whom this work is intended, that the question here outlined is not of my concern. There is no proposition to elucidate official Christian doctrine, whether by the help of Kabbalism or otherwise, nor to explore the Gospels and early Patristic literature in the hope of discovering alleged vestiges of Secret Jewish Theosophy. It has been suggested also that Christ Himself testified to the existence of a Tradition [3] in Israel and gave His judgment on its value ; but if so—and

---

[1] KABBALA DENUDATA, *seu Doctrina Hebræorum Transcendentalis et Metaphysica*, vol. i. *Apparatus in Librum Sohar, pars secunda*, pp. 3-5. It should be said that the last clause has been added by myself.

[2] " It is apparent from the many similarities in this Kabbalistic philosophy to the doctrines in the New Testament and early Patristic literature that both of the latter most probably have had a common germ and origin in the esoteric teachings of the Israelites, as well as in the more open and exoteric teachings of the Hebrew Holy Writings." Isaac Myer : THE PHILOSOPHICAL WRITINGS OF SOLOMON BEN YEHUDAH IBN GEBIROL, Philadelphia, 1888, 8vo, p. 7. This is cited as a point of view at its value, for which no brief is held. The letter of St. Jerome to Marcella, which dwells consecutively upon mysteries contained in the books of the Old and New Testaments, has been regarded sometimes as a case in point. All that can be said, however, is that it enumerates " ten Names by which God is known among the Hebrews," and the sole Kabbalistic connection resides in the fact that ten Divine Names—not identical throughout with those cited by St. Jerome—are allocated to the ten SEPHIROTH which constitute the Tree of Life in Kabbalism.

[3] " Thus have ye made the commandment of God of none effect by your tradition."— S. Matt., xv. 6.

for me it is more than doubtful—the purpose of the research to come is by no means to determine whether the later literature of Reception is to be included in the condemnation of the Divine Rabbi. But these assurances lead up to the point in view, and it is by this also that they are justified. A study of the Secret Doctrine or of Theosophy in Israel, as it is embodied in the Great Book of the ZOHAR and in other texts of Kabbalism, might be made assuredly on one or other of several plans; but as there can be no object in particularising further those which it is not intended to adopt, it shall be explained only that I have approached the subject from that point of view which is important to my own mind and in the one way that is possible, having regard to the nature of the work proposed. I have taken it as it is essentially, namely, a store-house of affirmed Secret Doctrine, and for the use of students of Secret Doctrine I design to present it, so to speak, at first hand—in all its important aspects—for the purpose of ascertaining—as already mentioned—whether it must remain with us merely as an historical landmark, or whether it conveys an understanding of things which, when considered in their true light, is of moment to us as mystics here and now. To complete the circle of these preliminary remarks, I will add that the plan thus outlined will be found in the outcome to include all that is of importance in any alternative scheme, for by the nature of the case there is no paramount doctrine under the ægis of the Old Covenant, no vital phase of Scriptural Tradition and no large event in the history of Israel about which we shall not learn in due course, and fully, the mind of Kabbalistic Theosophy.

There is one thing more which it may seem well to make clear as a point of fact: it is not of my design to produce a kind of *prolegomenon* which is intended to facilitate research when readers have recourse to the texts themselves and their developments. After due allowance has been made for the predilection and enthusiasms of a mystic who has taken the business of the Secret Tradition into his heart of hearts, I shall be glad if those whom I address will be content to believe on my testimony that the ZOHAR—being the text in chief—is one of the great books of the world, one also which stands alone and is comparable to nothing save itself; but I have no intention of recommending it to their particular and earnest consideration at full length. In the French translation—

whatever the value thereof [1]—it contains, roughly speaking, about 1,250,000 words, distributed throughout six very large volumes, and in the absence of a special dedication it will prove frankly unreadable. I am embodying an account of its essence on the great subjects of its concern—things which a careful collation has lifted out of the mass of material. Beyond these there is all the drift and scattermeal of rabbinical speculations, like a vast waste beyond the garden of the wise, arid as a field of quest, arbitrary beyond words as exegesis, out of all reason as thesis and ridiculous at every turn and corner of the streets of thought. I am confusing images or mixing metaphors rather of set purpose, to produce the kind of effect which is fitting to the kind of subject. If the ZOHAR may be likened otherwise to a temple of learning, then for ordinary critical minds the words inscribed on its porch are : " Abandon hope, all ye who enter here."

In attempting to educe from the body-general of the records that root-matter of Secret Doctrine which they claim to embody, we are brought quickly to a pause by the fact not merely of many inconsistencies characteristic of the text-major at large in a variety of lesser respects, but of the obvious manner in which the great ingarnering seems continually at issue with itself over matters of prime importance. It is easy to allow for those cases—and they are comparatively few—in which the doctors correct one another, whether or not they reach an agreement subsequently in the course of their long debates ; but we are confronted with irremediable variation over clear issues in the fontal source itself, while to establish those which distinguish this source from its subsequent

---

[1] It should be said that the value has been challenged and the translator himself placed in a lurid light, from the standpoint of Israel, by certain Jewish critics. It will be sufficient for most of my readers to consult the strictures and references of Dr. Robert Eisler in THE QUEST quarterly review, vol. xxiv. ; but there may be mentioned also the hostile judgment of Dr. Gerhard Scholem, who is reader in Talmudic and Kabbalah at the Jewish University in Jerusalem. The translator of the ZOHAR was a Jew who turned Christian and the consequent bias may have coloured the rendering of certain passages and exaggerated their Christian aspects ; but the question is whether the version at large—all faults, wilful and otherwise, notwithstanding—is or is not sufficiently representative of its original—if even by way of paraphrase—and that it is, or appears to be, seems indicated by the fact that it is quoted at need even by those whose voice has been raised against it, e.g., by Paul Vulliaud, LA KABBALE JUIVE, 2 vols., 1923. Like these, " we must even be content with what we have," until a better is offered. The ZOHAR is a most obscure text, and no translation is likely to escape criticism. For an historical example we may remember the animadversions of German scholarship on Adolphe Franck's rendering of certain Zoharic excerpts. In 1913 Dr. Abelson said that De Pauly's translation was indispensable, as the only complete one yet attempted : JEWISH MYSTICISM, p. 179. That is the exact position.

developments in the mind of later Kabbalism would demand the research of years. I mention these points only to indicate my intention to find—as we move forward—a middle way, wherever possible, between statements that exclude one another, even if in the last resource we must recognise that the Secret Doctrine issues in a mystery in all directions because there is no place at which it enters into expression fully, so that the adequate materials are never in our hands. When things appear mutually or commonly exclusive, it will be little to our purpose if we decide that one of them seems to have a preferential claim ; but we may get to our term if we can find a point of coincidence between the things which they tend to intimate, though they are scarcely expressed by any.[1]

According to the form of another school of symbolism, I will proceed now to open the Lodge of Research by affirming that I am approaching the Holy Kabbalah from a standpoint heretofore unattempted in the history of all its criticism, so that I am as usual without precedents, while I am also without any specific intention of creating them.[2] The remark is in a sense helpful, because those who are in favour of established ways and notions can take their proper warning before they go further. And again, in so far as it is possible, I should wish to exclude from the auditorium those who understand *Scientia Kabbalistica* as an art of making, consecrating and using talismans and amulets, as a magical mystery concerning the power of Divine Names, or as source and authentication of Grimoires and Ceremonial Rituals of Evocation. I can tell them at least that they will be saved from disappointment if they go elsewhere for enlightenment : here is no guide to the perplexed in the paths of occult arts. I mention this matter because there is a debased Kabbalism, improperly so called, which deals in these putative mysteries and claims some roots in the past, as if it belonged to the authentic Tradition of

---

[1] To give almost a frivolous example of disparities which arise in this way, the ZOHAR proper everywhere condemns Astrology, but the FAITHFUL SHEPHERD, a tract inserted at different points of the text, acknowledges one of its root principles.—Z., Pt. II, fol. 42a ; III, 191. It should be observed that throughout these notes the reference which follows immediately on the Part and Folio of the ZOHAR is always and only to the French translation, its particular volume and page. The ZOHAR reference is also to the codex used by the translator, De Pauly, unless stated otherwise.

[2] I do not refer here to what is sometimes called the Practical Kabbalah, in which are included the artificial methods of GEMATRIA, NOTARIKON and TEMURA, which are principles of exegetical interpretation. The reader may consult W. Wynn Westcott : AN INTRODUCTION TO THE KABBALAH, 1910. These methods are old : about the Magical Kabbalah, the antiquity must be left unsettled ; regarding its folly and iniquity there is no question.

Israel when it is not even a reflection. The mind of the
ZOHAR on the subject of pretended occult sciences will be
shewn towards the end of this study, so that there may be no
mistake hereon at the term of quest. I mention it at this
initial stage, so that there may be no mistake now.

I have termed the present chapter THE HIDDEN CHURCH OF
ISRAEL, but it is not in the sense of suggesting that there was
any formal incorporation,[1] much less that there were Secret
Religious Rites and Ceremonies in use among a company of
adepts; it was an entirely inward, spiritual and mystic
Church, for all purposes of which the official forms of the
external Holy Assembly would have been held to be of
sufficient efficacy, had the Temple, during the period when
the records came into existence, stood at Jerusalem, as it did
in the days of old.   One reason is [2] that the Secret Doctrine
was judged to be inseparable from the literal or written word;
it was developed to deepen its meaning and extend its office,
but never to make it void within its own measures or in the
place to which it belonged.[3]   Our first task is therefore to
ascertain what is established in the great texts concerning the
fact of Secret Doctrine; and at some later stage subsequently
we must take in succession the chief points of intimation on
doctrine and religion in Jewry, so as to elicit the sense of that
Tradition respecting each and all.   Lastly, we must find—if
this indeed be possible [4]—whether the Tradition has a central
root from which the great tree of the concealed knowledge
has grown up; whether also—as I have said—and how far
we are concerned or perhaps even are integrated therein as

---

[1] At the same time we do meet with a number of occasional instances, the suggestion
of which is almost as if the colleagues formed a College of Initiates.   Sometimes it
even looks as if there were almost a ceremonial manner of imparting Mysteries.   See,
for example, Z., Pt. I, fol. 133a; II, 124.   Again, it is said that the Mysteries are
guarded secretly in the hearts of those who possess them and communicated secretly
to each other.   *Ib.*, fol. 96b; I, 55c.   For further allusions, see *ib.*, fol. 133a; II, 124;
ib., fol. 155b; II, 212, shewing that what was known by one of the adepts was not
always familiar to another; *ib.*, Pt. II, fol. 8b; III, 6b; *ib.*, 14a; III, 61; *ib.*, fol. 168a;
IV, 116; *ib.*, Pt. III, fol. 187a; V, 489.

[2] In illustration of this, there is one similitude which says that the Written Doctrine
is the candle or lamp, while the flame is the Oral Law.—Z., Pt. II, fol. 166a; IV, 112.

[3] The thesis was that the written word of Scripture, in every passage and syllable,
was the word of the Living God.   The meanings, however, were many, but they are
usually reduced to three: (1) the historical sense, which corresponds to the Court of
the Temple; (2) the moral sense, which answers to the Holy Place; and (3) the
mystical sense, which is in analogy with the Holy of Holies.

[4] It is perhaps just to myself if I add in this place that, since I am not concerned with
compilations as such, there would have been no excuse for the present work if I had
not satisfied myself: (1) that such a root exists, and (2) that its nature can be set forth
clearly.   This has been implied already in several places.

mystics at this day. I should add that while the last point is obviously the most important and vital, it can be reached only by the mediation of the two others.

The question is therefore as to the fact of the Secret Doctrine and under what terms it is mentioned in the records. It is of course, broadly and generally, a method of interpreting Scripture,[1] but so far as this expression is to be understood in an ordinary sense—as an actual and logical construction of the letter—the interpretation, as I have indicated already, is of no value—for the most part, at least. It is to be taken or left in the sense of its own motive, which is to establish, at any and all cost, a Secret Doctrine on the foundation of the Old Testament ; and in the light of this it signified little that the Doctrine, in respect of exegesis, was arbitrary to the last degree : one would scarcely expect it to be otherwise, having regard to the Rabbinical mind. The point in chief for ourselves is that the mills of those lesser gods who are called Sons of the Doctrine produced and polished great things in their processes—pure and precious jewels of the spirit—as well as much dust and scoria from the matter which they passed through their hands. It is only as if casually that the word interpretation [2] can be held to apply in any solid sense : the Secret Doctrine is rather the sense below the sense which is found in the literal word—as if one story were written on the obverse side of the parchment and another on the reverse side. This is not an exact comparison, but it gives my meaning clearly enough for the purpose. There are hard things said from time to time about the outward sense and they must not be taken too seriously, for the letter was always precious, if only as a vesture ; but the difference between that which was

---

[1] The symbolism of the Secret Doctrine is extracted also from Scriptural words and phrases which antecedently seem far from the mark. The word "waters," as it is used sometimes in the TALMUD, is said to signify the Secret Doctrine, and when David cried : "Create in me a clean heart, O God, and renew a right spirit within me" (Ps. li, 10), he was praying for his heart to be opened by the study of Divine Mysteries. So also it is said : "Let the waters under the heaven be gathered together into one place" (Gen. i, 9). The waters refer to the Secret Doctrine, and the one place designates Israel, whose soul depends from that region to which Scripture alludes in the words : "Blessed be the glory of the Lord from His place" (Ezek. iii, 12). The "Glory of the Lord" signifies the Shekinah below and "from His place" signifies the Shekinah above. From this point of view, Shekinah is the Doctrine itself personified.

[2] The canon of interpretation is often exceedingly simple : for example, any reference to vegetation coming up out of the ground is explicable by symbolical vegetation, the one and the other being confused together, and either taken to explain the other. In Ps. lxxxv, 11, it is said that "truth shall spring out of the earth," and literal grass is held therefore to signify truth.

within and without is well illustrated [1] by a similitude which
says that those who interpret Scripture according to the
literal sense set the Sacred King and His Bride upon an ass,
while those who understand it according to the mystic sense
mount them nobly on a horse.[2] This notwithstanding, the
two belong to one another, because the Written Law is completed by that which is traditional,[3] and the latter issues from
the former as woman was brought forth from man : it can
exist only in union with the Written Law, and this it serves to
enlighten—by the hypothesis at least. We shall see at the
proper time that chief among the root-doctrines is that
Jehovah is one with Elohim in a sense which is very far from
the theological understanding of Scripture ; but it is held also
that the Written Law is the image of Jehovah, as the Oral
Law is of Elohim, meaning the Holy Shekinah, from which it
would follow that at heart they are two aspects of one and the
same Law. That which is oral is called the voice of the
turtle,[4] and it comes from the side of mercy ; it is also the
green wood, while the literal Law is the dry,[5] coming from
the side of judgment. But as a further instance of the unity
in both it is laid down that there are three things which are at
once hidden and revealed —being God, the Law and Israel
itself. The vulgar man sees only the material side, but the
initiate discerns also that which is imbedded within it. In
virtue of this bond of union, we meet with intimations occasionally in which terms are applied to the one that seem
referable rather [6] to the other. It is said, for example, that
the written Law is above and that which is oral below, as also
that the former penetrates and fructifies the latter.[7] That
which is without seems, however, to be clearly a manifestation

---

[1] The ZOHAR gives another illustration when it says that the Oral Law enlightens
the Written Law. Z., Pt. III, fol. 23a ; V, 61.
[2] Z., Pt. III, 275b ; VI, 47.
[3] The Written Law is designated in another place under the name of heaven, while
the Oral Law is called earth. On the surface this appears somewhat against the more
obvious sense and intention, but what is signified may be an obscure counterchange in
virtue of correspondences between things above and below, and this is a recurring
Zoharic doctrine.—Ib., Pt. I, fol. 247b ; II, 578.
[4] Z., Pt. III, fol. 4b ; V, 9.
[5] Ib., fol. 27b, and V, 76.
[6] According to the rabbi in Longfellow's GOLDEN LEGEND, all Bible lore is water
and MISHNA is a strong wine ; but according to the ZOHAR, it is the Written Law
which is wine ; the Oral, however, is not water but milk. I conclude that the one is
the lesser, the other is the greater salvation, according to the voice of the Doctrine.
See Z., Pt. I, fol. 240a ; II, 549.
[7] Z., Pt. II, fol. 200a ; IV, 200 ; also Z., Pt. II, fol. 206a and IV, 208.

of that which is within, though there is a sense also in which the Law was regarded as written on high ; but this I should understand to signify that the Oral Law passes into expression here and into realisation there. To conclude upon these analogies : the manifested part bears no comparison with that which is contained within ; that which is essential is called the Soul of Scripture ; the commandments are its body and the tales are the garments thereof. This is in the world below, while in that which is above the Ancient of Days is the Soul of soul in the Law ; the soul is that mystery which is called the Beauty of Israel ; the body is the Community of the Elect ; while the vesture is heaven and its region. Cursed be he, says the text,[1] who pretends that the recitals of Scripture have no other meaning than that which appears on the surface. Scripture, if this were the case, would not be the Law of Truth, the Holy Law and the Perfect Witness, more precious than gold and jewels. If it contained only simple stories and such vulgar elements—as of Esau, Hagar, Laban and Balaam's ass—it might be possible to produce something better, apart from all inspiration, after the manner of profane books ; but the truth is that every word of Scripture enshrines a Supreme Mystery, and is capable of sixty methods of interpretation.[2] This is a characteristic extravagance, but every one who has followed the quest of the mystic sense knows how manifold it is, and for this reason no doubt it has been testified that the original ZOHAR was at least a camel's load. That is like St. John saying : " I suppose that even the world itself could not contain the books that should be written," if all the acts of Jesus were reduced into a complete memorial.[3] I am very sure that the beloved disciple was guilty herein of no extravagant utterance, because Christ has been always in the world ; and I am not less certain that the extent of the ZOHAR has been understated, for the variations of inward meanings are numberless as the Sons of the Doctrine, and all may be true analogically, though some of them are brighter jewels, while the pearls of greatest price may be few enough. Whatever

---

[1] Z., Pt. III, 149b ; V, 386, 387.
[2] Ib., Pt. I, fol. 26a ; I, 161. It is said otherwise that there are sixty sections, which are the sixty queens of the SONG OF SOLOMON. The " young maids " without number are the HALAKHOTH, otherwise, things belonging to the outward, ceremonial Law, its customs and enactments—Ib., Pt. III, fol. 216a ; V, 548. Another statement concerns seventy modes of interpreting Scripture, all of which are true in their results. Ib., Pt. I, fol. 54a ; I, 310.
[3] St. John xxi, 25.

belongs to man at his highest belongs also to Christ : so too
the Divine Sayings are like the Divine Acts, and from the
first time of manifestation until that moment when God shall
be All in all, there is no end to either.

Now, it is said that the inner sense of the Law is not less
concealed than the world from which it emanates,[1] wherefore
the Mysteries known to the Sons of the Doctrine are guarded
secretly in their hearts.   Those who apply themselves to its
study receive as their inheritance the World to Come, as well
as that of Jacob, for it is the path of the Life Beyond.[2]   He
who is so dedicated and so consecrated is accounted as if he
had received its sweet and heavenly words on Mount Sinai
itself.[3]   It is the way of the Garden of the Sacred King and
the way of the King Himself.[4]   A certain price has to be paid
however, for it is said hyperbolically that the study of the Law
succeeds only in the case of him who kills himself for the Law,
meaning that it is a path of poverty and a poor man is considered as one who is dead.[5]

I have dealt so far with preliminaries, and if the next
question be how did the Secret Doctrine originate, the answer
seems that it was before the world was with God.   The sense
of this must be that it was implied in Elohim, whose image it
is, as we have seen.   Another explanation is that it is on the
side of mercy, and by mercy the world was made : it is the
beneplacitum termino carens.   We find, moreover, that God
created the world by joining thereto the Secret Doctrine.

---

[1] *Z.*, Pt. I, fol. 156b ; II, 215.

[2] *Ib.*, fol. 158a ; II, 220.   I should mention here that consecration to the study of
the Secret Doctrine brings down what is called the Supplementary Soul which Zoharic
Kabbalism attributes frequently to all pious Children of Israel who observe the Sabbath
in the plenary sense.   It remains with them during that day and returns thereafter
whence it came.   But it would seem that true Sons of the Doctrine are in permanent
enjoyment of this added part.   He who does not cultivate the mystic science is therefore in a state of deprivation.   The Soul is brought down by the voice of him who
studies the Secret Doctrine and it comes from the Land of the Living, making him
whom it overshadows equal to the angels.   When it is said in Ps. ciii, 20, " Bless the
Lord, ye His angels," the reference is to those who study the Doctrine and are called
God's angels on earth.   In the world to come they will have wings like those of the
eagle.

[3] *Ib.*, Pt. III, fol. 179b ; V, 471.

[4] *Ib.*, I, 224b ; II, 485.

[5] *Ib.*, Pt. II, fol. 158b ; IV, 95.   But against this, he who is dedicated to the study
of the Law opens the 50 gates of BINAH, corresponding to the letter YOD multiplied
by the letter HE.—*Ib.*, III, fol. 216a ; V, 548.   Now, YOD is the Sign of the Covenant
and therefore of the male principle, while HE—the letter of Shekinah—is that of the
female principle, which produces fruit to the male through intercourse ; and the
multiplication here in question alludes to the generations of mind as the fruit of study—
that is to say, of Divine Research.   The Study of the Doctrine is not a barren study,
but brings forth " the eternal brood of glory excellent."

The world was founded thereon, and it is added that so long
as Israel is consecrated to its research, so long will the world
be stable. When the lovers of truth [1] rise for its study at
midnight [2] the Holy One and all the just who are with Him
in the Garden of Eden listen to their voices.[3] The versicle
appertaining hereto is : "Thou that dwellest in the gardens,
the companions hearken to thy voice : come out to hear it." [4]
We may understand by this that those who work below are
really listening to the Voice which is above and that when
they hear it, it is the Mystery of Doctrine which they hear.
There is no need to add that the Voice is speaking in the
heart. The word BERESHITH, with which Genesis opens and
which has been rendered sometimes "in wisdom," not "in
the beginning," is said to signify the Secret Doctrine and its
part in the work of creation. The Scriptural allusion is :
"The Lord possessed me in the beginning of His way, before
His works of old. I was set up from everlasting, from the
beginning, or ever the earth was." [5] It will be observed that
this is personified Wisdom testifying on her own part, and
the application of the text by the ZOHAR in connection with
the beginning of things is, under the circumstances, rather
subtle. It goes on to affirm that this was the kind of beginning in which God created the heaven and earth, the basis of
which is His Covenant. Hence it is said also : "If the
Covenant which I have made existed not, there would be
neither day nor night, neither heaven nor earth." [6] All
accepted renderings of this passage from the Vulgate downward are quite different ; but the point to be remembered is
the allusion made to the Covenant in the particular connection, for we shall find at a much later stage that it is the

---

[1] Z., Pt. I, fol. 77b ; I, 455.

[2] I may mention at its value that the annotator of the French version—M. Lafuma-
Giraud— distinguishes between that which the ZOHAR designates Mysteries of Doctrine
and that which it calls Mysteries of Tradition. The first is the spiritual sense of Scripture and the second that of Tradition.

[3] The study of the Doctrine is held to call for adornment of body as well as attention
of mind. It was needful for the doctors who rose at midnight to clothe themselves
for the purpose of study, out of respect to Shekinah, who accompanies Students of
the Doctrine. Moreover, the study calls for serenity of mind, and it was held difficult
to ensure this in a reclining posture.—Z., Pt. I, fol. 72a ; I, 426.

[4] SONG OF SOLOMON, viii, 13. Z., Pt. I, fol. 77b ; I, 455.

[5] Prov. viii, 22, 23. Z., Pt. I, fol. 24b ; I, 153.

[6] This is Pauly's rendering of the ZOHAR, but the Authorised Version reads : "If
my covenant be not with day and night, and if I have not appointed the ordinances of
heaven and earth ; then I will cast away the seed of Jacob, and David my servant," &c.
Jer. xxxiii, 25, 26. Compare the Vulgate : *Si pactum meum inter diem et noctem, et leges
cæli et terræ non posui, equidem et semen Jacob et David, servi mei, projiciam*, &c.

sign manual or visible of one of the Divine Hypostases and it is also one of the keys to the whole Mystery of the ZOHAR. We are not, however, dealing with the question of creation at this point of our debate, and it has been mentioned only to indicate the seemingly eternal pre-existence of the Secret Doctrine.[1]   After what manner was it brought down to earth, so that it came to the knowledge of the elect? The thesis of possession and successive custody depends from a legend of Paradise, and this in its turn arises from the Scriptural reference to a BOOK OF THE GENERATIONS OF ADAM.[2] It is supposed by the ZOHAR to signify that there was a Secret and Supreme Book, the source of all, including the Hebrew letters[3]—presumably in that form under which they are manifested below. It expounded the Holy Mystery of Wisdom and the efficiency resident in the Divine Name of seventy-two letters.[4]   It was sent down from heaven by the hands of the angel Raziel[5] and Adam was entrusted therewith. Raziel is said to be the angel of the secret regions and chief of Supreme Mysteries.   The gift placed Adam in a superior position to that of any celestial being—possibly with the exception of the messenger, though indeed he may have carried that which he was not permitted to understand. Adam was made acquainted in this manner with Supernal Wisdom,[6] and the Celestial Choirs came down to be present when he read the book. He was cautioned, however, to conceal it, and he seems therefore to have studied it in silence, with recollection of the heart.   The book proved later on to

---

[1] See Book V, § 5, *passim.*

[2] Gen. v, 1.

[3] Z., Pt. I, fol. 37a *et seq.* ; I, 231—233.

[4] The Mysteries of this Name and the mode of its formation will be considered in their proper place.   There are said to be three books which are opened in heaven on the first day of the year.   The first is that which was transmitted to Adam, and this is the book of the just who are perfect.   The second has a part in heaven and a part on earth, but it is not otherwise described.   The third is the Written Law, which was designed for the first man and was presumably known of the heart, for it is not said that it was manifested at that time on earth.—*Ib.*

[5] Z., Pt. I, fol. 55b; I, 319, 320.   There is a legend of an old MIDRASH called the BOOK OF RAZIEL : it is said to have been developed by Eleazar of Worms and to have been reproduced in various debased forms by late Kabbalism.   There is also an imposture of Ceremonial Magic which passes under the name.   Compare E. V. Kenealy's notice of a Book of the Wisdom of Adam, received in an ecstasy and " full of mysteries and signs expressive of profound knowledge."   See THE BOOK OF GOD, pp. 243 and also *ibid.*, pp. 273 *et seq.*, for a rabbinical account of a staff given to Adam and supposed to signify the support of Secret Knowledge.

[6] The Sacred Name of 72 letters was explained in the GENESIS OF MAN by means of the 670 mysteries which it contains.   The Mystery of CHOKMAH discovered the 1500 keys which are not entrusted to any celestial being.

be like the LIBER GRADALIS or fundamental record concerning the Holy Graal, for it took unto itself wings at need, when Adam—his advantages notwithstanding—fell ultimately into sin. It was clasped in his hands when he was driven out of the Garden of Eden, but thereafter it vanished, and for long and long he lamented the loss of his treasure. Ultimately it was given back to him in answer to his tears and prayers,[1] by the angel Raphael : he returned to its study and bequeathed it to his son Seth, who entrusted it to later messengers, so that the Secret Doctrine might be spread through the world.[2] It became known as the BOOK OF ENOCH after passing through the hands of that patriarch,[3] and it is said that Abraham penetrated the glory of his Master by means of its mysteries. Moses, however, was the first man who attained perfection in its fullness,[4] and perhaps on this account it is not suggested that he derived his knowledge from a book, so that after Abraham we hear nothing of the secret text : it was a treasure of the patriarchal age. The External Law and the Secret Doctrine were both revealed on Mount Sinai, and as Moses transmitted the one to his nation at large so he communicated the other to certain elders, by whom it was handed on. But there are two remarkable passages designed to shew that the whole secret knowledge came down to the Zoharic period under the darkening of successive clouds. It is said that at the death of Moses the sun was eclipsed and that the Written Law lost its splendour. At the hour of King David's death

---

[1] The variant account in fol. 55b says that he smote his forehead when the work vanished and plunged up to his neck in the river GIHON, being the second river which flowed out from the " garden eastward in Eden." Gen. ii, 13. The result was that all his body was covered with wrinkles, so that he was no longer recognisable.

[2] A genealogy of this kind will recall the fabulous origins once ascribed to institutions like Freemasonry, the appeal made by alchemists to sages of antiquity and other fictions which deserve to be classed as monstrous. We must beware, however, of fixing wilful imposture on an archaic literature because its attribution is mythical : it should be remembered that we are dealing by the hypothesis with a body of Secret Doctrine, and an Oral Tradition is liable to the exaggeration of its antiquity : we must distinguish therefore between the possible fact of its existence at a more or less distant period and the growth of legend about it.

[3] There are several Enochian legends which offer curious points in themselves, but seldom connect with our subject. According to one account, Enoch became the great archangel Metatron ; according to another, he was exalted to the high heavens and made guardian of their treasures, including the 45 keys to the combinations of graven letters.—Z., Pt. I, fol. 56b ; I, 326. An apocalyptic BOOK OF ENOCH, believed to be a Hebrew text in its original state and belonging as such to the beginning of the Christian era, has been known in an Ethiopic translation since the year 1778, when a manuscript copy was brought from Abyssinia by J. Bruce.

[4] This is one of the theses, but we shall see that there was a certain Gate of Understanding which he failed to open.

the light of the moon diminished and the radiance of the Oral Law was tarnished. The consequence was that discussions and controversies began among the sages of the MISHNA, so that joy in the study of the Law has ceased for all future generations.[1] It was pursued previously in clear and full light, and there was that unanimity which comes from certitude among the Sons of the Doctrine ; but afterwards it was followed from afar in a state of doubt and separation, amidst wrangling of the schools, who saw only as in a glass and darkly. This state of things is sometimes symbolised by a division in the Divine Name, by the loss of the true method of pronouncing the Tetragram in conformity with its proper vowels, and so forth. Occasionally there are intimations of a new breaking of light, as when it is said that Ezekiel was less faithful than Moses, for he divulged all the measures of the king [2] ; but apparently those measures were not displayed before doctors who—whatever their zeal and sincerity—were unable to value them in understanding at their proper worth. It was otherwise in the days of Rabbi Simeon, for the glory of the mystic light was at its zenith in him, according to the ZOHAR, which, considering that he was the revealer in chief of its doctrines, exalts that master of wisdom above all the stars of heaven. It is added that from the day when Rabbi Simeon came out of his cavern [3] the Mysteries were secrets no longer for the colleagues, because the Hidden Doctrine had become no less familiar to them than it was to their precursors when it was revealed on Mount Sinai. But the time came for this great sun to set in the hour of the master's death ; and when afterwards his disciples and successors sought to reproduce the words which they heard from his lips, the attempt proved a failure.[4] The withdrawal of the Secret Doctrine is mentioned also, but with a suggestion of vestiges remaining over : these are to be consulted, notwithstanding

---

[1] Z., Pt. II, fol. 156a, b ; IV, 88.

[2] Ib., Pt. II, fol. 5a ; III, 19.

[3] The reference is to the TRACT. SABBATH, which contains the history of Rabbi Simeon, the reasons which led him to find refuge in a cave for twelve years and the circumstances under which he came out. See Michael Rodkinson : BABYLONIAN TALMUD, vol. i, c. 2. I cite this translation, which was done in America, because it is available to the English reader ; but its method of condensation has been a subject of hostile criticism, and the unexcised German rendering of L. Goldschmidt, begun in 1898, is preferred reasonably by scholars.

[4] This disposes of the ridiculous tradition that R. Simeon wrote anything in the cavern where he found a refuge from Roman imperial persecution.

their incompleteness, because the Doctrine is incorruptible gold, and even its shards are priceless.[1]

The next point which calls for our consideration here is whether the general references to the Secret Doctrine as a whole, apart from its various branches, offer any ground of presumption concerning its radical nature. Now, it is said that the Supreme Mystery is concealed in the Law,[2] that it is the Secret of the Law, meaning the Secret of the King—*Sacramentum Regis quod abscondere bonum est*—revealed only to those who fear sin, and that as to its nature, this is bodied forth by the Sacred Covenant concerning circumcision.[3] In other words, it is a Mystery of Sex. It was on account of this that Rabbi Simeon consecrated to the study of the Secret Doctrine the entire night in which the Heavenly Bride is united to her Heavenly Spouse, being the night of that day when the Law was revealed to the Israelites and the Covenant contracted between God and His people. The reason was that the Mystic Knowledge constitutes the jewels of the Heavenly Bride. We can understand this only on the hypothesis that the science in question is concerned at some stage or under some aspect with a most holy Mystery of Sex, as if some unknown path of splendour and path to the height can and may open therefrom. It is said that " the King's Daughter is all glorious within," and the ZOHAR explains that there is glory and glory, a glory of the male and a glory of the female principle.[4] It is said also, as if in connection with the pursuit of this path, that whosoever follows in the train of the Heavenly Bride on the night of union [5] shall be preserved from all evil for ever, in heaven and on earth—as if death and the second death had no power. He will enjoy celestial peace to the end of time. The counsel in this respect is : " Taste and see that the Lord is good." [6]

If the study of the doctrine adorns the Bride of Heaven with

---

[1] Z., Pt. I, fol. 216b, 217a ; II, 453–455. See also *Ib.*, fol. 9a ; I, 50, from which it follows that the Secret Doctrine is the explanation and unfoldment of all. This is founded on Ps. xix, 6 : " There is nothing hid from the heat thereof." But this was the Doctrine in its fullness.

[2] *Ib.*, fol. 236b ; II, 533.

[3] Z., Pt. I, fol. 237 ; II, 535. Cf. *ante* concerning a " Sign manual," p. 16.

[4] This is based on Ps. xlv. 13 : " The King's daughter is all glorious within," which the Zohar renders : " All the glory of the daughter of the King is within " ; and the Vulgate : *Omnis gloria ejus filiæ regis ab intus.* The words are held to designate the Community of Israel.

[5] Z., I, 9a ; I, 51.

[6] Ps. xxxiv, 8.

jewels, as we have just seen, it seems that it adorns also the souls of its students with all manner of graces and sanctities. When the ZOHAR affirms that their desert is far above anything which follows on mere works, there is no doubt that it gives expression to a great truth, though it may be one that is reserved only for the understanding of the elect. But in the ordinary sense the explanation is that it enables good works to be fulfilled with knowledge, under the operation of Divine Will. Those who study the Doctrine are set free from fear, whether of things in heaven or things on earth, whether of evils which may overwhelm mankind, because such students are grafted on the Tree of Life and are taught daily thereby. As regards things in heaven, the meaning is that the fear of God, which is the beginning of wisdom, has been absorbed by the love of God, which is wisdom in realisation, and the Divine Doctrine cannot be studied without imparting love for the Divine. To walk in the path of the Doctrine is therefore to follow the path of love : it is said otherwise to lead into the way of truth, so that we learn how the soul may return to its Master. It is not the work of a certain day or of a certain hour, but one of the day and the night. We come to understand in this manner that the study is a question of life, of living with the face towards Jerusalem, having the awareness of God in the heart, and herein is the *moyen de parvenir*, the counsel of real being. We shall understand also why it is added that he who neglects or forsakes the study of the Doctrine is not less guilty than if he separated himself from the Tree of Life, for he is leading the life of separation.[1]

The last considerations follow, as it seems to me, the ordinary course of thought in the direction to which they belong ; but the extracts out of which they arise are a counsel to those who would study the Secret Doctrine that there is needed a conscious union by intention, contemplation and the art of finding in the heart, so that the heart and mind of the student may concur in an ineffable union which is said to be consummated above. As to its nature we know enough to be certain that the night thereof is not of a festival below but of the eternal oneness in that Divine Darkness which is called otherwise in the records AIN-SOPH AOUR, the limitless and undifferentiated light. The festival of the Paschal Lamb

---

[1] Z., Pt. I, fol. 11a ; I, 62.

in the Calendar of Jewry is only a specific memorial on earth, so that what it is held to signify may be kept in the soul of Israel ; and this is not really an act of unreason : on the contrary, the intention is so to proceed here as if that which is remembered below is in particular remembrance above ; yet the union there is in the still rest and the changeless simplicity, being infinite and eternal therein. Lastly, the extracts out of which these things arise would be worse than idle words if the quest concerning their meaning could be carried no further.

It will be seen as we move forward on the strange path of our research that the Sons of the Doctrine were only from time to time, and as if by accident, concerned with reserving any common, or indeed any merely remote and arbitrary understanding of the Written Word in Israel ; that in short there was something, on the contrary, which—at least from their point of view—imposed a reasonable and even a zealous reserve, because it was pre-eminently one of those matters which the unprepared and sensual mind would wrest to its own destruction.

It has been necessary at this initial stage to establish the root fact of an alleged Secret Doctrine, in order to justify the long research which follows. An examination of the Doctrine itself and of its message to us, if any, belongs to a much later stage. Between these vital matters and the simple point of fact there intervenes all that belongs to the apparatus of the texts, including their external and critical history.

II.—FOLLIES OF OCCULT EXEGESIS [1]

As the Kabbalah claims to be a Tradition long received in secret by one generation from another and reduced at length into writing, so one of its legends informs us,[2] because of the bad state of the affairs of Israel—that is to say, after the destruction of Jerusalem—it is to be expected that its literary

---

[1] When it was found by experience that the Kabbalah had no office for the propagation of the Christian Gospel in Jewry, the subject at large fell almost unconditionally into the hands of occult students and schools. It comes about in this manner that, much against my own will, their views and pretensions will obtrude for consideration in brief at different stages of my research, so that they can be reduced to their proper value.

[2] It is an explanation offered by a commentator on the SEPHER YETZIRAH or BOOK OF FORMATION.

methods will offer difficulties to the ordinary student.[1] It has, indeed, proved so unintelligible upon the surface in some of its developments that, on the one hand, it has been considered merely meaningless jargon, while a few—like the late Macgregor Mathers—who claim that they have penetrated to its real sense have, on the other, found pleasure in believing that it is sealed to uninitiated persons, for whom it must ever remain a matter of curious and unrewarded research, though not perhaps wanting some gleams of unexpected suggestion. The first view suggests that more patience and greater pains were needed; the second, that the faculty for painstaking is a kind of peculiar election which is possible only to the few, and this appears unwarranted. As a fact, it is a pretence brought forward by expositors of Kabbalism belonging to occult schools of the last century, and it carries no other warrant than is characteristic of those schools.

Specialists in cryptography assure us, and we have even higher warrant in the testimony of reason itself, that no cipher writing devised by human ingenuity is incapable of solution, also by human ingenuity; but the assumption, of course, supposes good faith in the cipher: it must follow a certain method and conceal a definite sense. There is further no system of symbolism and no form of philosophical speculation, however complex, which will not surrender its secrets to the searchlight of analysis, provided always that the symbolism is systematic and that the speculation is methodised, however curious in its involutions. There are cryptic philosophies and concealed metaphysics, even as there is cryptic writing; but if they possess a meaning, it cannot escape ultimately the penetration of competent criticism, subject, however, to the distinction which must subsist of necessity between the sense of a cipher—which is unmistakable from the moment that it is disengaged—and the construction of a debate in jargon which in its minor issues may be open always to debate.[2]

There are, however, two considerations which arrest

---

[1] Obscurities, complexities and confusions do not point, however, to the existence of a double sense.

[2] The best example of a really cryptic literature is that concerned with Alchemy, and yet it is not cryptic in the sense of cipher-writing. It has a perfectly simple surface meaning; the concealment is the significance of certain conventional words and recipes. This also is its great difficulty. While cryptography must disclose its secret to skill and patience, it is nearly imposible to say what the word Vitriol, for example, may represent to any writer, if it be not the ordinary substance passing under that name.

attention on the surface of this debate. The first is whether cryptic philosophies are not inherently unmeaning, and unable therefore to disclose what, in fact, they do not possess ; or alternately, in the case that they are methodised after some manner, whether the mystery which they cover is not out of all proportion to the intellectual cost of unravelling it. Of these two points one at least must be determined according to individual predilection. For my own part, after spending many years among strange pathways of human ingenuity, I know certainly that Kabbalistic Theosophy does constitute a methodised system which is curiously inwrought, at least in its later development, and since *la science est une noblesse qui oblige*, I must bear testimony to this fact, which leaves the question of values over, even though an imaginative reader may transfigure the statement and interpret too liberally the narrow concession which I have made here to sincerity. About the second point it is extremely difficult to indicate even a personal opinion on esoteric philosophies at large. So far as knowledge is its own reward, I suppose that it may be worth the cost ; but if any department of research should be ruled out of the sphere of operation possessed by this truism, it is that of so-called occult science and philosophy. The labour involved by their study can repay those who undertake it only in a few cases. In the pursuit of its hidden " know-ledge " Campaspe is never finished. But it is precisely for this reason that an inquiry like the present may be held to deserve a welcome, because it offers all those who may be disposed to concern themselves with one important depart-ment of esoteric philosophy an intelligible statement of the issues and their central point of value which will save such persons the need of first-hand research. It is to be observed further and finally as a clearance of all the issues that in so far as the Secret Tradition of Israel, and in so far as the cryptic metaphysics and Theosophies of other schools and nations, offer grave difficulties, they are not those of a sense within the sense, but of the one and only meaning which should and can be attached to the *chaos embrouillée* of what I have termed their jargon language.

The importance of the Written Tradition of Kabbalism can be regarded only from two standpoints. There is that which it may possess for the Sacred Scriptures of the Jewish and Christian Religions and for the exoteric doctrines which more or less derive from these.[1] Under this first head may be included its significance, if any, for the science of Comparative Theology and for the history of human thought.[2] Besides such obvious and unquestioned grounds upon which it is entitled to consideration, there is another warrant in the interest which it possesses for a sincere and informed seeker after the authentic vestiges—if any—of hidden knowledge in the past. And here it is necessary to determine what is meant and involved by such knowledge, whether real or alleged. The study of the large literature which incorporates the secret pseudo-sciences and the occult philosophies is pursued by many persons from many motives, but few of these can, in the proper sense of the term, be regarded as esoteric and much less as mystical students. Nor, indeed, does the attempted practice of one or other of the " secret sciences " in any sense constitute a claim to that title. In a very large number of cases such occupations suggest titular distinctions which are not of a flattering kind. As I understand him, the true student of THEOSOPHIA in its widest meaning is seeking evidence for the existence of a knowledge—which in effect is hidden science—handed down from remote ages,[3] which knowledge

---

[1] From the conventional occult standpoint this is of more consequence than from that of ordinary exegesis. Adolphe Bertet, in his APOCALYPSE DU BIENHEUREUX JEAN . . . DEVOILÉE (Paris, 1861, p. 51), gives the position very clearly in respect of its arbitrary assumptions. " We find on every page of the five books of Moses Kabbalistic expressions which proclaim that everything must be taken in a figurative sense, yet in none of these books do we possess a complete treatise of initiation, whence it follows that prior to Moses oral tradition was alone charged with transmitting the secret of initiation." Bertet owed his inspiration and frequently his language to Éliphas Lévi. His dogmatic assertions are, moreover, of like value as those of his master. The Kabbalistic sense of the Pentateuch had to be invented before it could be found, and it happens that the " oral tradition " transmitted its " secrets " long ages after the books supposed to contain it had been reduced to writing.

[2] It is to be understood that this aspect of the Secret Tradition in Israel is beyond the field covered by my present undertaking, which is concerned with an examination of the literature to ascertain its mystical value.

[3] The chief aspects of this belief are, as might be expected, quite modern ; it cannot be shewn to have existed prior to the end of the eighteenth century, and even then it had taken no definite shape. One of its presentations was attempted by M. de Brière, who in his ESSAI SUR LE SYMBOLISME ANTIQUE DE L'ORIENT, *principalement sur le symbolisme Égyptien* (Paris, 1847), maintained : (*a*) A common origin for all religions ; (*b*) The existence of sacerdotal sciences as an exclusive patrimony of the priesthood ; (*c*) The existence among all eastern priests of a common idiom of high antiquity, which passed as a theurgic, magical and efficacious language ; (*d*) The reproduction of this language by hieroglyphics, which were also theurgic and magical ; (*e*) A dual sacerdotal method of expressing the principles of priestly sciences, and chiefly of Theology : (1) Imitation of words = hieroglyphs of the texts ; (2) Imitation of thoughts = images, idols, emblematic figures of gods ; (*f*) The existence of the sacred language and hieroglyphic writing among all peoples possessing sacerdotal sciences, the Phœnicians and Chaldeans for example. This speculation may be called suggestive ; but it has come to pass that after all the phantoms and all the oracles of dream we have heard the voice of Egyptology.

concerns, in Saint-Martin's language, an exposition of the relations between God, man and the universe, or the way of union between man and God. It has, according to its legend, assumed, for various reasons, the disguise of many veils ; it is not confined to one country or people, nor is it the interior sense of any single religion or of any single cycle in literature to the exclusion of all others. There are alleged traces of its existence in far-off times, among many nations, through all the chief religions : [1] it has been held even to lie behind the conventional occultism of Magic and the transcendental physics of Alchemy ; among Secret Traditions, Kabbalistic literature has been regarded sometimes as one of its most important vehicles.

From this standpoint the true message of the Kabbalah is not exegetical or historical ; it is not of systems, schools, or interpretations ; it is of a living and spiritual kind. Here is, indeed, the only vital point of view from which the subject can be regarded, and it redeems the whole circle of my present inquiry from the charge of vanity. It explains also why the research has been undertaken and why its results are offered at full length to those whom they concern.

Given this standpoint, Kabbalistic literature is indescribably momentous ; but so far, unfortunately, it has been maintained and unfolded, either on the warrant of alleged knowledge which cannot be made public,[2] and is therefore idle to proclaim, or on that of evidence which is without much title —if any—to consideration. If we take, for example, the expository literature of Kabbalism which has been written from the occult standpoint in any modern language, there is not a single work which does not break down at once in the hands of the most temperate criticism. Mathers, in England, translated many years since a small portion of the ZOHAR from a printed Latin version, and prefixed an introduction which takes the whole claim for granted, while he leaves on the mind of his readers an indistinct impression that Dr. Ginsburg, who errs on the side of hostility, is not only one of its supporters, but gives credit to the most fabulous side of Kab-

---

[1] As regards the Christian religion, see Eckartshausen concerning " a more advanced school," or " invisible celestial Church," to which the " deposition of all science has been confided." THE CLOUD UPON THE SANCTUARY, Letter I. Translated by Isabel de Steiger and introduced by myself. 3rd edition, 1919.

[2] I refer to the pretensions of certain societies which worked under pledges of secrecy, here and in Paris, towards the close of the nineteenth century.

balistic Legend.[1]   In America, Isaac Myer, whose learning—
undigested as it is—entitles him to respect, is forced on crucial
points to assume many things that are required for his hypothesis.[2]   In France the real questions at issue are scarcely
skirted in the tabulation attempted by Papus.[3]   In Germany,
which exhausts everything, I do not know that in any true
sense of the term the position has found a single defender.
I propose on my own part to determine, by the testimony of
its texts themselves, whether there is ground for believing
that the Kabbalah has been a channel of old Tradition, and if
this view must be abandoned, to place those who are willing
to follow me in possession of a method of regarding it which
will make its existence at least intelligible without taking anything for granted and without appealing to any source of
knowledge which is not fully in evidence—the latter for the
best of reasons, namely, that there is no such source.

III.—THE KABBALAH AND THE TALMUD

The post-Christian literature which is of authority in Israel
must be distinguished, of course, from the multifarious productions of its scholars and *literati* which it was the object of
rabbinical bibliographies, like those of Bartolocci and Wolf,[4]
to resume in brief.   In order to understand the place occupied
by the Kabbalah it is necessary to say something of that great
and authoritative collection which is known to everyone as
the TALMUD.   The latter is a large as it is also an ancient
growth.   Its starting-point has been placed by a moderate
criticism shortly before the birth of Christ,[5] and, to use a

---

[1] It is significant also that in THE KABBALAH UNVEILED Mathers classes THE HOUSE
OF GOD or of the Elohim and THE BOOK OF THE REVOLUTIONS OF SOULS—which are
late developments and commentaries—among the most important sections of the
ZOHAR.

[2] He assumes in fact the existence, antiquity and general but concealed diffusion of a
Wisdom Religion, a term borrowed from Modern Theosophy, and one which, in the
last analysis, is not entirely satisfactory to the mystic.

[3] LA KABBALE.   *Tradition Secrète de l'Occident.   Résumé Méthodique.*   Paris, 1892, 8vo.
There was a second edition, revised and enlarged, which I have not seen, the first being
conclusive as to the qualifications of the writer.

[4] The work of Bartolocci has been cited and Wolf's title is as follows : BIBLIOTHECA
HEBRÆA, *sive notitia tum auctorum Hebraicorum cujuscumque ætatis, tum scriptorum, quæ vel
Hebraice primum exarata, vel ab aliis conversa sunt, ad nostram ætatem deducta.*   4 vols.,
Leipsic and Hamburg, 1715, 4to.

[5] There are writers outside esoteric circles who ascribe a similar antiquity to the
Kabbalah, as, for example, the author of the article *s.v. Cabale* in the GRAND DICTION-
NAIRE UNIVERSEL DU XIXe SIÈCLE (Pierre Larousse), t. iii. Paris, 1867.   " In reality

somewhat conventional phrase, its two canons were said to have been less or more fixed in the fourth and sixth centuries, A.D.,[1] at which periods, although there are certain traces of a more esoteric doctrine, it cannot be shewn that Kabbalistic literature, according to the restricted sense in which the term is here applied, had as yet come into existence.[2] Put shortly, the sources of the TALMUD are said to be " the customs and regulations practised by the authorities in their administration of religious and civil affairs."[3] It is claimed that this source goes back to the period of Esdras, but the most that can be admitted is that materials embodied in the literature are older than their earliest collected forms. These materials were certain MISHNAYOTH, a term signifying repetitions—namely, notes of academical teachings, which received many subsequent additions.[4] Prior to the year 220, A.D., a considerable proportion of these was engarnered by Rabbi Judah the Prince,[5] by whom they were methodised carefully, short comments of his own being also added occasionally.[6] It follows that the collection received the impression of his peculiar views, from which other authorities differed. He endeavoured to destroy all rival MISHNAYOTH, but some of

---

the Kabbalah originated among the Jews five centuries before our era. Formed of the mixture of oriental ideas and Mosaism at the epoch of the captivity, it was elaborated silently, and in the main among the sect of the Karaites, but did not attain its definite development till the period of Philo and the schools of Alexandria." The inspiration here is Franck, but it must be added that the evidence is wanting. Philo, for example, cannot be cited as an indubitable witness to a Secret Tradition in Jewry.

[1] There may be mentioned, however, at its value a thesis in the JEWISH MESSENGER, July, 1837, according to which (1) the TALMUD has never been declared closed, (2) the MISHNA is an incomplete work, and (3) so also is the GEMARA.

[2] It is indeed obvious that nothing had come into writing. Professor Schiller-Szinessey testifies to a root-matter connected with the name of Rabbi Simeon and regarded as his in its source, but he offers no view as to the epoch when it began to assume a written form.

[3] THE BABYLONIAN TALMUD. English Translation. By Michael L. Rodkinson. Vol. i. New York, 1896, 8vo, pp. xv., xvi.

[4] In the HALAKOT OLAM it is said that Jewish teachers had little schedules or scrolls of parchment, in which they set down all the traditions, sentences, statutes, decisions and so forth which they learned from their masters, and that these scrolls were called the volumes of things secret. The work in question, i.e., עולם הליכות—see Habacuc iii, 6—is an introduction to Talmudic dialectic and formulæ. The author was R. Jescivah ben Joseph Hallevi, a Castilian who flourished before and after 1467. It was printed originally at Constantinople in 1510.

[5] He was the third patriarch of the Western Jews, and a legend says that, having converted the Emperor Marcus Aurelius, he compiled the MISHNA at the command of that Prince. See E. H. Palmer: HISTORY OF THE JEWISH NATION, London, 1883, pp. 204, 205. He has been called " redactor of the MISHNA." His birth is referred to circa 135, and he died in or near 220.

[6] For an old account of this labour, see David Ganz: GERMEN DAVIDIS, sive Chronologia Sacra et Prophana. Leyden, 1644.

them were preserved in secret and came to light after his death. In this way we have—

(*a*) The MISHNA, or repetition, being the methodised selection of Rabbi Judah.

(*b*) The TOSEPHTOTH, or additions, called also BARAITHOTH,[1] outsiders, or secondary matter, terms applied by the followers of Rabbi Judah to the rival MISHNAYOTH, by which the original collection is said in the course of time to have been almost extinguished. Their competitive claims were harmonised ultimately by later rabbis, and thus arose

(*c*) The GEMARA—*i.e.*, conclusion or completion.[2]

The union of the GEMARA and the MISHNA forms the TALMUD,[3] or instruction—from a word signifying " to teach " —of which there are two versions, the MISHNA being the same in each. The GEMARA collected by Jerusalem rabbis, representing the school of Tiberias and R. Johanon Ben Eliezer—*ob.* A.D. 279—with the MISHNA, forms the JERUSALEM TALMUD, and belongs to the end of the fourth century. The GEMARA collected by Babylonian rabbis, and especially by Rabina—*ob. circa* A.D. 420—R. Ashi—A.D. 353–427—and R. José, with the MISHNA, forms the TALMUD OF BABYLON, four times larger than that of Jerusalem.[4] It was begun in the fifth and completed in the sixth century, but even subsequently to this period much additional material was gathered into it.

It is exceedingly important that we should understand the position which is occupied by the great collections of the TALMUD in respect of the literature which is termed technically the Kabbalah. In the first place, this name, technical or conventional, as I have said, has suggested many errors of comparison. By the hypothesis of both literatures the TALMUD is Kabbalah even as the ZOHAR is Kabbalah, because both are matters of reception by tradition.[5] But to say that the

---

[1] And extravagances, in the sense of things extraneous.

[2] Simeon ben Yohai is represented as asserting that the study of the GEMARA was more meritorious than that of the MISHNA or the sacred Scriptures. But here a later predilection has sheltered itself under an earlier name. It may be noted that the term GEMARA came into use also as a description of the TALMUD.

[3] Strictly speaking, the term TALMUD applies only to the GEMARA, but it has obtained the wider application because the GEMARA is always accompanied by the MISHNA, the text being essential to the note.

[4] The proportion of the Babylonian GEMARA to the original MISHNA is about eleven to one.

[5] " In older Jewish literature, the name (Kabbalah) is applied to the whole body of received religious doctrine with the exception of the Pentateuch, thus including the

TALMUD is Kabbalistic in the sense of the ZOHAR is extremely misleading. The cycles are distinct and indeed divergent. There is no question as to the age and great authority of the one,[1] while some centuries of inquiry have not as yet determined the claims of the other. Moreover, could we assume the equal antiquity of both, the nature of the Tradition would be still generically different. The TALMUD is not in any sense of the term a Theosophical system :[2] it is law and commentary ; it is the construction placed by authority on the jurisprudence, ecclesiastical and political, of old Israel.[3] It is sociology, not metaphysics, even if it has admitted metaphysics and has accretions which might be termed mystical.[4] To place it by the arbitrary use of a conventional term in the same category as the literature which discusses the Mysteries of the Supreme Crown, the evolution of withdrawn " Divine Subsistence," so-called, into positive being, the emanation or forthcoming of the SEPHIROTH and the origin, metempsychosis and destiny of souls, is to make a foolish and deceiving classification. M. Isidore Loëb [5] offers us the equivalent of an admirable distinction between the two literatures in his observations upon the comparative position of the French and Spanish Jews at the period of the promulgation of the ZOHAR. Talmudic Israel was, he tells us, circumscribed by the circle of the Law : it had no horizon and no future ; it had no place in the life of philosophy.[6]

---

prophets and HAGIOGRAPHA, as well as the oral traditions ultimately embodied in the MISHNA."—AMERICAN ENCYCLOPÆDIA, iii., pp. 521, 522.

[1] I do not mean that there has never been a question, for the French ecclesiastic Morin, proceeding on the principle that the Jews cannot be believed in anything relating to the age of their literature, endeavoured to refer the MISHNA to the beginning of the sixth century and the GEMARAS to some two hundred years later.—EXERCITATIONES BIBLICÆ, Paris, 1660.

[2] Hence the conspicuous philosophical doctrines of the Kabbalah have no place therein. For example, the Sephirotic system, with which we shall be concerned later on, and the theory of emanation which it may suggest, cannot be traced in the TALMUD. Consult Edersheim : HISTORY OF THE JEWISH NATION, third edition, p. 406.

[3] It has been described as " a *corpus juris* in which the law has not yet been differentiated from morality and religion." See F. W. Farrar : LIFE OF CHRIST, illustrated edition, *n.d.*, p. 758.

[4] It is possible to institute a comparison between the TALMUD and the Kabbalah as between Freemasonry and late Western Occultism. The TALMUD is not Mysticism, but it became the asylum of some mystical traditions. Freemasonry is not an occult teaching, but under the standard of the Craft all occult arts of the eighteenth century found not only a refuge, but a field of work and of development. The way of entrance in the one case was the Haggadic morality : in the other it was the High Grades.

[5] LA GRANDE ENCYCLOPÉDIE, Paris, 4to, *s.v.* CABBALE, vol. viii.

[6] " In the immense collections which have come down to us from the fifth or sixth centuries of the Christian era, in the TALMUD as in the allegorical interpretations of the Bible, there is no trace of philosophical speculations. If we find reminiscences of the

The ZOHAR gave to Israel the splendid impulsion of the ideal ; it gave philosophy ; it created a wide horizon ; it brought the exiled Jew into correspondence with the thought of the world : it communicated the Eternal.

The first result of the confusion in question is to place a wrong construction upon Talmudic literature, to suggest that, as believed by some of the Kabbalah proper, it possesses a double meaning, and that we are to look below its literal sense.[1] It has been pointed out appositely that it would be as reasonable to admit a metaphysical construction in the Common Law of England, the deliberations of a Holy Synod in the collections of State Trials, and a theory of transmutation in Conveyancing. Yet this is what has been done actually in the case of the TALMUD by the one Kabbalistic expositor whose influence with certain groups of students in France and England was once so paramount as to have been considered almost beyond appeal. To Éliphas Lévi, who, as a fact, misstated so much and knew so little of post-Christian Jewish literature, we owe a grandiose presentation of the Talmudic system which does grave outrage to fact.[2] He lays down that the first TALMUD, the only truly Kabbalistic one, was collected during the second century of the Christian era by " Rabbi Jehudah Hakadosh Hanassi—that is, Judah the most holy and the prince "—who " composed his book according to all

---

Kabbalah, they concern, so to speak, the exoteric portion, or angelology ; the existence of the speculative part is shewn in these books solely by the reference to Mysteries contained in BERESHITH, or the first chapter of Genesis, and in the MERCAVAH, or Vision of Ezekiel."—S. Munk : LA PHILOSOPHIE CHEZ LES JUIFS, Paris, 1848, p. 8. The author was an informed and accomplished defender of the existence of Kabbalistic Tradition in Talmudic times. It should be added that the Talmudic references to the Work of Creation and the Work of the Chariot would, if collated, do something to excuse the opinion that such a Tradition was known as regards the fact of its existence ; but it was referred to only enigmatically, and its real nature does not transpire. While the TALMUD records occasionally that there were conversations between the doctors of Israel thereon, it does not report the utterances.

[1] Edersheim divides Talmudic traditionalism into two portions : HALAKHA = the legislative enactments of the Fathers ; and HAGGADA = free interpretation.—HISTORY OF THE JEWISH NATION, p. 136. Some of the Haggadic legends may possess an inner meaning, that is, they may be allegorical stories : the history of the salting of Leviathan is so absurd in its literal sense that one is driven out of mere generosity to suppose that it meant something which does not appear on its surface. Compare ISRAEL AMONG THE NATIONS, by Anatole Leroy-Beaulieu, p. 24. As HALAKHA is rule, *norma*, so HAGGADA is legend, saga, " a collection of miscellaneous utterances touching on every possible subject." The HALAKHA alone is law.

[2] LA CLEF DES GRANDS MYSTÈRES. Paris, 1861, 8vo, p. 351, *et seq.* See also Waite : MYSTERIES OF MAGIC. Second edition, London, 1897, 8vo, pp. 112–120. It is to be noted that the ZOHAR describes the HALAKHA, MISHNA and GEMARA as heavy and involved casuistry, the MISHNA in particular being likened to a hard rock.— Part I., fol. 27b, and Part III., fol. 279.

the rules of supreme initiation." He " wrote it within and without, as Ezekiel and St. John have it, and he indicated its transcendental sense by the sacred letters and numbers corresponding to the BERESHITH of the first six SEPHIROTH " [1] of Kabbalistic Theosophy, the subject-general of which belongs to a later stage. This asserted Sephirotic correspondence has no place in reality. The MISHNA comprises six sections,[2] of which the first concerns tithes, the beasts which it is unlawful to pair, the seeds which must not be sown together in the earth, the threads which must not be interwoven, the fruits which must not be gathered till the trees have passed their third year, and so forth. It is by no means chiefly, much less exclusively, agricultural, as Lévi, who had obviously not read it, represents. Nor has it any correspondence with KETHER, except on the fantastic ground that " in the notion of the Supreme Crown is contained that of the fructifying principle and of universal production." Any attribution could be accredited after this fashion.

The second book concerns the festivals of Israel, the meats which are prohibited on these, the days of fasting and so forth. Lévi makes no attempt to justify the attribution which connects it with CHOKMAH. The third book deals with marriage and divorce, or, in the words of Lévi, " it is consecrated more particularly to women and the fundamental basis of the family." It is allocated by Lévi to BINAH, the third SEPHIRA. The fourth book embodies a consideration of civil contracts, general jurisdiction, civil and criminal actions, penalties, &c. Éliphas Lévi says that it is superior to any code of the Middle Ages and accounts for the preservation of Israel through all its persecutions. According to the natural order of the SEPHIROTH, it corresponds with CHESED or Mercy ; but as it looks better under the attribution of Justice, the Sephirotic

---

[1] I should note that, long prior to Éliphas Lévi, Adrianus Relandus (ANALECTA RABBINICA, 1702) and Galatinus (DE ARCANIS CATHOLICÆ VERITATIS, 1656) supposed a second sense in the TALMUD. It was not, however, metaphysical or mystical, but was a concealment prompted by the necessities of a persecuting time. This supposition is not less idle than the other, for the first thing which prudence would have suggested would be to hide the real feelings of Talmudic Jews towards Christians, and these are not dissembled in the TALMUD. It embodies a number of stories which must not be construed literally, but, as in the case cited previously, they belong at most to the domain of allegory.

[2] The fifth section is missing from the PALESTINIAN TALMUD and it has fragments only of the sixth. See THE JEWISH ENCYCLOPÆDIA, vol. xii, s.v. TALMUD, and also for Mishnaic treatises which are wanting in the Babylonian collection.

system is reversed accordingly, and it is attributed therefore to GEBURAH. The fifth book, which is allotted to Mercy by this transposition, is concerned, according to the French transcendentalist, with consoling beliefs and things holy, which creates a completely false impression concerning it. As a matter of fact, it is dedicated to votive offerings. The sixth book treats of purifications, which Lévi terms " the most hidden secrets of life and the morality which directs it." [1] It belongs by his hypothesis to the SEPHIRA called TIPHERETH, which signifies Beauty.

It is procedures of this kind which have made occult criticism deservedly a byword among scholars.[2] The TALMUD has its correspondences with the Kabbalah, but they are of method rather than material. It is highly desirable to remember it in connection with the ZOHAR, but it is a consummate act of ignorance to confound and to regard them as written upon the same principle and with the same objects.

Another writer, who has been quoted previously and is governed by different sentiments of scholarship, the late Isaac Myer, makes an exceedingly proper distinction when he affirms that the Kabbalah and the ZOHAR " allow a great margin to speculative thought "—meaning that they are purely speculative, metaphysical and theosophical—while the TALMUD " deals with everyday life and humanity under the Law ; " that the one " starts from a spiritual point of view, contemplating a spiritual finality as regards the Law and its explanation," but that the other is " eminently practical in both its starting-point and end, having, in the face of ignorance, want of perception and natural waywardness of the

---

[1] The exegesis thus inaugurated loses nothing in the hands of later occult writers. For example, an occult *opusculum* observes that the key which alone will open the revelations of the Christian Scriptures and manifest their interior sense, " exists in a book proscribed by the Christian Church—the JEWISH TALMUD." See THE ASTRAL LIGHT, by Nizida. Second edition, London, 1892, pp. 50, 51. It is just to add that this work was not regarded as of consequence by the circle to which it appealed.

[2] Some criticism which is not the work of occultists deserves the same condemnation. C. W. Heckethorn, author of the SECRET SOCIETIES OF ALL AGES AND COUNTRIES (new edition, 2 vols., 1897), presumed to treat the subject of the Kabbalah in the absence of elementary knowledge. Thus, he tells us that the literal Kabbalah is called the MISHNA (vol. 1. p. 85), which, as we have seen, is traditional commentary on the legislative part of the Mosaic THORAH. So also Walton, in his eighth prolegomenon to the POLYGLOT BIBLE, observes that the terms KABBALAH and MASSORAH are applied to one science by the Jews. Richard Simon draws attention to this error, saying that the MASSORAH is the criticism of the Hebrew text.—HISTOIRE CRITIQUE DU VIEUX TESTAMENT, p. 498. Amsterdam, 1685.

masses, nothing but the strict observance of the Law in all its details in view." [1]

IV.—DIVISIONS OF THE KABBALAH

Before we can proceed with our subject it will be necessary to remove some further false impressions which, unlike the esoteric aspect attributed to the TALMUD, are not errors which characterise occult pretence and ignorance, and have consequently a wider sphere of operation. They concern the nature and applications of the Tradition which is supposed to have been perpetuated in Israel. For most popular writers, for most encyclopædias of the past which have not had recourse to a specialist, the Kabbalistic Art is simply the use of Sacred Names in the evocation of spirits,[2] or it is that at least above all and more than all.[3] We find it in sources of reference like the great dictionary of Calmet,[4] while it obtains to this day in many slipshod accounts which pass from book to book, without any attempt at verification on the part of those who reproduce them. It illustrates the importance which is attributed everywhere to Magic, for in the last analysis all pretended occult science and all its oral traditions are resolved by the popular mind into a commerce with supposed denizens of the unseen world. I have done full justice elsewhere [5] to the enormous influence exercised by the belief in this commerce, so that the vulgar instinct is not entirely at fault. In a higher sense than that of Ceremonial Magic the ends of all hidden science, as of all occult arts, are assuredly in the unseen, and as to the processes of evocation I have said already that they are largely Kabbalistic processes.[6]

---

[1] PHILOSOPHY OF IBN GEBIROL, p. 35. Compare W. B. Greene : THE BLAZING STAR, 1872, 12mo. " The MASSORAH is in every respect the converse of the KABBALAH. The MASSORAH is that which was openly delivered by the Rabbi ; the KABBALAH is that which was secretly and mysteriously received by the disciple," p. 29. It will be observed that this comparison appears to identify the MASSORAH and the TALMUD.

[2] Compare Frinellan : LE TRIPLE VOCABULAIRE INFERNAL (Paris, *n.d.*), p. 30 : " What is termed the Kabbalah is the art of commercing with elementary spirits."

[3] Sometimes, however, it is closely united with Astrology, and to speak of this occult art is considered equivalent to speaking of Kabbalistic matters. Such, apparently, was the notion of Démeunier, in L'ESPRIT DES USAGES ET DES COUTUMES DES DIFFÉRENS PEUPLES, *tom.* ii. lib. xi. London, 1776.

[4] DICTIONARY OF THE BIBLE. For convenience of reference, consult C. Taylor's translation, London, 1823, vol. i. *s.v.* Cabbala.

[5] THE BOOK OF CEREMONIAL MAGIC, *i.e.*, THE SECRET TRADITION IN GOËTIA, part i. c. i. p. 3 *et seq.* London, 1911, 4to. It must be admitted that the term Kabbalah was applied early in its history to some forms of mediæval magical practice.

[6] Refer to preface.

They are, however, either late and corrupt derivatives which are not the Esoteric Tradition, but applications, and hence accidents thereof; or, if we must admit that there were magical practices involving a conventional procedure and a formal Ritual prevalent among the Hebrews at a remote period,[1] which also were handed down, and are therefore entitled to be classed, in a sense, as Kabbalah, then that reception must be distinguished very carefully from the Kabbalah with which we are concerned here.[2] The Tradition of the BOOK OF FORMATION and the BOOK OF SPLENDOUR is not of Magic but of Theosophy. It has been described with enthusiasm by an almost unknown writer, in the following terms : " The Kabbalah claims to be that spontaneous philosophy which man, quoad man, naturally affirms now, always has affirmed, and always will affirm as long as man is man. The worlds confessed by the Kabbalah are worlds known to man, worlds upon which man has set the seal of his own nature, worlds related to man and of which man is the authentic form. There is nothing in the Kabbalah which is not found also in the nature of man." [3]

As we have proved it expedient to set aside the Kabbalah of the TALMUD in order to clear the issues, so also, or at least till a further stage of our inquiry, we must ignore the Kabbalah of Magic. We are dealing in part with an attempted explanation of the universe, but above all of the origin, nature and destiny of the human soul, which things are entirely distinct from processes of evocation and the art of dealing with spirits. The theurgic and talismanic use of Divine Names and the doctrine of efficacious words belong to a distinct category, and are liable to be encountered everywhere in Jewish Theosophy. As will be seen later on, there is no

---

[1] It is to these practices that I suppose Richard Simon alludes, when he says that " the ancient Jewish doctors brought many superstitious sciences from Chaldea," p. 93. This author can be hardly regarded as an authority on Kabbalistic questions ; indeed, he seems to confess (op. cit., pp. 116, 117) that he had not thought it worth while to expend time over " the ancient allegorical books of the Jews," such as the ZOHAR and the BAHIR.

[2] The opposite is held by an American writer, T. K. Hosmer, who says : " From this source all Jewry was overrun with demonology, thaumaturgy, and other strange fancies."—THE JEWS IN ANCIENT, MEDIÆVAL AND MODERN TIMES, London, 1890, pp. 222, 223. Speaking generally, it is most in consonance with the facts to regard the Magic which Europe received at Jewish hands as a debased application of Kabbalism.

[3] W. B. Greene : THE BLAZING STAR, p. 57. I am not endorsing the statement ; but it follows from the specific teaching of the chief storehouse of Kabbalism, the ZOHAR, that apart from the human form, permanence and organisation are impossible to finite existences, whence, also, it is the form in which God communicates Himself.

question as to the antiquity of these notions, but they do not concern us now.

In virtue of another error the subject-matter of the Secret Tradition is confused with certain exegetical methods by which a scriptural authority is found for it. These methods obtained very widely, and there is no doubt that many of their most curious results contributed to swell the volume of Tradition; but the method which deals with material, and occasionally may even supply it, must be held distinct therefrom. They were, however, a matter of reception, and as such are Kabbalah; but they are not the doctrinal Kabbalah, and in the attempt to methodise our subject these also must be held as embodying things distinct.[1]

It follows from the above discriminations that there are, broadly speaking, four separate groups or species of Tradition in Israel which, by virtue of the meaning of words, are entitled to rank as Kabbalah : [2]

1. The Administrative Tradition of the TALMUD, the authoritative regulations as to the laws, customs, ceremonies and civil life of the Jewish nation. The literature of this Tradition is of great historical value, but it has no place in philosophy.

2. The Magical Tradition of the Hebrews, very important to the sources of occult arts, very obscure in its history, very much exaggerated by those who write about it, possessing little literature prior to the fourteenth century of the Christian era, by which time some speculations affirm that it had lost most of its antique elements.[3]

---

[1] P. J. Hershon divides the Kabbalah into two parts, symbolical and real. The first teaches the secret sense of Scripture and the thirteen rules by which the observance of the Law is expounded Kabbalistically, *i.e.*, GEMATRIA, NOTARICON, THEMURAH, &c. The real Kabbalah he subdivides into theoretical and practical : the one is concerned with the Emanations and Worlds of Kabbalism, the Nature and Names of God, the Celestial Hierarchy and its influence on the lower world, the Mysteries of Creation and so forth ; the other deals with the mystical properties of Divine and Angelic Names and the wonders performed with these.—TALMUDIC MISCELLANY, London, 1880. The essence of Zoharic Theosophy escapes in this division.

[2] Wynn Westcott, in a work on NUMBERS, THEIR OCCULT POWER AND MYSTIC VIRTUE, observes (p. 11) that the word Kabbalah " includes the Hebrew Doctrines of Cosmogony and Theology as well as the Science of Numbers." The first he terms the Dogmatic and the second the Literal Kabbalah. The Kabbalistic Science of numbers is included in GEMATRIA. There is, however, no such Science ; there is only a curious and unprofitable art.

[3] The indefectible title of Magic to a place in Jewish Kabbalah is enforced by all modern occultists, who have helped very much to confuse the issues in question. So far back as the end of the seventeenth century the distinction between the magical Tradition and the philosophical or doctrinal was recognised by R. Simon (HISTOIRE

3. Certain exegetical and other traditional methods by which a secret sense was extracted from the letter of Holy Scripture. Very curious results were sometimes obtained by these solemn follies, which appear so childish and ridiculous at the present day.[1] They comprise :

(*a*) GEMATRIA, a cryptographical system, by which the letters of a word were converted into numbers, and the arithmetical value was used to explain its internal sense.

(*b*) NOTARIKON, from *Notaricum*, described as a system of shorthand, by which each letter of a word was taken as the initial of another word, or, conversely, the initial letters of an entire sentence were combined to form a word, which word was held to throw light on the sentence.

(*c*) THEMURAH or Exchange, that is, the transposition of letters in a given word or sentence.

It is obvious that the field of these methods is not confined to one language or one literature ; their application to the plays of Shakespeare might produce results which would exceed even the pretensions of any GREAT CRYPTOGRAM. It is a little humiliating to find an important subject and a fascinating literature connected with such diversions ; but we shall see later on that the peculiar views of the Hebrews upon the divine character of their language invested them with a certain speciousness, while, for the rest, our inquiry is fortunately not concerned with them. These methods are sometimes termed the Artificial or Practical Kabbalah.[2] Their antiquity, like that of the Hebrew vowel-points, is a debated question. By some critics their traces have been discerned

---

CRITIQUE DU VIEUX TESTAMENT. Amsterdam, 1685, 4to), who said : " There is another sort of Kabbalah which is more dangerous and forms part of that which is commonly called Magic. It is mere illusion, the prepossession of certain persons who believe that they can perform miracles by means of it." (p. 374).

[1] The Kabbalistic method of interpreting Scripture, " which reduces the sense of the sacred books to vain and ridiculous subtleties, the mysteries contained in letters, in numbers, and in the dismemberment of certain words," was supposed by Simon to have passed from the school of Platonism to that of the Jews, chiefly in Europe. There seems no ground for this view. He adds (*op. cit.*, p. 374) that this " speculative Kabbalah " was, in his own day, still highly esteemed by the Jews of the Levant.

[2] They assumed sometimes the most extravagant forms. For example, the middle letter of any sacred book was written in an unusual position or of an unusual size, and was regarded as possessing a deep spiritual meaning. See THE BIBLE HANDBOOK, by Joseph Angus, D.D., 1860, p. 499. " The modes by which the Kabbalah educes the secret meaning veiled under the words of the Hebrew scriptures are manifold, extending to every peculiarity of the text. Even in what we should regard as critical marks or as errors or fancies of some transcriber, as when a letter is written too large or too small, is inverted or in any way distinguished, an occult intent was presumed." *American Encyclopædia*, iii. 521, 522.

even in Holy Scripture.[1] One point, however, which should be noted especially is that recourse to such devices is met with comparatively seldom in the ZOHAR.

4. The Philosophical Tradition, embodied in the SEPHER YETZIRAH and the ZOHAR cycles. To this only, in the interests of clearness, should the conventional term Kabbalah be applied, and it is this also which is signified by every informed writer who uses it. It is divided by Kabbalists themselves into

(*a*) The Doctrine of Creation,

(*b*) The Doctrine of the Throne or Chariot—*i.e.*, the Chariot of Ezekiel's vision.[2]

These divisions are concerned respectively with the natural and the metaphysical world, and are sometimes termed collectively the Theoretical Kabbalah. There is a broad and rough sense in which it may be said that SEPHER YETZIRAH embodies the Doctrine of Creation, while that of the Chariot is to be sought in SEPHER HA ZOHAR. But we shall find that the latter is full of creation myths, while, although it is our chief source of Tradition on Chariot Theosophy, the doctrine is only imbedded therein, its methodical extraction and development being the task of later Kabbalists. The so-called theoretical Kabbalah is that which gave to Israel—at least in respect of opportunity—the intellectual horizon which was impossible to the Talmudic Jew, and it is this also which gave the Children of the Exile a place in western philosophy. When we hear that the Kabbalah once fascinated some of the great minds of Christendom, it is to this only that the statement can be applied.[3] It is this, finally, which it is the purpose of the present inquiry to elucidate.[4] It should be added that

---

[1] The TARGUM to the Prophets, called the official TARGUM, which passes traditionally under the name of Jonathan ben Uzziel, a disciple of Hillel the Great, in the days of King Herod, has recourse occasionally to a species of transliteration when dealing with certain obscure scriptural names. It has been referred to the third century.

[2] Both these divisions are mentioned in the MISHNA by name (CHAGIGA, xi. 2), and are said to be Secret Doctrine, but the MAASEH BERESHITH and the MAASEH MERKABAH there referred to are not a written tradition, nor does that of the written Kabbalah necessarily represent it. The ZOHAR identifies MERCABAH with the SEPHIROTH or Ten Emanations, which will be examined at a further stage.

[3] Drach distinguishes three uses of the term Kabbalah for which authority can be cited : (1) It is applied frequently by the TALMUD to the books of the Old Testament, outside the Pentateuch ; (2) The rabbins apply it to the Legal or Talmudic Tradition ; (3) It signifies especially the " mystic, esoteric, acroamatic portion of the Oral Tradition."—DE L'HARMONIE ENTRE L'ÉGLISE ET LA SYNAGOGUE. *Par le* Chevalier P. L. B. Drach, 2 vols., Paris, 1844, Vol. II., pp. xv–xxxvi.

[4] Some readers may think it desirable to include the division of the Kabbalah proposed by Papus in one of his publications, though it is, critically speaking, fantastic.

outside the cycle of the ZOHAR there is a considerable Jewish theosophical and mystical literature, of which the SEPHER YETZIRAH is an instance. It was this which led up to the ZOHAR, and was embraced thereby. But whether it was Kabbalistic in the sense of the latter is one of the disputes of scholarship.

The Kabbalah, in his opinion, was attributable to Moses, and the written word of Scripture is therefore naturally a part of the Tradition. We have thus : (*a*) The written word ; (*b*) The oral word ; (*c*) An intermediate portion, being rules insuring the preservation of the text, *i.e.* MASSORAH. The last is the body of the Oral Tradition ; the MISHNA and GEMARA are its life ; the SEPHER YETZIRAH and the ZOHAR are its spirit. Unfortunately Papus did nothing to elucidate and nothing to justify his thesis, and assumed, as he did too often, the most important points at issue. Moreover, the Massoretic annotations are not comprehended by the explanation offered. See TRAITÉ ELÉMENTAIRE DE SCIENCE OCCULTE, 5ᵉ édition, Paris, 1898.

BOOK II

SOURCE AND AUTHORITY OF THE
KABBALAH AND THE AGE OF
THE CHIEF TEXTS

BOOK II

SOURCE AND AUTHORITY OF THE KABBALAH

I.—DATE OF THE BOOK OF FORMATION

HAVING sought to distinguish the subjects proper of the Secret Tradition in Israel from certain side issues and a mass of overgrowth, we have to ascertain in the next place whether and how far we are warranted by evidence in regarding the texts which embody it as authentic memorials and its doctrines as part of a Tradition perpetuated in Israel from early times.[1] For this purpose it will be convenient to accept the literature as divisible into four classes—(1) The BOOK OF FORMATION; (2) The commentaries on that work which preceded the public appearance of the ZOHAR; (3) The ZOHAR itself; (4) The writings subsequent thereto.[2] The report of an Esoteric Tradition in Israel did not begin to circulate through Christendom till the fourteenth century, and this, as we shall see later on, is explained by the fact that the chief collection of its archives was unknown, at least generally, in Jewry itself till about 1290, A.D. This collection is that which is termed by Kabbalists the Work of the Chariot, represented by the ZOHAR. The Work of Creation—to

---

[1] It is pertinent to recall at this point what has been said in my prefatory words on the question of antiquity. The subject is approached here with that reservation in view, its determination being essential on what may be called the historical side. We must know under what circumstances the Tradition comes before us, whatever the final values.

[2] Solomon Munk, who still ranks high among French authorities on Kabbalism, tabulates the following classification in the DICTIONNAIRE DE LA CONVERSATION, s.v. KABBALE. (1) A symbolical portion, namely, mystical calculations, i.e., THEMURAH, GEMATRIA, NOTARICON, on which refer to Book I. § 4; (2) A dogmatic or positive part, which is, in fact, concerned with the hypothesis of spiritual essences, i.e., angels, demons, human souls and their transmigration; (3) A speculative and metaphysical part, namely, Sephirotic Doctrine and so forth. It is not an exhaustive classification, but there is no need to criticise it here. The Secret Tradition on its Theosophical side is not represented by a bare allusion to Sephirotic Doctrine.

which the SEPHER YETZIRAH [1] corresponds—was known, as
we have some ground for believing, to at least one Christian
student so far back as the middle of the ninth century, but
there was no consequence attached to it for Christendom.[2]
The SEPHER YETZIRAH is supposed to embody a Tradition
handed down from the time of Abraham, and there is no
doubt that the uncritical spirit of several centuries represented the patriarch as its author. This does not seem,
however, as some modern criticism has supposed loosely,[3] to
have been the view adopted universally by the Jewish learning
which accepted the document. That he received and he
transmitted it was held undoubtedly, but the work itself is not
pretended to have been reduced to writing till after the
destruction of Jerusalem, and tradition has ascribed its formal
authorship to Rabbi Akiba ben Joseph,[4] the pupil of R. Joshua
ben Hananiah,[5] who was himself the successor, as he was also
once the opponent, of Rabban Gamaliel.[6] There is nothing
flagrantly improbable in this attribution, though it reaches us
late in history. Akiba was a speculator with whose notions
the scheme of the SEPHER YETZIRAH was in complete accordance, and he is the reputed author of another work dealing
with the mysteries of the Hebrew Alphabet.[7] In his interpre-

---

[1] See THE BOOK OF FORMATION (SEPHER YETZIRAH). Translated from the Hebrew,
with Annotations, by Knut Stenring, 1923. The bibliography of the text is treated at
some length in an introduction prefixed by myself.

[2] Maimonides explains in his GUIDE OF THE PERPLEXED that MAASEH BERESHITH
corresponds to physical and MAASEH MERKABAH to metaphysical science. They have
been termed otherwise the History of Creation and the History of the Divine Throne.

[3] Dr. Edersheim, HISTORY OF THE JEWISH NATION, observes that it is properly
" a monologue on the part of Abraham, in which, by the contemplation of all that is
around him, he ultimately arrives at the conviction of the unity of God." 3rd ed.
p. 407. So also Ginsburg says that it professes to be a monologue of the patriarch.
It does nothing of the sort ; but the fifth chapter mentions " Abraham our father."
Of course, the legend of patriarchal derivation became stereotyped quickly. In the
twelfth century, R. Judah Ha Levi speaks of " the Book of the Creation which belongs
to our father Abraham."

[4] He is said to have perished in the Bar Cochba rebellion, A.D. 120, but this is wrong,
and the evidence points to his martyrdom twelve years later for transgressing the edict
of Hadrian against the practice of the Jewish religion. He was born A.D. 50.

[5] He was the leading Tanna of the period which followed immediately on the
destruction of the Temple. The Tanna was a Teacher of the Oral Law.

[6] He was the head of Palestinian Jews at the close of the first century and in the
opening years of the second.

[7] It is called the ALPHABET of R. Akiba, being the letters allegorically explained.
It was printed at Cracovia in 1597, with a *Commentarius Prolixus*. See Buxtorf's
BIBLIOTHECA HEBRÆA RABBINICA. Basilia, 1618–19, 4 vols. fol. An earlier edition
of the Alphabet appeared at Venice in 1546. See Bartolocci, iv. 274. Karppe suggests
that it was originally a method of teaching children to read. ÉTUDES SUR LES ORIGINES
ET LA NATURE DU ZOHAR, pp. 108, 109. Compare the analogous proposition that
SEPHER YETZIRAH was meant to serve as a Hebrew Grammar.

tation of Scripture he followed and exaggerated the principles
of Hillel the Great and Nahum of Giso.[1] He promulgated,
or at least gave the weight of his authority to the doctrine
that " every sentence, word and particle in the Bible has its
use and meaning." [2] His literary labours were also very
great, for to him is attributed the arrangement and redaction
of the HALAKHA.   Subsequent generations were so impressed
by his marvellous knowledge of divine things that he was
asserted to have discovered much of which even Moses was
ignorant, which, in the sense not intended, is indubitably true.
If we admit the existence of a Secret Tradition in Israel, we
shall not need to question that Akiba was initiated therein ;
if we admit the existence of the SEPHER YETZIRAH in the
second century, we can imagine no more probable author for
that work.[3]   Nor is the date essentially disagreeable to a
moderate criticism [4] ; it is merely unestablished for want of
overt evidence,[5] which begins only with the ninth century,
when there is barely tolerable reason to infer that it may have
been known by St. Agobard.[6] It is not possible from any
internal testimony to fix the work as belonging to the later
period, for obviously any book may be much older than the
date of its first quotation, while the fact, if established, that it
was known in France in or about the year 850 [7] would create a

[1] Hillel was of high authority among the Scribes and Pharisees in the days of King
Herod, and is said to have been familiar with the whole Traditional Law. Nahum
was the instructor of Akiba.

[2] Edersheim, HISTORY OF THE JEWISH NATION.

[3] Curiously enough, M. Nicolas admits the date necessary but not the authorship it
suggests, on the ground that Akiba was a rigid and head-strong doctor of the Law and
not likely to indulge in speculative lucubrations. This estimate, with which it is
difficult to agree, has also the authority of Franck, on the ground that the TALMUD
reproaches Akiba for his incommensurate notions of God ; but Franck is possibly
more influenced by his belief in the earlier origin of the work.—LA KABBALE, p. 87 et
seq. Whether Yetziratic notions of Deity are not inadequate also is another question.

[4] It has been argued that the language of the SEPHER YETZIRAH is a Hebrew wholly
analogous to that of the MISHNA.

[5] Dr. Schiller-Szinessy says expressly that the book no doubt belongs to Akiba,
" both in substance and form."—ENCYCLOPÆDIA BRITANNICA, 9th ed., s.v. MIDRASHIM,
a term derived from a root signifying to seek out or to question. Munk also takes
this view in the article s.v. KABBALE, contributed to the ninth volume of the DICTION-
NAIRE DE LA CONVERSATION ET DE LA LECTURE, Paris, 1833.

[6] The English reader may consult Taylor's translation of Basnage's HISTORY OF THE
JEWS, p. 590 et seq. London. 1708. Agobard was Archbishop of Lyons, and wrote
against trials by ordeal and other superstitions of his period. See the Abbé Migne :
DICTIONNAIRE DES SCIENCES OCCULTES, vol. i. col. 32. Despite this apparent en-
lightenment he figures among the persecutors of Jewry. See Basnage : HISTOIRE DES
JUIFS, t. v. pp. 1493, 1494.

[7] The evidence falls far short of demonstration, and is confined to two short passages
in the EPISTOLA S. AGOBARDI . . . DE JUDAICIS SUPERSTITIONIBUS. In the first, the
Jews are branded for their gross notions of the Deity, on the ground that they believe

presumption that it was in existence much earlier, since literature travelled slowly in those days.   We must remember also that a SEPHER YETZIRAH is mentioned in both TALMUDS, in connection with the doctrine that heaven and earth were created by a mysterious combination of letters, and that Franck characterises the attempt of some modern scholarship to distinguish two works under an identical title as founded in gross ignorance.[1] If, however, we do not place the work in Talmudic times, we may concede that it came into existence within a measurable distance of the stormy period in which the great Talmudic canons reached their term.

We have to distinguish in the next place between the date which may be surmised for the treatise and that which must perhaps be attributed to the notions embodied therein. Have we any ground for believing that the doctrine of the SEPHER YETZIRAH is older than the Egyptian captivity, as its legend affirms?   This question must be answered by an emphatic negative.   The doctrine under notice gives prominence to the sacred and divine character of the Hebrew alphabet, and we have no warrant for supposing that the art of writing was possessed by Abraham ; every probability is against it and every authority is agreed on this point.   But the SEPHER YETZIRAH contains, by implication at least, the doctrine of an occult power and sanctity inherent in certain Divine Names,[2] and we know that this belief is very old in humanity, that it is found at an early period in Chaldea, Akkadia and so forth.   It is ridiculous for modern intelligence, but it is of great antiquity, and as it belongs to those countries with which Israel was in contact, there is reason to

---

Him to be possessed of a bodily form, having distinct members and lineaments, including organs of seeing, hearing, speaking and so forth ; also that they note only one difference between the body of God and that of man who is in His image, namely, that the fingers are inflexible, because God effects nothing with his hands.   It seems certain that St. Agobard draws here from the DESCRIPTION OF THE BODY OF GOD.   In the second passage it is said : " Further, they believe the letters of their alphabet to have existed from everlasting, and before the beginning of the world to have received diverse offices, in virtue of which they should preside over created things."—S. AGOBARDI, LUGDUNENSIS EPISCOPI, OPERA OMNIA.   Patrologiæ Cursus Completus . . . accurante J. P. Migne.   Paris, 1851, p. 78 et seq.   This appears to indicate an acquaintance with SEPHER YETZIRAH, though obviously misconstruing its meaning, or is alternatively a reference to Akiba's ALPHABET, the date of which in its two extant versions seems highly conjectural.   The TALMUDS are also a possible source of the statement.   Karppe (op. cit., p. 129) affirms that St. Agobard quotes almost verbatim from the ALPHABET.
   [1] On this fact Franck insists very strongly, maintaining that these references demonstrate the existence of a work reserved to a few and that this work is identical with the SEPHER YETZIRAH as we now have it.—LA KABBALE, Paris, 1843, p. 75 et seq.
   [2] See Appendix IV.

think that it may have become part of the religious baggage of the Hebrew people long before any Master in Israel dreamed of the Sepher Yetzirah, the Alphabet of Akiba, or even the Mishna itself. Purveyors of occult reverie have attached themselves naturally and inevitably to this doctrine,[1] and we must allow that the most ancient document of Kabbalism [2] does embody in this subject something of Tradition from the past, perhaps even from the period of the Babylonian captivity, as the Talmud itself indicates. On the other hand, we have no evidence to shew that the doctrine of the Instruments of Creation is much prior to the date of the treatise which develops it; it has no history previously, and can be placed therefore at most in Talmudic—*i.e.*, in post-Christian—times. It should be added that the Sepher Yetzirah is part of a considerable literature of an occult or cryptic complexion covering the period between the Talmudic Age and the first report of the Zohar.[3]

II.—MODERN CRITICISM OF THE BOOK OF SPLENDOUR

The commentaries on the Sepher Yetzirah which preceded the publication of the Zohar make no claim on antiquity, and may be reserved for consideration in their proper place later on. The alleged traces of Kabbalism in writers of known dates also prior to that event may be left in like manner till we deal with the documents consecutively. We can proceed therefore at once to the several problems connected with the Book of Splendour. Chief among these

---

[1] And so also, it would seem, has one elementary form of modern Christian Mysticism. See, for example, the collection entitled Letters from a Mystic of the Present Day, by an anonymous writer. Second edition, London, 1889, pp. 205–207. " We seem to have to learn the *various* names of God before we can grasp *the* Name. *The* Name grasps us, while the others are various outer courts through which we come into the Sanctuary or Name of God ; in that name we find pasture wherever our outer life may take us." Compare Saint-Martin : L'Esprit des Choses, tom. ii. 65 *et seq.*

[2] I ought not, perhaps, to omit that Mayer Lambert, one of the French editors of the Sepher Yetzirah, affirms that it has nothing in common with the Kabbalah, by which he understands a mysterious explanation of the Bible drawn from the letters of the text and a metaphysical theory which connects God with the world through a series of emanations of Divinity. As regards its date, he agrees that it is one of the numerous Midrashim produced by the Talmudic period. It should be added that this definition of Kabbalism does not answer to the Zohar in any adequate or tolerable sense.

[3] See Phineas Mordell—in the Jewish Quarterly Review, 1913—on the tradition that Sepher Yetzirah was written by Joseph ben Uzziel towards the end of the fifth century.

are the questions : (1) Whether some modern criticism is
right in ascribing the ZOHAR to the thirteenth century as its
period, and to R. Moses Shem Tob de Leon as its author.
(2) Whether we have evidence that part at least of its doctrine
was in existence at a much earlier period, or, as its legend
states, at the time of the Roman Emperor Antoninus.
We shall get very little help from the insight of contemporary Israel as to either point. The SEPHER YETZIRAH was
known and accepted before documentary criticism can be said
to have been conceived or born ; and so also when the ZOHAR
was promulgated it was among a mixed audience who either
took or rejected it on *à priori* grounds. Those who loathed
the yoke of Aristotle, which Abraham ben David Ha Levi (*ob.
circa* A.D. 1126), Abraham ben Meïr Ibn Ezra (*circa* 1092–1167),
and Moses Maimonides (1131–1201) would have placed on
the neck of Jewry, accorded it a glad welcome.[1] All that
great section of Jewry which was addicted to Astrology and
Magic took it into their heart of hearts : it was neither Magic
nor Astrology, but it harmonised with their peculiar aspirations.   On the other hand, it was hated by the Aristotelians
because it did not consort with their methods.[2]   It is not till
recent times that we have any intelligent defence on the part
of Jewish thinkers—Konitz in 1815,[3] Franck in 1843, David
Luria in 1857,[4] Munk in 1859 ; or, on the other hand, a strong
and informed hostility, as that of Graetz [5] in Germany, to
quote only one instance.

[1] The contrariety of the two systems is best shewn by this fact. Myer says : " Its
opponents were almost universally Jewish Aristotelians, who opposed the ancient
secret learning of the Israelites because it was more in accord with the philosophy of
Plato and Pythagoras, and indeed most likely emanated from the same sources, the
Aryan and Chaldean esoteric doctrine."—PHILOSOPHY OF IBN GEBIROL, p. 12. It is
the fact only which is of value : Myer's explanation may be read in the light of Book ii.
§ 5.
[2] " When the Saracens became the patrons of philosophy . . ., the attention paid
both by Arabians and Christians to the writings of Aristotle excited the emulation of
the Jews, who, notwithstanding the ancient curse pronounced on all Jews who should
instruct their sons in the Grecian learning, . . . continued in their philosophical
course reading Aristotle in Hebrew translations made from the inaccurate Arabic, for
Greek was at this period little understood."—Gould : HISTORY OF FREEMASONRY,
London, 1885, ii. 66, 67 ; see also 69, 70.
[3] See Isaac Myer, *op. cit.*, pp. 20 *et seq.*
[4] See his KADMOOTH HA ZOHAR, which appeared at Johannesburg at or about the
date in question. It maintained that the completion of the ZOHAR was much prior to
that of the BABYLONIAN TALMUD and that some of its doctrines were cited by Babylonian
Geonim on the authority of a MIDRASH YERUSHALMI, which was in fact the ZOHAR.
[5] Perhaps it is more strong than it is well informed. I see no trace in Graetz of any
real acquaintance with the Kabbalah, about which he writes savagely and with the
indiscrimination which we connect with a savage. Thus, he terms the ZOHAR " a
notorious forgery," whereas the chief notoriety concerning it is that after nearly seven

In estimating the influence exercised by the Kabbalah upon certain minds of Christendom, the SEPHER YETZIRAH must be distinguished from the ZOHAR. The former has had no influence ; it was indeed introduced to our knowledge by a monk of exalted erudition and of eccentricity equally great, but it was not till the sixteenth century, and it found no sphere of operation. Some of its Sephirotic developments, the commentaries of Rabbi Abraham and Rabbi Azriel, met with a certain audience among a few men of learning ; but they can bear no comparison with the appeal made by the larger cycle. ' For Christian students the Kabbalah was either the ZOHAR itself or it was developments therefrom, and, as we shall see subsequently, the office attributed to it was almost exclusively evangelical : that is to say, the discovery that there had existed in Israel, from time immemorial, as it was alleged, a Secret Doctrine which appeared to contain analogies and even identities with fundamental dogmas of Christianity, put the Jews so clearly in the wrong, by their own shewing, that their conversion was deemed inevitable.[1] Thus, the antiquity of the Tradition was not at that time challenged in Christendom, and again it was not a period when documentary criticism was pursued with any keenness. The fourteenth century made the grave, but yet excusable, mistake of supposing that most people wrote the books attributed to them. They accepted the claim of the ZOHAR for much the same reason that they were persuaded of the antiquity of Homer. In the existing state of scholarship to have challenged one might have opened an abyss beneath the other, and could well have included all ancient literature in a common uncertainty. Of course, as time went on and the evangelical instrument proved to be of no effect, its validity began to be challenged, but even then it was scarcely on critical grounds. So also even at the inception of the enthusiasm, some sceptical voices

centuries of criticism scarcely two authorities can be found to agree in their estimate. Throughout this part of his history we encounter things uncertain described in the language of certitude, and things for which there is little evidence as if there were overwhelming testimony.
    [1] " Some Christians have also esteemed them (i.e., the Kabbalistic books and their connections) because they found them more favourable to the Christian religion than recent commentaries of the Rabbins. But they failed to consider that these same allegorical books are filled with an infinitude of ridiculous fables, and that Jewish superstition is much more clearly proved from them than are the Mysteries of our Religion. William Postel has imposed on several theologians in this matter, having pretended to find Christianity in the books of the ZOHAR."—Richard Simon : HISTOIRE CRITIQUE DU VIEUX TESTAMENT, p. 371.

were raised, but again from uncritical and predetermined motives.[1] The Christians who rejected the Zohar were like the Jews who rejected it—the latter because they were Aristotelians, the former because they were Christians, who saw no good in the Ghetto, and only the final impenitence of the lost thief in the erudition of Toledo.[2]

The credulity, or at least the disability, of early students has been atoned for amply in the spirit which has governed later critics of the Kabbalah. I must confess that in some cases they seem, after their own manner, to have prejudged the question much as that laborious bibliographer Julius Bartolocci prejudged it in the seventeenth century. It was offensive to the dignity of the Latin Church to suppose that there was a rival Tradition, full of illumination and wisdom, preserved unknown to the Church in the rejected House of Israel. By a similar sentiment it has seemed intolerable to modern notions that any cryptic literature should possess a real claim on attention. It is therefore said out of hand that the Kabbalah, represented by the ZOHAR, is a forgery of the thirteenth century. We must endeavour to comprehend precisely what is involved in this standpoint.

There are some literary fabrications which do not need a high degree of scholarship to expose them, for they may be said to betray themselves, often at every point. In the department of *belles lettres* it is sufficient to mention the so-called Rowley poems. These, as everybody is aware, were forgeries pure and simple, and their disguise is so entirely spurious that it can be peeled off without any difficulty. It is not necessary to add that they possessed their believers, and not further back than the days of the Bell edition of Chatterton, the race of Rowleyites had still a few survivals, for we find the editor describing their characteristics in terms which have a wider application than he was concerned with at the moment. A true Rowleyite, he says, is not open to

---

[1] Among writers who did not permit themselves to be deceived by the alleged instrument of conversion, a high place must be accorded to Petrus Galatinus and his DE ARCANIS CATHOLICÆ VERITATIS *contra Judæorum perfidiam*, first published in 1518.

[2] The connection between Christianity and the ZOHAR once found an occasional expositor in French occult circles. Consult Stanislas de Guaita : ESSAIS DES SCIENCES MAUDITES. *I. Au Seuil du Mystère. Nouvelle édition, corrigée.* Paris. 1890. " The ZOHAR has wedded the Gospel ; the spirit has fructified the soul ; and immortal works have been the fruits of this union. The Kabbalah became Catholic in the school of St. John," &c. A romantic criticism, inspired by Éliphas Lévi and utterly devoid of warrant.

conviction, and the statement obtains in the case of all pertinacious defenders of spurious literary productions. The position of the Rowley MSS. is fairly paralleled by that of many occult documents, among which, as typical instances, we may select the handboks of Ceremonial Magic. There are no works which betray themselves more transparently and abundantly than certain versions of the KEY OF SOLOMON and its connections, or the SACRED MAGIC OF ABRAMELIN THE MAGE, and yet they possessed their believers in England only some decades ago, enthusiasts for the good faith of their claims to a high antiquity or a Hebrew origin, as the case might be.

There are again some fabrications which possess a certain basis in fact, over which a mass of forgery has been arranged. One ready instance in point is found in the poems of Ossian, for which there was indubitably a nucleus of floating Gaelic tradition, and it was wrought into his production by MacPherson. The result may deceive for a moment even sound scholarship, but its full exposure is only a matter of time. In this case the epic of WALLACE was fatal to the possibility of Fingal. The Latin alchemical writings attributed to Geber might be regarded as typical instances in occult literature of this form of fraud, if we could accept Berthelot's view that they have scarcely any resemblance to the Arabic originals, for such originals exist.[1]

Finally, there are certain works which may or may not be fabrications, but either they incorporate so much genuine material belonging to the department of literature which they pretend to represent, or else are constructed so skilfully that the balance of probability is poised pretty equally concerning them, and it is almost impossible to arrive, by impartial methods, at the determination of their claims. I do not know whether there is any good instance in *belles lettres* of this kind of alleged fabrication. Hogg's JACOBITE RELICS OF SCOTLAND is perhaps the nearest approach to a parallel. That collection contains undoubtedly a large proportion of genuine material, but it is suspected that the Ettrick Shepherd supplied a proportion of the memorable garner by his own skill in

---

[1] See my SECRET TRADITION IN ALCHEMY, 1926, p. 117, for a note on Djaber texts which have come to light since Berthelot wrote. There is ground for believing that they—and not the texts edited by the French chemist—are the originals of the Latin Geber.

verse-craft, and criticism, though it has not concerned itself
seriously, is perhaps divided fairly on the question. In so-
called occult literature we have several signal examples of
such suspected writing which has not been found out to the
satisfaction of the impartial mind. For example, a few of the
Hermetic books, which are classed by scholars as productions
of the Alexandrian period, and therefore as post-Christian,
are held by others to represent traditions of considerable
antiquity, and I do not know that the case has been decided
for all time as regards one or two of these works. But the
most renowned of all the instances is that with which we are
here concerned—the Kabbalah itself. Destructive criticism
has maintained that its foremost work was forged by a single
writer, of indifferent claims to our intellectual consideration,
at the end of the thirteenth century. There is, as we shall
see, no positive evidence on this point which is worth naming,
and the presumptive evidence is not at all strong. There is
very good proof of late writing, but the theory of the fabrication of the ZOHAR by Moses de Leon puts an almost impossible burden on the shoulders of that questionable personage, and is generally the work of writers who have not
paid sufficient regard to the possible existence of much of the
traditional doctrine which is summarised in the ZOHAR at a
period preceding its appearance, perhaps even by some
centuries.

It must be recognised therefore that Kabbalistic literature
belongs to a suspected class, but how we are to regard its
impeachment is a different question. In respect of material
and usually as regards its motive, spurious literature belongs
to the most accountable class. It falls into line readily.
Where there are complex workings of the human mind, as in
the ZOHAR, there sincerity is usually present. The Kabbalah
is much too singular in its mechanism, and far too piecemeal
in its numerous texts, to be referable to a solitary author. So
far as there is evidence on the subject, that evidence tends to
shew that it grew, and that in its final state it was neither
wholly old nor entirely new, but doctrine more or less familiar
or following from familiar doctrine.[1] These facts are in

---

[1] This is very nearly the position of Solomon Munk, who maintained that the
ZOHAR and its connections, that is, the various tracts and fragments which enter into
the compilation, are not the inventions of an impostor, but that ancient documents
were used by the editor, including MIDRASHIM which are not now extant.—MÉLANGES
DE PHILOSOPHIE, JUIVE ET ARABE. Paris. 1859, p. 275 *et seq.* In spite of this,

course of open recognition in the academic circles which rule general opinion. Of this Dr. Schiller-Szinessy offered perhaps in his day the best evidence when he observed that " almost all that the latest critics have said concerning the age of the various TARGUMIM and MIDRASHIM," including the ZOHAR, " will have to be unsaid." [1]

III.—THE DATE AND AUTHORSHIP OF THE BOOK OF SPLENDOUR

The theory which accounts for the ZOHAR on the ground that it was written by Moses de Leon in the latter half of the thirteenth century does not depend merely on internal evidence : it is not exclusively an inference made by modern criticism from allusions to late events found here and there in the work ; it is not a presumption arising only from an alleged fact that the Spanish Jew who is suspected of the splendid imposture lived by transcribing copies of it ; [2] that it had never been heard of previously ; or that the original MS. from which R. Moses claimed to have drawn has never come to light. It is based upon supposed evidence which claims to be contemporary, or thereabouts, with the appearance of the ZOHAR itself. It may be highly probable that in the absence of such testimony, if it could pass muster, the same point would have been reached independently ; but the fact remains that, supposing the evidence has been construed rightly, then the chief charge against the ZOHAR is not a discovery of modern criticism at all ; it transpired without being sought for, and hence the case against the work is based both on external and internal grounds. It is not therefore at

---

Munk did not consider that the ZOHAR, at least in its present form, was anterior to the seventh century, but rather that the Kabbalistic developments which it represents took place in the thirteenth century, and were either influenced by Gebirol (1021–1070) or by sources common to both.—*Ibid.* pp. 276, 277.

[1] See the article on MIDRASHIM in the ninth edition of ENCYCLOPÆDIA BRITANNICA, already cited.

[2] It is accepted as such by all critics who depend on the account of the ZOHAR given in the SEPHER YUHASIN, but it seems to me that the statement has an air of fable. The ZOHAR is a very large work, and Moses de Leon must have employed a staff of copyists in order to transcribe it frequently. There is no evidence, however, that he employed any one ; but if he worked single-handed, he could not have " made large sums," as alleged, by so slow a process. It has been suggested alternatively that he profited much by the patronage of wealthy Jews, to whom he dedicated his books ; but as to this there is no conclusive evidence. It is merely an inference from the fact that he addressed several other works to co-religionists who were, *ex hypothesi,* his patrons.

first sight a weak case and must be sketched fully and frankly, that I may not be accused of any bias in the matter. At the same time it is my purpose to shew that the indictment breaks down altogether. Let us dispose first of all of the alleged external evidence. In the year 1566 there appeared in Hebrew at Constantinople a work entitled SEPHER YUHASIN, or BOOK OF GENEALOGIES, by R. Moses Abraham ben Samuel Zakut, who belongs to the second half of the fifteenth century.[1] Its point of view with regard to the ZOHAR is that the splendour of that work is truly an illumination of the world; that it contains deep secrets of the Law and of concealed Tradition in Israel; that it is conformed to the truth as regards both Written and Oral Law; that it embodies the sayings of R. Simeon ben Yohai, of the period of the Emperor Antoninus, under whose name it appears, but is really the work of his disciples; and that, finally, it did not become public till after the death of Nahmanides, namely, the second half of the thirteenth century.[2] It is therefore obvious that R. Moses Abraham must not be classed among those who opposed the ZOHAR, as some modern critics have attempted to shew.

It will seem almost incredible that in this work, which so defends the ZOHAR, a narrative should be found which appears to represent it as an imposture devised from mercenary motives by Moses de Leon, otherwise, Moses ben Shem-Tob; yet such at first sight is the case, and as such it has been accepted by those who impeach the work. The explanation is in reality simple; the narrative in question is a fragment, and the proof that its missing conclusion is really to the credit of the ZOHAR, and exculpatory as to the transcriber of that work, resides in the fact that the person whose adventures it relates became assured subsequently that the ZOHAR was not a splendid forgery, seeing that he embodied some of its principles in one of his own treatises. The most biassed of modern critics, Dr. Graetz, admits the force of this fact.

---

[1] That is to say, to the reign of Ferdinand and Isabella. He was a Jew of Salamanca, but he taught at Saragossa. When the edict of expulsion was published he retired into Portugal and was appointed Royal Historiographer by King Emanuel. The YUHASIN embraces the entire period between the creation of the world and the year 1500 A.D. It was in great repute among Latin bibliographers of Kabbalism and is cited continually by Bartolocci.

[2] Moses ben Nahman Gerondi, the Spanish Talmudist of Gerona, called also Ramban and Nahmanides, died in Palestine, circa 1270.

The narrative is concerned with the adventures of Isaac de Acco [1]—a disciple of Nahmanides—who laid claim to the performance of miracles by a transposition of Hebrew letters according to a system which he pretended that he had learned from the angels. It will be seen that he was therefore a visionary, unless a rougher criticism be held to apply. In any case, he was at Novara, in Italy, about 1293, when he heard that a Spanish Rabbin was in possession of the original ZOHAR MS., and, being very anxious to see it, he made a journey into Spain. He learned there by report that the erudite Moses Nahmanides was said to have transmitted the book to his son in Catalonia from Palestine,[2] but that the ship which bore it was driven by wind to Aragonia [3] or to Catalonia, and the precious volume came into the hands of Moses de Leon. At Valladolid Isaac de Acco made the acquaintance of the latter, who declared upon oath that he was in possession of the MS. and that it was at his home in Avila, where he would exhibit it to Isaac. They undertook a journey together with this object, but Moses de Leon died at Arevolo on the way.[4] His companion proceeded to Avila, and there prosecuted his inquiries among the relatives of the deceased. By one of these, namely, by David Rafon of Corfu, he was informed that Moses de Leon had been a spendthrift who derived great profit from his writings,[5] but neglected his wife and daughter,[6] while as for the ZOHAR he had made it up out of his own head. How far Isaac was impressed by this testimony does not appear explicitly ; but he next had recourse to a wealthy Rabbin of Avila, named Joseph, who communicated with the widow and daughter of Moses, offering for the maiden the hand of his son and a substantial dowry if they would produce the original MS. of the ZOHAR. The women had been left in poor circumstances, and there was every reason to suppose that they would comply gladly. They concurred, however,

---

[1] *I.e.*, Acre, besieged by the Sultan of Egypt in 1291. Isaac was one of the Jewish refugees from that city, and seems to have suffered imprisonment for a time.

[2] It is curious that the disciple should first learn that his master was in possession of such a treasure by a floating rumour from a great distance.

[3] The reference is probably to Alicante, as Arragon has no seaboard.

[4] So far the account represents Moses de Leon as acting with sincerity in the matter.

[5] It is obvious that the statement has no evidential character.

[6] There is evidence, on the contrary, (1) that when elected Rabbi of the Synagogue at Avila, his poverty was such that he could not defray the expenses of the journey, and (2) that his emoluments in that position did not enable him to support his family.—See SEPHARDIM, or the *History of the Jews in Spain and Portugal*, by JAMES FINN, 1841, pp. 303, 304.

in affirming that there was no such MS., that the dead man had composed the work out of his own head and written it with his own hand.[1] His quest having thus failed, Isaac de Acco left Avila and proceeded to Talavera, where he met with R. Joseph ben Todros, and Jacob, a pupil of Moses, both of whom, in reply to his inquiries, affirmed that the genuine ZOHAR was in the hands of Moses de Leon, as they had proved conclusively. The nature of the proof does not appear, and the account of Isaac breaks off abruptly in the middle of a sentence describing some testimony which he received at Toledo as to an ancient Rabbin, named Jacob, who had " testified by heaven and earth that the book ZOHAR, of which R. Simeon ben Yohai is the author * * *."

I have passed over purposely in this brief account several minor details which have awakened suspicion as to the honesty of the narrative, for it is unnecessary to confuse the issues. The point is that it closes with a solemn testimony to the authenticity of the ZOHAR, and by the course which he took subsequently Isaac de Acco must have concluded to abide by this. Assuming that the narrative is authentic, the evidence which was set aside as insufficient by the one person who has recorded it cannot be accepted by impartial criticism unenforced by other considerations. So far therefore as the account in the SEPHER YUHASIN is concerned, it is not proved that Moses de Leon wrote the ZOHAR " out of his own head."[2] R. Moses Abraham himself mentions an opinion that he did produce it under the guidance of the Writing Name, *i.e.*, by angelic revelation ; but I do not conceive that it is necessary to discuss this possibility.

The state of the case as it stands is confused, and most persons who have taken part in the controversy have been led into more or less contradiction. Those who have regarded

---

[1] Hence he did not employ transcribers, and whatever price he may have obtained for copies of the work he could not have multiplied many. If assiduous, he could have had no time for squandering ; if idle, no money to spend. Moreover, he must have had a copy of his invention from which to make his transcripts and there would have been that at least in the house, to be shewn and seen.

[2] Outside this document there is, moreover, no proof, so far as I am aware, that he was even connected with it as transcriber. If, however, he did act in this capacity, and as its editor, codifier, or what not, it is desirable to point out that the antiquity of the ZOHAR is not certified for this reason. Finally, speaking still under correction, the YUHASIN is the one authority by which we can fix so important a date as the death of Moses de Leon. Who was the Rabbi of this name and place, for whom Samuel, son of Isaac, transcribed a copy of the MOREH, *anno* 1452, which copy is still preserved in the Günglung Library, Paris ? It is numbered 771, according to Friedlander's preface to the third volume of his version of Maimonides, p. xiv.

Moses de Leon as nothing more than a transcriber have had to reckon as they could with certain damaging references to late events which are found in the ZOHAR, and their explanations are often quite worthless ; those who regard the transcriber as the concealed author have had to meet as they might the extreme difficulty of supposing that such a collection was the production of one individual, and that individual Moses de Leon. Their explanations also are of little value and are for the most part ingenious or other assumptions.

The internal evidence against the ZOHAR may be reduced under the following heads :

(1) It refers to the vowel points which are alleged to have been invented in post-Talmudic times.[1] (2) It quotes or borrows from a book entitled the DUTIES OF THE HEART, written by a Jew of Saragossa,[2] about the middle of the eleventh century. (3) It mentions two kinds of Phylacteries, or Tephilin, which fact is supposed to prove the late origin of the entire work.[3] (4) It quotes authorities posterior to its alleged period. (5) It is written in Aramaic, whereas at the period to which it is ascribed—meaning presumably that of R. Simeon—Aramaic was the vernacular, while Hebrew was made use of in religious writings.

These difficulties are met by defenders of the ZOHAR in the following way :

(1) The vowel points are not the invention of times posterior to the TALMUD ; the proof is that they are mentioned in the TALMUD, and there is no question that this work is long anterior to the thirteenth century, being the period of Moses de Leon. In the TALMUD they are said to have been a rule given to Moses the Prophet on Mount Sinai.[4] The pre-

---

[1] Elias Levita, a German Jew of the sixteenth century, was one of the first to affirm the late institution of the points, which he ascribed to the Jews of Tiberias about the beginning of the sixth century. In reply to this it has been advanced that at the period the schools of Judæa had been closed, and that Jewish learning was then centred at Babylon (see David Levi : LINGUA SACRA, part i. c. iii. § 1, London, 1785). Ginsburg, however, adopts the theory of Levita, subject to the modification that they were introduced by the Karaite, R. Mocha, at the end of the sixth century. David Levi, on the other hand, makes their reception by the Karaite Jews a proof of their antiquity, because they were " professed enemies to tradition and innovation." Unfortunately, there are no pointed Hebrew MSS. prior to the tenth century.

[2] R. Behai ben Joseph Ibn Bakoda.

[3] For a general description of the TEPHILIN, see Basnage : HISTOIRE DES JUIFS, tom. iii. pp. 752 *et seq.* Any dictionary will tell the unversed reader that the Phylactery was a strip of parchment inscribed with certain passages from the Pentateuch. It was worn on the forehead, otherwise on forehead and arm, during prayer.

[4] Treatise NEDAREEM, also BAB. MEGILLAH, BAB. BEROCOTH, and BAB. ERUBIN.

Christian existence of the point system, with the exception of a very few cases occurring in the Pentateuch, which, moreover, are not vowel-points, this is one thing, and must be left to those who affirm it ; its existence in early post-Talmudic times [1] is another, and all that is required in the present case to destroy the validity of this objection to the reasonable antiquity, as affirmed, of the ZOHAR.[2]

(2) The treatise on the DUTIES OF THE HEART is certainly a work of the eleventh century, but it is advanced that its author himself borrowed from the ZOHAR in an early form, the existence of which is traceable, from Talmudic references, under the name of MIDRASH of Rabbi Simeon ben Yohai.[3] It is said also that the author was a contemporary of Rabbi Abraham, who wrote a commentary of repute upon the BOOK OF FORMATION, but this personage, identified by some dreamers as the pretended instructor of Nicholas Flamel in the secrets of Alchemy, died at the close of the twelfth century. We may choose as we please between the alternatives offered, but the fact remains that the ZOHAR contains matter which is found in a work belonging to the eleventh century.

(3) The existence of two kinds of Phylacteries arose through a difference of rabbinical opinion as to the Scriptural passages to be used on them. The question is whether this difference of opinion occurred in the eleventh century and later, or whether it originated in earlier Talmudic times. Certain statements and inferences therefrom are set forth by defenders of the ZOHAR in support of the second view ; but the use of two kinds of Phylacteries before the tenth century has not been demonstrated.

This at its value is, moreover, the testimony of the ZOHAR, obviously reproducing current legend, or borrowing from the traditional storehouse of the TALMUD.

[1] See David Levi, *op. cit.*, who says that in several places of the BABYLONIAN TALMUD mention is made of " the distinction of the accents, and, in particular, of the accents of the law, which might be shewn and pointed at by the hand, consequently they must be visible marks or figures, and are to be understood both of the vowel points and accents." Though belonging to an early period of the controversy, Levi's defence is still worth reading. Basnage, tom. ii. p. 763, refers the invention to the eleventh century.

[2] The commentary of St. Jerome on Jeremiah has been regarded as positive proof that the vowel signs were not in existence at his day. A critical dissertation on their antiquity will be found in MÉMOIRES DE LITTÉRATURE DE L'ACADÉMIE DES INSCRIPTIONS ET BELLES LETTRES, *Tome* xx., pp. 22 *et seq.* It tends to prove that vowel-points existed in the middle of the third century A.D.

[3] According to Jellinek the great classic of the Kabbalah has passed under three names : (*a*) MIDRASH of Rabbi Simeon ben Yohai ; (*b*) MIDRASH : Let there be Light ! (*c*) ZOHAR, *i.e.*, Splendour or Light, after Daniel xii. 3.—DIE KABBALA, *oder die Religions philosophie der Hebraëi von Franck*. Leipsic, 1844. The MIDRASH is a symbolical narrative or account.

(4) The citation by the ZOHAR of late authorities belonging to the Amoraim school is met by representing it in its extant form as the growth of several centuries, which is true of much early Hebrew literature, canonical or not. The indirect strength of this view is considerable; but it is weakened by its supporters when they attempt to argue that had the ZOHAR been forged by Moses de Leon he would have avoided the citation of later authorities. The history of literary impostures points wholly in the opposite direction, and the objection demonstrates quite clearly that the work as we have it is later than its latest authority. For it to be otherwise is impossible. How the late authorities came to be included is a distinct matter.

(5) When Isaac de Acco set out on his quest for the original MS. of the ZOHAR, he is recorded to have said: " If it be written in the Jerusalem idiom it is genuine, but if in Hebrew it is not." The value of an objection to the ZOHAR founded on its use of Aramaic is here exhibited by the express statement of a Jewish witness referred to the thirteenth century.[1] It is argued furthermore, by its defenders: (a) That Aramaic is the language of the Targums, which are mystical; (b) That the uncanonical language is used to increase the symbolism, but this may be regarded as a subtlety; (c) That supposing the antiquity of the ZOHAR, the scribe of R. Simeon ben Yohai was undoubtedly the Rabbi Abbah whom it mentions, and he as a Babylonian must have been thoroughly conversant with Aramaic;[2] (d) That supposing the ZOHAR to be a forgery produced by Moses de Leon, he was more likely to have written it in Hebrew, which is the language of his other books.[3]

---

[1] Compare the article s.v. MIDRASHIM in the ninth edition of the ENCYCLOPÆDIA BRITANNICA, by Dr. Schiller-Szinessy, Reader in Talmudic at Cambridge. " The ZOHAR was begun in Palestine late in the second or early in the third century, A.D., and finished at the latest in the sixth or the seventh century. It is impossible that it should have been composed after that time and before the Renaissance, as both language and contents clearly shew."

[2] There is no evidence for the editorship of R. Abbah, but if anything Zoharic was committed to writing in the second century there might be ground for accepting the express statement of the LESSER HOLY SYNOD that the recorder was the son of R. Simeon, obviously and of course in respect only of that particular text.

[3] On the entire question compare Munk: MÉLANGES DE PHILOSOPHIE, JUIVE ET ARABE, pp. 280, 281. " The Aramean dialect of the ZOHAR is not that of Daniel and Ezra, of the Chaldaic Paraphrase of Onkelos and Jonathan, of the Targums, the Talmuds, the MIDRASHIM or the Gueonîm, but an incorrect and most corrupt mixture of all." Munk also sees traces in the ZOHAR of unfamiliarity with the language used. By this a double and altogether intolerable burden seems placed on the shoulders of its reputed forger. The question raised by Franck in 1843 remains still pertinent and still

From these objections and these answers the general conclusion must be that the internal evidence for the late origin of the bulk of the ZOHAR as it stands is not of any real force. The two tabulations have by no means exhausted the difficulties or the counter-evidence, as to which, even at the present day, Franck is in many cases the best and certainly the most lucid expositor.[1] Putting aside the alleged absence of Christian influence, if not of all reference to Christianity, his remarks on the absence of Aristotelian influence, and some points of the argument from the dialect in which the work is written, seem to possess as much force as they did originally in 1843. But the strength of the case in favour of the ZOHAR is also the strength of the chief objection against it. It does quote later authorities, but this may exhibit that it grew like the Talmudic writings and several of the canonical Hebrew books. It has been well urged that if contemporary with the TALMUD, the latter ought to have mentioned it, and it is replied that it does, not, however, under the catchword of its late name, but by the title of the Secret Learning, and by other titles which have been mentioned in this section. It would exceed my province to pursue the subject further. The minute considerations are of course highly technical, and there are some on both sides which it is wise to abstain from pressing. One of these is the argument that Moses de Leon was an unlikely person to have written such a work as the ZOHAR, because he was intellectually and morally unfit.[2] I have noted that he was unlikely, but possibilities of this kind can only be determined by the event. Many great books

---

unanswered :—How could Moses de Leon at the beginning of the fourteenth century treat matters of the most elevated order in an idiom which the most distinguished scholars had been for so long content merely to understand and which, on this hypothesis, had not produced a single work capable of serving him as a model ?—LA KABBALE, p. 104.

[1] On the opposing side there is negative force at its value in one contention of Karppe (op. cit., pp. 307, 308). He cites Juda Hadessi and his ESHKOL HAKOFER, written in 1148 and exhibiting vast knowledge of Jewish religious and philosophical tendencies. It inveighs bitterly against the anthropomorphisms of the Talmudists and cites everything of this nature in rabbinical literature, but it says no word about the ZOHAR, the inference being that if this great and occasionally most anthropomorphic collection had been in existence at his period Juda Hadessi must have known and could not have failed to cite it.

[2] Dr. Schiller-Szinessy shews that he was proud of the authorship of his books, and hence unlikely to conceal his hand in the composition of any ; but this argument also must not be pressed too far. The same writer terms him an inferior Kabbalist, and it seems admitted on all sides that his original books are poor in quality. From these works Jellinek has extracted passages which are parallel to others in the ZOHAR and some critics have thence concluded an identity of authorship. In any other branch of research such parallels would be held to prove nothing.

have been produced by those who were antecedently improbable, and after all, at the best, we know Moses de Leon only through his other writings and the alleged testimony of a hostile relative. There is no doubt that the ZOHAR was to some extent sprung upon the Jewish people at the period of its appearance. The manner of its reception was not unmixed; it received the kind of welcome which would be given to a work which may have been old as regards its materials, though unfamiliar—less or more—in its form, and this is sufficient to account for any silence of previous authorities, while in the shaping of those materials and the impressing of that form the individual who is supposed to have multiplied copies may have had a hand.[1]

IV.—THE AGE OF ZOHARIC TRADITION

It must not be supposed that the field of criticism is occupied entirely by a hypothesis of unmixed fraud, or that this hypothesis has fastened always upon the same person.[2] The most favoured delinquent is, of course, Moses de Leon, because he is reported to have circulated the ZOHAR, but occasionally he appears as the tool of other conspirators. Thus, Samuel Cahen maintained that the Zoharic writings were composed by a convocation of converted Rabbins, assembled for the purpose in a Spanish monastery, employing Moses as their publisher, and hence the Church itself might almost figure as

---

[1] And by those who accept this view it is considered that he interfered only to disfigure it. The view itself is not to be regarded as advanced altogether on my own behalf, for I have done little more than summarise and deduce from intimations on the part of apologetic writers, without feeling that it can be satisfactory to either side. A long debate is possible on the nature of alleged materials which were or might be old ; while if admitted as of fact, it does not follow that they give evidence of a Secret Tradition corresponding to that of the ZOHAR and perpetuated by reception from an early period. Some things were obviously familiar, including Yetziratic notions, and developments therefrom would have been welcome to certain rabbinical minds. It may be noted that the JEWISH ENCYCLOPÆDIA, *s.v.* ZOHAR, concludes that the text originated among Persian Jews of the eighth and following centuries. But the same epoch-marking work has a yet longer study, *s.v.* CABALA, from which it may be gathered (1) that the testimony of Joseph ben Judah in the second half of the second century seems to indicate the existence of an esoteric doctrine at that time in the world of Jewry and its connection with the name of Johanan ben Zakkai, who lived before and after the destruction of Jerusalem ; (2) that the apocalyptic literature " belonging to the second and first pre-Christian centuries contained the chief elements of the Kabbalah " ; (3) that one thousand years before the supposed date of SEPHER YETZIRAH the BOOK OF JUBILEES offers a cosmogony based like that on the letters of the Hebrew Alphabet.
[2] Basnage is inclined to refer the original ZOHAR to the tenth century, and, following Bartolocci (BIBLIOTHECA RABBINICA, t. iv. p. 82), represents Moses de Leon as in possession of several exemplars, which he amplified.—HISTOIRE DES JUIFS, t. ii. 781 ; t. v. 1775, 1776.

an accomplice.[1] Others, like M. H. Landauer,[2] argue that
the true author was Abraham ben Samuel Abulafia,[3] while the
voice of Graetz was raised in favour of the school of Abraham
ben David of Posquière—who belonged to the twelfth
century.[4] Isaac the Blind of Narbonne [5]—*ob. circa* 1219—is
also a favoured name, and to him it seems indubitable, in any
case, that Kabbalism owed something of development and of
impulse. Meanwhile this extreme opinion in all its varieties
is balanced by counterviews which also denaturalise the
literature. It may be suspected therefore with reason that on
both sides there is an error of enthusiasm : there are the
children of intelligence who look to find the Secret Doctrine
of Judea a mere transcript from that of Egypt, or whatever
land is for them the well-spring of all truth and all truly
sacred knowledge. These remember, for example, that
Abraham was in Egypt, and, accepting at once the fairy-tale
attribution of the BOOK OF FORMATION to the patriarch, conclude that this document is older than the RITUAL OF THE
DEAD. It is useless to reason with those whose confidence
is not shaken in the face of impossibilities, whose imagination
can bridge all gulfs in evidence by fantastic suppositions.
On the other hand, there is the crass criticism which rules off a
literature by a single stroke of the pen into the region of
forgery and imposture, as it rules off all psychical phenomena
into that of imposture or hallucination. It does not matter
that this criticism is always in disgrace. It proved Troy town
to be solar mythos till Troy town was excavated ; it under-
mined, as it believed, the Book of Daniel till fresh archæo-

---

[1] At the opposite extreme was Christianus Schœttgenius in his considerable work,
HORÆ HEBRAICÆ ET TALMUDICÆ *in Theologiam Judæorum Dogmaticam antiquam et
orthodoxam de Messia impensæ*, 2 vols., Dresden and Leipsic, 1733, 1742. See vol. ii.
Rabbinicorum Lectionum Liber Secundus, c. ii., *docens R. Simeonem filium Jochai, auctorem
Libri Sohar, Religionem fuisse Christianam*. There are eight heads to the argument, the
most important being that the ZOHAR contains the precise, orthodox doctrine concerning
the Messiah and His divine and human nature, and this not in one place or mysteriously,
but in many and openly. As regards Samuel Cahen, I know his fantastic story at
second hand only and have failed to trace its source, but it is buried somewhere in
what is called his " Great French Bible."

[2] He maintained the apocryphal nature of the Isaac de Acco story and that the
ZOHAR did not come into general knowledge till a much later period. See ORIENT
LIT., vi, 710–713, 1845–46.

[3] A prophet and Messiah of his period, A.D. 1240–1291, who is said to have termed
his system " a prophetical Kabbalah."

[4] He has been described as the chief Talmudic authority of his period in Southern
France, but most of his works are lost.

[5] That is, Isaac ben Abraham, referred also to Posquière. He has been termed
" father of the Kabbalah," and is supposed to have conferred on the Ten SEPHIROTH
those names by which they are known.

logical discoveries cast it into the pit which it had dug. It is truly not less stupid, and it is far less engaging, than the opposed excess.[1]

The antiquity of the Zohar does not depend so much upon the date of its documents as on that which may belong to its Tradition.[2] It is clear that the speculations, for example, of mediæval Rabbins, referred backward in virtue of a fabulous claim to the dawn of the Christian era, are in a worse position than the HIERARCHIES of pseudo-Dionysius, and that their importance, if any, will differ in kind rather than degree from that which must attach to a Tradition which interlinks with the far past.[3] We are therefore more concerned in ascertaining the state in which modern criticism has left the content of the ZOHAR than the form in which it is presented to us. The early students of the work, who accepted and defended its antiquity, did not make this saving distinction, and in many instances modern hostility does not make it either. Upon the surface of the history of Kabbalistic criticism the first presumption is, of course, unfavourable to any hypothesis of antiquity, because this would seem to have been admitted in days when scholarship was equipped insufficiently for the determination of such a question. In the light of fuller knowledge it will be thought that the claim has lapsed, or remains only as a pious belief prevailing among an uncritical minority, a few persons being always found whose mental bias predisposes them to the defence of exploded views. It happens, however, in the present case that an indiscriminate rejection is not much less superficial than an overcredulous acquiescence in a non-proven claim. Moreover, the history of debated questions of this kind teaches another lesson, and the closest approximation to truth is found usually in the mean of extreme views. Now, in the history of Zoharic criticism we find that the old students not only accepted the claim of the Tradition to antiquity, and were disposed to understand the

---

[1] In Kabbalistic criticism its typical representative is Graetz, and one can scarcely conjecture by what principle he was guided in his estimate of Moses de Leon. It is the height of exaggeration, the account in the YUHASIN transcendentalised till it almost exceeds recognition.

[2] According to Edersheim in his JEWISH SOCIETY AT THE TIME OF JESUS CHRIST, " there existed indubitably " at this epoch " a mass of doctrines and speculations which was concealed carefully from the multitude " and even, he adds, from ordinary scholars. He says also that it bore then, as it bears now, the name of Kabbalah.

[3] It should be added, however, that their importance and validity might be so great and unchallengable that the question of their date would pass into the background.

genealogy more or less literally, but that further they regarded
the books which contain both as belonging to certain dates
and produced by certain writers without much suspicion, on
the simple authority of the literature.[1]   Later scholars, on the
other hand, having found something to countenance the
modern origin of the documents, have overlooked frequently
the possible antiquity of their Tradition.   The question of
this antiquity as something which calls to be surveyed apart
from the date of publication will explain what I mean by
possible moderate and middle views in which the truth
should be sought.   If we fail entirely here we may regard the
case as closed, it being understood that essential values in
respect of *Theosophia Mystica* remain over.

I believe that a careful and unbiassed comparison of all the
evidence will lead us to conclude that there are elements of
old doctrine in the ZOHAR : their exact antiquity is, in part,
highly speculative, but it is quite sufficient to invest them
with considerable interest, from this point of view only.   Like
the SEPHER YETZIRAH, some of it may be even referable to
a comparatively remote period.   I refer here to Yetziratic
notions concerning the virtue of Divine Names, for this also
is found in the ZOHAR, as it is found abundantly in the
TALMUD : a residuum of its teaching concerning angels and
demons may be also an inheritance from Babylon.   All this,
however, is the negligible part of the ZOHAR, as it is the
negligible, if curious, part of Talmudic literature.   With
regard to the Scriptural exegesis which constitutes so large a
portion of it, we shall not offend possibility by supposing that
some of it may be an obscure transmission from Talmudic
times.[2]   If we take the hints and references found in the
Talmuds to the existence of a Mystical Tradition, and follow
them through the large mystical literature which intervened

---

[1] Some modern ecclesiastical historians, for no solid reason, incline to this view.
Thus, we have in Dean Hook's compilation, A CHURCH DICTIONARY (fourteenth
edition, London, 1887), the statement that the chief Kabbalistic author was Simeon
ben Yohai, and also that most of the heretics in the primitive Christian Church fell into
the vain conceits of the Kabbalah, particularly the Gnostics, Valentinians and Basilidians.
There is perhaps no more warrant for the second than the first view, but it has been
advanced warmly, as readers of Matter's HISTOIRE DU GNOSTICISME and of King's
GNOSTICS will not need to be told.   It is understood, however, that the day of these
works, in so far as the second can be said to have had a day, has some time ceased to be.

[2] In other words, we may follow the learned author of the article on the MIDRASHIM
in the ENCYCLOPÆDIA BRITANNICA, who says that the nucleus of the work is of Mishnic
times and that R. Simeon was its author in the same sense that R. Johanan was of the
PALESTINE TALMUD, namely, that he gave the first impulse to its composition.

between those works and the ZOHAR as we now have it, we shall be led not to the conclusion of the mere occultist and dreamer, that there was a great body of Secret Doctrine which became revealed gradually, but that there was a kernel of Tradition which was planted in the secret heart of Israel, which many watered and fostered, till the growth at length put forth, not without something of transformation and of suddenness, the strange flower of the ZOHAR. As regards form its most ancient part is probably the BOOK OF CONCEAL-MENT, but it is entirely improbable that any conspicuous portion could have existed in writing till after the sixth century, while the growth of most of it is probably much later and subsequent to the latest date which can be ascribed to SEPHER YETZIRAH.[1] It is advanced, as we have seen, by its defenders that the ZOHAR is a subject of reference in several texts both of the BABYLONIAN and JERUSALEM TALMUD under the name of the MIDRASH of Simeon ben Yohai, and the parallels between Talmudic sayings attributed to this Rabbi have been compared with the extant work in order to exhibit their identity. The existence of a text entitled MYSTERIES OF SIMEON BEN YOHAI before the middle of the eleventh century and possibly much earlier, is acknowledged by Dr. Graetz. It is reasonable therefore to conclude that early written and oral materials entered into the composition of the ZOHAR as we now possess it.[2] This is the most that can be urged, and this is sufficient to prove that no one person wrote it out of his own head.[3]

It must be confessed, on the other hand, that the legend

---

[1] I put forward this hypothesis because Dr. Schiller-Szinessy has not stated his reasons why it is impossible that it should have been later than the seventh century, and subject to the conclusiveness of those reasons. We may speculate what Dr. Szinessy would have thought of Israel Zangwill, had he read the epilogue to the CHILDREN OF THE GHETTO, in which it is remarked casually that the ZOHAR was "forged by a Spanish Jew in the thirteenth century." By the way, are copies of the ZOHAR likely to be found in a small room, used as a synagogue, outside Jerusalem and so poor that it is bare even of seats?

[2] An interesting article by M. Nicolas in Lichtenberger's ENCYCLOPÉDIE DES SCIENCES RELIGIEUSES, t. xi. s.v. CABALE (Paris, 1877), regards it as certain that the philosophical speculations which compose the Kabbalah generally began to form during the century which preceded the Christian era; but they were oral, imparted to a few only, and under the seal of secrecy. Unfortunately, the article is not trust-worthy, representing, as it does, the AIN SOPH doctrine to be part of the SEPHER YETZIRAH.

[3] Compare Blunt's DICTIONARY OF DOCTRINAL AND HISTORICAL THEOLOGY, which argues that the variety of style and the disjointed character of its contents shew that the ZOHAR is the growth of ages. But Blunt's work indicates no real acquaintance with the Kabbalah and its criticism.

which attributes its origin to R. Simeon ben Yohai seems to have made an unfortunate choice, for this great authority of the TALMUD represents a reaction against the tendencies attributed—rightly or not—to R. Akiba, and there is some evidence for believing that he did not investigate the hidden meaning of Scripture, but rather its rational principles. He is described by a modern writer as cold, exclusive and stoical. At the same time, if we accept the existence of a genuine Tradition which became incorporated in the ZOHAR, it is difficult to reject its leading and central figure.[1]

If we turn now for a moment to the unequipped standpoint of so-called modern occultism we shall see that so far we have no warrant for connecting the chief cycle of Kabbalistic literature with the high antiquity to which occultists incline.[2] While we leave them once more in full possession of the alleged virtue inherent in Divine Names, and perhaps with some elements of legend concerning angels and demons, we are forced to take all that remains a considerable distance into the Christian era. But the ZOHAR, although it embodies the entire content of Kabbalistic doctrine, is not the sole nor the earliest storehouse of that doctrine, and we have next to consider whether the antiquity of the metaphysical Tradition is to be inferred from its points of contact and correspondence with other theosophical systems which have prevailed in the past.

V.—ALLEGED SOURCES OF KABBALISTIC DOCTRINE

On the basis of considerations so far enumerated, it would appear that we are warranted in regarding some part at least of the materials incorporated by the ZOHAR as earlier than

---

[1] The author of the article CABALA in Herzog's REAL ENCYCKLOPÄDIE takes a middle view, namely, that the ZOHAR is not the work of Moses de Leon, nor is it of R. Simeon's period, though its doctrines are referable to him. It was completed in the eighth century. The evidence adduced for this view seems inconclusive, so far as the article is concerned.

[2] Take, for example, the following typical instance of the exaggerations which have found currency on this subject. " The origin of the Kabbalah is lost in the night of of time. Is it of India or of Egypt ? We do not know ; but it is certain that to Egyptians and Indians it was alike known. Pythagoras returned with it into Greece after his travels in the East, then the region of the light. One asks vainly whether its first revelation was divine or the product of inspiration."—Desbarrolles : LES MYSTÈRES DE LA MAIN, 14me édition, Paris, n.d. Desbarrolles knew nothing of the Kabbalah, but he reflected his friend Éliphas Lévi, who claimed knowledge but wrote frequently in the same distracted strain.

the period of their promulgation. We cannot say whether the SEPHER YETZIRAH is much anterior to the ninth century.[1] But both works are in connection with Talmudic times and, within the limits of the Christian centuries, there seems therefore to have been an esoteric tradition in Israel.[2] Whether it existed prior to Christianity itself is the next concern of our inquiry. At this point the difficulties begin to multiply, because the range of research is exceedingly large, and it has been covered in every direction by successive generations of hardy speculators. We must proceed step by step and shall do well to begin first of all by a general survey of the subject.

The doctrines of the Kabbalah have been referred for their origin to almost every philosophic and religious system of antiquity, and its points of alleged correspondence with each have been tabulated with some care. They have been derived from Akkadia, from India, from China, from ancient Egypt,[3] from Platonism and Neo-Platonism, from the categories of Aristotle, from early Christian Gnosticism.[4] The most reasonable conclusion which can be drawn, I think, from all this rival evidence—in so far as it can claim the term—is that it is not derived from any one of these sources specifically and exclusively, but rather that the human mind, when engaged on certain fundamental and perhaps insoluble problems of the universe, tends independently to reach conclusions that are similar and may even wear sometimes an aspect of literal identity ; that the Kabbalah is largely an outcome of such

[1] But we can say that one of the most pronounced opponents of Jewish Theosophy assigns it to early Gnostic times.—See Grätz : GESCHICHTE DER JUDEN, 11 vols., 1853–1870.

[2] One of the most credulous and also most pretentious exponents of the English school of Kabbalism in a debased occult interest states that, according to Hebrew Tradition, the doctrines of the oldest portions of the ZOHAR are antecedent to the Second Temple.—W. Wynn Westcott, SEPHER YETZIRAH. Translated from the Hebrew. Second edition. London, 1893. A third edition has been published recently, since the decease of the author.

[3] This is the view which obtained most widely among French occultists. " It is in Egyptian science," says Stanislas de Guaita, " carried from Mitzraïm by Moses at the exodus of the Sons of Israel, that we must discern the source of that Sacred Tradition transmitted among the Jews from generation to generation, by the oral way, down to the disciples of Simeon ben Yohai, who wrote, at the dictation of this master, about the second century of the Christian era, the GREAT BOOK OF THE LIGHT (ZOHAR)." —AU SEUIL DU MYSTÈRE, pp. 183, 184. The last statement is, of course, merely an assumption of the vital point at issue, and the speculations of the French Marquis are worth as much and as little as the rest of the rubbish-heap which used to pass in Paris for occult learning and criticism. It will be noted that R. Simeon is referred to the second instead of the first century.

[4] Even the so-called " Symbols of Pythagoras " have been approximated to Kabbalistic teaching. See COLLECTANEA HERMETICA, edited by W. Wynn Westcott, vol. v. id est, SOMNIUM SCIPIONIS, &c., London, 1894.

unaided research ; that its results are in the main *sui generis*, but that they offer points of contact with other attempts of the kind in all ages and nations ; and that they owe something to other traditions and memorials of the past, in part by filtration therefrom, but in part also because they belong thereto and were born among them. We must, of course, distinguish the fundamental part of the Kabbalah from its developments. Included in the first class are the doctrine of the Ten Emanations, that of AIN SOPH, of the MACROPROSOPUS and MICROPROSOPUS, some of which may go far back in the history of post-Christian Jewish literature, indeed almost to Talmudic times. They are mentioned of necessity here, but must be unfolded and explained later. The subsequent developments possess a complexion reflected from many sources, not excluding the scholastic philosophy of Christian Europe during the Middle Ages.[1] AIN SOPH is that final concept of the Deity which is reached by all true metaphysics ; it is not necessary to suppose that it was derived from Babylonian initiations during the exile of seventy years, or from Greek speculation at Alexandria : it may be regarded more probably as a product of the unfinished exile of Christian centuries, a fruit of first-hand reflection by the theosophical mind of Jewry on problems present to the mind, but not altogether untinctured by the debates which encompassed it at different centres of culture. It is the ultimate point of theosophical speculation possible to the human mind, at which the mind tends always to arrive. The doctrine of the SEPHIROTH is, in its turn, an intelligible form of another widespread device of old-world thought when it sought to bridge the gulf between finite and infinite, between absolute purity and that material world which, in one or other way, seems to have been regarded always as unclean. The MACROPROSOPUS and MICROPROSOPUS, whether late or early in Jewish literature, are late at least in the history of human speculation. They are an attempt to distinguish between God as He is in Himself and in His relation with His children. As might be expected, they are the most characteristic of Jewry and, as such, offer the least connection with any external system. Yet they have some points of contact. As regards each and all, given the times and the circumstances, the people and their places, they

---

[1] I refer here to the Kabbalistic schools of Isaac de Loria and Moses of Cordova.

are the kind of speculative doctrine which one might have expected *à priori*. The peculiar conventional forms under which they are conveyed were characteristic of the rabbinical mind, its own and no other's throughout. We shall find that some of them are crude and monstrous; but it happens that the Secret Tradition at its highest can be separated from its extravagant and materialistic developments.

When we remember the persistence of Tradition which has characterised the most persistent of all races, when we remember that the Jew of the Christian Dispensation may be said to have lived in the remembrance of his glory passed away, we can believe that he was encompassed by an atmosphere of legend on which his fervid mind was at work continually, out of which he never stepped, and it would be unreasonable to suppose that all his literature, like all his thought, was not tinctured profoundly by this his intellectual environment. But it is a wide and an unwarrantable step from the belief in such a natural and inevitable operation to a belief that Jewish Tradition must or may be referred to one distinctive source in the past, from which it was perpetuated by some conventional transmission, as occult writers suppose, and some others also who have no such bias towards the mysterious to intervene in apology for their opinion. We have no ground for affirming with Basnage [1] that old Egypt is the true nursery of the Kabbalah, though it is quite possible that Israel brought something from the Nile valley which does not appear in the Pentateuch. Nor are we justified in agreeing with a quondam Grand Master of the Ancient and Accepted Rite of Freemasonry, United States Southern Jurisdiction, when he suggests a direct communication of doctrine from the religion of Zoroaster [2] to Kabbalism which must be referred to the period of the exile. [3] That the Jews may have derived something from Babylon I have noted already, and amidst their chequered experience under Persian domination, after their final scattering, possibly the great body

---

[1] L. iii. c. xiv.

[2] For some tables indicating " the harmony and identity of the Chaldean philosophy with the Hebrew Kabbalah," see CHALDEAN ORACLES OF ZOROASTER, edited by *Sapere Aude*, London, 1895, pp. 8–11. The true value of such parallels is shewn by such frenzied developments as Archbishop Meurin's SYNAGOGUE DE SATAN, which will be noticed in Book X. § 18. *Sapere Aude* was a pseudonym adopted by Wynn Westcott in some English occult circles.

[3] MORALS AND DOGMA, Charleston, A.M. 5641, pp. 266, 267, and elsewhere throughout the compilation. Compare Matter: HISTOIRE CRITIQUE DU GNOSTICISME. It refers the Gnostic systems to the ZENDAVESTA and Kabbalah.

of Haggada may have received increment and colouring. More fantastic theorists have imagined that not only is there a Chinese Kabbalah, but that it is the source of that which was in Israel. That the great unknown empire, in which all things from Alchemy to the art of printing are said to have germinated, possessed and still possesses a body of traditional lore, of so-called secret teaching,[1] is mere commonplace on which there is no call to insist, and if some persons will be so foolish as to term this Kabbalah, as if in the sense of Israel, it is idle to dispute with them about the improper and confusing use of a mere word. That the book called YI-KING,[2] or MUTATION, contains an Esoteric Religious Tradition which has, as it is affirmed, some analogies with Kabbalistic doctrine, is neither surprising nor significant of anything except the irresistible tendency of the human mind to reflect after much the same manner, in all lands and times, upon mysteries that are everywhere the same, ever urgent, ever recurring. Such analogies do not prove, as dreamers would have us believe, the existence of a conventional Wisdom-Religion, unfolded through ages of initiation. In the natural order, the truly fundamental religion is the common ground of all, which stands in need of no formal perpetuation, as it is inborn in the heart and mind of humanity.[3] And yet the undoubted existence of the Mongolian race in Mesopotamia almost at the dawn of history may suggest that the Semite drew something from Mongolian Chaldea even in the days of Abraham,[4] as afterwards the Jew of Babylon may have had a certain contact with Confucianism in its earliest form. We may admit, readily and reasonably, that the Jew received everywhere and always retained the reception, provided that we leave him

---

[1] In conformity with which Bryant's ANALYSIS OF ANCIENT MYTHOLOGY (vol. i. p. 94) and Oliver's HISTORY OF INITIATION (pp. 79 *et seq.*) would have us believe that there were Mysteries in China " similar to those of India," which again were more or less the same as those that flourished subsequently in Greece.

[2] For some information concerning this work and its Kabbalistic analogies, see L'INITIATION, *revue philosophique des Hautes Études*, tom. xxxvii. No. 3, Dec., 1897. Paris. *S.v. Yi-King, Tao-see, Tao-te-King et la Numération*, pp. 266 *et seq.* Also Eugène Nus : A LA RECHERCHE DES DESTINÉS. Paris, 1892.

[3] I refer here to sacramental and not to natural religion so-called.

[4] " The power of the Mongol rulers of Chaldea, about the time of Abraham, was far more extensive than that of the contemporary rulers of Thebes and of the Delta, and the victories of the great eighteenth dynasty in Egypt, extending over some three centuries at most, form only a passing episode in the story of Asiatic civilisation, which dates back probably earlier than the time of the Pyramids, which was native and original, and from which Egypt borrowed much in the days of its greatest rulers."— BABYLONIAN DISCOVERIES, EDINBURGH REVIEW, April, 1898.

everywhere his own intellectual initiative, and bear in mr that the process was everywhere natural and informal, ne arbitrary and conventional.

Passing over the regions of wild surmise in which Odin the Norse God becomes identified with the Kabbalistic ABBA, the Supernal Father; Frea with AIMA, who is the Mother in transcendence; Thor with ARIK ANPIN, the Lesser Countenance; and the Supreme Being discerned behind the northern mythology with AIN SOPH; passing over also certain alleged Druidic correspondences into which it would be folly to enter,[1] we may take much the same view as before regarding the alleged Gnostic connections of the Kabbalah. We may concur with King when he argues that whatever the date of the ZOHAR in its present form, some of its traditions are similar to those taught in the schools of Babylon and Tiberias.[2] They are the same and they are also different, and the difference represents the growth of the intellectual thought of Israel, its proper native development under the various impulsions which it received between the period of Gnosticism and the period of the promulgation of the ZOHAR. We may acknowledge also that Marcus, as " a born Jew," transmitted something of his national heritage to the system which he produced. Yet Gnosticism is not Kabbalism, though there are occasional analogies between them, and something of common source may be attributable to both. M. Amélineau is nearer the truth when he speaks of a coincident development of the two systems.[3] There are analogies in nature and appearance between glass and rock-crystal, but glass is glass and a pebble is a pebble.[4]

---

[1] Pike, following his usual unacknowledged authority, affirms that the Druids were true children of the Magi, whose initiation came from Egypt and Chaldea, " that is to say, from the true sources of the primitive Kabbalah."—MORALS AND DOGMA, p. 103. The inspiration is Éliphas Lévi, who uses substantially the same terms.

[2] THE GNOSTICS AND THEIR REMAINS. Second edition. London, 1897.

[3] ESSAI SUR LE GNOSTICISME EGYPTIEN, ses développements et son origine Egyptienne. Par M. E. Amélineau, published in Annales du Musée Guimet, tom. xiv. Paris, 1887, but written so far back as 1882, the date affixed to the preface. Compare Edersheim, who believed that " Gnosticism, like later Jewish Mysticism, sprang from the contact of Judaism with the religious speculations of the farther East." Compare also the JEWISH ENCYCLOPÆDIA, which is disposed to recognise in the ZOHAR an influence referable to Vedanta Schools of Hindu Philosophy through Persian channels of Mohammedan Mysticism in the eighth century and later.

[4] The PISTIS SOPHIA has been considered the most valuable document for analogies between Gnosticism and the Kabbalah, but it is easy to exaggerate its evidence. King says that the doctrines are identical, and that it exhibits the leading principles of the Kabbalah ; but he does not seem to speak with any first-hand knowledge of Jewish Theosophy. The Gnostic text has been edited since his day by Mr. G. R. S. Mead, who neither establishes nor alludes to the alleged correspondences.

It is unphilosophical because unneedful to go far back and far off when the explanation of given facts lies near in time and place. "That is best which lies the nearest," says the poet, and, artists or dreamers, makers of verse or Kabbalistic commentators, we should shape our work of art or interpretation without drawing needlessly from things remote. The prototype of Yetziratic and Zoharic Theosophy is close to our hand in Jewry. The fusion of all systems which is a characteristic of the present day, has its parallel in that epoch of the past which witnessed the rise of Christianity. "At the time when John the Baptist made his appearance in the desert, near the shores of the Dead Sea, all the old philosophical and religious systems were approximating toward each other. A general lassitude inclined the minds of all toward the quietude of that amalgamation of doctrines for which the expeditions of Alexander and the more peaceful occurrences that followed, with the establishment in Asia and Africa of many Grecian colonies, had prepared the way. After the intermingling of different nations, which resulted from the wars of Alexander in three-quarters of the globe, the doctrines of Greece, of Egypt, of Persia, and of India met and intermingled everywhere. Many barriers that formerly had kept the nations apart were at last thrown down; and while the people of the West readily connected their faiths with those of the East, the latter hastened to learn the traditions of Rome and Athens. . . . The Jews and Egyptians, then the most exclusive of all peoples, yielded to that eclecticism which prevailed among their masters, the Greeks and Romans." [1] National ambition, however, rather than eclecticism influenced the Jews, and though it was impossible, having regard to their environment, that they should not be tinctured largely, it was their object to tinge other systems and not to modify their own, to shew that the ethnic philosophers owed everything to the Divine Doctrine of Palestine. Philo the Greek of Alexandria to some extent Hellenised the Hebrew religion that he might the better Judaise the philosophy of Hellas. [2] From this fusion there arose the nearest approach, if not in time and place at least in form and subject, to Kabbalistic Theosophy as regards its source in Jewry. There is no need in the present study, which

[1] MORALS AND DOGMA, p. 247.

[2] For an illuminating study of Philo's eclecticism, in the higher sense of this term, see H. A. A. Kennedy : PHILO'S CONTRIBUTION TO RELIGION, 1919.

is intended to simplify and not to enlarge the issues, that should do more than cite Aristobulus, who a century before had exercised a similar vocation. Philo, and the movement and mode of thought which he represents, cannot have been without an effect upon the literature of later ages in Jewry,[1] though the history of that influence and the mode of its transmission cannot be traced conclusively. We must not fall, however, into the error of supposing that the Kabbalah is Platonism derived through Philo and the Jewish school of Alexandria, or that it is Jewish Tradition modified by Philoism. When we find in the SEPHER YETZIRAH the alphabetical symbols of the Logos made use of by God in the formation of the universe, it is very easy to set it down to Greek influence, but the fact remains that the BOOK OF FORMATION is essentially and characteristically Hebrew, and this fact lifts it altogether out of the category of Platonic succession. Yet we know where to look for the explanation of certain points of contact. As regards the doctrine developed by commentators on the SEPHER YETZIRAH prior to the appearance of the ZOHAR, as regards the literature which makes contact with these, and as regards the ZOHAR itself, saying nothing of the later literature, which had recourse consciously and openly to Greek sources, the case is much stronger.[2] Philo insists on the antithesis between God and the material world, the infinite and the finite ; so, let us say, does the ZOHAR, which may be taken to stand for the literature. Philo affirms the absolute transcendency of God ; so does Zoharic doctrine. Philo regards

---

[1] I should observe here that Arthur Lillie, who once argued a process in the Buddhistic origin of Christianity, discovered in the ZOHAR not only the Trinity of Philo, but the Trinity of Buddhism, and he held that the Kabbalah " was one of the secret books of the Essenes."—MODERN MYSTICS AND MODERN MAGIC, p. 14. He testified also that it was " written down from tradition by one Moses de Leon," thus shewing that he was not aware of the existence of Kabbalistic books outside the ZOHAR. —*Ibid.*, p. 13. Finally, he affirmed that it is " a book of Magic."—MADAME BLAVATSKY AND HER THEOSOPHY, p. 194. After this we shall not be surprised to find that St. Paul was a Kabbalist.—*Ibid.* So also was Jacob Böhme, whose Three Principles, one of which was the " Kingdom of Hell," have something to do with the three supernal SEPHIROTH. For similar worthless speculations, see Lillie's BUDDHISM IN CHRISTENDOM.

[2] For example, the PORTA CŒLORUM of R. Abraham Cohen Irira, which forms the third part of Rosenroth's APPARATUS IN LIBRUM SOHAR, was written expressly to exhibit the correspondences between Kabbalistic dogmas and the Platonic Philosophy. Later on the same theme was taken up by Christian writers, some of whom connect the Kabbalah with Aristotle, and so we have works like Burgondo's PODROMUS SCIENTIARUM ARTIUMVE LIBERALIUM *ad ipsos Peripateticæ Scholæ et Kabbalisticæ doctrinæ purissimos fontes revocatus*, Venice, 1651. · So also at an earlier period Thomas Campanella in his DE SENSU RERUM ET MAGIA, Frankfort, 1620, joined Neoplatonism and Kabbalism in his attempt to explain the universe.

the Divine Nature as in Itself escaping definition and in Itself
without quality ; Kabbalism denounces those who would
attempt to describe God as He is in Himself even by the
attributes which He manifests. Philo's descriptions of God
are all negative : compare the LATENS DEITAS of the Kabbalah. Philo says that no name can be given Him ; all
Kabbalism agrees,[1] though its unfolded reveries confer many
Names on the Deity and explain their powers and meanings
Philo regards the Scriptural God as anthropomorphic, and
allegorises upon all the descriptions, attributions and manifestations of Deity in the Old Testament : compare the
doctrine of the Two Countenances, designed—as some have
supposed—to explain the same anthropomorphisms by their
exaggeration to a *ne plus ultra* degree. Philo regards the letter
of Scripture as a veil : so does the ZOHAR. Philo interprets
it literally or mystically according to his purpose : so does
Kabbalistic exegesis. Philo regards the visible world as the
gate of the world unseen ; he believes in the possibility of an
immediate contemplation of God, in the existence of an
archetypal world, and that things seen are a counterpart of
things unseen,[2] in all of which we are enumerating express
points of Kabbalistic doctrine. These analogies are too
numerous, too close, too consecutive, to leave any room for
doubt that the heads of Kabbalistic teaching pre-existed in
Israel, and we have further the explicit testimony of Philo as
to the fact of a Jewish mystic doctrine. Spontaneity, initiation,
subsequent influences, all remain unimpeded and all are
necessary to explain the existence of the ZOHAR and its connections, but its source is not Philo of necessity, much less
Philo exclusively : it is that which produced Philo. And
more than all, it is hardy, independent speculation, wearing
tradition like a veil which does not conceal its essential
individuality, and much nearer to ourselves at times in its
spirit than we should ever suspect from its form. Yet we may
suspect it on philosophical grounds, for however concealed

---

[1] It is to be understood also that the ZOHAR affirms a Divine Mode, wherein God
was alone with His Name ; but there was an antecedent and nameless state.

[2] There is a twofold correspondence in Kabbalism between superior and inferior
things : one transcendental, being that of phenomena with their archetypes in the
noumenal world, and one natural in the narrower sense of the term, being that which
is summed up in the axiom : " There is no herb on earth to which a certain star does
not correspond in the heaven." See Kircher : MUNDUS SUBTERRANEUS, ii. 401*b*.
The whole theory of Natural Magic is imbedded in this maxim. Compare ZOHAR,
one might say, *passim*, for it is a recurring doctrine.

behind the veil of symbolism, however distorted in strai
glasses of vision, the sentiments and aspirations of humanr
have ever a common root, and through the vehicle of Kab
balistic apparatus, under many covers and tinctured by many
fantastic colourings of art and artifice, we see that our own
yearnings and longings find expression, after their own
manner, in this book of the words of the exile. We acknowledge therefore with the poet how truly all the lore and the
legend is

" A part
Of the hunger and thirst of the heart,
The frenzy and fire of the brain,
Which yearns for the fruitage forbidden,
The golden pomegranates of Eden,
To quiet its fever and pain."

When the FAITHFUL SHEPHERD of the ZOHAR puts these
words into the mouth of the Father of universal Israel : " In
this world my Name is written YHVH and read ADONAI, but
in the world to come the same will be read as it is written, so
that Mercy shall be from all sides," [1] we see that here and
now, at this point of the twentieth century, we might express
differently the longing, the hope, the faith, for which this
symbol stands, but the old symbolism stands in its own way
for that which we all desire to express, and, furthermore, I
do not know that our modern terms would represent it better.
Herein is the justification of the ways of God to man and
herein the pious conviction of the believing heart that in the
great day of the Lord there shall be no scandal to His children ;
that in spite of the darkness of our ways we have held rightly
that He is light ; that though we write Mercy in our hearts
but read Law and its inflexible order in all around us, we shall
one day know that it is Mercy on every side, the highest
expression of the Law, or that Law is that order under which
Divine Love is manifested. It is in messages like this that the
abiding beauty and significance of the Kabbalah are contained, not in the beard of MICROPROSOPUS or in the number
of worlds suspended from the hair on the cranium of ARIKH
ANPIN. GEMATRIA and METATHESIS may be pastimes fit only
for ultra-serious children, but the voice of the Rabbis of the
ZOHAR expressing the language of the heart of Israel needs

---

[1] Cremona edition, part ii. fol. 106a.

no TEMURAH to expound its meaning; and it is by the ring of such utterances that the true believer of to-day is made conscious electrically that the Holy Synods were composed of men who are our brethren.

As this view disposes implicitly of any claim on a divine authorship, and places the theory of aboriginal Tradition among fables, so also it forbids us to suppose that Kabbalistic doctrines are the work of a single mind.

One feels instinctively, without any necessity of evidence, that these things are not and cannot be the unaided creation of Moses de Leon. They are a growth and a result. As, however, the ZOHAR assumed its present shape at a late period admittedly, it may by possibility have taken part of it at the hands of this Spanish Jew. That his other works are inferior is no argument. Cervantes produced many worthless romances before and after the sum of all chivalry. The GALATEA did not make DON QUIXOTE impossible. So also Beroalde de Verville wrote books on Alchemy which are despised even by alchemists, but he wrote also the MOYEN DE PARVENIR. Every *magnum opus* is antecedently improbable, and the intellectual distance between the SORROWS OF WERTHER and the second part of FAUST is like the void between AIN SOPH and MALKUTH, which it was the purpose of the SEPHIROTH to fill.

But if all masterpieces are antecedently improbable, it is true also that they are impossible without antecedents. There are certain dull old histories known to *literati* which were necessary to the plays of Shakespeare. So the formulation of the ZOHAR must have been preceded by much raw material, both oral and written, parts of which were no doubt incorporated without any change in their formulation. For example, the BOOK OF OCCULTATION bears all the marks of antiquity, no less considerable than that of the BOOK OF FORMATION.

There is, of course, a point beyond which the reasonable critic will not pass. So far as it goes we are on tolerably safe ground with the meagre testimony of St. Agobard—supposing that it is allocated correctly; with R. Simeon Ben Yohai we are on purely traditional ground, and it is not to be supposed for a moment that more authenticity resides in the *dramatis personæ* of the Holy Synod than in those of the TURBA PHILOSOPHORUM. I do not mean that such names are entirely pre-

texts, for they may possess an honest basis in legend, but tr
are not literal or historical. They occupy a middle positic
between the script of a shorthand reporter and imaginar,
conversations like those of W. S. Landor.

VI.—ISLAMIC CONNECTIONS OF THE KABBALAH

When the Jew of the Exile sought a consolation in Theosophy, and thus produced the higher part of Kabbalism, compounded of his traditions, his speculations, his external
receptions, his longings, the memories of his election and its
glory, we must bear in mind that all exotics adjust themselves
to their environment, not without certain changes even in the
most persistent types. Now, the Jew is an anthropological
exotic in all countries of the world, and just because his
persistence is so enormous that it is explained by a special law
of Providence, we find that in all countries he has been modified sufficiently to guarantee his survival. As in things
physical, as in matters of daily life, so in the intellectual order,
he lost nothing but he assumed much. The Jew of Salerno
differed from that of France, and the Jew of Spain offered
contrasts to both. Without attempting to add another
hypothesis to the scores extant as to the origin of Kabbalism,
I propose to indicate that this literature is naturally, if partially,
elucidated by the place in which it grew up, if it did not in
part originate.

Having made a reasonable allowance for spontaneity in
Jewish thought, and having noted its observed connections
and correspondences in distant times and places, it seems
fitting that we should look now to that which lay the nearest.
Without disputing or defending the opinion that Israel may
have possessed a Tradition handed down by the oral way from
comparatively early times, of which there may be barely
sufficient evidence to warrant a presumption that it existed
but not enough to determine what it was, let us begin by considering where the Kabbalistic books first began to circulate.
That was in Spain. Now, what was the environment of Jews
in the Peninsula at the period in question—let us say, from
the ninth century and onward? It differed considerably from
that which surrounded them in other countries of Western
Europe. Spain was for Israel not indeed a Garden of Paradise,

but a species of oasis in the great wilderness of the Exile,[1] for the simple reason that much of it was not then under Christian rule.[2] The Jew of Spain enjoyed comparative immunity ; he possessed even political influence ; he rose occasionally to high political power. It is not surprising therefore that Spain became a centre of Jewish literature and philosophy. Thence Jewish treatises passed into France and Italy under the Arabian equivalents of their authors' names, and were accepted as speculations or teachings of the learned among the Moslems. Avicebron is a case in point. There can be no doubt whatever that the learning of Mohammedanism exercised an influence on the Rabbins,[3] who reacted in their turn on the Moslem doctors.[4] The questions of priority and preponderance may be passed over, because they are of no importance here.

We have concluded already that the ZOHAR presents the theosophical thought of preceding centuries in Israel under a certain aspect of transformation. The traditional knowledge, of which we have evidence as to its existence in Talmudic times, had received many developments from many sources and under the influence of many minds. There is ground for supposing that the nucleus in Christian times is first heard of in Palestine, which indeed follows from its connection, once admitted, with R. Simeon ben Yohai. But despite the legend which represents the ZOHAR as sent from Palestine by Nahmanides, everything points to Spain and the South of France as the chief scenes in which the literature developed, and it is not unreasonable to suppose that it has been affected by the prevailing tone of mystical thought in one or both of these places. There is evidence to shew that such influence was at work outside the ZOHAR and prior perhaps to its existence in the form that it now possesses. In post-Zoharic Mysticism, and in the commentaries on the ZOHAR which are the work of Spanish Jews, it may be traced more fully and plainly. In no case does it justify the now exploded criticism which would

---

[1] See Finn's SEPHARDIM, already cited, c. xi., and especially pp. 142, 143.
[2] So also the necessities of Christian princes in Spain till the thirteenth century led them usually to protect the Jews.
[3] The translation of the TALMUD into Arabic by R. Joseph, disciple of Moses the sack-clothed, during the reign of Al-Hakim, Caliph of Cordova, in the tenth century, would be the best evidence which could be cited on this point, but the undertaking is no longer extant, if indeed it came into being.
[4] Islamic Mysticism is almost coincident with the mission of the great Islamic prophet. For example, the Ghoolat sect, famous for the "extravagance" of its doctrines, is referred to the time of Ali. See SECRET SOCIETIES OF THE MIDDLE AGES, London, 1846, pp. 29, 31.

make the ZOHAR merely a reproduction or echo of Arabian Theosophy, or would regard all Kabbalism as referable to Islamic Mysticism for its sole source, *plus* the Greek influence at work in Islam. This was the hypothesis of Tholuck. We are concerned only with a question of complexion and of tincture, and have other criteria by which to judge the true significance of the points of doctrinal resemblance between Sufi and Kabbalist concerning the hidden state of Deity, the operation of the Divine Will at the beginning of creation, the emanation of the world, &c. The analogies are interesting enough and the Orientalist who first specified them had everything to justify him at his period.[1] As it may not be uninteresting to cite a few cases in point derived from other sources, let us take a fact, one of many concerning which we possess impregnable testimony. About the middle of the fifteenth century, or, more exactly, from 1414 to 1492, there flourished a Sufi poet named Nuruddin Abdurrahmann, known as Jami of Herat, among whose works the SEVEN THRONES is most famous. One of the poems in this collection is entitled SALOMON AND ABSAL, a mystical story of earthly and heavenly love. In the epilogue to this poem, where the author unfolds his meaning, the following lines occur :

> The Incomprehensible Creator, when this world
> He did create, created first of all
> The First Intelligence, First of a chain
> Of Ten Intelligences, of which the last
> Sole agent is in this our Universe,
> Active Intelligence so called.

It may be admitted at once that if we are to accept the method and admit the quality of evidence which has satisfied heretofore the several authorities who have referred Kabbalism to definite sources in philosophy and religion, we may feel at liberty to infer from this passage that somewhere about the year 1450 a Sufic poet, so far away from Spain as Herat, was adapting, with slight variations of a verbal kind, the Sephirotic Doctrine of the Kabbalah [2] a century before the BOOK OF FORMATION and the ZOHAR came into circulation through the medium of print. I have chosen this instance because it proves nothing of itself on account of its lateness, but it gives a point of

---

[1] See F. A. D. Tholuck: SUFISMUS, *sive* THEOSOPHIA PERSARUM PANTHEISTICA, Berlin, 1831, c.v. *passim*. Also DE ORTU CABBALÆ, Hamburg, 1837.

[2] See Book V., § 2.

departure backward for tracing a possible connection between the mystical sects of Mohammedanism and the mystical sects of Israel.

With this let us compare for a moment the doctrine developed in the CELESTIAL DESATIR, which has been described as "a very early attempt on the part of the ancient Persians to form a cosmological theory." [1] The DESATIR, it should be observed, is a revelation addressed to the great prophet Abad, who has been identified incautiously with Abraham. "The nature of God cannot be known. Who can dare to know it but He (Himself)? The entity and the oneness and the personality are 'His very nature and nothing beside Him.'" From this Being proceeded by free creation "him whose name is BAHNAM, called Prime Intellect and First Reason," and through him "ASHAM, the second intellect," who created in turn the intellect of the next lower heaven named "FAMESHAM." From these proceeded the "Intellect of the heaven of KANIAN," or Saturn; of HARMUZD, or Jupiter; of BAHRAM, or Mars; of KHURSHAD, or the Sun; of NAHID, or Venus; of ZIR, or Mercury; and of MAH, or the Moon.

Here, again, we have the production of ten primary intelligencies, recalling the Sephirotic emanations, which themselves have planetary attributions.

Let us now take another step. At the beginning of the twelfth century, or actually in the year 1100 A.D., Abū Bakr Ibn Al-Tufail, a noted Arabian physician, poet, mathematician and Sufi philosopher, was born at Guadix in Spain, and he died at Morocco in 1186. His chief work is a species of philosophical romance called THE LIFE OF HAI EBN YOKDAN, *the self-taught Philosopher*. In this curious narrative we find Ibn Al-Tufail using a form of comparison which occurs almost verbatim in the Kabbalistic books. "The Divine Essence is like the rays of the material sun, which expand over opaque bodies and appear to proceed from the eye, though they are only reflected from its surface." We find also substantially : (*a*) The AIN SOPH of the Kabbalists under the name of that One True One ; (*b*) the reflection of this Being, dwelling "in the highest sphere, in and beyond which there is no body, a Being free from matter, which was not the Being of that One True One, nor the sphere itself, nor yet anything

---

[1] My knowledge is confined to the translation by Mirza Mohamed Hadi which appeared in successive issues of THE PLATONIST, vols. iii. and iv.

different from them both ; but was like the image of the sun as it appears in a well-polished mirror, which is neither one nor the other, and yet not distinct from them " ; (*c*) the immaterial essence of the sphere of the fixed stars ; (*d*) the sphere of Saturn—and so with the rest, in harmony with the scheme of the DESATIR, ending at this world, which is subject to generation and corruption, and comprehending all that is contained within the sphere of the Moon. None of the material essences were identical and yet none were different, either as regards the rest or in comparison with the One True One.[1]

The doctrine of Divine Absorption is the very essence of Sufism and Sufism is contemporary with Mohammedanism itself. It is also mainly pantheistic,[2] as may be gathered from its proposed object. Some refer it to India, others to a Gnostic origin, but the question does not concern us, for the significant fact is that this form of Islamic Mysticism was one of the environments of the Kabbalistic Jews to whom we are indebted for part at least of the ZOHAR. The influence of such environment was felt outside the Kabbalists, and was confessed even by the most inflexible of the sects in Jewry— that of the Kairites, or Literalists, who rejected all innovations in the primeval doctrine of Israel, who set no store by Tradition, and were thus as much opposed to the TALMUD as to Zoharic writings. The proof is their analogies, indeed one might say their fusion, with the Motozales, a sect of scholastic Arabs.[3] A Kairite Jew of the period allows that his brethren followed the doctrines of this sect, and they even assumed its name.

The purpose of the present section should not be misconstrued. Once more, it is by no means designed to indicate that the mystical sects of Mohammedanism are responsible for the peculiar scheme of the Kabbalah, or that the Sufi drew only from the rabbin. Such devices belong to a scheme of criticism which has passed fittingly away. If we know anything concerning the early connections of Sufism it is that they are Neoplatonic, and that the Gnostics of the early Shiite

---

[1] See the Improvement of Human Reason exhibited in the LIFE OF HAI EBN YOKDHAN. " Written in Arabick above 500 years ago, by Abu Jaafar Ebn Tophail." . . . *Newly translated from the original Arabick* by Simon Ockley, A.M. London, 1711.

[2] See, on this subject and generally, Professor Reynold A. Nicholson's STUDIES IN ISLAMIC MYSTICISM, 1921, especially Chapter II.

[3] Munk : LA PHILOSOPHIE CHEZ LES JUIFS, p. 10.

sects were attracted to it because of these connections.[1] But
to name Neoplatonism and Gnosticism is to cite analogies of
Kabbalism, however remote. To say that Sufism has been
referred to a woman who died at Jerusalem in the first century
of the Hegira is to say that Sufism began to live and move in
an atmosphere of Jewish Tradition. To say that Spain was the
forcing-house of the Kabbalists is to say that the theosophical
doctors of Jewry brushed arms with those of Islam, and to
deny that there was any consequence of such contact is to
deny Nature. Sufism was pantheistic and emanationist;
Kabbalistic emanationism was saved from pure pantheism by
the doctrine of Divine Immanence, and their literatures have
no real likeness ; but between the metaphysics of Divine Love
and the mystical absorption of Islam, and between the Kabbalistic return of the soul to God, or its union with the transcendent principle which never departs from ATZILUTH, and
the theory of ecstasy in Islam, it seems possible to suppose
that there was not only the connecting link of analogy between
all mystics but a bond even in history.[2]

VII.—INFLUENCE OF THE KABBALAH
ON JEWRY

There is perhaps no one at the present day, certainly no
Christian student of the subject, who is in a position to define
precisely what kind of profit accrued to the mind of Jewry
from the promulgation, let us say, of the ZOHAR—notwithstanding the statement, already cited, that it gave to Israel the
splendid propulsion of the ideal.

So far as it is possible to ascertain, the Kabbalah has
exercised only a very subsidiary influence upon the Children

---

[1] On this point the reader may consult with advantage an admirable account of
Islâmic Mysticism in A YEAR AMONG THE PERSIANS, by E. G. Browne. London,
1893. It makes no references to Kabbalism, with which the author seems unacquainted,
but it may be gathered from what it tells us of Sufic commentaries on the KORAN that
these, although pantheistic, have many points of contact with later Kabbalism. We
find not only the unmanifest state of Deity, but the attempt to explain why the contingent world (compare LIBER DRUSHIM) was evolved from " the silent depths of the
non-existent," the use of which term is so typical of AIN SOPH doctrine. See p. 129
for Browne's opinion that the early schools of Mohammedan philosophy in Persia
were adaptations either of Aristotle or Plato, and were also the scholasticism of Islam.
[2] Dr. Abelson speaks of a comparatively recent theory—or newer at least than
are theories of Neoplatonic and Gnostic sources—which " finds echoes of Persian
Sufism in the ZOHAR," but unfortunately he gives no references.—JEWISH MYSTICISM,
p. 119.

of the Exile—those excepted obviously for whom it was a path of devotion, a path of life in sanctity for the attainment of the Good and the One. We can point to certain enthusiasms for which it is partially responsible, among the crowd of Ghetto believers who understood only its aberrations, and they are those precisely which did their best to wreck Jewry and of which Jewry is now ashamed. The history of Abraham Abulafia, of Sabbataï Zevi and the founder of the Hassidim,[1] are typical cases in point which warrant us in saying that the Kabbalah gave spurious Messiahs to Israel.[2] It was perhaps the last instance of its open activity before it ceased to exercise any powerful influence, and with this also it would have begun if we cared to believe that Rabbi Akiba was the author of the Book of Formation, and that he was connected with the bogus or at least the frenzied mission of Bar Cochba. We have seen that there is no truth in the story ; but this notwithstanding it has, I fear, to be admitted that if a literature may be judged by its influence, that of the Kabbalah has been small on the external side, while it has encouraged false enthusiasm, and has been the warrant for direct imposture.[3]

So far as its operation was intellectual, there is tolerable ground for thinking that its field was the Christian rather than the Jewish mind.[4] And having established one useful point there is an opportunity here of making another. Kabbalistic influence on Christendom has been of two kinds, but it has

---

[1] *I.e.*, the new Order of the mysterious Baal Shem, which is said to have had its representatives even at the close of the nineteenth century in a number of Jewish communities and to have held the Zohar in high esteem.—Israel among the Nations, pp. 61, 40, 345. The sect had its chief hold among Russian and Galician Jews : the name signifies "pious ones." In the time of Judas Maccabæus, it meant the strict party among the Jews.—Edersheim, History of the Jewish Nation. Compare Scaliger's Order of Knights of the Temple, with which the sect has been identified. There is a long contemplation by Paul Vulliaud on Sabbataï Zevi and the Hassidim in La Kabbale Juive, Vol. II., pp. 139 *et seq.* The accounts of the original Hassidim are full of mythical elements.

[2] Zangwill in his Dreamers of the Ghetto was perhaps the first who brought this notion to the knowledge of the external and popular world.

[3] It has given also a few obscure sects to Jewry. A knowledge of Kabbalistic Mysteries was alleged to have imparted superhuman power to Löbele, chief Rabbi of Prague in his day ; to Jacob Franck, the Polish distiller, of whose followers the so-called Christian Jews of Poland represented a small survival ; and to his contemporary, Israel of Podolia, who established the New Saints and had a recipe for miracles by means of the name Tetragrammaton.

[4] Zangwill is not of this opinion. Referring to the period which antedated immediately the mission of Sabbataï Zevi, he says : " The Zohar—the Book of Illumination, composed in the thirteenth century—printed now for the first time, shed its dazzling rays further and further over every ghetto." But perhaps he follows here the principle that he has borrowed from Spinoza, " to see things *sub specie æternitatis.*" I wish the same principle had inspired him to lay less stress on the exact date of the Zohar.

been much more of one kind than another. It has been an influence exercised by a peculiar theosophical claim upon the students and the acceptors of such. But it has been much more the influence of possible missionary material on the missionary enterprise of the Christian Church. To begin at a late date—What gave the Kabbalah of the ZOHAR to the Latin-reading scholars of Europe? The *magnum opus* of Rosenroth—or more at least than all. What impelled Rosenroth? The " splendid spectrum " of the conversion of Jewry *en masse*. And now, if we sweep backward to the very beginning of the Christian interest in Kabbalism, almost coincident, in fact, with the appearance of the ZOHAR, and suppose that Raymund Lully was really, as it has been said that he was, the first Christian student of the Kabbalah, what was the life-long labour of that amazing seneschal of Majorca, and for what did he renounce the world? To wrest, as it has been said, from reluctant Nature the elusive Mastery of Nature, the Great Palingenesis of Alchemy? The Hermetic treatises ascribed to him may say Yes, but we know that they are ascribed falsely, and that this was by no means the ambition of Raymund Lully. But was it the attainment of a religion behind all religions? Nothing of the sort; that is modern fantasy. The work of Raymund Lully was apostolical and missionary, and it closed with martyrdom at Bugia, in a feverish attempt to evangelise " Mahound." What prompted the fiery energy of Picus de Mirandula, that he filled the Papal Court with the rumour and the wonder of Secret Jewish Tradition? The fact that he also regarded it as a way, revealed against all expectation and as if on the part of Divine Providence, by which the Princes of the Exile might be brought to the gates of the Eternal City and the Ghetto might be transformed into a Baptistry. Suppose, lastly, that Nicholas Flamel was really initiated by the BOOK OF ABRAHAM THE JEW," [1] so that Kabbalism connects integrally with Alchemy, what prompted the unostentatious scrivener of old Paris to make precious metals by occult arts when his wants were few and his trade sufficient for a modest man? Why, he also had the missionary spirit—witness his bequests, actual or fabulous, for the conversion of the heathen.

The inference is that the Kabbalah was imported out of

---

[1] See my SECRET TRADITION IN ALCHEMY, c. x.

Jewry to prove that Jewry might be Christianised if it were handled wisely according to the lights given in the Holy Synods.[1]

Now, I do not need to say that there are very few students of cryptic literatures at this late day of the world who would take any interest in the Kabbalah, regarded from this point of view. They are not, as a class, inspired by missionary zeal for any form of official religion, and their memorials, as they stand, do not manifest more than a distant respect for the great orthodoxies of Christendom. On the other hand, it is only in virtue of some immense misapprehension that the Esoteric Tradition of the Jews can be supposed to offer them the religion behind all religions. What it does offer them on the surface falls almost infinitely short. At its highest a bizarre but strenuous attempt to unriddle the universe, the most unaided of all metaphysics, the *systema mundi* excogitated in a darkened synagogue with the praying-shawl drawn over the eyes. What darkness to be felt in the void! What strange lights flashing in the darkness! In such a state Spanish Jew or Spanish Mystic of the Latin Church, Moses de Leon, if you will, or St. John of the Cross, exile of Babylon or recluse of the Thebaid, may enjoy a certain communication of the Infinite. But to say more than this is frenzy. And at its lowest, that is to say, on that side upon which it makes contact no longer with the infinite, but with the occult as it was understood by occultism at its zenith—let us say, in Victorian days—finite of all things finite : what sombre trifling unredeemed by a saving sense of triviality ; the physiognomy of the section Yithroh, the astrology of the processes of Gaffarel, the star messages of the Hebrew planisphere, the paper tubes of Éliphas Lévi ;[2] or, again, NOTARIKON, METATHESIS, GEMATRIA,[3] the arcana of the Extended Name, the virtues of AGLA and ARARITA for conjuring heaven and earth. It is

---

[1] One writer in modern times has even gone so far as to maintain that " Christian doctrine, except the Trinity, which is Platonic, issues wholly, with all its details, from the TALMUD. Christianity is son and brother of the TALMUD."—Alexandre Weill : MOISE, LE TALMUD ET L'ÉVANGILE, ii. 92. The statement sounds perilous, but M. Weill is not to be taken seriously. Compare *ibid.* ii. 91 : " The TALMUD is itself the most violent adversary of Moses," *i.e.*, the Moses of M. Weill. One paradox enables us to judge another.

[2] And the kind of Kabbalah which A. Lelièvre undertook to defend in his JUSTIFICATION DES SCIENCES DIVINATOIRES (Paris, 1847).

[3] Observe also the developments which these subjects received in works like the CABALLA ANAGRAMMATICA of Ranutius Longelus, *Placentiæ*, 1654—*ars mirabilis* indeed, as the author terms it.

here that occultism illustrates how it receives only what it can give and how it comes to pass that the interest of the occultist in the KABBALAH was less inspired by Zoharic Theosophy than by the magic garters of the KEY OF SOLOMON.[1] Hence writers like Papus in France found it necessary to include in their scheme of Kabbalism the sorry literature of the Gri-moires.[2] And they and he had nothing to tell us of the ZOHAR. But we do not find the Grimoires in Picus de Mirandula, or in Raymund Lully ; we do not find Mysteries of Magic in the KABBALA DENUDATA. The Lexicon of Rosenroth does not include the occult wonders of AGLA, nor does it tell us after what manner the Extended Name is compounded, by a child-craft of acrostics, out of three verses in Exodus. We do find all these in Agrippa, who wrote as a young man of things that he had heard and read, making a very dignified retractation of it all in his book of great excellence which unfolds their solemn vanity.

There remains, of course, the mystical side of Kabbalism, the return of the soul to God, and that path of ecstasy already mentioned, by which it was conceived that the soul might effect such reunion even in this life ; but it is precisely this side of which we see no effect whatsoever in Jewry, and it is also this which has been neglected by later occultism. For example, the present work is the first published in England which has any reference to the highest principle of the human soul in Kabbalism and the Instrument of Unification with the Divine. But it is here and only here that we encounter what gave to Israel " the splendid propulsion of the ideal " ; and it is here, as in all whatsoever of Zoharic Theosophy which led up and belongs thereto, that a justification shall be sought and found for an inquiry at large into a Secret Tradition in Israel and into the doctrine of the Holy Kabbalah.

---

[1] I am referring here to the past of the nineteenth century. It happens at the present time that the subject is dead in England and is almost extinct in France, not that French occultism has improved, but that it has varied the fashion of its follies.

[2] LA KABBALE, pp. 10, 16, 26, the last especially, where the reference to Molitor makes the author of the PHILOSOPHY OF TRADITION apparently responsible for the identification of the *claviculæ* and " magical MSS." as a serious branch of Kabbalism.

BOOK III

THE WRITTEN WORD OF KABBALISM:
FIRST OR YETZIRATIC PERIOD

BOOK III

THE WRITTEN WORD OF KABBALISM: FIRST PERIOD

I.—EARLY KABBALISTIC LITERATURE

It seems beyond controversy that there was a not inconsiderable mass of old theosophical speculation and doctrine once extant in Jewry, of which vestiges are to be found in the TALMUD, and that it is connected occasionally with brilliant and even with a few great names. It is this somewhat nebulous material which prepared a way for later developments, leading up in fine to the ZOHAR, and should scholarship forbid us to confer on its earlier stages the distinctive denomination of Kabbalism,[1] we must defer to scholarship, though with the mental reservation that if the question be more than of words it is at most one of stages of growth, for that which was of Mysticism in Israel between the period of the TALMUD and the period of the promulgation of the ZOHAR is that which in the course of its evolution became—as just intimated—the Kabbalah and ZOHAR.

The title of this section is obviously tentative or speculative, but the modest conclusions of the previous book are a sufficient warrant for supposing that there are evidences of Kabbalism, outside the SEPHER YETZIRAH, prior to the promulgation of the ZOHAR, and possessing in fact certain literary remains. It is indeed essential to the natural history of the later work that it should have had its antecedents and precursors in the world of texts. According to the most

---

[1] There can be, I think, little doubt that the Kabbalah was the " reception " of the BERESHITH and MERKABAH Mysteries mentioned in the TALMUD, or that this was the view always taken by Kabbalistic Jews. My readers should be referred at this point to an important study of the subject in THE JEWISH ENCYCLOPÆDIA, vol. iii., *s.v.* CABALA, under the names of Dr. Kaufmann Kohler, Rabbi of Temple Beth-El, New York, and of Dr. Louis Ginzberg, Professor of Talmud at the Jewish Theological Seminary of America, New York City.

acceptable view these were various MIDRASHIM which, in many cases, are no longer extant, and it is fair to suppose that such memorials must have exercised some influence.

So also the SEPHER YETZIRAH, whatever the date ascribed to it, was of high authority, and the respect in which it was held was of the kind which creates literature. We must beware, however, of assuming that there was an unbroken line of Kabbalists, maintaining and unfolding one and the same Tradition, from the second to the twelfth century, as some incautious writers have pretended. There was, however, " the mystical literature of the Geonic period." Whatever the date ascribed to SEPHIR YETZIRAH in its present form, we must regard as its prototype a work already mentioned under the title of the ALPHABET OF AKIBA,[1] while the predecessor of THE BOOK OF OCCULTATION, one of the most challengeable sections of the ZOHAR, must be sought in the anthropomorphic SHIUR KOMAH, i.e., THE MEASURE OF THE HEIGHT, or MEASURE OF BEING, in other words, the DESCRIPTION OF THE BODY OF GOD, a development of the various Scriptural places in which divine members are mentioned. It survives only in two fragments which are held to be not later than the eighth century. The dates of both these works are, however, conjectural, but there can be no doubt, as indeed there is no question, of their comparative antiquity, in respect of rootmatter. Connected with them are the GREATER and the LESSER PALACE, known also as DELINEATION OF THE HEAVENLY TEMPLES,[2] which, in common with the others, is not regarded by some modern critics as Kabbalistic, though it is allowed that all were instrumental in calling the Kabbalah into existence.[3]

In accordance with the exigencies of his standpoint, Dr

---

[1] There are two versions, of which A is considered older by Jellinek, while Graetz takes the opposite view. A third MIDRASH, on the ornamentation of the letters, is also referred to Akiba.

[2] Not to be confused with a work mentioned by Bartolocci under the name of R. Eliezer and dealing with the measurements of the earthly temple. The PIRKE HAIKLUTH, otherwise PIRKE MERKABAH, is an account of Seven Heavenly Temples or Palaces which must be visited in succession by the elect before they can enter the region of the Sacred Chariot. They would appear to represent stages of rapture and vision. Compare the Palaces of the ZOHAR.

[3] " By the difficulty," says Ginsburg, " in which they placed the Jews in the South of France and in Catalonia, who believed in them almost as much as in the Bible, and who were driven to contrive this system whereby they could explain the gross descriptions of the Deity and of the plains of heaven, given in these Haggadic productions." It may be affirmed indeed that one spirit informed the chief works of Kabbalistic complexion which preceded the ZOHAR.

Graetz, who may be taken to represent at his period all tha
is most acrid and uncompromising in hostility to Jewish
Mysticism, fixes the origin of Kabbalism, as to its date, in the
tenth century, and thus by implication denies the claim of the
SEPHER YETZIRAH to be included in its literature. He is
followed, as we have seen, by Ginsburg,[1] but it is not open
to question that the work is indispensable to the Kabbalah on
its artificial and external side, though it contributes nothing
to the heights and deeps of the HOLY ZOHAR. The tenth
century is, however, an important period in Jewish history
and Jewish letters, for at this epoch the quickening of the
Arabian mind was followed by that of Israel[2] and was sometimes eclipsed thereby. There was for the moment a lull in
persecution ; the Academies in the East flourished, and in the
West the internecine struggle of Christians and Moslems in
Spain insured a breathing space to the Children of the Exile.
Prior to that period, from the sixth century and onward, there
was a hiatus in the literature of Israel. The canons of the
Talmud were closed to all intents by the terror and peril of
the time, and the history of Israel became one of bitter struggle
for existence. A certain hazardous shelter was found under
Persian dominion, and ultimately the intellectual lamp of
Israel shone forth clearly and steadily during the Moslem
domination of Spain, which country—from that period till
the beginning of the thirteenth century—was like a second
Palestine to the Jew, and this land of refuge, under the tolerant
and enlightened sway of the Spanish Khalifs, became almost
as dear to his heart as the Land of Promise. Montpellier in
France and Salerno in Italy were famous for their Jewish
Schools, but that of Seville was, perhaps, more illustrious than
either. Spain also was a nursing-land of Kabbalistic literature,
and the traces of an Esoteric Tradition between the epoch
which produced the BOOK OF FORMATION [3] and that of the
BOOK OF SPLENDOUR must be sought chiefly therein, though
in the twelfth century something may be gleaned from
Southern France and earlier still from Hay Gaon, who

---

[1] Kitto's CYCLOPÆDIA, third edition, 1864, *s.v.* KABBALAH.
[2] Basnage, HISTOIRE DES JUIFS, livre vii. c. 4, tom. v. pp. 1503 *et seq.*
[3] Outside the dates and authorship ascribed by old Kabbalists to the SEPHER
YETZIRAH and the ZOHAR there are other treatises attributed to the early days of the
Exile. Thus tradition regards Eliezer Hagabite, son of Jose, a contemporary of Simeon
ben Yohai, as a Kabbalistic doctor and the author of a treatise on the thirty-two
qualities of the Law.

flourished in the eleventh century, a Babylonian, on the borders of the Caspian Sea.[1]

There is neither space nor occasion here to produce a bibliographical list, and indeed the materials at our command cannot be regarded as extensive, serving mainly to correct false and highly coloured impressions regarding the claims of Kabbalistic Tradition. The chief names of the period with which we are concerned are :

I. Rabbi Eliezer ben Hyrcanus, whose supposed mystical system, as presented in his PIRKE = *Capitula*, connects on the one hand with SEPHER YETZIRAH, and on the other with Zoharic teaching.[2] We have, in the first place, God subsisting prior to the creation of the world, alone with his Ineffable Name ; next, the creation, prior to the visible world, of the THORAH or Law, together with the Throne of Glory, the Name of the Messiah, Paradise, Hell and the Temple of Jerusalem, *i.e.*, the archetype of the earthly temple ; subsequently, the creation of the world by means of ten words. With this work may be connected the ancient MIDRASH CONEN,[3] which represents the THORAH as the foundation of the universe and the gage of its stability. It is a matter of conjecture whether these works are slightly later or earlier than the SEPHER YETZIRAH.

II. The Gaon R. Saadiah ben Joseph, *nat. circa* 892, *ob.* 942, head of the Persian Academy of Sura, was the author of a commentary on the SEPHER YETZIRAH preserved in the Bodleian Library and only printed recently in France, as we shall see in the third section of this book.

III. R. Abn-Yussuf Chasdai, a Spanish physician who died at Cordova between 970 and 990 A.D., was a Prince of the Exile and temporal head of the Jews in that city. He was also a political minister under two Khalifs. For the rest, he is said to connect the school of Hay Gaon with that of Gebirol ; but the dates do not correspond.

IV. The Gaon R. Shereerah—otherwise Sherira b. Hanina—

---

[1] Hay Gaon is said to have died A.D. 1038. Gaon was a title given to the heads of two Jewish Academies at Babylon.

[2] The first edition was printed at Venice in 1544, and a Latin version appeared at Leyden precisely one hundred years later. The PIRKE is held to have been written soon after A.D. 833.

[3] MIDRASH CONEN = מדרש כונן = *Expositio Stabiliens*. See Prov. iii. 19. It was the first treatise in a collection entitled ARZE LEVANON = *Cedri Libani*. See Ps. civ. 16. It appeared at Venice in 1601.

head of the Academy of Pherruts Schibbur [1] in the neighbourhood of Babylon, was perhaps more distinguished for the
violence with which he wrote against the Christians than for
his Kabbalistic knowledge. But Nahmanides [2] has preserved
his critical observations on the DELINEATION OF THE
HEAVENLY TEMPLES,[3] or more correctly on the fragments
which it embodies under the title of the PROPORTION OF THE
HEIGHT, otherwise called the DESCRIPTION OF THE BODY OF
GOD, which shew the Kabbalistic leanings of Shereerah and
create that antithesis to the anthropomorphism of these early
works which has been mentioned already as a keynote of the
higher Kabbalism. " God forbid," he exclaims, " that man
should speak of the Creator as if he had bodily members and
dimensions ! " This Rabbi was despoiled of his wealth
and hanged by order of Cader, Khalif of the race of the
Abassides.

V. The Gaon R. Hay, son and successor of Shereerah
as the head of the Babylonian School of Schibbur, is also
credited with a commentary on the SEPHER YETZIRAH, which
will be dealt with in its proper place. The interpretation of
dreams was one of the daily occupations of Jewish Academies,
and the skill exhibited therein, or the credulity of the times,
often purchased toleration and respect for the Rabbis at the
hands of the Khalifs. To Rab Hay is attributed a treatise on
this art, which was printed at Venice.[4] Outside his alleged
commentary on the BOOK OF FORMATION his voluminous
works have many Kabbalistic references, especially that
entitled THE VOICE OF GOD IN ITS POWER. It will be sufficient
to mention among these the doctrine of correspondences, of
man as a microcosm and a peculiar theory of mystical contemplation. He possessed enormous influence and became
subsequently the head of the Academy of Pumbaditha in the
neighbourhood of Bagdad. He died in 1038.

VI. Solomon ben Yehudah Ibn Gebirol, the scholastic
Avicebron and in all respects, Kabbalistic and otherwise, a
focus of intellectual and literary interest, was a contemporary
of the famous Nagrila.

---

[1] Or of Pumbaditha according to some authorities, including Graetz. He is
supposed to have died at the age of one hundred years, *circa* A.D. 1000.
[2] In his commentary on the THORAH.
[3] Attributed to R. Ishmael, apparently the doctor of that name whose sentences are
sometimes quoted in the TALMUD.
[4] Bartolocci : BIBLIOTHECA RABBINICA, ii. 387.

VII. R. Abraham ben David or Ben Dior Ha Levi, *ob. circa* 1180, the great orthodox apologiſt of the twelfth century, has been included in the chain of Kabbalism. He is described otherwise as a Spanish astronomer, hiſtorian and philosopher.

VIII. Moses Ibn Jacob ben Ezra,[1] one of the greateſt Jews of his time, was of Granada, and flourished in the earlier part of the twelfth century. His work entitled the GARDEN OF AROMATICS shews traces of the doƈtrine of Gebirol, but it appears by his COMMENTARY ON ISAIAH that he was in disagreement with this doƈtor. Basnage says that he did not rejeƈt the Kabbalah, though he knew its weakness, because he did not wish to be embroiled with contemporary writers.[2] He wrote upon the Divine Name and the myſtical attributes of numbers in conneƈtion therewith.

IX. The name of Juda Hallevi—*ob. poſt* 1140—who has some references to the SEPHER YETZIRAH in his work entitled KUSARI, of Jacob Nazir—referred to the second half of the twelfth century—of Solomon Jarki, of R. Abraham ben David, the younger, bring us to the thirteenth century and to the period of (*a*) Maimonides, who is reported, chiefly on the authority of R. Hayyim, to have turned Kabbaliſt at an advanced age but in any case conneƈts with the subjeƈt, and was acquainted at leaſt with the exiſtence of the twofold Myſtical Tradition, diſtinguished as that of the Creation and that of the Chariot ; (*b*) R. Azriel, of Valladolid, a famous commentator on the SEPHER YETZIRAH ; (*c*) Shem Tob Ibn Falaquera, a disciple of Maimonides, who conneƈts with Gebirol ; (*d*) R. Abraham Abulafia,[3] who wrote on the TETRAGRAMMATON, the myſticism of Letters and Numbers, and the Myſteries of the Law, but his works have not been published.[4] He endeavoured to combine the theoretical and praƈtical schools, but he was a quixotic adventurer and a Messianic enthusiaſt, whose opinions it is unnecessary to

---

[1] See ESSAYS ON THE WRITINGS OF IBN EZRA, in the TRANSACTIONS OF THE SOCIETY OF HEBREW LITERATURE.

[2] Basnage quotes Skinner's letters and Usher in support of this view, but he and they are in some confusion as to important dates in Kabbaliſtic hiſtory and literature. Graetz has a good account of Ibn Ezra, but it is unnecessary to say that his analogies with Kabbalism are not mentioned.

[3] See Frankel : MONATSHRIFT FÜR GESCHICHTE UND WEISSENSCHAFT DES JUDENTHUMS, vol. v. p. 27, Leipsic, 1856. Graetz has also a long account of Abulafia, designed to ridicule the mental condition to which he refers the Kabbalah.

[4] They include also THE FOUNT OF LIVING WATERS, of which there is a Latin version in the Vatican. Graetz extends the number of his works to twenty ; Bartolocci knew only of three.

determine. It may be noted also that he exhibits some Christian tendencies.

Those who maintain the authenticity of Kabbalistic Tradition find something to their purpose in all these writers and personalities ; but they often proceed on a misconception. What, for example, is more likely to lead an unpractised student astray than the treatise of Abraham ben David Ha Levi—*ob. circa* 1150—by the mere fact of its title ? It is called SEDER HA KABBALAH, the Order of the Tradition.[1] As a fact, it is the least mystical of all productions, and though I have termed its author a great orthodox apologist, he had a strong Aristotelian leaven. The occasion of his book was a Sadducean heresy prevalent in Castile and Leon, and represented by a work of Abu Alphrag, which maintained that the true synagogue was to be found among the Sadducees. The SEDER HA KABBALAH vindicates the authority of the orthodox claim under the two heads of succession and universality, or community of doctrine among all the synagogues. It embraces the entire history of the Jewish Church and the perpetuation of Mosaic doctrine, which is the tradition named in the title.[2] The work of Abraham ben David Ha Levi is perhaps greater than was the occasion which called it forth. The Jews were divided among themselves upon many questions, of which Sadducean pretentions were certainly not the most important. The great distinction of the time for the purpose of our own inquiry was between the Jews who had adopted Aristotelian principles and the Jews who opposed the innovation. The enlightenment and culture were incontrovertibly on the side of the former ; the fascination of bizarre thought, and its occasional flashes of a great mystical light, in a word, all that we connect with the ideal of rabbinical Israel, went, however, into the opposite scale. There were important names on both sides. For the rest, Rabbi Abraham and his SEPHER exercised a large influence : his contemporary, Maimonides, who survived him by almost a quarter of a century, was described by the enthusiasts of his period as " the elect of the human race," and by a play upon his name it was said of him

---

[1] It was the prototype of several later productions, such as that of Ghedalia on the CHAIN OF THE KABBALAH, the YUHASIN of Zakut, famous in connection with the ZOHAR, and finally TSEMACH DAVID = *Germen Davidis*, already quoted. The last was the work of R. David Ganz, a treatise on sacred and profane history from the beginning of the world.

[2] Bartolocci : MAGNA BIBLIOTHECA RABBINICA, i. pp. 18 *et seq.*

that "from Moses to Moses there was no one like unto Moses." The rival school was to some extent represented by Avicebron, and some of those who assert that the ZOHAR incorporated Traditions belonging to preceding centuries are content to rest their case on the writings of this poet and philosopher. The evidence, however, is in a very confused state. On the one hand, the system of Avicebron has many Aristotelian traces ; on the other hand, it has been asserted that Maimonides has much to connect him with Avicebron, though he was not acquainted with his works, while, further, the great masterpiece of the Talmudic Jew of Cordova, entitled THE GUIDE OF THE PERPLEXED, offers many indications of his sympathy with doctrines which are no other than those of the Speculative Kabbalah.[1] In a general sense, however, those who wished to introduce Aristotelian principles into Jewish philosophy belonged to that school which subsequently opposed the ZOHAR,[2] as, for example, Joseph ben Abraham Ibn Wakkar of Toledo, at the beginning of the fourteenth century,[3] while those who accepted the ZOHAR belonged to that school which connects with Avicebron, among whom was Rabbi Abraham ben David of Posquière, to whom one section of modern criticism attributes the invention of the Kabbalah, and Isaac the Blind—ob. circa 1219 —with his disciples Azriel and Ezra, whose supposed alternative claim is favoured by Ginsburg.[4] The Kabbalistic interests of this school are outside all debate ; it prized the SEPHER YETZIRAH, and one of the most important commentaries on that treatise was produced within it.

When we investigate the claim made with regard to Avice-

---

[1] There does not seem, however, the slightest ground for supposing, with Isaac Myer, that Maimonides was acquainted with the ZOHAR. On the contrary, there is more perhaps to be said for the conjecture of S. Munk that the ZOHAR quotes, or rather borrows, from Maimonides. See MÉLANGES, &c., p. 278. Among the Kabbalistic correspondences of Maimonides are (1) His recognition of a secret sense in Scripture ; (2) Of the inaccessible nature of God ; (3) Of the universe as an organic whole. The student should consult also an interesting NOTICE SUR LA CABALE DES HÉBREUX, prefixed by the Chevalier Drach to the second volume of his work already cited on the HARMONY BETWEEN THE CHURCH AND THE SYNAGOGUE. He establishes (a) That where Buxtorf supposes the TALMUD (Tract ROSH HASHANAH) to allow the same authority to the Kabbalah as to the text of Moses, the reference is really to the spiritual power of the Synagogue ; and (b) that the alleged mention of the mystical Kabbalah by Maimonides is a misconception (L'HARMONIE, ii. xvi. xvii. xviii.). It is certain, however, that Maimonides mentions a Lost Tradition.
[2] In which, however, Munk traces Aristotelian influences.—MÉLANGES, pp. 278, 279.
[3] See the English translation of Steinschneider's JEWISH LITERATURE, p. 114.
[4] Who follows Graetz literally.

bron, we must not be discouraged at finding that writers like Isaac Myer have much enhanced the extent and kind of his Kabbalistic connections. We meet, it is true, the doctrines of the Inaccessible God, of intermediaries between God and the universe, of the emanation of the world and even of the universal knowledge attributed to the pre-existent soul of man by most Jewish Mysticism. But what we should like to discover in a Theosophist of the eleventh century is some distinct trace of typical Zoharic doctrine, let us say, that of Shekinah, not mere Yetziratic references, Sephirotic correspondences and so forth. The two latter are to be expected at the period, and in this case the former is wanting. There remains, however, sufficient to concern us, perhaps even to warrant the inclusion of Gebirol among precursors of Zoharic Kabbalism, and a short account of this author may be appended as a conclusion to this section.

At that period when the influence of Arabian imagination was infused into the romantic literature of Western Europe, Scholastic Philosophy and Theology were imbued with the tincture of Arabian thought; but as, on the one hand, this tincture was received sometimes without much consciousness of its origin, so, on the other, influences were occasionally credited to Arabian sources which were in reality referable only to Spanish Jews living under the protection of the Khalifate during the Moslem domination of the Peninsula. A case in point was the once renowned Avicebron, whose identity with Solomon ben Yehudah Ibn Gebirol, a Jew of Cordova, was first demonstrated by Munk in the early part of the nineteenth century.[1] His chief treatise, entitled the FOUNTAIN OF LIFE, became widely diffused in a Latin version ascribed to the middle of the twelfth century. Albertus Magnus, St. Thomas of Aquin and Duns Scotus, all cited it; and it is said to sum the philosophy of the thirteenth century. According to Renan, Avicebron preceded the school of Arabian philosophy which arose in Spain. He wrote philosophy in Arabic and poetry in Hebrew; the Jews valued his poetry, but his speculations were not in repute among them; the Christian scholastics debated his metaphysical notions, and knew nothing whatever of his verses. By both classes of

---

[1] MÉLANGES DE PHILOSOPHIE JUIVE ET ARABE. The hostile school of Zoharic criticism has not done sufficient credit to Munk for his discovery, but he was not a *persona grata* among them on account of his theory that the ZOHAR was founded on genuine ancient MIDRASHIM. This school has almost passed away.

admirers he was celebrated respectively as the greatest philosopher and the greatest poet of his time. But the nominalists denounced him; realists like Duns Scotus entailed on him their own condemnation; while he is said to have exercised an influence upon mystics of the Middle Ages, he was proscribed by the University of Paris at the period of the publication of the ZOHAR on the ground that he favoured Aristotle. When the school of Averroes arose he was unknown among it; at a later period he was unknown to Maimonides; he was unknown also to the encyclopædic learning of Picus de Mirandula; and on the threshold of the Reformation his memory may be said almost to have perished at the pyre of Giordano Bruno.

Avicebron was born about the year 1021 at Malaga; he was educated in the University of Saragossa, and he died at Valencia in 1070. He was patronised by Nagdilah—*i.e.*, Samuel-ha-Levi ben Josef Ibn Nagréla—a Prince of the Exile, who was also Prime Minister of Spain under the Khalifate of Habus. Nagdilah was the centre and mainspring of Jewish learning in that country, and it has been proposed that through him the Sacred Tradition of the Hebrews was communicated to Avicebron at a period when the ZOHAR and its connections were still in course of formation. It seems certain, in any case, that some of the conceptions and the system incorporated in the literature may be found in his writings, more especially in the FOUNTAIN OF LIFE and the CROWN OF THE KINGDOM. The first is affirmed to be the earliest known exhibition of " the secrets of the Speculative Kabbalah." [1] The second, composed towards the end of his life, is a hymn " celebrating the only one and true God, and the marvels of His creation."

The existence of Zoharic tradition previously to the time of Moses de Leon, the reputed forger of the ZOHAR, has been rested, among other supports, on the writings of this Spanish Jew, and he seems to have been acquainted indubitably with the BOOK OF FORMATION. In the second book and twenty-second section of the FOUNTAIN OF LIFE this passage occurs : " Hence it hath been said that the construction of the world was accomplished by the inscription of numbers and letters

---

[1] There is some confusion here, as the SEPHER YETZIRAH is certainly speculative if contrasted with the so-called Practical Kabbalah, which was mainly the working of miracles by the use of Divine Names.

in the air," which is in obvious analogy with a fundamental notion of the Kabbalistic work in question. The table of the Thirty-Two Paths, which arises out of the BOOK OF FORMA-TION, was the theme of one of his poems. Whether the later Kabbalists derived from Avicebron or both from a common source cannot be determined conclusively, but having regard to the Jewish indifference for his philosophical writings, and to the probable existence of a vast mass of floating Esoteric Tradition, there can be no doubt as to the direction in which probability points.[1]

The connection between Avicebron and the Kabbalah is not sufficiently explicit upon the surface of the FOUNTAIN OF LIFE to have attracted the attention of scholars like Ernest Renan : while Kabbalistic critics refer the system which it develops to the ten SEPHIROTH, others suppose it to be based on the ten categories of Aristotle, a pantheism analogous to that of the early realists.[2] " On the one hand," says Renan, " his application of Peripatetic principles to Mosaic doctrine alarmed the theologians ; on the other hand, his concessions to orthodoxy concerning the creation and the free will of the Creator did not satisfy the extreme Peripatetic Jews." Of his alleged Kabbalistic connections Renan was either unaware, as suggested already, or they were ignored by him.

An impartial examination of the FOUNTAIN OF LIFE makes the pantheism of Avicebron perhaps less apparent than his Kabbalistic correspondences. So far from identifying the universe with God, it establishes no uncertain contrast between them. In order to bridge the abyss, and to make it conceivable that one derived being from the other, he supposes nine intermediaries, *plus* the Divine Will, " through which the Absolutely Existing, Which is above number," is " attached to Its corporeal universe." The analogies that this conception offers to Sephirotic Doctrine are self-evident and do not need enforcing, even if an impartial judgment must pronounce the philosophy of Avicebron to be of Greek rather than Jewish complexion. It is clear at least that FONS VITÆ, which is a dialogue after the manner of Plato, is tinctured deeply by Hellenic thought.

---

[1] Graetz takes the opposite view, saying that the Kabbalah borrowed many principles from Ibn Gebirol. He offers, of course, no evidence on the subject.

[2] The nature and names of the SEPHIROTH will be explained fully in Book V, §§ 2 and 3. At the present stage, and in respect of a few further preliminary allusions, the reader is referred to the first three plates which illustrate this volume.

Modern scholarship has recognised three chief schools which led up to Zoharic Kabbalism : (*a*) that of Isaac the Blind, to which belongs Azriel, with his celebrated commentary on the SEPHER YETZIRAH ; (*b*) that of Eliezar of Worms, which is largely of the theurgic order ; and (*c*) that of Abulafia, which to some extent united the preceding two and made use of theurgic formulæ combined with contemplation to achieve union with God—that is to say, the exteriorisation of mental images for the attainment of an end which is of all things inward and apart from the forms of mind.

II.—THE BOOK OF FORMATION

The attribution of SEPHER YETZIRAH to the patriarch Abraham is imbedded in the text itself of that minute tract which is regarded by most scholars as the chief nucleus of all Kabbalism. Depending from this there arose inevitably the rabbinical legend which affirms that Abraham transmitted it orally to his sons, by whom it was perpetuated in turn till certain " sages of Jerusalem " committed it finally to writing, so that the Tradition might not perish, even when the chosen people seemed themselves on the eve of perishing. We are acquainted already with this story and are in a position to gauge its value, which lies indeed upon the surface. It is the claim on a Secret Tradition *ab origine Symboli*, personified, so to speak, and it is carried back further still by the ZOHAR. It belongs to the mythos of successive custodians for the transmission of that which was itself a myth, so far as the claim on antiquity is concerned.

At the period when we hear first of the existence of such a tract it may have been old already, and most old books have fables designed to explain them. Those who take the fables historically convert honest legend into something approaching farce. We must be content therefore to say that the first Christian reference to SEPHER YETZIRAH may belong to the ninth century ; it has been held also that it is quoted in the TALMUD ; but criticism has proposed an alternative text under the same title and that the subject of Talmudic reference is no longer extant.[1] However this may be, there is no question

---

[1] The treatise SANHEDRIM contains the following passage : " By means of combining the letters of the Ineffable Names as recorded in SPR ITsIRH "—meaning the Sealing Names enumerated in the first chapter, being permutations of IHV—" Rava once created

that the BOOK OF FORMATION may have antedated its first citation in literature by a generation, a century, or an age. It should be realised that we do not know, and that those who judge the question dogmatically on either side deserve to be classed as intemperate. Let us look now a little more closely at the work itself. It is divided into six chapters, the first being concerned with the office of the SEPHIROTH in creation and the remaining five with what have been termed the Instruments—namely, the letters of the Hebrew Alphabet. It was after the revelation of these Mysteries to Abraham that he received the manifestation of God and that the Covenant was instituted. According to the expression of the original, God " bound the twenty-two letters " on the tongue of the patriarch and discovered to him His secret.[1]

There are two points which require to be noted at this preliminary stage of the Yetziratic myth. One is the absolute distinctness between God and the instruments of creation,[2] whether numbers or letters,[3] which is established by this early Kabbalistic work. Separated from all number and transcending all expression, He is represented as a Faithful King sojourning in eternity and ruling the SEPHIROTH for ever from His holy seat. The second point concerns the emanation of the SEPHIROTH, to which, in preference to their creation, later Kabbalism inclines. There is little on the face of the BOOK OF FORMATION to countenance this view, though the latest

---

a man and sent him to Rav Zeira. The man being unable to reply when spoken to, the Rabbi said to him, Thou art a creature of the company "—or those initiated in the Mysteries of Necromancy—" return to thy dust." It seems idle to suggest that this allusion is not to the tract which has been known for centuries and has been edited on so many occasions. As a fact, however, the reference is in reality to HILKOT YETZIRAH, a magical work belonging to the Talmudic period.

[1] SEPHER YETZIRAH, chap. vi.

[2] Hence C. G. Harrison was in error when he implied that pantheism is involved in the Sephirotic system, and when he proceeds to argue that " it takes no account of the element of illusion which is necessarily implied in the theophanic doctrine."— See THE TRANSCENDENTAL UNIVERSE, London, 1894, pp. 86, 87. Cf. Alexander Weill : LOIS ET MYSTÈRES DE LA CRÉATION CONFORMÉS À LA SCIENCE LA PLUS ABSOLUE. Paris, 1896. The writer refers to a work under a similar title which he issued forty years previously, purporting to be the translation of a Hebrew MS. by a master of Kabbalah. " This writing is distinguished from all rabbinical and philosophical treatises by proclaiming the identity of the Creator with His creatures, based on the text of Genesis itself." Weill was a fantasiast who pretended to separate the frauds and contradictions which Esdras and his assistants introduced into the Pentateuch from the real work of Moses. Cf. the same author's MOÏSE, LE TALMUD ET L'EVANGILE. Paris, 1875, tom. i. p. 99. According to Franck, the last word of the system developed by SEPHER YETZIRAH is the substitution of absolute unity for every species of dualism.— LA KABBALE, p. 159.

[3] See Appendix III.

translation makes use of the word " emanate " in one place only, *i.e. Cap.* I, v. 6. A literal rendering would be " go forth " ; for they appear as the instruments and servants of the King of Ages, informed by Whose word they do actually go forth " and returning, fall prostrate in adoration before the Throne." [1] It is said, however, that their end is bound to their beginning, as the flame is bound to the firebrand, and perhaps the principle of emanation is contained implicitly in this statement. We have no reason for rejecting a construction which has been adopted invariably, but it is just to draw attention to the fact that the first work which mentions the SEPHIROTH leaves this point in obscurity, while it depicts God as the active Former, Artificer and Maker, Who graved, sculptured and builded. In Masonic terms, He became and was the Great Architect of the Universe ; and anthropomorphism is postulated therefore at the very root of being.

The first SEPHIRA—classified therefore as ONE—is described as the Spirit of the Living Elohim, the Living God of Ages, eternal and for ever. It is said otherwise that the Spirit of the Holy One is Voice, Spirit and Word. Two is the Breathing of the Spirit, described otherwise as Air ; the twenty-two letters depend herefrom and each one of them is Spirit. THREE is the moisture which comes from the Breath—otherwise, Water from Air : herewith God sculptured and engraved the first lifeless and void matter. He built TOHU, the line which circles snake-like about the world,[2] and BOHU, the concealed rocks imbedded in the abyss whence the waters issue. This triad of the Spirit, the Breath and the Water corresponds to the conception formed subsequently of the Atzilutic or Archetypal World.[3] FOUR is the Fire which comes forth from the Water : with this God sculptured the Throne of Honour, the SERAPHIM, the OPHANIM or Celestial Wheels, the Holy Animals—*i.e.*, the Four Living Creatures— and other Ministering Spirits. Within their dominion He established His habitation.

When this numeration is combined with those which follow immediately, namely, FIVE and SIX, there is formed a second triad, which comprises the conception of BRIAH, the

---

[1] SEPHER YETZIRAH, chap. i. See the BOOK OF FORMATION. Translated from the Hebrew, by Knut Stenring, already cited.
[2] Compare the " green line "—*linea viridis*—which encircles the world in the CONCLUSIONES KABBALISTICÆ of Picus de Mirandula : see p. 446 of the present work.
[3] On the Four Worlds of Kabbalism, see Book V, § 3.

archangelic world of late Kabbalism. It should be remembered, however, that the BOOK OF FORMATION is concerned only with the sphere of operation tabulated subsequently as the Third World of Kabbalism. As each SEPHIRA was supposed at a later period to contain all the SEPHIROTH, so there was a superincession of the Four Worlds, which were all contained in each. The arrangement of the SEPHER YETZIRAH does not conform with this and indeed excludes it; for the numerations from five to nine inclusive muſt be held to represent the Yetziratic World, while the tenth and laſt numeration corresponds to ASSIAH—otherwise, the World of Aĉtion. FIVE is the seal with which God sealed the Height when He contemplated it above Him. He sealed it with the name IHV. SIX is the seal with which He sealed the depth when He contemplated it beneath Him. He sealed it with the name IVH. SEVEN is the seal with which He sealed the Eaſt when He contemplated it before Him. He sealed it with the name HIV. EIGHT is the seal with which He sealed the Weſt when He contemplated it behind Him. He sealed it with the name HVI. NINE is the seal with which He sealed the North when He contemplated it on His right. He sealed it with the name VIH. TEN is the seal with which He sealed the South when He contemplated it on His left. He sealed it with the name VHI. The ten numerations are classed finally together under the one title of "Ineffable Spirits of God." The Sealing Names are combinations of three letters, successively transposed, which enter into the name TETRAGRAMMATON.

The SEPHER YETZIRAH was published at Mantua in 1592, but the Latin translation of Poſtel had preceded it by ten years.[1] The Mantua edition was accompanied by five commentaries.[2] Another Latin version will be found in the colleĉtion of Piſtorius; it is ascribed to Reuchlinus and Riccius. In 1642 a further edition was published at Amſterdam in Hebrew and Latin by Rittangelius. It was issued by

---

[1] The full title of this curious little volume is ABRAHAMI PATRIARCHÆ LIBER JEZIRAH, sive Formationis Mundi, Patribus quidem Abrahami tempora præcedentibus revelatus, sed ab ipso etiam Abrahamo expositus Isaaco, et per Profetarum manus poſteritati conservatus, ipsis autem 72 Mosis auditoribus in secundo divinæ veritatis loco, hoc eſt in ratione, quæ eſt poſterior authoritate, habitus. Vertebat ex Hebræis et commentariis illuſtrabat 1551, ad Babylonis ruinam et corrupti mundi finem, GULIELMUS POSTELLUS, Reſtitutus. Parisiis, 1552.

[2] It contained also two recensions of the text, the differences between which are regarded by some authorities as considerable and by others as unimportant variants. Karppe (op. cit.; p. 138) terms them très divergents.

Meyer at Leipsic in 1830, with a German translation and notes, and at Frankfort, 1849, with a German translation and commentary,[1] by L. Goldschmidt. In 1887 the Parisian occultist Papus made a French translation, to which he added the Thirty-two Paths of Wisdom and the Fifty Gates of Intelligence. With laudable sincerity he admitted later on that this was superseded by Mayer Lambert in 1891.[2]

There is a question at its value which remains over for consideration, and this is how we are to account for the importance attributed in certain circles to such a work as the SEPHER YETZIRAH. Did its defenders believe that the combination of ALEPH with all the other letters and all the rest with ALEPH, BETH with all the others and all the rest with BETH, &c., &c., actually produced the universe? That is an insupportable assumption for any class of persons except possibly occult fantasiasts in the ecstasy of aberration which seems to have been their normal mode during the second half of the nineteenth century. Did they regard the letters as symbols of forces and hold that SEPHER YETZIRAH teaches that the universe originated in their orderly combination? That is tolerable speculation for the same class in its lucid intervals, having regard to its equipment, though it does not demand the apparatus of a Secret Tradition to secure its transmission from Abraham to Eliphas Lévi and from Lévi to Westcott and Mathers. But did they consider that the letters represent occult powers of a fixed, determinable character, and that initiation into the real meaning of Kabbalistic Tradition would discover their nature, explaining thus the secret behind the arbitrary doctrine of a virtue inherent in words and letters? Having known most of the groups, personally and otherwise, I have never met with any maker of reveries who took such a view, or had anything to substantiate it if he did. In the absence of light on this point one can conclude only that it is the arbitrary doctrine in question which accounts for the interest taken in the SEPHER YETZIRAH, outside that which it represents for pure scholarship, about which something has been said in an introduction

---

[1] The AMERICAN ENCYCLOPÆDIA, iii. 521, 522, mentions the Amsterdam edition of 1642, with a Latin translation, but does not connect it with Rittangelius.

[2] Other translations are those of (1) Isidor Kalisch, New York, 1877 ; (2) Edersheim in an Appendix to his JEWISH MESSIAH, 1886 ; (3) Wynn Westcott, 1887 and 1893, which I have described as paraphrase ; (4) Phineas Mordell, Philadelphia, 1914 : it reduces the genuine text to twenty-four paragraphs ; and (5) Rabbi A. B. Joseph, 1923.

prefixed by myself to the most recent English translation, being that of Mr. Knut Stenring, cited already in a note. I do not propose to retrace this ground and hence refer thereto. In conclusion, if the ZOHAR absorbed the SEPHER YETZIRAH as to its essence, it must be added that the older text brought nothing to the later which is part of its Theosophy at the highest.

III.—CONNECTIONS AND DEPENDENCIES OF THE BOOK OF FORMATION

Were there evidence to warrant us in believing that Moses de Leon did actually, as his hostile relative is reported to have affirmed, write the ZOHAR bodily " out of his own head," there would be substantial evidence still that the Kabbalistic system which it contains was not his invention at the root. The existence of the SEPHER YETZIRAH is part of this evidence, which appears, however, more fully and more strongly in the commentaries and developments of that work. We have seen already that when it came to be printed at Mantua, the BOOK OF FORMATION was accompanied by five such connections, which at the same time do not exhaust the list that might be given in a complete bibliography. The best known is unquestionably the SEPHER SEPHIROTH, or " Commentary on the Ten SEPHIROTH by way of Questions and Answers," the work of R. Azriel ben Menahem ; that of Rabbi Abraham has been regarded as the most important from an esoteric standpoint, while the earliest in point of time is the work of Saadya Gaon [1] in the tenth century. Another, which has been attributed to Hay Gaon in the early part of the eleventh century, would rank next in antiquity, but it has been rejected usually as spurious in respect of date and attribution. Commentaries are ascribed also to R. Moses Botarel,[2] R. Moses ben Nahmann,[3] R. Abraham ben David Ha Levi the younger and R. Eleazar. Of these personalities the first and last are subse-

---

[1] That is, Saadiah Ben Joseph, Gaon of Sura. The JEWISH ENCYCLOPÆDIA suggests that Saadia is " an artificial Hebrew equivalent " of his Arabic name Sa'id. GAON is a title which distinguished the heads of the two Academies at Babylon, those of Sura and Pumbedita, as we have seen. It arose late in the sixth century. The plural is GEONIM.

[2] He describes the Kabbalah as a most pure and holy philosophy, but exhibits no acquaintance with the ZOHAR. He belonged to the fourteenth and fifteenth centuries, and was instructed in the Secret Tradition by Jacob Sefardi.

[3] Bartolocci, iv. 267.

quent to the period when Moses de Leon is supposed to have been at work on the ZOHAR, and the two others have been cited to shew that the novelty of that work " is of form rather than material."

The commentary of R. Saadya Gaon is one of those which was published in Hebrew at Mantua, together with the SEPHER YETZIRAH [1]; but it was written originally in Arabic, and a copy is preserved in the Bodleian Library. After remaining in MS. for over eight hundred years this Arabic original was at length printed at Paris, together with a French translation, in 1892. In the introduction prefixed to his version, M. Lambert observed that Saadya Gaon appears as a Theosophist in his commentary, which is almost equivalent to saying that the first expository treatise on the SEPHER YETZIRAH possesses a Kabbalistic complexion, though the author has been regarded as a purely rationalistic writer. It must be confessed, however, that Saadya offers little connection with Zoharic doctrine. We have noted that the SEPHIROTH of the SEPHER YETZIRAH shew scarcely any trace of an emanational system. For Saadya Gaon there is one intermediary between God and the world, but this is the physical air and not the transcendental numerations. In this air God is present everywhere, and it penetrates all bodies, even the most compact. Of the doctrine of AIN SOPH there is also no real trace. It is recognised however, on the one hand, that we cannot have an adequate notion of the Divinity or His correspondences with the world, but, on the other, that some approximate idea may be obtained as to the latter and that they may be shewn forth by means of figures and comparisons. One of these illustrations tells us that God is the life of the world as the soul is the life of the body, and as in man the soul is all-powerful, so God is omnipotent in the world. He is also its Supreme Reason, and as in man the rational faculty is the guide of life, so the Divine Power is directed by the Divine Reason. Above this elementary form of Natural Theology the commentary never soars, and we are warranted in saying that the work, as a whole, has little inherent interest, though it is valuable as a historical document.

Unlike the SEPHER YETZIRAH, which makes no reference to pneumatology, Saadya Gaon devotes a certain space to the

---

[1] See p. 90.

consideration of the soul in man ; and here, in a sense, he connects with Zoharic Kabbalism, though he rejects metempsychosis utterly, for he recognises the soul's five aspects or divisions and calls them by their conventional names, which names, however, occur in the Talmud.[1]   They will be tabulated at a later stage.   Unfortunately, his classification is exceedingly clumsy, and he begins by following Plato in the recognition of three faculties—reason, concupiscence and anger.   On account of reason the soul is called NESHAMAH ; on account of concupiscence it is called NEPHESH ; and on account of anger it is called RUAH.   The two other names, HAÏA (living) and YEHIDAH (unique), refer to the vitality of the soul and to the fact that no other creature resembles it. We shall see that the Zohar knows nothing of such material attributions.

The doctrine concerning Divine and Angelic Names is also a subject of some references which are important to our inquiry because they establish the fact that Saadya Gaon did not ascribe to them any thaumaturgic virtues.   The names of the angels vary according to the events which they are commissioned to accomplish, and in like manner those referred to the Deity are descriptive of His operations.   In the Work of Creation He terms Himself ELOHIM ; when ordaining the Covenant of Circumcision He is called EL SHADDAI ; He is the I AM in connection with the wonders of the ten plagues ; and He is JAH when producing the great miracle of the Red Sea.[2]   As it is with the names of God and the angels, so is it with those of the stars, which vary according to their qualities —namely, their greater or lesser brilliance, their hot or cold natures, &c.

When explaining that the SEPHER YETZIRAH is concerned with created things and how they came into being, there is a

---

[1] Despite his hostility to reincarnation, as understood by the Kabbalah, he accepts the pre-existence of souls and teaches that the resurrection of the body will take place when all souls destined for earthly life have passed through it.   Here is one example of Zoharic doctrine, pure and simple, but it has been reflected from the past into the later text.

[2] The ZOHAR teaches that the Divine Name AHIH, which signifies I AM, indicates the unification and concealment of all things in such a manner that no distinction can be established between them.   The words ASHR AHIH, THAT I AM, represent God on the point of manifesting all things, including His Supreme Name. On the other hand the Name or Title AHIH ASHR AHIH, I AM THAT I AM, refers to the Deity, or is that Name assumed by Him, on the occasion of the manifestation of the Cosmos, when God is called JEHOVAH.—Zohar iii. 65*b*, Mantua.   Compare the French translation, v. 179.

reference to the ten categories—namely, substance, quantity, quality, relation, place, time, powers, position, activity, passivity ; and if these are to be regarded as referring to the numerations of the SEPHER YETZIRAH, it is clear that Saadya Gaon understood the latter as an Aristotelian philosopher. With these categories, the ten commandments are also forced to correspond in an arbitrary manner. For example, that against adultery answers to the category of position, for the act itself is a position and a contact.

Lastly, in his analysis of the Hebrew Alphabet, the commentator seeks to account for its sequence. ALEPH is the first sound pronounced—*i.e.*, it is vocalised at the back of the tongue. SHIN is vocalised in the middle of the mouth and MEM on the lips. Unfortunately for the analogy, MEM precedes SHIN in the alphabet, and indeed the design of the speculation seems past conjecture.

About the commentary ascribed to Hay Gaon there is considerable confusion, which Isaac Myer increases by representing that it deals with the BOOK OF CONCEALMENT, instead of that of FORMATION. There are no historical notices and no traces whatsoever of the former text before the appearance of the ZOHAR, in which it was first made known. The tract of Hay Gaon needs only to be mentioned in passing on account of its disputed authenticity. Other works attributed to him are not above suspicion, but it may be admitted in a general way that he had more distinct Kabbalistic connections than Saadya. The condemned commentary deals largely with the Mysteries of TETRAGRAMMATON and gives perhaps for the first time the curious quadrilateral method of writing it by means of letters and circles, to which so much importance has been attributed by modern occult writers.[1] The commentary of Abraham ben David Ha Levi,[2] the younger of that name and a contemporary of Maimonides, whom he attacked bitterly, is included also in the Mantua edition of the BOOK OF FORMATION, and was used largely by Rittangelius in that of Amsterdam, 1642.[3] The uttermost

---

[1] By Éliphas Lévi above all, who reproduces its diagram with additions which are merely fantastic (DOGME DE LA HAUTE MAGIE, section dealing with the Kabbalah), and elsewhere (LA SCIENCE DES ESPRITS) illustrates these additions by a Kabbalistic document which I think also is one of his specimens of invention.

[2] Bartolocci, i. 15. His birth is referred to *circa* 1110, and he is supposed to have suffered the death of a martyr in or near 1180.

[3] LIBER JESIRAH (Hebrew and Latin) *qui Abrahamo patriarchæ adscribitur, una cum commentario Rabbi Abraham* F. D. (*i.e.*, Ben Dior, *i.e.*, Daur and also Rabad) *super* 32

confusion prevails with regard to the personality of the author, who, on the one hand, is frequently identified with the writer of the SEDER HA KABBALAH, and is, on the other, the subject of many contradictory myths prevailing in occult circles. Éliphas Lévi, who cites a passage from his treatise as a proof of the authenticity and reality of his own " discovery " of the *Magnum Opus*,[1] makes a great deal of mystery concerning it and its rarity, but he has used evidently the edition of Rittangelius, which is perfectly well known and attainable in almost any national library.

We have recognised that the commentary of Saadya Gaon can scarcely be termed Kabbalistic ; we have agreed to set aside another which abounds in Kabbalistic material because its date and attribution have been challenged ; in the work of R. Abraham, however, there are Zoharic elements which admit of no question, and it is indeed to the school which he represents that Graetz and others have referred the authorship of the BOOK OF SPLENDOUR. There is the peculiar distinction between upper and lower SEPHIROTH which is not only characteristic of the Zoharic period, though it is not found in the ZOHAR, but offers a connecting link between R. Abraham and the late Kabbalism of Isaac de Loria.[2] Moreover, there is the doctrine of the Unknowable God, of " the Cause of Causes which is not apprehended by any one outside Itself," being void of all distinction and all mode of existence. The doctrine has not assumed that final shape in which it is presented by the ZOHAR, and its notion of the Divine Being appears to be, if possible, more concealed and latent than the conception of AIN SOPH, the NON ENS, which Itself is distinguished by R. Abraham from KETHER, the Crown of Creation, on the remarkable ground that " the accident is not

---

Semitas Sapientiæ . . . *Translatus et Notis illustratus à Joanne Stephano Rittangelio* . . . *Amstelodami*, 1642. The thirty-two Paths referred to at the beginning of the SEPHER YETZIRAH are given in Latin and Hebrew, each followed immediately by the commentary of R. Abraham, likewise in Latin and Hebrew. Then comes the explanation of Rittangelius, which sometimes extends to many pages, quoting various authorities, including the ZOHAR and its Supplements. After the Paths, we have the SEPHER YETZIRAH itself, in Latin and Hebrew, with the editor's commentary, also in both languages. It should be added that the entire commentary of R. Abraham is not given by Rittangelius, who is content with presenting that part only which is devoted to the Paths of Wisdom.

[1] RITUEL DE LA HAUTE MAGIE, c. 12, where the Hebrew passage cited is completely unintelligible. It has been rectified in my annotated translation, s.v. TRANSCENDENTAL MAGIC. *Cf.* LA CLEF DES GRANDS MYSTÈRES, pp. 233, 234.

[2] There is no doubt that the ten SEPHIROTH were an evolved system in the time of the Yetziratic commentator.

made from the essence, nor the Res from the Non Res or Non Ens," thus occasioning an insoluble difficulty as to the emanation of the manifest universe. This view offers a strong contrast to Zoharic Theosophy. Otherwise, the Ain Soph of our commentator is described in terms which are almost identical with Zoharic teaching. "Neither unity nor plurality can be attributed to It, because unity cannot be ascribed to that which is incomprehensible in its essence," the reason being that number is an accident belonging to the world of extension, place and time.

Among minor Zoharic contrasts, it may be noted that a more peculiar importance is attributed to the letter Aleph than to the Beth with which Genesis opens ; it is the form of all the letters, and all the Paths of Wisdom are contained therein, but after an universal mode. There are traces also of the peculiar angelical system which was destined to receive so much elaborate extension from expositors of the Book of Splendour.

Before dismissing this commentary we may note the alleged connection of its author with that Abraham the Jew [1] who belongs to the literature of Alchemy. The testament of this mysterious personage transformed the legendary Nicholas Flamel from a simple scrivener into a seeker after the Great Work—a search, moreover, which his story represents as crowned with high success. The memorial in question was addressed to the nation of Israel, dispersed by the wrath of God in France, by one who styled himself "Priest, Prince, Levite, Astrologer and Philosopher." The description which constitutes our sole knowledge concerning it is given in another testament, that of Nicholas Flamel, and I have shewn elsewhere that this memorial cannot be regarded as authentic. [2] Belonging as they do to Alchemy, there is no ground here to discuss their respective claims ; but it is well to say that the attempt made by Éliphas Lévi to identify the Abraham of Flamel with the commentator on the Sepher Yetzirah not only institutes a connection between Alchemy and Kabbalism which is unwarrantable in itself but has no colourable evidence to cite in its own support, as there is no trace whatever of any alchemical meaning in the Hebrew commentator. Abraham

---

[1] This title is used by Bartolocci in his bibliography to describe numerous writers who cannot be identified more closely.
[2] See my Secret Tradition in Alchemy, 1926, c. x., pp. 137 et seq.

the Kabbalist belongs, moreover, to the twelfth century, while Flamel was two hundred years later, and the book which he mentions could scarcely have existed in Jewry, even on the Lévi hypothesis, for such a space of time without something transpiring concerning it.

As a literary and philosophical work the first place among dependencies of the SEPHER YETZIRAH seems assigned correctly to the commentary of Azriel. Its author was born at Valladolid in or about the year 1160 and died in 1238. According to some authorities he was a pupil of Isaac the Blind,[1] but others say that his teacher was R. Jehuda, son of Rabad. He became in turn the instructor of R. Moses Nahmanides, who also belongs to the chain of Yetziratic tradition.[2]

Azriel is said to have travelled much in search of Secret Wisdom, but it was an age when men of learning were frequently wanderers, and it was perhaps less recondite motives which actuated him. He connects with the Kabbalistic system which was expounded by the school of Gerona, and there are no real grounds for supposing that he acquired knowledge elsewhere, but he added the result of his own reflections. Many works have been attributed to him, of which some are lost and some have remained in MS. THE EXPLANATION OF THE TEN SEPHIROTH *by way of Questions and Answers* must have helped to shape the metaphysical speculations of the Kabbalah and may well enough have originated more than it derived.

The teachings of Azriel aroused the opposition of the Aristotelian Jews, and it is thought by Isaac Myer that the logical form of his commentary was a concession to this school of thought. Whatever its motive, the fact, broadly taken, is of importance to our inquiry: it shews that the Sephirotic notion in its earliest development could not have been that of the categories, since it had to be conformed to the principles espoused by the disciples of Aristotle. The Jewish *literati* followed various schools, and the influence attributed to the Stagirite has been perhaps exaggerated. The votaries of the so-called Secret Wisdom were a small minority. Platonism, as it is needless to say, was very little known in the

---

[1] Was in evidence A.D. 1190 to *circa* 1210. He taught the doctrine of metempsychosis and a few fragments of his writings are still extant.

[2] And brought, as Graetz admits, the influence of his great reputation to bear upon its fortunes.

West at the period in question, though it appears in later Kabbalism.

As regards both matter and form, Azriel's commentary has been the subject of high praise. It contains the doctrine of AIN SOPH, which is not in the SEPHER YETZIRAH, and it has express views on the emanation of the SEPHIROTH, which are said to be contained in AIN SOPH and of no effect when separated. Their emanation was possible because it must be within the omnipotence of Deity to assume a limit. The essence and the real principle of all finite things is the Thought of the Supreme Being ; [1] if that were withdrawn, they would be left as empty shells, and this is true not only of the visible world but of the intermediaries between God and the creation. With his philosophical speculations the Kabbalist mingles something from the fantastic region, attributing, for example, to the SEPHIROTH [2] certain symbolical colours. KETHER is " like the Concealed Light," or the light which is veiled in darkness, the comparison intended being probably that of a luminous mist. BINAH is sky-blue, because BINAH is the great sea of Kabbalism. CHOKMAH is yellow, CHESED white and GEBURAH red ; TIPHERETH is white, red, or pink, NETZACH is whitish-red and HOD reddish-white. JESOD is a combination of the previous triad, while MALKUTH is like the light which reflects all colours. Azriel countenances also the Sephirotic division of the human body which is found in later Kabbalism.

Moses ben Nahman, or Nahmanides, was born in 1194 at Gironne. Before he made acquaintance with the Kabbalah he is said to have had a prejudice against it, but he was afterwards an enthusiastic student both of its speculative and practical parts, and by his writings and influence contributed much to its development. His Kabbalistic EXPLANATION OF THE LAW was completed in 1268, and among his many other works that called the GARDEN OF DELIGHT, and another on the SECRETS OF THE THORAH, are full of theosophical speculations.[3] He left his native land to settle in Palestine, where he

---

[1] *Cf.* ZOHAR, Pt. I. fol. 74a ; I. 440.

[2] According to the ZOHAR the colour attributions are as follows : KETHER, black, white, or colourless ; TIPHERETH, purple ; MALKUTH, clear sapphire.

[3] His other works include an epistle on the use of matrimony in exercising the fear of God—no humorous suggestion being intended ; a work on the nature of man, from the text of II. Samuel, vii. 19 ; a BOOK OF FAITH AND CONFIDENCE ; another on Wars ; and yet another on the Pomegranate. These are not professedly Kabbalistic,

died, apparently at a great age, but at what precise time is not known : it was *circa* 1270.

The commentary on the SEPHER YETZIRAH which passes under the name of R. Eliezer of Worms seems to have been the work of a German Jew of Germesheim,[1] one of the greatest Kabbalists of his period. That he was the instructor of Moses Nahmanides, as some authorities have stated, is, however, a mistake, as Basnage has indicated, for he belongs to a later date. His works, which are wholly Kabbalistc, are (1) THE VESTMENT OF THE LORD, but this has never been printed. (2) THE GUIDE OF SINNERS, exhorting them to repentance and amendment of life (Venice, 1543). (3) A TREATISE ON THE SOUL, cited by Mirandula in his thesis against astrologers. (4) An explanation of Psalm cxlv. (5) A commentary on SEPHER YETZIRAH, appended to the Mantua edition of that work. The author flourished before and after the middle of the fourteenth century. Commentaries on the SEPHER YETZIRAH are referable or ascribed —as the case may be—to R. Aaron the Great,[2] under the title of BOOK OF THE POINTS ; R. Judas Ha Levi[3] ; Sabbatai Donolo[4] ; Judah ben Barzillai[5] ; and Isaac the Blind. The Bodleian has a manuscript entitled MISHNAT, by Yosef ben Uzziel, which has been classed as a commentary on SEPHER YETZIRAH, but is said otherwise to be a supplement to the text itself. See JEWISH ENCYCLOPÆDIA, *s.v.* Joseph ben Uzziel.

---

like the TREASURE OF LIFE, the TREASURE OF THE LORD, the GARDEN OF DELIGHT (mentioned in the text above), or the mystical epistle on the thing desired. As regards the practical part of the Kabbalah, he treated it with grave consideration, including its arts of necromancy, the evocation of evil spirits and the methods of their control.

[1] Basnage : HISTOIRE DES JUIFS, c. vii. t. v. p. 1859. See also Bartolocci, i, 186, 187.
[2] Bartolocci, i. 15.
[3] See his work entitled KUSARI.
[4] Edited by M. Castelli. Florence, 1880. He was an Italian physician and astrologer, who was born in 913 and died subsequently to 982. He is known otherwise as Shabbethai b. Abraham b. Joel.
[5] Edited by M. Halbertstamm. Berlin, 1885. The Judah in question was a Spanish Talmudist of Barcelona, who flourished at the end of the eleventh and early in the twelfth centuries.

BOOK IV

THE WRITTEN WORD OF KABBALISM:
SECOND OR ZOHARIC PERIOD

BOOK IV

THE WRITTEN WORD OF KABBALISM: SECOND PERIOD

I.—THE BOOK OF SPLENDOUR: ITS CONTENT AND DIVISIONS

THE cycle of the SEPHER YETZIRAH lies within a small compass; the text is extant in several languages; and its most important dependencies will be found in Latin translations.[1] It has been available therefore to students and inquirers at large, even if they were unacquainted with Hebrew. The SEPHER HA ZOHAR, on the other hand, is not only large in itself but has considerable supplementary matter belonging to a later period and an extensive connected literature. Moreover, it is written—for the most part—in Aramaic, "the Jerusalem idiom" of Isaac de Acco; and only three short tracts imbedded in the general text are extant in Latin. Between the thirteenth and twentieth centuries it was therefore a sealed book for the great majority of scholars, till a full-length version appeared in French—as we have seen—within recent years.[2] Prior to this event great confusion had obtained in regard, firstly, to the content of the work and, secondly, to the comparative importance of its various divisions.[3] Part of this must be attributed to the ambitious design of Rosenroth's historical collection. The KABBALA

---

[1] The first printed edition appeared at Mantua in 1562 and contained two recensions, the second being longer and embodying important additions.

[2] The Italian reader may be referred also to an analysis of the Zohar by the Abbé de Rossi, which appeared in his DIZIONARIO STORICO DEGLI AUTORI EBREI. The writer follows Morin as to the late date of the work.

[3] The case of Basnage may be mentioned as that of a well-informed writer, whose history of the Jewish people from the time of Jesus Christ to his own date—the beginning of the eighteenth century—is memorable in several respects, yet whose knowledge of the ZOHAR does not even extend so far as it might have been taken by Rosenroth. He terms (*Livre* iii. p. 775) the BOOK OF CONCEALMENT the first part of the work, and seems to regard it as comprised simply in that and the two Synods. In a word, he had not read the preface to KABBALA DENUDATA, vol. ii.

DENUDATA, by attempting to cover much too wide a field, gives no adequate idea of the work which it is meant to elucidate. It attributes an exaggerated importance to three tracts introduced into the body of the ZOHAR and to late commentary on these ; the apparatus in the form of a lexicon which fills most of the first volume, though it has a methodical appearance, is little more than a chaos, in which late and early expositors are bundled together after the uncritical manner of the period ; in a subsequent section undue prominence is given to some personal discussions and correspondence between the Editor and Henry More, the English Platonist ; finally, the second volume includes an enormous treatise on the doctrine of the Revolutions of Souls by a Kabbalist of the seventeenth century. With all its defects the KABBALA DENUDATA remains of prime value, but it would have been beyond all price had a clearer genius governed its arrangement. As it is, the class of persons who have proved to be most concerned with the subject have been content to follow the lead of Rosenroth, by accepting a little tract called the BOOK OF CONCEALMENT as the fundamental part of the whole ZOHAR, and the developments of that tract as entitled to the next highest consideration. There are, of course, several sources of information which might have corrected this false impression—the work of Franck in France and that of Ginsburg in England, to name two only—but it has endured notwithstanding, and a notable example to the point is found in an enlarged edition of a compilation by Dr. Papus. There a bibliographical appendix states that "the only complete translation" of the ZOHAR is the work of M. H. Chateau,[1] whereas the enterprise in question is confined only to the tracts rendered into Latin by Rosenroth, and these have been available for years in the English version of Mathers. The BOOK OF OCCULTATION—or CONCEALMENT—and its Zoharistic commentaries are only accidents of the ZOHAR, and they furnish no notion of the scope of that vast Theosophical Miscellany. I should add that from an esoteric standpoint the ZOHAR itself is only an accident of the Kabbalah—an

---

[1] LE ZOHAR, *Traduction française et Commentaire de* M. H. Chateau. The bibliographical annotation accredits the translator with *minutieuse érudition* and adds that he has carefully collated the Hebrew texts, the Latin and the other versions. The work is poorly produced, it bears no trace of the scholarship imputed to it and the commentary is of no real value. Moreover, the title itself deserves to be called fraudulent.

accident in the life of the alleged Tradition, much as, from the standpoint of Latin Christianity, the New Testament is not the exclusive foundation of the Church but an event in her development.

The ZOHAR proper, as stated in my preface, purports to be a commentary on the Pentateuch, and to indicate its scope, prior to any presentation of my own, I will vary my general rule of confining quotations from modern authors to footnotes and summarise an account of Ginsburg : " The ZOHAR does not (apparently) propound a regular Kabbalistic system, but dilates upon the diverse doctrines of this Theosophy, as indicated in the forms and ornaments of the Hebrew alphabet, in the vowel points and accents, in the Divine Names and the letters of which they are composed, in the narratives of the Bible and in the traditional and national stories. The long conversations between its author, R. Simeon ben Yohai, and Moses, which it records ; the short and pathetic prayers inserted therein ; the religious anecdotes ; the attractive spiritual explanation of Scripture passages, appealing to the hearts and wants of men ; the descriptions of the Deity and the SEPHIROTH under the tender forms of human relationship, comprehensible to the finite mind, such as father, mother, primeval man, matron, bride, white head, the great and small face, the luminous mirror, the higher heaven, the higher earth, &c., which it gives on every page, made the ZOHAR a welcome text-book for the students of the Kabbalah, who, by its vivid descriptions of Divine Love,[1] could lose themselves in rapturous embraces with the Deity."

We are placed by this quotation in a position to understand, firstly, after what manner the literature of Kabbalism affected the fervid imagination of the rabbinical Jew and the kind of influence which it had on him, well illustrated in one of its aspects by the fascinating and terrible histories of Messianic enthusiasm and illusion, as already noted, but in another by Zoharic Theosophy at its highest development. We can understand, secondly, how much there is to correct in the pretence of a French speculation which once fixed upon the ZOHAR as embodying traditional knowledge of a religion

---

[1] It is in this respect that the ZOHAR suggests analogies with Christian Mysticism as well as Arabian Sufism. For the rest, my readers must be dissuaded from supposing that Ginsburg's summary is adequately representative of the work, for it contains no reference to the Doctrine of Shekinah or the Zoharic Mystery of Sex.

behind all religions.[1] No system responds less readily to what is involved in such a conception. No person would be less disposed than the conventional occultist, present or past, to accept Kabbalistic notions of religion, were he really acquainted therewith, after due allowance has been made for Zoharic and other reveries which connect with occult beliefs, as these seem in their turn to connect magnetically with everything unsound in faith and unreasonable in doctrine. That God is immanent in the material world is a much simpler and more rational hypothesis than to establish intermediaries between finite and infinite, which create innumerable difficulties without resolving any, while on another side of the subject we have better means of excusing the anthropomorphisms of the Bible, than their *reductio ad absurdum*, which has been regarded as implied in the Kabbalistic Doctrine of the Two Countenances.

The ZOHAR proper—apart, that is to say, from all supplements and interpolations—is divided into five parts, corresponding to the five Scriptural Texts on which it is supposed to be a commentary, namely, Genesis, Exodus, Leviticus, Numbers and Deuteronomy. The first two are complete to all intents and purposes, the third and fourth have certain missing portions, while of Deuteronomy there is little more than fragments. The extant work, as printed, is in three parts only, of which the last comprises all that remains of the Commentary on the three later books of the Pentateuch. Each part is subdivided into various sections, separately entitled, *e.g.*, SECTIO BERESHITH, SECTIO TOLDOTH NOAH, and so forth. There is no call to enumerate them in this place. There are twelve sections of alleged interpretation in respect of Genesis, ten on Exodus, nine each on Leviticus and Numbers, and five only on Deuteronomy, manifestly imperfect as such. The Commentary on Genesis is followed by certain Appendices, being I, HASHMALOTH = OMISSIONS; II, TOSSEFTOTH = ADDITIONS; and *sub voce* Appendix III, two important Supplements, comprising extracts from MIDRASH HA NEELAM = SECRET MIDRASH, and SITHRE THORAH = SECRETS OF THE LAW. The following independent texts are introduced between certain sections of the Commentary on Exodus and sometimes within the sections themselves, namely : *post* § I,

---

[1] According to Éliphas Lévi, " all religions have issued from the Kabbalah and all return thereto."

MIDRASH HA NEELAM (continued); *post* § III, RAAIAH MEHEMNAH = FAITHFUL SHEPHERD; *post* § V, SEPHER HA BAHIR = LUMINOUS BOOK, and SITHRE THORAH (continued); *post* § VI, FAITHFUL SHEPHERD (continued), and IDRA DE MASCHCANA = ASSEMBLY OF THE SANCTUARY; *post* § VII, SIPHRA DI ZENIOUTHA = BOOK OF CONCEALMENT. The Commentary on Exodus has also three Appendices, two embodying ADDITIONS and one containing an independent tract on PALACES. The sections of Exodus have, moreover, certain MATHNITIN = REPETITIONS interpolated. Others follow § I of the Commentary on Leviticus, while §§ VII, VIII and IX are reinforced by further continuations of the FAITHFUL SHEPHERD. The Commentary on Numbers has the following independent texts introduced between its sections: *post* § II, FAITHFUL SHEPHERD (continued), and IDRA RABBA KADISHA = GREAT HOLY ASSEMBLY; *post* § III, FAITHFUL SHEPHERD (continued); *post* § VII, FAITHFUL SHEPHERD (continued), and certain MISCELLANIES. Among the fragments of Deuteronomy, § I is followed by a further instalment of the FAITHFUL SHEPHERD, while portions of this work constitute the extant sections numbered III, V and VI. To § X is appended IDRA ZOUTA KADISHA = LITTLE HOLY ASSEMBLY.

With this very simple and unpretentious collation there may be compared the analytical scheme of Rosenroth, which remains of bibliographical interest after the lapse of more than two centuries. The ZOHAR is divided thereby into internal and external parts, which are tabulated at length as follows.[1]

I. The internal parts are those which are collected together in one edition.[2] They are:

(*a*) The text of the ZOHAR, properly so called. Apart from all its additions this is not of unmanageable dimensions.

(*b*) SIPHRA DI ZENIOUTHA, or BOOK OF CONCEALMENT —otherwise, that of MODESTY.

(*c*) The IDRA RABBA, or GREATER SYNOD.

---

[1] KABBALA DENUDATA, vol. ii. pp. 8 *et seq.*
[2] So far as it is possible to estimate the intention of this statement there is no correspondence with fact. The BOOK OF CONCEALMENT and IDRAS are certainly not internal parts of any Commentary on the Pentateuch, and in the ZOHAR they are not combined with the text proper so as to form one scheme therewith. It may be said on the contrary that all interpolations are casual, while the Appendices to the part of Exodus might change places with those of Genesis, and so of the rest.

(*d*) The IDRA ZOUTA, or LESSER SYNOD.

(*e*) SABAH DI MISHPATIM, the *Discourse* or *Story of the Ancient One in section* MISHPATIM.

(*f*) MIDRASH RUTH, or COMMENTARY on the Scriptural book of that name. These are fragments only.

(*g*) SEPHER HA BAHIR, the RENOWNED or ILLUSTRIOUS BOOK, sometimes called BOOK OF BRIGHTNESS.

(*h*) TOSSEFTOTH = ADDENDA, or ADDITIONS.

(*i*) RAAIAH MEHEMNAH, or the FAITHFUL SHEPHERD.

(*j*) HAIKLUTH, *i.e.*, PALACES, MANSIONS, or ABODES.

(*k*) SITHRAI THORAH, or *Mysteries of the* THORAH, *i.e.*, the LAW.

(*l*) MIDRASH HA NEELAM, or SECRET COMMENTARY.

(*m*) RAZÉ DERAZIN, or SECRET OF SECRETS.

From this account are omitted the following tracts and fragments, because they do not appear in the Mantua edition of *circa* 1558, known as the LITTLE ZOHAR : [1]

(*a*) MIDRASH HAZEETH, or *Commentary on the Song of Solomon.*

(*b*) PEKOODAH, or *Explanation of the Thorah.*

(*c*) YENOOKAH, or the *Discourse of the Youth.*

(*d*) MAAMAR TO HAZEE, or the *Discourse* beginning, Come and See.

(*e*) HIBBOORAH KADMAÁ, or *Primary Assembly.*

(*f*) MATHNITIN, or Repetitions = *Traditional Receptions*, according to Rosenroth.

The ground on which these portions are set aside appears insufficient, as the sections *e, f, g, j,* and *m* in the first tabulation are also wanting in the Mantua edition. The GREAT ZOHAR, the Cremona edition (1558–60), contains all the treatises enumerated in both the above lists. I am not aware that any superior authority resides in the Mantua ZOHAR. [2]

II. As understood by Rosenroth, the external parts are those superadded to the earlier editions. These are :

(*a*) TIKKUNIM HA ZOHAR, or SUPPLEMENTS of the BOOK OF SPLENDOUR, called also the ANCIENT SUPPLE-

---

[1] The GREATER ZOHAR being that of Cremona. Blunt's DICTIONARY OF DOCTRINAL AND HISTORICAL THEOLOGY makes a ludicrous confusion over this point, representing the GREATER ZOHAR as the Commentary on Genesis and the Lesser as the BOOK OF CONCEALMENT.

[2] A Hebrew translation in MS. by Barachiel ben Korba is preserved—it is said—in the Public Library of Oppenheim.

MENTS, to distinguish them from further and later additions.

(*b*) ZOHAR HADASH—the NEW ZOHAR, containing matters omitted in the printed editions. This has four parts.

(1) The text of the ZOHAR itself, scattered through which is the supplement of the tract MIDRASH HA NEELAM, part of which appears in the original work.

(2) TIKKUNIM HADASHIM, or *New Supplements.*

(3) ZOHAR SHIR HA SHIRIM, or EXPOSITION OF THE SONG OF SONGS, appertaining to the ZOHAR.

(4) ZOHAR AIKE, or *Exposition of Lamentations,* appertaining to the ZOHAR.

In the above tabulations are contained everything of the ZOHAR that has come down to us.[1] It may be thought that its authenticity did not increase with its bulk, but on this subject no canon of criticism can be said to have emerged.

For the better comprehension of the cycle Rosenroth recommends :

(*a*) SEPHER DEREK EMETH, that is, the *Way of Truth,* being various readings in the ZOHAR arranged according to the Mantua edition.

(*b*) BINAH IMRI, or *Words of Understanding,* being an elucidation of difficulties in Zoharistic vocabulary.

(*c*) ZOHAR CHAMAH, or SPLENDOUR OF THE SUN, a short commentary which follows the Mantua edition.

(*d*) PARDES RIMMONIM, or GARDEN OF POMEGRANATES, by R. Moses of Cordova, an explanation of numerous texts in the ZOHAR and TIKKUNIM.

(*e*) MEQUR CHOKMAH, or FOUNT OF WISDOM, forming a continuation or new part of the WAY OF TRUTH.

(*f*) MARAH KOHEN, or the VISION OF THE PRIEST, a synoptic work, the greater part of which appears in KABBALA DENUDATA, vol. ii. part i.

(*g*) ZER ZAHAB, or a CROWN OF GOLD, used largely in the apparatus of Rosenroth.

(*h*) PATHACH AINIM, or GATE OF THE EYES, for the Biblical quotations in the ZOHAR and TIKKUNIM.

Rosenroth also recommends and reproduces largely the manuscript treatises of Isaac de Loria, compiled by R. Hayyim

[1] KABBALA DENUDATA, ii. p. 9.

Vital, and further acknowledges his indebtedness to two other unprinted works, a Kabbalistic commentary on the whole Law and a treatise entitled CHESED ABRAHAM.

The ZOHAR proper, the conversations of Simeon ben Yohai with the prophets by whom he was visited, with the disciples by whom he was surrounded and of these, as we have seen, with each other, is not a work that is to be judged by the same standard as certain symbolical portions which have been incorporated therewith, and to which Christian students of Kabbalism have given so much prominence. There are extravagant speculations and wild exegesis, but it is uncontaminated by monstrous symbolism; it has occasionally a touch of Nature to indicate its kinship with humanity, and condescends even at times to a Rabelaisian episode.[1] Finally, it does not betray any trace of that secret meaning, otherwise double doctrine, that hypothetical sense withdrawn far down below any primary inward sense, which has been sometimes ascribed loosely to its entire content, by those who would and do likewise discern a latent transcendental philosophy in Pantagruelism.[2]

We have seen that in a certain manner—somewhat occasional and informal—the ZOHAR is a commentary on the Pentateuch, and it is to be understood and passed over that as such it is not only casual and occasional, that not only has it nothing in harmony with the simple sense of Scripture, but that for us in the western world and at this age of the world it opens abysses where dark clouds hang out and fire of madness flashes, more often than deeps of meaning which resound with pregnant messages. It would serve no purpose to enlarge upon this fact, which applies to so much of Kabbalistic interpretation. The governing principle affirmed is the existence of several senses in the written word. These are enumerated differently, and there seems no reason why they should not be extended; but they are reducible broadly under three heads, which are compared by the ZOHAR to the garment, the body which is within it and the soul which is within the body.[3] They are to be distinguished in all cases

---

[1] Many rabbinical histories, fables and apologues are narrated in it, sometimes elucidating a knotty point of Scripture, as, for example, whether the destruction of animal life at the Deluge may indicate that the beasts also sinned, sometimes recounting the death of a just man, sometimes describing visions and narrating tales of wonder.

[2] Following the lead of Éliphas Lévi, especially in LE SORCIER DE MEUDON.

[3] See *ante*, Book I, § 1, pp. 11–13. They do not emerge in the text.

from those speculations on hidden significance to which reference has been made above. The design of Theosophy in Israel was to magnify the election of Israel by exalting its title-deeds, but that of the expositors in question was to represent the Sons of the Doctrine as the custodians of a Liberal Theology which made all election void.

" There are those unwise," says the ZOHAR, " who behold how a man is vested in a comely garment, but see no farther, and take the garment for the body, whereas there is something more precious [than either], namely, the soul. The Law has also its body. Some of the commandments may be called the body of the Law, and the ordinary recitals mingled therein are the garments which clothe this body. Simple folk observe only these garments, *i.e.*, the narrations of the Law, perceiving not that which they hide. Others more instructed do not give heed to the vestment but to the body which it covers. And there are the Wise, the servants of the Great King, who dwell on the heights of Sinai and concern themselves only with the soul, which is the foundation of all and the true Law. These shall be ready in the coming time to contemplate the soul of that soul which breathes within the Law." [1]

This passage illustrates what is meant by an added depth and significance which the Kabbalah would read always into the Bible,[2] and does, moreover, at least from time to time. It offers, I think, also an instance of intellectual humility in the great rabbins of the Exile, who confessed on occasion to a sense in Scripture which exceeded their own loving penetration,[3] so that after all subtleties of exegesis, all the symposiums of synods, the Word of God issued in a mystery, and the key of this mystery was the reward of the just and wise man in the world to come.

The necessity of the manifold sense follows from the insufficiency of the letter. Simple recitals and common words suggest only the human lawgiver; if these were the sum of the THORAH, it would be possible to equal, perhaps even to excel it. Moreover, the sayings of Esau, Hagar, Laban, of

---

[1] Zohar, part iii. fol. 152b, Mantua edition. De Pauly, v. 391.
[2] I mean, of course, *ex hypothesi*. The extracted sense was too often a ridiculous illusion.
[3] Isaac Myer supposed that the higher soul of the THORAH signifies God Himself, but no doubt it is the Divine Sense of the Word which gives knowledge of the Word Itself.

Balaam and Balaam's ass, cannot be " the Law of Truth, the Perfect Law, the faithful witness of God." [1] And hence a hidden meaning, in which is the true Law, was supposed to save Israel from scepticism, and it may have postponed rationalistic criticism in Jewish circles for some centuries. It led of course into extravagance ; the second sense became in its turn inadequate and one more concealed was inferred. So also, besides a general latent meaning, there was that more particular triple significance attributed to each several word. As the possibilities suggested by such a method are boundless, it is unnecessary to say that these senses were never methodised, or that the ZOHAR does not unfold in a consecutive form either the allegorical or mystical meaning. It gives glimpses only, and it may be for such reason that the original ZOHAR is said to have been a camel's load. That original was a latency in the minds of Kabbalistic rabbins, but it was never written with pen.

As the ZOHAR establishes the necessity of the concealed meaning on the insufficiency of the outward, and as the sense of such insufficiency is indubitably a late event in the history of sacred documents, we have full evidence for deciding the value of that claim which it makes elsewhere to a high anti-quity for its interpretation. Had the Jew never come in contact with culture outside Judea he would never have conceived the " Tradition," and the kind of culture which helped him to the sense of insufficiency is not to be looked for in old Egypt or in Babylon, but in the Hellenised thought of the late Roman Empire at the international clearing-house of Alexandria. [2]

As the doctrinal, theosophical and mystical content of the ZOHAR will be the concern of several ensuing divisions of this study, it is obvious that the reference is to these on all important questions of subject-matter in the great text as well as its *additamenta*. That which remains over may be called accidental and casual, in the spirit of which description we may glance at the Commentaries in search of occasional side-lights. Summary is out of the question here, and so is also analysis : the office of these belongs to hypotheses on cosmo-

---

[1] Mantua edition, Part III. fol. 149*b*. De Pauly, V. 390. Compare *ante*, Book I, § 1, p. 13.
[2] It does not follow that the Kabbalah is Platonism or Neoplatonism. It was the consequence of a contact, but the growth and increase were fostered in the mind of Jewry.

logy, to myths of Paradise, Creation and the Fall of Man—to these and the sequence at large of those other matters which are to be treated at some length later on. The purpose of the present survey is therefore to offer gleanings and illustrative instances, drawn from there and here.

In the PRELIMINARIES attached to Genesis and the work of exposition thereon, a tradition is cited which says that whosoever just men undertake a journey together and discuss on their way subjects belonging to the Secret Doctrine they are favoured by visits of Holy Ones who dwell in the world beyond.[1] When Rabbi Eleazar and Rabbi Abba were travelling to call on Rabbi Yosse, they were accompanied by an unknown porter who carried their baggage. But when they began to commune one with another on things appertaining to the Mysteries of Law and Doctrine, it came about that he interposed between them, asking pregnant questions and preferring points of debate. It did not take long to discover that he was one endowed with knowledge ; but when he spoke of the Sabbath and its keeping, of the day and the night thereof, of the Liturgy belonging to the Sabbath, of Divine Hypostases and the Seventy Names of God, they saw also that his science was greater than theirs. They came down from their saddles to embrace him, and would have mounted him on one of their horses, seeing that he rode upon an ass. He refused them, however, but resumed his discourse otherwise, opening deeps and heights in the hidden themes of Wisdom, explaining the secret influence exercised by names on the lives of men, telling strange things and new concerning the Temples at Jerusalem, but over and above all on the mystical union between Moses and her who is called Shekinah throughout the great record. It is said that they halted again and again dismounted, but this time it was to fall on their faces before him. When they looked up, however, it was to find that he had vanished from their eyes. Who was this Master in Israel and Keeper of Hidden Doctrine, to them unknown and clothed in weeds of service ? They had asked many times, and he had answered nothing ; but it was inferred or assumed at the end that he was Rab Hammenouna the Ancient, who had returned for their inspiration and enlightenment from the world beyond.

---

[1] Z., Pt. I, fol. 7a ; I, 37.

THE HOLY KABBALAH

I have cited this gracious Story to shew that thus early in the BOOK OF SPLENDOUR it is about the great things of speculation, as if faring through a land filled with wells of refreshment and running with Streams of light. I might indeed have begun earlier, as the ZOHAR itself begins, and told how a conference opens on page one of the mythos concerning the Rose of Sharon, and after what manner the deeply-imbedded meanings of the Song of Solomon are unfolded through its length and breadth. The Rose is the Community of Israel; but the Rose is red and white, and in the first of these States the elect people abide under the ministry of judgment, while in the second they are encompassed by thirteen ways of mercy.[1] For in another aspect the Rose is a Cup of Blessings, as it is also a Chalice of Redemption. Great doctors of the Christian Church have written many commentaries on the immortal Song, and it has been expounded by notable mystics down even to this day; but the ZOHAR on the Rose and the Lily—*flos campi et lilium convallium*—and the ZOHAR on CANTICUM CANTICORUM has not been known to any, howsoever late or early. A most amiable clergyman of the Church Catholic and Anglican has given us, not so long since, an extended thesis on the MYSTICAL WAY, and this is the Way of the Song.[2] It is all for our delectation, and in his agreeable company the path is travelled pleasantly; but it is a path of moonlight refreshed by draughts of water, while those who walk with the ZOHAR go forward in sunlight and strong wine is poured into their cups.

There is also a travellers' tale as the last Story of all on matters appertaining to Genesis—after what manner must be left to those who are concerned. It tells how two other Masters were faring on the way to Cappadocia, intending to visit Rabbi Simeon, and they refer as they go to a Sacred Tradition by which man is directed to meditate on the glory of God before he begins to pray. They had learned already, it may be—as others before and since—that there is a prayer in the silence which dispenses with the prayer of words and is itself a contemplation in the heart. They knew otherwise, no doubt, that the study of the Secret Doctrine and communing one with another thereon constitute a prayer of

[1] Z., Pt. I, fol. 1a; I, 3.
[2] VIA MYSTICA: A Devotional Treatise on the Life of Prayer. By the Rev. Jesse Brett, 1925.

works; and we have seen how it lifts *ex hypothesi* the veil between two worlds. That which they confessed to each other was, however, of a diverse order, namely, that prayer is in place of sacrifice, the obvious—though unexpressed—reason being that true prayer is love. And seeing that it opens the fountains above and below, with the well-springs on every side, we find among the sayings of the time one perfect utterance at least. It affirms that the Holy One, blessed be He, drove Israel into exile among the Gentiles for the sole and only reason that the nations of mankind at large might be gladdened by the presence of the Chosen People which draws down blessings on the world below from that World of Benedictions which is above.[1] It follows in the radiant dream that Israel suffered crucifixion to aid in the salvation of the world.

Very early in the Commentary on Exodus we are delving again for treasure in the herb-sweet earth of the Song,[2] and that which is brought to the surface belongs to the Mystery of Union between the Voice and the Word. There have been intimations on the same subject much earlier in the ZOHAR, on thought as the origin of all things, on the inward contemplation of the Holy One before He made the worlds, on the uttering of the Voice, which brought forth or manifested the thought, and on creation as the Word expressed. The Commentary ends also on the Keynote of Thought in the Holy One, the mysterious joy thereof and the light which flows out therefrom. It drew together the forty-two letters comprehended by one of the extended Sacred Names, and out of the relation established in this manner it is affirmed that the world came forth. They fared to some purpose in those days, did the Doctors of Hidden Law, whether they went on horses or whether an ass bore them, for in these words, brief and plain as they are, is found at full length the Doctrine of Divine Immanence, the Presence of the Father Almighty—by and within the Word—in all that lives and is.

It is said in the first leaves of the Commentary on Leviticus that faith completes the Sacred Name, and a little further on that from the thought of the Holy One come forth those ways and paths which lead to a knowledge of the Name and

---

[1] Z., I, 244a ; II, 566.
[2] Song of Solomon, iv. 8.

to perfection thereby and therein.[1] We are told also that it were better for a man never to have been born than to live without uniting the Sacred Name on earth.[2] The secret of such union belongs to the study of the Law,[3] which is the work of men of faith, the reference being not to the Expounded Law delivered *coram populo* but to that of the Secret Doctrine, which in another place is identified with and affirmed indeed to constitute the Name of the Sacred King.[4] But prayer and good works are said otherwise to promote unity in the Name of God,[5] and this is the intention which should occupy the priest when he proceeds to the work of sacrifice.[6] We shall see later on that there has been a division brought about between the four sacramental letters comprised in the Hebrew Name which we are accustomed to render Jehovah, and there is a very true sense in which it is the work of man to make an end of this separation. On the surface, however, the mythos develops its symbolism after a diverse manner, while so far as the Commentary on Leviticus is concerned, we are in the presense of another and highly figurative Mystery. The Complete Name is Jehovah Elohim, and the work which devolves on all Sons of the Doctrine is to make evident on earth that Jehovah is indeed Elohim, even as these Divine Hypostases are One in Heaven. We shall see, also later on, that the kind of union is that between male and female.[7] It is affirmed elsewhere that the Glory of the Sacred Name must be the end of all our works [8]; but this is the Glory of Union. A part in the Sacred Name is allotted to those who possess the Hidden Law, the reason being that they possess God therein. The meaning is that those who live the Doctrine are those alone who possess it, and God is the life of these. We shall realise therefore the sense in which it is defined presently, and shall not fail to understand that the Sacred Name is revealed by successive stages.[9] It is revealed in proportion as it is lived and becomes alive within us—a

---

[1] Z., III, 4b; V. 9, and III, 5b, V. 13.
[2] *Ib.*, 7a; V. 18. Meaning of course by the mode and manner of life which is led here below.
[3] *Ib.*, 12b; V. 37. It is to be understood that those who study the Law to a real purpose are those who live thereby.
[4] *Ib.*, 21a; V. 56.
[5] *Ib.*, 26a; V. 67.
[6] *Ib.*, 32a; V. 86.
[7] *Ib.*, 46b; V. 129.
[8] *Ib.*, 51b; V. 139.
[9] *Ib.*, 65b; V. 179.

simple question of growth, but very deep withal. We shall understand in like manner when it is affirmed further that the Name is hidden and revealed at once,[1] because there is ever "a deep below the deep and a height beyond the height" of its knowledge, while for ever they grow therein who study and exemplify that Doctrine which is both the Name and Law.[2] It is added in fine that those who practise charity do cry forth the Sacred Name daily. The explanation is not only that offices of love are channels of grace and power, which are also modes and aspects of the Name of God, but that the work of love is an uttering forth of the Name, and there is indeed no other way given unto man by which he shall express it on earth.

And now as to that veridic parable at large, the messages of which have been drawn from so many pages. In part at least only implied—since the Secret Doctrine emerges in sudden flashes through a mist of clouded light—but in part at least shadowed forth, there is a correspondence established in Zoharic Theosophy between the four letters of the Sacred Name—יהוה—and certain diverse parts or aspects of the soul in man about which we shall hear at full length at a proper point in the sequel. The letter י = YOD is in analogy with YEHIDAH, a spiritual state or mode in the ascending scale of inward being, and with all that is postulated above it, the human *singularitas*, the Christian apex of the soul and Divine Selfhood. The ה = HE primal answers to NESHAMAH, the sovereign reason within us, above material mind; the ו = VAU or VAV connects with RUA'H, which is normal intellectuality, the rational principle; and HE final with NEPHESH, the side on which humanity is related to the animal world. It is the lower *vitalitas*, and is not as such the physical body, which is, however, its vehicle. When a man lives in the light and law of his Higher Selfhood he has built up the Divine Name within him and has become it within the measures of his humanity. Here is theosophical symbolism which may seem at its highest, but it does not enlighten that of the Commentary on Leviticus, unless we are able to look below the surface and realise that there is a marriage of male and female proclaimed by the consonants which form the

---

[1] Z., III, 65b; V. 179.
[2] *Ib.*, 71b; V. 195.

Sacred Name of Four Letters, יהוה, whence it follows that whosoever affirms Jehovah does affirm Elohim also ; that he who completes the one within him completes the other, is a witness in his own person that Jehovah is Elohim and makes their union perfect. As our *Theosophia Magna* unfolds, we shall learn also that there is a supernal part of our nature which does not come down to earth, but abides in Heaven and God ; that it is possible to be united therewith according to the Secret Doctrine ; while if this is accomplished it will follow that what corresponds at the height of our being to the Divine Hypostasis Jehovah has entered into bonds of marriage with that which makes answer to the Divine Hypostasis Elohim. In the light of this hypothesis and its symbolism we shall understand what is meant by the Commentary on Leviticus when it speaks of the Divine Name being complete on earth as it is in Heaven and in Heaven also as on earth. The completion is accomplished below by a true Son of the Doctrine in his own being ; but when it is fulfilled therein, for himself and for those about him, before whom his light shines forth, it is seen by the eyes of faith—as at a gate and threshold of knowledge—that the Name is indeed perfect on all planes of being.[1]

The Commentary on Numbers is full of occasional lights on great subjects. We know that the Israelites in the desert were fed by manna which God sent down from heaven ; but a time came when that stiff-necked generation loathed the light food and cried for material fleshpots. The opportunity offered to parable is not lost on the ZOHAR in its consideration of Exodus ; but it is in the present place that we hear more especially of a supersubstantial bread which on a day to come shall feed the elect and fill them.[2] The mystery of this *panis vivus et vitalis* is hidden in the Tree of Life, which is said to be above, while the Averse Mystery of the meat demanded by Israel is contained in the Tree of Death, and this is said to be below.[3]

We hear more than once in the ZOHAR that the Archangel Michael sacrifices the souls of the just on the Supernal Altar

---

[1] It is said elsewhere in the ZOHAR that the Sacred Name is peace.—Z., III, 176b ; V. 459. It is understood that peace is union.

[2] Z., III, 156a ; V. 399. Compare III, 208a ; V. 530, which says that the manna sprang from the dew above which came down from the Hiddenness of all the Hidden Ones and was the food of higher angels.

[3] *Ib.*, III, 157a ; V. 405. See also *ante et post.*

of Burnt Offerings ; but once only in the text—and it happens to be in this Commentary—is it said that some souls go up, as of their free will and by their own high intent, to make a holocaust of themselves, amidst rejoicing in the Supreme Light which shines forth from the Holy King.[1] For us, at least, it reads like a parable of the union in its last and highest mode, when God becomes All in all for the individual soul. It was revealed to certain Masters in Israel by one who was unknown, who had asked and received water to quench his thirst. After such manner is the reward of the just unfailing and comes quickly, as a cloud of stories makes evident throughout the radiant pages. So also he who gives bread in God's Name on asking may receive a star. Hereof is the sweetness of the Law, about which it is declared a little later that its works are holy, heavenly and mild withal.[2] It is life and the blessing of life for those who are consecrated thereto, as if each had received it himself on Mount Sinai. He has indeed and certainly, because Sinai is also within. It is said elsewhere that the Hidden Law is the Tree of Life and that this Tree is Knowledge,[3] meaning that which is Science of Unity, not of divorce and separation like the Tree of Death. As there is a School of Doctrine on earth which cultivates this Knowledge, so is there a Heavenly School above which is in the state of science attained and is said therefore to be nourished by the Tree of Life. Of those enrolled therein we hear from time to time ; but the Commentary on Numbers tells us that some children who die in tender years are admitted to its teaching, in one or other of the classes—for example, a son of R. Juda, whom two Pillars of the Doctrine brought into that Sacred Conclave and into the presence of its Chief.

In the fragments on Deuteronomy we hear more of the Heavenly Bread, which is Fruit of the Tree of Life, and learn that it is not alone eaten by those in the Heavenly School but by those of the School on earth,[4] meaning that *Summa Scientia* is not beyond attainment here and now. At the end of all, in the last of all the sections, we are brought back to that which is the subject-matter of discourse in the first leaves. I refer to the Mystical Rose and its connotations *ab origine symboli*.

---

[1] Z., III, 157b ; V. 407.
[2] *Ib.*, III, 179b ; V. 471.
[3] *Ib.*, III, 182a ; V. 474.
[4] *Ib.*, III, 260a ; VI. 5.

It is still the Community of Israel, which is likened to a Rose composed of six Petals. There is, however, one new and eloquent affirmation—that Israel is united with the Rose when it is united with the Supreme King. It is another way of saying that Jehovah is Elohim and that Jehovah Elohim is the Complete and Perfect Name. But more than all it is the proclamation of an unity possible on earth as it is actual and eternal above.

It will be understood that my extracts have been made with the object of shewing that there are strange lights and pregnant theses here and there in the ZOHAR proper, apart from anything that it may prove qualified to communicate on those subjects of formal doctrine which remain for our examination at a subsequent stage of this study. If it be said that the miscellany has been made to appear at its best, an adequate answer and one offered in sincerity would be that much more might have been quoted without invading the ground of later themes. For the rest, I have called it a medley, and after the manner of a medley the ZOHAR combines with things precious some others and many that are of little or no value, and not a few which to us, and to Jewry itself at this day, must appear indescribably foolish. They are in much the same position as its modes of scriptural interpretation, and as stated already, it would be idle to suppose that these can have the least exegetical importance. I speak of them obviously as a whole, and do not mean that they hold up no lamps which light up there and here some dark and doubtful path. It must be understood, moreover, by those who are addressed especially, that modes and scheme and purview are essentially Jewish, supposing the exclusive claim of Israel to Divine Election and therefore the last source to which any one so disposed could look for confirmation of the romantic notion that a transcendental doctrine of absolute religion has been handed down from the far past. That which is transmitted in the ZOHAR, but in fragments only, is a Secret Doctrine peculiar to Israel, and it makes contact with the deep things of universal religion, the religion behind religion of Max Müller, in so far as it offers vestiges of inward experience on the union of the soul and God, because the records of this experience are everywhere in the world, in all ages, in all the great religions, and it counts its living witnesses among us at this day.

Understood as it actually is, a thesaurus of Jewish Theosophy, Jewish visionary doctrines, Jewish yearning and aspirations, which, because Jewry is part of humanity, is in contact at a thousand points with the aspiration and yearning of the whole heart of the world, it is a priceless memorial; but it loses all significance in the attempt to misplace it. Because it is theosophical although Jewish, it has otherwise its points of connection with other theosophical systems, and not infrequently with matters which are beyond the range of that which is usually understood by this word, with the things of Mysticism, as, for example, in its transcendental speculations on the identity of subject and object in God and, as I have intimated above, in the mystical experience of the soul. It has other and obvious connections with past speculations and the systems into which they have been drawn. It enters, for example, into that strange doctrine of correspondences which we meet everywhere in the domain embraced by the higher understanding of the term Magia. It might be described indeed as the extended mystery of correspondence. "Whatsoever is found on earth," says the ZOHAR, "has its spiritual counterpart on high and is dependent on it. When the inferior part is influenced, that which is set over it in the upper world is affected also, because all are united." From this doctrine the art of Talismanic Magic must be called a logical consequence, and so far as that which passes under the denomination of occult philosophy is based on this postulated law, so far it belongs to Kabbalism in the kinship of descent. Elsewhere it is said : " That which is above is in the likeness of that which is below, and the likeness of that which is below is in the sea "—meaning that the sea reflects the inferior heaven—" but all is one." [1] This is, of course, identical with the pseudo-Hermetic maxim : *Quod superius est sicut quod inferius, et quod inferius est sicut quod superius, etc.* Apart from its context, this citation from the EMERALD TABLE might have been a Zoharic dogma. We know, however, that the law of correspondences is in Zosimus the Panopolite as well as in the Secret Tradition of Israel.

It may be added that the ZOHAR took the SEPHER YETZIRAH into its heart of hearts, dwelt upon it, extended, magnified, almost transformed its symbolism. The Hebrew letters

---

[1] ZOHAR, Cremona, Part II, fol. 9a. Cf. Part I, fol. 91a : " As it is in all things below, so is it above."

which figure in the earlier tract as the instruments of creation are for it the ciphers or vestures of the Written Law, the expression of the THORAH, and the THORAH is the archetype of all the worlds. Whether or not we are able to agree with Franck that the SEPHER YETZIRAH ends where the ZOHAR commences, and that they are exact complements of each other, it is certain that the instinct of those early students who singled out the BOOK OF FORMATION from the rest of pre-Zoharic MIDRASHIM was not at fault in regarding it as the head and source of Kabbalism.

But, in conclusion, as there was an occultism and Mysticism in Israel prior to the SEPHER RAZIEL and to the ZOHAR, so both were incorporated in the latter; both in the process underwent a species of transmutation, and as I venture to think the process, like that " sea-change " of the poet, produced something more strange and rich. There are, at least, flights of mystical thought and aspiration in this great book of Theosophy which are unknown to Ibn Gebirol and Ibn Ezra, and are more direct and strong in their appeal to the inner consciousness of man at this epoch of the twentieth century than anything in the famous commentary of Azriel or in the School of Isaac the Blind. And to confess this is to confess out of hand that the ZOHAR has still a message for the mystic. Perhaps all that is of value therein would be contained within a few leaves ; but, as said of the choicest poems of Coleridge, they should be bound in pure gold.

II.—THE BOOK OF CONCEALMENT

Passing now from the Commentaries on the Pentateuch to the texts and fragments which are, so to speak, imbedded therein, or thereunto added, it seems reasonable in the first place to pass those in review which, owing to Latin translations, have represented the ZOHAR at large for most readers during a space of some two hundred and fifty years. They differ generically from the *corpus* of the great text and from the other additions or supplements because their subject-matter is " veiled in allegory and illustrated by symbols." For the time being, moreover, we have finished with things belonging to discussion and debate, and are entering a realm of revelation. The statement obtains throughout, though it happens that two of the tracts in question are expository of

the third, which ranks therefore first in the sequence. But he
who expounds is he also who reveals, that is to say, Rabbi
Simeon ben Yohai, while the office of his auditors is to learn,
mark and digest inwardly—not to question and dispute. I
refer to SIPHRA DI ZENIOUTHA, with its sequels, the IDRA
RABBA and IDRA ZOUTA. Their places have been indicated,
from which it follows that the BOOK OF CONCEALMENT or of
OCCULTATION,[1] to which so much prominence has been given
from the days of Rosenroth, is not as some have supposed,
the beginning of the great cycle entitled the ZOHAR, nor is it
the most important part, or perhaps any part that is vital, at
least from my own standpoint. In the Sulzbach edition,
produced by Rosenroth, it begins at fol. 176b and ends at
fol. 178b of the second volume. Several editions are either
paged in correspondence with one another or refer readers to
the pagination of previous codices. Among early printed
texts that of Lublinensis follows the Cremona edition, which,
though used by Rosenroth for his references, was regarded
by him as inferior to the simultaneous or slightly prior edition
of Mantua. The latter he terms invariably *Codex correctus*.
From the silence of certain writers on the subject of the ZOHAR
proper it might be judged that it was not regarded as of great
exegetical or indeed any other importance ; but there is a
simpler explanation, which is not far to seek : it was known
to them only by excerpts prior to 1906–1911. The BOOK OF
CONCEALMENT, on the contrary, though small in its dimensions, was of the highest consequence, the presumed root and
foundation of the ZOHAR,[2] and also the most ancient portion
of that collection. The last view is not, on the whole, unlikely.[3] It has been said further that it is a theogony comprised in a few pages, but with developments more numerous
than the TALMUD.[4] In a word, for occult dreamers of the
past in France and England, the BOOK OF CONCEALMENT and
the BOOK OF FORMATION are the fountain-heads of all Kabbalism. The Hebrew term which is rendered Mystery, Concealment, or Modesty by Isaac Myer, is given as Concealed

---

[1] A literal translation would be BOOK OF MODESTY—of course in the sense of
concealment.
[2] Mathers : KABBALAH UNVEILED, p. 14. .He was unfortunately not qualified to
speak.
[3] Myers : QABBALAH, p. 118.
[4] Éliphas Lévi : LE LIVRE DES SPLENDEURS, preface, p. ii. ; MYSTERIES OF MAGIC,
2nd ed., p. 97. The comparison of one who was unacquainted with both cycles of
literature.

Mystery by Mathers, without affirming that the version is literal. For SIPHRA DI ZENIOUTHA Rosenroth renders LIBER OCCULTATIONIS.[1] The work is concerned, however, with the manifestation of the Divine Being, as the term of His conceal- ment in the eternity which preceded manifestation. The first chapter deals with the development of what is termed the Vast Countenance, the image of the Father of all things, the MACROPROSOPUS, when equilibrium had been established in the universe of unbalanced forces. This Countenance, which is referred to KETHER, or the Crown—first of the ten SEPHIROTH—is compared to the tongue of a balance, *lingula examinis*. When equilibrium obtained, the Coun- tenance was manifested, the Ancient of Days appeared, God issued from His concealment.[2] This symbolism of the balance depicting the harmony of the universal order is a key-note of the treatise, which, in its own words, is the book describing " the libration of the balance." The balance is suspended in the place which is no place, that is to say, in the abyss of Deity, and it is said to be the body of MACROPROSOPUS, referring to the SEPHIROTH Wisdom and Understanding,[3] which are the sides of the balance. The Countenance, of which no man knoweth, is secret in secret, and the hair of the head is like fine wool hanging in the equili- brium. The eyes are ever open, and the nostrils of the Ancient

---

[1] Rabbi Loria says that it refers to things which are secret and should be kept secretly, and compares Prov. xxv. 2, " The Glory of God is to conceal the word." But he supposes also an allusion to the circumstances under which the work is reported to have been composed—namely, during the concealment of R. Simeon for twelve years in a cave.

[2] See COMMENTARIUS GENERALIS METHODICUS . . . è *Libro Emek Hammelech* in KABBALA DENUDATA, vol. ii. pp. 47 *et seq.* of the second part. For casual and mis- cellaneous references to the Divine Head, see Z., Pt. I, fol. 65a ; I, 381. *Ib.*, fol. 232a ; II, 515. *Ib.*, fol. 251b ; II, 591, 592. *Ib.*, Appendices, III, fol. 6a ; II, 689. *Ib.*, Pt. II, fol. 192b ; IV, 79, quoted from a BOOK OF ENOCH. *Ib.*, fol. 268b ; IV, 302. *Ib.*, Pt. III, fol. 7b ; V, 21. *Ib.*, fol. 10b ; V, 30. *Ib.*, fol. 48b ; V, 135. *Ib.*, fol. 66b ; V, 183. *Ib.*, fol. 119b ; V, 306. For the Doctrine of Countenances, see *Ib.*, Pt. II, fol. 61b ; III, 271. *Ib.*, fol. 64a ; III, 283. For the Great Adam, see *Ib.*, Pt. I, fol. 134b ; II, 132. *Ib.*, Pt. III, fol. 48a ; V, 132.

[3] " For Wisdom is on the right, upon the side of Benignity ; Understanding is on the left, upon the side of Severity ; and the Crown is the tongue in the centre which abideth above them."—K. D., II, p. 48. The meaning of the symbolism is that an equili- brium between Justice and Mercy must be assumed before the universe, having man for its object, could become possible, and the source of this notion must be sought in BERESHITH RABBAH—a Haggadic Commentary on Genesis, of historical and exegetical importance. It is ascribed by tradition to the third century, but modern scholarship is disposed to place it a little later than the TALMUD of Jerusalem. Compare also the teaching of the pre-Zoharic MIDRASH CONEN, according to which the Grace of God prevents the opposing forces out of which the world was created from mutual destruction.

One arc as two doors whence the Spirit goes forth over all things. But the dignity of all dignities is the beard of the Countenance, which also is the ornament of all. It covers not only MACROPROSOPUS as with a vestment, but the SEPHIROTH Wisdom and Understanding, called here the Father and the Mother,[1] descending even unto MICROPROSOPUS—of whom we shall hear shortly—and it is divided into thirteen portions, flowing down as far as the heart, but leaving the lips free. Blessed is he, says the text, who receiveth their kisses! From the thirteen portions there descend as many drops of purest balm, and in the influence of all do all things exist and all are concealed.

In addition to the manifestation of MACROPROSOPUS, the BOOK OF CONCEALMENT shews how the Most Ancient One expanded into MICROPROSOPUS, to whom is referred the name TETRAGRAMMATON, whereas " I am " is that of the first Ancient.[2] The letter YOD, which is the first of TETRAGRAMMATON, corresponds to the SEPHIRA Wisdom, the supernal HE to Understanding, and the union of these twain brought forth MICROPROSOPUS, corresponding to the six SEPHIROTH from Mercy to the Foundation inclusive, and referred to the letter VAU.[3] It follows, according to this text, that the primal manifestation of Deity, which is connected with the conception of the Crown, has no other name than that which proclaims His self-existence, as if—according to a French commentator—the Hebrew Jehovah were in some sense a reflected God. MACROPROSOPUS, although manifesting in the Crown, is still regarded as ever hidden and concealed, by way of antithesis in respect of MICROPROSOPUS, who is both manifest and unmanifest. When the life-giving influx rushes forth from the Ancient One, amid the intolerable refulgence of that great light the likeness of a head appears. The distinction between the two Countenances is the distinction of the profile and the full face, for whereas the God Who comes forth is revealed in so doing, the Great Countenance is only declared partially, whence it is obviously inexact to speak of MICROPROSOPUS as a reflection[4] : He is rather a second manifestation, taking place in the archetypal world.

---

[1] *I.e.*, ABBA and AIMA.

[2] This is at issue on the surface with what may be called the ZOHAR proper, for which YAH = יה is the Divine Name of KETHER. The fact is that allocations vary in different texts of the medley.

[3] The HE final is referred to the tenth SEPHIRA, or MALKUTH.

[4] This is a device of Éliphas Lévi and connects with his method of interpretation.

From the sides of the Lesser Countenance depend black locks, flowing down to the ears; the eyes have a three-fold hue, resplendent with shining light; and a three-fold flame issues from the nostrils. The beard, considered in itself, has nine portions, but when that of MACROPROSOPUS sheds down its light and influence they are found to be thirteen. Though the Ineffable Name is referred to the Vast Countenance, it is said also that the manifestation of MICROPROSOPUS is represented by the ordinary letters of the Tetragram, his occultation by the transposition of the letters.

The BOOK OF CONCEALMENT is described in its closing words as the withdrawn and involved Mystery of the King, and as it is added that " blessed is he who cometh and goeth therein, knowing its paths and ways," there is urgent need for some explanation of its significance. This, as we shall see, was unfolded in rabbinical commentaries, which are confessedly posterior to the period of the public promulgation of the ZOHAR. There are, moreover, two works possessing the same authority as the BOOK OF CONCEALMENT, and they constitute extensions at large of that work, being also expository, though there is good reason to demand—like Byron, referring to Southey—that their explanations should be themselves explained. The first of these will be the subject of some consideration in the next section.

The SIPHRA DI ZENIOUTHA is preceded in the ZOHAR by a fragment entitled אידרא דמשכנא = IDRA DE MASCHANA, i.e., ASSEMBLY OF THE SANCTUARY, introduced at an arbitrary point [1] and followed by a brief colloquy between Rabbi Eleazar and Rabbi Abba, who affirms (1) that he has recorded its Mysteries by command of the Sacred Lamp, otherwise R. Simeon, for the use of the Colleagues; (2) that the Mysteries will abide henceforth in concealment, the inference being that the Light of the Oral Law has passed away; (3) that R. Simeon appeared to him in a dream and communicated certain secret teaching concerning the Divine Son or VAU, begotten from the Father and the Mother, represented by the letters YOD and HE, as we have seen otherwise. It will be seen that the ASSEMBLY OF THE SANCTUARY is misplaced obviously in the IDRA sequence, being inserted prior to the text which the ASSEMBLIES are designed to expound. In the fragment itself

---

[1] Z., Pt. II, fols. 122b–123b; III, 471–477.

there is nothing to shew that it forms part of a colloquy or of any discourse whatever. It opens with a statement on the authority of an instruction drawn from a supposed treatise entitled MYSTERY OF MYSTERIES and is concerned more especially with the Face and Head of the Son, the Word which comes from His mouth and the sound of His voice. The brief colloquy by way of supplement may be the vestige of a third IDRA, not otherwise extant, and the ASSEMBLY OF THE SANCTUARY may be part of a text after the manner of SIPHRA DI ZENIOUTHA and dealing obviously with the same symbolism.

III.—THE GREATER HOLY SYNOD

The BOOK OF CONCEALMENT has been simplified to the utmost in the preceding account. It must be added that it stands almost alone in the great body of texts, an anonymous revelation, without antecedents or history; it quotes no rabbinical writers and has no references by which a clue to its date may be obtained. It has, however, two characteristics which give it the appearance of a much older document than those which follow it immediately, and are designed, as intimated already—outside its monstrous symbolism—to develop and expound it. These are its rudeness and the multitude of its obscurities—even for a Zoharic document. The first translator, Rosenroth, supplies explanations placed within brackets, but even with these it is in an exceedingly faulty state. The treatise now under consideration is in several respects different. It possesses almost a literary aspect, begins in narrative form, methodises the ensuing dialogues in a manner which is perfectly explicit and stands in need of few emendations. It exists, however, to unfold further the barbarous allegories of the preceding book, and were it possible to admit any alleged motive behind it as something more than the subtlety of a later interpreter, it would still be incumbent to recognise that it has no message for us at this day rather than to describe it as repellent to modern taste, a fact which has been noted by at least one sympathetic critic who was himself a suggestive writer.[1] The first point which calls for notice otherwise is that the GREATER SACRED SYNOD claims Rabbi Simeon Ben Yohai as the author of the BOOK OF CONCEALMENT, and itself contains the discourses of this

---

[1] Éliphas Lévi : LA CLEF DES GRANDS MYSTÈRES.

Master in Israel, delivered in a field beneath trees in the presence of his disciples, namely, Rabbi Eleazar, his son; Rabbi Abba; Rabbi Jehuda; Rabbi Jose, the son of Jacob; Rabbi Isaac; Rabbi Hiskiah, the son of Rav; Rabbi Hia; Rabbi Jose; and Rabbi Jesse. Some of these are historical names belonging to the period which succeeded the destruction of Jerusalem.

For an account of Rabbi Simeon himself we must have recourse to TRACT SABBATH of the TALMUD, Babylonian recension, which contains a narrative that may be reproduced here in substance :

" On a certain occasion R. Jehudah, R. Jose and R. Simeon were sitting together, and with them also was Jehudah, the son of proselytes. R. Jehudah opened the conversation, saying : ' How beautiful are the works of this nation (the Romans). They have established markets ; they have built bridges ; they have opened bathing-houses.' Whereupon R. Jose was*silent. But R. Simeon ben Yohai answered, saying : ' All these things have they instituted for their own sake. Their markets are gathering-places for harlots ; they have built baths for their own enjoyment, and bridges to collect tolls from those who cross them.' Jehudah, the son of proselytes, repeated this conversation, and it came to the ears of Cæsar, who proclaimed : ' Jehudah, who extols us, shall be extolled ; Jose, who said nothing, shall be exiled to Saphoris (i.e., Cyprus) ; Simeon, who has disparaged us, shall be put to death.' R. Simeon and his son then went out and hid themselves in the lecture-hall, but afterwards in a cave, where a miracle took place, a date-tree and a spring of water being raised up for them. They laid aside their garments and sat covered with sand up to their necks, studying the whole time, and assuming their vestures only at prayer-time, for fear that the same might wear out. In this wise they spent twelve years in the cave, when Elijah came to the opening, and said : ' Who will inform the son of Yohai that Cæsar is dead and his decree is annulled ? ' Hereupon they left the cave." [1] The secret wisdom embodied in the ZOHAR is supposed to have been the fruit of the long seclusion enforced upon R. Simeon by the Roman decree.

The TALMUD mentions expressly the learning obtained

during this period, but without specifying its kind. According to the tradition of Kabbalists, the BOOK OF CONCEALMENT was the first form in which it was reduced to writing. The discourses of the GREATER SACRED SYNOD were recorded by Rabbi Abba and so also in the case of the LESSER SYNOD. When exposition was about to begin a voice heard in the air revealed that the Supernal Assembly had gathered in heaven to hearken, and the commentators add that not only the souls of the just were marshalled round the speakers, coming from their rest in Paradise, but that the Holy Shekinah of the Divine Presence descended.

The explanations and developments concern the world in its void state before the manifestation of the Supreme Countenance, the conformations of that Countenance, or MACROPROSOPUS, as also of MICROPROSOPUS, the Lesser Countenance, and after what manner the inferior depends from the superior. It must be said that the expounding and the extension neither are nor assume to be explanatory in the sense that they unfold any real significance of the symbolism. As a fact, the treatise ends, like all treatises concerned—shall I say, at a venture?—with Mysteries of Initiation, by testifying that he is blessed who has known and beheld the concealed words and does not err therein. In an account like the present, which does not even pretend to be synoptic, it is impossible to attempt a tabulation of the typology with which the GREATER SYNOD is concerned, and it should be noted in this connection that a few modern writers on Kabbalism who have claimed to speak magisterially and as if from within a secret circle of knowledge, may have shewn us glimpses in one or two rare instances—and then according to their individual hypotheses —of the system on which the symbolism is constructed, but have done nothing to elucidate and therefore recommend it to our understanding. It must be added that while the text is hard to approach from the side of its literal sense, the alleged esoteric aspects are matters of curious speculation only.

The unbalanced forces of the universe, the world in its void state, are considered under the symbolism of the kings who reigned in Edom before a king was raised up to rule over the children of Israel, that is to say, before the emanation of MICROPROSOPUS.[1] At that time there was neither beginning

---

1 The Kabbalah represents the present universe as preceded by others which passed away quickly. According to Basnage, this notion occurs also in the TALMUD, where

nor end, and the Edomite kings were without subsistence. According to Rosenroth this signifies the fall of creatures partly into a state of rest, such as that of matter, and partly into one of inordinate activity, such as that of the evil spirits, in which case we are dealing not so much with cosmology as with the legends of souls. So also when the GREATER SYNOD represents the Ancient of Ancients creating and producing the essence of light, the same interpreter, who speaks with the authority of knowledge as regards the literature of Kabbalism, observes that the reference is to the Law,[1] in other words, to the letters of the alphabet, by the transpositions of which the Law was recorded subsequently. For the rest, symbolism of this order is not simplified by its multiplication, and the record of Rabbi Simeon's discourses is only the BOOK OF CONCEALMENT dilated in a glass of vision. Compare, for example, the description of MACROPROSOPUS with the indications on the same subject contained in the previous section. " White are His garments as snow, and His aspect is as a face manifested. He is seated upon a throne of glittering brightness, that He may subdue. The whiteness of his bald head is extended into forty thousand worlds, and from the light of the whiteness thereof shall the just receive four hundred worlds in the world to come." The Vast Countenance itself is said to extend into three hundred and seventy myriads of worlds. The brain concealed within the skull is the Hidden Wisdom, and the influence of this Wisdom passes through a channel below and issues by two and thirty paths.[2] The hair of MACROPROSOPUS radiates into four hundred and ten worlds, which are known only to the Ancient One.[3] The parting of the hair is described as a path shining into two hundred and seventy worlds, and therefrom another path diffuses its light, and in this shall the just shine in the world to come. When the

---

it is said, with characteristic crassness, that when God was alone, in order to kill time, He diverted Himself by the formation of divers worlds which He destroyed forthwith. These were successive attempts at creation, by which Deity became experienced and at last produced the existing physical order.—HISTOIRE DES JUIFS, t. ii. p. 712. Compare also the PIRKÉ of R. Eliezer, according to which the basis of the existing universe is the repentance of God over His previous failures. We have seen that this work is referred to an early period of the ninth century. For other Zoharic references to the subject see ZOHAR ii. 20a, Mantua.

[1] Understood as the essence of the light.

[2] It is therefore the influx of KETHER descending through the Tree of Life even to MALKUTH, understood as the Kingdom of this world.

[3] An intimation of Divine Knowledge which is withdrawn in the hiddenness of Divine Being.

forehead of MACROPROSOPUS, which is the benevolence of all benevolence, is uncovered, the prayers of the Israelites are received, and the time of its uncovering is at the offering of evening prayer on the Sabbath. The forehead extends into two hundred and seventy thousand lights of lights abiding in the Supernal Eden. For there is an Eden which shines in Eden: it is withdrawn in concealment, and is unknown to all but the Ancient One. The eyes of the Vast Countenance differ from other eyes, having neither lids nor brows, because the Guardian of Supernal Israel knows no sleep. The two eyes shine as a single eye, and were that eye to close even for one moment the things which are could subsist no longer.[1] Hence it is called the open eye, ever smiling, ever glad. In the nose of MACROPROSOPUS one of the nostrils is life and the other is the life of life. With regard to the Beard of the Vast Countenance, called otherwise the decoration of all decorations, neither superiors nor inferiors, neither prophets nor saints, have beheld it, for it is the truth of all truths. Its thirteen forms are represented as powerful to subdue and to soften all stern decrees of the judgments. Thirteen chapters of the GREATER SYNOD are devoted to the consideration of this subject, including the number of the locks in each portion, the number of hairs in each lock and the number of worlds attributed to them. This ends the discourse concerning MACROPROSOPUS, and the treatise proceeds thence to the consideration of the Lesser Countenance. The conformations of MICROPROSOPUS are disposed from the forms of the Vast Countenance, and His components are expanded on either side under a human form. When the Lesser Countenance gazes on the Greater, all inferiors are restored in order, and the Lesser is vaster for the time being. There is an emanation from the Greater towards the skull of the Lesser, and thence to numberless lower skulls, and all together reflect the bril-

---

[1] Compare, in Southey's CURSE OF KEHAMA, Part X, the episode of Parvati placing her hands on the eyes of Seeva.

> " Thereat the heart of the universe stood still ;
> The Elements ceas'd their influences ; the Hours
> Stopt on the eternal round ; Motion and Breath,
> Time, Change, and Life and Death,
> In sudden trance opprest, forgot their powers,
> A moment, and the dread eclipse was ended ;
> But, at the thought of Nature thus suspended,
> The sweat on Seeva's forehead stood,
> And Ganges thence upon the World descended,
> The Holy River, the Redeeming Flood."

liance of the whiteness of this emanation towards the Ancient of Days. From the brain of MACROPROSOPUS an influence descends, from the hair an outpouring of splendour, from the forehead a benevolence, from the eyes a radiance, from the nostrils a spirit and the spirit of life, from the cheeks gladness, and all these fall upon the Lesser Countenance. From the brain of MICROPROSOPUS there are emanations of wisdom, emanations of understanding and emanations of knowledge; in each lock of the hair of MICROPROSOPUS there are a thousand utterances; his forehead is the inspection of inspection, and when it is uncovered sinners are visited with judgment. For the lesson of the GREATER SYNOD is that wrath may dwell with MICROPROSOPUS, but not in the Ancient of Days. So also the eyes of the Lesser Countenance possess lids : when the lids are closed judgments subdue the Israelites and the Gentiles have dominion over them. But the eyes, when they are open, are beautiful as those of the dove, for they are then illuminated by the good eye. With one of those pathetic touches which soften occasionally for a moment the un-yielding lines of Kabbalistic symbolism, it is said that two tears dwell in the eyes of the Lesser Countenance, and the Holy of Holies, when He wills to have mercy on the Israelites, sends down these two tears to grow sweet in the great sea of wisdom, and they issue therefrom in mercy upon the chosen people. The special seat of severity in MICROPROSOPUS is the nose, and judgment goes forth therefrom, unless the forehead of the Vast Countenance is uncovered, when mercy is found in all things.

As in the case of the Ancient of Ancients, the discourse appertaining to the beard of MICROPROSOPUS fills many chapters, full of strange scholia on various passages of Scrip-ture, and details minutely the conformations of its nine divisions, what it conceals of the Lesser Countenance, what it permits to be manifested, with observations on the descent of a holy and magnificent oil from the beard of MACROPRO-SOPUS and a general description of the correspondences and differences of the two adornments.

It should be observed that the body of MICROPROSOPUS is androgyne, and at this point the symbolism is concerned largely with the sexual organs. A modern symbologist has said that Nature is not ashamed of her emblems,[1] and there is

---

[1] Gerald Massey on phallic symbols, in a letter contributed to the SPIRITUALIST.

no doubt that for the Kabbalist the body of man was peculiarly sacred, whence for him there would be nothing repellent in dealing exhaustively with its typology. But it will be unnecessary in a descriptive summary to do more than allude to this. The student who desires to pursue the subject may be referred to the French version.

The sum of the whole treatise can be given in the words of the original. " The Ancient of Ancients is in Microprosopus ; all things are one ; He was all things ; He is all things ; He will be all things ; He shall know no change ; He knoweth no change ; He hath known no change." [1] Thus God in manifestation is not really separable from God in concealment, and if the symbolism depict Him in the likeness of humanity, it is by way of similitude and analogy.

At the conclusion of the GREATER SYNOD, we are told that three of the company died during the deliberations, and that the survivors beheld their souls carried by angels behind the " veil expanded above." [2]

Amidst all its obscurity and uncouthness there are sublime touches in this treatise. The Kabbalah is perhaps the first of all books which appeared in the western world reciting with no uncertain voice that God is altogether without mutation and vicissitude—that wrath and judgment are of man alone, placing thus a new construction on the divine warning : " Judge not, lest ye be judged " ; and shewing also the higher significance of the not less divine promise : " I will repay." Never for the true Kabbalist could this mean that God would repay the sinner in his own spirit, outrage for outrage, hate for hate. The repayment of God is the compensation of everlasting justice or the gift of everlasting bounty. In a sense the writers of the ZOHAR anticipated some liberal conclusions of modern eschatology.[3] Amidst the firebrands of the Papal Church, it promulgated for the first time the real meaning of the forgiveness of sins. It is in the sense of such intimations and not in its body of extravagant symbolism that

---

[1] IDRA RABBA, seu Synodus Magna, sectio xxxix. par. 920, in KABBALA DENUDATA, t. ii. Compare De Pauly's translation, Vol. V, p. 365 : " The Ancient of Ancients and the ' Little Figure,' these are one and the same ; it was and shall be all. It is not subject to transformation ; it has never changed and will not change for ever ; it is the centre of all perfection."

[2] Ibid., § xlv. par. 1138.

[3] Franck summarises the position as follows :—Nothing is absolutely evil, nothing is accursed for ever, not even the archangel of evil, for a time will come when his name and angelic nature will be restored to him. LA KABBALE, p. 217.

the Holy Assembly of Rabbinical Israel may speak to us at
this day.

IV.—THE LESSER HOLY SYNOD

Similar in its chief characteristics to the more extended discourse which precedes it, the LESSER HOLY SYNOD, or IDRA
ZOUTA, is termed by Rosenroth the Swan's Song of Simeon
ben Yohai, a supplement to the subjects not discussed
exhaustively in the Greater Assembly. As the master's death
is recorded at the end of the treatise, the translator's words
must be understood of the instruction it contains and not of
its setting. The SYNOD consists of the survivors from the
former Conclave, with the addition of Rabbi Isaac. Simeon
begins by affirming that it is a time of grace : he is conscious
of his approaching end ; he desires to enter without confusion
into the world to come ; and he designs to reveal those sacred
things in the presence of Shekinah which have been kept
secret hitherto. Rabbi Abba is appointed as scribe, and
Simeon is the sole speaker. The discourse still concerns
MACROPROSOPUS and MICROPROSOPUS, with the correspondences between them ; but it sketches only the subject of
Concealed Deity and deals at length with the manifestation
of the Lower Countenance. In both cases, as indeed would
be expected, it repeats, substantially and verbally, much of
the preceding Synod ; but it gives some additional imagery,
as, for example, concerning the three heads of MACRO-
PROSOPUS, " one within the other and the other above the
other," and at a later stage a very considerable extension of
symbolism regarding the first manifestation of the Ancient
One under the form of male and female, which is, in fact, the
emanation or " forming forth " of the supernal SEPHIROTH—
CHOKMAH, or Wisdom, and BINAH, or Understanding. So
also the instruction concerning MICROPROSOPUS, when it is
not a close reflection of the GREATER SYNOD, deals with His
androgyne nature and His union with the Bride, who cleaveth
to the side of the male until she is separated, *et accedat ut
copuletur cum eo*, face to face. Out of this comes the Kabbalistic
doctrine of the sexes, so much in advance of its time, in whatever Christian century we may elect to place the literature,
namely, that male and female separated are but an incomplete
humanity, or, as the text expresses the idea, are but half the body;

that no blessing can rest on what is mutilated and defective; that no divided being can subsist for ever or receive an eternal dowry, " for the beauty of the female is completed by the beauty of the male." [1] The conjunction of the supernal male and female is said to be in the place called Zion and Jerusalem, which further on are explained to signify Mercy and Justice. " When the Bride is united to the King in the excellence of the Sabbath, then are all things made one body." And then the most Holy God sitteth on His throne, then all things enter and are integrated in the One Undivided, Perfect and Holy Name. " When the Mother is united to the King, the worlds receive a blessing and are found in the joy of the universe." [2]

About this point the discourse of Simeon ceases and Rabbi Abba, the scribe, still in the act of writing and expecting that more should follow, heard nothing. But afterwards a voice cried : " Length of Days and Years of Life " ; and yet another : " He seeketh Life from Thee." A fire abode in the house the whole day : when it burned no longer, Rabbi Abba saw that the holy light, the holy of holy ones, had been wrapped away from the world : he lay upon his right side and a smile shone upon his face. Rabbi Eleazar, the son of Simeon, rose up and taking his hands, kissed them. " But I," says Abba, " licked the dust under his feet." It is added that during his obsequies the bier of the deceased saint was raised in the air, and fire shone about it, while a voice cried : " Enter in unto the nuptial joys of R. Simeon."

It will be seen that in spite of a monstrous symbolism the Kabbalistic narratives have at times the touch of Nature which gives them kinship with this world of ours. Whether it has pearls of great price to offer from the world within is another question, as to which we are now only at the beginning of our research.

V.—THE DISCOURSE OF THE AGED MAN

The prominence given by Rosenroth to the BOOK OF CON-CEALMENT and its sequels was not without its warrant, as they are certainly the most arresting, I might almost say sensational, of the tracts imbedded in the ZOHAR. Those which remain

---

[1] IDRA ZOUTA, *seu Synodus Minor*, § viii. *passim*. The foundation of this mysticism concerning the nuptial state must be sought in Talmudic literature.
[2] *Ibid.*, § xxii. par. 746 *et seq.*

to be examined will be taken now in the order in which they
are placed in KABBALA DENUDATA, and their more sober
interest will appear by the short analyses which will accompany
their tabulation. The first to be enumerated is that contained
in Section MISHPATIM (*Historia de sene quodam in sectione* MISH-
PATIM). The term SABAH signifies ancient man and MISHPAT
is judgment, referring to Exodus, from the beginning of c. xxi.
—" Now these are the judgments "—to the conclusion of
c. xxiv. The discourse occurs in the Cremona edition, pt. ii.
fol. 43 ; in the Mantua, vol. ii. fol. 94 ; in the Sulzbach,
vol. ii. 94*a*.[1] The Section MISHPATIM opens with a conference
between Rabbi Simeon ben Yohai and a certain aged man,
not otherwise identified, on the subject of the ordeals and
metempsychosis of the soul, to which there are allusions at
some length in the BERESHITH division of the ZOHAR—otherwise the first part. It breaks off, however, abruptly, giving
place to another conference which takes place at an inn between
the same or a second aged man and two Sons of the Doctrine
who have met together by accident. It is described in a
colophon as a recital relative to Rabbi Yebba the Ancient,
who is moved to reveal at great length the Mystery of the
Soul, its nature, modes or parts and the law which governs
its transmigrations. It is the most important and elaborate
study of these subjects in the extant text, and Isaac de Loria's
yet more complex treatise on the REVOLUTIONS OF SOULS is a
development of the Section MISHPATIM. But as there has
been occasion to note previously, the study of the soul in
Kabbalism belongs to a later stage of our research, and it must
be sufficient to state here that in the discourse under consideration the psychic nature of man is regarded under a
sevenfold aspect, whereas other theses reduce it to three and
by one it is extended to ten. The facts are worth stating at
the present point, not only as an illustration of the discourse
out of which they arise, but because they suggest a working
canon of criticism in the case of those writers in the past who
speak of a concealed sense in the ZOHAR and other Kabbalistic texts. It is not to be supposed that when Rabbi
Yebba and other doctors divide and subdivide the soul they
mean anything else than to distinguish the successive states
and modes which are possible therein and may become actual.

---

[1] In De Pauly's translation see Vol. III, pp. 377–441.

In a word, it means what it says, just as Modern Theosophy does when it affirms that there are seven principles in man. The concealed sense of the ZOHAR, as indicated heretofore, is the extraction of some method from its vast and confused mass, which at first sight may appear inextricable. If and when the discrepancy between the variously divided aspects of the soul in man have been harmonised, we shall have reached the concealed sense of the Commentary and its connections as regards our inward nature. We may attain it in this case by assuming that the involved discourse of Rabbi Yebba describes the development of mystical experience and the ascent of the soul in sanctity according to a tabulation of seven stages, ending—as it states literally—in the realisation of Divine Union. The text says that a flame of fire comes down from the Supernal World and is joined to the Community of Israel, " that union may be perfect." [1]

At an early stage of the conference we hear of a Hidden Palace which is called the Palace of Love, and it is affirmed that the Heavenly King kisses the holy souls who arrive therein.[2] " And Jacob kissed Rachel " [3] is a text which alludes hereto. Thereafter, the Holy One—blessed be He—raises them into exalted realms and there rejoices with them, as a father with his beloved daughter. It is obvious, however, that the Beatified Life of this Palace is not the life of union, though it may be called a vestibule. It is a place of beatitude in the Beloved Presence. The distinction is vital, though its significance is likely to escape those who are in the Court of the Mystical Temple but not in its Holy Place, who have conceived the Vision but not the Ineffable Union. It may be noted in this connection that, according to Rabbi Yebba, the Most High has hidden in each word of Scripture a Supreme Mystery which constitutes the soul of that word. But the profane man sees only the external body of the word, meaning the literal sense. On the other hand, for those who have eyes the external word is an envelope through which the soul is seen.[4] This is illustrated a little later on after another manner, when the inward meaning is likened to a beautiful virgin shut up in a palace, who contrives a little chink that

---

[1] Z., II, 114a ; III, 440.
[2] Ib., 97a ; III, 389.
[3] Ex., xxix, 11.
[4] Z., II, 98b ; II, 397.

her lover when he passes may have a glimpse of her beauty. There are many who go to and fro, but he only who has the eyes of love can see her. It is the same with Holy Scripture, which reveals its hidden secrets only to those who love it : the uninitiated go by on the other side and observe nothing.[1] Outside these deeper aspects and the subject-general of the text, there are occasional intimations which will carry their simple messages as directly at this day as when the ZOHAR first shed light on the greater exile of Jewry and all its thorny paths. We are told, for example, that penitence cancels everything, looses all that binds, annuls all decrees and breaks all chains.[2] It is said also that man's conduct here below forms a window in his brain, and if he lives in a state of grace the glass of that window remains polished and diaphanous, so that his intelligence is a faithful reflection of the Most Holy Intelligence which is above. But the man of evil life clouds his window.[3] Finally, as an example of notions that offer a strange contrast to all that obtained and was current about Theosophical Jewry when the ZOHAR emerged, there is that which is said on the place of children in the world to come, namely, that there is a sojourn reserved for them which is higher than that of the just made perfect.[4] It is added that children die young to become the defenders in heaven of those who remain on earth.

VI.—THE LUMINOUS BOOK

Excerpts of considerable length, purporting to come from a work entitled SEPHER HA˙ BAHIR, or LIBER ILLUSTRIS, are given in the Cremona edition of the ZOHAR at the places which here follow. Part I., col. 76, 79, 82, 86, 88, 104, 110, 112, 122, 125, 127, 130, 137, 138, 185, 241, 462. Part II., col. 145 and 259. Part III., col. 151, 176, 301 and 333. They are omitted in the so-called LITTLE ZOHAR of Mantua, but reappear in Rosenroth's Sulzbach edition and in those of later date which are based thereon. In 1651 these excerpts were brought together into a volume and published at Amsterdam, which was at that period a great stronghold of Jewry. A

---

[1] Z., II, 99a ; III, 399.
[2] Ib., II, 106a ; III, 422.
[3] Ib., II, 110a ; III, 433.
[4] Ib., II, 113b ; III, 439.

reprint of this volume appeared at Berlin in 1706.[1] Some interesting but complex questions are involved in the consideration of this work, which is thus known to us only by quotations. It is alleged on the one hand to be of higher antiquity than any Kabbalistic book and hence of superior importance to the SEPHER YETZIRAH itself; on the other it is affirmed to be a manifest forgery, included in the condemnation of the ZOHAR, and by implication also the fruit of the inventive faculty of Moses de Leon. Between these extreme views there is placed that which considers the extant extracts unauthentic but believes in the existence of an old Kabbalistic treatise, under the same title, which is now lost. An examination of the ascertainable facts does not, I think, prompt and much less impose agreement with any one of these opinions, and a more modest, indeterminate conclusion will be the safest to form. In other words, there is evidence that the SEPHER HA BAHIR was in existence prior to the promulgation of the ZOHAR,[2] but there is no evidence that it preceded it by a considerable period, and there are no means of knowing whether or not the extracts which occur in the ZOHAR represent the original work. In the absence of evidence to the contrary it must be assumed that they do.

It is to be regretted that most English and French students have passed over the fragments of the SEPHER HA BAHIR as they have passed over the ZOHAR proper, and for the same reason, namely, because they were not available by translation until comparatively recent years. It would have been interesting to know whether the Kabbalistic legend which has gone abroad concerning it would have remained acceptable, had such persons been in a position to improve their equipment over certain points of fact. Of that legend one aspect appears in the bibliography of their spokesman Papus. It indicates, however, no first-hand research, reproducing information of which Molitor is the avowed source. In his METHODISED SUMMARY OF THE KABBALAH the quondam President of all Martinism ascribes the SEPHER HA BAHIR,

---

[1] See BIBLIOTHECA HEBRÆA on Wolf, especially p. 906. It was a mere pamphlet in quarto, the BAHIR occupying 10 pp., followed by a tract on Wisdom which accounted for a further three.

[2] Because it was denounced as a forgery by Rabbi Meir ben Simon in the first half of the thirteenth century, thus antedating the period at which hostile criticism places the public appearance of the ZOHAR. Graetz ascribes the forgery to Rabbi Azriel, on what grounds may be gathered from the general warrant of his Kabbalistic criticism.

which he renders LIGHT IN THE DARKNESS, to R. Nehunya ben Ha-Kanah, the master of R. Ishmael ben Elisha, a high-priest, who flourished during the half-century preceding the birth of Christ. Each, however, was a Tanna of the first and second centuries.[1] Some notable sayings of his are preserved in Talmudic collections, but it is quite certain that he left nothing in writing. This notwithstanding, other works are also ascribed to him, namely :

(*a*) Letter on Mysteries or Secrets concerning the advent of Messiah, His Divinity, Incarnation and Resurrection. This epistle was addressed to his son, who is said to have embraced Christianity. It betrays the hand of a Christian, and there can be no question in any case that it is a late production. Paulus de Heredia Hispanus translated it into Latin and dedicated it to Henry of Mendoza, legate of the King of Spain.

(*b*) SEPHER HA-KANAH, the Book of the Fragments of the Temple, but this is attributed also to Ismael (Samuel) ben Eliezer. It deals with the generation of Christ, embodying apocryphal narratives taken from the Talmud, and the real author was Abigdor Kanah, who belongs to the fifteenth century.

(*c*) A Kabbalistic Prayer, to be recited by pupils on entering or leaving the gymnasium.

(*d*) SEPHER HA-PELIAH, which is also the work of Abigdor.

(*e*) SEPHER HA-MINHAD, concerning the Mystery of the Name of God, a work akin to the BAHIR ; but I have met with no opinion as to its date or history.

An alternative aspect of Kabbalistic legend concerning the LUMINOUS BOOK may be used to colour the pretension that the Zoharistic quotations do not represent the original. It is affirmed to be of such profound occult significance that it has been preserved among the hidden treasures of Israel, *in manus Cabbalistorum Germanorum*, says Wolf,[2] quoting Shem Tob. Buxtorf,[3] Bartolocci,[4] and Buddæus [5] relate the same story, and not one of them challenges the excerpts found in the ZOHAR, receiving them explicitly as genuine, while all agree likewise that the BAHIR was regarded by Kabbalists as their

---

[1] Nehunya's name occurs in one of the BAHIR fragments, where, however, he is cited as an authority and by no means as responsible for the work itself.

[2] BIBLIOTHECA HEBRÆA.

[3] BIBLIOTHECA HEBRÆA RABBINICA.

[4] BIBLIOTHECA MAGNA RABBINICA.

[5] INTRODUCTIO AD HISTORIAM PHILOSOPHIÆ HEBRÆORUM.

oldest document. The question of authenticity was renewed in comparatively recent times by Simon, who, speaking of the book printed in Holland, observes : " It does not appear that this is the ancient BAHIR of the Jews, which is much more extended and has not yet been printed." [1] Obviously this is neither the language of criticism nor of knowledge ; we may infer that Simon was unacquainted with the fact that the Amsterdam publication did little more than collect the Zoharic extracts, and that he might not have challenged the extracts had he been aware of that circumstance. Bartolocci mentions a general opinion that manuscript copies of the BAHIR were to be found in many Continental libraries and particularises one such codex as contained in the Vatican collection. Wolf bears witness to others, but as to their claims and content it would seem that they await examination to this day.

The impeachment of the Zoharic excerpts naturally became part of the general charge against the ZOHAR itself ; the theory which ascribed that work to Moses de Leon was exceedingly comprehensive and made a clean sweep of everything included therein. It finds an almost exact parallel in the consistent application of those principles which are held to prove the Baconian authorship of the Shakespeare plays : serving equally well for Marlowe, Massinger and all Elizabethan literature, that literature directly or indirectly is attributed to Bacon. Legend says as we have seen, that the complete ZOHAR was originally a camel's load, and were the whole of it now extant no doubt the Jew of Leon would still have been its exclusive creator. Raymund Lully is credited with the authorship of five hundred separate treatises : a list may be seen in the first volume of an unfinished and impossible attempt to collect them into a folio edition, the editor supplying not only the precise years but the months in which they were composed. What Raymund did, as they say, could not have been impossible to R. Moses. But, as a fact, the *doctor illuminatus* wrote only a low percentage out of all that gorgeous range, and reasonable criticism regards the alleged spendthrift Israelite as a possible compiler and polisher who may have played a little at " writing out of his own head," and that is all, not, however, because it allocates the ZOHAR as the work

---

[1] HISTOIRE CRITIQUE DU VIEUX TESTAMENT.

of Simeon ben Yohai, or even of R. Abba, but because it regards R. Moses as human.

Graetz, the German historian of Jewry, whose distinctive views of Kabbalistic literature once obtained much vogue, lays down a principle of criticism which ought to be written in capitals at the head of most impeachments of the ZOHAR, namely that it is not compulsory for a hostile critic to be more careful in his arguments than those who plead in defence. Without seeking to determine what is compulsory in criticism, it may be observed that there is also no binding law to enforce serious consideration for a scholar who adopts that principle. What Graetz did openly has been done tacitly or unconsciously by others. Taking the case now under notice, I do not know of one instance in which the challenge of authenticity has been accompanied by an assigned reason, beyond the fact that it was heard of first in the thirteenth century : it is part of the programme to get rid anyhow of anything which goes to shew that the whole ZOHAR was not written at the period of Moses de Leon. The reason is not far to seek : the excerpts from the BAHIR, if genuine, involve the existence not merely of purely Kabbalistic but of typically Zoharic teaching prior to that date : as this proves too much for the imposture theory, they are set down as part of the imposture. One critic who espouses the antiquity of the ZOHAR has, however, rejected the BAHIR. He says : " The SEPHER HA BAHIR, attributed to Nehunya ben Ha-Kanah, contemporary of Hillel the Elder and Herod the Great, is often cited. Various fragments, manifestly unauthentic, still pass for extracts from this book." [1] Perhaps so ; but why, if so ? It is for some determinate and material reason that one looks and waits in vain, failing which the identity of the ZOHAR quotations with the original can be accepted as a tolerable hypothesis, because no reason has been given to the contrary. It is quite another thing to affirm that they are the work of Nehunya, or that they are older than the SEPHER YETZIRAH. Placing this cosmogony somewhere between the fourth and the ninth century, as our personal feeling prompts ; regarding the ZOHAR itself as, at least, a gradual growth between the close of that period and the date of its publication, the BAHIR can

---

[1] Adolphe Franck : LA KABBALE, ou la Philosophie Religieuse des Hébreux. Paris 1843. If the unauthentic nature follows from the fact that it is falsely attributed, then the SEPHER YETZIRAH belongs to the same category.

he accepted as a production of the formative age of the work which is made to quote it until evidence to the contrary has been produced. When the extracts were inserted therein we do not know ; absent from the Mantua edition, which was simultaneous with that of the Cremona codex which contains them, it is possible that they were first added when the ZOHAR was prepared for press under the supervision of R. Isaac De Lattes, that unknown but " highly learned Jew unsurpassable in all the branches of knowledge required," whom the publisher describes. In this case, they have no connection with Moses de Leon.

There is, of course, little unanimity in hostile or indeed any Kabbalistic criticism. As, on the one hand, a defender of the ZOHAR challenges the BAHIR excerpts, so the latter have been exalted as the prototype and actual inspirer of the former work. This view, though in any case of little moment, involves at least the existence of the BAHIR prior to the alleged period when the ZOHAR was produced out of the head of Moses de Leon, like Minerva out of the head of Jupiter, ready made and at one leap. Morinus, who has left on the whole a sensible review of the subject, founds his opinion that the BAHIR was a product of the thirteenth century, on the silence of writers prior to that date, and especially of Moses Nahmanides, a Kabbalistic Jew of Jerusalem, whose literary labours belong to the period before and after 1250. Morinus, however, is wrong on the point of fact, as the work is mentioned *sub voce* Midrash R. Nehunya ben Ha-Kanah in the Commentary of Nahmanides on the Pentateuch (Gen. i.). See the JEWISH ENCYCLOPÆDIA, *s.v.* BAHIR. According to Wolf the first reference to the BAHIR is made by R. Shem Tob, who was a contemporary of Moses de Leon, but belonging to a younger generation. This, however, is a mistake also, because R. Azriel, the author of a distinguished treatise on the Sephirotic system, and born, as we have seen, about 1160, in his commentary on the Song of Songs which is ascribed sometimes to Nahmanides, quotes the BAHIR, though not under its own name but under that of .YERUSHALMI. The proof is that the Italian Jew Recanati, contemporary of Moses de Leon, used these quotations, and, misled by the name, inferred that they were from the JERU-SALEM TALMUD, but afterwards discovered them in the BAHIR, to which a Palestinian origin is ascribed. By how much the lost treatise antedated Azriel we have no ground for conjecturing ; but the position of Wolf and Morinus is destroyed by the fact here recorded, which leaves the BAHIR where we should be disposed to place it, between the date when the SEPHER YETZIRAH is first mentioned and the first report of the ZOHAR.

The name BAHIR is referred to Job xxxvii. 21 : " And now men see not the bright light which is in the clouds," according to the Authorised Version, or according to Dr. Durell's amended rendering, " And now men see not the light which is above (or within) the clouds, &c." [1] The subject-matter of the book, which—like the great bulk of the ZOHAR—is in the form of a dialogue between certain illuminated doctors, includes the mystery inherent in Divine Names, and it contains a very full exposition of the celebrated SHEMAHAM-PHORAS, or Expounded Name of Deity. Some of it therefore at least must be relegated to the side of waste and scattermeal, to which extent we can sympathise with the instinctive dislike of Franck to accept the excerpts by which it is known among us. Facts, however, must have precedence of predilections, and though the later history of the doctrine of Divine Names may well make an admirer of the higher Kabbalism regret such a connection, it is far older than that of the SEPHIROTH, not to speak of the Two Countenances in the BOOK OF CONCEAL-MENT and its dependencies. Setting aside certain references to the parts or modes of the soul and the mythos of the Fall, it must be confessed that the other fragments are involved as theses and almost barren of suggestion ; yet a few points may be noted here and there. A tradition is cited concerning a Sacred Palace in which are four Living Creatures who are the holiest of all angels and also the most ancient : they are in correspondence with the four letters of the Sacred Name and constitute therefore its image.[2] They are also a connecting link between the world above and that which is below, presumably because of their relation to the Divine Name, which unifies height and deep. Elsewhere a comparison is drawn between those Mysteries of Scripture which are concealed from all but initiates and the Mysteries of God hidden within His own being.[3] We are assured on the authority

---

[1] Compare the Vulgate version : *At nunc non vident lucem ; subito aer cogetur in nubes, et ventus transiens fugabit eas.*

[2] Z., II, 82b ; III, 344.

[3] *Ib.*, II, 83b ; III, 346.

of Rabbi Abba that three meals muſt be eaten on the Sabbath Day, the firſt while it is yet night, and this is in honour of Shekinah ; the second in honour of Him Who is the Ancient of Days ; the third to the glory of Him Who is begotten of Wisdom and Underſtanding, according to the doctrine of the IDRAS. By these meals are the people of Israel set apart from the pagan nations, and those who neglect them shall have no part in the Sacred Palace where dwell the Living Creatures.[1] It is added hereto that the Sabbath is the Name of the Holy One, which explains why the elect who observe it carry titles of admission to the presence of those angels who are in its image and likeness. We shall discern also a certain sequence of symbolism when it is said elsewhere that the Sabbath is a day favourable to the ſtudy of the Hidden Law, for that which belongs to the Name belongs also to the Law [2] : it is under such auspices that the seventy modes of interpreting Holy Writ are revealed to initiates.[3] The laſt word on the subject tells us that whosoever observes the Sabbath fulfils the whole Law, from which point of view it might be said that its yoke is easy and its burden light.

It remains to say, on the authority of Wolf at its value, that William Poſtel is reported to have rendered the BAHIR into Latin ; but, if so, I can find no record that the version was ever printed, nor is there any indication of its whereabouts in manuscript form.

VII.—THE FAITHFUL SHEPHERD

The Zohariſtic treatise bearing this title records conversations between Simeon ben Yohai and Moses, who appeared to the great light of Kabbalism and gave him many inſtructions and revelations. Elijah took part in the conference, and the witnesses included not only Abraham, Isaac, Jacob, Aaron, David and Solomon, but God Himself. This indicates that in spite of the exalted doctrine concerning AIN SOPH, the ZOHAR recurs occasionally to the same anthropomorphic conceptions that are found in the Talmud. Ginsburg says : " The chief object of this portion is to shew the twofold and allegorical import of the Mosaic commandments

---

[1] Z., II, 88a, 88b ; III, 360, 361.
[2] " The Law is the Name of the Holy One."—Ib., II, 90b ; III, 366.
[3] Ib., II, 89a ; III, 362.

and prohibitions, as well as of the Rabbinical injunctions and religious practices which obtained in the course of time." THE FAITHFUL SHEPHERD is longest by far of all the supplementary texts which have been brought into the ZOHAR proper, and it has been shewn where and how the various portions have been distributed in the codex followed by the French translator. It may be added now that they are dispersed through the Cremona edition in the following order : Part I., col. 98, 104, 126, 207, 211, 214, 247, 322, 343, 346, 378, 483 ; Part II., col. 72, 100, 106, 165, 203, 281, 328 ; Part III., col. 1, 26, 32, 42, 45, 47, 56, 57, 79, 101, 122, 134, 144, 147, 171, 187, 209, 214, 218, 233, 235, 277, 289, 329, 332, 339, 343, 394, 400, 404, 408, 413, 422, 429, 430, 431, 432, 433, 434, 447, 451, 456, 457, 458, 459, 460, 461, 466, 468, 472, 519, 534. As regards their authenticity, Franck classes these excerpts along with those of the BAHIR, but, as in that instance so in this, he gives no account of his suspicions, which may be taken, however, to follow from a personal conviction that much of the ZOHAR is really attributable to the period of Simeon ben Yohai and the disciples who came after him. In either case, the DISCOURSE OF THE FAITHFUL SHEPHERD is important to our purpose in several respects. Its views on vicarious atonement and on the Messiah to come will enable us to appreciate its contribution—if any—to the profound Salvation mythos ; some of its moral teachings will illustrate its ethical position ; its references to the Shekinah will cast light on this *Theosophia magna* of Kabbalism ; while its speculations on angels and demons might shew the Zoharistic foundation for the later system of pneumatology which was developed by Isaac de Loria. They are reserved, however, for consideration at their place in later sections.

The discourse introduces two phases of vicarious atonement, the first of which is effected through the sufferings of just men in a general sense, or in the aggregate.

" When the righteous are afflicted by disease or other sufferings in atonement for the sins of the world, it is so ordered that all the sinners of their generation may obtain redemption. How is this demonstrated ? By every member of the physical body. When all these are suffering through some evil disease, one of them is afflicted [*i.e.*, by the instrument of the leech] so that the others may recover. Which member ? The arm. It is chastised by the blood being drawn

from it, which ensures healing in all other members of the
body. It is in like manner with the children of the world;
the members are in relation with each other even as those of
the body. When the Holy Blessed One willeth the health of
the world, He afflicts a just man therein with pain and sickness
and heals the rest through him. How is this shewn? It is
written: But He was wounded for our transgressions, He
was bruised for our iniquities: the chastisement of our peace
was upon Him, and with His stripes we are healed (Isa. liii. 5).
'By his stripes,' as by the bruises [incisions] made in bleeding
the arm, are we healed, that is, recovery is insured to us as
members of one body." [1]

Here, it will be said, the Kabbalah recognises the great and
fruitful doctrine of the solidarity of humanity. We may
register full agreement: it is one of those instances wherein
Jewish Theosophy has forestalled some modern ideas. But
if we take the illustration which it gives, we shall see that it is
fantastic in character; the affliction of a diseased rabbi does
not as a fact benefit his neighbour physically, and only on the
most arbitrary hypothesis can we suppose that the patience
with which he may suffer will reflect credit on any one but
himself and on those in his immediate circle, who may profit
by a bright example. Let us glance, however, at a more
particular illustration which follows in the text immediately.

"This is also exemplified in the history of Job. For the
Holy Blessed One, seeing that the entire foundation was sinful,
and how Satan appeared to accuse them, said unto Him:
'Hast thou considered my servant Job, that there is none like
him in the earth' (Job i. 8), 'to save his generation through
him?' This may be illustrated by the parable of a shepherd
who beheld a wolf approaching to rend his sheep and destroy
them. What did this shepherd? Being wise, he gave unto
the wolf the strongest and stoutest bell-wether, even that
which the flock was accustomed to follow, and while the wolf
was bearing it away, the shepherd hurried with his sheep to a
place of safety, and then returning rescued the bell-wether
from the wolf. So does the Holy Blessed One deal with a
generation: He surrenders a righteous man into the power
of the accuser for the salvation of the generation through him.
But when such an one is strong like Jacob, it is said: A man

---

[1] ZOHAR, Cremona ed., part iii. fol. 101a.

wrestled with him (Gen. xxxii. 24). But he (Satan) will be
unable to prevail, and in the end he will supplicate the
righteous man to release him (*Ibid.* 26), for the righteous man,
chosen by the Holy Blessed One, is too strong for the evil
one and bears the most cruel afflictions willingly for the
redemption of his generation ; whence also he is held as their
saviour, and the Holy Blessed One constitutes him shepherd
over all the flock, to feed them in this world and to rule over
them in the world to come." [1]

The clumsy and inadequate parable which thus represents
the Almighty flying from Satan as the shepherd flies from a
wolf, and in accordance with which the just man is at first
compared to a bell-wether and afterwards to the shepherd of
a flock, is something more than a literary failure. Theologians have, I believe, found some trouble in locating the
accuser of Job, and it is perhaps most accurate to say with the
poet that " He, too, is God's minister " ; but the Zoharic
commentary on Job makes Satan in most respects a match
for the Almighty, Who must have recourse to a stratagem in
order to save His people. The Kabbalah on the problem of
evil is therefore, in this place, neither illuminating nor
reassuring : it is, in fact, no better than childish. " The
ancient pillars of the world [the intellectual luminaries of
Israel] differ," says the same disquisition, as to the nationality
of Job. One affirms that he was a righteous Gentile who was
chastised for the atonement of the world. At a certain time
R. Hammarumnah met the prophet Elijah and said to him :
How is it to be understood that the righteous man suffers
while the wicked one has joy of his life ? He answered,
saying : The just man of few sins receives his punishment for
these in this world, and hence it is that he suffers here ; but
the man whose sins are many, while his good deeds are few,
receives recompense for the latter in this world and hence
has the joy of life." [2]

In this instance the Kabbalah offers an explanation which,
however manifestly crude, is in close correspondence with
findings of Latin Theology. The latter goes even further, and
affirms that not only the sporadic good actions of those who

---

[1] Z., Cremona ed., part ii. fol. 100*b*.
[2] Z., Cremona ed., part ii. fol. 106*b*. Compare the Mantua edition, I, 6, 8, where
it is said that the pure man is in himself a true sacrifice and that the just are the expiation
of the universe.

are wicked habitually but all natural goodness can find their reward only in this world. The Kabbalah is disfigured seldom by methodised enormities of this kind. There are times also in which it loses its grotesqueness for a moment, and by some not unhappy reference to Scripture illustrates an elementary spiritual truth, as, for example, concerning the change necessary to sinners.

"Those who are oppressed with sin need a change of place, a change of name and a change in their actions, even as it was said unto Abraham : Get thee out of thy country (Gen. xii. 1.) Here is a change of place. And : Neither shall thy name any more be called Abram, but thy name shall be Abraham (Gen. xvii. 5). Here is a change of name. A change of deeds : he changed from his former evil actions to good actions." [1] The Christian Theosophist might develop the significance of this quotation in connection with the new name of the Apocalypse, the new name received in confirmation, ordination and the monastic and conventual life. But such analogies, though suggestive, are of slender value ; and the change mentioned in the FAITHFUL SHEPHERD offers no point of mystical importance : it concerns only an initial aspect of spiritual life.

The Zoharistic speculations on Shekinah are a great treasury of mystical symbolism, but their study at full length belongs to a much later stage. It is said in the FAITHFUL SHEPHERD that the relation of Shekinah to other lights of creation is like that of the soul to the body, but she—for this Divine Manifestation is presented under a feminine aspect— "stands to the Holy Blessed One as the body stands to the soul." The Shekinah is the vestment of the Almighty. But the discourse of the Faithful Shepherd adds that all are one, that is, God is one with His manifestation. This may be illustrated by the profound spiritual doctrine of the Christian Eucharist : the bread is the vestment of Christ, the mode of His manifestation in His Church ; but Christ, by the hypothesis of the doctrine, is one with the veil which He assumes. It is otherwise in man, says the FAITHFUL SHEPHERD. "His body is earth, but the soul is called reason. The one is death, the other is life." The death, however, is obviously emblematic or figurative. It is to be understood as imprisonment,

---

[1] Z., Cremona ed., part ii. fol. 98b.

the limitation of walls and fetters. " But the Holy Blessed One is life, and Shekinah also is life. Whence it is written : She [meaning Shekinah, but the Scriptual reference is to Wisdom] is a Tree of Life to them that lay hold upon her " (Prov. iii. 18). The Shekinah of Kabbalism is not, however, merely the visible splendour which shone in the Holy of Holies. The FAITHFUL SHEPHERD affirms that the Holy Blessed One is concealed in the Mysteries of the THORAH and is known or manifested by the commandments, for these are His Shekinah and this is His image. Herein are high intimations, and they do not need the gift of the mystic to understand and appreciate. It is one of those instances in which a depth is opened within or beneath the sacred tales of Jewry. We may not at this day feel disposed to accept literally and, so to speak, physically the alleged manifestation in the Temple; here the Zohar helps us to something truer and profounder than the letter of the legend, and we acknowledge gladly that the little people of Palestine, encompassed by the idolatrous nations, had truly something of the divine in the law which was given them. The passage continues : " As He is humble, so is Shekinah humility ; as He is benevolent, so is she benevolence ; as He is strong, so is she the strength of all the nations of the world ; as He is the truth, so the truth is she ; as He is the prophet, so is she the prophetess ; as He is righteous, so is she righteousness ; as He is King, so is she Queen ; as He is wise, so is she wisdom ; as He is intelligent, so is she His intelligence ; as He is the crown, so is she His diadem, the diadem of glory. Therefore the masters have decided that all those whose inward part is not like unto the outward semblance shall have no admission to the House of Doctrine. As the image of the Holy Blessed One, whose interior He is, whose outward splendour is Shekinah ; He, His interior internally, she His exterior externally, so that no difference subsists between her the outward and Him the inward,[1] as she is an outflow from Him, and hence all difference is removed between external and internal, and as, further, the inner nature of YHVH is concealed, therefore is He only named with the name of Shekinah, that is to say, Adonai ;

---

[1] It follows that She is He, She as God in manifestation and He the God in hiddenness ; She Who is attained and Known, He Who is unknown, except as we know in Her. Cf. Z., Part ii, fol. 118b ; III, 456.

hence the Masters tell us on the part of the Holy One : Not as I am written [YHVH] am I read." [1]

The connection instituted between Shekinah and MALKUTH, in the light of the alleged unity of God and the vestment which conceals Him, suggests the identity of the divine and the universe ; but it is only in the sense of immanence. The Kabbalah, in its great moments, knows that all things are One and even that the One is All ; but at others it is in some respects the very opposite of pantheism.

Our quotations must close with two references to angels and demons in the FAITHFUL SHEPHERD. The first concerns the great Presence-Angel Metatron, who—in this text—is the sole occupant of the Briatic world, as the supernal Adam is of that of ATZILUTH. He is the garment of Shaddai. According to some his form is that of a boy, while others ascribe to this angel a female aspect. This shews a connection with Shekinah, and indeed Metatron, with the difference of an added letter, signifies the cohabiting glory. [2] There are secondly certain reveries concerning Samael, or Satan, and his wife Lilith. The first was once a servant of the Holy Blessed One and the second a maid of Matroneetha. [3] Their ultimate destruction is hinted ; but meanwhile Lilith is the devastation of the world and the lash in the hands of the Holy Blessed One to strike the guilty. So she, too, is God's minister.

VIII.—HIDDEN THINGS OF THE LAW

The extant fragments of this tract were tabulated by Rosenroth as follows in the Cremona edition of the ZOHAR : Part I., col. 221, 258, 262, 370. [4] Part II., col. 250. Dr. Ginsburg discovered others in the Amsterdam codex, to which his references are made. The words SITHRE THORAH signify SECRET DOCTRINE, otherwise, Mysteries of the Law and its Hidden Things. The title belongs, therefore, to the Tradition at large rather than to a single text which claims to treat thereof. The tract itself has no history outside the ZOHAR, and it does not seem that a line of it is extant elsewhere. A note of the French editors affirms it to be demonstrably

---

[1] Z., Cremona ed., part ii. fol. 106a. Myer, PHILOSOPHY OF IBN GEBIROL, p. 341.
[2] ZOHAR, part iii. fol. 106b.
[3] Z., Cremona ed., part iii. fol. 134b.
[4] In the French paraphrase see II, 720–734 ; III, 328 et seq., 367–373.

impossible that it is earlier than the tenth century; but whether it is much anterior to the Mantua and Cremona codices is an alternative speculation which may not be devoid of likelihood. The question is not of my concern and can be left to stand at its value, nor is SITHRE THORAH calculated to detain us long, as I conceive it unnecessary to give examples of its Scriptural exegesis, which is at once monstrous and puerile. It has, however, some occasional lights, even if they shine among clouds, and there is much on the evolution of the SEPHIROTH, but it belongs to another section. There is one rather curious reverie which has been thought to distinguish certain stages of mystical vision. It is said that the glory of the King is discovered in three colours.[1] The first is above and so far away that no eye can perceive it in its clearness; but it is distinguished (dimly) by contracting the range of vision [*i.e.*, by half opening the eye]. It is of this Divine Manifestation that Scripture says: Jehovah appeared to me far off.[2] The second colour is seen when the eye is hardly opened at all. The clearness of the light could not be endured otherwise. Of this it is written: What seest thou?[3] The third colour is that bright luminous flash which cannot be suffered at all, except between the rolling of the eyes when the lids are closed altogether and the eyes move in their sockets. There can be seen then in that rolling the light as of a luminous mirror; but the colour thereof can be comprehended only by him who beholds the shining with eyes shut, and as if in recollection, whence it is written: The hand of the Lord was upon me[4]; and: The hand of the Lord was upon me in the evening.[5] It is added on the authority of another sacred text that all prophets stood in need of an explanation to make their visions intelligible, save Moses only, who could look on highest Divinity.[6] No doubt the Kabbalists had visions and means of inducing visions, as well as modes of contemplation and occasional deeper states which pass under

---

[1] Z., I, Appendix III; II, 720, 721.
[2] Jer. xxxi. 3. The Authorised Version reads: The Lord hath appeared of old unto me. Compare, however, the Vulgate: *Longe Dominus apparuit mihi.*
[3] Jer. i. 11. The prophet, however, did not see the will of God but a rod of an almond-tree.
[4] Ezek. xxxvii, 1.
[5] Ezek. xxxiii, 22.
[6] See Numbers xii. 7, 8, and especially: With him will I speak mouth to mouth, even apparently, and not in dark speeches. But the Vulgate seems stronger, clearer, and corresponds better with the mind of SITHRE THORAH: *Ore enim ad os loquor ei, et palam, et non per ænigmata et figuras Dominum videt.*

this name. So also had Böhme, St. John of the Cross and all the seers and mystics; but this delineation confuses cause and effect, while it offers no intelligible result.

The discourse proceeds, however, to another illustration of colour symbolism in the case of the three angels who appeared to Abraham.

" It is written : And lo, three men stood by him.[1] These are the three angelic emissaries, clothed in human forms, which come down to this world, and shew themselves to the children of men. They correspond to the three colours of the rainbow : white, red and green. The white is Michael, because he is the right side ; the red is Gabriel, because he is the left side ; and the green is Raphael. And these three colours are those of the rainbow, because it is never seen otherwise than with them.[2] . . . Thereby also was the Shekinah revealed to Abraham. . . . It is written also : And they that be wise shall shine as the brightness of the firmament.[3] They shall shine with a light which is enkindled by igniting a splendour. That brilliant light which is hidden, the spark of all sparks, of all lights, is therein invisible and hidden, concealed and made known, seen and not beheld. This shining light came out from the Supreme Fountain of enlightenment, which is shewn in the day and hidden at night. It illuminates the ordinances of the Law and all colours are concealed therein. . . . Those three colours which are beheld below are in the likeness of colours that are above and are unseen by eyes of flesh. The light is called by the Name YHVH." [4]

The account in Genesis, upon which this pretends to be a commentary, is exceedingly perplexing, and to say that the three men are three angels clothed in the light of Shekinah scarcely removes the difficulties. The explanations of Christian interpreters may not be satisfactory and may not call for recital ; but in this place the colour symbolism of SITHRE THORAH leads only to a disquisition on Divine Names and Titles, and this leads nowhere.[5]

---

[1] Genesis xviii. 2.
[2] This point should interest ethnologists.
[3] Daniel xii. 3.
[4] Z., Part I, Appendix III ; II, 722, 723. See also Isaac Myer, *op. cit.*, pp. 427, 428, for another form of paraphrase.
[5] The fact remains, however, and is important for the whole Zoharic subject, that when God manifests on earth He appears in the form of Shekinah. Latin theology postulates a Christ form.

For the rest, SITHRE THORAH delivers intimations there and here not only in disquisitions but also in occasional short passages and mere sentences, of which a few are worth noting. We are taken back by one of them to that colour symbolism which so far has profited little and are told that even as white is the foundation of colours, while all return therein, so is there a White Light of the Spirit, even a Light of Mercy, from which other lights emanate—meaning sacred qualities and virtues—that belong to the Divine Order. It is mysterious and concealed, is perceived by no one who depends on bodily vision and is reserved for the just alone.[1] Those who seek to know it should meditate on the precepts of the Law by day and by night.[2] We are reminded of another passage in the ZOHAR, which affirms that the world was made by Mercy, derived from the Supernal Loving Kindness abiding in the world above. It is another way of saying not alone that Mercy is greater than Judgment, but is that which moves therein and rules in all. It seems to me that we shall remember this and keep it in our hearts when we have forgotten about the three angels which appeared to Abraham, the colours to which they correspond, and that the words ADONAI ELOHENU ADONAI are composed of fourteen Hebrew letters.[3]

We are told elsewhere that the Scriptural ordinance to sanctify the Sabbath Day is not merely, as we have seen, the synthesis of all other Scriptural commandments and earns the same merit as the observance of all, but that it lifts up those who do so into a realm of everlasting memory.[4] The explanation is that forgetfulness is found only below, but in the world above that which we are is known, that which we were is with us and the future stands revealed.

It is affirmed finally that the letter ALEPH calls upon us to proclaim the unity of God, and this is clear at least, because its numerical value is one. But the text goes on to tell us that ALEPH is a letter of prohibition as well as of command, since it forbids us to acknowledge the identity of the true God with any pagan divinities. There is added, and the point may be commended to " occultists " of all classes, that the same letter

---

[1] Z., II, 78b ; III, 328, 329.
[2] Joshua i. 8.
[3] Z., Appendix III, SITHRE THORAH ; II, 723.
[4] Z., II, 91a ; III, 370.

forbids us to be seduced by Magic and the art of evoking the dead.[1] In the absence of this information it is unlikely that I should have cited the passage.

IX.—THE SECRET COMMENTARY

We know that Scott provided headings to many chapters of his romances by pretended quotations from old plays which existed only in his imagination, and it happened occasionally that these mythical excerpts contained stronger lines than some of his acknowledged versecraft. Those who believe— if indeed any are left at this day—that Moses de Leon wrote the ZOHAR out of his own head may account in a similar manner for certain fragments of unknown treatises which are found only in that work. Of some of these it may be said also that they are more curious here and there than is the ZOHAR proper. As we have seen, the student world of Kabbalism agreed in the past to exalt the BOOK OF CONCEALMENT over other discourses attributed to Simeon ben Yohai; but for the purposes of our present inquiry it must be confessed that not a little interest attaches to the SECRET COMMENTARY. The extant fragments of MIDRASH HA NEELAM are found in the Cremona edition at the following places : Part I., col. 257, 260, 261, 264, 265, 268, 269, 272, 273, 276, 296, 370. The field which they cover is chiefly that of the destiny of souls, future punishments and rewards, the resurrection of the body, the Paradise above and its relation to the Paradise below, and the doctrine concerning angels and demons. But these subjects are reserved for consideration in their proper places subsequently. It is possible, however, to offer here and now a few of the intimations concerning the soul and its destiny, as they will not detract from that which is designed to follow. At the beginning of the MIDRASH, or more properly at that point which is cited first in the ZOHAR,[2] we hear not alone of the soul in glory, because it ascends thus into heaven, but that this splendour is called a visit of the Holy One, meaning therefore that the soul is encompassed by the Divine Presence. But it is only a light which is reflected thereupon by an event to come, for it is said presently that the Holy One comes to the soul, accompanied by Abraham, Isaac and Jacob. There

---

[1] Z., II, 91a ; III, 368, 369.
[2] Ib., Part I, Appendix III ; II, 675 et seq.

is the authority of Rabbi Eleazar for an assurance that the souls of the just desire after that moment when they will leave the vanities of this world and enjoy the life to come; but the picture presented at this stage of the MIDRASH is more than normally anthropomorphic; and even when it is said a little later that the soul's joy in heaven is in the contemplation of the glory of God and in the nutriment of higher lights, it does not rise definitely above this level or in any wise approach the Thomist conception of the Beatific Vision, though it is unchallengeable that in the last resource, and howsoever transmuted, this also is the doctrine of separation impressed with everlasting seals. It should be added that texts outside the SECRET COMMENTARY present a different view.

Meanwhile the suggestion that Light in the celestial world becomes the nourishment of those who have been admitted therein takes us back to a subject on which we have dwelt previously, namely the Supersubstantial Bread, and it happens to be unfolded for our further consideration in the SECRET MIDRASH.[1] The epoch under discussion by various Masters in Israel is that which will follow the resurrection, a time when the Holy One will be in union with His creatures, the just will be conscious of His inward presence, and they shall know Him as if they saw Him with their eyes—an intimation which differs from all that so far has preceded. It has been handed down that at this time He Who is Holy and Blessed will prepare a Feast for the righteous, that is, a spiritual nourishment, defined as the splendour of Shekinah between the Cherubim on the Mercy-Seat. A later intimation says that it will be a food of joy, experienced by contact with the Holy One, otherwise, rejoicing in His joy.[2] There is also a wine reserved for the righteous from the creation of the world, and it is said to signify Hidden and Immemorial Mysteries which will be revealed in the age to come.

It will be seen that in this very suggestive passage the MIDRASH offers a great advance upon the monstrous Talmudic allegory of the salted leviathan, even if it be objected that the cream and marrow of the rabbinical discourse is summed up in a single sentence which affirms that " it hath not entered into the heart of man to conceive what God hath prepared

---

[1] *Loc. cit.*, § TOLDOTH ; II, 713–715.
[2] There is a reference at this point to Ps. xxxiv.

for those who love Him." [1] Isaac Myer has sought to increase the significance by an indication that the word " wine " refers Kabbalistically to " the mysterious vitality and spiritual energy of created things," an opinion based on its investigation by NOTARIKON, for Wine = 70 = SOD, or secret. [2] However this may be, there is a more pregnant explanation on the part of the MIDRASH itself, according to which the leviathan of Isaiah and the TALMUD, the behemoth of Job and analogous rabbinical legends are things written for the crowd, which understands only material rewards and punishments. We know, however, what is the faith of the just and whither their aspirations tend, namely, " to rejoice with God, with a joy that shall be wholly spiritual."

For the rest, what is evident in other texts is evident also in the SECRET COMMENTARY : that the study of the Doctrine and the Study of its Secret Law was the consolation in chief which was sought by Sons of the Doctrine through the exile of the Christian centuries. The Temple was destroyed, and it was not possible to offer sacrifices ; but always the Law remained, and the reward of dedication thereto was that of the world to come, understood as the Mountain of the Lord, the Mountain of Delight and Felicity. [3]

X.—MINOR TRACTS OF THE ZOHAR

We have now passed in review the more important MID-RASHIM and fragments which have been incorporated with the ZOHAR proper. It is far beyond the province of this analysis to offer an account in full of all that remains over, of texts and pieces particular to the Cremona edition, of the Ancient and Later Supplements and the additional content of ZOHAR HADASH. A few items only can be noticed briefly for the sake of comparative completeness.

A.—THE OMISSIONS

We have seen that certain השממות = HASHMATOTH = OMISSIONS are comprised in the first Appendix to Part I. of the ZOHAR, being the Commentary on Genesis. Of these the first cannot be identified and the rest—with one exception,

---

[1] Is. lxiv. 4 ; I. Corinthians ii. 9.
[2] PHILOSOPHICAL WRITINGS OF IBN GEBIROL, p. 358.
[3] Z., Part I, Appendix III ; II, 680.

about which something muſt be said later—form part of the
HIDDEN LAW, the LUMINOUS BOOK and the FAITHFUL
SHEPHERD. These texts, or their extant portions, having
been reviewed already, the present note has reference only to
a few leaves of Appendix I.[1] The subjeĉts of consideration
include : (1) The White Head in the BOOK OF CONCEALED
MYSTERY, to which the Divine Name יהוה = JEHOVAH is
allocated in place of יה = JAH, according to the Holy
Assemblies. (2) The Glory of the Lord—that is to say,
Shekinah—which was revealed in the Tabernacle is identified
with what is termed the Sea of Wisdom in the Supernal
World, meaning the SEPHIRA CHOKMAH = Wisdom; but
we shall find that the Shekinah in Transcendence is referable
to BINAH = the Sea of Underſtanding. (3) It is said that the
Sun and Moon are placed under the presidency of two powerful angels, otherwise Planetary Spirits of old magical lore ;
that Esau was under solar dominion, while Jacob was under
lunar influence ; and that for this reason the one would rule
over nations here on earth, but the other in the world to
come. (4) It is affirmed yet once more that the true Sacrifice
of Expiation is the ſtudy of the Law, that is, the Secret
Doĉtrine.

B.—THE ADDITIONS

The various TOSSEFTOTH = ADDITIONS or ADJUNCTIONS,
which occupy the second Appendix of Part I., are in the same
position as the OMISSIONS, being extraĉts from the same
MIDRASHIM already enumerated, one only excepted.[2] A
paragraph under the title of ADDITIONS is found also in
Appendix I., so that there are two left for our consideration
in this place. In one of them [3] the Great Sea is again identified
with Wisdom instead of Underſtanding ; but it may be
remembered in this conneĉtion and recurring to my previous
note that the qualities and titles of Wisdom in the Old Testament are referred to Shekinah throughout the ZOHAR, from
which it follows that Wisdom and Underſtanding, otherwise,
CHOKMAH and BINAH, the second and third SEPHIROTH in
the Tree of Life, are in a ſtate of union, which is obvious by
the nature of things ; and it is shewn elsewhere in the ZOHAR

---

[1] Z., Part I, fol. 251b–253a ; II, 591–597.
[2] Ib., Part I, fol. 283b, 284a ; II, 657, 658.
[3] Ib., fol. 278a ; II, 646, 647.

that this union or marriage produces a Son, who in fact is Divine Knowledge. By the second we learn that two spirits are provided for just men, one which animates them in this world, and one in the world to come, both now in being and presumably in joint activity. The affirmation is important, because we shall see later, on other authority than a mere gloss or annotation, that the highest part of the human soul never leaves the Supernals.

There are also ADDITIONS which constitute the first and third Appendices to the Commentary on Exodus.[1] That of Appendix I. is a conference of some length on the Celestial Tabernacle, and in certain editions of the ZOHAR it is printed as part of the eleventh and last section into which the Commentary itself is divided. The subject-matter claims to be derived from a book entitled SUPREME MYSTERIES. The Tabernacle above is built upon twelve thousand worlds, while the Tabernacle below corresponds by its material images to the Celestial Chariot ; but it is in the likeness also of the Tabernacle of Adonai, even as this is in analogy with the higher Tabernacle of Jehovah. In this connection it is affirmed that the Divine Name Jehovah designates the male principle in Deity, while the Divine Name Adonai signifies the female principle ; but it is added that these two are one, a pregnant doctrinal point which may be noted for future reference as regards the Mystery of Sex. It is affirmed at a later stage that the holocaust ascends to the Infinite, or to That Which is without end or beginning, a Supreme Will, more mysterious than all other Mysteries : its name is Nothing. This also should be noted, awaiting that time when we shall be called to consider the Majesty of God in Kabbalism. As regards the recurring subject of the holocaust, it is said that man was intended originally as an offering to the Supreme Spirit, but man fell and animals were substituted in consequence. The ADDITIONS of Appendix III. are drawn in part from the SEPHER HA BAHIR and in part from ZOHAR HADASH. Among subjects of consideration in those which remain over it must be held sufficient to mention (1) express prohibitions in respect of Magic, Sorcery, the Evocation of the dead and the practice of Astrology ; (2) a discourse on the creation of Paradise, the Pillar which is based thereon and

---

[1] Z., Part II, fols. 235b–244b and 269b–296a ; IV, 261–273 and 307–318.

goes up to the Throne of Glory, or the sapphire firmament which is above and the splendour which fills the Blessed Place when the Holy One comes down to visit the just therein ; (3) a dogmatic affirmation that the tradition according to which the Law delivered to Moses on Mount Sinai was by him transmitted to Joshua and by the latter to certain Elders, alludes to the Oral Law, whereas Deuteronomy xxxi. 9, concerning transmission through the sons of Levi, refers to the Written Law.[1]

C.—REPETITIONS

There are two only which call for notice here, and one of these especially because it has reference to that Mystery of Faith which is cited continually in the ZOHAR, as we shall see in due course, though its nature never emerges in clear language. It is said in the first MATHNITIN = REPETITION [2] that those who would penetrate the Mystery must hearken concerning the well by which Moses sat and helped the daughters of Reuel to water their father's sheep.[3] On the side of external things it is the well of Jacob,[4] but on the inward side it is Adonai, even Adonai Jehovah, the Lord God,[5] and that Lord Who is Master of all the earth.[6] It is certified that this figurative well conceals a sacred spring, the Name of which is Jehovah Tsabaoth. The well in fine is the Ark of the Covenant which belongs to the Lord of all.[7] It may be thought that this is an involved way of affirming that the Mystery of Faith is revealed only in God ; but we shall find in proceeding that Adonai is a name of Shekinah, that Shekinah is described emblematically as a well and is also the Ark of the Covenant. In this case Shekinah is the Mystery of Faith.[8]

The second MATHNITIN [9] claims to describe a hierarchic

---

[1] The *additamenta* or Accessions are scattered as follows through the Cremona codex : Part I, cols. 83, 87, 145, 176, 188, 189, 203, 222, 259, 265, 295, 303, 318, 367, 371, 487, 513 ; Part II, cols. 48, 107, 120, 163, 238, 358, 426 ; Part III, cols. 50, 82, 97, 98, 117, 149, 155, 163, 177, 184, 186, 191, 274, 331, 441.
[2] Rendered Traditional Receptions by Knorr von Rosenroth.
[3] Exodus ii. 15-19.
[4] Genesis xxix. 2-10.
[5] The reference cited is to Deuteronomy, iii. 24 : O Lord God (Adonai Jehovah), Thou hast begun to shew Thy servant Thy greatness, and Thy mighty hand.
[6] The text quotes Daniel ix. 17 : And cause Thy face to shine upon Thy sanctuary that is desolate, for the Lord's sake.
[7] Exodus ii. 16.
[8] Z., II, 12b, 13a ; III, 56, 57.
[9] *Ib.*, III, 73b, 74a ; V, 200, 201.

order in the empire of the Demon and would be remitted to another section if its symbolical imagery could be made intelligible. It is mentioned here because it introduces Metatron, the Great Angel of the Presence, and because above all he is said to bear a sword which changes every instant from male to female and from female to male. So far as a sword is concerned, the statement is mere nonsense ; but we shall find that Metatron himself transforms in the same manner. He belongs therefore to the Zoharic Mystery of Sex, and so also does Shekinah, who is called Adonai. It is to be inferred, therefore, that the two REPETITIONS—which reveal rather than repeat—are concerned with this subject, *sub nomine* Mystery of Faith. The point may be noted at this stage in view of future references.

D.—THE SECRET OF SECRETS

The single fragment which is extant of RAZE DE RAZIN is found in Part II. of the Cremona edition, beginning at col. 134.[1] It treats, firstly, of the connection between the soul and the body ; and, secondly, of physiognomy, which must be a subject of future reference in the final consideration of so-called " occult science " and the judgment of the ZOHAR thereon. It may be worth while, however, to say in the present connection that Kabbalistic physiognomy proves, as might be expected, to have little connection with any accepted principles to which this empirical subject may be supposed to have attained, and is, indeed, purely arbitrary and conventional. Lavater, the physiognomist in chief and reputed inventor of the art, was something of a Theosophist, but he borrowed nothing, as probably he knew nothing, of the ZOHAR and its connections. Four general types of the human countenance are distinguished by the text in chief, and these are referred to the faces of the Four Living Creatures in Ezekiel's vision.[2] We have thus the leonine, the bovine and the aquiline types, and another, less easy to characterise, but corresponding to the " living creature " which " had the likeness of a man." The approximation of any individual to a given type depends upon his intellectual and moral rank. Physiognomy, however, according to the SECRET OF SECRETS,

---

[1] See also ZOHAR HADASH, fol. 56a, in the Venice edition.
[2] Compare Z., Part II, 73b-75a, Section JEIHRO.

" does not consist in the external lineaments, but in the features which are drawn mysteriously within us. The features of the face vary, following the form which is impressed on the inward face of the spirit. The spirit only produces all those physiognomical peculiarities which are known to the wise, and it is through the spirit only that the features exhibit meaning. When spirits and souls pass out of Eden they possess a certain form which is afterwards reflected in the face." M. Gabriel Delanne, in his day perhaps the most interesting if not most persuasive writer on the French theory of reincarnation, would say that the Zoharic fragment here refers undoubtedly to the " perisprit "—of the Kardec school of spiritism—which he holds to be the plan or type upon which the body of the man is fashioned. The SECRET OF SECRETS pretends also that every feature in a given countenance indicates to those who can read therein whether it is possible or not for the possessor to be initiated into Divine Mysteries.[1] It is, perhaps, unnecessary to say that the fragment does not disclose the rules which governed the sages in their discernment, so that the Kabbalah is not likely to be of much practical use to the few persons who may be inclined to include physiognomy within the charmed circle of any secret wisdom.

E.—THE DISCOURSE OF THE YOUTH

The little history which has passed under this name will be found in the Cremona edition of the ZOHAR, Part II., comprised in a few columns, 91 et seq., which follow shortly after the BOOK OF CONCEALMENT.[2] It is the account of a rabbinical prodigy, the son of R. Hammenouna, but living at the period in question with his widowed mother in a certain village. One day two disciples of R. Simeon ben Yohai, namely, R. Isaac and R. Judah, passed through this village on a journey and paid a visit to the widow. When her son returned from school she wished to present him to the rabbis, to receive their blessing, but he declined to approach them, after the unamiable manner of prodigies. The reason assigned in the narrative is that he discerned by the odour of their garments

[1] In the writings of the Gaon R. Shereerah and other literature preceding the appearance of the ZOHAR we meet with notions of physiognomy and chiromancy of a parallel kind. They recur in the SUPPLEMENTS of the ZOHAR.

[2] See, however, the French translation, where it appears in Part III., sect. BALAC, fols. 186a–191b.

that they had not recited the requisite " Hear, O Israel ! " in honour of the unity of God. He did not disdain, however, to converse at the table, delivering sundry discourses (1) On the symbolism of washing the hands, a function of some mystery, because it is written : So they shall wash their hands and their feet, that they die not (Ex. xxx. 21), that is, Aaron and his sons, when entering the tabernacle of the congregation ; (2) On grace before meat ; (3) On the Shekinah ; (4) On the utterance of Jacob : " The Angel which redeemed me from all evil, bless the lads " (Gen. xlviii. 16) ; and on other matters. The cautious critic might not be prepared to deny that the invention of this history was beyond the genius of R. Moses de Leon. However, the discourses impressed the disciples of Simeon ben Yohai, to whom they gave account of the adventure and paid subsequently a second visit to the lad, who unfolded to them further Secrets of the Law, concerning the heave offering,[1] the Mystery of Bread and Wine, and on grace after meat. When again the facts were reported to the Lamp of Knowledge, he was of opinion that the lad would not continue on earth, for the Holy One would call him to Himself.

F.—THE MANSIONS OR ABODES

We have made acquaintance with a work anterior to the appearance of the ZOHAR in which there is a methodical description of heaven. It must not be confused with the equally methodical treatise which, under the above title, termed in the original HIKLVTh = Palaces, gives account of the structure of Paradise and the infernal region, as an Appendix to the Commentary on Exodus. There will be something to say of it in connection with the soul in Kabbalism. We shall see also that many Palaces and several series of Palaces will be found in the text and its supplements, for example, in the Cremona edition, Part I., col. 116 *et seq.* ; Part II., col. 358 *et seq.*, and col. 438. According to one tabulation the mansions are seven in number and were the original habitations of the earthly Adam. After the Fall of man they were reconstituted and became the abode of the saints. Rabbi Simeon testified otherwise to nine Celestial Palaces which are of no definable form, being the Thought

---

[1] Numbers xv. 19.

of the Holy One. He should have said rather that they are forms of Divine Thought.[1]

The term which signifies Mansion, Temple or Palace, is applied by later Kabbalism to MALKUTH, in which TIPHERETH is said to be concealed as in a palace. So also the name Adonai [ADNI], Lord, is the Palace of TETRAGRAMMATON, because it is the same number as HIKL = PALATIUM = 65. This name is attributed to BINAH, and in an especial manner to KETHER, on the authority of the ZOHAR proper, for HIKL, Palace, is the place in which HKL, that is, the All, is contained, seeing that KETHER includes the whole world of ATZILUTH, because the Supernals are in unity. In another sense the term is applied to the SEPHIROTH generally. In the plural, HIKLVTh = Palaces are the branches of the SEPHIROTH in the inferior worlds. The Palace of the Holy of Holies corresponds, says Rosenroth, to the Three Supernals.

The ZOHAR proper has also a good deal to tell us concerning the seven heavens, one above the other, like the layers of an onion. " Each heaven trembles with fear of its Lord, through Whom they all exist and all are taken away. Over all, the Holy Blessed One holds all in His power." There are further seven earths below, arranged after the same manner. " These earths are disposed according to their names, and between them is the Garden of Eden and Gehenna." They are inhabited by creatures of whom some have four faces, some two, while others are single visaged, like humanity. They are not the children of Adam; some of them are clothed in skins and others in shells, " like the worms which are found in the earth." It would serve no purpose to enlarge upon monstrous inventions of this kind. The concealed meaning which some dreamers once supposed them to possess is again evidently the plan upon which they are based, and to understand them is to know the method by which they can be calculated out, so to speak. For example, we have just seen that ADNI is the mansion of YHVH; by counting the numbers of these Names it appears why the Kabbalists said this, but we do not discover that it served any reasonable purpose until we find elsewhere in the medley that ADNI is God in manifestation, while YHVH stands for God in concealment. It emerges then at long last that the

---

[1] Z., Part II, fol. 269a; IV, 302.

Immanent and Transcendent are One God; and as—according to the ZOHAR—ADNI = ALHIM = SHEKINAH, we enter into a deeper sense of the doctrine that Jehovah is Elohim, or that God and His Shekinah are One. And this is THEOSOPHIA at the highest.

G.—THE COMMENTARY ON RUTH

It should be understood in the first place that the Zoharic extracts are drawn from MIDRASH RUTH, which is to be distinguished from RUTH RABBAH, otherwise MIDRASH ZOUTA. They are found in SITHRA THORAH, SEPHER HA BAHIR and MIDRASH HA NEELAM; but expert knowledge has been required to distinguish them from the text of those tracts, which do not refer to their source. There are, secondly, views and notions expressed in the MATHNITIN of Appendix III to the first part of the ZOHAR which depend from MIDRASH RUTH, or, at least, are found therein. The subject-matter of the extracts may be tabulated briefly thus : (1) The libations of water made at the Feast of Tabernacles signify the grace and favour which the Holy One will pour upon the world when impurity has passed from earth.[1] (2) Wine is an emblem of Severity or Fear, and Milk of Mercy.[2] (3) Their point of meeting is Peace.[3] (4) The world was created by means of ten words, and among them are Lover and Beloved, Joy and Mirth—one of the ever-recurring testimonies to the irrepealable optimism of the ZOHAR, for which the good things of the Lord are ever in the Land of the Living.[4] (5) The word sacred belongs to all books of Scripture, but to the Song of Solomon in a peculiar manner : it is also the most beautiful book, even as the citron is fairest of all trees.[5] (6) Its versicles are subject to two hundred and sixteen interpretations, and they were communicated on one occasion by R. Eliezer to R. Abba.[6] (7) There is a Paradise on earth as well as a Paradise on high, and there is a celestial GEHENNON, even as there is a GEHENNON below. The hell which is above is the abode of Jews who have neither kept the Law nor

---

[1] Z., Appendix I, fol. 265b ; II, p. 627.
[2] Ib., 270a ; II, 637, 638.
[3] Ib.
[4] Ib., fol. 275a ; II, 643.
[5] Ib., fol. 282 ; II, 653.
[6] Ib., Appendix III, 4b II, 678.

repented of their sins ; the earthly hell is the place of the shadow of death, an eternal terror.[1]

My analysis of the ZOHAR, regarded as a literary document, has reached its utmost limit, and these specimens of extraneous or interpolated texts—howsoever we may choose to term them—must be held to serve for the whole. It should be added that a few only are omitted. Though he regarded the Mantua edition as *Codex correctus*, Rosenroth ingarnered all the tracts and fragments embraced by that of Cremona when he produced his own careful codex ; but it must be remembered that the ZOHAR had in all probability grown under the hands of transcribers and makers of glosses during the space, approaching three centuries, which elapsed between its first promulgation and the date when it was first printed. We have no means of knowing how much of it was contained actually in the alleged script of Moses de Leon. The suspicion under which it has remained may be accounted for partly by its frequent quotation of unknown works which have been considered fictitious ; but the ZOHAR was edited prior to the persecution of the Jews inaugurated by the atrocious edict of Ferdinand and Isabella, and many documents existing in Spain may have been destroyed during that fiery epoch. Again, it is impossible to say that Continental libraries contain no MSS. by which the excerpts of the ZOHAR might be justified. The unprinted literature of Jewry has been catalogued by various bibliographers, but no critical knowledge of its contents is possible by recourse to bibliographies. Let us take, for example, the passages from a commentary on the Song of Solomon, which is peculiar, as we have seen, to the Cremona *editio princeps*. These excerpts have not, I believe, been identified ; but there is a manuscript in the Vatican Library which is mentioned by Buxtorf under the very same title, namely, MIDRASH HAZEETH.[2] It is the work, as he tells us, of an unknown author, but a uniform tradition assigns it to a Tanaite commentator, *circa* A.D. 100. The existence of such a work, of course, predicates nothing ; but why should a commentary on the Song of Solomon be called MDRSh

---

[1] Z., fol. 2b ; II, 686, 687. It should be mentioned that Rosenroth specifies passages drawn from MIDRASH RUTH in the Cremona edition of the ZOHAR, Part III, cols. 114, 124, 130, 174, 181, 184, 332, 530.

[2] Among later MS. commentaries, also in the Vatican, Bartolocci mentions that of R. Abraham ben Isaac Tze'mach Levi, the physician, and that of R. Immanuel ben Solomon written towards the end of the fifteenth century.

ChDzITh, which is understood as a reference to Proverbs xxii. 29 ? I speak under correction, but I know of no ground except in the idiosyncrasy of an author, and I am inclined to infer therefore that the same catchword would not have been used by two writers, but that the editor of the Zohar quoted the alleged Tanaite treatise.

XI.—THE ANCIENT AND LATER SUPPLEMENTS

The sudden appearance in public of a momentous work which either has or purports to have remained in concealment for several centuries may be expected to lead to the discovery or manufacture of continuations or connections thereof, and thus we have two series of Zoharic writings subsequent to the BOOK OF SPLENDOUR and distinguished as its Ancient and Later Supplements. When productions of this kind multiply their authenticity does not tend to assume a stronger guise, and the documents with which we shall deal in this section the reader will do well to regard as without determined claims. I should add, however, that considerable importance and authority have been ascribed always by Kabbalists to the ANCIENT SUPPLEMENTS, and according to Franck they have been known as long as the ZOHAR itself. They contain explanations of the term BRAShITh by R. Simeon ben Yohai after seventy different ways, and hence the work is divided into seventy chapters, with eleven further chapters added at the end. It was printed by Jacob ben Napthali at Mantua in 1557 under the editorship of Immanuele di Benevento, and appeared again at Cracovia.

Among notable matters in these ANCIENT SUPPLEMENTS we find the attribution of the members of the human body to the SEPHIROTH, whence the practical Magic of the West may have obtained later on its notion of Divine and Angelic Names ruling those members.[1] The apex of the head and brain is referred to KETHER, the brain as a whole to CHOKMAH, the heart to BINAH, the back and breast are attributed to TIPHERETH, the arms to CHESED and GEBURAH, the legs to NETZACH and HOD, the generative organs to JESOD, the feet to MALKUTH. Later Kabbalism recognises other corre-

---

[1] According to the ZOHAR itself the erect figure of humanity exhibits the letters of the TETRAGRAM superposed one upon the other. Part II, 42a, Mantua.

spondences, the arbitary nature of which is obscured sometimes by an appearance of methodical precision.

There are better things than this in the Supplements to the
Zoharic books, and it may be well supposed that some out of
all the seventy ways of interpreting the much-debated word
which is rendered " beginning " in Genesis should be suggestive as well as curious. A single instance must, however,
suffice. " ' In the beginning God created.' This is the soul
when it emerges from the bosom of its mother and is taught
thereof. ' And the earth was without form, and void, and
darkness was upon the face of the deep ' (Gen. i. 2), because
the eyes of the soul were closed. Hath it opened its eyes ?
' And God said : Let there be light.' Hereafter man is
gathered in from this world, and this then is written about the
soul. ' And God said, Let the waters under the heaven be
gathered unto one place, and let the dry land appear.' When
the soul is removed from a man his body remains even as
' dry land.' "

That French school of occultism which was once beginning
to recognise in the plays of Shakespeare a veiled scheme of
initiation has, it must be admitted, an influential precedent in
the biblical exegesis of the ZOHAR, of which the above passage
seems to be a very neat instance, arbitrary beyond all words,
and yet not without a certain grace of notion.

One of the most celebrated quotations from the ANCIENT
SUPPLEMENTS is, however, the Prayer of Elijah, though it
belongs only to the prefatory part.[1]

" Lord of the universe, One alone art Thou, but not
according to number. Thou art the most sublime of all that
is sublime, the most withdrawn of all things concealed, and
conception cannot attain Thee. Thou hast produced ten
forms which we call SEPHIROTH, and Thou guidest by means
of these the unknown and invisible as well as the visible
worlds. In them Thou dost veil Thyself and, permeated by
Thy presence, their harmony knows not change. Whosoever
shall regard them as divided one from another, it shall be
accounted unto him as if he dismembered Thy unity.
These ten SEPHIROTH are developed in successive gradations,
so that one is long, another short and the third intermediate
between them ; but Thou art He who ruleth them, and

---

[1] Namely, the beginning of the second preface.

whether from above or below art guided Thyself by none. Thou haſt provided the SEPHIROTH with garments which serve human souls as intermediate phases ; Thou haſt veiled them with bodies, so-called in comparison with their encompassing veſtures, and taken together they correspond to the members of the human form. . . . Thou art the Lord of worlds, Foundation of all foundations, the Cause of all causes ; Thou doſt water the Tree from that source which spreads life everywhere, as the soul spreads it through the body. But Thou haſt Thyself neither image nor form in all that is within or without. Thou didſt create heaven and earth, that which is above and that which is below, with the celeſtial and terreſtial hoſts. All this didſt Thou do that the worlds might know Thee. . . . Yet no one can conceive Thee in Thy reality ; we confess only that apart from Thee, whether above or below, there can be no unity, and that Thou art Lord of all. Each SEPHIRA possesses its allotted name, after which angels are also called, but none describes Thyself, the One alone, Who doſt all names inform, to all impart their force and their reality. Didſt Thou withdraw therefrom, they would be left like bodies devoid of souls. Thou art wise, yet not with positive wisdom ; thou art intelligent, but not with a definitive intelligence, nor haſt Thou a fixed place ; though all these things are attributed to Thee, so that man may conceive Thine omnipotence and may be shewn how the universe is guided by means of severity and mercy. If therefore a right or a left side or if any centre be named, it is only to exhibit Thy government of the entire universe by comparison with human aƈtions, but not because any attribute can be really imputed to Thee corresponding either to mercy or severity."

The diſtinƈtion between God and His attributes, and hence between God and the SEPHIROTH, which in a manner are His attributes emanated, is insiſted on elsewhere in the Supplements by the help of a ſtriking illuſtration :

" Woe unto those whose hearts are so hardened, whose eyes so blinded, that they regard God as the totality of His attributes ; they are like unto a madman who should describe the King as the totality of his insignia. Behold a king wears his insignia only that he may be known through them, and verily, the King of Kings, the Concealed of all the hidden, the Cause of all causes, is disguised in a splendid garment so only that He may be known thereby, and thereby may impart to the dwellers on this earth a conception of His sacred nature." [1]

This distinction has at first sight an appearance of considerable profundity, but perhaps in the last analysis it is rather childish than otherwise, for it is obvious that even in our finite humanity there is a latent and unseen nature behind all its manifested characteristics. Man is not exhausted by any description of his attributes, and to insist that this is true also of God seems scarcely necessary.

From what has been quoted above it will be seen that the ANCIENT SUPPLEMENTS are identical in their teachings with the ZOHAR itself, as they are in resemblance throughout, from a documentary and literary standpoint; and some affirm that the original work had existed from time immemorial at Fez in Africa. [2] We have no means of checking this statement, nor is there any authority for supposing with Isaac Myer that the tracts were brought thither by disciples of Rab Hay, the Gaon of the Sages of Chirvan on the Caspian Sea. [3] There is, on the other hand, no need to say that hostile critics make use of weak points in the ANCIENT SUPPLEMENTS as if there were no distinction between these and the ZOHAR proper.

In the section on the bibliographical content of the BOOK OF SPLENDOUR we have seen what is broadly embraced by the NEW ZOHAR—ZOHAR HADASH—namely, a sequel to the HIDDEN COMMENTARY, certain additional Supplements, a Commentary on the Song of Solomon, and another on the Book of Lamentations. It was published at Cracow in 1703, or subsequently to the KABBALA DENUDATA, by Isaac ben Abraham of Neustadt. Its history seems entirely unknown. It may be noted also that later still Isaac ben Moses of Satanow, though otherwise of some literary repute, is said to have produced a forged ZOHAR which may have deceived a few persons, but it was unmasked speedily. It is difficult to conceive what is meant by the denomination "forged" in connection with a memorial which has been so described from the beginning by hostile critics, and I have failed to find particulars of the work.

[1] SUPPLEMENT, 21.
[2] Compare the statement which rests on the authority of the SUPPLEMENTS, that the revelation in full of the ZOHAR is reserved for the end of time. It will be the work of Moses. The prediction is utilised by Karppe (op. cit., p. 323) to picture Moses de Leon, the alleged concealed author, as bringing forward himself and his work as a new prophet bearing a new revelation.
[3] PHILOSOPHY OF IBN GEBIROL, p. 47.

BOOK V

THE DOCTRINAL CONTENT OF THE KABBALAH IN RESPECT OF GOD AND THE UNIVERSE

BOOK V

THE DOCTRINAL CONTENT OF THE KABBALAH

I.—THE MAJESTY OF GOD IN KABBALISM

FROM a study of the documents at large, their age and general nature, from the names, traditional and otherwise, connected with these, but leaving over expositors of the Secret Tradition in its later developments, the research passes now to the Tradition itself, which is the subject-matter of the next four Books. The first will be dedicated to the Kabbalistic idea of God and the evolution of the universe ; the second to the soul in man and the hypothesis of extra-mundane spiritual essences ; the third to a consideration of the ways of God with man, from Paradise to the resurrection state ; and the fourth to those deeper questions which are concerned with the Holy Shekinah and the Mystery of Sex.

A conventional division of Kabbalistic doctrines into metaphysical and physical has been proposed from time to time, and it serves for purposes of tabulation ; but it must not be held to signify that there is a clear line of demarcation in virtue of which the literature branches off into divergent paths, much less that the Kabbalah offers a natural history of the universe. Its physics, so far as it can be said to have any, are transcendental physics. Admitting of no separation between God, Man and Nature,[1] the science which explains them is likewise one, and the best manner of studying it is to follow its view as to the eternal order. It begins in that Absolute which it is the purpose of all fundamental wisdom to make known or communicate to man ; it attempts to exhibit the transition from the Absolute to the related, from the noumenal to the phenomenal, and to establish a chain of

---

[1] That is to say, the mystic communication is permanent, but the pantheistic doctrine of identity is quite foreign to the real position of Kabbalism.

correspondence between the infinite and the finite. It is, however, more than a philosophical attempt to bridge over the gulf which separates the timeless from the temporal; that is the side on which it·connects with philosophy, as understood commonly. The intermediaries of the transition are, moreover, the ladder of ascent by which man returns to the Divine ; and hence it is more than an explanation of the universe : it is, speaking correctly, a sum of religion, and as it is founded, no matter how, on those Scriptures which Jew and Christian have recognised equally as the peculiar revelation of God, the text-book of true religion, we shall see readily what depth and mystery are sought to be infused by the Kabbalah into the Bible. We shall realise also that it is described most adequately as a system of Theosophy, an application of the wisdom of Israel to the Mystery of God, beginning, as we might have expected, with a confession that it is unsearchable, that beyond our highest conceptions of all that is most divine, as beyond so many veridic illusions, there is the unknown and unknowable God.[1]   Even in the mystical communication possible between the divine and man, which is an old doctrine of Jewish Mysticism, long anterior to the ZOHAR, at least in its present form, the essence escapes our apprehension. We can indeed know God, but not as He is in Himself, our knowledge being made possible—*ex hypothesi* —through the manifestation of the Deity, and this takes place after two manners—by the mediation of the Law of Nature, that is to say, in the physical universe ; and by the Law of Grace, which is the manifestation of God in his relation with the souls of his elect.   It will be seen that both these methods are sacramental, and the sacramental system is the outward vesture or form of all Mysticism. For the Kabbalistic Jew the Law and the Covenant were signs or mysteries capable of a plurality of interpretations, while the whole outward world was omen and metaphrasis. It is to be expected therefore that in the written word we must look for another meaning than is conveyed by the outward sense. It was also a part of Jewish mental bias to look for an inward significance which

---

[1] According to the ZOHAR, it is impossible to know that which there is in this Principle, for it never stoops to our ignorance and is above even wisdom. See THE LESSER HOLY SYNOD, when treating, for example, of the *Caput quod non est caput . . .*, *quod non comprehenditur Sapientia nec intellectu*. KABBALÆ DENUDATÆ TOMUS SECUNDUS, p. 528. Compare De Pauly's version in SEPHER HA ZOHAR, Vol. VI, p. 83.

was opposed to the external, and strikes unfailingly the modern observer as strained and unnatural.

In the eternity which preceded either of the manifestations that have been mentioned, the Deity was withdrawn into Himself and subsisted after a manner which transcends entirely the conception of human faculties.[1] It is said that the Glory of the Holy One is so sublime and so highly exalted that it remains eternally secret : no man can penetrate the deeps of Divine Wisdom. The place of its exaltation is unknown to men and angels [2] ; and this is held to be intimated by the prophet when he said : " Blessed be the Glory of the Lord from His place." The Names which are ascribed to the Deity in this abyssal condition are not Names which present either the condition or the Divine Nature : they are conventions of the philosophical hypothesis ; they are terms which serve to indicate that God, prior to manifestation, is nameless, even as He is beyond reach.[3] He is the Ancient One, and the most Ancient of all the Ancients, but this describes only the eternity of His subsistence ; and He is the Hidden of all the Hidden Ones, but this concerns only His concealment. We are led in this manner to the Doctrine of the Infinite, as it finds expression in the ZOHAR on the Mystery of AIN SOPH, or the Divine Essence abiding in the simplicity and undifferentiation of perfect unity. The Latin equivalent is *fine carens*,[4] that is to say, without end ; but it includes also by the separate significance of the word AIN, an abstract conception of nothingness, as a last attempt to register the ineffable nature of an infinite mode.[5] AIN SOPH is under-

---

[1] The tract entitled THE FAITHFUL SHEPHERD, which forms part of the ZOHAR, says, on the authority of R. Simeon ben Yohai, that before God created the archetypal idea which underlies the form of the world, He was alone, without form or similitude, and hence there could be no cognition of Him. See RAAIAH MEHEMNAH, in the Cremona edition of the Zohar, pt. ii. col. 73. Compare De Pauly's version, Vol. III, p. 192. There was, of course, no intelligence to comprehend Him ; but the idea behind the confusion may be that the supposed period of God's immemorial rest is now beyond realisation by the human mind. We are unable to think of a state or period in which the world was not, but God alone. It is to be understood, however, that the essence of the subject escapes not only in this attempt to simplify, but also in the Zoharic position. God in the uttermost transcendence is eternally in this state which is postulated here as prior to creation.

[2] Z., Pt. I, fol. 103a ; II, 18. See also Ezek. iii. 12.

[3] The interrogative pronoun *Who ?* is ascribed by the ZOHAR to this state of the Supreme. Earlier Mysticism speaks of God being alone with his Name, *i.e.*, the DIVINE TETRAGRAM, which, according to Maimonides, preceded the whole creation.

[4] *Apparatus in Librum Sohar pars prima*, KABBALA DENUDATA, vol. i. p. 81.

[5] Zoharic teaching affirms this point specifically. We have just seen, according to the FAITHFUL SHEPHERD, that prior to the creation of the world, God was alone, formless and resembling nothing. It is added that in this state it is forbidden to

Stood, moreover, as the limitless mystery of Divine Thought, the centre of all and the secret of all secrets.[1]   The pregnant references to this state of Deity are comparatively few in the ZOHAR,[2] and we have seen that it is unknown to the BOOK OF FORMATION which preceded it.   The first developments are in commentaries on that work and in the School of Isaac the Blind.[3]

According to the BOOK OF CONCEALMENT, His dwelling is the place which is not a place, or more literally, *locus qui non est*. We are here on familiar ground, with many echoes of the past about us, and it may seem even for a moment that the ZOHAR is translating pseudo-Dionysius into its own terms of symbolism.[4]   The *Non-Ens* dwelling in the *Non Est* is a metaphysical subtlety which seeks, by successively stripping off every attribute pertaining to manifest existence, to attain some idea of unmanifest, unconditioned, abstract being.   It is the TRACT ON MYSTICAL THEOLOGY in another form of language, but after all varied slightly, and behind this little book of the supposed Areopagite lies all the field of Neoplatonic speculation.   But after the ZOHAR there came its commentators, with power to methodise and materialise all that came into their hands, and among them is R. Moses of Cordova,[5] who affirms that the Cause of Causes is called AIN SOPH because His excellence is without bound, and there is nothing which can comprehend Him.   This is mere repetition ; but it must

---

represent Him by any image, even by His Holy Name, or by any letter or any point.— ZOHAR, ii., 42*b*, Mantua.

[1] Z., Pt. I, fol. 21a ; De Pauly, I, 129. LIBER OCCULTATIONIS, *seu Mysterii*, c. i. § 5. KABBALA DENUDATA, vol. ii. p. 348. Compare, however, De Pauly's rendering, vol. iv. p. 137.

[2] They are pregnant, however, because of TSURE, being the Supernal part of the soul.

[3] It is important to establish this point because of confusions created on the subject by several writers. In those portions of the ZOHAR which were translated into Latin by Rosenroth he has added interlinear commentary which gives a false impression as to the recurrence of the doctrine throughout the text. Franck (LA KABBALE, pp. 173-176) introduces the term AIN SOPH in the course of a Zoharic excerpt which is by no means direct translation. Lastly, Mathers (THE KABBALAH UNVEILED, 1887), who failed to render even Rosenroth's Latin correctly, produces the latter's annotations with additions of his own and increases the confusion further,

[4] The antecedents of Zoharic doctrine in past theosophies are of necessity outside my whole proposition, except where occasion offers a brief intimation from sources ready to the hand. There are obvious limits to a study of this kind. Such an undertaking, moreover, would demand qualifications to which I make no claim, and it is somewhat late on my part to serve another apprenticeship. Special proficiency is not required, of course, to recognise in how many quarters the great vistas open.

[5] PARDES RIMMONIM, *i.e.*, *Paradise of Pomegranates*, Tract iii. c. i. Moses of Cordova belonged to the more modern school of Kabbalists, and his treatise is exegetical, not authoritative in Kabbalism.

be admitted that later Kabbalism has occasional developments of consequence respecting AIN SOPH. It was located above KETHER in the Sephirotic Tree, and this first SEPHIRA—sphere or numeration—was regarded as the Throne of Ineffable Deity. It is added that AIN SOPH dwells in the hiddenness thereof.[1]

It will be seen that the Kabbalistic conception is one which is familiar to later forms of speculative philosophy under the name of the Absolute, a term, in the last analysis, which is not wanting in similar intellectual difficulties, or, rather, symbolises our intellectual recognition of that which exceeds our intelligence.[2] In this Absolute resides the essence or potentiality of all[3]; it is not accurate to say that it is the Subsistent Principle which underlies the objective state termed existence, because existence is a condition of the finite and the created, though there is a true and real sense in which God is held to encompass and indwell the whole visible world.[4] AIN SOPH is the subsistent state of Deity itself,[5] whence it follows that there is from the Kabbalistic standpoint a manifested state of the Divine Nature, and this is certainly not the visible world. How this manifestation occurs will be indicated in the next section.

It will be obvious that all ordinary notions of a personal God are transcended by this *Non-Ens* or *Non-Ego* of the Kabbalists. It is absolutely simple, unity without any multiplication, above all number, above Wisdom, which, as we shall see, is, however, one of its first emanations. It is also without sex, and it is therefore, strictly speaking, inaccurate to make use of the masculine pronouns in reference thereto. According to Moses of Cordova, the angels are

---

[1] See KABBALA DENUDATA : *Apparatus in Librum Sohar, Pars Prima*, p. 81.

[2] See, however, Dr. Noah Porter : THE HUMAN INTELLECT, London, 1868, who argues that in its proper definition the Absolute becomes knowable. Our idea of the Absolute belongs, nevertheless, to that region of our consciousness which Herbert Spencer terms indefinite and escaping formulation.

[3] Hœne Wronski, whose mathematical transcendentalism was once at least of high authority with French students of Kabbalism, affirms that the reality of the Absolute is the first principle of reason, and in the absence thereof every assertion made by reason would be valueless. On this principle, as on an indispensable condition, he establishes "absolute philosophy" in his work entitled APODICTIQUE.

[4] According to the ZOHAR, God is immanent in all that has been created or emanated, and yet is transcendent to all.

[5] It has been described absurdly by S. L. Macgregor Mathers as "negative existence." See THE KABBALAH UNVEILED, which embodies a translation of three Zoharic texts from the Latin of Rosenroth, as already noted. So far back as 1867 Herbert Spencer established clearly in his FIRST PRINCIPLES that "the Unconditioned must be represented as positive and not negative."

neither simple nor without multiplication in comparison with it. The book entitled FAITHFUL SHEPHERD [1] says : " Woe unto him who makes God to be like unto any mode or attribute whatever, even if it be one of His own ; but woe still more if he make Him like unto the sons of men, whose elements are earthly, and so are consumed and perish ! There can be no conception attained of Him, except in so far as He manifests Himself when exercising dominion by and through some attribute. Abstracted from this there can be no attribute, conception or ideal of Him. He is comparable only to the sea, filling some great reservoir, as, for example, its bed in the earth, wherein it fashions for itself a certain concavity, so that thereby we may begin to compute the dimensions of the sea itself."

To sum up now on the whole subject, the ZOHAR testifies (1) that God is essentially without form, [2] but in His manifestation He is seen or discerned under different aspects, according to a scale of degrees, which will be unfolded hereafter in a study of the Paths of Wisdom. (2) That the most secret of all Mysteries is that which is called Nothing, [3] being the Most Holy Ancient, from whom the Light flows forth. [4] This notwithstanding, it is affirmed (3) that in the essence of the Infinite there are neither intentions nor lights, nor brightness, [5] and the explanation is that although every light emanates therefrom, they are not in that state of clear shining which would enable man to grasp the nature of the Infinite : it is a Supreme Will. (4) That, again this fact notwithstanding, the holocaust, which has for its object an union effected with the Holy of Holies, ascends to AIN SOPH, because all perfection

---

[1] Quoted in BETH ELOHIM, or the HOUSE OF THE GODS, *Dissertatio* i. c. i.   See KABBALA DENUDATA, vol. ii. ; *Partis Tertiæ Tractatus* i., *i.e.*, *Pneumatica Kabbalistica*, p. 187.   But see De Pauly's translation, Vol. III, p. 193.   It is much shorter and affirms that the forms under which God manifests are merely subjective.

[2] Z., Pt. I, 275a ; II, 644.   The text derives its authority in the usual amazing manner from the SONG OF SOLOMON, vii. 11, 12 : " Come, my beloved, let us go forth into the field ; let us lodge in the villages.   Let us get up early to the vineyards ; let us see if the vine flourish."   This is contrasted with a Talmudic story concerning the son of Zoma, one of the four persons who penetrated into the Mysterious Garden ; but he remained on the hither side of the vineyard, which is taken to mean that he did not enter the Paths of Supreme Wisdom.

[3] *Ib.*, 64b ; III, 283.   It is founded on Ex. xvii. 7 : " They tempted the Lord, saying, Is the Lord among us, or not ? "—which is supposed to contain a distinction between the Ancient and Jehovah, contrary of course to the unity of God, whether manifest or unmanifest.

[4] *Ib.*, 43b ; III, 194.

[5] *Ib.*, Pt. II, 239a ; IV, 267.

must tend to fusion with the Mysterious Unknown,[1] which is
the Object of all desires, though in AIN SOPH there are no
desires, even while they subsist only by reason thereof.
(5) That AIN SOPH is symbolised by the letter ALEPH.[2] It
seems to follow that later Kabbalism was well within the
measures of the symbolism when it posited AIN SOPH as a
Hidden Light above KETHER, at the head of the Sephirotic
Tree.

II.—THE TEN SEPHIROTH

Having postulated the existence of the Absolute and the
Unconditioned, the next concern of the Kabbalah is the mode
of the manifestation of that withdrawn and inconceivable
nature. Having attained its ultimate and fundamental conception of the Deity by the process of elimination to which
reference has been made already, it was inevitable that the
attribution of absolute reality to that which had been stripped
of all realism should have produced as a result something
which was outside intellectual comprehension, the fact
notwithstanding that its methodical and elaborated antithesis
of anthropomorphism was as much a convention of the human
mind as that which it sought to replace. The intellectual
difficulty became a ground for exaltation of the conception
at the expense of the human mind by which it had been
devised so laboriously.[3] Now, the Jew was confronted by
at least two problems which called for the exercise of his
further ingenuity as regards the *latens Deitas* of AIN SOPH.
He had to account for the bond of connection between this
abyss of the Godhead and the visible universe, having man
for its mouthpiece ; but so far this is only the common
problem of all philosophy which begins and ends in the unconditioned. He had further a problem peculiar to his own
inheritance and election, and this was to establish another
bond of connection between the absolute transcendency of
AIN SOPH, apart from all limitation, outside all human
measurement, isolated from all relationship, and the anthropomorphic Lord of Israel, whose stature and measurements were
not beyond the ingenuity of rabbinical calculations, and most

---

[1] Z., Pt. II, 26b ; V, 74, 75.
[2] *Ib.*, 257a ; V, 597.
[3] The ZOHAR says that it is called AIN, not on the ground of nonentity, but, it
may be inferred, because that which is wholly outside our knowledge is for us as
nothingness.

of whose members are mentioned with sufficient fullness and frequency in the sacred writings for any devout student to possess a clear notion of the " body of God," and to describe it, did he please, and we have seen already that he did, with considerable minuteness, in a book dedicated to the question. For the moment, however, we are concerned only with the first problem, namely, the difficulty of conceiving why the abyssal state in which God unmanifest had been sufficient from eternity to Himself should at any period have had another mode superadded to it. I say superadded by convention based on the notion of sufficiency ; it is not an adequate term to make use of in such a relation, to which no terminology is suitable. The *non ens* dwelling in the *non est* is like the cipher of the decimal system [1]; of itself it is nothing, and its extension produces nothing ; so also it is not possible to add to it, but it gives power to all numbers. The solution offered by Kabbalism does not differ materially from that which has been given by other philosophies and religions which postulate a First Cause. It is, in a word, the movement of the Divine Will. " In this," says Myer, " the Unknown Absolute, above all number, manifested itself through an emanation in which it was immanent, yet as to which it was transcendental." [2] We are dealing here with a system of speculative philosophy, and, traditional or otherwise, it must not be supposed to be free from the disabilities of other philosophies or from the crudities of its particular period. The Kabbalistic hypothesis supposes an eternity antecedent to this initial operation of the Divine Will, and in the latent subsistence of AIN SOPH it would appear an inconsequence to assume that there was either will [3] or consciousness possible.[4] Both, however, by a common and almost inevitable anachronism, are attributed to AIN SOPH, despite the warning of the ZOHAR already quoted : " Woe unto him who shall compare Him with any mode or attribute, even with one of his own." [5] The later commentators on the

---

[1] The circle is, in fact, a Kabbalistic symbol of AIN SOPH.
[2] PHILOSOPHY OF IBN GEBIROL, p. 266.
[3] The ZOHAR, however, says expressly that " in the beginning was the will of the King."
[4] " Exceeding comprehension it must be regarded as the *non-Ego* rather than the *Ego*. All that is in man depends from it, but it transcends consciousness ; it transcends what we conceive by the terms personal and individual." Myer : PHILOSOPHY OF IBN GEBIROL.
[5] Z., Pt. II, RAAIAH MEHEMNA, col. 73, Cremona edition. See also Mantua edition, Pt. II, 42b.

ZOHAR either do not recognise or are content to ignore the difficulty. Thus a treatise entitled THE ROYAL VALLEY, by Rabbi Naphthali Hirtz, says : " Blessed be His Holy Name ! Before anything was, He, by His simple will, proposed to Himself to fashion the worlds. For the King is not given without the people, as it is written in Proverbs xiv. 28 : ' In the multitude of the people is the King's honour.' And it is the nature of the supreme Goodness to dispense good. Now, if the world were not, on whom could He bestow it ? " [1] The exegetical literature, treatises like GATES OF LIGHT, indicate that the exertion of Divine Will in the production of the emanations is a path so secret that no creature, not even Moses himself, can understand it.[2] At the same time, that will is *beneplacitum*, or good pleasure, and *beneplacitum termino carens*, without end or limit. Hence the motive by which the universe is accounted for is the same motive which communicates the mercy of God to them that fear Him, after which it will be unnecessary to say that optimism is a fundamental characteristic of Kabbalism, or that, according to the ZOHAR, this is, in some respects, the best of all possible worlds, as affirmed by Robert Southey.

Seeing then that the transition of the Divine Being from the state of the *non ens* was accomplished, like the conversion of man from the condition of a merely material creature, by an operation of the mystery of will, we have next to ascertain something of the nature of such process, and we are brought back in this manner to the word which I have had occasion to cite already, namely, emanation.[3] The Kabbalah repudiates implicitly the axiom *ex nihilo nihil fit*, for the *non ens* dwelling in

---

[1] KABBALA DENUDATA, tom. ii., *partis primæ tractatus secundus*, § 1, *De Mundo Infinito primo*, p. 152.

[2] KABBALA DENUDATA, tom. i., *Apparatus in Librum Sohar pars prima*, pp. 691, 692.

[3] In which the idea of pantheism is almost always, but not, I think, of necessity, involved. There is, of course, a certain sense in which that notion is not escaped even on the hypothesis of creation, and further there is a higher sense of pantheism from which no true Theosophist could wish to escape. But as regards Jewish Mysticism, while there is always some doubt in what way it made use of the term emanation, there seems to me no question that its system does not answer to what is commonly understood by pantheism, though it has often a pantheistic aspect. God was all for the Kabbalist, as he is for the Christian, and yet no Theosophical Jew, any more than the orthodox Christian theologian, would admit that God was one with the material world. When, therefore, Solomon Munk : DICTIONNAIRE DE LA CONVERSATION, says that the Kabbalah issued from the amalgamation of oriental pantheism with the religion of the Hebrews, we can accept this only by supposing that the pantheism in question had suffered a peculiar alteration.

the unconditioned State, wherein is neither time nor place,[1] is the fullness which contains the all. *Ex plenitudine ista omnia fiunt.* In this Divine Plenitude pre-existing eternally was the sub-stance of all the worlds, which therefore came forth from God. Hence the Kabbalistic system is broadly one of emanation.[2] When it is said that emanation is not its only foundation, for it rests also on the identity of thought and existence,[3] or other-wise the doctrine of Divine Immanence, there is much in the literature which combines to enforce this view, after due allowance has been made for the confusion and obscurity of the originals.[4] But that which is more to our purpose and rests on Zoharic authority is that the idea of emanation belongs more especially to the Divine Nature unfolding from within Itself, that it may be revealed ultimately to and within an external universe, the relation of which to God is not that of a symbolic globe held in a king's hand, nor even a veil or a vesture, but rather a cosmic sacrament, of which He is the inward power and He the abiding grace. For the rest, at the moment it is enough to say that after the World of Emanation there is a Kabbalistic World of Creation.

The first consequence which followed the operation of Divine Will was the manifestation or unfolding of the Divine Attributes—in a word, the transition of Deity from the latent to the active mode, so far as any of these terms can be used in respect of a State where there was no universe in which mani-festation could take place, no created intelligence to cognise it, and no objective for action. As in the postulated State of latency, God was above all number, so in the subsequent activity He is held to have produced numbers, and the decade— in the sense of the SEPHIROTH—is brought forth from AIN SOPH. We must not be so crude as to suppose that mere arithmetical numerals are here intended : it was powers, forces, vitalities, virtues, attributes, principles, which were thus produced or unfolded, and these are the ten SEPHIROTH,

---

[1] " The No-Thing is not, however, an absolute negative or void, but some-Thing unknown to man." Myer : PHILOSOPHY OF IBN GEBIROL, p. 378. It should be added that Nahmanides was one of the few Kabbalists who maintained creation *ex nihilo.*

[2] In Book III, § 2, we have seen that this statement is subject to a reservation regarding the most ancient document of the Kabbalah, and it should be noted in this connection that at least one capable writer has rejected the general view, and does not regard the Kabbalah as a system of emanation. See Joel : PHILOSOPHIE RELIGIEUSE DU ZOHAR.

[3] Isaac Myer : PHILOSOPHY OF IBN GEBIROL, p. 266.

[4] That is to say, the terms emanation, creation, formation and such like, signifying distinct ideas, are used somewhat indiscriminately by the Kabbalists.

which arc tabulated as follows with their curious conventional titles : [1]

I. כתר = KETHER, the Supreme Crown.
II. חכמה = CHOKMAH, Wisdom.
III. בינה = BINAH, Intelligence or Understanding.
IV. חסר = CHESED, Mercy, otherwise גדולה = GEDULAH, Magnificence or Benignity and Greatness.
V. גבורה = GEBURAH, Severity, Judgment, Awe, Power.
VI. תפארת = TIPHERETH, Beauty.
VII. נצח = NETZACH, Victory.
VIII. הוד = HOD, Glory.
IX. יסוד = YESOD, the Foundation.
X. מלכות = MALKUTH, the Kingdom.

The conjunction of CHOKMAH and BINAH produced a quasi-emanation called DAATH, knowledge, but it is not one of the SEPHIROTH.[2]

To these ten emanations or numerations various profound meanings are attached ; indeed, the study of the Kabbalistic system of the SEPHIROTH [2] constitutes a research by itself, and one which is full of complexity ; but we are not engaged here in its exhaustive presentation or with more than its elementary symbolism.[3] We are concerned, in a word, not with what it may have been designed to conceal for the benefit of a presumed circle of initiates, which is the claim implied by the ZOHAR, but with what it was intended to explain, and this explanation may offer some warrant for concluding that outside it there is only a wider province of fantasy.

Beyond a certain point it is not allowable to suppose a double meaning in any literature ; the theory of many-sided allegories does credit chiefly to the ingenuity of the critic,

[1] Azriel, in his work on the Song of Solomon, terms them " measures and organs," and in the ZOHAR itself they appear as divine emanated essences.
[2] A term derived from a word signifying " to number," though late Kabbalists offer other etymologies, as, for example, the Greek σφαῖρα. The singular is SEPHIRA. The emanations are regarded as vessels, receptacles of the Divine Power and attributes as they developed, and there is no doubt that these vessels were usually considered spherical. See especially the treatise BETH ELOHIM concerning KETHER, in which the idea of circularity is involved. The author of the GATES OF LIGHT refers the term to the Hebrew word signifying sapphire, which stone, on account of its brightness and purity, is a symbol of the SEPHIROTH. Other rabbinical authorities have supported this view. See Jellinek : BEITRÄGE ZUR GESCHICHTE DER KABBALA. Leipsic, 1851.
[3] See Appendix I.

and of its general value we have had a typical instance in Talmudic exegesis.[1]

The initial purpose of the Sephirotic system was undoubtedly to provide intermediaries between the Deity and the material world. It is that of all doctrines of emanation. But while we set aside conjectures for which no warrant is produced we must be careful not to fall into the opposite error. To bridge the gulf between the finite and the infinite, and to effect a correspondence by stages between the inconceivable purity of the Divine Nature and the uncleanness attributed to matter by all the old Theosophies, was not the sole purpose of the Sephirotic system, a point which is sometimes missed by the merely academical critic.

It is affirmed by hostile writers, for example, by Dr. Ginsburg,[2] that as the earliest Kabbalistic literature does not contain the doctrine of AIN SOPH, so also it wants that of the SEPHIROTH; but it is above challenge that the germ of the Sephirotic scheme must be sought in SEPHER YETZIRAH. The ten numerations of that treatise are, in fact, SEPHIROTH, and it seems quite impossible to maintain a contrary opinion.[3]

III.—THE DOCTRINE OF THE FOUR WORLDS

The Sephirotic system was concerned first of all, as I have indicated, with the mystery of Divine Evolution. From that unsearchable condition which is above consciousness, by a mysterious operation, the Uncreated Will moved forthward, and certain manifestations or relations of Deity became established. By a kind of flowing forth or emanation, there were produced Four Worlds in succession,[4] and as it happens that the developments of these are chiefly in later Kabbalism,

---

[1] After an exhaustive study of modern esoteric literature, I doubt much whether even French occultism of the late nineteenth century really concerned itself with the discovery of a concealed sense in the Kabbalah. It is a sufficient exercise of patience to codify and harmonise the outward sense, which is assuredly not removed. Take, for example, the conception of AIN SOPH : even the fantasiast Éliphas Lévi does not look for any notion more withdrawn than that of Divine Latency therein. The inner meaning of the Kabbalah is its proper and single sense, which has been confused by an obscurity of style and subject.

[2] More especially in his article, *s.v.* Kabbalah, contributed to the third edition of Kitto's CYCLOPÆDIA OF BIBLICAL LITERATURE.

[3] William Postel, the first translator of SEPHER YETZIRAH, indubitably regarded the Ten Numerations as identical with the SEPHIROTH of more evolved Kabbalism.

[4] The earliest description of these Worlds is found in a TREATISE ON EMANATION—MASSEKET ATZILUTH—which belongs to the twelfth century and has been described as the earliest literary product of the Speculative Kabbalah.

being very elaborate therein, it is desirable to see exactly what is said upon the subject in the fountain text. The references are in summary form as follows : (1) There is a Sephirotic degree entitled MALKUTH, and it seems clear that to what world soever this name is allocated, one SEPHIRA alone is signified, being that which is tenth in numeration and is actually called MALKUTH,[1] signifying the Kingdom. (2) It is testified that Scripture makes use of the three expressions " to create, to form and to make "[2] in allusion to the three worlds which are below the World of Emanation.[3] It follows that the Four Worlds are those of Emanation, Creation, Formation and Manifestation, otherwise Action, the material universe, or as it is called by Rosenroth *Mundus Factionis*.[4] The Hebrew equivalents are ATZILUTH, BRIAH, YETZIRAH and ASSIAH. (3) The union of God and His Shekinah takes place as we shall see in ATZILUTH,[5] the World of Emanation, where there is no separateness ; the angels of BRIAH form the body of Shekinah,[6] when she descends therein, and this World is called the region of the Throne. It is said that the princes of Israel, the wise, the intelligent, the zealous, heroes, men of truth, prophets, just men and kings are all from the World of Emanation, but there are others from the World of Creation, whereof Shekinah is the sacrifice. This is not to be taken literally, as there can be no call to say. (4) There is also a reference to three Worlds of Divine Hiddenness.[7] The first can be neither seen nor discerned and is known only to Him Who is concealed therein ; I suppose that this alludes to AIN SOPH. The second is attached to the first and the Holy One is manifested therein : it is presumably ATZILUTH. The third is the beginning of division, signifying created intelligence, and is the world of

---

[1] Z., Pt. I, 18a ; I, 112. MALKUTH is supposed to be designated by the word " bow," when it is said : " I do set my bow in the cloud."—Gen. ix. 13.

[2] *Ib.*, Part I, fol. 179b ; II, 298.

[3] I conceive that this must be understood in a dual sense. Divinity in the world of ATZILUTH is God in the Hiddenness and yet moving towards manifestation, because this Deific mode not only can be but is conceived, however remotely, by the human mind. Beyond is the unknowable mode of AIN SOPH, from which it emanates. But there is a state of emanation in ATZILUTH, although it is a World of Unity, for God and His Shekinah in Kether are brought forth, so to speak, into CHOKMAH and BINAH as ABBA and AIMA, the Father in Supernal Wisdom and the Mother in Supernal Understanding.

[4] KABBALA DENUDATA : *Apparatus, Pars Prima*, p. 12.

[5] Z., Pt. III, fol. 109b ; V, 276.

[6] *Ib.* The Angel METATRON is called the vesture of Shekinah.

[7] *Ib.*, fol. 159a ; V, 411, 412.

the superior angels : it is therefore BRIAH, according to later Kabbalism.

For the Sons of the Doctrine the Four Worlds of their conception were understood not only in their first or universal sense but in a manner particular to themselves, from which point of view the worlds in their synthesis are symbolised, in later Kabbalism, by the Hebrew word פרדס = *Pardes*, signifying a Garden and understood as that of Paradise, the consonants of which—as we have seen—are the initial letters of four words signifying (*a*) the literal sense of the word of Scripture = פשוטה ; (*b*) the symbolical sense = רמן ; (*c*) the allegorical sense = דרוש ; and (*d*) the mystical or Kabbalistic sense = סוד.[1] It was a question of correspondence and went to show in the eloquent manner of symbolism that the Divine Word is truly Divine in all its stages and that its study is an ascent from the world of manifested things to that of Deity.   So also it was out of the literal sense of Scripture that the doctors derived their exalted notion of things unseen and of Him Who reigns not alone in the world to come but in this which we see with our eyes, Who fills them both and by Whom the soul is replenished on all the planes of being.

Now it follows from the Kabbalism of every period that these Four Worlds are subdivided into those ten spheres which are called SEPHIROTH or Numerations, and have been tabulated already in brief.   Their further consideration will follow, but we are concerned at the moment with the way in which these spheres are allocated to the Worlds of Kabbalism. Now the ZOHAR speaks of three Supernal Degrees or Divine Hypostases, and the first of them is called KETHER.[2]   It is said also that when the world of manifest things was in the state of TOHU, God revealed Himself therein under the Hypostasis SHADDAI ; when it had proceeded to the condition called BOHU He manifested as the Hypostasis TSABAOTH ; but when the darkness had disappeared from the face of things He appeared as Elohim.   Hereto appertain the words : " And the spirit of God moved upon the face of the waters," [3] understood as a reference to the sweet and harmonious voice

---

[1] KABBALA DENUDATA : *Apparatus Pars Prima*, p. 12.   The Sons of the Doctrine made up the worlds in their minds, and—for us at least—this is the sense of their claim that the story of creation is the history of the chosen people.

[2] Z., Pt. I, fol. 22b ; I, 139.

[3] Gen. i. 2.

heard by Elijah and termed : " The Voice of the Lord is upon the waters." [1] This signifies the completion of the Sacred Name Jehovah. Hence in the vision of Elijah it is said that " the Lord (Jehovah) was not in the earthquake " : it was SHADDAI. He was not in the fire : this was TSABBAOTH ; but He was in the still small voice, being that of the Spirit of Elohim, and the Name of Jehovah was complete. [2] It is said also that this Name is composed of four letters, [3] the relation of which to the Divine Essence is like that of the limbs to the human body [4] ; but this notwithstanding, the Hypostases are three only. Now, as KETHER is the first it is to be inferred that CHOKMAH and BINAH constitute the other two, and the world of ATZILUTH or Emanation will be completed in these. They are symbolised by the three bars of the Hebrew letter SHIN, [5] which also exhibits their essential unity. We may regard the point as determined by one further statement, according to which the First Light is symbolised by the Crown and the Second Light or Hypostasis forms the second SEPHIRA. These lights appeared to Abraham, [6] and the third, which was seen by Jacob, [7] proceeds from the two first. [8]

It has been necessary to enter at some length into this involved subject because later Kabbalism has complicated almost inextricably the Worlds of the ZOHAR. [9] I proceed now to establish the following Sephirotic division as that which represents the mind of the original text. To the First World of ATZILUTH are referred KETHER, CHOKMAH and BINAH ; to the Second World of BRIAH are allocated CHESED, GEBURAH and TIPHERETH ; YETZIRAH comprises NETZACH, HOD and YESOD ; while ASSIAH is MALKUTH, as I have said earlier in this study. The ten SEPHIROTH are contained therefore within the Four Worlds.

According to the ZOHAR, the SEPHIROTH are comparable to chariots for the Degrees of the Divine Essence, and the word Degrees, which is used very frequently in the text, illustrates after a simple manner the idea of gradations in the nature of the Presence, as the spheres of manifestation proceed further from the Head of the Tree. The Supernal World contains the highest Degrees of which the human mind can

---

[1] Ps. xxix. 3.
[2] I Kings xix. 11, 13.
[3] Z., Pt. I, fol. 16a ; I, 97.
[4] Ib.
[5] Ib., Pt. III, 194a ; V, 503.
[6] Gen. xviii. 1.
[7] Gen. xxxii. 31.
[8] Z., Pt. I, fol. 21a, b ; I, 130, 131.
[9] See APPENDIX II.

conceive by the intellection of faith, and KETHER, CHOKMAH, BINAH form an unity therein. It will be seen from previous extracts that BRIAH is the World of created intelligence, though it would seem that its content flows over into YETZIRAH. The Third and the Fourth World are not described, though they are implied obviously, in the ZOHAR, and their names indicate that as in BRIAH God created the forms of consciousness to which He could manifest Himself by Divine Modes, so in YETZIRAH He produced the pattern, idea or archetype of the visible and material cosmos, referred to ASSIAH. The names allocated to the ten SEPHIROTH are on their surface conventional and arbitrary—at least in certain cases. We can recognise that MALKUTH is appropriate in respect of the visible world, and that KETHER is the crown or summit of the entire Sephirotic system. Mercy and severity will be found to explain the reason why they are ascribed to certain SEPHIROTH when arranged as what is called the Tree of Life in Kabbalism. YESOD has a deep significance which we shall come to understand later; but the names of NETZACH and HOD = Victory and Glory are without interpretation, even in later Kabbalism, which can be said to be of moment.

The source of Zoharic information respecting the ten SEPHIROTH or Numberings is—as we have seen—in the SEPHER YETZIRAH or BOOK OF FORMATION.[1] The sequence, however, seems arbitrary to the last degree, and I have found nothing in the ZOHAR which can be held to connect therewith. It should be observed that the names allocated to the SEPHIROTH are wanting in the early text, nor do I pretend to say when or in what work they are met with for the first time. Something will depend on the date to which we assign the ZOHAR itself: if it is earlier than the earliest commentaries on the SEPHER YETZIRAH—for example, that of Ha Levi—it may have been—for all that I know to the contrary—the authority for the ten names. We have met with a story which refers their invention to Isaac the Blind, and this shall stand at its value, because it has been said also that the ZOHAR itself was either his product or that of his school at Posquières.

It should be remembered further that the SEPHIROTH are

---

[1] The little text is mentioned twice in the ZOHAR. See Pt. II, fol. 187b, where it is quoted to prove that the SEPHIROTH are not eleven but ten, and *Ib.*, fol. 289a; IV, 315, where its authorship is referred to the patriarch Abraham, in accordance with Tradition. The English reader may consult the translation of Knut Stenring, *s.v.* THE BOOK OF FORMATION or SEPHER YETZIRAH, 1923.

represented as good and evil equally, which seems reasonable in respect of that world of dimensions wherein both principles manifest. The ZOHAR has developments of its own on this subject and something must be said of them later. The diagrams which represent the SEPHIROTH in the form of the Tree of Life are unknown to THE BOOK OF FORMATION, nor can they be deduced therefrom. Here also the origin is doubtful, but a certain form is met with in the ZOHAR, or perhaps it would be more accurate to say that it is implied continually therein. Passing to this work, I will give the indications suggesting the arrangement mentioned. There is firstly the Middle Pillar and there are the Right and Left sides, corresponding to Mercy and Severity. CHOKMAH is on the right of KETHER and BINAH on the left.[1] CHESED is the right and GEBURAH the left arm. NETZACH and HOD are the right and left hips, for the Tree in this case has become a human figure. The right side is life and the left is death.[2] The Pillars of Mercy and Severity are thus completed, according to the scheme of the Tree. The Middle Pillar is one of the Hypostases in the Divine Essence, and it is called the Perfect Pillar.[3] The light of the right side, which is active, enters therein, and so does the passive light of the left. The Word issues from this union, an allusion to the Divine Son, Who, according to another text, is begotten by ABBA and AIMA, the Holy Father and the Holy Mother in the World of the Supernals. Elohim forms the Middle Pillar and therein are the union and fecundity of the waters above and below, meaning Sephirotic degrees.[4] Children, life and the means of existence come therefrom [5]: it is " mine eldest son, Israel." [6] It is to be understood therefore that Israel is in the likeness of the Highest. The four rivers of Eden seem to be CHESED, GEBURAH, NETZACH and HOD.[7] The Middle Pillar is the Tree of Life, and perhaps the two other Pillars are together the Tree of Knowledge of Good and Evil—but it is all speculation and all is high convention, as well as a jumble of notions. There is no evil when these are united with the Central Pillar, which is called the seventh day,[8] the Sabbath and the tent of peace.[9] The Central Pillar is Shekinah. It is the peace in

[1] Z., Pt, fol. 26b ; I, 164, 165.
[2] Ib., Pt. I, fol. 22b ; I, 139.
[3] Ib., Pt. I, fol. 16b ; I, 101.
[4] Ib., fol. 17a ; I, 103.

[5] Ib., fol. 24a ; I, 149.
'Exodus iv. 22.
[7] Z., fol. 28a ; I, 165.
[8] Ib., fol. 47b ; I, 276.

[9] Ib., fol. 48a ; I, 279.

particular between the light of the right side and that which in another place is called the darkness of the left.[1] The TALMUD and the MISHNAH come from the Middle Pillar.[2] There are many alternative allocations, as for example, when the Middle Pillar is called the Son of YOD but also the HE, which is BINAH.[3] The Middle Pillar is otherwise the Master of the House.[4] It is said of the right arm that it draws the immensity of space in love, like the arm of the male drawing the female.[5] The law of faith is on the right side.[6] The left arm draws the immensity of space in rigour.[7] The serpent constitutes the left arm and thence emanates the impure spirit. It is the side of water and the side of sadness. These engender darkness and the way of escape is by the harmony which can be instituted between the Mercy or Grace of CHESED and the Severity of GEBURAH.[8] The left side is without pity in the state of separation,[9] yet she who is Matrona according to another allocation is the left side, as well as the Middle Pillar : she is the latter apparently because she is the ground and state of union, and it is known that she is the Mother of Mercy.[10] A day will come when the left side shall disappear and good will obtain only.[11] It is said further that the Mercy and Severity of CHESED and GEBURAH are united in TIPHERETH.[12] The Holy Degrees are declared to emanate from the holy side and the impure degrees from the impure side.[13] It follows that the ZOHAR bears out the thesis of SEPHER YETZIRAH when this work describes the SEPHIROTH as the abyss of good and evil. It gives no explanation which will help us to understand this, though it speaks in one place of the union between good and evil [14] as a secret or mystery and indicates in another that there is a sense in which the left side is on the way of attainment.[15] It was possibly the difficulties arising from the allocation of evil to spheres in which God was present everywhere [16] that led some later Kabbalists to

---

[1] Z., fol. 254a ; II, 599.   [2] Ib., fol. 255a ; II, 601.
[3] Ib., Pt. II, fol. 115b ; III, 445. We shall see that from one point of view this is supported by an independent text, one of the most ancient imbedded in the ZOHAR ; but the text-general presents a different aspect.

[4] Ib., III, 272a ; VI, 37.
[5] Ib., Pt. I, fol. 64a ; I, 375.
[6] Ib., Pt. II, fol. 82a ; III, 342.
[7] Ib., Pt. I, fol. 64a ; I, 375.
[8] Ib., Pt. II, fol. 103b ; II, 21.
[9] Ib., fol. 198b ; II, 387.

[10] Ib., fol. 250a ; II, 584.
[11] Ib., Pt. II, fol. 190a ; IV, 175.
[12] Ib., Pt. III, fol. 233a ; V, 563.
[13] Ib., I, 203b ; II, 409.
[14] Ib., Pt. II, fol. 34a ; IV, 166.
[15] Ib., 60b ; IV, 268 ; and 114b ; III, 443.

[16] The mystery deepens when it is affirmed that there is no other God comprised outside the ten SEPHIROTH, and that Shekinah, Who is a Divine Hypostasis, dwells in each SEPHIRA.—Z., Pt. III, fol. 109b ; V, 276.

suppose that the ten SEPHIROTH were repeated in each of the four worlds ; but this development does not really deal with the point at issue, and as there is no further light thereon we must be content to pass it over, remembering that, almost in the words of the text, the Middle Pillar draws the right and left sides, the good and the evil together, in which union evil dissolves as such and the good obtains entirely under the name of Benignity—which is that of the Middle Pillar. It is a question of transmutation.

The conventional Tree of Life connects the SEPHIROTH together by means of lines which are called paths, being twenty-two in number, and these in connection with the SEPHIROTH themselves constitute the thirty-two paths of the SEPHER YETZIRAH. As there are several forms of the Tree according to different commentators, I have reproduced those which are regarded as of authority. They do not seem to represent the mind of the ZOHAR, and I have therefore added one which seems to be more in consonance, especially regarding the Supernals.[1] Serving only to reconcile several statements to which no vital consequence attaches, I am of opinion that the accepted forms are generally speaking preferable. We must remember that late Kabbalism arose to account for the difficulties, omissions and discrepancies which prevail in the fountain text, and though I have had occasion to make various strictures, these are without prejudice to the fact that the work as a whole was done with sincerity and zeal, whence it is helpful in respect of occasional conciliation and from time to time as reasonable extension and inference. There is one point, however, in which I believe that my diagram is more within the logic of the symbolism than are its alternatives in the printed text-books. It is a question of the right and the left sides, which are always presented from the observer's standpoint, so that CHOKMAH is on the right of him when he is looking at the figure, while GEBURAH is on his left. On the contrary, what seems intended obviously in the ZOHAR is right and left in the order of procession on the Tree, or on the path of descent into manifestation. The distinction may seem unimportant at first sight, but it has enabled me to rectify the position of the consonants belonging to the Sacred Name in respect of certain SEPHIROTH, so that it is

---

[1] The reference is to the plate which forms the Frontispiece.

justified by a particular allocation, as well as by the reason of things.

I will now summarise the correspondences of the ten Sephiroth in succession. Kether is the crown or head of the Tree.[1] It is the first Hypostasis but not apparently the First Cause or Cause of causes.[2] The meaning seems to be that the First Cause contains within itself two Hypostases, understood as male and female.[3] Jehovah manifests with Shekinah in the degree of Kether.[4] In contradiction hereto it is said that the first and third Sephiroth are united as male and female.[5] It is said also that Kether and Chokmah are never in separation.[6] This is true, however, of the whole Supernal Triad, or First Three Sephiroth.

As regards Chokmah, it is by the sublime and impenetrable mystery of this Sephira that the world exists [7] and all other mysteries depend therefrom.[8] It is the second Sephira or Hypostasis and is called Man [9] : otherwise, it is ABBA, the Father. The house is built by Chokmah ; [10] it was concealed like the Supreme Point before the creation,[11] and it is called Yod.[12] It is Eternal Wisdom,[13] and therein is concealed the Eternal Thought, which is the Great Voice,[14] meaning the still small voice which is the House of Eternal Wisdom. In contradiction to these indications it is said to be the Sister, meaning thereby Shekinah.[15] It is also Daughter and Mother. It is the beginning of all.[16]

Binah is intelligence or understanding,[17] and its number is said to be fifty because of the Gates of Understanding.[18] It is the concealed world,[19] and motherhood is its image.[20] It is also penitence,[21] the degree of the moon,[22] the mystery of the Supreme World,[23] and the Community of Israel.[24] The letter He is allocated to Binah, and it is then described as the only Daughter [25] or alternatively AIMA, the Mother. It is

[1] Z., Pt. I, 21b ; I, 131.
[2] Ib., fol. 22b ; I, 138.
[3] Ib., fol. 22b ; I, 139.
[4] Ib., Pt. III, fol. 242b, 243a ; V, 581.
[5] Ib., fol. 31b ; I, 196.
[6] Ib., Pt. II, fol. 11b ; III, 51.
[7] Ib., fol. 3b ; I, 18.
[8] Ib., fol. 7 ; I, 38.
[9] Ib., fol. 21b ; I, 131.
[10] Ib., fol. 29a ; I, 183.
[11] Ib., fol. 30a ; I, 188.
[12] Ib., fol. 31a ; I, 194.
[13] Ib., fol. 31b ; I, 195.
[14] Ib., fol. 50b ; I, 293.
[15] Ib., fol. 111b, 112a ; II, 50, 51.
[16] Ib., Appendices III, Secrets of the Law ; II, 732.
[17] Ib., fol. 71a ; I, 420.
[18] Ib., fol. 106a ; II, 34.
[19] Ib., fol. 154a ; II, 206.
[20] Ib., fol. 158a ; II, 220.
[21] Ib., Appendices II, Secrets of the Law ; II, 662.
[22] Ib., Pt. II, fol. 11b ; III, 51.
[23] Ib., fol. 43b ; III, 194.
[24] Ib., fol. 85a ; III, 349.
[25] Ib., Pt. III, 6a, 27b ; V, 76.

the Throne of Mercy and the celestial fire which descends, as MALKUTH is the Throne of Justice and the fire which goes up.[1] It is the sweetness of God [2] and constitutes the mystery of the Levirate.[3] The House is built by CHOKMAH and is established by BINAH.[4]

CHESED is the male side [5] and the patriarch Abraham is referred thereto.[6] The Divine Name Jehovah is attributed to CHESED [7] and it is even called in one place the first degree of the Divine Essence. It is merit, as demerit is GEBURAH.[8] It is the place of revelations [9] and it is the twin sister who came into the world with VAU,[10] but this allocation is contrary to the general trend of the symbolism. The VAU is the son of YOD and HE; it unites to the HE, symbolising CHOKMAH, and itself represents BINAH.[11] What, however, it represents really is the six lower SEPHIROTH.

GEBURAH or PACHAD is sometimes used in a good and sometimes in an evil sense [12]; the world is based thereon— in the sense that severity is indispensable—but it could not subsist without Mercy.[13] It is said also to be the repentance of God [14] and it seems even to connect with Samael.[15] It was by GEBURAH that Jerusalem was destroyed.[16]

TIPHERETH is beauty; [17] it is the heart of the Sephirotic Tree and is called Heaven.[18] It is also glory.[19] NETZACH and HOD come from the celestial river.[20] NETZACH is in correspondence with the Covenant,[21] according to one attribution. NETZACH and HOD represent also the two Messiahs [22] mentioned by the TALMUD. In the macrocosmic human figure YESOD is the organ of generation, and it receives

---

[1] Z., Pt. III, fol. 34a (FAITHFUL SHEPHERD); V, 89.
[2] Ib., fol. 161b; V, 416.
[3] Ib., fol. 215b (FAITHFUL SHEPHERD); V. 547.
[4] Ib., Pt. I, fol. 52b; I, 203.
[5] Ib., fol. 94a; II, 282.
[6] Ib., fol. 152b; II, 123.
[7] Ib., fol. 173b, 174a; II, 282.
[8] Ib., Pt. 8, Appendices I, fol. 265a (SECRETS OF THE LAW); II, 626.
[9] Ib., Pt. II, fol. 119b; III, 460.
[10] Ib., Pt. III, fol. 776; V, 210, 211.
[11] Ib., fol. 247b (FAITHFUL SHEPHERD); V, 585. It must be remembered that the FAITHFUL SHEPHERD is a text imbedded in the ZOHAR and—as here—is not always in harmony therewith, while it contradicts also other imbedded texts.
[12] Ib., Pt. I, fol. 160a; II, 228.
[13] Ib., fol. 180b; II, 311.
[14] Ib., fol. 163a; II, 237.
[15] Ib., fol. 36a; I, 223.
[16] Ib., fol. 151a; II, 196.
[17] Ib., fol. 34a; I, 211.
[18] Ib., fol. 31a; I, 195.
[19] Ib., Pt. II, fol. 79b; III, 332.
[20] Ib., Pt. III, fol. 68a; V. 186.
[21] Ib., Pt. I, fol. 24b; I, 152.
[22] Ib., Pt. III, fol. 243a, 243b (FAITHFUL SHEPHERD); V, 581.

light from the supreme SEPHIROTH.[1] It is said to issue from the right and left sides—meaning that it draws from both—as MALKUTH issues from YESOD. MALKUTH is connected with Israel, regarded as Son of the King.[2] It is the rainbow, or at least the arch thereof.[3] It is also the lower firmament.[4]

The following points may be drawn together in conclusion : All Supreme Degrees and all SEPHIROTH are one, and God embraces all the SEPHIROTH. The law is CHESED. BINAH is repentance,[5] and MALKUTH is confession. God and the ten crowns are one [6]—a notable statement, which substitutes a doctrine of identity for that of mere emanation. To ascend to the Paradise above, it is necessary that souls should cleave to the Middle Pillar.[7] There is an unity of the ten SEPHIROTH, and [8] there is joy in the world when order reigns among them.[9] Finally, the Holy One manifests in the SEPHIROTH for those who comprehend them.[10]

The doctrine concerning the three Divine Hypostases is obviously that of a Trinity in Kabbalism, and the heads of this subject must be considered in the next place in view of developments towards the end of my study, not to speak of the Christian implicits suggested by the simple expression. There are three that bear testimony in ATZILUTH, and these three are one. They are described after many manners, as, for example, when it is said that they are three lights, which form a single light.[11] But the chief symbolism is drawn from the Sacred Name, being YOD, HE, VAU, HE, = Jehovah. YOD is the Father, HE is the Mother and VAU the begotten Son.[12] At the moment we will not affirm that these ineffable

---

[1] Z., Pt. I, fol. 30b ; I, 191.
[2] Ib., Pt. III, fol. 223a (FAITHFUL SHEPHERD) ; V, 563.
[3] Ib., Pt. I, fol. 18a ; I, 112.
[4] Ib., fol. 33b ; I, 209.
[5] Ib., fol. 286a (SECRETS OF THE LAW) ; II, 662.
[6] Ib., Pt. III, fol. 70a ; V, 190.
[7] Ib., Pt. II, fol. 211a ; IV, 219.
[8] Ib., fol. 67a ; III, 298. See also Pt. III, fol. 28a ; V, 80.
[9] Ib., Pt. II, fol. 78b ; III, 329.
[10] Ib., Pt. I, fol. 241a ; II, 554.
[11] Ib., I, fol. 17b ; I, 103.
[12] An important analogous intimation occurs early in the ZOHAR. The Scriptural reference is " Let there be light" (Gen. i. 3), which in Hebrew is יהי אור, the first word being the verb in the imperative. It should be remembered here that Hebrew is read from left to right. This word, YOD, HE, YOD, is regarded as a symbol of the three Divine Hypostases occurring at the opening of Genesis and designed to shew that the three are one. The first YOD is the Heavenly Father, the HE is the Divine Mother, while the third Hypostasis is indicated by the second YOD and proceeds from the first two.—Z., I, 16b ; I, 99, 100.

personalities are referable to KETHER, CHOKMAH and BINAH
—as might seem probable—because later considerations will
intervene to correct this view.   Let us remember only that
the Zoharic Trinity constitutes a Divine Family in the World
of Heaven.   Like the Christian Trinity, the letters which are
their symbols are called one on account of the unity of God.

We are now in a position to advance a step further.   YOD
and HE are the Supreme Mystery,[1] for ever impenetrable.[2]
On the YOD are all things based,[3] and it is never in separation
from the HE.[4]   As the prototypical male principle, it has
man for another symbol.[5]   HE is the female principle,[6] and
it has woman therefore as its emblem; it signifies many
mysteries,[7] and its true name is Shekinah.   Because the letter
HE is duplicated in the Sacred Name it is said to terminate
both the first and second parts thereof.[8]   The world was
created by the HE,[9] or alternatively by the YOD and HE in
the perfection of their concurrence.[10]   The VAU is the " free
Son," [11] and it is this which diffuses all blessings.[12]   The YOD
unites with the HE, as male with female, and gives birth to
the VAU as Son.[13]   The three dwell together in unity.[14]   VAU
is the Eternal World.[15]

So far in respect of three Divine Hypostases ; but there is
the HE final which completes the Sacred Name, and this is
called the Daughter.[16]   It is said of this Daughter [17] that the
HE came down to earth.[18]   The first He is liberty above and

---

[1] Z., Pt. I, fol. 159a ; II, 225.

[2] Ib., fol. 232b ; II, 517.

[3] Ib., Pt. III, fol. 10b ; V, 31.

[4] Ib., fol. 279b ; VI, 54.

[5] Ib., fol. 34a ; V, 89.

[6] Ib.

[7] Ib., Pt. II, fol. 180b ; IV, 152.

[8] Ib., Pt. III, 89b ; V, 240.

[9] Ib., fol. 298a ; VI, 125.

[10] Ib., Pt. II, 22b ; III, 13.

[11] Eccles. x, 17.

[12] Z., Pt. I, 124b ; II, 98.

[13] Ib., Pt. II, 123b ; III, 472.

[14] Ib., Pt. III, 92a ; V, 245.

[15] Ib., fol. 252b ; V, 591.

[16] Ib., Pt. I, fol. 27b ; I, 174.

[17] Ib., fol. 354b ; II, 600.   There is another symbolism as follows :   When the letter
YOD is written at length in Hebrew it is composed of YOD, VAU and DALETH.   YOD
is the Father of all, VAU—as seen already—is the begotten Son, and DALETH is the
Daughter—that is, the Daughter of Matrona.   The imagery is confused on the surface,
as this Daughter is said to proceed from the Father and the Son, whereas it is certain
in the sense of things and is plain from the text elsewhere that the HE primal of the
Sacred Name produces in union with the YOD not only the Son, being VAU, but his
Sister, who is also her Daughter and in the natural succession of the Divine Name is
therefore the HE final.—Ib., Pt. III, 10b ; V, 31.   It is not of much consequence to
the purpose in view whether it is possible or not to harmonise distinct symbolisms
on this subject : it is sufficient that they help to formulate the Kabbalistic notion of
the Trinity in the Supernal World.   As a fact, however, the Daughter proceeds from
the Son in precisely the same sense as Eve proceeded from Adam, for the Daughter
originally abode within the Son, in a state of ineffable union, and was brought forth
afterwards from Him.

[18] Ib., Pt. I, 354b ; II, 600.

the second is liberty below.[1] The High Priest depends from
the HE which is above but the ordinary priest from that HE
which is below.[2] It follows that two letters of the Name
belong ·to the male principle—namely, YOD and VAU—two
also to the female, being HE primal and final. The engendering of a whole world depends on these two principles.[3] The
second HE will rise from the earth, meaning that it will be
united with the Divine Hypostases in the world of transcendence.[4] The VAU will be united to the HE,[5] and when the
VAU is thus attached, as a bridegroom to the Bride, there will
be union everywhere—between the YOD and the HE above,
between the VAU and the HE final.[6]

The abodes of these symbolic personalities is our next
question. Now, it is said that the YOD is CHOKMAH, while
the HE is BINAH,[7] this being repeated in another place, where
it is added that they sustain the VAU, but without intimating
the location of this letter or of the second HE which is represented as in union therewith.[8] For information on these
points we must transfer our attention from the ZOHAR proper
to some of the additional materials with which I have dealt
already in the previous book.

The tracts in question are THE ASSEMBLY OF THE SANC-
TUARY, THE SECRET BOOK—otherwise, BOOK OF CONCEAL-
MENT—THE GREAT AND HOLY ASSEMBLY and THE LESSER
HOLY ASSEMBLY.[9] We can pass over the first of these, as
Rosenroth was guided wisely in omitting it ; it seems contradictory and inextricable in its symbolism and is speaking
roughly a sort of summary appendix to much that has preceded in a better and fuller form. THE SECRET BOOK comprises a discourse concerning The White Head,[10] the Ancient,

---

[1] Z., Pt. II, fol. 183a ; IV, 109. [5] Ib., fol. 119a ; II, 76.
[2] Ib., Pt. III, 89b ; V, 240. [6] Ib., Pt. III, 267b ; VI, 23.
[3] Ib., Pt. II, fol. 228a ; IV, 250. [7] Ib., Pt. II, fol. 123b ; III, 478.
[4] Ib., Pt. I, 116b ; II, 66. [8] Ib., Pt. III, fol. 153b ; V, 394.

[9] THE ASSEMBLY OF THE SANCTUARY is inserted towards the end of Part II, § 6,
and occupies folios 122b to 123b. THE SECRET BOOK, called sometimes in translation
THE BOOK OF CONCEALED MYSTERY, follows Part II, § 7, and occupies folios 176b to
179a. THE GREAT AND HOLY ASSEMBLY is placed at the end of THE COMMENTARY ON
NUMBERS, § I, Z., Pt. III, folios 127b to 145a. THE LITTLE HOLY ASSEMBLY follows
THE COMMENTARY ON DEUTERONOMY, § 10, Z., Pt. III, folios 287b to 296b.

[10] Z., Pt. III, fol. 128a ; V, 334. The White Head is also without beginning and
without end before its reign was established and the Crown, that is, KETHER, was
assumed. The reference would seem therefore to AIN-SOPH AOUR, which pours
down into KETHER, and we shall see that the White Head is called AIN. At this
point the ZOHAR and the mystical theology of pseudo-Dionysius the Areopagite join
hands. It should be understood, however, that the White Head is not AIN-SOPH, but
the first procession therefrom.

or the Great Countenance. The same subject is continued in
THE GREAT AND HOLY ASSEMBLY, and he who is symbolised
therein is the Master with the white mantle and resplendent
visage ; he is called also Holy of Holies.

Connected by means of a white thread [1] or bond of union
with the Great Countenance, there is that which is called the
Lesser Countenance, Little Form or Figure, which presents,
however, a complete aspect of humanity and is extended
through many symbolical worlds. The distinction between
the two heads is that in this case the hair and beard are black.[2]
The Lesser Countenance has eyelids, because it has periods of
sleep,[3] a complete visage in manifestation, because severity is
one of its attributes ; and a distinctive name, being Lord,
whereas the Great Countenance is called AIN,[4] or Nothing,
because it draws or is emanated from AIN SOPH, though it is
located certainly in KETHER. These points notwithstanding,
it is laid down (1) that the Lesser Countenance emanates from
the Greater,[5] (2) that the Greater metamorphoses into the
Lesser,[6] (3) that the latter is actually the former, as if seen
through a curtain,[7] and more specifically that they are one and
the same.[8] The body of this Sacred Form is described fully
and is that of the male perfect in all its members.

Of this Form there is a counterpart of perfect womanhood,
and these two were primordially side by side, till the Ancient
of Days put the Lesser Form to sleep and detached the female
principle,[9] whose name is Matrona, Bride, Daughter, Betrothed
and Twin-Sister—for the Zoharic allegories institute strange
marriages in the world above. The object of separation was
that the Bride might come to the Bridegroom and, in the
great sacrament of matrimonial union, that they might
become one body and as if one flesh.[10] All is mercy in this

---

[1] Z., fol. 128b ; V, 335, 336.
[2] Ib., Pt. III, fol. 132a ; V, 346. The authorities are THE SONG OF SOLOMON, v. 11 :
"His locks are bushy, and black as a raven," and Dan. vii. 9 : "The hair of his head
like the pure wool," or as the ZOHAR gives it, "whitest and purest wool." It is to be
noted, however, that when severity operates the hair of the White Head becomes
black.
[3] Ib., fol. 136b ; V, 359.
[4] Ib., fol. 129a ; V, 337.
[5] Ib., fol. 131b ; V, 345.
[6] Ib., fol. 135a ; V, 354.
[7] Ib., fol. 128b ; V, 335.
[8] Ib., Pt. III, fol. 141a ; V, 365. See also THE LITTLE HOLY ASSEMBLY, ib., fol. 288a ;
VI, 82, and fol. 292a ; VI, 99.
[9] Ib., Pt. III, fol. 142b ; V, 368.
[10] Ib., fol. 143b ; V, 369.

union ; [1] it constitutes the Law of the Sabbath ; and it is this
that God blessed and sanctified.[2] The sacred organ of intercourse is called YESOD [3] on the male side, and it has access to
the concealed and mysterious region on the female side which
is called ZION.[4] It is a holy place and all the holiness of the
male enters therein.[5]

The reference to YESOD shews that the Lesser Form is
extended through the Lower SEPHIROTH. It is the Begotten
Son or VAU,[6] whose place we have been seeking on the Tree ;
and as its name is DAATH [7] or Knowledge, being a semi-
SEPHIRA which represents the junction point of the influences
flowing from CHOKMAH and BINAH, the inference is that the
Lesser Countenance or Head is located there, while the feet
are established on MALKUTH, as later Kabbalism affirms. We
have learned also where the Daughter and Bride dwells, being
side by side or face to face in union with her Celestial Spouse.
But she is the HE final of the Divine Name and we shall learn
at a later stage that her present dwelling is in MALKUTH.

We are now in a position to establish the Doctrine concerning the Tree with as much clearness as is possible considering the subject. According to the symbolism of the
IDRAS, the Great Countenance is in ATZILUTH and it encompasses therefore the three Supreme SEPHIROTH, which are
KETHER, CHOKMAH and BINAH. It is located, as I have said,
in KETHER, where it is at once male and female, these principles
being brought forth subsequently, the male principle into
CHOKMAH and the female into BINAH, who produced between
them DAATH, which is the Divine Son. We have therefore in
the Sephirotic Tree : (1) The first Divine Manifestation proceeding from AIN-SOPH and so interpenetrated thereby that
it bears sometimes the same name. In so far as it is postulated
in KETHER, it is not differentiated into male and female, but
these are implied, and according to other testimony the
Shekinah is certainly there. (2) But when the Sacred Ancient
wished to establish all things, He constituted male and female

---

[1] Z., fol. 143a ; V, 368.
[2] It is said that Matrona dwells in the Supernal Sanctuary—that is to say, in BINAH—
and in the Jerusalem which is manifested on earth—that is to say, in MALKUTH ; and
it is because she is united to the male in the unseen world that she is joined in manifestation with man. This is defined as the quintessence of all faith, for all faith is comprised
in this mystery.—Z., Pt. III, fol. 143b ; V, 370.
[3] Ib., fol. 296a ; VI, 118.   [5] Ib., fol. 296b ; VI, 119.
[4] Ib., fol. 290b ; VI, 92.   [6] Ib., fol. 291a ; VI, 94.
                        [7] Ib.

in His supreme region,[1] namely, the Father and Mother, owing to Whom all is made male and female. These are the second Divine manifestation in CHOKMAH and BINAH.[2] (3) The third is in the lower SEPHIROTH, as Son and Daughter, Brother and Sister, King and Queen. According to later Kabbalism, the Great Countenance is MACROPROSOPUS, the soul of the greater world, while the Lesser Countenance or Figure is MICROPROSOPUS, the soul of the lesser world, and ADAM PROTOPLASTES, his Bride being the archetypal Eve. They form together the *habitaculum* of all created intelligences, the hierarchies of consciousness ; and we can therefore sum up the whole subject by saying that THE BOOK OF MYSTERY and the IDRAS are a great allegory of man and his analogues coming forth from God. Male and female they were implied and conceived in Him ; male and female He manifested Himself on account of them ; male and female they came forth in Him and from Him ; male and female they abide above and below ; male and female they return in fine to Him, as we shall see fully and clearly in its proper place.

In conclusion, as to the Four Worlds, the consideration of which and of the Ten SEPHIROTH belongs essentially to the Majesty of God in Kabbalism, I must add that there is a Zoharic Theosophy of the Word, but how the term should be referred in respect of the Divine Hypostases is not easy to determine. The name of Elohim is allocated thereto,[3] but this is a title of Shekinah. Again, it is said that the Word was manifested in the Sanctuary, because it was indispensable to the existence of the latter on earth that the Divine should be present therein ; [4] but that which we know to have appeared between the Kerubim on the Mercy Seat was the Presence in the form of Shekinah. In the paraphrase of Onkelos the term MEIMRA was substituted for Jehovah, Who is thus identified with the Word ; but in the ZOHAR it is held that the Word in Scripture is designated under the term BERE-SHITH, because in order to fulfil the work of creation this term was engraven " under the form of a turnstile," [5] representing the six great celestial directions, being the four cardinal points, together with height and depth. The Word seems also to be specified under the name Sabbath ; [6] it had

---

[1] Z., Pt. III, fol. 290a ; VI, 90.
[2] *Ib.*, Pt. III, fol. 290b ; VI, 92.
[3] *Ib.*, Pt. I, fol. 16b ; I, 99.

[4] *Ib.*, fol. 74a ; I, 439.
[5] *Ib.*, fol. 3b ; I, 18.
[6] *Ib.*, Pt. I, fol. 32a ; I, 199.

birth by the union of the active and the passive light, the latter being called darkness, and it discovers to us the Supreme Mysteries.

The Supreme Principle and the Word are distinguished as two, though at the root they harmonise as one.[1] It is said : " While the King sitteth at his table, my spikenard sendeth forth the smell thereof." It is to be understood here that the King means the Supreme Principle while the spikenard signifies the Word, Who is king below and has formed the world below on the model of the world above. Thought and the Word are held to be of the same essence ; seen through the medium of one region, this essence appears as Thought, but through another as the Word. The doctrine of Israel is placed between two voices,[2] one of which constitutes the Supreme Mystery, but the other is more accessible. The first is the Great Voice, " the voice out of the midst of the darkness." It is interior, imperceptible, without cessation or interruption. Thence cometh the Secret Doctrine, which —in its manifestation—is called the Voice of Jacob, and this voice is heard. The Voice of Jacob is placed between the interior, imperceptible voice and that Word which resounds abroad and which I should identify with the Written Law. The Great Voice is the House of Eternal Wisdom and is female, as a house should always be. The Word is the House of the Voice of Jacob, that being apparently the literal and this the esoteric doctrine. When the Song of Solomon testifies that the voice of the turtle is heard in our land, the reference is to that voice which emanates from Him Who is the inward essence of all.[3] It is the Voice that utters the Word—as for example, the Word which ordained circumcision for Abraham, so that he might be made perfect. The Voice is added or joined to the Word—meaning that what is conceived in thought passes into expression, whether of speech or action—and this is held to be indicated by the appearance of the Lord to Abraham, when that tent before the door of which the patriarch was seated signified the Supreme World, on the threshold of which he rested, to receive the light thereof.[4]

---

[1] Z., fol. 74a ; *ib.*, 439.
[2] *Ib.*, fol. 50b ; I, 292, 293.
[3] *Ib.*, fol. 97b, 98a ; II, 5.
[4] Further intimations on the Word in Kabbalism will be found in the fifth section of the present Book.

In dismissing this section, the reader is asked to observe that it offers, thus early in our subject, some vital intimations on the root-matter of the Secret Doctrine, as this has been enshrined in the Secret Tradition of Israel. As proposed more than once already, it is that which is embodied in the distinction, relation and union of male and female ; but—as there should be no need to say—such root-matter is a metaphysical foundation and far removed from anything that belongs in public ways of life to the idea of sex.

IV.—THE PATHS OF WISDOM AND GATES OF UNDERSTANDING

In the Latin collection of Pistorius the marrow of philosophical Kabbalism is presented in the form of certain terse propositions or dogmas,[1] according to one of which the ways of eternity are thirty-two—*Via æternitatis sunt triginta duo.*[2] These are the Paths of the SEPHER YETZIRAH, namely, the ten SEPHIROTH and the letters of the Hebrew alphabet. The doctrine concerning them is a dependency of this fundamental treatise, but of much more recent date, and without even an imputed authorship. It tabulates the special graces and illuminations which may be communicated to man from above by means of these channels, and is not unimportant, because it shews that Kabbalism, even on its most speculative and formal side, had a practical application to the human mind, and was not a purely arbitrary system. It is outside the province of this work to offer translations to the student, but as in the present instance it would be difficult to summarise the tabulation more briefly, I shall give it *in extenso*, premising only that it has been translated more than once into English, and is indeed available in a number of European languages.

I. The first path is called the Admirable Intelligence,[3] the Supreme Crown. It is the light which imparts understanding

---

[1] They are extremely interesting theses of Picus de Mirandola, which will be found in Book VII.

[2] They are referred to the SEPHIRAH CHOKMAH and are termed channels, at once hidden and revealed. In the FAITHFUL SHEPHERD, CHOKMAH is called the highest of all paths, embracing and including all that are beneath it, and the influx of all is derived therefrom. The same treatise connects with CHOKMAH the words in Job xxviii. 7 : " The bird hath not known the path, neither hath the eye of the vulture beheld it."—KABBALA DENUDATA, *Apparatus*, i. 601, 602.

[3] Stenring gives Mystical Intelligence, following the French version of Comtesse Calomira de Cimara.

of the beginning which is without beginning, and this also is the First Splendour. No created being can attain to its essence.

II. The second path is called the Illuminating Intelligence. It is the Crown of Creation and the splendour of the Supreme Unity, to which it is most in proximity. It is exalted above every head and is distinguished by Kabbalists as the Second Splendour.

III. The third path is called the Sanctifying Intelligence and is the foundation of Primordial Wisdom, termed the Creation of Faith. Its roots are אמן. It is the mother of Faith, which indeed emanates therefrom.

IV. The fourth path is called the Arresting or Receiving [1] Intelligence because it arises like a boundary to receive the emanations of the higher intelligences which are sent down to it. Herefrom all spiritual virtues emanate by the way of subtlety, which itself emanates from the Supreme Crown.[2]

V. The fifth path is called the Radical Intelligence, because it is more akin than any other to the Supreme Unity and emanates from the depths of the Primordial Wisdom.[3]

VI. The sixth Path is called the Intelligence of Mediating Influence, because the flux of the emanations is multiplied therein. It communicates this affluence to those blessed men who are united with it.[4]

VII. The seventh path is called the Hidden Intelligence, because it pours out a brilliant splendour on all intellectual virtues which are beheld with the eyes of the spirit and by the ecstasy of faith.

VIII. The eighth path is called the Perfect and Absolute Intelligence. The preparation of principles emanates therefrom.[5] The roots to which it adheres are in the depths of the Sphere Magnificence, from the very substance of which it emanates.

IX. The ninth path is called the Purified Intelligence. It

---

[1] Receptacular is an awkward variant which has been used by more than one translator.

[2] Westcott, following the text of Rittangelius, makes this rendering: " The fourth path is named Measuring, Cohesive, or Receptacular ; and is so-called because it contains all the holy powers, and from it emanate all the spiritual virtues with the most exalted essences ; they emanate one from the other by the power of the primordial emanation," *i.e.*, KETHER.

[3] Or, " the primordial depths of CHOKMAH."—Westcott, SEPHER YETZIRAH, p. 28.

[4] According to Comtesse de Cimara, the sixth path is the Intelligence of Separated Emanation.

[5] According to Westcott " it is the means of the primordial."—*Ibid.*, p. 29.

purifies the numerations, prevents and stays the fracture of their images,[1] for it establishes their unity, to preserve them from destruction and division by their union with itself.[2]

X. The tenth path is called the Resplendent Intelligence, because it is exalted above every head and has its seat in BINAH : it enlightens the fire of all lights and emanates the power of the principle of forms.[3]

XI. The eleventh path is called the Fiery Intelligence. It is the veil placed before the dispositions and order of the superior and inferior causes. Whosoever possesses this path is in the enjoyment of great dignity ; to possess it is to be face to face with the Cause of Causes.[4]

XII. The twelfth path is called the Intelligence of Light,[5] because it is the image of magnificence. It is said to be the source of vision in those who behold apparitions.

XIII. The thirteenth path is called the Inductive Intelligence of Unity. It is the substance of glory, and it manifests truth to every spirit.[6]

XIV. The fourteenth path is called the Illuminating Intelligence.[7] It is the institutor of arcana, the foundation of holiness.

XV. The fifteenth path is called the Constituting Intelligence, because it constitutes creation in the darkness of the world.[8] According to the philosophers, it is itself that darkness mentioned by Scripture (Job xxxviii. 9), cloud and the envelope thereof.

XVI. The sixteenth path is called the Triumphant and Eternal Intelligence, the delight of glory, the paradise of pleasure prepared for the just.

XVII. The seventeenth path is called the Disposing Intelligence. It disposes the devout to perseverance and thus prepares them to receive the Holy Spirit.[9]

---

[1] Or, " proves and corrects the designing of their representations."—*Ibid.*

[2] Or, " disposes their unity with which they are combined without diminution or division."—*Ibid.*

[3] " Causes a supply of influence to emanate from the Prince of Countenances."—*Ibid.*

[4] Westcott gives an entirely different version : " It is the essence of that curtain which is placed close to the order of the disposition, and this is a special dignity given to it that it may be able to stand before the face of the Cause of Causes."—*Ibid.*

[5] Or of Transparency, in the French version.

[6] " It is the consummation of the truth of individual spiritual things."—Westcott.

[7] Otherwise, Luminous Intelligence.—De Cimara.

[8] " It constitutes the substance of creations in pure darkness."—Westcott, p. 30.

[9] Stenring terms it " the path of Life and Death."

XVIII. The eighteenth path is called the Intelligence or House of Influence,[1] and thence are drawn the arcana and the concealed meanings which repose in the shadow thereof.

XIX. The nineteenth path is called the Intelligence of the Secret or of all spiritual activities. The fullness which it receives derives from the highest benediction and the supreme glory.

XX. The twentieth path is called the Intelligence of Will. It prepares all created beings, each individually, for the demonstration of the existence of the primordial glory.

XXI. The twenty-first path is called the Rewarding Intelligence of those who seek.[2] It receives the divine influence, and it influences by its benediction all existing things.

XXII. The twenty-second path is called the Faithful Intelligence, because spiritual virtues are deposited and augment therein, until they pass to those who dwell under the shadow thereof.[3]

XXIII. The twenty-third path is called the Stable Intelligence. It is the source of consistency in all the numerations.

XXIV. The twenty-fourth path is called the Imaginative Intelligence. It is the ground of similarity in the likeness of beings who are created to its agreement, after its aspects.

XXV. The twenty-fifth path is called the Intelligence of Temptation or Trial, because it is the first temptation by which God tests the devout.

XXVI. The twenty-sixth path is called the Renewing Intelligence, for thereby God—blessed be He!—reneweth all which is capable of renovation in the creation of the world.[4]

XXVII. The twenty-seventh path is called the Natural Intelligence, whereby the nature of everything found in the orb of the sun is completed and perfected.[5]

XXVIII. The twenty-eighth path is called the Active Intelligence, for thence is created the spirit of every creature

---

[1] Westcott adds : " By the greatness of whose abundance the influx of good things upon created beings is increased."—*Ibid.*

[2] Westcott gives " the Conciliating Intelligence," and De Cimara " the Intelligence of Desire."

[3] Westcott's rendering reads : " by it spiritual virtues are increased, and all dwellers on earth are merely under its shadow."—*Ibid.* The version lacks discernment.

[4] " All the changing things which are renewed by the creation of the world."—*Ibid.*, p. 31. But this seems nonsensical.

[5] " The twenty-seventh path is the Exciting Intelligence,' and it is so called because through it is consummated and perfected the nature of every existent being under the orb of the sun, in perfection."—*Ibid.* A redundant rendering.

of the supreme orb, and the activity, that is to say, the motion, to which they are subject.[1]

XXIX. The twenty-ninth path is called the Corporeal Intelligence ; it informs every body which is incorporated under all orbs, and it is the growth thereof.

XXX. The thirtieth path is called the Collective Intelligence, for thence astrologers, by the judgment of the stars and the heavenly signs, derive their speculations and the perfection of their science according to the motions of the stars.

XXXI. The thirty-first path is called the Perpetual Intelligence. Why is it so called ? Because it rules the movement of the sun and the moon according to their constitution and causes each to gravitate in its respective orb.[2]

XXXII. The thirty-second path is called the Assisting Intelligence, because it directs all the operation of the seven planets, with their divisions, and concurs therein.

The comparatively modern accent of this tabulation will occur to the reader, but its quotation was necessary to exhibit the intellectual profit believed to follow from the study of Kabbalism, and still more that it was in the last resource the understanding of man methodised,[3] embracing, as such, the entire circle attributed to human knowledge.[4] After what manner the Paths correspond to their various affirmed offices, how they communicate the powers and graces which abide therein, and for what reason they bear their distinctive titles, must remain open questions. The thesis concerning them constitutes a body of dogma, and is to be taken or left as such. The Paths are those of the Tree and its SEPHIROTH.

---

[1] This path is omitted both in the text of Rittangelius and in Westcott's version.

[2] According to Éliphas Lévi, this verse contains the secret of the Great Work of Alchemy. The reason assigned is that path thirty-one corresponds to the Hebrew letter SHIN (Sh), which represents the magic lamp, or the light between the horns of Baphomet. " It is the Kabbalistic sign of God or the Astral Light, with its two poles and equilibrated centre." The sun mentioned in the paragraph represents gold, the moon silver, and the planets correspond to the other metals.—LA CLEF DES GRAND MYSTÈRES, p. 234. It is needless to say that the SEPHER YETZIRAH and its developments have nothing to do with Alchemy. As regards the Great Work and Lévi's pretended discovery of its secret, see my annotated translation of his TRANSCENDENTAL MAGIC, pp. 345–347.

[3] " Man is the Kabbalistic balance," according to W. B. Greene.—THE BLAZING STAR, p. 51.

[4] However, it fell, as may be expected, into superstitious uses and became a kind of theosophic divination, based on the first chapter of Genesis, wherein the name Elohim is mentioned thirty-two times. The consultation of this chapter was accompanied by prayers extracted from the divine name in question, and, according to Kircher, by suitable ceremonies.

A word must be added concerning a still more arbitrary Kabbalistic classification, entitled the FIFTY GATES OF UNDERSTANDING. It is referable to BINAH, the third SEPHIRA, and is an attempt—as developed—to sketch the outlines of universal science, to embrace, as Éliphas Lévi observes, all possible departments of knowledge and to represent the whole encyclopædia. At the present day such fantastic experiments have something more than a ghostly aspect. There is, however, no intention to methodise human science after the manner of Raymund Lully and his *Ars Magna Sciendi*. I infer also that, in spite of the exalted themes which are included in the scheme, it concerns only intellectual knowledge, acquired by the external way, and thus constitutes a kind of scholastic introduction to the Paths of CHOKMAH or of Wisdom,[1] by which the holy men of God may, as Kircher observes, after long toil, long experience of divine things and long meditation thereon, penetrate to the concealed centres.[2] The principle of the enumeration must be sought in the symbolism of the Hebrew word כל = KOLL, which signifies All, and the consonants of which are equivalent to the number fifty.

The Gates of Understanding, considered as an introduction to the Paths of Wisdom, which diverge, as we have seen, from CHOKMAH, are essential *ex hypothesi* to the higher knowledge approached by these.[3] It would serve no purpose to enumerate them all categorically ; they begin with the first matter, the Hyle or Chaos, proceed through the various elements of ancient science to the theory of composite substances, thence to organic life and the physical, intellectual and psychic nature of man, afterwards to the heaven of the planets, that of the fixed stars and the *primum mobile*, then to the nine orders of the angelic world, and, finally, to the supermundane and archetypal world, that of AIN SOPH, unseen by mortal eye, transcending human intelligence. It is said that Moses did not attain to this, the fiftieth, gate, and some stress seems to be laid on the point, one would think a little superfluously, as it is obvious that what is beyond all finite capacity

---

[1] According to Papus, the thirty-two paths are deductive like the SEPHER YETZIRAH itself, which starts from the notion of God and proceeds thence to natural phenomena, while the fifty gates are established on the inductive principle, ascending from Nature to Deity.—LA KABBALE, p. 132.

[2] Athanasius Kircher : ŒDIPUS ÆGYPTIACUS, Rome, 1623, *Pars Prima*, p. 321.

[3] They are called gates, because no one can attain to the paths unless he enters by these.—*Ibid.*

must have been beyond the law-giver of Israel. We shall meet however with a more particular and indeed curious explanation at a later stage.

The scheme in full of the Gates of Understanding is late in Kabbalism; it is found in the treatise entitled THE GATES OF LIGHT,[1] which is full of references to the mystery of the word כל = KOLL (All). All created things, it explains, have come out of these gates, so that in a sense their knowledge connects with the mystery of universal generation, in reference to which it may be observed that the addition of the feminine letter H = 5 to the word KL = 50 gives KLH = the Bride of MICROPROSOPUS, the Lesser Countenance, whence follows the whole mystery of spiritual generation in man, for KLH = BRIDE, connects with כנסת = KNST = Church, *i.e.*, the Church, ECCLESIA ISRAEL, and brings us back to that place called mystically Zion and Jerusalem, in which the Divine is communicated to man, as seen in an earlier section. It is by living gleams of suggestion after this kind that the dull art of GEMATRIA is lighted up from time to time, or is refreshed and fructified by the waters of Secret Doctrine. We seem to be contemplating from a distance some greater subject than an arid tabulation of sciences, more especially when it lies far apart from any method of attainment; and it happens that we shall come later on to the Gates of Understanding in the light of another Mystery and shall enumerate the intimations of the ZOHAR apart from the formulæ of later Kabbalism.

V.—THE DOCTRINE OF COSMOLOGY

If the Four Worlds of Kabbalism are held in a very true sense to correspond with a path in consciousness by which the mind of the dedicated seeker after Divine things may pass from the " sacred and beautiful Kingdom " of the literal sense or the surface of the Word of God, and through world on world of experience may attain at last that place or state of realisation where all meanings are unified in the light of the Eternal Word, we shall find no difficulty in understanding those who devised this analogy when they go on to tell us not only that *Deus non pars est sed totum*—as Raymund Lully expressed it—but that all whatsoever of the realms in which

---

[1] By R. Joseph Gikatilla ben Abraham.

He is immanent or is held to have revealed Himself are part of that law of election in virtue of which those who are drawn by God are journeying in Him for ever. So is the spiritual history of Israel the sole concern of Scripture, from the moment when Elohim said " Let there be light," that the minds of the chosen might be enlightened. The same motive manifests, as a fact, through all the story of creation, nor was there other reason needed for the Kabbalist to account for God passing from the withdrawn state of AïN-SOPH to the manifestation which begins in KETHER and reaches its limit in MALKUTH.

The thesis of creation is as follows, but I should explain that I am drawing from many quarters of Zoharic texts and simplifying at every point, so that no remediable difficulties may be left in respect of expression. We are not concerned at the moment with the respective share in the work taken by any or all of the three Divine Hypostases. It will be more intelligible at this point to speak of the cosmos in a general sense, as created by the Holy One, which is indeed a recurring affirmation of the ZOHAR. When therefore the Holy One, Who is the Mystery of all mysteries, willed to manifest Himself, He constituted in the first place a point of light, which became the Divine Thought [1]—that is to say, in its application to the purpose then in view. Within this point he designed and engraved all things, but especially that which is termed the Sacred and Mysterious Lamp, being an image representing the Most Holy Mystery. [2] About the nature of this mystery, situated—if one may so speak—at the heart of all the manifested world, we may derive some light of speculation at a later stage. Here indeed is one of those allusions through which a vista opens into the unwritten Secret Doctrine. It follows in the meantime that the universe was created by and from thought. [3] The authority for this revelation is the prophet Elijah, and the development is an excursus on the

---

[1] Z., Pt. I, fol. 2a ; I, 8. See *ib.*, II, 98a ; III, 395, where it is said that the words " Lord my God " (Ps. civ, 1) are the foundation of the mystery concerning the unity and indivisibility of the world at the moment when it was conceived in the Supreme Thought.

[2] We shall see that this is identical with what is called so frequently the Mystery of Faith, and it is to be distinguished therefore from what is called otherwise the Lamp of God, being simply the general notion of merit.—*Ib.*, III, 28b ; V, 80.

[3] It may be noted here—though the statement belongs to another part of the text— that thought and the word by which it is formulated are of the same essence : seen under one aspect, this essence appears as thought and under another as the word,

words : " Behold Who hath created these things." [1]   In the beginning, however, that is to say, in the point of Divine Thought, the creation was only in the subject of the Divine Mind, or—as the text says—it existed, yet existed not.   In other words, it was hidden in the Divine Name, and it would seem to follow that this also was hidden.   The symbolism of the thesis is very curious and deep withal herein.   The Sacred Name of God presupposes those who can pronounce, or at least conceive it. [2]   In this sense the Name exists for man and as antecedent of necessity thereto are the letters which are images of the Word.   Now the world is said to have been created by the help of the Hebrew letters, [3] whence it follows that these were produced in the first place—or rather their archetypes.   They are said to have emanated from one another, [4] presumably on account of the fact that it is possible to reduce them to a few primitive simple forms.   After their emanation, the Sacred Letters, the Great Letters—the letters that are above, of which those on earth are a reflection— remained in concealment for a period which is specified as 2,000 years before the Holy One proceeded further in His work. [5]   When He willed so to do the letters came succes- sively before Him, to shew cause why each one of them should be utilised as an instrument in the task.   This is mere comedy in the literal understanding and is one of the curiosities of literature in its form of expression, as it is all easy to say ; but let us mark what issues therefrom.   The letter BETH was chosen, but not because it is the initial of the word BARA, meaning to create, nor yet because it is that of BERESHITH, or " In the beginning," with which the BOOK OF GENESIS opens, but because it is the initial letter of the word BARACH, which signifies to bless. [6]   It serves therefore to illustrate the ineradicable optimism of Jewish philosophical thought, which maintains that in the root-sense all is " right with the world," because for ever and ever God is " in His heaven."

which may really mean that, for the processes of the human mind, they are inseparable.— Z., Pt. I, fol. 74a ; I, 439.   It is obviously, as we have seen, the transition from conception to expression.

[1] Isaiah xl. 26.
[2] In other words, it is recognised that manifestation can be only to consciousness.
[3] Z., Pt. I, fol. 204a ; II, 411.
[4] *Ib.*, fol. 2a ; I, 9.
[5] *Ib.*, fol. 2b ; I, 12 *et seq.*
[6] See the Talmudic treatise entitled HAGHIGHA, cap. II, which affirms that the world was created by the letter BETH.   But a counter-affirmation on the authority of another rabbi substitutes the letter HE.

It is indeed something more than optimism, which is often a characteristic rather than a ground in reason ; it is something more than instinct ; it is an apprehension in consciousness, the beginning of a work in knowledge. It is so permeating and so paramount that there are moments when the catholic sense of goodness seems to cast down the last barrier, and one or another rabbi thinks in his zeal that even the punishment of the Gentile in the world to come shall be for this or that period or season, but not world without end. It is in virtue of *beneplacitum termino carens* that the letter BETH was used in creation, and I care not by what devious or grotesque path of thought such a truth is reached, so long as it emerges at last on the Pisgah height with such a sun shining in the eyes.

The ZOHAR is like the Hebrew Scriptures, canonical and sub-canonical : it is sealed with sanctity. The writers had passed that sacred initiatory degree in which the soul looks for " good things of the Lord in the land of the living " : [1] they had come to see with their own eyes. Amidst the sorrows and rogations of the Greater Exile, their hearts never faltered nor failed over that faith which opens into sight, or in that hope which begins already to realise itself in participation. The ZOHAR is therefore like Osiris : it is " true of voice," and is inspired on every page, not only with the sense of immortality but with that of a conscious communion subsisting ever and continually between the Holy Assembly that is above and the Assembly which has attained holiness below. There is hence a consolation throughout it which seems—for the most part—to be implied only under veils by the Law and the Prophets.

The Divine intention to make use of the letter BETH, for the reason stated, does not concern further the mind of the ZOHAR,[2] because it has done its work in delineating the motive of the worlds, shewing that the instrument of creation was the power to bless all things. The intention was further to manifest the Divine Name therein as an Indwelling Presence of the universe and as a glory standing above the four quarters thereof. The procedure is symbolised by reciting that the Holy One engraved in the ineffable world those letters which

---

[1] Ps. xxvii. 13.
[2] I ought to say that there is one instance of recurrence to the general notion when the story of the letters and their pleading is mentioned, with variations respecting the letters RESH and TETH ; but they do not now concern us.—Z., Pt. I, fol. 204a ; II, 411.

represent the Mystery of Faith, being YOD, HE, VAU, HE, the synthesis of all worlds above and below.[1]   God represents the central point and the cause of all things, concealed and unknown for ever, being the Supreme Mystery of the Infinite.[2] It is that point of Divine Thought which has been mentioned previously, and from it there issues a slender thread of light which is itself concealed but contains all lights, receiving vibrations from Him Who does not vibrate and reflecting light from Him Who does not diffuse light—that is, the mysterious point, or God centralised in thought on the world about to be produced.   The slender light—*lumen exile*— gives birth to a world of light, which enlightens the other worlds.   It is affirmed that when the central point—the thread of light and the light-world—are united, then is union perfect.   This is the office of the Great Name shadowed forth in part, but the primordial elements which were produced at the beginning of creation were without feature—as it is said that " the earth was without form and void," [3] like " the sign drawn by a pen overcharged with ink," and it was by the grace of the Sacred Name of forty-two letters that the world assumed shape.[4]   All forms emanate from these letters, which—in a manner—are the crown of TETRAGRAMMATON— that is to say, the Sacred Name of four letters already enume- rated.   By their combinations, their superposition, and by the figures thus obtained above and below, the four cardinal points had birth, with all other images.   The letters of the Sacred Name were the moulds of the work of formation, and as such they were arranged in a reverse order to that which obtains here.

Many things, however, were united or drawn together in the mind of the Holy One for the perfect purpose of His providence in respect of all that which was to come into being. He contemplated in His foresight the Mystery of the Law, and because it was impossible for the world to subsist without

---

[1] The Mystery of Faith is once more the hidden doctrine that there is male and female above, as there is male and female below.

[2] Z., Pt. II, fols. 126b, 127a ; IV, 5, 6.

[3] Gen. i. 2.

[4] Z., Pt. I, fols. 30a, 30b ; I, 189.   The name of forty-two letters is an expansion of TETRAGRAMMATON, for if the consonants of that Name are written at length thus— YOD, HE, VAU, HE = ‎ן‎, ‎וו‎, ‎ן‎, ‎ויו‎, their sum in numbers is forty-two.   After what manner the letters themselves are extracted to make up the expanded Name it is scarcely worth while to consider, being not only outside our subject but of no consequence in itself.   I will refer, however, to Athanasius Kircher : ŒDIPUS ÆGYPTIACUS, Tomus III, pp. 261 *et seq.*

it,[1] He created that Law to rule in all things above and below, and to sustain them. But because of the Law, in which the possibility of transgression is implied, He created also repentance [2] as a path of refuge in Himself, of return at need to Him. But the Law is said to be contained in the Sacred Name and to be summarised by the Decalogue, the ten sections of which correspond to ten other Names. These appear to be described alternatively as ten creative words,[3] which are reducible to three, for it is said : " With the Spirit of God, in wisdom and in understanding." [4] The end in view was that God might manifest Himself and be called by His Divine Name.[5]

It is easy to say that all this is arbitrary in the extreme, and certainly many developments, which I forbear to cite, represent the casuistry of words pushed into a region of distraction ; yet one is inclined to think that almost any peg will serve to support a discourse on Divine Things—though some devices are to be preferred before others—and if it be found to serve the purpose it is then a good peg. Whether it so does depends upon the quality of thought which is extracted in such strange manners as these, and of course it has to be realised that the peg is only a pretext—whether Jewish Theosophy understood it as such or not. From the manner in which the Secret Doctrine is externalised in the ZOHAR one cannot help feeling that some of its authors knew this in their day, and in no very different manner from that in which I realise it now. The changes are rung after many manners by the great bells of tradition when they peal out the work of creation. The truth which emerges from the far-spreading tissue of reveries is the operating efficacy of the Divine Will in all the manifest universe, together with that which may be

---

[1] Z., fol. 207a ; II, 429.

[2] *Ib.*, fol. 290a ; II, 670.

[3] *Ib.*, Pt. II, fol. 14b ; III, 66, 67. It is said, however, elsewhere that the words by the help of which the world was made were not established until it pleased God to create man. The intention was that he should be dedicated to the study of the Law, by which the world subsists. In this study man is said to sustain creation.—*Ib.*, Pt. II, fol. 161a, b ; IV, 101. In this manner the ZOHAR seems to stultify itself intentionally, establishing a contradiction in terms, as if to indicate that its concern was not with cosmology *per se* but with a mode of regarding creation imposed on the elect. Alternatively it might be intimating that the mind creates its world.

[4] Exodus xxxi. 3.

[5] Z., Pt. I, fol. 2a ; I, 8. It is to be noted in this connection that this Name was not revealed to the angels, which is one instance only of a recurring pretension that man was in a position of superiority to all other hierarchies of being.—*Ib.*, Pt. III, 78b ; V, 214. See also *ib.*, Pt. I, fol. 25a ; I, 157.

held to be within the measures of the Doctrine of Correspondences, which obtains everywhere in the Secret Doctrine
—whatever the schools thereof—and has been reflected thence
into systems which cannot be included in the same category.
It would seem further to have been discovered at first hand
by a few seers—as, for example, Jacob Böhme [1] and perhaps
Swedenborg. It is the erection of an inevitable anthropomorphism into a philosophical doctrine, though when I say
this I may be sanctifying the seeming limitation. It is at least
true that man is, for all concern of man, the measure of the
whole creation, and if the testimony of creation is true—as
Leibnitz would have held—then that which we discern
intellectually is in the likeness of the truth of things. But
this is the Doctrine of Correspondences.

Nature, according to the ZOHAR, is the garment of God [2];
it is that in which He appears and wherein He is veiled, so
that we can look upon Him and know Him in His vestured
aspect ; but it is not the body of God—which is more properly
Shekinah, at least in one of her aspects—and it is still less God
manifest. It is that which He took upon Himself for the
purpose of appearing. Prior to the period when the Divine
Name was formulated for the ends of creation He was apart
from the kind of definition implied therein and this non-
defined state is termed " Who " by the ZOHAR, as in the
words : " Behold Who hath created," [3] while the product of
creation is called " That " : " Behold Who hath created
That "—or these things. The Hebrew words are respectively
MI and ELAH. The product specified was not, however, for
the ZOHAR, that which we understand by creation but the
Elohim below,[4] who thus came into being when the letters
emanated from each other. The explanation is that by the
pairing of ELAH and MI the Sons of the Doctrine contrived

---

[1] A comparison between Böhme's MYSTERIUM MAGNUM, which is a commentary
on Genesis, and the ZOHAR on the same text would bring out some extraordinary
parallels and would increase the zeal of speculation concerning the glass of vision into
which the German mystic looked. It was assuredly a glass which was common in
several respects to other seers besides himself. His intimations on the first estate of
man, on the making of woman, on Paradise and the Mystery of the Fall offer recurring
analogies with Jewish Theosophy.

[2] Z., Pt. I, fol. 2a ; I, 8.

[3] Isaiah xl. 26.

[4] It is not difficult to follow the reverie, though it seems involved at first sight. In
the transcendence God and Elohim are inseparable, being male and female, and the
first movement towards the production of a manifested universe was to send forth
their living images below. That which was of the nature of God became of the nature
of the Cosmos.

to obtain the word Elohim, and out of this verbal juggle arise the following conclusions : (1) Even as in creation Mɪ, or Who, the Unnamed, remains always attached to ELAH == That, so (2) in God these two descriptions are inseparable, and (3) it is, thanks to this mystery, that the world exists. We have here at the very inception of the ZOHAR that identification of Jehovah and Elohim which we shall find of such capital importance at a later stage of our research. At the moment we have only to observe that what I have called the juggle educes a doctrine of Divine Immanence in the cosmos of manifested things. Apart from this there could be neither the things themselves nor the harmony which produces the music, the accord, the grace, the beauty of creation. It was to make known this doctrine that Elijah once shewed himself to Rabbi Simeon on the sea-shore, after which he took flight, as the text says, and the Master of Kabbalism saw him no more, leastwise at that time.[1]

The passage of Isaiah which I have quoted twice already is affirmed elsewhere to express the whole work of creation. By " Who " above and " That " below has all been made.[2] When we read in yet another place that Scripture was the Architect under God,[3] the reference is also to Elohim, either in the vesture of the Written Law or in that of the Secret Tradition. But I have spoken of the word BERESHITH and how it is rendered sometimes " in Wisdom," which is recognised by the ZOHAR on the authority of the Chaldaic Paraphrase of Onkelos. But Wisdom is regarded more correctly as the analogical interpretation of the Word,[4] and it is added that the world exists owing to the " sublime and impenetrable mystery of CHOKMAH." It follows that creation is a work of wisdom, operating by means of benediction. He Who is ineffable, according to the Secret Doctrine, He Who is mysterious and unknown,[4] delineates Himself in vesture, as a priest assuming pontifical clothing. He unfolds Himself in the Voice of Blessing and passes continually from the unknown into the range of apprehension by means of this Voice, uttering the speech of wisdom.

But God said : " Let there be light," and it is affirmed that

---

[1] Z., Pt. I, fol. 2a ; I, 9.
[2] Ib., fol. 29b, 30a ; I, 186.
[3] Ib., Pt. II, fol. 161a, 161b ; IV, 100, 101.
[4] Ib., Pt. I, fol. 3b ; I, 18.

all celeStial legions and powers emanate therefrom. When
firSt manifeSted, its brilliance filled the world from end to
end ; but when God foresaw the number of the guilty He
concealed and rendered it inaccessible.[1] The sweet smell of
the spikenard in the SONG OF SOLOMON signifies the celeStial
light,[2] while it is said elsewhere that it is designated by the
word goodness.[3] This is an illuStration of the way in which
from many ingenuities of interpretation some appealing
lesson is educed. Again, it does not signify that the methods
are artificial in their nature ; Zoharic Theosophy is in a very
marked and particular sense an illuStration beforehand of
Matthew Arnold's idea that God has put " a heap of letters "
into the hands of man and has bade him make with them
" what word he would." The diStinction between Arnold's
hypothetical case and the one now under notice is that in
place of a painful consciousness on the part of humanity
through the ages that the true Word has never been formed
with the letters, the rabbinical maSters believed that their
sacred ciphers produced true words invariably and could be
used in any manner which would extract a refulgent and
Divine idea. BERESHITH has served on more than a single
occasion in this manner, but its capacities are not exhauSted,
and so also in respect of the firSt created light. If that word
signifies goodness, it means also Perfect Love,[4] the Grand
and Divine Love, that Love of man for God, the correspondence of which is God's Perfect Love for man. This
Love of the Divine in man is not grounded on the self-
queSting hope of personal benefit, but is something conStant
in affliction and in joy, rooted in the perfection of God.
Hereof is the ground of union between the Divine Creator
and the creature divinely fashioned by the hands of Him.[5]
And because of this union the word Light is said also to be
the symbol of Unity.[6] It is in the sense of all these considerations that our world is held truly to form the centre of
that which is celeStial and to be surrounded by doors which
open thereon.[7] Like all the Streets of thought, all paths and

---

[1] Z., Pt. I, fol. 30b ; I, 190, 191.   [3] Ib., fol. 7a ; I, 3b.
[2] Ib., fol. 30a ; I, 188, 189.   [4] Ib., fol. 11b ; I, 66.
[5] The authority is THE SONG OF SOLOMON, i. 2 : " Let him kiss me with the kisses
of his mouth " ; and these words are held to express the perfect and eternal joy which
all worlds shall experience in their union with the Supreme Spirit. The condition of
this union is said to be the prayer of man.—Z., Pt. I, fol. 44b ; I, 262.
[6] Ib., fol. 12b ; I, 70.   [7] Ib., fol. 172a ; II, 275.

vistas of the cosmos, the portals in their tens of thousands
open on God.

I must append hereto the symbolism of a certain myth
which connects with the primæval formulation of the Divine
Name and has its origin in the TALMUD.[1] As developed in
the ZOHAR, it presents another aspect of that point of Divine
Thought about which we heard at the beginning of this
section. It concerns a mysterious stone called SCHETHÍYÂ
which was originally in the Throne of God [2]—that is to say,
it was a precious stone or jewel —and was cast by Him into
the abyss, so to form the basis of the world and give birth
thereto. One might say otherwise that it was like a cubical
stone or altar, for its extremity was concealed in the depth,
while its surface or summit rose above the chaos. It was the
central point in the immensity of the world, the corner-stone,[3]
the tried stone, the sure foundation, but also that stone which
the builders rejected.[4] The last allocation, however, passes
understanding, as by the hypothesis of the legend it was used
in the building from the beginning. Finally—but this is not
less inscrutable—it was that stone which served Jacob as a
pillow and thereafter for an altar.[5] It was the good stone,
the precious stone and the foundation of Zion.[6] The Tables
of the Law were made from it,[7] and it is destined for the
salvation of the world.[8] Jacob called it the House of the
Elohim,[9] meaning that the Hypostasis to which this name is
attributed transfers her residence from the world above to
that which is below.[10] It is like the *lapis exilis* of the German
Graal legend, and of Alchemy according to the Second
Raymund Lully, for it appears to be a slight stone ; it is
supposed to have been carried by Aaron [11] when he entered
the Holy Place, and it was held in the hands of David when
he desired to contemplate close at hand the glory of his Master.[12]

---

[1] See the tracts called YOMA and SANHEDRIN.
[2] Z., Pt. II, fol. 222a, 222b ; IV, 243.
[3] *Ib.*, Pt. I, fol. 231a ; II, 511. See also Job xxxviii. 6.
[4] Ps. cxviii. 22. See also Z., III, 152b ; V, 392.
[5] Z., Pt. I, fol. 72b ; I, 429.
[6] *Ib.*, fol. 231a ; II, 512.
[7] *Ib.*, fol. 231b ; II, 514.
[8] *Ib.*, fol. 231a ; II, 512.
[9] Genesis xxviii. 22.
[10] Z., Pt. I, fol. 231a ; II, 512.
[11] Leviticus xvi. 3. The reference is merely to Aaron's entry, and does not tolerate
the suggestion indicated.
[12] Z., Pt. I, fol. 72a ; I, 427.

In a sense it fell from heaven, like the stone from the crown of Lucifer, and again it was overturned by the iniquity of man, until Jacob restored it to an upright position. Solomon was also one of those who restored it, and thereon he built the Sanctuary [1] We may not know how to harmonise these references which seem to exhaust all that is said of the stone in the Old Testament, but its connection with other ard less fabulous elements belonging to the Zoharic myth of creation resides in the fact that this stone was inscribed with the Divine Name before it was cast into the abyss.[2] For the rest, it seems part of the inherent notion that the world was created for Israel and that the story of its making is a part of the story of election. So is it said in one place that the world did not obtain stability until Israel received the Law on Mount Sinai [3]; that God created the worlds after He had delivered the Law; that He ended his work in the Levitical Law, which is the basis of the world, and is therefore that legendary stone with which we have been dealing, for the Secret Doctrine is a Sabbath; and that Abraham is also the foundation, the one just being on whom it rests, by whom it is made permanent, and who nourishes all creatures.[4] It would be not less idle work to try and harmonise these references than to shew that they are not to be taken blindly. They are things that stand by themselves, unrelated one to another, and they serve their purpose as such, being loose lines of thought turning the student's attention in one direction. If we look in this direction and read with the heart therein, I think that we may come to understand how the mystic stone is the central point of the world and how at this point there is the Holy of Holies.[5]

---

[1] Z., fol. 91b; I, 429.

[2] Ib., Pt. II, fol. 91b; III, 370.

[3] Ib., Pt. I, fol. 89a; I, 511. Within the measures of the romantic hypothesis, it is obvious that the world was created for the elect of Israel, for it is the scene in which their election finds its field of action. The fantasy would obtain more widely in its application to that greater Israel which is the elect of all ages and peoples.

[4] Ib., Pt. II, fol. 86b; I, 498.

[5] Ib., Pt. I, fol. 231a; II, 511.—There is also the stone " cut out without hands " of Dan. ii. 34, and it is said in the ZOHAR to represent Him Who is " the shepherd, the stone of Israel " (Gen. xlix. 24). It is the Community of Israel—that which shall be called the House of God (ib., xxviii. 22). The stone of Jacob is that stone which forms the bond of union between the Divine Essences—blessed on the right, blessed on the left, blessed above and below. According to THE FAITHFUL SHEPHERD, Z., Pt. III, fol. 279b, the stone of Daniel was engraved with the letters of TETRAGRAMMATON, and it is not to be identified with the stone of Moses, being that rock which he smote twice.—Num. xx, 8–11.

I have spoken of the Word in its relation to the Divine Transcendence. It is said that the six days were created thereby, being lights emanating from the Word and illuminating the world. It is also the Divine Seed from which manifest things came forth. The specific affirmation is, however, that the world was created by the Word united to the Spirit,[1] that which operated being the sound of the Word as a voice which spoke and it was done. For the dispensation of the light this Word was joined with the Father, the light itself proceeding from the Father and being as such incompatible with matter.[2] In the union of the Father and the Word it became accessible thereto, seeing that henceforward it proceeded from both. Before the manifestation of the Word the light proceeding from the Father formed seven letters, which—in some inscrutable sense—were without body and for this reason were inaccessible to matter. When the sacred, nebulous, clouded fire which is called " darkness upon the face of the deep "[3] appeared for the transmutation of matter, seven other letters were formed, also from pure light and hence inaccessible to matter, like the first seven. When the Word manifested, the remaining eight letters were formed, and then the whole alphabet was rendered accessible by the casting down of that barrier which separated matter from the celestial rays. It is for this reason that, according to Scripture, Elohim said : " Let there be light."[4] The firmament was made likewise and the waters were separated from the waters, or the light above from the light below.[5] It was subject to this separation that matter became susceptible of light, and I infer that a spiritual mystery is here indicated which might be comparable to the distinction between material light of reason and that of the higher mind. Now, the Word is said to be designated by the name Elohim.[6]

---

[1] It is taught that the one is not without the other, and the authority is Ps. xxxiii, 6 : " By the word of the Lord were the heavens made and all the hosts of them by the breath of his mouth."—Z., Pt. I, fol. 156a ; II, 213, 214.

[2] Z., Pt. I, fol. 16b ; I, 98 *et seq.*

[3] Gen. i. 2.

[4] *Ib.*, v. 3.

[5] Z., Pt. I, 16b ; I, 100.

[6] The greater light which God made to rule the day is a symbol of Jehovah, while the lesser which rules the night is the Word, regarded as the end of thought.—*Ib.*, fol. 20a ; I, 123. It is said elsewhere that if the world had been the work of the Divine Essence called Jehovah, everything would have been everlasting therein, but being the work of the Divine Essence called Elohim, it is all subject to destruction. This curious statement arises from Ps. xlvi. 9, but it has been pointed out that in this Psalm the

The firmament constituted the line of division : thereunto matter could ascend and thereunto could the light come down ; but while it is thus a limit in both directions, the firmament is also a bond of union between the one and the other, so that both are united thereby in Elohim.   It is said also that the Word assumed the form of the alphabetical signs, presumably because it is in this form that thought passes into written expression.[1]   The six days of creation are lights emanating from the Word for the illumination of the world.[2]   It is thanks, in fine, to the Word that the waters of the celestial river flow for ever to irrigate the worlds that are below.[3]

So far therefore concerning the work of God in creation and the instruments appertaining thereto.   But there are certain final intimations which belong more especially to our subject and lead therein.   When the Holy One created the world He engraved the Mystery of Faith in letters of sparkling light ; He engraved it above and below, because it is the same Mystery and because the world below is the mirror of that which is above.   By means of the Mystery of Faith He created the worlds.   Now, in another place it is asked : What worlds ?   The answer is matrimonial unions.[4]   These are the worlds which God does not cease from creating.   It follows that creation, as the story is told, is a veil of the sex mystery ; it follows also that something is understood of which physical union is the shadow as this is known here : the intimations concern union as the result of a law, which law is literal on the plane of expression and mystical on a higher plane.   Another Key is given in these words : The union of the male and female principle engendered the world [5]—as indeed it was impossible that it should do otherwise within the measures of Zoharic symbolism.   So also in the emanation of the letters, ALEPH and BETH are postulated, from which two come forth the rest of the alphabet, and hence

---

Divine Name used is not Elohim but Jehovah.   In the text itself a debate follows and there is a divided view.—*Ib.*, fol. 59b ; I, 337.

[1] Z., Pt. I, fol. 21a ; I, 129.

[2] *Ib.*, fol. 31b ; I, 196.   The ZOHAR is sometimes like scholastic philosophy in its lighter moments, and seeing that the six days of creation are mentioned by Genesis but not the six nights which are implied therein, it inquires what has become of the latter and concludes that God holds them in concealment for some good purpose of His own.

[3] *Ib.*, fol. 33b ; I, 208.

[4] *Ib.*, fol. 89a ; I, 511.

[5] *Ib.*, Pt. II, fol. 228a ; IV, 250.

it is said that these two are male and female.[1]   Here is a
further reason why BETH was the instrument of creation, as
already explained.   Another story intimates that God took
the "heap of letters" in His hands and began to make
worlds therewith over and over, but they had no consistence,
the reason being that the Covenant had not yet been made.[2]
The world under the law of circumcision must be understood
as a specific dispensation within the manifest order, and the
destroyed worlds are previous dispensations which arose and
decayed unceasingly.   This is illustrated when it is said that
their destruction was because those who dwelt therein did not
accept the commandments of the Doctrine.   It is not that
God undoes His works, but the works undo themselves by
refusing salvation.   Why, it is asked, should God put an end
to those children whom, according to tradition, He created
by the Second Hypostasis, called HE ?[3]

   It is only under the Law and the Doctrine, or in virtue of
that Inward Covenant of which circumcision was once the
shadow, that man is hereby made male and female by the
Elohim, which is another manner of saying that the cosmic
harmony is established in him.   We shall see in a later
division that he was created prototypically in the likeness of
the world below and in that of the world above.   He was
also so made that he represents the Celestial Lover and
Beloved, Who are symbolised by the letters YOD and HE,
and are united by VAU.[4]   In another form of symbolism he
was designed to be the Spouse or Beloved of God who was
never to be separated from the Lover.   So proceeds the
mystery with which we are concerned from stage to stage of
unfoldment ; but we are at present concerned only in seeing
how it belongs to all.

---

[1] Z., Pt. I, fol. 30a ; I, 187.   It is said elsewhere that the letters expressing the male
principle are not susceptible of transformation, while those expressing the female
principle can be counterchanged by means of certain combinations.—Ib., Pt. II,
fol. 134a ; IV, 29.   Which letters are male and which are female, we are not told.   A
note to the French version suggests that the uneven are masculine and the even feminine,
which is theoretically plausible but is not borne out in fact because it is certain that
HE, the fifth letter, is female in the ZOHAR, while the sixth or VAU is masculine.

[2] Ib., fol. 25a ; I, 154.

[3] Ib.

[4] Z., Pt. I, fol. 26a ; I, 161, 162.

BOOK VI

HIERARCHIES OF SPIRITUAL BEING

BOOK VI

HIERARCHIES OF SPIRITUAL BEING

I.—THE SOUL IN KABBALISM

WE have ascertained the heads of Kabbalistic instruction as to the essential nature of God, the transition from the Divine Unmanifest into the manifestation of Divinity, the extension of the powers and attributes thus developed through the archetypal, creative, formative and material worlds, the Kabbalistic hypothesis of creation and the doctrine of transcendental and natural science. It remains for us to present in brief outline the doctrine of spiritual essences according to Jewish Theosophy. This is one of the favoured and certainly most recurring subjects found in the ZOHAR, as it is that also which was destined to receive fuller development than any other in the later literature of Kabbalism. The history of its growth is also worth noting. Pre-existence and the subdivision of the spiritual nature in man are found in the TALMUD, but the SEPHER YETZIRAH has nothing to tell us on the subject, and there is very little in the first commentators on that treatise. It may be said, with considerable truth, that the book and its connections were concerned rather with the physical forces which produced the universe ; but the commentaries at least are sufficiently discursive to have included it in their scheme if they had anything to say upon the subject. It remains therefore that the curious and involved speculations with which we are dealing here are in the main a later growth. The distinction between a holy intelligence and an animal soul in man is found in the BOOK OF CONCEALMENT,[1] which, so far

---

[1] " When the inferior man descends (namely, into this world) there are found (in him) two spirits, according to the supernal form. Man (therefore) is constituted from the two sides, the right and the left. As from the right side he has a holy mind, as from the left an animal soul." The extension of the left side was the consequence of the Fall.—BOOK OF CONCEALMENT, c. iv. par. 7–9. This is according to the Latin version of Rosenroth, his expansions in brackets included. Compare, however, De Pauly's translation, Vol. IV, p. 143, as follows : " When ' Adam ' came here below the

as can be judged from its form, is among the most ancient portions of the ZOHAR. The latter cycle may be regarded, broadly speaking, as the chief source of metapsychical hypotheses in Kabbalism proper. The indications contained therein became a vast and ponderous system in the schools of Isaac de Loria and Moses of Cordova. This system has exercised at all times a particular influence on writers who have approached Kabbalism from an occult standpoint, and—chiefly, perhaps, because it has been made available in Latin by Rosenroth—has superseded that of the ZOHAR itself. Franck states that it is not Kabbalism proper, and affirms very truly that it is full of distorted rabbinical reveries, but it cannot be denied that the roots are in older texts. The later speculations are in other words developed from the ZOHAR, and the following slight sketch contains the general elements of the subject.

Belief in the soul's immortality, which is not found in the Pentateuch or the prophets, was held by the Israel of later times in connection with that of the resurrection of the body, and appears freely in the TALMUDS.[1] Makers of occult speculations, who remember that Moses was learned in all the wisdom of the Egyptians, conceive it to be impossible that he should have known nothing of doctrines which were known to all Egypt, and they hold accordingly that he communicated them secretly to a circle of initiation, by which they were perpetuated in the oral way. Others incline to the notion that they were acquired by the Jews in Babylon. In the Græco-Egyptian period it was, of course, impossible that the learned rabbins of Alexandria should not have been acquainted with the great speculation of a future life. In one way or another it was inevitable that the Jews should have acquired it, which they did accordingly, and the particular date or circumstances are a minor question, about which there can be no certainty. The doctrine, as taught by the TALMUD,

---

Celestial Figure had two spirits, one on the right destined to man and the other on the left destined to animals. But after the sin of Adam the left side was so extended that it penetrated even to man."

[1] " The immortality of the soul and the resurrection of the body figure in the TALMUD as tenets of the Synagogue. They form the thirteenth and last article in the profession of faith of Maimonides."—Leroy-Beaulieu, ISRAEL AMONG THE NATIONS, p. 17. This is not quite accurate, as that article concerns the resurrection only. " I firmly believe that there will be a resurrection of the dead, at the time when it shall please the Creator, blessed be His name ! "—M. Freidlander, TEXT BOOK OF THE JEWISH RELIGION. 4th ed. London. 1896.

though recognising five divisions of the soul having names
familiar to Kabbalism, is comparatively of a simple kind : it
does not possess, for example, that philosophical aspect which
we find in Philo, and even those who dwell upon Greek
influence in early Kabbalism must admit that its pneumatology,
after allowing for pre-existence, shews very little trace of
Platonism.[1]

It should be understood that the story of the soul in Kabbalism is part of that central doctrine which the ZOHAR calls
the Mystery of Faith, or at least the one is in close connection
with the other and they arise together.[2]   I shall proceed at
once to my subject and consider it under four heads, being
(1) Pre-existence, (2) The parts of the soul, (3) The soul in the
world to come, but here only in respect of the blessed state,
and (4) Reincarnation.   The doctrine concerning Sheol will
call for separate treatment.

As regards pre-existence, I will establish first what may be
termed the general thesis, with that which belongs thereto,
and will then illustrate it by such distinctions and variations
as may seem to deserve mention.   When the Holy One willed
to create the universe, He formed [3]—and apparently in the
first instance—those souls which were intended subsequently
to dwell in human bodies.[4]   The place of their tarrying is said
in more than one place to be the Paradise below, which is the
Earthly Paradise or the Lower Eden.[5]   This is also an abode
of disincarnate souls who have entered that path which leads
to the blessed life ; but it is not their final home.[6]   Like the
Christ of Nazareth, the ZOHAR seems to know that there are

---

[1] For a good summary of Kabbalistic pneumatology the German student may consult,
inter alia, Leiningen's LEELENLEHRE DER QABALAH.   Leipsic.   1887.

[2] It speaks at once for the genesis and term of the mystery : there is that which must
be done in heaven, brought down amongst the similitudes of earthly things and finally
restored to heaven.

[3] This is the method of expression in the place from which I derive, but the idea,
in its more adequate Zoharic expression, is not one of formation ; it is rather of begetting.   The point is that souls are affirmed to have a father and mother, and they are
produced in virtue of the union between male and female.   The basis of the idea is
Gen. i. 24 : " Let the earth bring forth the living creature," this " creature " being
held to mean the soul of the first celestial man.—Z., Pt. II, fol. 12a ; III, 53.   The
fundamental point to be noticed is that the ZOHAR teaches the pre-existence, as it does
also the foreknowledge of the soul.

[4] *Ib.*, fol. 96b ; III, 387.   " Each has its form like that of the body which it is
destined to animate."

[5] Z., Pt. II, fol. 11a ; III, 48.   It is also said poetically that souls are formed in
Paradise of the four winds which breathe therein, but the reference is really to that
psychic vesture which gives form to the soul.—*Ib.*, fol. 13b ; III, 59, 60.

[6] Z., Pt. II, fol. 11a ; III, 48.

many mansions in the House of the Father. Before they left the presence of the Maker, all souls—meaning those destined to incarnate under the obedience and election of Israel—were conjured to keep the precepts of the Law.[1] While they await incarnation in Paradise they are clothed with bodies and have countenances like those which they are destined to possess hereafter, but these vestures are of course of a psychic or spiritual kind.[2] When the time arrives for embodiment each soul in its turn is called before the Holy One and is told which physical envelope to inhabit.[3] Paradise is a place of blessing, and it may be that " from the gold bar " thereof it has leaned out and seen no reason to descend of its own accord, or to quit present happiness, as it is said, " for bondage and temptation." It is assured, however, that from the day of its creation it had no other mission than to come into this world.[4] It submits therefore and is stripped of the paradisaical body, that it may be clothed with veils of earth. It takes the road of earth sorrowing [5] and proceeds into the exile of human life.

Souls descend in a pre-established order of succession, though there are certain exceptions.[6] As in all the great events of human life and the universe the precedence must be taken by Palestine, it is held that descent to earth reaches its term therein, and this invariably, after which the souls are thence

---

[1] Z., Pt. I, fol. 223d ; II, 520. See also Pt. III, fol. 13a ; V, 38, and Pt. II, fol. 161b ; IV, 101, where the soul is pledged to the study of the Law and the attainment of the Mystery of Faith.

[2] *Ib.*, Pt. II, fol. 150a ; IV, 70. There is no real joy for the soul, save in the body of Paradise ; in that of earth it is shut out from communication with the Supreme Mysteries. See also *Ib.*, Pt. I, fol. 90b, 91a ; II, 515, 516.

[3] *Ib.*, Pt. II, fol. 96b ; II, 388.

[4] *Ib.* Seeing that the Earthly Paradise is the house of pre-existing souls and the place to which they return after death, it might seem that the Fall which took place therein was in the prototypical humanity, or ADAM PROTOPLASTES of later Kabbalism, in whom all souls fell, as Recanati maintained. He speculated also that they are detached from the parent body in succession for incarnation on earth. This is not Zoharic symbolism but individual reverie. There is a sense in which the man of the Eden myth was ADAM PROTOPLASTES, as the first of human beings, but the prototypical ADAM PROTOPLASTES is the Divine Son, conceived in DAATH and so extended through the Lower SEPHIROTH that He stands on MALKUTH.

[5] It is even declared that all which is learned by man as a consequence of his habitation here below was known previously by him in the world above, but this is apparently the case—more especially or only—with those who love the truth and are righteous in earthly life. My authority is the COMMENTARY ON LEVITICUS, and it puts an end to the question of freewill by adding that those who are wicked below have been already set aside by God, their incarnation being delayed through frequent enforced visits to the abyss. So also those who are headstrong here were headstrong prior to their incarnation.—Z., Pt. III, fol. 61b ; V, 169. This was said in the presence of Rabbi Simeon and was suffered to pass unchallenged.

[6] *Ib.*, Pt. II, fol. 101a ; III, 407.

distributed to the whole world.¹ What is much more important is that all souls awaiting incarnation are arranged in pairs ; the one which is destined to animate a male is by the side of one who is to animate a female, so that those who are united below have been united previously above,² because, according to Scripture, there is nothing new under the sun. They descend also together, but they pass into the charge of an angel who presides over the pregnancy of women and they are then separated.³ Sometimes the male soul animates a man first, sometimes the reverse.⁴ When the time of marriage comes, the Holy One unites them as before and proclaims their union. After the espousals, and apparently when intercourse has taken place, they become—mystically speaking—one body and one soul. If, this, however, is the law, we shall see later on that it is illustrated chiefly by exceptions.⁵ At the moment I will mention only a variant of the last notion, which says that, prior to their descent on earth, all souls form an unity, and are part of the same mystery ; separation into male and female takes place by reason of incarnation, but they are again made one in marriage.⁶ This recalls the Adamic legend and would seem its application to the history of individuals above and below.

I have now given the general thesis, supplemented by counter-theses, but it should be realised that it is drawn from several places. Among questions which must be left open when the text is collated at large there is that which locates the soul prior to incarnation in the Paradise below, as I have said. Other accounts substitute the superior Eden,⁷ and

---

¹ Z., Pt. I, fol. 205b ; II, 424. The exceptions correspond to the ideas of those who are born out of due time. It is said that male souls come from the Tree of Wisdom and female souls from an Inferior Tree, but it is a sporadic suggestion which is at issue with recurring notions.—Ib., Pt. II, fol. 101a ; III, 408. It is explained in another place that just souls attached to the Sacred King by true love are longer than others in coming to this earth.—Ib., Pt. III, fol. 68a, b ; V, 186.

² This is the blessed union.—Ib., fol. 91b ; I, 520. But it is to be understood almost unquestionably that the allusion, here and elsewhere, is always to the souls of Israel.

³ Ib.

⁴ It is not said that a mistake ever occurs, though this is recognised by one form of occultism and is held to account for certain sex-aberrations. I have not found any Kabbalistic warrant for the opinion. See Éliphas Lévi, in my translation of his TRANSCENDENTAL MAGIC, Its Doctrine and Ritual, 1923, pp. 109, 110.

⁵ As the Zoharic considerations on the subject of sister-souls who have been, so to speak, mismarried bear ample witness.

⁶ Z., Pt. III, fol. 43b ; V, 121. See also ib., Pt. I, fol. 85b ; I, 493, 494, where it is stated that whether or not a man shall meet in this life with the soul predestined to himself in union, even from the beginning, depends on his own desert.

⁷ Ib., Pt. III, fol. 43a ; V, 120. Here it is said that when the soul is in the act of

according to one of these the descent for a period into the Earthly Garden takes place just prior to incarnation. The time is thirty days.[1] One of the alternatives has no explicit concern with either Paradise but affirms that from an epoch which preceded the creation of the world all souls have been in the presence of the Holy One and there remain till they are called to go down on earth.[2] According to tradition all emanate from the same region and during their sojourn in heaven they share in the government of things above and below.[3] There are also certain souls which are kept in the hiddenness and are guarded in a particular manner. When these enter into earthly bodies they have power to reascend into heaven without dying.[4] Of such were Enoch and Elias. Speaking for the majority of cases, there is some trouble in effecting a harmonious junction between the soul and its earthly envelope[5]; it is not definitely established therein until after thirty-three days, and for the first seven it goes in and out continuously. One reason seems to be that circumcision does not take place till the thirtieth day and that for three days thereafter the body is in a state of suffering.[6] These reveries are drawn out of two texts : " She shall then continue in the blood of her purifying three and thirty days," [7] which is of course a reference to the purification of women after childbirth ; and : " It shall be seven days under the dam," [8] which is a reference to the birth of animals—bullocks, sheep, or goats. The " blood of her purification " is in some obscure way the blood of circumcision.[9]

---

descending towards this world it visits the Earthly Paradise, where it sees the souls of the just who have left this life. It goes also to SHEOL and sees the souls of the wicked. These are object-lessons, and the inference is that they may act as a guide in life. It is said in another place that the Soul is from the Sanctuary on high.—*Ib.*, Pt. I, fol. 205b ; II, 424. It is that Temple which is mentioned in Ex. xv. 17, as " the Sanctuary, O Lord, which Thy hands have established."—Z., Pt. I, fol. 7 ; I, 38.

[1] According to another account, they pay only a flying visit—also for purposes of inspection.—*Ib.*, Pt. III, fol. 13a, b ; V, 39.

[2] *Ib.*, Pt. II, fol. 282a ; IV, 310. It was especially the union of male and female souls which existed before creation. The time of intercourse corresponds to midnight on earth. It is an union in the contemplation of God and the joy thereof brings forth other souls, which are those of Gentiles who become converts to Jewry.

[3] *Ib.*, Pt. III, fol. 68a ; V, 186.

[4] *Ib.*, fol. 68b ; V, 186, 187. See also *ib.*, fol. 182b, 183a ; V, 475, 476.

[5] It is said to be attached to the body by one end only. The soul and its envelope develop simultaneously, meaning that their union becomes more perfect, but care of the soul is needed for this purpose, just as the body needs care. The soul, however, is in the care of heaven.—*Ib.*, Pt. I, fol. 197a ; II, 381.

[6] Z., Pt. III, fol. 43b ; V, 121, 122.

[7] Leviticus xii. 4.

[8] Ex. xxii. 30.

[9] Z., Pt. III, fol. 43b, 44a ; V, 122.

Hereof is the ZOHAR in one of its exceptional moods ; but these things are weariness, and I will conclude therefore on pre-existence with one further reference. It is said that the souls of the patriarchs pre-existed in the thought of God before the creation and were connected in the other world, whence they came forth in their due day.[1] The text apposite hereto is : " The flowers appear on the earth," [2] meaning that the souls of the patriarchs appear in this world. One would say that these souls were the thoughts of God dwelling in divine men, but if we debated the subject, we should see, I think, that the ZOHARIC hypothesis really comes to this ; that the soul-world is a world of thought in God ; that the thought precedes the Word, as it is shewn to have done in respect of creation generally ; and that souls are uttered forth continually, passing ultimately into expression in flesh.

Though it is closely connected with pre-existence, the mode followed in the generation or creation of souls is hypothetically at least independent and there are important reasons why it should be postponed for consideration till I treat of the mystery of sex in Zoharic Theology. I proceed therefore to the parts or divisions of the soul. It is taught in a summary way that man is composed of three things [3] : Life, or NEPHESH ; Spirit, which is RUAH or HAÏÂ ; and Soul, that is, NESHAMAH. By these he becomes " a living spirit "— a term, however, which is applied more especially to NESHA-MAH. They are called also three degrees, or vital spirit, intellectual spirit and soul proper.[4] NEPHESH is the fallible part, for sin is suggested neither by RUAH nor NESHAMAH.[5] It is said elsewhere and more plainly that the vital spirit sins, but not the soul. The three degrees are superposed one upon another in the order already given, [6] and NESHAMAH is attached

---

[1] Z., Pt. I, fol. 1a ; I, 5.

[2] Song of Solomon ii. 12.

[3] Z., Pt. I, fol. 27a ; I, 169. The " living spirit " is said to proceed from the mouth of Shekinah, who is called " living soul." Here is another aspect of souls being uttered forth by the Divine, and seeing that this is the Shekinah in transcendence, who is (a) the Third Hypostasis and (b) the Mother = AIMA, in the Supernal SEPHIRA BINAH, we shall understand the kind of union which subsists between her and the Father, who is ABBA in CHOKMAH. There is the Divine Thought in KETHER : it is formulated as if mentally in CHOKMAH : and it is uttered in BINAH, producing the living intelligences, who are therefore begotten into the higher Paradise.

[4] Ib., Pt. I, fol. 205b, 206a ; II, 424.

[5] Ib., Pt. III, fol. 16a ; V, 46. It is said, however, elsewhere that the defilement of Nephesh defiles Ruah and Neshamah.—Ib., Pt. II, fol. 182a ; IV, 155.

[6] Ib., Pt. II, fol. 206a ; II, 425.

to God [1] ; but all these are not the imprescriptible possession of every person in life : the higher parts are earned by serving the Master. [2]

Unfortunately, this thesis—which may seem intelligible enough in itself—leads to very grave complications in respect of that which pre-existed and that which constitutes man a living being in manifestation. It is said that some persons are judged worthy to possess a NESHAMAH, others a RUAH only, while yet others have a NEPHESH and nothing more. [3] These last, by reason of their deficiency, are attached to the impure spirit. [4] The NEPHESH alone is imprescriptible, or necessary to the man's existence. [5] If he comports himself worthily with this gift another spirit is poured into him, which is like a crown of NEPHESH, and this is RUAH. The man is then illuminated by light from a superior region and is in a position to discern the laws of the Secret King. If he still continues worthy he receives the crown of RUAH, the name of which is NESHAMAH ; but it is called also Soul of God. Now, it seems obvious that it is this only of which pre-existence, paradisaical life and the Divine Vision can be predicated, and the point is therefore that—contrary to the very clear doctrine concerning the descent of souls—NESHAMAH does not come down and incarnate at birth in any human being. [6] It seems in this case to be mere fantasy with which we have been dealing previously.

There is, however, an attempt elsewhere to harmonise these disparities, for it is said that when the soul, meaning NESHAMAH, leaves the celestial region and comes down

---

[1] Z., Pt. III, fol. 25a ; V, 64.

[2] Ib., Pt. I, fol. 206a ; II, 424.

[3] Ib., fol. 25a ; V, 65.

[4] We have to check this by other statements as follows : (a) Man is endowed with a NEPHESH in the first place and it is given him as a preparation for leading a holy life.—Ib., Pt. I, fol. 206a ; I, 424. (b) The three degrees constitute one soul and are attached one to another.—Ib., Pt. III, fol. 70b ; V, 191. But in further contra-distinction hereto, another ruling suggests that the possession of NEPHESH and RUAH leaves man useless for the purposes of Shekinah in captivity and of Moses who abides with her.—Ib., Pt. I, fol. 28a ; I, 175, 176. But the reason seems to be that they are unskilled in the Secret Doctrine.

[5] Z., Pt. III, fol. 70b ; V, 191, 192.

[6] Alternatively, the successive addition of higher parts of the soul must be understood as gifts of grace, and there is authority for this view in the text, though I do not propose to consider it, as the multiplication of aspects beyond what is actually needed must tend only to the reader's confusion. I have registered the fact for the use of those who would carry their research further. When it is said elsewhere that NESHAMAH cannot sin, the reference—from such point of view—is to a state of attained sanctity in which lapse is—by this statement—impossible, meaning unlikely. It has become not less difficult to sin than before it was to abstain from sin.

towards earth it is joined to the intellectual spirit ; afterwards both are joined to the spirit of light—that is, NEPHESH.[1] The spirit of light and the intellectual spirit dwell together and depend one upon the other ; but the soul is independent of both. Another thesis is that when man proposes to live in purity, heaven comes to his aid, granting him the holy soul, by which he is purified and sanctified ; but if he be unworthy and will not live in purity, he is animated only by NEPHESH and RUAH. It is obvious that this fails to concur with the earlier statement, which represents RUAH as a gift to be earned ; but we can read between the lines of contradiction and conclude that the real intention is to represent the permanent part of man as descending and overshading the personality, when this is born into the world ; it draws nearer with his growth and improvement ; and it may be, so to speak, incorporated with him, or it may not. Understood thus, the speculation will stand at its value : it is a primitive crudity of materialism, but the ZOHAR sometimes exceeds such notions and ascends into a clearer region.

Before giving two or three casual examples, I will cite another classification because of the extraordinary consequences which follow.[2] NEPHESH is the soul which forms the body and presides over the propagation of beings ; RUAH is the soul which causes NEPHESH to act and determines its kind of action[3] ; NESHAMAH is the supreme force issuing from the Tree of Life.[4] These three degrees separate after death, each returning to the place from which it was brought. NEPHESH is presumably of the earth earthy, for it is said to remain in the tomb[5]—but any statement seems to serve which is made on the spur of the moment ; RUAH passes to

---

[1] Z., Pt. I, fol. 62a ; I, 365. According to Adolphe Franck, NEPHESH throughout the Old Testament signifies the body of man, so long as it is alive.—LA KABBALE, p. 61. It is identified with the PSYCHE by ADUMBRATIO KABBALÆ CHRISTIANÆ, which is one of the rare supplements to Rosenroth's KABBALA DENUDATA. It is here regarded as the vitality inherent in the natural and instrumental body, and it is vegetative and sensitive in its nature. There seems to be no Zoharic authority for the other definitions.

[2] Z., Pt. I, fol. 287b, Appendix II, containing TOSSEFTA or ADDITIONS : I, 664.

[3] Late Kabbalism sometimes termed RUAH the Spirit, meaning the human soul itself. It was held to extend through the body, to be rational and self-subsisting, but its mode of comprehension was by intermediaries and not direct. It was also the seat of good and evil, and hence of the moral attributes.

[4] NESHAMAH is understanding in late Kabbalism, the individual intellect communicated by the Catholic and Divine Intellect.

[5] Z., Pt. I, fol. 287b ; I, 664, 665. This statement is subject to considerable modification in other places.

the Earthly Paradise, where the High Priest Michael offers it as a holocaust to the Holy One and it remains in the joy of Paradise[1] ; NESHAMAH ascends on high.[2] What purpose has been attained by its experience below does not appear in the text : it cannot sin, and it is not in search of merit. There is no need to add that—here again—this version of the tripartite personality, postulating independent survival in three separate directions—for NEPHESH is alive in the tomb— cannot be reconciled with the alternatives that have gone before. I conclude that the Secret Doctrine in Israel was unsettled on the subject of the soul and its divisions, that there is no guide for the perplexed therein, and that we shall come in the end to recognise only one truly and pregnant Secret Doctrine in Jewry, which is the secret concerning sex.

Among several intimations which are better than formal attempts to classify there is one which says that man acquires the soul of soul by fear of the Lord and by wisdom. He acquires the soul by penitence. Abraham represents the soul of soul ; Sarah is the soul ; Isaac is the intellectual spirit ; and Rebecca is the vital spirit.[3] Another speculation desig- nates NEPHESH as the soul in a state of sleep, and this definition seems excellent. RUAH is the soul in a waking state, by which I understand the earlier stages of becoming alive to things above. It is said that these two do not differ in essence. Above them is NESHAMAH, which is the soul proper.[4] These grades of the spirit of man are the image of the Mystery of Wisdom, and to fathom them is to discover that Wisdom. When NESHAMAH is pre-eminent in man he is called holy.

The parts of the spiritual personality are by no means exhausted in any triadic enumeration,[5] for ascent in the

---

[1] This also is qualified ; it remains in the Paradise for a period and then returns whence it came, because the spirit—*i.e.*, RUAH—goes back to God Who gave it.
[2] It returns to the Tree of Life, because it came therefrom.
[3] Z., Pt. I, fol. 264a ; II, 622.
[4] *Ib.*, fol. 83a, b ; I, 480, 481.
[5] A more simple extension than here follows is given in Pt. II, fol. 158b ; IV, 95, where it is said that the soul has five names, being NEPHESH, RUAH, NESHAMAH, HAÏA and YEHIDAH. This is an extract from THE FAITHFUL SHEPHERD. But—as we have seen—HAÏA is sometimes a synonym for RUAH. Isaac Myer gives the following definition : " YE'HU-DAH, the only one, is the *personality* of man ; HAÏA is the life in man ; NESHAMAH the soul or intellect ; RUAH the spirit ; NEPHESH the animal soul or vital *dynamics*, the *anima*.—PHILOSOPHY OF IBN GEBIROL, p. 397. Such a classification makes for confusion only as the distinctions do not correspond to separable aspects of human nature. Late Kabbalism said that YEHIDAH is individuality—the unity or correspondence by which man becomes like unto his First Cause. HAÏA is a condition of unity between the particular and catholic intellect, the union apparently

grades of sanctity can provide additionally to these and in succession : (1) a soul from the world of emanation on the side of the Daughter of the King [1] ; (2) a soul from the world of emanation on the side of the Son of the King [2] ; (3) a soul from the side of the Father and the Mother [3] ; and (4) a soul which reflects the four letters of the Sacred Name Jehovah.[4] This is one specimen extension, but there are others, some of which I will omit and some are transferred to their proper place elsewhere. I may add here, however, that there is a casual supplementary soul [5] added to the Students of the Doctrine on the Sabbath Day, after which it returns whence it came. It appears to be a sacred soul issuing from the Tree of Life, and it is adapted to the works of the recipient. An alternative account attaches it to all good Israelites who fulfil the Law, whether they are students of the Doctrine in the deeper mystical sense or not.

The state of the soul in the world to come is described in several ways, as we should expect assuredly ; but those which concern the blessed life of the departed can be harmonised, or at least there is nothing of essential discrepancy. When the good soul is preparing to leave this world, and while it is suspended from the body only at the larynx, it beholds three angels, to whom the dying man confesses his sins.[6] These spirits engarner the souls of the just and they accompany the glorious Shekinah, for no man leaves this world without seeing the Shekinah at the last moment of life.[7] The soul prostrates itself before her and praises God.[8] It seems then to enter a cavern wherein is a door leading to the Earthly Paradise[9] ; there it encounters Adam, the patriarchs and all the just, who rejoice with her and she is admitted within the Garden. Either then or previously, she has been furnished

---

of our life with that life which is Divine. Franck says that it is the vital spirit, that its seat is in the heart, and that it is distinct from the principle of animal life.—LA KABBALE, p. 235.

[1] Z., Pt. II, fol. 94b ; III, 379.

[2] Ib., the authority being : " Ye are the children of the Lord your God."— Deut. xiv. 1.

[3] Z., fol. 94b ; III, 379, 380. The versicle appertaining hereto is " breathed into his nostrils the breath of life ; and man became a living soul."—Gen. ii. 7.

[4] A man in possession of this soul is the image of the Heavenly Master. Of him it is said : " And have dominion over the fish of the sea."—Gen. i. 28.

[5] See Z., Pt. II, fol. 88b ; III, 361—among many other places.

[6] Z., Pt. I, Appendix III, SECRET MIDRASH, fol. 3b ; II, 677.

[7] Ib.

[8] Ib., fol. 2b ; II, 676.

[9] Ib., Pt. I, fol. 127a ; II, 103. See also fol. 287b ; II, 664.

with an envelope other than the fleshly body but still having the form thereof.[1] It is said as to this that the days of life are a vesture, and the days of man's life on earth are his vesture in the world to come, in so far as he has lived them worthily.[2] The odours given forth daily in the Garden of Eden perfume the precious vestments woven out of the days of man.[3] This again is a clear issue at its value, but it is superseded in other accounts and it complicates its own position by adding that there is one vesture [4] for NESHAMAH, another for RUAH, and one finally of an external and scarcely perceptible kind for NEPHESH [5]—all formed from the days of life. At the same time the commandments of the Law are the vesture of NESHAMAH.[6]

In this way we are taken to another point of spiritual progression which may be perhaps without prejudice to what has gone before. When the soul of a man who has been consecrated to the study of the Law during life quits this world, it goes up by the roads and pathways of the Law,[7] so that his knowledge is a guide in attainment, while the souls of those who have neglected such study go astray in the paths which lead to the region of GEBURAH, where they suffer punishment.[8] In another manner of symbolism the Law goes before the soul when it rises into the celestial regions, and it opens to him all the doors.[9] The Law remains with the soul till the day of resurrection, when it will take up the defence of the soul. This is again in reference to the Students of the Law,

---

[1] Z., Pt. I, fol. 91a ; I, 516.

[2] See post, p. 285 ; and Z., Pt. I, fol. 224a, b ; II, 482–484.   It is said elsewhere that the soul cannot have two vestures at one and the same time, even as the spirit of good and the spirit of evil cannot dwell together.   The heavenly envelope is assumed, or the soul is clothed therewith, when that of earth is decomposed as well as laid aside. It is a curious theory of vehicles, but it rests—ex hypothesi—on the authority of Rabbi Simeon.   The object of Samael is to hinder man from receiving the garment of heaven, and this he can do until the fleshly body has dissolved.—Ib., Pt. I, fol. 169b, 170a ; II, 441.   But the reference is apparently to NEPHESH.   The RUAH is itself not at rest ; it is only after the complete return of the earthly part to earth that it is drawn back to the Holy Spirit Which gave it.

[3] Ib.

[4] It is admitted that the wise in doctrine have not reached a full agreement on the subject, yet the number of vestures is three.—Ib., fol. 225a ; I, 485.

[5] Because, notwithstanding previous testimony, NEPHESH is bound up with the body in its tomb for twelve months only, after which it goes wandering and enters into communication with those who are still incarnate, to inquire respecting their sufferings and to pray at need for them.—Ib., Pt. II, fol. 141b ; IV, 48.

[6] Presumably NESHAMAH is so clothed with righteousness because it cannot sin.

[7] Ib., fol. 175b ; II, 290.   See also fol. 27a ; I, 170.

[8] Ib., Pt. I, fol. 175b ; II, 290.

[9] Ib., fol. 185a ; II, 329.

and it is said that after their resurrection they will preserve intact all knowledge which they had during their antecedent life.[1] Indeed such knowledge will be extended, so that they will be able to penetrate mysteries which were concealed from them previously.[2] It would seem also that those who are dedicated to the study of the Law on earth will be so occupied also in the world to come, and this apparently apart from the resurrection life.[3]

I will make an end of these economies by condensing one more parable of the soul.[4] There are Seven Palaces on high containing the Mystery of Faith, and I understand these as seven stages of union, like a tower going up to God. In case I am correct herein, it is said that six of them are accessible to the understanding of man, but the seventh is secret and forms part of the Supreme Mysteries.[5] The reason is the old reason, namely, that " eye hath not seen " ; and considering that in this state the union is altogether ineffable, it may be worth while saying that we have no title to term it absorption, identity, or by any other word which is within the measures of things expressible. There are also Seven Palaces below, and among these one is superior to the rest, as it holds both from heaven and earth. For the rest, they are postulated in relation to certain grades of advancement in the world to come. When the souls of the just leave material life they enter the first Palace and are occupied with preparations for the next stage of their experience, but there are no particulars.[6] The second Palace [7] is the sojourn of those who have suffered

---

[1] Z., fol. 185a ; II, 330.

[2] Ib.

[3] Ib. When stripped of its conventions, the real meaning which issues from these extracts is that the pursuit of the Law is the following of the will of God and that the union hereafter therewith is a penetration of the Divine Mystery, in which the soul progresses for ever.

[4] Ib., fol. 38a ; I, 235.

[5] Ib.

[6] Z., Pt. I, fol. 38b ; I, 236.

[7] There are several systems of Palaces described by the ZOHAR ; there are those in which speech prevails but in others thought or intention. The latter are more exalted in order, presumably because silence is better than speech, seeing that it stands for the contemplation of God in the heart. I do not find for what reason per se or in what manner, but the object of all the Palaces above is to preserve Shekinah in the world below. The variant accounts are somewhat confusing, as it is not invariably too easy to see whether the subject of discourse is the Palaces which are above or those which are below. (See, for example, Z., Pt. I, fol. 38a ; I, 236.) It is said (Ps. xxvii. 4) : " That I may dwell in the House of the Lord all the days of my life, to behold the beauty of the Lord, and to inquire in His Temple." The beauty of the Lord is held to designate the Palaces above, but the word " beauty " is rendered " delights " by the ZOHAR. The Temple means the Palaces below. The seven superior Palaces are

morally and physically in the present world, but have given
daily thanks to their master, this notwithstanding, and have
not neglected prayer.[1] The Messiah descends into this abode
and thence he draws souls into the third Palace. It is the
place of those who have suffered extremely in earthly life as
the result of serious disease. It contains also the souls of
young children and of such as have shed tears over the
destruction of the Temple. They are consoled by Messiah,
who brings them into the fourth Palace, where are the souls
of all those who have shared the sorrow of Zion and those
also who have been slain by heathens. The fifth Palace is the
sojourn of true penitents, who have restored their souls to a
state of purity, and of those who have sanctified the Name of
their Master by going to meet death for His glory.[2] There
also are the souls of those who have repented on their death-
beds, since the Doctors of Kabbalism insist no less on the
possibility of saving the situation of life thus at the last moment
than do the Doctors of the Latin Church : for the one and
the other the great fatality resides in final impenitence. The
sixth Palace is the sojourn of the souls of ZELATORES who
have proclaimed the Master's unity, and have loved Him
with a true love.[3] The seventh Palace is that which I have
called superior in respect of the rest ; it is also more secret
and mysterious. It is not unlike that glimpse of the Beatific
Vision which according to Catholic Theology is seen for a
moment by souls on the threshold of purgatory, or it is like
the vision of Shekinah which is granted *in articulo mortis*,
according to Kabbalism—as we have seen. The soul on its

---

(1) the basis and beginning of the Mystery of Faith ; (2) the abode of Faith ; (3) the
place in which worthy souls are offered in sacrifice ; (4) the place of judgment, whether
propitious or otherwise ; (5) the Palace of Love ; (6) the Palace of Mercy ; and
(7) the Holy of Holies and final end of souls.—See TRACT PALACES, being Appendix II.,
Z., Pt. II, fol. 244b, 261a ; IV, 277–294. There are also Seven Palaces of Prayer,
provided with doors by which the prayers of man ascend to the Great Master. The
first corresponds to the " paved work of a sapphire stone."—Ex. xxiv. 10. It leads to
the heaven of heavens. The second is like " the body of heaven in its clearness " (*ib.*).
The third is a Palace of pure untinctured light, having a point of golden splendour.
The fourth is a Palace of 70 lights, while the splendour of the fifth is like that of the
lightning and thunderbolt, combining purple with many colours. The sixth is the
Palace of Will, and it diffuses 12 lights ; its mystery is expressed by the words : " Thy
lips are like a thread of scarlet " (SONG OF SOLOMON iv. 3). It is also the Palace of
Love. But the seventh Palace is devoid of all form ; it constitutes the Mystery of
Mysteries ; and it is separated from the other habitations by a veil. Herein sojourns
the Infinite Will.—Z., Pt. I, fol. 41b–45b ; I, 248–265.
¹ Z., Pt. I, fol. 38b ; I, 237.
² *Ib.*, fol. 39a ; I, 239.
³ *Ib.*, I, 240.

.departure from earth enters this Palace for a moment—though there seems no assignable reason and though it is not said to see anything : it is then immediately relegated to that place of sojourn which corresponds to its state at death. It will be noted that the parable has no logical consistence—as it has no concurrence with previous accounts : if those who have suffered martyrdom for the glory of God have a particular abode assigned them, it is obvious that others who have died naturally, for example, have no title therein ; and so of the rest. Were it worth while to exercise one's mind on the subject, it might be suggested that souls which have reached a certain grade in life do not pass through the Palaces below that grade, while those who are below work upward and attain that grade after a given period in the world to come. But the ZOHAR is really concerned only with enforcing the idea of ascent in the scale hereafter, and the logic of its fiction is of no consequence in comparison with the main object. It is therefore idle to rectify on our part ; let us realise rather that the ZOHAR is establishing another point of correspondence between the lesser and greater world. We have seen how early in the Christian centuries it forestalled the modern doctrine of macrocosmic evolution, and this now is a story of evolution in the microcosm, working on the basis of six periods corresponding to those of creation ; and as the latter was followed by a period of rest, so is the seventh Palace a place of secrecy and mystery, suggesting a Sabbatic state. But above it there is the other and ineffable order of Supernal Palaces, and beyond the present epoch in created things there is the Messianic age to come, in which the story of the world and man reaches its end for Zoharic Theosophy, as it does in the Apocalypse for Theosophy according to Christ.

The idea of reincarnation in Kabbalism has been the subject of much confusion in the modern occult schools, which have depended, firstly, on the vague and incorrect vestige of elucidation offered by Adolphe Franck [1] and, secondly, on the obvious misstatements of Éliphas Lévi. [2] It is dismissed by

[1] LA KABBALE, pp. 244–247. There is postulated in the first place the fact of metempsychosis in Kabbalism on the authority of Z., Pt. II, fol. 99b, and afterwards the author gives a very imperfect account of the Zoharic doctrine concerning overshadowing, impingement, or embryonic states of souls, with which I am proceeding to deal.

[2] See A. E. Waite : THE MYSTERIES OF MAGIC : *A Digest of the Writings of Éliphas Lévi*, second Edition, 1897, where it said that a multiplicity of incarnations has never been recognised by Kabbalists of the first order.—pp. 131, 132.

the one in a few paragraphs and the other states that the doctors of traditional science in Israel did not admit the subject. On the contrary, there is a clear system of reincarnation scattered throughout the ZOHAR, but it calls to be distinguished from those later developments with which I must deal otherwise.

To some extent the doctrine hinges on questions of paternity, for it is stated plainly that when a man has failed to have children in this world, the Holy One will send him back, and many times at need, to fulfil what has been neglected, so that he is compared to a plant which is removed continually from the ground and located elsewhere—in the hope that it will do better.[1] Reincarnation is not, however, an universal law, or at least it is contingent in other cases than the particular case which has been just specified. Those who have accomplished their mission during a single sojourn on earth rest near to the Holy One ; those who return are those who have not finished their work, whether it be that of parentage or otherwise.[2] It is rather obvious that the perfect fulfilment of the Law was a matter of great difficulty, and we know that St. Paul regarded it as an intolerable burden ; we know also that failure in certain points voided the entire fulfilment ; and the inference would seem to be that reincarnation for the doing of that which had been previously left undone and for the undoing of that which was amiss formerly must, by the hypothesis, have been the rule rather than the exception. Hence it is said in one place that the words " seeing that he also is flesh "[3] signify that the spirit of man, meaning his soul, will be many times reclothed with flesh, until the time comes when the soul shall be susceptible of receiving the spirit of God. In order that the significance of the expression should not remain doubtful, it is added that the Holy One will some day ransom the world and will grant the spirit in question to men generally, so that they may live eternally.[4] This is said to be shewn by the words : " For as the days of a tree are the days of my people,"[5] and also : " He will swallow up death in victory : and the Lord God will wipe away all tears from

---

[1] Z., Pt. II, fol. 186b ; II, 337.
[2] Ib., fol. 187b ; II, 341.
[3] Gen. vi. 3.
[4] An allusion apparently to the permanence of the resurrection state.
[5] Is. lxv. 22.

off all faces ; and the rebuke of His people shall He take away from off all the earth : for the Lord hath spoken it." [1] Reincarnation or transmigration would seem also to be the invariable fate of the Gentiles. The souls of Pagans who deliver up their bodies in the Holy Land are not received in heaven : they wander about in the universe, transmigrate many times and finally return to the unclean place whence they came. [2] The souls of Israel which leave the body outside Palestine have also transmigrations and wanderings before reaching the region assigned them. [3] If this is to be taken as definite—and I do not think that the view is revised subsequently—one side of the law of reincarnation depends upon a merely external accident. [4] It will be useful to remark here that the ZOHAR knows nothing concerning spaces of time intervening between death and rebirth ; the question does not seem to have arisen within their consciousness ; the period elapsing may have been variable, as it is regarded in Eastern doctrine ; but the new event is sometimes at least immediate. Seth, for example, was animated by the soul of Abel, which thus returned to earth. [5] At the birth of Benjamin, however, his soul left the body of his mother, which it had animated previously. [6] At the death of Rachel, her soul animated the son of Benjamin. [7] It seems to follow that in each case there were two souls at one time in the same body. It is said further that Phineas received the soul of Nadab and Abihu, who were alive at the time. [8] Rabbi Simeon testifies that this is a mystery, meaning that their soul did not find refuge under the wings of Shekinah, because they left no children and had thus diminished the figure of the King.

I have spoken already of the place—whatever it is, for it is indeed described variously—in which souls are reserved, awaiting the period of their primary embodiment in flesh ; and I have mentioned the notion that at the Messianic period

---

[1] Is. xxv. 8.
[2] Z., Pt. II, fol. 141a ; iv. 46.
[3] Ib.
[4] See *post*, p. 320, regarding final reincarnation, which must take place in Palestine.
[5] *Ib.*, Pt. I, fol. 55a ; I, 315. Adam is said to have called his son Seth to mark the end of a situation, the consonants of his name being the two last letters of the alphabet.
[6] Z., Pt. I, fol. 155b ; II, 211.
[7] *Ib.*
[8] *Ib.*, Pt. III, fol. 216b ; V, 550. The suggestion is difficult to follow and would scarcely deserve the pains. It is added that when Phineas slew Zimri and Cozbi the tribe of Simeon were keen on avenging the death of their chief ; the soul of Phineas fled and the two wandering souls took possession of its vacant place.

the fount of souls will be exhausted, leading to the creation
of entirely new cohorts.[1] But it is said also that there will
come a time when old souls, meaning souls in migration, will
be renewed for the renewal of the world.[2] Each of these
souls who have been incarnated previously will be united to
a new created soul, as it is written : " And it shall come to
pass that he that is left in Zion, and he that remaineth in Jerusalem, shall be called holy, even every one that is written
among the living in Jerusalem." [3] We see by these extracts
that reincarnation according to Kabbalism is complicated by
several considerations and that the word impingement or
overshadowing would be a better description of that which
occurred in certain cases. The subject is not developed in the
text itself, and it came into the hands of later Kabbalists who
manufactured mighty systems thereon. The testimony of
Isaac de Loria in his BOOK OF THE REVOLUTIONS OF SOULS is
an instance of the lengths to which it could be carried and I
shall have to deal with it at a later stage.[4]

The question of resurrection in connection with reincarnation created difficulties of its own. It was alleged that in the
case of souls who take flesh several times the body which shall
rise will be that in which the soul has succeeded in taking root,
meaning presumably that it has fulfilled the Law in perfection.[5]
Those bodies in which the soul fails to reach its ends are like
dried up trees which fall to dust, and they will rise no more.
There is some subtlety in this as a way out of the difficulty
created by the idea of resurrection in connection with the idea
of rebirth. But it will be observed that nothing is said as to
those who have been rooted only in wickedness. I may add
that the Zoharic doctrine of the world to come and the
recompenses and punishments therein is quite independent of
any reincarnation hypothesis and cannot be adjusted thereto.
The two notions were developed almost certainly in complete
independence of each other. As regards resurrection, there
is a variant of the above view, according to which the soul
will return into the last body that was animated, but the previous bodies will rise also and will be animated with new
souls. " If these bodies have fulfilled meritorious works "—
I give the literal words in this instance—" they will continue,

---

[1] Z., Pt. I, fol. 28b; I, 179.   [3] Is. iv, 3.
[2] Ib., Pt. I, fol. 119a; II, 76, 77.   [4] See Book IX, § 1.
[5] Z., Pt. I, fol. 131a; II, 114.

but if not they will return again to dust," and as no purpose will have been served, this reverie does not seem less than imbecile.[1] Some incidental points may be summarised as follows. On the basis of the words : " One generation passes away, and another generation cometh," [2] it is said that the generation which comes is that also which has passed.[3] Reincarnation is sometimes despite the soul and sometimes apparently otherwise.[4] In one place it is formulated in the terms of uttermost simplicity by affirming that souls are sent for a second time on earth, that they may repair faults committed on the first occasion.[5] They come back also through the workings of Grace, as for example when husband and wife have been sterile through no fault of theirs in a previous lifetime[6] ; on the next occasion they will be enabled to fulfil the Law, though it is not suggested that they will do so one with another. This implies that the axiom once an Israelite always an Israelite obtains automatically, and though I have not had occasion to mention it previously, it may be said now that what may be called the primordial generation of the chosen people insures this—supposing that rebirth occurs. There is another point : reincarnation is good because good reasons are, by the hypothesis, behind it ; but as it is not good in itself, it is well to be spared therefrom. In conclusion, rebirth befalls those who do not study the Law, the inference being that those who do and who at the same time fulfil the other precepts do not suffer transmigration.[7]

II.—ANGELS AND DEMONS

We have seen that the world of BRIAH is that of Creation so-called, that is, of the emanation of creative forces. These forces are Elohim, and in this sense BRIAH is therefore the Elohistic world. It is called also the world of archangels, but

---

[1] Z., Pt. I, 131a ; II, 114.
[2] Eccles. i. 4.
[3] Z., Pt. I, fol. 268b. LUMINOUS BOOK or BOOK OF BRIGHTNESS ; II, 635.
[4] Z., Pt. II, fol. 96b ; III, 387, 388.
[5] Ib., Pt. II, fol. 54a ; III, 244.
[6] Ib., fol. 109a ; III, 429, 430.
[7] Ib., Pt. III, fol. 178b, THE FAITHFUL SHEPHERD ; V, 464. According to the testimony in this text, incarnation may take place thrice, because of the words : " Lo, all these things worketh God oftentimes with man."—Job xxxiii. 29. The ZOHAR renders the passage : " Behold what God doeth in respect of each man, even to the third time." Compare the Vulgate : *Ecce haec omnia operatur Deus tribus vicibus per singulos.*

this is in later Kabbalism. It would not be exact to say that the archangels are Elohim, much less that Michael, Raphael, Gabriel, Metatron and so forth are deities according to the Kabbalah.[1] In a general way it may be affirmed perhaps that the intelligent forces of the Briatic World, when assumed, so to speak, by the Divine World, can be regarded as Elohim, in the speculations of later rabbinical minds. Thus, according to Kabbalism, the three men who appeared to Abraham in the vale of Mamre to announce the destruction impending over the cities of the plain were three archangels, but they were also Adonai, the Lord, for they were forms assumed by Divinity. Even at the risk of forestalling some part of that which is to come, it seems important to register at this stage that Shekinah is Elohim as well as Adonai, according to recurring testimony of the Zohar, and that she under God made the world by Chesed, which is the highest of Briatic Sephiroth, and it is in this sense that Briah is the Elohistic world.

Of the hierarchy of spiritual beings outside humanity we meet with various classifications by different rabbinical writers, and they are not to be regarded as mere inventions, for they have their roots or vestiges in Talmudic times. As regards the descending or demonological scale, later authorities do not hesitate to contradict Zoharic statements. It should be understood that what follows depends from Zoharic expositors and not from the Zohar itself. They are tabulated on the Tree of Life and the Four Kabbalistic Worlds, which are complicated, moreover, by assuming an evolution of the Ten Sephiroth in each. The archangels of Briah, corresponding to the extension in question through that world, are usually enumerated as follows :

    I. Metatron, Angel of the Presence, World-Prince, corresponding to Kether.[2]

    II. Raziel, the Herald of Deity, corresponding to Chokmah.

---

[1] Isidore Loëb, however, describes Metatron as a species of *Demiourgos*, following presumably the heterodox opinions of the Talmudic R. Acher. Franck also regards him as a Divine Hypostasis.

[2] When written with a Jod (MITTRVN), the name Metatron signifies Shekinah ; without that letter it signifies the angel who is " legate of Shekinah," also called NGHR = Boy, and hence Metatron has been said to be a boy-angel.—Kabbala Denudata, *Apparatus*, i. 528. We shall see later that he has other and more pregnant titles.

III. TSAPHKIEL, Contemplation of God, corresponding to BINAH.
IV. TSADKIEL, Justice of God, corresponding to CHESED.
V. SAMAEL, Severity of God, corresponding to GEBURAH.
VI. MICHAEL, Like unto God, corresponding to TIP-HERETH.
VII. HANIEL, Grace of God, corresponding to NETZACH.
VIII. RAPHAEL, Divine Physician, corresponding to HOD.
IX. GABRIEL, Man-God, corresponding to YESOD.
X. SANDALPHON, Messias, the second phase of Metatron, corresponding to MALKUTH.

The world of YETZIRAH or Formation is said to be that of the angels, who are divided into nine choirs, which are very nearly identical with the hierarchy of pseudo-Dionysius, whose scheme has become part of Christianity.[1] Those who attribute a high antiquity to Kabbalistic Tradition say that Dionysius drew from the oral doctrine of Israel ; others pretend that Dionysius and the Kabbalah both derive from Neoplatonism ; but Greek and Hebrew thought had come to know one another before the date of the Areopagite. Dionysius, perhaps, may be taken to represent the point of contact between Hellenism and Jewry after modification by Christianity. The Kabbalah may represent, but at a much longer distance, in the form of its extant literature, the point of contact between Hellenism and Israel unmodified by Christianity.

According to the most usual attribution the choirs of YETZIRAH are as follows :—

I. HAYYOTH HA KADOSH, the holy living creatures, or animals of Ezekiel and the Apocalypse, corresponding to KETHER and to the Christian Seraphim.
II. OPHANIM, or Wheels, also mentioned in Ezekiel, corresponding to CHOKMAH and the Cherubim.
III. ARALIM, or Mighty Ones, corresponding to BINAH and the Thrones.
IV. HASHMALIM, or Brilliant Ones, corresponding to CHESED and the Dominations.
V. SERAPHIM, or Flaming Serpents, corresponding to GEBURAH and the Powers.

[1] It should be remembered, however, that unlike Christian angelology, that of the ZOHAR represents the divine messengers as altogether inferior to man and most certainly to the souls of the just, which ascend higher and attain a superior rank. See the Mantua edition, iii. 68b.

VI. MELACHIM, or Kings, corresponding to TIPHERETH and the Virtues.

VII. ELOHIM, or Gods, corresponding to NETZACH and the Principalities.

VIII. BENI-ELOHIM, or Sons of God, corresponding to HOD and the Archangels.

IX. CHERUBIM, the. Seat of the Sons, corresponding to JESOD, the Foundation, and the Angels.

The tenth order required to complete the Sephirotic attribution is found in the ISHIM, or beatified souls of just men, corresponding to MALKUTH and the great multitude of the redeemed seen by St. John in the Apocalypse.

These orders are also summarised in the notion of a third Adam, YETZIRAH, represented by the MALKUTH of the Yetziratic world, man in the likeness of the angels—in a word, the ADAM Microprosopus of the IDRAS.

The world of ASSIAH, or of matter, is that into which Adam descended at the Fall, and beneath it is the abode of evil spirits, the Shells, Envelopes and CORTICES of the later Kabbalah.[1] It contains the orders of retrograde spirits corresponding by inversion to the angels of YETZIRAH and the arch-fiends corresponding after the same manner to the archangels of the Briatic world.[2] They are usually enumerated as follows :

I.—THAUMIEL, the doubles of God, said to be two-headed and so named, because they pretend to be equal to the Supreme Crown. This is properly the title of the averse SEPHIRA corresponding to KETHER. The cortex is CATHARIEL, according to the Supplements of the ZOHAR. Satan and Moloch are said to be the arch-demons, but the attributions are hopelessly confused throughout, partly owing to the obscure classifications of the ZOHAR and the contradictions of later Kabbalists.

II.—CHAIGIDIEL, a term connecting with the significance of *placenta*, or, according to other authorities, with that of obstruction, in the sense of an impediment to the heavenly influx. This averse SEPHIRA corresponds to CHOKMAH. Its cortices are the OGHIEL or GHOGIEL, which cleave to illusory

---

[1] For some information on Kabbalistic demonology, see DIE KABBALA : *ihre Hauptlehren und ihr verhältniss zu Christenthum.* Innsbruck, 1885.

[2] But there are also many material correspondences which are not of shells and demons.

or material appearances in opposition to those of reality and wisdom. This explanation is, of course, very late. The arch-demon is said to be ADAM BELIAL, and so again is Beelzebuth. The Dukes of Esau are connected with this number.

III. SATHARIEL, the concealment of God, meaning that this averse SEPHIRAH, unlike BINAH or Intelligence, hides the face of mercy. In the Supplements of the ZOHAR it is termed SHEIREIL, from the hirsute body of Esau. The Dukes of Esau are referred alternatively to this number, instead of to the averse correspondence of CHOKMAH, by the same work. LUCIFUGE is said to be the arch-demon, but this is obviously not a Kabbalistic term : it is known, however, to the grimoires and to some late demonologists of the Latin church.

IV. GAMCHICOTH, or GOG SHEKLAH, disturber of all things, the averse correspondence of CHESED. According to the Zoharic Supplements the cortex seems to be AZARIEL. The arch-demon is ASTAROTH in late Kabbalism.

V. GOLAB, or burning, in the sense of incendiarism. This is the averse correspondence of GEBURAH and the antithesis of the Seraphim or Fiery Serpents. The cortex is USIEL. The arch-demon of late Kabbalism is ASMODEUS.

VI. TOGARINI, wranglers, because, according to Isaac de Loria, this averse correspondence of TIPHERETH strives with the Supernal GEBURAH. The cortices are called ZOMIEL and the arch-demon is BELPHEGOR.

VII. HARAB SERAP, dispersing raven, referring to the idea that this bird drives out its young, the averse correspondence of NETZACH. The cortices are the THEUMIEL and the arch-demon is BAAL CHANAN.

VIII. SAMAEL, or embroilment, corresponding to HOD, the supernal Victory. The cortices are THEUNIEL according to the Supplements of the ZOHAR, and ADRAMELEK is the name assigned to the arch-demon by late writers.

IX. GAMALIEL, the obscene, in averse correspondence with JESOD, which signifies generation of the higher order. OGIEL, which other classifications attribute to the averse correspondence of CHESED, seems to be the cortex mentioned in the Zoharic Supplements, and the arch-fiend is LILITH, according to late Kabbalism.

X. LILITH [1] is, however, according to another tabulation,

---

[1] According to the ZOHAR she is a stryge who slays infants.

the averse correspondence of MALKUTH, with whom later
Kabbalism connects NAHEMA,[1] the demon of impurity.

In Zoharistic doctrine, however, the chief personalities of
ASSIAH are SAMAEL, who is to some extent the averse Adam
Kadmon, and his bride LILITH. The Sephirotic attributions
are obscure and incomplete, but in a general way it is said
that as in the Holy Kingdom so is it in that of iniquity,[2] as in
the circumcision so also in the uncircumcision. SAMAEL is
said to be the uncircumcised and his bride is the prepuce,
which, it adds significantly, is the serpent.[3]

I have given space to this portion of the psychical hypotheses of Kabbalism, most of which is post-Zoharic, not
because it is of inherent importance, or can be regarded otherwise than as a disfigurement of the metapsychical doctrine,
but because we shall have later on to give account of the
connection between the Kabbalah and Ceremonial Magic,
and the doctrine of angels and demons is necessary to the
understanding of this connection.[4] It should be added that
not only is a methodised doctrine of the Celestial and Infernal
Hierarchies not found in the ZOHAR, but there is no adequate
material for the construction of such a doctrine.

---

[1] A succubus who brings forth spirits and demons after intercourse with men, says
the ZOHAR, which in various places develops this idea further.
[2] Hence the true name of Satan is said to be that of YHVH reversed.—Pike, MORALS
AND DOGMA, p. 102. He is reproducing Éliphas Lévi.
[3] R. Simeon ben Yohai in TIKKUNIM, or Supplements, No. 18. See BETH ELOHIM,
by R. Abraham Cohen Irira, c. ii., KABBALA DENUDATA, ii., Part 3, Tract 1, i.e.,
PNEUMATICA KABBALISTICA, pp. 188 et seq.
[4] The TALMUDS abound with legendary history and teaching on this subject, for they
are like a storehouse of folk-lore as well as of jurisprudence. It has been even proposed
that the mediæval notion of vampirism is to be traced to Talmudic fables concerning
stryges. See A. Brierre de Boismont, DES HALLUCINATIONS, &c. Second ed.,
p. 395. Paris. 1852.

BOOK VII

WAYS OF GOD WITH MAN

BOOK VII

WAYS OF GOD WITH MAN

I.—THE MYTH OF THE EARTHLY PARADISE

IN some previous chapters I have been content to lead up
as I could to certain intimations which have formed part of
each concerning that Mystery of Sex which is called Mystery
of Faith and Supreme Mystery in the ZOHAR; but in the
present consideration it will be with us even from the beginning. It is a matter of some difficulty to disassociate the
subject from that Divine Personality—the Indwelling Glory—
which is the central figure of the Aramaic text and the full
discussion of which I have decided for good reasons to
postpone till much later in our study. It must be remembered
in the first place that there are two Gardens of Eden which
are in communication one with another, while the one leads
to the other.[1] The one is the Mystery of Sex as it was
established or rather formulated originally on this lower
earth, by the hypothesis of the Secret Doctrine, but this
Garden was ravished; the other is a Mystery in Transcendence, as it subsists in the Eternal World, the World of the
Supernals. In the symbolism of the whole subject, the ward
of both is womanhood; she is the Garden in transcendence
and she is also the Garden [2] below, or alternatively their

---

[1] According to later Kabbalism, the Superior Paradise is referrable to BRIAH in
respect of souls and to YETZIRAH in respect of angels, but this is manifestly opposed
to Zoharic teaching, by which it is allocated to BINAH and is therefore in the Supernal
World of ATZILUTH. The Inferior Paradise is in ASSIAH according to both forms of
Kabbalism. We have seen also that the Higher Eden is the abode of souls awaiting
incarnation and that the Lower Eden is, so to speak, the threshold of entrance into the
life of earth. So also on the return journey through the gate of death the Lower
Paradise is a tarrying-place for the souls of the just before they ascend higher, that is
to say, into the Supernal Eden, where perfect liberation is enjoyed.—Z., Pt. III, fol.
196b; V, 506.
[2] According to Franck, Paradise is always termed by the Kabbalists either עדן גן =
the Garden of Eden or עולם הבא. = the World to Come and never פרדס = PARDES =
Garden, this being the word of the modern Kabbalists.—LA KABBALE, p. 57. GAN

mystery is she ; and their image amidst the exile and penitence of this present order is also woman—woman in her betrothals, woman in her espousals, woman as wife, mother, daughter and sister.   We shall see at a later stage that all these designations are titles of Shekinah—as the Divine Personality which I have mentioned—and she can be regarded from two points of view, being (1) as woman in the archetype and (2) as the Mystery of Sex.   Speaking essentially, these two are reducible to one.   But the male is not without the female, nor is the woman apart from man in respect of this mystery, which includes all.   It is that of God in His concealment—being, however, the concealment of KETHER and not that of AIN SOPH—of God also as He is manifested in the Secret Doctrine, and of prototypical humanity.   It is the mystery of the Traditional Fall of man and of all the banishments which the elect are postulated as having suffered ; but as it is owing to this mystery that each one of us is incarnate here so is it also through this that we return homeward into the refuge whose name is Shekinah : it is with us at this day in the bondage of our mortality, but it is also the law of our liberation.   The Zoharic Legend of the Earthly Paradise may be held to formulate the mystery, but without expounding it.   The Paradise above is called " the Sanctuary, O Lord, which Thy hands have established." [1]   The Paradise below has the Holy of Holies for its image and both are at the centre of the earth, called Zion and Jerusalem—the place and house of peace.[2] As regards the making of man we know that there are two accounts in Genesis, one dovetailed into the other, a fact which the Zoharic doctors did not realise, and with the difficulties which thus arose they dealt as they could.   According to the Elohistic text man was made in the likeness of the Elohim—that is to say, male and female, for which reason we shall see that Shekinah—whose title is Elohim—is presented as male on a few very rare occasions, but so invariably other-

---

EDEN is applied in the Zohar both to BINAH and MALKUTH as the Sephirotic locations respectively of the Superior and Inferior Eden.

[1] Z., Pt. I, fol. 7a ; I, 38.

[2] See *note*, p. 210.   The Palace or Paradise below is modelled on the pattern of that which is above, for the Divine Presence in MALKUTH, as the Kingdom of this world, does not differ from the Divine Hypostasis in BINAH, which is the World to Come. The Lower Garden was formed and planted by the Holy One, that He might have joy with the souls of the just who dwell therein ; but the Garden which is placed in the transcendence, under the Wings of Shekinah, is the place of contemplation for souls in the sweetness of the Lord, and herein is the Blessed Vision.—Z., Pt. II, fol. 127a ; IV, 8.

wise as female that the alternative has the aspect of a mere blunder or a wilful confusion of issues. In so far as she represents the Mystery of Sex, it might be said that she is of both sexes, is male on the right side of the Tree of Life— which is the masculine side—and female on the left side. But the myth of the Earthly Paradise is a Jehovistic text, and by its hypothesis Adam, being the male in distinction from the female, or having the female latent within him, was made in the first place. Now, it is said that when the Holy One created Adam He exhorted him to walk in the way of goodness and revealed to him the Mystery of Wisdom, by aid of which he could attain even to the Supreme Degree.[1] He gave him also the Law and taught him His ways.[2] This is not, however, Adam in distinction from Eve but refers to humanity in its two primordial forms : so also in respect of what follows. Man was crowned with celestial crowns and was so formed that he could rule over the six directions of space ; he was perfect in all things and bore the seal of the heights on his countenance. The angels encompassed him and honoured him, revealing mysteries relating to the knowledge of their Master. But he on his part beheld all Supreme Mysteries and all wisdom—exceeding, as we have seen already, the science of the angels—and he knew the glory of God. The intention was that he should remain united in heart and mind to Him Who was his model, thus being preserved unchanged, like God Who is the synthesis of all things and in Whom all is unified.[3] If it be said that this is mere fantasy in distraction, because man, by the hypothesis of the legend, did not know good or evil and much less one from another, I can point out only that authorised Christian doctrine on the same subject is in the same case precisely, since it is obvious (a) that in such state no person can be accountable for disobedience, or (b) if he be so accountable he is at least aware that obedience is on the side of goodness and its opposite on that of evil : but this spoils the postulate. The unreason is of course to treat a pure myth as if it were literal history. By so much, however, as we elect to exalt the state of man in Paradise, by

---

[1] Z., Pt. I, fol. 140b ; II, 147.
[2] Ib., fol. 199a ; II, 338.
[3] Z., Pt. I, fol. 321e, 221b ; II, 470. It is said also that God encompassed Adam with glory from on high (ib.), meaning the resplendent vesture or vehicle in which he was manifested before he was clothed with skins as one consequence of his Fall.

so much our construction crucifies further the story with which it professes to deal.[1]

In respect of the Garden itself, we learn that the whole world is watered by that mysterious river which went forth out of Eden—meaning the Paradise that is above.[2] It came from a secret place on high, and brought life to things below.[3] This place is symbolised by the letter BETH, when it appears for the first time in Genesis. The meaning is that this letter contains all letters in its womb, even as the river vivifies all things else. The secret place resembles a narrow path along which it is difficult to travel, but there the treasures of the world are hidden. The river brings sanctity from on high ; and when the Kingdom of Heaven shall have come under the form of first-fruits of the earth, the latter will be raised and made equal with Heaven. One might call this a keynote for the whole doctrine of cosmology, except that a keynote of one or another kind seems to emerge everywhere. Holiness is life, and the world subsists by holiness. If this, its correspondences and analogues, were not the beginning, middle and end of Zoharic Theosophy, I should have no cause to write about it, because it would not belong to the Secret Doctrine of God, which is my concern in the old literatures.

As regards the formation of Eve from the side of Adam, we meet in the ZOHAR with another presentation of a tradition which is found in many places of legend.[4] Adam and Eve were joined side by side originally. The explanation—which is given in one place only, or perhaps I should say rather that there is no alternative—is after the most inscrutable manner of the text—i.e., that they were not face to face because as yet

---

[1] We are told in Gen. ii. 15, that " the Lord God took this man, and put him into the Garden of Eden to dress it and to keep it." With this it is interesting to contrast the Zoharic ideas of those duties which fell to Adam in his original state of radiance. He was set to offer sacrifices in the Garden, and for such purpose an altar is postulated therein, which he profaned by his Fall, and so became a tiller of the ground.—Z., Pt. I, fol. 57b ; I, 331. It is said in another place that he was set to grow roses. These things occurred by the hypothesis before the institution of blood offerings ; we can infer therefore that the sacrifices of Adam were offerings of aspiration, and I think that what is indicated is part of the Mystery of Union. We shall see otherwise the kind of altar that was profaned by the Fall ; it is simply another aspect of the mystery of womanhood—that Garden which man was given to cultivate.—Ib., Pt. II, fol. 109a ; III, 430. The roses were children of Shekinah, because she is the Rose of the World, and under another aspect is herself the Garden.

[2] Ib., fol. 30b ; I, 192.

[3] In other terms, it brought the celestial waters, and thus gave birth to the plants and fruits which flourished in the Garden.—Ib., fol. 59b ; I, 348.

[4] Z., Pt. I, fol. 35a ; I, 216.

" the Lord God had not caused it to rain upon the earth." [1]
This is on the authority of Rabbi Simeon, who forgot, as one
might think, for a moment that the same verse adds : " And
there was not a man to till the ground." Too much attention
muſt not be given to inconsiſtencies of this kind—whether or
not some means of escape happens to be found subsequently—
as the purpose of the ZOHAR is always to make known a point
of its Secret Doctrine which can be hooked on to a text, and
the context—for this purpose—is seldom held to signify.[2]
The point in this case is (a) that man being superior to all the
works of creation,[3] the union of man and woman muſt be
modelled on that of Nature—meaning, however, the Arch-
Nature that is above ; but (b) their union face to face could
not be accomplished till after that of heaven and earth, which
was manifeſted by rain. It is obvious that a spiritual myſtery
is indicated, and one that is part of the intercourse which
conſtitutes the transcendental unions. The physical basis is
of course that the sex-union of humanity takes place in an
opposite position to that of all the animals, which was certain
to suggeſt deep symbolism to ZOHARIC doctors, though they
do not formulate the contraſt. Another intimation is that in
their original ſtate not only was Adam made male and female
but so also was the woman attached to his side.[4] I suppose
that this notion is the antechamber or threshold of that
" Supreme Myſtery " which is believed to be expressed in the
words : " Male and female created He them." [5] It is said
to conſtitute the glory of God and to be the object of faith.
In the root-nature it is regarded as inaccessible to human
reason, perhaps in the sense that it has not entered into the
heart of man to underſtand what God has prepared for those
who love Him, or, from another ſtandpoint, it is a matter of
experience and not of dissertation. By this myſtery was man
created, as well as the heaven and the earth. It is inferred
that every figure which does not represent male and female

[1] Gen. ii. 5.
[2] As a matter of fact, the discrepancy is recognised speedily, and the same maſter of
doctrine explains that there was no man because Eve had not yet been created, and man
was as if non-exiſtent, seeing that he was incomplete in her absence. The laſt point
is not a subtlety of the moment, but a doctrine which obtains everywhere regarding
our human nature.—Z., Pt. I, fol. 35a ; I, 217.
[3] Ib., fol. 34b ; I, 216.
[4] Z., Pt. III, fol. 117a ; V, 301.
[5] Gen. i. 27.

has no likeness to the heavenly figure.[1] We shall see in due course that the Holy One does not make His dwelling except where male and female are united, and there only His benedictions are disposed. This is why Scripture says : And God " blessed them and called their name Adam, on the day when they were created." [2]

It is recognised by the ZOHAR in no uncertain manner that the condition of side to side was one of imperfection, because it was not a true union in the likeness of heaven ; the latter is eye to eye and beyond it there is another state, in which heaven and earth pass away, like all the former things, since the distinctions of THIS and THAT are at an end. Eve was joined to Adam until he was put to sleep,[3] and here the text dwells especially on the fact that the place of his entrancement was that place where the Temple was built subsequently.[4] As regards the formation of Eve, it is said that " He took one of his ribs," and here the ZOHAR develops a great subtlety, inferring that the second pronoun alludes, like the first, to Jehovah Elohim. It says, further, that the plural " ribs " signify the virgins of MATRONA, meaning her maids of honour, one of whom was taken to be the " helpmeet " for Adam.[5] However this story is forgotten soon afterwards and yet others are substituted ; but I do not think that we need attach importance to any.

When the time came for man and woman to be joined face to face the text which here follows is applied to the intercourse : " They stand fast for ever and ever, and are done in truth and uprightness." [6] The reference is to the state of true nuptials, ineffable in the holy transcendence, when between the male and the female, as between the wings of the two cherubim, the glory of Shekinah manifests, when within and without are over and there is neither marrying nor giving in marriage because those which were once in separation have entered into the heaven of union. The words

---

[1] Meaning the Great Adam, the Cosmic Son, himself a reflection of what subsists but is not explicated in the World of ATZILUTH.

[2] Gen. v. 2.

[3] Z., Pt. I, fol. 34b ; I, 215.

[4] Ib., fol. 31b ; I, 215.

[5] Ib., fol. 28a, b ; I, 176–178. The reference is to Gen. ii. 21. It is even said that " bone of my bones and flesh of my flesh " (Gen. ii. 23) are words that signify Shekinah, so close is the connection recognised between the Indwelling Glory who is the guide of man on earth and the womanhood which is part of him.

[6] Ps. cxi. 8.

"Stand fast" are said to designate male and female, whose union here below will subsist through all eternity in the world that is above.[1] It consists in a sacred union face to face, for Zoharic similitudes seldom transcend this, though it is only the court of the Temple, where the Lover and Beloved are still clothed in their vestments. The words : " There went up a mist from the earth, and watered the whole face of the ground "[2] signify the desire of the female for the male, and here it is added cryptically that man was taken from his place and transplanted, or changed about, that man and woman might attain perfection. Now, it is claimed in one place that the sleep of Adam signifies the captivity, so that it is another episode in the long history of creation ; but it is to be questioned whether these scattered intimations can be drawn into a true memorial.

A word must be added concerning the Trees of the Garden, though I do not know that the Secret Doctrine offers lights of the first magnitude on this subject. The Tree of Life is identified with the Doctrine,[3] presumably in its inward form, or that which is inculcated by the surface sense and by the sense within : it is the Holy Law, which offers aspects of truth in all its interpretations. The fruits of this Tree subsist for ever and give life to all[4] ; it gave life in particular to the twelve tribes who issued therefrom.[5] It covers those vessels which are pure souls with its wings. It is Knowledge in the true sense, which is supernal, the Knowledge that is above reason : those who are attached thereto possess life in the world to come as well as life in this world.[6]

The Tree of the Knowledge of Good and Evil is reputed to have been a vine and the forbidden fruit was the grape,[7] as to which it is added elsewhere that Scripture interdicts wine and fermented drink : but this is obviously untrue. It is said also to be the female principle,[8] which, I suppose, may mean when it is unsanctified and in the state of separa-

---

[1] Z., Pt. I, fol. 35a ; I, 217.
[2] Gen. ii. 6.
[3] Z., Pt. I, fol. 106b, 107a ; II, 36.
[4] Ib., Pt. II, fol. 2a ; III, 3. They are sweeter than honey.—Ib., Pt. I, Appendix 3 ; II, 730.
[5] At the end of time the purified Israel will depend from this Tree only.—Ib., Pt. III, fol. 124b ; V, 322.
[6] It is the centre of all life.—Z., Pt. II, fol. 11a ; III, 48.
[7] Ib., Pt. III, 158b ; V, 410, fol. 127a ; V, 327.
[8] Ib., Pt. I, fol. 36a ; I, 223.

tion.[1] Among the fables concerning it there is that which
relates how it invited many spirits to revolt before they were
furnished with bodies, meaning possibly in the state of pre-
existence about which we have heard previously. When so
furnished, these spirits conceived a plan to descend on earth
and assume possession thereof. God classed therefore the
spirits in two categories, the good being placed on the side
of the Tree of Life and the evil on that of mixed knowledge.
He provided the first with bodies, but when the time had
come to do likewise in respect of the second, the Sabbath
interrupted the work of creation [2]—otherwise there would
have been wreck and ruin from end to end of the world. By
this intervention the Holy One provided the remedy before
the evil, advancing—that is to say—the hour of the Sabbath,
so that evil spirits had the mortification of seeing good spirits
invested with desirable bodies, whilst they in their deprivation
were impotent. It would seem to follow that the desire of
the evil side is towards sex, but in the iniquity to which it may
be debased. The infernal hosts are therefore in a state of
inhibition, arrestation and unsatisfied longing.

Generally as regards both Trees, the Secret Doctrine looks
forward not only towards that time—and because of it is glad
in all its aspects—when the elect will depend no longer on the
Tree of Good and Evil, when they will not be subject longer
to a Law which legislates on things permitted and forbidden,
on clean and unclean things.[3] Our entire nature will be
drawn in that day from the Tree of Life and there will be no
further debates about the evil and impure, for concerning
this state to come it is written : " I will cause . . . the impure
spirit to pass out of the land." [4] Herein is the rest which
remains for the people of God and the fruition is herein of
those good things of the Lord which are gathered into the
Land of the Living.[5] Now, there is a strange thing said in
another place which seems to connect with the subject and to
issue therefrom in a mystery that seems yet like a path of light.

---

[1] As a matter of fact, the passage referred to, which is curious in all respects, seems
to suggest that the Tree of Knowledge is that evil woman who is the wife of Samael
and intercourse with whom is incest, idolatry and murder. It is the averse side of the
Sex Mystery.

[2] Z., Pt. I, fol. 14a ; I, 82.

[3] Z., Pt. III, 124b ; V, 322.

[4] Zechariah xiii. 2.

[5] The Tree of Knowledge being the Tree of Death, in contrast to the Tree of Life.—
Z., Pt. III, fol. 157a ; 405.

Between the spirit of good and the spirit of evil " she must stand who is called woman," and they shall then abide in harmony or in the turning of the evil to account on the part of goodness. It is by the help of woman that the spirit of good preponderates over that of evil. After this manner does the Mystery of Faith proceed from more to more in the law of its self-unfoldment.

In conclusion, I infer that the Tree of Life is over the female principle in the state of *sacramentum ineffabile*, preserving all who are attached to it from death for ever.[1] My reason is that when it is said of the other Tree that those who are attached to it cleave also to death, the text quoted is : " Her feet go down to death ; her steps take hold on hell." [2] As this is woman on the side of the devil, so is the other womanhood also, but on the side of God.

II.—THE SERPENT, SON OF THE MORNING, AND FALL OF THE ANGELS

An adequate study of Kabbalistic speculations on the subject of angelology, the fall of the angels and the hierarchy of demons which came about as a consequence would begin in Talmudic literature and would be itself an undertaking of no inconsiderable magnitude, for behind that literature lies all oriental belief. I do not pretend to know what remains to be said on the subject when I recall the vast histories which have been written already, counting only from the days of Van Dale at the end of the seventeenth century.[3] It is fortunate that such an inquiry does not belong to our subject for there is very little in the Zohar or its expositors which is important hereon from the standpoint of Secret Doctrine, though there is a mass of curious speculation and ingarnering of bizarre superstition. It would be arid and wearisome to collect it without commentary of any kind, and as certain tabulations have been made in a previous Book I shall confine

---

[1] Here it is fair to mention that in one place the letter VAU is said to be the Tree of Life.—*Ib.*, fol. 121a ; V, 309. But the point is that VAU in the perfect state—which I have called *sacramentum ineffabile*—is in union with the second HE of the Sacred Name, as we have seen already.

[2] Prov. v. 5.

[3] Antonio van Dale : DISSERTATIONES DE ORIGINE ET PROGRESSU IDOLATRIÆ . . . *et de Divinationibus Idolatricis Judæorum.* Quarto, pp. 762. Amsterdam, 1696. It offers a mass of information on angels and demons according to Jewish ideas, on false Messiahs and on the magical side of Kabbalism.

my remarks under a few general heads, to elucidate things which led up to the Fall of Man and some which followed therefrom. I suppose that in the first place a word must be said upon the subject of evil and how it is regarded in the text. It seems to follow expressly or by implication from several statements—some of which have been cited previously—that there is at least a sense in which God is the Author of evil.[1] A system being given in which not only do all things come from God but He is present immanently in all, it is not unnatural to accept the direct consequences without debate or refinements, and in this particular respect no difficulty is created thus in the Kabbalistic mind. The Pauline consciousness that all Nature groaneth and travaileth, the sense of suffering in all animate beings had never entered therein, though there was a very keen sense of the burdens on election in Israel. It is admitted quite freely, and indeed the notion is implied in several places, that the Holy One has created both the just and the unjust,[2] or still more plainly that He formed man of a spirit of good and a spirit of evil. The exoneration resides in the fact that evil is of service to good, because good turns evil to account.[3] Moreover, God created a certain Tree, the eating of which meant that the full understanding of the evil side of things entered into the life of humanity; but the saving clause is that it imparted also the knowledge of good. There can be no question—and we have seen already—that from this point of view the Tree of the Trespass is a synonym or image of the Written Law, for this is prohibition above all things, which defines evil and separates that which is so imputed from what is recognised as good. It is understood, however, that the definition is on the formal side and stands therein at its value, without reference to essentials.[4]

---

[1] We have seen also that there is no difficulty in the SEPHER YETZIRAH on the subject, and it is this primitive text which is responsible for Sephirotic Theology throughout the ZOHAR proper. The evil which is created by God is to be distinguished, however, from that which man works on his own part. It is woe to those who make themselves wicked. This is on the authority of Is. iii. 11. It is ruled, however, that " He hath made everything beautiful in His time " (Eccles. iii. 11), because He is glorified by the works of the just and the occasional good acts of the wicked.—Z., Pt. II, fol. 11a ; III, 47.

[2] Ib.

[3] Ib., Pt. I, fol. 49a ; I, 283.

[4] The exoneration in chief is, however, in a discourse of R. Simeon, who maintains that merit and demerit would have been equally impossible for man if God had not (1) created the Spirit of Good and the Spirit of Evil, and if He had not (2) composed our nature of both.—Z., Pt. I, fol. 23a ; I, 142. The Spirit of Good and the Spirit of Evil are on the right and left of man. If the last lives in puri v, the first acquires an

There is no tabulated account of the Hierarchy of the Blessed Angels in the ZOHAR, but we hear generically of great hosts and cohorts, battalions of guardians, usually for purposes of honour—as when angels accompany Shekinah on some of her missions [1]—and there are also clouds of messengers. It is specified that METATRON is the leader of the Invisible Host and that his place is immediately beneath the throne of God [2]; but we are told nothing of legions, like those of the Nine Choirs of Dionysius,[3] though there are divisions and subdivisions with correspondences of this kind in late Kabbalism. As regards the Infernal Hierarchy there are various categories consisting of angels who kept not their first estate and of demons generated in several ways.[4]

They are specified as comprising ten degrees or ten crowns below [5] and corresponding as such to numerous hierarchic grades,[6] separated in appearance yet communicating one with another, being ramifications of a single tree. There are ten crowns to the right and ten also to the left,[7] for there is a right and there is a left side in the empire of the demons, this being modelled throughout on that of God.[8] There is even an infernal triad in correspondence as such with the Sacred Triad that is above, and the observance of the Paschal Lamb was instituted to break its bonds.[9] There are averse Seraphim in the form of serpents, emanating from the evil serpent.[10] There are finally seven averse Palaces corresponding, on the

ascendency over the second, so that both combine to protect him in all his ways.—*Ib.*, fol. 165b; II, 250. The Spirit of Evil is in a state of incompleteness unless man nourishes him by sin.—*Ib.*, fol. 201a; II, 398. Apparently, those who thus nourish their master are maintained in turn by him, whence the happiness and prosperity of the Gentiles is a fruit of the union between Samael and his prostituted wife.—*Ib.*, Pt. II, 11a; III, 47. It is admitted, on the other hand, that evil is stronger than good.—*Ib.*, Pt. III, fol. 263b; VI, 24. But even the demon contains a particle of sanctity, without which he could not exist.—*Ib.*, Pt. II, fol. 203b; IV, 205.

[1] It is mentioned, for example, that 42 sacred angels, commissioned for her service, came down with SHEKINAH when she accompanied Israel into Egypt. Each bore a letter of the Divine Name of 42 letters.—*Ib.*, fol. 4b; III, 15.

[2] *Ib.*, fol. 294b; IV, 318. It is here that METATRON is said to be the name assumed by Enoch when he was raised to heaven.

[3] It is just, however, to say that Picus de Mirandula, in his CONCLUSIONES KABBALISTICÆ, manages to extract nine hierarchies in the following order: KERUBIM, SERAPHIM, CHASMALIN, ARALIM, TARSISIM, OPHANIM, ISHIM, MELACHIM and ELOHIM, but it is a purely arbitrary classification. See Book X, *s.v.* PICUS.

[4] Speaking generally, the Empire of the Demons is supposed to be under the presidency of three chiefs or princes, who are described as three impure branches, from which depend seventy minor branches, and these are the leaders or angels of the seventy Gentile nations.—Z., Pt. III, fol. 194a; V, 503.

[5] Z., Pt. I, fol. 167a; II, 256.
[6] Z., Pt. I, 277a; II, 296.
[7] *Ib.*, Pt. III, fol. 207a V, 527.
[8] *Ib.*, Pt. II, fol. 37b; III, 179.
[9] *Ib.*, Pt. II, fol. 40b; III, 189.
[10] *Ib.*, fol. 247b; IV, 281.

one hand, to the Palaces that are above [1] and on the other to the seven names which are attributed to the tempting spirit : Satan, Impure, Enemy, Stumbling-block, the Uncircumcised, Wicked, Crafty.[2]

What I may call the metaphysical account is as follows :

When the passive light, designated as darkness in Scripture, was joined to the active light on the right side,[3] following the ordinary arrangement of the Sephirotic Tree, many celestial legions—concluding that there was antagonism between the modes—in place of harmony or equilibrium by virtue of the Middle Pillar—declared themselves for the light of the left side and made ready to revolt against the other. When the Middle Pillar manifested the Perfect Unity of God, the good legions renounced the struggle and submitted, but those which were evil [4] persisted and gave birth as a consequence to hell. In this manner discord was introduced into the world on both sides, and the sense of the text seems to suggest that its vibrations remained on that of the good powers, though apart from any spirit of rebellion. The Scriptural allusion is : " And God made the firmament, and divided the waters which were under the firmament from the waters which were above the firmament," [5] a text which does duty on many sides of interpretation, and signifies, in this sense, that He separated the discord which had its source in the angels who kept not their first estate from that which was introduced into the world by those who were cast into the abyss. Both disruptions had, however, their result below ; but that which belonged to the first class redounded to the glory of heaven, had this as its end in view and disappeared apparently when the end in question was reached. This is so far concerning one category of souls rejected from heaven and enchained below. There was another class, the downfall of which was consequent on the Holy One assembling several legions of superior angels and advising them that He intended

---

[1] Z., fol. 245a ; IV, 278.
[2] Ib., fol. 363a ; IV, 295, 296.
[3] Ib., Pt. I, fol. 17b ; I, 105.
[4] The inference seems to be that, belonging to the passive side, their potentiality for evil was greater than that of the active side, though it subsisted also in this, or the imputed conspiracy could not have been shared by the intelligences of both sides, as the case was apparently. It is said also elsewhere that the " Sons of God " (Gen. vi. 2) were angels of the evil side who were in a state of perversity from the beginning.— Ib., fol. 270a ; II, 638.
[5] Gen. i. 7.

to create man.[1] They appear to have replied by quoting the Psalmist when he said : " Nevertheless man being in honour abideth not : he is like the beasts that perish." [2] Thereupon the Holy One stretched forth a finger and burned these blessed legions, after which He called others into His presence and made the same statement, to which they answered on their part : " What is man that Thou art mindful of him and the son of man that Thou visitest him." [3] The Lord explained that man should be made in His image and would be superior to those whom He addressed. It does not appear what happened to these legions.[4] There were, moreover, those Sons of God who " saw the daughters of men that they were fair," [5] and they included Aza and Azael, who entered into a dispute with Shekinah on the advisability of creating Adam, seeing that he would end by sinning with his wife, to which Shekinah replied that before they could make accusations of this kind it must be postulated that they would prove more chaste in their own persons.[6] This was the conclusion for the moment ; but the children of God had recourse to the daughters of men and " took them wives of all that they chose." [7] The result was that Shekinah stripped them of their sanctity and of all part in eternal beatitude,[8] which had been the case also with the rebellious angels belonging to the first category : these are burnt eternally in Sheol.[9] According to one version Aza and Azael became enamoured of the evil daughters of Cain,[10] but the text says also that the Sons of Elohim or of God were actually Sons of Cain. We can take our choice among alternatives over matters of no consequence. Elsewhere it is affirmed that before the corruption of the

---

[1] Z., Pt. III, fol. 207b, 208a ; V, 529.

[2] Ps. xlix. 12.

[3] Ps. viii. 4.

[4] It must be confessed that these ridiculous fables have neither an inward sense nor an outward light. We know that Latin Christianity has a legend of the Fall of the Angels which connects that event in some clouded manner with the scheme of human redemption ; but it speaks with the tongue of seraphs in comparison with these inventions, in which the superior sense of the hierarchies is punished by burning and expulsion.

[5] Z., Pt. I, fol. 23a ; I, 141.

[6] Certain codices of the ZOHAR cause the Shekinah to intimate at this point that Adam will indeed end by sinning with a single woman, but it will prove also with her that he will be able to repair the fault, while the lost angels will sin with many women and will be deprived of all reparation.

[7] Gen. vi. 2.

[8] Z., Pt. I, fol. 25b ; I, 157.

[9] Ib., fol. 17b ; I, 108.

[10] Ib., fol. 37a ; I, 230.

world all men were called Sons of Elohim.[1] When Aza and Azael were cast down, they assumed bodies on earth and were imprisoned therein.[2] It was subsequently—according to this version—that they were seduced by women and are alive at this day, still instructing men in the Art of Magic, which they had begun to teach soon after their descent. They were chained on certain black mountains, which Laban and Balaam frequented for instruction in the forbidden art.[3] There were in all five orders of intelligence which seem to have been cast out of heaven, and some of them were incarnated as men.[4] These were the Giants of Genesis, the NEPHILIM, the descendants of AMALEK, the Intruders of the TALMUD, and so forth. It is on record that they caused the destruction of the Temple.

There is a distinction made in the ZOHAR between the serpent mentioned in Genesis and him who rode thereon. It is said that the serpent was female and was she who is called the Prostituted Woman.[5] She was the wife of him who rode upon her back,[6] and this was Samael the death-angel. It comes about in this manner that there is male and female on the evil, even as on the sacred side [7]—though in a rough and general sense the right side is sometimes said to be masculine and the left feminine. Samael is the tempter-spirit whose purpose is to put man to the test, and his other name

---

[1] Z., Pt. I, fol. 37a; I, 230.

[2] Ib., fol. 58a; I, 334. They belonged to that class who appeared under the form of men, and it was possible therefore for them to exist on earth. They assumed bodies to come down and because of their revolt they could not unclothe to reascend. By their union with women they engendered giants, the " mighty men of old," and " men of renown," mentioned in Gen. vi. 4. Compare, however, the previous section, p. 268.

[3] Z., Pt. III, fol. 208a; V, 530. According to another version Naamah, the sister of Tubal Cain, was from the side of Cain the murderer; she was a seducer of men and spirits, including Aza and Azael, who again were of the children of God mentioned in Genesis. She became the mother of demons and is still abroad in the world, exciting the desires of men, more especially in dreams of the night. She is associated with Lilith, of whom we shall hear shortly in connection with the Fall of Adam. It is testified by this tradition that demons are subject to death in the same way as human beings, but this must apply to the progeny and not to the first parents, as Samael, Lilith and Naamah are still in activity.—Z., Pt. III, fol. 55a; I, 317.

[4] Ib., fol. 25a; I, 156. See also TARGUM of Jonathan to Gen. vi. 4.

[5] Ib., APPENDICES, Pt. III, SECRETS OF THE LAW; II, 727. See also ADDITAMENTA (TOSSEFTA); II, 734. It is she whose " feet go down to death."—Prov. v. 5.

[6] It is said also that the adulterous woman by whom the world is seduced is the sword of the destroying angel.—Z., Pt. III, fol. 231b; V, 571.

[7] Ib., Pt. I, 153a; II, 201. They are impurity taking shape as such; and from their union issue powerful spiritual leaders who are spread abroad in the world and defile it. Samael mounted on the serpent's back is a symbol of the evil side of sexual intercourse—that is to say, after the manner of the beasts.

is the End of Darkness, which is equivalent to " the end of all flesh." [1] But when the ZOHAR speaks of the spirit of evil generically, it affirms that this is an old and insensate thing [2]—much as European folk-lore was accustomed to represent Satan as a poor and witless creature who is cheated easily in the end. When the serpent was condemned to go upon her belly this means that God took away those feet which are the support of the body, and here the text affords one of its profound intimations when it goes on to say : But Israel, who would not be supported by the Law—which was built up to encompass it, as the hills stand round Jerusalem—has lent feet to the serpent for the support of her.

As there is a serpent below which is still at work in the world, so there is a sacred serpent above which watches over mankind in all the roads and pathways and restrains the power of the impure serpent.[3] It is one of the adornments of the heavenly throne. From the kind of union which is predicated concerning Samael and the evil serpent, they seem to pass easily one into another, and it is presumably in this way that we hear of a great serpent—the dragon of later Kabbalism—which was cast into the abyss with his legions when the Sacred Name of forty-two letters was first graven upon the seal of God. But the abyss subsequently gave up the demons and the surface of the earth was covered with darkness till celestial light illuminated the world.[4] This spirit of evil has chiefs and messengers under his orders, intervening in all acts of man ; yet the serpent can only defile the soul by special authorisation therefrom.[5] Hence Israel still suffers on account of the impurities which came from the side of the first serpent ; from the impurities of ill-doing spirits ; and from those of demons ; but especially from the impurities of that particular reptile which is called " the other god " and is identified with AMALEK.[6] He is said to be the cause of all uncleanliness in the world, in all the degrees thereof. He is apparently on the male side and as such is an assassin, while his wife is a mortal poison, because she incites to idolatry. It is curious in this connection that the name Samael—םמיאל—is held to signify

---

[1] Z., Pt. I, fol. 152b ; I, 201.

[2] Ib., fol. 179a ; II, 307. The reference is to the " old and foolish King " of Eccles. iv. 13. See also Z., Pt. II, fol. 33b ; III, 163, and Pt. III, fol. 219a, THE FAITHFUL SHEPHERD ; V, 553, from which it seems to follow that the demon is a fool.

[3] Z., Pt. I, fol. 243b ; II, 563.   [5] Ib., fol. 152b, 153a ; II, 200, 201.

[4] Ib., fol. 30b ; I, 190.   [6] Ib., fol. 28b, 29a ; I, 181, 182.

the " venom of God." He is also the Angel of Death, who destroys men with a single drop of poison. AMALEK is apparently his synonym. There are said, however, to be two demons, *sub voce* AMALEK and the Divine malediction of the first serpent applies to both.

For the rest, demons are the excrement of the earth and are designated by the word TOHOU, while BOHOU signifies that part of the world which is free from demons.[1] It follows that the first state is that of the infernal cohorts, so confused with matter that they formed one body therewith. A separation was accomplished by the fire which is referred to under the name of darkness, when it is said that " darkness was upon the face of the deep." [2] But to make the clarification complete, the Holy Spirit brooded upon the face of the waters.[3] It is added that so long as the purification was unfinished, the spirit of the demon still interposed between heaven and matter, to deprive man of the pure vision of God [4]—another suggestion that the history of creation is one of states of the soul. Unfortunately the ZOHAR—amidst all its casual information of this kind—does not furnish one per cent. of the materials necessary to elucidate it at length, and the same remark applies to the general history of election of which it is a part, so that this phase of the Secret Doctrine cannot be developed.

We shall meet with the Serpent and Samael again in the next chapter and shall ascertain after what manner they enter into the Mystery of Sex. As a conclusion to this part, it seems desirable to say that the Zoharic prince of demons is never compared to the morning star or to any other luminary in heaven. I do not remember that the word הילל=Day-Star= Lucifer occurs anywhere in the text as a synonym of Satan. Finally, the world will not be set free from the serpent until the coming of Messiah the King, who will cast down death for ever.[5] As to what may happen thereafter, the mind of the doctors is divided, which it seems to have been invariably

---

[1] There is apparently a light of the world below which is in separation from the world above, and this is said to generate demons without number.—Z., Pt. I, fol. 156b ; II, 214. As regards TOHOU and BOHOU, it may be useful to compare Book VI, § 2.

[2] Gen. i. 2.

[3] *Ib.*

[4] Z., Pt. I, fol. 16a ; I, 94–96.

[5] Z., Pt. I, fol. 113b, 114a ; II, 58, 59. The authority is Is. xxv. 8 ; Zech. xiii. 2. The point is that Samael is the death-angel, and it is one of those places in the ZOHAR where he and the serpent on which he rides are identified on account of their union.

on all matters that concern eschatology. We shall have to take back into our hearts every primitive form of thought before we shall consent to believe that the Holy One, blessed be He, created the tempter-spirit so that He might put man to the test[1] ; but this is one of the theses, as we have seen, and it follows in course " that he is also God's minister." Perhaps it is for this reason that there is a counsel not to affront the demon, since in virtue of such an imposed office he would be saved, like the executioner. Moreover, as the infernal male and female principles symbolise the Sex Mystery in the deeps of corruption, we have to remember that even in these deeps it is a reflection of the Mystery that is on high, and to say that it may not be without an inward element of redemption seems to connect with the truth of things, working towards a justification of the Divine Ways in all the quarters of the universe.[2] *Si descendero ad infernum, ades.* One of the fragmentary texts incorporated with the ZOHAR affirms there- fore that even the evil spirit will be restored at the end of days.[3] The inference is extracted with an all too common perversity out of the words : " He brought back all the goods, and also brought again his brother Lot." [4] The imputed authority matters nothing and the idea which has begotten the interpretation signifies everything. I have indicated that the ZOHAR as exegesis was conceived and born in a house of distraction.

III.—THE FALL OF MAN

Matthew Arnold was of opinion that it was impossible to dispense with Christianity or to be satisfied with it in the current and accepted forms. A similar impression has been created through all the Christian centuries by the Myth of Paradise, and especially that part of it which concerns the Fall of Man[5] ; but it will be understood that I am not

---

[1] Z., Pt. I, Appendix III, THE SECRET MIDRASH, fol. 2a ; II, 686.

[2] Between good and evil the mediating and reconciling principle is held to be woman- hood, and hence it is said—in rather cryptic language—that the Spirit of Good and the Spirit of Evil can only abide in harmony so far as the female is between them, she having part in both. It is then only that the Spirit of Good, which constitutes pure joy, attracts the female and thus preponderates over the Spirit of Evil.—*Ib.*, fol. 49a ; I, 284. Cf. *ante*, p. 269.

[3] *Ib.*, SITHRE THORAH, Pt. I, fol. 287b ; II, 664.

[4] Gen. xiv. 16.

[5] There is a feeling at the present day in certain schools of interpretation that the idea of a genuine difference between man in the first estate of Paradise and in the exile of the world beyond has no authority in Scripture and that it was adopted by the

alluding to persons for whom it is folk-lore or fable. As to these there is no difficulty : it is only among those who regard it as in some sense a veil of man's spiritual history that the problems offered by this myth are of real consequence, and it is these naturally who have expended their skill in seeking to construct it rationally. Very few have done otherwise than distort the materials placed in their hands, so that if it is hard to be satisfied with the plain story, it is impossible to accept the attempts by which the literal body has been buried, so that it might be raised a spiritual body. The resurrections are worse than the form which used to move among us in some manner of the life of faith. I believe that at this day the Latin Church imposes on its members an acceptance of the simple story, exactly as it is given in Genesis, so that it is a clear issue and deserving of our respect as such.[1] It is to be taken or left ; those in the faith take it amidst silence in the heaven of faith, though there may be many wry faces turned to the wall for concealment ; the rest leave it no doubt. I have spent many years among the mystics who have made excursions into this subject and have produced their various versions, " to perplex the sages " and others. The versions stand at their value, and I do not know that there is much to choose between them, from those of St. Augustine to Saint-Martin. Readers who are acquainted with the theses of Jacob Böhme on the Paradisaical state will remember that Adam, in his system, began to degenerate before the specific occasion of his Fall is supposed to have arisen and, as part of his declension, that a state of inactivity supervened.[2] One consequence was that Eve had to be removed from within him and manifested in a mode of separation. I do not know how this is harmonised with the Lord God's statement that

---

Church early in the Christian centuries as a working hypothesis of doctrine. However this may be, the ZOHAR has very plain instruction on the subject, and the present section of our research, taken in connection with that on the Myth of Paradise, will show that a life of glory and divinity was followed by a life of shame. The word Fall is of course technical and as such particular to Christian Theology, with all its cloud of developments, but about that which is meant thereby no question will be found in the ZOHAR.

[1] It makes a clean sweep of the whole fantastic mass of private interpretation and throws us back on the first principles of the story, forbidding us to exercise our personal and putative wisdom above that which is written. While it is not possible to accept the asylum offered, there is no desire to make salvage in respect of the baggage which has been " heaved over among the rubbish."

[2] It is said that the " tincture " of Adam was quite wearied: THE THREE PRINCIPLES, c. 13. The reason is given at length in MYSTERIUM MAGNUM, c. 18, being his hunger to eat of good and evil, not indeed in the mouth but with the imagination.

" it is not good that the man should be alone," [1] nor does it perhaps signify. In any case the provision of a helpmeet did not save him, for in the obscure providence of the dealings woman was the occasion of his literal fall. The Zohar also recognises a gradual degeneration of Adam,[2] because apparently the workings of the beast "more subtle than any" were in process prior to the manifest temptation of Eve. I do not know why a time-limit should be drawn about the story so closely, but it is stated more than once that Adam fell on the very day of his creation,[3] the notion being drawn in the usual inscrutable manner from this text of Isaiah : " In the day shalt thou make thy plant to grow, and in the morning shalt thou make thy seed to flourish," [4] though the reading differs in the Zohar.

It appears that the original union of man, male and female, was apart from fleshly sensation, and it was therefore an union in modesty.[5] When Adam said : " This is now bone of my bones and flesh of my flesh " [6] he was seeking to dispose Eve in favour of such intercourse, because they were one only. It was out of this that the temptation is represented as having arisen, for immediately after these words of tenderness the spirit of evil awoke, to substitute carnal pleasures for its own profit in place of pure affection.[7] The object was also to sully the sanctity above by defiling man below in the first place.[8] As regards what Theology would call the matter of the sin, there is no need to say that the apple is not understood literally.[9] It is called sometimes—as we have seen—the fruit of the vine, that is to say, grapes ; but this is a veil also and is to be understood as the explanation of a certain Mystery of Knowledge, which Knowledge belongs to the dominion of

---

[1] Gen. ii. 18.

[2] Z., Pt. II, fol. 262b ; IV, 295.

[3] Ib., Pt. I, fol. 35b ; I, 219. According to Jacob Böhme, the period was forty days. We shall see elsewhere that the First Sabbath followed the decree of expulsion.

[4] Is. xvii. 11. The Zoharic rendering is : " The day that you have planted, your seed shall produce only wild fruits."

[5] There is an obscure suggestion that children were born to Adam in the Garden of Eden, that is to say, souls, and if they had come with him out of the Garden, man would have had eternal life. He was expelled, however, to engender children outside. —Z., Pt. I, 60b, 61a ; I, 356.

[6] Gen. ii. 23.

[7] Z., Pt. I, fol. 49b ; I, 287.

[8] Ib., fol. 52a ; I, 301.

[9] After the Fall of Man, it is said that the Tree of the Trespass was banished from Paradise, which sounds fantastic ; but the whole Tree is allegorical and moves with man through the places of his exile. See the Cremona ed., Pt. I, fol. 126b.

sex. These are the fruits that are said elsewhere to be agree-able, on the authority of Genesis, but they trouble the spirits of those who make bad use of them, as Noah did in the case of his own vine.[1] He who rode upon the serpent, the Tempter-Spirit or Samael,[2] who is said also to have descended from heaven so mounted, as if he were an accredited messen-ger, approached Eve and testified that the Holy One created the world by help of the Tree of Knowledge ;[3] that by eating thereof and so only was He able to create the world ; and that if the woman ate of it, on her own part, she would attain the same power.[4] In a work so multifarious as the ZOHAR and so free of all responsibility created by the precedents of its own sections, it will be understood how there are alternative accounts as to the kind of temptation. In another case it is said that Eve was seduced by the peculiar atmosphere of the demon which encompassed the mythical fruit, as if it lay in a hot bed ;[5] but this is additional detail rather than alternative. In a third there is exactly the kind of intimation which we should expect in relation to the mystery which the text reads into the myth : it was a seduction arising from the bewray-ment of love, which had not appeared in the world till Adam and Eve were set toward one another, face to face ;[6] it was also an outcome of the blind turning towards conception and generation ; so that in this sense Eve was made victim as a result of her own womanhood. By reason of one or another cause, she decided to taste the fruit, which had the faculty of opening the eyes, in those who approached it, meaning in things concerning the Tree itself.[7] The result was a division between life and death,[8] as if the peace-insuring Middle Pillar had been removed from the Sephirotic Tree and Shekinah had ascended to KETHER, leaving the SEPHIRA MALKUTH

---

[1] Z., Pt. I, fol. 192a ; II, 356. See also Deut. xxxii. 32 : " Their grapes are grapes of gall, their clusters are bitter." And see Z., Pt. I, fol. 36a ; I, 225.

[2] *Ib.*, fol. 35b ; I, 221. It is said that all creatures took fright when he appeared.

[3] The allusion is to the Mystery of Faith and Sex ; the universe was a work of generation, and in this sense therefore the testimony of Samael was true, but that to which it was a preface proved—by the hypothesis of the legend—a lying travesty of the true practice.

[4] Z., Pt. I, fol. 36a ; I, 222.

[5] *Ib.*, Pt. II, fol. 203b ; IV, 205.

[6] *Ib.*, fol. 231a ; IV, 253. It is suggested again in this place that Adam and Eve began to engender children from the moment that they were put face to face.

[7] *Ib.*, Pt. I, fol. 36a ; I, 224.

[8] *Ib.*, fol. 36a ; I, 225. The threatened death seems always to have been understood spiritually. It is said elsewhere that " the Serpent takes away the higher souls—NESHAMOTH—of all flesh."—Z., Cremona ed., Pt. I, fol. 28a.

without God in the world. There was division also between the Voice and the Word, so that the Voice spoke yet the Word was not uttered.[1] God was asleep therefore in the heart of man. To speak of events like these in whatever immemorial past is of course to remind the Sons of the Secret Doctrine how it fares with them in the actual present ; and so it is added that since Israel has been in captivity the Voice has been divided from it, whence the Word is audible no longer.[2] The inference is that the Word remains in the heart, but the lips which should speak are paralysed.

Recurring to the substitution of a mystical vine for the apple-tree, another tradition certifies that Eve pressed grapes and gave the juice to her husband. The opening of their eyes was to behold all the ills of the world.[3] I suppose that I need not specify in what sense these grapes are to be understood as a sex-symbol, and it follows that she shewed Adam how they might be enjoyed. Obviously, according to this version—*Traditum est genitales partes adæ existere,* in some sense, at that period, though neither he nor his wife had as yet been clothed with skins, which are understood sometimes as material bodies. They discerned also their nakedness, and of this fact there are several explanations, the most important of which must be cited. In the act which constituted the trespass they lost that celestial lustre and decoration of sacred letters which had covered them previously and they clothed themselves with leaves of the same Tree of which they had eaten—that is to say, with leaves of the vine or fig ! [4] They knew now all secrets of the lower world—*vel infra cingulum*—and seeing that the leaves of the Tree were the most pleasurable of that region, they sought to acquire force therein by the means thereof.

---

[1] Z., Pt. I, fol. 36a ; I, 225. It was the consequence of separating life from death, the analogy of which is separation between man and woman by the chastisement of the *menses,* so that she is in hiding like the moon, which is taken away from the heaven of stars for a week from month to month. But I question whether the symbolism is true in this case, for as the phenomenon concerned is a line of demarcation in sex between woman and the world of animals, it is in the proper sense a dignity rather than a punishment.

[2] The suggestion comes from Ps. xxxix. 2 : " I was dumb with silence. I held my peace, even from good."

[3] Z., Pt. I, fol. 36b ; I, 226.

[4] These leaves are said in more than one place to signify demons, meaning probably the evil side of fleshly desires. It is difficult not to think that the Doctors of the Secret Law who invented a cloud of parables to explain the parables of Scripture in its literal sense had a meaning behind this grotesque woof of symbolism, and sometimes it shines through the texture.

Another account renounces symbolism utterly, so that he who runs may read. " And when the woman saw that the tree was good for food and pleasant to the eyes . . . she took of the fruit thereof, and did eat." [1] These words are held to designate the first union of Adam and Eve. [2] " She consented originally to union as a result of her reflections on the values of conjugal relations and by reason of that pure affection and tenderness which united her to Adam." [3] But the intervention of the serpent had as its result that Eve " gave also to her husband with her," which means that their conjugal relations changed and that she filled him with carnal desires. [4] Henceforth desire was first on the part of the woman, she alluring the man. This evil notwithstanding, the acts performed between them subsequently were in correspondence with those which obtain above, for the Spirit of Evil imitates the Spirit of Good, and that which it occasions below in malice the spirit of good fulfils in holiness above. This correspondence implies, however, " a sublime mystery," which is said to exceed the capacity of most men. [5] When Adam and Eve had sinned the Holy One stripped off the cuirass formed by the light of the sacred letters with which they had been invested : it was then they saw that they were naked. [6] Previously the cuirass had shielded them from all attacks, whilst they were free therein. " And they sewed fig-leaves together and made themselves aprons." [7] This means that they betook themselves to the delights of the lower and material world, leaves of the Tree of Good and Evil, fleshly pleasures and the consequences thereof. [8] But it is to be observed that the evil is not without the good in the Tree of Knowledge : it was the profanation of a Great Mystery, but the seeds of redemption remained. It is for this reason that

---

[1] Gen. iii. 6.

[2] Z., Pt. I, fol. 49b ; I, 287.

[3] I have put this sentence literally, to shew that the early Victorian accent existed prior to the congeries of motives and manners belonging to that period. This statement is by allusion to that which remains after due allowance has been made for the habit of paraphrase which beset the French translator De Pauly.

[4] Z., Pt. I, fol. 49b ; I, 287, 288.

[5] Z., Pt. I, fol. 49b ; I, 288. It is obvious *ex hypothesi* that the correspondence existed previously in the putative spiritual intercourse already mentioned, and the fact that the likeness remained in the alleged grosser union constituted its title to redemption. That the Sons of the Doctrine practised that which they regarded as the path of its transmutation we shall see later.

[6] *Ib.*, fol. 53a ; I, 307.

[7] Gen. iii. 7.

[8] Z., Pt. I, fol. 53b ; I, 307.

the Zohar discerns a promise of salvation hidden in the words : " And the Lord God commanded the man, saying, Of every tree of the garden thou mayest freely eat : but of the Tree of the Knowledge of Good and Evil, thou shalt not eat of it : for in the day that thou eatest thereof thou shalt surely die." [1] The interpretation itself is extracted against all simple sense and reason ; but the fact remains that the Sons of the Doctrine recognised a way of escape.[2]

A third version affirms that the forbidden fruit signifies woman herself,[3] and the versicle appertaining hereto is : " Her feet go down to death ; her steps take hold on hell." [4] But we know that the extract applies only to a " strange woman," and the application must have reference to intercourse in unredeemed bonds of the body of death, as if the *ficus religiosus* of the Tree of Life had become the barren figtree which Christ cursed, or as if the letter of the Law remained without one vestige of its spirit. Woman is also signified by the Garden,[5] when it is said : " And a river went out of Eden to water the Garden." [6] Prior to the trespass this river penetrated into the woman and irrigated her waters. It is added—obscurely enough—that when men are in such a degree of sanctity there is perfect unity, and of this unity it is said : " In that day there shall be one Lord, and His Name one." [7] Subsequently to their sin the Holy One clothed Adam and Eve with vestments belonging to flesh alone.[8] The suggestion is that previously the flesh was glorified by

---

[1] Gen. ii. 16, 17. This was prior to the creation of Eve, according to the literal account in Genesis and therefore, as a technical point, it is to be noticed that he alone was commanded and he alone forbidden.

[2] Z., Pt. I, fol. 35b ; I, 219.

[3] *Ib.*, fol. 35b ; I, 220. The Tree is said, moreover, to signify man. *Ib.*, fol. 35b ; I, 222. It must follow in the sense of things that, in this case, the forbidden fruit is an act common to man and woman. It is not less certain that in the logic of such symbolism the Tree of Life is another postulated act performed by male and female according to a law and life of perfection. I must add, after weighing all the counter-symbolism, that we must be on our guard how we accept in all its literal bearings the somewhat casual and certainly isolated suggestion that the forbidden fruit was woman. It is true in a certain sense, but that sense postulates the kind of relations between the woman and the serpent, between the man and Lilith, of which we hear otherwise, and which is the recurring symbolism. I think, in conclusion as to this matter, that woman was the forbidden fruit in the same way that she is said to be the Garden of Eden. Here again there is a sense in which the statement is true assuredly : she is the Garden in the Kingdom of Malkuth and she is meant to become the Garden in Binah when man has been redeemed in her and she in man ; but this is high mysticism and would be nonsense according to the letter, if it were so taken.

[4] Prov. v. 5.
[6] Gen. ii. 10.
[5] Z., Pt. I, fol. 35b ; I, 221.
[7] Zech. xiv. 9.
[8] Z., Pt. I, fol. 36b ; I, 226, 227.

light of the spirit; but what is stated otherwise is that they had garments of light, thanks to which they were raised above the higher angels—who had recourse to them in order to enjoy light.[1] A non-Zoharic tradition declares that the beauty of Adam was reflected from the glorious Throne, while the beauty of Eve was such that no creature could look on her. Even Adam could not do so till after the trespass, when both lost their supernatural loveliness.[2]

According to yet another account, the sin of Eve was one of separation, and this would no doubt have been endorsed by the Böhme school of Christian Mysticism. Separation, on the other hand, according to the ZOHAR, designates death.[3] This is on the one side, and on the correlative it is said elsewhere that when Adam ate of the Tree of Good and Evil he provoked the separation of woman from man.[4] On the day of transgression both heaven and earth sought to flee away, because they were established only on the covenant of God with man, as it is written: "If my covenant be not with day and night, and if I have not appointed the ordinances of heaven and earth,"[5] &c. When Adam forsook the way of faith and the Tree which is the synthesis of all trees, he lapsed from a region of stability into one susceptible of variation, exchanging life for death.[6] The Tree of Life preserves all who are attached to it from death for ever. Humanity was made originally in the likeness of the Elohim, which likeness was obscured by the Fall, so that the faces of men were transformed, with the result that they began to fear the beasts who had been afraid previously of them.[7]

I will put separately another intimation which is distinct

---

[1] Z., Pt. I, fol. 36b; I, 226, 227. Towards the close of the ZOHAR, Rabbi Eleazar, in the course of a discussion with another doctor of the Secret Law, allows that Adam and Eve were clothed with garments of skin before the Fall, but they were then glorious vestments which became gross subsequently. He adds that their eyes were opened by the trespass to the material form of this world, whereas previously they had beheld in all things only the celestial side.—*Ib.*, Pt. III, fol. 261b; VI, 11.

[2] *Ib.*, Pt. III, fol. 83b; V, 227. The physical beauty was theirs afterwards and is the subject of several allusions.

[3] *Ib.*, Pt. I, fol. 12b; I, 70, 71.

[4] *Ib.*, fol. 53a; I, 306. The intention may be to signify that the union of physical intercourse is of times and seasons only, but above it there is a spiritual union, once enjoyed by man, and this is unceasing, like that of Jehovah and Elohim. We have seen that this union is postulated in a pre-natal state, and it may well be that the myth of the Earthly Paradise is an allegory thereof, embodying a delineation of things which led up to the life of earth.

[5] *Ib.*, fol. 56a; I, 321, 322. Jer. xxxiii. 25.

[6] *Ib.*, Pt. III, fol. 107a, b; V, 269, 270.

[7] *Ib.*, Pt. I, fol. 71a; I, 419.

from these and belongs to a variant order of symbolism, though it seems to me a moral consideration rather than a secret doctrine. It depends from the reverie that innumerable pleasant odours are diffused for ever throughout the Garden of Eden, to prepare the precious vestments of the soul which are formed from the good days spent by man on earth.[1] "And they knew that they were naked."[2] This means, according to tradition, that they were aware of being without the precious vestures which are formed of stainless days.[3] As a result of the trespass, no such day was left to Adam, and it is in this sense that he was naked.[4] When he repented, the Holy One clothed him with other garments, but they were not garments of days.[5] If, however, the garments of skin are on the whole to be understood as vehicles of manifestation, material in place of spiritual bodies, the question of nakedness remains in the absence of a covering belonging to the origin of artifice. Alternatively, if the bodies were not already of flesh, in what sense did the trespass open the eyes of Adam and Eve to the fact that they were naked? There are two places in which the garments of skin are said to be robes of glory with which they were clothed by God, in which they left Paradise, in virtue of which they resembled those who are on high, and wherein they were ultimately buried.[6]

There is one more point of view before I come to the suggestion in chief of the story. It is said that when Adam sinned the evil serpent cleaved to him and defiled him, as well as all future generations.[7] The serpent was able to penetrate

---

[1] The Earthly Paradise is a place of sojourn for the departed on the return whence they came.

[2] Gen. iii. 7.

[3] Z., Pt. I, fol. 224a, b ; II, 482, 483.

[4] It is rather an unhappy similitude, for so long as he had not eaten of the Tree of Knowledge, he was incapable of good days, and furthermore—according to another myth—that which was stripped from him was a robe of glory, wherein he had no need for the vesture of stainless days.

[5] Z., Pt. I, fol. 224a ; II, 483.

[6] Ib., Pt. II, fol. 39a, 39b ; III, 184, 185. They were permeated with the odours of Paradise. See also ib., Pt. III, fol. 261b ; VI, 11, already quoted.

[7] Ib., Pt. I, fol. 53b ; I, 309. As regards the serpent, it is said—Cremona cd., Pt. I, fol. 28a—that Samael descended with all his hosts, and he sought upon the earth a companion like unto himself, but it had an appearance even as a camel. This curious comparison is based on the fact that the Hebrew G M L means camel when certain vowel points are added to these consonants, and reward or recompense with others. The significance of this is developed in the PEKUDE section of the ZOHAR, commenting on Gen. xxiv. 64 : " And Rebeccah lifted up her eyes, and when she saw Isaac, she lighted off her camel." The camel is here said to signify the mystery of death, referred to in Prov. xix. 17 : " That which he hath given will He pay him again." The connecting idea is, firstly, that reward, in the sense of retribution, came into the world by

secretly into man's interior, and Adam submitted to this so that he might know the mysteries of things below. The serpent shewed him all the pleasures of the world [1]—presumably as Satan took Christ into a high mountain whence He beheld all the Kingdoms. These intimations depend from a thesis which recurs many times in the ZOHAR. It is testified by the colleagues that the Fall of man was one of sin with a woman,[2] in the normal sense which attaches to this expression. It is added almost immediately that sexual desires have caused all evils, but a correction or modification follows in the course of debate—namely, that in themselves they are good or evil according to the spirit which inspires them. Now, seeing that it is to Eve that sin of a sexual order was first imputed, the question is who instructed or initiated her? The answer is that the serpent—meaning Samael—had " criminal relations " with her and injected his defilement into her,[3] Adam not being affected until she communicated in turn to him.[4] She cohabited with Samael, who corrupted her and by him she became with child, bringing forth Cain.[5] It is obvious that this is in clear contradiction to the text of Scripture, which says : " And Adam knew his wife Eve ; and she conceived, and bare Cain." [6] But the anomaly is so glaring that it must be assuredly of set purpose, or, in other words, that to develop the sexual nature of the Fall the history on which it is founded is ignored at need. The ZOHAR is content equally to contradict itself, for it

the serpent, and, secondly, that the peculiar nature of the Fall is indicated by the alleged hidden sense of the term camel, which represents the *pudenda*. Compare Cazotte's DIABLE AMOUREUX, where the impure demon is revealed at last with the head of that animal.

[1] Z., Pt. I, fol. 52a ; I, 301.

[2] *Ib.*, Pt. I, fol. 23a ; I, 142. This transpires in the course of a conversation, already mentioned, between Shekinah and the two fallen angels Aza and Azael. Some of the codices add, as we have seen, that with woman man will repair his fault, which is a very important statement from the standpoint of the Mystery of Faith, and involves the reintegration of nuptial union in the order of Divine things.

[3] *Ib.*, fol. 54a ; I, 311.

[4] *Ib.*, fol. 126a ; II, 101.

[5] *Ib.*, fol. 37a ; I, 230. The story of this cohabitation is of Talmudic origin and will be found in the TRACT SABBATH, among other places. It is also of general rabbinical authority otherwise, and is stated by R. Abraham de Seba in his commentary on the Pentateuch. The MIDRASH RUTH affirms that both Adam and Eve were defiled by the serpent. Finally, it is mentioned categorically in the PARAPHRASE of Jonathan ben Uzziel (Gen. iv. 1) that when Adam knew Eve his wife she had conceived already of the angel Samael. Apparently as a result of the dual intercourse, she brought forth Cain, who is said to have resembled the beings who are above, not those who are below. Eve is also recorded to have said : " I have gotten a man, an angel of Jehovah," and not : " I have gotten a man from the Lord " (Gen. iv. 1).

[6] Gen. iv. 1.

affirms in another place that Adam was defiled by the impure spirit before his union with Eve, and the son whom he begot in this State of impurity was from the left side : so was Cain born. But when Adam repented he engendered a son from the right side : so was Abel born.[1] It is of course arbitrary to postulate such repentance between the two nativities, rather than before or after. All that we know from the text of Genesis is that at the birth of Cain, Eve was of opinion that she had " gotten a man from God." [2] Another account, on the authority of Rabbi Eleazar, recurs to the earlier thesis, specifying that Cain was begotten from the serpent but that after intercourse with Adam, Eve conceived again, and so brought two sons into the world—one of the works of the serpent and one of the works of Adam. The image of Abel was from on high and that of Cain from below.[3]

We have not finished, however, with the complications of this subject, for another Story recites that the relations of Samael continued for a long time with Eve, who bore him many children—presumably after the expulsion from Paradise.[4] They were not in human likeness. So also, after the death of Abel,[5] Adam separated from his wife and began to receive visits from two female demons, with whom he had relations, and engendered those evil spirits and demons which infest the world.[6] It is pointed out that there is no need for surprise at this, because every man in his dreams sees such women occasionally, observes them smiling at him, and if

---

[1] Z., Pt. I, fol. 54a ; I, 311.

[2] Gen. iv. 1.

[3] Z., *ib*. It will be seen that this is at issue with the PARAPHRASE of Jonathan. According to ZOHAR HADASH, § YITHRO, the seduction of Adam by Lilith and of Eve by her companion Samael caused our mortal condition. This is the sense in which death was brought into the world, " and all our woe." *Ex hypothesi*, the springs of generation were tainted.

[4] Z., Pt. I, fol. 53a ; I, 315, 316.

[5] It is taught, much after the manner of Christian Theology, that if Adam had never sinned man would never have tasted death as the condition of his entrance into the world beyond. But Christian Theology does not encourage us to suppose that in such case the union of Adam and Eve would have produced children—so far at least as I am aware. On the other hand, the separation of the sexes was primarily for this purpose, according to Kabbalism.—See Z., Pt. III, 159b ; V, 412. I should add that in another place one of the doctors maintains that Adam and Eve would have remained alone in the world in the unfallen State, but another answers him that they would have engendered children emanating from the Holy Spirit.—*Ib.*, Pt. I, fol. 61a ; I, 356, 357. See also Pt. III, fol. 189a ; V, 495, 496.

[6] Z., Pt. I, fol. 54b ; I, 314. The Talmudic Story is different in this sense, that the sin of Adam in eating of the forbidden fruit was punished by an excommunication which lasted 130 years, and it was thereafter that he began to engender children in his own image.

they excite his concupiscence they conceive and bear demons. I suppose that one of these demons was the black Lilith and the other Naamah, who are both mentioned in the ZOHAR, though not actually in this connection. We shall see shortly that presumably another Lilith was the wife of Adam in Paradise. Adam remained separated from his true wife for one hundred and thirty years, continuing to engender, and so long as he was defiled by the infection of the impure spirit, he had no desire for union with Eve. It returned, however, when he purified himself, and he begot " a son in his own likeness, after his image "—that is to say, Seth.[1] Dwelling still upon the mystery behind sex, the ZOHAR generalises on this matter, saying that so long as man follows the path which leads to the left side, his desire is towards the impure only, but the just who walk in the right way have children worthy of themselves. The important point to fix in our minds is that the Fall of man was not the result of human intercourse taking place between Adam and Eve but of some aberration in sex variously described, most accounts being exclusive one of another. There is an alternative not mentioned previously which balances the copulation of Eve and Samaël by the relations subsisting for a long period of time between Adam and Lilith amidst all the splendours and perfections of Paradise, prior to the creation of the helpmeet. It was to substitute human for impure pleasures that she was taken ultimately from the side of Adam, and from this point of view we discern another sense in which it was " not good that the man should be alone." [2]

---

[1] Z., Pt. I, fol. 5a ; I, 316.

[2] *Ib.*, fol. 34b ; I, 216. There are many scattered references to this female demon, who—in one of her forms—appears to have been of the Melusine and mermaid type, for when it is said that " God created great whales " (Gen. i. 21), the reference is to Leviathan and his wife Lilith.—*Ib.*, fol. 34b ; I, 213. She is a *negotium perambulans in tenebris*, for she goes abroad in the night.—*Ib.*, fol. 34b ; I, 214. She is the instigator of punishments, clamouring daily for their infliction.—*Ib.*, fol. 106a ; II, 33. She is said to preside over all fish who are charged with missions to this world—presumably other amphibious demons, though the ZOHAR says that they are called " the first-born in the land of Egypt " (Ex. xii. 29). The sacred angels of the waters that are above were separated by God from the emissaries of Lilith in the waters below. It may be noted here that she is distinct from the " adulterous woman " who was the wife of Samael, as the latter is to be distinguished from Leviathan.—*Ib.*, Pt. II, fol. 35a, b ; III, 169, 170. She is termed " servant " in one place, which is in opposition to that servant who is Shekinah. The latter is like the conjugal Venus and presides over the birth of children, but Lilith devours them.—*Ib.*, fol. 96a, b ; III, 387. Also *ib.*, fol. 111a, b ; III, 435. She is the mother of demons.—*Ib.*, fol. 267b ; IV, 301. She is the most terrible of all evil spirits, but she took refuge in the deep when God created and adorned Eve.—*Ib.*, Pt. III, fol. 19a ; V, 51, 52. See also *ib.*, Pt. I, fol. 169b ;

To illustrate further that, from the first page of Genesis to the last of the prophets, the importance of Holy Writ is in its adaptation to the history and election of Israel, it is said that when the Tables of the Law were broken, it was then man perceived that he was naked [1]—as he was literally, according to the account in Exodus. It is said further that the words : " They heard the voice of the Lord God," is an allusion to the voice of God on Mount Sinai. And finally : since the Day when Adam fell the world was in a condition of poverty [2] until the arrival of Noah, who—having offered a sacrifice— restored it to the normal state. Now, it is obvious that there had been sacrifices previously—*e.g.*, the acceptable offering of Abel. There must have been therefore something particular about that of Noah—I mean, in the mind of the ZOHAR—and we shall see in the next chapter that there was something particular also about his drunkenness, which was an exploration of Divine Mysteries. We know the indignity which befell him, and I shall shew presently the kind of sin which led, *ex hypothesi*, to the Deluge. I believe that all these allusions touch upon the same mystery.

The ZOHAR contains no suggestion of importance in respect of the expulsion from Eden or the Flaming Sword.[3] Adam is said to have chanted the 92nd Psalm in his flight and the Sabbath intervened to protect him, so that he was not entirely driven out until the end of that day. I do not know what purpose this version is supposed to serve ; but the Secret Lamp of Israel did not diffuse always the same light. The way of the return to the Garden was barred, lest worse evils might be brought upon the world.[4] The " Flaming Sword which turned every way " [5] signifies angels set over

---

II, 266.—Pt. II, fol. 114b ; III, 442.—Pt. III, fol. 222b ; V, 562. A Talmudic legend relates that Lilith was created from the same earth as Adam and refused in the end to serve him through pride respecting her origin. I should mention that the word which the Authorised Version renders " screech-owl " in Is. xxxiv. 14, and the Vulgate *lamia* is Lilith in the original Hebrew, the root of which is a word signifying night. Rabbi Elias recognised four mothers of demons, namely, Lilith, Naamah, Ogeret and Mahalath.

[1] Z., Pt. I, fol. 28b ; I, 181.
[2] *Ib.*, fol. 63b ; I, 371.
[3] A certain supposed confusion of pronouns in the Hebrew text of Gen. iii. 24. enables the ZOHAR to suggest that it was not the Lord God who drove out Adam but rather that the latter expelled the Divine Being, presumably from his own heart and also, as a manifest Presence, from that world which man had ravaged by his trespass.— Z., Pt. I, fol. 53b ; I, 307.
[4] Z., Pt. I, fol. 53b ; I, 308.
[5] Gen. iii. 25.

the chastisement of man in this world.[1] Now, there is no true grace herein and there is no mystery ; but if the temptation and the Fall signify an aberration of sex, a declension or a materialisation therein, there is no question that the Tree of Life is the perfect way of nuptials ; and the ascent of the Sephirotic Tree, which—according to the Secret Schools—is a return into union, we shall find at the proper time to be a journey in the graces and glories of the Sacred Shekinah, who presides over the intercourse which, if begun on earth, is completed in the World of the Supernals. For there is a grade of perfection attainable in these Mysteries which was known to the Sons of the Doctrine, and in view of it they said that a day shall come when the world will be avenged of the serpent : [2] this will be the day of the coming of the Tree of Life, which will obtain the remission of sins and will enchain the serpent. The male and female will be united in the Garden of Eden as they were before the Fall. But now the nakedness of the natural Adam is a nakedness of good works and of obedience to the commandments of the Law—understood as that Secret Doctrine which is concerned with the Mystery of Faith.[3]

IV.—THE LEGEND OF THE DELUGE

THE way of human generation [4] had replaced the higher intercourse which is outlined faintly, at a far distance and amidst all confusion by the Secret Tradition, and so outlined only in deference to the covenants expressed and implied, because it is admittedly a mystery that cannot be revealed to

---

[1] It is said also to have symbolised the trials with which God overwhelms man, that he may be restored to the way of goodness.—Z., Pt. II, fol. 167a ; IV, 114.

[2] Z., Pt. I, fol. 145b ; II, 173, 174. It is an exceedingly suggestive intimation, and its seeming Christian implicits are plain, almost on the surface. The world will remain in the toils of the serpent until that day shall come when a woman who is comparable to Eve and a man corresponding to Adam shall vanquish not only the serpent but the angel of death and destruction who rides thereon.

[3] It is quite extrinsic to my subject at this point, but as there will be occasion for a subsequent reference, I may add here that Adam and Eve were interred together in a cave having a door which opened on the Garden of Eden ; and there also some of the patriarchs were buried.—Z., Pt. III, fol. 164a ; V, 423. There are several other references.

[4] It should not be inferred that the way of human generation is ever reduced in its importance or tampered with in its high symbolism. This is why I have termed it important to observe that the Fall of man was not a sin of natural intercourse with a woman. Under certain prescribed conditions, that is rather the way of his return into the true likeness of God—though not so much for what it is in itself as for that which it intimates.

the world. The way of humanity had become a sacred way, a sacrament in virtue of its correspondence with things above, in virtue also of its reflections from that which was the design of Nature when it came forth resplendent at its first birth.[1] Had this been maintained there would have been no path of regeneration, for men would have walked in union, as Enoch walked with God. It is implied more especially that in the birth of Seth [2] human generation was uplifted into the sacramental world, and the path of nuptials was followed by the saints of old in accordance with a practice of wisdom which will be indicated hereafter—towards the end of the present study. But it was not the way of the world, and we have next to consider those stages of the downward path which led up to the Deluge, as this is understood in Zoharic Theosophy. It will be found that the mystery of sex belongs thereto, but it is here on the averse side.

In the explanation of this cataclysm the text dwells naturally on the wickedness of man and has the authority of Scripture that it was very great over the whole world. The particular mystery of iniquity indicated by the ZOHAR is peculiar thereto. The patience of God was extended until the evil began to take that form which is described as the spilling of blood vainly on the earth.[3] The sex aberration here designated will be understood by the expression used. It is the crime attributed to Onan, and the Zoharic doctrine affirms that no man who is sullied in this manner shall enter the Heavenly Palace or behold the face of Shekinah.[4] The Shekinah is driven away thereby, and because of its prevalence the world fell into corruption, in part through the sin itself and for the rest by the absence of Shekinah. It was as if the principle of life had been withdrawn or that the loss of the head caused the body to decay. The world had become like

[1] The point is that the ZOHAR postulates a mystery of spiritual intercourse belonging to the state of Paradise and in the body of our present life a natural intercourse which can be raised into a sacrament of things Divine : between these was a sexual iniquity described in the language of earthly lust and constituting the Fall of Man.

[2] Because he only—according to the ZOHAR—was in the image and likeness of his father, who was in the likeness and image of God.

[3] Z., Pt. I, 56b ; I, 326.

[4] Ib., fol. 57a ; I, 327. I believe that some *Theologia Moralis* of the Latin Church is not in agreement with the ZOHAR respecting the nature of the offence recorded in Gen. xxxviii. 9, and offers a particular alternative which there is no need to specify. I mention the matter because the alternative probably represents an old understanding of the subject. For the rest, it may be suggested that the specific enormity is possibly the veil of a larger complex and would include aberrations connected with the cities of the plain and Lesbos.

an unclean woman who has to hide in the presence of her husband.[1] Yet this was not the last state, for a time came when corruption reached such a point that there was neither shame nor concealment longer. The sin of Onan is held to have corrupted the earth as well as man,[2] *quia semen fundebat in terram.* Now, the waters above represent the male principle, while the female principle answers to the waters below, which is a very simple allegory of posture in the act of intercourse. The sin postulated was concerned with the waters of the male principle and it was necessary therefore that the whole contaminated earth should be purified by those of the Deluge.[3] But the waters above, which are spiritual, and the spiritual waters below both concurred therein, for the floodgates of heaven were opened and the fountains of the great deep were broken up.

One explanation of the vicious state of the world is that at the Deluge period it had as yet not been purified fully from the infection of the serpent.[4] The generation was also without faith —more especially concerning the secret subject matter of that which is called the Mystery of Faith. Men were attached to the leaves of the Tree of Good and Evil, meaning the spirit of the demon.

There is something very strange implied in the symbolism of the Ark, and one is inclined to ask : What was this Ark, or who ? It is a symbol of the Ark of the Covenant, and Noah had to be shut up in such a vessel here below because this comes to pass also in respect of the Mystery which is on high.[5] He could not be so inclosed until God had entered into a covenant with him.[6] He was then able to save the world, and this corresponds with the Supreme Mystery. It is said that Noah walked with Elohim, Who is the Covenant of Peace in the world : he was predestined from the day of creation to be shut up in the Ark. But it is unbecoming for a wife to

---

[1] Z., Pt. I, fol. 61a ; I, 359, 360.

[2] *Ib.,* fol. 61a, 61b ; I, 359, 360. This, however, is qualified later on, when it is said that the earth is called corrupt when man is in a state of decadence.—*Ib.,* fol. 62a ; I, 363.

[3] *Ib.,* fol. 62a ; I, 363, 364.

[4] *Ib.,* fol. 63b ; I, 371. The complete purification took place for a moment at the foot of Mount Sinai.

[5] It is obvious that the meaning of this passage is not on the surface. It will be seen from what follows that the Noetic Ark was feminine, because it was a house for those who were saved from the waters of the Deluge, and we know already that a house is always feminine.

[6] Z., Pt. I, fol. 59b ; I, 349.

receive any one as a guest at her house without the consent of her husband, so when Noah proposed to enter the Ark, it was necessary that Jehovah, the Spouse or Master of the House, should authorise his union therewith.[1] It was therefore at the invitation of God that he so entered. The reason is found in the words : "For thee have I seen righteous before me in this generation."[2] But Elohim is the celestial Bride, who is Shekinah, and it was by her permission, as Bride, Wife and Mistress of the house, that he had a permit to leave the Ark when the Deluge was over. It would seem that in some mystical sense he had dwelt within her precincts. After leaving those hospitable quarters, Noah made a present to the lady of the house, but it reached her by the mediation of her Spouse, because Scripture tells us that it was to Jehovah and not to Elohim that Noah erected an altar and offered sacrifice thereon. It was direct, however, from the lady of the house that Noah received his reward, because it is said that Elohim blessed Noah and his children, saying : "Increase and multiply and fill the earth."[3] It follows, as we shall see otherwise, that Shekinah presides over the fruit of nuptials, as well as over the nuptials themselves. In respect of the altar itself, it may be remembered that the ZOHAR has occasional references to an offering made by Adam and to that on which he sacrificed. The Deluge either destroyed or overturned everything, and when the time came for Noah to sacrifice on his part he is supposed to have raised up for this purpose the overthrown altar of Adam.[4] We see that his sacrifice is connected, though obscurely enough, with that Mystery of Sex which is the subject of allusion throughout. This would seem to be the case with every kind of burnt-offering, and it is even said that Leviticus i. 17, should be translated to signify that the holocaust is a woman and as such an agreeable odour to God.[5] The Authorised Version, reads : "A burnt sacrifice, an offering made by fire, of a

---

[1] Z., Pt. I, fol. 67a ; I, 394 ; and *ib.*, fol. 70b, 71a ; I, 418.
[2] Gen. vii. 1.
[3] Gen. ix. 1. The name which the Authorised Version and the Vulgate translate "God" is "Elohim" in the Hebrew. But the name in Gen. viii. 20, 21, which is translated "Lord" in the Authorised Version and Vulgate is Jehovah in the original.
[4] Z., Pt. I, fol. 69b, 70a ; I, 412.
[5] The translators point out that the ZOHAR in this passage alters the sense of Scripture by substituting other vowel-points. But the question for us is whether it succeeds in conveying its own designed intimation. We shall see in due course that Shekinah, the Divine Woman, is termed more than once the Sacrifice of the Holy One.

sweet savour unto the Lord." It is admitted at the same time that the victim of the holocaust is male, according to the text, a male without blemish. It is admitted also that the word translated " burnt " is correct according to the literal sense ; but if this were its true meaning it is argued that the orthography would have been different. The real purpose of the holocaust was the union of the male and female principles, as these should never be in separation. Noah offered a sacrifice because he represented the male principle which the Holy One united to the Ark, the latter representing the female principle.[1]

There are two other points which may be mentioned for the sake of completeness, and the first of these is that the Holy Land was not covered by the waters of the Deluge.[2] An authority is found in the words : " Thou art the land that is not cleansed, nor rained upon in the day of indignation." [3] The second is that the Deluge came to be called the waters of Noah, because he prayed for himself only and not for the world. I believe that this idea attaches to a Talmudic story, for there is no indication in Genesis of especial prayer on the part of Noah. The thesis is, however, that had he chosen he could have prevailed with God to spare the whole creation.[4]

We know from Genesis that Noah planted a vineyard, and according to one Zoharic opinion he transplanted the vine which had grown in the Garden of Eden ; but whether this signifies the Tree of Knowledge does not transpire—except by inference from the legends. According to another view, he moved an ordinary vine of earth to a more favourable place. The fact that Noah pressed the grapes—as Eve is said also to have done—partook of the juice and so became drunken, is affirmed to contain a mystery of wisdom.[5] We have seen that *ex hypothesi* the lady of all our race was making an experiment of knowledge, and we shall understand further that what followed was an intoxication after its own kind. So also Noah was concerned with an experiment, having set himself to fathom that sin which had caused the fall of the first man. His intention was to find a cure for the world,

---

[1] Z., Pt. I, fol. 70a ; I, 413.
[2] *Ib.*, P. II, 197a ; IV, 192.
[3] Ezek. xxii. 24.
[4] Z., Pt. III, fol. 14b, 15a ; V, 43. The manner in which he saved the world, as we have seen that he was supposed to do, proved wanting therefore in the seals and characters of perfection.
[5] Z., Pt. I, fol. 73a ; I, 433.

" in place of Eve and her poison " [1]; but he became drunken by laying bare the Divine Essence without having the intellectual strength to fathom it. This is why Scripture says that he was drunken and was uncovered within his tent. The meaning is that he raised a corner of the veil concerning that breach of the world which ought always to remain secret. The physical symbolism is obvious in this place. Moreover, the tent of Noah was really the tent of the vine.[2]

I do not pretend that the last sentences are intelligible from any point of view, nor that the materials as a whole of this section convey anything of especial importance beyond the postulated experiment made by Noah for the purpose of restoring the Mystery of Sex to its proper place in the spiritual life of man. The rest only continues the tale of lapse and degradation from the perfect union signified by the state of Paradise. I will add here a few vestiges of symbolism on the subject of the confusion of tongues, which was the next event of importance after the Deluge. The builders of Babel are said to have found a book containing certain Mysteries of Wisdom, which book had belonged to the generation destroyed by the Deluge.[3] The text is very loosely worded and it might seem at first sight that it was the primeval memorial of secret knowledge which, as we have seen, was transmitted to Adam and thence to the chiefs of the people, leaders of sanctity in the early generations. I do not think that this is the case, but that it was rather a record of magical art as this was attained by Enos, according to another Zoharic account.[4] It is said that his knowledge and ability in occult science exceeded that of his predecessors from Adam downward, and this is the sense in which we are to understand the scriptural statement that he, Enos, began to " call upon the name of the Lord " [5]—that is to say, he used the Divine Name to compel

---

[1] But not of course Eve apart from the serpent's poison. I cannot help feeling that it would have been a great relief to the Sons of the Doctrine and a material simplification of their system, if they had not been compelled to follow the legend of Genesis which ascribes the Fall to the woman.

[2] Z., Pt. I, fol. 73b ; I, 434. The Ark was the means of transmitting the true knowledge concerning the Mystery of Sex from one epoch of the world to the other. Certain " literati " of the early nineteenth century, like Jacob Bryant, the Rev. G. S. Faber, Godfrey Higgins and Edward Davies seem to have recognised that it conveyed somehow certain profound Mysteries of Knowledge, but of what nature they had no conception.

[3] Ib., fol. 76a, b ; I, 449, 450.

[4] Ib., fol. 56a ; I, 323.

[5] Gen. iv, 26. The Authorised Version reads : " Then began men to call upon the Name of the Lord "—apparently at the time of the birth of Enos, or soon after. The

spirits in accordance with the recognised procedure of magical operations. The progress of this science ended by assuming such proportions that the wicked generation of the Deluge expected to escape Divine chastisement by recourse thereto. With the help of its mysteries they prepared even to make war on the Holy One, which was also the intention of those who planned the tower of Babel.[1] Like their predecessors, they had great trust in Magic : it was enough for them to pronounce words and things were accomplished. But the project had its source in a limited knowledge concerning the Mystery of Ancient Wisdom,[2] and I conclude therefore that there were two primeval books recognised in the legend—one that of Adam and the other one of knowledge which was either evil in itself or could be converted readily to evil.[3] At the dispersion which arrested the building those concerned therein lost even their partial knowledge. The confusion of tongues was of course a punishment adjudged[4] ; but the apocryphal prophecy of Sophonia assures us that at the end of days the Lord will change the tongues of all the people into a pure tongue, so that all may invoke His Name and all pass under His yoke in one spirit.[5] This is quoted by the ZOHAR and is, I think, the only instance in which it cites a scriptural text outside the greater canon.

V.—THE COVENANT WITH ABRAHAM

The considerations arising in the ZOHAR out of the history of Abraham fall into two sections, the first of which is con-

---

Revised Version agrees, but the Vulgate translates the verse in the sense of the Zohar : *Iste—i.e.*, Enos—*cœpit invocare nomen Domini.* I should mention that the ZOHAR always recognises the claim of Magic as the art of a secret power, but, as we shall see more fully, it is condemned in all its branches and all its modes.

[1] Z., Pt. I, fol. 75b *et seq.* ; I, 445, n.

[2] *Ib.*, fol. 76a ; I, 447.

[3] It must be admitted that this does not agree with a statement in fol. 76a ; I, 446, where it is said that the celestial book containing the Mystery of Wisdom was transmitted by Adam to other men who penetrated this Mystery, and seem to have imitated God thereby ; but this is not in agreement with the succession of the keepers of the treasure, already enumerated.

[4] The union between thought and the word already mentioned seems to have been symbolised by the original existence of one language only. When men became separated from God, unity was no longer possible among themselves. The plan of Babel was elaborated with ingenious perversity, as the builders desired to quit the celestial domain for that of Satan and so substitute a strange glory for the glory of God.

[5] But the Vulgate rendering of the PROPHETIA SOPHONIÆ reads, *Quia tunc reddam populis labium electum, ut invocent omnes in nomine Domini, et serviant ei humero uno.* This is rendered by the revised Douay version : " Because then I will restore to the people a chosen lip, that all may call on the name of the Lord, and may serve Him with one shoulder."

secutive, coherent in a certain sense and of great length, but it is not of our especial concern, while the second, on account of its content, is scattered throughout the text and is of prime importance to the subject of this study. The first may be said to open with an interpretation of the call that came to the patriarch, in answer to which he left " the land of his nativity, in Ur of the Chaldees " [1] and entered into the land of Canaan. The journey was literal no doubt for the doctors in Kabbalism and stood as such at its value, but it was also a mystical travelling, and in this respect it belongs to a higher currency. Abraham had been endowed with a spirit of wisdom [2] and by the use of its talents had attained a knowledge of the celestial chiefs [3] who govern the various divisions of the habitable world.[4] He had gone further also than this, having discovered that Palestine was the centre of the earth, as well as the point of departure in its creation. He had not as yet ascertained by what chief it was ruled but concluded that such a president must be head over all the cohort. The study of the Holy Land was therefore the intent of his journey and he drew for the purpose on all his stores of astrological knowledge, but still was unable to penetrate the essence and importance of that Supreme Power which ruled the worlds innumerable and was postulated in his mind as the Spiritual Chief of Palestine. When at the end of his resources, however, the Holy One manifested on His own part, counselling that he should enter into himself, learn how to know himself and forsake all the false occult sciences to which he had recourse previously. This is another sense in which he was to come out of his own country. The words : " Go into a land that I will shew thee " [5] mean that Abraham was to be occupied henceforth only by those things which God would make known to him, though the essential nature of the Supreme Power which rules the world could not be included in the revelation, being above human understanding. It was there-

---

[1] Gen. xi. 31 ; xv. 7.
[2] Z., Pt. I, 77b, 78a ; I, 457.
[3] It is not quite certain whether this carries the implicit that he was addicted to the kind of Magic which is an art of dealing with spirits and is usually called ceremonial because it follows a ritual and prescribed verbal formulæ. If so, the sequel shews that he was held exonerated in virtue of his intention.
[4] Z., Pt. I, fol. 78b ; I, 457.
[5] Gen. xii. 1. The direction to leave his country signified that he should abandon his studies of the moral influences connected with different regions ; to leave his kindred was to abandon the science of astrology ; to leave the house of his father was to cease from the manner of life observed therein.—Z., Pt. I, fol. 78b ; I, 458.

fore a journey in the Divine obedience rather than one of the soul in God ; but this path of conformity is itself a ladder of sanctity, by which man can be united to the Holy One, and is indeed the one way of our ascent. Abraham went up this ladder stage by stage [1] until he attained that point which was designed in his case, as it is written : " And Abram journeyed, going on still toward the South " [2]—being the Holy Land, wherein he was to reach the highest degree of holiness. But it is said that there was famine therein, which means that the country was not as yet consecrated, and he proceeded therefore to Egypt which is assimilated to the spiritual Garden of the Lord,[3] for it is written : " As the garden of the Lord, as the land of Egypt." [4] Abraham knew the mystery of this Garden,[5] the degrees of which are in correspondence with those that are below—that is to say, with Egypt, which is therefore said to be assimilated. But the nearer that he drew to Egypt the more did he cleave unto God. This notwithstanding, as the journey had not been authorised divinely, he was destined to suffer therein in respect of Sarah.[6] It is stated in this connection that Abraham had lived so modestly with his wife, and in such holiness, that he had never looked upon her face previously. Only as they drew near to Egypt did she raise a corner of her veil, and then he saw that she was fair.[7] In Egypt he found a great centre of the occult arts and again betook himself to their study, but this time he penetrated the secret of evil without being led away thereby. He returned thence to his own grade or degree, which is indicated by the words [8] : " And Abram went up out of Egypt . . . into the South " [9]—meaning the inward height of his

---

[1] Z., Pt. I, fol. 80a ; I, 468.

[2] Gen. xii. 9.

[3] Z., Pt. I, fol. 81b ; I, 469.

[4] Gen. xiii. 10.

[5] The knowledge of Abraham was the consequence of his absolute faith in God.

[6] Gen. xii. 14–20. It is said that the Holy one was seeking to prove Abraham and for this reason allowed him to act on his own initiative in visiting Egypt.—Z., Pt. I, fol. 82a ; I, 474.

[7] Sarah was under the protection of Shekinah and during the night that she passed in the palace of Abimelech she was accompanied by angels belonging to the superior degrees, who gave thanks to God.—Z., Pt. I, fol. 82b : I, 476. See also ib., fol. 81b ; I, 470, by which it appears that the beauty of Sarah was a reflection of the Divine Presence. I may mention here that the verbal economy or subterfuge to which Abraham had recourse in respect of his wife and sister occasions no comment in the ZOHAR, although it enlarges on the account and adds miraculous elements. It is affirmed that the description of Sarah as Abraham's sister was a description of Shekinah, who was with her.

[8] Ib., fol. 83a ; I, 478.   [9] Gen. xiii. 1.

sanctity. From this time forward he knew the Mystery of Supreme Wisdom and became the right hand of the world. This is indicated by the words : " From the South even to Beth-el," ¹ which is the integral stone—that stone of the world and Jacob, about which we have heard already. Abraham—in other words—had attained what the ZOHAR understands by perfect faith. But he was yet to proceed further, " going on still toward the South," ² rising from grade to grade, as one experiencing the infinite and winning his aureole.³ So did the Holy One become his patrimony, and after Abraham was parted from Lot he " dwelled in the land of Canaan," ⁴ which is the place of faith.

When the time comes for the ZOHAR to speak of Melchizedek King of Salem it says that his offering of bread and wine symbolised the world above and the world below.⁵ The sense in which he was " priest of the Most High God " is that in the sanctification of himself he raised the world below to the height of that which is above. For once, as it seems to me, the ZOHAR has exceeded its own measures at this point and has announced a spiritual truth, the full purport of which it did not realise. Concerning the mission of the priesthood it gives, however, a proper definition when it says that this conjoins the world below to that which is above by an indissoluble bond.⁶

I believe that I have indicated sufficiently the qualities of interpretation which appertain to the first section in the history of Abraham ; but the second covers that period which opens with the making of the Covenant between God and the patriarch, or the whole of his later history. The subject at this point passes from personal narration to the " token " or signing the Covenant and the mystery foreshewn thereby.⁷

The characteristic physical sign of all Israel on the male

¹ Gen. xiii. 3.
² Gen. xii. 9.
³ Z., Pt. I, fol. 83b ; I, 482.
⁴ Gen. xiii. 12.
⁵ Z., Pt. I, fol. 87a ; I, 502. It seems to follow that according to another manner of Zoharic symbolism bread and wine signify male and female. The bread and wine of Melchizedek were also symbols of nutriment and blessings for the world.—Ib., fol. 87b ; I, 505.
⁶ Ib., fol. 87a ; I, 502.
⁷ I have called Abraham throughout by his name in its later form, but it is said that the addition of the letter HE, by which Abram was transformed, was not added until he had suffered circumcision, and it was thereafter that the Shekinah became attached to him.—Z., Pt. I, fol. 93a ; I, 529. The letter HE was added also to the name of Sarah, as a symbol of the female principle.—Ib., fol. 96a ; I, 546, 547.

side has issued in the ZOHAR from the region of arbitrary ordinance into that of most sacred symbolism. If at first it was a hygienic observance or one that might act as an aid to continence, it has become in the Secret Tradition a seal of purity, and though it is not expressed it is implied indubitably by the text that it had reference also to the purity of womanhood, because her protection was therein. The proof is that, according to the ZOHAR, the male side of humanity in its separation from the female had no true title to the name and prerogative of man. There is little need to add that the woman was not without the man, but this is not discussed in the ZOHAR, for, with all its illuminations and its strong tendencies towards the liberal side, it represents the last development of a purely oriental religion.[1] It remains that while the masculine shares in humanity, it is true man only in union with womanhood.

When Abraham was circumcised[2] he separated himself from the impure world and entered into the Sacred Covenant, into that Covenant on which the world is based ; and seeing that he so entered, it follows that the world is founded on him. Expanding this fantasy it is affirmed sometimes that Genesis opens with the words : " By Abraham God created," &c., and therefore the Covenant of circumcision is the origin of heaven and earth.[3] The HE added to the name of Abram after he had fulfilled the ordinance is said to symbolise the five books of the Law, which are the records at length of the Covenant. But that which begins on earth is raised gloriously into heaven and prolonged through all the worlds. The Sign of the Covenant constitutes the foundation of the Sacred Name and of the Mystery of Faith—the root of the notion being probably the shape of the letter YOD with which the Name commences, or this at least is the material root. It is said further that the Sacred Sign of the Covenant is fixed at the base of the Throne, between the two thighs and the trunk[4] —a reference to the SEPHIRA YESOD, when this is placed on

---

[1] It is said, however, that the Covenant implies the union of the two principles.—Z., Pt. II, fol. 26a ; III, 127.

[2] *Ib.*, fol. 91b ; I, 519.

[3] Z., Pt. I, fol. 93a ; I, 529.

[4] When it is said in Gen. xxi. i : " And the Lord visited Sarah," the Divine Name used in the Hebrew is Jehovah, but according to the ZOHAR it was that Degree of the Divine Essence which was symbolished by the VAU. It is added that all is contained in the mystery of VAU, and thereby all is revealed.—Z., Pt. I, fol. 117b ; II, 69.

the Tree.[1] As the sun enlightens the world, so the Sacred Sign enlightens the body ; as a buckler protects man, so does this : no evil spirit can approach him who preserves it in purity.[2] By the fact of circumcision man enters under the wings of Shekinah.[3] He who preserves the Sign as I have just said, and fulfils the commandments of the Law, is righteous from head to foot, and his life in continence is his title to a part in the world to come.[4] It is said also that so long as a man is uncircumcised, he cannot unite himself to the Name of the Holy One ; but after circumcision, he enters that name and is joined therewith.[5] Those who do not preserve the sign in purity make separation, in a manner, between Israel and the Heavenly Father.[6] All the forces of Nature centre in the organ of the Covenant, and in the metaphysical principle of the Covenant it is said [7] that there was subsequently hidden and enclosed that light created when God said : " Let there be light " [8]—the alleged reason being that it symbolises the fructifying principle, *qui semen injicit fœminæ*. It is this which is called in Scripture " the fruit of a tree yielding seed." [9]

It is counselled :. " Suffer not thy mouth to cause thy flesh to sin," [10] and the exhortation is understood as a restraint placed upon speech lest this should generate evil thoughts, calculated to soil the consecrated flesh which is marked with the Seal of the Holy Covenant. When the Psalmist says : " The firmament sheweth His handiwork," [11] it is to the Mark of the Covenant that reference is made—that is " the work of His hands." So also those other words : " Wherefore should God be angry at thy voice and destroy the work of thine hands ? " [12]—are an allusion to those who keep the Seal in purity. In yet other terms, the firmament publishes the names of those holy men who have lived in chastity, and our part is to plead for their intercession with God, Who hears them always. Their names are written in the Book of God, which

---

[1] Z., Pt. I, fol. 149b ; II, 190. It is very difficult to allocate sporadic symbolism of this kind to its proper source elsewhere in the text, but the allusion is almost certainly to the extension of the Divine Son through the lower SEPHIROTH, having the head in DAATH, as explained in a previous section.

[2] *Ib.*, fol. 8a ; I, 45, 46.

[3] *Ib.*, fol. 95a ; I, 543.

[4] *Ib.*, fol. 162a ; II, 235. The text is : " Blessings are upon the head of the just."— Prov. x. 6. But the head of the just signifies the Sign of the Covenant.—Z., *in loco cit.*

[5] *Ib.*, fol. 89a ; I, 510.

[6] *Ib.*, fol. 189b ; II, 348.

[7] *Ib.*, fol. 1a ; I, 4.

[8] Gen. i. 3.

[9] Z., Pt. I, fol. 1a ; I, 4.

[10] Eccles. v. 6.

[11] Ps. xix. 1.

[12] Eccles. v. 6.

is the great firmament of stars : they are the company which follow the Heavenly Spouse.[1]

It is said otherwise concerning the Sign of the Covenant that holy flesh is marked with the letter YOD,[2] referring to the obvious analogy between the " organ of sanctity " and this letter, when circumcision has been performed upon the first. The letter YOD symbolises also the configuration of the celestial river which is the source of souls. The words : " Sanctify unto me all the firstborn, whatsoever openeth the womb among the children of Israel," [3] is a commentary on the letter YOD, which is the first-born of all the heavenly sanctities.[4]

Finally, there is a curious train of thought which requires to be followed carefully.[5] " Through wisdom is an house builded." [6] This is termed an allusion to the mystery expressed in those other words : " And a river went forth from Eden to water the garden." [7] It is said further : " Thy tabernacle is holy," [8] but our English rendering is not literally the same. This tabernacle is termed the union of all. The verse in question enumerates three enclosures, one within the other—the Courts, House and Tabernacle—and the ZOHAR says, unexpectedly enough on the surface, that whosoever subjects his son to the holocaust of circumcision may be assured that the Holy One will draw the child to Himself and make his abode in the innermost of these enclosures, while the father will earn no less merit than if he had offered all other sacrifices in the world and had raised up the most perfect altar. The explanation of these things can rest only, as I have said, in a most profound understanding of the Mystery of Sex, and the final place of that Mystery is indicated by the correspondence alleged in another part between the Sign of the Covenant and the Sacred Crown.[9]

---

[1] Z., Pt. I, fol. 8b ; I, 48.
[2] Ib., fol. 13a ; I, 74.
[3] Ez. xiii. 2.
[7] Gen. ii. 10.

[4] Z., Pt. I, fol. 13b ; I, 79.
[5] Ib., fol. 94b ; I, 539.
[6] Prov. xxiv. 3.

[8] See Ps. lxv. 4 : " Even of Thy Holy Temple." Compare, however, the corresponding passage in the Vulgate, Ps. lxiv. 5 : Sanctum est templum tuum.

[9] Z., Pt. I, fol. 95a ; I, 542. The following points may be gathered from other parts of the text : (1) The mark of the Covenant is imprinted above as well as on man below ; but this is probably a reference to the mark on the Throne, already given. (2) The Kingdom was removed for a period from David because he had not preserved the sign in perfect purity. (3) He who so keeps it has nothing to fear from severity—i.e., judgment—being united thereby to the Name of the Holy One. (4) He who defiles it cannot aspire to the mark of God, which is royalty and Jerusalem. (5) The

It was said at the beginning of this section that the history of Abraham is for the ZOHAR the actual story concerning the father of nations, and this obtains throughout; but for the great theosophical commentary its living value lies in the way of its understanding as an inward text of election, applicable to every soul in Israel.

VI.—OF MOSES, THE MASTER OF THE LAW

The Biblical story of Moses issues in a mystery, for he "whom the Lord knew face to face," [1] having died in the Lord on Mount Nebo, was also by Him buried, and "no man knoweth of his sepulchre unto this day." [2] But, according to the ZOHAR, the story of Moses begins in a mystery also, for he, about whom it is said that "there arose not a prophet since in Israel like unto Moses," [3] was not in his conception after the manner of men who had preceded or of those who came after him. The distinction belongs more properly to another part of my subject and will be found therein. I will therefore say only that his parents—the "man of the house of Levi" [4] and she who was "a daughter of Levi" [5]—had their hearts uplifted unto Her who is called Shekinah, second of the Divine Hypostases—at the time of that union when it is said that "the woman conceived and bare a son." [6] The consequence of this was that Shekinah reposed on the nuptial bed of his parents. [7] He was therefore born, "not of blood, nor of the will of the flesh, nor of the will of man" merely, "but of God" [8]; and even from the day of his birth the Shekinah never quitted him. [9] He ascended into that region

---

sign is the gate of the body, to hold which in sanctity is to find the gate of heaven always open.—Z., Pt. I, fol. 94a; I, 535, 536; and fol. 150b; II, 193. But that to which all this applies is surely the idea which lies behind circumcision.

[1] Deut. xxxiv. 10.   [2] Ib., v. 6.   [3] Ib., v. 10.
[4] Ex. ii. 1.   [5] Ib.   [6] Ib., v. 2.

[7] See Z., Pt. II, fol. 11a–12a; III, 48–52. It is said in the most cryptic manner of the text that the "man of the house of Levi" was the angel Gabriel, who is called "man," as it is written: "Even the man Gabriel, whom I had seen in the vision at the beginning" (Dan. ix. 21). The house of Levi signifies the Community of Israel—referring probably to the School of Sanctity above in the SEPHIRA BINAH. The daughter of Levi is the soul. The meaning is that the parents of Moses stood for these symbolically.

[8] St. John i. 13.

[9] The father of Moses is said to have been espoused to Shekinah—apparently in the sense that she was attached to or overshadowed him. Otherwise he would have been unworthy to beget the Lawgiver. But it is added that the daughter of Levi whom he espoused was the Shekinah—perhaps in the sense of being her symbol below.—Z., Pt. II, fol. 19a; III, 92.—Ib., Pt. I, fol. 120b; II, 83.

where she is said to extend her wings,[1] as it is written : " He did fly upon the wings of the wind." [2] The Lawgiver is affirmed, moreover, to have been the first man who attained perfection, even as Messiah will be the last [3] ; but there are good reasons—*e.g.*, the story of Abraham—from the standpoint of Zoharic Kabbalism, why it was requisite to qualify this statement, and so it is said elsewhere that he was not perfect in all things, the reason being that he was separated from his wife.[4] There is no authority in the Pentateuch on this subject, but there is that of Talmudic Tradition which says that they ceased to cohabit. It is probably an arbitrary inference from the fact that neither she nor his two sons, Gershom and Eliezer, are mentioned in Exodus or elsewhere after they were brought back to Moses, " when he encamped at the Mount of God " in the wilderness of Sinai.[5] So it is said otherwise that the Lawgiver attained the degree of BINAH but not that of CHOKMAH [6] ; in other words, he did not open the 50th Gate of Understanding which gives upon the path of DALETH, leading from BINAH to CHOKMAH in the Sephirotic Tree.

It is difficult, however, to judge clearly as to the earthly espousals of Moses, according to the ZOHAR, for we learn elsewhere that he separated himself from Zipporah by the ordinance of God, that he might be joined to the heavenly light of Shekinah.[7] Hence it is intimated elsewhere, on the authority of Rabbi Simeon, that to attribute children to him was in some sense beneath his dignity, as he had entered into spiritual espousals.[8] It is a question of the Mystery of Faith and a case of extraordinary exception from the prevailing mind of the ZOHAR, which makes children according to the flesh an indispensable title to union with the glory of that

---

[1] Z., Pt. II, fol. 78b ; III, 329.
[2] Ps. xviii. 9.
[3] Z., Pt. III, fol. 260b ; VI, 7.
[4] *Ib.*, Pt. I, fol. 234b ; II, 523. The explanation is that in order to perfection tnere must be union not alone with that which is above but also with that which is below. A Talmudic Tradition on the subject will be found in the Tract SABBATH, but this is at issue with the ZOHAR as it reckons the fact of his separation among his titles of honour.
[5] Ex. xviii. 5.
[6] Z., Pt. III, fol. 223a ; V, 564.
[7] Z., Pt. III, fol. 180a ; V, 472.
[8] *Ib.*, Pt. II, fol. 69b ; III, 308. The argument is purely casuistic, pretending that Scripture attributes the children of Moses to the mother only, and afterwards—on the authority of Rabbi Simeon, wresting Ex. xviii. 5—maintaining that Jethro brought his own sons to Moses.

Second Hypostasis which stands for the nuptials that are above. It should be understood at this point that the Mystery of Faith consists, according to the French translation of the ZOHAR, " in the union of God with a Female whom He fructifies, after the manner of the union of male and female." This is true assuredly, yet it is only a part of the Mystery, or rather it is the doctrinal aspect, and arising therefrom is a practical side about which we receive intimations at many points of the text, though it enters into complete expression nowhere. Its real nature is the sole end of our research. To conclude as to the marriages of Moses, there was a moment when God said to the Lawgiver : " Let it suffice thee " [1] ; but that which was sufficient, says the ZOHAR, [2] was the prophet's union with Shekinah, to Whom he was nearer in truth than hands and feet, for—as we have seen—they were not in separation prior to his birth in this life. So also he was under the guidance of no angel and no messenger from heaven but under that of God Himself, [3] because God and His Shekinah are one. He represented the male principle, [4] though in virtue of his union with Shekinah he was the light of the moon, the moon being his symbol, for albeit that she and God are one—as I have said—she shines in the light of the Eternal Sun of Justice, more especially in her manifestation below, or in the work of her providence concerning the children of men. It is by Moses that the men of this world are held to have found salvation, for he communicated the vital spirit of the Tree of Life. If Israel had not sinned this spirit would have been preserved for ever in Israel. [5]

There was no servant so faithful as he who is called in the Secret Tradition the Faithful Shepherd. He knew all the celestial degrees and was never tempted to join himself otherwise than to the Highest. [6] His fidelity was greater than that of Ezekiel, for the latter is said to have divulged all the treasures of the King. [7] This statement is not explained by the ZOHAR, [8] but I suppose that it refers to what is called

---

[1] Deut. iii. 26.
[2] Z., Pt. III, fol. 260b ; VI, 7.
[3] Ib., fol. 286b ; VI, 72. This is held to follow from the words : " And he said unto Him, If Thy Presence go not with me, carry us not up hence."—Ex. xxxiii. 15.
[4] Z., Pt. II, fol. 37b ; III, 178.
[5] By virtue of the gracious Law contained in the First Tables.
[6] Z., Pt. I, fol. 76a ; I, 447.
[7] Ib., Pt. II, fol. 5a ; III, 19.
[8] Except indeed to say that if Ezekiel so acted he had authority from the Holy One.

Kabbalistically the Work of the Chariot, being that of Ezekiel's vision, and it seems to me that in this respect the later prophet may be held to deserve exoneration. The title of Moses was that he kept the Secret Law secretly, transmitting it only to the elect,[1] and that he made public the Exoteric Law, which does not contain the Mystery of Faith. In this sense he is called the elder son of Adam,[2] and the reason—which is not readily translatable—is *quia verenda patris sui operaverat*. It is the keeping of the Mystery.

I pass now to the promulgation of the Law, and it would seem that Moses ascended Mount Sinai clothed in the vesture of Shekinah, being that cloud which he entered and in virtue of which it was possible for him to go up.[3] The intention of the Law was to place man under the domination of the Tree of Life,[4] which means that there would have been no mysteries, the Law in this aspect being the Spouse of God, and therefore it is Shekinah herself, or the Mystery of Faith expounded. It is that Mystery which is beheld in contemplating the face of Shekinah, in the state which is eye to eye.[5] If this intention had been fulfilled, there would have been no distinction of an Oral and Written Law, and the question is therefore as to what intervened so that another order followed, contrary to the design of Providence. Now, it is affirmed by the ZOHAR that a change took place in Israel at the foot of Mount Sinai,[6] and this is insisted upon so frequently in terms which never vary as to the alleged fact that one cannot help feeling some principle is involved, some unstated matter of Secret Doctrine. It is testified that Israel was joined anew to the Tree of Life, so that it beheld the heavenly splendours and realised their lights ; it experienced the ineffable joy which fills the hearts of those who desire to know and understand the Supreme Mysteries. The nation was reclothed by the Holy One with that cuirass formed from the letters of His Sacred Name which was the protection of Adam and Eve before their fall. The serpent could cleave no longer to Israel, and it is affirmed to

---

[1] Z., Pt. I, fol. 28b ; I, 179.   [3] *Ib.*, Pt. II, fol. 99a ; III, 398.

[2] *Ib.*   [4] Z., Pt. III, fol. 261b ; VI, 10.

[5] *Ib.*, Pt. II, fol. 40b—THE FAITHFUL SHEPHERD ; III, 189.

[6] *Ib.*, Pt. I, fol. 52a, b ; I, 302, 303. See also *ib.*, fol. 36b ; I, 226. It may be that an arbitrary mode of reasoning is all that lies behind this subject. In the view of the Zoharic doctors, there was something so great and beyond all experience of fallen human nature which it was designed to promulgate in the first Tables of the Law that for them it was the Law of Paradise, and its proposed reception by Israel involved for them a restitution of the paradisaical state.

have disappeared from the world. We muſt underſtand all this as a refleċtion rather of the Divine Intention in its union with the covenant made by the people on their part : " All that the Lord hath spoken we will do." [1] They were washed also and sanċtified. To go beyond this point is unreason, and I know not how the ZOHAR, regarded as commentary, can poſtulate such exaltations of Israel either on the basis of the text or of that which followed.[2] For we muſt remember that in the absence of Moses, and in the uncertainty as to what had become of him, but—*ex hypothesi*—in the absence otherwise of all temptation, Israel adored the golden calf ; the old evil order was thus reinſtated, and I conclude that the serpent returned. It is to be underſtood further that the riot of the feaſt which followed the idol-worship signifies a sexual orgy, so that she who presides over the Myſtery of Sex in sanċtity was driven from the people, and her secret was taken from them. When therefore Moses came down from the mountain carrying the Tables of the Law he broke them in the presence of the people, which, according to Scripture, was because " his anger waxed hot " [3] ; but it is underſtood otherwise in the ZOHAR. The thesis is that the original Tables conſtituted the liberation of all,[4] meaning the separation from that serpent who is called " the end of all flesh." [5] They were formed originally from a single block of sapphire, but God breathed upon them and the precious ſtone was divided into two parts.[6] They were created prior to the world by the coagulation of the sacred dew which is said to fall on the Garden of Apples.[7] They were written before and behind, and were symbolised by the loaves of proposition.[8] It is

---

[1] Ex. xix. 8.

[2] The canon of criticism seems to be reached by the contraſt of two passages of Scripture : " And Israel saw that great work which the Lord did " (Ex. xiv. 31)—which the French translation of the ZOHAR renders : " And Israel saw the mighty hand of the Lord," following apparently the Vulgate (*et manum magnam quam exercuerat Dominus contra eos*)—this being reputed to mean that Israel was able to contemplate the celeſtial splendour and enjoy the vision of the supernal lights. The other passage is this : " And when Aaron and all the children of Israel saw Moses, behold, the skin of his face shone, and they were afraid to come nigh him " (Ex. xxxiv. 30). As to the value of the contraſt, it is enough to point out that the firſt text belongs to the period when the Red Sea had juſt been crossed and has nothing to do with the sojourn at the foot of Mount Sinai, which was reached three months after (Ex. xix. 1).

[3] Ex. xxxii. 19.

[4] Z., Pt. I, fol. 63b ; I, 371.

[5] *Ib.*, Pt. I, fol. 63b ; I, 371. It is underſtood that one consequence of this separation would have been that there should be no more death.

[6] *Ib.*, Pt. II, fol. 84a, b ; III, 347.

[7] *Ib.*, fol. 84b ; III, 348.

[8] *Ib.*, Pt. III, fol. 271b ; VI, 27, and fol. 273 ; VI, 39.

noted in another place that the writing thereon was like black fire on white fire,[1] while according to yet another it would appear that the stones were transparent[2] : the writing in front, or on the obverse side, was read from behind, and that on the reverse, or behind, was read from in front.[3] It is an allusion to the inter-connection of the written and oral Law. The Tables were given to Moses on the Sabbath Day. It is recorded by Scripture[4] that they were cast from the hands of Moses and were broken, and here it is explained by the Zohar that this was because the letters took flight[5]—a device designed to point out that no writing remained upon them which could possibly be seen by Israel in contemplating the fragments. The Tables were broken because Israel was not worthy to profit by them,[6] and that which was shattered is said to have been not only the written but the inward and oral Law.[7] The meaning is that the higher order of liberation and mercy which included these, the revelation of the secret union, was taken henceforth into concealment. The malediction brought upon the world by the trespass, and removed for a moment as the people passed under the shadow of Mount Sinai,[8] descended again upon them. The Tables came out of that region from which all liberties issue and on which they all depend.[9] Over the mystical mountain they diffused a sweet odour, because the sanctities of the world of sanctity inhered therein ; but this passed away when the golden calf was set up for the worship of the nation.[10]

It is recognised by the Zohar that the second Tables embodied another record, which was the Law of opportunism, the Law of mine and thine—of prohibition and denial, being that of bondage. It was sacred after its own manner, because it was a shadow of the first intention, but it reflects at a very far distance. I do not know whether it is affirmed

---

[1] Z., Pt. II, fol. 226b ; IV, 248.

[2] Ib., fol. 84b ; III, 348. See also fol. 84a ; III, 347.

[3] Ib., fol. 84a ; III, 347.

[4] Ex. xxxii. 19. According to the Zohar, they fell of themselves from his hands.— Z., Pt. II, fol. 195a, b ; IV, 188.

[5] Ib.

[6] Ib., Pt. I, fol. 26b ; I, 167.

[7] Ib., fol. 28b ; I, 181. "And the Lord said unto Moses, . . . I will give thee tables of stone, and a law, and commandments which I have written.—Ex. xxiv. 12. According to the Zohar, the word "law" signifies that which is written, while the word "commandments" refers to the Oral Law.—Ib., Pt. III, fol. 40b ; V, 109.

[8] Ib., fol. 26b ; I, 22b.

[9] Ib., Pt. III, fol. 6b ; V, 17.

[10] Ib., fol. 61b ; V, 170.

literally that it is a work of the Tree of Knowledge, but this must be held to follow from numerous impressive intimations. And the Secret Doctrine, with all the Oral Law by which that Doctrine is encompassed, is the Tree of Life ; but the art of its mastery is long, and of all the Sons thereof, of all the heirs at law, I suppose that only Rabbi Simeon could have been said to possess it in the fullness.[1] We know that after him the reign of certitudes was over and the great quest in the hiddenness was pursued in the attitude of groping, not erect as heretofore with the light of sure enlightenment shining from a meridian sun on the heads of the initiates. There is much more that could be said upon this subject, but I feel that my purpose is served. I would add only that amidst the clouded splendours and substitutions of the surface sense we can understand readily the great and pressing need for that study of the inward meaning which is imposed everywhere in the ZOHAR on those who would enter into the real heritage of the elect. To sum up therefore : Moses gave other Tables to Israel, and these were from the side of the Tree of the Knowledge of Good and Evil, from which the Law emanates. The other Tables emanated from the Tree of Life.

I should add that the Written Law seems to be represented by the word DAATH, or Knowing [2] : it is completed by that which is traditional. The Doctrine is sometimes called CHOKMAH, or Wisdom, and sometimes BINAH, or Understanding.[3] The Traditional Law has come out of the Written Law, as woman was brought forth from man, according to the Mystery of the Garden—but this we have seen already. It can exist only in unison with the Written Law ; but I think that the Zoharic treatment of the latter shews that it was regarded rather as a beast of burden—that ass of a certain comparison—already cited—on which the King and Queen of the Secret Mysteries must never be set to ride.[4] There is,

---

[1] I mean, of course, since the days of patriarchs and prophets. As regards the work of this Tree of Knowledge, the Law—from this point of view—was to preserve the species of the chosen people according to the mode of human generation in the world beyond the mystical Garden of Eden ; but the work of the Tree of Life, for those who would dwell beneath it, was one of mystical generation and fruition. It is not suggest d that the Sons of the Doctrine attained the secret in its fullness : they raised a corner of the veil.

[2] Z., Pt. I, fol. 48b ; I, 282.

[3] The reason given is that it has been formed by the " Complete Name "—i.e., Jehovah Elohim, being the Divine Male and Female.

[4] It was like the mule in THE HIGH HISTORY OF THE HOLY GRAAL—" a beast on God's side."

however, one more memorable point concerning the Oral Law, and this is that although it is a balm of life for the just, for the unjust it is a mortal poison.[1] I believe that as much has been said concerning the Elixir of Alchemy. The aphorism is not therefore *vel sanctum invenit, vel sanctum facit*, yet I think that there is a heart of the Doctrine in which the good must fill us entirely, as the student enters more deeply into its understanding. But the sorrow of it is that after eating of the Tree of Knowledge through the years and the ages we are still untutored children, knowing little in the essential manner either of good or evil.

I have reminded my readers already that Moses was interred outside the Holy Land and that "no man knoweth of his sepulchre unto this day."[2] But this sepulchre, according to the ZOHAR, signifies the MISHNA.[3] The Secret Doctrine was interned in the written word—that end of all revelations.[4] But the tradition says that the inner meaning—like the spirit of Moses—remained with the elders and was handed on secretly. The Scripture mentions that "the children of Israel wept for Moses in the plains of Moab thirty days."[5] They might have mourned him, had they known, through the triumphs and the exiles continued thenceforward, for they lost the Secret Doctrine of which he was the personification. It was withdrawn when he left, as if into a secret sanctuary, and no voice issued therefrom until the days of Rabbi Simeon. He was even as a Rose of Sharon which blossomed on the ruins of Jerusalem in the days of Vespasian. I wonder not that there was sorrow on occasions amidst the Sons of the Doctrine, as with Marius over the ruins of Carthage. Moses was the life of the Doctrine, and hence it is affirmed that when he ascended to the height of Pisgah "his eye was not dim, nor his natural force abated."[6] It is recorded also of his figure in its prime that this resembled the sun in its splendour [7] —so perfectly did his moon reflect that glory.

One legend says, however, that he did not die,[8] though the

---

[1] Z., Pt. I, fol. 268a ; II, 633, 634.
[2] Deut. xxxiv. 6.
[3] Z., Pt. I, fol. 27b ; I, 175.
[4] The MISHNAH is the maid-servant who takes the place of the mistress.—*Ib.*, fol. 28b ; I, 175.
[5] Deut. xxxiv. 8.
[6] Deut. xxxiv. 7.
[7] Z., Pt. I, fol. 28a ; I, 177.
[8] *Ib.*, fol. 28a ; I, 176, and *ib.*, Pt. II, fol. 174a ; IV, 129.

text repeats it on an authority which is not its own, and it adds —rather in the manner of a casuist—that no man does who is graced by faith. As a fact, the authority is the MIDRASH RABBA on Deut. xxxiv., and the ZOHAR quotes it again in another place but in a less questioning mood. Perhaps there is a deeper heart of meaning than transpires on the surface, for if we accept the Secret Doctrine on the subject of Moses and the Law there is an aspect of failure about the great mission of the Lawgiver. His stiff-necked generation prevailed against him to the extent that he could fulfil only the shadow of that which he proposed. His intention was to deliver the truth which makes men free, but they were fit only for a substitute. Now, this is set forth very curiously in a single passage of the text, where it is affirmed that Moses sought to bring the Shekinah out of exile, but he failed.[1] The Shekinah signifies here the Secret Doctrine and this implies that the First Tables were written *ad clerum*, but the context was destined to remain in exile so long as Israel was incorporated as a people in its own place and land, while there is no suggestion that the debates of the Doctors brought Shekinah into liberation.[2] It is said therefore, in yet another place, that Moses will return on earth at the end of time to complete his mission by revealing the True Name of Shekinah[3] which is also in the hiddenness, and there is no pretence that it was known to the Doctors. Those whom he brought out of Egypt he will then lead into knowledge. This is why it is exclaimed by Job : " The Lord hath given and the Lord hath taken away : Blessed is the name of the Lord." [4] That will take place which was to have been fulfilled at first : the elect will be set free from the death-angel by the true Tables of the Law. Meanwhile Moses obtained the degree of BINAH—as we have seen—but not that of CHOKMAH. His death was from what is called in the ZOHAR the other side, which means the right side, the left being the side of the serpent.[5] It was not caused by the sin of Adam but by the operation of a

---

[1] Z., Pt. I, fol. 28a ; I, 176.
[2] On the contrary, so long as the Shekinah is in captivity, she is never left by Moses.—*Ib.* That which he did on earth was, however, to attract her to Israel.—*Ib.*, fol. 68a ; I, 400.
[3] *Ib.*, fol. 28b ; I, 180. See also, for the return of Moses, *ib.*, Pt. II, fol. 255a ; I, 602.
[4] Job i. 21.
[5] Z., Pt. I, fol. 53a ; I, 306.

Supreme Mystery. It is also recorded of Joshua that he did
not die through his own sinning, but through the serpent's
counsel to Eve, and this is said to be expressed in the words :
" His servant Joshua, the son of Nun, a young man, departed
not out of the Tabernacle." [1]

VII.—THE TEMPLES IN JERUSALEM

Looking back upon the chequered history of their nation
and on the purport of its life generally, the mystical doctors
of Israel did not fail to discern the uplifting of strange portents
in their spiritual sky, the full significance of which was not
rightly to be recognised beforehand, supposing that they
were real prognostics. It is only after the event that most of
us become wise in this manner. In retrospect the portents
were everywhere ; in retrospect the world's creation, the
great myth of the Garden, the judgment of the Flood, and
the rest of the Divine Providences were like tocsins and
trumpet voices concerning all that was to follow. Not alone
were the seeds therein, but it was Israel delineated throughout.
Abraham might turn to the South and again he might turn
therefrom, but the reason in either case was of that or of this
to come in respect of the twelve tribes. Yet it was not only
to come ; already it was in a sense there, so that the stories of
old look weirdly in a light which suggests that they were
recorded before the events with which they are supposed to
deal. The occurrences of the past were also fateful in
respect of later things that were to come. For example,
when the Tables of the Law were broken by Moses, this is
said to have occasioned the ultimate destruction of the First
and Second Temples.[2]

There are two aspects under which the Temples come
before us in Zoharic texts, and as happens so often, they do
not harmonise together, while it is impossible rather than
difficult to believe that an adjustment can be effected between
them. I will collate them under what may be called the
motives attaching to each. There is firstly that wherein
there is no shadow of vicissitude as to the glory and the
plenary grace which inhered in the design and execution of
Solomon's Holy House.   The Inner Sanctuary constituted the

---

[1] Ex. xxxiii. 11.   [2] Z., Pt. I, fol. 26b ; I, 167.

heart of the world ;[1] the Shekinah dwelt therein after the manner of a virtuous and faithful wife who never leaves the abode of her husband.[2] It was therefore well with Israel during this period. The building plan was sketched by a supernatural hand and was delivered—as we are aware—to David, by whom it was shewn to Solomon.[3] The Temple was erected on seven pillars,[4] the craftsmen following the design, point by point, until the work was finished.[5] There was a sense in which they followed blindly, but there was also another sense in which the work was self-executed. This is suggested by the silent nature of the building, about which we hear in Scripture.[6] The analogy is that of creation, for the world evolved of itself, with God as the beginner of the work.[7] Hence David said : " Except the Lord build the house, they labour in vain that build it." [8] The meaning is that the Lord designed the Temple and the work went on of itself. It is said also : " Except the Lord watch the city, the watchman waketh but in vain." [9] This is Jerusalem in its building. The moon is symbolised as shining at the full during the whole period.[10] The Temple was built for the union of the King and Matrona,[11] God and His Church in Israel. Of the structure in its completeness we are told that the earth inhabited by the Gentiles encompasses the Holy City, which is the centre of the habitable world ; the town encircles the Holy Mountain ; the Mountain surrounds the session-house of the Sanhedrin ; this in its turn stands about the Temple ; and the Temple encompasses the Holy of Holies, where dwells the Shekinah and where are the Propitiatory, the Kerubim and the Ark of the Covenant.[12] The Holy of Holies itself was built on that foundation stone which, as we know already, is held to form the central point of the world. It is identified with the celestial throne of Ezekiel, and in

---

[1] Z., Pt. I, fol. 84b ; I, 487.
[2] Ib.
[3] Ib., Pt. II, fol. 164a ; IV, 107.
[4] Ib. It was guarded by the archangel METATRON.
[5] Ib., Pt. I, fol. 74a ; I, 438.
[6] " And the house, when it was in building, was built of stone made ready before it was brought thither : so that there was neither hammer nor axe nor any tool of iron heard in the house, while it was in building."—1 Kings vi. 7.
[7] Z., Pt. II, fol. 226a ; IV, 247.
[8] Ps. cxxvii. 1.
[9] Ib.
[10] Z., Pt. I, fol. 150a ; II, 190.
[11] Ib., Pt. III, fol. 74b ; V, 203.
[12] Ib., fol. 161b ; V, 416.

appearance it was like a sapphire.[1] Solomon is said to have united Matrona to the Supreme King by the building of the Temple and there was joy everywhere, both above and below.[2] The Temple itself is understood as the spiritual union of male and female apart from any fleshly union.[3] It symbolises therefore the Mystery of Sex at its highest, and this is a point to be memorised in respect of all these reveries.

Here is the first picture, but the alternative as follows is drawn from the FAITHFUL SHEPHERD and not the ZOHAR itself. The First and Second Temples were transitory things in their nature; they should have been the work of God Himself, but because of Israel's sin in the wilderness, the First Temple was built by Solomon, and hence it did not subsist.[4] Contrary to the former intimation, the Lord was not its builder. So also at the epoch of Ezra, again on account of sin, the Second Temple was erected by men and there was no ground of subsistence. It follows that so far no holy house has been built in reality at all,[5] nor has even the city of Jerusalem been as yet constructed. The world is still awaiting that promise of the Lord : " I, saith the Lord, will be unto her a wall of fire round about, and will be the glory in the midst of her." [6] There are suggestions however which go much further than mere questions of substitution. It is said that from the day when the Holy One raised the Supreme Sanctuary the celestial favours were never manifested in the terrestrial Temple, built of stones and mortar.[7] I suppose that here is the house not made with hands which is termed elsewhere a place of spiritual nourishment which the kingdom of heaven accords to those in need of it and that sanctuary which brings all the poor under the shadow of Shekinah.[8]

The Temple of Solomon was a symbol of penitence as well as a house of prayer, and its destruction signifies an impenitent state.[9] The cause of its destruction is said otherwise to have been the separation of the HE and VAU in the Divine Name

[1] Z., Pt. I, fol. 71b, 72a ; I, 425. See Ezek. i. 26 : " And above the firmament that was over their heads was the likeness of a throne, as the appearance of a sapphire stone." This stone, according to the ZOHAR (ib.), signified the celestial throne, and the throne of the vision signified the Traditional Law, while " the appearance of a man " who sat thereon was the Written Law.

[2] Ib., Pt. III, fol. 74b ; V, 203.
[3] Ib., Pt. II, fol. 258b ; IV, 292.
[4] Ib., Pt. III, fol. 221a ; V, 559.
[5] Z., Pt. III, fol. 221a ; 539.
[6] Zech. ii. 5.
[7] Z., Pt. II, fol. 108b ; III, 427.
[8] Ib., Pt. I, fol. 208a ; II, 434.
[9] Ib., Pt. III, fol. 75a ; V, 204.

as the result of sin.[1] The people were sent into exile and the Shekinah was driven out.[2] The VAU went in search of the HE, but she was in a distant place ; it looked towards the sanctuary, but it was burnt ; it looked for the chosen people, but they were in exile ; it turned towards the source of benedictions, but this was dried up.[3] It is said otherwise that the destruction of the First Temple dried up the sources of the Shekinah above and that of the Second Temple those of the Shekinah below.[4] All light was clouded, so that the saints of this world were no longer enlightened.[5] During the exile in Babylon the wings of the Mother in Transcendence did not cover her children ;[6] there was therefore a separation between the YOD and first HE of the Divine Name. The reference is of course to the spiritual state of Israel, and behind it lies a strange spiritual understanding of the Fall of man. During the present and greater exile the Divine Name is divided now as it was divided then,[7] albeit that which it signifies is one eternally above. In another form of symbolism the First Temple was destroyed because it wanted light,[8] which was absent also from the Second Temple, but in a still greater degree, the Second Temple signifying the fleshly union of male and female.[9] The priests of the First Temple ascended on the walls of the Sanctuary, holding their keys in their hands and said to God : Hereunto we have been Thine administrators ; henceforth take back Thy possessions.[10] The sun turned away from the moon and enlightened it no longer ; there was no day without maledictions and sufferings.[11]

These are the lamentations of the ZOHAR over its Holy Places and Houses ; but another day will come when the moon shall resume its primal light.[12] It will be that period

---

[1] Z., Pt. I, fol. 122a ; V, 316.
[2] Ib., fol. 75a ; V, 204.
[3] The reason was that the male was united no longer to the female.—Ib.
[4] Ib., Pt. I, fol. 255a ; II, 601.
[5] Ib., Pt. II, fol. 9b ; III, 40.
[6] Ib., fol. 9b ; III, 39, 40.
[7] Ib., fol. 9b ; III, 41.
[8] Ib., fol. 179b ; IV, 150. The obvious commentary hereon is that Shekinah, by the hypothesis at least, was reigning on the Mercy Seat.
[9] Z., Pt. II, fol. 258b ; IV, 292.
[10] Ib., Pt. I, fol. 202b, 203a ; II, 406. This is " the burden of the valley of visions."— Is. xxii. 1.
[11] Ib., fol. 181a, b ; II, 315.
[12] Ib., fol. 181b ; II, 316.

mentioned in Scripture : " Behold, My servant shall deal prudently, he shall be exalted and extolled and be very high." ¹ The reference is to the Messianic epoch, when the world will be restored, impurity will disappear therefrom, and death shall be cast out for ever. The Holy One will remember His people Israel and the Temple shall be rebuilt.² Formerly it was based on severity and wrath, but it will be restored in charity and will be founded thereon.³ Meanwhile, since the destruction of the Sanctuary here below, the Holy One swore never to enter the Jerusalem above until Israel returned into the Jerusalem below.⁴ No blessings have gone forth, either in the world above or in that which is below, for these worlds depend on one another.⁵ The consolation of the elect is however that, in the absence of a place of sacrifice, devotion to the study of the Law will bring the forgiveness of sin more readily than the burnt-offerings of old." ⁶

VIII.—THE COMING OF MESSIAH

There is no question that the Kabbalistic teaching concerning a Deliverer to come should begin by a consideration of Talmudic intimations on the subject ; for these are many and important within their own measures. There is unfortunately no space for such an extension of the materials already in my hands, but there are several sources of information which are open to any reader, and indeed the whole subject is available if he can have recourse to the French rendering of the JERUSALEM TALMUD ⁷ and even to the unscholarly English version of the BABYLONIAN TALMUD ⁸ which appeared some years since in America. Outside this question of the past, the first thing for us to realise on our own part is that there is not one line, and much less one page,

---

¹ Z., Pt. I, fol. 181b; II, 316; Is. ii. 13. See also Gen. xxiv. 2.
² Ib., Pt. I, fol. 134a ; II, 128.
³ Ib., Pt. II, fol. 59a, b ; III, 263, 264.
⁴ Ib., Pt. I, fol. 231a ; II, 511.
⁵ Ib., fol. 70b ; I, 415.
⁶ Ib., APPENDICES III, SECRET MIDRASH, fol. 6a ; II, 680.
⁷ M. Schwab : LE TALMUD DE JÉRUSALEM, 11 vols., Paris, 1871-1889, 8vo. See also LE TALMUDE DE BABYLONE, traduit par l'Abbé Chiarini, 2 vols., Leipsic, 1831. It embodies a condensed account of both recensions and may serve some general purpose.
⁸ New edition of the BABYLONIAN TALMUD : English Translation. Original Text edited, formulated and punctuated by Michael L. Rodkinson, vol. I, TRACT SABBATH, 1896. In all 18 volumes, various years.

in the ZOHAR which can be constructed according to its proper
sense on the assumption that a Messiah has appeared already
in Israel, while there is consequently nothing that can be
applied to a Second Advent of the Christ of Nazareth. These
things are dreams, and recent pleadings on the subject are if
possible of less consequence than those of the old scholars
who filled Europe with their debates in the sixteenth and
seventeenth centuries.[1] The points of analogy between
Kabbalistic and Christian doctrine are many and eloquent in
their way, but they belong to another order. There is an
attractive hypothesis with which I shall attempt to deal later
on, and its whole design is to construct Zoharic Theosophy in
a direction opposite hereto, or not only in a Christian sense but
in one which would place the texts under the particular
obedience of Latin Theology ; and I who, of all things else,
would desire, were it possible, to look through such enchanted glasses, have concluded that there is no evidence, so I
would therefore warn others. It should be added in justice
to the interests at large that the Roman Church is much too
wise to lend countenance—officially or extra-officially—to the
interesting view, which is therefore the outcome of private
zeal only.

The first question which concerns us is that of Messianic
expectations in mystical Israel. The elect—and if these are
more especially the Sons of the Doctrine it is in the sense that
the greater imitate the lesser, meaning the race of chosen
people—the elect must hope always for the coming of the
man of holiness,[2] for it is said : " I will wait upon the Lord,
that hideth His face from the house of Israel, and I will look
to Him." [3] He is the man in transcendence, the man who is
allocated in one place to the SEPHIRA CHOKMAH,[4] but the
point is of great complexity and its elucidation belongs to a
subsequent part of our research. It is said further that He is
the " man more precious than fine gold " who is mentioned

---

[1] See Benedictus Poscantinus : DIALOGUM DE MESSIA, Venice, 1548, and Antonius
Hulsius : IN THEOLOGIAM JUDAICAM DE MESSIA, Bremen, 1580. There is a still
earlier work, but I can only claim to know of a report concerning it : EPISTOLA R.
Samuelis Judæi missam ad Isaac, Mantua, 1475. It claims to have been translated from
the Arabic by a Dominican, Alphonsus Bono-Homo, and is an argument from the
prophets that Jesus Christ was the Messiah expected by Jewry.
[2] Z., Pt. I, fol. 204a ; II, 413.
[3] Is. viii. 17.
[4] I should mention that this reference depends on certain SUPPLEMENTS, which are a
later addition to the ZOHAR.

by Isaiah ; [1] and it is on record also that He shall be raised above all the inhabitants of the world, who will adore Him, prostrated in His presence.[2] As a further witness respecting His eternal generation, the Spirit of Elohim which brooded over the face of the waters is sometimes regarded as the Spirit of Messiah, who has washed His robes in heavenly wine from the creation of the world.[3] He is also the sacred moon on high, having no other light than that which it receives from the sun above ; [4] but it is to be noted that the Shekinah is also symbolised by the moon and this has led to a precarious and indeed impossible identification of the Messiah as the Shekinah incarnate. It might be said on the same evidence that Solomon was an incarnation of Messiah and Moses also, for both had the moon as a symbol.

According to MIDRASH TALPIGOTH, the Messiah will bring eternal peace, which of course was understood by the Israelites as peace for Israel, *plus* that which may follow extermination for all who did not enter by conversion into the House of Jacob. It is said in the ZOHAR that, according to tradition, wherever Solomon is mentioned in the Song of Solomon this King of Peace is designated.[5] Conversion at the Messianic period will be apparently on a great scale, because all the nations of the world will gather about the King Messiah when He shall be manifested,[6] seeing that these words of the Scripture must be fulfilled : [7] " And in that day there shall be a root of Jesse, which shall stand for an ensign of the people ; to it shall the Gentiles seek ; and his rest shall be glorious." It will be a time for the revelation of mysteries which the will of God has concealed through the ages, but as the day of the King approaches even little children shall know the Mysteries of Wisdom.[8] It will be also a time of union, for in the Sabbatic millenary the Holy One will accomplish union between souls.[9] All the blessings of Israel will be realised in Israel,[10] which will form one people only on earth, " and I will make them one nation in the Lord." [11] The meaning seems to be that all nations shall become one nation of the Holy One ; but the great war of the world will precede this.

---

[1] Is. xiii. 12.
[2] Z., Pt. I, fol. 107b ; II, 39.
[3] *Ib.*, fol. 240a ; II, 548.
[4] *Ib.*, Pt. I, fol. 238a ; II, 540.
[5] *Ib.*, fol. 29a ; I, 182, 183.
[6] *Ib.*, Pt. II, fol. 172b ; IV, 127.
[7] Is. xi, 10.
[8] Z., Pt. I, fol. 118a ; II, 71.
[9] *Ib.*, fol. 119a ; II, 77.
[10] *Ib.*, fol. 145b ; II, 172.
[11] Ezek. xxxvii. 22.

It is unfortunate that the annotations to the French ZOHAR are largely polemical in character and elucidations which would have been valuable on difficult points of fact are too often wanting. It would seem at first sight that there are several Messiahs to come. There is he who is to be the Son of Ischaï, said to be master of all, by whom the earth is nourished.[1] There is secondly the Son of Ephraïm, of whom it is testified that he will be driven back from Rome.[2] Three personalities are mentioned, each of them once or twice only, and it is suggested in the notes—but without offering a reason—that the second is identified with the third Messiah, who is the Son of Joseph. The fourth is the Son of David,[3] and both are mentioned in the TALMUD;[4] but one of the " Omissions " given in the first appendix to the first part of the ZOHAR affirms that the last two are one.[5] Certain MIDRASHIM are said to agree, but the distinction for what it is worth remains perfectly clear in the Talmudic references, according to which the Son of Joseph will suffer a violent death[6] and will be succeeded by the Son of David. Elsewhere in the ZOHAR it is denied that the Son of Joseph will be killed because he is compared to an ox and evil has no hold over him.[7] It is of this Messiah that it is said in Scripture : " He was wounded for our transgressions . . . and with his stripes we are healed."[8] On the contrary, the fact that he will die is reaffirmed a few folios subsequently. It is said also that one of these alternative deliverers is poor and mounted on an ass, while the other is the first-born of a bull.[9] They are the two Kerubim stationed before the Garden of Eden ; the Flaming Sword is METATRON,[10] but at this point the symbolism passes into a wilderness of confusion where it

[1] Z., Pt. I, fol. 29b ; I, 185, 186. Eternal life is possible through him only. The authority cited is 1 Kings xx. 31, and a supposed statement therein that " the son of Ischaï lives upon the earth," but it is not to be found.

[2] Z., Pt. II, fol. 120a ; III, 461. See also Part III, fol. 153b ; V, 394.

[3] The Son of David is said to be the SEPHIRA NETZACH, while the Son of Ephraim is HOD.—Ib., Pt. III, fol. 243a, b ; V, 581.

[4] Tracts ABODA-ZARA, SUCCA, YEBAMOT and SANHEDRIN.

[5] Ib., Pt. I, fol. 267b ; II, 633.

[6] The ZOHAR agrees in one place, but adds that he will rise again.—Ib., Pt. III, fol. 203b ; V, 520. See also Ib., Pt. I, fol. 267b ; II, 633, from which it follows that there is one Messiah and that he will suffer death. But this is contradicted in Pt. III, fol. 279a ; VI, 52, where a distinction is made between the Son of David and the Son of Joseph, who will be slain.

[7] Ib., fol. 276b ; V, 48.

[8] Is. liii. 5.

[9] Z., Pt. III, fol. 279a ; VI, 52, 53.

[10] Ib., Pt. I, fol. 267b, 268a ; II, 633.

is impossible and would serve no purpose to follow it. I do not know that we need come to any decision as to the number of Messiahs ; it does not look in the ZOHAR as if they can mean States of one personality, which is the opinion of the editors, for in another place the text explains by an accident what is meant by a previous identification : it is said that the Messiah who is the Son of Joseph will be united—that is, in his mission—to the Son of David but will be slain.[1] The one is the conqueror of the great Rome and the other of the little Rome [2]—whatever the distinction between these cities may signify. The number 60 is fixed for the manifestation of the first and the number 6 for that of the second.[3] I do not pretend to explain the mysticism of these numbers, but I note that the number 6 is represented by VAU and the Son of David is connected with this number.[4] It is obvious that it is convenient for purposes of Christian interpretation to identify the Son of David and Joseph, as Jesus of Nazareth was both.[5] I should add in this connection that the words : " Lowly and riding on an ass, and upon a colt the foal of an ass," [6] which are referred to Messiah are not understood literally, for the ass represents that demon which shall be curbed by the King to come.[7]

The time of the coming of Messiah will be when all souls who are kept in the treasury of souls against the day of their incarnation shall have actually come hither in flesh.[8] Thereafter it would seem that new souls will be incarnated in Israel. Then shall the chosen people deserve to find—and shall not fail herein—the beloved and sister-soul predestined to each from the beginning of creation. It is in allusion to this that the Scripture says : " A new heart also will I give you, and a

---

[1] Z., Pt. III, fol. 203b ; V, 520.

[2] Ib., fol. 252a ; V, 589.

[3] Ib., fol. 252a ; V, 590.

[4] Z., fol. 203b ; V, 520. The letter VAU—as we have seen—is said to symbolise the Eternal World.—Ib., fol. 252b ; V, 591.

[5] The Chevalier P. L. B. Drach concludes that the TALMUD speaks of the suffering Messiah as Son of Joseph and of the victorious Messiah as Son of David ; but the evidence which he quotes from the TRACT SUCCA seems, on the whole, against him.— DE L'HARMONIE ENTRE L'ÉGLISE ET LA SYNAGOGUE, T. 1eie, pp. 184, 185.

[6] Zech. ix. 9.

[7] Z., Pt. III, fol. 238a ; V, 577. The explanation given is that the demon, who is called the ass, can be made subject with the Sacred Name SHADDAÏ. This reference and extract belong to THE FAITHFUL SHEPHERD. It follows that Messiah, who connects with the Ox symbolically, will overcome the ass or demon, and hence it is forbidden in Deut. xxii. 10, to yoke an ox and an ass together.—Z., Pt. III, fol. 207a ; V, 528.

[8] Ib., Pt. I, fol. 28b ; I, 179.

new spirit will I put within you."[1] And again : "It shall
come to pass that I will pour out my spirit upon all flesh ;
and your sons and your daughters shall prophesy, your old
men shall dream dreams, your young men shall see visions."[2]
The Intruders[3] shall be exterminated at the time when this
shall be accomplished, which is said to be of old tradition.[4]
To this period there is referable also that text of Genesis which
says that Adam and Eve were " naked and not ashamed,"[5]
the reason being that the Intruders are the cause of luxury
and when they disappear all leaning towards incontinence will
vanish in like wise.[6] Now all this is utterly stultifying
disquisition and mania of interpretation in the literal sense,
so far as it can be said to have any ; and yet through all one
feels that the Secret Doctrine is sealing and veiling the
simplicity which is of all grace in Nature and Mystical Art.
It is a change come over the dream of Israel, so that it shall
enter into its own on all the planes and in all the worlds by
the help of the " right spirit " renewed within them. This
is the Spirit of Messiah,[7] as it is written : " Renew a right
spirit within me."[8] And as we know that the Christ Who
is to come in each one of us, Who is of Nazareth and of all
the local habitations of the mastery, Who is son of David,
son of Joseph, Heir of the true legitimacy, stands ever at the
door and knocks, that rectified period is the one when all
portals shall open, so that He shall be welcomed in all the
ways. Out of the heart and the mind shall the Intruders be
cast once and for all, and the soul shall find the Spouse. We
might come to a pause at this point on the subject of the
Messiah in Israel, according to the lights and shadows of the
Secret Doctrine. It is a forecast of that time when the
Mystery of Union which is now a Mystery of Faith shall have
entered into realisation in experience on this earth of ours :

---

[1] Ezek. xxxvi. 26.
[2] Joel ii. 28.
[3] The reference is primarily to the mixed crowd which followed Israel during the
Exodus from Egypt and were not afterwards separated from the chosen people.
There are recurring allusions, and in one place it is said that these aliens were souls in
transmigration from antecedent, destroyed worlds.—Z., Pt. I, fol. 25a ; I, 155.
[4] See next section.
[5] Gen. ii. 25.
[6] It will be seen therefore that the alien people are understood spiritually as the
prompters towards evil which are within us.
[7] It is also the Spirit of God which " moved upon the face of the waters " (Gen. i. 2).
It is to this Spirit that David aspired.—Z., Pt. I, fol. 192b ; II, 357, 358.
[8] Ps. li. 10.

as in the world above there is no distinction between Shekinah and the Holy One, so in that which is below there will be such a spiritual communion between the Lover and the Beloved that the voice of the turtle, which is the Song of Solomon, shall be heard everywhere, and of that time it may be said : " The male with the female, neither male nor female."

There are, however, some further points which, being of an external kind, are of the shadows rather than the lights, though there is one which is a light of symbolism, so it shall stand first in the sequence.

In the time of the letter HE [1]—that is, when the HE shall rise from the earth—God will fulfil that which is mentioned in Isaiah. The reference is to c. lx, at the end of verse 22, and it reads in the Authorised Version : " I the Lord will hasten it in his time " ; [2] but the Zohar gives : " I am the Lord ; and it is I who will hasten these marvels when the time thereof shall have come." When Israel was driven from its abode the letters of the Sacred Name were separated one from another, if it be permissible so to speak ; the HE was separated from the VAU, and hence the Psalmist said : " I am dumb with silence." [3] When the VAU is separated from the HE the Word is stilled. The day of the letter HE is the fifth millenary—the period of Israel in exile. When the sixth millenary comes, the VAU shall raise up the HE, and Israel shall be lifted also from the dust.[4] After six hundred years of the sixth millenary the Gates of Supreme Wisdom shall open, and the springs of Wisdom shall begin to pour upon this world, which will make ready to enter worthily into the seventh millenary, and this latter will constitute the Sabbath of creation.

Assuming that we have a proper point of departure for calculation, we have in another place [5] the exact year of the

---

[1] Z., Pt. I, fol. 116b, 117a ; II, 66–69.

[2] The Vulgate agrees : *Ego Dominus in tempore ejus subito faciam istud.*

[3] Ps. xxxix. 2.

[4] To understand this passage, it is necessary to remember that, according to more than one Zoharic testimony, the second HE of the Divine Name יהוה = Jehovah, fell, as I have mentioned in Book VI, § 3, with a promise to recur in the future, when we pass to the consideration of Shekinah. We have seen also that the second HE is the Daughter and that whereby she will be raised is the VAU, or Son. It is well to observe here how remote these intimations are from the Christian scheme which is based on the resurrection of the Son.

[5] Z., Pt. I, fol. 119a ; II, 75, 76.

Messiah's advent. When sixty years shall have elapsed after the sixth century of the sixth millenary, it is said that heaven shall visit the daughter of Jacob. In the seventieth year the King Messiah shall be revealed in the province of Galilee. The portents will be as follows : (1) The rainbow—which is now tarnished, because it serves only as a memorial that the world will be destroyed no more by a deluge—will shine with very brilliant dyes, like a betrothed lady adorning herself to enter into the presence of her spouse.[1] (2) A star will rise in the East and swallow up seven stars in the North.[2] (3) Presumably after a period, a fixed star will appear in the middle of the firmament and will be visible for seventy days. It will have seventy rays and will be surrounded by seventy other stars.[3] (4) The city of Rome will fall to pieces [4]—an intimation which should be of moment to the hot gospel of certain protestant second-advent preachers, whose vestiges remain among us. (5) A great King will rise up and will conquer the world.[5] There will be war against Israel, but the chosen people shall be delivered. According to one account, the seventy celestial chiefs who rule the seventy nations of the earth will marshal all the legions of the world to make war on the sacred city of Jerusalem, but they will be exterminated by the power of the Holy One.[6] It is written : " And the house of Jacob shall be a fire, and the house of Joseph a flame, and the house of Esau for stubble." [7] As such stubble, by such fire and flame shall the nations perish. Thereafter the King Messiah will cause Jerusalem to be rebuilt ; [8] the Holy One will remember that Covenant which He has made with Israel ; and in such day will David be also raised up.[9] The Messiah will draw to him the whole world ; it shall be so to the end of the century ; and then the VAU shall be united with the HE.[10] It will be the period of true bridals ; the Messiah will bring about union between the Palaces above and below, as also between EL and SHADDAI.[11]

The soul of Messiah is pre-existent in common with all souls, and its present place, according to the prevailing opinion, is in the Garden of Eden, but the testimony is not in

[1] Z., Pt. I, fol. 72b ; I, 429, 430.
[2] Ib., fol. 119a ; II, 76.
[3] Ib., Pt. III, fol. 212b ; V, 536.
[4] Ib.
[5] Ib., fol. 212b ; V, 537.
[6] Z., Pt. II, fol. 58b ; III, 260, 261.
[7] Obadiah, v. 18.
[8] Z., Pt. III, fol. 212b ; V, 536.
[9] Ib., Pt. II, fol. 72b ; I, 430.
[10] Ib., fol. 119a ; II, 76, 77.
[11] Z., Pt. II, fol. 253a ; IV, 286, 287.

full accord and it must be left open as to whether this is the Eden above or that which is below. Wheresoever it be, there is a most secret place in the hiddenness which is called the Bird's Nest, and therein he abides.[1]   In the Paradise there is also a certain place which is called the Palace of the Sick ; [2] the Messiah enters therein and calls upon all the diseases, sorrows and troubles of Israel in exile to assail himself, and this comes to pass accordingly.   Were it otherwise there is no one who could suffer the penalty due to his misdeeds. Hence it is said : " Surely he hath borne our griefs, and carried our sorrows." [3]   So long as Israel dwelt in the Holy Land, and sacrifices were offered therein, Israel was preserved thereby from all maladies and penalties : now it is the Messiah who bears them—as it is affirmed, for the whole world ; but I fear that this can be understood only as the world of Israel.[4]

I have left one statement till the last, that it may stand for the present by itself, because we shall recur thereto at a point which is still far away.   It is said, almost at the beginning of the ZOHAR, and in that part which is called PRELIMINARIES,[5] that God created man with the object of preparing for the advent of the Lesser Countenance—that Divine Son corresponding to the letter VAU, about Whom we have heard in several of the previous sections.   It is obvious that this is Messiah, and if the fact is not in undiversified agreement with a few other intimations, about which we have heard also, there will be an opportunity to contrast them in the proper place, and perhaps also to reach a conclusion on the subject.

IX.—THE DOCTRINE CONCERNING SHEOL

If there be any subject on which it might seem reasonable to expect something like unanimity of opinion on the traditions of Kabbalism, I should have thought that it would have been the question of rewards and punishments in the world to come—the latter perhaps more especially.   The very contrary happens to be the case, and it is the more difficult to account for as by no extension of language can the question

---

of the temporal or eternal punishment reserved for dis-incarnate souls be regarded as a real part of the Secret Doctrine. It seems to me that the Doctors testified very often with unmeasured words of enthusiasm and that the emotion of the moment gave the inward meaning to the written word much more frequently than any abstruse law of interpretation. I will speak first of that which is held to occur at the time of death and then of punishment in SHEOL, with special reference to its duration.

Many things which are hidden from the mind and heart of man so long as the body is in health are beheld by the soul when it is hovering between life and death.[1] Three messengers descend who begin to count up the days that he has lived, the sins that he has committed, and all the works which he has accomplished here below. The dying man confesses with his lips to the facts so related and signs the *procès-verbal* with his own hand, psychic or not, as you please.[2] Thereon is he judged, for Zoharic Theology, like that of the Latin Church, recognises a particular as well as a general judgment at the end of time. On quitting this lower world the man gives account to his Master on the basis of the record which has been mentioned. Having crossed the threshold, he recognises many persons whom he knew on earth. As we have seen otherwise, he beholds also Adam seated before the Garden of Eden, so that he may rejoice with those who have observed the commands of their Master. Adam is ever encompassed with a multitude of the just who have learned how to avoid the path going down to hell and who have been gathered into the abode of Paradise.[3]

---

[1] Z., Pt. I, fol. 79a ; I, 462. This is held to be the " spiritual interpretation " of Job xxxvii. 7, which reads thus in the Authorised Version : " He sealeth up the hand of every man ; that all men may know His work." In the Revised Version there is the following variant of the last words : " That all men whom He hath made may know it." *Cf.* the Vulgate : *Qui in manu omnium hominum signat, ut nesciunt singuli opera sua.* But the ZOHAR reads : " He causes every man to sign with his own hand, that each may know His acts."

[2] The thesis is that sins are committed while spirit is united to body, and the account must be taken therefore before their separation is completed.—Z., Pt. I, fol. 79a ; I, 463. Zoharic pneumatology is sometimes almost inextricable, but we may remember that, according to one testimony, NESHAMAH cannot sin, whence it cannot be under the judgment ; NEPHESH remains with the body for twelve months, and it would seem therefore that it is RUAH only which enters into reward or punishment as a result of the particular judgment ; that in contrast hereto, we must further remember that all parts of the inward personality are one, by another account, so that the ZOHAR, like Latin doctrine, recognises fundamentally only (1) body and (2) soul. The so-called parts are therefore states of soul.

[3] *Ib.*, fol. 65b ; I, 386.

Another account says that when the soul leaves this world, it is stopped by a number of angels who preside over the offices of severity, and is prevented from passing through that door by which it would attain a place on high if the person has left no pledge on earth, meaning no son.[1] Those who would enjoy the inheritance of God and be united with Him for ever in the land of life must have produced male issue, so that the Divine Law may continue to have its servants through all generations.[2]

It is said also elsewhere that the day of death is the day of the Lord.[3] When the Holy One desires that the soul should return to Him, it does so return if worthy.[4] In the case of the just man his approach by the gate of death is proclaimed in the Garden of Eden throughout the thirty days which go immediately before the event.[5] During these days the soul is separated nightly from the body and ascends to heaven for the purpose of inspecting the place reserved for it in the world to come.[6] It follows also from a tradition mentioned by the ZOHAR that at the actual hour of death man is allowed to see his departed relations and friends, that he recognises these and that they appear to him with the same countenances which they wore here below.[7] If the man is worthy, his relations and friends salute him full of joy; in the contrary case, he beholds only the guilty whom he has known and who are expiating their offences in hell. They are all plunged in sadness. Relations and friends accompany the soul into the other world and shew him the place of his reward or punishment. This is one side of the story,[8] but another is that when the

---

[1] Z., Pt. I, fol. 115b; II, 63.

[2] This is the higher side of the desire which prevailed in Israel towards the increase and predominance of the people; it was not alone that they might inherit the earth but that the Law might prevail therein. The production of children was therefore for the glory of God. It was a continuous building of houses not made with hands which might become meet for His habitation. Here is one sense in which the Zoharic Mystery of Sex was a Great Mystery of Sanctity and a Divine Work in the world.

[3] Z., Pt. I, fol. 217b; II, 457.

[4] There is firstly a purgation by fire according to fol. 217b; II, 457, for those who are imperfect and yet not deserving of entire condemnation. The purgatorial state of catholicism is therefore recognised.

[5] Z., Pt. I, fol. 217b; II, 457.

[6] Ib.

[7] Ib., fol. 218b; II, 463. The point is of interest in connection with death-bed visions in Jewry at the period to which the text is referable.

[8] It is said also that the highest place in the world to come is kept in reservation for those who have (a) penetrated the mysteries of their Master and (b) learned how to cleave to Him during life. It follows that the illumination of mind by Divine Things has a greater reward than works, but the works are necessary.—Ib., fol. 130b; II, 111.

souls of those who have studied the Doctrine relinquish the body which is composed of the four elements they ascend into heaven—or into that part and region which is allocated to the Four Living Creatures.[1] The more general thesis is that the spirit which man attracts during life will draw his soul after death. Should it have been the Holy Spirit he will be raised thereby into the higher realms, and there—incorporated in the legion of sacred angels—he will become a servant of the Holy One.[2] He enjoys in the world above that light which he has desired here on earth. It is called " the splendour of light in reverberation," [3] reflected by that which is in the region above all regions. Souls are clothed in what is characterised as the Mantle of the Master, in the absence of which they would be incapable of approaching the light and contemplating it.[4] I suppose that this mantle is that which is called vestments in another place. These are said to be stored in a certain Palace, each being adapted to that soul for which it is reserved.[5] All the good works which have been performed by him or her are, so to speak, embroidered thereon. The soul is not clothed, however, until the thirtieth day after death, because the sins committed on earth have to be expiated during this period, indifferently by bad and good. It is an expiation by fire and a passage through a river of fire.[6] There is, moreover, a punishment of the body in the grave [7] for a period of twelve months,[8] during which the so-called animal spirit—or NEPHESH—is attracted

---

[1] Z., Pt. I, fol. 27a, b ; I, 170.

[2] Ib., fol. 100a ; II, 8. The authority is : " I will give thee places to walk among these that stand by."—Zech. iii. 7. Cf. Vulgate : *Et dabo tibi ambulantes de his qui nunc hic assistunt.* The Zoharic version is : " I will give thee access among those who stand before me."

[3] Z., Pt. I, fol. 65b, 66a ; I, 387.

[4] Ib., fol. 66a ; I, 388.

[5] Z., Pt. II, fol. 210a ; IV, 217. The vestments seem to be different from that which Latin theology terms " the form of the soul " and from that which occultism— or its derivatives—calls the astral and psychic body. They are rather the soul's clothing in its literal sense, corresponding in things above to that worn by the High Priest in the ceremonies of the Sanctuary. I note further that in the Earthly Paradise souls are clothed with good works but in the Paradise above they are clothed more gloriously, namely, with purity of intention, rightness of heart and prayers.—Ib., fol. 210b ; IV, 218.

[6] Ib., fol. 211b ; IV, 221.—Pt. I, fol. 201a ; II, 397.

[7] Ib., Pt. III, fol. 53a ; V, 144.

[8] Ib., Pt. I, fol. 225a ; II, 487. The NEPHESH knows also the sufferings of survivors but cannot go to their aid. After the twelve months it is clothed with that envelope to which I have referred previously and passes on wings through the world, learning from the RUAH the misfortunes which befall man and seeking to communicate with these so that they may pray for the evil to be averted.

thereto and suffers therewith ; but the juſt are not subjeɗ to this.   As there does not seem to be any purgation in view the intervention of this ordeal is idle.

And now with regard to those who go down into hell I will endeavour to tabulate the diſtinɗions and counter-diſtinɗions under two heads, collating firſtly those ſtatements which predicate the everlaſting nature of their torments.   It is laid down that the Holy One forgives every man who repents of his sins ; but it is woe to those who will not and who persiſt in their evil conduɗ.   They will be precipitated after death into hell and will not issue therefrom through all eternity.[1]   The same idea is expressed analogically in another place as follows.   The souls of those who defile their bodies, and of the evil generally, go down into hell and never come forth therefrom.[2]   Of these it is said : " As the cloud is con-sumed and vanisheth away : so he that goeth down to the grave shall come up no more." [3]   But the ZOHAR here under-ſtands the grave—SHEOL—in the sense of hell, againſt the obvious meaning of the verse.   Again, to fall into the hands of him who is called the Angel of Vindication is defined to be death in eternity.[4]   These inſtances will suffice as to one aspeɗ of the subjeɗ, and it will be observed that they are sufficiently unqualified.[5]

As much can be said of those in the opposite category, though if possible they seem more salient.   There are only two extraɗs which need especially concern us ; the firſt is an unqualified ſtatement that the guilty are chaſtised in the fires of hell, but that they are not damned for all eternity.[6]   Indeed the period has been fixed by tradition at twelve months, being that of the sufferings of Job.[7]   This is the firſt ſtatement, and

---

[1] Z., Pt. I, fol. 66a ; I, 389, 390.

[2] *Ib.*, fol. 77b ; I, 455.

[3] Job vii. 9.

[4] Z., Pt. I, fol. 94a ; I, 535.   The Angel of Vindication is DOUMÂ, and the Gentiles seem to be his viɗims *en masse* (*ib.*), while that which is the proteɗion of Israel againſt him and his consequences is the Sign of the Covenant, on the underſtanding that it is preserved in purity.

[5] Respeɗing punishment in the other world, man was not considered to have attained his majority—and therefore to be capable of punishment—till he had reached the age of thirty years.—*Ib.*, fol. 118b ; II, 74.

[6] Z., Pt. II, fol. 21b ; III, 105.   There is some undemonſtrable way in which this ſsurance and its consolation are drawn from Is. xxxiii. 12 : " And the people shall be as the burnings of lime : as thorns cut up shall they be burned in the fire."   But the ZOHAR gives " thorn-bush " and inſtitutes a comparison with the burning but uncon-sumed bush on Mount Sinai.

[7] And also of NEPHESH with the body.—Z., Pt. I, fol. 130b ; II, 111.

the second is that at the end of time all the guilty will be saved, with the single exception of Canaan.[1] It is said that this mystery is not unknown to those who are familiar with the highroads and bypaths of the Secret Doctrine.[2] We are acquainted with the pre-Zoharic tradition respecting Caanan, which is part of a sex-mystery. It belongs to the same realm of reverie as the mystery which presided over the marriage of Bathshebah and Uriah before she was espoused to David.[3] It is added that those who know this mystery will be in a position to see why the Holy Land was given as a patrimony to Canaan before the coming of the Israelites.

The question is whether there is any middle term by which we can reconcile the two series of conflicting testimonies, and if it be granted beforehand that the Doctors of the Secret Law, as they are reported in the ZOHAR, were frequently very loose in their statements, we may find what we seek almost at the end of the great text.[4] There, on the authority of yet another tradition, it is affirmed that there are various compartments in hell, one beneath another, and corresponding to the different degrees of culpability found among men. The lowest of all bears the name of ABADDON, and the man who is cast therein is lost through all eternity, because it has no door through which he can go out therefrom. It is about this place that it is said : " As the cloud is consumed and vanisheth away : so he that goeth down to the grave—SHEOL—shall come up no more." [5] This notwithstanding, says the ZOHAR, we learn otherwise from Scripture that " He sends down into hell and again He brings forth therefrom." [6] The first of these verses refers to the lowermost pit and the second to one of those places from which escape is possible.[7] Canaan is not located and the darksome picture of the deep below the deep is relieved by the unconscious grotesquerie which testifies that the denizens of this region are those who,

---

[1] Z., Pt. I, fol. 73b ; I, 435. See also fol. 114b ; II, 60, 61, where it is argued that all men will be acquitted at the celestial judgment.
[2] Ib.
[3] Ib., fol. 73b ; I, 436.
[4] Ib., Pt. III, fol. 285b, 286a ; VI, 67.
[5] Job vii. 9.
[6] I Sam. ii. 6. The French translators follow the Vulgate, which says, *Liber Primus Samuelis, quem nos Primum Regum dicimus.*
[7] But as a travesty of the whole situation—as we shall see immediately—the abysmal hell is reserved to punish acts of irreverence. I make a point of this because one is inclined to speculate whether Rabbi Simeon—who is the supposed speaker—was not secretly insinuating the opposite of that which he expressed.

prompted by disdain, have omitted the word AMEN which completes the forms of prayer.

Two other points deserve to be mentioned in this connection as they tend to shew that the ZOHAR might have furnished some useful material to the pious author of HELL OPENED TO CHRISTIANS. It is said [1] that the impure soul which is cast into SHEOL is sometimes drawn out therefrom and carried through celestial realms, with this cry going before it : " Such is the lot of those who transgress the commandment of their Master." It is then returned to its place. There may be some justice in adding that this moral diversion is meted out in that part of the text which limits the period of damnation to twelve months, after which the soul is remitted to a suitable region. Here is the first point, and the second is a brief picture [2] of souls located in Paradise proceeding to view ceremonially the chastisement of the guilty. So does eschatology reproduce itself independently in the minds of its makers. I do not suggest that the ZOHAR in this place is really a post-Thomist text or that St. Thomas Aquinas was acquainted with the Zoharic COMMENTARY ON EXODUS, but I say that the same notion is found in both.

In conclusion as to the whole matter : (1) There are three chiefs in hell, acting as overseers of those who are doomed for murder, incest, and idolatry.[3] If this is to be taken literally, Barabbas would have left the premises without a stain upon his character ; but the inference is doubtless that greater crimes stand at the head of a long list in their respective sequences. (2) The chastisement is by fire and ice,[4] but an elucidation in another place [5] explains that the waters which fall from above are cold as ice, while the fire which comes up from below is water which burns. (3) The souls of the heathen will never come out of hell.[6]

I suppose that things more ridiculous have never been said on the subject of retribution, but there are gleams here and there of a better sense. It is recorded for example that those who have been guilty on earth but have been also punished

---

[1] Z., Pt. I, fol. 130b ; II, 111.

[2] Ib., Pt. II, fol. 212a ; IV, 221, 222. As regards both these points they constitute solitary statements in the text, but the second is on the authority of Rabbi Simeon, by which I mean that it is imputed to him and occurs in one of his discourses.

[3] Ib., Pt. III, fol. 237a, THE FAITHFUL SHEPHERD ; DE PAULY, V, 576.

[4] Ib., Pt. I, fol. 238b ; II, 542.

[5] Ib., fol. 68b ; I, 405.

[6] Ib., fol. 4b of Appendix III, to Pt. I, i.e., SECRET MIDRASH ; II, 687.

on earth will not suffer in eternity if they have shewn resignation here.[1]   And I observe rather frequently a disposition in the doctors to lean towards human mercy and to forget very often even their sentence on the heathen in general.   There is a feeling that all men will be acquitted at the general judgment,[2] and there is one place from which it seems to follow that Satan himself will become again an angel of light.[3]   So is the " broken circle " made whole by fits and starts.

There are the following supplements and alternatives which have suggestive points, and they serve, moreover, the unintended purpose of proving that eschatology in the ZOHAR is in a state of complete flux : all views were possible and the alternatives of all views.   The souls of those who die impenitent go forth naked and find no envelope,[4] but it is set forth pretty plainly elsewhere that some kind of vesture is essential to personal existence.   They suffer punishment in hell, but many of them are saved at the end of time, being those who intended to repent but did not get to the work. They take up their task in SHEOL and its gates are opened subsequently in their respect.   There is nothing more agreeable than this to the Sacred King, a view that is illustrated amply in another place.   It is laid down furthermore that even those who are just and nearly approach perfection go down into hell (1) because all have been guilty of some offences at least ; but (2) because it is theirs to bring forth those very sinners who had proposed to repent in this life and have succeeded only on the other side of the grave.[5]   So and continually does the ZOHAR lean towards mercy, as I have said, though it holds out little hope for persons who have planned no atonement : [6] they remain in the place of perdition for ever.[7]   This is the case especially with those who have led a life of debauch ; they do not have respite on the Sab-

---

[1] Z., Pt. I, fol. 108a ; II, 42.

[2] Ib., fol. 114b, 115a ; II, 60, 61.

[3] It is even said that while we are to be on our guard against the attacks of the demon we are not authorised to treat him with contempt.—Ib., Pt. II, fol. 237b ; IV, 265.   See also Pt. III, fol. 265b ; VI, 19.

[4] Ib., Pt. II, fol. 150a ; IV, 70.

[5] Ib., Pt. III, fol. 220b ; V, 558.   We have seen already that intention is greater than works and the uttermost sacredness is ascribed thereto.   It may be said therefore that the ZOHAR is inclined to pave the way to God with good intentions rather than the road to hell, as the old proverb puts it.   But it is implied of course that such intentions pass continually into work ; it is a question therefore rather of a permanently right direction of heart and mind.

[6] Ib.

[7] See Pt. II, fol. 150a, b ; IV, 70, 71.

bath—like the rest of the damned.[1] However, another thesis shows that the flames of hell are stilled of necessity on that day.[2] By these and all other considerations we are justified in applying the most liberal sense to the vague suggestions that all men—Jew and Gentile—will enter ultimately into some kind of salvation and that hell will give up all its prey at the end of days, whether demons and the prince of demons or men, including Canaan.

One last word : the doctors of the ZOHAR countenanced prayers for the dead, one of them asking another to visit his tomb for seven days following his burial, there to plead for his soul.[3]

X.—CONCERNING RESURRECTION

Seeing that the doctrine of physical resurrection remains to our confusion as something of a blot on the 'scutcheon of Catholic Theology—though it was almost inevitable for the period in which it grew up—it may be reasonable to ascertain that which is advanced on the subject by Zoharic Theosophy. We shall find that it is pleased to be particular—I was about to say—in no common degree ; but my readers may judge for themselves.   It will be thought, and this naturally, that a Secret Doctrine which offers no enlightenment on the subject —in the sense that we should attach to this term—is scarcely one that can appeal to the modern mind and much less that of the mystic ; but I trust that I have done nothing throughout the present study to reduce the difficulties, or—if it should be preferred—the impossible nature of much that has been transmitted from this source.   To say otherwise would be to pose as unserious.   We are concerned, however, in reality only with the root-matter of the Tradition and we have yet to reach a decision thereon.   If the central testimony should prove of moment, it is of little importance—however regrettable otherwise—that there should be a considerable accretion of waste and drift from all sources encrusted over

---

[1] Z., Pt. II, fol. 150b ; IV, 72.
[2] Ib., Pt. I, fol. 14b ; I, 84.
[3] Ib., fol. 217b ; II, 458.   It is testified also that the faithful departed pray for those who are alive, without which the latter would be unable to subsist for a single day, or even part of a day.—Ib., Pt. II, fol. 16b ; III, 75.   This is another side of a very clear Christian reflection—the intercession of the just above for those who need help below.

it.[1] I believe that so far in our quest we have come across much that is at least of a certain value, while the curiosities—taken as such—are not in themselves idle. In respect of physical resurrection we shall find, in the first place that it is physical above all things, and as the Sons of the Doctrine happen to be acquainted with the *modus operandi* of the whole process, we may have great expectations on the wonder-side, and though we can scarcely look to be edified, the lessons in other respects may not be without significance.

I should record in the first place that it must be left as an open question whether the Gentiles are included in the scheme of resurrection.[2] This is negatived categorically in one place,[3] while in another it is added by way of re-expression that only the circumcised will subsist at that dreadful day.[4] But even here there are reservations, for certain persons belonging to the past of Israel—persons conspicuous for their ill-doing—are regarded as blotted out completely, so that for them there is neither judgment nor rising.[5] The restrictions would be still greater if several casual statements were to be construed literally—as when it is said, for example, that resurrection is by the merit of chastity.[6] The vesture of holy days—about which we have heard—is a particular aid of the just ; [7] but as it is certain that many of the wicked will also come to judgment it is possible that evil days may serve in their case, while making for their condemnation of course.[8]

---

[1] The point is that the root-matter is not one of metaphysical speculation or dogmatic teaching merely : it is a practice connected with a theory, the latter on account of the practice belonging to a category apart.

[2] For example, when it is said without qualifying the statement that the guilty will rise with the just, will do penance and will enjoy thereafter the light of God, there can be no question that the reference is to Israel alone.—Z., Pt. I, Appendix III, MATHNITIN ; II, 711.

[3] The words are that God will command His Servant who is charged with the work of resurrection not to restore their souls to the Gentile peoples.—*Ib.*, fol. 181b ; II, 317. The servant is METATRON.

[4] *Ib.*, Pt. II, fol. 57b ; III, 256.

[5] *Ib.*, Pt. I, fol. 69a ; I, 406. The allusion is especially to the sin of Onan, the enormity of which is ever present to the mind of the Doctrine. See also fol. 66a ; I, 390.

[6] *Ib.*, fol. 220a ; IV, 234. The remark should perhaps be taken in the sense of the previous extract.

[7] Another account tells us that when a man has maintained his soul in its pristine purity, on leaving this world many lights are poured upon him and he is preserved against the day of resurrection in a hidden Palace of Love where the King of Heaven kisses the holy souls.—*Ib.*, Pt. II, fol. 97a ; III, 389. The Scriptural authority is Ex. xxi. 9, very curiously adapted : " He shall deal with her after the manner of daughters." It follows that all souls in respect of God are held to be female by the ZOHAR, and the kind of Divine Union here adumbrated is remarkably like that which we meet with in many recognised aspects of Christian Mysticism.

[8] Z., Pt. I, fol. 224a, b ; II, 483, 484.

The general thesis of the subject is put very clearly as follows : When circumstances required it, a simple morsel of wood—the reference is to Aaron's rod—was transformed by the Holy One into a thing having body and life. With how much the more reason will He change into new creatures those forms which possessed previously a vital spirit and a holy soul, fulfilling the commandments of the Law, consecrated to its study.[1] It is the same bodies that have existed heretofore which will be resuscitated, as it is written : " Thy dead men shall live ; "[2] and they will be animated by the same souls.[3] There is a sense, however, in which they will be formed anew, but they will have the aspects of old and will be therefore recognisable.[4] The new formation is more especially a Divine act of healing, so that the lame and the blind will be disqualified thus no longer.[5] This will be effected by the rays of that primitive sun[6] which shone at the beginning, embracing the whole world from one extremity to the other.[7] After God had beheld the generations of Enoch, with those of the deluge and confusion of tongues, He concealed this light, which had curative properties. Its future restoration as stated signifies the restoration and enlightenment of Israel. It is said that " in that day shall there be one Lord, and His Name one."[8]

We should read between these lines to our destruction, did we seek to spiritualise any of the statements made : there is nothing so full as their literalness, and the details to which I have alluded rise up here and there for our complete confusion. The resurrection of the dead will take place in the order of their interment :[9] if a wife was the first to be buried, it is she who will rise first, and this rule seems to prevail through the

---

[1] Z., Pt. II, fol. 28b ; III, 135, 136.
[2] Is. xxvi. 19.
[3] Z., Pt. I, fol. 130b ; II, 112.
[4] Ib., Pt. III, fol. 91a ; V, 243.
[5] Ib., see also Pt. I, fol. 203b ; II, 410. The robes of glory, or psychic vestures and vehicles with which the disembodied soul is clothed in the state of beatitude, being psychic garments, would, by the hypothesis, serve in the transfiguration of the risen physical body, though there would not be two envelopes one within the other, this idea being set aside by the ZOHAR, as we have seen.
[6] The Gentile nations will be consumed by its fire.—Ib., fol. 203b ; II, 410.
[7] Ib., fol. 203b ; II, 410. The light of this concealed sun encompassed Moses as an infant among the bulrushes ; it surrounded him on Mount Sinai, whence the children of Israel could not look upon his countenance ; and in some sense it remained with him for the rest of his life.—Ib., fol. 31b ; I, 198.
[8] Zech. xiv. 9.
[9] Z., Pt. III, fol. 164a ; V, 423.

ages, with an exception in favour of those who died in the desert : the trumpet will sound for these sooner than for the earliest of humanity.[1] When the great day approaches it will be the task of METATRON to embellish or glorify the bodies in the sepulchres and presumably to prepare them for rising ; [2] but when the hour sounds the Holy One will cause a dew to fall, and it is thanks to this that the event itself will be accomplished. It will be a dew of light and it will emanate from the Tree of Life.[3] There is, however, a special dispensation in respect of students of the Doctrine. Whether or not without prejudice to those who died in the desert, it is those who will be raised first,[4] and they will bear witness in favour of the rest. The instrument in their case will be a wind which shall be the synthesis of all winds.

These things stand at their value, but there is a sort of central fact—ex hypothesi—which may be held to explain everything : each man who is born into the world is provided with an imperishable bone in his present physical body, and it is from or on this that his organisation will be built up anew at the time of the resurrection [5]—it is like the rib taken from the side of Adam. The bone in question will be to the risen body that which the leaven is to the dough. So is it sown a natural body and raised miraculously enough, though scarcely—on the evidence—spiritually. Now, it is said in one place that by virtue of the dew of light, already mentioned, the resurrection of bodies will be as the upspringing of flowers ; [6] but this is the poetry of the subject, and there is another side of the question. It was essential for the peace of the doctors that such an event as resurrection should take place only in Palestine, and it became necessary to devise a particular scheme for the great majority of Israel dying outside the precincts of that sacred land. This was done by

---

[1] Z., Pt. III, fol. 168b ; V, 437.

[2] Ib., Pt. I, Appendix III, MATHNITIN, fol. 6a ; II, 705. But it is MATRONA who preserves souls until the resurrection.—Ib., Pt. III, fol. 222b ; V, 561.

[3] Z., Pt. I, fol. 130b, 131a ; II, 113. It is said elsewhere that at the time of resurrection (1) the waters of that heavenly fountain which is represented by the letter YOD will flow forth afresh ; (2) the 32 paths of communication between things above and below will be open freely ; and (3) all letters of the Sacred Name will be complete, which has not been the case in the world heretofore.—Ib., fol. 10a ; I, 42.

[4] Ib., fol. 175b, 176a ; II, 290, 291. The risen bodies of these will subsist always, because the Law will be their protection.

[5] Z., Pt. I, fol. 69a ; I, 406. See also Appendix III to Pt. I, SECRET MIDRASH ; II, 716.

[6] Ib., fol. 130b, 131a ; II, 113.

postulating that, after their reconstitution, the bodies of such persons will be transported underground to the Holy Land, and there only will they receive their souls.[1] The complete resurrection will begin in Galilee.[2] Souls will come down through the gates of heaven and rejoin their bodies.[3] At first it will be a day of severity, for the Holy One will demand an account of all actions prior to the separation of soul and body ; the books of record will be opened and the chiefs of severity will stand ready to act.[4] But Israel is a nation of the elect ; the guilty who rise with the just will do penance and thereafter will enjoy the Divine splendour.[5] It is even testified—as we have seen—that the tempter-spirit will be transformed,[6] though whatever is understood by extermination is meted out to him in other passages.[7] The Holy One will bless the bodies of the just and will render them like the body of Adam in the state of Paradise. Such souls will bring with them the higher lights which nourish them during their sojourn in heaven, between the death and the rising, and those lights will make their bodies radiant.[8] Soul and body in fine shall know their Master.[9] A great festival will follow ; but in place of the salted leviathan promised to the elect by the TALMUD the refection will be spiritual, because those who are truly just have no need to eat or drink but are nourished by the splendour of Shekinah.[10]

I am no doubt exceeding the restricted province which I have chosen, but it seems to me difficult to deny that Zoharic eschatology is tinctured by that of the Christian scheme, as presented by the Latin Church. Subject to the distinctions— not always maintained—on the question of the duration of punishment, all souls at death go to the place prepared for them and the judgment connected with the resurrection

---

[1] Z., Pt. I, fol. 131a ; II, 115.

[2] Ib., Pt. II, fol. 10a ; III, 42.

[3] Ib., Pt. I, Appendix III, SECRET MIDRASH ; II, 712.

[4] Ib., Pt. I, fol. 201b ; II, 401. It is said also that the " Serpent will rise up to bite and man shall tremble in all his members."—Ib.

[5] Ib., Pt. I, Appendix III, MATHNITIN ; II, 711.

[6] Ib., Appendix III, SECRET MIDRASH ; II, 716. The passage is a good example of the ZOHAR in its most cryptic mood. " The tempter spirit and his two daughters will be transformed. Formerly he was called Lot, meaning malediction, but hereafter he will be called Laban, meaning white."

[7] In one place it is said merely that he will disappear.—Ib., Pt. I, fol. 131a ; II, 114.

[8] Ib., Pt. I, Appendix III, SECRET MIDRASH ; II, 696.

[9] Ib., II, 713.

[10] Ib., p. 714.

determines once and for all the state of humanity for ever. There is neither change nor vicissitude thereafter. The just in their risen bodies will behold the Divine, so that the earth shall be filled with the knowledge of God.[1] In this world— as it now is—they are in a state of imperfection, but after the resurrection they will be perfect and will rejoice with Shekinah.[2] Their bodies will be like the splendour of the firmament, or like silver that has no alloy.[3] So will the earth be renewed.[4]

---

[1] Z., Pt. I, Appendix III, SECRET MIDRASH; II, 713. *Ib.*, p. 696. It is affirmed also that those bodies shall be unto them as a lasting habitation.—*Ib.*, Pt. I, fol. 80, Cremona ed. Again—*ib.*, fol. 66—the body shall be made wholly, even as it was formerly—meaning the body of Adam unfallen—that it may be like unto the holy angels.

[2] *Ib.*, p. 698.

[3] *Ib.*, Pt. I, Appendix III, SECRET MIDRASH; II, 699.

[4] *Ib.*, p. 697. I will mention in this connection for the students of numerical mysticism that the number 40 seems to be a resurrection or renewing number.—*Ib.*, Appendix III, SECRET MIDRASH; II, 715, 716, where the recurrences of the number in the Old Testament are tabulated. It will be remembered that the Ascension of Christ occurred 40 days after the Resurrection.

BOOK VIII

THE HIGHER SECRET DOCTRINE

BOOK VIII

THE HIGHER SECRET DOCTRINE

I.—THE MYSTERY OF SHEKINAH

THERE is a very true sense in which the Secret Doctrine of the ZOHAR must be said to centre in that Mystery, whatsoever it may be, which lies behind the wonder and glory of Shekinah —a recurring, and speaking literally, incessant subject of reference in adoring honour throughout the great text. There is a very true sense furthermore in which it may be said that out of this Mystery all Kabbalism seems to issue and, moreover, goes back therein. It would have been very reasonable, if indeed it had been possible, to have opened my study of the Doctrine with this subject; but it would have involved entering at once into its most recondite and difficult part, one also which might have made the whole undertaking insuperable for the general and not too critical reader.[1] As it is, I must proceed carefully, not only on account of the difficulties but because the Keys of the Mystery open into a region about which there are grave motives for speaking with considerable reserve, when it is possible to speak at all. It is here, if anywhere in our subject, that we shall find whether as mystics we are coming into something which may be our own in the matter of Jewish Theosophy or whether we must relegate it to the curiosities of past speculation that are not of our vital concern.

---

[1] The old maxim of the mystical alchemist, Khunrath, seems to obtain in every direction without variation or reduction : *Sigillum Naturæ et Artis simplicitas*, and I quote it here, as I have quoted it on several occasions elsewhere, to indicate that it is one which applies in a paramount manner to the root of the Secret Doctrine in Israel ; for the vast body of cryptic writing and the practice concealed behind it arose out of that one verse in Scripture which says : " So God "—that is to say, Elohim—" created man in His own image, in the image of God created He him ; male and female "—defining the nature of the image—" created He them."—Gen. i. 27. The difficulty therefore to which I have alluded above is not in respect of the fact wherein the Doctrine centres but in the complications of its development and in the details of the practical part.

" The sole object with which the Holy One, blessed be He, sends man into this world is to know that Jehovah is Elohim."[1] Herein is also all true joy of heart.[2] Now, it is in this manner that I open the high conference respecting the Mystery of Shekinah, which is a Mystery of man and God, of man in the likeness of the Elohim, of the relation between things above and things below, of intercourse for union upon earth performed in the spirit of celestial union, and the transmutation of one by the other for the work of God in the world. In this union abides the Mystery of Faith, which is the synthesis of the whole Law—Written and Oral Law—and of all that exists whatsoever. But union is not identity,[3] whence it is said further that Jehovah and Elohim are distinct, not synonymous, though together they form an unity.[4] It must be remembered in the first place that Elohim is a title of Shekinah and so also is Adonai,[5] in which sense—but presumably for us in manifestation—she is called the Mirror of Jehovah.[6] Like the First Matter of the Great Work in Alchemy, Shekinah is almost myrionymous in respect of her designations, but, almost without exception, the ascriptions are feminine. She is now the Daughter of the King ; she is now the Betrothed, the Bride and the Mother, and again she is sister in relation to the world of man at large.[7] There is a sense also in which this Daughter of God is—or becomes—the Mother of man. In respect of the manifest universe, she is the architect of worlds, acting in virtue of the Word uttered by God in creation. In respect of the myth of Paradise, the Shekinah is the Eden which is above, whence the river of life flows forth

---

[1] Z., Pt. II, fol. 161b, 162a ; IV, 101, 102. There is also a marriage of the two names in Kabbalism, producing the Sacred Name of nine letters, the consonants succeeding one another alternately, thus—יאהלוהחים : YOD, ALEPH, HE, LAMED, VAU ,HE, HE, YOD, MEM.—Ib., iv, 151. It is said also : " And the Lord God formed man " (Gen. ii. 7)—i.e., Jehovah Elohim, the male principle united to the female, according to the ZOHAR. Man is said to be grafted on Elohim, as the latter is grafted on Jehovah.—Ib., Pt. II, fol. 260a ; IV, 293.

[2] Ib., Pt. III, fol. 8b ; V, 23.

[3] Ib., Pt. II, 162a ; IV, 102.

[4] Cf. Deut. iv. 35 : " Unto thee it was shewed, that thou mightest know that the Lord He is God "—or, as the ZOHAR quotes it, that Jehovah is Elohim. It will be observed that the Scriptural text does not tolerate the Zoharic dogma, though ex hypothesi one of its sources.

[5] Z., Pt. I, fol. 101a ; II, 10.

[6] Ib., Pt. II, fol. 124b ; III, 482.

[7] Ib., Pt. I, fol. 81b ; I, 470. See also Pt. III, fol. 297b ; VI, 124, for Shekinah and Matrona ; Pt. I, 276a, SEPHER HA BAHIR, OTHERWISE, LUMINOUS BOOK or BOOK OF BRIGHTNESS ; II, 644, for Daughter of the King ; and Pt. II, fol. 100b ; III, 406, for all the synonyms.

that waters the Garden below, and this is also Shekinah as she is conceived in external things—or Bride, Daughter and Sister in the world below. Considered in her Divine Womanhood, in the world of transcendence, she is the Beloved who ascends towards the Heavenly Spouse, and she is Matrona who unites with the King, for the perfection of the Divine Male is in the Divine Female. Hence it is said that the perfection of Jehovah is in Elohim.[1] She is a trinity in respect of her title as Elohim, for there is an Elohim in transcendence—concealed and mysterious—an Elohim that judges above and one who judges below ; but these three are one.[2] As such, the Oral Law is her image, while the image of Jehovah is the Written Law[3]—a distinction at once eloquent and pregnant, for the Inward Law is life, while the Outer is the body of life. So also she is the waters that are above the firmament in respect of her title of Elohim, but she is the waters below the firmament when she manifests as Adonai.[4] As Elohim she is the Middle Pillar,[5] and all the various aspects of the one thing that is needful from the standpoint of the Secret Tradition are collocated, their seeming exclusiveness notwithstanding, to shew that she abides in all, is at once above and below, without even as within. She is that Divine Presence which walked in the Garden of Eden in the cool of the evening, which went before Israel in the desert and protects the just man who has fulfilled the precepts, dwelling in his house and going forth with him in his journeys.[6] As Elohim, in fine, she is the middle degree of the Divine Essence [7] corresponding to the Pillar of Benignity in the Tree of Life.

Now, in all the references cited up to this point the intention of the ZOHAR has been to shew in the most positive and unqualified way that the Shekinah—as affirmed already in the present section—is female in essential aspect, whether as the Bride of God in that transcendent state wherein there is no distinction between her and the Holy One,[8] or whether as the

---

[1] Z., Pt. III, fol. 5a ; V, 11.
[2] Ib., Pt. II, fol. 257a ; IV, 290.
[3] Ib., fol. 161b ; IV, 102. Elsewhere the ZOHAR seems to say that the Kabbalah is actually Shekinah and that the MISHNA is its humble servant.—Pt. III, fol. 279b.
[4] Ib., Pt. I, fol. 17b, 18a ; I, 108.
[5] Ib., fol. 278a, THE FAITHFUL SHEPHERD ; II, 647. See also fol. 241a ; II, 552.
[6] Ib., Pt. I, fol. 76a ; I, 448.
[7] Ib., fol. 150b ; II, 194.
[8] " She and God are one."—Ib., Pt. II, fol. 118b ; III, 456.

tutelary guide of humanity.[1] But in preparation for another
part of our subject it is necessary to glance at certain alternative allocations which appear in the ZOHAR. The Shekinah
is the Liberating Angel who delivers the world in all ages,[2]
who is ever near to man and never separated from the just.[3]
Of her it is said : " Behold, I send an angel before thee, to
keep thee in the way, and to bring thee into the place which I
have prepared." [4] But it is stated that this Liberating Angel
manifests as male and female, being male when it dispenses
the celestial benedictions on the world below, because it then
resembles a male nourishing the female ; but when charged
with offices of judgment it is called female, as a woman who
carries her child in the womb of her.[5] It is said elsewhere
that those who understand these male and female attributions
know the great wisdom.[6] But the exposition as to this
wisdom is given much later on, when it is stated that MATRONA
is feminine in so far as she is not in union, but in that state she
is identified with the male principle, and this is how the
interchange of sex in divine things must be understood
throughout.[7] So also METATRON, who is an aspect of
Shekinah, is indifferently male and female, changing inces-
santly according to the vibrations of the union.[8] Now, it is
said that Shekinah is to METATRON what the Sabbath is to the
weekdays.[9] In other words, she is rest and the rapture of
rest, yet it is that rest in which there is the intercourse of
spiritual union. The same vibrations which are mentioned
in the case of METATRON constitute the beatitude of the soul
in heaven.

There are two points which should be memorised on this
subject. At the apex of the union between male and female—
which is to be understood only in a spiritual sense—the sex
distinction has ceased : it can be only from this point of view

[1] See Z., Pt. II, fol. 207a ; IV, 210.
[2] Ib., Pt. I, fol. 228b ; II, 502.
[3] Ib., fol. 230a ; II, 508.
[4] Ex. xxiii. 20.
[5] Z., Pt. I, 232a ; II, 516. The " Flaming Sword which turned every way, to keep
the way of the Tree of Life " (Gen. iii. 24) is a symbol of this Angel and of Shekinah
in the dual sex of both. Mercy is always counted as masculine and severity or judgment
as feminine.
[6] Z., Pt. II, fol. 100b ; III, 406.
[7] Ib., Pt. III, fol. 31a ; V, 84. It is said distinctly that, in this respect, whether the
feminine or masculine form is used by Scripture, the same degree is always and only
designated.
[8] Ib., fol. 73b ; V, 201.
[9] Ib., fol. 243b ; V, 581.

that the Shekinah is mentioned sometimes as if she were on the male side. Here is the first point, and the second is that in charaſteriſtics and in mission, she is always typically female ; it is she who comprises all women in her myſtery,[1] and this is why—as we shall see—she does not abide except with him who is united to a woman.[2] In conclusion, so far as there is a dual aspeſt on the sex side in the notion of Shekinah, it may be noted that the Divine Name Adonai would answer to the male aspeſt, Shekinah to the female and Elohim to the combination of both. There is, however, no Zoharic authority.

We have next to consider her relation to the letters of Tetragrammaton. The HE which is above, meaning the firſt HE of the Sacred Name, is the symbol of the Shekinah in transcendence, while the HE final represents the Shekinah below, or in manifeſtation, conneſted with the idea of MAL-KUTH [3]—underſtood as the world of ASSIAH. According to one account, she has been in manifeſtation so long as the world was created.[4] She is, however, above and below at one and the same time—there encompassed by twelve sacred legions and the supreme HAYOTH, or Living Ones, here by the twelve sacred tribes of Israel.[5] The YOD and the HE conſtitute the Father and the Mother : these are Jehovah and Elohim.[6] She is the Mother, MATRONA, above and MATRONA or Mother below.[7] From the conſtant and ardent love of HE for YOD there issues VAU, conceived and born of HE, who also nourishes VAU. But VAU came into the world with a twin siſter bearing the name of Grace ; the two took root on earth and conſtituted the HE final—a reference to the meta-physical conception of their affirmed union. Then and thus was the VAU united to the HE, meaning the second HE of the Divine Name.[8] It follows that there is a descent of VAU into

---

[1] Z., Pt. I, fol. 228b ; II, 501.
[2] *Ib.* The task of lighting the Sabbath candles devolved on the matrons, because they are in the service of MATRONA. The aſt was regarded as an earneſt (a) of long life for the husbands and (b) of a holy poſterity for both, as well as (c) great personal rewards for themselves.—*Ib.*, fol. 48b ; I, 281.
[3] *Ib.*, Pt. I, fol. 27b ; I, 174, where it is said also that the HE final is the child of the firſt HE.
[4] *Ib.*, fol. 85a ; I, 489.
[5] *Ib.*, fol. 159b ; II, 227.
[6] *Ib.*, fol. 28a ; I, 177. That is to say, in CHOKMAH and BINAH, as we have seen by the evidence colleſted in Book V, § 5, especially p. 226.
[7] *Ib.*, Pt. III, fol. 10b ; V, 31.
[8] *Ib.*, fol. 77b ; V, 210, 211.

manifestation, but there should be no need to add that this notwithstanding the Vau has its place in the Supernal World and so also has the final He, because it is obvious that the Divine Name must be perfect above before it can manifest below, and from this point of view, though there is no Zoharic authority, and other allocations are paramount, the place of the He final is with the Vau in Daath.[1] As the He in manifestation, the Shekinah is the repose of beings below and in transcendence of beings above,[2] referring more especially to souls who have attained beatitude, which is defined as the vision of her.[3] The Vau is the male child or the Son.[4] The Yod of the Sacred Name is ever united to the primal He, and when the Vau is also joined thereto it is union everywhere, including that which should obtain between the Vau and the He final.[5] Owing to the present state of the world, we shall see that this union has been broken. In a withdrawn sense the Yod of the Sacred Name designates the Supreme Thought, while the He designates Shekinah, as the Heart of Love in that Thought.[6] To conclude as to the Divine Name, its consonants bear the vowel points of the Name Elohim,[7] from which two things seem to follow : (1) That the intimate union between Jehovah and Elohim is here indicated by the silent eloquence of verbal symbolism, and (2) that the degree or hypostasis, or that part of the Divine Nature with which man is in communion on earth, is that which the Secret Tradition understands as Shekinah. It is she who enables the Name to be expressed on earth, or God to be realised in the heart. I conclude that in the perfect state, the manifestation of the He final on earth would be in espousals with Vau, but there is separation in the present order until that which now hinders shall be taken out of the way.[8]

The next point which is posed for our consideration is the

---

[1] I have put this on record in respect of the Sacred Name in the Supernals, but it need not concern us further. In the scheme of Divine Names allocated to the ten Sephiroth by late Kabbalism, Jehovah is referred to Chokmah.

[2] Z., Pt. III, fol. 108a, b ; V, 274.

[3] Ib., Pt. II, fol. 40b, The Faithful Shepherd ; III, 189, 190.

[4] Ib., Pt. III, fol. 118b ; V, 305.

[5] Ib., fol. 267b ; VI, 23.

[6] Ib., fol. 230a ; V, 570.

[7] Ib., Pt. I, fol. 90a ; I, 511, 512. Otherwise this Divine Name has the pointing of Adonai.

[8] My reference is to the period, foretold in the Zohar, when the Vau shall raise up the He.

place of Shekinah in the Sephirotic Tree, and it will be well to state at the inception that the attributions throughout Kabbalism seem almost as many as the references, though there is only one which is predominant. She is the Middle Pillar—as we have seen—the Pillar of Benignity, extending from KETHER to MALKUTH,[1] and she takes up the SEPHIROTH to God, or into the place which is no place, beyond the infinite height and depth, the infinite of all directions embraced by the Tree. This is the place of AIN SOPH.[2] The Middle Pillar is described otherwise as the trunk of the Tree,[3] it being understood that the root is in KETHER, so far as the genesis and legend of the soul are concerned ; but it is in MALKUTH in respect of the return journey to God, which is a journey through the Shekinah, or under her glorious leading. Shekinah is, in another form of symbolism, the body of the Tree ; [4] and the elect—summarised as Israel—are the cloud of witnesses forming the branches. But it is said also that she is the crown of the Middle Pillar,[5] the synthesis of all the SEPHIROTH and of every Sacred Name expressed or implied in the wisdom of the Secret Doctrine. She is to God that which the vowel point is to the letter—a thing not distinct therefrom but the means of its utterance. She is further the crown of the seven lower SEPHIROTH, and this would account for the allocation of the semi-SEPHIRA DAATH or Supernal Knowledge to the centre of the influence coming from CHOKMAH and BINAH, as tabulated by later Kabbalism.[6]

---

[1] This is likely to cause some mental confusion, for which the text is too often responsible. We have seen that, according to the IDRAS, the Son or VAU is extended through the three worlds which are below the world of ATZILUTH, and He is called also the Middle Pillar ; but He is in union with the HE final, or Bride, therein. I have spoken in the present tense, but this was during the perfection of the manifest world. They are in separation now, for the HE is fallen to earth—that is, to MALKUTH—and has to be raised by the VAU. It is never said that the VAU also has fallen, but as the method and terminology chosen to illustrate the notion are an adaptation of the Myth of Paradise symbolism, the VAU is certainly involved, as Adam in the calamity of Eve. The undoing of the evil rests also with her—as the ZOHAR itself intimates in one place. The whole account is an allegory of man and woman involved by a fatal construction respecting the Mystery of Sex but intended to redeem the trespass, with the life belonging thereto.

[2] This is a matter of inference from one isolated statement, which says that Shekinah in her ascent draws up the ten SEPHIROTH, and it is a matter of logic that thither where she draws them is beyond KETHER. Now, beyond KETHER is AIN SOPH by the hypothesis of the Tree.—See Z., Pt. I, fol. 24a ; I, 149, where it is said that when she rises towards God she causes all the ten SEPHIROTH to go up with her.

[3] Ib., Pt. I, fol. 241a ; II, 552.

[4] Ib., fol. 241b ; II, 555.

[5] Ib., Pt. II, fol. 158a ; IV, 94.

[6] This again leads to confusion, for we have seen that the head of the Son is in DAATH. I am not, however, attempting to harmonise the innumerable statements

Now, we know that there is an appendix to the SEPHER YETZIRAH concerning 50 Gates of Understanding—referred to BINAH, also by late Kabbalism; but this ascription is countenanced by the ZOHAR when it is said that these Gates are in the region of the Supreme Mother, who gives power to the Mother below [1]—a reference to the Shekinah in transcendence and in manifestation. This determines absolutely that the Shekinah is in BINAH and that the first HE of the Divine Name is also therein. It is said further that the side of severity emanates from her, though she is not herself severity,[2] and we know that the Pillar of Severity is on the left side of the Tree, at the head of which is BINAH.[3] " Shekinah emanates from the left side." [4] The 50 Gates are another symbolism concerning the return of man to the heights by the operation of Shekinah, as by a journey through the great distance, for the first gate is in matter and the last is in God Himself; but this gate was not, according to tradition, opened by Moses—presumably because another tradition affirms—as we have seen—that he ceased to cohabit with his wife on earth. It is to be observed that it is a Gate in BINAH, so that God is attained by man in and because of Shekinah, for which reason her number is said to be 50,[5] though from another point of view she is not contained in number.[6] There are, however, various allocations. Two Supernals, namely CHOKMAH and BINAH, are disposed on the right and the left, and these are said to be united in Shekinah.[7] But the complete integration in her of all branches of the Sephirotic Tree will not take place till He comes Who shall be called Man, that is, Adam or SHILOH.[8] It follows that

---

and counter-statements. Our object is to study the bent of the symbolism, and the glaring discrepancies—seeing that they speak for themselves—must take care of their own differences.

[1] Z., Pt. III, fol. 262a ; VI, 12. As regards the number 50 which is allocated otherwise to Shekinah, it should be noted that the jubilee year, occurring once after every 49 years, is allocated to the Divine Mother in BINAH, as the Sabbatic year—occurring every 7 years—is referred to the Mother below—that is, the Shekinah in manifestation, so that her number on earth is 7.—See ib., fol. 108b, THE FAITHFUL SHEPHERD ; V, 274.

[2] Ib., fol. 262b ; VI, 13.

[3] That is to say, in the ordinary diagrams of the Sephirotic Tree—left and right referring to the observer.

[4] Z., Pt. III, fol. 275b ; VI, 44. But this is looking towards the observer—as, for example, when he is faced by the two Countenances of the IDRAS. See Bk. V, § 5.

[5] Z., Pt. III, fol. 108b, THE FAITHFUL SHEPHERD ; V, 274.

[6] Ib., Pt. II, fol. 164b ; IV, 108.

[7] Ib., fol. 165a ; IV, 109.

[8] Ib., Pt. I, fol. 25b ; I, 160.

there is a sense in which Shekinah is in CHOKMAH,[1] and it is supposed to be of her that it is said : " She openeth her mouth in wisdom." [2] For the purpose of this attribution wisdom is the letter HE and all depends therefrom.[3] The Shekinah in this relation is called concealed and visible, conciliating the mysteries above and the mysteries below.[4] Her hiddenness is in respect of the Supreme Degree of the Divine Essence, which exceeds understanding. She herself is revealed in wisdom by the mode of the Law of Mercy, so that she is Mercy on one side although Severity proceeds from her on the other. As the mouth which is opened with wisdom, she is the HE final of the Sacred Name, and this is the word which emanates from wisdom.[5] Again it is said that Elohim is seated on the right side, suggesting that the Shekinah is in CHOKMAH—according to the familiar diagrams. Moreover, wisdom is the glory of and is revealed in the Tabernacle [6]—that is to say, by Shekinah. We must deal with this as we can, seeing that in another place Elohim, who is Shekinah, is said definitely to designate BINAH.[7] Fortunately the harmony between these statements is given elsewhere in the ZOHAR itself, when it is said that the mother below is sometimes called the Betrothed and sometimes Sister. If she comes from the side of the Father she is called CHOKMAH, but if from that of the mother she is BINAH.[8] The truth is that Shekinah is on both sides of the Tree, and the explanation is that she is the spirit of all the Holy Assem-

---

[1] Because she is indubitably present in things that are united in her ; because, in so far as she represents sex conceived transcendently, she is male and female ; and because—as we have seen—in the Supernals there is no distinction between her and the Holy One.

[2] Prov. xxxi. 26. The reference is to a virtuous woman—accentuating in this manner the feminine aspect of Shekinah. We ought, I think, to remember in this connection that, in the physical order, it is woman who conceives, contains and brings forth both male and female—a point which must have been present assuredly to the minds of Zoharic doctors.

[3] But the attribution is casual or transient and as such fantastic. There is no question that in the natural allocations of the Tree it is the YOD that is in CHOKMAH, and for this—as we have seen—there is full evidence. Compare THE ASSEMBLY OF THE SANCTUARY, Z., Pt. II, fol. 123b ; III, 478.

[4] Ib., Pt. I, fol. 145a ; II, 171.

[5] Ib., Pt. I, fol. 145a ; II, 171.

[6] Elsewhere the Tabernacle is said itself to be Shekinah.—Ib., Pt. III, fol. 114 ; V, 285.

[7] Ib., Pt. I, fol. 263a, SECRETS OF THE LAW ; II, 620. It is all a very simple question of transposing the diagram and bearing in mind what follows above.

[8] Ib., Pt. III, fol. 77b ; V, 212. She is known by many names, as we are told in another place—sometimes as an angel simply, sometimes as the angel of Jehovah and sometimes even as Jehovah.—Ib., Pt. I, fol. 113b ; II, 58.

blies above and below.[1] It is in this sense and this only that CHOKMAH is sometimes said to be female and is that Mother who is allocated alternatively to BINAH, while she is Daughter, Sister and Bride in the worlds below. There is also a question of the unity which obtains throughout the Supernals. For the same reason she is now located in her manifestation at the foot of the Middle Pillar—that is to say, in the fallen world; but we have seen that she is also at the head and is therefore in KETHER—that is to say, as AIMA ELOHIM, covering the Supernals with her wings. Hence it is mentioned that the Holy One is covered by His Shekinah, both within and without.[2] I conclude that there are the Father, the Mother and the Begotten Son, being CHOKMAH, BINAH and DAATH, overshadowing the lower SEPHIROTH, though other allocations are made and stand at their value. These three are symbolised by YOD, HE and VAU in the Sacred Name, while the HE final, the Bride in manifestation, is in MALKUTH since the legendary Fall, but so that the kingdom of this world may become in the fullness of the Messianic day the Kingdom of Heaven. Outside these there is KETHER, and it should be noted in this connection that Jehovah abides, in the deep hiddenness, with Shekinah in that Supernal SEPHIRA.[3] The seeming attribution of feminine descriptions to the Shekinah in her threefold aspect, so far from leading to confusion, really provides the key. She is the catholic nature of womanhood in all degrees and grades. In so far as everything proceeds from KETHER, it is in virtue of the union between God and His Shekinah therein. That which was produced is male and female also, being the Father and Mother in CHOKMAH and BINAH, but because of this twofold procession there is a sense in which these two may be called Son or Word and Daughter. They beget on their own part the King and the Queen below, Lover and Beloved, the Son and Shekinah in manifestation. But the Supernals are in unity, and this is why the ZOHAR is

---

[1] Z., Pt. III., fol. 103b; V, 262.
[2] *Ib.*, Pt. II, fol. 159a, THE FAITHFUL SHEPHERD; IV, 96. The Shekinah is represented also by the initial letter of the word Sabbath, but this would be, I think, the Shekinah below, because of the Sabbatic year already mentioned.
[3] This is a most important point and is on the authority of THE FAITHFUL SHEPHERD.—Z., Pt. III, fol. 243a; V, 581. It determines affirmatively a suggestion which I made in considering the symbolism of the White Head, as this is found in THE BOOK OF MYSTERY and the IDRAS. There is no aspect of the manifest Godhead in which the Male is without the Female, but the distinction is lost in AIN SOPH, about which nothing can be posited, except that it is shewn forth in KETHER.

so careless seemingly in its allocation of Shekinah, so that it is in CHOKMAH or BINAH as the one or the other mood happens to prevail. There are moments even when it looks as if Father, Word and Spirit abide in the SUPERNAL SEPHIROTH.[1] We must beware, however, of being misled by apparent correspondences with Christian Trinitarian doctrine and must remember in this connection that the Zoharic hypotheses are never spoken of as proceeding eternally one from another. The Word, for example, is strictly a time concept, postulated in respect of creation and preceded by the indwelling thought of God.

Shekinah herself in the state of distinction which—as we have seen—is affirmed concerning her, is either the first of created things or may be such when she assumes the vesture of METATRON.[2] In the state of ineffable union and in that conception which lies behind her name, she can be only eternal like the Holy One, save in so far as the Holy One, postulated in KETHER, is also a time conception in respect of AIN SOPH, the Inaccessible God, compared with Whom even the world of ATZILUTH is a conditioned state, and its conditioning is in respect of manifestation.

I have mentioned in another connection the work of Shekinah in creation. In her office as architect of the world, the Word was uttered to her, was by her conceived and brought or begotten into execution. We have seen that Shekinah below concurred with the architect above and was also a builder—in what sense does not signify, nor is it explained by the ZOHAR.[3] In so far, however, as creation is the history of the elect symbolised, it is obvious that the work remains unfinished till the great day of restitution, and coincident therewith is the history of Shekinah herself. On the manifest side it begins in the Garden of Eden—in that Garden which is she, according to another symbolism [4]—and it continues for the Theosophical Jew through the whole period of the

---

[1] Z., Pt. III, fol. 10b ; V, 31.

[2] *Ib.* We have seen that METATRON is the vesture of SHADDAI, but this Divine Name, with those of Adonai, Elohim and Shekinah herself, are evidently interchangeable. See Z., Pt. III, fol. 231a ; V, 571, in respect of METATRON, by which it appears that they are so related because the numerical value of the one name is the same as that of the other.

[3] *Ib.*, Pt. I, fol. 22a, b ; I, 136-138. It is said, however, that she is the object of the mysteries relative to the works of creation.—*Ib.*, Pt. III, fol. 231a ; V, 571.

[4] The counterpoise to this is that Shekinah was the companion of human exile when Adam and Eve were expelled from the Garden—as we shall see immediately.

Greater Exile. I have mentioned that it was Shekinah who walked with Adam in Paradise under the title of Lord God,[1] that is to say, of Jehovah Elohim, the union above communicating to the union below and prescribing the first law of life. This is the Shekinah in manifestation. But we know that the trespass followed and that our prototypical parent was driven out of the Garden. This might appear to mean that he was cast out from under the wings of Shekinah ; but he was not deserted in his need, for she followed him into the captivity of the senses. This is one side of the Zoharic doctrine that Shekinah suffered with mankind,[2] but it is put much more explicitly when it is said : " Therefore the man was driven out and the Mother was driven out with him." [3] This was the primal captivity, and many captivities followed, wherein Shekinah shared ; for it is said that she is the sacrifice which God has placed on His right and on His left hand, and about Him.[4]

There was separation between the King and Matrona in respect of the outer world and so came about a separation in the Divine Name, for the final HE was detached and came down on earth, the source of graces coming with her.[5] Though it is forbidden to separate the Heavenly Bride and Bridegroom, even in thought, it is this which has come to pass by reason of the sufferings of Israel,[6] with whom Shekinah was destined—as we have seen—to endure even from the beginning.[7] " When Israel is in exile the Shekinah is also in exile. It is for this reason that the Holy One will remember Israel," meaning that He remembers His covenant, " which is Shekinah." [8] The symbolical position is summed up in the

---

[1] Z., Pt. I, fol. 76a ; I, 448.

[2] *Ib.*, fol. 120b ; II, 84, 85.

[3] *Ib.*, fol. 22b ; I, 137. The authority is : " Behold, for your iniquities have ye sold yourselves, and for your transgressions is your mother put away."—Is. l, 1.

[4] *Ib.*, fol. 256a ; II, 603.—*Ib.*, Pt. III, fol. 109a ; V, 275.—*Ib.*, Pt. I, fol. 24a ; I, 149. Sometimes it is a question of drawing into the deeps and heights of Divine Union. Sometimes it is the same conception symbolised by the female offering all her members and all the parts of her personality to the corresponding members and parts on the male side.

[5] Z., Pt. I, fol. 254b ; II, 600. The point is expressed in a very curious way—namely, that the world could not exist until the HE final detached itself from the other three letters of the Divine Name and descended on earth. The authority seems to be : " I have said, Mercy shall be built up for ever " (Ps. lxxxix. 2), which the ZOHAR renders : " The world shall be built by mercy." *Cf.* Vulgate : *In aeternum misericordia aedificabitur in caelis.*—Ps. lxxxviii. 3.

[6] Z., Pt. II, fol. 9a, b ; III, 39.

[7] *Ib.*, Pt. I, fol. 120b ; II, 84.

[8] *Ib.*, Pt. I, fol. 120b ; II, 84. Compare Deut. xxx. 3 : " The Lord thy God will turn thy captivity, and have compassion upon thee."

statement that the second HE was obscured and fell,[1] becoming a symbol of penitence.[2] The meaning is that she is with the elect, for better, for worse, for richer, for poorer ; [3] and as in their attainments so is she with them in their sins, though not after the same manner, for she is then on the wrath side. Her shame is the defiled body of man.[4] Again, she is in separation from the King owing to the wickedness of man, and though she does not leave him the sin of Israel causes her to turn away.[5] To sum up on this subject, she was driven out of the Garden of Eden with Adam, like a wife sent away by her husband ; but it was for the salvation of the world.[6]

In glancing at the concurrent history of Israel and that of Shekinah, considerable care is needed to distinguish between the allusions to her who is enthroned in BINAH, never leaving the Supernals, and the exiled servant of God,[7] for there is a Shekinah called servant and a Shekinah called Daughter of the King.[8] The one is above the angels, like her who in Christian doctrine is called *Regina Angelorum*,[9] and in respect of all other lights of creation is that which soul is to body, though in relation to the Holy One she is as the body to the soul, notwithstanding that she and God are one.[10] She is the Mistress of the Celestial School, called the Abode of the Shepherds, and this is a school of METATRON, understood as a vesture or form assumed by Shekinah.[11] In another aspect of symbolism she is that great and wide sea mentioned in Ps. civ. 25, and she embraces the whole world, which is concentrated in her.[12] She is the jubilee above—presumably on account of joy.[13] All this is in the world of procession or

---

[1] Z., Pt. II, fol. 9b ; III, 40.
[2] *Ib.*, fol. 114b ; III, 442.
[3] *Ib.*, Pt. III, fol. 74a ; V, 202.   She is weighed down by the sin of Israel.—*Ib.*, fol. 28a ; V, 79.
[4] *Ib.*, fol. 75a ; V, 204.
[5] *Ib.*, fol. 155a, b ; V, 397.
[6] *Ib.*, Pt. I, fol. 237a ; II, 535, 536.   It is written : " O Lord our God (Jehovah Elohim), other lords beside Thee have had dominion over us ; but by Thee only will we make mention of Thy Name," or—as the ZOHAR has it—" but, thanks to Thee, we have remembered Thy Name only."—Is. xxvi. 13.   This verse is held to contain the Supreme Mystery of Faith.   JEHOVAH ELOHENOU is the source of highest mysteries, and when Israel attains perfection it will make no distinction between Jehovah and ELOHENOU.   It is forbidden to separate these Names even in thought.   Yet is there separation now on account of the sufferings of Israel, and because it is apart from God.—*Ib.*, Pt. II, fol. 9a, b ; III, 38-40.
[7] Z., Pt. III, fol. 223a ; V, 563.
[8] *Ib.*, Pt. II, fol. 94b ; III, 378.
[9] *Ib.*, fol. 116b ; III, 450.
[10] *Ib.*, fol. 118b ; III, 456.
[11] *Ib.*, Pt. III, fol. 197a ; V, 508.
[12] *Ib.*, Pt. I, fol. 236a ; II, 530, 531.
[13] *Ib.*, fol. 252a ; II, 593.

emanation—the hypostatic world, which is ATZILUTH.[1] But Shekinah is said otherwise to receive a body in YETZIRAH [2] and so is empowered to manifest in ASSIAH, wherein—among other titles—she is the Lady of Battles,[3] who also obtains remission of the sins of Israel, after the manner of the *Agnus Dei qui tollit peccata mundi*.[4]

The Shekinah is held to connect in a particular sense with the patriarchal age. It was after his circumcision that the letter HE was added to the name of Abram and it was also thereafter that he was united—as we have found—with Shekinah.[5] Most of the divine visions beheld by Abraham were visions and manifestations of Shekinah,[6] who dwelt constantly in the tent of Sarah, and this is why Abraham—as we have seen—on appearing in the presence of Pharaoh, described Sarah as his sister, not as his wife, his reference being really to Shekinah, who bears this title in respect of man and who accompanied Sarah.[7] When he went to the rescue of Lot,[8] on leaving his house, Abraham beheld Shekinah lighting the way before him and encompassed by many celestial legions.[9] She was present when Isaac blessed Jacob ; [10] it was she who conferred upon Jacob the name of Israel,[11] and she was with him when he set up the mystic stone as a pillar.[12] When seeking a wife it was with Shekinah that Jacob united his intention, and hence it is said—in characteristic Zoharic symbolism—that when he married Rachel he united heaven and earth.[13] Shekinah, however, did not ignore or forget Leah but—as the Holy Spirit—inspired her, so that she knew respecting her part in the bearing of the twelve tribes.[14] Rachel died when the progenitors of these tribes were completed and her place was taken by Shekinah, but after the death of Leah she removed to the house of Bala, so that she might be near Jacob, though she could not dwell in his house because—as we know—she resides only where

---

[1] Z., Pt. III, fol. 109a ; V, 276.
[2] *Ib.*
[3] *Ib.*, fol. 75b ; V, 205. It is of course obvious that Shekinah as Daughter of the King did not fall into sin and hence her exile is willing, or she is empowered, as this text says. But that of which she is prototype—incarnate womanhood—did—*ex hypothesi*—fall, and that son who is incarnate manhood fell with her.
[4] Z., Pt. I, fol. 191b ; I, 353.
[5] *Ib.*, fol. 93a ; I, 529.
[6] *Ib.*, Pt. II, fol. 105a ; II, 27.
[7] *Ib.*, fol. 111b ; II, 50.
[8] Gen. xiv. 14.
[9] Z., Pt. I, fol. 112b ; II, 55.
[10] *Ib.*, fol. 144b ; II, 168.
[11] *Ib.*, fol. 173b ; II, 283.
[12] *Ib.*, fol. 148b ; II, 186.
[13] *Ib.*, fol. 153a ; II, 203.
[14] *Ib.*, fol. 157a ; II, 216.

the man is united to the woman.[1] When Jacob lost Joseph he lost the Shekinah also, either because joy had left him, and she dwells only with the glad heart, or because it is said that he ceased to cohabit with his wife, as a mark of grief and desolation.[2] The part of joy returned to him after reunion with his son and presumably also Shekinah, for she accompanied Jacob and his family into Egypt, and forty-two sacred angels destined for her service came down with her, each bearing a letter belonging to the Divine Name of forty-two letters.[3] So long as Joseph was with the Israelites the Shekinah was with them also, and they were not enslaved by the Egyptians ; but when the day came for him to die, it is said that she departed,[4] and we know how it was with the people until the advent of Moses. It was he who attracted again the Shekinah to Israel[5] ; it is said that she never quitted him from the day of his birth[6] ; but more even than this, one of the doctors affirms that the father of Moses was espoused to Shekinah, or alternatively that both father and mother aspired towards her in their hearts during the intercourse which was followed by his conception.[7] This is what is meant by the statement, already cited, that the Shekinah reposed upon the nuptial bed of the parents of Moses.[8]

The nature of the union which subsisted between Moses and Shekinah is set out very curiously, for it is said that in a manner she had three husbands, namely, Jacob, Joseph and Moses. But the first abode with his wives on earth and was only united with her after his death. The espousals were not dissolved between her and Joseph until the bones of the latter were interred in Palestine. It was for this reason that Moses carried them out of Egypt, and they accompanied the children of Israel during the wanderings in the desert. It was somehow in virtue of their presence that Moses was united to Shekinah, so that she cohabited with him, and in connection with this it is observed that he detached himself from his wife—a very strange intimation if the Indwelling Glory abides only with man in so far as he is wedded in the ordinary and lawful sense.[9] Indeed in another place the fact

---

[1] Z., Pt. I, fol. 175b ; II, 289.
[2] Ib., fol. 197a, b ; II, 381, 382.
[3] Ib., Pt. II, fol. 4b ; III, 15.
[4] Ib., I, fol. 184a ; II, 327.
[5] Ib., fol. 67b, 68a ; I, 400.
[6] Ib., fol. 120b ; II, 83.
[7] Ib., Pt. II, fol. 19a ; III, 92.
[8] Ib., fol. 11b ; III, 49.
[9] Ib., Pt. I, fol. 21b, 88a ; I, 133–135. I am only giving a very slight sketch of the whole subject, which would seem to the general reader a record of utter unreason.

Stated is not counted to Moses exactly as righteousness.[1] The whole point rests on that Talmudic tradition which we have met with concerning the separation of Moses from Zipporah.[2] Another account, which is in opposition to much that has preceded, says that the Holy One espoused Matrona to Moses, and this was the first time that she made contact with the world below.[3] We may compare herewith the remark on the Daughter of God in another place, where it is said that until she became a Bride, no one spoke with God face to face [4] : it is another reference to the espousals of Moses, contradicting her alleged union with Abraham and Jacob and her presence in the world before its creation. The meaning is that Shekinah was united with Moses after a new and more intimate manner than had been the case previously, just as God revealed Himself to the lawgiver in another way and in a sense under a New Name. The exodus brought about by Moses occasioned, moreover, the manifestation of Shekinah before the people of Israel, she being the pillar of fire by night, as Jehovah was that of cloud by day.[5] According to another account, she was also a cloud, and it was through this cloud that Moses passed on his ascent of Mount Sinai.[6] Finally, and most important of all, Moses caused Shekinah to manifest in the Ark of the Covenant over the Mercy-Seat, between the figures of the Kerubim. The Tabernacle was erected to serve as her residence ; and at the moment when it was set up by Moses, there was another erected in the world above. What seems to have happened, however, was that the Mosaic Tabernacle became the residence of METATRON, who connects so curiously with Shekinah.[7] The latter was also that cloud which abode on the tent of the

---

The fact that the bones of Jacob were interred in Palestine means that they belonged to the " celestial beings " : it was otherwise with those of Joseph, and he was still counted as belonging to the earth. The bones are symbols of the celestial legions, and these only needed to be interred in Palestine. The Sons of the Doctrine did not know that a man in the position of Joseph would have been embalmed after his death. A still more inscrutable suggestion is worded literally as follows : " Moses cohabited with Shekinah, who is symbolised by the moon, even while the spirit dwelt in his body, and he subjected her to his desires."—*Ib.*, fol. 22a ; I, 134. After his death he ascended to the degree of the Jubilee, which—as we have seen—is BINAH and the Shekinah in transcendence therein. She who was the spouse of Moses was the Shekinah in manifestation, and it is said that after his death she returned to Jacob. With all this compare *ante*, Book VIII, § 6, where it is said that Moses failed to open the 50th Gate of Understanding because he had ceased to live with his wife.

[1] Z., Pt. I, fol. 234b ; II, 523.
[2] See *Tract Sabbath.*
[3] *Ib.*, Pt. II, fol. 145a ; IV, 59.
[4] *Ib.*, fol. 22b ; III, 115.
[5] *Ib.*, Pt. III, fol. 191b ; V, 499.
[6] *Ib.*, Pt. I, fol. 176b ; II, 293.
[7] *Ib.*, Pt. II, fol. 143a ; IV, 54.

congregation while the glory of the Lord filled the Tabernacle.[1] Alternatively it was a cloud that rose up to veil her presence, and dissolved when she went forth. It is called smoke by the ZOHAR, which also gives the reason, according to its own fantastic symbolism—namely, that Shekinah had been drawn into this world by the fire which burns in the hearts of the patriarchs.[2] The male principle or Jehovah is said further to have spoken from the Tabernacle by the intermediation of Shekinah, who is the female principle.[3] The Tabernacle itself—as we have seen—is Shekinah under another aspect,[4] much as the tent of Sarah is so called on occasion, because she and the Divine Bride dwelt therein.[5] The Shekinah considered as the Tabernacle is in pledge for the sins of man.[6]

We know by the scriptural account that in the temple of Solomon the Shekinah continued to repose between the wings of the Kerubim.[7] She is described as resident throughout the Holy of Holies,[8] yet is connected in an especial manner with the western wall of the temple.[9] The Holy of Holies was guarded moreover by METATRON [10] and was built for the union of the King and MATRONA. It is written : " Those of the country shall utter cries, and the angels of peace shall weep bitterly." [11] This is the Zoharic version of Isaiah xxxiii. 7. It refers to the weeping of the angels when the Sanctuary was destroyed and the Shekinah was exiled into a foreign land.[12] She underwent transformation and assumed another form than that which she had worn previously. So also the Spouse of Shekinah—referring to the VAU of the Sacred Name, she in manifestation being the second HE—reduced that light which enlightens the world,[13] as it is written : " The sun at his rising shall be covered with darkness, and the moon shall give no light." [14]

These are naturally the heads, and such only, of the history of election in Israel and the glory of all in connection there-

[1] Ex. xl, 34, 35.
[2] Z., Pt. I, fol. 1, 76b ; II, 294.
[3] Ib., fol. 239a ; II, 545.
[4] Ib., Pt. III, fol. 114a ; V, 285.
[5] Ib., Pt. II, fol. 116a ; III, 447.
[6] Ib., Pt. I, fol. 101b ; II, 11.
[7] Ib., Pt. III, fol. 114a ; V, 285.
[8] Ib., Pt. II, fol. 16b ; III, 76.
[9] Ib., Pt. III, fol. 161b ; V, 416.
[10] Ib., fol. 164a ; IV, 107.—Ib., Pt. III, fol. 74b ; V, 203.
[11] Cf. Vulgate : Ecce videntes clamabunt fores, angeli pacis amare flebunt. The Authorised Version is : " Behold, their valiant ones shall cry without : the ambassadors of peace shall weep bitterly." The Revised Version agrees.
[12] Z., Pt. I, fol. 203a ; II, 407.—Ib., fol. 182a ; II, 319.
[13] Ib.
[14] Is. xiii. 10.

with. In the Second Temple the Shekinah had no part,[1]
though by the hypothesis of the subject she had followed her
people into the exile of Babylon and helped them to remember
Zion by its sad waters. Albeit the Sons of the Doctrine had
their dark moments during that day of a thousand years or
over which followed the destruction of Jerusalem, at some
period of which the ZOHAR entered into record, and though
some of their sayings in these moments haunt the heart with
their catholic sense of unavailingness, the mood and its clouds
lifted ever and unerringly. Deeper still in their own hearts
they knew that they had not been deserted, that on account
of the Betrothed of God Israel was not forsaken by Him.[2]
Were they not conscious also—I think in my soul, most
surely—as by all the waters and in all the Babylons of the
greater exile, they made up their dream of Shekinah, that she
was more vitally and efficaciously with them than she had
been with patriarchs of old ; that she was married to them
not less closely than to Moses, prince of lawgivers ; and that
she was realised better as a presence than when she sat between the Kerubim ? Ever in BINAH her celestial fire abode
on the Throne of Mercy [3] for those who dwelt in her covenant,
and by her mediation an union was still possible, as indeed
actual, between the Holy One and the Community of Israel.[4]
This is one of the senses in which the souls of Israel are said
to be attached to Shekinah.[5] That is not true therefore *quod
unus doctor dixit in excessu suo :* " Israel is dead for the Shekinah
which is above by the destruction of the First Temple ; it is
dead a second time for the Shekinah which is below by the
destruction of the Second Temple." [6] And again : " The
destruction of the two Temples dried up the sources of the
Shekinah above and below." [7] She and Israel are in exile
together, in sorrow and loss together,[8] and the path of
penitence trodden by the one is the path of emancipation for
both. Meanwhile, " the earth is the Lord's, and the fullness
thereof ; the world, and they that dwell therein " ; [9] but the
fullness thereof is a reference to Shekinah, as an ample moon
enlightened over its surface by the sun. She is full also of

---

[1] The First Temple was destroyed, because light failed therein, but the Second
Temple seems never to have had the light.—Z., Pt. II, fol. 95b ; IV, 150.
[2] *Ib.*, Pt. III, fol. 115b ; V, 297.   [6] *Ib.*, Pt. I, fol. 26a ; I, 164.
[3] *Ib.*, fol. 34a ; V, 89.   [7] *Ib.*, fol. 255a ; II, 601.
[4] *Ib.*, fol. 37b ; V, 102.   [8] *Ib.*, Pt. II, fol. 189b ; IV, 175.
[5] *Ib.*, Pt. I, fol. 25a ; I, 154.   [9] Ps. xxiv. 1.

celestial benefits, like a treasury ; and in her manifestation to Israel she is a treasury which belongs to the Lord.[1] Moreover, the exile of Shekinah with Israel, and her residence among other peoples, has its train of extrinsic consequences in the peace and benefits which are enjoyed by the latter.[2] This is the sense in which it is said that other nations have attracted the Shekinah towards them.[3] Indeed her perfection is throughout the whole earth and her benedictions are over all the world,[4] for Elohim is a Mystery of Life[5] and the Source of all life. She never separated from man so long as he observed the commandments of the Law ;[6] but in connection with this we must take and qualify freely a number of counter-statements : (1) Every sin committed in public drives away Shekinah from the earth ;[7] (2) the generation of Noah sinned in the sight of the whole world, and the Shekinah was far from the world ;[8] (3) when owing to the wickedness of the world the latter has been left by Shekinah it is deprived of all defence, and the severity of justice reigns therein ;[9] (4) after the guilty have been exterminated the Shekinah returns.[10] It is obvious that these statements do not obtain generically on the literal side ; the consequences, like the acts, are individual, or, in the case where they are collective, it is only in a restricted way.

To sum up : the wounds of the world and the wounds of the Church in the world may be wide and deep ; but the Church and the world go on, for ten persons in the House of Prayer constitute the body of Shekinah ;[11] and there is a very much truer sense than was ever conceived by the ZOHAR in which those ten are never wanting : the elect are everywhere the true Israel, and it is thanks to Israel that Shekinah resides on earth, Israel being its bodyguard.[12] In thousands and tens of thousands of cases, all the wide world over, it is true and glorious that man acknowledges the kingdom of heaven and submits thereto ; that the Shekinah rests upon his head, assisting him in the quality of witness ; that she testifies before the Sacred King how this man proclaims the Divine Unity—or, in other words, that Jehovah is Elohim—above

[1] Z., Pt. I, fol. 67a ; I, 395, 396.
[2] Ib., fol. 84b ; I, 488.
[3] Ib.
[4] Ib., Pt. I, fol. 166a ; II, 251.
[5] Ib., fol. 227b ; II, 497.
[6] Ib., Pt. I, fol. 231a ; II, 516.

[7] Ib., fol. 57b ; I, 333.
[8] Ib.
[9] Ib., fol. 68b ; I, 406.
[10] Ib.
[11] Ib., Pt. III, fol. 126a ; V, 324.
[12] Ib., Pt. I, fol. 61a ; I, 358.

and below, twice every day ; [1] that so far as these are concerned the earth is perfect and all joy is found therein.[2]   Thus
is Jerusalem rebuilt for ever in the heart ; the Shekinah goes
up into the high mountain and announces its reconstruction
to the patriarchs.[3]   In these also she herself is delivered,[4] and
they dwell together henceforward in the Holy Land.[5]   It is a
foretaste of that time when all peoples shall enter under the
wings of Shekinah,[6] as also of the day to come when evil
shall be exterminated entirely and there shall be the same
solemnity of festival as when the Holy One, blessed be He,
created heaven and earth.[7]   Let us therefore join our voice
to those of the doctors who say that the Covenant with
Shekinah will endure for ever.[8]

Before attempting to place a reasonable interpretation on
the materials that are now in our hands, it is necessary to
complete the collection by certain additional particulars
which to some extent stand by themselves.

The created Law is called the garment of Shekinah [9]—a
vesture, as METATRON is also, being perhaps the same vesture.
It follows that she herself is something that dwells within it—
as, for example, the Traditional, Oral and Secret Law which
is not disclosed to the rank and file of believers because of the
wickedness of the world.   When the Created or External
Law is broken below it is as if the sinner rent or removed the
vestments of Shekinah, while alternatively those who observe
the commandments have the same merit as if they clothed
the Shekinah with garments.[10]   Such is the work of sanctity
in the higher conventions, according to the reverie of Israel.
The MISHNA is the servant of Shekinah [11] and is also that helpmeet for man which is promised in Scripture.[12]   Whether this
interpretation could be elucidated by explaining in what sense
the MISHNA—as part of the story of Israel—may be said to
have tempted men, understood as those who are elect or are
at least capable of election, and may have led them into the
exile of the Fall, is another question ; but the *tour de force* is
not attempted in the ZOHAR.   It might be affirmed truly that

---

[1] Z., Pt. II, fol. 160b ; IV, 99.
[2] *Ib.*, Pt. I, fol. 61a ; I, 357.
[3] *Ib.*, Pt. III, fol. 173b ; V, 451.
[4] *Ib.*, Pt. II, fol. 216b ; IV, 229.
[5] *Ib.*, fol. 222a ; IV, 242.
[6] *Ib.*, fol. 69b ; III, 308, 309.—Is. ii. 2, 3.

[7] *Ib.*, Pt. I, Appendix III, SECRET MIDRASH ; II, 714.
[8] *Ib.*, Pt. III, fol. 257a ; V, 597.
[9] *Ib.*, Pt. I, fol. 23a, b ; I, 143.
[10] *Ib.*, Pt. I, fol. 23a, b ; DE PAULY, I, 143.
[11] *Ib.*, fol. 27b ; I, 174.
[12] Gen. ii. 18.

it took him further and further into the bondage of the letter. The text itself says only that the MISHNA was the spouse of Israel during his adolescence,[1] spouse also during his exile, though sometimes for and sometimes against him. The marriage was imperfect at best. During the adolescent period the MISHNA was pre-eminent over MATRONA, so that the King and MATRONA were separated from the Celestial Spouse.[2] It was the servant who took the place of the mistress. Perhaps the meaning is that the literal explanation in its excessive development clouded the spiritual sense of holy doctrine;[3] but if it be this, it is also more. Who then is the mistress? The answer, according to the ZOHAR, is that the Oral Law is the image of Elohim, and this we know to be Shekinah.[4]

There is one practical application of all this cloud of doctrine, and it may be summarised in a few words. It is prayer that attaches man to Shekinah, and as the Holy One is united constantly to her, it follows that by prayer man is attached to the Holy One.[5] All the angels open their wings to receive the Shekinah by prayer, and those on earth who wish their prayers to reach heaven should unite themselves with the Shekinah.[6] Whereas the gates of the palaces to which prayers ascend commonly have numerous guardians, those of the palace of Shekinah have none, and prayers enter unhindered.[7] It will seem at first sight that she occupies in Kabbalism the same position of intercessor which is ascribed to the Blessed Virgin by the devotion of the Latin Church, yet having regard to Shekinah's incorporation with the Divine Hypostases, I incline to think that the analogy is misleading. In view of all that has been done to Christianise Kabbalism by every good means, and by so many that are bad intellectually, one has to be very careful about reading Christian implicits into the text of the literature.[8]

---

[1] Z., Pt. I, fol. 27b ; I, 174.   [2] *Ib.*, fol. 27b, 28a ; I, 175.

[3] We have had one example previously to shew that the sense of darkness and uncertainty alternated with the sense of light. The successors of Rabbi Simeon were not like that doctor himself, who had apparently William Postel's key of things kept secret from the foundation of the world. They were rather like the second circle of Brothers of the Rosy Cross, of whom it was said to be doubtful whether they were admitted to all things. It is clear, by their own confession, that they did not understand all things.

[4] Z., Pt. II, fol. 161b ; IV, 102.   [5] *Ib.*, Pt. I, fol. 24a ; I, 148, 149.

[6] *Ib.*, fol. 279b, 280a ; II, 648.   [7] *Ib.*, fol. 24a ; I, 148.

[8] Undesigned Christian reflections are another matter, and I have mentioned a few out of many possible examples.

There is a question whether my next and last point of analysis had better be taken here or in a later chapter; but as I have mentioned Christian implicits, and as what I have to say seems to connect with this subject, I will incorporate it under that motive, though it has also other issues. We have come across already in our quest many allusions to the Divine Father, the Divine Son, being two of the Christian Hypostases, and as we know that the Shekinah in transcendence is also the Divine Mother, the question arises naturally whether this is the Holy Spirit, the Third Person of the Christian Trinity.[1] Those who are acquainted with Theology will know that the Third Person is not recognised as feminine, though there has been a tendency in several modern departments of semi-Christian Transcendentalism to regard the Holy Spirit in this light and thus complete the triad of the Divine Family. They forget, however, that neither in the East nor the West—under the ægis of the Greek or Roman Orthodoxy—is the Son held to proceed from the Father and the Spirit, but on the contrary that the last is postulated as proceeding from the Father and the Son. Albeit the *Filioque* clause of the Nicene Creed was a ground of division between the two branches of the Church Catholic, as not of apostolical authority, I have heard that it is not denied otherwise in the Greek Rite. One alternative would be the co-equal and co-eternal procession of the Son and the Spirit from the Divine Father, and the symbol in this case would be a triangle with the apex upward, not in the reverse position which characterises Latin Theology. Now it cannot be said that either doctrinal position represents the mind of Kabbalism. We have seen that Jehovah Elohim, Spouse and Bride, Father and Mother, God and His Shekinah are in KETHER in a state of oneness, without separation and without distinction. There are very few references to this state in the ZOHAR. I have intimated indeed that there is only one which can be quoted with complete certainty in the wording, but I am justified thereby in saying that it is a state corresponding to that of parentage. They reproduce themselves immediately below as ABBA and AIMA, referred to CHOKMAH and BINAH.

---

[1] I have said that it arises naturally, but I do not mean that we should do much in this manner to complete the Christian Triad in Kabbalism. Readers who have followed my study up to this point will find little ground for comparison between Those who dwell in the Sephirotic Supernals and Father, Son and Holy Ghost in the Heaven of St. Thomas Aquinas, or other of the Latin Doctors.

But as in the Supernals the Divine Persons are not in a state of separation, so the male and female in these SEPHIROTH are one with those which are in KETHER. It follows that Shekinah is on both sides of the Tree, as I have said elsewhere in this section, and it is difficult to postulate in such a triad either a time conception or passage from subject to object. But the Trinity was working towards manifestation, and the result was that ABBA and AIMA begat the Son, who is VAU in DAATH, from which His personality was extended through six of the lower SEPHIROTH. They begat also the Daughter and Bride, at first implied in the Son, but afterwards separated and extended with him through the three worlds below ATZILUTH. Later Kabbalism locates the conception of YOD in CHOKMAH, excogitated as King and Father ; HE in BINAH, as Queen and Mother ; VAU posited in the Six Briatic and Yetziratic SEPHIROTH from CHESED to YESOD inclusive, but enthroned especially as the Son in TIPHERETH ; while the HE final is in MALKUTH. So far as I have been able to see, the particular variations of arrangement are not destitute of Zoharic authority. It must be recognised perhaps that there are two separate arrangements of the Tree of Life in the text. There is that which I have followed, drawing largely from THE BOOK OF MYSTERY and the three IDRAS, and there is its alternative which can be extracted—not without some confusion—from other parts of the collection. According to this the Father and Mother are in KETHER, the Son Who is the Word is in CHOKMAH, the Daughter and Bride is in BINAH. Now the Divine Name attributed to KETHER is JAH, formed of JOD and HE primal belonging to the TETRAGAM. It is said to be the Unknown God for whom the Name in question is that which the Propitiatory was for the Tabernacle—a summary of the male world above and the female world below. It is the Name of the Ancient of Ancients ; it is the synthesis of all things below and above. It follows in the arrangement that the VAU is referable to CHOKMAH and the HE final to BINAH, who descended to MAKLUTH, as the Bride or Shekinah in manifestation. Once more, Shekinah is really in every part as well as on both sides of the Tree, being the Mistress of the height and the deep, President over the four quarters of the universe of created things and all that led up thereto.

Now the French editor and translator of the ZOHAR have an arrangement peculiar to themselves, by virtue of which

YOD or the male principle, understood as the Father, is allocated to KETHER ; HE, understood as Shekinah, is in CHOKMAH ; while VAU in BINAH is the Holy Spirit. The Christian Trinity is thus complete, though the question of procession is left to account for itself as it may. The attribution is part of a scheme for decoding the mystery of Shekinah along a particular line in connection with Zoharic doctrine respecting Messiah, and it will be considered in full later on. The question which arises here is whether Shekinah, by us allocated to BINAH, is or is not the Holy Spirit. The editor and translator maintain that she is not, and the fact that two opinions are possible on the subject implies that the ZOHAR is either not at one with itself or utters an uncertain voice. There are many references, and perhaps there is a mean between them. It is manifest in the first place that the Holy Spirit is personified in the ZOHAR, and a preliminary point is whether we can find authority for this in the Old Testament. " Take not thy Holy Spirit from me," [1] says David, and according to Isaiah the people of Israel vexed God's Holy Spirit.[2] He asks also : " Where is He that put His Holy Spirit within him ? " [3]—meaning Moses, adding that " The Spirit of the Lord " caused Moses to rest. I do not know whether these can be called personifications, but they exhaust the allusions in the Old Testament which are connected with the distinctive qualification of " holy." We know that " the Lord put his spirit upon them " ; [4] that " the spirit rested upon them and they prophesied " ; [5] that Joshua was " a man in whom is the spirit " ; [6] that God hardened his spirit " ; [7] that " the spirit came upon Amasai " ; [8] that David gave to Solomon all the designs for the temple " that he had by the spirit " ; [9] that by His spirit God " garnished the heavens " ; [10] that God sends forth His spirit; [11] that there is a spirit poured from on high,[12] and Isaiah also says that " the Lord God and His spirit hath sent me," i.e., on the prophet ; [13] that " the spirit of the Lord God is on me," i.e., Isaiah ; [14] that the spirit took up Ezekiel ; [15] and that according to Zechariah God sent in His spirit by former prophets.[16] There is a sheaf of other

[1] Ps. li. 11.
[2] Is. lxiii. 10.
[3] Is. lxiii. 14.
[4] Numbers xi. 29.
[5] Ib., xi. 26.
[6] Ib., xxvi. 18.
[7] Deut. ii. 30.
[8] 1 Chron. xii. 18.
[9] Ib., xxviii. 12.
[10] Job xxvi. 13.
[11] Ps. civ. 30.
[12] Is. xxxii. 15.
[13] Is. xlviii. 16.
[14] Is. lxi. 1.
[15] Ezek. iii. 12.
[16] Zech. vii. 12.

allusions, but enough has been quoted for the purpose in hand. They may be kept in mind by the reader in connection with the Zoharic allusions which will follow hereon. He shall decide for himself—as I have no wish to adjudicate—whether there is more explicit personification in the Kabbalistic text, and if so whether it is to be accounted for by (1) natural development of ideas ; (2) Jewish tendencies prior to the TALMUDS, represented roughly by Philo and, as such, a possible common source for Kabbalistic Jew and Christian ; (3) Talmudic evidence ; or (4) the atmosphere of Christian doctrine in which the Kabbalistic Jew lived and moved for the most part and which he can have scarcely failed to absorb in some degree.

I will take first of all those references which are either dubious or appear to suggest that the Holy Spirit is not synonymous with Shekinah.

The ZOHAR asks : what is signified by the words : " And the Spirit returns to Elohim who gave it ? " [1]   The answer is that one of the words designates Shekinah, that word being אלהים = Elohim, while another word designates the Holy Spirit, i.e., the word רוח == " spirit." It might seem therefore that the Holy Spirit is not Shekinah but is in close connection therewith, like a breath that goes forth and returns.[2] It does not signify for our purpose that the ZOHAR is making a false interpretation—seeing that the spirit mentioned in Scripture is that of man. Again, it is said that when man is circumcised he is joined to the sacred crown of Shekinah and the Holy Spirit rests upon him.[3] In another place three spirits are distinguished : (1) The Spirit below, which is called the Holy Spirit ; (2) the Spirit of the Middle Way, which is that of Wisdom and Understanding ; (3) the Spirit which sounds the trumpet and unites the fire to the water, this being the Superior, Concealed and Mysterious Spirit, whereunto are suspended all sacred spirits and all luminous countenances.[4] Now, it is stated, after the prevailing manner of the ZOHAR, which cannot postulate a triad apart from an inward unity, that these three are one and that

---

[1] " And the spirit shall return unto God who gave it."—Eccles. xii. 7.   Authorised Version, for which the Revised Version substitutes : " And the spirit returns." Cf. Vulgate : Et spiritus redeat ad Deum, qui dedit illum.

[2] Z., Pt. II, fol. 97b ; III, 390.   [3] Ib., Pt. III, fol. 14b ; V, 42.

[4] Ib., Pt. III, fol. 26a ; V, 73, 74.

they form a holocaust which is the Holy of Holies.[1] This, however, is explained elsewhere to be Shekinah, for—as we have seen—she is the sacrifice which God has placed on His right and His left hand, and about Him.[2] Again, " she is the sacrifice of the Holy One," and prayer is the holocaust which in turn is offered to her.[3] Once more, it is said that when the Shekinah resided in the Holy Land the impure spirit took flight and found refuge in the abyss, while the Holy Spirit was diffused throughout the world, so that the one would seem to be associated closely with the other, if we can presume that there is indeed distinction.[4] In this connection the Holy Spirit is spoken of as the cloud that covered the Tabernacle ; but the same cloud has been identified otherwise with Shekinah and with Metatron. It will be seen so far that it would be difficult to quote anything more indecisive. There is, however, one memorable passage which I have reserved to the last, and must cite almost *in extenso*. " A tradition tells us that at the hour when Moses, the true prophet, was about to be born into the world, the Holy One caused the Holy Spirit to come forth from the Tabernacle "—elsewhere that which seems to be the abode of Shekinah in transcendence. God entrusted all power thereto and innumerable keys of power, together with five diadems, the splendour of which enlightened a thousand worlds. " The Sacred King exalted the Holy Spirit in His palace and set Him above all celestial legions "—even as Shekinah is placed above all angels. " These were in great amazement, for they saw that the Holy One was resolved to change the face of the world by the intermediation of the Holy Spirit." They began to inquire concerning " Him," and were told to prostrate themselves, because " He " would descend one day among men, and the Law—till then hidden—should be revealed. They did homage accordingly, and thereafter the Holy Spirit ascended towards the King. The three letters, MEM, SHIN and HE, belonging to the name of Moses, offered their worship also ; and then the Holy Spirit, in fulfilment of what had been fore-

---

[1] Z., Pt. III, fol. 26a ; V, 73, 74.
[2] *Ib.*, Pt. I, fol. 24a ; I, 149.
[3] *Ib.*, fol. 256a ; II, 604.
[4] *Ib.*, Pt. II, fol. 269a ; IV, 303. I may add that when Joseph saw Benjamin with the rest of his brethren, as related in Gen. xliii. 16, he is said by the ZOHAR to have discerned by the Holy Spirit (a) that Benjamin would have part in the Holy Land, and (b) that the Shekinah would reside therein. Whether this tends to identification or to the opposite might be difficult to affirm.—See *ib.*, Pt. I, fol. 202b ; II, 405.

told, came down to earth, bearing the arms necessary to smite Pharaoh and his entire country. On reaching this world He found the Shekinah already here, radiant of aspect and spreading light through all the house.[1] It will be observed that the last sentence looks like an unqualified and conclusive distinction, though in its absence and from what has preceded in the extract one would have said that the Holy Spirit was actually a synonym of Shekinah. We hear nothing more, however, of any office in distinction, for that which henceforward abode with the Lawgiver was not the Holy Spirit but the glory of his Spiritual Spouse, who had been with him from his beginning on earth.

Let us now take the evidence in the contrary sense, proceeding in the same manner and remembering that there is only one testimony at most on the negative side of the subject.

In the first place, it is said—as we have seen indeed already—that the Holy Spirit inspired Leah concerning her work in connection with the foundation of the twelve tribes ;[2] but we know otherwise that it is Shekinah who presides over birth, seeming to be in analogy with the chaste and conjugal Venus. In connection with the daughter of Jethro—who was the father-in-law of Moses—the Holy Spirit is affirmed to have been always with Moses,[3] which we may read in the light of another statement—that the Shekinah was associated with the orders which Moses gave to the experts charged with building the Tabernacle, because such work could not be accomplished properly without the inspiration of the Holy Spirit.[4] The association of Shekinah meant the enlightenment of the Holy Spirit. Here again is at least the close connection in virtue of which the one is not without the other, and the kind of nearness is illustrated more clearly by another passage which speaks of that day when God shall pour upon us the Holy Spirit of His Shekinah.[5] It would seem again to be the breath of Shekinah. Once more it is said that the Holy Spirit is called ZOTH,[6] being the name which designates the sign of the Sacred Covenant imprinted on man ;[7] but we

---

[1] Z., Pt. II, fol. 53b, 54a ; III, 241, 242.
[2] Ib., Pt. I, fol. 157a ; II, 216.
[3] Ib., Pt. II, fol. 13b ; III, 61.
[4] Ib., Pt. II, fol. 179b ; IV, 149, 150.
[5] Ib., Pt. III, fol. 219a ; V, 555.
[6] זאת = This, in its opposition to הלזו or ההוא = That, understood as on the evil side. The ZOHAR cites a number of Biblical passages.
[7] Z., Pt. I, fol. 228a ; II, 498.

shall see that this sign is connected especially with Shekinah. So also when Balaam lifted up his eyes,[1] he is supposed to have beheld Shekinah resting with poised wings above the twelve tribes of Israel, and to have questioned how he could prevail against them, seeing that the Holy Spirit was thus their stay and their protection. There seems no doubt that this is an equivalent of identification.[2] It is only at the end of the ZOHAR that we obtain a still more decisive voice on the affirmative side. The question is one of alleged or suggested criminal relations between Esther and Ahasuerus, which are characterised as slander, the ZOHAR adding that " she was clothed with the Holy Spirit," [3] as it is written : " Esther put on her royal apparel "—or, as the passage renders it, " clothed herself with royalty." The interpretation follows immediately thus : " The Holy Spirit—this is the Shekinah with which Esther clothed herself." [4] It is an opportunity for a favourite form of testimony, and the great text adds : " Woe to those who feed upon the husk of the Law, while the grain of wheat is the mystical sense." It will be observed that, if words signify anything, this is not less than an unqualified and conclusive identification. If anyone will read over with care similar to my own the references which I have provided now on both sides of the question, I believe that they will conclude with me, as against the one definite statement on the negative side, that there is a cumulative affirmative evidence crowned by a most clear affirmation : " The Holy Spirit—this is the Shekinah."

When therefore the editor and translator of the ZOHAR allocate this Spirit to BINAH, it means that they are referring the Shekinah thereto, as I have done also, even if their design is in the opposite sense. But this Spirit is not the Third Person in the Blessed Trinity of Christendom, though it is impossible that it should not have aspects of likeness, in so far as the root of both doctrines is in the Holy Scriptures of Israel. I conclude on the authority of the text itself—which for once I must repeat at this point—that " from the constant and ardent love of HE " in BINAH " for YOD " in CHOKMAH " there issues VAU " in DAATH, conceived and born of HE,

---

[1] Num. xxiv. 2.
[2] As a fact, it is actually more than a simple equivalent.
[3] Z., Pt. III, fol. 275b ; VI, 47.
[4] Ib. See Esther v. 1.

by which also it is nourished.[1] " But VAU came into the world with a twin-sister bearing the name of Grace," which is CHESED, because Grace is Mercy. " The two took root on earth and constituted the HE final "—that is to say, in MALKUTH—because the male is not without the female—as we shall see—either above or below. " Thus was the VAU united to the HE " final. But in the completion, the perfection and harmony of the Divine Name, letter by letter and letter within letter, all these are one at the root : there would be separation proclaimed in the Divine Nature if YOD, HE, VAU, HE did not bear witness to His unity.[2]

The most important consideration which arises out of the whole subject is after what manner we are to regard essentially this Cohabiting or Indwelling Glory which is termed Shekinah in Scripture and in the sacred texts of the ZOHAR. We know that it dwelt between the Kerubim in the Tabernacle or Ark of Moses, and the Kerubim are said to have been male and female, types in the Sanctuary of Israel of things manifested on earth as types in their turn of the union that is above. When a mean is taken between all the cloud of references, it calls for no gift of interpretation to discern what lies with uttermost plainness on the surface ; but we have explained nothing which is vital if we say that Shekinah is the principle of Divine Motherhood—that is, the feminine side of Divinity, implied in the logic of our symbolism when we speak of the Fatherhood in God. It is a case of being true to our symbols, and though this is of consequence intellectually, it remains thereat. If we turn to the analogy which subsists in virtue of the symbolism between womanhood above and that which is found below, we shall not proceed much further if there is brought home to us merely the notion that the office of the mother on earth is made sacred in a sense that is above the hallowed sense of Nature by the conception of its archetype in heaven. It has been present to us through all the Christian centuries in the popular and most catholic devotion to the Queen of Heaven, which, like so many other popular interests,

---

[1] Z., Pt. III, fol. 77b ; V, 210, 211.

[2] The passage is important to my purpose, but it must be admitted that it is exceedingly confused. The meaning may be that in the extension of VAU through the worlds below ATZILUTH, the head of the Son is in DAATH—as we have seen otherwise—while that of his Bride and Sister is in CHESED, which, however, is on the male side of the Tree. I do not pretend to explain fully how the descent of the Son and Daughter constituted the HE final, for the VAU is distinct from the HE. But this has been touched upon in a previous note.

but those more especially that are consecrated by the greatest of all the Churches, adumbrates a vital truth in the spiritual life and a first principle in the world of reality. It has been a very sincere and whole-hearted devotion in those who have been drawn thereto ; but the particular doctrine of miraculous and virgin birth, though eloquent and suggestive within its own measures, creates a clear line of demarcation between subject and object, so that there is a world-wide distinction between the honour paid to her who is ever outside ourselves and the adoration of Him Who is never understood essentially until He is realised within. Now, there are no prayers to Shekinah in the official liturgies of Jewish religion ; but in the Secret Church of Israel, frequented in spirit and in truth by the Sons of the Doctrine, she is either the House of Prayer or else abides therein, and we have seen that her doors are open to prayers for ever. She was the great object of prayer, though it is to be questioned whether it was by the way of prescribed forms : it was rather by that prayer in the stillness of unexpressed thought about which we hear in the ZOHAR. The reason is ready to our hands, and the first light which may be said to fall on our subject is that the Shekinah is an Indwelling Glory. The Latin Kabbalists made use of the term *cohabitans* by an imperfect understanding on their own part of the mystery involved—that is to say, by a consideration of the external side which obtains in espousal-relations on earth. The proper word is *inhabitans*, for it is said that the Shekinah dwells in man,[1] being in the hearts of those who seek after good works zealously.[2] And more definitely : Man is the House of Shekinah.[3] The beginning of this inhabitation is when man makes a firm effort towards self-amendment, for by such turning the Shekinah is drawn towards him,[4] and to this condition are applied the words : " I am my beloved's and his desire is towards me." [5] Those with whom she dwells are those who are humbled and even broken by suffering.[6] Yet does she reign only where there is joy rather than sadness, an allusion to the support of trials with resignation. The suffering is, however, more especially that of which the root or cause is in love, being the state of those who are consumed by the love of the Divine : these

---

[1] Z., Pt. I, fol. 166a ; II, 250.
[2] *Ib.*, Pt. II, fol. 128b ; IV, 11.
[3] *Ib.*

[4] *Ib.*, Pt. I, fol. 88b ; I, 509.
[5] Song of Solomon vii. 10.
[6] Z., Pt. I, fol. 181a ; II, 315.

are the Brothers of Shekinah.[1] Again, it is said that the work of Shekinah below is comparable to that which the soul accomplishes in the body : more accurately still it is the same work,[2] and this enables us to understand in what sense she is termed the soul of the Tabernacle below,[3] which Tabernacle is the sacred body of man.

I have called these intimations a first light, but I have not intended to exaggerate their value as such. I speak as a mystic ; we have heard for two thousand years that God is within and His kingdom, yet the world remains comparable rather to the wilderness without the Holy City than to the blessed Zion ; and if Shekinah is offered to us in the secret literature of Jewry as that aspect of the Divine Nature or Principle which is realisable by the heart of man, I do not see that we have added anything to our subject. It is idle to decode books of Secret Doctrine unless they have something more definite to tell us concerning the way, the truth and the life. So also it is beautiful to hear that whosoever wrongs a poor person is guilty of wrong to Shekinah, because she is the protectress of the poor ; [4] but we know too well already about things which grieve the Spirit. I might multiply these quotations, and it would serve no greater purpose ; the question would remain then which remains now : the Secret Doctrine of Israel either covers a mystery of knowledge wherein there lies possible a mystery of certitude in experience or it is a temple in a waste of thought, far from any city of refuge and filled only with confused rumours or raving of empty words. Now, I have performed many arid journeys in my time and have returned with an empty wallet ; but if this had been one of them I should not have written its itinerary in the present study of the ZOHAR. There have been recurring intimations there and here in these pages concerning a Mystery of Sex ; it is imposed upon me now to affirm that this is the Mystery of Shekinah ; and the nature of such Mystery corresponds—according to its veiled claim—with the definition which I have just given concerning a knowledge and an experience. The point and centre of the whole subject is the Indwelling Glory ; it is declared everywhere,

---

[1] Z., Pt. I, fol. 181a ; II, 315.
[2] *Ib.*, Pt. II, fol. 140b ; IV, 45.
[3] *Ib.*
[4] Z., Pt. II, fol. 86b ; III, 355. See also Is. lvii. 15.

but everywhere also it is concealed : one aspect of its presentation—amidst great hiddenness of wording—suggests that the entrance of the High Priest into the Holy of Holies belongs to the Mystery of Sex [1] ; but I do not propose to pursue this intimation, as it seems to me like that fiftieth gate which was not opened by Moses, and, moreover, the fitting time is not yet. I will resume rather the conference by saying that, according to the ZOHAR, the union of male and female is Modesty,[2] and that the title to behold the face of Shekinah is one of purity.[3] It seems true therefore to say that she is the Law of the Mystery, and the ZOHAR quotes concerning her, " When thou goest, it shall lead thee ; when thou sleepest, it shall keep thee ; and when thou awakest, it shall talk with thee." [4] The study of this Law is life eternal.[5] Considered as a law, it implies a covenant, and of this covenant Joseph is said to be the image, because of his continence in respect of Potiphar's wife.[6] Having tabulated these premises and thus secured a point of departure, we have to approach again the great text and see after what manner it will shed light on the research.

It is specified that Shekinah dwelt with Israel prior to the captivity, meaning probably the captivity in Babylon, and the sin which brought about this exile was equivalent to the uncovering of the hidden physical centre of Shekinah. I am speaking here under great difficulty and am somewhat exchanging terms, for this Minerva and Diana of Israel is a woman, like Isis, and her veil is not to be lifted. The French translators finish the quotation under notice with the help of the Latin tongue, and it reads : *Traditum est . . . genitales partes Shekinæ existere.*[7] This also is a sacrament, but we can understand the meaning by assuming that Shekinah in such a connection signifies the Secret Doctrine in so far as it was a mystery of sex, and the ZOHAR goes on to particularise the alleged sin as a crime of incest, by which we must understand some illegal and reprobate application of the sex doctrine. It matters nothing to our subject if on the surface of Scripture the accusation seems without warrant : to justify the hermeneutics of the ZOHAR would be a task as much beyond my

---

[1] Z., Pt. III, fol. 66b ; V, 182. The hour of entrance is when the Sacred King is united to MATRONA.
[2] *Ib.*, fol. 145b ; V, 375.
[3] *Ib.*, Pt. II, fol. 60b ; III, 268, 269.
[4] Prov. vi. 22.
[5] Z., Pt. I, fol. 175b ; II, 290.
[6] *Ib.*, fol. 184a ; II, 327.
[7] *Ib.*, fol. 27b ; I, 173.

province as beyond my powers of pleading.[1] But we begin to see in this manner the kind of problem that has been taken in hand.

It is said further that the Mystery of Shekinah comprises all women, and this—as we have seen—is why she does not abide except with him who is united to a woman.[2] She is fixed definitely in the house of man when he marries, *et quum fœderis suum signum in locum ponit*.[3] This is why the HE and the VAU follow each other in the alphabet—VAU being the symbol of the male and HE of the female principle. Husband and wife are one, and a ray of celestial grace covers them ; it descends from CHOKMAH, penetrates the male principle, and the latter communicates it to the female.[4] We can understand therefore in what sense her shame is the defiled body of man,[5] and how she is weighted by the sin of Israel.[6] The reason is that she is a virgin betrothed to the Middle Pillar,[7] and of her it was said by Adam in the great day of his perfection : " This is now bone of my bones and flesh of my flesh," [8] which is to affirm that in one of her aspects she is the type of stainless womanhood ; but she passes ever into espousals below—as she is ever in espousals above—for the fulfilment of herself in humanity, and of all humanity in her. The evidence is that when there is a just man on earth the Shekinah cleaves to him and does not leave him henceforth.[9]

It will be observed that in order to gain the particular point at a given moment the ZOHAR is valiantly careless of that which goes before, as of that which may be designed to come after. The history of the Fall of man through the intermediation of woman, acting under the virus of the serpent, is by no means the history of Shekinah, unless under a special aspect and as a remote reflection ; but when it is sought to shew that she is nearer to the elect than hands and

---

[1] As a matter of fact, the idea is drawn from the TALMUD, which enumerates various cases of the crime in question, but the reference in the ZOHAR is to be understood spiritually, as of an assault on Shekinah, who—as we have seen—is the sister of all men. From all modern points of view and feeling, this kind of symbolism is unfortunate and disconcerting enough ; but I think that the Sons of the Doctrine, if they had been challenged on the subject, would have replied with Gerald Massey that Nature is not ashamed of her emblems.

[2] Z., Pt. I, fol. 228b ; II, 501.
[3] *Ib.*, fol. 94a ; I, 536.
[4] *Ib.*, fol. 94a ; I, 537.
[5] *Ib.*, Pt. III, fol. 75a, b ; V, 205.
[6] *Ib.*, fol. 28a ; V, 79.
[7] *Ib.*, Pt. I, fol. 28a ; I, 178.
[8] Gen. ii. 23. The interpretation of this text in this strange manner is like an opening into a great vista of the Secret Doctrine.
[9] *Ib.*, fol. 66b ; I, 391.

feet are near, it is difficult to find anything more complete in its correspondence than such words as "bone of my bones and flesh of my flesh," [1] and the use of the text—so long as it is apart from the context—happens to be a true one, though it is about as literal in its application as is the tale of the Garden of Eden.   So also when the ZOHAR wishes to apply that idea of a "field which the Lord hath blessed" [2] to the Mystery of Sex, it is not above saying that the King who "tills the field" [3] or is "served by the field" is the Shekinah, sex-contradiction notwithstanding.   The object is to indicate that the dwelling of Shekinah in the house of those who are married is to bring about the descent of souls to animate children under her presidency. [4]   But perhaps there was never an instance so much to our purpose as the statement that on the day when the Song of Solomon was revealed below, the Shekinah descended [5]—as if for the first time, though we know that she had been with man from the beginning and had shared in the whole creation.   The object, however, is to shew that this glorious canticle is the world's history of her in man, the beginning and end of all that belongs to the union, the Mystery of the Lover and the Beloved throughout the ages of election.   It is the summary of Holy Scripture ; it is the work of creation, the mystery of the patriarchs, the exile in Egypt, the exodus of Israel, the Decalogue and manifestation on Sinai, the emblem of all events during the sojourn in the desert, thence to the entrance into the Holy Land and so forward to the building of the Holy Temple.   It is also a summary of the Mystery contained in the Sacred and Supreme Name, of the dispersal of Israel through the nations, of its deliverance to come, the resurrection of the dead and the events leading up to that day which is called the Sabbath of the Lord.   In a word, it contains all that hath been, is and ever shall be, for it is the story of that Isis who is Shekinah, from the first verses

---

[1] Gen. ii. 23.
[2] *Ib.*, xxvii. 27.
[3] Eccles. v. 9.   The Authorised Version says : "The King is served by the field." Cf. Vulgate : *Et insuper universæ terræ rex imperat servienti*, and the Douay rendering : "Moreover there is the King that reigneth over all the land subject to him."— Eccles. v. 8.
[4] Z., Pt. I, fol. 122a ; II, 91, 92.
[5] *Ib.*, Pt. II, fol. 143b ; IV, 55.   The putative authority is I. Kings viii. 11 : "So that the priests could not stand to minister because of the cloud ; for the glory of the Lord had filled the house of the Lord."

concerning the kisses of his mouth to the laſt rapture on the mountain of spices.[1]

Now, it is said that there is desire on the part of man to be united with the Mother in transcendence as well as with the Mother below, to attain her by perfeƈtion and to be blessed on account of her.[2]   We know that this is a desire for Divine Union because Jehovah is Elohim, and in case such teſtimony should not be found full or sufficient, the ZOHAR adds else-where that the memorable words : " 1 am that I am " signify in their inward sense : " I, the Holy One, blessed be He, am the Shekinah."[3]   It is certain that the ſtate of union is not only deeper than the ſtate of vision but differs generically therefrom, and I cannot say that I have found plenary Zoharic authority for the attainment of Divine Union in that proper sense of the term which is to be desired by the heart of the myſtic.   But the implicits are in many places, for we have seen that Shekinah is within.   It is more often vision which is promised to the blessed in the world beyond, to gaze upon the face of Shekinah,[4] as in a subſtituted ſtate of union, and the title muſt be earned in this life by the following of the path of purity.[5]   It is affirmed in reference to this that those only who quit the lower world in the grace of Shekinah are judged worthy of eternal life.[6]   So also there are some who do not die as men die commonly, but are ravished by the attraƈtion which Shekinah exercises on their souls.[7]   The Mother in transcendence is, however, like the Mother below, and spiritual communion with her is in so far as man has become a house or abode by attaching himself to the female : it is then that the Divine Mother pours down her blessings on both.[8]

There is—in the true sense of this term—a spiritual union below for the Sons of the Doƈtrine, so that they are encom-passed by two females [9]—the wife who is on earth and the Unseen Helpmate.   After what manner her presence is

---

[1] Z., Pt. II, fol. 144b ; DE PAULY, IV, 55, 56.   It should be underſtood that while I have not given an aƈtual translation of the passage I have kept faithfully to its sense. My readers may recognise with myself at this ſtage that, with due regard to the logical inviolability of diſtinƈt schools of symbolism, all Sufic imagery concerning the Lover and Beloved belongs to Shekinah and might have come forth with all its adornments from the Secret Tradition in Israel and its intimations on MATRONA and TABOONAH.
[2] It is a queſtion of integration in the Zoharic law of correspondences.
[3] Ib., Pt. I, fol. 23a ; I, 140.
[4] Ib., Pt. II, fol. 40b ; III, 189.
[5] Ib., fol. 60b ; III, 268, 269.
[6] Ib., Pt. I, fol. 82a ; I, 473.
[7] Ib., fol. 16b ; II, 99.
[8] Ib., fol. 50a ; I, 292.
[9] Ib.

realised never transpires definitely in the text, but—as there is no need to say—it is by spiritual apprehension only. Curiously enough, this does not appear at its best in connection with views on the nuptial state itself but in discourses of the Sons of the Doctrine on the Traditional Law : they are conscious then of the presence of Shekinah and testify respecting it continually with no uncertain voice. It must be said that the women of Israel are never present at the debates,[1] but their place in the house insured that of the Divinity. When, however, the master of the Law was going by himself upon a journey, and when, technically speaking, the male was to be apart from the female, he was not for that reason in a state of separation from Shekinah, supposing that he had prayed to the Holy One before starting,[2] in order to maintain the union between male and female abroad as well as at home. Another condition was that he must watch over all his actions in every phase of life :[3] otherwise he might be separated from his Spiritual Companion, putting a stop to the union and rendering himself an incomplete being.

It is scarcely desirable at this stage to speak of anything so obvious and familiar as the known characteristics of oriental imagery, to recall for example the personifications of Wisdom in the books ascribed to King Solomon ; but the literary vestures of these experienced two curious developments. The titles and offices of the Hebrew CHOKMAH were raised bodily from their setting and transferred to the Blessed Virgin by the compilers of the Roman Breviary, while through another channel they passed over to the Gnostic SOPHIA and by a last transition into the Virgin Wisdom of Jacob Böhme and the later mystics of his school. The correspondences between Shekinah and the Christian Mother of God are rather plausible on the surface and may be deceptive to that extent, because shallow analogies still deceive many ; but even the unusual predispositions which led up to the French translation of the ZOHAR have not permitted its editors to postulate that Shekinah is a veil of Mary. The correspondences between the Indwelling Glory and the Virgin Sophia of Böhme are so much closer that they cannot fail to create an impression that

---

[1] I remember, however, that there is a solitary exception in favour of an innkeeper's daughter, who was present when her husband exhibited his knowledge of the Hidden Law before a company of adepts.—Z., Pt. II., fol. 166a ; IV, 111.

[2] Z., Pt. I, fol. 49b ; I, 289.   [3] Ib., fol. 50a ; I, 289.

the German Theosophist owed something to this source. There is nothing in his life to suggest that he was taught in any secret schools or was in communication with persons who were acquainted with the Secret Doctrine in Israel, though there were many Kabbalistic scholars at his period. There is one possible alternative—that the root-matter of Jewish tradition in the Scriptures of the Old Testament developed in his own consciousness, to some extent after the same manner as it did in that of the Sons of the Doctrine, so that in his case, as in others without number, it proved that true men and seers spoke the same language because they belonged to the same region of thought. They saw also in the same glass of vision. But the question, however interesting, is not of our real concern.

We have now considered the Shekinah in the light of all her attributes. I do not believe that I have omitted a single reference of the least importance found in the text of the ZOHAR, while all have been regarded critically. The conclusion reached is that Shekinah, as the president of a Mystery of Sex, is the direction in which we must look if—as labourers in this strange field—we are to obtain our wages. The other intimations are excellent and agreeable in their way, but that which we seek, in what is for us an untrodden region of thought, is some new message, which is not to be found in the other offices, qualities and virtues that characterise the Holy Guide of Jewry. I suppose that, here in conclusion, I have no real need to say that the Secret Doctrine in Israel is not one of sex only, though intimations concerning the latter are found everywhere. Eschatology, for example, is not of this order, nor are the parts of the soul in man, but with these things and with several others that are like them I have dealt at their value.

II.—THE MYSTERY OF SEX

I am entering in this division upon that part of my task which is at once most important and difficult. It may be an open question whether I should begin at the highest point of the research and thence work downward or take the opposite course and so—as the proverb counsels—proceed from small beginnings to the greater end. That is best which seems the simplest, and I have therefore chosen to work upwards from below. I will cite in the first place certain great axioms of the whole subject—as these have been proclaimed on the authority of the masters. It is testified that the union of the male and female must be a perfect union in the Mystery of Faith.[1] There is also another testimony, and this is that the title to behold the face of Shekinah is one of purity,[2] the scholium on which—though it lies far away in the text—is that modesty is the union of the male and female ;[3] and it may be remembered in this connection that the most cryptic of all texts in the ZOHAR—containing the mysteries of Divine Personalities—is called THE BOOK OF CONCEALMENT OR OF MODESTY. These things being so, we may consider in the next place what is said on the subject of espousals, as these are known on earth. There is one definition which is in keeping with the Tradition at large, and this is that marriage is the union of the Sacred Name here below [4]—that is, its completion in each person. The thesis appertaining hereto is that circumcision is the symbol of all purity in sexual intercourse ;[5] that Israel is placed on this account in purity as a starting-point and enters under the wings of Shekinah.[6] This sacred sign of the Covenant constitutes the root-matter of the Sacred Name and of the Mystery of Faith.[7] As the sun enlightens the world, so the sacred sign enlightens the body ; as a buckler protects man, so does this : no evil spirit can approach him who preserves it in purity.[8] But as the advantage is greater with which the children of Israel begin their earthly life, so is the responsibility greater if they make the Covenant of no effect in their own persons.

Now, the Sacred Name is never attached to an incomplete man, being one who is unmarried, or one who dies without issue.[9] Such a person does not penetrate after death into the vestibule of Paradise,[10] on account of his incompleteness. He is like a tree that is rooted up, and he must be planted anew— that is to say, he must suffer rebirth, as we have seen, in order

---

[1] Z., Pt. I, fol. 101b ; II, 11.
[2] Ib., Pt. III, fol. 213a ; V, 542 ; ib., Pt. II, fol. 60b ; III, 268, 269.
[3] Ib., Pt. III, fol. 145b ; V, 375. Man is perfect only when he comprises male and female ; it is then that he fears sin and then that the title of modest is conferred upon him. But here is the sum of the whole subject passing into expression at the highest.
[4] Ib., Pt. III, fol. 7a ; V, 18.
[5] Ib., Pt. I, Appendix III, SECRETS OF THE LAW ; II, 721, 722.
[6] Ib., fol. 95a ; I, 543.   [9] Ib., Pt. I, fol. 48a ; I, 278.
[7] Ib., Pt. II, fol. 3b ; III, 10.   [10] Ib., fol. 66a ; I, 388 ; ib., fol. 48a ; I, 278.
[8] Ib.

that the Sacred Name may be completed in all directions.[1]
The command to increase and multiply, which means the
procreation and engendering of children, is to spread the
radiance of the Sacred Name in every direction, by collecting
spirits and souls which constitute the glory of the Holy one—
above and below. Whosoever fails to apply himself to the
fulfilment of this command diminishes the figure of his Master
and prevents it descending here below.[2] The last statement
refers of course to the making of man, male and female, in
the likeness of the Elohim. It is said also that the paucity in
the descent of souls is the reason why Shekinah does not
come down into this world,[3] with which is to be compared
the affirmed presence as the Indwelling Glory throughout the
whole creation. God blessed Adam because they were made
together male and female, and blessings are found only where
male and female are united for the fulfilment of the purpose
of creation,[4] which—according to the counsel of the Elohim—
was to increase, multiply and replenish the earth. It was not
good for man to be alone because this end was in a state of
frustration. It may be even that the Zoharic legend concerning male and female being originally side by side is only a
veiled way of indicating that they were not in the marital
estate.[5] Afterwards they were face to face, signifying the
fulfilment of the precept.

I have now dealt briefly with what may be called the
principles at issue, and we have next to see after what manner
those who exalted so highly the nuptial state gave instruction,
so to speak, on its practice here below. The doctrine was that
no marriage is made on earth before it is proclaimed in
heaven, and that the Holy One accomplishes unions in the
world above before the descent of souls on earth.[6] About

---

[1] *Ib.*, Z., Pt. I., fol. 66a; I, 388; *ib.* fol. 48a; I, 278. [2] *Ib.*, fol. 272b; II, 641.
[3] Z., Pt. I, fol. 272b; II, 641. The reference is really to her manifestation and not
to her immanence. She stands at the door and knocks, but those who should welcome
her in keep fast their precincts and tyle their portals. This, however, is symbolism;
it is more true to say that we fail to realise her presence in our consciences.
[4] *Ib.*, Pt. I, fol. 165a; II, 245.
[5] I have put this tentatively, as I wish to leave some conclusions in the hands of my
readers; but there is no question that Zoharic teaching is clear on the point, not only
in what it implies but in what is expressed frequently. Whether there was ever such
an epoch in the history of the human soul is another question. We must remember
that the object of the soul's legends is not the delineation of putative histories, but the
symbolical administration of possibilities inherent in the soul. That which is indicated
here is a transcendental union between the Lover and Beloved, of which the nuptial
union on earth is a type and to which it may be a path of approach.
[6] *Ib.*, fol. 229a; II, 503.

the last point we shall see at a later stage. In practice the Sons of the Doctrine were separated as far from the un-initiated world of Israel as the chosen people at large were separated *ex hypothesi* by the fact of their circumcision. There is a particular sense in which it is held that the union here below between husband and wife is the work of the Holy One, and herefrom, as from other considerations, arises the sanctity and necessity of that act which is implied by the word union.[1] After what manner the Divine is said to intervene therein, or perhaps I should say to overshadow it, is indicated by the theory that man is formed below on the model of that which is above.[2] It follows that he who, in Zoharic terminology, suffers his fount to fail and produces no fruits here—whether because he will not take a wife, whether his wife is barren, or whether he abides with her in a way that is against Nature—commits an irreparable crime.[3] " It is vain . . . to sit up late "[4] are words that designate those who do not marry till an advanced age, for it is woman who constitutes the repose of man.[5] Hereof, according to the text, is the peace of espousals, and in further variation of the testimony which recurs continually, it is added that man shall participate in the world to come because he has entered during this life into the joy of living honourably with his wife.[6] The reason is that soul as well as body shares in the *gaudium inexprimabile* by which children are engendered. This is the eroticism which characterises the ZOHAR, according to commentators : but as the Doctors of the Law beheld the Supreme Mystery in sex, it is obvious that whatever belongs thereto is explained thereby.[7]

And now as regards the practice, the thesis is that whoever

---

[1] Z., Pt. I, fol. 186b ; II, 337.

[2] *Ib.*, fol. 186b ; II, 338.

[3] *Ib.*

[4] Ps. cxxvii. 2.

[5] Z., Pt. I, fol. 187a ; II, 340. See also Pt. III, fol. 108a ; V, 274, where it is said, on the authority of Rabbi Eleazar, son of Rabbi Simeon, that the HE is the repose of beings above and below—above being the rest of the Shekinah in transcendence and below of the Shekinah in manifestation.

[6] *Ib.*, Pt. I, fol. 90b ; I, 515 ; *ib.*, Appendix III, SECRET MIDRASH, fol. 14b, 15a ; II, 694 ; *ib.*, fol. 187a ; II, 340.

[7] It is about the worst word that could be selected by a scholar and a critic who is alive to the issues of his subject. Coventry Patmore's young lady thought that the sacrament of marriage was rather a wicked sacrament, but the Zohar raises it into realms of which Christian Churches have never dreamed, though I have met with some rare aspects of Latin Theology which seem to indicate that a Redeemer may live hidden therein.

sanctifies himself at the moment of intercourse shall have children who will not fear the tempter-spirit. This is the consequence respecting the fruit of marriages, but there is also a consequence within the measures of the union itself, so that it is raised from the physical into a spiritual degree, from the mode of Nature into the mode of Grace.[1] The fulfilment of a particular precept is the condition attaching hereto and this is the raising of the heart and mind on the part of the Lover and Beloved, to the Most Holy Shekinah, the glory which cohabits and indwells, during the external act.[2] The *absconditus sponsus* enters into the body of the woman and is joined with the *abscondita sponsa*.[3] This is true also on the reverse side of the process, so that two spirits are melted together and are interchanged constantly between body and body. The sexes are then interchanged also in a sense, as the sex of METATRON is said to be transformed momently before the veil of palms and pomegranates on the threshold of the Inmost Shrine in the Supernals.[4] In the indistinguishable state which arises it may be said almost that the male is with the female neither male nor female : at least they are both or either. So is man affirmed to be composed of the world above, which is male, and of the female world below.[5] The same is true of woman.

Now according to the ZOHAR those words in the Song of Solomon : " Thy breasts are better than wine "[6] refer to that wine which provokes joy and desire ; and seeing that— in an alternative manner of language—all things are formed above according to a pattern which is reproduced faithfully below, it is held to follow that when desire awakens beneath it awakens also on high.[7] Herein lies the sanctity of espousals

---

[1] It is added significantly that herein the Holy One exercises such providence over man that he may not be lost in the world to come.

[2] There are many references, but perhaps the most signal is Z., Pt. I, fol. 50a ; I, 290.

[3] *Ib.*, Pt. II, fol. 101b ; III, 410.

[4] This intimates what, by the hypothesis, can be accomplished in nuptials, through the purification of body and mind, towards the union of souls. The statement in the ZOHAR on which my words are based seems to contain the elements of the whole mystery on the manifest side and after what manner that which is now only mutual in a complete distinction may be unified by experience in consciousness. I am somewhat veiling my meaning because it is not possible to speak *ad clerum*.

[5] Z., Pt. II, fol. 173b ; IV, 128.

[6] In the majority of Scriptural quotations the translator of the Zohar has done his best to conform his rendering to the Vulgate : it was of course unlikely that he would follow any other version, and I am stating the fact only to shew that he has seldom translated *de novo*. Our Authorised Version of I, 2, reads : " Thy love is better than wine," and the Vulgate : *Quia meliora sunt ubera tua vino*.

[7] Z., Pt. I, fol. 70a, b ; I, 415.

on earth and herefrom depends the need for exalting that
sanctity and all that belongs to espousals into the highest
grade.   There are however two classes whose respective
duties differ with the degrees of their election; there are
those who are termed ordinary mortals, meaning the rank
and file of the chosen people, but there are also the Sons of
the Doctrine, chosen among the chosen out of thousands.
The counsel imposed on the first class is to sanctify their
conjugal relations in respect of the time thereof, which is
fixed at midnight, or forward from that hour, the reason
being that God descends then into Paradise and the offices of
sanctity are operating in the plenary sense.   But this is the
time when the counsel to the Sons of the Doctrine is that they
should arise for the study of the Law, for union thereby with
the Community of Israel above and for the praise of the
Sacred Name of God.[1]

The Sons of the Doctrine are described as reserving conjugal relations for the night of the Sabbath, being the moment
when the Holy One is united to the Community of Israel.[2]
The thesis is that God is One and as such it is agreeable to
Him that He should be concerned with a single people.
Out of this arises the question as to when man may be called
one, and the answer is that this comes about when the male
is united to the female in a holy purpose : it is then that man
is complete, is one and is without blemish.[3]   It is of this that
the man and the woman must think at the moment of their
union ; it is in uniting bodies and souls that the two become
one ; man in particular is termed one and perfect ; he draws
down the Holy Spirit upon him and is called the Son of the
Holy One, blessed be He.[4]   According to Rabbi Simeon, the

---

[1] Z., Pt. III, fol. 81a ; V, 224.
[2] Ib., Pt. I, fol. 14a, b ; I, 82.   Ib., Pt. III, fol. 81a ; V, 224.
[3] Ib.
[4] Ib., fol. 81b ; V, 224.   The intention here seems obvious, and it is to shew that
beyond that process indicated by Gen. ii. 24, when it is said that " they shall be one
flesh," there is another and higher process, in the fulfilment of which it is possible that
they shall be one soul.   The one is not, however, without the other, and this is a point
to be marked because the contrary idea may be presented to some minds.   The following curious speculation should be noticed in this connection.   It is affirmed that the
words : " In the beginning God created " (Gen. i. 1) conceal the same mystery as
those other words : " And the rib which the Lord God had taken from man made
He a woman " (Ib., ii. 22).   In " God created the heaven " the two last words conceal
the same mystery as the words : " And brought her unto the man " (Ib., ii. 22).   In
" God created the heaven and the earth " the three last words conceal the same mystery
as " bone of my bones " (ib., ii. 23).   All designate " the earth of life."—Z., Pt. I,
fol. 50b ; I, 293, 294.   But it is said also that the words " the heaven " signify Shekinah

relations of the patriarchs with their wives were actuated by a Supreme Mystery.[1] So long as Jacob was unmarried, God did not manifest to him clearly, and this mystery is familiar to those who are acquainted with the ways of the Law. After marriage he arrived at the perfection which is above, as distinguished from the perfection which is below, and God manifested to him clearly.[2] The explanation seems to be that the Supreme Wisdom is a Mystery of Sex,[3] as intimated on my own part previously.

Out of these considerations there arose a very curious question, of which I must speak at some length because—in its way—it is a characteristic development on the practical side and, within certain measures, it carries our subject further. The principle is that the male must be always attached to the female for the Shekinah ever to be with him.[4] All holiness might be practised, the Secret Doctrine might be studied by night and by day, and the illuminations thereof might overflow the intellectual part ; but failing fulfilment of this radical counsel a man was not on the way which leads into true life.[5] He was in that condition in which " it is not good for man to be " [6]—alone, like Adam in the Garden.[7] But those who had the precept at heart and were therefore complete men, by their union with women on earth, remind us in one particular of many Sons of Israel and Students of Doctrine in the Middle Ages : they were travellers in search of wisdom ; and they were also men of affairs, workers in the vineyard of this world as well as in the Garden of God. The ZOHAR is full of their little journeys and these, so far as possible, were taken one with another, that the Secret Doctrine might be studied on the way and that the presence of Shekinah might be secured thus for their consolation, protection and instruction as they fared forward. Great adventures befell them in the sense of the Mysteries of Doctrine, for strange

---

above, while the words " and the earth " denote Shekinah below, whose union shall be as perfect on a glorious day to come as the union of the male and the female.—Z., Pt. I, fol. 50b ; I, 295.

[1] Ib., Pt. I, fol. 133b ; II, 126.   [3] Z., Pt. I, fol. 150b ; II, 193.
[2] Ib., fol. 150a ; II, 192.   [4] Ib., fol. 49b ; I, 289.
[5] There was otherwise a certain dispensation for the Sons of the Doctrine in respect of the fruit of intercourse. On the assumption that there was no issue they appear to have been spared the penalty of return into incarnation.
[6] Gen. ii. 18.
[7] He was held to be in a state of sickness, and as such was to be isolated from the offices of the altar. Only a man completed, and in this sense made perfect, by union with a woman, could offer sacrifice.—Z., Pt. III, fol. 5b ; V, 12.

people went about in those days carrying, unknown to one another, the treasures of hidden knowledge. It was after all an unincorporated fraternity, and though it looks differently there and here, initiation was by a segregating principle, not by communication from a common centre of knowledge. The son of an instructed doctor might have advanced a great distance unknown to others, while occasionally an isolated student entered by his own reflections, and by grace descending into the heart, into the golden chain of tradition, so that he was not less in an illuminated state than if he had sat at the feet of Rabbi Simeon through the days and the years.

Now, journeys in search of wisdom or in the prosecution of business—which, it may be mentioned, was often of a humble kind—meant separation from the wife of the doctor's household, and this would seem at first sight to involve separation from Shekinah.[1] To remove this difficulty it was held sufficient (a) that the doctor should pray to the Holy One before starting, and (b) should watch over all his actions during the period of absence from home.[2] He would not be separated then from his spiritual companion, nor would he put that stop to the union between male and female which would render him an incomplete being. It was understood further that the counsel which prevailed abroad must prevail at home also, so that what was inculcated was really a precept of life. I feel that this might have been almost taken for a point of departure in respect of the Cohabiting Glory, if considerations of a different kind had not intervened. It occurs early in the ZOHAR—as a fact, in the first section—and concerning the Great Presence it postulates the dwelling of Shekinah with man.[3] The word cohabiting seems to be the correct word here, though it was obviously in an inward

---

[1] The position is a little fantastic, because in such case the same danger might arise from the isolation of a single hour : moreover, the notion discounts the whole value of unions realised in spirit and in truth, appearing to make physical contiguity more important than that nearness of heart which spatial considerations do not help or hinder. But the question seems raised in reality because it is an opportunity to enforce a practice of inward dedication after the best manner of the ZOHAR. As usual, the peg answers because it supports this lesson.

[2] Z., Pt. I, fol. 49b, 50a ; I, 289.

[3] It is said elsewhere that Shekinah never separates from man so long as he observes the commandments of the Law.—Z., fol. 232a ; II, 516. The authority is : " Behold I send an angel before thee, to keep thee in the way " (Ex. xxiii. 20) ; and : " I will send an angel before thee " (ib., xxxiii. 2). This is held to be the Liberating Angel to whom Jacob made allusion (Gen. xlviii. 16), who watches over man, who receives blessings from above and distributes them below.—Z., Pt. I, fol. 230a ; II, 508 ; and fol. 228b ; II, 502.

sense only that the Shekinah accompanied the Sons of the Doctrine in their recurring voyages and ventures. If not indwelling, she was their overshadowing grace and power ; but they seem to have been conscious of a certain marriage state—spiritually realised—in their relation with her, though it was of course collective and not personal. Alternatively, there is a sense in which it was peculiar and catholic at one time, and this is an important point of analogy between the Holy Guide of the Sons of the Doctrine and that Christ Who is the Spouse of the soul. That this, however, is *per se* an insufficient ground for the identification of the two Divine Principles we are likely to see at the end. I need not add that the Shekinah appears throughout this section of the symbolism as distinctively feminine.

Recurring to the text, after having made these lawful inferences therefrom, the ZOHAR—with Rabbi Simeon as the mouthpiece of its teaching—is comprehensive and precise in its justice after the manner which obtains throughout. It is not in virtue of the man being side by side with the woman, as the legend depicts him previously, that Shekinah abides with man.[1] We have seen that this ancient mode was before all things imperfect. The man and the woman must be face to face, at once in the continuity and restrictions of the sacred mystical act. So also when, after days and weeks of travel, the Son of Doctrine returns to his home he must procure nuptial gratification to the wife of his heart, seeing that he has had the advantage of mystical union in his absence with the Companion or Helpmate who is on high.[2] In the deepest understanding of the subject, the one belongs to the other, that which is without being Zoharically as that which is within, and all the correspondences being aspects of one thing seen and done upon different planes of being. The external and expressed reason is, however, twofold : (1) be-

---

[1] See, among other places, Z., Pt. I, fol. 49a ; I, 284. I suppose that the reason is obvious from the Zoharic standpoint : contiguity is not union. It is obvious also, or should be, that we are not considering a Siamese-Twins symbolical legend. What lies at the heart of the story, regarded as hypothetically something of the far past, would be very difficult to decide if it were to be regarded as one of fact. It belongs to " the hunger and thirst of the heart " after a way to the blessed life through earthly espousals. Surely the Sons of the Doctrine must have found in their own marriages pearls of great price which their heirs have lost now, and of which we have not even dreamed. And yet we continue to hear rough things about the position of womanhood in Israel, sometimes even from converted Jews like that Chevalier Drach who chaffered and trafficked in his conversion—as it seems to me, more than enough.

[2] Z., Pt. I, fol. 50a ; I, 290.

cause there is Talmudic authority that conjugal relations on returning from a journey constitute a good work [1] and (2) every pleasure resulting from a good work is shared by Shekinah.[2] Furthermore, it is in such pleasure that the peace of the house is maintained, for the ZOHAR is much too modest and inclined spiritually to have any shyness over the physical and emotional facts of daily life. The Scriptural authority, obtained after the usual manner, is contained in the words : " Thou shalt know that thy tabernacle shall be in peace ; and thou shalt visit thy habitation, and shalt not sin." [3] To abstain from conjugal relations in such a case would be indeed sinful, depreciating the work of the Companion on high, who cleaves to the man, but thanks only to his own union with his wife.[4] If subsequently there be fruit of this intercourse, the Heavenly Companion will provide a holy soul for the new-born child, the Shekinah being that Covenant which is termed : Covenant of the Holy One. The rule on return from a journey must be fulfilled therefore with the same zeal as the ordinance laid down by the wise regarding the restriction of conjugal relations to the day of the Sabbath, and it is apparently the only recognised exception thereto in the matter of times and seasons, unless of course an exception is made by Nature.

Finally, and this, which is assuredly a most strange, and within my experience of the sacred literature, an unique counsel, has been cited already : when man has in view the Shekinah [5] at the moment of his conjugal relations the pleasure which he experiences is a meritorious work. The reason—which has been explained also—is that the union below is an image of the union that is above. The mystery of the whole subject is the now familiar dogma that the Mother in transcendence abides with the male only in so far as he has constituted himself a house by his attachment to the female : there must be a local habitation, an union below to offer a point of contact with the union that is on high, and

---

[1] See Talmud, Tract YEBAMOTH.
[2] Z., Pt. I, fol. 50a ; I, 290. She who suffers with Israel enters into joy with him.
[3] Job v. 24.
[4] Z., Pt. I, fol. 50a ; I, 290.
[5] It is part of the contemplation of the absent and higher beauty in union with that beauty which, albeit lower, is present, manifest and is or may become sacramental. It is a memorial also that the union which is of time has, or may attain, a part in the union which is eternal, described in one place as the contemplation of the beauty of Shekinah, already mentioned.—*Ib.*, Pt. II, fol. 116a ; III, 448, 449.

then the Divine Mother pours down her blessings therefrom—
that is to say, on male and female in equal measures.[1] So is
the male below said to be encompassed by two females, and
all the ways of blessing in the two worlds are open before
him.[2] He reads the Secret Doctrine in the womanhood on
earth, and it is read to him by her who sits between the Pillars
of the Eternal Temple with the Book of the Secret Law lying
open on her sacred knees.[3]

Among its lesser objects the counsel concerning the
Sabbath Day and the relations therein offers proof to the
spirits of the evil side respecting the superiority of those on
the side of goodness, meaning mankind, who being provided
with bodies can fulfil the duties of procreation.[4] Whosoever
has intercourse with his spouse, on what day soever, must
obtain her consent beforehand with words of affection and
tenderness ; failing consent, he should proceed no further,
for the act of union must be willing and not constrained.[5]
Nuptial intercourse is interdicted during the day because of
the words : " And he lighted upon a certain place, and
tarried there all night, because the sun was set." [6] Subject
to these and the rest of the provisions, some of which I have
omitted, because of their difficulties of expression,[7] it is
affirmed that blessed are those who sanctify the Sabbath Day
by intercourse with their wives ; for the Sons of the Doctrine
it is a work consecrated to the Holy One, because the union
of Matrona with the heavenly King has for its object to send

[1] Z., Pt. I, fol. 50a ; I, 291.   It is said also that Shekinah does the will of the master
of the house.—Ib., fol. 236b ; II, 532.   The reference on the surface is to Moses.
[2] Ib., fol. 50a ; I, 292.
[3] It is important to note here what is involved by the illustration as a whole—
namely, that man in his union with woman becomes a house in which the Divine
Presence can dwell. Let us take another illustration, which is excellent and indeed
admirable in its symbolism. The eye of man is said to be an image of the world ;
the white of the eye is an image of the great ocean by which earth is encompassed,
and the latter is represented by the " internal circle " of the eye. Within this there is
another circle, and it is called the image of Jerusalem, centre of the whole world.
Finally there is the pupil, which corresponds to Zion, and this is the abode of Shekinah.—
Ib., fol. 226a ; II, 490, 491. So also there are the parts of human personality—physical
and mental parts—and there is the conscious centre wherein is the Divine Presence,
awaiting realisation within us. The thesis is that marriage is a condition of realisation.
[4] Z., Pt. I, fol. 14a, b ; I, 82, 83.
[5] Ib., fol. 49a, b ; I, 286.
[6] Gen. xxviii. 11. Z., Pt. I, fol. 49b ; I, 286.
[7] In view of the sanctity which the Zohar attributes to the sex-act under the obedience
of purity—which is marriage—there was a prohibition respecting its performance in
nuditate personarum. Those who ignore it are subject to the visitation of demons and
will produce epileptic children obsessed by Lilith. This is the case more especially
if the light of a lamp is used. I do not know whether this has Talmudic authority.—
Z., Pt. I, fol. 14b ; I, 83.

down holy souls into this world, and the colleagues on earth
seek to attract these sacred souls into their own children.[1]
The theory of conception is that the Holy One and His
Shekinah furnish the soul, while the father and mother
provide the body between them [2]—heaven, earth and all the
stars of heaven being associated in the formation, together
with the angels.[3] By the desire which the man experiences
for the woman and the woman for the man at the moment of
their intercourse, their seeds are interblended and produce a
child which is said to have two figures, one within the other.
The child in this way draws life from father and mother, and
this is why there should be some kind of sanctification for all
classes at the moment of conjugal union, so that the child
about to be born may be perfect and complete in figure.[4]
The Secret of Divine Generation is however a Secret of the
Doctrine and is reserved for the initiated therein ; it is
apparently they alone who draw down the holy souls which
are the fruit of the union between God and His Shekinah.
But there are various kinds and generations of souls, some
being superior to others, and when the desire—apparently of
the ordinary man—provokes in an equal degree the desire of
the male soul for the female soul, the child born of this union
will have a soul superior to that of other men, since its birth
has come about by desire of the Tree of Life.[5]

These things are clear issues at their value, and in looking
at them from the standpoint of Israel we must make allowance
for national exclusiveness in what is said about holy souls
which can only become incarnate in Jewry. We must make
allowance also for that which by inference from the teaching
might be supposed to befall the barren woman. In conclusion as to this part, it is affirmed that the Sons of the
Doctrine, knowing the Mysteries of the Doctrine, turned all
their thoughts to God, and their children were called Sons of
the King.[6] But those whose marital relations were not

---

[1] Z., Pt. I, fol. 50a ; I, 290.   Ib., Pt. II, fol. 89b ; III, 363.
[2] Ib., Pt. III, fol. 219b, THE FAITHFUL SHEPHERD ; V, 556.
[3] Ib.
[4] Ib., Pt. I, fol. 90b ; I, 514, 515.
[5] Ib., fol. 209a ; II, 437.   This also is important because of that which it implies.
The frigid, uninspired unions of *pro forma* marriages are, by this hypothesis, useless
for the higher purposes : there must be mutual and equilibrated desire, upspringing
from love, and such desire must be transmuted by the tincture of Divine Aspirations.
[6] Here then is the counsel of espousals : *Mens sana in corpore sano et spiritus Deo
adhaerens ;* but such cleaving is in virtue of love uplifted through all the worlds.—See
Z., Pt. III, fol. 78a ; V, 213.

encompassed with sanctity caused a breach in the world above.[1]

The religion of earthly espousals, if I may so term it, is the part in manifestation of that which is called so frequently the Mystery of Faith, and I will proceed next to the consideration of what is intimated there and here on this subject. In the words " male and female created He them " [2] there is expressed the Supreme Mystery which constitutes the glory of God, is inaccessible to human intelligence and is the object of faith. By this mystery was man created, as also the heaven and the earth.[3] It is inferred that every figure which does not represent male and female has no likeness to the heavenly figure. This is why Scripture says that God " blessed them and called their name Adam in the day when they were created." [4] The Scriptural authority for the affirmation that there is a Mystery of Faith is drawn from several sources, but without exception on the *lucus a non lucendo* principle, as it is impossible to conceive where it lies in the texts or what it can be on the evidence of their surface meaning. I will group a few of them together and let them speak for themselves. (1) " O Lord, Thou art my God ; I will exalt Thee. I will praise Thy Name ; for Thou hast done wonderful things ; Thy counsels of old are faithfulness and truth." [5] (2) " And his hand took hold on Esau's heel." [6] (3) " Thus the heavens and the earth were finished, and all the host of them," [7] *et seq.* This is said to be the Great Mystery. (4) " I will sing unto the Lord, for He hath triumphed gloriously : the horse and his rider hath He thrown into the sea," [8] *et seq.* Among the intimations which rest upon the ZOHAR there are many which seem designed almost obviously to confuse the issues and misdirect research thereon. The Mystery is said to consist in the examination of good and evil and then in cleaving to the good.[9] It is

---

[1] It is said also that woman is the image of the altar, from which it seems to follow in the symbolism that man is the priest, and then of the oblations there should be no need to speak. It is said further, in this connection, that divorce makes a breach in the altar—in the altar below, because there is separation between male and female, and in the altar above, by the Kabbalistic hypothesis of correspondence between things above and below.—Z., Pt. II, fol. 102b, 103a ; III, 415. See also *ib.*, Pt. III, fol. 78a ; V, 213.

[2] Gen. i. 27.
[3] Z., Pt. I, fol. 55b ; I, 320.
[4] Gen. v. 2.
[5] Is. xxv. 1.
[9] Z., Pt. II, fol. 34a ; III, 166.

[6] Gen. xxv. 26. Z., Pt. I, fol. 199a ; II, 387.
[7] Gen. ii. 1.
[8] Ex. xv. 1.

said again to be contained in the fact that Zion constitutes the foundation and beauty of the world and that the world draws its nourishment therefrom.[1] There is Zion, which is severity, and there is Jerusalem, which is mercy ; but the two are one.[2] We may say in respect of both that goodness and mercy are on the male side of the Sephirotic Tree, while evil and severity are on the female side ; that these two must be united by the Middle Pillar : that this is entering under the wings of Shekinah ; and that when they are thus joined, goodness, joy and beauty are found everywhere. We shall speak in this manner the characteristic language of the ZOHAR and might deserve the blessing of Rabbi Simeon ; but we shall not have advanced our subject by one line or syllable belonging to a line. We must therefore go further and test the values of a few less obdurate extracts.

There are forty-nine gates of compassion which connect with the mystery of the perfect man, composed of male and female, and with the Mystery of Faith.[3] These are the Gates of Understanding referable to BINAH,[4] wherein dwells the Spouse in Transcendence, who is Shekinah ; but there is a fiftieth Gate which Moses did not open, according to the legend. This Gate is the Mystery of Espousals in the Divine

---

[1] Z., Pt. I, fol. 206b ; II, 427. Ib., fol. 186a ; II, 335.
[2] Ib.
[3] Ib., Pt. II, fol. 139b ; IV, 41, 42.
[4] It seems desirable at this point to collect the references to these Gates which occur throughout the text, so that there may be no misunderstanding on the subject. The indications are these in summary : (1) It is through 50 openings of the mysterious heavenly palaces that the Word of YOD—which, as we have seen, is in CHOKMAH—penetrates to the HE (in BINAH).—Z., Pt. I, fol. 13b ; I, 79. (2) There is one Gate which is the synthesis of all Gates and one Degree which is the synthesis of all Degrees ; by this Gate and Degree do we enter into the glory of the Holy One.—Ib., fol. 103b ; II, 19. (3) This Gate is unknown because Israel is in exile, and the result is that all the Gates are shut.—Ib., fol. 103b ; II, 20. (4) The 50 Gates of Understanding are or may become salvation for the whole world.—Ib., Appendix I, OMISSIONS ; fol. 260a ; II, 611. (5) The Gates emanate from or are referable to the side of severity.—Ib., Appendix III, SECRETS OF THE LAW ; II, 723, 724. (6) It is owing to the evil Samael that Moses could enter only 49 of the 50 Gates of BINAH.—Ib., Pt. II, fol. 115a ; III, 443. (7) The union of the Father and the Mother produced 5 lights, which gave birth in their turn to the 50 Gates of Supreme Lights.—Ib., ASSEMBLY OF THE SANCTUARY, fol. 122b, 123a ; III, 473. (8) The light of the Mother above reaches us by 50 Gates.—Ib., fol. 137b ; IV, 37. (9) He who devotes himself to the study of the Law opens the 50 Gates of BINAH, which correspond to the YOD multiplied by the HE.—Ib., Pt. III, fol. 216a ; V, 548. (10) By such multiplication Moses attained these Gates.—Ib., fol. 223b ; V, 565. (11) In the absence of these Gates Israel would have remained always in the bondage of Egypt. They are in the region called the Supreme Mother, who gives power to the Mother below.—Ib., fol. 262a ; VI, 12. It will be seen that the subject is left at a loose end and does not emerge in fact ; but it becomes clear at least that the Zoharic Gates of Compassion belong to another mode of Understanding than was evolved by late Kabbalism, as summarised in Book V.

World. Another reference tells us that there are Seven
Degrees above which are superior to all others, and they
constitute the Mystery of Perfect Faith.[1] The attachment of
Israel to the good side is attachment to the Supreme Mystery,
the Mystery of Faith, so that Israel is one therewith.[2] By the
hypothesis that the Mystery of Faith is a Sex Mystery, the
practice of perfection therein, on the terms already indicated,
should give a title to the knowledge of these Degrees and
thereby the Mystery of Faith would pass into a perfect Mystery
of Experience. Probably these Seven Degrees are identical
with the seven firmaments the purpose of which—as we are
told elsewhere—is to reveal the Mystery of Faith.[3] They
are called also Seven Palaces.[4] There is a kingdom to come
after that which is termed symbolically the end of the world ;
it is a sacred region, and this also is said to constitute the
Mystery of Faith ;[5] but we have heard otherwise that the
advent of Messiah means perfect conformity in the nuptial
state, above as well as below.

It has been necessary to make these citations ; but it will
be seen that the most which they tell us is (1) the fact that
there is a Mystery of Faith, and (2) that it is concerned with
the union of male and female. We may take the question one
step further by the collation of some final references. The
priestly garment with fringes [6] and the phylacteries on head
and arms [7] designate the Supreme Mystery, because God is
found in that man who wears them.[8] It is the Supreme
Mystery of Faith. A spring which flows unfailingly is
another image of the Mystery,[9] and we shall remember in
this connection the sex-interpretation placed on the river
which came forth from Eden to water the Garden—in which
man was created male and female—and which was afterwards
parted and became into four heads. A well fed by a spring
also symbolises the Mystery of Faith, because it symbolises
the union of male and female,[10] and here again we shall
remember (1) the " fountain of gardens," [11] (2) the " garden
inclosed " which is " my sister, my spouse," [12] (3) the

---

[1] Z., Pt. I, fol. 204b ; II, 414.
[2] Ib., Pt. I, fol. 205a ; II, 217.
[5] Z., Pt. II, fol. 134a, b ; IV, 30. The Feast of the Paschal Lamb is said to contain
the Mystery of Faith.—Ib., fol. 135a ; IV, 32.
[6] Numbers xv. 38.
[7] Deut. xi. 18.
[8] Z., Pt. I, fol. 141a ; II, 150.
[12] Ib., iv. 12.

[3] Ib., fol. 85b ; I, 494.
[4] Cf. Book IV, § 10, p. 176.
[9] Ib., fol. 141b ; II, 151.
[10] Ib., fol. 141b ; II, 152.
[11] Song of Solomon iv. 15.

" fountain sealed," [1] and (4) the " well of living waters and
streams from Lebanon." [2]   Whoever contemplates such a
well is said to contemplate the Mystery of Faith.[3]   The moon
is said finally to be another image, and we know that this
luminary is a symbol of Shekinah.[4]

I conclude on all the evidence that the doctors of the
Zohar had no intention of communicating under the formula
which they used so often more than a broad and general
definition of what their convention symbolised.

Again therefore we must go further, and the key to the
matter before us will be found, under another form of symbolism, by the collation of two passages which are separated
widely from each other.   It is affirmed [5]—as we have seen—
that when the Yod is united to the He they give birth to that
river concerning which it is said : " And a river went forth
from Eden to water the Garden." [6]   The other extract tells
us that from the union of the male and female—meaning, of
course, in the transcendence—come all souls which animate
men.[7]   The inference is that the Eden-river is that of life, or

---

[1] Song of Solomon iv. 12.
[2] Ib., iv. 15.
[3] Z., Pt. I, fol. 141b ; II, 152.
[4] Ib., fol. 142a, b ; II, 157.   As I have by no means exhausted the references and
as so much seems to be implied in the formula, I will make a further selection as follows :
(a) That the Supreme Mystery, which is synonymous with the Mystery of Faith, is
the law of the whole world is taught in the words : " These are the three sons of Noah :
and of them was the whole earth overspread " (Gen. ix. 19), as if the Zohar were
indicating that the event in question marked a new epoch in the mode of generation.—
Z., Pt. I, fol. 73a ; I, 432.   (b) The Mystery of Faith is represented by Jacob.—Ib.,
fol. 138b ; II, 143.   (c) Every word in Scripture conceals the Supreme Mystery of
Faith, because all the works of the Holy One are based on equity and truth.—Ib.,
fol. 142a ; II, 154.   (d) The Supreme Wisdom is by implication the Mystery of Sex.—
Ib., fol. 150b ; II, 193.   (e) The Mystery of Faith and all celestial sanctities emanate
from the union of male and female principles.—Ib., fol. 160a ; II, 229.   (f) One
Mystery of Supreme Wisdom is that the world's salvation must issue from the union
of Juda and Thamar, as if there were a secret sanctuary somewhere in the world which
overwatched that true legitimacy belonging to the line of David.—Ib., fol. 188b ;
II, 344.   (g) The union of the worlds above and below is of the Mystery of Faith.—
Ib., fol. 206b ; II, 426.   (h) The Supreme Mystery concealed in the Law is the Secret
of the Lord, and this is a secret of the Holy Covenant.—Ib., fol. 236b ; II, 533.   (i) The
Cup of Blessings comprises the Mystery of Faith, which Mystery embraces the four
quarters and the Sacred Throne.—Ib., fol. 250b ; II, 585.   (k) The Sacred Reign to
come constitutes the Mystery of Faith—meaning union sanctified everywhere.—Ib.,
Pt. II, fol. 134a ; IV, 30.   (l) The Mystery of Faith is to know that Jehovah is
Elohim.—Ib., fol. 161a ; IV, 100.   As I have now omitted only references that are
trivial or obscure and calling for considerable explanation, the two collections are in
all respects adequate and it will be seen that they are quite clear as to the nature of the
Mystery, whether it is qualified as Supreme or characterised as that of Faith.
[5] Z., Pt. I, fol. 95b ; I, 545.
[6] Gen. ii. 10.
[7] Z., Pt. II, fol. 70a ; III, 310.   It is said here that the creation of man in the likeness
of the Elohim is an allusion to the Mystery of the Male and Female Principles.

synonymously it is the river of souls,[1] and in this case we shall understand that the Higher Eden is the place of Divine Nuptials, while the Garden which was watered by the river was the place of nuptials below. We have found this illustrated already by various speaking images—as, for example, in the higher degree by the analogy instituted between Shekinah and the Seed of Solomon,[2] the tent of grace,[3] and so forth ; but in the lower degree by the identification of the Garden with womanhood.[4] We are not left, however, to mere inferences on the subject, for it is said elsewhere that at the moment of the union of the Spouse and Bride all souls came forth from the celestial river.[5] The one is " the Sanctuary, O Lord, which Thy hands have established " and the other is the repose of man.

It is said elsewhere—and we have seen indeed already— that souls are produced by the union of male and female,[6] whence it follows that they have a father and mother—*ex hypothesi* in God—even as their bodies have when they enter into incarnate life. We learn also that all souls emanate from the celestial region called JAH, which is explained to be the Unknown God.[7] As seen already, this name is for God that which the Propitiatory is for the Tabernacle—a summary of the male world above and the female world below.[8] We can understand now in what sense the Shekinah is termed so often the Supreme Mother ; we can understand also why it is joy of heart [9] to know that Jehovah is Elohim and why the attainment of such knowledge is the object with which the Holy One sends man into this world.[10] It is said—as we have seen also—that this is the Mystery of Faith which is the synthesis of the whole Law. It is said further that Eden is

---

[1] It is the river of life and of souls in the sense that it issues from the letter YOD, regarded as the organ of the Covenant in the Supernal World—*semen superinexprimabile.* Sometimes this idea is expressed almost literally.

[2] Z., Pt. II, fol. 66b ; III, 292.

[3] *Ib.*, Pt. I, fol. 101b ; II, 11, where the tent of Sarah is understood as the tent of Shekinah, or as Shekinah herself. There are other instances : The Jerusalem above is said to be designated a tent in Is. xl. 22, and to signify Shekinah.—*Ib.*, Pt. II, fol. 65b ; III, 288.

[4] It was also the Synod of Israel.—*Ib.*, Pt. I, fol. 63a ; I, 369.

[5] *Ib.*, Pt. I, fol. 207b, 208a ; II, 432. They came forth male and female, descending confusedly. This intimation is of some importance in the legend of the soul.

[6] See Z., Pt. I, fol. 207b, 208a ; II, 432, among other places.

[7] *Ib.*, Pt. II, fol. 165b ; IV, 111. The reference is to KETHER, where Jehovah is in union with Elohim, or God and His Shekinah are one. We have seen that the letters YOD and HE primal of the Divine Name are allocated to this SEPHIRA.

[8] *Ib.*   [9] *Ib.*, Pt. III, fol. 8b ; V, 23.

[10] Z., Pt. II, fol. 161b ; IV, 101, 102.

the Mother above and the Garden which was watered by the river coming forth out of Eden is the Shekinah or Mother below, while the river itself is the Middle Pillar of the Sephirotic Tree.[1] It follows that descent into manifestation is by the central path which communicates between KETHER and MALKUTH. It is the path of Shekinah, and when it is testified that she was destined from the beginning to suffer with Israel [2] this means that the nuptial intercourse which was infinite and holy in the world above, which was pure, spiritual and holy for a period—*ex hypothesi*—in the world below, descended through what is termed the Fall of man into the region of the shells, or the order of animal things. The physical sign of the Covenant is held to symbolise Shekinah [3] because it symbolises the path of purification by which man may return into the perfection of spiritual union.[4]

We have heard that the Supreme Mystery of Faith is the union of Jehovah and Elohim, which union is the source of all other Mysteries. We have heard also that when Israel shall become perfect, it will make no distinction between Jehovah and Elohim—the male with the female being neither male nor female. It follows that the Supreme Mystery and the Mystery of Faith are one and are also the Mystery of Union of Male and Female in the Divine Nature, behind which I infer that there is a Mystery of Experience in man.

Let us now take another legend of the soul which is not quite in consonance with some things that have preceded, as it postulates a continual generation as fruit of the eternal union between the Father and Mother in transcendence [5] in place of a creation of souls once and for all, prior to the

---

[1] Z., Pt. I, fol. 26a, b ; I, 164.

[2] *Ib.*, fol. 120b ; II, 84. It is said here that Shekinah is the first of all that is, which is affirmed also of METATRON.

[3] *Ib.*, fol. 278a, b, THE FAITHFUL SHEPHERD ; II, 647. So also it is said, as we have seen, that the Covenant with Shekinah will endure for ever.—*Ib.*, Pt. III, fol. 257a ; V, 597.

[4] I ought to mention here that in one place only of the text it is said that in forming the prototypical Eve and placing her face to face with man, it was intended that the union between male and female should be accomplished after the same manner as that of Jehovah with Elohim, or in the absence of any fleshly and impure sensation.—Z., Pt. II, fol. 258b ; IV, 291, 292. This seems to me an allusion to a pre-natal state, for things must be referred to their natures : the spiritual unions are one thing and have their own end ; the physical union is another and Nature insures thereby the perpetuation of species.

[5] Hence it is said that man—understood as male and female—is the synthesis of Jehovah and Elohim.—Z., Pt. III, fol. 48a ; V, 134.

evolution of the created universe. That which follows is more in consonance with the Mystery of Faith, and is in fact one of its aspects. It is said that at every birth new souls are created and detached from the Celestial Tree.[1] Thanks to these new souls, the legions of heaven are increased,[2] for which reason the Scripture says : " Let the waters bring forth abundantly the moving creature that hath life," [3] meaning the waters of the celestial river which has its source in the Holy and Eternal Alliance.[4] It should be understood that this Alliance, which is the union of Jehovah and Elohim, has its correspondence below in the Covenant between God and man on the basis of circumcision—as symbolising the great postulate concerning purity. The Scripture adds : " And fowl that may fly above the earth," [5] because at the moment when the newly-created soul traverses the heavenly region called " living "—meaning the Land of Life—it is accompanied by many angels, who have followed it from the time that it was detached from the Tree of Heaven.[6] Those who abstain from practising the precept " Increase and multiply " diminish—if it be permitted so to speak—the Celestial Figure, centralisation of all figures : they arrest the course of the celestial river and defile the Holy Alliance.[7] We have seen that this is a sin against God Himself ; the soul of such a man will never penetrate into the vestibule of Paradise and shall be repulsed from the world above.[8] After this manner does the ZOHAR indicate yet again that from the beginning of the sacred text it is concerned with the history of man rather than the external cosmos and, by inference, with the history of Israel rather than of man at large. We on our part are in a position to understand it in a higher sense as

---

[1] It is repeated also that all souls issue from the celestial region called JAH, which is the source of wisdom. This is called the Holy Spirit, and all souls are comprised therein.—*Ib.*, Pt. II, 174a ; IV, 129. According to another version, those souls which animate men issue or emanate from Him Who is called the Just.—*Ib.*, fol. 70a ; III, 310.

[2] *Ib.*, Pt. III, fol. 168a ; V, 434, and elsewhere.

[3] Gen. i. 20.

[4] They are the waters of CHOKMAH and BINAH, the YOD and the HE in their union, or alternatively—according to another form of the symbolism—they are those waters proceeding from KETHER under the presidency of the Divine Name JAH.

[5] Gen. i. 20.

[6] This notion is expressed in one place only and seems only semi-poetical adornment.

[7] Z., Pt. I, fol. 273a, a, Appendix I, BOOK OF BRIGHTNESS ; II, 641.

[8] *Ib.*, fol. 48a ; I, 278. The guilt of such abstinence is exaggerated in the prevailing manner of the ZOHAR, and if we come to discriminate thereon we shall remember that the man returns—*ex hypothesi*—to this life in another body and has the chance to do better.

the catholic history of souls ; it is this on the inner side, though it is cosmic history of course on the surface of the outward sense. This also is the construction of the ZOHAR, which naturally does not deny that on the literal side the first chapters of Genesis are the story of creation ; but the vital or palmary interest rests in the internal sense—as if the one were a question of accidents and the other of essence.

The souls of all Gentiles emanate from the demons under circumstances which are not explained in the ZOHAR.[1] The suggestion is sometimes that they are from the left side of the Tree ; but the question is exceedingly obscure,[2] because God and His Shekinah are everywhere in the Tree of the SEP-HIROTH, and though there is a sense in which God is allowed to have created evil, the position is by no means maintained with any consistency throughout. It was left for late Kab-balism to contrive its own way of escape from the difficulty, for which purpose it conceived the idea of postulating ten SEPHIROTH in each of the four worlds, as also in each SEPHIRA. There is practically no warrant for this in the original text, though there is a trace of some septenary repetition of SEPHIROTH in the individual SEPHIROTH. The case of those who were converted from Paganism to Jewry and fulfilled the whole law thereafter raises another question : it was necessary that they should be reconciled on all the planes or it would serve no purpose to receive them into the fold ; and it was therefore postulated that after undergoing circumcision they entered under the wings of Shekinah and were separated from the side of the Demons.[3] They did not participate, in the world to come, in the full beatitude of the elect who were such by their right of birth ; they remained under the wings of Shekinah, but the latter was like a chariot for Israel, in which Israel passed higher, namely, into the Land of the Living. The Gentiles had no part in the Heavenly Tree and could not therefore return to it.[4] The view is naturally at

---

[1] It is affirmed elsewhere, on the contrary, that they come from the Divine World ; but the question is negligible, as anything that is found in the ZOHAR on the subject of unbelievers is antecedently known to be worthless. The literal statement is that, all differences notwithstanding, human souls come from heaven.—Z., Pt. I, fol. 13a ; I, 77.

[2] There is one place at least in which the right and the left side seem to be two paths of coming out into manifestation apart from any Sephirotic notion.—Z., Pt. I, fol. 160a ; II, 229.

[3] Ib., fol. 13a ; I, 76.

[4] The records are obscure and contradictory, but I have suggested previously that the Sephirotic Tree is really the Tree of Life, and there may be a sense intended in which

issue with much that has preceded ; but the question does not concern us in any important way.

Returning to the generation of souls, it is said that there are three souls in the superior degrees ; [1] the first is the Supreme Soul, which is unintelligible even to beings on high : it is the Soul of all souls, it is concealed eternally and all depends therefrom. The second soul is the female principle, and by the union of these two Divine Works are manifested to the whole world, even as all acts of the human soul are manifested by the human body. The third soul is that of all holy souls emanating from the Male and Female in the transcendence.[2] The multiplication of symbolical modes for the expression of the same speculative doctrines is disconcerting enough and sometimes tends to confusion, but the meaning is in no sense remote, as it happens in the present instance. We see in the first place the root-postulate belonging to the Mystery of Faith—that the union of male and female in the Ineffable Persons causes conception and birth everlastingly ; that what are born are souls ; that these descend, and that they are male and female. One account

---

the Tree of the Knowledge of Good and Evil is also Sephirotic in its attributions, the good being the right and the left the evil side. Zoharic Kabbalism recognised, moreover, an averse Tree under the title of Inferior Crowns, in analogy with the Crowns that are above, namely, the true SEPHIROTH. The salient allusions are as follows : (a) There were ten averse Crowns and they were in analogy with ten varieties of Magic, all understood as infernal, for the ZOHAR very properly recognises no distinction between Black and White in the occult arts.—Z., Pt. I, fol. 167a ; II, 257. (b) The Inferior Crowns are ramifications of one and the same Tree.—Ib., fol. 177a ; II, 296. (c) The Law of Correspondence obtains in these things, for—as we have seen—the empire of the demon is modelled on that of God.—Ib., Pt. II, fol. 37b ; III, 179. (d) There is further a demoniacal triad in imitation of that Triad which is Supernal.— Ib., fol. 40b ; II, 189. (e) There are also inferior palaces corresponding to the Palaces that are above and—like these—they are seven in number.—Ib., fol. 245a ; IV, 278. (f) There are hierarchies of demons answering to the Hierarchies of Blessed Angels— Seraphim to Seraphim, and so forth.—Ib., fol. 247b ; IV, 281. (g) The titles of the averse SEPHIROTH are the same as those above—Wisdom and so forth, all the qualities being illustrated by their opposites.—Ib., Pt. III, fol. 70a ; V, 190. (i) It is said finally, and this is a further light on another subject which has been under consideration just previously, that there are ten averse SEPHIROTH on the right and ten upon the left, even as in the Holy World. Here is another way of understanding the right and left side in the ZOHAR. I do not affirm that there is a single ruling idea throughout the references, yet if there be, the modes of expression are not less obscure than they are otherwise misleading.—Ib., Pt. III, fol. 207a ; V, 527.

[1] Ib., Pt. I, fol. 245a, b ; II, 570, 571.

[2] Though there has been no occasion to dwell upon it, seeing that I am not concerned with the maintenance of orthodox theological views or their opposites, I think that the reader has abundant proof in his hands by this time that the Zoharic system as a whole is no more emanationist than pantheistic. That which proceeds from AïN-SOPH into the complete concealment and yet comparative manifestation of the Three Supernal SEPHIROTH may be called an emanation from AïN-SOPH, but as it is a question of Divine Essences, that is an orthodox view at its value. In the present instance the symbol is one of begetting, which is not synonymous with emanation.

says that at the moment of earthly marriage the souls must sort themselves out, each male soul discovering the female who was its companion before incarnation ; but this is so rough and crude that it is set aside tacitly, without, however, establishing any general law in its place.   The implicit is of course that the male body contains a male soul and that the soul of a woman is female, though there is an obscure sense in which any soul is male to any material body but is female to the degree which is above it.[1]   Another implicit can be recognised which is more to our purpose—that he who abides in the true way will meet in marriage with the woman-soul which was his pre-natal companion.[2]   If he has deviated it may happen that the woman predestined to him is espoused to another ; but in the event of his repentance a time will come when the alien male will disappear, thus yielding the woman to her true mate.[3]   In a scheme like this it is obvious that there must be fatalities and mischances innumerable when it comes to be worked out : among others there is that in virtue of which a male soul will come into this world without a sister-soul, and presumably *vice versâ*.   It is held that such a person will not marry and cannot therefore have children ; but in the event of his keeping the Law and proving worthy, he will find the means of rehabilitation in another earthly life.   In the alternative case, he will be judged un-worthy of a new transmigration.[4]   It is part of the Divine Plan for the salvation and felicity of man that a sister-soul is not permitted to remain the wife of another.[5]

The considerations with which I have been dealing lead up to other dreams that are significant of the concern of Israel on another and higher side of the sex mystery.   It is not to be supposed, the union of humanity below according to the manner of flesh being, at least in its consecration, a reflection of the Divine Union, that there should not be an union of souls in the world to come, so that in the beatitude of the true

---

[1] Z., Pt. I, Appendix III, MATHNITIN ; II, 703.

[2] See on the general subject *ib.*, Pt. III, fol. 283b, 284a ; VI, 64, 65.   Also, *ib.*, fol. 43b ; V, 120, 121, and Pt. I, Appendix III, MATHNITIN ; II, 703.

[3] See on the general question *ib.*, Pt. III, fol. 283b ; V, 64.   And on this special point, *ib.*, Pt. II, fol. 229a ; II, 503.

[4] We have seen that reincarnation is not in itself desirable but that it is justified—*ex hypothesi*—by adequate reasons.   It follows from the above statement that there is a less favourable alternative.   That which is suggested or proposed is, however, only a sporadic or casual notion, and it is quite out of harmony with much that goes before and comes after.

[5] This is discounted somewhat fully in other places of the text.

region of life they should not continue to reflect the Supernal Work and its Mystery. This is why, as we shall see, the union between God and the soul is so often in the sense of vision, though there are indications of deeper stages. That which is substituted is the union in heaven of souls who have been espoused on earth—being those who were espoused previously before the world began.[1] When it is said that the Blessed Vision is the sight of Shekinah and the contemplation of her Divine Face,[2] we are to understand apparently that the union of sister-souls is under her eyes and in her presence. It is said that in the heights of heaven there is yet another union of two born of love and for ever inseparable.[3] It is contemplated by those who have part in the life to come. The way which leads to the Tree of Life, the Tree which is kept by the Kerubim and the Flaming Sword, are the Grand Matrona herself. She is the way of the Sacred City, the way of the Heavenly Jerusalem, the intermediary of communication between things above and below in both directions : she is the perfect Mediatrix, to whom all the Divine Powers are confided.[4] The intimation is vague, but as the contemplation

---

[1] It is a recurring subject of reference and we see that the triad obtains here as otherwhere. There are (a) Pre-natal union ; (b) Union on earth and (c) Union in the risen life of the spirit. Two things are to be observed, firstly, that we hear nothing concerning marriage-life after the resurrection, or in that state wherein the perpetuation of a physical envelope seems to pronounce separation for ever between God and man, so far as all that is understood by Mysticism respecting the union is concerned ; but, secondly, following all the analogies, there can be no doubt that the risen bodies will enter into the life of intercourse, because they are complete bodies.

[2] Z., Pt. II, fol. 40b, THE FAITHFUL SHEPHERD ; III, 189, 190. But there are other references.

[3] Ib., Pt. II, fol. 50b ; III, 229.

[4] Ib., fol. 51a ; III, 230. The same Divine Powers were said to be entrusted to Enoch when he became METATRON, concerning whom I will now collect the following references : (a) He is charged with the government of the earth.—Z., Pt. I, fol. 143a ; II, 161. (b) He sets all his legions in motion by the power of a single letter in his name—presumably any letter, as none is specified.—Ib., Appendix III, MATHNITIN ; II, 705. (c) He is the Serpent above.—Ib., Pt. II, fol. 28a ; III, 134. (d) This is explained by ib., Pt. I, fol. 27a ; I, 171, which says that he is favourable to man when he is transformed into a wand—e.g. that of Aaron or Moses—but as a serpent he is against man. (d) The river which went out of Eden to water the Garden (Gen. ii. 10) is Enoch, who is called otherwise METATRON ; but it is the Lower Eden and not that in the Supernal World. It is the place called PARDES, which name—according to Franck—was never so used in the ZOHAR.—Ib., fol. 27a ; I, 168, 169. (e) He is to the cohorts above apparently that which is Samael to the cohorts below.—Ib., Pt. II, fol. 42a ; III, 191. (f) He is called Server and he embraces the six directions of space.—Ib., fol. 94a ; III, 377. (g) It is said that souls proceed from the side of METATRON and from the side of Shekinah, but it does not seem to be by the way of generation, as between male and female.—Ib., fol. 94b ; III, 379. (h) He is also called " Young Man," and it was he who dwelt in the Tabernacle of Moses.—Ib., Pt. II., fol. 143a ; IV, 54. (i) He helped to build the Tabernacle.—Ib., fol. 159a ; IV, 96. (j) He guarded the Temple of Solomon.—Ib., fol. 164a ; IV, 107. (k) The School of

of Matrona sanctified nuptials below, so is the path by which
the elect enter into the higher nuptials as if they ascended that
Middle Pillar of the SEPHIROTH which is so often said to be
she. We can proceed therefore to glance at another question
of those palaces for which the ZOHAR has a natural attraction,
while their number is most usually seven. When souls leave
the lower world they enter into a certain palace which is
above, if they carry the proper warrants, and therein those
which are male are again united to the female, in which union
they radiate light as in sparkles.¹ This palace is said to be
the throne of Faith and, I infer, is the place of its mystery.
Yet another story of palaces tells us that there are four which
are exclusive to women, or at least to holy mothers, but it
is forbidden to reveal their nature.² During the day the
females are separated from the males ; but the spouses are in
union at night, and in their mutual embrace the lights of both
dissolve into a single light. The conclusion reached on this
subject is that blessed is the lot of the just, male as well as
female, for they shall enjoy all delights in the world to come.³

We are led on in this manner to the great mystery of the
subject, as to which there are several testimonies. It rests on
the witness of a testament bequeathed by Rabbi Eleazar the
Great ⁴ that when the Holy One comes down into Paradise

METATRON is the School of the Holy One.—*Ib.*, Appendix III, fol. 287a ; IV, 314.
(l) The curtain of the Tabernacle was his symbol.—*Ib.*, fol. 293a ; IV, 317. (m) He
is like Michael, for he offers the souls of the just to God.—*Ib.*, Pt. III, THE FAITHFUL
SHEPHERD, fol. 29a, b ; V, 81. (n) There is an obscure suggestion that he may be
the Angel of the Sun, and it is said also that he draws milk for his purification from his
mother, as if she were the MATRONA in BINAH and he were the Begotten Son or VAU.—
Ib., fol. 64b ; V, 177. (o) He has the Keys of Heaven.—*Ib.*, fol. 171b ; V, 445.
(p) During the exile, he has the government of the House ; he is the rainbow, and he
is called SHADDAI.—*Ib.*, fol. 215b ; V, 547. (q) He is old and he is again young.—*Ib.*,
fol. 217a, b ; V, 530. (r) He is the Man of the Lesser Countenance ; that is to say,
he is the tenth SEPHIRA, MALKUTH ; and here we must remember that there is a
sense in which the VAU came down to earth in union with the HE final.—*Ib.*, fol. 223b ;
V, 565. (s) As otherwise noted, he is the vesture of SHADDAI.—*Ib.*, fol. 231a ; V, 571.
(t) As noted also, he is to Shekinah that which are the week days to the Sabbath—as
if he were activity and she rest.—*Ib.*, fol. 243b ; V, 381. (u) He is poor in exile—
that is to say, in the exile of Israel, and his nourishment is prayer.—*Ib.*, fol. 278a ;
V, 51. I have omitted only a few minor allusions and one fantastic comparison which
would tend to confuse the issues. Apart from the stultifying intervention of the Enoch
motive, I think that these extracts tend very clearly towards the identification of
METATRON with the Son who is extended through the worlds below ATZILUTH, and
who is not exactly in union with Shekinah and yet not apart from her during the fall
and exile of the elect. At times—perhaps generally—they are distinct from one another ;
at times they are found together ; and their end is complete union.
¹ Z., Pt. II, fol. 246a ; IV, 279.
² *Ib.*, Pt. III, fol. 167b ; V, 434.
³ *Ib.*
⁴ It is not clear whether this means the son of Rabbi Simeon.

at midnight the male souls are united to the female ; fecunda-
tion follows from the joy which they experience in the
contemplation of God, and they bring forth other souls [1]
which are destined to occupy the bodies of Gentiles who will
become converts to the Law of Israel.[2]   In another place this
is explained after a different manner : the souls born of
celestial unions are reserved in a palace, and when a man is
converted one of them takes flight and comes under the
wings of Shekinah, who embraces her—because she is the
fruit of the just in their intercourse—and sends her into the
body of the convert where she—or he—remains, and from
that moment the convert acquires the title of just.[3]   This is
the mystery of those words in Scripture : " The fruit of the
just is the Tree of Life." [4]   There is, however, by yet another
testimony, a general sense in which the Holy One affects the
union of twin-souls so that they may engender other souls,
themselves animated by those sacred forces which are above
them.[5]

The fact that these passages are all less or more irreconcilable is of no consequence ; the object is to indicate the
nature of beatitude in the world above, and they are all
independent fables belonging to the motive, inspiration or
casual spur of the moment : [6] no one would have been more
astonished possibly than a Son of the Doctrine, had he heard
that they were to be collated and harmonised, were that
possible.

There are a few minor points which may be mentioned at
this stage.   It is said that all depends on thought and intention ; holiness is attracted by good thought ; but he who
defiles himself by thought, and he who at the moment of
fulfilling the act of intercourse with his wife thinks of another
woman changes the Degree above—the Degree of Holiness—
into one that is impure.[7]   We may compare the elective

---

[1] I must not omit to mention that this is contradicted in THE FAITHFUL SHEPHERD,
which says that in the world to come there is neither eating nor drinking, that there
are no conjugal relations, and that the beatitude of the just—as we have seen—is to
contemplate the beauty of Shekinah.—Z., Pt. II, fol. 116a ; III, 448, 449.

[2] *Ib.*, Pt. III, fol. 168a ; V, 434.   [4] Proverbs xi. 30.

[3] *Ib.*   [5] Z., Pt. I, fol. 186b ; II, 337.

[6] I must except, however, conditionally at least, one other quality of testimony
which seems to suggest that the way of the generation of souls has been always by
conception and birth, following intercourse.

[7] Z., Pt. I, Appendices III, SECRETS OF THE LAW ; II, 730.   Yet it would seem
permissible on occasion to think of another, because in cohabiting with Leah, Jacob
thought of Rachel, though unintentionally, as it is said.—*Ib.*, p. 731.

affinities of Goethe, for the child born of such union is called a substituted son : soul and body are held alike to be substituted. The second point is that there are rare occasions when conjugal relations seem forbidden, even on the Sabbath, and periods of famine are a case in point : [1] the child born at such a season will be from the side of the demon. Lastly, there is the question of virginity—by which I mean among women.[2] That such a condition on earth should be considered as tolerable, much less as a title of sanctity, never entered into heart or mind of any Son of the Doctrine. The only Zoharic reference to virgins in an exalted state specifies that the third among several legions is composed of celestial virgins who are in the service of MATRONA and adorn her when she is presented to the King : these are her maids of honour. It is a very simple transfer of an earthly image ; but the legion does not consist of human souls.[3]

We are now at the end of our inquiry into the Mystery of Sex, so far as the statements in the text are concerned, and that which remains is to determine whether the path which was followed by the early Kabbalists may have led them into any experience of a spiritual kind that is implied rather than expressed in the records before us. I will suppose that they followed the counsel on which those records insist, and as it involved a distinct mode of procedure in connection with an important fact of life, the insistence, as it seems to me, must indicate that in the experience of things the method had proved of practical service. In other words, they had found that there is a mystery of nuptials of which it has not entered into the heart of man to conceive in the ordinary ways and under the common motives of desire.[4] There is one beautiful point to observe in this connection—that their mystery lay within the pure offices of Nature, under all the accepted warrants. Those who conceived it had fulfilled already the Law in respect of marriage ; they sought no new way of the physical kind ; they were not lovers at white heat on the

---

[1] Z., fol. 204a ; II, 412, 413. The consequence threatened seems arbitrary, as usual, but—according to Rabbi Simeon—a Supreme Mystery is involved. Ordinary sense would assume that the regulation was a question of doing penance.

[2] *Ib.*, Pt. II, fol. 131b ; IV, 23.

[3] *Ib.*, Pt. II, fol. 131b ; IV, 23.

[4] We must remember that there is no lawful act of life and no law of Nature which cannot be raised above its own degree by the consecration of motive, or otherwise that the will of man in all its authorised ways and places can be united to the Divine Will.

quest of the ideal beloved ; [1] they were not in search of an excuse for setting aside old pledges and old bonds ; they were content with that which they had ; they made use of the elements which had been given already into their hands, like true craftsmen and masters. The genesis of their practice is of course outside our knowledge : it may be that those who sought to make all things holy in their life had sanctified by intention of their own the fulfilment of that Law which told them to "increase and multiply," and that which they experienced in its sanctification may have developed subsequently the sequence of theosophical speculations with which I have been dealing ; alternatively, it may be that they had come across teaching in unfrequented paths, something handed down from the past. I know nothing of written records on the subject outside the ZOHAR ; but I do know that there is some vestige of teaching in the East [2] which is communicated on rare occasions, though I believe that it is concerned with the act itself rather than with the fruit thereof, and it is not the kind of secret which the East keeps to itself exclusively. Two things followed in respect of Kabbalistic doctrine and practice. Marriage for the mystical Jew had become a sacrament, and I care nothing if scholarship— supposing that it were to take up the question—should decide in its wisdom that the Zoharic notion of marriage owes something to the sacramental system of the Catholic Church. I reject the proposition in advance—for what my view is worth—and I do not think that it will be put forward ; but it would signify nothing if it were true. There has been no failure so great on the register of Latin orthodoxy as its consecration of marriage ; there has been nothing that is so skin deep, nothing so reluctant and half-hearted. It never did a wiser thing, a greater or a truer, than when it instituted the seventh sacrament ; how it ever came to do it is another question, having regard to all the conflict of interests, the so-called counsels of perfection, the intolerable and melancholy burden brought over from Theban deserts and everything that has been collected into that strange edifice which is termed the Paradise of Palladius.[3] The result has been that

---

[1] More correctly, they had an inward, spiritual and godly ideal, on which they dwelt, and by which they seem to have accomplished transmutations below.

[2] It is precisely the same teaching as that of the ZOHAR, though not of course in the same terms.

[3] Dr. E. A. Wallis Budge : THE PARADISE OR GARDEN OF THE HOLY FATHERS . . .

after nearly two thousand years of so-called Sacramental Rites there is nothing less consecrated either in the East or West than are the offices of earthly marriage. On the other hand, the ideal presented in the ZOHAR stands for true and life-long consecration on the highest plane : it is not the ceremonial of a moment which puts a kind of ecclesiastical veneer over something that was less or more abhorred. Here is the first point, and the second in all simplicity is added on the hypothesis, at its value, that the ideal did more than exist on paper and may represent the practice of a secret school. We are told by the records that the fruit of the mystical intercourse was the begetting of children from what is called the Holy Side, as against the side of the demons, and I believe that this was a Kabbalistic way of accounting for the literal fact that children born of such unions belonged to another category than we are accustomed to meet with in the streets and byways of daily life all the world over, or—for that matter—to be familiar with in our own homes. They were Children of Grace, rather than what we call Nature, though Grace is only Nature better understood.

There is one word more : of the personal consequences which befell the Sons of the Doctrine in their delineated life of espousals we hear nothing directly, but the claim is that they came to realise the Divine Presence in their hearts as the general recompense of their consecrated lives. They were not ascetics and they were not solitaries : truly they were a company of scholars in the city and along the countryside, in village and in wilderness. For them the world of Nature was Grace externalised ; the Presence was about them therein, and they attained it after their own manner—which was one of very life and testimony—each of them in his proper heart and mind. I conclude that they had found the true meaning of the words : " It is not good for man to be alone." [1] and that there is a very secret path in which " the joy of living honourably with his wife " [2] may bring the completed man—male and female—into the

---

Compiled by Athanasius Archbishop of Alexandria, Palladius Bishop of Helenopolis, Saint Jerome and others. Translated out of the Syriac. 2 vols., 1907. I do not wish to be understood as making a sweeping condemnation ; I speak chiefly of processes and atmosphere. There are other respects in which the text is worthy to rank with THE GOLDEN LEGEND.

[1] Gen. ii. 18.
[2] See page 380.

spiritual city of joy, great city of praise,[1] wherein is the joy of the Lord.[2]

So the souls go up male and female into the world beyond : if they are prepared souls, they find one another ; and the union that is everlasting begins in the light of God.

---

[1] Jer. xlix. 25. [2] Is. xxix. 19.

BOOK IX

THE WRITTEN WORD OF KABBALISM: THIRD PERIOD

BOOK IX

THE WRITTEN WORD OF KABBALISM: THIRD PERIOD

I.—EXPOSITORS OF THE ZOHAR

THE works—already cited—which are recommended by Rosenroth as assisting to a better comprehension of the ZOHAR fall under two heads—namely, those which are designed to elucidate technical matters and those which may claim to be original expository treatises. In the first are included WORDS OF UNDERSTANDING, which is actually a Zoharic lexicon or vocabulary; the GATE OF THE EYES, which is concerned with the Scriptural passages in the ZOHAR and ANCIENT SUPPLEMENTS; and the ZER ZAHAB—by the hypothesis, a Golden Crown, a wreath of gold, but it is not otherwise described than the title itself indicates, the reason being that the APPARATUS of Rosenroth borrows various extracts from its pages. The second section contains the famous GARDEN OF POMEGRANATES, the WAY OF TRUTH, with its sequel the FOUNT OF WISDOM, and a digest of the ZOHAR proper, entitled the VISION OF THE PRIEST. Outside these there are a few texts which may be regarded as extensions or developments of Zoharic doctrine, but more especially of that part which is concerned with spiritual essences. The scope of this inquiry excludes the discussion of such technical matters as the claims of word-books and anthologies of Biblical quotations : they will be found by those who are concerned in the *Apparatus* of Rosenroth. To mention them in this place will be therefore sufficient, and we may proceed to the consideration of those commentaries and developments which arose out of the ZOHAR and to the names, illustrious in later Kabbalism, which are connected with these.

A.—Moses of Cordova

Assuming that the ZOHAR first became known in Spain towards the end of the thirteenth century, there was a lapse of two hundred and fifty years, according to the dates fixed by modern scholarship, before any literature followed thereon. Hence this literature may be regarded largely as a consequence of the Cremona and Mantua editions. Franck says [1] that two Zoharic schools were founded about the same time in Palestine, namely, the middle of the sixteenth century, the first by Moses of Cordova and the second by Isaac de Loria. On the other hand, Bartolocci [2] and Basnage [3] agree in assigning Moses of Cordova to the fourteenth century. The earlier date would be of importance to the history of Kabbalism, because certain side issues of documentary criticism, untouched in this study, depend upon it ; but, as it happens, there is no question that Moses ben Jacob, called Remak, was born in 1522 and died on June 25, 1570. He is the first commentator on the ZOHAR, for Joseph ben Abraham Gikatilla, called the divine Kabbalist and Thaumaturge, who was of the time of Ferdinand and Isabella, was a writer on the SEPHIROTH, and connects with the SEPHER YETZIRAH rather than Zoharic Theosophy, though he refers to the Kabbalistic Work of the Chariot.[4]

As his name indicates, Moses of Cordova was a Spaniard, but he travelled to Palestine, and it is conjectured that he was instrumental in founding the Academy of Sapeth in Upper Galilee, nine miles from Bethsaida. In either case he was one of its teachers and helped to make it illustrious, for he was regarded by his fellow theosophists as the greatest light of Kabbalism since Simeon ben Yohai. Franck says that he adhered to the real significance of the original monuments of Kabbalism ; but, although this appears worthy of praise, the French critic seems to complain that R. Moses was wanting in originality. However this may be, the work by which he is known is of high authority in Kabbalism. It is entitled the

[1] LA KABBALE, p. 4.
[2] BIBLIOTHECA MAGNA RABBINICA, t. iv. p. 230.
[3] HISTOIRE DES JUIFS, livre vii. c. 24, t. v. p. 1942.
[4] He was born in Old Castile anno 1248 and died at Peñafiel circa 1305—perhaps somewhat later. His views on the relation between the Divine Names JHVH and Elohim shew that he was unacquainted with the doctrine of Shekinah, as this is found in the ZOHAR.

GARDEN OF POMEGRANATES (*Pardes Rimmonim*), referring to the versicle in the Song of Solomon, iv. 13 : " Thy plants are an orchard of pomegranates." Basnage says that, after the manner of Kabbalists, he discovers whatsoever he pleases in that single sentence.[1] The pomegranate, with its innumerable seeds, is a favourite object for symbolism, and the garden, orchard, or paradise has produced a wealth of imagery for all Mysticism. Here, in a general sense, it is the treasury of Scriptural meanings, and the Hebrew word by which it is described having four consonants, these meanings are classified as four : פרדם = PRDS ; the P signifies the literal sense, R the mystic sense, D the enigmatic sense, and S the secret and concealed sense.

Dwelling upon these involved meanings, as may be imagined, the GARDEN OF POMEGRANATES [2] is an obscure and difficult treatise, and the attempt made by Rosenroth to dismember it for the purpose of his APPARATUS, while it gives no idea of its contents, creates a lively image of its complexity. The attribution of the letters of TETRAGRAMMATON to the SEPHIROTH, the mystical meaning of words deprived of their context, the names applied to SEPHIROTH, the superincession of these and their union with AIN SOPH, the Mystery of the Throne and of Shekinah, primæval TOHU and BOHU, the unknown darkness—these are specimens here and there of the subject-matter. But as the heart of the Kabbalist, in opposition to the ascribed character of his nation, was fixed with peculiar intentness on the eternal destinies of Israel and not on temporal concerns, so his chief interest was the soul, ever recurrent in his writings, as if it were impossible to atone sufficiently for the silence of his sacred books. There is hence no need to say that a special tract in the GARDEN OF POMEGRANATES [3] is dedicated to the subject of the soul, discussing the region from which it emanates, its purpose in the world, the profit of its creation, its union with matter, its superiority over the angels, its chief divisions, their relation one with another, the SEPHIROTH to which they are referred, the places to which they resort after death, the absence of one or both

---

[1] HISTOIRE DES JUIFS, l. vii. c. 24, vol. v. p. 1943.
[2] It appeared at Cracow in 1591, and Samuel Gallico published an abridged version under the title of ASIS RIMMONIM, which is cited often by Rosenroth, but I have failed to trace its date.
[3] Namely, Tract xxxi., translated in the KABBALA DENUDATA, *Apparatus in Librum Sohar pars secunda*, i. 100 *et seq.*

of the higher divisions in many individuals—following Zoharic doctrine—and the good and evil angels accompanying each human being. The tract devotes also a very curious chapter to the *simulacrum* which presides at generation, a phantasmal image of humanity which descends on the male head *cum copula maritalis exercetur inferius*. It is affirmed to be sent from the Lord, and no procreation can take place without its presence. It is not, of course, visible, yet might be seen if licence were given to the eye. This phantom or *imago* is prepared for each man before he enters the world, and he grows in the likeness thereof. With the Israelites the *simulacrum* is holy, and it comes to them from the Holy Place. To those of another religion it descends from the side of impurity, and hence the chosen people must not mingle their seed with that of the Gentile.[1]

Another curious speculation is founded on that thesis of the ZOHAR, according to which the good works performed by a person in this world become for him vestments of price— as we have seen—in the world to come. Here was a poetic sentiment which had to be methodised and made literal inevitably by a late Kabbalist. When a man who has performed many good works falls away finally from righteousness and is lost, what becomes of his earlier works ? Though the sinner may perish, they, says R. Moses, remain, and if there be a just man walking in the ways of the Supernal King, yet wanting something in his vestments, God will supply the deficiency from the good works of the impious one. The preference is given to those who, taken in their youth, have been unable to fulfil all the precepts of the Law.

B.—ISAAC DE LORIA

Of this Kabbalist Bartolocci and Basnage have very little to tell us, and it is not necessary to say that he is ignored by writers like Graetz. He is referred by Basnage to the seventeenth century [2] and by Franck to that which preceded it. As a fact, he was born at Jerusalem of German parentage in 1534, and he died at Sapheth or Safed in 1572, having pub-

---

[1] This fantasy rests on the authority of the ZOHAR, which states that the *simulacrum* is an emanation of the celestial form of each man, *i.e.*, JECHIDAH.—Mantua edition, iii. 107.

[2] HISTOIRE DES JUIFS, l. vii. c. 31, p. 2089, vol. v. He was a pupil of David ibn Abi Zimri, and has been regarded as the greatest rabbinical doctor at his period in Germany.

lished nothing himself except some Aramaic poems. The substantial authenticity of the great body of his doctrines collected by his disciple, R. Hayyim Vital, has not been challenged, however, and Franck bases thereon his hostile judgment of Loria,[1] on the ground, firstly, that he was, like Moses of Cordova, not original ; and, secondly, that he departed from Zoharic Kabbalism to indulge in his own reveries, a criticism which stultifies itself. It is certain, however, that Loria—otherwise Luria—did innovate or extend, and that this is also his title to interest. He is not a mere echo or reflection, and he makes good reading because he is a wild fantasiast. Rosenroth terms him the eagle of the Kabbalists. It is, of course, impossible to say how far his scribe and disciple, R. Chaïm, may have developed his developments and elaborated his fantasies. Subject to one reservation, as will appear shortly, the vast thesaurus which represents both made its first printed appearance in KABBALA DENUDATA, where the excerpts, embodying whole treatises, fill some three hundred quarto pages.[2] They include :

I. The first tract, so called, of the LIBER DRUSHIM,[3] *i.e.*, BOOK OF DISSERTATIONS, forming the second volume of the collection. It occasioned a curious correspondence between Rosenroth and Henry More, who was surprised, as he expresses it, by the unexpectedness of its doctrine, but found much with which he could sympathise, as we shall learn later on in the book devoted to Christian students of the Kabbalah.

II. A commentary on the BOOK OF CONCEALMENT,[4] forming the second tract in the sixth volume of the collection. It is not given in its absolute integrity—*cujus maximam partem infra exhibemus*, says Rosenroth.[5]

III. The BOOK OF THE REVOLUTIONS OF SOULS,[6] forming the first tract in the fifth volume of the collection, which seems to have been even larger than the ZOHAR itself—in fact, almost the camel's load of the legend. A portion of this tract is said to have been printed in DE PERCUSSIONE SEPULCHRI, at Venice in 1620, together with DE PRECIBUS, recalling a further

---

[1] The modern orthography is Luria and the full name Isaac ben Solomon Ashkenazi Luria. I have followed that of Rosenroth for the convenience of those who may have occasion to consult his great collection.

[2] A printed edition in full appeared at Volkiev in 1772.

[3] KABBALA DENUDATA, *Apparatus* . . . *pars secunda*, i. 28 *et seq.*

[4] *Ibid.* ii. *pars secunda, tractatus quartus*, pp. 3 *et seq.*

[5] In the *Præfatio ad Lectorem*, p. 16, vol. ii.

[6] KAB. DEN. ii., *partis tertiæ tractatus secundus pneumaticus*, pp. 234 *et seq.*

subject treated in the collection.   I have been unable to trace
the volume or to find any particulars concerning it.[1]

The LIBER DRUSHIM is a metaphysical introduction to the
Kabbalah, which discusses a variety of subtle and abstruse
questions much after the manner of scholastic philosophy,
and there is no doubt that Isaac de Loria might have diffused
a great light of reasoning at Salamanca, had he been a Christian
Doctor instead of a Jewish Rabbi.   His first point, as he tells
us, is one over which Kabbalists, late and early, had out-
wearied themselves already, namely, for what reason were the
worlds created and was their creation of necessity ?   Assuredly
from the period of the Angel of the Schools, the halls of
Salamanca, of Padua, of Louvain and the other seats of
scholastic learning, had echoed with similar debate.   Perhaps
the Kabbalists owed something to the Scholastics, perhaps
they drew both from one another.   The Wisdom of the Exile
was encompassed on all sides by the great debate of Christian
speculation.   It would be interesting to discriminate the
extent of interchange between them and to determine whether
the plummet of Kabbalism sounded lower depths than the
schoolmen ; but I doubt whether the dimensions of a volume
would suffice for this one excursion.   Let me indicate therefore the answer of Isaac de Loria, and perhaps some student
at large among scholastic quartos will find illuminating
parallels in the Scholastics.[2]   The answer is that God cannot
fail of perfection in all the works and names of His magnificence, His excellence and His glory ; but unless those works
had been brought from potentiality into act they could not
have been termed perfect, as regards either works or names.
The Name TETRAGRAMMATON signifies perpetual existence,
past, present and future, in the condition of creation before
the creation, and thereafter in the immutability of things.
But if the worlds had not been created, with all that is in
them, it could not have signified thus the continuity of
existences in every instant of time, and TETRAGRAMMATON
would have been an empty formula.   How very curious is
the treachery of this reasoning, which ascribes to a Name of
the Deity an existence independent of the intelligent creatures
whose convention it is !   But we should probably find many

---

[1] This is the subject of my reservation on the previous page.
[2] He must go further, however, than B. Hareau in his treatise DE LA PHILOSOPHIE
SCHOLASTIQUE.   Paris.   1880.

parallel treacheries among scholastic reasoners, were there any one at hand to disinter them. So also the name of ADONAI, or the Lord, involves the idea of ministers or servants, and if there were no ministers God could not be called by this title. But after the creation of the worlds and the production of the divine works from potentiality into accomplishment, God has fulfilled His perfection in every operation of His powers, and in all His Names without any exception.

The next point discussed by LIBER DRUSHIM is why the world was created at the time and moment that it was, and not at an earlier, or, for that matter, at a later epoch. The answer is that the Supreme and Most Excellent Light is infinite, exceeding comprehension and speculation, and that its concealed foundation is far from all understanding. Before anything was produced by emanation therefrom, there was no time or beginning therein. This is the solution of the difficulty which is offered by most official theology, and it could have no aspect of novelty at the late period of Isaac de Loria. It may be affirmed in a general way that when Kabbalists touch any common ground of speculation they surpass their epoch but seldom in profundity or subtlety, I might add also in the adequacy of their views, though metaphysical sufficiency was not, of course, to be expected on any side.

But it is not often and it is not for long that works like LIBER DRUSHIM confine themselves to the common ground of speculation, and the Kabbalist in this instance passes speedily into the transcendental region of the SEPHIROTH, including the manner of their emanation, another question, as he tells us, which has involved all Kabbalists in controversy. In so far as such speculations are of consequence to our purpose, they belong to an earlier stage and have been noted at least therein. Do they proceed from one another in the simplicity of a successive series, or is their emanation in columns? We have found that there is authority for both views and also for a third, which represents them as a series of concentric circles. These questions, says R. Isaac, are hard and difficult to determine, but he offers a solution on the ZOHAR, namely, that before the order of things was instituted, they were disposed one over the other, but after that time in three pillars, those of Mercy and Severity, with the central column of which KETHER is the summit and MALKUTH the base.   The hypothesis of circles adopted by a German expositor in CŒLUM SEPHIROTICUM is thus implicitly set aside.

In subsequent chapters the SEPHIROTH are considered under a dual aspect, namely, as regards the portion of Divine Light contained in each and as regards the containing vessel, while these again are distinguished into an ambient and an inward Light, and an external and internal vessel.   The existence of many worlds prior to the Sephirotic emanations is affirmed, herein following, as we have seen, both Talmudic and Zoharic tradition.   Finally, several classifications of the SEPHIROTH are considered in the last chapter.

The study of LIBER DRUSHIM may be recommended to those —if any remain among us—who have been taught to regard the Kabbalah, on so-called " occult " authority, as a doctrine of certitude, whereas it is largely empirical, its leading theorems giving rise to as much disputation regarding their proper meaning as the principles of any other speculative philosophy.

The commentary on the BOOK OF CONCEALMENT, as might be expected, is written undesignedly on the *lucus a non lucendo* principle.   It does not yield readily to an analysis of contents, as it takes various paragraphs of the text and exposes their meaning consecutively, with the help of the IDRA RABBA and IDRA ZOUTA.   The peculiar designation of the treatise is said to arise out of Proverbs xxv. 2 : " It is the glory of God to conceal a thing," [1] and *Ibid.* xi. 2 : " With the lowly is wisdom." The second reference explains why it is termed both the BOOK OF CONCEALMENT and that of MODESTY.   On the authority of the Zohar, section PEKUDE, the balance symbol, which has made this treatise so famous in Kabbalism, is affirmed to represent the Male and Female principles, which indeed follows from the developments of the LESSER HOLY SYNOD. The male denotes Mercy, the right-hand Pillar of the SEP-HIROTH, and the female Severity, the Pillar on the left hand. These principles are termed the Father and the Mother, and in the Hebrew Alphabet are referable to JOD and HE.   The Father is perfect love and the Mother perfect severity.   The latter had seven sons, namely, the Edomite Kings, who had no foundation in the Holy Ancient One. [2]   These are empty

---

[1] Or according to the Vulgate : *Gloria Dei est celare verbum.*
[2] See Book IV, § 3, p. 141.

lights dispelled by the source of lights concealed within the Mother. Male and female are conformations of the Holy Ancient One, corresponding to KETHER, and represented mystically by three heads signifying : (*a*) the Unmanifested Wisdom, which is so withdrawn that it is as though it were not, in contradiction to that which is manifested in the thirty-two paths ; (*b*) the Supreme Crown, which is the Holy Ancient One ; and (*c*) the Head which neither knows nor is known, namely, AIN SOPH. Thus on the one side of KETHER is CHOKMAH, or Wisdom : this is the Father; while on the other is BINAH, the Mother or increment of Understanding; and above is the *latens Deitas*.

These instances of Loria's skill in developing and distorting the Zoharic symbolism of the three supernal SEPHIROTH must suffice as a specimen of the whole commentary, which, it may be added, does not proceed—in this its Latin version, beyond the first chapter of the BOOK OF CONCEALMENT. Loria affirms, as the sum of the whole mystery, that man in his prayers should fix his mind upon the foundation of all foundations, that he may derive to himself a certain influence and benediction from the depths of that source. In this manner the obscurities of Kabbalism are redeemed at times by the simplicity and depth of the lesson which is extracted from them.

THE BOOK OF THE REVOLUTIONS OF SOULS is obviously of more living consequence than an obscure exposition of so obscure a work as SIPHRA DI ZENIOUTHA ; but it is difficult to give account of it in a small space because the system which it develops is involved, even for a Kabbalistic work. The greatest importance has been attached to it by speculators like Éliphas Lévi, who made no distinction between Zoharic and later doctrine.

The basis of its scheme is the doctrine of the BOOK OF CONCEALMENT and its expository synods concerning the Seven Edomite Kings who emanated and passed away prior to the production of the present universe. In these Kings there was good as well as evil, and a separation therefore was made, that which was good being used for the material of the Four Kabbalistic Worlds as they are now constituted. Each of these Worlds, according to Isaac de Loria, has its MACRO-PROSOPUS, Supernal Father, Supernal Mother, MICROPROSOPUS and Bride, all derived from the Seven Kings. A like origin is attributed to souls, and they are disposed similarly in the Four Worlds, some corresponding to the Bride, some to MICROPROSOPUS, some to the Father Supernal, some to the Supernal Mother and some again to MACROPROSOPUS in the World of ASSIAH. The totality of these souls constitutes Psyche in ASSIAH, which in reference to the Supernal Personalities of that World has therefore five parts : the Psyche in the Psyche, or NEPHESH of ASSIAH, the *mundus factivus ;* the medial spirit, or RUAH of the *Psyche factiva ;* the *mens,* or NESHAMAH ; the *vitalitas,* or HAÏA ; and the *singularitas,* individuality, or YEHIDAH, all belonging to the *Psyche factiva,* or NEPHESH of ASSIAH. There is a similar distribution through the Three Superior Worlds, RUAH and its five-fold division being referred to YETZIRAH, NESHAMAH to BRIAH, CHIAH to ATZILUTH, and JECHIDA, possibly to the World of Unmanifest Deity which is beyond ATZILUTH ; but Loria's system is not extended above the measures of the Tree of Life. Each of the five divisions is again attributed as follows in the Sephirotic scheme :

    I. NEPHESH to MALKUTH, the Kingdom, *i.e.,* the Bride.
    II. RUAH to the SEPHIROTH of MICROPROSOPUS.
    III. NESHAMAH to the Mother, *i.e.,* BINAH.
    IV. CHIAH to the Father, *i.e.,* CHOKMAH.
    V. YEHIDAH to KETHER, *i.e.,* the Crown.[1]

We are now in a position to appreciate the standpoint of Franck when he observed that Loria added his own reveries to Zoharic teaching. The developments have at the same time been considerably simplified in this digest.

All these souls were contained in the Archetypal or Protoplastic Adam at the time that he was formed, some corresponding to the head, others to the eyes, and so with all the members. But these souls are those of the Israelites, who are *gens unica in terram.* We must look elsewhere for the origin of the nations of the world. The recrements, the evil and rejected parts of the Edomite Kings are the *cortices* or shells which compose the averse Adam Belial, evolved by our late expositor from rare Zoharic allusions to the SEPHIROTH

---

[1] It follows that each of the Four Worlds has the Four Worlds within it, and the Ten SEPHIROTH tabulated in the authentic Tree of Life. Other Loria speculations shew each SEPHIRA as containing all SEPHIROTH. Compare Book VI, § 2, p. 254. There is perhaps a certain vestige of this notion in the ZOHAR.

of the shadow. When the Adam and Eve of Genesis partook of the forbidden fruit, their fall confounded the good with the evil of the *cortices*, that of Adam with the male shells of Samael or Adam Belial, and that of Eve with the evil of his bride Lilith, the *spurcities* of the serpent; for the serpent had commerce with Éve according to Issac de Loria, which is a recurring but not invariable doctrine of the ZOHAR. It was after this fall that the nations of the world were produced from the shells. This is the doctrine which certain dreamers of the late nineteenth century accepted by implication when they spoke of the connection between later Kabbalism and the Secret Traditions on which their devotion was fixed. To put the position tersely, the souls of the Israelites were distributed in the members of the protoplastic Adam, regarded in his mystical extension through the four worlds, and the souls of the Gentiles in the members of Adam Belial, belonging to the Averse Tree. It is not seemingly affirmed that if man had remained in perfection he would have procreated according to the way of Nature and brought an Israel of super-election into the world; but the Fall at least was responsible for the souls of the nations taking flesh on earth. Liberation from the foulness and venom of the serpent—as things are— is by generation and death only, whereby the good is separated from the evil, until all nations of the world shall have been brought forth from the evil and the Israelites from the good kind.

From the time when the good and evil were thus confounded two things have been necessary: (1) that the good man should be separated from the evil; (2) that the portion of the good should be restored. The first is accomplished by observation of the prohibitive precepts of the Law, and the second by that of the affirmative. Both classes must be accomplished in all their number, and in thought, word and deed, by every soul, whose revolutions therefore must continue until the whole Law has been fulfilled. This Law must be studied also in each of its four senses, failing which the revolutions of the deficient soul will further be prolonged. This scheme seems to apply exclusively to the Israelites, as the nations of the world can be destined only to return whence they came, and Adam Belial is obviously not under the Law. The scheme, however, is subject to a certain mitigation, as revolution proper is sometimes replaced by *status embryonatus*.

Revolution is the entrance of a soul into the body of an infant at birth, to experience the pain and trial prepared for that body. The alternative condition is the entrance of a soul into the body of a grown man, who must be at least thirty years old,[1] *i.e.*, when he is obliged to fulfil the precepts. The *status embryonatus* is entered either (*a*) because the soul in question has something to fulfil which was neglected in the preceding revolution ; or (*b*) for the benefit of the man who is impregnated, *i.e.*, to justify and direct him. Revolution occurs (1) for the cleansing of sin ; (2) for the fulfilment of a neglected precept ; (3) for the leading of others into the right way, in which case the returning soul is perfect in justice ; (4) to receive the true spouse, who was not deserved by the soul in the prior revolution. Four souls may revolve in one body, but not more, while the *status embryonatus* may associate three alien souls with a single man, but again no more. The object of all revolutions and all Kabbalistic embryology is the return of the Israelites into the stature of the first Adam, all having been involved in his fall since he included all.

The Kabbalistic doctrine of revolution according to Isaac de Loria is not Zoharic doctrine—though it has a certain ground therein—nor is it a scheme of reincarnation peculiar to any other school of theosophy in the past or at the present day. In so far as it differs from the ZOHAR, it would be unreasonable to regard it as a fuller light of any old Tradition ; it is greatly curious, yet fitly described as a reverie, written by R. Hayyim Vital out of the head of Isaac de Loria, and perhaps owing something to the scribe.

C.—NAPTHALI HIRTZ

This German Kabbalist, who is known otherwise as Napthali Herz ben Jacob Elhanan, was born at Frankfort-on-the-Main in the second half of the sixteenth century, but he is said to have lived in Palestine and presumably died there at an uncertain date, few biographical particulars being extant concerning him. His work, entitled THE VALLEY OF THE KING, was made great use of by Rosenroth, who gave, firstly, a compendium of its content [2] in the form of one hundred and

---

[1] The Jewish age of reason.

[2] So far at least as the first part is concerned, being that which was printed at Amsterdam, 1648, under the title of EMEK HA-MELEK. The second part, or GAN HA-MELEK, has remained in manuscript.

thirty KABBALISTIC THESES,[1] arranged with considerable
perspicuity ; in the second place, the first six sections of the
treatise, designed as an introduction to the ZOHAR for the
better comprehension thereof ; [2] and, thirdly, all that part of
it which is concerned with the BOOK OF CONCEALMENT and
the two Synods as a commentary on these works.[3]   A large
part of the ROYAL VALLEY is included therefore in KABBALA
DENUDATA, the excerpts extending over several hundred
pages.   Its author belonged to the school of Isaac de Loria,
and he appears to have traversed a portion of the ground
covered by the Lorian MSS. of R. Hayyim Vital.   After the
same manner that these develop and exaggerate Zoharic
metapsychical teaching, so the ROYAL VALLEY extends Kabbalistic cosmology, and classifies it in correspondence with the
parts or divisions of the human soul, as these are found in the
ZOHAR.   The *mundus prior* of Kabbalism, *i.e.*, the emanation
of the Seven Edomite Kings, is termed the world of NEPHESH,
and it was destroyed with the souls belonging to it because
evil prevailed therein.   The actual world is that of RUAH, in
which good and evil are confused, but good comes out of the
evil and at last all shall be good.   Then a new world shall
succeed, being that of NESHAMAH, and this will be the Sabbath
of Grace.   It follows therefore that the present order must
pass away, and this is symbolised by the death of the second
Hadad, the eighth Edomite King, as recorded in 1 Chron. i.
50, 51.   In the day of this destruction the spirits of impurity,
namely, the shells, shall be burnt up entirely, God will
establish a new creation and will bring forth from His glorious
light the mystery of the NESHAMAH of His Great Name.
The dominion of this NESHAMAH is the King who shall reign
over Israel, and in that day the Lord shall be one, and His
Name one.

The hypothesis of the creation of the world begins with
the contraction of the Divine Presence, producing that space
which is termed primæval air.   " Before the emanations
issued forth and the things which were created, the
Supreme Light was extended infinitely.   When it came into
the Supreme Mind to will the fabrication of worlds, the issue
of emanations and the emission as light of the perfection of

---

[1] KABBALA DENUDATA, *Apparatus in Librum Sohar pars secunda*, i. 150 *et seq.*
[2] *Ibid.* ii. 152 *et seq.*
[3] *Ibid.* ii. *partis secundæ tractatus quartus*, pp. 47 *et seq.*

His active powers, aspects and attributes, then that Light was in some measure compressed, receding in every direction from a particular central point, and thus a certain vacuum was left in mid-infinite, wherein emanations might be manifested."

It is to this treatise that Kabbalism owes the curious conception of the evolution of SEPHIROTH by a process of explosion, through the excess of light which distended them. From the fragments of the broken vessels originated the Four Worlds, the shells both good and evil, and myriads of souls. This notion is fundamentally similar to that of Isaac de Loria, and becomes identical in its developments. As it is impossible to compress the scheme of the treatise within the limits that are here possible, I will add only that the ROYAL VALLEY regards KETHER as containing *in potentia* all the remaining SEPHIROTH, so that originally they were not distinguishable therefrom. " Precisely as in man there exist the four elements in potence but undistinguishable specifically, so in this Crown there were all the remaining numerations." It is added that in the Second World, called that of restoration, KETHER became the Cause of Causes and the Ancient of the Ancients. We see therefore that, according to this late school of Kabbalism, the first attempt at manifestation by the *latens Deitas* went utterly astray, and that the evil of the whole world is the result of the failure of God—a peculiar reverie which is found also in the Talmud.

D.—ABRAHAM COHEN IRIRA [1]

This Spanish Jew was another and late follower of the school of de Loria, but tinctured by Platonic philosophy, which he sought to harmonise with Kabbalism in his GATE OF THE HEAVENS.[2] His other treatise is BETH ELOHIM, the HOUSE OF GOD, containing three dissertations in exposition of the doctrines of Loria, but founded upon and citing at considerable length the metapsychical portions of the FAITHFUL SHEPHERD, the PEKUDE section in the ZOHAR, and the

---

[1] The name is given in the form adopted by Rosenroth and as such familiar. It is otherwise Abraham Cohen de Herrera and accurately Alonzo de Herrera, who was of Spanish birth, but died at Amsterdam in 1631.
[2] KABBALA DENUDATA, *Apparatus . . . pars tertia*, t. i.

ANCIENT SUPPLEMENTS of that work.[1] So much space has been given already to Kabbalistic psychology that it will be permissible to dismiss this writer in a few words. The first dissertation in the HOUSE OF GOD rests chiefly on Zoharic utterances attributed to R. Simeon ben Yohai, who is termed the mouthpiece of holiness and the angel of the Lord ; it recites the emanation of the SEPHIROTH according to the received doctrine, develops the system of the hierarchy of evil spirits, who are termed *cortices*, or shells, and of the ten sinister or impure Numerations—otherwise, the AVERSE SEPHIROTH. It examines also in a special chapter the opinion of R. Isaac de Loria concerning eleven classes of shells, and of R. Moses of Cordova concerning the connection of the angels with the celestial bodies, and concerning their physical vestments. The second dissertation treats of the different angelical orders and the seven heavens, while the third deals with elementary spirits and the nature of the soul.

We have seen that the HOUSE OF GOD has been included unaccountably by some occult writers [2]—who did not know their subject—among the books which constitute the ZOHAR, but it is a commentary or development, of considerable importance in its own sphere, yet neither possessing nor claiming any pretension to antiquity. Both works were written in Spanish and remained in manuscript till they had been translated into Hebrew, in which form they appeared at Amsterdam in 1665.

E.—ISSACHAR BEN NAPTHALI

This expositor of Kabbalism seems to have been a contemporary of Loria, and, like him, was a German. His chief work, the VISION OF THE PRIEST, was printed at Cracovia in 1559.[3] It is a synopsis of the entire ZOHAR, or, more properly, a methodised analysis of its contents, distributed under a number of titles, each of which is sub-divided according to the Mosaic books. It has been found almost impossible to make use of it for the purposes of this study, and it is indeed designed only for the assistance of the scholar who may

---

[1] KABBALA DENUDATA, ii. *partis tertiæ tractatus I.*, pp. 188 *et seq.*

[2] As, for example, S. L. MacGregor Mathers in the introduction to his KABBALAH UNVEILED.

[3] Translated in the KABBALA DENUDATA, ii. *pars prima ejusque tractatus primus*, p. 1. *et seq.*

desire to consult the ZOHAR on a given subject.   The other
works of R. Issachar are of similar character, and are, in fact,
those technical treatises mentioned at the beginning of the
present section as outside the scope of the present inquiry.   I
find no particulars concerning him, even in the JEWISH
ENCYCLOPÆDIA, which fails to follow up a cross-reference *s.v.*
Napthali Herz ben Issachar.

II.—THE BOOK OF PURIFYING FIRE

When a given order of mystical symbolism, possessing
distinct objects and a sphere of application more or less
defined, is applied to the purposes of another order, we may
expect to derive some curious results from the analogy thus
instituted if we can get to understand the method, though, as I
have indicated, this superincession of typology tends to be
somewhat dazing in its results.   The treatise entitled ÆSH
MEZAREPH, which signifies Purifying Fire, is an instance of
the application of Kabbalistic apparatus to the purposes of
Alchemy, and is, so far as I am aware, the sole instance of its
kind.   In this connection, however, we shall do well to
remember that Hermetic and Kabbalistic philosophy are
ascribed by some authorities on occultism to a common
source,[1] while the rabbinical influence on Alchemy is
illustrated by such inventions as that about Rabbi Abraham
and Flamel, not to speak of a work under the title of THE
PHILOSOPHICAL STONE, which is attributed idly to Saadiah by
Moses Botrel, and is known only by a single quotation.   A
few metallic allusions are to be found in the ZOHAR, which
recognises the existence of an archetypal gold, and regards the
metals generally as composite substances.   But these references are almost less than incidental, and it is needless to say
that there is no cryptic chemistry whatever in the great
theosophical storehouse.

The treatise on Purifying Fire is said to have been written
in Aramaic Chaldee.   It was made use of so largely by
Rosenroth in his LEXICON that practically the whole work is
affirmed to have been rendered into Latin in the pages of

---

[1] Thus Thomas Vaughan (Eugenius Philalethes), see Book X, § 11, affirms in his
MAGIA ADAMICA that the learning of the Jews, *i.e.*, their Kabbalah, was chemical, and
that Flamel's BOOK OF ABRAHAM THE JEW is the best proof thereof.   See A. E. Waite:
THE WORKS OF THOMAS VAUGHAN, London, 1919, pp. 171, 172.

Kabbala Denudata.[1] It was reconstructed from this source in the early part of the eighteenth century by an Unknown Hermetic Student, styling himself a Lover of Philalethes, and was by him put into an English vesture.[2] In the year 1894 this translation was included in a series of Hermetic reprints under the editorship of Dr. Wynn Westcott.[3] The preface and notes which accompany this edition appear under the denomination of *Sapere Aude*, being one of his pseudonyms, and have certain points of interest. No information is given, however—and of course none was to be expected—as to the Chaldee original, either by the English translator or his modern editor.

There is further no evidence available by which we can fix with any degree of precision the period at which this treatise was composed.[4] It is subsequent, of course, to the promulgation of the Zohar, which it quotes frequently. It is subsequent to the Garden of Pomegranates by R. Moses of Cordova, a treatise belonging to the middle of the sixteenth century, which it quotes also. It borrows processes from R. Mordechai, a Kabbalistic alchemist, whose date I have failed to discover,[5] and it refers to the Latin treatises of Geber. We may conclude that it does not antedate Rosenroth by any considerable period, and that it may be placed conjecturally at the beginning of the seventeenth century, or a little earlier. Finally, it contains expressions which are common to most of the Latin alchemists, and were by them derived from the Greeks, such as, " He that is wise may correct natures." It does not possess the interest or importance which would attach to a chemico-Kabbalistic treatise of the Zohar period,

---

[1] The authority—such as it is—is that of Dr. Westcott, but no one has seen the original since Rosenroth, and the statement represents therefore not merely a personal speculation, but one of a hazardous kind.

[2] Æsh Mezareph, or Purifying Fire. A Chymico-Kabbalistic treatise collected from the Kabbala Denudata of Knorr von Rosenroth, London, 1714. Perhaps it should be added that the translator's pseudonym is an allusion to Eirenæus Philalethes, a famous English adept of the seventeenth century, whose identity, like that of his admirer, has never been discovered.

[3] Collectanea Hermetica, vol. iv. London, 1894.

[4] It is mentioned by Claverus in his Observations on the Most Useful Things in the World, 1706, pp. 72 *et seq.* He gives an account of it designed to shew that the Jews accommodated the Kabbalistic Sephiroth to Chrysopœia, *i.e.*, the Art of Alchemy. He states also that the Jews hold the Æsh Mezareph in such high esteem that they consider no Christian worthy of reading it.

[5] A number of writers, mostly Kabbalistic, are classed under this name in the bibliography of Bartolocci, but there is no alchemist among them, the statement obtaining also for the Jewish Encyclopædia, its cross-references included.

and I have not been able to find any evidence on the authority ascribed to it.[1]

In the supplement to his KEY OF THE GREAT MYSTERIES, Éliphas Lévi gives, firstly, what he calls the fragments of the ÆSH MEZAREPH, terming it one of the most important books of Hermetic science ; secondly, the complements of its eight chapters, being further fragments which he claims to have discovered ; thirdly, a hypothetical restitution of the original.[2] The methods of the brilliant French occultist are well illustrated in each case. It should be observed that the fragments are designed to exhibit the difficulties and the weariness which his researches have spared to his readers, and to illustrate the conscientious and serious nature of his studies. The first section proves when examined not to be fragments of the ÆSH MEZAREPH, but a loose paraphrase which has a very slender correspondence with the original. The second section, which is similarly paraphrase, is substantially to be found in Rosenroth and the English version. The hypothetical reconstruction serves only to shew that Lévi, like every one else, never saw the original which some have said is still extant, or he would not have so misplaced his ingenuity. Lastly, he attributes the work to Rabbi Abraham of the Flamel mythos, thus investing it with an antiquity which is contradicted by its own references.[3]

Before indicating, however briefly, the heads of its contents, it is necessary to observe that ÆSH MEZAREPH must be for the ordinary student only a curious memorial of the connections instituted between two orders of cryptic symbolism. It is described by its latest editor as " suggestive rather than explanatory," and he adds that its alchemical processes are not set forth " in such a way that they could be carried out by a

---

[1] Dr. Gerhard Scholem published an interesting and important study of ALCHEMY AND THE KABBALAH in the MONATSCHRIFT FÜR GESCHICHTE UND WISSENSCHAFT DES JUDENTUMS in 1925 and reprinted it subsequently as a pamphlet. He affirms that after examining every Kabbalistic text which came within his reach, it is certain that Alchemy and Kabbalism cannot be reconciled, if only because gold is the perfect metal for the one and silver for the other. As to ÆSH MEZAREPH, it is concerned with producing silver rather than gold, but it is not a treatise on actual processes of transmutation. Its Kabbalistic parts may be *circa* sixteenth century. It should be noted that, according to the ZOHAR, II, 147b ; IV., 65, gold is superior to silver.

[2] LA CLEF DES GRANDS MYSTÈRES. See RENSEIGNEMENTS *sur les grands mystères de la philosophie hermétique*, pp. 405 *et seq.*

[3] Firstly, in the title, which reads, *Fragments de L'ASH MÉZAREPH du Juif Abraham ;* secondly, in the hypothetical recomposition of the treatise which connects it with the mystical book possessed by Flamel. The ÆSH MEZAREPH is entirely anonymous, and is included as such in the bibliography of Wolf, ii. 1265.

neophyte ; any attempt to do so would discover that something vital was missing at one stage or other." The fact is
so true of all alchemical literature that it does not need stating,
and the Æsh Mezareph has the common difficulties of purely
Hermetic books complicated further by the system of Gematria
and the Sephirotic correspondences of metals.

On the correspondences here indicated the treatise is based
mainly, and it is in this sense that the mysteries of alchemical
transmutation are said to " differ not from the superior
mysteries of the Kabbalah." The Sephiroth of the material
world are identical with those of the archetypal, and they are
the same in the mineral kingdom. The alchemical root of
the metals corresponds to Kether ; all metals originate
therefrom, as the other Sephiroth are all emanations from
the Crown. The metallic root is concealed, and so also is
the Crown. Lead is referred to Chokmah, which proceeds
immediately from Kether, as Saturn from the metallic root.
Tin has the place of Binah, Silver that of Chesed, and these
three are the white metallic natures. Among the red, Gold is
is in correspondence with Geburah, Iron with Tiphereth,
and the hermaphroditic Brass with Netzach and Hod.
Quicksilver is referred to Jesod, and " the true Medicine of
Metals " to Malkuth. The attribution will appear in some
cases a little conventional, and it depends upon a curious use
of Scriptural authority. However, the writer adds : " If any
one hath placed these things in another order, I shall not
contend with him, inasmuch as all systems tend to the one
truth." In illustration of this, he cites another attribution,
as follows :

" The three Supernals," namely, Kether, Chokmah and
Binah, " are the three fountains of metallic things." " The
thick water," that is, Mercury, " is Kether, Salt is Chokmah
and Sulphur is Binah." These are the Three Principles of the
alchemists. This attribution, says the treatise, is " for known
reasons." Chesed, Geburah and Tiphereth correspond as
before to Silver, Gold and Iron ; Netzach is Tin, Hod is
Copper, Jesod is Lead, while Malkuth is the " Metallic
Woman," the " Luna of the Wise " and the " Field into
which the seeds of secret minerals ought to be cast, that is,
the Water of Gold." The attribution in either case has a
concealed sense which " no tongue may be permitted to
utter." It seems to follow that superficial explanations

offered at one and another point should not be taken literally, as, for example, that Silver is referred to CHESED " on account of its whiteness, which denotes Mercy and Pity." The KAMEA or Magical Squares of the planets are given in connection with each of the seven metals, but not always correctly in the printed copies.

The peculiar genius of the work is illustrated in the third chapter, where Daniel's vision of the beast with ten horns is interpreted alchemically by the help of *gematria*.[1]

III.—THE MYSTERIES OF LOVE

With the sole exception of Abraham Cohen Irira, the succession of Kabbalistic writers whom we have thus passed in review never descended to the use of a vulgar tongue. To that exception we must now add the case of R. Juda, son of Isaac Abravanel, better known under the designation of Leo the Hebrew. His inclusion in an account of developments which find their place in Kabbalism is to be justified only as an example of the distance which was travelled at times. Leo is, comparatively speaking, early, though I have placed him later, for it is only at a far distance that he offers any link with the ZOHAR, which obviously he had never seen. He was born in the kingdom of Castile shortly after the middle of the fifteenth century, and it is even stated that he broke away from all Jewish tradition by becoming a Christian. At the same time there are two additional points by which he is forced upon our notice : in the first place, he has been a favourite subject of allusion with some modern esoteric writers, and should not be overlooked therefore in a work which is compelled to recognise the recurring fact of occult interest in Kabbalism ; in the second place, his dialogues on love have been more popular than any Kabbalistic treatise—actual or imputed. According to the best opinion, they were written originally in Italian : in any case, they appeared in this language at Rome in the year 1535. They were reprinted at Venice in 1541. Then they were translated into Latin by Sarrazin, being published, according to Wolf, in 1564 at Vienna. This version, which has been praised for its elegance, was included by Pistorius in his famous ARTIS

---

[1] For another excursus of my own on ÆSH MEZAREPH the reader may consult THE SECRET TRADITION IN ALCHEMY, Appendix II, pp. 377-394.

CABALISTICÆ SCRIPTORES, Basle, 1587. They were rendered twice into Spanish, the first version, and the only one of my acquaintance, being that of Juan Costa, in 1584. Lastly, there have been at least three French translations, namely, by Pontus de Thiard, 1580; the Seigneur du Parc Champerrois; and Alexander Weill, 1875.

Though he wrote, as it is said, in Italian, Abravanel was Portuguese by birth, but was removed by his father to Spain and thence to Italy, through the edict of Ferdinand and Isabella. This was in 1492. His first refuge was Naples, where he entered the king's service; but the king died and his realm fell into the hands of Charles VIII., after which the "Spanish Jew" became once more a wanderer. Some say that he retired to Sicily, afterwards to Corfu and Ponilles, and, finally, to Venice, where he died in 1535. Others relate that he fixed his abode at Genoa, and there practised medicine with honour for a long period. As to the change, real or pretended, in his religious opinions there is also serious confusion. Basnage says that he was a man of a mild nature who mixed familiarly with Christians, but inveighed against them in his writings, especially against the priests and the Pope.[1] Pistorius, on the other hand, represents him as a converted Jew.[2] He is the subject of high praise, based on intimate knowledge, in the bibliography of Bartolocci.[3]

The interest in Leo the Hebrew can be only of a mystical kind, and it is on this basis presumably that he was included by Pistorius in his ambitious and unfinished attempt to engarner the signal treatises of Kabbalism. Even so, it is difficult to see that such a text has any title to a place among records of the Secret Tradition in Israel. We look in vain for the essential doctrines of Jewish Theosophy, as these are enshrined in the ZOHAR; we have in their place the elegant sentimentalism which characterised Italian literature at the period; we are reminded now of Boccalini, and now of the declamatory Latin exercises of Palingenius. The machinery of the dialogues, if they can be said to possess machinery, belongs to classical mythology; the allusions, the illustrations,

---

[1] HIST. DES JUIFS, l. vii. t. v. pp. 1898, 1899.
[2] So also does Drach in his notice of the Kabbalah in L'HARMONIE ENTRE L'ÉGLISE ET LA SYNAGOGUE.
[3] BIBLIOTHECA RABBINICA, iii. 86. There is no mention of his conversion in the notice, but the original edition of the Dialogues describes their author as *di natione Hebreo et di poi fatto Christiano*. There seems to be good evidence against the testimony.

the images are echoes of Greek and Latin poets ; when the philosophical authority is not Aristotle, it is Plato ; there is only one direct reference to the Kabbalah in the whole three hundred folio pages which the dialogues occupy in Pistorius, and it is then a slender allusion to successive renewals of the world, which suggests that the author had misconceived the " restoration " of the BOOK OF CONCEALMENT. As against this there is not one trace of characteristic Hebrew thought or influence ; there is nothing which would lead us to suspect a Jewish authorship, except such negative evidence as the absence of any Christian reference. If the work can be said to recall anything outside the *belles lettres* of the sixteenth century in Italy, it is certain Sufic poets adapted to the under-standing of Venetian ladies in the days of the Doges. And here, indeed, is the true secret of its popularity. It is not only so pleasing, so educated according to the lights of its period, so correct in its sentiment and breathing too often so little but mere sentiment, so refined in its amorous passion and so much above reproach, that it does not contain a single indelicacy or a single recondite thought, until it passes towards the heights of its subject, as the undertaking draws to a close. One of its French translators has thought it worth while to append a glossary of its difficult words, but it has no difficulties and its words are simplicity itself. It has many passages which even at the present day may be called delightful reading, and it is redeemed from the commonplaces of senti-ment by tender suggestions of shallow allegory. The Philo and Sophia of the dialogue are enough by their mere names to suggest transcendentalism to an occult student, and more than one criticism has supposed it to be concerned *ab initio* and only with the love of God. As a fact it discerns in all things the activity, the influence and the power of the master passion, and another of the secrets of its popularity in the warm-blooded world of the South is that however much love is transcendentalised in the dialogues, it is always sexual, as it is throughout the ZOHAR. So also the philosophy of this love is the doctrine of delectation and felicity. Delectation is union with the beloved, and the good and the beautiful are identified in words that recall the light metaphysics of Cousin and the blessed life of Fichte.

The general definition of love is that it is a vivifying spirit which permeates all the world, and a bond uniting the entire universe. But the proper definition of the perfect love of man and woman is the concurrence of the loving with the beloved to this end, that the beloved shall be transformed into the lover. When such love is equal between the partakers it is described as the conversion of the one into the other being. Below such human love in apotheosis, there is not only that which subsists among mere animals, but in things insensible, in the hypothetical first matter, in the elements and in the heavenly bodies, which are drawn one to the other and move in regular order by the harmonious impulse and interaction of a reciprocal affection.

Hereof is the form and the spirit, and—for the rest—though I have spoken plainly, this Book of Love and its Mysteries moves forward to deeper things, when the knowledge of God is presented, as regards language and images, under a transcendentalised sexual aspect. God is loved in proportion as He is known, and as He cannot be known entirely by men, nor His wisdom by the human race, so He cannot be loved as He deserves, for such an exalted sentiment transcends the power of our will. The mind therefore must be content to know God according to the measure of its possibility and not that of His excellence. The knowledge and love of God are both necessary to beatitude, for He is the True Intellectual Agent with Whom consists felicity, which is not to be found in the knowledge of all things, but in the One alone Who is Himself all others. This felicity does not consist in the cognoscitive act of God, which leads to love, nor in the love which succeeds such knowledge, but in the copulation of the most interior and united Divine Knowledge, for this is the sovereign perfection of the created intellect, the last act and happy end in which it finds itself rather divine than human. Such copulative felicity with God cannot be continuous, however, during our present life, because our intellect is here joined to the matter of our fragile body.

It may be added that Leo the Hebrew, like Raymund Lully, accounts for the self-sufficiency of the Divine Nature on the ground that the love, the lover and the beloved are all one in God; that God alone is the end of all love in the universe; and that His love towards His creatures is the stimulation of a desire of good for their sake and not for His own. It may be inferred also that a mystical meaning is not improbably contained in such speculations as that of the sleep of love, of amorous contemplation, of the graving of the image of the beloved in the thought of the lover, and of the ravishment of this state. In other terms and in another setting, it could be said that all this belongs to the root-matter of highest Mysticism. It is here and there like a door which opens on the Infinite ; but it is to be feared that if Abravanel had conceived something in the mind on these great subjects, he had not conceived in the soul.

IV.—MINOR LITERATURE OF KABBALISM

We have now completed our study of the chief Kabbalistic writings to which any currency has been given ; but we have by no means exhausted the literature either before or after the appearance of the ZOHAR. It has been classified in chronological order, but otherwise uncritically enough, in a special list by Bartolocci at the beginning of his vast work, and those who desire to pursue the subject further will there see how impossible it is to deal with in this place. It is, moreover, outside the purpose of our inquiry. A few names, however, may be mentioned which are to some extent typical of the minor literature of Kabbalism.

When the ZOHAR was on the verge of the historical horizon, in the reign of Alphonso X., we find at Toledo Rabbi Mevi, the son of Theodore, Prince of the Levites of Burgos. Though a Kabbalist and a light of Kabbalism, he opposed Nah-manides, thus shewing that at a comparatively early period there was little unanimity among the doctors of Theosophy and the voices of Tradition, on the subject of Tradition or Theosophy. His book is entitled BEFORE AND BEHIND, which is supposed to indicate that he had approached the Kabbalah from every point of view.[1]

Side by side with philosophical Kabbalism the spurious practical part, the ARS KABBALISTICA, never wanted its pro-fessors. As neither worse nor better than the rest we may mention R. Chamai of Arragon, in the early part of the fifteenth century. One of his practical secrets was the determination of the sex of an unborn child by placing the nuptial couch from North to South, thus indicating respect

[1] Bartolocci, BIBLIOTHECA MAGNA RABBINICA, iv, 18 ; Basnage, HISTOIRE DES JUIFS, v, 1773.

for the majesty of God, which resides between East and West, and might suffer dishonour by marital intercourse taking place in the same direction. Such consideration, it was deemed, would not go without its reward in the birth of male children.[1]

In the reign of Ferdinand and Isabella, and a victim of their edict of expulsion, flourished Joseph Gikatilla, called the divine Kabbalist and the Thaumaturge, who wrote on the attributes of God, the Divine Names and the SEPHIROTH.[2] He has been mentioned already.

At the period of Picus de Mirandula Kabbalists abounded in Italy, many of whom were refugees from persecution in Spain and Portugal. Picus in his APOLOGIA affirms that his demonstrations of Christian dogma in Jewish Theosophy effected the conversion of a Kabbalist named Dattilius. As it is one of few instances on record, the sincerity of the change may be allowed to pass unchallenged.[3] Long afterwards, that is to say, in 1613, Samuel Nahunias, a Jew of Thessalonica, but residing at Venice, also abjured Judaism and wrote the PATH OF FAITH. So also, about 1672, Mordekai Kerkos composed a treatise directed against the Kabbalah ; but it has not been printed. Basnage hints that such an action at that period seemed scarcely less subversive in Israel than to embrace Christianity. On the other hand, Judas Azael, about the same period, contributed to the literature of the Tradition by his THRONES OF THE HOUSE OF DAVID, a treatise dealing with the Fifty Gates of Understanding, while in Germany Nathan of Spire, better known, however, for a treatise in praise of the Holy Land, produced a Kabbalistic commentary on Deuteronomy iii. 13, under the title of MEGILLAH HAMNEOTH. In Holland, a few years previously, the famous Manasses composed his work on the resurrection of the body, which connects with Jewish esoteric theology

---

[1] Bartolocci, BIBLIOTHECA MAGNA RABBINICA, ii, 840 ; Basnage, HISTOIRE DES JUIFS, v, 1895.

[2] *Ibid.* v, 1899.

[3] In the sixteenth century Paul Elhananan became a convert to Christianity, and in his MYSTERIUM NOVUM sought to prove from the Kabbalah that Jesus of Nazareth was the true Messiah. Petrus Galatinus also abjured Judaism ; so did Johannes Fortius, who wrote on the mystical meanings of the Hebrew Letters. Paul de Heredia was a convert of the fifteenth century. Bartolocci (iv, 420) mentions Louis Carret, a Frenchman of the sixteenth century, who in his VISIONS OF GOD defended the truth of the Catholic faith by means of the Kabbalah. Later names are Aaron Margalita, whose many works attempted to Christianise the Kabbalah. There are also Rittangelius, the editor of the SEPHER YETZIRAH, who turned Protestant ; and Prosper Ruggieri, the astrologer.

by its defence of metempsychosis ; and Isaac About, a Brazilian settled in the Low Countries, translated the PORTA CŒLORUM of Abraham Cohen Irira from the original Spanish into Hebrew.

These meagre memoranda, which do not pretend to represent a serious study, may close with the name of Spinoza, who connects also with Kabbalism, though it must be confessed that the tincture which he exhibits is little more than the memory of early reading.

BOOK X

SOME CHRISTIAN STUDENTS OF
THE KABBALAH

BOOK X

SOME CHRISTIAN STUDENTS OF THE KABBALAH

I.—INTRODUCTORY

So far as our inquiry has proceeded no theosophical system would seem less connected with what is known conventionally as Magic than is the Kabbalah to all outward appearance. That there was, however, an imputed connection, there can be and is no doubt, for side by side with the Secret Tradition in Israel, as understood and set forth here, there was a so-called Practical and Thaumaturgical Kabbalah which not only belongs to Magic but has helped to create its forbidden arts in the West, as stated summarily in an early part of the present work. We owe our mediæval witchcraft chiefly to this source ; we owe also our mediæval demonology ; and the Jew, hounded out of Spain by the iniquitous edict of Ferdinand and Isabella, left to the Inquisition and its devildom another pretext for extermination, more fuel for the burning— in a word, the tremendous legacy of sorcery. The Jew was avenged in the magician.

When enumerating the alleged branches of Esoteric Tradition in Israel I endeavoured to distinguish that of Magic from Theosophy. While the traces of Theosophical Tradition are met with nowhere in remote antiquity, those of Magic abound : be it observed that the reference is to rumour and vestige, not to records at large, since these are mostly late. It was to be expected that the newer order of ideas should become interfused with the older. But the SEPHER YETZIRAH and the ZOHAR are not Magic, and that which drew the Christian students of the literature and made them seek to fathom the Kabbalistic Mystery was assuredly its Theosophical, transcendental indeed, but not its thaumaturgic part.

We are on the track here of another misconception which prevails among that class of thinkers who have discovered moſt reason to concern themselves with the claims of the Kabbalah. It is useless for the expositors of occult views and their too easy disciples to continue, as they have done in the paſt, appealing to Chriſtian authorities as to great names supporting their notion of the subjeſt. Those who accepted and those who vindicated the authenticity of the Secret Tradition had never dreamed of a religion behind all religions, nor did they look to Sanſtuaries of Egypt for any light but that which perchance was carried into it by the descendants of Abraham. Persons of the class referred to have fallen into two major among many minor errors. In the firſt place, they cite as Chriſtian Kabbaliſts various alleged authorities, within and without the myſtical circle, who have no claim to the title ; in the second place, they misconſtrue entirely the position of those whose title itself may be beyond any challenge. Over and above these points, many names, great and otherwise, which it looks well to engross on the deeds of a brief for the defence, bear witness only to prevailing ignorance.

The purpose of the brief ſtudies which follow is to demonſtrate these faſts, which are not without importance and are therefore an integral part of my scheme. They are not biographical sketches, and they are not bibliographical notes. They are designed to exhibit that among the names commonly cited in conneſtion with Kabbalism, some should be removed from the liſt ; some belong to a Quixotic attempt at discovering an *eirenicon* for Chriſtendom and Jewry ; some are not worth citing, because, despite their imputed authority, they have nothing of moment to tell us ; and some, a bare residuum, with a handful of recent writers, may be left on the otherwise vacated benches.

II.—RAYMUND LULLY

The name of Raymund Lully has been cited as that of a considerable authority on the Kabbalah, as upon several other departments of secret knowledge. It is time to affirm that few ascriptions seem to possess less foundation in faſt. It muſt be said, firſt of all, that there is indubitable evidence for diſtinguishing between two persons at leaſt who bore this name : otherwise it was assumed for a second time at a later date. The original Raymund Lully was that seneschal of Majorca whose legend is narrated in a monograph on the *doctor illuminators* which I wrote in recent years.[1] He was born during the first half of the thirteenth century.[2] The second Raymund Lully was an alchemist.[3] His legend, enshrined in the deceitful memorial of a so-called Abbot of Westminster,[4] was unknown, so far as I can trace, till the beginning of the seventeenth century,[5] but the works by which he is distinguished from his prototype are certainly much earlier, possibly by two centuries.[6] There is a third and modern legend, which bears all the marks of invention on the part of its narrator, Éliphas Lévi, and this identifies the two personages by prolonging the life of the first through the instrumentality of the Great Elixir.[7] It is described as a popular legend, but Raymund Lully and his namesake were never of enough importance to impress the imagination of the people. The first was known chiefly as a scholastic reformer and a Christian evangelist, martyred for an ill-judged attempt at the propagation of the faith among the Mussulmen of Africa. The second has been described as a " Jewish neophyte," the denomination on its surface suggesting a proselyte of the gate. This is therefore the personality which would connect naturally with Kabbalism. The second Raymund connects, however, exclusively with Alchemy, and his works are evidence that he did not renounce the Christian faith.[8] It is to him must be attributed those Keys,

---

[1] RAYMUND LULLY, *ILLUMINATED DOCTOR, ALCHEMIST AND CHRISTIAN MYSTIC,* 1922.

[2] The dates attributed to some of his works, if accurate, would shew that he was separated from his successor by more than a century, but they are in a sad state of confusion, and all popular sources of information are misleading. See, for example, Blackie's *Popular Encyclopædia, s.v.* Alchymy.

[3] See my SECRET TRADITION IN ALCHEMY, 1926, pp. 131, 132.

[4] TESTAMENTUM CREMERI, *Abbatis Westmonasteriensis, Angli, Ordinis Benedictini.*

[5] It was published at Frankfort in 1618, by Michael Maier, being the third tract of TRIPUS AUREUS, *hoc est tres tractatus chymici selectissimi.* In 1678 it reappeared in MUSEUM HERMETICUM *Reformatum et Amplificatum,* and is known in English by a translation of that collection, edited by myself, 2 vols. London. 1893.

[6] They contain a few personal memoranda, but of a mythical order.

[7] With material derived from Éliphas Lévi, and a pyrotechnic terminology from M. Huysman, a bizarre work entitled LE SATANISME ET LA MAGIE, by Jules Bois, compresses all the legends into one small pellet of fable which, published in 1895, was, I suppose, the last memorial on the subject of Raymund Lully till the Catalan poet of that name began to attract attention from the students of early Spanish literature.

[8] Witness the address to the Deity at the head of the TESTAMENTUM *Magistri Raymundi Lullii* (Mangetus : BIBLIOTHECA CHEMICA CURIOSA, i. 707, 708) ; the last words of its theoretical division—*Laus honor* et *gloria Jesu (ibid.* 762) ; the TESTAMENTUM NOVISSIMUM, addressed to King Charles : *Ideo mi Carole dilecte, te in filium sapientiæ dilectissimum ut*

Compendiums, Testaments and Codicils of Alchemy which are found in all the great collections of Hermetic treatises. He was so far imbued with the apostolic spirit of his predecessor that his great ambition was to engage some Catholic monarch in another barren crusade for the recovery of the Holy Sepulchre. According to his legend he transmuted into gold sufficient base metal for the minting of six million nobles, and gave it to an Edward, King of England, on condition that the latter assumed the Red Cross. The king did not keep his promise, and the adept escaped as he could from the extortion of further projections.[1]

The confusion of the two Raymunds is perhaps more excusable among occultists than for ordinary biographers. That Alchemy connects with Kabbalism, or that Kabbalism became identified with Alchemy, the treatise on Purifying Fire stands forth to bear its witness ; but the alchemist *per se* is not, as we have seen, a Kabbalist, and there is no single word of Kabbalism in the Hermetic treatises of Raymund Lully the second. The doctor of Majorca does connect artificially with the esoteric tradition of the Jews, by the arbitrary use of certain words and methods, though he was not a proselyte of the gate ; but his intellectual system is a mechanical introduction to the sciences, and has no title to the name, having nothing to do with a tradition, exoteric or esoteric, Jewish or Gentile. It has, moreover, no mystical foundation, and is concerned wholly with an educational method. It is untrue therefore to say that Raymund Lully was one of the grand and sublime masters of transcendent science, as Éliphas Lévi describes him. In the ARS MAGNA SCIENDI and the ARS NOTORIA there is as much occult significance as in the scholastic jest concerning *chimæra bombinans in vacuo*. The NOTARY ART of Solomon, which Robert Turner first printed in English, connects remotely with Kabbalism, and the ARS NOTORIA of Raymund Lully has a verbal connection, and no more, with this enchiridion of Jewry. It is the same with the treatise entitled DE AUDITU KABALISTICO, an *opusculum Raymundinum*, or particular application of the method of Lully, which has been ignorantly included among his works. The name alone

---

fidei catholicæ ampliatorem eligam ; and again : *Accipe igitur in nomine sanctæ Trinitatis et æternæ Unitatis,* &c. *(ibid.* p. 790).

[1] See my *op. cit.,* caps. iv, v and vi. It contains a full discussion of the two Raymunds.

is occult, and its selection is beyond conjecture.[1] The work proves on examination to be a late offshoot of the great vacant pretentious system which enabled those who mastered it to dispute on all subjects with success, though perhaps without knowledge of any. Some great minds were captivated by it, but such captivities are among the weaknesses of great minds. The best that can be said for the ARS MAGNA is that it was discoursed upon by Cornelius Agrippa, that it was tolerated by Picus de Mirandula, and that the encyclopædic mind of Athanasius Kircher had embraced it sufficiently to produce a *summa magna* on the subject in one of his vast folios. And of these facts, at the present day, not one possesses a consequence. The chief philosophical mission of the first Raymund Lully was to protest against the school of Averroes ;[2] his chief practical work was the exhortation of prelates and princes to found schools for the study of languages so as to facilitate the conversion of the heathen ; but there were few who heard or heeded him. It was only after his death that his system obtained for a time a certain vogue. The collapse of the process of his beatification is one of the escapes of the Latin Church, because it would have helped to accredit a system which began and ended in words. It was not, as it has been described erroneously, an universal

---

[1] It is fair to say that Franck takes the opposite view, but with what qualification for judgment may be gathered from the fact that he accepts the attribution to Lully of the work mentioned above. He says that Lully was the first to reveal the name and existence of the Kabbalah to Christian Europe, for which there is no ground in fact ; he thinks that it would be difficult to determine how far Lully was " an initiate of this mystical science " or the precise influence which it exercised on his doctrine. " I refrain from saying with a historian of philosophy (Tennemann) that he borrowed thence his belief in the identity of God and Nature " (I think that Tennemann has here misconstrued his author), " but it is certain that he had a very high idea of it, considering it a divine science, a veritable revelation addressed to the rational soul, and it may perhaps be permissible to suppose that the artificial processes used by Kabbalists to connect their opinions with the words of Scripture, such as the substitution of numbers or letters for ideas or words, may have contributed in no small degree to the invention of the Great Art. It is worthy of remark that more than two centuries and a half before the existence of the rival schools of Loria and Cordova, at the very time when some modern critics have sought to place the origin of the Kabbalah, Raymund Lully makes already a distinction between ancient and modern Kabbalists." The passage on which Franck seems to depend for his general view is as follows : *Dicitur hæc doctrina Kabbala quod, idem est secundum . . . Hebræos ut receptio veritatis cujuslibet rei diviñitus revelatæ animæ rationali . . . . Est igitur Kabbala habitus animæ rationalis ex recta ratione divinarum rerum cognitivus. Propter quod apparet quod est de maximo etiam divino consequutivè divina scientia vocari debet.* This extract is derived from the *Opus Raymundinum* already mentioned.

[2] I am speaking throughout here of him who was Lully of the schools, whether or not he was also that Catalan poet, whose title to greatness has emerged of recent years, under the auspices of scholars who are content so far to know nothing of ARS MAGNA.

science, or a synthesis of knowledge ; it was chaffer and noise ; its egregious tabulations are a mockery for the modern under-standing. Even the martyrdom of this eccentric Spanish enthusiast had a strain of the folly of suicide, if the martyro-logists have told it truly. It had, however, its defenders, and it had in time its miraculous legend. So also, and for the space of some centuries, there was a quiet and intelligible cultus of Raymund Lully in the Balearic Islands, which, like other local sanctities, seems even at the present day to be some-thing more than a memory.

I should add, in conclusion, that there are works by or attributed to the original Raymund Lully[1] which have no connection with his ARS MAGNA SCIENDI, as they have none with imputed occult science : they belong to a higher cate-gory. When we turn over the vast, uncompleted collection of his OPERA OMNIA, and dwell, as the devout student will do, on certain passages concerning the eternal subsistence of the lover and the beloved in God, concerning contemplation in God—*quomodo omnis nostra perfectio sit in perfectione nostri Domini Dei*—and the deep things of Divine Union, we begin to discern the existence, so to speak, of a third Lully, who has qualities which recommend him to our admiration that are wanting in the *Doctor illuminatus*, though he invented *Ars Magna*, and in the *Doctor alchemisticus*, even if he transmuted metals.[2]

III.—PICUS DE MIRANDULA

Magical legend has availed itself of the name of Mirandula, and on the warrant of his Kabbalistic enthusiasm has accredited him with the possession of a familiar demon.[3] His was the demon of Socrates which a late Cardinal Archbishop brought within the limits of natural and clerical orthodoxy.[4] His marvellous precocity furnished a thesis to the ingenuity of the late Gabriel Delanne, for, as with the music of Mozart and as with the mathematics of Pascal, it remains a ground of speculation how this Italian Crichton acquired his enormous

---

[1] The reference is here to the Catalan poet and the author of BLANQUERNA.
[2] See my *op. cit.*, c. vi. Some texts cited therein have been translated since into English from their Catalan originals by Professor Peers, but apart from all reference to Lully of the ARS MAGNA and the Hermetic Lully.
[3] Migne's DICTIONNAIRE DES SCIENCES OCCULTES, t. ii. col. 308.
[4] See Manning's brochure, *s.v.* THE DAIMON OF SOCRATES. London, 1874.

erudition. Delanne would assure us [1] that he brought it with him at his birth, that it was an inheritance from a previous life and that Picus de Mirandula Kabbalised in a college of Babylon. On the other hand, Catholic writers, for whom his studies are unsavoury, affirm that he was swindled by an impostor who sold him sixty bogus MSS. on the assurance that they had been composed by the order of Esdras. " They contained only ridiculous Kabbalistic reveries." These MSS. have been enumerated and described by Gaffarel, and his monograph on the subject will be found, among other places, in the bibliography of Wolf.[2] As Mirandula, who was born on February 24th, 1463, and died mentally exhausted in 1494, is the first true Christian student of the Kabbalah, it is important to know what he derived from his studies in this respect. Now, unfortunately, we are met at the outset with a difficulty only too common in such inquiries. Of the Kabbalistic Conclusions arrived at by Picus de Mirandula, and actually bearing this name, there are two versions extant ; there is that which we find in the collected editions of his works, both late and early, reproduced in the garner of Pistorius with a voluminous commentary by Archangelus de Burgo Nuovo, and there is that which we find with another commentary, though curiously by the same writer, in a little volume, published at Bologna in 1564—prior to the collection of Pistorius which belongs to 1587—and again at Basle in 1600.[3] The evidence is in favour of the first version, but nothing attaches to the question : it is that in any case which came to be known and used, the Bologna codex being so utterly obscure that I have not seen it mentioned. We may accept either without prejudice to the point which it is here designed to establish, and that is the nature of the enthusiasm which prompted Picus de Mirandula. In the first place, though he speaks of Magic in terms which may be held to indicate that he possessed a tolerant and open mind as to some of its claims and, like a learned man as he was, did not regard

---

[1] See in particular ÉTUDE SUR LES VIES SUCCESSIVES, *Mémoire présenté au Congrès Spirite International de Londres* (1898), *par Gabriel Delanne*, p. 61, where Mirandula is a case in point.

[2] Joh. Christophori Wolfii : BIBLIOTHECA HEBRÆA . . . *Accedit in calce Jacobi Gaffarelli* INDEX CODICUM CABBALISTIC. MSS. *quibus* Jo. Picus, Mirandulanus Comes, *usus est.* 1715. The Index in question is reprinted from the Paris edition of 1651.

[3] *Archangelus de Burgo Nuovo agri Placentini :* APOLOGIA PRO DEFENSIONE DOCTRINÆ CABALÆ, &c. Ostensibly a reply to an impeachment of Mirandula by Peter Garzia.

it from the standpoint of Grimoire Sorcery, he is not to be considered as a disciple of any alleged Higher Magic. The only department of the putative Secret Arts which he has treated at any length is Astrology, and to this he devoted a long and undermining criticism, which in some of its salient parts is as good reading as Agrippa's VANITY OF THE SCIENCES, and on its special subject takes much the same point of view. We should not expect therefore that he betook himself to the esoteric speculations of Jewry because he was attracted by supposed supernormal powers ascribed to Divine Names, because he intended to compose talismans, or because he desired to evoke. I must not speak so confidently as to possible fascinations in the direction of GEMATRIA and THEMURAH, for his was a subtle and curious intelligence which found green spots or rather enchanted cities of mirage in many deserts of the mind, and he might have discovered mysteries in beheaded words and achroamatica in acrostics. There is, however, no proof that he did. The bibliographical legend which represents him purchasing MSS. on the assurance that the prophet Esdras had a hand in their production will disclose his probable views as to the antiquity of Kabbalistic literature. He took it, we may suppose, at its word, and the legend indicates also that he was persuaded easily : it was a common weakness in men of learning and enthusiasm at the period. On the other hand, it is more than certain that he did not regard this antiquity as a presumption that the Kabbalah was superior to Latin Christianity ; the wisdom which he found therein was that of Christian doctrine : [1] when he hung up his famous theses in Rome and offered to defray the expenses of every scholar who would dispute with him, those theses included his KABBALISTIC CONCLUSIONS, but that which he sought to establish was a *via media* between Jewry and Christendom. When he turned the head of Pope Julius with Secret Mysteries of the THORAH, the enthusiasm which was communicated for a moment to the Chair of Peter was, like Lully's, that of the evangelist. The *servus servorum Dei* found other zeal for his ministry, and the comet of the schools blazed itself out. The KABBALISTIC CONCLUSIONS alone remain to tell that Rome had a strange dream in the evening

---

[1] The existence of Christian elements, or at least of materials which might be held to bear a Christian construction, is admitted by several Jewish writers of the post-Zoharic period.

of the fifteenth century.[1] They lie in a small compass and, as I believe that it will be of interest to shew what Picus de Mirandula extracted from his sixty MSS., I will translate them here for the reader. It ought perhaps to be premised that Éliphas Lévi rendered some of them in his own loose fashion and published them with a suggestive commentary, in LA SCIENCE DES ESPRITS,[2] ascribing them to the collection of Pistorius but without mentioning the name of Mirandula. He gave also what purports to be the Latin originals, but these he has polished and pointed. To do justice to his skill, they are occasionally much better than the quintessential Kabbalism of Picus, but as they are neither Picus nor the Kabbalah, I shall not have recourse to them for the purposes of the following version, except by some references in footnotes.

Kabbalistic Conclusions

I.

As man and the priest of inferior things sacrifices to God the souls of unreasoning animals, so Michael, the higher priest, sacrifices the souls of rational animals.

II.

There are nine hierarchies, and their names are CHERUBIM, SERAPHIM, CHASMALIM, ARALIM, TARSISIM, OPHANIM, ISHIM, MALACHIM, and ELOHIM.

III.

Although the Ineffable Name is the quality of clemency, it is not to be denied that it combines also the quality of judgment.[3]

IV.

The sin of Adam was the separation of the kingdom from the other branches.

V.

God created the world with the Tree of the Knowledge of Good and Evil, whereby the first man sinned.[4]

---

[1] They appeared originally at Rome in 1486, the volume being entitled : CONCLUSIONES PHILOSOPHICÆ, CABALISTICÆ ET THEOLOGICÆ. Picus wrote also CABALISTARUM SELECTIONES, which seems to have been printed for the first time at Venice in 1569.

[2] Part II, c. iv. pp. 147 *et seq.*

[3] As Lévi puts it tersely : *Schema misericordiam dicit sed et judicium.* He utilises it to denounce the doctrine of everlasting punishment.

[4] Hence Lévi infers that the sin of Adam was educational.

VI.

The great North Wind is the fountain of all souls simply, as other days are of some and not all.[1]

VII.

When Solomon said in his prayer, as recorded in the Book of Kings : " Hear, O Heaven," we must understand by heaven the green line which encircles all things.[2]

VIII.

Souls descend from the third light to the fourth day, and thence issuing, they enter the night of the body.[3]

IX.

By the six days of Genesis we must understand the six extremities of the building proceeding from Brashith as the cedars come forth out of Lebanon.

X.

Paradise is more correctly said to be the whole building than the tenth part. And in the centre thereof is placed the Great Adam, who is TIPHERETH.

XI.

A river is said to flow out from Eden and to be parted into four heads signifying that the third numeration proceeds from the second, and is divided into the fourth, fifth, sixth, and tenth.[4]

XII.

It is true that all things depend on fate, if we understand thereby the Supreme Arbiter.[5]

---

[1] I have given this literally without pretending that it has much meaning. Lévi reduces it to *Magnus aquilo fons est animarum*, explaining that souls enter this world to escape idleness. Archangelus de Burgonuovo, in his *Cabalistarum Selectiora, Obscurioraque* DOGMATA affirms that *Aquilo* signifies GEBURAH, the fifth SEPHIRA. SEE Pistorius : ARTIS CABALISTICÆ SCRIPTORES, 1587, p. 753.

[2] Lévi renders this *Cælum est Kether*, which does not, at first sight, seem to represent it. See, however, CONCLUSION 48, and note thereto.

[3] This is mangled by Lévi, who seems to have misunderstood its meaning. For the night of the body he substitutes the night of death.

[4] CONCLUSIONS 9, 10, 11 signify, according to Lévi, that the history of the earthly paradise is an allegory of truth on earth.

[5] Lévi gives, *Factum fatum quia fatum verbum est*, an admirable specimen of polishing.

XIII.

He who shall know the Mystery of the Gates of Understanding in the Kabbalah shall know also the Mystery of the
Great Jubilee.[1]

XIV.

He who shall know the meridional property in dextral
co-ordination shall know why every journey of Abraham was
always to the south.[2]

XV.

Unless the letter HE had been added to the name of Abram,
Abraham would not have begotten.[3]

XVI.

Before Moses all prophesied by the stag with one horn
(*i.e.*, the unicorn).[4]

XVII.

Wheresoever the love of male and female is mentioned in
Scripture, there is exhibited mystically the conjunction of
TIPHERETH and CHIENSET (or CHENECETH) ISRAEL, or BETH
and TIPHERETH.[5]

XVIII.

Whosoever shall have intercourse with TIPHERETH in the
middle night shall flourish in every generation.[6]

XIX.

The letters of the name of the evil demon who is the prince
of this world are the same as those of the name of God—
TETRAGRAMMATON—and he who knows how to effect their
transposition can extract one from the other.[7]

---

[1] The significance evaporates in Lévi's shortened recension, *Portæ jubilæum sunt*.
He explains the Jubilee as the joy of true knowledge.

[2] Lévi's explanation is feeble, namely, that the South is the rainy quarter, and that
" the doctrines of Abraham, *i.e.*, of the Kabbalah, are always fruitful."

[3] *Per additionem* HE *Abraham genuit*, this being " the feminine letter of the Tetragram."

[4] *I.e.*, says Lévi, they saw only one side of truth : Moses is represented bearing two
horns.   Lévi adds that the unicorn is the ideal.

[5] Lévi substitutes *Mas et fæmina sunt* TIPHERETH ET MALKUTH, and gives a sentimental explanation which has no connection with Kabbalism.   It is to be observed,
for the rest, that the fruitful union on the Tree of Life in Kabbalism is between
CHOKMAH and BINAH.

[6] Lévi interprets by distinguishing the marriage of mere animals, human or otherwise,
from the true human and divine marriage of souls, spirits and bodies.

[7] Lévi substitutes *Dæmon est Deus inversus* and argues with characteristic logic that
could the former be said to exist, then God as his opposite could certainly have no
existence.

XX.

When the light of the mirror which shines not shall be like the light of the shining mirror, the day shall become as the night, as David says.[1]

XXI.

Whosoever shall know the quality which is the secret of darkness shall know why the evil demons are more hurtful in the night than in the day.

XXII.

Granting that the co-ordination of the chariots is manifold, nevertheless, in so far as concerns the mystery of the PHYLACTERIES, two chariots are prepared, so that one chariot is formed from the second, third, fourth, and fifth, and these are the four Phylacteries which VAU assumes ; and from the sixth, seventh, eighth and ninth, a second chariot is made, and these are the Phylacteries which HE final assumes.[2]

XXIII.

More than the quality of penitence is not to be understood (or applied) in the word (which signifies) " He said." [3]

XXIV.

When Job said : " Who maketh peace in his highest places," he signifies the austral water and boreal fire, and their leader, concerning which things there must be nothing said further.[4]

---

[1] This apparently puzzled the commentator, so he invented a substitute which partly reproduces an apocryphal saying of Christ.

[2] That is to say, CHOKMAH, BINAH, CHESED and GEBURAH form the chariot, seat, or throne of the third letter of the Tetragram ; while TIPHERETH, NETZACH, HOD and JESOD constitute the chariot of the fourth letter. This is the explanation of Archangelus ; but it is not Sephirotic doctrine according to the ZOHAR, nor is it reflected from Picus into later Kabbalism. Moreover, VAU is TIPHERETH, and TIPHERETH cannot be used to build a chariot for HE final, which is MALKUTH. The idea is that the Phylacteries were like chariot wheels on which the soul ascends in prayer ; but it is rather nonsense symbolism.

[3] This is the best rendering which I can offer of the obscure original—*Supra proprietatem pænitentiæ non est utendum verbo dixit.* It is quite certain that its intention is not represented by Lévi's substituted aphorism *Pænitentia non est verbum*, which he translates, " To repent is not to act." According to Archangelus de Burgonuovo, the meaning is that he who seeks the forgiveness of sins must not have recourse to the Son, nor to the Holy Spirit. The proof offered is that the word rendered *dixit* belongs to the Son, and that which stands for *dicens* to the Holy Ghost. This refers to certain sayings of Christ. Forgiveness is to be sought from the Father. The Kabbalah is not, however, a commentary on the New Testament.

[4] Lévi substitutes : *excelsi sunt aqua australis et ignis septentrionalis et præfecti eorum. Sile.*

XXV.

BERESHITH—*i.e.*, in the beginning He created, is the same as if it were said : " In Wisdom He created." [1]

XXVI.

When Onkelos the Chaldean said : BECADMIN—*i.e.*, with or by the Eternals, he understood the Thirty-two Paths of Wisdom. [2]

XXVII.

As the first man is the congregation of the waters, so the sea, to which all rivers run, is the Divinity. [3]

XXVIII.

By the flying thing which was created on the fifth day we must understand angels of this world, which appear to men, and not those which do not appear, save in the spirit. [4]

XXIX.

The name of God, composed of four letters, MEM, TSADE, PE, and final TSADE, must be referred to the Kingdom of David. [5]

XXX.

No angel with six wings is ever transformed. [6]

XXXI.

Circumcision was ordained for deliverance from the impure powers wandering round about.

XXXII.

Hence circumcision was performed on the eighth day, because it is above the universal bride.

---

[1] Pointed by Lévi, this appears as *In principio, id est in* CHOKMAH.
[2] This is given boldly by Lévi as *Viæ æternitatis sunt triginta duo.*
[3] Lévi sums the idea by writing *Justi aquæ, Deus mare*, and shews in his annotation how God becomes man and man God after his familiar Voltairean fashion.
[4] Lévi gives, *Angeli apparentium sunt volatiles cæli et animantia*, which exceeds the Kabbalistic idea. I do not think it was intended to say that birds are angels of the outer form, but that the flying things created on the fifth day are symbols of the angels who have appeared to men, wearing the likeness of humanity, as to Abraham and to Lot, not those seen in the interior state and in vision.
[5] Lévi reads Daniel.
[6] Meaning, says Lévi, that there is no change for the mind which is equilibrated perfectly ; but this is mere ingenuity.

XXXIII.

There are no letters in the entire Law which do not shew forth the secrets of the ten numerations in their forms, conjunctions and separations, in their curves and direction, their deficiency and superfluity, in their comparative smallness and largeness, in their crowning, and their enclosed or open form.[1]

XXXIV.

He who comprehends why Moses hid his face and why Ezekias turned his countenance to the wall, the same understands the fitting attitude and posture of prayer.[2]

XXXV.

No spiritual things descending below can operate without a garment.[3]

XXXVI.

The sin of Sodom was the separation of the final branch.

XXXVII.

By the secret of the prayer before the daylight we must understand the quality of piety.

XXXVIII.

As fear is outwardly inferior to love, so love is inwardly inferior to fear.

XXXIX.

From the preceding conclusion it may be understood why Abraham was praised in Genesis for his fear, albeit we know by the quality of piety that all things were made from love.

XL.

Whensoever we are ignorant of the quality whence the influx comes down upon the petition which we put up, we must have recourse to the House of Judgment.[4]

---

[1] *Literæ sunt hieroglyphicæ in omnibus*, according to the shorter recension of Lévi.

[2] *Absconde faciem tuam et ora*, writes Lévi, connecting the praying shawl in his comment with the veil of Isis !

[3] *L'esprit se révêtent pour descendre et se dépouille pour monter*, says Lévi elsewhere in his writings. Here in his annotation he reasons that, as we cannot live under water, so spirits without bodies are unable to exist in our atmosphere.

[4] Literally, *Domum Naris ;* and hence Lévi's abridgment is *Nasus discernit proprietates*, which he defends from the BOOK OF CONCEALMENT.

XLI.

Every good soul is a new soul coming from the East.[1]

XLII.

Therefore Joseph was buried in the bones only and not in the body, because his bones were virtues and the hosts of the Supernal Tree, called ZADITH, descending on the Supernal Earth.

XLIII.

Therefore also Moses knew no sepulchre, being taken up into the Supernal Jubilee and setting his roots above the Jubilee.

XLIV.

When the soul shall comprehend all that is within its comprehension, and shall be joined with the Supernal Soul, it shall put off from itself its earthly garment and shall be rooted out from its place and united with Divinity.[2]

XLV.

When prophecy by the spirit ceased, the wise men of Israel prophesied by the Daughter of the Voice.

XLVI.

A king of the earth is not manifested on the earth until the heavenly host is humbled in heaven.[3]

XLVII.

By the word אֵת = ATH, which occurs twice in the text : " In the beginning God created the heaven and the earth," I believe that Moses signified the creation of the intellectual and animal natures, which in the natural order preceded that of the heaven and the earth.

---

[1] The distinction between new souls and old is developed at some length by Isaac de Loria. Éliphas Lévi overlooks this point and has recourse to a sentimental explanation. He takes occasion also to deny that reincarnation was taught by the best Kabbalists ; but he is not quite correct as to his facts.

[2] Lévi gives *Anima plena superiori conjungitur,* and understands this to mean that a complete soul is united with a superior soul, whereas the reference is undoubtedly to the Divine Soul.

[3] The version of Lévi is an entirely different aphorism, namely, *Post deos rex verus regnabit super terram.*

XLVIII.

That which is said by Kabbalists, namely, that a green line encircles the universe, may be cited appropriately as the final conclusion which we draw from Porphyry.[1]

XLIX.

Amen is the influence of numbers.[2]

We have seen that a rival series of Kabbalistic Conclusions has been referred to Picus, and so also the number of the above series is occasionally extended to seventy. The collection of Pistorius contains only those which have been cited, and they are possibly intended to connect with the Fifty Gates of Understanding, less the one gate which was not entered by Moses. To develop any system from these aphorisms would appear almost impossible, and this difficulty has occurred to earlier critics, despite the labours of their commentator, Archangelus de Burgo-Nuovo, who was himself a Christian Kabbalist, but disputatious, verbose, and with predetermined theological motives.

IV.—CORNELIUS AGRIPPA

The untimely death of Picus de Mirandula took place in the early childhood of another Christian Kabbalist, Cornelius Agrippa of Nettersheim, born at Cologne in 1486. It is to him that we owe the first methodical description of the whole Kabbalistic system, considered under the three heads of Natural Philosophy, Mathematical Philosophy and Theology. Agrippa is therefore of importance to our inquiry, and his three books, entitled DE OCCULTA PHILOSOPHIA, are practically the starting-point of Kabbalistic knowledge among Latin-reading scholars of Europe. It is needless to say that his treatise enjoyed immense repute and authority. We must remember, however, that it is professedly a magical work,

---

[1] According to Lévi, the Kabbalists represent KETHER as a green line encompassing all the other SEPHIROTH. I do not know his authority, but Azriel, in his commentary on the SEPHER YETZIRAH, says, as we have seen, that KETHER is the colour of light seen through a mist. I assume that this is not green, though Zoharic observations on the rainbow seem to indicate that some Kabbalists at least were colour-blind. It should be noted that Norrelius in his PHOSPHORUS ORTHODOXÆ FIDEL, 4, Amsterdam, 1720, translating from an elegy on R. Simeon ben Yohai, given in the SEPHER IMRE BINAH, explains that the *linea viridis* is the new moon.

[2] An affirmation of the mind, an adhesion of the heart, a kind of mental signature, says Lévi.

by which I do not mean that it is a Ritual for the Evocation of Spirits, but that it unfolds the philosophical principles upon which all forms of Magic were supposed to proceed, and this is so true that the forged FOURTH BOOK, which was added to it soon after the death of Agrippa, and does provide a species of Magical Ritual, is so much in consonance with the genuine work that it might have been almost by the same hand. We must expect therefore that the magical side of Kabbalism, that which deals with the properties and virtues of Divine Names and so forth, is developed much more fully than the cosmology of SEPHER YETZIRAH or the Divine Mysteries of the ZOHAR. We have to remember also that, albeit Agrippa was the first writer who elucidated the Kabbalistic system, he was better acquainted with the philosophy of Greece and Rome than with that of the later Hebrews. He was in a position, however, to understand and expound the Mysteries of Divine Names and the NOTARICON connected therewith. Of the literature itself he gives no information from which we could infer his textual knowledge ; he does not mention the SEPHER YETZIRAH or the ZOHAR, both of which were then only accessible in manuscript, and I am inclined to think that his acquaintance with Kabbalistic subjects was formed chiefly through the CONCLUSIONES CABALISTICÆ of Mirandula, which, as we have seen, appeared at Rome in the year of Agrippa's birth. It should be added also that there are serious errors in his division of the Hebrew alphabet which would not have been made by one who was acquainted with any authoritative source of knowledge, as, for example, the BOOK OF FORMATION, not to speak of mistakes without number in the lettering of Divine Names, when the time came for his work to be printed.

It is noticeable in this connection that the doctrines of occult virtues residing in words and names is expounded on the authority of the Platonists.[1] It is only in the scales of the twelve numbers, dealt with somewhat minutely in the second book, that a Kabbalistic system is developed, but this has remained a chief source of information among writers on occult subjects up to this day.[2] The most important gleanings

---

[1] It should be noted, however, that he preceded the chief Hellenising schools of later Kabbalism.

[2] On the general question of Agrippa's connection with Kabbalism, see Frederich Barth : DIE CABBALA *des Heinrich Cornelius Agrippa von Nettersheim*, Stuttgart, 1855.

are, however, in the third book, devoted to Theology and the doctrines, mainly Kabbalistic, concerning angels, demons and the souls of men, but creating correspondences with classical mythology wherever possible. Thus, AIN SOPH is identified with the Night of Orpheus and the Kabbalistic Samael with Typhon. The ten SEPHIROTH are described as vestments, instruments or exemplars of the Archetype, having an influence on all created things from high to low, following a defined order.

It would serve no purpose here to attempt a summary account of the instruction, while tables of commutations shewing the extraction of angelical names would require elaborate diagrams. My object is to note rather than illustrate exhaustively the character of Agrippa's exposition, which is concerned largely with the so-called Practical Kabbalah, and very slightly with the theosophical literature. It brought him no satisfaction, and before his troubled life drew to its disastrous close he recorded his opinion that the Kabbalistic art, which he had " diligently and laboriously sought after," was merely a " rhapsody of superstition," that its mysteries were " wrested from the Holy Scriptures," a play with allegory proving nothing. As to the alleged miracles wrought by its practical operations, he supposes that there is no one so foolish as to believe in any such powers. In a word, " the Kabbalah of the Jews is nothing but a pernicious superstition by which at their pleasure they gather, divide and transpose words, names and letters in Scripture ; and by making one thing out of another dissolve the connections of the truth." What was done by the Jews for the literature of the Ancient Covenant was performed, he goes on to say, for the Greek documents of Christianity by the Ophites, Gnostics and Valentinians, who produced a Greek Kabbalah, as Rabanus, the monk, later on attempted with the Latin characters.

I do not know that a modern writer could have put the position more clearly, but its chief value to ourselves lies in its clear exhibition of the author's limits in respect of Kabbalistic knowledge. He was acquainted with its artificial side and with that only. Agrippa adds another argument which also, from its own standpoint, could not be expressed better : " If Kabbalistic Art proceed from God, as the Jews boast, and if it produce to the perfection of life, the health of men and the worship of God, as also to the truth of under-standing, surely that Spirit of Truth which has left their synagogue, and has come to teach us all truth, would not have concealed it from His Church even until these last times, and this the more, seeing that the Church knows all things which are of God, while His Mysteries of Salvation are revealed in every tongue, for every tongue has the same power, if there be the same equal piety ; neither is there any name, in heaven or on earth, by which we can be saved, whereby we can work miracles, but the one Name Jesus, wherein all things are recapitulated and contained."

Of course, in the last analysis this argument proves too much. There is either a peculiar virtue in Divine Names or there is not. If there be, the Christian cannot well deny it to Jehovah ; and if there be not, any thaumaturgic doc-trine of the Great Name in Christianity is a subtlety no less idle than the TETRAGRAMMATON or the SCHEMAHAMPHORASH. We know, however, that, in so far as names represent ideas, they are moving powers of the intellectual world ; when they are used without inspiration and without knowledge they are dead and inert, like other empty vehicles. The Kabbalistic Jews believed that they could dissect the name without losing the vital essence which informs it, and they erred therein. The name of Jesus spells grace and salvation to millions, but it spells nothing when lettered separately and nothing when it is transposed. To say otherwise is to rave.

V.—PARACELSUS

Among the great names of occultism which are cited in support of the influence exerted by the Kabbalah and the authority which it possessed, that of Paracelsus is mentioned. We are given to understand, for example, by Isaac Myer, that it is to be traced distinctly in the system of the great German adept.[1] Statements like these are themselves a kind of Kabbalah, which are received by one writer from another without any inquiry or any attempt at verification. In this way we obtain lists of authorities, references and testimonials which seem at first sight to carry great weight, but they will bear no examination and defeat their own purpose when they

---

[1] PHILOSOPHY OF IBN GEBIROL, p. 171.

come into the hands of a student who has sufficient patience to investigate them. In the present instance we have to remember that Paracelsus occupies an exceptional position among occult philosophers ; he was not a man who respected or quoted authorities ; he owed very little to tradition, very little to what is understood commonly by learning.[1] If we take his alchemical treatises and compare them with Hermetic literature, we shall find that they are quite unlike it, and that he was, in fact, his own alchemist. When he concerns himself with Magic, he has few correspondences which will enable him to be illustrated by other writers on this subject : again, he was his own magician. And as regards the question of the Kabbalah, if we discover, on examination, that he has something to say concerning it, we should expect that it would be quite unlike anything that went before him, and quite foreign to the known lines of Kabbalism. Once more, we should find that he would prove to be his own Kabbalist. In every department of thought he illustrated his characteristic maxim : *Alterius non sit qui suus esse potest*. It must be added also that any contributions which he offers are seldom helpful. They do nothing to elucidate what is obscure in previous authorities, and they constitute new departures which are themselves in need of explanation.

Nearly two centuries elapsed between the death of Moses de Leon, the first alleged publisher of the ZOHAR, and the birth of Theophrastus of Hohenheim, and though no attempt to print it took place till some forty years after his turbulent life closed sadly at Strasburg, or wherever it occurred actually, there can be no doubt that it was accessible in manuscript, or that Paracelsus, had he known Aramaic, could have made himself acquainted with its contents. It seems certain, however, that he never acquired the language from which it had not been translated, and that his knowledge of the Kabbalah would be limited to what he could gather from authors who wrote in Latin or some current tongue ; but his own works shew that he was at very little pains of this kind. As to this, it is only necessary to collect the few references on the subject which they contain.

The study of Magic and the Kabbalah is enjoined several times on the physician, and old medical authorities are scouted

---

[1] He is said, indeed, to have boasted that his library would not amount to six folio volumes.—Gould's HISTORY OF FREEMASONRY, vol. ii. p. 77.

on the ground that they were unacquainted with either.[1]
The " Cabala " is in one place identified with Magical
Astronomy,[2] which, I presume, refers to the Paracelsic theory
concerning stars in man and the stars of disease, and connects
with the contextual statement that all operations of the stars
in all animals centre at the heart.   It is identified also with
Magic itself, of which it forms a part.[3]   But from indications
given in another place, Kabbalistic Magic seems to have
signified some obscure operations with the faculties of the
astral body.[4]   Subsequently this point is exposed more
plainly, when the Kabbalistic Art is said to have been built
up on the basis of doctrines concerning the sacramental
body, which appears after the death of the corruptible, and
accounts for the phenomena of spectres, visions, apparitions
of a supernatural character, &c.[5]   The art of judging what is
concealed by certain outward signs—in a word, the theory of
signatures—is said to be the Kabbalistic Art, " once called
' caballa,' afterwards ' caballia.' "   It has also been termed
falsely Galamala, from its alleged author—of whom one has
heard nothing otherwise—and is of Ethnic origin, having
been transmitted to the Chaldæans and the Jews, by whom
it was corrupted, " for the Jews were exceedingly ignorant
in all ages."[6]   Finally, the use of certain prayers and *signacula*
—*i.e.*, talismans in the cure of diseases is connected with the
Kabbalah.[7]

These meagre instances exhaust the three folio volumes
which constitute the Geneva collection of the works of
Paracelsus, and shew little relation even to the debased and
thaumaturgic side of the Secret Tradition in Israel.   I should
add, however, that there is a short section entitled CABALLA,
which forms part of a treatise on the plague, but it is concerned with the official elements of early science and with the
alchemical principles, Salt, Sulphur and Mercury.   There is
a reference also in one place to some " books of the Caballa,"
apparently the work of Paracelsus and in this case presumably
no longer extant.   By the student of Paracelsus that loss may

[1] DE CAUSIS ET ORIGINE LUIS GALLICÆ, Lib. iv. c. 9, OPERA OMNIA, Geneva,
1658, vol. iii. p. 193, *b*.   Also *De Peste*, Lib. ii., *præfatio, ibid.*, vol. i. p. 408.
[2] DE PESTILITATE, Tract. i., *ib., ib.*, p. 371, *b*.
[3] DE PESTE, Lib. i., *ib., ib.*, p. 405, *b*.
[4] DE VITA LONGA, Lib. i. c. 6, *ib.*, vol. ii. p. 56, *b*.
[5] DE NATURA RERUM, Lib. viii., *ib. ib.*, p. 101, *b*.
[6] PHILOSOPHIA SAGAX, Lib. i., *ib.*, vol. ii. p. 565, *b*.
[7] DE VULNERIBUS, Lib. v. in CHIRURGIA MAGNA, Pars. iii., *ib.*, vol. iii., p. 91 *b*.

be regretted, but it is not of moment so far as the Kabbalah proper is concerned, for it is evident that this term, like many others, was made use of in a sense which either differs widely from its wonted meaning, or is the lowest form of that meaning. The Kabbalah for Paracelsus, when it is not something quite fantastic and unimaginable, is a species of Practical Magic, and here we shall do well to remember that the adept of Hohenheim flourished at a period when the spurious literature of Clavicles and Grimoires was abroad already in the world.

It is very difficult to judge Paracelsus, and many false statements have been made concerning him by friends and enemies. But it is well to know that he was not a student of the Kabbalah in any sense that we should care to associate therewith.

VI.—JOHN REUCHLIN

As these sketches are not constructed biographically, there will be no difficulty in regarding the subject of the present notice as the representative of a group, which group illustrates most effectively the standpoint and purpose of our inquiry as regards the Christian students of the Kabbalah. They have been mentioned already in my preface. The missionary enthusiasm which may be said to have begun with Mirandula, which, if Lully had been a Kabbalist, would have been already at fever heat in the *doctor illuminatus* of Majorca, which ceased only in the early part of the eighteenth century, assumed almost the aspect of a movement between the period of Reuchlin and that of Rosenroth. It was not a concerted movement ; it was not the activity of a theosophical society or a learned body ; it was not actuated by any occult interests, and perhaps still less by those of an academic kind. The shape which it assumed in its literature was that of a deliberate and successive attempt to read Christian dogma into the written word of Kabbalism. It does not appear so strenuously in the work of Rosenroth as it does in the collection of Pistorius,[1] because in the days of the KABBALA DENUDATA there was, perhaps, more reason to hinder such intellectual excesses. Nor is it so strong in the writings of Reuchlin as in those of Archangelus de Burgonuovo. It is impossible

---

[1] ARTIS CABALISTICÆ, *hoc est, reconditæ theologiæ et philosophiæ Scriptorum*, Tomus I., Basiliæ, 1587.

to survey the vast treatises, extending in some cases to hundreds of folio pages, by which the enthusiasm is represented, and it is fortunately not necessary. We have only to establish their proper connection with Kabbalism and to shew that it has been so far misconceived by occultists of the past.

We are justified in regarding Éliphas Lévi as to some extent a mouthpiece in his day of modern occult thought : it is to him more than to any one that such thought owes its impulse towards the Jewish Tradition as to a so-called absolute of philosophy and religion, " the alliance of the universal reason and the Divine Word." [1] It was he who first pretended that " all truly dogmatic religions have issued from the Kabbalah and return therein," that it has " the keys of the past, the present and the future, etc." [2] In order to " receive initiation " into this great tradition he has counselled us, among other books, to have recourse to the " Hebrew writers in the recollection of Pistorius." [3] Following this direction, occultists have been taught to regard the famous Basle folio as a storehouse of genuine Jewish Tradition. No impression could well be more erroneous. The works engarnered by Pistorius are neither the Jewish tradition nor valid commentary thereon. It is well also to add that they are not the work of occultists or of persons who believed that " Catholic doctrine," or Lutheran, is " wholly derived " from the Kabbalah. The writers are of three types : I. The Jew who had abjured Israel and directed his polemics against it. He is represented by Riccius, and his presence is fatal to Lévi's standpoint. Lévi recommended the Christian to become a Kabbalist; Riccius thought it logical for the Kabbalist to turn Christian.[4] II. The born Christian, who believed that the Jew was in the wrong for continuing in

---

[1] DOGME DE LA HAUTE MAGIE, p. 95, 2me édition, Paris, 1861 ; TRANSCENDENTAL MAGIC, p. 20 ; MYSTERIES OF MAGIC, second edition, p. 502.

[2] See my translation of the DOGME ET RITUEL, *s.v.* TRANSCENDENTAL MAGIC : *its Doctrine and Ritual*, second edition, 1923, pp. 24, 25.

[3] *Ibid.* Students who know the collection of Pistorius will be aware that a large part of it is Christian in authorship, and that, with the exception of PORTA LUCIS and a version of SEPHER YETZIRAH, none of its treatises was written originally in Hebrew.

[4] After his conversion this German repaired to Padua, where he taught philosophy with great credit. He was invited back to Germany by the Emperor Maximilian. He belongs to the sixteenth century. His chief work treats of CELESTIAL AGRICULTURE. It occupies nearly two hundred pages in the folio of Pistorius and offers very curious reading to those who can tolerate it at this day ; but it is to be noted that the ZOHAR is not cited through all its length.

Judaism when the Kabbalah taught—as it was argued—the doctrine of the Trinity, the Divine Word and so forth. He also is in opposition to Lévi, who thought that the Jew was in the right because the germ of all dogmas could be found in the traditions of Israel. This type is represented by Reuchlin,[1] who is learned, laborious and moderate, but also by Archangelus de Burgonuovo, who does frequent outrage to good sense, and seems to regard the Kabbalah as a note-book to the New Testament. Reuchlin toyed with Lutheranism ; Archangelus was a Catholic prelate. III. The purely natural mystic, who might be either Jew or Gentile, who has no Kabbalistic connections worth reciting, and to whom Christianity does not seem even a name. He is represented by a writer who, as a fact, was born a Jew and seems to have been included by Pistorius because of his supposed conversion. I refer to Abravanel, whose PHILO-SOPHY OF LOVE is the subject of special mention by Éliphas Lévi as if it were a text-book of Kabbalism. The DIALOGUES have been dealt with already, and here it is enough to say that their citation annihilates Lévi, because a student of the Kabbalah might as well be referred to an " Art " of Ovid Spiritualised.

As regards Pistorius himself, the only point at which he makes contact with occult follies is in the fact that his enter-prise was undertaken, among other reasons, as a counterblast to the superstitions which the Kabbalah had promoted in Christendom ; a reference, we may presume, to the juvenile budget of Agrippa and to the increasing grimoire literature. The Kabbalistic studies of the editor began in his boyhood ; but, so far from leading him to the boasted certitude of Lévi, he passed under their escort into Protestantism, and there was conferred upon him the august distinction of figuring as one of the deputies charged to present the Lutheran Con-fession of Faith to the Diet of Augsbourg. Having registered the fact itself as an illustration of the quality of his progress towards the Absolute, it is of course permissible to regard his sympathies with the attempted purgation of the Church in a spirit of clemency, perhaps even of interest, or to confess, at least, that they were excusable on the ground of natural

---

[1] A successful politician, diplomatist and man of the world. He also belongs to the sixteenth century. Some account of his life will be found in Basnage, t. v. pp. 2059 *et seq.*

infirmity, seeing that he was for long subjected to persecution, fostered by a monkish inquisitor, because he had saved the books of Jewry from confiscation and burning throughout all Germany. In place of them, as opportunity afforded, they burnt DE VERBO MIRIFICO and DE ARTE CABBALISTICA, contributions of Reuchlin to the right understanding of the Secret Tradition in Israel.[1] The treatises remain all the same as witnesses of the standpoint of Christian students in the sixteenth century, and they help to warrant us in affirming that the largest Latin collection of Kabbalistic writers, outside KABBALA DENUDATA, contains no evidence in support of any occult hypothesis.

I must by no means leave this brief and confessedly inadequate notice of Reuchlin and his connections without a word of reference to his learned pupil, J. A. Widmanstadt, whose collection of Hebrew manuscripts, for the most part Kabbalistic, is one of the great treasures of the Library of Munich. In the course of his life-long studies he gave special attention to the ZOHAR and to the theurgic side of Jewish Tradition.

VII.—WILLIAM POSTEL

A philosophical, or rather an occult legend has gathered in an unaccountable manner round the name of William Postel, and it is supplemented by a popular legend which has depicted this peaceable, though perhaps somewhat puerile monk in a vestment of thaumaturgic splendour. The philosophical legend we owe almost exclusively to Éliphas Lévi, and to a few later writers in France who have accepted his leading and, with him, appear to be impressed honestly by Postel's well-intended but too often inane writings, among which is included a KEY OF THINGS KEPT SECRET FROM THE FOUNDATION OF THE WORLD. Postel was the son of a poor Normandy peasant: by his perseverance and self-denial he contrived to obtain an education, and became, on the authority of his chief admirer, the most learned man of his time. " Ever full of resignation and sweetness, he worked like a labouring man to insure himself a crust of bread, and then returned to his studies. Poverty accompanied him always, and want at times compelled him to part with his books ; but he acquired

---

[1] They will be found in the collection of Pistorius.

all the known languages and all the sciences of his day ; he discovered rare and valuable manuscripts, among others the Apocryphal Gospels and the SEPHER YETZIRAH ; he initiated himself into the mysteries of the transcendent Kabbalah, and his frank admiration for this absolute truth, for this supreme reason of all philosophies and all dogmas, tempted him to make it known to the world." [1]

So far Éliphas Lévi, whose undeniable influence upon all modern occultism has done more than anything to exaggerate the true philosophical position of Jewish secret literature and to place some of its supposed expositors in a false light. The redeeming point of Postel is his exalted piety ; the points to be regretted are his extravagance, his transcendental devotion to a religious and homely nun of mature years, and his belief that he underwent a process of physical regeneration by the infusion of her spiritual substance two years after her death.[2] To the Council of Trent, convened for the condemnation of heresies connected with the Reformation, he addressed a benevolent but unpractical epistle, inviting it to bless the whole world, which seems outside the purpose of a deliberative assembly considering doctrinal questions. The result of these errors of enthusiasm was that Postel was shut up in some convent, a course dictated possibly as much by a feeling of consideration, and even of mercy, towards a learned man unfitted for contact with the world, as by the sentiment of intolerance. The seclusion, in any case, offered him the kind of advantages that he most needed, and he died in peace, having retracted, it is said, everything that was disapproved by his superiors.

As seen already, Postel connects with Kabbalism by the great fact that he discovered and made known in the West that celebrated BOOK OF FORMATION which contains some of its fundamental doctrine.[3] He expounded also its principles in a species of commentary to which I shall recur shortly.[4]

---

[1] HISTOIRE DE LA MAGIE. Paris, 1860, liv. v. c. 4, p. 347. See also my annotated translation, s.v. HISTORY OF MAGIC, second edition, 1922, p. 336.

[2] Ibid., p. 250.

[3] " Postel was the first, to my knowledge, who translated into Latin the most ancient and, it must be confessed, the most obscure, monument of the Kabbalah ; I refer to the BOOK OF FORMATION."—A. V. Franck, LA KABBALE, p. 16. He adds : " So far as I am in a position to judge of this translation, which at least equals the text in obscurity, it appears faithful in a general way."

[4] We have seen that tradition refers also to him a Latin translation of the ZOHAR, for which Franck sought vainly in the public libraries of Paris.

His own doctrine has also some remote traces of analogy with Zoharistic tradition, but its summary by Éliphas Lévi is loose and inexact, like all literary and historical studies undertaken by this modern adept.

"The Trinity," his interpretation begins, "made man in Its image and after Its likeness. The human body is dual, and its triadic unity is constituted by the union of its two halves ; it is *animus* and *anima ;* it is mind and tenderness ; so also it has two sexes—the masculine situated in the head, and the feminine in the heart. The fulfilment of redemption must be dual therefore in humanity ; mind by its purity must rectify the errors of the heart, and the heart by its generosity must correct the egoistic barrenness of the head. Christianity has been comprehended heretofore only by reasoning heads ; it has not penetrated hearts. The Word has indeed become man, but not till the Word has become woman will the world be saved. The maternal genius of religion must instruct men in the sublime grandeurs of the spirit of charity ; then will reason be conciliated with faith, because it will understand, explain and govern the sacred excesses of devotion." [1]

The particular fatuity of Postel was that he recognised the incarnation of this maternal spirit in the person of the pious nun before mentioned. Éliphas Lévi, who took no illuminations and no enthusiasms seriously, terms this spiritual ardour a lyrical puerility and a celestial hallucination, but there is no lyrical element in the Latin of Postellus, and, whatever the source of the hallucination, the lady died making no sign. Into the question of their subsequent reunion after a manner which recalls the *status embryonnatus* of Kabbalistic abnormal psychology, it would be ridiculous here to enter. From the period of its occurrence the mystic always termed himself *Postellus Restitutus ;* it is reported that his white hair became again black, the furrows disappeared from his brow, and his cheeks reassumed the hues of youth. Derisive biographers explain these marvels as derisive biographers might be expected, as if, Lévi well observes, "it being insufficient to represent him as a fool, it was necessary also to exhibit this man, of a nature so noble and so generous, in the light of a juggler and charlatan. There is one thing more astounding than the eloquent unreason of enthusiastic hearts, and that

---

[1] HIST. DE LA MAGIE, liv. v. c. 4, p. 348.

is the stupidity or bad faith of the frigid and sceptical minds which presume to judge them." [1]

A less unsympathetic historian than those confounded by Lévi reduces the doctrines of Postel under two heads, (1) " That the evangelical reign of Jesus Christ, established by the apostles, could not be sustained among Christians or propagated among infidels except by the lights of reason," which appears wholly plausible. (2) That a future King of France was destined to universal monarchy, and " that his way must be prepared by the conquest of hearts and the convincing of minds, so that henceforth the world shall hold but one belief and Jesus Christ shall reign there by one King, one law and one faith." Given universal monarchy as a possibility of the future, no Frenchman who is true to his traditions would assign it otherwise than to a King of France. However, one or both of these propositions led the biographer in question to infer that Postel was mad, and I cite this conclusion less on account of its essential merit than because it afforded Lévi the opportunity for a rejoinder of characteristic suggestiveness. " Mad, for having dreamed that religion should govern minds by the supreme reason of its doctrine, and that the monarchy, to be strong and lasting, must bind hearts by the conquests of the public prosperity of peace! Mad, for having believed in the advent of His Kingdom, to Whom we cry daily : Thy Kingdom come! Mad, because he believed in reason and justice on earth! Alas, it is too true, poor Postel was mad!" He wrote little books at intervals which, I must admit frankly, are almost impossible to read, and in the case of the SEPHER YETZIRAH the printer has done his best to make the difficulties of Postel's translation absolute ; but as I have promised to speak of the commentary which accompanies the version, I must say at least that it should be described rather as a collection of separate notes. Franck recommends no one to be guided by the views which it expresses, but they scarcely suggest leading, as they contain nothing of real importance, and some of them are almost childish. Among the points which may be noted are :—(a) Defence of the lawfulness and necessity of the concealment of sacred things ; (b) A pertinent and useful distinction between the terms creation, formation and making,

---

[1] HIST. DE LA MAGIE, liv. v. c. 4, p. 348.

as used in the SEPHER YETZIRAH ; (c) The antiquity of the belief in ten spheres of the heavens ; (d) The recourse to numerical mysticism, to shew why the SEPHIROTH are, in the words of SEPHER YETZIRAH, " ten and not nine," the necessity of the number ten being shown by the progression from the unit to the quaternary, as follows :—1 + 2 + 3 + 4 = 10. And this, according to a mystical mode of calculation, brings us back to the unit, even as the external universe brings back the soul to God ; (e) The attribution of angelic choirs to the SEPHIROTH, thus shewing that Postel's study of the Kabbalah was not confined to the one document which he is known to have translated.

Of Postel's original writings, that entitled DE RATIONIBUS SPIRITUS SANCTI *Libri Duo,* 1543, seems on the whole the most soberly reasoned ; if, unfortunately, it has no connections with the Kabbalah, it has at least some with good sense. It is useful also for those—if any remain among us, except in France—who are disposed to be influenced by Lévi, and hence to regard Postel as an adept of their mysteries. While it is quite true that he was more than fanciful in his notions, which are extravagant in the philological as well as the conventional sense of that term, it is not at all true that he had set aside or exceeded the accepted doctrinal views of his period, nor does he appear to have possessed a specific light on given points of teaching which can be regarded as considerable for his period. He upheld, for example, the doctrine of eternal damnation, and justifies it in such a manner that no room is left for the conjecture that he was not saying what he meant. For the rest, Postel was a good and single-minded Christian, who, in spite of his CLAVIS ABSCONDITORUM A CONSTITUTIONE MUNDI, and in spite of the panegyrics of Éliphas Lévi, had no knowledge whatsoever of any so-called BOOK OF THOTH, and had never dreamed of looking for a doctrine of absolute religion beyond the Seat of Peter.

VIII.—THE ROSICRUCIANS

Among many adventurous statements advanced concerning this mystical Fraternity, we are not infrequently told that it gave a great impetus to the study of the Kabbalah. The assertion is so far from being founded on any accessible fact, that one is tempted to rejoin that it gave no impetus to anything except a short-lived curiosity and a certain pleasant fantasia in romantic fiction.[1] The truth is that no statement should be hazarded on either side. In the first place, the historical evidence for the existence of the Order, though it points to certain conclusions, is in a very unsatisfactory state,[2] and were any knowledge of another kind conceivably still in existence it would be in the custody of those unlikely to commit themselves. I have never met in literature with an express statement designed to indicate knowledge and to represent authority which could bear investigation. On the contrary, I have found invariably that those which most assumed the complexion of certitude were only the private impressions of persons who had no title to conviction, nor even a sufficient warrant for an estimable opinion by their acquaintance with the exoteric facts. I have therefore to say that there is no known student of the Kabbalah,[3] with one tentative and barely possible exception, who can be cited on evidence as the member of a Rosicrucian Fraternity, laying any claim to antiquity. It is of course well known that there have been, as there still are, various corporate societies, some semi-Masonic, as in England, some occult, as in France, which have formulated their particular interests and purposes by adopting the name. There is no great mischief in such adoption, provided the limits of the pretension are clear, and, with the exception of recent impostures which have appeared there and here in America, this, I think, has been the case.

The few great names of the past which connect with Rosicrucianism and at the same time with Kabbalism are not to be identified with the Fraternity, except on a common ground of sympathy.[4] Such was Thomas Vaughan. More-

---

[1] See, however, my BROTHERHOOD OF THE ROSY CROSS, 1924, in which the history and claims of the Order, more especially on their external side, are examined in an exhaustive manner.

[2] It is open therefore to numerous fantastic constructions, one of the most curious being that placed on it by Mrs. Henry Pott, in FRANCIS BACON AND HIS SECRET SOCIETY, London, 1891. See c. xii. especially, and compare Clifford Harrison, NOTES ON THE MARGINS, London, 1897, p. 49 : " There is every good reason to suppose that the founder of Inductive Philosophy was a Rosicrucian."

[3] The term is sometimes used loosely in connection with the Rosicrucians, as if meaning a tradition of any kind. Thus, Mr. W. F. C. Wigston speaks of " German philosophers and writers . . . who each and all held up Freemasonry as a branch of their own Rosicrucian Kabbalah."—THE COLUMBUS OF LITERATURE, p. 203, Chicago, 1892. The Rosicrucian Kabbalah, understood in this sense, was Divine Magia.

[4] In a paper read before the Quatuor Coronati Lodge, and published in its transactions, Dr. Wynn Westcott, Supreme Magus of the English Rosicrucian Society,

over, the memorials which we possess of it, especially those belonging to the eighteenth century, indicate that it was engrossed mainly by alchemical processes. The barely possible exception mentioned, namely, the one case in which a well-known student of the Kabbalah, or rather a well-known expositor of Kabbalistic subjects, may have received initiation into a Rosicrucian Order going back through the last century, is Éliphas Lévi. It is not perhaps improbable that he received initiation of some kind, though I must be disassociated with all clearness from the pretence of a certain French occultist, who claimed access to secret sources of information, namely, that the scattered groups of Rosicrucian Societies were reorganised by Éliphas Lévi, presumably about the year 1850. But this solitary instance, supposing that it could be called valid, does not save the situation, more especially as I shall establish more fully later on that Éliphas Lévi, though he obtained a reputation among occultists as a Kabbalist, was not entitled to it by any tolerable acquaintance with the literature which contains the Kabbalah. The point of fact has been noted, as the need arose, already in preceding pages.

IX.—ROBERT FLUDD

The name of Robert Fludd stands high among esoteric philosophers and " philosophers by fire " in England ; he was a man of wide learning, of intellectual ambition, of exalted spiritual faith. He was also a theosophical writer in the catholic sense of the term. If we add to this that he is an accessible figure, not too remote in time, and that a short pilgrimage in Kent will lead us to the site at least of that house in which he lived and died, it will not be difficult to understand the fascination which he has exercised on many who, for the rest, have never dared to stir the dust from his folios. I have had occasion already in more than one work to account for this Kentish " philosopher by fire," and as there is only a single mystery in his life, on which no one is likely to give light, I shall not need here to retrace ground that has been travelled.[1] The one mystery is whether he did ultimately enter the Fraternity of the Rose-Cross. It is

---

describes Rosicrucianism as a new presentation of Gnostic, Kabbalistic, Hermetic and Neo-Platonic doctrines. At the beginning, middle and end, it happens to have been nothing of the kind.

[1] See HAUNTS OF THE ENGLISH MYSTICS, No. 1, in THE UNKNOWN WORLD, vol. i. pp. 130 *et seq.* Also THE BROTHERHOOD OF THE ROSY CROSS, 1924, cap. x.

clear from the first tracts which he wrote in defence of this Order that he had not been then initiated into its mysteries.[1] Perhaps so much energy and devotion earned its reward in the end, as there is ground for supposing was the case with his friend Michael Maier, who espoused the same cause in Germany. But we do not know, and modern occult writers who pretend that he was a Rosicrucian are either misled or are romancing.

His connection with Kabbalism is, however, the only point with which we are concerned here, and as to this there is no doubt of his proficiency along certain lines, for he occupied himself a great deal with vast cosmological hypotheses, which were drawn to some extent from this source. He was forty years of age when the Rosicrucian controversy first gave opportunity to his pen, and the COMPENDIOUS APOLOGY, which he published in reply to Libavius, a German hostile critic, exhibits his Kabbalistic studies. I must add also that it gives evidence of his besetting intellectual weakness, an inordinate passion for the marvellous, which leads him to dwell unduly on the thaumaturgic side of Jewish Secret Knowledge. Having given the usual Legend of the Tradition, its reception by Moses from God and its oral perpetuation till the time of Esdras, he divides the Kabbalah into two parts. There is firstly that of Cosmology, dealing with forces operating in created things, both sublunary and celestial, and here he expounded also on philosophical grounds the arcana of the written law. This division, he observes, does not differ materially from the Natural Magic in which Solomon is recorded to have excelled, and he adds that the magical powers of natural things, concealed in their centre, can be brought forth by this species of Kabbalah. The second division is entitled MERCAVAH, which contemplates things Divine, angelical powers, Sacred Names and *signacula*. It is sub-divided into NOTARICON and THEOMANTICA. NOTARICON treats of angelical virtues and names, of demoniacal natures and of human souls; THEOMANTICA investigates the Mysteries of Divine Majesty, of Sacred Names and pentacles. Those who are proficient therein are invested with strange powers, can foretell future things,

---

[1] Perhaps the *Valete Nostrique Memores estote* of the *Epilogus Autoris ad Fratres de Rosea Cruce* may create a different impression in the minds of some readers. See APOLOGIA COMPENDIARIA, Leyden, 1616.

command entire Nature, compel angels and demons, and perform miracles. By this art Moses worked his various signs and wonders, Joshua caused the sun to stand still, Elijah brought fire from heaven and raised the dead to life. But it is a gift of God, through His Holy Spirit, which is granted only to the elect.

It will be seen that this classification presents not the exalted if bizarre traditions of the ZOHAR, but the debased and superstitious apparatus of SEPHER RAZIEL and of later Kabbalism, ignored if not unknown by writers like Rosenroth. In folios which followed the COMPENDIOUS APOLOGY the Kabbalistic connections of Fludd's philosophy are implicit and suggestive rather than patent and elaborated, and I think are positive proof that he had no acquaintance with the ZOHAR. In his Cosmology of the Macrocosmos,[1] which deals with its metaphysical and physical origin, he has recourse chiefly to Platonic and Hermetic writings, and although many other authorities are cited, nothing is borrowed from Kabbalists, except indeed the TETRAGRAMMATON, which figures within a triangle in one of the illustrations. The complementary treatise on the Microcosm recalls Kabbalism in its doctrine of angels and demons. Slight correspondences may be traced in his other writings ; but they indicate no real knowledge. In discussing the properties of numbers [2] (i.e., the SEPHIROTH) and the Divine Names attributed to these, the diagram which accompanies the remarks shews that he misconstrued totally the Kabbalistic scheme of emanation. So also some later observations concerning METATRON and the positive and negative sides of the Sephirotic Tree [3] suggest no special knowledge. When replying to Father Mersenne, Fludd defends what he terms his Kabbalah, but the term is used loosely and has certainly very little to do with the Kabbalah of Jewry.[4] It may be observed, in conclusion, that the Kentish mystic was pre-eminently a Christian philosopher, and, like other subjects, that of the Esoteric Tradition in Israel was approached by him from the Christian standpoint.

---

[1] *Utriusque Cosmi Majoris scilicet et Minoris* METAPHYSICA, PHYSICA *atque* TECHNICA HISTORIA, 2 vols., Frankfort, 1617 and 1629.
[2] PHILOSOPHIA SACRA *et vere Christiana, seu Meteorologica Cosmica,* 1626.
[3] MEDICINA CATHOLICA, *seu Mysticum Artis Medicandi Sacrarium,* 2 vols., Frankfort, 1629, 1631.
[4] DE SOPHIÆ CUM MORIA CERTAMINE, 1629.

X.—HENRY MORE

The Cambridge Platonic philosopher is regarded by Basnage as a great Kabbalist and his contributions to KABBALA DENUDATA as in some sense discovering the sentiment and spirit of Jewish Theosophy.[1] Franck, on the contrary, regrets their inclusion by Rosenroth on the ground that they are personal speculations which are not at all in harmony with Kabbalistic teaching.[2] While there can be no question that the just view belongs to the later critic, More is thinly interesting because of his enthusiasm and earnestness. His point of view is also of importance to our inquiry, because his name belongs undeniably to the literature of English Mysticism—or at least its outskirts. Let us begin therefore by stating that he approached the subject as a Christian who desired the conversion of the Jews, who regarded the Kabbalah as a fitting instrument to effect it, and not in the case of the Jews only, but even of Pagans. He came therefore to its study and elucidation not as an investigator of things esoteric, not as a seeker for an absolute doctrine of religion, nor even for a higher sense of Christianity, but like Picus and Postel and Reuchlin, or like his correspondent and editor Rosenroth, as one imbued with an evangelical spirit.[3]

The introduction of More to the Kabbalah was brought about, as it has been supposed, by means of Isaac de Loria's LIBER DRUSHIM. There is no reason to believe that he could or did undertake an independent study of the ZOHAR, and hence as his contributions to the subject are all prior to the appearance of KABBALA DENUDATA, it follows that his acquaintance was not exhaustive, nor was it altogether good of its kind. At the same time, his study of LIBER DRUSHIM called forth a well-reasoned letter from his pen, addressed to Rosenroth,[4] in which the description of the SEPHIROTH under the form of spheres is condemned as a fiction of the later rabbis and their relation to the denary is affirmed. The critical position of the writer is established, however, by the attribution of the Pythagorean denary to a Kabbalistic origin.

---

[1] HISTOIRE DES JUIFS, Livre iii. c. 10, tom. ii., p. 786.
[2] Ad. Franck : LA KABBALE, p. 22.
[3] And desiring the *Ecclesiæ emolumentum,* as the same correspondence shews.
[4] EPISTOLA AD COMPILATOREM, *Apparatus in Librum Sohar, Pars secunda,* pp. 52 *et seq.* KAB. DEN. t. i.

This letter was accompanied by a number of questions and considerations in development of the debated point and other difficulties, all which are duly printed by Rosenroth, to whom space seemed no object, together with his AMICA RESPONSIO, which cites the authority of the ZOHAR in support of the circular form of the SEPHIROTH.[1] More replied with an ULTERIOR DISQUISITIO and an accompanying letter, in which he announces his belief that he has hit upon the true Kabbalah of the Jewish BERESHITH. This epistle is in English and quaintly worded. The conclusion entreats Rosenroth to intimate to his readers " how beneficiall this may prove for the preparing of the Jews to receive Christianity, the difficultyes and obstacles being cleared and removed by the right understanding of their own Cabbala."

There is no need to follow this friendly discussion, which, it must be confessed, becomes exceedingly tedious in the ULTERIOR DISQUISITIO. More, however, contributed another thesis in exposition of the Vision of Ezekiel, *i.e.*, a Kabbalistic Catechism and a refutation of the doctrine that the material world is not the product of creation *ex nihilo*, in which last the Platonist seems scarcely to have understood the Kabbalah.

Of all these the most interesting is the MERCAVÆ EXPOSITIO, which contains nineteen postulates, fifty-two questions arising out of the text of Ezekiel and the replies thereto. It affirms, (*a*) That all souls, angelical and human, that of Messiah included, were created at the beginning of the world; [2] (*b*) That the material world in its first estate was diaphanous, or lucid; (*c*) That it had two chief elements, the Spirit of Nature and the vehicle of the Holy Spirit; (*d*) That it was divided into four parts, which are the Four Worlds of the Kabbalists; (*e*) That all souls were at first enclosed in ATZILUTH, but were subject to revolution in the other Worlds; (*f*) That souls which the Divine decree has sent into ASSIAH, but are free from willing sin, are sustained by Divine Virtue, and will assuredly return to ATZILUTH; (*g*) That in ATZILUTH the souls and the angels are absorbed wholly in the Beatific Vision, but that in BRIAH they have a tendency to external things; (*h*) That the soul of Messiah in ATZILUTH made such progress in the Divine Love that it

---

[1] In *Caput* ii., *Consideratio tertia, ibid.*, p. 91.
[2] For this there is Talmudic as well as Zoharic authority.

became united with the Eternal Word in a Hyper-Atzilutic or Hypostatic manner, and was thus constituted Chief of all souls and King of the Four Worlds, an event which took place at the beginning of the Briatic World, the special heritage of Messiah. At this point the Christian Kabbalist introduces the compact of the cross and dissolves all connection with the scheme of Jewish Theosophy.

The MERCAVÆ EXPOSITIO contains numerous references to another work of More, entitled CONJECTURA CABBALISTICA,[1] which preceded his correspondence with Rosenroth. It is a presentation of the literal, philosophical and mystical, or divinely moral sense of the three initial chapters of Genesis. It was received, so the author assures us, neither from men nor angels, and as a fact the " conjecture " illustrates the criticism of Franck, for it has very little in common with any ancient or modern Kabbalah ever received in Jewry. The literal section is a bald paraphrase of the scriptural account of the creation and fall of man. The PHILOSOPHIC CABBALA is established on the denary after the following fantastic manner :—

The Archetypal World = Monad, 1.
The First Matter = Duad, 2.
The Habitable Order = Triad, 3.
The Making of the Starry Heavens = Tetrad, 4.
The Making of Fish and Fowls, or Union of the Passive and Active Principle = Pentad, 5.
The Making of Beasts and Cattle, but chiefly of Man = Hexad, 6.

What becomes of the rest of the denary does not appear. In his first estate Adam was wholly ethereal, and his soul was the ground which was blessed by God, whereby it brought forth every pleasant tree and every goodly growth of the heavenly Father's own planting. The Tree of Life in the garden of man's soul was the essential will of God, while the Tree of Knowledge was the will of man himself. We have here the keynote of the allegory, which is merely pleasing and altogether unsubstantial. It may be noted, however, that the sleep which fell upon Adam was a lassitude of Divine

---

[1] A CONJECTURAL ESSAY *of interpreting the Mind of Moses according to a threefold Cabbala, viz., Literal, Philosophical, Mystical, or Divinely Moral*, London, 1662. The attempt was dedicated to Cudworth.

Contemplation. The MORAL CABBALA recognises two principles in man, namely, spirit and flesh. It gives apparently a synopsis of the work of regeneration, depicting, firstly, the spiritual chaos, when man is under the dominion of the flesh; next, the dawning of the heavenly principle, corresponding to the *Fiat Lux;* but the analogy in most instances seems at once weak and laboured. For example, the fruit-bearing trees are good works, the manifestation of the sun is the love of God and our neighbour, and so forth. On the whole, it may be concluded that More's connection with the Kabbalah is an interesting episode in the life of an amiable scholar, but it was without real increment to either.

XI.—THOMAS VAUGHAN

With the questionings, difficulties and tentative expositions of Henry More it will be useful to contrast what is said on the subject of Kabbalism by his contemporary Eugenius Philalethes, otherwise Thomas Vaughan. It will not be forgotten by students of the byways of literature in the seventeenth century that the two writers came into collision in pamphlets. When Vaughan began his theosophical labours by the publication of two tracts on the nature of man and on the universal Spirit of Nature, More, who was after all more Platonist than mystic and had scant tolerance for mystical terminology, published some acrimonious observations concerning them, to which the Welsh mystic replied in satires with the polemical virulence of his period. The dispute itself deserves nothing less than oblivion, but Thomas Vaughan has been regarded, and not, I think, with exaggeration, as the chief mystic, theosopher and alchemist, with one exception in the last respect,[1] produced at his period in England; and as he died nearly twenty-five years before the appearance of KABBALA DENUDATA, the source and extent of his Kabbalistic knowledge will help us to fix the state of scholarship in England on the subject before the formation of the group of Cambridge Platonists. Vaughan, in his early works, confesses himself a disciple of Agrippa,

---

[1] The exception is Eirenæus Philalethes, that truly " Unknown Philosopher," with whom Eugenius has been so often identified, and from whom of late years he has been so often and carefully distinguished by myself, that it is unnecessary in this connection to say anything concerning him, except that his numerous works have few points of contact with Kabbalism.

and the THREE BOOKS OF OCCULT PHILOSOPHY [1] represent
the general measure of his knowledge concerning the Esoteric
Tradition of the Jews, while the opinion which he had
formed thereon must be referred to the Retractation of his
master, that admirable work on the VANITY OF THE SCIENCES
AND THE EXCELLENCE OF THE WORD OF GOD. I must not
say that he shews no independent reading ; he quotes on
one occasion a passage in PORTA LUCIS [2] which is not to be
found in Agrippa, and there are one or two other instances, [3]
but for the most part he is content to represent his model
and his first inspirer. If my readers accept this judgment,
they must interpret his own statement that he spent some
years in the search and contemplation of the Kabbalah
reflectively and not bibliographically, which further will
assist them to see how the peculiar Mysticism of Thomas
Vaughan can offer distinct points of contact with the ZOHAR
without that text-book of Kabbalism, then untranslated,
having been read by the mystic, except in some Latin extracts.

In his discourse on the Antiquity of Magic we find him
alive, like the students who had preceded him, to the
distinction between a true and a false Kabbalah. The
latter, described after the picturesque manner of his period,
as the invention of dispersed and wandering rabbis " whose
brains had more of distraction than their fortunes," consists
altogether " in alphabetical knacks, ends always in the letter
where it begins and the vanities of it are grown voluminous."
But in respect of the " more ancient and physical traditions
of the Kabbalah," Thomas Vaughan tells us that he embraces
them for so many sacred truths. [4] He recognises also a
metaphysical tradition in which the greatest mystery is the
symbolism of Jacob's Ladder. " Here we find two extremes—
Jacob is one, at the foot of the ladder, and God is the other,
Who stands above it, *emittens formas et influxus in Jacob, sive
subjectum hominem.* The rounds or steps in the ladder signify
the middle nature, by which Jacob is united to God." [5] With
this symbolism he contrasts the " false grammatical Kabbala "
which " consists only in rotations of the alphabet and a

---

[1] Translated into English one year after the appearance of Vaughan's first treatises.
[2] Concerning the restraint of superior influences occasioned by the sin of Adam.
[3] Of which some are sufficiently erroneous, as, for example, in MAGIA ADAMICA,
when he states that MALKUTH is the invisible, archetypal moon.
[4] THE WORKS OF THOMAS VAUGHAN, edited by A. E. Waite, London, 1919, p. 167.
[5] *Ibid.,* pp. 169, 170.

metathesis of letters in the text, by which means the scripture hath suffered many racks and excoriations." The true Kabbalah only uses letters for artifice, thas is, with a view to concealment.[1] Of the physical side of the genuine Tradition he gives an unfinished presentation in alchemical language, which is transfigured, however, for Thomas Vaughan regarded Alchemy as at once a spiritual ?nd physical science, having its operations in the infinite as well as in the mineral kingdom. For him the SEPHIROTH are ten secret principles, of which the first is a spirit *in retrecesso suo fontano*, while the second is the Voice of that Spirit, the third is another Spirit which issues from the Spirit and the Voice, and the fourth is " a certain water " proceeding from the third Spirit, and emanating Fire and Air.[2] It will be seen that the reflections of the Welsh mystic on the apparatus of Kabbalism are not elucidating, and while recording the Sephirotic attributions of the SEPHER YETZIRAH are not fully in consonance therewith.

We shall be inclined, on the whole, to confess that Vaughan's connection with Kabbalistic texts is like his communications with the brethren of the Rosicrucian Order. He knew nothing of the latter " as to their persons," so he tells us in his preface to a translation of the FAMA and CONFESSIO of the Fraternity, and it was mainly by report and consideration on things heard at second hand that he was aware of Mysticism in Jewry. As time went on and he outgrew the simple leading-strings of Cornelius Agrippa, so he strayed further from Kabbalistic interests, and though he never lost the fascination betrayed in his earlier works, he passed far away over fields of Spiritual Alchemy, where no ÆSH MEZAREPH could help him. When he published EUPHRATES, *or the Waters of the East*, in 1655, he shews no longer any trace of the Tradition in Israel. In LUMEN DE LUMINE, which appeared some four years earlier, there are, however, a few references to the subject, and one indeed constitutes an adumbration of the Christian Kabbalah as impressed on the curious mind of the mystical royalist. The pretext by which it is introduced is a speculation concerning the " Fire-Soul," or informing spirit of the earth, which is described as an influence from the Almighty derived through

---

[1] WORKS OF THOMAS VAUGHAN, p. 171.   [2] *Ibid.*, p. 168.

the mediation of *terra viventium*. The mediating being thus described darkly, is said to be the Second Person, and that which " the Kabbalists style the Supernatural East." To explain this symbolism Vaughan adds : " As the Natural Light of the sun is first manifested to us in the East, so the Supernatural Light was first manifested in the Second Person, for He is *Principium alterationis*, the Beginning of the ways of God, or the First Manifestation of His Father's Light in the Supernatural Generation. From this *Terra Viventium* or Land of the Living comes all Life or Spirit." [1] The Kabbalistic warrant of this notion is the axiom : *Omnis anima bona anima nova filia Orientis.*[2] The East in question is CHOKMAH, which is contrary to Kabbalistic statements, and CHOKMAH is the Son of God. This also is opposed to the Sephirotic ascriptions with which we are familiar, but there is some trace in early Kabbalistic writers of an attribution of the Three Supernals to Father, Son, Bride, with which later rabbins are said—a little egregiously—to have tampered so as to elude its Christian inferences. In either case Vaughan is interesting as a strange light of Christian Mysticism rather than as an expositor of the Kabbalah.

XII.—KNORR VON ROSENROTH

It is, perhaps, more interesting to ascertain the motives which led the editor of KABBALA DENUDATA to the consideration of Jewish Theosophy than those of any other student of the subject. To Christian Knorr von Rosenroth the occultist of Victorian days owed nearly all his knowledge of the ZOHAR, for the bibliographical writers who preceded him give only meagre notices of that Kabbalistic *magnum opus*, and it is not even mentioned by, *e.g.*, Cornelius Agrippa. Now Rosenroth occupies a position which " occult " persons like Mathers and Westcott, as well as their inspirer Lévi, have failed to remark, because they seem to have known nothing about their chief illuminator in the theosophy of Israel. I propose to shew that he was actuated by the same missionary enthusiasm which characterised all Christian expositors who

---

[1] LUMEN DE LUMINE, London, 1651, pp. 80–82.
[2] CONCLUSIONES KABALISTICÆ, No. xli. Vaughan also cites the obscure eighth conclusion of Mirandula, and says that the third light is BINAH, the Holy Ghost.— *Ibid.*, p. 83.

preceded him,[1] but I shall begin by enumerating one or two
points which indicate that he may have had one occult
connection. Born in the year 1636, a German noble bearing
the title of baron, he appears on the scene of history shortly
after public curiosity had almost died out on the subject of
the Rosicrucian mystery. Joachim Junge, Johann Valentin
Andreas and Ægidius Gutmann, three persons to whom rival
theories have attributed the invention of that Mystery,[2] were
still alive ; Robert Fludd, the English apologist of the
Faternity, was on the threshold of death, but had not yet
passed away ; Thomas Vaughan was a schoolboy ; Eirenæus
Philalethes had just written his INTROITUS APERTUS to shew
the adepts of Alchemy that he was their brother and their
peer ; [3] Sendivogius had exhausted his projecting powder
and was living in seclusion, an aged man, on the frontiers of
Silesia ; [4] John Baptist van Helmont, who long before had
testified that he had seen and touched the Philosopher's
Stone—of a colour like saffron in powder, but heavy and
shining like pounded glass [5]—had christened his son Mercurius ; and Mercurius van Helmont, the contemporary and
friend of Rosenroth, divided his laborious existence between
a tireless search after the secret of transmuting metals and
the study of the Kabbalah. Rosenroth, Kabbalist like
Helmont, was, like Helmont, probably a chemist—in the
sense of the seventeenth century—and on the crowded title-
page of his great work, we find it described as *Scriptum
omnibus philologis, philosophis, Theologis omnium religionum, atque
philochymicis quam utilissimum.* The justification is that the
Loci Communes Cabbalistici include a *Compendium Libri Cabba-
listico-Chymici, ÆSCH MEZAREPH dicti, de Lapide Philosophico.*
I have had occasion in the sixth book to give some account of
this treatise.

We have reason therefore to suppose that Rosenroth was
infected—slightly or otherwise—with the alchemical zeal of

---

[1] It was indeed, both before and after, the conventional *raison d'être* of almost every
work on the subject. See, for example, Beyers' CABBALISMUS JUDAICO-CHRISTIANUS
Detectus Breviterque Delineatus. Wittemberg, 1707.

[2] REAL HISTORY OF THE ROSICRUCIANS, by A. E. Waite, c. viii., especially pp. 220–
222. Compare my later work on THE BROTHERHOOD OF THE ROSY CROSS, consulting
the references to these names in the Index.

[3] See *Præfatio Authoris,* which appears in all editions of the INTROITUS APERTUS *ad
Occlusum Regis Palatium.*

[4] A. E. Waite : THE SECRET TRADITION IN ALCHEMY, p. 295.

[5] In his treatise DE VITA ETERNA.

his friend, the second generation of an alchemical family. We may suspe&, however, that he was more theosophift than Hermetift ; we are told also that he loved meditating on the Holy Scriptures and that he knew them by heart. Like his countryman Khunrath, he was a Lutheran, and Éliphas Lévi would have said of him, as of the author of AMPHITHEATRUM : " herein he was a German of his period rather than a myftical citizen of the eternal kingdom."[1] In matters of religion his peculiar bent is determined by the fa& that he wrote an EXPLANATION OF THE APOCALYPSE, about which I will forbear from wearying my readers. More to our purpose is a dialogue on evangelical hiftory, in which a Kabbaliftic catechumen proposes queftions on the four Gospels and a Chriftian replies. With this also we may conne& a treatise entitled MESSIAS PURUS, in which the life of Jesus Chrift, from his conception to his baptism, is explained according to the do&rines of the Kabbalah. In a word, the motto of his correspondent Henry More was that also of Rosenroth : " May the glory of our God and His Chrift be the end of all our writings ! " In conformity with this he begins his enumeration of the reasons which juftify the appearance of a Latin version of the ZOHAR [2] by affirming that at a period when the divisions of Chriftendom are traceable to diversity of philosophical opinions and metaphysical definitions it muft be important to inveftigate a philosophical syftem which flourished during the age of Chrift and his apoftles, and from which fountain the sacred oracles have themselves drawn largely. In the preface to his translation of three texts of the ZOHAR he founds his opinion that Kabbaliftic dogmas may be of Divine revelation on the ground of their san&ity and sublimity, as well as their great use in explaining the books of the Old and New Teftaments. He affirms also that, unlike later Jewish writings, the ZOHAR does not contain a single utterance againft Chrift. Finally, after enumerating twenty-four reasons why the Jews should enjoy toleration at Chriftian hands, he mentions the chief things which will assift their conversion. They include, of course, the ordinary common-places of piety and the ordinary devices of proselytism, but there is ftress laid upon the promotion of the ftudy of Hebrew

---

[1] HISTOIRE DE LA MAGIE, Introdu&ion, p. 33. Paris, 1860. See also my translation, s.v. THE HISTORY OF MAGIC, second edition, 1922, p. 29.
[2] APPARATUS IN LIBRUM SOHAR, Pars Secunda, pp. 3 et seq., KAB. DEN., Tom. i.

and Chaldaic, and on the translation of the New Teſtament into those languages.[1] The disquisition is conventional enough, but it is important because it indicates, firſtly, the projeƈt which was ever near to the heart of Rosenroth, and, secondly, how little he dreamed either of an esoteric Chriſtianity or of a withdrawn Wisdom-Religion, how little he looked to find in Kabbaliſtic doƈtrine a deeper sense of Chriſtian doƈtrines, or indeed anything but their consecration in the eyes of Jewry, by demonſtrating that they were to be found in the ZOHAR. He did not wish the Chriſtian to become a Kabbaliſt, but he longed very much for the Kabbaliſtic Jew to become a Lutheran. He is said to have endured great sacrifices, outside the vaſt labour involved, over the publication of KABBALA DENUDATA, but there is no need to add that it missed its aim entirely ; it has enabled a few ſtudents to get a confused notion of the ZOHAR, and it has in this way done immense service to occultiſts by furnishing material for their reveries : it is outside probability that it ever brought a single Jew into the Church of Chriſt, and as Rosenroth failed in his public aim, so at the close of his life he had the misfortune to see his daughter depart from the reformed religion and embrace, under the influence of her husband, the faith of the Catholic Church. Taken altogether the ſtory of Chriſtian Rosenroth has a touch of heroism and tragedy, and seeing that with all its faults his gift to scholarship is one of permanent value, so it is, I think, a useful task to indicate the circumſtances under which he gave it and the motives by which he was prompted.[2]

---

[1] With this description the reader may compare a little treatise which belongs to KABBALA DENUDATA, though unfortunately it is met with very rarely in extant copies, *i.e.*, ADUMBRATIO KABBALÆ CHRISTIANÆ, *id eſt Syncatabasis Hebraizans, sive Explicatio ad dogmata Novi Foederis pertinens, pro formanda hypothesis, ad conversionem Judæorum proficientis*. It is an addendum to the second volume, separately paged, and is in the form of a dialogue between a Kabbaliſt and a Chriſtian philosopher. It has been translated of recent years into French. Even at this day the little work seems to me of singular intereſt, and it is written with limpid clearness. The disquisition on the parts or grades of the soul in man may be noted in this conneƈtion as a case in point.

[2] At a later date the same motives inspired two small treatises—the work of other writers—which are intereſting in their way, and are worth mentioning for the benefit of ſtudents who may wish to pursue the subjeƈt. (1) PHOSPHORUS ORTHODOXÆ FIDEI *Veterum Cabbaliſtarum, seu Teſtimonia de Sacro-Sanƈta Trinitate et Messia Deo et Homine, ex pervetuſto Libro Sohar deprompta, qua nunc primum Latiné reddita, suisque et R. Johannis Kemperi Judæo-Chriſtiani animadversionibus concinné explicata, Judæis æque ac Chriſtianis speciminis loco edidit Andreas Norrelius Suecus, qui item commentarios Kemperianos suis illuſtravit notis.* Amſtelodami, 1720. This has been cited previously, but by name only. The prolegomena are concerned with the praise of R. Simeon ben Yohai, shewing the authority of the ZOHAR and its superiority to the Talmud on the ground that its author

I should add that over the antiquity of Kabbalistic doctrine
and literature he was by no means credulous for his period,
seeming indeed to admit that there may have been an admixture of late material with the ancient fragments of the ZOHAR.
He regarded the BOOK OF CONCEALMENT as the oldest and
most important of its treatises, and this is the only one in
which he was inclined to recognise the direct authorship of
R. Simeon ben Yohai. Of the rest, some may have been
the work of R. Abba and some of the school which succeeded
these masters.

XIII.—RALPH CUDWORTH

The honoured name of Ralph Cudworth, perhaps the
greatest theosophist of his age on the side of scholarship, is
still a memory in English theological literature of the higher
type, though, except among rare students, the TRUE
INTELLECTUAL SYSTEM OF THE UNIVERSE is remembered
rather than read. It is a mine of Platonism, learning and
sapience, and more than this, it is a deeply reasoned treatise
of its period in opposition to the atheism of that period ; its
points are established victoriously, and turning over the
leaves of the colossal folio one almost regrets that the difficulties of the seventeenth century disturb us no longer and
that their solutions no longer help us. It must be confessed
that Cudworth connects but superficially with Kabbalism, and
the connection, such as it is, need not detain us long. The
chief thesis of the INTELLECTUAL SYSTEM is that behind all

flourished before Judah the Prince. The Talmud is quoted (p. 10), to prove that
R. Simeon studied the Kabbalah in the cave, and that he and his son wrote the ZOHAR
therein, or that part of it which is in the Jerusalem dialect. The Hebrew portions are
referred to other authorships (p. 16). The translated matter is chiefly from the
FAITHFUL SHEPHERD, and follows the Mantua edition of the ZOHAR. (2) LUX IN
TENEBRIS, *quam Zohar Antiquum Judæorum Monumentum, genti suæ occoccatæ præbet, in
denissimis rerum divinarum tenebris, ad mysterium SS. Trinitatis eo facilius appræhendendum, et
Majestatem Christi Divinam non pertinaciter oppugnandam, et Honorem Spiritus Sancti Recen-
tiorum more non fœdandum . . . Studio M. Nicolai Lutkens* (without place or date, but
about the same period as the treatise of Norrelius). In the first two chapters there is
an attempt to prove that the Mystery of the Trinity is concealed in Leviticus xvi. 18,
and Deut. vi. 5. The third chapter investigates Gen. xix. 24—*De Domino qui a Domino
pluit*, in the same interest. The fourth chapter treats of the Lord God of Hosts,
Is. vi. 3 ; and the fifth of the Lord God, *ib.* xlviii. 16. The sixth chapter seeks to prove
that the three supernal SEPHIROTH were names and characters under which pre-Christian
Jews distinguished the Three Persons of the One Divine essence. (3) Compare
with these DIATRIBE PHILOLOGICA *de R. Simeone Filio Jochai auctore Libri Sohar, in qua
viri celeberrimi Christiani Schoettgenii Dissertatio docens R. Simeonum Filium Jochai Religionum
fuisse Christianum modeste examinatur et contrarium potius evincitur, auctore Justo Martino
Glæsenero, Hildesiæ*, 1736. A pamphlet of twenty-two pages.

the tapestries and embroideries of pagan mythology there is the doctrine of monotheism, and that civilised man in reality has never worshipped but one God, whose threefold nature was a " Divine Cabbala " or revelation, successively depraved and adulterated till it almost disappears for Cudworth among the " particular unities " of Proclus and the later Platonists.[1] Among the cloud of witnesses who are convened in support of this view are included the later Rabbinical writers, the HALACOTH of Maimonides, the OLAT TAMID = PERPETUAL OFFERING of Moses Albelda (sixteenth century), the IKKARIM or PRINCIPLES of Joseph Albo (fifteenth century), the commentaries of R. David Kimchi (1160–1235), and the book NITZACHON, references and extracts which at least serve to shew that this Christian divine had attempted some curious exploration in the world of Hebrew literature. His conclusion was " that the Hebrew Doctors and Rabbins have been generally of this persuasion, that the Pagan Nations anciently, at least the intelligent amongst them, acknowledged One Supreme God of the whole world, and that all their other Gods were but Creatures and Inferior Ministers, which were worshipped by them upon these two accounts, either as thinking that the honour done to them redounded to the Supreme, or else that they might be their Mediators and Intercessors, Orators and Negotiators with Him, which inferior Gods of the Pagans were supposed by these Hebrews to be chiefly of two kinds, Angels and Stars or Spheres, the latter of which the Jews as well as Pagans concluded to be animated and intellectual." The question at the present day is chiefly archaic or fantastic, but it has its interest, for it serves to illustrate the strange contrast which exists between the Hebrew mind at the period of Maimonides and at that far distant epoch when the song of the Psalmist described the idols of the Gentiles as " silver and gold, the work of the hands of men."

In addition to the TRUE INTELLECTUAL SYSTEM OF THE UNIVERSE Cudworth published some sermons and a discourse on the TRUE NOTION OF THE LORD'S SUPPER,[2] afterwards translated into Latin by Mosheim, with a confutation representing the consubstantial doctrine of Lutheran theology,[3]

---

[1] For the purposes of this notice I have used the original edition of the TRUE INTELLECTUAL SYSTEM OF THE UNIVERSE, London, 1668.
[2] London, 1676.
[3] This translation appeared in 1733.

and yet again enlarged upon by Edward Pelling in his DIS-COURSE ON THE SACRAMENT. The drift of the thesis is represented sufficiently by the summary of the first chapter : " That it was a custom of the Jews and Heathens to feast upon things sacrificed, and that the custom of the Christians in partaking of the Body and Blood of Christ once sacrificed upon the Cross, in the Lord's Supper, is analogous thereto." It is outside my province to pronounce upon this view, but as a Christian Mystic who holds that sacramentalism is the law of Nature and the law of Grace, it may be remarked in passing that no theory which reduces the Eucharist to a memorial or a religious banquet can be mystically acceptable. Cudworth was by no means a mystic, and the most that his subject afforded was an opportunity to give further evidence of his unusual erudition, and it may be added of no inconsiderable skill in its management. The thesis is mentioned here because it has recourse so frequently to the Rabbinical writers, to the glosses of Nahmanides, the writings of Isaac Abravanel, the MISHNA, the commentary on that work by Rabbi Obadiah, the scholiasts on Judges, rare MSS. of Karaite Jews and so forth. The Zoharic writings are not quoted, but it was because they contained nothing bearing on the matter in hand : had occasion arisen, no doubt Ralph Cudworth would have given evidence of passable familiarity with that great cycle of Kabbalistic literature.

XIV.—THOMAS BURNET

With the Cambridge school of Platonists the name of Thomas Burnet, some time master of the Charterhouse, connects by association rather than the similarity of intellectual pursuits. He entered Christ's College in 1654, when Ralph Cudworth was master, while Henry More was just in his fortieth year. It was probably to the last-named divine that he owed his slight knowledge of the subject which entitles him to mention in this place. The amicable discussion between More and the editor of KABBALA DENUDATA appeared, as we have seen, in that work in the year 1677, but the INTERPRETATION OF THE MIND OF MOSES had preceded it by a number of years. When Burnet published his TELLURIS THEORIA SACRA, he gave no evidence of interest in Platonic or Kabbalistic subjects : it has been described by Brewster as a beautiful geological romance. It is, of course, concerned with the Mosaic scheme of creation, and the more important work which followed it, dealing as it does with the ancient doctrine concerning the origin of things, is really its extension or sequel.[1] In this interesting volume, written elegantly in Latin of the period, *tout un grand chapitre*, as the bibliography of Papus describes it, is devoted to the Kabbalah. As hinted already, it bears no evidence of original research, or indeed of any first-hand knowledge, but it is justifiable by our purpose to ascertain how a literature which fascinated, though it did not convince, the Cambridge Platonists, impressed the liberal mind of a bold and not unlearned thinker belonging to the next generation. We find, as might be anticipated, that Burnet raises no question as to the wisdom of Moses, by which he understood what all other Kabbalistic students have understood also, a knowledge of natural mysteries derived from the Egyptian education of the Jewish lawgiver. He differs, however, from Kabbalists by questioning seriously how much of this wisdom came down to the Israelites. Assuming some tradition of the kind, there could be no doubt that it was depraved in the lapse of time.[2] In particular, the Kabbalah, as we now possess it, abounds in figments of imagination and in nugatory methods. From this statement of a general position, which may be regarded as common ground of criticism, he proceeds to a more detailed examination, and reaches conclusions which are not likely to be challenged at the present day. The debased character of Jewish Tradition in some of its developments must be recognised by those, critical and otherwise, who maintain most earnestly its mystical and theosophical importance.

If we attempt, says Burnet, to separate anything which may remain uncorrupted in the Kabbalah, to divide the genuine from the spurious, we must first of all purge away that numerical, literal, grammatical part which seeks to extract arcane meanings from the alphabet, the Divine Names and the word-book of the Scriptures. The magical and superstitious element must be also purged away. We should bear further in mind, and this, I think, is the most

---

[1] ARCHÆOLOGIÆ PHILOSOPHICÆ, *sive Doctrina Antiqua de Rerum Originibus*, LIBRI DUO, *editio secunda* (the best), London, 1728.
[2] *Fœdissime licet à Neotericis corrupta et adulterata.*

sensible of several secondary points raised in the criticism, that the enunciation of common notions in uncommon language cannot be accepted as any true Kabbalah. The warning which it implies was not less needed a mere genera- tion ago than in the days of Thomas Burnet. The delight in unintelligible language because it is unintelligible was as characteristic of Victorian occult writers, even as of gloom- wrapped Hades according to the Ritual of the Dead, and it is a tendency which has an inscrutable foundation in the entire subject. It would seem indeed that the sphinx who propounds the arcana in terms as monstrous as herself needs only a commonplace to overwhelm her, as in the case of Œdipus.

In accordance with his intention Burnet proceeds to divide the Kabbalah into the Nominal and Real. The first is that which he has specified as worthless—GEMATRIA, TEMURAH, NOTARICON, VOCABULA. Its devices, he says, are the diver- sions of our children, and in truth it would seem hard to decide whether intellectual superiority and philosophical seriousness should be ascribed to rabbinical anagrams or to the apparatus of " Tit : Tat : To." In any case, " they do not belong to sane literature, much less to wisdom."

So far we can accept readily the judgment of Burnet, but there was no novelty in the line taken, even so far back as the second half of the seventeenth century. When he comes, however, to consider what he has agreed to regard as the real Kabbalah, his insufficiency is evident, and his slender knowledge, drawn only from KABBALA DENUDATA, when it does not arrest his judgment, leads him into manifest error. Thus, he tells us that the real Kabbalah contains two things which are important for our consideration, the doctrine of the SEPHIROTH and that of the Four Worlds, but he com- plains that the conception which underlies the former does not appear clearly. With the help of the Lexicon of Rosen- roth he decides finally that they are emanations from God.[1] He sets forth what he can glean from that source concerning KETHER and CHOKMAH, and then surrenders the inquiry in the hope of finding more intelligible statements concerning the Four Worlds.[2] He concludes, however, that the con-

---

[1] Elsewhere, he attempts to consider their significance in connection with the axiom—*ex nihilo nihil fit*.

[2] He mentions in addition to the SEPHIROTH and the Four Worlds, the thirty-two Paths of Wisdom, from the SEPHER YETZIRAH and its commentary, and the Fifty Gates

demnation of all the pseudo-mystics of Kabbalism, Theosophy and Hermeticism is that of the unbelievers who continued to love the darkness rather than the light when the light was come already into the world.[1] He assumes, as might be expected, that the BOOK OF OCCULTATION is the most important part of the ZOHAR and, glancing at the commentaries of Isaac de Loria and of Hirtz on the tract in question and its developments, confesses his inability to understand either from text or interpreters what is meant by the symbolism of the Vast and the Lesser Countenance. "We are all of us liable some time or other to be distracted by reasoning, but it is a common complaint of the mind among Orientals to be distracted by allegories."

To sum his general position : We know from Maimonides that the Hebrews once possessed many mysteries concerning things divine, but that they have perished.[2] It is at the same time scarcely possible that all foundation should be wanting to the Kabbalah, yet if its doctrines were openly and clearly set forth, it is hard to say whether they would move us to laughter or astonishment.

Thomas Burnet has higher claims on our tolerance than his ability as a critic of Kabbalism, and his mind was not of that order which could be expected to understand or sympathise with the aspirations embraced by Theosophy. He was one of the rare precursors of liberal Theology, and he is said to have closed the path of his promotion by venturing to express an opinion that the story of the Garden of Eden should not be understood literally. In a later treatise on the FAITH AND DUTIES OF CHRISTIANS,[3] he is thought to have excluded so much which seemed to him doubtful or unimportant in accepted doctrine that it is questionable whether even Christianity remained. A posthumous work on eschatology and the resurrection [4] maintained that the punishment of the wicked would terminate ultimately in their salvation. I should add that some pretended English versions of the Archæological Philosophy do not represent the original, and in particular omit altogether the Kabbalistic section.

---

of Providence " through which Moses attained his marvellous science, and concealed the same in the Pentateuch," *i.e.*, according to the Kabbalists.
[1] John iii. 19-21.
[2] THE GUIDE OF THE PERPLEXED. Part i, c. 71.
[3] DE FIDE ET OFFICIIS CHRISTIANORUM.
[4] DE STATU MORTUORUM ET RESURGENTIUM.

XV.—SAINT-MARTIN

The life and doctrine of Louis Claude de Saint-Martin, the Unknown Philosopher, who at the end of the eighteenth century and amidst the torch-lights of the Revolution diffused in France the higher spirit of Mysticism, having been the subject of my studies elsewhere,[1] I shall refer to him here only as the recipient of an Esoteric Tradition through Martines de Pasqually, the genesis of which remains undetermined, though it was termed Rosicrucian by his initiator, and has been designated Swedenborgian subsequently by one of his interpreters in France. It is a Tradition which differs from other presentations of Theosophical Doctrine, and it has little in common with what we know or may infer concerning Rosicrucian teaching. In the RÉINTEGRATION DES ÊTRES of Pasqually,[2] and in the Catechisms of the Masonic Rite propagated by him, which are also most probably his work, the Tradition is presented in a crude manner. It was developed by Saint-Martin, who indeed brought to it a gift of genius which was wanting in his instructor. Now, Saint-Martin was a man who cared very little, and does not scruple to say so, for purely traditional doctrines, at least as traditional, nor did he shew much deference towards doctors of authority therein. He considered books at best a makeshift method of instruction, though he wrote many ; he preferred learning at first hand from God, Man and the Universe. Till he came under the influence of Jacob Böhme he neither quoted nor possessed "authorities," with the exception of the Scriptures. He drew, of course, from the source of his initiation, but he never mentions it in any clear manner, except in his correspondence and his life-notes, both published posthumously. There is nothing to indicate that he had read Kabbalistic literature : there is every presumption that he did not. Some of his lesser doctrines possess notwithstanding a certain Kabbalistic complexion. There is that in particular concerning the Great Name which I have developed at some length in a study to which I have referred, but it has lost all

---

[1] See A. E. Waite : THE LIFE OF LOUIS CLAUDE DE SAINT-MARTIN, *the Unknown Philosopher, and the Substance of his Transcendental Doctrine*, London, Philip Wellby, 1901. See also my SAINT-MARTIN, *the French Mystic*, 1922.

[2] It is right to say that Kenneth Mackenzie, in his CYCLOPÆDIA OF FREEMASONRY, attributes to him three published works which, so far as I am aware, are unknown.

touch with Kabbalism in the hands of Saint-Martin. So also he has a complex system of mystic numbers which might suggest the Rabbinical NOTARIKON, but it is entirely out of line with all anterior speculations on this subject, and makes the question of its origin one of the problems in his history.[1] I conclude that Pasqually, whom I take to have been a sincere and perhaps even a saintly man, as his Masonic school was almost a seminary of sanctity, derived from a source which retained some filtrations of Kabbalism, and that they were brought over by Saint-Martin without any historical associations whatever.[2] He has therefore little title to be included among defenders and expounders of Kabbalistic doctrine, which would have come as a surprise to himself. This was done, however, by French occult writers [3] belonging to so-called Martinist and other groups of the late nineteenth and early twentieth centuries, and by Dr. Papus especially, who seemed anxious to annex anyone, from Shakespeare to the author of SUPERNATURAL RELIGION.

XVI.—ÉLIPHAS LÉVI

Between the period of Saint-Martin and that of Alphonse Louis Constant, who is the subject of this notice, the French literature of Kabbalism may be said to have been initiated rather than to have received a new impetus by the publication of Adolphe Franck, to whose views on the subject of post-Christian religious philosophy among the Jews, I have made frequent reference already.[4] I have indicated also that its superficial value remains unimpaired after the lapse of eighty years, and indeed modern criticism has in certain definite respects reverted unawares to his standpoint, as regards not only the antiquity of Zoharic Tradition but of much of the body of the ZOHAR. Franck's work has, of course, its limitations, and it is known that his excerpts from Kabbalistic books were subjected to severe strictures in Germany ; but for an accomplished and luminous review of the whole

---

[1] It is not impossible that it derives from his first school and therefore from Pasqually, who was sole instructor therein.

[2] That man is superior to the angels, and may even instruct them, is, I think, the most convincing instance in Saint-Martin of such a filtration. This notion is found in the ZOHAR, and developed by some of its commentators.

[3] More especially in the case of the so-called facetious allegory LE CROCODILE, in which it may be said safely that there is not a single trace of Kabbalism.

[4] LA KABBALE ou la Philosophie Religieuse des Hébreux. Par Ad. Franck, Paris, 1843.

subject nothing of later date can be said to have superseded it. Its analyses of the SEPHER YETZIRAH and of the ZOHAR, together with its delineations of correspondences between the philosophical school of Kabbalism and the schools of Plato, of Alexandria, of Philo, created French knowledge on the subject, and together with the researches of Munk, published some few years subsequently, have been the main source of that knowledge down to recent times, the part of dream and reverie being provided by the writings of Éliphas Lévi. As regards both methods and motives, Franck and Lévi are located at opposite poles. The first was an academic writer having no occult interests ; the second claimed not only initiation but adeptship, not only the ordinary resources of scholarship focussed on a literary and historical problem but all advantages which could be derived from an exclusive possession of its master key.

Among the lesser difficulties of recent Kabbalistic criticism the proper allocation of Alphonse Louis Constant in the throng of students and expositors was not without its gravity till I sought on my own part to reflect some light thereon. Whether in France or in England few had approached the subject with sympathies in the direction of occult arts and speculations who did not owe their introduction to Éliphas Lévi. I speak, of course, of the period subsequent to 1850,[1] and I may add that few persons thus initiated did anything but read the interpretations of their first leader into the obscure body of dogma which comprises the Esoteric Tradition of the Jews. If it be necessary, therefore, to make void rather

---

[1] Although the treatise of Franck had, as we have seen, preceded Lévi's interpretations by several years. So far as I can recollect the professed adept never referred to the sympathetic criticism and defence of the more academic writer. Prior to 1843 the most extraordinary ignorance must have prevailed upon the subject in France, since it was possible for a distinguished philosopher to write as follows :—" When Christian philosophy made its appearance in the world it crushed Paganism and Theurgy, and in the second century humanity was made subject to a severe régime, which set aside Mysticism. It did not reappear till the fourteenth and fifteenth centuries in certain schools of Italy and Germany. This new Mysticism, called Kabbalah, from a name known already in the schools of Alexandria, but since entirely disappeared, and signifying oral tradition, issued from the bosom of the scholastic, and acted with the instruments of the scholastic, as formerly the neoplatonist Porphyry evoked with Platonic words. The Kabbalah of the fifteenth century put in operation bizarre formulæ, magic squares and circles, mysterious numbers, by the power of which the demons of hell and the divinities of heaven were compelled, as it was pretended, to appear in obedience to the wand. Hence the mystical ecstasies of Raymund Lully, who attracted such zealous partisans and furious enemies, causing blood to flow ; hence the delirium which brought Bruno to the stake." Victor Cousin : COURS DE PHILOSOPHIE, Paris, 1836. It would seem impossible to record a greater number of inaccuracies, or to display more signal ignorance, within the dimensions of a paragraph.

than reduce largely the authority attributed to Éliphas Lévi, I muſt expeɕt even now to alienate the sympathy of his remaining French admirers ; but this is only a queſtion of the moment, and so far as it is possible to take a plain course in the matter there can be no need for hesitation.

I do not think that Lévi ever made an independent ſtatement upon any hiſtorical faɕt in which the leaſt confidence could be reposed. He never presented the sense of an author whom he was reviewing in a way which could be said to reproduce that author faithfully. As in the one case he embroidered hiſtory by the help of a decorative imagination, so it occurred frequently that he attributed to an old author the kind of sense which it would be intereſting to find in old authors, but it is not met with except by the mediation of a magician with the transmuting power of Abbé Conſtant. He takes, for example, a perfeɕtly worthless little book by Abbot Trithemius, which does not refleɕt the opinions of that learned Benediɕtine, but is simply a trifle addressed to a German prince explaining how some persons in antiquity diſtributed the government of the world among certain planetary intelligences, ruling successively and reassuming rule in rotation. He inveſts it with the importance of a grand and sublime achievement of prophetic science, whereas it does not shew half the acumen of our empirical friend Noſtradamus, and is equalled in any year of grace by the almanacks of Raphael and Zadkiel. Here is an inſtance of what Lévi reads into an author. Nor do we need to depart from this unhappy little treatise to teſt Lévi's reliability over an express matter of faɕt. He tells us that the forecaſt of Trithemius closes with a proclamation of universal monarchy in the year 1879. Trithemius says nothing of the kind, but modeſtly remarks that the gift of prophecy, so generously attributed to him by his reviewer, would be required to discern anything beyond that period. I mention this matter, to which I have drawn attention long since,[1] because it is necessary to exhibit the quality of mind which was brought by Éliphas Lévi to the illumination of Kabbaliſtic and occult literature. The deliberations of the Holy Synods will be found to have suffered many transfigurations through the medium of their interpreter, and any matter of

---

[1] MYSTERIES OF MAGIC, a Digeſt of the Writings of Éliphas Lévi. Second and revised edition, 1897.

sharp fact in the hands of this unaccountable juggler is brought over into the realm of myth.

I need not dwell upon the miserable plight of every Hebrew quotation in those works which he may be supposed to have passed for press. No ordinary carelessness would account for such blunders, nor need they be explained by supposing that he was utterly ignorant of their language. His acquaintance must have been slender enough, but it is not necessary to be proficient in Hebrew or indeed in Chinese to ensure the accuracy of a few excerpts. The excerpts in Éliphas Lévi " no one can speak and no one can spell." But even in simpler matters his blunders are incredible. He gives the three mother-letters of the Hebrew alphabet inaccurately,[1] which for an accredited student of SEPHER YETZIRAH is almost as inexcusable as if an English author erred in enumerating the vowels of our own language.

The instance, however, which seems impressive and even final, occurs in a posthumous work entitled the BOOK OF SPLENDOUR.[2] Of this the first part is intended as a compressed translation of the GREATER HOLY SYNOD. Now, Lévi says that the deliberations of this Conclave are contained in a Hebrew treatise entitled IDRA SUTA, and these words appear accordingly at the head of his version. But the IDRA SUTA, or more correctly ZOUTA, is the name of the LESSER SYNOD, while IDRAH RABBA is that appertaining to the record of the Greater Assembly. What should we think of the qualifications of a commentator on the books of the Old Testament who informed us that the word BERESHITH was applied to Deuteronomy ?

That in spite of his slipshod criticism, his careless reading and his malpractices in historical matters the writings of Éliphas Lévi are not without a certain interest is true up to a certain point. What seems to distinguish him from all other occult writers is not his knowledge as occultist, but the peculiar genius of interpretation which he applied to that knowledge, the surprising results which he could obtain from an old doctrine, even as from an old author. They were not reliable results ; they were not in harmony with any secret knowledge ; they represented the standpoint of the

---

[1] LA CLEF DES GRANDS MYSTÈRES, Paris, 1861, pp. 199, 200.
[2] LE LIVRE DES SPLENDEURS, *contenant le Soleil Judaïque* . . . *Études sur les Origines de la Kabbale*, &c., Paris, 1894.

agnostic rather than the transcendentalist ; and they afflicted the transcendental standpoint in consequence, but they wore the guise and they spoke the language of occultism, and it is they which have fascinated his students, they which once multiplied his admirers, they also which imparted at their period a new impulse to the study of occult speculations. This is equivalent to saying that the influence of Éliphas Lévi does not make for a proper understanding of occult reveries, and as concerns the Kabbalah that it reads a meaning into the Esoteric Tradition of Israel which is not in harmony therewith.

Let us take, for example, his inverted text of the first chapter of Genesis, for which he claims a Kabbalistic foundation.[1] It is needless to say that it neither has nor could have any rabbinical authority and that it first occurred to the imaginative mind of a Frenchman in the second half of the nineteenth century. As it exceeds quotation in this place I must refer the reader to the work in which I have rendered it at length.[2] It may be described shortly as replacing the history of creation by God with that of God's creation by man. It is, if you prefer it, the evolution of the God-idea in humanity. As an exercise of ingenuity it is notable and high diversion, but the point at which the sober critic must diverge from the interpreter is that " this occult Genesis was thought out by Moses before writing his own."

Let us take another case which, though it brings us to the same question, is more perhaps to our purpose, because it is a construction placed upon Zoharic symbolism. For Éliphas Lévi the MACROPROSOPUS or Great Countenance of the ZOHAR is the evolution of the idea of God[3] from the shadow divinities represented by the Kings of Edom. MICROPROSOPUS is the grand night of faith. The one is the God of the wise, the other the idol of the vulgar. The one is the great creative hypothesis, the other the dark figure, the restricted hypothesis. As it is to the Lesser Countenance that the name of TETRA-GRAMMATON is attributed,[4] it follows that the secret of the ZOHAR is the alleged utterance of the adept to the recipiendary of the Egyptian Mysteries : " Osiris is a black god." MICRO-

---

[1] LA CLEF DES GRANDS MYSTÈRES, pp. 334 et seq. MYSTERIES OF MAGIC, second edition, London, 1897, pp. 108 et seq.

[2] i.e. : THE MYSTERIES OF MAGIC, first and second editions, London, 1886, 1897.

[3] It follows that he was either unacquainted with the hypothesis of AIN SOPH or elected to ignore it.

[4] The letter VAU and that only is referable to the Divine Son.

prosopus is, however, " neither the Ahriman of the Persians nor the evil principle of the Manichæans, but a more exalted concept, a mediating shadow between the infinite light and the feeble eyes of humanity ; a veil made in the likeness of humanity with which God Himself deigns to cover His glory ; a shadow which contains the reason of all mysteries, explaining the terrible Deity of the prophets, who threatens and inspires fear.   It is the God of the priests, the God who exacts sacrifices, the God who sleeps frequently and is awakened by the trumpets of the temple, the God who repents having made man, but, conquered by prayers and offerings, is appeased when on the point of punishing." [1]

That this interpretation has attracted a few unversed students who did not have the texts before them may be no cause for surprise.   It was pleasant to make acquaintance with a supposed esoteric tradition in which all theological difficulties seem to dissolve together.   While on the one hand it might be little short of incredible that the Kabbalah should conceal so reasonable and elegant a doctrine, the putative symbolism was on the other so plausibly accounted for that it encouraged an easy acceptance.   When we come, however, to the analysis of text and construction we find that the one does not warrant the other and that the evolution of the God-idea in humanity had no more occurred to the authors of the Zohar than it would have occurred, e.g., to Grant Allen to write a Book of Occultation.   It is not a case in which it is necessary to tax space and patience by the exhaustive demonstration of a negative.   The validity of the construction is seen by the text with which it is connected.   We know how much was read by Fitzgerald into Omar Khayyám, but his verses are literal and line upon line compared with the high fantasy of Lévi's Zoharistic analysis.   As an example of this it is sufficient to refer the student who may desire an express case for comparison to the forty third section of Idra Rabba as it stands in the Latin version of Rosenroth and the excursus on Justice in the Book of Splendour which follows, says Éliphas Lévi, the text of Rabbi Simeon.   It is mere illusion and mockery.[2]

Another extreme instance is the fantastic inversion of the Sephiroth which gives despotism an absolute power as the dark side of the supreme power in Kether ; blind faith as

---

[1] Le Livre des Splendeurs, pp. 69, 70.   [2] Ibid., pp. 86 et seq.

the shadow of eternal wisdom in CHOKMAH; so called immutable dogma, which is at the same time inevitably progressive, as the antithesis of active intelligence in BINAH; blind faith again as the inversion of spiritual beauty in TIPHERETH; divine vengeance as opposed to eternal justice in GEBURAH; willing sacrifice as the shadow of infinite mercy in CHESED; abnegation and voluntary renunciation as opposed to the eternal victory of goodness in NETZACH; eternal hell as opposed to the eternity of goodness, presumably in HOD; celibacy and sterility as opposed to the fecundity of goodness, presumably in JESOD; while MALKUTH, corresponding to the number of creation, is said to have no negative aspect, because celibacy and sterility produce nothing.[1] Without dwelling on the carelessness of the arrangement, in part sephirotic and in part transposing and abandoning the sephirotic series, or on the failing ingenuity which repeats the same contrasts, I may point out that advanced views on the transfiguration of dogmas and on vicarious atonement are not the findings of illuminated rabbins in the middle ages or earlier but belong to the excursions of modern thought, and that since arbitrary tabulations and artificial contrasts are easy exercises, and can be varied to infinity—more especially when the text itself is scouted—we may appreciate the contrasts here created by the evidence which supports them and that is simply the magisterial affirmation of the interpreter.

It remains to say that Éliphas Lévi represents the invention of a new and gratuitous phase in the study of the Kabbalah, undertaken neither as an object of research nor as a part of the history of philosophy. The students whom we have considered heretofore have been either Christian propagandists or writers by the way whose connection with the subject is unsubstantial; but the standpoint of Lévi is that there is a religion behind all religions and that it is the veiled mystery of Kabbalism, from which all have issued and into which all return. Christian doctrine, in particular, is unintelligible, apart from the light cast on it by the deliberations of the Holy Assemblies. Now it is precisely this standpoint, its derivatives and connections, that created French occultism in the generation which followed Lévi. In the past the magician was content to evoke spirits, the alchemist to produce gold when he could, the astrologer to spell the dubious

---

[1] LE LIVRE DES SPLENDEURS, pp. 74 *et seq.*

messages of the stars, the Kabbalist of sorts to be wise in anagrams and word-puzzles, but these things were regarded henceforward as parts of a greater mystery, and in a very true sense Éliphas Lévi was the magus who opened before his readers the wide field of this imaginary view. He had no antecedents in scholarship but he drew suggestions from there and here in the texts, and he wrote it all up and he coloured it. The more he wrote and the more he coloured there is no need to say that his delineations diverged the further from all likeness to his sources, and so of all claims thereon. This is illustrated in a plenary sense by his posthumous MYSTÈRES DE LA KABBALE, 1923, and by his letters to Baron Spedalieri which have been printed through the moons and the years in LE VOILE D'ISIS of Paris.

XVII.—TWO ACADEMICAL CRITICS

Having regard to the fact that, as already stated, there has been always in England a small number of persons who have been interested, mostly through sympathy with subjects called esoteric, in the study of the Kabbalah, it may appear incredible that there are no memorials of their interest between the period of Thomas Vaughan and the year 1865, a space of two centuries. There is a similar hiatus in the merely academical interest represented by Burnet. I do not say that there have been nowhere any references to Kabbalism ; they may have made up in number what they wanted in learning and authority ; and a few curious gleanings might be gathered from early editions of the larger encyclopædias ; but as there has been no mystical student who wrote anything of moment concerning it, so there has been no scholar apart from such interests who has treated the subject seriously. The work of Dr. Ginsburg, once so well known that even now it scarcely needs description, may be said to have marked an epoch, because it was the first clear, simple and methodised account of Kabbalistic doctrine and literature. It leaves naturally much to be desired, as it arose in an informal manner out of a meeting of some literary society in Liverpool, and the nucleus of the short paper produced for the occasion in question was afterwards expanded into a slender volume. It is a meagre measure that is thus allotted to so large a subject, but it was as much as might be warranted by the existing interest, which is determined sharply by the fact that no second edition was needed until quite recent years. There is good reason to believe that it did not represent Dr. Ginsburg's knowledge at the period, yet it went much further than encyclopædic or theological notices. Dr. Ginsburg is entitled to a place among Christian students of the Kabbalah because of his conversion in 1846, and I purpose in this brief notice, which is concerned mainly with a standpoint, to connect him with the name of a writer who belonged to his period in France. Both were accomplished Hebrew scholars ; both of Jewish origin. Dr. Ginsburg did much valuable work in connection with the Trinitarian Bible Society, while M. Isidore Loëb, so far as I am aware, remained in the faith of Jewry, and it is therefore only by way of contrast with his English prototype that I am warranted in referring to him in this place. There was a period of a quarter of a century between the two writers, and as their point of view is in general respects similar and indeed suggests that the French critic may have profited by the English, it is interesting to note the one matter over which they diverge, namely, the authorship of the Zohar.

It has been objected against Dr. Ginsburg that he draws chiefly from Continental writers, reflects their views and shews little independent research. His quotations from the Zohar are, it is said, derived from Franck, and are open therefore to the harsh criticisms passed on them many years ago in Germany. These matters are perhaps of slight importance to those who are in search of elementary knowledge, whose purpose is served well enough by the translations of Franck and for whom a digest of fairly informed criticism is about the best text-book possible. The fact itself made Dr. Ginsburg's little treatise the English representative of a particular school, being that of the hostile judgment which refers the Zohar to the authorship, more or less exclusive, of Moses de Leon. In England Dr. Schiller-Szinessy's article on the Midrashim in the ninth edition of the Encyclopædia Britannica, referring the nucleus of the book to Mishnic times and regarding Simeon ben Yohai as author in the same sense that R. Johanan was author of the Palestine Talmud, has helped to create another and more qualified manner of regarding the Zohar. The critical objections of Dr. Ginsburg derived from the work itself have

been disposed of in the majority of cases, and the few which
still remain can establish nothing conclusively. They have
been noticed briefly elsewhere in the present work. The fact
that M. Isidore Loëb, who so closely reproduced Dr. Ginsburg, abandons the theory of unqualified imposture, signifies
that some progress was made with the subject towards the
end of the nineteenth century, and as it is one of the purposes
of the present study to place the evidence of this and analogous
facts before the English reader, I feel warranted in giving
space to the following synopsis of M. Isidore Loëb's essay,
as it may not be accessible to some who are acquainted with
that of Dr. Ginsburg. There is a literary excellence in the
one which is fairly precluded by the circumstance that called
the other into being, and it is a matter of regret that the sole
contribution of M. Loëb towards the elucidation of Kabbalistic literature occurs in LA GRANDE ENCYCLOPÉDIE. M.
Loëb was, however, for some time president of the publication
committee of the French Society of Jewish Studies. His
other literary work comprises a monograph on Jewish
chroniclers, a table of Jewish calendars, and some observations
on the situation of the Israelites at his period in Turkey,
Serbia and Roumania. In the essay with which we are
concerned he records the opinion that the term Kabbalah
may not be anterior to the tenth century and that the claim
to antiquity which it signifies is supported by no written
monument. It seems difficult in the nature of the case that
it should be so substantiated. M. Loëb, however, makes a
very proper distinction between the metaphysical or mystical
Kabbalah and the gross thaumaturgy connected with the
practical branch. To the original elements of the first he
ascribes, like all critics, a high antiquity, but not, as it need
scarcely be said, of a kind which would permit it to be
regarded as the perpetuation of an indigenous, much less
an uncorrupted Tradition. As we have had occasion to
see, this claim is no longer made by any competent student
of the subject. For M. Loëb the Kabbalah is a part of the
age-old reverie which seeks to explain the disparity between
an infinite God and a finite world by means of intermediate
creations through which the Divine Power descends, diminishing in its spiritual qualities as it removes further from its
source, and becoming more imperfect and material. The
difficulty is removed by this anthropomorphic process much

in the same manner as the difficulty of a *terra firma* for the elephant which supports the universe is disposed of in Indian cosmology by assuming the tortoise. In other words, it is not removed at all. At the same time the explanation of Emanationist Mysticism, which is not all Mysticism, as M. Loëb seems to assume, is not in the last analysis open to greater objection than any other speculative attempt to bridge the gulf between finite and infinite. Passing from this consideration the French critic discovers the foundation of Kabbalistic Theosophy in the Scriptural personification of Wisdom, and the chief elements of its symbolism in the prophetical books, about which points there is no question whatever, and they are matters of common knowledge. So also he refers correctly the name or catchword of the ZOHAR to Daniel xii. 3. He cites the number of the beast in the Apocalypse, as every one has cited it before him, in illustration of GEMATRIA; but he raises a less hackneyed point by suggesting, on the authority of Munk, that TEMURAH was employed by Jeremiah. He does better service by reminding us that the Essenians attached great importance to symbolical angelology, and that each individual of that obscure fraternity was required to remember accurately the names of the angels. It is, however, among the Jews of Alexandria that, following several previous authorities, he discovers the main germs of Kabbalistic Mysticism; but in this connection he cites only the Platonic doctrine of the Logos, its influence on the Greek Septuagint and on the Chaldee version of the Old Testament.

On the whole, I do not think that M. Loëb's critical faculty, or indeed his erudition, is at all comparable to his graceful synthetic talent. To cite a crucial instance, he dismisses one testimony to Kabbalistic Tradition by saying: "Despite the contrary assertions of the TALMUD, we refuse to believe that Johanan ben Zoccai (*sic*) or his contemporaries devoted themselves to mystical doctrines or secret things." It is to the second century that he refers the "ravages" of Gnosticism among the Jews of Palestine, and cites various subtleties of the doctors which arose at that period. He sketches the decline of the Palestine Schools and the rise of those of Babylon, "the traditional country of Magic." He cites from Rab, the Babylonian of the third century, that passage which I have mentioned elsewhere, and confesses that it is another germ of the mediæval Kabbalah, that is, the doctrine of the SEPHIROTH. With a rapid pen he runs over the great impetus given to Jewish literature under Arabian influence from the middle of the seventh century. He refers to the ninth century that all-important treatise entitled THE MEASURES OF THE STATURE OF GOD, which is, in fact, as we have seen, the first form of the Zoharistic MACROPROSOPUS, and is mentioned apparently by Agobad. He places the ALPHABET of Akiba, dealing with the symbolism of the Hebrew letters, about the same period, together with a crowd of apocalyptic treatises, including PIRKE of R. Eliezer, which has an elaborate doctrine of Pneumatology. Among all these he distinguishes the SEPHER YETZIRAH as occupying a place and deserving a rank apart. He admits its comparative antiquity, seeming to regard it as immediately posterior to the TALMUD, which he affirms to have been finished A.D. 499. He describes it as a philosophy and a gnosis, and supposes it to have been written in Palestine under the direct influence of Christian and Pagan Gnosticism. The opinion is interesting, but, of course, entirely conjectural, and as the doctrine of emanation is not clear in the SEPHER YETZIRAH, we should not accept hastily the theory of an influence which assumes it. When he observes further that its fountain-heads must be sought in Azriel's Commentary on the SEPHIROTH and in the BAHIR, I fail to understand the grounds on which he attributes a superior antiquity to those works. He assigns to the ZOHAR itself a Spanish origin, but does not press the authorship of Moses de Leon. Among the fine points of his criticism is a picture of the pure Talmudists of the period of Maimonides, especially those of the Peninsula and the South of France, living under the influence of Arabian philosophy, without philosophical doctrine, without perspective, having only the literature of the Law, and the anthropomorphic Mysticism of the Jewish Schools of Northern France, between which the Kabbalah rose up as a mediator, " completing Talmudism by philosophy, correcting philosophy by Theosophy, and anthropomorphic Mysticism by philosophic Mysticism."

XVIII.—THE MODERN SCHOOL OF FRENCH KABBALISM

Éliphas Lévi died in 1875, having founded, as it must be admitted, a new school of occult philosophy, not in its way without a certain brilliance but built on sands of dream. For the ten years which preceded his death he had made no outward sign. There are mendacious rumours of the initiations which were offered him and of the Rites which he remodelled ; but all that is known certainly is that he collected around him a small group of private students who looked up to him as their master, regarded his fantastic speculations almost in the light of revelation and, following his leading, accepted the Kabbalah as a great synthesis of religious belief. It was not till another ten years, after his death, had elapsed that any visible result of his influence became manifest. During that period a marked change had come over speculative thought there and here in Paris ; many of the younger generation broke away from the traditions of positivism and materialism, and, without returning to the Church, passed off in the direction of occultism, and occultism moderated by science became a characteristic of the succeeding epoch. When about the year 1884 the Theosophical Society opened a lodge in Paris and began the publication of a monthly magazine, some few of the French occultists gathered round it, and one of the most noticeable in the group was Gérard Encausse, the young *chef de laboratoire* of an eminent doctor celebrated in connection with one of the schools of hypnotism. His first contributions appeared in the pages of Le Lotus and his first work, on the elements of occult science, so called, was published under the auspices of the Society. A rupture took place, however, and the seceding members, abandoning for the moment their interest in *la métaphysique orientale*, established, so to speak, a school of western occultism, of which Dr. Encausse became the moving spirit and Éliphas Lévi the most immediate inspiration of the past. The ostensible characteristics of this school were Neo-Martinism and Neo-Rosicrucianism, but the conceptions associated with these names suffered developments which effaced their original outlines. So also the admired masterpieces of Éliphas Lévi became a point of departure quite as much as a guide. It is, broadly speaking, nevertheless, the work of Lévi which was continued, and along with other occult interests the study of the Kabbalah was revived under the reflected impulsion of his enthusiasm. It was in no sense an exhaustive and still less a critical study ; it began by taking too much for granted and its textual knowledge was negligible. There was, however, no writer of this group who had not something to tell concerning Jewish Theosophy, while its activity engendered consequences of much the same kind outside its immediate circle.

The two names which most call for notice in this connection are Dr. Gérard Encausse and Stanislas de Guaita. The literary and occult antecedents of the first writer are Saint Yves d'Alveydre, Fabre d'Olivet, Éliphas Lévi and Adolphe Franck. From the first he derived a systematic view of Jewish history, from the second his notion of esoteric mysteries concealed in the Hebrew language, from Lévi unfortunately a burden of historical suppositions, and from Franck an academic precedent for the modified antiquity of Kabbalistic literature. On the other hand, Stanislas de Guaita belonged to a literary school of occultism and as such he connects with Sar Péladan. I propose to consider the position of both these writers in short sub-sections and to connect them with a third who is governed by very different motives and principles.

A.—Papus

The word Papus signifies physician, and according to a commentary of Éliphas Lévi on the Nuctemeron of Apollonius, it is the title of a genius belonging to the first hour of that mystical period, understood, in Lévi's words, as "the day of the night." It is also the pseudonym adopted by Gérard Encausse, head of the French Martinists and once leader of occult activity in Paris. Papus became a voluminous writer, methodical and laborious, and some of his work had value along its own lines. From the beginning of his literary life he was occupied with Kabbalistic questions, and so far back as the year 1887 he made the first French translation of the Sepher Yetzirah, which appeared in the theosophical review Lotus. It is not a satisfactory version and was superseded speedily by that of Meyer Lambert, as Papus recognised himself. He appears to have depended on the Latin text in the collection of Pistorius which renders throughout the words "ineffable Sephiroth" as Sephiroth præter ineffabile, thus making the Book of Formation responsible for the Theology of Ain Soph, and it is a point of critical importance that it is not to be found therein.

In 1892 Papus published a methodical summary of the

Kabbalah, together with a bibliography, which is again open to criticism. The bibliography was constructed upon the most debatable of all principles, viz., the increase of numerical importance by adventitious elements which are not Kabbalistic at all, and again by the inclusion of works which were evidently unknown to the writer, with results that are occasionally ludicrous. Thus, in the one case, among books in the French language, we find Figuier's ALCHEMY AND THE ALCHEMISTS, which contains no reference to the Kabbalah ; Saint-Martin's CROCODILE, a clumsy satire open to the same objection ; Eckartshausen's CLOUD ON THE SANCTUARY, also non-Kabbalistic ; and a number of esoteric romances which have as much claim to insertion as Baudelaire's translation of Poe.[1] In the other case, Dr. Papus, who was only superficially acquainted with English, classified among Kabbalistic writings Massey's translation of Du Prel's PHILOSOPHY OF MYSTICISM, my own LIVES OF ALCHEMYSTICAL PHILOSOPHERS, Dr. Hartmann's WHITE AND BLACK MAGIC, a catalogue of second-hand books issued by George Redway, and, unfortunate above all other instances, the once celebrated SUPERNATURAL RELIGION. The bibliography of works in the Latin language is better done, though it contains some useless numbers.

As regards the treatise itself, it is little more than a series of tabulated quotations from Franck, Loëb, de Guaita, Kircher and so forth, with a number of serviceable diagrams derived from similar sources. It was passable at its period as a French introduction to the subject for the use of French occultists. But it made the mistake of attributing importance to the debased Hebrew influences found in the literature of Ceremonial Magic. Having appreciated in another section the claim of the clavicles to recognition in Kabbalistic literature, it is here only necessary to say that in the work under notice there is no attempt to justify their inclusion, which is explained by the sympathies of the author, who in this connection owes something to the French version of Molitor.

Dr. Papus had also a bias common to the majority of French

---

[1] Another instance is Julien Lejay : LA SCIENCE OCCULTE APPLIQUÉE à l'économie politique, in a volume of composite authorship, entitled La Science Secrète. I may observe, however, that this volume contains a paper on the Kabbalah by Papus, subsequently embodied in his larger work. Outside this, the only reference to the subject is in an essay by F. C. Barlet, which refers the origin of the Kabbalah to the fourth century.

and English occultists of Victorian days, and by this bias he was led irresistibly to prefer the imperfect equipment of past authority to the result of modern scholarship. In Egyptology he knew no higher name than that of Court de Gebelin ; in problems of Hebrew philology his great master was Fabre d'Olivet ; and hence, on the one hand, we shall not be surprised to find that he regarded P. Christian as a source of serious information concerning Egyptian Mysteries of Initiation, or, on the other, that he considered the Hebrew of the Mosaic books to be identical with the idiom of ancient Egypt.[1] The position of writers who base their views on language-studies undertaken at the beginning of the last century is not more reasonable than would be that of a person who should attempt now to defend the antiquity of the Rowley poems. But it might be scarcely worth while to speak of it were it not for the consequences that it involves, at least in the case of Papus, as, for example, his views on the descent of Esoteric Tradition from Moses and its identity with the Mysteries of Egypt.

I have said sufficient to indicate that the historical aspect, so far as it exists in Papus, is altogether unsatisfactory, and there is indeed no need to reckon with it. As regards the special motive of our own inquiry, the standpoint of Papus is that the Kabbalah is the keystone of all the Western Tradition of Transcendentalism ; that the alchemists were Kabbalists, and so also all mystical fraternities, whether Templars, Rosicrucians, Martinists or Freemasons ; that the source of the Kabbalah was Moses and that Moses drew from Egypt, whence the Kabbalah is the most complete summary in existence of Egyptian Mysteries. Why those mysteries

---

[1] He was not alone among French writers of his day in taking a similar view. M. Edouard Schuré, in LES GRANDS INITIÉS, Esquisse de l'Histoire Secrète des Réligions, Paris, 1889, maintains that, " owing to the education of Moses, there can be no doubt that he wrote Genesis in Egyptian hieroglyphics, having three senses, and confided their keys and oral explanations to his successors. In the time of Solomon it was rendered into Phœnician characters, and after the captivity of Babylon into Aramaic Chaldean characters by Esdras. The esoteric sense was lost more and more, and the Greek translators had a very slight acquaintance therewith." In this case it may have been the remnant of such knowledge which made the Jews so hostile to the Septuagint. M. Schuré continues : " Jerome, despite his serious intention and his great mind, penetrated only to the primitive sense when he made his Latin translation. The secret sense does, however, remain buried in the Hebrew text, which plunges by its roots into the sacred tongue of the temples," and the writer affirms that it flashes forth at times for the intuitive, that for seers it " shines forth once more in the phonetic structure of the words adopted or created by Moses," and that by the study of this phoneticism, by the keys which the Kabbalah furnishes, and by comparative esotericism, " it is permitted us at this day to reconstruct the veritable Genesis." Pp. 180, 181.

should have an absorbing claim on our respect does not appear from Papus, but the sub-surface understanding is undoubtedly that a Tradition of Absolute Religion has been perpetuated from antiquity, and with all his dissemblings and palterings, with all the hindrance of his scepticism, that also is Lévi's standpoint, as we have seen in an earlier section.

B.—Stanislas de Guaita

Associated with the literary work and much of the active propaganda of Dr. Gérard Encausse, the name of the Marquis Marie-Victor-Stanislas de Guaita, though scarcely known in England, was valued in occult circles of Paris, and his death at the early age of thirty-six years occasioned profound sorrow. It will perhaps be unnecessary to state that he was a disciple of Éliphas Lévi, whose works he regarded as constituting " the most cohesive, absolute and unimpeachable synthesis that can be dreamed by an occultist." If we add to this that De Guaita is described by Papus as occupying beyond contradiction the first rank among the pupils of Lévi, we shall have a fair knowledge of his position. He began his literary life as a poet, and in that character connects with the school of Baudelaire. His occult preoccupations appear, however, in his verses, and he soon devoted himself exclusively to occult subjects. His works entitled THE THRESHOLD OF MYSTERY, THE SERPENT OF GENESIS and THE KEY OF BLACK MAGIC were admired for their " magisterial form," which recalls that of his master. He expounded Kabbalistic Tradition and considered that in " Neo-Mosaic Christianity, explained by the Holy Kabbalah and Alexandrian Hermeticism (under certain reserves), the absolute truth must be sought in all knowledge." [1]

At an early period of his enthusiasm Stanislas de Guaita founded a Kabbalistic Order of the Rose-Cross, comprehending three Grades, to which entrance could be obtained only after successful examination, while the possession of the three Grades of the Martinist Order—an invention of Papus— was an indispensable preliminary condition. When the numerical strength of the association had attained the limits

---

[1] From a *Lettre inédite* quoted in L'INITIATION, tom. xxxviii., No. 4, Jan., 1898, pp. 12, 13.

prescribed by its constitution, it was closed rigorously by decision of the Grand Master. De Guaita is termed an erudite orientalist by his friends, who mention also the Hebrew folios which enriched his library.[1] Finally, it is recorded that he believed himself more thoroughly possessed of the Kabbalah than all others. But if we may accept the authority of Dr. Marc Haven he seems to have distinguished two species of Kabbalah, the first a science which no one could teach and no one could learn, except with the most arduous toil and by years of sacrifice, for it is " more rugged than Wronsky, more diffuse than Spanish Mysticism, more complex than Gnostic analysis." And after all it appears to be only a pseudo-Kabbalah. The other is apparently the Kabbalah as presented by William Postel, Nicholas Flamel, Khunrath, Saint-Martin and so forth. I must confess that this distinction is a puzzle. I know well enough that Saint-Martin was not a Kabbalist, except in the most phantasmal sense and by a most remote derivation. I know that Flamel the alchemist, if he ever wrote anything, was concerned with the transmutation of metals and not with the mysteries of AIN SOPH. It is, however, the Kabbalah of such Kabbalists that is said to illuminate the pages of de Guaita and to have inspired his active works.

Despite therefore his accredited erudition, the author of the SERPENT OF GENESIS has no message for the student of Kabbalism : the ZOHAR has its difficulties, by which he was clearly intimidated and the work had not been translated. But the kind of distinction which de Guaita sought to establish offers at least one point of interest. Postel, Flamel, Khunrath, Saint-Martin, are names which stand in his mind for Kabbalistic Christianity, for that marriage of the Zohar and the Gospel to which he refers expressly.[2] He differs therefore from his fellow propagandist Papus, who exhibits few Christian sympathies and is attached more consistently to the doctrine of Éliphas Lévi. But in de Guaita, as in Lévi, it is not orthodox Christianity, as understood, on the one hand, by Mirandula and Postel or, on the other, by Rosenroth, with

---

[1] *Op. cit.*, pp. 32 *et seq.*

[2] "The ZOHAR has wedded the Gospel ; the spirit has fructified the soul ; and immortal works have been the fruits of this union. The Kabbalah became Catholic in the school of St. John, the master of masters, incarnate in an admirable metaphysical form . . . the absolute spirit of the science of justice and love which vivifies internally the dead letter of all the orthodoxies."—LE SERPENT DE LA GENÉSE, p. 183.

which his Kabbalah is connected, but Christianity permeated by Gnostic elements, and this is the special characteristic of modern occult students who have taken any interest in the light cast on the religion of Jesus by the post-Christian developments of Jewish Theosophy. Thus, the missionary enthusiasm of the early Christian Schools of Kabbalism, and the Messianic dream constructed by Jewry out of the elements of the ZOHAR, have been exchanged for an attempt to go back upon the path of doctrinal development and to discover in analogies between the Kabbalah and the Gnostics a practicable thoroughfare into debated regions of esoteric religion. As disappointment waited on the mistaken ardour of the first zealots, so it was equally in store for the revived zeal in Kabbalism.

C.—LÉON MEURIN, S.J.

Having to establish some points of accidental connection between the Kabbalah and Freemasonry, it seems possible to include among Kabbalistic students the most fantastic investigator of this subject, once Archbishop of Port Louis. It is true that his large treatise, FREEMASONRY THE SYNAGOGUE OF SATAN, is a product of the troubled dream of the Papacy concerning the *Liberi Muratori* and can be saved only—if saved indeed at all—by the sincerity of its intention from a place in bogus literature ; it is true also that it connects with a squalid imposture long since unmasked ; but it shews a considerable acquaintance of the superficial order both with Kabbalistic Doctrine and Masonic Symbolism ; and it is worth noticing how the Tradition of the Jews was appreciated at the end of the nineteenth century by a Catholic critic who was also an ecclesiastic of some eminence and a member of the Society of Jesus.

It is unnecessary to say that it is an entirely hostile criticism. "In place of the orthodox synagogue and the true doctrine of Moses which God Himself inspired, modern Kabbalists represent the paganism with which certain Jewish sectarians became imbued during the captivity of Babylon. We have only to study their doctrine and to compare it with those of civilised nations in antiquity—Indians, Persians, Babylonians, Assyrians, Egyptians, Greeks and so forth—to become assured that the same pantheistic system of emanation is inculcated by all. We find everywhere an eternal principle producing a primeval triad and thereafter the entire universe, not by creation but by substantial emanation. Hence we are compelled to recognise a close connection between Kabbalistic philosophy and ancient paganism which is difficult to explain except by the inspiration of the same author, in other words, the Lying Spirit who is the enemy of mankind."

The entire treatise may be regarded as a development of this paragraph, which, it must be confessed, is the view that would be taken inevitably by the Latin Church. We have seen that under the auspices of Christian Kabbalists, with Picus de Mirandula as their mouthpiece, there was for one moment a sign of *rapprochement* between the Church and Jewish Tradition ; but it was impossible in the nature of both, and the Church was saved then, as it has been saved occasionally since, as if by some happy intuition which preceded any real knowledge of the interests at stake.

The general position being thus defined, Mgr. Meurin proceeds at a later stage to develop his impeachment by exhibiting the fundamental error of all pantheism, that, namely, which concerns the transition of the Infinite to the Finite, which wears, he tells us, for any serious thinker, the aspect of a fraudulent device. Basing his argument on the well-known verse in WISDOM : " Thou hast ordered all things in measure, and number, and weight," he advances that we must seek in these the distinction between the Infinite and the Finite, for such categories do not exist in God, or rather they are " elevated above themselves and lost in a superior unity." Creation out of nothing is the only rational solution of the grand problem concerning the origin of a world which is governed by number, weight and measure, a doctrine which assumes no passage from Infinite to Finite, since it does not derive the universe from the divine substance by an emanation of any kind. " It is true that *ex nihilo nihil fit*. But in the creation there is not only the *nihilum ;* there is also the *Omnipotens*, and it is untrue to say that with nothingness and the all-powerful, nothing can be made. *Ex nihilo nihil fit a Deo* would be a false axiom."

In a study like the present it would be out of place to discuss the points at issue between emanationists and creationists. We have seen that the Kabbalah is by no means utterly and only a system of emanation : it is a medley which tends occasionally in that direction ; but it has also a world of creation and a creation myth. The doctrine of orthodox religion on a question of fundamental philosophy is in no danger from a certain element of confusion in such reveries. But the whole controversy concerns a *res ardua et difficilis*, as Isaac de Loria would have termed it, which fortunately cannot produce a single consequence of importance to the human mind, though it is precisely to such arid speculations that official orthodoxy has always attached an eternal consequence for the soul.

Mgr. Meurin remains, however, the consistent and correct exponent of the Church which he represented, and so far as this Church is concerned he has registered, as we must admit fully, the non-Christian nature of Kabbalistic doctrine. We may go further and allow that in other places he scores occasionally a logical point against it. We have, for example, such notions as the commencement of thought in AIN SOPH which precedes the emanation of understanding in the Three Divine Supernals, thus reversing the psychological order, as the prelate observes, besides formulating an absurdity concerning the one Being in whom there is no beginning. It may well be that in the last analysis these things are to be understood more profoundly than is suggested by their surface meaning, but they are crude and misleading enough in their outward sense.

XIX.—THE KABBALAH AND ESOTERIC CHRISTIANITY

A discussion of points of contact between Christianity and the Mystical Tradition of the Jews should not proceed without some reference to a scheme of mystical Christianity which obtained for a period a certain vogue in English esoteric circles and met with especial commendation from certain Kabbalistic students. I refer to the New Gospel of Interpretation, founded on illuminations received, or believed to have been received, by Anna Bonus Kingsford, and developed since her decease, not always well and wisely, by her collaborator and co-recipient, Edward Maitland, long since also passed away. The text-books of this movement were, firstly, a small collection containing the illuminations, and, secondly a formal treatise which, under the title of THE PERFECT WAY, constituted a philosophical development and historical verification of the doctrines received by the seeress. The late McGregor Mathers dedicated his pretentious and inexact translation of certain Zoharistic books from the Latin of Rosenroth to the authors of this treatise on the ground that it was " one of the most deeply occult works that has (*sic*) been written for centuries." The dedication described it also as an " excellent and wonderful book," touching much on the doctrines of the Kabbalah and laying great value upon its teachings. It was welcomed in terms of still higher appreciation by Baron Spedalieri, of Marseilles, the disciple of Éliphas Lévi, who regarded it as " in complete accord with all mystical traditions, and especially with the great mother of these, the Kabbalah." In connection with this appreciation the respectable French occultist observed : (*a*) That Kabbalistic Tradition as we now possess it is far from genuine, and was much purer when it first emerged from the sanctuaries. (*b*) That when William Postel and his brother Hermetists predicted that the literature containing the Secret Tradition of the Jews would become known and understood at " the end of the era," they meant that it would be made the basis of " a new illumination," reinstating that Tradition in its purity. (*c*) That this illumination and this restoration have been accomplished in THE PERFECT WAY. He adds : " In this book we find all that there is of truth in the Kabbalah, supplemented by new intuitions, such as present a body of doctrines at once complete, homogeneous, logical and inexpugnable. Since the whole tradition thus finds itself recovered or restored to its original purity, the prophecies of Postel and his fellow Hermetists are accomplished ; and I consider that from henceforth the study of the Kabbalah will be but an object of curiosity and erudition, like that of Hebrew antiquities."

If this be the case, the inquiry with which we have been occupied at such considerable length is only prolegomenary to the New Gospel of Interpretation, and our concluding words should be simply to direct the student who is in search of the true meaning of Esoteric Tradition in Israel to the doctrines contained in this last word of revelation. Indeed, such a course would seem at first sight the only one which could be followed. I must add, however, that the opinion expressed by Baron Spedalieri produced no consequence, that the Kabbalistic School of occultists in England did not follow the lead thus indicated, and did not endorse the opinion, while the New Gospel of Interpretation took no permanent hold on the occult or any other prevailing thought of the time. I infer also that Baron Spedalieri's statement as to the adulteration of the genuine Tradition in the Hebrew Kabbalah was not traversed seriously, but for its recovery occultists of the period were disposed to look backward towards Egypt rather than to any form of supplementary revelation.

I do not propose to recite here even the leading aspects of the system of Esoteric Christianity developed in THE PERFECT WAY, for the work is well known and its substance has been made accessible in many forms, thanks to the untiring devotion of Edward Maitland. It does offer some points of contact with the Tradition of the Kabbalah, especially as to the dual nature of God, or the Divine-Feminine, and "the multiplicity of principles in the human system"; but it would be easy to exaggerate their extent, as also, in some less conspicuous cases, their importance. The traceable references are few and superficial. We may find, for example, the Kabbalistic doctrine of AIN SOPH and His emanations in the statement that "God unmanifest and abstract is the Primordial Mind, and the Kosmic universe is the ideation of that Mind," but it is not a far-reaching correspondence. So also the conception of Macroprosopus reflected in Microprosopus is sketched thinly by the following passage. "In 'the Lord' the Form-less assumes a form, the Nameless a name, the Infinite the Definite, and these human. But, although 'the Lord is God manifested as a man' in and to the souls of those to whom the vision is vouchsafed, it is not as man in the exclusive sense of the term and masculine only, but as man both masculine and feminine" (MICROPROSOPUS it will be remembered is androgyne), "at once man and woman, as is Humanity itself." I should add that the "new Gospel" maintained the divinity of the Kabbalah on the ground of the purity of its doctrine of correspondences, which shews that "this famous compendium belongs to a period prior to that destruction by the priesthoods of the equilibrium of the sexes which constituted in one sense the Fall." With this statement of its Divine origin may be brought into contrast the interpretation of the claim made by the Kabbalah as to the manner of its delivery. "When it is said that these Scriptures were delivered by God first of all to Adam in Paradise, and then to Moses on Sinai, it is meant that the doctrine contained in them is that which man always discerns when he succeeds in attaining to that inner and celestial region of his nature where he is taught directly of his own Divine Spirit, and knows even as he is known." As THE PERFECT WAY and its connections assume to be the outcome of a similar quality of discernment, it follows, of course, that it is a recovery of " the doctrine commonly called the *Gnosis,* and variously entitled Hermetic and Kabbalistic."

I should add that many thoughtful persons have found in THE PERFECT WAY a "fountain of light, interpretative and reconciliatory," and that some of its interpretation indicates a suggestive quality of genius ; yet it was not free at the beginning from the fantastic element, and it depends largely on philological arguments which are more than fantastic. Also at the close of Maitland's life he wrote much which must have been regretted by his friends, bringing his earlier work into discredit by exaggerated claims concerning it. Taking it as a whole, THE PERFECT WAY can be regarded only as a series of suggestions and intuitive glimpses concerning the postulated hidden sense of several sacred scriptures.

XX.—THE KABBALAH AND MODERN THEOSOPHY

The attempt which was made in the year 1875, by the foundation of the Theosophical Society, to extend and centralise the study of Oriental Occult Philosophy, has, in spite of its chequered history, succeeded to a large extent in that object. If we remove from consideration certain claims advanced by the founders, and if we regard the Society rather as it assumed once at least to regard itself, namely, as an organisation designed to promote a neglected branch of knowledge, we have only to survey its literature during the past fifty years to see how large a field it has succeeded in covering. No unbiassed student will be inclined to overlook this fact, and as the Theosophical Society possesses at least this aspect of importance, it will be useful to ascertain how far the expositions of eastern philosophy which we owe to it connect with the subject of our inquiry.

It may be said in a general manner that the correspondences

which I have established already were recognised from the beginning of the movement and, so to speak, at its fountain-head. The cosmology and metapsychics of Jewish Esoteric Tradition were regarded, roughly speaking, by Madame Blavatsky as reflections or derivatives from an older know-ledge and a higher teaching which has existed from time immemorial in the farthest East.[1] Beyond or outside this broad affirmation and representative point of view one does not trace a sufficient warrant in knowledge for the expression of particular opinions. The author of Isis Unveiled and The Secret Doctrine had an enormous budget of materials, but not very carefully selected. On the one hand, she offers information which we are not able to check because we do not know her authorities ; on the other she makes statements occasionally with which it is difficult to agree. Thus, she distinguishes between the ordinary, or Judaistic, and the universal, or Oriental Kabbalah. If little be known of the one, there is nothing, at least nothing that is definite, known of the other. " Its adepts are few ; but these heirs elect of the sages who first discovered ' the starry truths which shone on the great Shemaïa of the Chaldæan lore ' have solved the ' absolute ' and are now resting from their grand labour." [2] That is a statement which, of course, we cannot check, and for any critical study of the Jewish Kabbalah it can therefore carry no weight. It may be taken to indicate a feeling at its value among certain occultists that the Hebrew tradition has been perverted.[3] It may be accepted also as evidence that because the term Kabbalah signifies an oral reception it has come to be used in connection with almost any unwritten knowledge. Such a course is very inexact and misleading ; but the same abuse of words is found in Paracelsus and many later writers. It serves, however, a purpose not intended

---

[1] As might be expected, some of her followers did not fail to go further, *e.g.*, the late W. Q. Judge, who was able to affirm categorically that Abraham, Moses and Solomon were members of an ancient lodge of adepts from whom this high teaching has been handed down. The Ocean of Theosophy, New York, 1893, c. 1. " Echoes " of this kind " from the burnished and mysterious East," to quote Judge terminology (Echoes from the Orient, p. 5, New York, 1890), did not find response among theosophical writers in England.

[2] Isis Unveiled, i., 17.

[3] Another theosophical writer, however, maintains that " the collection of writings known as the Bible constitutes but one of a number of records which are all derived from and based upon one unifying system, known at times as the Ancient Wisdom Religion, or Secret Doctrine." W. Kingsland : The Esoteric Basis of Christianity, Part I., p. 15, London, 1891.

ьy those who use it : it distinguishes between scholar and
sciolist. The statement which we cannot check is, however,
usually accompanied by the statement that we can. In the
present case we are told that the BOOK OF OCCULTATION is
" the most ancient Hebrew document on occult learning," [1]
and I doubt much whether this would be countenanced by
any student who was acquainted with the strong claims of
the BOOK OF FORMATION, to say nothing of the literature
which belongs to Talmudic times. It is added that SIPHRA
DI ZENIOUTHA was compiled from another and older work
which is not named, but it is stated that there is only one
" original copy " in existence, and that this is " so very old
that our modern antiquarians might ponder over its pages
an indefinite time, and still not quite agree as to the nature of
the fabric upon which it is written." [2] Till antiquaries are
furnished with the opportunity they will be tempted to
overlook this claim. With both these classes of statement
we may contrast the affirmation that is not evident in itself
and is supported by doubtful reasoning. Thus we are told
of Oriental Kabbalists who assert that the traditions of their
science are more than seventy thousand years old, concerning
which claim it is observed that modern science cannot prove
it to be false ; but the question is whether Kabbalists, oriental
or otherwise, can produce evidence in support of its truth.
We may pass over the writer's personal pretension to a first-
hand acquaintance with Kabbalistic books once indisputably
in existence, but now regarded as lost. Of such is the
Chaldæan Book of Numbers,[3] which, according to another
authority, is a companion to the ÆSH MEZAREPH,[4] but is
declared in ISIS UNVEILED to be a part of the great Oriental
Kabbalah, namely, the patrimony of the persons previously
described as having " solved the absolute." [5] To the lesson
which is taught by observations of this kind we may add the
borrowed view which rests on bad criticism, as, for example,
that the TALMUD is " the darkest of enigmas even for most

---

[1] ISIS UNVEILED, i., 1.
[2] Ibid.
[3] This work is said to be much superior to the ZOHAR. SECRET DOCTRINE, i., 214.
It is, in fact, the only real Kabbalah, ib., iii., 170. It appears to be now in possession
of certain Persian Sufis (ib.), an interesting statement which I have not, however, felt
authorised to make use of in Book II., § 6, of this study.
[4] This is Westcott's opinion. Madame Blavatsky adds that the SEPHER YETZIRAH
is also a portion of the Book of Numbers.
[5] Op. cit., i., 579.

Jews," [1] thus attributing a mystical sense to the commentaries on the exoteric laws of Israel, the value of which attribution has been exhibited already.[2]

It would serve no purpose to enumerate any further challengable assertions which rest more or less exclusively on the good authority of Madame Blavatsky. It will be sufficient to refer to her views upon the authenticity of the ZOHAR.[3] On the one hand the author is said to be R. Simeon ben Yohai;[4] again, it was " edited for the first time " between A.D. 70 and 110;[5] and yet again, it was written, as it now stands, by R. Moses de Leon, the original being lost, though at the same time its contents were " scattered through a number of minor MSS." R. Moses had Syriac, Chaldaic, and Christian Gnostics to help him. Such opinions are without any warrant for criticism.[6]

---

[1] Isis Unveiled, i., 17.

[2] The best test of Madame Blavatsky's first-hand knowledge of the subject is the fact that she calls the Liber Drushim of Isaac de Loria a part of the Talmud, and thence proceeds to exhibit the Sephirotic doctrine as a characteristic of that collection. Secret Doctrine, i., 438. The symbolism of the Lesser Countenance is also referred to the Talmud. Ibid., i., 350.

[3] It is not perhaps surprising that she should regard the Zohar as not sufficiently esoteric. Ibid.

[4] Ibid., iii., 92. She says also that it was on account of his possession of the " secret knowledge " that R. Simeon was forced to take refuge in the cave. After this version of the matter of fact we shall not be surprised to learn that St. Peter was a Kabbalist (ib., iii., 125), that the Comte de St. Germain had access to unknown Vatican MSS. on the Kabbalah, which MSS. contain information regarding the Central Sun (ib., ii., 237), or that the Zohar is " called also the Midrash," as if the last term were particular, and not generic (ib., iii., 167).

[5] Ibid., iii., 167.

[6] Ibid., i., 114, 230; iii., 167.

BOOK XI

THE KABBALAH AND OTHER CHANNEL OF SECRET TRADITION

BOOK XI

THE KABBALAH AND OTHER CHANNELS OF SECRET TRADITION

I.—THE KABBALAH AND MAGIC

It was intimated at the outset of our inquiry that certain speculations, belonging to the more immediate past, do not consider any single system as the exclusive depository of supposed hidden knowledge; a variety of channels are recognised, and by the network of communications subsisting between these channels the secret arts are methodised and their identities and analogies exhibited. There is an enormous divergence of opinion as to what may and may not constitute a path of the postulated Secret Tradition, individual predilection exercising, as will be understood, no inconsiderable influence. We may conclude in a general manner that the Tradition being ubiquitous by the hypothesis is thought to have assumed its forms everywhere and at all times. There was, for example, no exoteric religion which did not possess *ex hypothesi* an esoteric interpretation [1] and there was no esoteric interpretation which did not connect that religion with all that is signified more especially here by secret teaching. For this hypothesis an integral connection of Kabbalism with other systems belonging to remote periods would be evidence enough that it had its root in the Secret Tradition; but, without denying altogether that there may be a certain warrant for a not dissimilar view, we have found that many of the resemblances may be accounted for in a more natural and spontaneous manner. As, however, it was in the western world that Kabbalism grew up and flourished,[2] it is

---

[1] John Yarker : NOTES ON THE SCIENTIFIC AND RELIGIOUS MYSTERIES OF ANTIQUITY, p. 5.

[2] If the derivation of the ZOHAR from R. Simeon ben Yohai be admitted, Palestine was, of course, the birthplace of that work. Dr. Schiller-Szinessy, who defended this derivation, accepted also what follows therefrom.

necessary to observe its connections—real or supposed—with other channels by which an arcane knowledge is believed to have been communicated to the West. These are Magic, Alchemy, Astrology, the occult associations which culminated in Freemasonry, and, finally, an obscure sheaf of hieroglyphs known as Tarot cards. There is also a side question as to whether devotional Mysticism, apart from any formal initiation, shews any trace of Kabbalism over and above that of unconscious analogy. Like the several studies which have preceded it, the object of this eleventh book is rather to correct crude misconceptions than to establish novel views. Far too much stress has been laid upon the common basis of occult arts and reveries, while those who look for their enlightenment more especially to Kabbalistic apparatus have been predisposed unduly to discern Kabbalism at the root of all. We shall see that in most instances the connection was accidental, a matter of adornment, late in its introduction, or chiefly of the historical order. The paramount exception to this statement is the first subject with which we have to deal here. There is no doubt that Ceremonial Magic in the West [1] owes its typical processes and its peculiar complexion to Kabbalism, though it would be folly to pretend that without Kabbalism there would have been no Western Magic.[2]

I propose in the present section to restrict the use of the term Magic within the narrow limits of its common acceptation. To take it in its pretended higher sense,[3] as equivalent to Divine Wisdom, might make it seem almost superfluous to inquire whether it connects with a Tradition which lays claim to the same definition. The question as it is understood here is rather historical than metaphysical, and is concerned only with the western world. The White and Black Magic of the Middle Ages constitutes a kind of spurious practical

---

[1] " The Kabbalah is the source of all the vain imaginations which form the basis of Magic, and many Jews devoted to the Kabbalah are also addicted thereto, abusing the Names of God and the angels for the performance of things supernatural." Moreri : GRAND DICTIONNAIRE HISTORIQUE, Tom. ii., s.v. *Cabale*. Amsterdam, 1740.

[2] The strength of the connection is exhibited by the modern literature of occult *colportage* in France. LA GRANDE ET VÉRITABLE SCIENCE CABALISTIQUE is still *la Sorcellerie dévoilée*, and it is under such titles that mutilated reprints of the GREAT ALBERT, the LITTLE ALBERT and the RED DRAGON have appeared in obscure by-ways of Paris, usually without place or date. Similar productions of the eighteenth century also exhibit it : see the anonymous TÉLESCOPE DE ZOROASTRE *ou Clef de la Grande Cabale divinatoire des Mages, s.l.*, 1796.

[3] It would be unwise to deny altogether that there is such a higher sense, but such attempts to present it as Dr. Franz Hartmann's MAGIC WHITE AND BLACK are coloured too highly to possess historical value.

THE KABBALAH AND MAGIC

Kabbalah which represents Jewish esoteric doctrine debased to the purposes of the sorcerer, and it is necessary that we should estimate it at its true worth, because it has been the subject of misconception not only among uninstructed persons but even professed expositors.

A study of the Zoharistic writings, their developments and commentaries will shew that the ends proposed by the Speculative Kabbalah are very different from evocations of spirits, the raising of ghosts, discovery of concealed treasures, the bewitchments and other mummeries of Ceremonial Magic. The Kabbalah does, however, countenance, as we have seen, the doctrine of a power resident in Divine Names,[1] and it is in fact one of the burdens of its inheritance. Of the antiquity and diffusion of that doctrine there can be no doubt; in one or other of its forms it has obtained almost universally, and, like all universal beliefs, behind the insensate character which it exhibits externally there may be—by mere possibility—an inward reason which accounts for it. Without attempting an inquiry in which we are not unlikely to be baffled, it is sufficient to indicate here that at the sources to which Kabbalistic Tradition is referred, namely, Akkadia, Chaldæa and Babylonia, this doctrine prevailed: it was no doubt brought away from Babylon by the Jews, and they carried it with them into the dispersion of the third exile. It inspired a whole cycle of bizarre legends concerning Solomon and his marvels. More than this, it may be said to be connected directly with Kabbalistic symbolism concerning the divine powers and qualities attaching to the Hebrew Alphabet. The worlds were made, so to speak, by the instrument of a single letter, and four letters are the living forces which actuate them. There can be therefore no question that every Kabbalist accepted, symbolically at least, the doctrine of the power of words. It must have passed very early into unfortunate applications [2]; Sacred Names were written on amulets and talismans which were used to heal diseases, to

---

[1] See the important chapter on the Name of God in J. Leusden's PHILOLOGUS HEBRÆUS, 1672.

[2] The SEPHER RAZIEL, referred falsely to Eleazer of Worms, and posing as an angelic revelation to Adam and Noah, has been mentioned. With its long catalogues of angelic names, its talismans and philtres, its double seal of Solomon, its mystical or occult alphabetical symbols, its figures for the government of evil spirits, and its conjurations by means of Divine Names, this work constitutes one of the storehouses of Mediæval Magic, besides being broadly representative of the Practical Kabbalah at large.

avert evil chances and so forth.[1] But it was a part also of the
Chaldæan doctrine that a ceremonial utterance of the Divine
Name could, in some obscure way, influence the God to
whom it was attributed. Above all, the demons and evil
spirits became subservient to the power of such words.
Here is the germ of which the last development, or rather
the final corruption, is to be found in the French and Latin
Grimoires of Black Magic.

It was, broadly speaking, somewhere about the fourteenth
century that a Latin literature rose up in Europe, passing
subsequently into the vernaculars of various countries, containing processes for compelling spirits by means of Divine
Names which are corruptions of Hebrew terms.[2] The
processes pretend to be translated from the Hebrew, but, if
so, the originals are either not extant or have been altered out
of all knowledge. The chief of them is known as the KEY
OF SOLOMON, of which there are two recensions, more correctly regarded as distinct works under an identical title.[3]
Among the points which should be observed concerning
them is the fact that while they are concerned with all classes
of spirits, good and evil, for every variety of purpose, but
mostly illicit, they contain no formulæ for dealing with the
dead, and this, I think, indicates their Jewish origin, for the
Jews had very strong feelings as to the sacred nature of the
repose of the human soul. Out of these two works there was
developed subsequently a variety of processes, more distinctly
spurious, which did enter into Necromantic Mysteries. They
begot also many variations adapted for the use of Christian
operators, and containing Sacred Words the efficacy of which
would not have been acknowledged by a Hebrew.

It is one thing to note the existence of this literature and to
confess its derivation ; it is another to exalt collections like

---

[1] So far as regards the early Christian centuries, the question is settled by a reference
in the thirty-third Sermon of Origen by way of commentary on St. Matthew, wherein
allusion is made to a book of exorcisms or adjurations of demons passing under the
name of Solomon, which was no doubt the prototype of later KEYS and GRIMOIRES.
[2] Jean Wier, a demonologist of the sixteenth century, in his HISTOIRES, DISPUTES
ET DISCOURS des Illusions et Impostures des Diables, originally in Latin, gives a list of
magical works current at his period under great names of the past, and points out that
their art has depraved the most secret interpretation of the Divine Law, known as
Kabbalah among the Jews.—See the reprint of this work, Paris, 1885, 2 vols., i., 175.
[3] A text passing under this name was condemned in a Decree of Pope Gelasius. See
Antonius van Dale : DE ORIGINE ET PROGRESSU IDOLATRIÆ, Amsterdam, 1696, p. 558.
See also the Jewish Encyclopædia, Vol. XI, s.v. SOLOMON, concerning MAFTEAH
SHELAMOH, a book of incantations, said to have been extant in Hebrew so late as 1697
and supposed to be the original of the Latin CLAVICULÆ SALOMONIS.

the KEY OF SOLOMON into embodiments of genuine Kabbalistic Tradition. It is an insult to the rabbins of the Holy Synod to suggest their connection with the puerilities and imbecility of Ceremonial Magic. This, however, has been done in England and was being done until recently in France.[1] The professed Kabbalistic occultists of the latter country have ascribed a superior importance and an additional aspect of mystery to the worthless CLAVICLES of Solomon, by representing that they are the only written memorials of a most secret oral branch of Practical Kabbalism, instead of the final debasement of a perfectly traceable, if not rationally accountable, doctrine concerning Divine Names. Papus observes : " The practical part of the Kabbalah is barely indicated in a few manuscripts scattered through our great libraries. At Paris, the *Bibliothèque Nationale* possesses one of the finest exemplars, of which the origin is attributed to Solomon. These manuscripts, generally known under the name of CLAVICLES, are the basis of all the old Grimoires which circulate in country places (the GREAT ALBERT and LITTLE ALBERT, RED DRAGON and ENCHIRIDION) and of those which once drove priests into mental alienation by sorcery." The statement does not exhibit much acquaintance with the works which it mentions ; the ENCHIRIDION in its earliest forms owes little to the KEYS OF SOLOMON, and the GRIMOIRE OF HONORIUS is not more concerned with sorcery than are Rituals like the RED DRAGON. Finally, the intellectual and moral difference between the Clavicles and their derivatives is so slight that it is scarcely worth labouring. As regards their scope and intention, the Clavicles are themselves Grimoires. I have indicated the possibility that behind the ancient doctrine of the virtue resident in certain theurgic words and formulæ there may be concealed a Secret of Lower and Averse Sanctuaries ; so also the apparatus of Ceremonial Magic may be a travesty and disfigurement of practices known also to Occult Sanctuaries ; but no one is on the track of these mysteries who begins by mistaking *signum* for *signatum* on the one hand or the mutilated reflection for the original on the other.

---

[1] There is some ground for supposing that the first express attempts to identify Magic with Kabbalism must be referred to Germany. There are numerous earlier examples, but Welling's OPUS MAGO-CABBALISTICUM, Hamburg, 1765, is a good instance, and it is also a work of some interest.

The general fact remains that it was by a perversion of the Kabbalah that we have obtained Grimoires, and that the student of Jewish Tradition must tolerate this fact as best he can.[1]

I should prefer to ignore altogether this so-called practical part of the Kabbalah, but so much importance having been attributed to it by modern occultists, it seems necessary for the sake of completeness to say something briefly of its materials and its method in their later developments. It was concerned above all with the Names of God, firstly, as they are found in Holy Scripture, and, secondly, as their mysteries were unfolded by means of Kabbalistic processes. It attributed certain names of power to the ten SEPHIROTH, and these were regarded as analogous to the divine forces and attributes associated with these.

The Divine Name connected with KETHER was that signifying the essence of the Deity, EHEIEH (AHIH). That of CHOKMAH is JOD, JAH, or TETRAGRAMMATON, commonly rendered Jehovah (JHVH), and susceptible of twelve permutations, similar to the sealing names of IHV in the SEPHER YETZIRAH. These permutations are called Banners by Kabbalists. The title JEHOVAH ELOHIM (JHVH ALHIM) is attributed to BINAH and signifies God of Gods. EL (AL) is referred to CHESED, and its meaning, according to Rosenroth, is God of Grace and Ruler of Mercy. GEBURAH is in correspondence with ELOHIM GIBOR, the strong God Who avenges the crimes of the wicked. ELOAH VA DAATH is the Divine Title of TIPHERETH (ALVH V DATh); JEHOVAH or ADONAI TZABAOTH (ADNI TsBAVTh), the God or Lord of Hosts, is connected with NETZACH; ELOHIM TZABAOTH, of similar meaning, belongs to HOD; SHADDAI EL CHAI (ShDI AL ChI), the omnipotent living God, is referable to JESOD; ADONAI MELEKH (ADNI MLK) to MALCHUTH. But the ten SEPHIROTH are connected with the ten numbers,

---

[1] A work belonging to this class, but more elaborate and interesting than most of them, goes to shew that a Jew in possession of the " Holy Traditions of the Kabbalah " and also of the secrets of practical Magic, bequeathed the first to his elder and the second to his younger son. What happened when there were more than two sons does not appear.—See the BOOK OF THE SACRED MAGIC, translated by S. L. MacGregor Mathers, London, 1898. The original is an MS. in the Arsénal Library, Paris, and belongs to the 18th century, but it claims to have been written in Hebrew in the year 1458, which claim, by the internal evidence, is manifestly imposture. Even its Jewish authorship is unlikely. Mathers, who had a certain erudition but was devoid of critical judgment, accepted every claim advanced by this work, as he accepted that of the KEY OF SOLOMON.

and hence there was an occult power resident in numerals analogous to that which was inherent in Hebrew letters ; the Divine Names belonging to the SEPHIROTH were those also of the scale of the denary ; but over and above these there were other names referred to numbers based on the number of the letters which gave expression to these names. Thus, the number one was represented by the single letter JOD, understood as a Divine Name, and not in its alphabetical order, in which it is equivalent to ten. The number two was represented by JH and AL ; the number three by ShDI = Shaddai ; the number four by JHVH and AHIH ; five by ALHIM, to which I presume that Christian Kabbalism added JHShVH = JEHESHUAH or Jesus ; six by ALVThIM and AL GBVR ; seven by ARARITA and AShRAHIH ; eight by ALVH V DATh and JHVH V DATh ; nine by JHVH TsBAVTh, ALHIM GBVR, and JHVH TsDQNV ; ten by ALHIM TsBAVTh and by the extended TETRAGRAMMATON JVD HE VAV HE. It may be added in this connection that according to Cornelius Agrippa simple numbers were used to express divine things, numbers of ten were for celestial, numbers of one hundred for earthly, and numbers of a thousand for things to come. The Divine Names and their qualifications were also tabulated in reference to the twenty-two letters.

Of these Names the greatest power and virtue were attributed to TETRAGRAMMATON, which was the root and foundation of all and the ruling force of the world ; its true pronunciation, as already seen, was one of the secrets of the Sanctuary and for Kabbalistic Magic was the master key of all successful operation. With this was connected the name of 72 letters obtained by the Kabbalistic computation of the numbers of the letters of TETRAGRAMMATON after a conventional manner, as follows :—

$$\left.\begin{array}{r} \text{Jod} = 10 \\ \text{Jod He} = 15 \\ \text{Jod He Vau} = 21 \\ \text{Jod He Vau He} = 26 \end{array}\right\} = 72$$

After the Divine Names come those of the Orders of Angels and chiefs of the hierarchy, concerning which something has been said already in the section on ANGELS AND DEMONS. It would serve no purpose to enumerate all the complicated apparatus developed in this connection. The ten archangels and the ten angelic orders corresponded to the ten Divine Names connected with the SEPHIROTH and the Name of 72 letters had 72 other angels attributed thereto, whose names were extracted by a conventional device from Exodus xiv. 19, 20, 21. There were angels of the cardinal points, rulers of the four elements, angels of the planets, angels of the Divine Presence, and in opposition to all these there were also evil spirits, princes of Devils, held to be " offensive in the elements," and so forth. This apparatus passed bodily over to the Ceremonial Magic of the Middle Ages, which the debased Kabbalah may be said to have constituted and ruled throughout, and it is for this reason that Western conventional Magic has so little connection with folk-lore.

It is to be understood that so far I have presented developments of later Kabbalism, the elements of which pre-existed, however, in Israel, and this laid down we have finished with one aspect of the occult subject in its relation to the Secret Tradition of Israel. Beyond this, and much more important —that is to say, from a theosophical standpoint—there is the fact that the voice of the ZOHAR testifies in no uncertain manner as to the view concerning Magic, its connections and derivations, held by all true Sons of the Doctrine and imposed by inference on those who might seek to come after them, following in their path. This notwithstanding, we may find here and there in the long sequence of debate that the same standpoint is not maintained invariably on specific details, and there are certain statements which might lend colour to an opinion that the root-matter of one and another department of occult experiment may be found therein. It is said, for example, that there is a mystery known to the holy thaumaturgists concerning the miraculous powers which inhere in the sacred celestial letters and that if these are written inversely, after a certain manner, the extinction of the guilty can be brought about thereby.[1] Now it is to be observed that the so-called celestial characters are not those which are written with the hand by human scribes, but are the Great Letters, alive and givers of life, emblems of all intelligence and therefore endowed with understanding. By the Zoharic hypothesis, they existed before the creation and—as we have seen in its

---

[1] Z., Pt. I, fol 67b ; I, 398.

place—one of them was concerned therewith. The explanation of this fable is that, for all the sages of Israel, thought must pass into expression, because that which is done in heaven must be done also on earth. The Sons of the Doctrine must reflect therefore in their hearts on the Secret Doctrine, as the Divine Thought was turned upon itself in the eternity which preceded creation; but it must pass also into expression, because at length the creation was formulated, and this expression enters into record by means of letters. These are further the elements of that Law by which the world was made, and the use of their reflections on earth was another instance of accomplishing below that which is performed on high. After what manner the holy thaumaturgists brought down the celestial letters for the purpose under consideration, or for any other, is not told in the story, and I suppose that for sane persons there can be no question that the intimation must be understood allegorically, though I am not proposing to explain after what manner—as the unexpressed meaning exceeds my purpose. For the rest, I am certain that the ZOHAR was unknown to the adepts of magical workings; it reflects there and here some practices which obtained in Jewry, and the TALMUDS are a source of sporadic information to whose who would pursue the subject.

The general thesis of the ZOHAR is that the art of Magic came from the sages of the East,[1] and as it is said by the Scriptures that the wisdom of Solomon surpassed that of the Egyptians, as well as of all the East,[2] it seems to be understood that he drew from some superior source, in respect of occult " science." The intention is not, however, either to exonerate the science or to justify the king in this branch of his learning. He seems to have pursued it when he fell away from justice, but it was otherwise during the building of the Temple[3] : then he beheld wisdom face to face and had no need of occult arts. That of the Egyptians is regarded

---

[1] Z., Pt. I, fol. 223a ; II, 478.

[2] I Kings iv. 34. It is very difficult to understand the purpose of the ZOHAR in this reference. Somehow Shekinah was his teacher, but it is not certain, and the question is scarcely worth pursuing.—See Z., Pt. I, fol. 223a, b ; II, 478–481.

[3] Ib., fol. 150a ; II, 190. There is more on the subject which need not be quoted here. We have seen in our study of the Deluge-Myth that Magic is older than the Deluge : it existed also during the patriarchal age. Laban was the greatest magician in the world, and by the aid of his idols learned all that he wished to know.—Ib., Pt. I, fol. 164b ; II, 243.

as the lowest of all,[1] presumably because the subjugation of Israel is said to have been its chief object, and it failed at the end therein. It was not, however, mere trickery ; the wands which changed into serpents became actual serpents, not only in dream or vision, and those of Aaron which devoured them were actual in like manner.[2] The Egyptian masters had acquired ten degrees of Magic, corresponding to the averse or evil SEPHIROTH, the Inferior Crowns,[3] which rule in all Magic. In virtue of his communications with the abyss, Pharaoh himself was skilled more highly in occult practices than any of the magicians he employed.[4] Abraham seems to have been drawn in this direction, and when he first went into Egypt it was for the profound study of Egyptian occult art, though not as one who was seduced or one who became attached thereto.[5] He penetrated the secret of evil only to reascend towards the good. As regards the later children of the East and their wisdom, there is a sense in which Abraham was himself a fountain of knowledge, for the presents made by him to the children of his concubine seem to have been a medley of true knowledge and occult arts, which were taken eastward and deteriorated in the course of the centuries.[6] There is thus a vestige of truth in the eastern wisdom, but it is combined with impure Magic. The source of all magical power, howsoever it may be derived through individual persons, is the first serpent, who is the impure spirit, and the theory is that in order to attract this spirit the magicians must begin by defiling themselves, apparently by sex acts against Nature.[7] The workings are facilitated by the fact that the impure spirit bestows himself for nothing, so that the path to the abyss looks easier than the path to the heights. The authority for this statement is not fortunately the Secret Tradition in Israel but a Book of Magic said to have been transmitted to Solomon by the demon Asmodeus.[8] It

---

[1] Z., Pt. I, fol. 223b ; II, 481. " It is designated under the name of the maid-servant seated behind the mill."

[2] Ib., Pt. II, fol. 28a ; III, 134.

[3] Ib., fol. 30b ; III, 145. Ib., fol. 35b ; III, 171. " All the streets of Egypt were full of magicians, and in each house were to be found articles belonging to the works of Magic."

[4] Ib., Pt. II, fol. 37b ; III, 179. Also, fol. 52b ; III, 236.

[5] Ib., Pt. I, fol. 83a ; I, 478.

[6] Éliphas Lévi makes a great point of these " presents." See my rendering of THE HISTORY OF MAGIC, p. 48. See also Z., Pt. I, fol. 133b ; II, 127.

[7] Z., Pt. I, fol. 125b ; II, 100.

[8] Ib., Pt. II, fol. 128a ; IV, 10. The very opposite is taught in the Grimoires concerning evil spirits, of whom it is said that this kind of creature gives nothing for

affirms also that the Holy Spirit demands a price, must be bought and the cost is high. The ZOHAR explains that this price is one of effort for the purification of heart and soul, that the aspirant may be made worthy of serving in the Tabernacle of the Spirit. The present state of the art is defined at the end of the ZOHAR when it is said that Magic has been abolished by the Holy One.[1] In other words that has prevailed which is always above Magic, namely faith, this being friendship with God, whereas Magic is friendship with the demon.[2]

The term Magic is sufficiently general to answer for some other arts and practices included in the department of pseudo-occult science. Astrology stands to some extent apart, and it is perhaps for this reason that it is a subject of distinct and particular condemnation. The thesis is that it is a lying science, understood as the prediction of future events of the human order by the constellation rising at nativity, and the consequent pretension that the day, hour and minute of each man's birth exercises an influence on his future.[3] When God directed Abraham to look up to heaven, it was a counsel to forsake Astrology, this having predicted apparently that he would die without children, whereas God promised him a posterity not less numerous than those stars which in this matter seemed to have been in combination against him.[4] The point is, and it appears fully elsewhere, that Abraham had studied Astrology, presumably in Egypt; that he was wrong in fact, was told to neglect the study and have faith in the Divine Name, when a son would be given to him.[5] When it was said in the Scriptures that Abraham believed in God,[6] this means in contradistinction from the testimony of stars, and this faith was imputed to him for righteousness. At the same time it is not denied that many things are indicated

---

nothing. Whatsoever is evoked, for example, must be satisfied on its own part ; if it be a question of obtaining some hidden treasure, a coin must be thrown to the fiend who assists in securing it.

[1] " The Holy One, blessed be He, has caused Magic to disappear from the world, in order to prevent men, under the seduction thereof, from forsaking the fear of God."— Z., Pt. III, fol. 299b ; VI, 128. It is like a final message of the text. I observe that Parisian occultism, after all its futilities, false-seeming and ignorant ascriptions respecting Kabbalistic Magic, has preserved a discreet silence since the publication of the ZOHAR in its own language.

[2] *Ib.*, Pt. II, fol. 52b ; III, 237. It is said that Pharaoh was unacquainted with this truth and had found no confirmation of the doctrine that the Divine Name Jehovah, as formulated by Moses, had dominion over the whole earth.

[3] *Ib.*, Pt. I, fol. 78a ; I, 458.   [5] *Ib.*
[4] *Ib.*, fol. 90b ; I, 514.   [6] *Ib.*

by the course of the stars in heaven; but the Holy One changes them according to His will.[1] Here is one aspect of the admission in respect of the subject; another says that, according to an old book, there are times when the moon is hollowed, and souls born at this period will be overwhelmed with sufferings and poverty, without reference to their personal deserts.[2] On the other hand [3] those who come down into incarnate life when the moon is full will enjoy all earthly prosperity. The ZOHAR explains that in the first case the souls are those whom the Holy One loves the most and allows to suffer in this world, so that they may be purified from stain.[4] . . . This notwithstanding, the lunar intimation remains correct and Astrology is justified by the hypothesis.

The subject of occult reverie suggests that of demonology, as to which there is much information scattered throughout the text, and it may be well to summarise the Zoharic doctrine of evil spirits—apart from the Fall of the angels, already dealt with, and outside the methodical developments of later Kabbalism. Speaking generally, the evil spirit is a serpent, and he who rides on the serpent is Samael.[5] The wife of Samael is that adulterous woman who seduces humanity at large.[6] It is suggested that demons existed prior to the creation, but there came a time when in company with all other maleficent and impure spirits, they were authorised to go about the world and ravage therein.[7] Their abodes are in ruins, in great forests and in deserts.[8] They are all emanations from the serpent, and this is why the evil spirit reigns in the world.[9] These are apparently one class, and another are the scourges which Adam engendered during those years when he was in separation from his wife.[10] A third class

---

[1] Z., fol. 90b; I, 514.

[2] Ib., fol. 180b, 181a; II, 313, 314. When it is said that the moon is hollowed, the meaning is that it is sometimes waxing and sometimes waning, through the wiles of the old serpent.—Ib.

[3] There is another point: the ancient and prevailing connection of angels and certain stars is admitted by the ZOHAR, which holds also that angel succeeds angel, and in some manner that does not transpire this putative fact places human temperaments under the ascendant of that constellation which happens to preside at birth. It will be seen that the principles on which Astrology rests do not seem to be denied, and that the " lying science " is the attempt to calculate the influences and predict thereby. The authority in the present instance is THE FAITHFUL SHEPHERD.—Z., Pt. II, fol. 42a; III, 191, 192.

[4] Ib.

[5] Ib., fol. 35b; I, 221.

[6] See Book VII, § 3.

[7] Ib., fol. 169b; II, 265, 266.

[8] Ib.

[9] Ib.

[10] See Book VII., § 3.

arises from the fact that when the soul is apart from the body during sleep the impure spirit may attach itself to the latter, or in other words, that female demons may cohabit therewith.[1] They conceive and bring forth children as a result of the union. Such demons are in the likeness of man but without hair on their heads.[2] It would appear that holy men, or people having holy souls, are not less liable than others to be thus defiled in the body. I do not know whether these three categories correspond to those of the MISHNA, some of whom resemble angels while some are like men and others are comparable to beasts.[3] They are versed occasionally in the oral law for the better misdirection of mankind.[4] Another account says that there are many hierarchic degrees in the kingdom of the demons. Every three groups have at their head a chief placed in charge of one or other nation of the earth.[5] These chiefs in their turn are overruled by superiors entrusted with the direction of the stars, so that each nation is indirectly under the influence of a certain star, which, it will be seen, is another astrological intimation. Hence the destiny of one nation is never like that of another.[6] The reign of these chiefs will continue till the Holy One shall Himself come down and govern here below.[7] Most curious of all is the intimation that if these degrees or groups are disintegrated there will be found at the centre a sacred kernel which draws all, even the impure side.[8]

Having regard to the consideration allotted to the interpretation of dreams by the Old Testament, it would surpass expectation if the ZOHAR rejected the possibility, more especially with the authority of the TALMUD to support the affirmative view. It does something, however, to reduce the rank of dreams. They are the gross form of that which the soul sees when it is separated from the body. The soul then discerns things as they actually are, while the body perceives

---

[1] Z., Pt. I, fol. 169b ; II, 266, 267.
[2] Ib.
[3] An exact description of the Infernal Hierarchies according to the Grimoires—not that they are borrowing from the ZOHAR but because the province of images is restricted.
[4] So also one of the demons in Goëtic Theurgy is supposed to give true answers respecting things human and divine.
[5] Z., Pt. I, fol. 177a ; II, 296.
[6] Ib., fol. 177b ; II, 297.
[7] Ib. This has been mentioned previously in other terms. It does not seem to differ from the doctrine of Latin Theology.
[8] The logical consequence is realised in another place, where it is said that this vestige or kernel can never be lost utterly.

them only in a form corresponding to its own degree.[1] Every dream is regarded as an admixture of truth and falsehood [2] ; but the moSt curious thesis of all is that a dream is realised according to the interpretation placed upon it : should this be favourable,[3] favours will overwhelm the man, but in the contrary case he will be weighed down by adversity. The reason is that the word governs,[4] and it follows that no dream muSt be disclosed to any one by whom the dreamer is not loved. There are in all three degrees—dream, vision and prophecy : the greateSt of these is prophecy.[5]

Now it so happens that the Doctrine of Signatures, of which we seem to hear firSt in Paracelsus—so far as Latin-writing Europe is concerned—and which was derived from him into the theosophical syStem of Jacob Böhme, is a doctrine of Kabbalism, and though the Zoharic allusions are few and far between in respect of actual definition, they enable us— with the aid of their developments—to conclude that the mental environment of Paracelsus included some reflections from Zoharic sources. According to the sage of Hohenheim, there are elements and signatures of elements [6] ; a science of the signatures exiSts, and it teaches how heaven produces man at his conception, how also he is conStellated thereby.[7] Stones, herbs, seeds, roots and all things whatsoever are known by their signatures, that which lies within them being discovered thereby.[8] In respect of man, signature has three species, which are chiromancy, physiognomy and proportion.[9] The ZOHAR has a good deal to tell us on the firSt two, while

[1] Z., Pt. I, fol. 194a ; II, 367.
[2] Ib., fol. 183a ; II, 322.
[3] Ib., fol. 183a ; II, 323.
[4] Ib. I think that this is the only place in which a definite, over-ruling power is attributed to the formulation of thought in speech, apart from those words which—like Divine Names—are supposed to be essentially potent. The explanation is probably that the dream-interpreter was in a kind of prophetic State ; but this is to be diStinguished from the ceremonial and magical use of words, as—for example—when it is said of the pre-diluvian sorcerers that, with the aid of the mySteries contained in their secret book, it was enough for them to utter words and the desired things were accomplished.—Ib., fol. 76a, b ; I, 449.
[5] Ib., fol. 183a ; II, 323, 324.
[6] PHILOSOPHIÆ AD ATHENIENSES LIBER II, Textus x, p. 247.
[7] EXPLICATIO TOTIUS ASTRONOMIÆ : Interpretatio Alia, p. 666.
[8] Ib., IN SCIENTIAM SIGNATAM PROBATIO, p. 669.
[9] Ib., s.v. DE MASSA ET MATERIA ex qua Homo factus eSt, p. 666.—See OPERA OMNIA, Vol. II, Geneva edition, 1658. See also my HERMETIC AND ALCHEMICAL WRITINGS OF PARACELSUS, Vol. II, pp. 268, 294, 295, 305. The 9th book DE NATURA RERUM treats at considerable length de signatura rerum naturalium.

it has a supplement, so to speak, concerning chara&er and hair.[1] I do not know how the findings would appeal to those arti§ts of our own day who deal in such subje&s ; but it is desirable to point out that—within the consciousness of Kabbali§tic do&ors—such things were no part of the decried occult sciences ; they were matters of observation arising from that do&rine of correspondences which obtained in all dire&ions. I append the following particulars, gleaned from there and here, without pretending to know whether they have points of concurrence with later readings of chara&er on the same bases, or whether they differ therefrom. I should expe& that the ZOHAR would be found peculiar to itself— here, as in more important matters.

There are seven considerations regarding hair and the dispositions indicated thereby : (1) Hair which is crisp or frizzy and inclined to §tand up signifies a choleric temper ; the heart is tortuous like the hair, and such a person should be shunned. (2) Straight and silky hair is usually that of a good companion, one who succeeds in business—if not undertaken alone. He is prudent respe&ing Supreme My§teries, but cannot hold his tongue about matters of daily life. (3) Hair that is coarse and §traight signifies one who does not fear God, but works evil knowingly. He will become better, however, if he reaches an advanced age. (4) A man having black and glossy hair will succeed in material things, but he mu§t work alone. (5) The success of a black and dull-haired man is rather of an intermittent kind, and he may quarrel with his business associates ; should he take to the §tudy of the Holy Law, he will make progress therein. (6) A prematurely bald man will do well in business ; but he will be crafty, avaricious, hypocritical and one who makes a pretence of religion. (7) A man who grows bald in the natural course of years will undergo great changes otherwise ; if he has been of good condu& previously, he will now be bad, but he will turn into paths of virtue if he has been so far an evil liver. I dare not furnish particulars, but these ascriptions are referable to my§teries belonging to certain Hebrew letters. Since some of the conclusions are a little hard and arbitrary—under the reserve of sacred letters—it shall be added that certain alternative readings at a later §tage do not

---

[1] The general references are to Z., Pt. II, fol. 70b to 78a ; III, 311–328, and *ib.*, fol. 284b to 288b ; IV, 312–315.

endorse them entirely ; but from this secondary account it will be sufficient to cite a ruling in respect of auburn hair. On the understanding that it is curly, the head which wears it will fear sin, will feel compassion for all in misfortune and will have the welfare of others as much at heart as his own.

Physiognomy is a larger subject, and being treated at some length, I shall be content with a few typical examples. The man whose forehead is low and flat acts without thinking, is fickle in notions, believes himself wise and understands nothing. His tongue is like a biting serpent. The man who has deep wrinkles on his forehead which are not in parallel lines, and which are replaced when he speaks by parallel and less deep wrinkles, is to be shunned under most circumstances, as he seeks nothing but personal interests and will keep no secrets. A large and full forehead denotes the best kind of personality, capable of acquiring knowledge with the least pains and successful in all search after spiritual felicity. In money questions he may succeed at one time and fail at another, but he is not solicitous regarding material things. The man with blue eyes has a tender heart and one that is free from wickedness, but he follows his own ends and is careless proportionally about wrong done to others. He seeks pleasure but not of an unlawful kind, yet if he should fall into evil ways, he would remain therein. A man with green, shining eyes is touched with madness, believes himself superior to others and lets them know it ; he will not prevail against enemies, and he is inapt for the Mysteries of the Law. A man with clear but yellowish eyes is passionate, though often sympathetic towards the sufferings of others ; yet is he cruel in his anger, and he also cannot keep secrets. A man with dark grey eyes will succeed in the Mysteries of the Law, and if he perseveres in its study he will make steady progress therein : he will also prevail over enemies.

The distinctive marks of the countenance are modified by conduct, and differ from general inherited types, which correspond broadly to the four living creatures of Ezekiel's vision. There are those which are distinctively human, those which are leonine, bovine and in aspect like that of the eagle. There are also four types which are said to be imprinted by the soul, being : (1) That of the virtuous man, who is distinguished by a small horizontal vein on either temple, the one on the left being bifurcated and crossed by another small, vertical vein. (2) That of a man who returns to his Master after leading a bad life. He is repulsive at first, but others are finally drawn towards him; he does not care to be looked straight in the face, because he thinks that his past may be legible : he is alternately pale and yellow. He has one vein descending from right temple to cheek, another under the nose and this joins with two veins on the left cheek. These last are united by another vein, but the last will disappear when the man is habituated to a virtuous life. (3) That of a person who has fallen off completely from the good way. He has three red pimples on either cheek and some faint red veins beneath them : should he be converted the pimples would remain but the veinlets vanish. (4) That of a man who has been incarnated a second time, to repair the imperfections of his first sojourn on earth. He has a vertical line on the right cheek, near the mouth, and two deep lines on the left cheek, also vertical. His eyes are never bright, his health is poor, and the cutting of his hair and beard changes his appearance completely. Thick lips are those of the evil speaking. If a medium lower lip is cleft the person will be of violent temper, but he will succeed in business. Unusually large ears are a sign of stupidity and even of tendencies to mania ; persons with very small and well-shaped ears are awakened in mind and yearn for knowledge.

I need some indulgence for bringing in these details, and I will forbear from dwelling on chiromancy, except to say that the lines of the hand are believed to shew forth great mysteries, including those of the fingers. On the contrary I might not be forgiven by the few who know if I omitted to certify that a man with two great hairs between the shoulders is one who swears without ceasing and to no purpose. The presence of three such hairs is the sign of a happy nature. To make an end of these fantasies, he who has been guilty of adultery and has not done penance is identifiable by an excrescence with two hairs, below the navel. If he repents, the swelling will remain but the hairs will fall off.

Hereof is the ZOHAR when it makes an excursion into by-ways beyond its province, and it is likely enough that those who take palmistry and physiognomy seriously will regard the indications as worthless, even from their standpoint. It is none of my own concern. The lesson in general

concerning the occult arts is another matter, and it counts
to the text for righteousness ; it stands also much better in
its own context than can be made to appear herein. For the
rest, even when it says that they are lying, the ZOHAR does
not deny the arts ; they come from the pit and are deceptions
belonging to the pit, but they are not vagrant trickeries. There
is the greater reason to eschew them, and the work of condemnation has more than prudence or scriptural ordinance
behind it : there is the sense mystical of the essence and truth
of things. The Book of the Secret Law in Israel puts forth
its arms to draw those for whom it was written, among the
Academies and Synagogues of the past, from the world of
pictures, wherein the images of mind are multiplied and
superposed one upon another, into the inward ways of
thought, into a true refuge, where—in processes of silent
prayer and contemplation—the mind is released from images
and the Glory of the Indwelling Presence is seen and understood in the heart.

II.—THE KABBALAH AND ALCHEMY

Some reference has been made to the subject of Hermetic
Tradition when considering the Kabbalistic treatise entitled
PURIFYING FIRE. We have seen that Hermetic and Kabbalistic Philosophies are ascribed frequently to a common
source, and this has been the case with sympathetic as well as
hostile critics. The question, however, is complicated, and
though I should hesitate to differ from a consensus of informed authorities,[1] I am not less sure that as regards the
branch of Hermetic Philosophy which is known under the
name of Alchemy, we should be exceedingly careful about
making and accepting statements. We must begin first of
all by distinguishing the earlier books ascribed to Hermes
Trismegistus, and not concerned with the transmutation of
metals,[2] from such late compositions, to make use of no

---

[1] In a pamphlet entitled THE SCIENCE OF ALCHYMY, by " Sapere Aude," Fra. R.R.
et A.C., the " sages of mediæval Europe " are said to have derived their knowledge
of this subject, (1) from the Arabs, (2) from the heirs of the traditional lore now
identified by the name " Kabbalah," (3) from ancient Egypt. Of these alleged sources,
the first only is historically true in the sense that the Arabian alchemists derived from
Byzantium : the other notions belong to the slush of occult reverie.

[2] Compare, however, the anonymous preface to the first English translation of the
DIVINE POIMANDER, that of Dr. John Everard, 1650. Here the possession of " the
great Elixir of the Philosophers " is ascribed to Hermes Termaximus. See also

Stronger term, as the EMERALD TABLE and the GOLDEN TREATISE. When Isaac Myer affirms that many of the doctrines of the Kabbalah, more or less veiled, may be found in the books attributed to Hermes Trismegistus,[1] the reference obtains only, and can be intended only, to the DIVINE POIMANDER, the ASCLEPIOS and other tracts, the existence of which can be traced about or prior to the fourth century, A.D. We may search the Greek alchemists in vain for any doctrinal connection with these works, though Hermes is included among great names of antiquity which are associated with the making of gold, and there are also other references to this mystical personage. While we must discount altogether such extreme opinions as that of Isaac Casaubon, who represents the earlier Hermetic treatises as the work of a Kabbalistic adept who was probably a Jew of Alexandria,[2] we have general reasons for admitting that there were points of contact between Neo-Platonism and the Kabbalah,[3] as seen in an earlier section. The connection of Alchemy with Hermes is not through the Hermetic books of the Neo-Platonic period, and its Kabbalistic correspondences must also be sought elsewhere. Among the writings of Zosimus the Panopolite, which belong to the third century,[4] there is a quotation from the TRUE BOOK OF SOPHE THE EGYPTIAN concerning the Divine Lord of the Hebrews and the powers of Sabaoth, which affirms that there are two sciences and two

---

Westcott's observations prefixed to his verbatim reprint of Everard, COLLECTANEA HERMETICA, vol. 2, London, 1894.

[1] THE PHILOSOPHY OF IBN GEBIROL, pp. 166, 167.

[2] M. Berthelot observes, however, that " the *rôle* attributed to the Jews in the propagation of alchemical ideas recalls that which they enjoyed at Alexandria during the contact of Greek culture with the culture of Egypt and Chaldea. It is known that the Jews exercised an influence of the first importance in this fusion of the religious and scientific doctrines of the East and of Greece, which presided at the birth of Christianity. The Alexandrian Jews were for one moment at the head of science and philosophy."—LES ORIGINES DE L'ALCHIMIE, Paris, 1885.

[3] Le Chevalier I. A. de Goulianov in his ESSAI SUR LES HIÉROGLYPHES D'HORAPOLLON, &c., Paris, 1827, connects Hermetic and Kabbalistic Tradition on the fantastic ground that Enoch, who plays such an important part in the revelation, of the Kabbalah, is identical with the Edris of the Orientals and with Hermes (p. 48).

[4] As Louis Figuier's popular work, entitled L'ALCHIMIE ET LES ALCHIMISTES, was once quoted freely by occultists, and is still presumably in the hands of some of them, it will be well to point out that he classes all Byzantine literature of Alchemy as apocryphal, and the work of monks belonging to the 8th, 9th, and 10th centuries. There was never much excuse for this opinion, and it is only necessary to add that since the researches of Berthelot it has become impossible. I may add that, throughout, Figuier's work is most inaccurate as regards its facts, and of no consequence as to its opinions and inferences. Consult, on the point involved, the third edition, p. 6, Paris, 1860.

wisdoms, that of the Egyptians and that of the Hebrews, the second being rendered " more solid by Divine Justice." ¹ Both come from remote ages; they do not investigate material and corruptible bodies; their generation operates independently of any foreign action, sustained by prayer and Divine Grace. Then comes the following significant passage, which accounts for the philosophical work of Alchemy being likened to that of God in the creation. " The symbol of chemistry is drawn from creation (in the eyes of its adepts) who save and purify the divine soul enchained in the elements, and, above all, who separate the divine spirit confounded with the flesh. As there is a sun, the flower of fire, a celestial sun, the right eye of the world, so copper, if it become flower (that is, if it assume the colour of gold) by purification, becomes then a terrestrial sun, which is king on earth, as the sun is king in the sky." ² There is no doubt that this is a very important citation.³ It shews why early Hermetic books came to be regarded as alchemical in later times, and it institutes a striking parallel between Egyptian and Jewish science. But that the latter is the science of the Kabbalah there is no evidence to cite. So also a reference to the LABYRINTH OF SOLOMON which occurs among the remains of still earlier Greek alchemists is a mediæval interpolation.⁴ In short, the celebrated Byzantine collection, which is so far the source of all Alchemy, shews no traces of acquaintance with any Jewish Secret Tradition. The same observation applies to the early Arabian and Syriac alchemists who drew from Greek sources, though some extracts from Zosimus, with analyses, in a Syriac MS. possessed by the University of Cambridge, mention the talismans of Solomon, referred to the seven planets, and the power which they exercise over demons. When we add to this that in spite of such evidence for the connection between Alchemy and the Kabbalah as is offered by the late ÆSH MEZAREPH there is nothing, as already seen, to support it in the ZOHAR,⁵ it must be inferred

---

¹ COLLECTION DES ANCIENS ALCHIMISTES GRECS, *livraison* ii., p. 206.
² *Ibid.*
³ See, however, my SECRET TRADITION IN ALCHEMY, pp. 80, 81.
⁴ COLLECTION DES ANCIENS ALCHIMISTES GRECS, *livraison* ii., p. 206.
⁵ Dr. Gerhard Scholem, who has been cited in a previous note, gives an extract from SEPHER HA BAHIR, adding that it is used in the ZOHAR, but is garbled therein. The extract says that gold is called זהב because it contains the three principles. They are not, however, those of Alchemy, the letter ZAIN corresponding to a principle called human, HE to the soul and BETH to the balance between them. So also Dr.

that these two Esoteric Traditions grew up for a long period in independence of one another.[1] Furthermore, there is no trace of any science of transmutation in ancient Egypt, and it is worth noting that the claim of Alchemy rose into prominence precisely at that period when certain Chinese ports were first thrown open to western commerce. If it be true, as it has been affirmed, that Alchemy flourished in China from a remote period, that it possesses a literature, and that the terminology of this literature offers analogies with that which prevailed afterwards in the West, it may well be that we must look to the furthest East for the cradle of what is usually understood by Hermetic Science, namely, that of transmutation.[2] The subject is far too large to enter on in this place, but we shall do well to remember that the doctrine of the Macrocosm and the Microcosm, the analogy between spiritual and material, the Zoharistic symbolism of the balance, have all been traced to the oldest sacred books of the Chinese.[3] The analogies may not be so striking as the persons who have discovered them have thought; as to this, we have no real means of deciding; but they indicate at least the possibility of a common source for both Esoteric Traditions at a centre not as yet acknowledged and at a very far epoch of the past.

Of course, as time went on, and as alchemical literature

Scholem cites ZOHAR I, 249b–250a ; II, 23b–24b ; II, 147a, 148a ; and II, 171. But again they are not alchemical in the sense of alchemical symbolism, as this is known among us by the witness of its western literature. We hear of the solar rays shining straight on mountain summits in the days of Solomon and turning earth to gold ; of gold, silver, copper and iron being made of the four elements ; of gold under the presidency of Gabriel and silver under that of Michael ; of silver corresponding to mercy and gold to severity ; of gold representing joy ; and of seven kinds of gold, the seventh of which is celestial, illumines all and cannot be contemplated by the eye. All this is not Alchemy, and I agree with Dr. Scholem when he says otherwise that the Hermetic Quest was one thing and that of Kabbalism another.

[1] It is fair, however, to state that the Leyden papyrus which contains the earliest known process of alchemical sophistication forms part of a Gnostic and Theurgic collection. On this point, see Berthelot's COLLECTION DES ANCIENS ALCHIMISTES GRECS, *livraison* Ie., pp. 6 *et seq.* Albert Poisson, whose THÉORIES ET SYMBOLES DES ALCHIMISTES is a contribution of consequence to the elucidation of Hermetic Art, observes that " Alchemy among the Greeks was, by reason of its very origin, mixed up with Magic and Theurgy. Later on, thanks to the philosophic Arabs, this science became purified, and it was not till the fifteenth or sixteenth century that it allied itself afresh with the occult sciences properly so called. Thenceforth a considerable number of alchemists demanded the Key of the Great Work from the Kabbalah, Magic and Alchemy."—*Op. cit.*, p. 27. Paris, 1891.

[2] See THE CHINESE, by Dr. W. A. P. Martin, New York, 1881.

[3] The most accessible work of reference is Isaac Myer's PHILOSOPHY OF IBN GEBIROL, Appendix B. I mention this hypothesis so that it may be taken for what it is worth. See Book II, § 5. But see also my SECRET TRADITION IN ALCHEMY, cap. v.

developed in Europe, a connection undoubtedly arose with the Kabbalah.[1] The ÆSH MEZAREPH is one of its evidences ; some Kabbalists became alchemists ; a few alchemists studied the Kabbalah. But it is still a slight and occasional connection, which we must be careful not to exaggerate : there is also very little trace of it prior to the seventeenth century,[2] when writers like Fludd concerned themselves with both subjects, and Khunrath[3] introduced Kabbalistic symbolism into the pictorial emblems of transmutation.[4]

The best proof of these statements is the literary history of the ÆSH MEZAREPH itself. Mathers in his pretentious manner observes that it is "known to few, and when known is understood by still fewer."[5] If this were its position in the year 1887, it may be added that when Alchemy most flourished in the West, the treatise had never been heard of, being first mentioned by Rosenroth at the end of the seventeenth century. Prior to that date there is no case within my knowledge of its quotation by any alchemist, and although KABBALA DENUDATA was described on its title-page as *Scriptum omnibus philologis, philosophis, theologis omnium religionum, atque* PHILOCHYMICIS *quam utilissimum*, I believe that only one alchemical writer concerned himself with it after the appearance of its fragments among the *Apparatus in Librum Sohar*. This was the "Lover of Philalethes," already cited, who collected and translated the fragments in 1714 and also published in the same year A SHORT ENQUIRY CONCERNING THE HERMETIC ART,[6] which introduces certain citations from ÆSH

---

[1] "Alchemy, a science of observation, could not profit in any way by its alliance with the Kabbalah, which was purely a speculative science."—Poisson, THÉORIES ET SYMBOLES DES ALCHIMISTES, p. 28.

[2] Poisson refers this confusion of one occult science with another mainly to Paracelsus, but I have given proof already of the very slender connection between this adept and the Esoteric Tradition of the Jews.

[3] AMPHITHEATRUM SAPIENTIÆ ÆTERNÆ, with which compare the second tract of the TRINUM CHEMICUM, Strasbourg, 1700.

[4] There is a treatise entitled THE AZOTH OF THE PHILOSOPHERS which passes under the name of Basil Valentine, and has suggested a connection with Kabbalism to a few, because the term AZOTH is composed of the first and final letters of the Greek, Latin and Hebrew alphabets. It has been called into requisition accordingly, but the foundation is exceedingly slight. Moreover, the term is at least as old as pseudo-Geber, while the treatise attributed to Basil Valentine is of doubtful authenticity, and was excluded from the collection of Mangetus.

[5] THE KABBALAH UNVEILED, Introduction, p. 15. He belonged to the second class.

[6] Reprinted in Wynn Westcott's COLLECTANEA HERMETICA, vol. 3, London, 1894 ; the preface, which is not by the editor, states that the SHORT ENQUIRY was "written with special reference" to ÆSH MEZAREPH, but there seems no foundation for this view. The little tract is largely a collection of opinions and quotations, not always

MEZAREPH and connects them with the symbolism of the Doves of Diana first introduced into Alchemy by Eirenæus Philalethes.

It follows, however, from what has been stated previously that the literary connection between the Kabbalah and Alchemy does not begin so late as the first quarter of the eighteenth century [1]; and though ÆSH MEZAREPH seems to have been cited methodically by only one writer, the influence of KABBALA DENUDATA may be traced in Germany soon after its publication by means of an anonymous tract which pretends to treat of the Chemical Kabbalah [2] (*cabala chymica*) and has these words on its headline. This little work is incidentally of importance in more than one respect. On p. 16 there is a curious *Figura Cabalæ*, where the light from *Ens Entium* falls on a bearded figure holding the compass in the right and the square in the left hand, thus giving two characteristic symbols of Emblematic Masonry in connection with the secret arts at a date when such a connection would scarcely be expected on the Continent by modern scholarship. There are also some observations worth noting on the subject of regeneration which are useful for the mystical aspects of Alchemy.[3] Unfortunately the correspondences between the Kabbalah and transmutation seem to be confined to the title which I have quoted.

Some information on the subject might be expected— among works of the past—in Hoefer's HISTORY OF CHEMISTRY,[4] which claims to include an exposition of Kabbalistic doctrines concerning the Philosophical Stone;

derived from the best sources, for its author appears to regard Edward Kelley and Elias Ashmole as of equal authority with the acknowledged adepts of Alchemy.

[1] I except such slender analogies as the correspondence traced by *Sapere Aude* between the three worlds of Jean D'Espagnet and the four worlds of the Kabbalists. See HERMETIC ARCANUM, Collectanea Chemica, vol. 1 (Westcott's Edition), London, 1893.

[2] CABALÆ VERIOR DESCRIPTIO : *das ist, Brundliche Beschreibungund Enveisung aller naturalischen und uber naturalischen Dingen boiedurch das Verbum Fiat das alles erschasun* . . . Hamburg, 1680. There was a later edition, Frankfort, 1761.

[3] A work of similar pretensions is F. Kiern's CABALA CHYMICA : *concordantia chymica, Azoth Philosophicum Solificatum*, Mülhausen, 1606. Here the term Cabala is simply a catchword derived from Paracelsus, and is used in this sense by a compiler belonging to the group of Paracelsian exponents, of whom Benedictus Figulus and Alexander von Suchten are the names now most remembered or least forgotten.

[4] Ferdinand Hoefer : HISTOIRE DE LA CHIMIE *depuis les temps les plus reculés jusqu'à notre époque ; comprenant une analyse detaillée des MSS. alchimiques de la Bibliothèque Royale de Paris ; un exposé des doctrines cabalistiques sur la Pierre Philosophale*, etc., 2 vols., Paris, 1842, 1843. Mr. H. C. Bolton observes that this work is superseded so far as MSS. are concerned by the researches of Berthelot. See A SELECT BIBLIOGRAPHY OF CHEMISTRY, Smithsonian Miscellaneous Collections, Washington, 1893, p. 119.

but the term proves on examination to be used in the loose
sense of the period, and out of two very large volumes
there are only two pages devoted to the subject of the
Kabbalah.[1] The authorship of the SEPHER YETZIRAH is
attributed to R. Akiba and that of the ZOHAR to R. Simeon.
It is affirmed also that Jewish and Arabian alchemists possessed
an old knowledge of Kabbalistic books, and that they were
held by adepts in as much honour as those of Hermes Trismegistus. The evidence is unfortunately wanting, and as M.
Hoefer maintains also that the science of transmutation was
pursued in ancient Egypt, it would be unsafe to accept his
opinion unsupported by other authority.[2]

Before dismissing the Kabbalistic connections of Alchemy,
a word must be said concerning two works which have been
supposed to be examples of that connection, and to which
some importance has been attached.[3] Both have the advantage, which they share in common with Khunrath and his
AMPHITHEATRUM, of precedence over the publication of
Rosenroth's KABBALA DENUDATA, and one is prior to any
printed edition of the ZOHAR. It will be needless to say that
neither shews an acquaintance with ÆSH MEZAREPH, nor do
I observe in their contents anything to connect them with the
Sephirotic attribution of metals which is characteristic of that
work. One is a treatise by Joannes Augustinus Pantheus, a
Venetian priest, entitled ARS ET THEORIA TRANSMUTATIONIS
METALLICÆ, cum Voarchadumia Proportionibus, muneris et
iconibus rei accomodis illustrata. It was published at Venice in
April, 1530.[4] Following the author himself, the Hermetic
Lexicons interpret Voarchadumia, (a) as "a liberal art gifted
with the virtues of occult science," a definition which leaves
something to be desired ; (b) as the Kabbalistic science of
metals. It is further a species of alchemical metallurgy,

---

[1] T. i., pp. 242–244.
[2] There is indeed one authority cited, namely, the APPARATUS of Rosenroth, KAB.
DEN., i., 441–443, and this is a quotation from the ÆSH MEZAREPH, c. 7.
[3] There are others naturally in the large literature of Alchemy, but they are not of
Hermetic value, and, as in all cases, the Kabbalistic connection is thin and elusive.
Such is the PHILOSOPHIA SALOMONIS, or Secret Cabinet of Nature, a German anonymous
treatise published at Augsburg in 1753. Here the Royal Stone of Alchemy is connected with the art of King Solomon, but there is no Kabbalistic knowledge, and the
work is quite worthless. See also : Cabala : SPIEGEL DER KUNST UND NATUR IN
ALCHYMIA, Augsburg, 1690, remarkable for its curious folding plates.
[4] Rare in the original edition, but rendered accessible by the reprint in Lazarus
Zetner's THEATRUM CHEMICUM, Argentorati, 1613, etc., second edition, 1659. See
vol. ii., pp. 459 et seq. A Paris edition of the tract is mentioned also, date 1550.

concerning " auriferous metallic veins " ; it explains " the intrinsic fixed form and the natural yellow colour of gold " ; it distinguishes the heterogeneous, combustible, volatile parts, and exhibits how the same may be conducted to the grade of perfection. It defines, lastly, the Matter of the work as " a heavy, corporeal, fixed, fusible, ductile, tinged, rarefied and arcane substance of Quicksilver or Mercury, and of an incombustible Metallic Sulphur, educed and transmuted into true gold by means of cementation."[1] It will be seen from this specimen of style that the work is very nearly unreadable, even for an alchemical treatise, and it will be enough for the present purpose to note the fact of its existence and to observe that it seeks to throw light on the mysteries of transmutation by calculations of GEMATRIA. It exercised no influence, and no importance can be ascribed to it.

The other work is much better known to fame and it offers several interesting, and so far unsolved, problems to the student. This is the MONAS HIEROGLYPHICA of Dr. John Dee, first published in 1564, and containing an analysis of the planetary symbols attributed to the metals.[2] Thus, the symbol of Mercury ☿ is composed of the crescent ☽, which is the sign of silver, the circle ☉, which is that of gold, and the cross representing the four elements. Special alchemical importance is attributed to their union in the sign which represents the fundamental matter of the philosophers as well as metallic quicksilver. It will be seen that this is not in any sense information which helps to connect Alchemy with Kabbalism, though it is important for the obscure question of the symbolism and history of astronomical signs.[3]

I may observe in conclusion that there is one possible connection between Alchemy and Kabbalism which would appear to be overlooked by all those who have instituted a comparison between them. It is supplied by the obscure but subsisting analogies between the ancient document of Latin

---

[1] See the anonymous English translation of Martinus Rulandus : LEXICON ALCHEMIÆ, sive Dictionarium Alchemisticum, the edition of 1612. This translation, without date or place, was restricted to six copies, and includes a large SUPPLEMENT to the Alchemical Lexicon of Martinus Rulandus. The explanation of Voarchadumia occurs on p. 438.

[2] For the astrological aspect of this analysis, see some curious speculations in Alan Leo's PRACTICAL ASTROLOGY, second edition, n.d.

[3] For information and references see § xliv. of the ECLAIRCISSEMENT ASTRONOMIQUE appended to M. Bailly's HISTOIRE DE L'ASTRONOMIE ANCIENNE, 2nd edition, Paris, 1781.

Alchemy known as TURBA PHILOSOPHORUM [1] and the two Synods of the ZOHAR. I am not, of course, referring to the accidental similarity of form, though, having regard to the history of the TURBA, this accident is certainly a feature of interest. There are statements and allusions in this obscure colloquy, more especially regarding the four elements of ancient chemistry, which offer curious points of contact with Kabbalism. When we add to this that some scholars— including Berthelot—have referred the TURBA in the guise that we at present possess it to a Hebrew original, now lost, and that its date, so far as it can be assigned, is somewhere between the promulgation of the BOOK OF FORMATION and the ZOHAR, enough has been said in indication of a possibility upon which there is no need, as indeed there are few materials, to insist further. [2]

III.—THE KABBALAH AND ASTROLOGY

The Victorian schools of French and English Kabbalism were inclined, as remarked already, to claim that all " occult sciences " are rooted in the Secret Tradition of Israel ; but it seems more correct to infer that the Kabbalah has been engrafted on some of them, and in this manner we have

---

[1] See TURBA PHILOSOPHORUM, or Assembly of the Sages, called also the Book of Truth in the Art, and the third Pythagorical Synod . . . Translated from the Latin . . . By A. E. Waite, London, 1896. I must confess that I have no theory as to the two previous Synods.

[2] It is due to my readers, and to the subject, to confess that I have not made an exhaustive examination of alchemical literature in reference to its connections with Kabbalism. I have made myself acquainted with all sources which have been cited by those who affirm them, but as their observations have not been based upon a wide study of the alchemists, it is possible that future researches may discover something which has, so far, been overlooked on both sides. I should note also that, according to M. Berthelot, " the Kabbalah was bound up during the middle ages with Alchemy, and the connection goes far back," that is, to the Leyden Papyrus as well as to the Greek alchemists. But I infer that this great authority has, so far as the mediæval period is concerned, received only a derived impression, or that at least his notion of the Kabbalah has been obtained as such notions most commonly are. All his instances as to the earlier connections must be rejected decisively. Some of them, such as the LABYRINTH OF SOLOMON, have been dealt with already ; others are mere names— Abraham, Isaac, Jacob and the word Tsabaoth " in papyri of the same family as No. 75 of Reuvens." It is further obvious that a reference by Zosimus to Solomon and his wisdom establishes no Kabbalistic analogy. Finally, when the Greek alchemist traces the revelation of the Sacred Art from the Egyptians to the Jews, " who published it to the rest of the world," we must remember that this view belongs to a period which referred all science and philosophy to the chosen people on the principle of Aristobulus and Philo, so that this also proves nothing. Les Origines de l'Alchimie . . . Observe that Watt's BIBLIOTHECA BRITANNICA, ii., 179 n, gives a reference to a work by H. C. van Byler, entitled, TRACTATUS CABBALISTICO—CHYMICO—PHILOSOPHICO—MAGICUS. Cologne, 1729, but I am not acquainted with its contents.

Kabbalistic Astrology, as we have also Kabbalistic Alchemy. To determine the superior accuracy of either view we must have recourse exclusively to history and literature. It is only in the instance of Ceremonial Magic that the voice of both is unanimously in favour of a Kabbalistic origin as regards the western world. From *a priori* considerations we shall be disposed to believe that the case of Astrology will prove something like that of Alchemy, namely, that its history and literature contain little to connect it essentially with Jewry, outside the casual traditions and express condemnation of the ZOHAR. It has the air of an exact science and seems to suggest few possible analogies with the speculations of a theosophical system. There are two facts, however, which are above challenge, firstly, that the Jews were much addicted to Astrology,[1] and, secondly, that the prophetic science of the stars, as it is known in the West, has derived something from later Hebrews. Against these must be placed two other facts, not of less significance, namely, that ancient Israel contributed very little to the science of astronomy, that Jewish astronomical writings belonging to the Christian centuries draw chiefly from Arabia, and that as regards Astrology in Jewry, during the Kabbalistic period, it was imbedded in fantastic notions and puerile processes. We are not called to deal here with the history of the art : we know that Josephus traces it to Seth and assures us that he himself had visited the two famous Pillars reported to have survived the deluge, and on which all the rules of Astrology are said to have been engraved. Josephus may have been deceived easily, or he may have been tempted to claim for his nation on the warrant of a fable the precedence in a study to which the notion of learning was attached. Seth and the Pillars set apart, we know also that antique Chaldea was a great centre of Astrology, that it flourished among the Babylonians, that it was practised in Egypt ; and it is natural to suppose that the Jews must have had their share in the knowledge of each of these peoples. There may have been even a Kabbalah

---

[1] The question whether the art was condemned by the Law of Israel has been a subject of some debate, and we have made acquaintance with Zoharic intimations on the theosophical side of the subject. Perhaps the best opinion considered that it was. See on this point the CONCILIATOR of Menasseh ben Israel *sive de conventia locorum S. Scripturæ quæ pugnare inter se videntur*, Frankfort, 1633, p. 142. It was debated also by Gaffarel, writing from the Christian standpoint. He contrived to defend the art by distinguishing it into two branches.

of astrological procedure communicated to Christian times.[1] All this, however, is beside the real question; we are not justified in looking for the ZOHAR or its influence in Jewish writings on mathematics or natural philosophy, for the simple reason that the ZOHAR does not connect seriously with these subjects. We are at liberty, however, to ask ourselves one question. Astrology works upon data which are very obscure in their history,[2] and there are doctrines connected with it which even to the "occult student" may seem insufficiently grounded. It would be interesting to ascertain whether they have any Kabbalistic correspondences, notwithstanding the condemnation of the ZOHAR. As to the data, I suppose that no one has attempted to institute a parallel, but it has been thought that some astrological theorems may have a connection with Kabbalistic apparatus. Let us see therefore what is said upon this subject by its students.

The attribution of metals to the SEPHIROTH in ÆSH MEZAREPH suggests planetary attribution, and a tabulation has been constructed by Papus,[3] following the authority of Kircher :—

1. KETHER corresponds to the Empyrean.
2. CHOKMAH   „   „   Primum Mobile.
3. BINAH   „   „   Firmament.
4. CHESED   „   „   Saturn.
5. GEBURAH   „   „   Jupiter.
6. TIPHERETH   „   „   Mars.
7. NETZACH   „   „   Sun.
8. HOD   „   „   Venus.
9. JESOD   „   „   Mercury.
10. MALKUTH   „   „   Moon.

It is possible, as ÆSH MEZAREPH affirms, that "all systems tend to the one truth," but this scheme is not in accordance with either of its own attributions. These are followed by

[1] P. Christian affirms that there was, but he offers no evidence in support of his assertion that the SPECULUM ASTROLOGIÆ of Junctin was a kind of synthesis of the astrological labours of the "Arabian and Hebrew Kabbalists."—HISTOIRE DE LA MAGIE, l. vii., Clefs générales de L'Astrologie, p. 579.

[2] The history, moreover, has never been elucidated by any writer on the subject. Mr. W. Gorn Old's NEW MANUAL, 1898, does not attempt to account for the grounds on which the old judgments are based.

[3] For Papus consult LA KABBALE, already cited frequently ; for Kircher ŒDIPUS ŒGYPTIACUS. The synopsis of the Kabbalah in this rare work has been translated recently into French.

Rosenroth ; but R. P. Esprit Sabathier, in that strange little treatise on Kabbalism which once exercised so much fascination on French students of the subject, refers Mars to GEBURAH and Mercury to HOD.[1] When there is no unanimity we must infer that there is no point of importance involved and that attributions and tabulations of this kind are less or more conventional and can have little application to Astrology itself. In modern times, however, all divinatory practices, which in every case possess or suggest astrological connections,[2] have received some kind of Kabbalistic attribution. Thus, the planetary correspondences of the figures used in geomancy have been adjusted to the SEPHIROTH ; Kabbalistic principles have been applied to chiromancy ; physiognomy alone, possibly because it has never had much attention at the hands of professed occultists, seems an exception to this rule, although, as we have seen previously, there is direct warrant for it in the ZOHAR.[3]

The most accessible information on Astrology among the Jews is in the CURIOSITIES of James Gaffarel, who based his observations on a direct knowledge of its chief rabbinical exponents during the Christian centuries.[4] To reduce what he says to a sentence, the Jewish astrologers read the heavens like a book, they regarded it as a book, and, for the purposes of methodising its contents with a view to its interpretation, they collected the stars into hieroglyphic characters, which were, in fact, the Hebrew alphabet. Their process was therefore not an astrological process, but more correctly one of divination, and as to its value, we have only to glance at the Hebrew planisphere furnished by Gaffarel to see how arbitrary was the nature of the arrangement. At the same time it suggests a correspondence with the fundamental

---

[1] See L'OMBRE IDÉALE DE LA SAGESSE UNIVERSELLE, 1679. A reprint of this work has appeared in Paris. The original is rare, and there is no copy in the British Museum ; but the reader may consult the Table given by Papus at pp. 80, 81 of his treatise on the Kabbalah, where the attribution in question will be found.

[2] Thus, the PRINCIPLES OF ASTROLOGICAL GEOMANCY became the subject of a special treatise by Franz Hartmann, M.D. (London, 1899), while Rosa Baughan compiled a curious medley of Chiromancy and Astrology under the title of THE INFLUENCE OF THE STARS.

[3] Physiognomy has been, of course, connected with Astrology, and an old work published about the beginning of the seventeenth century under the title of BOOK OF PALMISTRY, PHYSIOGNOMY AND NATURAL ASTROLOGY illustrates this connection. See also A TREATISE ON ZODIACAL PHYSIOGNOMY, by John Varley, London, 1828.

[4] A summary of Gaffarel's information, with some pertinent criticisms, will be found in Éliphas Lévi's RITUEL DE LA HAUTE MAGIE. See also TRANSCENDENTAL MAGIC, part ii., and MYSTERIES OF MAGIC, pp. 248, 252, 253, 254. Second edition, 1897.

notion of SEPHER YETZIRAH, though the fact has not been observed by any previous writer. There could be nothing more natural for those who believed that the heavens and the earth were made by the inscription of letters in the air than to discover these letters in the configurations, apparently fortuitous, of the starry heavens.[1] In place therefore of the unmeaning mythological figures of pagan antiquity they imagined the twenty-two elements of the divine word manifested to the chosen people, and the imagination once justified by the apparent delineation of the characters, it became part of the scheme of the universe.[2] To read the sense of the heavens so that they could give the meaning thereof was an operation no less sacred in its intention, mysterious in its methods, and strange in its results[3] than the application of Zoharistic processes to the disentangling of the mystical meaning beneath the letter of the Scriptures. This is the true Kabbalistic Astrology,[4] based on a Kabbalistic Doctrine which is its justification and of which it is in turn the logical development. Outside the SEPHER YETZIRAH, it has the countenance of the ZOHAR itself. But it has little in common with the science of the stars, as this has been pursued in the western world; it can offer nothing in evidence of its considerations, even as Astrology in the West has nothing to tell us concerning the Kabbalistic Mystery of AIN SOPH. It is better therefore not to confuse further the complicated issues of occult arts by the suggestion of fantastic influences and unrealisable communications.[5]

It will be anticipated of course that a literature so large as

---

[1] These are the Celestial Letters mentioned previously, or at least their cosmic counterparts.

[2] This is the Zoharic notion, and it was claimed that by means of the signs and figures in the heavens most profound secrets and mysteries could be discovered. So regarded, the stars and constellations are a subject of contemplation and a source of mysterious delight for the sage.—Zohar, ii., 76a, Mantua.

[3] Compare those other strange results in Symbolical Astrology of which Ruysbroeck the Mystic speaks in the BOOK OF THE TWELVE BEGUINES, Latinised by Surius under the title De Vera Contemplatione. Needless to say this Astrology is not judicial. The late Mr. Hargrave Jennings has also some pleasing fantasies on the " astronomy of the mind " in THE INDIAN RELIGIONS, pp. 207 et seq., London, 1890.

[4] Which Astrology, as Lévi observes rightly, must be distinguished from what is commonly understood by Judicial Astrology. See MYSTERIES OF MAGIC, p. 247.

[5] As an instance of the extraordinary lengths to which speculations of this kind have been carried, outside astronomical connections, see Dr. J. Lamb's HEBREW CHARACTERS DERIVED FROM HIEROGLYPHS, London, 1835. The hieroglyphics in question are " re-constituted," and various doctrines, passages and words of the sacred writings are interpreted by recourse to them. But it happens unfortunately that scholarship had yet to do its work in the light of the Rosetta Stone.

that of the Jews and embracing, as we said at the inception of our inquiry, so wide a range of subjects could not have grown up without contributing anything to the knowledge of the heavens. In the third century the Jews of Babylon have been called famous as doctors and astronomers and; partly for this reason, are said to have been in high credit at the Persian Court during the reign of the usurper Artaxerxes. Samuel Lunaticus, to whom astronomical tables are attributed, the head of the Academy of Naharden, is an instance in point, and R. Ada, also of Naharden, is another. Abba Aricha, better known as the Babylonian Rav, founder of the Academy of Sora, was an early student of astronomy, and names might be multiplied easily. Side by side with medicine and the interpretation of dreams, Astrology was pursued by eastern Jews of the tenth and eleventh centuries. In 1150, or thereabouts, R Avi Joseph wrote a treatise on the intelligences which move the heavens and concerning the judgment of the stars. Aben Ezra, about the same period, is a considerable name among astronomers of Jewry as well as in doctrine and philosophy. Abraham Chiia and Abraham Nasi are also contemporary students of the same art. In the second half of the thirteenth century, during the reign of Alphonso X., King of Castile, himself called the astrologer, the rabbins were in estimation for their knowledge of the heavens, and the Tables attributed to Alphonso were the work of a Jew whom he employed. In the fifteenth century the family of Alcadet produced two astronomers, and Abraham Zacut, author of the SEPHER YUHASIN, was another student of the subject in the days of Ferdinand and Isabella.

Meagre as are these indications, having regard to the fact that astronomy was pursued usually in connection with the judgment of the stars, i.e., with Judicial Astrology, they are sufficient to establish that this occult practice is to be found in Jewry during most of the Christian centuries.

The reader who desires to become acquainted with the first principles and procedure of Jewish Astrology may consult the CURIOSITIES of Gaffarel, whose information is drawn from R. Moses, R. Aben Ezra, R. Jacob Kapol ben Samuel, &c. This learned but pedantic writer rejected what is called Kabbalistic Astrology, with its Sephirotic attributions [1]; but

---

[1] So far as I am aware, no astrological work developing these connections has ever been printed in any European language, but books like John Bishop's MARROW OF

the system which he develops is not less fantastic, and is that indeed which I have described briefly in an earlier part of the present section. It would be out of place to extend references, for, as on the one hand Sephirotic Astrology is set aside even by so determined a Kabbalist as Gaffarel, so, on the other, the secrets of the Hebrew planisphere and the mysteries of stellar writing do not connect with the practice of the art in the West.

It may be added that a contemporary writer, Mr. W. Gorn Old, has published a Kabbalistic Astrology [1]; but it is merely a process of divination, like that attributed to Cagliostro, which was developed at great length and applied to the science of the stars by P. Christian.[2] It is obvious that the use of the term Kabbalistic in such a connection is merely a *façon de parler*, unfortunately in very common use. This is made further evident by the parallel application of the term Hermetic, not only as an analogue, but an actual equivalent. Mr. Old's process is affirmed to have been " in use among the ancient Kabbalists," but this is merely speculative and an inference from certain alleged Tarot connections.

IV.—THE KABBALAH AND FREEMASONRY

The researches and findings of Masonic scholarship notwithstanding, occult reverie has not emerged altogether from the old maze of fables concerning the origin of Speculative Freemasonry. Even now, in France and England, it is thought by uncritical writers to have a past extending behind it into remote ages. In one or another sense it is still a survival of the Ancient Mysteries ; but this term is used in a general sense, not as signifying only the initiations of Egypt, of Greece, or of Rome, but rather the secret power and intelligence which is thought to have been present behind the philosophical associations of all ages and most civilised countries. During the Christian period the knowledge which would otherwise have perished was preserved *ex*

ASTROLOGY, London, 1688, with its list of the governing angels of the signs and the planets, suggest Kabbalistic connections through the vehicle of Ceremonial Magic.

[1] KABALISTIC ASTROLOGY, *or Your Fortune in your Name*, by Sepharial, London, n.d. (? 1892). It has been mentioned in a previous note.

[2] In his HISTOIRE DE LA MAGIE, books ii., iii., and vi. Also in L'HOMME ROUGE DES TUILERIES. Some account of Cagliostro's Method will be found in Grand Orient's MANUAL OF CARTOMANCY, &c., of which several editions have appeared.

hypothesi among successive occult fraternities, some known to history, such as Templars and Rosicrucians, the rest working in complete silence. Corporately or otherwise, they were all affiliated with each other, and Symbolical Freemasonry forms the last link in the western chain of transmission.

As there is little need to say, no presentation of this hypothesis has been able to survive analysis, and it is left at most with a possible connection between Masonry and Rosicrucianism, a little before and after the Grand Lodge epoch of 1717. The evidence is, however, inconclusive, or at least unextricated.[1] This being the state of the case, and the claim on antiquity which is made for Freemasonry by some of its unwise votaries not having been urged by the institution on its own behalf outside the Rituals, there is nothing *prima facie* to accredit the idea that it has been ever a channel of any Secret Tradition except its own, or to warrant us in supposing *a priori* that it should have any distinct analogies with Kabbalism. And as a fact its position in this respect is much like that of Alchemy, seemingly fortuitous, a question of subsequent introduction, as much imputation as reality, a varnish rather than a permeating tincture, and yet, like all such positions, interesting. To establish my point, I must refer to the fact that since Masonry appeared on the historical plane, occultists and even mystics have tended towards it, that it has received them all amiably, and that—now, of course, in the past—all have elaborated the system in accordance with their particular notions. During the prevalence of the passion for Rites we know that alchemists, Swedenborgians,[2] Martinists, theurgists, astrologers, all invented new Grades and new Orders, and as at this period there were also Kabbalists, so in one or two instances we hear of Kabbalistic Rites, especially of Rites and Grades which exhibit Kabbalistic influences. As Freemasonry is not Swedenborgianism, as it is not Alchemy, as in spite of Elect Cohenim, the Evocations and Rituals of Pasqually, and the pretended marvels of Schrœpfer, it is not

[1] See, however, my BROTHERHOOD OF THE ROSY CROSS, *cap.* xvi, pp. 443–446 ; also my EMBLEMATIC FREEMASONRY, II, pp. 21–45.
[2] The history of the Swedenborgian Rite being exceedingly obscure, and yet possessing considerable occult interest, it may be observed that some account of it was published at New York in 1870 by Samuel Beswick. It is not to be trusted, however, on the score of accuracy.

Theurgy or Magic, nor—unless at its root—the Mysticism of any of the true Mystics, so it is not Kabbalism, but it has been put to use in Kabbalistic as in other interests.

It must be added that the few Kabbalistic Degrees which have left any record behind them beyond their name, and the uncommon swiftness with which they passed into extinction, give no evidence of acquaintance with Jewish Esoteric Tradition. They represent the Kabbalism of the period. There is no need to speculate as to its quality in most cases ; it has bequeathed its literary remains in Grimoires and Grand Clavicles, in the spurious thaumaturgic processes of Abramelin, and in amusing Kabbalistic correspondence with the Seigneur Astaroth,[1] the lees and lavations of rabbinical conduits. As it will be well to enforce these statements by means of documentary evidence, I will add an account of one Kabbalistic Grade which may be taken to represent the whole. It is otherwise among the best of its kind.

A degree of Knight of the Kabbalah once existed among those innumerable developments of the Fraternity which were termed high by their disciples and spurious by some who resented innovations, and especially those which led to nothing. It has long since fallen into disuse. The object of the Candidate, according to the Catechism of the Degree, was " to know, by means of numbers, the admirable harmony which subsists between Nature and Religion." It defines the Kabbalist as a man who has acquired the Sacerdotal Art and the Royal Art by the communication of Tradition. The device was *Omnia in numeris sita sunt.* The Master of the Lodge in which the Degree was communicated seems to have been called President of the Sanhedrim and Rabbi. The mystical significance of numbers [2] was developed by the Catechism in a somewhat curious manner, which it may be worth while to summarise.

I = in the moral order, a Word incarnate in the bosom of a virgin, otherwise, Religion ; in the physical order, a spirit embodied in the virgin earth, or Nature. It is the

---

[1] See D'Argens : LETTRES CABALISTIQUES, *ou Correspondance Philosophique* . . . *entre deux Cabalistes*, &c., 7 vols., La Haye, 1754.

[2] The numerical mysticism of the Kabbalah is based, of course, on the SEPHIROTH ; most of its developments are very late, and possess a magical complexion, for which reasons they do not enter into the scheme of this study. Those who are concerned may consult an attempt to simplify chronology by Kabbalistic figures in Michael Aitsinger's PENTAPLUS REGNORUM MUNDI, Antwerp, 1579. On the general subject, see Petrus Bargus : MYSTICÆ NUMERORUM SIGNIFICATIONIS LIBER, Bergomi, 1585.

generative number in the order of Divinity—apparently a false symbolism, because the monad neither generates nor is generated, whence Éliphas Lévi says more correctly that the monad supposes the duad, and thence, through the triad, all numbers are evolved.

II = in the moral order, man and woman ; in the physical, active and passive. It is the generative number in created things.

III = in the moral order, the three theological virtues ; in the physical, the three principles of bodies. The reference here is to Salt, Sulphur and Mercury, thus indicating the Hermetic connections of this Grade. Three also denotes the triple Divine Essence.

IV = the four cardinal virtues, the four elementary qualities—another Hermetic reference—and it is, moreover, the most mysterious of numbers, because it contains all the Mysteries of Nature.

V = the quintessence of religion, and the quintessence of matter—which again is alchemical. It is also the most occult number, " because it is enclosed in the centre of the series." The precise meaning of this last statement does not appear, but it may possibly refer to the pentagram as one of the emblems of the Grade.

VI = the theological cube and the physical cube. It is the most salutary number, " because it contains the source of our spiritual and corporeal happiness." Is this a reference to the symbolical adultery of the first man whereby the coming of the Liberator was necessitated ?

VII = the seven sacraments and the seven planets. It is the most fortunate number, " because it leads us to the decade, the perfect number."

VIII = the small number of the elect, or the wise. It is the most desirable number, " because he who possesses it is of the cohort of the Sages."

IX = the exaltation of religion and the exaltation of matter. It is the most sublime number, because Religion and Nature are both exalted thereby.

X = the ten commandments and the ten precepts of Nature. It is the most perfect number, " because it includes unity, which created everything, and zero, symbol of matter and chaos, whence everything emerged. In its figures it comprehends the created and uncreated, the beginning and end,

power and force, life and annihilation. By the study of this
number we find the relations of all things, the power of the
Creator, the faculties of the creature, the Alpha and Omega
of Divine Knowledge.

XI = the multiplication of Religion and the multiplication
of Nature. It is the most multiplying number, " because
with the possession of two units, we arrive at the multiplication of things."

XII = the twelve articles of faith ; the twelve apostles,
foundation of the Holy City, who preached throughout the
whole world for our happiness and spiritual joy ; the twelve
operations of Nature ; the twelve Signs of the Zodiac,
foundation of the *Primum Mobile*, extending it throughout
the universe for our temporal felicity. It is thus the most
solid number, being the basis of our spiritual and corporeal
happiness.

The numbers after twelve were left to the discernment of
the Candidate. The Catechism shews also that this putative
chivalry concerned itself with the Universal Spirit of Alchemy
and even with the quadrature of the circle. The history of
the Knights of the Kabbalah is unfortunately involved in
obscurity ; but it will be seen that it was Christian and
Catholic, which furnishes a resemblance to other and later
institutions professing similar purposes and having similar
religious sympathies.[1]

Had the Book of Occultation been made in the eighteenth
century the theme of a Masonic Grade, had the Lodge represented the Tree, the Master in the East Kether, and the
officers the remaining Sephiroth ; had the Ritual been
constructed from the Zohar and the Catechism from the
Apparatus of Rosenroth, all this would have proved nothing
as to the Kabbalistc connections of Masonry. Within
comparatively recent years a powerful Masonic Order
underwent a species of development in this direction through
the labours of Albert Pike, and it would almost seem that he
had a mind to transform the Ancient and Accepted Scottish
Rite into a seminary of occult study. There may be many
of its own brethren at the present time in whom this statement
will excite only incredulity ; but it is not the less certain that

---

[1] Among the degrees collected by the French Mason Peuvret, there was that of
Maçon Cabbalistique. The Metropolitan Chapter of France specified the 80th
Grade of its mammoth collection on paper by the title of Chevalier de Cabale.

Albert Pike was more than an ardent admirer of occult philosophies, or that he pursued the subject into regions of which Masonry has no conception. He was seconded also by numerous like-minded persons who occupied high dignities in the United States' Southern Jurisdiction. The evidence of all these things is to be found (*a*) in his transformation of the Rituals, (*b*) in the vast body of instruction which he compiled, chiefly from sources in occult literature, for all Grades of the Order. No person who is acquainted with MORALS AND DOGMA can fail to trace the hand of the occultist therein, and it is to be observed that, passing from Grade to Grade in the direction of the highest, this instruction becomes more and more Kabbalistic. It matters little that the sources from which Pike drew were of the worst rather than the best, or that, though a man of wide reading, he was not a critic ; for we are concerned only with a tendency and its development. He accepted *en bloc*, for example, the construction placed on Kabbalism by the most unsafe of all its expounders, Éliphas Lévi, from whom he translated verbatim at great length, and, following his professed habit, with no specific acknowledgment, while for the rest his only source of further information was KABBALA DENUDATA, of which, however, he shews no analytical knowledge, seeming to regard LIBER DRUSHIM as entitled to rank in authority with SIPHRA DI ZENIOUTHA. In spite of these limitations he made available an amount of information on occult subjects with which no previous scheme had ever provided Masonry. Yet with all his strenuous efforts the seal of occultism was not impressed effectually on the Ancient and Accepted Scottish Rite, and it remains therefore that the Oriental Rite of Memphis, Ancient and Primitive,[1] and that of Misraïm,[2] with its long Kabbalistic Class or Series of Degrees, are the only sections of high-grade Masonry which claim a distinct purpose of an occult kind : it is not necessary to say that in England, at least, they have failed in obtaining recognition

---

[1] See Marconis et Moultet : L'HIÉROPHANTE, *développement complet des Mystères Maçonniques*, Paris, 1839. LE RAMEAU D'OR D'ELEUSIS, another work by Marconis, is also interesting as the views of an amiable but somewhat moonstruck student upon the Mysteries in connection with Masonry.

[2] A history of this institution, with all the fabulous and indeed mendacious elements which might be expected, was written by Marc Bédarride and published in two volumes at Paris, 1845, under the title, DE L'ORDRE MAÇONNIQUE DE MISRAÏM, *depuis sa creation jusqu'à nos jours*, &c.

as acceptable developments of Masonry, and both have passed into abeyance.[1] We see therefore that Kabbalistic influence is confined to so-called High Grades. It would be absurd to discuss the possibility of its presence in the Blue Lodges or seek to interpret the Legend of the Master Grade in connection with Jewish Tradition, outside at least the allegory of the Lost Word. The symbols, however, which are familiar to the initiates of these Lodges do connect with Kabbalism, if not with other forms of occult philosophy ; but the presence of the Seal of Solomon among the heirlooms of the Brotherhood being, so far, unaccountable, it is useless to insist on the connection, because nothing logically follows from it. So far as history is concerned, Kabbalism and Masonry once joined hands in the sphere of the Higher Grades, and as a historical fact this is interesting, but that it is otherwise significant must be left to those who affirm it.

V.—THE KABBALAH AND THE TAROT

It is known to innumerable persons who are not occult students at the present day that the Tarot is a method of divination by means of seventy-eight symbolical picture-cards, to which great antiquity and high importance have been attributed by several expositors. Their literary history is also fairly well known. They were mentioned first by the French archæologist Court de Gebelin at the close of the eighteenth century, and were attributed by him to an Egyptian origin. Much about the same time the subject was taken up by a professed cartomancer, named Alliette, who wrote a great deal about them in several illiterate tracts, and endeavoured to trace their connection with Egypt through the Jewish Kabbalah. The inquiry then fell into neglect, except in so far as Continental fortune-tellers were concerned, until the year 1855, when Éliphas Lévi made his first contribution to occult subjects.

In 1857, J. A. Vaillant [2] endeavoured to prove their Chinese

---

[1] The fourth Series of the Rite of Misraïm is designated Kabbalistic.

[2] HISTOIRE VRAIE DES VRAIS BOHÉMIENS. As a notice of the gipsies this work is exceedingly good for its period ; its Tarot speculations are worthless, and its philological arguments absurd. M. Vaillant described the Tarot as " the synthesis of ancient faith, a deduction from the sidereal Book of Enoch " (412). Its origin he affirms to be lost in the night of time (413). He mentions the Kabbalah only to establish its connection with Cabul ! (p. 54).

origin [1] and transmission by means of the gipsies; their connection with these nomads was adopted subsequently by Lévi, who gave great prominence to the Tarot in all his writings up to the year 1865. The subject was taken in hand also by P. Christian, who published a large HISTORY OF MAGIC in 1870. He developed still further the Egyptian hypothesis, but no statement which he makes can be accepted with the least confidence. In the year 1887 I was the first who introduced the claims of the Tarot to English readers in a digest of the chief works of Éliphas Lévi. A contribution to the inquiry was made shortly after by the French occultist Papus, whose volume entitled the TAROT OF THE BOHEMIANS, though of no critical value on the historical side, remains an elaborate summary of all the arguments which have been produced from the standpoint of occult reverie and invention in France.

The point which concerns us here is, of course, the alleged Kabbalistic connections. Éliphas Lévi says that the Tarot cards are a key to the Esoteric Tradition of the Jews, and " the primitive source of Divine and human Tradition "; he institutes an analogy between the symbols of its four suits and the four letters of the Divine Name TETRAGRAMMATON, and between the ten SEPHIROTH and the ten small cards belonging to each sequence. He gives also the correspondences between the twenty-two Trump Cards and the letters of the Hebrew Alphabet, for which he quotes the authority of " divers Kabbalistic Jews," the fact notwithstanding that there is no trace of any reference to the Tarot by Kabbalistic writers of the past. It must be admitted, on the other hand, although the historical evidences cannot be said to exist, and have been supplied from treasures of imagination, that the Tarot is actually, as it is claimed to be, of considerable importance symbolically. I may be permitted to register also my feeling that it has Kabbalistic connections, some of which were broadly outlined by Éliphas Lévi.

---

[1] Occult writers mostly favour Egypt as the birthplace of the Tarot, and this is consistent with their views on the origin of the Kabbalah. So Mons. Z. Lismon has published a version of the cards under the title of LIVRE DE THOT, *Jeu des 78 Tarots Egyptiens*, with explanatory booklet. Compare R. Falconnier: LES XXII. LAMES HERMÉTIQUES DU TAROT DIVINATOIRE, which pretend to be re-constituted exactly according to " the sacred texts and translation " of the Magic of old Egypt! Of more recent times the Masonic littérateur Oswald Wirth has produced two versions of the Trumps Major, while in England a complete set, of symbolical and artistic value, has appeared under my own auspices.

There is, moreover, a Jewish Tarot of great rarity which
has never been published ; but it belongs to the worst side
of so-called Practical Magic.

Unfortunately, the interpretations of Tarot symbolism
which have been attempted by various writers are worthless,
in the first place because they have proved themselves incapable of conducting an historical inquiry ; they have allowed
affirmation to take the place of evidence ; they have regarded
a hint as a sufficient ground of conviction ; they have made
conjecture certitude. Setting aside Court de Gebelin, who
was merely an inquirer hampered by the limitations of his
period ; setting aside Lévi, who seldom made an accurate
statement about any matter of fact ; observe how Papus
pursues his inquiry into the origin of the Tarot. It is by an
appeal to writers who preceded him, as if their authority
were final ; to Court de Gebelin, who was a groper in the
dark during the childhood of archæological research ; to
Vaillant, with his fascinating theory of gipsy transmission
which is about as conclusive as Godfrey Higgins on the
CELTIC DRUIDS ; to Lévi, whose " marvellous learning " is
so much and so unsafely insisted on by the whole French
school. Papus contributes nothing himself to the problem
on its historical side except an affirmation that " the game
called the Tarot, which the Gypsies possess, is the Bible of
Bibles."

In the second place, the supposed Hebrew symbolism of
the Tarot, which, in justice to Papus, is laboriously elaborated
—though apart from all inspiration—becomes disorganised
if there is any doubt as to the attribution of its Trump Cards
to the Hebrew Alphabet. Now there is one card which bears
no number and is allocated therefore according to the discretion of the interpreter. It has been placed in all cases
wrongly, by the uninstructed because they had nothing but
their private judgment to guide them, and by some who
claimed to know better because they desired to mislead. It
happens, however, that they also were at sea. I may go
further and say that the true nature of Tarot symbolism is
perhaps a secret in the hands of a very few persons, and outside that circle operators and writers may combine the cards
as they like and attribute them as they like, but they will
never find the right way. The symbolism is, however, so rich
that it will give meanings of a kind in whatever manner it

may be disposed, and some of these may be suggestive, though illusory none the less. The purpose of this short paper is therefore to shew that published Tarots and the methods of using them may be serviceable for divination, fortune-telling and other trifles ; but they are not the key of the Kabbalah, and that the Royal Game of Goose may be recommended with almost as much reason for the same purpose. Papus was therefore misdirecting his many followers when he advertised his involved readings as the " Absolute Key to Occult Science."

VI.—THE KABBALAH AND MYSTICISM

On the one hand the history of Kabbalism is so imbedded in that of mere occultism, that it is scarcely known or admitted in any distinct connection. On the other hand, to the pure mystic, there is so much in the Kabbalistic system which is extrinsic to the subject of Mysticism, that there is a temptation to underrate its influence, though herein is its test of value, and it is a palmary purpose of the present long research to produce the materials and in fine pronounce upon them. I am offering at this point a few preliminary considerations only, based on the fact that Western Mysticism was the channel of a great Tradition in Christian Times.

It is to be observed here and now that the correspondence and difference may perhaps be brought into harmony if it be permissible to regard Mysticism in two ways—as a philosophical doctrine, or rather body of doctrine, that is to say, an ordered metaphysics, held intellectually,[1] but also as a mode of conduct practised with a defined purpose, in a word, as mystical doctrine and mystical life, it being understood that the doctrine is rooted in first-hand experience derived from the course of life. The practical mystic is the saint on the path of his ascent into the mystery of Eternal Union, concerning whom it is consonant with the purpose of our present inquiry to speak at the moment only with great reservation, seeing that the Mysteries of Divine Life do not fall within the limits of historical research. I conceive that the sum of Kabbalistic instruction is not without service to the disciple

---

[1] And this would be the correspondence of the ZOHAR with Mysticism. For example, the doctrine of ecstasy is assuredly found therein, but not in the same way that we find it in Ruysbroeck or St. John of the Cross. It is more especially a rationalised system of mystical thought.

of this secret path, because of the Zoharic doctrine that a science of Holy Unity, into which all things return as all come forth therefrom, can be attained by man.[1] *Invenit sanctum*. Like all other studies, and perhaps not more so than any other methodised Theosophy, it has, moreover, a certain office in the *sanctum facit*. For that far larger class to whom the possibility of great sanctity is denied, who are in search rather of a guide for thought upon questions of fundamental philosophy, I conceive that the Kabbalah—but obviously, like other metaphysics—has useful and reassuring lights. It is a source of intellectual consolation that one of the most barren of all the ways pursued by the human mind has its own strange flowers and fruit. It is also, as I have sought to shew, something more than an inheritance from the past, even an inheritance that has been transmitted from a period far back in human history. The ZOHAR at least has the power of stirring those depths in the human heart which are beyond the " plummet of the sense " ; it seems occasionally to " strike beyond all time, and backward sweep through all intelligence," and to say this, is to confess that it is of the eternal soul speaking, here under the common influence of right reason, there in ecstasy and vision, and again, as it would seem in somnambulism or even in frenzy. Now, the speech of the human soul, in what state soever, is not without a message to the mystic, be it even in certain cases a word of warning only. There is no need to add that on its Theosophical side the Kabbalah connects assuredly with Mysticism.[2]

With occultism, of course, it is not without connection on the theurgic side throughout all its history, as the doctrine of Names and their power exhibits but too well. The difference between occultism and Mysticism is much more than that of a Latin equivalent for a Greek term, as might appear at first sight. We are all acquainted with the distinction which is made between the magnetic and hypnotic sleep. They have

---

[1] Zohar, I., 51*a*, Mantua.

[2] M. Anatole Leroy Beaulieu says that the Jew is not inclined to Mysticism, and seems never to have been so. " Judaism has always been a law, a religion of the mind, an intellectual creed, not favourable to mystic transports or divine languors." He denies also that Kabbalism was indigenous in Jewry. " The mysteries of the Kabbalah, and those of the Hassidim, the neo-Kabbalists, seem to have been a foreign importation ; according to the best judges, the Kabbalah itself is not rooted in Judaism."—ISRAEL AMONG THE NATIONS, translated by Francis Hillman, London, 1895, p. 292. This view shews little first-hand acquaintance with the subject.

much in common, but they are pathologically separate, having diverse characteristics and a divergent mode of induction. Sleep, however, is obtained in both, and this is their superficial and obvious point of union—so superficial and so obvious that the ordinary observer would scarcely fail to identify them, while they have been identified also on grounds which are not precisely those of ordinary observation. Between occult arts and mystical science there is the common and rather banal point of union which is created by the inherent notion of secrecy. Beneath this fantastic resemblance there is the more important fact that they both profess to deal with inner and otherwise uninvestigated capacities of the human soul. In the case of occultism it is, however, for the kind of end which we connect with the notions of Magic. For example, Talismanic Magic, so called, is ostensibly the art of infusing a supposed recondite spiritual power into some object composed artificially. This is an operation of occult art because it deals with a power which is, by the hypothesis, of a secret or generally unknown nature and applies it in accordance with the formulæ of a concealed instruction. A knowledge of the capacities which are latent in human nature may suggest Mysticism, which is the development of such capacities in the direction of Divine Union. There is usually, however, no person less really mystic than the occultist conventionally understood, while the mystic on the path of attainment in the life of sanctity is exploring the world of grace, not that of psychic power.

The end of Mysticism is the recovery or attainment of consciousness in God, and there are two exotic Kabbalistic doctrines which not only connect therewith but belong thereto. The first is found—but once only—in the ZOHAR and has been referred to in these pages : it is the doctrine of TSURE, of the supernal part of the soul, which does not leave the Supernals, but from beginning without beginning to endless end is rooted in God for ever. The second is in later Kabbalism and is expressed tersely by Rosenroth in one pregnant Latin sentence : *Linea autem media ascendit usque ad* AYIN SOPH. The ascent of the soul to God is by the Middle Path in the Tree of Life, and the soul is led thereby not only to the World of the Supernals but to the deep beyond the deep and the height beyond the height, which is the abyss and height of Deity. So does the Holy Kabbalah join hands with the Mysticism of all the ages, and so is it part of our inheritance.

[It should be added that TSURE, which signifies Prototype and corresponds to ATZILUTH, is said to be connected with NESHAMAH by "an invisible thread," constituting a bond of union which is also a path of ecstasy. NESHAMAH ascends thereby and attains therein—namely, union with the supernal part.]

BOOK XII
FINAL CONSIDERATIONS

BOOK XII

FINAL CONSIDERATIONS

I.—DEVELOPMENTS OF LATER KABBALISM

THE circulation of the ZOHAR by Rabbi Moses de Leon at the end of the thirteenth century—he being its concealed author, according to one section of opinion—proved unquestionably as great a surprise to the community of Israel as it was to the Christian scholars when they came to know of it later. I speak here with a qualification because our first information concerning Zoharic MSS. comes to us from Picus de Mirandula towards the end of the fifteenth century, and we have seen that his was the first voice which testified to the presence of Christian elements therein. On the other hand, the Jewish expositors belong to the sixteenth century and later ; but I speak of those who are of repute, and if any one wishes to go farther into the matter there are the great rabbinical bibliographers to tell of things unprinted which are among the treasures of the Vatican and other libraries of Europe.[1] Speaking generally—as I have mentioned elsewhere—the impetus of studies in both directions must be sought in the Cremona and Mantua editions of the ZOHAR. So far as the records are concerned, it must not be said that there is a very large literature on either side ; but a few sons of Israel had recourse to the wonderful memorial with as much zeal as Mirandula and his successors. To the better Kabbalistic Jew it offered an illimitable field of development and the indulgence of that particular sort of metaphysical speculation which was dear to his heart at the period. There

---

[1] The most important of the older bibliographies are (1) Johannes Buxtorf : BIBLIOTHECA RABBINICA *novo ordine alphabetico disposita*, 8vo, Basle, 1613. (2) Bartolocci : BIBLIOTHECA MAGNA RABBINICA : *De Scriptoribus et Scriptis Rabbinicis*, 4 vols., Folio, Rome, 1678–92. (3) Imbonatus : BIBLIOTHECA LATINA-HEBRAICA (a sequel to No. 2, by the editor of Bartolocci's work, most of which was published posthumously), Folio, Rome, 1694. (4) O. Christoph. Wolf : BIBLIOTHECA HEBRÆA, 4 vols., 4to, Leipzic, 1715.

could be no greater opportunity, for I have indicated that the ZOHAR assumes throughout a more or less perfect familiarity with the chief heads of its subject, and it is not therefore concerned with presenting a formal system of the Secret Doctrine. The later Kabbalists provided that which was wanted there and here out of their own heads, with the help of any *flotsam* and *jetsam* of theosophical reverie which was passing from mouth to mouth in and about the Academies from Sapeth to Beaucaire. We know that about the middle of the eighteenth century two sects arose in Jewry, claiming the ZOHAR as their authority in chief. One was the sect of Pietists or New HASIDIM, which rejected the TALMUD, together with external forms, and was zealous in the practice of Contemplative Prayer, as recommended by the ZOHAR to those who are in search of inward knowledge concerning Divine Mysteries. It was incorporated for the quest of perfection along these lines.[1] Solomon Maimon has left some particulars concerning the vagaries of these enthusiasts, who were followers of Israel Baal Shem[2]: it survived bitter persecution on the part of orthodox Jewry and was still active in Poland at the middle of the nineteenth century. It is now, I believe, in dissolution rather than decline. The second was the sect of Zoharists who belonged to the same country and were also anti-Talmudic. It was established by Jacob Frank, and it embraced Christianity.[3] I mention these matters, because they shew the kind of influence exercised by the ZOHAR at one period in a particular locality. Of its secret influence on remote continental Jewry, in places like Galicia above all, we shall probably never know, so that the later developments of Kabbalism are without adequate records.

---

[1] I am reflecting current opinion of the eighteenth and nineteenth centuries, but assuring my readers that there is no call for inquiry either as to the kind of perfection or the particular practice of prayer. While it is true that the end of both was spiritual communion with God, the anticipated fruits of this were the gift of prophecy and power to work miracles. Moreover, those who had attained the height of Hasidism acted as mediators between God and the rest of humanity.

[2] Israel ben Eliezer Ba'al Shem Tob, who acquired extraordinary repute as a teacher and yet more as a healer in Podolia, *circa* 1740 and onward.

[3] There is an excellent account of Frank in THE JEWISH ENCYCLOPÆDIA, V, 475–478, to which readers may be referred. He was born in Podolia about 1726 and died in 1791, the work being carried on by his beautiful daughter Eve, who became " the holy mistress " and " the leader of the Sect." At the beginning its conversion to Christianity was in view of a coming Messianic religion. After the death of Eve in 1816, the Frankists of Poland and Bohemia are said to have been transformed gradually "from feigned to real Catholics, and their descendants merged into the surrounding Christian population."

It would serve little purpose to extend this study by additional summaries of contributions made in the sixteenth and seventeenth centuries to the understanding of the ZOHAR. There were scholiasts and expositors outside those who have been considered in the ninth book : some of them produced lexicons dealing with obscure and " foreign " words found in the text ; some wrote commentaries on particular sections ; some analysed the Kabbalistic system presented in the ZOHAR. In respect of one and all it may be said that for those—if any should remain—who believe in a floating Tradition transmitted from mouth to mouth among the later doctors of Israel, it would be advisable that they should not regard the memorials to which I refer as its representatives in written form. As indicated already in respect of a few examples, that which they did was to reproduce current speculation, to which they added their own. Had the debates at Salamanca been reduced into what FAMA FRATERNITATIS R. C. calls " a true memorial," the later Kabbalists—supposing their admission to the conclave—might have added their quota, and it might have been according to the law and order respecting the rule of debate ; but it would have remained within these measures, a sequence of excursions in theses, with an open field in regard to counter-theses. All the contentious voice of certitude notwithstanding, I have not found that the additional literature of Zoharic Kabbalism possesses a higher claim. It seems above all other things certain that on the higher doctrines of the ZOHAR, on Shekinah and the Mystery of Sex, it offers nothing at all.

In comparatively recent days, we have been told by responsible writers that the ZOHAR itself made its own way among the Jews rapidly ; that " even representatives of Talmudic Judaism began to regard it as a sacred book " ; and that " Zoharic elements . . . crept into the liturgy of the sixteenth and seventeenth centuries." [1] But again the higher teaching did not unfold, or I at least have failed to trace its development. There were poets who arose in Jewry and adopted there and here some elements of Zoharic symbolism ; but it was that part which is called by the unhappy name of erotic symbolism, the notion of the Lover and Beloved brought down into terms of sense. Of the soul's supernal

---

[1] JEWISH ENCYCLOPÆDIA, xii, *s.v. Zohar.*

part, which does not leave the Supernals, the poets do not speak, nor do those who were doctors in their day and called Masters in Israel. Of AIN SOPH as a mental proposition or a doctrine of Transcendental Theology we hear from time to time, and may become fairly well acquainted with it on the historicity side ; but of experience of the soul in God beyond the forms and images, beyond the names and attributes, there is again nothing. The considerations belong to debate and the expositions have their place in systems, unlike the brief and pregnant sentences in some of the early texts, which speak in comparison from the centre and the great vistas open. They open, that is to say, for some of us, and for one at least of these, confessing in humility, there is new realisation of his own formulary, far in the past years, that the soul comes forth from that centre, and the centre draws it back.

A word may be said in concluding this section on some works of modern scholarship which are considerable and important in their way. When my first study on the Secret Tradition in Jewry was passing through the press, Dr. S. Karppe published at Paris in 1901 his own elaborate ÉTUDE SUR LES ORIGINES ET LA NATURE DU ZOHAR, which approached the subject from a standpoint very different to my own, but was at the same time a valuable contribution to our knowledge of Jewish Theosophy, and I noted with satisfaction that there were various debated points on which, working thus independently, we had reached the same conclusion. Dr. Karppe's study was designed for the scholar and the philosopher, while my own, as explained, was intended, primarily at least, for the theosophical student. The Jewish Mysticism which led up to and preceded the ZOHAR was very fully presented by him, but of the influence exercised by that work and of its after history he had nothing to tell us. On the other hand, the scheme of my own treatise led me of necessity to pass somewhat lightly over pre-Zoharic Theosophy, over Saadyah, Ibn Gebirol, Judah Ha Levi, Aben Ezra, Maimonides, &c., because they did not affect materially the mystical thought of Europe, and give prominence to Kabbalistic literature in its later phases, to the Christian students of the subject, and to its influence upon other proposed channels of Secret Tradition in Europe. Among the points of agreement between Dr. Karppe and myself may be mentioned the common recognition of the heterogeneous nature of the ZOHAR, which justified me in terming it a medley; of the specifically Jewish character of Zoharic Mysticism, which justified me in denying that it is referable exclusively to any one school of thought outside Jewry; of the rapid deterioration of the Kabbalah, subsequent to the appearance of the ZOHAR, into a thaumaturgic system; of the undue prominence which has been given to the commentaries on the ZOHAR and the false impressions which have been the result; of the preconception which governed the mind of most Christian students of the literature, by which they were led to regard it as an unacknowledged depository of Christian doctrine; of the absence in the SEPHER YETZIRAH of any distinctive pantheism or emanationism. There was also considerable similarity, both of thought and treatment, in the development of the Kabbalistic and typically Zoharic doctrines concerning God and the universe, more especially concerning AIN SOPH and creation *ex nihilo*. It would be easy to multiply these instances, nor less easy to furnish numerous points of divergence; for, on the other hand, Dr. Karppe laid too much stress, as I think, on his distinction between the early Jewish Mysticism and that of the Zoharic period, not because such a distinction is either non-existent or unimportant in itself, but because I cannot find that it has been challenged by any qualified writer. And I must, of course, as a mystic, take exception to the conception of Mysticism expressed or implied throughout the whole work. Mysticism is not a double doctrine, whether of monotheism for the initiate and of many deities for the vulgar, or of any other such antithesis as priestcrafts may have devised in the past; but it is outside possibility to do more in the present place than refer to this point and register the bare fact that the students to whom personally I appeal would join issue with Dr. Karppe now, as they must have done then, respecting all that follows from his conception, whether it be a matter of simple definition, such as that Mysticism is a reprisal of faith against science, or of historical criticism, as for example when he observes that the Doctrine of Ecstasy is almost unknown to Jewish Theosophy, a statement, however, which the author himself abundantly, though not explicitly, modifies at a later stage of his study. The student will notice also a tendency in certain instances to pass over questions of criticism as if there had never been a dispute regarding them: on the one hand the commentary of Hay

Gaon is made use of as if no scholar had challenged its authenticity; and, on the other, the late date of the BAHIR is taken for granted. Criticism may not have said its last word on either subject, but Dr. Karppe ignores the criticism. The work has been long out of print and was tabooed matter from the beginning for the occult circles of Paris, which had eyes only for visions evoked on the subject by the wand of Éliphas Lévi. It was not until after two and twenty years that the next exposition of importance appeared in France, entitled LA KABBALE JUIVE,[1] by M. Paul Vuillaud, and was in a plenary sense of appeal and interest. I had published my second work on Israel and its Secret Doctrine so far back as 1914 and had turned from research thereon into higher fields of Mysticism, when M. Vuillaud brought me back for a season into the old paths of speculation, reminding me of things innumerable and casting new lights as I travelled. It must be said that he brought me also not a little satisfaction which might be called malicious, as I thought of *les écoles esotériques* of Paris; of their devotion to Éliphas Lévi, the *grand Kabbaliste* : of his egregious MYSTÈRES DE LA KABBALE ; of the excellent Dr. Papus, who had brushed those Mysteries also with the " extreme flounce " of Mrs. Browning and her AURORA LEIGH ; but last of all, Chateau, who took off the Latin vesture of Rosenroth's extracts and having clothed them in French was held to have " translated " the whole ZOHAR. To the confusion of all there was one knocking now at their gates who carried titles of knowledge and had a mind to cast out traffickers in spurious wares from the precincts of the Kabbalistic Temple. *Les écoles* sent Karppe to Coventry, and I suppose that M. Vuillaud will have watched with diversion that conspiracy of silence which awaited him also in those directions.

It is impossible in a short notice to say anything adequate or that can rank even as descriptive of so large a work : I can note only here and there, but with difficulty even then, for one tends to be drawn into side issues through predilection arising from old familiarity with the same paths. An early chapter on Generalities of Jewish Mysticism is full of such temptations, while another is the question of so-called Kabbalistic precursors and the position among them, for

---

[1] The sub-title is *Histoire et Doctrine*, 2 vols., 1923.

example, of Ibn Gebirol. I should like to compare at some length what is said of him from this point of view with the study of Isaac Myer, long ago now in America. But my readers must be at the pains for themselves, because Vuillaud's chapter on SEPHER YETZIRAH must set all these aside : it proves representative enough, though there is little that can be called new. Those who are acquainted with Mr. Knut Stenring's version, introduced some time since by myself, will find it very much to their purpose. M. Vuillaud's conclusion is that SEPHER YETZIRAH is not a " preface " to SEPHER HA ZOHAR, but that the two works belong to one and the same tradition, the first being more explicit than the second and a summary of certain Kabbalistic themes, " notably that of Divine Revelation considered under the form of symbolical writing, and of emanation and cosmic evolution, contemplated from the mystical as well as the natural standpoint and developed in the order of harmonious analogy." The possible authorship of Elisha ben Abuyah is passed over—*pace* Dr. Robert Eisler—with a mocking reference, in dismissing a hypothesis of Epstein which regards the tract as designed for the instruction of youth.

The antiquity of the ZOHAR is considered in a long excursus which embodies an acute analysis of salient points in hostile criticism and seems to dispose of them effectually. They are taken in succession and examined in their different aspects, variously put forward as their champions followed one another, from the date of the vowel-points—which are mentioned, as we have seen, in the ZOHAR—to the antiquity of the first intimations on AYIN SOPH and the SEPHIROTH. Thereafter follows the story of Isaac de Acco and the quest which he attempted concerning the great text—as it has been given on my own part, and with much the same results. M. Vuillaud concludes, like some others, including Professor Schiller-Szinessy, that the ZOHAR is not a forgery by R. Moses de Leon ; that it is a collection of many texts referable to various dates ; that the arguments against it are of anything but irresistible force ; that it represents an ancient Tradition, a school, and is the " authentic expression " of old Jewish wisdom, notwithstanding " interpolations, suppressions and changes " in the actual form, which things are an outcome of successive developments. M. Vuillaud goes further, citing unquestioned writings under the name of R. Moses, to the confusion of hostile critics. As regards De Pauly's French version of the ZOHAR, he is aware of its omissions and mentions one of them at least. This notwithstanding, his " critical essay " is dedicated with lively affection and gratitude to Émile Lafuma-Giraud, whose editorial labours gave us the French ZOHAR, after the death of its translator. Moreover, one of his longest extracts [1] from the text follows the De Pauly version, though elsewhere he appears to translate on his own part.

I have dealt with matters about which my readers are most likely to desire the views of a recent expositor in the field. For the rest, M. Vuillaud gives studies on Sephirotic Doctrine ; on the relation of Kabbalah to Pantheism ; on Shekinah the Indwelling Glory and Metatron the Angel of the Presence ; on Messianic Theosophy, more especially in the Zoharic School, the sects which have arisen therefrom, the Sabbataï Zevi movement and the excesses of later 'Hassidim. A chapter on the influence exercised by the Kabbalah on its earlier Christian students recalls my own monographs, though I miss a few names which are not without consequence to myself : the folios which they brought into being are still on my shelves. One of the most curious considerations, developed at some length, deals with the Kabbalah and Freemasonry. For Banamozaga and some few others, " Masonic Theology "—so dignified—is identical, we are assured, with the Secret Tradition in Israel. Certain authors of note and all the posse of zanies are quoted in this connection, not without rudimentary realisation at least of a distinction between the two classes and of the more important, if obvious, fact that the said Theology is after all *peu de chose*. M. Vuillaud has a good time, and offers as much to his readers among all the follies and nonsense ; but he is apparently not a Mason, has not been at work seriously and misses the root-matter of the whole correspondence, such as it is, and such as I have sought to develop it, here and elsewhere, in my own case. He misses, moreover, a wider occasion for distraction, being unacquainted with High Grades, their Rites and their Orders, which claim derivation from Kabbalism.

The volumes are written in a curiously discursive style, which does not mean that the author is diverging continually

---

[1] *Op. cit.*, Vol. I, pp. 272–274.

from his main issues, but he is very much at ease about them, is never in haste to proceed and finds an opportunity always to look at the various aspects. It may be said that the theme throughout is one of Zoharic Kabbalism, while the impression left on the reader is that which it is designed unquestionably to convey, namely, that the best evidence for the age of the Secret Tradition for which the word Kabbalism stands in the language of Jewry is the *milieu*, the environment, the atmosphere amidst which Christianity itself happened to be born and in which it grew at the beginning. The cosmic matter and nebulæ—so to speak—that are crystallised in the main Kabbalistic text is the age-long story of the theosophical mind of Israel, in Palestine, in Babylon, and at that great meeting-place of life and thought, Alexandria.

It does not appear that M. Vuillaud is himself a Son of Israel, and though he is well and sympathetically acquainted, he is not exactly a Son of the Doctrine. He has described his work exactly in the parenthesis beneath its title : it is a critical essay, having apprehension as such ; but I do not find evidence that he is aware anywise of a life and reality deep in the heart of the Doctrine. His contemplation of Shekinah—as Our Lady of Israel comes before us in the ZOHAR—offers proof of this : it is well enough done and is not apart from sympathy ; but as it begins so also it remains, an enlightened critical appreciation. Of Zoharic Sex-Doctrine he says little, and that there is anything pregnant in its intimations he does not dream. The work taken as a whole is a study of that which environed the central thing rather than of the thing itself. This is why it is so informing externally, but why also—as it seems to me—there is something deficient, and that something belongs to the secret life of the subject.

As regards Germany it has been stated that there are schemes in the making, including translations of the BAHIR and SEPHER YETZIRAH, but I have not heard of any considerable critical work on the literature at large or its chief representative text. It remains to add that Jewish scholarship in England has not been drawn especially towards the subject of Kabbalism : so far back as fifteen years ago, Dr. J. Abelson said that " works in English are unfortunately very few," and the statement obtains to-day as it did at that time. There is, however, his own extended study on the IMMANENCE OF GOD IN RABBINICAL LITERATURE, which appeared in 1912 and should be consulted for the doctrine of Shekinah, the significance of MEMRA and the Rabbinical Theosophy of the Word. It was followed some twelve months later by a small volume on JEWISH MYSTICISM, which has chapters on SEPHER YETZIRAH —referred in all likelihood to the sixth century—the ZOHAR, Ten SEPHIROTH and the soul in man. It is held incontestable that the ZOHAR is considerably later than the second century and that much of it is a development of doctrine " embodied in the TALMUD and MIDRASHIM " ; but " it could not possibly be the production of a single author or a single period of history."

I am brought in this manner to include among those final considerations which mark the term of our research a summary note on the present position of scholarship respecting its broad subject : there will be drawn thus into a focus the occasional lights and beacons which have shone upon our path in its travelling. They belong, however, only to the external side. As regards the documents of Kabbalism, that which was foretold by Dr. Schiller-Szinessy has substantially come to pass, and all that was said once about MIDRASHIM which embody the Secret Tradition is in course of re-expression from another and very different standpoint. The German school of Dr. Graetz, whose English exponent was Ginsburg, has passed utterly away, and the Zoharic writings are regarded now as a growth of several centuries, not apart from a certain root in Talmudic times. Their connection with R. Simeon ben Yohai remains where we should have expected, in the realm of legend and unlikely to emerge therefrom : it is not flouted, but no hypothesis is pledged thereto. The final shape assumed by the ZOHAR—in a word, its reduction according to the extant and only form—may not be much anterior to the first reports concerning it. Some of the increment and some or all of the redaction may be attributable by a bare possibility to Moses de Leon ; but I conclude that every statement concerning this personality must be taken under all reservation, the account in SEPHER YUHASIN having little, if any, evidential value.

The period of R. Akiba is not unwarrantable or repugnant as a date of the SEPHER YETZIRAH, or some earlier form of that document ; but the extent to which it anteceded the ninth century remains at present conjectural. And now in respect of content, the SEPHER YETZIRAH and ZOHAR incorporate beliefs which in some form or other belong to all occultism : they are part of the burden of Kabbalism, but they go back through the ages and would or might have been acquired by the Jew in his early settlements and successive captivities. Outside these, the *corpus doctrinale* of the ZOHAR, in so far as it is fantastic commentary on Scripture has—within my knowledge—invoked no special research and may be in its procedure of no assignable date. Having no concern in arbitrary systems or artifices apart from system, the inquiry has not been pursued on my own part. In so far as the *corpus doctrinale* consists of metaphysical subtleties, theosophical reveries or great spiritual lights, they are regarded, generally speaking, as post-Talmudic, but sometimes with occasional roots in a further past. If I speak for myself and look upon the Kabbalistic writings broadly, they appeal to me in the first place as documents of humanity, but among such as memorials of Israel and its peculiar genius, possessing their connections with other systems and other modes of thought, but by correspondence, by affiliation, by filtration, by causal identity, rather than by historical descent. The ZOHAR in particular is one of the chief Theosophical Manuals of the human mind, full of greatness and littleness, of sublimity and folly, but testifying continually in its higher intimations to a doctrine of certitude, attained at first hand by inward experience and not merely by a path of debate. The interest which it aroused on its appearance has in some measure survived all criticism, and the work itself has lived down even the admiration of its believers. It is to be accounted for naturally and historically as a genuine growth of its age ; but while it is not an " imposture " or a " forgery "—as it used to be called crassly in days that are fortunately dead as well as beyond recall—so also it is not a *clavis absconditorum a constitutione mundi* or the key of all veridic secret knowledge, as old follies have termed it. In particular it contains no vestiges of that Doctrine of Secret Religion, belonging to time immemorial and behind all Religion, which some of its expositors claimed once to find therein. It is secret in the sense of Theosophical Doctrine in Jewry, appealing to an elect school among that elect people and no further ; it supposes and involves the whole claim of Jewry. The existence of a Hidden Doctrine of Religion perpetuated from antiquity lies plainly upon the surface of the ZOHAR, but it happens to be that of the immortal medley and not that of the expositors to whom I refer and all or sundry of their so-called esoteric schools. Nor is it the Religion behind Religion of the late Professor Max Müller, or a highway or byway of Secret Doctrine according to Madame Blavatsky. It is none of these things and none of their shadows and reflections in the modern varieties of occult belief. It belonged to the Sons of the Doctrine who kept the Written Law that they might come to know of the Oral ; and as to those who were denied for ever an entrance to its Holy Temple, they were all the nations of the world, the Gentiles outside the Covenant. The Doctrine stood, in other words, behind one Religion, one and no other. That which by the hypothesis lies therefore at the back of all Religions cannot be proved by recourse to Kabbalistic literature ; and had this notion been rested thereupon it would be to that extent discounted. The question, however, does not stand or fall by the Kabbalah.

There is reached here and now one term of our research, but another remains over and belongs to the last section of this book, that is to say, whether—the Sons of Doctrine notwithstanding and all their dream of special and exclusive election—there is not something in the Secret Doctrine of Israel at its highest which belongs to all Religion, at the highest of that, and is therefore as much of our concern in this day as it was of the Holy Assemblies in that of R. Simeon, according to the Sacred Tradition.

II.—THE ALLEGED CHRISTIAN ELEMENTS

I have made some occasional allusions, as required by the matter of the moment, to those particular interests, circumstances and dedications in religion under which the ZOHAR assumed the vesture of the French language.[1] It has been

---

[1] We have seen that the French translation was the work of Jean de Pauly, leaving over the question whether this was an assumed name, as alleged by hostile criticism in certain Jewish quarters. It was published posthumously by M. Emile Lafuma-Giraud, who completed and corrected it, with the help of other Rabbinical scholars. As an example of personal views, their titles and their warrants, it may be noted that in De Pauly's judgment the three IDRAS—being the ASSEMBLY OF THE SANCTUARY and the GREATER and LESSER HOLY ASSEMBLY or SYNOD—are referable to the second or third century before Christ. M. Lafuma-Giraud says justly that this is rejected by all critical learning. His own conclusion is that the ZOHAR as a whole embodies very old materials, combined with much that is of comparatively modern authorship.

owing to a group of *literati*, incorporated—so to speak—for the purpose and actuated by an old and time-honoured zeal for its interpretation in a Christian sense [1] —at least as regards the chief elements of the text. I have indicated also at need the personal gratitude with which I should welcome a proof in this direction. I believe in my heart that the mystery of the Christ in Palestine is the Mystery of a Holy Sanctuary, hidden in the heart of the Providence which moves humanity forward; but it is not my intention to say anything on this subject unless and until I shall have opened another path in the mystic quest. It is one thing, however, to confess, under every prudent qualification, to such a view, but it is another to affirm that the ZOHAR, written long after the advent of Christ, is a secret storehouse of Christian Doctrine, confessing under veils to the Divine Mission of the Master of Nazareth. The bias of the translator in this direction was in several cases so strong that some paraphrasings, in which Christian predilections obscured the true sense, have been excised and redone by revisers. The supplementary task of annotation, which is partly the work of De Pauly but in the main that of his editor, is a storehouse of debate on the whole subject, and it goes even so far as to suggest that a considerable portion of the text, or of its codification at a given period, was the production of a Christian school which, in some undemonstrable manner, lay hidden in Jewry. Under these circumstances it is not surprising that the translation has been challenged in Jewry.

It is not worth while to follow out a speculation of this kind unless the canon of criticism on which it rests should be found to speak with authority, and this is by no means the case. But seeing that the ZOHAR does not correspond internally to that which it would appear on the surface, namely, verbatim reports of debates held in the first century of the Christian era,[2] but is—on the contrary—a work of

---

[1] The claim is not only the old claim but the expression is almost identical when it is said that Christian Teaching is neither more nor less than a continuation of Jewish Tradition, and that the ZOHAR—as the reflection of that Tradition within certain measures—formulates plainly, amidst all its obscurities, the doctrine of the Trinity and of the Man-God, Who came upon earth 2000 years ago. See EPILOGUE to the French translation, fol. 6.

[2] An occasional *lapsus memoriæ* determines the value of the implied claim in the negative, as we should expect antecedently, when the unknown editor is found reminding readers of that which has been written or said previously. The ZOHAR is a literary document and bears the marks of its making.

various periods and multifarious authorships, having further
a certain rough method and sequence preserved moderately
throughout, a certain unity of purpose, there is nothing
improbable in the idea that it was the work of an exegetical
school—if only for the very innocent and candid reason that
Kabbalism supposes Kabbalists. My reference is here to the
text itself, apart from the additional documents which are
brought in at various points. Speaking rather in a tentative
and fluidic sense than in one that is dogmatic and formal, I
believe personally that some of these [1] have their roots in a
further past than can be claimed for Commentaries on the
Pentateuch, at least in their extant form. It is, however, no
part of my concern to insist on the question of antiquity,
either in respect of the fact or its importance. The existence
of a Secret Tradition in pre-Christian times is beyond my
province of research, [2] as I do not happen to have taken all
knowledge for my subject. Herein, as in my other writings,
I am dealing only with an epoch of Christendom. If it could
be shewn that the ZOHAR did not antecede the twelfth or
thirteenth century in any part of the collection, even this
substituted antiquity would be adequate for my purpose, if I
found that its intimations offered aspects of importance within
the measures of Secret Tradition.

There was assuredly a Secret School of Kabbalism, and
it is a subject of incessant reference in the ZOHAR under the
general title of Sons of the Doctrine. Whether it was an
incorporated school—as we should understand the expression
at this day—is another question. It is said in one place that
man is renewed or reborn by every new idea respecting the
Secret Doctrine [3]—almost as if the latter constitutes a sequence
of principles, presupposed and wholly understood, out of
which many developments might issue. It was not consequently always a matter of Tradition. Granting that there
was this common or general root, not only were fresh lights

---

[1] On the other hand it is thought that some are later still, and one has been even
ascribed to the fourteenth century. If this be correct, it follows of course that they
were added by the editors of the first printed editions, and it is of common knowledge
that these varied in respect of their contents.

[2] Having stated this fact on the score of sincerity, it may be well to add that an
exhaustive study of the Kabbalah itself, whether or not as a branch of Secret Tradition,
would have to be made in connection with that of comparative religion, again demand-
ing qualifications on which I can make no claim, not to speak of space for its development which would be impossible, here at least.

[3] Z., Pt. I, fol. 5a ; I, 25.

possible but their discovery became a source of joy—where and whensoever it arose, with whomsoever it might be for a mouthpiece.[1] The disciples of the ZOHAR held open minds, giving ready—even rapturous—welcome to any new idea, if it carried the proper warrants. But it is said further, and not in full consonance with what I have just intimated, that the message must be one of a master—meaning presumably that he must either be known as such or must prove himself.[2] It was a case, however, that by his own words ye shall know him. A stranger in the course of some journey, a poor and outwardly despised person, might so exhibit his titles, when he was recognised and acclaimed on the spot.[3] It follows that the masters, as such or otherwise, were not always known to one another, so that if the Society of the Secret Doctrine was after any manner incorporated, it must have been scattered widely and propagated by a process of segregation—if I may so call it—by instruction or communication from master to disciple, from father also to son. As to the latter classes the counsel was one of silence, because he who pronounces sentences without having attained the grade of a master of sentences would produce only misfortunes.[4] Under the guide of ordinary reason, one would say that this must be interpreted intellectually, as of the misfortunes of ignorance, mistakes and mental mischances, or confusions arising therefrom. However, Rabbi Simeon ben Yohai cautioned his auditors on one occasion never to pronounce a word touching the Secret Doctrine without being entirely certain as to its exactness.[5] To do otherwise might cause the death of legions. This is an alleged consequence which calls to be understood literally, and I mention it because—although it can be nothing but a grotesque hyperbole of speech [6]—it

---

[1] For example, in the section MISHPATIM, which contains the discourse of Rabbi Yebba the Ancient, as we have seen, that master of Theosophy is treated at first with derision, for he is unknown and appears anonymously, with some crooked questions in his mouth ; but before he has finished the colleagues have thrown themselves more than once at his feet, with tears in their eyes, protesting that had they come into the world for no other purpose than to hear his words, their existence would not have been useless.—Z., Pt. II, fol. 99a ; III, 398. They were hearing new things.

[2] Ib., Pt. I, fol. 5a ; I, 27.

[3] Ib.

[4] Some of the incidents to which allusion is made here are quite in the dramatic manner ; perhaps it is only to our modern minds that they betray the literary hand, but this is how they impress at least one sympathetic mind. The section MISHPATIM is again a case in point, but there are several instances.

[5] Z., Pt. I, fol. 5b ; I, 27.

[6] There are analogies on the other side of the scale, as, for example, when it is said

looks for a moment as if the great teacher of Kabbalism were quoting the penal clause of a pledge by which the Sons of the Doctrine were bound together. It reads like the vengeance threatened in the obligations of secret societies— if their mysteries are betrayed by recipients. Another counsel was to examine the Secret Doctrine attentively before it was given out or taught, so that all error might be avoided.[1]

Being, *ex hypothesi*, originally oral doctrine which passed— in so far as it did pass—at a much later period into writing, it was obviously stored in memory, by the implicit of the claim ; and the glaring inconsistencies which are met with ever and continually throughout the text of the ZOHAR are really a rather strong presumptive testimony to this kind of transmission. If Rabbi Moses de Leon had, as it used to be suggested, conceived and begotten the whole colossus of words out of his own head, he would not have fallen out with himself in quite such an obvious manner—even if we grant that forgeries have an ill-starred manner of betraying them-selves there and here, so that they are for the most part a miscarriage rather than a making. But while accepting under all necessary reserves the general idea that the ZOHAR embodies some ancient MIDRASHIM [2] which are less or more complete and is, for the rest, a late compilation made up from similar sources, it must be recognised that it bears in an extraordinary degree the marks of compilation—as I have said. In connec-tion with my present point it would be possible to quote several cases in which the imaginary *turba philosophorum* seem to have been making up the Secret Doctrine as they went along at the moment. It is better to face these facts, but it may be added that they and the late editing—otherwise so transparent—leave untouched that which is necessary to my purpose, being the existence of old material belonging to the

---

that the Holy One, blessed be He, comes down into three of the Heavenly Schools— one of them being that of Rabbi Simeon—and listens to the expositions of the Secret Law. Moreover, a new idea produced with authority concerning the Doctrine ascends to the Ancient of Days and is ornamented with 370,000 crowns, after which it becomes a heaven. Others are metamorphosed into lands of the living.—Z., Pt. I, fol. 4b, 5a ; I, 22, 23, 25.

[1] *Ib.*, Pt. I, fol. 5a ; DE PAULY, I, 28.

[2] This was the opinion of S. Munk in MÉLANGES DE PHILOSOPHIE JUIVE ET ARABE, as far back as 1859, but the work as a whole, " in the form under which it has been transmitted," is not older than the thirteenth century, and its authors lived in Spain. The last point seems to rest on the evidence of a single word, and, according to the French edition of the Zohar, it fails thereon. Munk, however, recognised that certain doctrines—as, for example, that of the microcosm—go back to the ninth century.

Secret Doctrine. It may be of the tenth century and it may be earlier ; some vestiges may even go back to pre-Christian times, but this does not signify.[1] The literature of Alchemy made a great and new beginning, somewhere about that period, or when it assumed a Latin garb : the literature of the Holy Graal was posterior by some two centuries ; the other written testimonies to a Secret Doctrine under the aegis of Christendom were products of a still later period. What was the message of Theosophical Jewry in comparison with the alternative messages ? As a purpose in literature, does it connect with the other and the later purposes, as a school with some other schools in respect of the end proposed—or is it of itself and no other ? The Mystery of the Graal is of the mystical body of Christ ; the Mystery of Alchemy is many-sided, but on one very late side it is of the body of man in its transmutation ; the Mystery of Rosicrucianism—at the highest—is one of Divine Union, but here again there is more than a single aspect and one is the body of resurrection ; the Mystery of Speculative Masonry is of the building up of man into a spiritual house, meet for the inhabitation of God. And the Secret Doctrine of Israel concerns a Mystery of Sex summarised as the mystical body of Shekinah, while it includes the shadows and outlines of a science of perfection, of union also therein, so that amidst all variations of process, distinction in symbolism and diversity as to root-ideas in doctrine, the question is answered by saying that it is not only in analogy but in living concurrence with other witnesses.

As such, it is to my own mind a matter of considerable consequence that it is not a Christian witness, while acknowledging that if it were it would be of consequence even greater, though of another kind ; and my task in the present chapter is to shew that the case on the contrary side presented by those who have put forward the French version of the ZOHAR—whatever its value otherwise—is a case unproved.

Now, the points at issue between Israel and Christendom on the subject of Messiah are obviously of a very simple

---

[1] I mean that it does not matter so far as my purpose is concerned. As explained in my preface, I have been trying for some years past to hold up a certain glass of vision which tends to shew that the same term of research was sought everywhere in the secret literary schools and in two Instituted Mysteries belonging to the Christian centuries. It is not essential that Kabbalism, being a non-Christian system, should be linked into the chain, but it is important if it does enter therein, whether late or early in its origin.

kind, so far as the ground is concerned, for unless the Christ of Nazareth—as His story appears in the records—had (1) offered, or (2) had been represented as offering, at least some considerable proportion of the marks and seals by which He might be entitled to acknowledgment, the claim could not have been (1) proffered on His own part, or (2) sustained on that of His believers. Otherwise, the expectation of Jewry was one thing and the event another, or there would have been no colourable basis for His rejection in the natural reason of things. I suppose that the time has gone past when it was thought possible to affirm that Jesus, Son of Mary and putative Son of the carpenter Joseph, was antecedently likely or tolerable as the Deliverer to come and that it was owing to wilfully hardened hearts, to eyes that were blinded wilfully, that He was not recognised as such. It is not less true that any claimant was, in a sense, antecedently improbable, because of the complete vagueness characterising every intimation by which He is supposed to be foreshadowed. As it so happens—justly or unjustly—Israel expected a Deliverer who would be a mighty warrior before the face of the Lord Who sent him and before the faces of the nations whom he was to scatter, who was to deliver the Gentiles into the hands of Jews, that the one might be sacrificed by the other to that Samael who is the master of the Gentiles. In other words, they expected a personality as much and as little promised in prophetic literature as it was foretold that He who was to come would be crucified between two thieves who are the Written and Oral Laws, would rise up on the third day and would ascend into Heaven. Jewry was entitled to its dream in proportion to the sincerity of its expectation, whether this was warranted or not; the little company of disciples, whom the events of the crucifixion had scandalised, were entitled no less to theirs, when after the resurrection they received their Christ as the Lord of Glory, and so far as the present consideration is concerned, the question on either side is not of our business further.

The speculative thesis before us is that by the evidence, expressed or implied, of SEPHER HA ZOHAR the Messiah has come. So far as expression is concerned this thesis is manifestly untrue, while so far as implication goes I am very certain that the text is on the opposite side. It contains no particle of real evidence concerning that imputed sect in

Jewry which—under the title of Sons of the Doctrine—had confessed to the Christ of Nazareth and were putting forward their views under veils. It is clear, in the first place, that if such evidence exists it lies within the veils, as it is not suggested that it is part of the surface sense, and hence the question is reduced to its minimum so far as circumstances will permit. In the second place, I have to shew that it is not contained in the hidden sense.

Let me solicit my readers at the outset to recall and recur at need to all that which has been ingarnered and to the conclusions reached in preceding chapters : (1) On the Sephirotic allocations of the consonants comprised in the Divine Name, but especially those of the VAU and final HE ; (2) On the feminine nature and offices, the betrothals and espousals of Shekinah above and below, but on those in particular which concern our Lady of Providence in her manifestation here on earth, the companion and guide of our exile ; (3) on the relation of Shekinah to the Holy Spirit ; and (4) on the coming of Messiah. We found that the VAU is the begotten Son of the YOD and HE, being ABBA and AIMA abiding in CHOKMAH and BINAH ; that He is extended through three Kabbalistic Worlds below the Supernals in ATZILUTH ; that He came into the world with a twin-sister, namely, the HE final, who was also his predestined spouse ; that she was at first latent within Him but was afterwards drawn forth and put with Him in the nuptial state, that is to say, face to face, like Adam and Eve ; that she descended or fell to earth, as Eve also fell, and is to be raised up by the VAU hereafter ; that the Shekinah and Holy Spirit are in a condition of superincession ; and that the Messiah is he who has been expected always, a warrior and king to come.

The counter-thesis requires very careful tabulation, for it is scattered through a great many notes and is not presented formally. I shall connect it with two subsidiary points, which will illustrate further the uncritical bias with which we are called to deal.

In respect of Shekinah and Messiah it is maintained that the former designates the Second Degree of the Divine Essence, otherwise the Second Person, in CHOKMAH—and is also the Word. The Shekinah in transcendence is the Word before incarnation and below is the Word made flesh. It is stated in the ZOHAR that Shekinah does become incarnate, and in so doing assumes the form of man. The incarnation of Messiah is by operation of the VAU, and the ZOHAR indicates that there is unity between God and the Redeemer. This incarnation of the HE, or Word, is recognised by Rabbi Simeon. The Messiah is METATRON, or the body of Shekinah —which is said to be the same thing. The Lesser Countenance of the IDRAS designates the Word incarnate on earth, and the Greater Countenance is the Word prior to manifestation in created things. One passage of the ZOHAR is declared to have no meaning unless the incarnation is admitted, while it is held that another announces the mystery in formal words. Finally, it is believed that there is an allusion to Mary the Mother of Messiah and to her son Jesus Christ when it is affirmed—as we have seen otherwise—that " the world will remain under the domination of the serpent until the coming of a woman like unto Eve and of a man like unto Adam, who shall vanquish the evil serpent and him who rides thereon." [1]

As I have presented and collated these points, so that they may carry their own message with all the force that is possible, they would look rather plausible on the surface, if we knew nothing of the state of things as the result of our research. I feel that the whole question is determined already in a negative sense by my readers as well as myself, but I will analyse the various clauses, so that no false impression may be possible.

(1) We have seen that the Shekinah is on both sides of the Tree ; that it is in CHOKMAH as well as BINAH, because the Supernals are in unity ; that it is in KETHER for the same reason. (2) We have seen that the Holy One uttered forth the Word and that the Builder—who is Shekinah—acted thereon : there is thus a distinction between God, His Word and the Architect, but again the Three are One, because all is one in ATZILUTH. The affirmation that Shekinah in transcendence is the Word before manifestation and below is the incarnate Word is made on several occasions, but unfortunately in respect of extracts which carry no conviction because they do not convey the intended message. It is said, for example, in the ZOHAR that the daily morning sacrifice [2] is signified in the words of Isaiah which it renders : " And the Lord shall keep thee always in repose " ; [3] but this

---

[1] Z., Pt. I, fol. 145b, 146a ; II, 174.
[2] Ib., Pt. I, fol. 141a ; II, 151.
[3] The Authorised Version reads : " And the Lord shall guide thee continually."— Is. lviii, 11. Compare the Vulgate : *Et requiem tibi dabit Dominus semper.*

sacrifice of the morning-tide is held by the French editors to
mean the Shekinah above, while the afternoon sacrifice
signifies the Shekinah in manifestation.   Now, if this is
correct—as it may be—there is no reference to the Word
and much less to the Word made flesh.   We find further in
the ZOHAR a fantastic etymology of the word Sabbath,[1]
according to which it is identified with that only begotten
Daughter who is Shekinah below.   This is for our delectation ; but as an instance of their canon of criticism the
editors have recourse to the TALMUD, where they find that
the Sabbath came secretly into the world, unlike other gifts
of God to Israel, and thence they conclude that the only
Daughter is the only Son and was born secretly in flesh.
(3) It is never said in the ZOHAR that the Shekinah becomes
incarnate and much less that then it assumes the form of
man.   The passage referred to specifies that the letter VAU
is a symbol of the body of man in an erect position, and adds
cryptically : [2] " Hence God willed that Shekinah should be
present at the building of the Tabernacle " by Moses.   The
editors argue that if this does not mean what they postulate
there is no sense in the passage.   The second alternative is
preferable to the arbitrary construction.   (4) The ZOHAR
does not say that the incarnation of Messiah is operated by
the VAU.   The passage in question is dealing with Gen. xix. 33,
concerning the first-born daughter of Lot : " And he perceived not when she lay down, nor when she arose."   The
word which corresponds to " arose " in Hebrew " is aug-
mented by a VAU," to shew that the child whom she conceived
was to constitute the stem of Messiah.[3]   (5) The incarnation
of the HE or Word is not recognised by Rabbi Simeon, who
is referring only to the descent of Shekinah into Egypt,[4]
accompanying Israel and guarded by 42 angels, as we have
seen elsewhere.   (6) METATRON is not identified with
Messiah.[5]   It is said in the place referred to that the " eldest
servant " [6] of Abraham is the image of METATRON, who is
the servant sent by his Master.   (7) The reference to the
Lesser and Greater Countenances is purely arbitrary.   The
passage out of which it arises says (a) that the Little VAU
shall awaken to unite and renew the souls in migration, and

[1] Z., Pt. I, fol. 23b ; I, 146, 147.   [4] Ib., Pt. II, fol. 4b ; III, 15.
[2] Ib., Pt. II, fol. 181a ; IV, 152, 153.   [5] Ib., Pt. I, fol. 181b ; II, 316.
[3] Ib., Pt. I, fol. 110b ; II, 48.   [6] Gen. xxiv. 2.

(*b*) that at the period in question God shall send down new souls to earth.[1] The editors add that the Great VAU is the Holy Spirit above and the Little VAU the Holy Spirit below— after descent to earth—but I know of no place in which the VAU is said to descend except in connection with the HE final and then what is stated is not in consonance with the prevailing symbolism. The VAU must descend also to raise up the HE final. (8) Another passage which is affirmed to have no meaning unless it relates to the incarnation of Shekinah is as follows : " A tradition tells us that when the Holy One, blessed be He, regards the world and finds that the works of men are good here below, the Sacred Ancient is revealed to the world in the form of the Lesser Countenance, so that all men may see God and be blessed thereby." [2] Whatever the meaning may be, the construction offered by the editors is impossible, as the Lesser Countenance is the VAU in its extension through the worlds, and this is not the Shekinah. (9) Here also is the passage which is held to announce the said incarnation formally : " I have found in the book of King Solomon that אשר = ASHER was born in the Heavenly Palace of Delight from the embrace of two other Supreme Degrees. . . . It is a prediction that אהיה= EHEIH will engender ASHER." [3] The reference is to the words : אהיה אשר אהיה = I am that I am, and the text itself explains that it is dealing with the revelation of the Sacred Name in successive degrees : (1) EHEIEH, (2) ASHER EHEIEH, (3) JEHOVAH. The revelation was to Moses. (10) The alleged allusion to Mary and her Son Jesus in the words quoted above is negatived by the fact that the Blessed Virgin was the mother of Christ, whereas Eve happens to have been the wife of Adam.[4] It is a pity to create analogies over things which have no similitude.

I will mention only one thing more on this part of the subject. The HE final comes down to earth and has done so from the beginning of things, according to the ZOHAR. If we could suppose for a moment that there is authority in the

---

[1] *Z.*, Pt. I, fol. 119a ; II, 77. The period is that of Messiah the King in his triumph, when the VAU shall be united to the HE, when the sons of Ishmael shall make war on all other nations about the precincts of Jerusalem. The reference to new souls shews also that it is just before the great resurrection. As regards the Greater and Lesser VAU, the ground and nature of the distinction do not appear.

[2] *Ib.*, Pt. III, fol. 15a ; V, 44.

[3] *Ib.*, 116, fol. 65b ; V, 179.

[4] *Ib.*, Pt. I, fol. 145, 146a ; II, 174.

text for an actual incarnation of the HE—that is, of Shekinah—she could appear only as a woman, or the whole symbolism would be falsified. There is indeed one passage in which the Daughter of the King is said to have taken flesh [1] but Metatron was her body, even as Shekinah herself is said in another place to be the body of the Holy One. It is flesh of the Land of Life and not of earth. If any personality symbolised by any consonant of the Sacred Name is really expected by Kabbalism to assume the limitations of mortality in the bonds of the body of earth, that consonant is VAU, and what is meant can be only the incarnation of the Begotten Son, who is assuredly the Lesser Countenance of the IDRAS. At this point I will remind my readers of that which was stated at the end of Book VII, § 8, concerning the coming of Messiah. [2] There on the authority of the ZOHAR we have seen that the creation of man was designed to prepare a way for the advent of that Divine Personality. [3] The memorable passage is passed over by the French editors without a word of comment, owing no doubt to their unfortunate and impossible predilection for Shekinah as Christ. They could have done much better with the alternative materials, so far as the logic of symbolism is concerned. They would not of course have made out a case in favour of Jesus of Nazareth as Messiah of the ZOHAR, because it is obviously the intention of the text to shew that its New Adam, the Deliverer to come, is not without an Eve who is at once his sister and spouse, who has had an office in creation through all ages. For this feminine personality there is no room in the Christian scheme, because, although I regard Shekinah as practically identical with the Blessed and Holy Spirit, the suggestion that this latter is in the relation of wife to Messiah or belongs to the side of womanhood means that Latin Trinitarian doctrine calls to be revised and the French editors seem evidently under the obedience of Rome in respect of official religion.

Having reached this point, we can deal shortly with their views on the subject of the Holy Spirit, Which is identified with the VAU of the Sacred Name and is located in BINAH. There is one passage in the ZOHAR where, in consonance

---

[1] Z., Pt. II, fol. 94b ; III, 378, 379.
[2] See p. 324.
[3] Z., Pt. I, fol. 19b ; I, 119. I am sorry to add that the subject is connected with the notion of an infernal " shell " or " mark "—Lilith, or one of her type—said to be the cause of epilepsy in children.

with much that precedes and comes after, the VAU is said to issue from the HE in transcendence, while the second HE issues from the VAU.[1] The first clause of this statement is understood as the Holy Spirit proceeding from the Word and the second as intimating that the Messiah or Christ takes flesh by the operation of the Holy Spirit. The real intention is that which recurs everywhere—namely, to indicate that the union of YOD and HE primal causes the HE as Mother to conceive and beget of YOD, the Father and Spouse, that which is Son of both, namely, the VAU, who comes into being carrying the second HE latent within him; but this is subsequently removed from him in a profound Adamic sleep and they dwell as spouses in unity. As there is no need to say, it would be difficult to find symbolism in more complete opposition to Christian Trinitarian doctrine or to the Christian scheme of the Incarnation. By an accident of things, we are reminded in another note that the Holy Spirit is compared to the light of the moon; but we know that the moon is Shekinah, and the Holy Spirit is therefore the light of Shekinah which seems to correspond with its office—otherwise but analogically indicated when it is implied that the Spirit is the breath of Shekinah. As regards that place in the ZOHAR where the Indwelling Glory is plainly identified with the Holy Spirit,[2] the difficulty is disposed of by saying that it is a transcriber's mistake; but to justify this, even in a preliminary sense, the error would have to be characteristic of one codex only, *plus* any edition or manuscript which may have derived indubitably therefrom. Now we have seen that the trend of all collated extracts seems towards identification rather than distinction, or to something so like it that the two principles pass one into another and are interchanged continually, while in respect of the single extract which makes distinction absolute, I should be not less or more in order—perhaps even more—if I suggested, on the contrary, that the copyist's mistake is there. I do not adopt such devices; the ZOHAR is a contradictory collection; but I abide by the consensus of intimations.

If, however, we wish for even more typical specimens of the true value attaching to the annotations on their polemical side, we must have recourse to what is said about the Eucharist.

---

[1] Z., Pt. I, fol. 193b; II, 365.
[2] See Book VIII, § 1, p. 366.

According to the ZOHAR, there is a wine which is the synthesis of all joys,[1] an ancient and sacred wine which was known to Jacob,[2] Joseph and David.[3] METATRON in the personality of Enoch is said to have administered it to the patriarchs.[4] It is not connected with the wine carried by Melchizedek, but—according to the French editors—we have here an allusion to the mystery of transubstantiation. So also the unleavened bread, which is called bread of affliction in the Old Testament, and is therefore the very antithesis of Eucharistic Bread, is declared in the ZOHAR to represent the female in separation from the male,[5] who would be presumably represented by the yeast. Such separation means of course affliction for Kabbalism. There is, however, some undemonstrable way in which this understanding of unleavened bread is held to mean the Eucharist—in which case it can be only that of the Latin Rite, where the bread is in separation from the wine. There is also a Zoharic reference to the offering of bread and wine, the one representing joy and the right side, while the other is the left and is therefore affliction, though it is not specified in the text.[6] This, say the editors, exposes clearly the Mystery of the Blessed Sacrament. We are prepared in such manner for the last suggestion which I feel called to mention here. At the death of Rabbi Simeon, his son, Rabbi Eleazar, overcome with grief, exclaims that " all the colleagues should drink blood." [7] This indicates the " offering of the Holy Sacrifice and proceeding to transubstantiation."

Under all these considerations, not to speak of many others of similar purport and intention, we can understand that the Kabbalistic Community of Israel is identified with the Church of God, in the sense of the Christian Church. When it is said to be above, it is the Church Triumphant and Glorious in Heaven ; below it is the Church militant on earth ; but it is left to the reader's discrimination whether it is centred at Rome.

---

[1] Z., Pt. I, fol. 142b ; II, 157.

[2] Gen. xxvii. 25.

[3] Z., Pt. III, fol. 189a ; V, 496.

[4] Ib. Seven firmaments, seven palaces, six directions, and five pathways issue from this wine.

[5] Ib., Pt. I, fol. 157a ; II, 216, 217.

[6] Ib., Pt. II, fol. 29a ; III, 139. I suppose that when any sacred text speaks of bread and wine, our Christian pre-occupations on the subject will look inevitably for Eucharistic analogies. I was on the watch myself anxiously at the beginning of my Zoharic studies, but I suffered disappointment only.

[7] Ib., Pt. III, fol. 296b ; IDRA ZOUTA, VI, 120.

I am sure that the work of annotation has been done by the French editors with sincerity and even with zeal, but on the side of their palmary concern it has not been done with insight. There seems to me nothing more unfortunate in the long story of attempts to construe the Kabbalah in a Christian sense than the presentation of Shekinah as Christ and, as I have indicated, without dwelling thereon, another way was possible—by no means satisfactory, but not at least ridiculous. Our Blessed Saviour has been placed in many anomalous positions by those who seek to glorify Him and desire that His cause should prevail, but in none surely which is quite so curious as this.

III.—CONCLUSION ON JEWISH THEOSOPHY

As regards the message of the Secret Doctrine in Israel, apart from the body of texts, those who seek in the ZOHAR for a deeper knowledge—outside dogmatic affirmations, already cited—concerning the term of mystical experience, as it has reached expression in the great texts of mystical literature, will not find what they need in the plain and simple way that they are likely to need it, though I believe that the experience is there. It follows, however, a perilous path of symbolism ; but there is this further to be said—that, perhaps more than most others in the great schools, the Doctors of the Hidden Law realised that it has not entered into the heart of man to conceive what God has prepared for those who love Him. They must have known at least how the experience transcends expression, as the mournful failures of mystical literature bear witness on every side. I take it that this is why the union of male and female—which is their adopted form of symbolism—the more it is raised into transcendence is the deeper covered with veils. On the sanctification of the natural act and the path therein, they speak with reasonable fullness, all things perhaps considered. They are explicit also on the correspondence between things above and below therein, but without a word or part of a word which tells of the end attained. This is not to say that the term of Divine Union is never indicated ; but we shall see by collating the allusions that if they are spoken from the centre, at least in the wording itself, the centre seems very far away. In the first place, as to that path which may lead to the Mystery of Union : the thesis is that the just aspire to contemplate the delights of the Lord and in Him their delights are found : [1] it is in the Lord Himself, and so only, that they desire to rejoice. The counsel in symbolism is that those who seek to contemplate the Mystery of Sacred Union shall consider the flame which springs from a lighted candle. Two colours will be perceived, one being white and the other a kind of blue. The one is above and the other is the pedestal of the first : they are united and yet distinct.[2] Here is an analogy borrowed from a material object and indicating something which is postulated concerning the state of integration in God. The path is one of holiness,[3] for it is by the ascent of this as by a ladder that man is able to be joined with the Holy One. Hence God said to Abraham : " Get thee out of thy country." [4] Here was a call from earthly into spiritual life. The necessity of this call and the departure which follows thereon resides in the fact that whatsoever is produced in this world is in a state of separation ; union exists only in the world above, according to the words : " From thence it was parted and became into four heads." [5] This is held to be the doctrine of distinction, diversity and inevitable separateness in the way of manifestation. The path is followed in the faith which precedes experience, and the postulate of this faith abides in the recognition of unity in heaven, on earth and in all the worlds. Those who can realise along this line are counted among the just whose will is done by the Holy One.[6] The ZOHAR in this place is either written more wisely than its makers knew or we have a hint of Secret Doctrine and even of experience which never passed fully into expression. The essential of progress in the path is that man shall apply himself to the study of the Law and shall cleave thereto, so that he may be judged worthy of being united to the Tree of Life.[7] This is another symbol of the union, for as a tree is composed of leaves, branches and trunk, so are the souls which emanate from the Tree of Life grafted in the Holy One.[8] But there are distinctions, states and stages, and for this reason some souls may be compared to the leaves and some to the branches ; yet a common faith unites them and makes of them one tree.

[1] Z., Pt. I, fol. 219a ; II, 465.
[2] Ib., fol. 51a ; I, 296.
[3] Ib., fol. 79b ; I, 465.
[4] Gen. xii. 1.
[5] Gen. ii. 10.
[6] Z., Pt. I, fol. 191b ; II, 355.
[7] Ib., fol. 193a, b ; II, 364.
[8] Ib.

Prayer is an aid on the path, and there are two kinds of prayer held to be indicated by David when he speaks of the words of his mouth and the secret meditation of his heart.[1] The one is the prayer of words and the other is the prayer of silence, the state of the latter being very deep, according to the Zohar. It is foretold that " I will multiply thy race as the sands of the sea, the multitude of which is innumerable," [2] and this refers to the state of silent, unexpressed and inexpressible prayer, for which reason it is said to conceal the Mystery of Perfect Union in the Divine Essence.[3]

While the intellectual idea of a final union between the soul and God emerges with tolerable clearness in the sense that a state is suggested which seems to exceed that understood by the Blessed Vision of Theology, the evidence is as usual rather out of harmony with itself and does not correspond always with the two primary dogmas which belong to the root-matter of the whole subject. It is said in the first place that in their intercourse the Holy One and the Community of Israel are called one,[4] as also that there is no separation in the joy of heaven,[5] yet there are other modes of expression which are less clear in their nature. That of integration in the body of the heavenly King must be counted in this class,[6] and again it is said that the Master is in the midst of those who love Him,[7] which corresponds more probably to the state of eye to eye than to that of oneness.[8] Perhaps the clearest intimation is in a short commentary on the words, " Let him kiss me with the kisses of his mouth," [9] which are held as referring to the union of all spirits with the Supreme Spirit, called otherwise the condition of grand, perfect and eternal joy.[10] Imperfect spirits will enter into perfection by its means,

---

[1] Z., Pt. I, fol. 169a ; II, 264, 265.—Ps. xix. 14.

[2] Gen. xxxii. 12.

[3] Z., Pt. I, fol. 169a ; II, 265. It is said in another place that man must not raise his voice in prayer higher than is necessary, or he is not likely to be heard. The reason is that true prayer is made in silence. There is an obscure suggestion also that the prayer of silence is spoken by the Divine Voice within us. So also the later mystics say that Christ prays in us.—Ib., fol. 209b, 210a ; II, 440.

[4] Ib., Pt. III, fol. 93b ; V, 248.

[5] Ib., fol. 4a ; V, 7.

[6] Ib., Pt. II, fol. 87a ; III, 358.

[7] Ib., Pt. II, fol. 211a ; IV, 220.

[8] The words, " to behold the beauty of the Lord, and to inquire in His Temple " (Ps. xxvii. 4) are contrasted with, " Then shalt thou delight thyself in the Lord " (Is. lviii. 14), to shew that the latter signifies a deeper state of union ; but those who attain hereto are very few in number.—Ib., Pt. I, fol. 219a ; II, 465.

[9] Song of Solomon, i. 2.

[10] Z., Pt. I, fol. 44b ; I, 262.

and spirits that would be otherwise apart from life will diffuse a great brilliance by its aid.[1] This mystery is expressed also in those other words of Scripture : " And Jacob kissed Rachel." [2] It is obvious therefore that the analogy is one of human union, and it is said cryptically that the perfect union above is accomplished only in so far as seed shall be communicated by the Seventh Palace above to the Seventh Palace below.[3] It is then perfect, and blessed is he who knows how to effect it, for he is loved above and below : [4] he is the just man who is the foundation of the world.[5] In the state of perfect union all is concentrated in the Supreme Thought, the forms and images disappear, and this Thought animates and enlightens all.[6]

I have left until the present concluding section the suggestions which it is my intention to offer on the Mystery of Sex in Kabbalism, as it seemed desirable to isolate my own views from the evidence or intimations of the text. It will be observed that the Mystery in its unfolding comprises (1) the doctrine concerning an union between male and female principles postulated as inherent in Deity and illustrated as to its nature by analogies in physical humanity, which analogies have to be checked by (2) the doctrine of the essential unity between Jehovah and Elohim, Who are the male and female principles in question. The analogy breaks at this point and is not restored by (3) the hypothesis that Adam and Eve were

---

[1] Z., Pt. I, fol. 44b; I, 262. This union is said to depend entirely on the prayer of man.

[2] Gen. xxix. 11.

[3] Z., Pt. I, fol. 45a, b ; I, 263.

[4] Ib., fol. 45b ; I, 263, 264.

[5] Prov. x. 25.

[6] Z., Pt. I, fol. 45b ; I, 264, 265. There are the following additional allusions on the subject of union and its correlatives : (a) By following the ascending path of the SEPHIROTH, there is reached that supreme place where all is united and all henceforth is one.—Ib., fol. 18a ; I, 111. (b) So long as severity rules this world there is no union, the reason being that union is mercy, peace and the covenant. It is thought to be proved by the words : " And God remembered Noah " (Gen. viii. 1).—Z., Pt. I, fol. 69b ; I, 409, 410. (c) True unity depends on attachment to the Supreme King. When the river which went forth out of Eden was divided into four heads, this signified separation in manifest things ; but it was in union at the source itself.—Ib., fol. 74b ; I, 440, 441. (d) A sacred union is attained at times in prayer.—Ib., Pt. II, fol. 57a ; III, 254. (e) Those who dwell in the higher region are united in joy and never separated.—Ib., Pt. III, fol. 4a ; V, 7. (f) Lastly, the union of God in Himself— which is the ground of all other unions—is believed to be exhibited perfectly in the words—JEHOVAH ELOHENOV JEHOVAH (Deut. vi. 4). ELOHENOV is the root mentioned in Is. xi. 1 : " And there shall come forth a rod out of the stem of Jesse, and a branch shall grow out of his roots." The final JEHOVAH is the pathway here below ; in order to know the Mystery of Union it is indispensable to follow the pathway.—Z., Pt. III, fol. 7a ; V, 20.

originally side by side, which hypothesis is grounded on certain monstrous births that occur from time to time in humanity and are a yoking but not an unity. Nor is it restored by a literal understanding of Genesis, according to which Eve was dormant in Adam, not active and conscious within him, for in the latter case he could not have been said to be alone. There is finally no intention of maintaining the correspondence, because (4) the original generation of souls was in separation as male and female, and (5) this distinction will continue to be maintained in the eternal world by the mode of simple reunion in companionship, *plus* a transcendental intercourse the rapture of which is increased by a visual contemplation therein of God and His Shekinah, Who is also God. (6) But an important content of the Mystery is the generation of souls as a result of Divine Intercourse, and this is imitated on earth by incarnate man, as it (7) will continue to be imitated in heaven, where the union of created souls will produce fruit after their own kind.

We are not concerned with applying tests of value to the metaphysical part of the doctrine, for its collation with other doctrines leads to insuperable difficulties, some of which have been illustrated by the lights of later Kabbalism. There is, however, the doctrine of experience, and I wish to say that if we accept Zoharic teaching on its own warrants, then the imitation on earth of that which is operated in the transcendence, being done—if I may so express it—in the sense of God's ineffable union, did not unreasonably become, in the eyes of those who not only held the doctrine but performed the practice, a work of sanctification. Now, the question is where it may have brought them. The ZOHAR is silent hereon, except in so far as it testifies with no uncertain voice to the presence of Shekinah in the houses of the Holy Doctors of the Law. But this presence followed them in their travels abroad, and there is one allusion at least to a state in which it was realised invariably as indwelling in the soul.[1] It seems to me that these are three qualities of intimation as to a Divine Realisation in consciousness resulting from the manner of life laid down as indispensable thereto. In this case the Sons of the Doctrine walked not only by faith but by experience, and it follows that the mystery in its practice had a consequence within themselves as well as in their children.

---

[1] Z., Pt. I, fol. 166a ; II, 250.

More than this cannot be said on the evidence which lies
before us, and of the issue which came of the unions thus
adumbrated it is obvious that we can say nothing. One of
the Instituted Mysteries tells us in its moving ritual that the
children of philosophers belong to philosophy, and we may
believe—if we can and will—that in the case under notice
they were worthy of their high calling and birthright.

In what manner does this Secret Doctrine of Israel affect us
as mystics in the twentieth century? There is firstly the
doctrinal side, and it will be seen that those among us who
belong to the Christian Tradition, more especially on the
orthodox side, must be conscious that they are moving
through the great text as through a strange world of images—
vestiges of many pantheons, many systems of the past, and
legends of the soul in man. I have mentioned already that
the Theological Doctrine of the Trinity must complete its
own symbolism, if it is to be held as a product of the logical
mind, and that therefore the Eternal Father is *ex hypothesi* the
Eternal Mother, or in the sense and reason of things there
could be no generation of an Eternal Son. The Zoharic male
and female in the Deity cannot be therefore repugnant to the
Trinitarian. Beyond this point the Kabbalistic system moves
farther and farther, as it proceeds, from the field of Christian
Theology. If it were not complicated by irreconcilable
elements in the medley of texts and testimonies, so that on
the one hand we have the creation of souls *en masse*, as if by
the conventional *Fiat*, and on the other their unceasing
generation as the result of Divine Communion, to say nothing
of minor alternatives, there is much that is suggestive in the
second dream, and for those who feel able to accept any
definite hypothesis on the subject it may have an appealing
aspect. We know also that the tradition of souls being
created, generated or otherwise evolved in pairs is old and
far diffused. I am not sure that it does not belong to " the
hunger and thirst of the heart " after something like a timeless
sanction of human relations ; but it is difficult to regard it
either as part of a secret doctrine or as convincing *per se* if it
were.[1] The kind of reunion which constitutes the beatitude

---

[1] A distinction on Secret Doctrine is desirable in this connection, it being understood
that I am speaking *ex hypothesi* on both sides of the subject. There is that which is
based on experience and is kept secret because the nature of the experience is regarded
as a thing to conceal from public knowledge. If an Order of Alchemists discovered a
very simple process of transmuting metals, they might keep it secret presumably for

of the Elect who experience the rapture of intercourse—one with another—in the sight of God is rather like an houri's paradise conducted on monogamic lines, and it looks a little strange, moreover, in the face of its contrasts at other points in the text.[1] I refer to the continued study of the doctrine by the Elect in the Lower Paradise and by the Community of Israel gathered into the transcendence of BINAH.[2] I do not say that these ideas of a Paradise of espousals and a College of transfigured adepts are absolutely exclusive, but I am equally certain that they were never meant to dwell together in unity. The nuptials of Rabbi Simeon at the close of the Lesser Holy Assembly were, one feels, of another order[3] than most of the psychic marriages proclaimed in the ZOHAR. When, however, the scheme is detached to some extent from its setting, it is worth while formulating its irreducible minimum as follows : (1) The Communion of the Divine Duality, Ineffable Male and Female, in the Supernal World, generates human souls, male and female, in Its own likeness, who assume flesh—according to a law of succession. (2) They are intended to find one another in earthly life and to enter into marriage therein ; but there are various interventions which postpone and even seem to frustrate the general design : yet it is accomplished unfailingly in the case of those who keep the Law. (3) The souls return into the spiritual world and are reunited for ever therein. (4) The keeping of the Sex Law, which is part of the Secret Doctrine, insures the pro-creation of those who may be called the Children of the Doctrine, assuredly a " peculiar people."

It would not be worth while to place on record a personal opinion if it were not one which I feel is likely to be shared—in the detached manner that I design to put it forward. If we draw together from all sources whatever the soul's

---

their own benefit. If they discovered a simple way to compose an elixir of life which would confer physical immortality, they might keep it secret out of mercy to mankind. This is one side of the question, and the other is speculative doctrine, which there is no true reason to reserve from others, more especially as it seldom differs essentially from independent analogous forms and is usually not new at all.

[1] It is beautiful and moving, however, within its own measures, and the heart goes out to greet it.

[2] This is a subject of continual reference and is a clear issue in respect of departed souls gathered into the Lower Paradise. Israel in the Supernal World offers points of difficulty in most allusions. It is even described as a Degree of the Divine Essence uniting all legions above.—Z., Pt. III, fol. 197a ; V, 507. Presumably it is the history of souls in perfect union, almost in the state of absorption.

[3] See IDRA ZOUTA, ib., fol. 296b ; VI, 121, and Pt. I, fol. 218a ; II, 461.

legends, her travels and metamorphoses, into a single store-house of memorials, I question very much whether we should find in our collection a more tolerable proposition at its value, and I make this qualification because I am not suggesting that either one or another is convincing. I do not know of any light on the mystery of man's beginning in his inward state which carries the seals of mastery, for the literature of mystical attainment, the records of our precursors on the path which leads to God, have nothing to testify thereon, as it is not the concern of their experience. Each school reproduces therefore the accepted teaching of its time and place.[1] The ZOHAR shews in its own manner that the end is like the beginning, and if it be only a tale of faërie, it is one of grace as such.

Having said what is possible on this part of the subject, there arises in the next place that which must be called indubitably the most important question of all, and though it is one that is difficult to approach it would be quite impossible to pass over and not miss the whole point of the present study. I have said at the beginning of this chapter that the form of symbolism adopted in respect of Divine attainment by the doctors of the Hidden Law is that of male and female in their union ; it begins here on earth and it is raised into all the heavens ; *mutatis mutandis*, it is the same kind of intercourse on all the planes,[2] and all planes or worlds are in communication one with another, not merely by the analogy which obtains but in a manner which is represented by the recurring image of the world above being married to the world below. We have seen that he is called perfect and blessed who knows how to effect such an union, and this so far as the individual is concerned can be only by fulfilling

---

[1] The inference is obvious and is, I think, utterly true. If we take the Christian records, that part of them which deserves to be called mystical is either a study of conditions, processes, practices leading to the term in God or it is concerned with experience attained in the term. The first may depend from dogma—*e.g.* the idea that an ascetic path is of Divine counsel—but it does not explain the counsel or ordinance ; the second is a realisation of the Divine in consciousness and has nothing to do with vision, as when Dr. John Pordage seems to have seen the Trinity manifest in arbitrary forms. The deep mystical state is imageless and is not a light on theological teaching.

[2] I hope that the qualification will be quite clear to my readers. The body of man was the most sacred thing for Kabbalists and there is absolutely no question that it was in perfect analogy with the body of heaven in its clearness : they were not afraid of their symbolism and they accepted all its consequences. The result was what on the surface is called gross physicalism ; but there is sufficient evidence that when they happened to drop their symbolism, or to adopt another form, they realised that the things of the spirit are understood spiritually.

that which he is appointed to do under the provisions of the Secret Law. My hypothesis is that in so doing he became conscious of what—for want of a better expression—I must term the cosmic union, in which the personal act would be merged, so that he shared in the loving intercourse which obtains, according to Kabbalism, above and below. By this also the worlds are bound together, God is united to creation and the soul of man partakes within its proper measures—and under the reserves of all the veils by which he is covered during the life of earth—of that universal and divine communion.

I have said that there are intimations of this state in eastern teaching, by which I mean India, but that—so far as I am aware—they have not passed into writing. It was testified also in the past—once at least—by a spiritual alchemist that he was acquainted with the mystery of his art but had never proceeded to the practice because he had not found a woman who could help him in the work.[1] So also when Thomas Vaughan speaks of " the conjugal mystery of heaven and earth " I believe that he had some notion of these workings, whether as the result of experience or merely in an intellectual way, by the study of concealed literatures.

It would be possible to carry these considerations much further, but I do not feel that they are meant for presentation at length in this place. The suggestion is that, expressed in very plain language, there is something to be fulfilled between man and woman by a marriage of Nature and Grace of which the sacramental aspect sometimes attributed to earthly marriage is the merest shadow and vestige. We have seen what Zoharic Theosophy adumbrates on this work ; I have found vestiges of the same testimony in the allegories of some alchemical books,[2] and there are other traces of the experience or of notions concerning the experience in the Philadelphian

---

[1] The question is whether this is the open door of the Hermetic Mystery—*introitum apertus ad occlusum regis palatium*—in so far as the literature is apart from experiments in the mineral kingdom. It was once suggested that the key was to be sought in something done between operator and subject, after the manner of the trance-state induced by mesmerism. In *The Hidden Church of the Holy Graal* I have sought to establish certain crude analogies between the spiritual work in Alchemy and that in the Eucharist ; it obtains within its own measures, but everything depends on the true meaning of the breaking of the Host into the Chalice.

[2] The LIBER MUTUS, first published at Rupella in 1677, and reprinted in Mangetus, BIBLIOTHECA CHEMICA CURIOSA, is of some importance as a case in point, but the allegories are in pictures only. I have called it elsewhere THE BOOK OF THE SILENCE OF HERMES.

mystical school of the late seventeenth century in England.[1] It is better—for the moment at least—that those who feel drawn in this direction, with clean hearts and minds turned towards God, should follow out the needful researches for themselves in the literatures to which I have alluded. They may come to see that the analogy instituted by the Latin Church between those who are joined in wedlock and the union of Christ with His Church has a deeper meaning than has been discerned in the public ways ; that in certain grades of consecration the spouse and the beloved on earth do stand for Christ the Lover of the soul and for the soul in that nuptial union which is called the mystical marriage in great and holy texts ; the *absconditus sponsus* may be under veils of the living man, and the *sponsa* may realise in the person of her own consciousness that the soul is indeed the bride.

I am the last person in the world to enforce practical conclusions, but if those who are prepared thereto within and without—and this not too late in life—were to enter the nuptial state and fulfil it consistently, as also with high reverence, in the sense of the ZOHAR, I think that the world might be changed and that a generation to come born of such unions might be children of a risen life.

For the rest, in conclusion, it will be seen that I have not put forward the Secret Doctrine in Israel as one who regards its part major as of great Theosophical and high mystical importance, though I hold its memorials not merely as of living interest but as belonging to that kind which does not die ; for at the back of all its reverie, the strange fantasia of symbols and images, there is the pulsating heart of a dedicated humanity, set in and out of season to justify the ways of God to those who could see through its particular glass of vision. I speak as one who has found God in many strange ways of thought, and—what is perhaps more unusual—in very simple and homely ways. I look to go further, for much that has never been spoken or said, and so remains for expression, is not indeed beyond it. But the Kabbalistic Jew, dreaming of liberation and of union under the grievous yoke of his law, giving it the wings of interpretation and rising himself thereon,

---

[1] From this point of view and otherwise, all the writings belonging to the Philadelphian school demand consideration anew, including Robert Roach's IMPERIAL STANDARD OF MESSIAH TRIUMPHANT, THEOLOGIA MYSTICA of John Pordage, the works of Jane Lead, and the rare PHILADELPHIAN TRANSACTIONS.

is of my own lineage in the spirit, of my kinship in the heart of quest. His Fall of man is no mere dream, because it is highest symbolism. His myth of Paradise has a voice speaking within it from a far home of the consciousness : though the eyes of flesh may be dazzled and the longing of sense may sink when the glories of our end are published, I know that, be it ever so splendid, there is no place like home. The Jew's Covenant in the flesh is assuredly, in Zoharic understanding, one of God's most true Covenants ; the Master Who seals us within does often seal us without, whence peers and co-heirs have always known one another in every place of the world, and every sign-manual of heaven is honourable and worship-ful, since it sets apart to His service. The outward and inward Law is like the book of our life itself, *intus et foris scriptus ;* there is nothing so allusive in the whole world of images ; it is illustrated in all our ways—without in the rule of our conventions, without in the external veneer of our too imperfect conformities, without in the age-long tale of our schooling and self-schooling ; but within in our hungers and raptures after the " good things of the Lord in the Land of the Living," in the thirst after righteousness which we cannot attain ourselves and can scarcely formulate, in the ineradicable covetousness with which we would grasp at what God has prepared for those who love Him. The beauty of the courts of the Temple—Temple of Solomon and Zerubbabel—its Holy Place and the Holy of Holies beyond, has eaten up our hearts with desire. Do we not also expect the coming of Messiah, while confessing to the Messiah Which has come, Whose star we have seen in the East, nor yet in the East alone but all the quarters of Heaven, through the ages and nations ? Son of Issachar, Son of David, Son of Joseph, true legitimate and true King for ever, do we not know that for us He has never come without until He has come within ? *Domine, non sum dignus ut intres sub tectum meum :* yet are we His stable in Bethlehem, yet is He born in us. *Sed tantum dic verbo*—O Word of Words, speak it in the inward silence—*et sanabitur anima mea.* And the legend of the soul in Kabbalism, at however far a distance, flashes and reflects within us its changing aspects of that long, strange journey of old taken by those who came forth, and perchance are still coming, taken by those who go back ; God-speed them in both respects, and give to those who seek it safe conduct and the blessed end. Yes, there is truth in Kabbalism, all its contradictory messages notwithstanding ; the contradictions themselves are but turnings of the glass of mind, hither and thither, to encompass all directions—opposites included, and included the pairs of these. But the great message of all is the message of the Indwelling Presence, though it comes to us who are mystics under unwonted forms and in a peculiar radiance of vesture. The Divine Fatherhood is one side of the shield of faith and the other is Divine Motherhood. Whether we regard it as doctrine handed down from an immemorial past—few of us can so regard it—or whether we decide in our excess that it was conceived by Moses de Leon and born of his brain and pen, it is a wonderful heritage of mind which has come into our hands, and perhaps at this day it has a greater message for us than it had ever for our brothers in Jewry. I could almost wish that this Moses were the one and very man, for I do not think that in the wide world there would be the same kind of greatness as his. But taking things as they are, and by what we know of his writings, there is nothing so unlikely.

It follows that I have not put forward the Secret Doctrine in Israel as one who believes that it is literally what it claims to be in respect of antiquity, though I have made evident that in my opinion the ZOHAR incorporates old MIDRASHIM. It makes no claim except as to Oral Tradition, and about this I have no opinion. It follows also that I have not put it forward as a sum total of wisdom, written or unwritten ; but I do believe that in the expounded Mystery of Sex—so far as it is indeed expounded—it suggests a great experiment which—" once in time and somewhere in the world "—may have been practised in hidden sanctuaries that were homes of man and woman. The doctrine of sex in the ZOHAR is that *desideratum* which I mentioned at the beginning, a Key general to the House of Doctrine : all other teaching in the great Theosophical Miscellany may be said to encompass it, as the Divine Names and SEPHIROTH stand about the figure of the Cosmic Christ in the eloquent diagram of Khunrath. It is the central root which I have mentioned, and from this root the Tree of Knowledge grows. As the ZOHAR intimates, it becomes the Tree of Life. At this end of our travelling, we have reached what was set before us when our quest was undertaken first, namely, a *terminus ad quem*, from which we

can look over the strange path that we have followed, surveying it under one light. Shekinah is the high light which
shines thereon. We have seen that this Lady of Mediation
is the President over that nuptial intercourse which I have
described as begun on earth and completed in the World of
the Supernals. The return journey of the soul is performed
therefore under her light, in and by her grace, with the
sustenance of her mysterious power. For us at this day she
can be a Principle only, but it is Divine as such ; and after
what manner—if indeed other than this—she was understood
by Sons of the Doctrine during earlier days of their exile
through the long centuries of Christendom, we must be
content to leave. It would be a satisfaction to find the
answer, but it is not of our vital concern : enough if we have
convinced ourselves—and this, I think, we have done—that
the central testimony signifies as authentic and true of voice.
It follows in fine therefore that SEPHER HA ZOHAR, the BOOK
OF SPLENDOUR, has something to tell us at this day which
calls to be heard by those who have ears. God preventing,
I do not affirm that it offers an only way, since ways are many
to the height. From the beginning of things He has called
man and woman in all the states of life, in childhood and
virginity, in espousals and widowhood ; and He Who makes
all things one has called the Lover and Beloved, that they
may go up hand in hand and become one in Him. Hereunto
is that which can be said in the public places, and for all that
remains over—*Sacramentum Regis abscondere bonum est.*

There are things, however, which also remain over outside
the Mystery of Sex, and they recall me to that question which
has been mentioned and left open, whether, namely, there is
something in the Secret Doctrine of Israel which belongs to
all Religion and is no man's patrimony by virtue of official
belief or election as a peculiar people. The doctrine that we
come forth from the Centre and that the Centre draws us
back is formulated rarely in Kabbalism and never in clear
terms ; but it is implied or adumbrated continually, and it
belongs to the higher understanding of all Religion. That
Centre is AYIN SOPH according to the ZOHAR, and it is the
Font and Source of all. Whether it indicates that the soul
returns thereto arises for determination in the next place :
if so it can be only by virtue of something inherent and essential in the soul's nature. The nature of that something is

defined in affirming that God is within and His Kingdom. But this is common to all Religions understood at their highest. It is formulated by the ZOHAR in the Doctrine of TSURE, that most pregnant intimation concerning the prototypical soul in ATZILUTH, the supernal part of soul which does not leave the Supernals. This is the inward Kingdom of God and this the God Who is within. There is also a very eloquent shewing forth of the return journey in the figurative language of the Tree. We know that AIN SOPH is situated in the Symbolism above the Tree, the head of which is the Supernal SEPHIROTH. We have found also that the Central Pillar in the Tree of Life is the line of the soul's ascent, that the Sons of the Doctrine go up thereby on the way of return to God. This means and can mean only the realisation of TSURE, or the soul's union with the soul's Divine Part which itself is in union always with the Divine in the universe. The God Who is within is God. There is one thing more : the Atziluthic State of the soul is not the end of its progression, and an ineffable horizon expands from one dogmatic affirmation which is formulated once and once only. On my own part, I cite it for the second time, as it was met with in the Latin of Rosenroth : *Linea autem media ascendit usque ad* AIN SOPH. It follows that the soul goes on, an eternal " travelling in the subject," as I have called it elsewhere.

If it be said that these high things were conceived only in the mind by Sons of the Doctrine, my appeal is to all records of Mysticism, on the faith of which it is to be affirmed that the proper part of man is to conceive in the mind if he seeks to conceive in experience. The mode, moreover, is not defined by the evidence : in other words, the records may connote experience, as well as debate about it. However this may be, that which confronts us in Kabbalistic *Theosophia Magna* is a modality of soul in attainment which is second to none in the whole of mystical testimony, and *per contra* it exceeds all. It is the State beyond the summit of the Mount of God, an ascension into the great silence beyond all modes and forms.

After the rapture of Metatron, that great Angel of the Presence, vibrating on the threshold of Godhood; after KETHER, where Jehovah is united with Elohim; after *Mysterium* Shekinah, presiding over Sacred Births and Divine Marriages, there is set before us as the last estate of man and

the last word concerning it, AIN SOPH, that which is conceived in the mind and realised from far away in the heart
respecting unknowable darkness at the *centrum concentratum*
of light unknown, a state beyond all being, the soul at that
centre, and after all the warfare in manifold lives of quest, the
soul at rest therein.   We have made a long journey, and there
is nothing now to follow : there is to be said only, in the
humility of certitude, that it has been worth all the toil.   I
testify that the mind which conceives this end of being,
beyond all being, in the eternal nowhere and the ineffable
nought of nought is already there, in that unsearchable
inward part which does not leave the Supernals, even where
linea media contemplationis suae ascendit usque ad AIN SOPH.

APPENDICES

APPENDIX I

SEPHIROTIC DEVELOPMENTS

It has been said that later Kabbalism complicated almost inextricably the Four Worlds of the ZOHAR, one and the chief reason being that it attempted to methodise the inchoate and contradictory elements which are drawn into the fountain text. It is not unlikely that a lively apprehension on the subject may have been communicated to the general reader by an exceedingly simplified summary of the Worlds and their SEPHIROTH in the third section of my Fifth Book. For the benefit of those who may feel concerned about subsequent developments according to the mind of Kabbalism, I shall be justified perhaps in devoting a few pages to the following sketch, derived from various sources. We have seen that AIN SOPH passed, by the hypothesis, from latency into activity, still subsisting, however, in a state which is inconceivable humanly, being that of pure abstract thought. The concentration of this thought is depicted in KETHER, which is also Divine Will in primordial manifestation. The Supreme Crown [1] is, symbolically speaking, the base or sphere of the Divine Consciousness from which it would follow that self-knowledge cannot be postulated in respect of AIN SOPH itself. But this is contradicted explicitly in another text. By the second manifestation abstract thought entered into or developed the relationship of time, so that it could be regarded as that which was, which is and is to come. Lastly, it established a relation with Nature—that is to say, its development produced the universe.

By a slight extension of the symbolism KETHER is regarded also as the Throne of the Ancient of Days,[2] and as the Divine

---

[1] In the treatise entitled GATES OF LIGHT it is said that the name of KETHER is applied to the first SEPHIRA because even as a crown encircles the head so does KETHER encircle every SEPHIRA. It is the world of " Direction," which encompasses all things. This statement involves the view that the SEPHIROTH were emanated as a series of concentric circles.

[2] The term Throne is applied to several of the SEPHIROTH. Thus MALKUTH is the Throne of Judgment, TIPHERETH that of Mercy. Sometimes, however, BINAH is

Consciousness is the veil of the subsistent state, AIN SOPH is represented further as the central point of KETHER, regarded as a sphere, while the circumference is infinity, which is, as it were, the Divine Vestment. The later Kabbalists explain further that this is because KETHER has no vessel or receptacle wherein it may be contained.[1] Hence also it is beyond all cognition. The BOOK OF FORMATION affirms, however,—as we have seen—that the properties of all the SEPHIROTH are infinite.[2] As the vessel of the Divine Consciousness, which itself is contained by nothing,[3] KETHER comprehends all things : [4] it is the egg in which reposes the germ of the universe, to borrow the symbolism of another system. In particular it encompasses the remaining SEPHIROTH, which are the sum of all things. The Word of God circulates in all, and KETHER is, in a special sense, the Spirit of the Living God.

The second SEPHIRA is Wisdom, which, however, is held to be of a middle quality, for the highest of all, the truly celestial Wisdom, can be referred only to KETHER. That of CHOKMAH is, notwithstanding, so transcendent that no creature can attain it. It was concealed from Moses, and the Wisdom for which Solomon was magnified belongs to an inferior order, which connects with the lowest of the SEPHIROTH. The SEPHIRA CHOKMAH is described by the BOOK OF FORMATION as the Breath of the Spirit of God.

---

termed the Throne of Mercy, because it is as a seat under the supernal dilections. TIPHERETH is called also the Throne of Glory when it receives the influence of the Thirty-Two Paths of Wisdom. See Bk. V, § 4. The same name is applied to MALKUTH, because it is the seat of TIPHERETH. The term Throne taken simply signifies MALKUTH, and BRIAH, which is the seat of MALKUTH.—KABBALA DENUDATA, *Apparatus in Librum Sohar*, s.v. *Thronus*, vol. i. p. 483, citing the GARDEN OF POMEGRANATES, by R. Moses of Cordova. These points are cited only to shew the chameleon character of the symbolism, at issue too often with the Tree of Life itself.

[1] See *Morals and Dogma of the Ancient and Accepted Scottish Rite*, compiled by Albert Pike, Grand Commander of the Southern Jurisdiction, U.S.A. The authority is not stated, but it is derived from THE ROYAL VALLEY, by R. Napthali Hirtz.

[2] SEPHER YETZIRAH, c. I, par. 4.

[3] This appears paradoxical, but just as Fichte and Carl du Prel have maintained that the human ego is not wholly embraced in self-consciousness, so KETHER is presumably the vessel of the Divine Consciousness in the sense that it receives an influx therefrom, by a reflection from AIN SOPH to its centre. Readers may remember the Universal Solvent which yet could be contained in a phial, a diverting incident in one of the TALES OF THE GENII. According to THE ROYAL VALLEY, AIN SOPH had full consciousness and appeciation, prior to their actual existence,of all the grades and impersonations contained unmanifested within Itself.

[4] There is hence, as Isaac de Acco observes in his treatise on THE ENLIGHTENMENT OF THE EYES, an unity of the ten SEPHIROTH in themselves, which unity is concentrated always in AIN SOPH. It must be admitted, perhaps, that this idea is contained implicitly in the Zoharic statement that AIN SOPH is the beginning and end of all degrees in the creation.

BINAH, Intelligence or Understanding, is represented symbolically by the same fundamental authority as the moisture of the Breath of the Spirit. It is the highest SEPHIRA with which man can establish correspondence, but it contains at the same time one mystery which was also concealed from Moses. The root of all roots and the foundation of all foundations is communicated thereby to man, who could otherwise have no knowledge of the antecedent states of the Divine Nature.[1]

Magnificence or Mercy, GEDULAH or CHESED, the fourth emanation, is the warmth or fire contained within the moisture breathed forth by the Spirit of God. It expresses the Eternal Love and Compassion, connecting with life and vitality. It is the base of that *beneplacitum termino carens* which is ascribed to CHOKMAH and supposes implicitly the free will of the Divine Agent. It follows from this as a consequence that the universe was made or emanated, not because anything was wanting to the Divine completeness, but out of the fullness of goodwill, though some of the later Kabbalists, especially Isaac de Loria,[2] are not of one mind as regards the last point. Symbolically speaking, CHESED is therefore the SEPHIRA by which God constituted the world, operating through the Holy Shekinah.

The fifth SEPHIRA is GEBURAH, signifying Judgment, Justice, Judicial Power, known also as PACHAD, or Fear. It is the Supernal Tribunal, before which no creature can subsist. The treatise entitled SCHAARE ZEDEK excepts, however, those valiant heroes of the Lord who have overcome their concupiscence.

TIPHERETH, or Beauty, the sixth SEPHIRA, is, in a sense, the conjunction of Mercy and Judgment and summarises the Divine goodness : it is the heart of the Pillar of Benignity. It is to be noted that VAU, the letter which symbolises the Divine Son extended on the Tree of Life as on a Great Cross

---

[1] All things, according to the commentary of Isaac de Loria, in a certain and most abstruse manner, consist and reside and are contained in BINAH, which projects them and sends them downwards, species by species, into the several worlds of Creation, Formation and Fabrication. BINAH is hence represented as a great reservoir or ocean ; it is the source of prophetic inspiration, as CHOKMAH is that of revelation. We have seen that it is more especially the Shekinah in transcendence, at once her essence and abode. We have seen also that the world was made by Shekinah, and she made it in the spirit of CHESED, the fact notwithstanding that she belongs more especially to the Severity side in the Tree of Life.

[2] See LIBER DRUSHIM, a metaphysical introduction to the Kabbalah, KABBALA DENUDATA, vol. i. pt. 2.

of Manifestation, is denominated TIPHERETH, because it contains all things, exercises dominion in all and is invested with
all Sacred Names.[1]

But the Divine Benignity is manifested by the Victory
signified in NETZACH, the seventh SEPHIRA. There are three
rays diffused from the splendour of Providence—Benignity,
Beauty and Victory. When they shine and are diffused over
the SEPHIROTH the whole world is filled with joy and perfection, for the Divine goodness itself looks forth upon all
creatures, and all the worlds are in fullness and completeness.[2]
This SEPHIRA is also termed Eternity.

The eighth SEPHIRA, HOD, signifies Glory, Adornment,
Splendour. In combination with NETZACH it is called the
armies of Jehovah, and these two SEPHIROTH signify two hills
of Zion, on which the dew of Hermon falls. All the salu-
tations and praises contained in the Psalter of David belong
to this emanation. It is the place of praise, the place of wars
and victories, and of the treasury of benefits.[3]

JESOD, the Basis or Foundation, the ninth SEPHIRA, is the
storehouse of all forces, the seat of life and vitality, and the
nourishment of all the world.[4]

MALKUTH is the tenth SEPHIRA, signifying Dominion,
Royalty, Kingdom. In the LESSER HOLY SYNOD it is termed
" the Mother of all the Living." According to later Kabbalism, it is the final manifestation, emanation or development
of the Divine Nature taking place in the Divine World, and
is therefore that point at which the more external orders make
contact with the supernal.[5] This is unintelligible as it stands,
but it should be understood that the commentators and
interpreters represent the Sephirotic Decade as repeated

---

[1] The authority is SCHAARE ORAH, § V.
[2] APPARATUS in Librum Sohar. KABBALA DENUDATA, s.v. Superatio, i.e. Netzach,
pp. 589 et seq., citing SCHAARE ORAH.
[3] Ibid. s.v. Decus, Gloria, i.e. HOD, pp. 268 et seq., deriving from the same work.
According to the ZOHAR, NETZACH and HOD correspond to extension, multiplication
and force, and thence issue all the forces of the universe, for which reason these
SEPHIROTH are also termed the Armies of the Eternal. Zohar, iii., 296a, Mantua.
[4] KABBALA DENUDATA, Apparatus, s.v. Fundamentum, i.e., JESOD, pp. 439 et seq.
The authority is PARDES RIMMONIM. The key of the symbolism is given by Rosenroth
as follows, but without comment, as if it lay beyond his measures : In personis FUNDA-
MENTUM denotat membrum genitale utriusque sexus.
[5] Hence it is said that the tenth SEPHIRA is the SHEKINAH, that is, the place of the
manifestation of Deity. But this is the Lower Shekinah, represented by the final HE
of the Divine Name. It should be added that when the text describes MALKUTH as a
final manifestation in the Divine World it follows that ATZILUTH, the World of Deity,
contains the whole Sephirotic Decade. It is the prototype and the witness above of
that which abides below.

through each of the Four Worlds, and the reference in this place is therefore to MALKUTH in ATZILUTH, the World of Deity. To increase complications and confusions there is the Decade in each SEPHIRA.

To this brief general description, which rests on the authority and reproduces the words of the Kabbalists, I will now add the heads of a modern interpretation, which is, of course, conjectural and a personal point of view, but has a reasonable aspect and illustrates, perhaps unawares, the office of Divine Thought in the Zoharic evolution of the universe, as well as embodying later intimations.

AIN SOPH, the Unknowable and Absolute, manifests through the efflux of the spiritual and material universe, using the SEPHIROTH as its media. The first emanation symbolises Abstract Thought, the Absolute assuming consciousness to manifest outwardly. The second emanation represents the association of abstract ideas in the intellect, which association is Wisdom. The third emanation is Mind receiving the impression of the abstract ideas. These three constitute the Spirit of the World. The second triad of SEPHIROTH, Mercy, Judgment and Beauty, includes the principles of construction and symbolises the abstract dimensions of matter, length, breadth, depth and their double polarity. CHESED and GEBURAH are the centripetal and centrifugal energies between the poles of the dimensions. In their junction with TIPHERETH they represent all ethical life and perfection. They correspond to the Soul of the World. The third triad is dynamic; its SEPHIROTH signify the Deity as universal potentiality, energy and productive principle. They answer to the idea of Nature, the *natura naturans*, however, and not the *natura naturata*. The tenth SEPHIRA, or MALKUTH, represents the Concrete, and is the energy and executive power of the Abstract Intellect.[1]

---

[1] Summarised from Isaac Myer's PHILOSOPHY OF IBN GEBIROL, § xiii.

APPENDIX II

THE FOUR WORLDS IN LATER KABBALISM

IF scholiasts and commentators have complicated the Worlds of the ZOHAR, it must be granted that they had at least the will to methodise, and it is possible therefore to present a summary of their views in a brief conspectus. The visible world was for them the last consequence in the development of the attributes of God, while the SEPHIROTH were symbols of those attributes, and the manner of their unfoldment is like a history of Divine Evolution. It is affirmed, for example, that God called Himself Wisdom in CHOKMAH and Intelligence in BINAH; that in CHESED He assumed the character of Greatness and Benignity, in GEBURAH of Severity, in TIPHERETH of Beauty, in NETZACH of Victory, in HOD of our Glorious Author, and in JESOD of our Support, all worlds and vessels being maintained thereby; while in MALKUTH He adopted the title of King. We must recall again, however, in this connection that the Sephirotic Decade is in each of the Four Worlds, according to later Kabbalists, and therefore that this enumeration belongs to ATZILUTH in a primary sense, whereas in the realms below it obtains by derivation only. From the World of Deity, the Archetypal World and World of Emanation, the Divine Virtues were projected downward and there was produced a Second World, that of BRIAH or Creation, regarded as the World of highest finite intelligence, technically that of the archangels. Thereafter the prolongation was continued into a Third World, that of YETZIRAH, or Formation, the abode of angelic choirs. Though further removed from Supreme Perfection, there is not a taint of the material in this place of incorporeal beings. It is otherwise with ASSIAH, the World of Action, the fourth product of the tenfold emanation, for this is the region of matter, the earth of man in particular, and also the dwelling of those demons which are called shells or *Cortices* by the later Kabbalists. In common with many other systems of unqualified or qualified emanation this material world is regarded as the gross purgations of the upper regions. It should be observed in such connection that the SEPHIROTH or Virtues which permeate the four systems deteriorate as they proceed further, and that the corruption of the infernal world, the formless region and the seven hells of Kabbalism are apparently the extreme limits of the outpouring which begins in KETHER. Thus, in order to explain the imperfections found in the world-craft of a perfect Author the degeneration of His infinite energy is not disdained as a resource. It is easy to criticise such a system, or to set it down as beneath criticism; but, again, the disability is common to the dreams of all emanationists, even when they invoke creation at one point or other of their reverie. It remains to say that we have the authority of the ZOHAR for regarding the demons as products of the will of God and designed for a specific purpose.[1]

Broadly speaking, the Four Worlds of the later Kabbalah may be regarded as corresponding in the physical order :

(*a*) ATZILUTH, to the Primum Mobile.
(*b*) BRIAH, to the sphere of the Zodiac.
(*c*) YETZIRAH, to the planetary chain.
(*d*) ASSIAH, to the world of the four elements.

Thus, astronomy is at the basis of the conception—or is at least incorporated therein.

The doctrine of the Four Worlds originated between the period of the SEPHER YETZIRAH and that of the promulgation of the ZOHAR, and it received many increments from commentators on the latter work. It is first met with in the BOOK OF EMANATION, which is a product of the school of Isaac the Blind. This treatise is ascribed, doubtfully enough, to R. Jacob Nazir, who belonged to the second half of the twelfth century. Its distribution of the Four Worlds differs from the above tabulation, as, for example, by referring the souls of the just to BRIAH, the archangelic world. It should be added that the ZOHAR recognises also a distribution of the SEPHIROTH into Three Worlds—(1) Intelligible, (2) Moral, (3) Natural.

---

[1] We have already seen that, according to the BOOK OF FORMATION, the ten SEPHIROTH are the infinite of evil as well as of good.

APPENDIX III

THE INSTRUMENTS OF CREATION

THE doctrine of AIN SOPH may be assigned a high place among old theosophical dreams; the Sephirotic system may not suffer by comparison with other emanation reveries and may even challenge all; the metaphysics of the Two Countenances is crude on the surface and in the texts from which it depends is perhaps the most barbaric and unintelligible of all symbolism; but a considerable profundity of meaning may be discerned within it: there have been attempts in this direction. The cosmology of SEPHER YETZIRAH, with its development in the ZOHAR, belongs, however, to more purely fantastic aspects of Kabbalistic dream, and yet in its later form there lies something behind it which suggests—in the language of Jacob Böhme—"a deep searching" of the Divine Mind. I do not propose to add anything on this part of the mythos; but the very curious and indeed bizarre scheme of the SEPHER YETZIRAH in respect of the Hebrew Letters may be tabulated by way of supplement to what has been set forth previously.

We have seen that the World of BRIAH is that of Creation, but whatever reservations may be inferred from later Kabbalistic writers on the axiom *ex nihilo nihil fit,*[1] we have seen also that their use of the term Creation does not at all correspond to the sense of Christian cosmology, because that which they called Nothing evasively was the plenitude in which the All lay latent. Further, the World of BRIAH was not that in which anything material was formed, emanated, or otherwise brought into actual being; it was rather the Elohistic World, that of Panurgic force and intelligence, which became formative in YETZIRAH, but did not produce matter except in the Fourth World. Now the materials used and shaped, or, perhaps, more properly speaking, the instruments, the matrices of the material world, were in all simplicity the letters of the Hebrew alphabet, as explained previously.

---

[1] According to Myer, the speculative or metaphysical Kabbalah is an attempt to harmonise Hebrew monotheism with the "fundamental principle of ancient philosophy," namely, the axiom quoted above. PHILOSOPHY OF IBN GEBIROL, p. 230. This was also the design of Maimonides in his GUIDE OF THE PERPLEXED.

According to SEPHER YETZIRAH, God imparted to them form and weight by combining and transforming them in divers manners, ALEPH with all the rest and all the rest with ALEPH; BETH with all and all with BETH; and so of the rest.[1] Some hundreds of permutations were obtained in this manner, which *ex hypothesi* are the origin not only of all languages but of all creatures. As these permutations can also, by a later hypothesis, be reduced to a single Name, that of TETRA-GRAMMATON, otherwise JOD, HE, VAU, HE = Jehovah or Yahwe, it is said that the entire universe proceeds from this Name.[2] The reader will discern at once the nature of the device, which may be methodised by a simple process :

The world came forth from God :

But the name of God is יהוה ;

Therefore the world came forth from יהוה.[3]

The fundamental letters of the BOOK OF FORMATION are not, however, those which compose the Divine Name : they are *Aleph* (א), *Mem* (מ) and *Shin* (ש), distinguished as the Three Mothers and corresponding to Air, Water and Fire. The heavens are formed of Fire, the Earth is of Water, and the Air of the Mediate Spirit.

Their correspondences are : in the year, the torrid, frigid and temperate seasons ; in man, the head, belly and breast.

Besides the Three Mothers there are seven double letters—*Beth* (ב = B), *Ghimel* (ג = G), *Daleth* (ד = D), *Kaph* (כ = K), *Pe* (פ = P), *Resh* (ר = R) and *Tau* (ת = T, Th). These seven signs stand in the Book of Formation for :—

Life		Death
Peace		Strife
Knowledge		Ignorance
Wealth	and their opposites	Poverty
Grace		Sin
Fruitfulness		Sterility
Dominion		Slavery

[1] SEPHER YETZIRAH, c. ii. par. 4. Cf. the Talmudic teaching that the present world was created by God with the letter HE and the world to come with the letter JOD.

[2] And thus the Name in its realisation—understood in the heart and mind—gives all knowledge according to the Kabbalists. Compare Éliphas Lévi, who reduces the doctrine to an axiom : " All knowledge is in a word, all power in a name ; the intelligence of this name is the Science of Abraham and Solomon." CLEFS MAJEURES, Paris, 1895.

[3] It will be unnecessary to point out that this is a logical *non sequitur*, but it must be added that for the Kabbalistic Jew the True Name of God, as indeed of any existence, was a manifestation of its essence and, as such, inseparable therefrom.

Their correspondences in the universe are :—

East	Depth
West	North
Height	South

and the Holy Palace, fixed in the centre and sustaining all things. When the seven double letters had been shaped by the Deity, He combined and created therewith the planets in the heaven; the days in the year—*i.e.*, the seven days of creation; and the gates in man—*i.e.*, eyes, ears, nostrils and mouth.

There are, finally, twelve simple letters, having the following correspondences in man and the world :—

HE	= ה, E	= Sight	= N.E.
VAU	= ו, V	= Hearing	= S.E.
DZAIN	= ז, Z	= Smell	= E. Height
CHETH	= ח, Ch	= Speech	= E. Depth
TETH	= ט, T	= Digestion	= N.W.
YOD	= י, I	= Coition	= S.W.
LAMED	= ל, L	= Action	= W. Height
NUN	= נ, N	= Motion	= W. Depth
SAMEK	= ס, S	= Wrath	= S. Height
AIN	= ע,	= Mirth	= S. Depth
TSADE	= צ, Ts	= Meditation	= N. Height
QUOPH	= ק, Q	= Sleep	= N. Depth

By means of the twelve simples there were created the Signs of the Zodiac, the twelve months and the twelve directors of man—*i.e.*, the two hands, the feet, the two kidneys, the liver, the gall, the spleen, the colon, the bladder and the arteries.

I must leave my readers to decide how this bizarre system is to be interpreted. It has been regarded by one or two critics who have neither mystical nor occult leanings as a serious attempt to devise a philosophical cosmology ; [1] but for myself I must confess that I do not see in what manner it is superior to the familiar fable of the elephant and the tortoise. There are those, of course, who discern in it a secret meaning, who remember, for example, that the letters of the Hebrew Alphabet stand also for numerals, and do not fail to cite the

---

[1] Dr. Alfred Edersheim seems to speak in this sense in his HISTORY OF THE JEWISH NATION *after the Destruction of Jerusalem*. I have used the third, posthumous edition, revised by the Rev. H. A. White, M.A. London. 1896. See p. 408.

scriptural statement that God made everything by weight, number and measure.

Indeed, the SEPHER YETZIRAH may be regarded as a commentary on this declaration. As a rule, however, I think that the Kabbalists, like other makers of systems, arcane and otherwise, meant that which they said, and if they did not say all that they meant the unexpressed residuum was along the lines of the sense expressed. When they affirmed therefore that the world was made by means of the letters of the alphabet, they really meant what they stated ; but if it be asked whether they understood by those letters the symbols of hidden powers, it may be inferred that they did, perhaps beyond question, having regard to the reason of things. The letters are, in this case, more than mere symbols : they are vessels or manifestations of concealed virtues. The sense is therefore true *ex hypothesi* in a literal and transliteral manner.

The warrant of the hypothesis must be sought in the Talmudic system, which believed that the body of the sacred text was divine like the sense which was its soul, which soul had, even as man himself, an inner spirit, the highest of all, namely, the concealed meaning. Now, the letters of the alphabet were the materials of the textual body, to the care and preservation of which the traditional science of the Massorah was devoted.[1] For the mystical Jew, who discerned strange abysses of mystery in the smallest peculiarities of the THORAH, there was a weird fascination in the fact that all the wonders and sanctities of the Law and the Prophets resulted from the diverse combinations of twenty-two letters, and he came to regard this handful of conventional hieroglyphs as so many sacraments or instruments by which Divine Wisdom was communicated to man. In a word, for

---

[1] The MASSORAH was concerned with the body of the text, the rules as to reading and writing the THORAH, and special considerations on the mystical sense of the sacred characters. It belongs therefore to the criticism of the Hebrew text. It was also, as already seen, that which was delivered openly by the rabbins in contradiction to that which was supposed to have been communicated secretly. Thus it taught the true reading of doubtful passages, the true pronunciation of uncertain words, the correct subdivisions of the books, and so forth. Buxtorf's work entitled TIBERIAS (Basiliæ, 1620, 4to) deals with the MASSORAH. Compare Molitor's PHILOSOPHY OF TRADITION. Some French writers belonging to the occult school pretend that its exoteric formulæ were designed to conceal every trace of a secret sense in the THORAH. See MISSION DES JUIFS, p. 646, by Saint-Yves d'Alveydre, who follows Fabre d'Olivet in LA LANGUE HÉBRAÏQUE RESTITUÉE. The MASSORAH compiled from MSS., alphabetically and lexically arranged, has been published by C. D. Ginsburg. 3 vols. London. 1880-85.

him they ceased to be conventions ; a Divine Revelation required a Divine Language to express it, and the alphabet of that language was a derivation from the noumenal world, vessels of singular election, instruments of Deity, from which it was an easy transition to suppose that such channels of spiritual grace and life must have fulfilled some exalted office in the shaping of the universe itself.

APPENDIX IV

DIVINE NAMES

It is not my intention to produce a monograph on the Names and Titles of God in Kabbalistic and Rabbinical literature : it would be unlikely to serve any purpose of those whom I address. There is a sufficient study of the subject in the JEWISH ENCYCLOPÆDIA, Vol. IX, pp. 160–165, with the necessary references to other places in the collection. The following bare indications are added to elucidate allusions in my text. TETRAGRAMMATON, the so-called Ineffable or Unpronounceable Name, is the Name of Four Letters, יהוה = YHWH = YAHWEH or YAHAWEH, the Jehovah of our incorrect rendering, which Hebrew scholarship has characterised as philologically impossible. It is *Nomen Ineffabile*, that is to say, inexpressible, because the vowels thereto belonging are now unknown, having passed out of memory after the destruction of the Temple in the year 70 A.D. There is an explanatory Talmudic tradition that the utterance of the Sacred Name was prohibited at the death of the High Priest Simeon the Righteous. When it is said that the pointing of Adonai or Elohim is substituted by Massoretic practice for the lost vowels, this does not mean that there was an attempt to pronounce the Name with their aid but that one of the alternatives was to be used instead. It will be remembered that God is made to say in the ZOHAR : My Name is written YHVH but is read Adonai.

As regards the Sacred Name of Twelve Letters, which has been mentioned once in my text, according to one explanation it is formed as follows : הקדוש ברוך הוא = *Sanctus Benedictus Ille* ; but another derives from the word אמן = Amen, in Isaiah, lxv, the letters of which represent *ex hypothesi* אדני המלך נאמן = *Dominus Rex Fidelis*. There has been reference also to a Name of Forty-two Letters, which is accounted for in various ways : (1) by inscribing other Divine Names letter by letter at full length ; (2) by the fact

617

that the first eight words in Genesis total forty-two letters ; (3) by tabulating forty-two Divine Titles which do not rank as Names, but are held to represent all the attributes of God, and regarding their initials as composing the Extended Name. I have made a selection only as it is obvious that there is no end to devices of this kind. Finally, the ZOHAR refers on more than one occasion to SHEM HA MEPHORASH, and this is the Sacred Name of Seventy-two Letters. It happens that Exodus xiv. 19–21, has this number of alphabetical symbols in each of the three verses and thus can provide not only a triple illustration of the Super-extended Name but the three can produce when combined no less than seventy-two other distinct Names. It need not be said that there are other methods of extraction, and Athanasius Kircher offers us the benefit of all which he has met with or selected to throw light on ŒDIPUS ÆGYPTIACUS. There are printed works and manuscripts which deal yet more fully with the subject. All the Hierarchies of pseudo-Dionysius and all the pan-Dæmonium of Magical Black Grimoires are taxed to extend their tabulations. I leave it therefore at this point and with it the whole subject, to those who are concerned.

APPENDIX V

PHASES OF THE SOUL

THE Kabbalistic division of the soul into five parts has been given in Book VI, with the necessary elucidations. The following variant occurs in the DISCOURSE OF THE ANCIENT ONE, and it is given here because of its importance as a point of junction between Zoharic formulations on the subject and those of subsequent expositors. The soul in its various phases was distributed through all the worlds of Kabbalism, and every phase was held to contain all the others. It will be seen that this unmanageable complexity is justified by a text imbedded in the ZOHAR itself.

" When the child of man is born into this world there is appointed to him natural life (NEPHESH) from the side of the animals, the clean side, from the side of the Holy Wheels (the AUPHANIM, a Kabbalistic order of angels, assigned by some attributions to CHOKMAH). Should he deserve more there is appointed to him a rational spirit (RUAH) from the side of the Holy Living Creatures (HAYYOTH HA KADOSH, another order of angels, commonly attributed to KETHER by later Kabbalism, which seems, however, inconsistent with this tabulation). Should he deserve even more there is appointed to him a higher spirit, NESHAMAH, from the side of the Thrones (i.e., ARALIM, the order of angels ascribed to BINAH, whence come the higher souls, according to the BERESHITH section of the ZOHAR proper). These three are the mother, the male servant and the handmaid, even the Daughter of the King. Should he deserve yet more there is appointed to him an animal soul (NEPHESH) in the way of ATZILUTH (that is, the lowest essence of the supernal portions of the soul, again in late Kabbalism), from the side of the Daughter, YEHIDAH, the only one (YEHIDAH is the quintessence, the highest nature of the soul, under TSURE), and the same is called Daughter of the King. If he still deserve more, there is appointed to him the rational spirit (RUAH) of ATZILUTH, from the side of the

Central Pillar (that is, Benignity, the middle Pillar of the Sephirotic Tree), and he is called the Son of the Holy Blessed One, whence it is written : ' Ye are the children of the Lord your God (Deut. xiv. 1). And if he deserve even more there is appointed to him a higher spirit (NESHAMAH) from the side of ABBA (the Supernal Father, attributed to CHOKMAH in the Atzilutic world) and of the Supernal Mother (AIMA, attributed to BINAH in the same world), whence it is also written : ' And He breathed into his nostrils the breath of life ' (literally, souls of life, Gen. ii. 7). What is life ? It is JAH (the Divine Name attributed to KETHER by another Zoharic text), whence we have heard : ' Let everything that hath breath (i.e., life, i.e., all souls) praise the Lord ' (i.e., JAH), Ps. cl. 6). And in it is TETRAGRAMMATON (i.e., J.D.V.D., i.e., JHVH) perfected. But if he deserve still more there is appointed to him JDVD, in its plenary fullness, the letters of which are JOD, HE, VAU, HE : HEH, VAU, HEH, JOD, which is man in the path of ATZILUTH, and he is then said to be in the likeness (simulacrum) of his Lord, whence also it is said : ' And have dominion over the fish of the sea ' (Gen. i. 28)) ; that is, he shall rule over all the heavens and over all the AUPHANIM and SERAPHIM, over all the Hosts and Powers, above and below. When therefore the child of man deserves the NEPHESH from the side of the Daughter YEHIDAH, this is to say : ' She shall not go out as the men-servants do ' " (meaning probably that he shall serve God in His house for ever, Exod. xxi. 7).[1]

---

[1] Zohar, ii. 94*b*, Brody ed.

INDEX

God, 351 ; ascent of Shekinah, 347 ;
a World of Hiddenness, 197 ; Font and
Source of all, 600 ; Ain-Soph Aour, 20,
208. *See also* 566, 601, 602.
Aitsinger, M., 550.
Akiba, R., traditional author of the
SEPHER YETZIRAH, 42 ; claims of the
attribution, 43 ; his mystical ten-
dencies, 64 ; his death, 42. *See also*
81, 540, 572.
Al (El). *See* Divine Names.
Albelda, M., 481.
Albo, J., 481.
Alchemy, rabbinical influence on, 424 ;
the Flamel legend, 108, 109, 424, 426 ;
alchemical allusions in the ZOHAR,
536 ; Alchemy and the SEPHIROTH,
427, 428 ; Alchemy and Paracelsus,
456 ; general connection with Kab-
balism, 534–542. *See also* v, 22, 579.
Alliance, Eternal. *See* Covenant.
Alphabet, Mysteries of, 16. *See also*
SEPHER YETZIRAH and Instruments of
Creation.
Alphabet of Akiba, 42, 45, 88.
Altar, 264, 293, 294, 389.
Al Tufail, 78, 79.
Amalek, 274, 275, 276.
Amelineau, M. E., on the coincident
development of Gnosticism and Kab-
balism, 69.
Ancient, Ancient of Days, Ancient of
Ancients. *See* Vast Countenance.
Angels, the Hierarchies according to
Mirandula, 445 ; according to pseudo-
Dionysius, 271 ; according to later
Kabbalism, 254–256. *See also* 263, 269–
277, and s.v. Pneumatology.
Angus, Joseph, on exegetical methods, 36.
Apple, 279–283 ; Garden of Apples, 307.
Apron. *See* Vestures.
Aquinas, St. Thomas, 95, 330, 362.
Arabian Philosophy, 76.
Archangelus de Burgo Nuovo, Com-
mentary on Mirandula, 443 ; excerpts
from, 446, 448 ; his apparent view of
the Kabbalah, 460.
Architect, under God, Shekinah as, 342,
582.
ARIK ANPIN. *See* Vast Countenance.
Aristobulus, 71.
Aristotle, yoke of, in Jewry, 46 ; influence
on Abraham b. David Ha Levi, 93 ;
alleged influence on Avicebron, 94, 97 ;
Saadya Gaon, an Aristotelian philo-
sopher, 106 ; Azriel opposed by the
Aristotelian party, 109.
Ark of the Covenant, 172, 292, 313, 356,
368.
Arnold, Matthew, 227, 277.
Asher, 584.
Asmodeus, 526.
ASSIAH. *See* Four Worlds.

Astral Light, 32, 217.
Astrology, not essentially connected with
the Kabbalah, 542, 543 ; much studied
by the Jews, 543 ; Astronomy and the
SEPHIROTH, 544, 545 ; summary of
Jewish Astrology, 545–548 ; Jewish
Astronomy, 547 ; Sephirotic Astrology
according to Gaffarel and modern
occultists, 547, 548 ; Astrology con-
demned by Picus, vii ; its condemna-
tion by the ZOHAR, 9, 527, 528.
Atonement, 158.
ATZILUTH, xv, 197, 206.
Augustine, St., 278.
Averroes, 96, 441.
Avicebron. *See* Gebirol.
Aza and Azael, 273, 274.
Azriel, R., on the SEPHIROTH, 98 ; on the
SEPHER YETZIRAH, 103, 109, 110. *See
also* 498.

BAAL-SHEM, Order of, 81, 564.
Babel, 295, 296.
Bailly on the Astronomical Signs, 541.
Bakoda, R. Behai ben Joseph ibn, his
treatise on the DUTIES OF THE HEART,
55, 56.
Balaam, 274, 368.
Balance, 136.
Bar Cochba, his Messianic mission, 42, 81.
Barth, F., on Kabbalism in Cornelius
Agrippa, 453.
Bartolocci, Julius, his rabbinical biblio-
graphy, 3, 26 ; his prejudgment of the
Kabbalah, 48 ; on Abraham ben David
Ha Levi, 93 ; on the Commentary of
R. Saadya Gaon, 103 ; on other com-
mentators of the SEPHER YETZIRAH,
111 ; on the commentators of the
Canticle of Canticles, 178 ; on Abra-
vanel, 429 ; on the minor literature of
Kabbalism, 178. *See also* 91, 103, 412,
432.
Barzillai, Judah ben, on the SEPHER
YETZIRAH, 111.
Basnage, on the date of the original
ZOHAR, 59 ; importance of the tenth
century for Israel, 89 ; on R. Eliezer's
Commentary on the SEPHER YETZIRAH,
111 ; his slight knowledge of the
ZOHAR, 115 ; on Talmudic references
to former creations, 141, 142 ; on the
date of Moses of Cordova, 410 ; on
that of Isaac de Loria, 412 ; on Henry
More, 470. *See also* 43, 55, 67, 92, 142,
410, 411, 429.
Ben Dior Ha Levi, 92.
Benjamin, 251.
BERESHITH RABBA, 136.
BERESHITH, Mystery of, 15 ; Zoharic
explanations of, 211, 221, 227 ; accord-
ing to Mirandula, 449 ; according to
Henry More, 471.

A CATALOG OF SELECTED
DOVER BOOKS
IN ALL FIELDS OF INTEREST

A CATALOG OF SELECTED DOVER
BOOKS IN ALL FIELDS OF INTEREST

CONCERNING THE SPIRITUAL IN ART, Wassily Kandinsky. Pioneering work by father of abstract art. Thoughts on color theory, nature of art. Analysis of earlier masters. 12 illustrations. 80pp. of text. 5⅜ x 8½.   23411-8

ANIMALS: 1,419 Copyright-Free Illustrations of Mammals, Birds, Fish, Insects, etc., Jim Harter (ed.). Clear wood engravings present, in extremely lifelike poses, over 1,000 species of animals. One of the most extensive pictorial sourcebooks of its kind. Captions. Index. 284pp. 9 x 12.   23766-4

CELTIC ART: The Methods of Construction, George Bain. Simple geometric techniques for making Celtic interlacements, spirals, Kells-type initials, animals, humans, etc. Over 500 illustrations. 160pp. 9 x 12. (Available in U.S. only.)   22923-8

AN ATLAS OF ANATOMY FOR ARTISTS, Fritz Schider. Most thorough reference work on art anatomy in the world. Hundreds of illustrations, including selections from works by Vesalius, Leonardo, Goya, Ingres, Michelangelo, others. 593 illustrations. 192pp. 7⅛ x 10¼.   20241-0

CELTIC HAND STROKE-BY-STROKE (Irish Half-Uncial from "The Book of Kells"): An Arthur Baker Calligraphy Manual, Arthur Baker. Complete guide to creating each letter of the alphabet in distinctive Celtic manner. Covers hand position, strokes, pens, inks, paper, more. Illustrated. 48pp. 8¼ x 11.   24336-2

EASY ORIGAMI, John Montroll. Charming collection of 32 projects (hat, cup, pelican, piano, swan, many more) specially designed for the novice origami hobbyist. Clearly illustrated easy-to-follow instructions insure that even beginning papercrafters will achieve successful results. 48pp. 8¼ x 11.   27298-2

THE COMPLETE BOOK OF BIRDHOUSE CONSTRUCTION FOR WOODWORKERS, Scott D. Campbell. Detailed instructions, illustrations, tables. Also data on bird habitat and instinct patterns. Bibliography. 3 tables. 63 illustrations in 15 figures. 48pp. 5¼ x 8½.   24407-5

BLOOMINGDALE'S ILLUSTRATED 1886 CATALOG: Fashions, Dry Goods and Housewares, Bloomingdale Brothers. Famed merchants' extremely rare catalog depicting about 1,700 products: clothing, housewares, firearms, dry goods, jewelry, more. Invaluable for dating, identifying vintage items. Also, copyright-free graphics for artists, designers. Co-published with Henry Ford Museum & Greenfield Village. 160pp. 8¼ x 11.   25780-0

HISTORIC COSTUME IN PICTURES, Braun & Schneider. Over 1,450 costumed figures in clearly detailed engravings—from dawn of civilization to end of 19th century. Captions. Many folk costumes. 256pp. 8⅜ x 11¾.   23150-X

CATALOG OF DOVER BOOKS

STICKLEY CRAFTSMAN FURNITURE CATALOGS, Gustav Stickley and L. & J. G. Stickley. Beautiful, functional furniture in two authentic catalogs from 1910. 594 illustrations, including 277 photos, show settles, rockers, armchairs, reclining chairs, bookcases, desks, tables. 183pp. 6½ x 9¼. 23838-5

AMERICAN LOCOMOTIVES IN HISTORIC PHOTOGRAPHS: 1858 to 1949, Ron Ziel (ed.). A rare collection of 126 meticulously detailed official photographs, called "builder portraits," of American locomotives that majestically chronicle the rise of steam locomotive power in America. Introduction. Detailed captions. xi+ 129pp. 9 x 12. 27393-8

AMERICA'S LIGHTHOUSES: An Illustrated History, Francis Ross Holland, Jr. Delightfully written, profusely illustrated fact-filled survey of over 200 American lighthouses since 1716. History, anecdotes, technological advances, more. 240pp. 8 x 10¾. 25576-X

TOWARDS A NEW ARCHITECTURE, Le Corbusier. Pioneering manifesto by founder of "International School." Technical and aesthetic theories, views of industry, economics, relation of form to function, "mass-production split" and much more. Profusely illustrated. 320pp. 6⅛ x 9¼. (Available in U.S. only.) 25023-7

HOW THE OTHER HALF LIVES, Jacob Riis. Famous journalistic record, exposing poverty and degradation of New York slums around 1900, by major social reformer. 100 striking and influential photographs. 233pp. 10 x 7⅞. 22012-5

FRUIT KEY AND TWIG KEY TO TREES AND SHRUBS, William M. Harlow. One of the handiest and most widely used identification aids. Fruit key covers 120 deciduous and evergreen species; twig key 160 deciduous species. Easily used. Over 300 photographs. 126pp. 5⅜ x 8½. 20511-8

COMMON BIRD SONGS, Dr. Donald J. Borror. Songs of 60 most common U.S. birds: robins, sparrows, cardinals, bluejays, finches, more–arranged in order of increasing complexity. Up to 9 variations of songs of each species. Cassette and manual 99911-4

ORCHIDS AS HOUSE PLANTS, Rebecca Tyson Northen. Grow cattleyas and many other kinds of orchids–in a window, in a case, or under artificial light. 63 illustrations. 148pp. 5⅜ x 8½. 23261-1

MONSTER MAZES, Dave Phillips. Masterful mazes at four levels of difficulty. Avoid deadly perils and evil creatures to find magical treasures. Solutions for all 32 exciting illustrated puzzles. 48pp. 8¼ x 11. 26005-4

MOZART'S DON GIOVANNI (DOVER OPERA LIBRETTO SERIES), Wolfgang Amadeus Mozart. Introduced and translated by Ellen H. Bleiler. Standard Italian libretto, with complete English translation. Convenient and thoroughly portable–an ideal companion for reading along with a recording or the performance itself. Introduction. List of characters. Plot summary. 121pp. 5¼ x 8½. 24944-1

TECHNICAL MANUAL AND DICTIONARY OF CLASSICAL BALLET, Gail Grant. Defines, explains, comments on steps, movements, poses and concepts. 15-page pictorial section. Basic book for student, viewer. 127pp. 5⅜ x 8½. 21843-0

THE CLARINET AND CLARINET PLAYING, David Pino. Lively, comprehensive work features suggestions about technique, musicianship, and musical interpretation, as well as guidelines for teaching, making your own reeds, and preparing for public performance. Includes an intriguing look at clarinet history. "A godsend," *The Clarinet*, Journal of the International Clarinet Society. Appendixes. 7 illus. 320pp. 5⅜ x 8½. 40270-3

HOLLYWOOD GLAMOR PORTRAITS, John Kobal (ed.). 145 photos from 1926-49. Harlow, Gable, Bogart, Bacall; 94 stars in all. Full background on photographers, technical aspects. 160pp. 8⅜ x 11¼. 23352-9

THE ANNOTATED CASEY AT THE BAT: A Collection of Ballads about the Mighty Casey/Third, Revised Edition, Martin Gardner (ed.). Amusing sequels and parodies of one of America's best-loved poems: Casey's Revenge, Why Casey Whiffed, Casey's Sister at the Bat, others. 256pp. 5⅜ x 8½. 28598-7

THE RAVEN AND OTHER FAVORITE POEMS, Edgar Allan Poe. Over 40 of the author's most memorable poems: "The Bells," "Ulalume," "Israfel," "To Helen," "The Conqueror Worm," "Eldorado," "Annabel Lee," many more. Alphabetic lists of titles and first lines. 64pp. 5³⁄₁₆ x 8¼. 26685-0

PERSONAL MEMOIRS OF U. S. GRANT, Ulysses Simpson Grant. Intelligent, deeply moving firsthand account of Civil War campaigns, considered by many the finest military memoirs ever written. Includes letters, historic photographs, maps and more. 528pp. 6⅛ x 9¼. 28587-1

ANCIENT EGYPTIAN MATERIALS AND INDUSTRIES, A. Lucas and J. Harris. Fascinating, comprehensive, thoroughly documented text describes this ancient civilization's vast resources and the processes that incorporated them in daily life, including the use of animal products, building materials, cosmetics, perfumes and incense, fibers, glazed ware, glass and its manufacture, materials used in the mummification process, and much more. 544pp. 6⅛ x 9¼. (Available in U.S. only.) 40446-3

RUSSIAN STORIES/RUSSKIE RASSKAZY: A Dual-Language Book, edited by Gleb Struve. Twelve tales by such masters as Chekhov, Tolstoy, Dostoevsky, Pushkin, others. Excellent word-for-word English translations on facing pages, plus teaching and study aids, Russian/English vocabulary, biographical/critical introductions, more. 416pp. 5⅜ x 8½. 26244-8

PHILADELPHIA THEN AND NOW: 60 Sites Photographed in the Past and Present, Kenneth Finkel and Susan Oyama. Rare photographs of City Hall, Logan Square, Independence Hall, Betsy Ross House, other landmarks juxtaposed with contemporary views. Captures changing face of historic city. Introduction. Captions. 128pp. 8¼ x 11. 25790-8

AIA ARCHITECTURAL GUIDE TO NASSAU AND SUFFOLK COUNTIES, LONG ISLAND, The American Institute of Architects, Long Island Chapter, and the Society for the Preservation of Long Island Antiquities. Comprehensive, well-researched and generously illustrated volume brings to life over three centuries of Long Island's great architectural heritage. More than 240 photographs with authoritative, extensively detailed captions. 176pp. 8¼ x 11. 26946-9

NORTH AMERICAN INDIAN LIFE: Customs and Traditions of 23 Tribes, Elsie Clews Parsons (ed.). 27 fictionalized essays by noted anthropologists examine religion, customs, government, additional facets of life among the Winnebago, Crow, Zuni, Eskimo, other tribes. 480pp. 6⅛ x 9¼. 27377-6

FRANK LLOYD WRIGHT'S DANA HOUSE, Donald Hoffmann. Pictorial essay of residential masterpiece with over 160 interior and exterior photos, plans, elevations, sketches and studies. 128pp. 9¼ x 10¾. 29120-0

THE MALE AND FEMALE FIGURE IN MOTION: 60 Classic Photographic Sequences, Eadweard Muybridge. 60 true-action photographs of men and women walking, running, climbing, bending, turning, etc., reproduced from rare 19th-century masterpiece. vi + 121pp. 9 x 12. 24745-7

1001 QUESTIONS ANSWERED ABOUT THE SEASHORE, N. J. Berrill and Jacquelyn Berrill. Queries answered about dolphins, sea snails, sponges, starfish, fishes, shore birds, many others. Covers appearance, breeding, growth, feeding, much more. 305pp. 5¼ x 8¼. 23366-9

ATTRACTING BIRDS TO YOUR YARD, William J. Weber. Easy-to-follow guide offers advice on how to attract the greatest diversity of birds: birdhouses, feeders, water and waterers, much more. 96pp. 5³⁄₁₆ x 8¼. 28927-3

MEDICINAL AND OTHER USES OF NORTH AMERICAN PLANTS: A Historical Survey with Special Reference to the Eastern Indian Tribes, Charlotte Erichsen-Brown. Chronological historical citations document 500 years of usage of plants, trees, shrubs native to eastern Canada, northeastern U.S. Also complete identifying information. 343 illustrations. 544pp. 6½ x 9¼. 25951-X

STORYBOOK MAZES, Dave Phillips. 23 stories and mazes on two-page spreads: Wizard of Oz, Treasure Island, Robin Hood, etc. Solutions. 64pp. 8¼ x 11. 23628-5

AMERICAN NEGRO SONGS: 230 Folk Songs and Spirituals, Religious and Secular, John W. Work. This authoritative study traces the African influences of songs sung and played by black Americans at work, in church, and as entertainment. The author discusses the lyric significance of such songs as "Swing Low, Sweet Chariot," "John Henry," and others and offers the words and music for 230 songs. Bibliography. Index of Song Titles. 272pp. 6½ x 9¼. 40271-1

MOVIE-STAR PORTRAITS OF THE FORTIES, John Kobal (ed.). 163 glamor, studio photos of 106 stars of the 1940s: Rita Hayworth, Ava Gardner, Marlon Brando, Clark Gable, many more. 176pp. 8⅜ x 11¼. 23546-7

BENCHLEY LOST AND FOUND, Robert Benchley. Finest humor from early 30s, about pet peeves, child psychologists, post office and others. Mostly unavailable elsewhere. 73 illustrations by Peter Arno and others. 183pp. 5⅜ x 8½. 22410-4

YEKL and THE IMPORTED BRIDEGROOM AND OTHER STORIES OF YIDDISH NEW YORK, Abraham Cahan. Film Hester Street based on *Yekl* (1896). Novel, other stories among first about Jewish immigrants on N.Y.'s East Side. 240pp. 5⅜ x 8½. 22427-9

SELECTED POEMS, Walt Whitman. Generous sampling from *Leaves of Grass*. Twenty-four poems include "I Hear America Singing," "Song of the Open Road," "I Sing the Body Electric," "When Lilacs Last in the Dooryard Bloom'd," "O Captain! My Captain!"–all reprinted from an authoritative edition. Lists of titles and first lines. 128pp. 5³⁄₁₆ x 8¼. 26878-0

CATALOG OF DOVER BOOKS

THE BEST TALES OF HOFFMANN, E. T. A. Hoffmann. 10 of Hoffmann's most important stories: "Nutcracker and the King of Mice," "The Golden Flowerpot," etc. 458pp. 5⅜ x 8½. 21793-0

FROM FETISH TO GOD IN ANCIENT EGYPT, E. A. Wallis Budge. Rich detailed survey of Egyptian conception of "God" and gods, magic, cult of animals, Osiris, more. Also, superb English translations of hymns and legends. 240 illustrations. 545pp. 5⅜ x 8½. 25803-3

FRENCH STORIES/CONTES FRANÇAIS: A Dual-Language Book, Wallace Fowlie. Ten stories by French masters, Voltaire to Camus: "Micromegas" by Voltaire; "The Atheist's Mass" by Balzac; "Minuet" by de Maupassant; "The Guest" by Camus, six more. Excellent English translations on facing pages. Also French-English vocabulary list, exercises, more. 352pp. 5⅜ x 8½. 26443-2

CHICAGO AT THE TURN OF THE CENTURY IN PHOTOGRAPHS: 122 Historic Views from the Collections of the Chicago Historical Society, Larry A. Viskochil. Rare large-format prints offer detailed views of City Hall, State Street, the Loop, Hull House, Union Station, many other landmarks, circa 1904-1913. Introduction. Captions. Maps. 144pp. 9⅜ x 12¼. 24656-6

OLD BROOKLYN IN EARLY PHOTOGRAPHS, 1865-1929, William Lee Younger. Luna Park, Gravesend race track, construction of Grand Army Plaza, moving of Hotel Brighton, etc. 157 previously unpublished photographs. 165pp. 8⅞ x 11¾. 23587-4

THE MYTHS OF THE NORTH AMERICAN INDIANS, Lewis Spence. Rich anthology of the myths and legends of the Algonquins, Iroquois, Pawnees and Sioux, prefaced by an extensive historical and ethnological commentary. 36 illustrations. 480pp. 5⅜ x 8½. 25967-6

AN ENCYCLOPEDIA OF BATTLES: Accounts of Over 1,560 Battles from 1479 B.C. to the Present, David Eggenberger. Essential details of every major battle in recorded history from the first battle of Megiddo in 1479 B.C. to Grenada in 1984. List of Battle Maps. New Appendix covering the years 1967-1984. Index. 99 illustrations. 544pp. 6½ x 9¼. 24913-1

SAILING ALONE AROUND THE WORLD, Captain Joshua Slocum. First man to sail around the world, alone, in small boat. One of great feats of seamanship told in delightful manner. 67 illustrations. 294pp. 5⅜ x 8½. 20326-3

ANARCHISM AND OTHER ESSAYS, Emma Goldman. Powerful, penetrating, prophetic essays on direct action, role of minorities, prison reform, puritan hypocrisy, violence, etc. 271pp. 5⅜ x 8½. 22484-8

MYTHS OF THE HINDUS AND BUDDHISTS, Ananda K. Coomaraswamy and Sister Nivedita. Great stories of the epics; deeds of Krishna, Shiva, taken from puranas, Vedas, folk tales; etc. 32 illustrations. 400pp. 5⅜ x 8½. 21759-0

THE TRAUMA OF BIRTH, Otto Rank. Rank's controversial thesis that anxiety neurosis is caused by profound psychological trauma which occurs at birth. 256pp. 5⅜ x 8½. 27974-X

A THEOLOGICO-POLITICAL TREATISE, Benedict Spinoza. Also contains unfinished Political Treatise. Great classic on religious liberty, theory of government on common consent. R. Elwes translation. Total of 421pp. 5⅜ x 8½. 20249-6

MY BONDAGE AND MY FREEDOM, Frederick Douglass. Born a slave, Douglass became outspoken force in antislavery movement. The best of Douglass' autobiographies. Graphic description of slave life. 464pp. 5⅜ x 8½. 22457-0

FOLLOWING THE EQUATOR: A Journey Around the World, Mark Twain. Fascinating humorous account of 1897 voyage to Hawaii, Australia, India, New Zealand, etc. Ironic, bemused reports on peoples, customs, climate, flora and fauna, politics, much more. 197 illustrations. 720pp. 5⅜ x 8½. 26113-1

THE PEOPLE CALLED SHAKERS, Edward D. Andrews. Definitive study of Shakers: origins, beliefs, practices, dances, social organization, furniture and crafts, etc. 33 illustrations. 351pp. 5⅜ x 8½. 21081-2

THE MYTHS OF GREECE AND ROME, H. A. Guerber. A classic of mythology, generously illustrated, long prized for its simple, graphic, accurate retelling of the principal myths of Greece and Rome, and for its commentary on their origins and significance. With 64 illustrations by Michelangelo, Raphael, Titian, Rubens, Canova, Bernini and others. 480pp. 5⅜ x 8½. 27584-1

PSYCHOLOGY OF MUSIC, Carl E. Seashore. Classic work discusses music as a medium from psychological viewpoint. Clear treatment of physical acoustics, auditory apparatus, sound perception, development of musical skills, nature of musical feeling, host of other topics. 88 figures. 408pp. 5⅜ x 8½. 21851-1

THE PHILOSOPHY OF HISTORY, Georg W. Hegel. Great classic of Western thought develops concept that history is not chance but rational process, the evolution of freedom. 457pp. 5⅜ x 8½. 20112-0

THE BOOK OF TEA, Kakuzo Okakura. Minor classic of the Orient: entertaining, charming explanation, interpretation of traditional Japanese culture in terms of tea ceremony. 94pp. 5⅜ x 8½. 20070-1

LIFE IN ANCIENT EGYPT, Adolf Erman. Fullest, most thorough, detailed older account with much not in more recent books, domestic life, religion, magic, medicine, commerce, much more. Many illustrations reproduce tomb paintings, carvings, hieroglyphs, etc. 597pp. 5⅜ x 8½. 22632-8

SUNDIALS, Their Theory and Construction, Albert Waugh. Far and away the best, most thorough coverage of ideas, mathematics concerned, types, construction, adjusting anywhere. Simple, nontechnical treatment allows even children to build several of these dials. Over 100 illustrations. 230pp. 5⅜ x 8½. 22947-5

THEORETICAL HYDRODYNAMICS, L. M. Milne-Thomson. Classic exposition of the mathematical theory of fluid motion, applicable to both hydrodynamics and aerodynamics. Over 600 exercises. 768pp. 6⅛ x 9¼. 68970-0

SONGS OF EXPERIENCE: Facsimile Reproduction with 26 Plates in Full Color, William Blake. 26 full-color plates from a rare 1826 edition. Includes "The Tyger," "London," "Holy Thursday," and other poems. Printed text of poems. 48pp. 5¼ x 7. 24636-1

OLD-TIME VIGNETTES IN FULL COLOR, Carol Belanger Grafton (ed.). Over 390 charming, often sentimental illustrations, selected from archives of Victorian graphics—pretty women posing, children playing, food, flowers, kittens and puppies, smiling cherubs, birds and butterflies, much more. All copyright-free. 48pp. 9¼ x 12¼. 27269-9

PERSPECTIVE FOR ARTISTS, Rex Vicat Cole. Depth, perspective of sky and sea, shadows, much more, not usually covered. 391 diagrams, 81 reproductions of drawings and paintings. 279pp. 5⅜ x 8½. 22487-2

DRAWING THE LIVING FIGURE, Joseph Sheppard. Innovative approach to artistic anatomy focuses on specifics of surface anatomy, rather than muscles and bones. Over 170 drawings of live models in front, back and side views, and in widely varying poses. Accompanying diagrams. 177 illustrations. Introduction. Index. 144pp. 8⅜ x11¼. 26723-7

GOTHIC AND OLD ENGLISH ALPHABETS: 100 Complete Fonts, Dan X. Solo. Add power, elegance to posters, signs, other graphics with 100 stunning copyright-free alphabets: Blackstone, Dolbey, Germania, 97 more—including many lower-case, numerals, punctuation marks. 104pp. 8⅛ x 11. 24695-7

HOW TO DO BEADWORK, Mary White. Fundamental book on craft from simple projects to five-bead chains and woven works. 106 illustrations. 142pp. 5⅜ x 8. 20697-1

THE BOOK OF WOOD CARVING, Charles Marshall Sayers. Finest book for beginners discusses fundamentals and offers 34 designs. "Absolutely first rate . . . well thought out and well executed."–E. J. Tangerman. 118pp. 7¾ x 10⅝. 23654-4

ILLUSTRATED CATALOG OF CIVIL WAR MILITARY GOODS: Union Army Weapons, Insignia, Uniform Accessories, and Other Equipment, Schuyler, Hartley, and Graham. Rare, profusely illustrated 1846 catalog includes Union Army uniform and dress regulations, arms and ammunition, coats, insignia, flags, swords, rifles, etc. 226 illustrations. 160pp. 9 x 12. 24939-5

WOMEN'S FASHIONS OF THE EARLY 1900s: An Unabridged Republication of "New York Fashions, 1909," National Cloak & Suit Co. Rare catalog of mail-order fashions documents women's and children's clothing styles shortly after the turn of the century. Captions offer full descriptions, prices. Invaluable resource for fashion, costume historians. Approximately 725 illustrations. 128pp. 8⅜ x 11¼. 27276-1

THE 1912 AND 1915 GUSTAV STICKLEY FURNITURE CATALOGS, Gustav Stickley. With over 200 detailed illustrations and descriptions, these two catalogs are essential reading and reference materials and identification guides for Stickley furniture. Captions cite materials, dimensions and prices. 112pp. 6½ x 9¼. 26676-1

EARLY AMERICAN LOCOMOTIVES, John H. White, Jr. Finest locomotive engravings from early 19th century: historical (1804–74), main-line (after 1870), special, foreign, etc. 147 plates. 142pp. 11⅜ x 8¼. 22772-3

THE TALL SHIPS OF TODAY IN PHOTOGRAPHS, Frank O. Braynard. Lavishly illustrated tribute to nearly 100 majestic contemporary sailing vessels: Amerigo Vespucci, Clearwater, Constitution, Eagle, Mayflower, Sea Cloud, Victory, many more. Authoritative captions provide statistics, background on each ship. 190 black-and-white photographs and illustrations. Introduction. 128pp. 8⅞ x 11¾. 27163-3

CATALOG OF DOVER BOOKS

LITTLE BOOK OF EARLY AMERICAN CRAFTS AND TRADES, Peter
Stockham (ed.). 1807 children's book explains crafts and trades: baker, hatter, cooper,
potter, and many others. 23 copperplate illustrations. 140pp. 4⅝ x 6.   23336-7

VICTORIAN FASHIONS AND COSTUMES FROM HARPER'S BAZAR,
1867–1898, Stella Blum (ed.). Day costumes, evening wear, sports clothes, shoes,
hats, other accessories in over 1,000 detailed engravings. 320pp. 9⅜ x 12¼.   22990-4

GUSTAV STICKLEY, THE CRAFTSMAN, Mary Ann Smith. Superb study surveys broad scope of Stickley's achievement, especially in architecture. Design philosophy, rise and fall of the Craftsman empire, descriptions and floor plans for many
Craftsman houses, more. 86 black-and-white halftones. 31 line illustrations.
Introduction 208pp. 6½ x 9¼.   27210-9

THE LONG ISLAND RAIL ROAD IN EARLY PHOTOGRAPHS, Ron Ziel.
Over 220 rare photos, informative text document origin (1844) and development of
rail service on Long Island. Vintage views of early trains, locomotives, stations, pas-
sengers, crews, much more. Captions. 8⅞ x 11¾.   26301-0

VOYAGE OF THE LIBERDADE, Joshua Slocum. Great 19th-century mariner's
thrilling, first-hand account of the wreck of his ship off South America, the 35-foot
boat he built from the wreckage, and its remarkable voyage home. 128pp. 5⅜ x 8½.
40022-0

TEN BOOKS ON ARCHITECTURE, Vitruvius. The most important book ever
written on architecture. Early Roman aesthetics, technology, classical orders, site
selection, all other aspects. Morgan translation. 331pp. 5⅜ x 8½.   20645-9

THE HUMAN FIGURE IN MOTION, Eadweard Muybridge. More than 4,500
stopped-action photos, in action series, showing undraped men, women, children
jumping, lying down, throwing, sitting, wrestling, carrying, etc. 390pp. 7⅞ x 10⅝.
20204-6 Clothbd.

TREES OF THE EASTERN AND CENTRAL UNITED STATES AND CANADA,
William M. Harlow. Best one-volume guide to 140 trees. Full descriptions, woodlore,
range, etc. Over 600 illustrations. Handy size. 288pp. 4½ x 6⅜.   20395-6

SONGS OF WESTERN BIRDS, Dr. Donald J. Borror. Complete song and call
repertoire of 60 western species, including flycatchers, juncoes, cactus wrens, many
more–includes fully illustrated booklet.   Cassette and manual 99913-0

GROWING AND USING HERBS AND SPICES, Milo Miloradovich. Versatile
handbook provides all the information needed for cultivation and use of all the herbs
and spices available in North America. 4 illustrations. Index. Glossary. 236pp. 5⅜ x 8½.
25058-X

BIG BOOK OF MAZES AND LABYRINTHS, Walter Shepherd. 50 mazes and
labyrinths in all–classical, solid, ripple, and more–in one great volume. Perfect inexpensive puzzler for clever youngsters. Full solutions. 112pp. 8¼ x 11.   22951-3

PIANO TUNING, J. Cree Fischer. Clearest, best book for beginner, amateur. Simple repairs, raising dropped notes, tuning by easy method of flattened fifths. No previous skills needed. 4 illustrations. 201pp. 5⅜ x 8½.   23267-0

HINTS TO SINGERS, Lillian Nordica. Selecting the right teacher, developing confidence, overcoming stage fright, and many other important skills receive thoughtful discussion in this indispensible guide, written by a world-famous diva of four decades' experience. 96pp. 5⅜ x 8½.   40094-8

THE COMPLETE NONSENSE OF EDWARD LEAR, Edward Lear. All nonsense limericks, zany alphabets, Owl and Pussycat, songs, nonsense botany, etc., illustrated by Lear. Total of 320pp. 5⅜ x 8½. (Available in U.S. only.)   20167-8

VICTORIAN PARLOUR POETRY: An Annotated Anthology, Michael R. Turner. 117 gems by Longfellow, Tennyson, Browning, many lesser-known poets. "The Village Blacksmith," "Curfew Must Not Ring Tonight," "Only a Baby Small," dozens more, often difficult to find elsewhere. Index of poets, titles, first lines. xxiii + 325pp. 5⅜ x 8¼.   27044-0

DUBLINERS, James Joyce. Fifteen stories offer vivid, tightly focused observations of the lives of Dublin's poorer classes. At least one, "The Dead," is considered a masterpiece. Reprinted complete and unabridged from standard edition. 160pp. 5³⁄₁₆ x 8¼.   26870-5

GREAT WEIRD TALES: 14 Stories by Lovecraft, Blackwood, Machen and Others, S. T. Joshi (ed.). 14 spellbinding tales, including "The Sin Eater," by Fiona McLeod, "The Eye Above the Mantel," by Frank Belknap Long, as well as renowned works by R. H. Barlow, Lord Dunsany, Arthur Machen, W. C. Morrow and eight other masters of the genre. 256pp. 5⅜ x 8½. (Available in U.S. only.)   40436-6

THE BOOK OF THE SACRED MAGIC OF ABRAMELIN THE MAGE, translated by S. MacGregor Mathers. Medieval manuscript of ceremonial magic. Basic document in Aleister Crowley, Golden Dawn groups. 268pp. 5⅜ x 8½.   23211-5

NEW RUSSIAN-ENGLISH AND ENGLISH-RUSSIAN DICTIONARY, M. A. O'Brien. This is a remarkably handy Russian dictionary, containing a surprising amount of information, including over 70,000 entries. 366pp. 4½ x 6⅛.   20208-9

HISTORIC HOMES OF THE AMERICAN PRESIDENTS, Second, Revised Edition, Irvin Haas. A traveler's guide to American Presidential homes, most open to the public, depicting and describing homes occupied by every American President from George Washington to George Bush. With visiting hours, admission charges, travel routes. 175 photographs. Index. 160pp. 8¼ x 11.   26751-2

NEW YORK IN THE FORTIES, Andreas Feininger. 162 brilliant photographs by the well-known photographer, formerly with *Life* magazine. Commuters, shoppers, Times Square at night, much else from city at its peak. Captions by John von Hartz. 181pp. 9¼ x 10¾.   23585-8

INDIAN SIGN LANGUAGE, William Tomkins. Over 525 signs developed by Sioux and other tribes. Written instructions and diagrams. Also 290 pictographs. 111pp. 6⅛ x 9¼.   22029-X

CATALOG OF DOVER BOOKS

ANATOMY: A Complete Guide for Artists, Joseph Sheppard. A master of figure drawing shows artists how to render human anatomy convincingly. Over 460 illustrations. 224pp. 8⅜ x 11¼.   27279-6

MEDIEVAL CALLIGRAPHY: Its History and Technique, Marc Drogin. Spirited history, comprehensive instruction manual covers 13 styles (ca. 4th century through 15th). Excellent photographs; directions for duplicating medieval techniques with modern tools. 224pp. 8⅜ x 11¼.   26142-5

DRIED FLOWERS: How to Prepare Them, Sarah Whitlock and Martha Rankin. Complete instructions on how to use silica gel, meal and borax, perlite aggregate, sand and borax, glycerine and water to create attractive permanent flower arrangements. 12 illustrations. 32pp. 5⅜ x 8½.   21802-3

EASY-TO-MAKE BIRD FEEDERS FOR WOODWORKERS, Scott D. Campbell. Detailed, simple-to-use guide for designing, constructing, caring for and using feeders. Text, illustrations for 12 classic and contemporary designs. 96pp. 5⅜ x 8½.
25847-5

SCOTTISH WONDER TALES FROM MYTH AND LEGEND, Donald A. Mackenzie. 16 lively tales tell of giants rumbling down mountainsides, of a magic wand that turns stone pillars into warriors, of gods and goddesses, evil hags, powerful forces and more. 240pp. 5⅜ x 8½.   29677-6

THE HISTORY OF UNDERCLOTHES, C. Willett Cunnington and Phyllis Cunnington. Fascinating, well-documented survey covering six centuries of English undergarments, enhanced with over 100 illustrations: 12th-century laced-up bodice, footed long drawers (1795), 19th-century bustles, 19th-century corsets for men, Victorian "bust improvers," much more. 272pp. 5⅜ x 8¼.   27124-2

ARTS AND CRAFTS FURNITURE: The Complete Brooks Catalog of 1912, Brooks Manufacturing Co. Photos and detailed descriptions of more than 150 now very collectible furniture designs from the Arts and Crafts movement depict davenports, settees, buffets, desks, tables, chairs, bedsteads, dressers and more, all built of solid, quarter-sawed oak. Invaluable for students and enthusiasts of antiques, Americana and the decorative arts. 80pp. 6½ x 9¼.   27471-3

WILBUR AND ORVILLE: A Biography of the Wright Brothers, Fred Howard. Definitive, crisply written study tells the full story of the brothers' lives and work. A vividly written biography, unparalleled in scope and color, that also captures the spirit of an extraordinary era. 560pp. 6⅛ x 9¼.   40297-5

THE ARTS OF THE SAILOR: Knotting, Splicing and Ropework, Hervey Garrett Smith. Indispensable shipboard reference covers tools, basic knots and useful hitches; handsewing and canvas work, more. Over 100 illustrations. Delightful reading for sea lovers. 256pp. 5⅜ x 8½.   26440-8

FRANK LLOYD WRIGHT'S FALLINGWATER: The House and Its History, Second, Revised Edition, Donald Hoffmann. A total revision–both in text and illustrations–of the standard document on Fallingwater, the boldest, most personal architectural statement of Wright's mature years, updated with valuable new material from the recently opened Frank Lloyd Wright Archives. "Fascinating"–*The New York Times*. 116 illustrations. 128pp. 9¼ x 10¾.   27430-6

PHOTOGRAPHIC SKETCHBOOK OF THE CIVIL WAR, Alexander Gardner. 100 photos taken on field during the Civil War. Famous shots of Manassas Harper's Ferry, Lincoln, Richmond, slave pens, etc. 244pp. 10⅝ x 8¼. 22731-6

FIVE ACRES AND INDEPENDENCE, Maurice G. Kains. Great back-to-the-land classic explains basics of self-sufficient farming. The one book to get. 95 illustrations. 397pp. 5⅜ x 8½. 20974-1

SONGS OF EASTERN BIRDS, Dr. Donald J. Borror. Songs and calls of 60 species most common to eastern U.S.: warblers, woodpeckers, flycatchers, thrushes, larks, many more in high-quality recording. Cassette and manual 99912-2

A MODERN HERBAL, Margaret Grieve. Much the fullest, most exact, most useful compilation of herbal material. Gigantic alphabetical encyclopedia, from aconite to zedoary, gives botanical information, medical properties, folklore, economic uses, much else. Indispensable to serious reader. 161 illustrations. 888pp. 6½ x 9¼. 2-vol. set. (Available in U.S. only.) Vol. I: 22798-7
Vol. II: 22799-5

HIDDEN TREASURE MAZE BOOK, Dave Phillips. Solve 34 challenging mazes accompanied by heroic tales of adventure. Evil dragons, people-eating plants, blood-thirsty giants, many more dangerous adversaries lurk at every twist and turn. 34 mazes, stories, solutions. 48pp. 8¼ x 11. 24566-7

LETTERS OF W. A. MOZART, Wolfgang A. Mozart. Remarkable letters show bawdy wit, humor, imagination, musical insights, contemporary musical world; includes some letters from Leopold Mozart. 276pp. 5⅜ x 8½. 22859-2

BASIC PRINCIPLES OF CLASSICAL BALLET, Agrippina Vaganova. Great Russian theoretician, teacher explains methods for teaching classical ballet. 118 illustrations. 175pp. 5⅜ x 8½. 22036-2

THE JUMPING FROG, Mark Twain. Revenge edition. The original story of The Celebrated Jumping Frog of Calaveras County, a hapless French translation, and Twain's hilarious "retranslation" from the French. 12 illustrations. 66pp. 5⅜ x 8½. 22686-7

BEST REMEMBERED POEMS, Martin Gardner (ed.). The 126 poems in this superb collection of 19th- and 20th-century British and American verse range from Shelley's "To a Skylark" to the impassioned "Renascence" of Edna St. Vincent Millay and to Edward Lear's whimsical "The Owl and the Pussycat." 224pp. 5⅜ x 8½. 27165-X

COMPLETE SONNETS, William Shakespeare. Over 150 exquisite poems deal with love, friendship, the tyranny of time, beauty's evanescence, death and other themes in language of remarkable power, precision and beauty. Glossary of archaic terms. 80pp. 5$\frac{3}{16}$ x 8¼. 26686-9

THE BATTLES THAT CHANGED HISTORY, Fletcher Pratt. Eminent historian profiles 16 crucial conflicts, ancient to modern, that changed the course of civilization. 352pp. 5⅜ x 8½. 41129-X

CATALOG OF DOVER BOOKS

THE WIT AND HUMOR OF OSCAR WILDE, Alvin Redman (ed.). More than 1,000 ripostes, paradoxes, wisecracks: Work is the curse of the drinking classes; I can resist everything except temptation; etc. 258pp. 5⅜ x 8½. 20602-5

SHAKESPEARE LEXICON AND QUOTATION DICTIONARY, Alexander Schmidt. Full definitions, locations, shades of meaning in every word in plays and poems. More than 50,000 exact quotations. 1,485pp. 6½ x 9¼. 2-vol. set.
Vol. 1: 22726-X
Vol. 2: 22727-8

SELECTED POEMS, Emily Dickinson. Over 100 best-known, best-loved poems by one of America's foremost poets, reprinted from authoritative early editions. No comparable edition at this price. Index of first lines. 64pp. 5³⁄₁₆ x 8¼. 26466-1

THE INSIDIOUS DR. FU-MANCHU, Sax Rohmer. The first of the popular mystery series introduces a pair of English detectives to their archnemesis, the diabolical Dr. Fu-Manchu. Flavorful atmosphere, fast-paced action, and colorful characters enliven this classic of the genre. 208pp. 5³⁄₁₆ x 8¼. 29898-1

THE MALLEUS MALEFICARUM OF KRAMER AND SPRENGER, translated by Montague Summers. Full text of most important witchhunter's "bible," used by both Catholics and Protestants. 278pp. 6⅝ x 10. 22802-9

SPANISH STORIES/CUENTOS ESPAÑOLES: A Dual-Language Book, Angel Flores (ed.). Unique format offers 13 great stories in Spanish by Cervantes, Borges, others. Faithful English translations on facing pages. 352pp. 5⅜ x 8½. 25399-6

GARDEN CITY, LONG ISLAND, IN EARLY PHOTOGRAPHS, 1869–1919, Mildred H. Smith. Handsome treasury of 118 vintage pictures, accompanied by carefully researched captions, document the Garden City Hotel fire (1899), the Vanderbilt Cup Race (1908), the first airmail flight departing from the Nassau Boulevard Aerodrome (1911), and much more. 96pp. 8⅞ x 11¾. 40669-5

OLD QUEENS, N.Y., IN EARLY PHOTOGRAPHS, Vincent F. Seyfried and William Asadorian. Over 160 rare photographs of Maspeth, Jamaica, Jackson Heights, and other areas. Vintage views of DeWitt Clinton mansion, 1939 World's Fair and more. Captions. 192pp. 8⅞ x 11. 26358-4

CAPTURED BY THE INDIANS: 15 Firsthand Accounts, 1750-1870, Frederick Drimmer. Astounding true historical accounts of grisly torture, bloody conflicts, relentless pursuits, miraculous escapes and more, by people who lived to tell the tale. 384pp. 5⅜ x 8½. 24901-8

THE WORLD'S GREAT SPEECHES (Fourth Enlarged Edition), Lewis Copeland, Lawrence W. Lamm, and Stephen J. McKenna. Nearly 300 speeches provide public speakers with a wealth of updated quotes and inspiration—from Pericles' funeral oration and William Jennings Bryan's "Cross of Gold Speech" to Malcolm X's powerful words on the Black Revolution and Earl of Spenser's tribute to his sister, Diana, Princess of Wales. 944pp. 5⅜ x 8⅜. 40903-1

THE BOOK OF THE SWORD, Sir Richard F. Burton. Great Victorian scholar/adventurer's eloquent, erudite history of the "queen of weapons"—from prehistory to early Roman Empire. Evolution and development of early swords, variations (sabre, broadsword, cutlass, scimitar, etc.), much more. 336pp. 6⅛ x 9¼. 25434-8

AUTOBIOGRAPHY: The Story of My Experiments with Truth, Mohandas K. Gandhi. Boyhood, legal studies, purification, the growth of the Satyagraha (nonviolent protest) movement. Critical, inspiring work of the man responsible for the freedom of India. 480pp. 5⅜ x 8½. (Available in U.S. only.) 24593-4

CELTIC MYTHS AND LEGENDS, T. W. Rolleston. Masterful retelling of Irish and Welsh stories and tales. Cuchulain, King Arthur, Deirdre, the Grail, many more. First paperback edition. 58 full-page illustrations. 512pp. 5⅜ x 8½. 26507-2

THE PRINCIPLES OF PSYCHOLOGY, William James. Famous long course complete, unabridged. Stream of thought, time perception, memory, experimental methods; great work decades ahead of its time. 94 figures. 1,391pp. 5⅜ x 8½. 2-vol. set. Vol. I: 20381-6 Vol. II: 20382-4

THE WORLD AS WILL AND REPRESENTATION, Arthur Schopenhauer. Definitive English translation of Schopenhauer's life work, correcting more than 1,000 errors, omissions in earlier translations. Translated by E. F. J. Payne. Total of 1,269pp. 5⅜ x 8½. 2-vol. set. Vol. 1: 21761-2 Vol. 2: 21762-0

MAGIC AND MYSTERY IN TIBET, Madame Alexandra David-Neel. Experiences among lamas, magicians, sages, sorcerers, Bonpa wizards. A true psychic discovery. 32 illustrations. 321pp. 5⅜ x 8½. (Available in U.S. only.) 22682-4

THE EGYPTIAN BOOK OF THE DEAD, E. A. Wallis Budge. Complete reproduction of Ani's papyrus, finest ever found. Full hieroglyphic text, interlinear transliteration, word-for-word translation, smooth translation. 533pp. 6½ x 9¼. 21866-X

MATHEMATICS FOR THE NONMATHEMATICIAN, Morris Kline. Detailed, college-level treatment of mathematics in cultural and historical context, with numerous exercises. Recommended Reading Lists. Tables. Numerous figures. 641pp. 5⅜ x 8½. 24823-2

PROBABILISTIC METHODS IN THE THEORY OF STRUCTURES, Isaac Elishakoff. Well-written introduction covers the elements of the theory of probability from two or more random variables, the reliability of such multivariable structures, the theory of random function, Monte Carlo methods of treating problems incapable of exact solution, and more. Examples. 502pp. 5⅜ x 8½. 40691-1

THE RIME OF THE ANCIENT MARINER, Gustave Doré, S. T. Coleridge. Doré's finest work; 34 plates capture moods, subtleties of poem. Flawless full-size reproductions printed on facing pages with authoritative text of poem. "Beautiful. Simply beautiful."–*Publisher's Weekly.* 77pp. 9¼ x 12. 22305-1

NORTH AMERICAN INDIAN DESIGNS FOR ARTISTS AND CRAFTSPEOPLE, Eva Wilson. Over 360 authentic copyright-free designs adapted from Navajo blankets, Hopi pottery, Sioux buffalo hides, more. Geometrics, symbolic figures, plant and animal motifs, etc. 128pp. 8⅜ x 11. (Not for sale in the United Kingdom.) 25341-4

SCULPTURE: Principles and Practice, Louis Slobodkin. Step-by-step approach to clay, plaster, metals, stone; classical and modern. 253 drawings, photos. 255pp. 8⅛ x 11. 22960-2

THE INFLUENCE OF SEA POWER UPON HISTORY, 1660–1783, A. T. Mahan. Influential classic of naval history and tactics still used as text in war colleges. First paperback edition. 4 maps. 24 battle plans. 640pp. 5⅜ x 8½. 25509-3

CATALOG OF DOVER BOOKS

THE STORY OF THE TITANIC AS TOLD BY ITS SURVIVORS, Jack Winocour (ed.). What it was really like. Panic, despair, shocking inefficiency, and a little heroism. More thrilling than any fictional account. 26 illustrations. 320pp. 5⅜ x 8½. 20610-6

FAIRY AND FOLK TALES OF THE IRISH PEASANTRY, William Butler Yeats (ed.). Treasury of 64 tales from the twilight world of Celtic myth and legend: "The Soul Cages," "The Kildare Pooka," "King O'Toole and his Goose," many more. Introduction and Notes by W. B. Yeats. 352pp. 5⅜ x 8½. 26941-8

BUDDHIST MAHAYANA TEXTS, E. B. Cowell and others (eds.). Superb, accurate translations of basic documents in Mahayana Buddhism, highly important in history of religions. The Buddha-karita of Asvaghosha, Larger Sukhavativyuha, more. 448pp. 5⅜ x 8½. 25552-2

ONE TWO THREE . . . INFINITY: Facts and Speculations of Science, George Gamow. Great physicist's fascinating, readable overview of contemporary science: number theory, relativity, fourth dimension, entropy, genes, atomic structure, much more. 128 illustrations. Index. 352pp. 5⅜ x 8½. 25664-2

EXPERIMENTATION AND MEASUREMENT, W. J. Youden. Introductory manual explains laws of measurement in simple terms and offers tips for achieving accuracy and minimizing errors. Mathematics of measurement, use of instruments, experimenting with machines. 1994 edition. Foreword. Preface. Introduction. Epilogue. Selected Readings. Glossary. Index. Tables and figures. 128pp. 5⅜ x 8½. 40451-X

DALÍ ON MODERN ART: The Cuckolds of Antiquated Modern Art, Salvador Dalí. Influential painter skewers modern art and its practitioners. Outrageous evaluations of Picasso, Cézanne, Turner, more. 15 renderings of paintings discussed. 44 calligraphic decorations by Dalí. 96pp. 5⅜ x 8½. (Available in U.S. only.) 29220-7

ANTIQUE PLAYING CARDS: A Pictorial History, Henry René D'Allemagne. Over 900 elaborate, decorative images from rare playing cards (14th–20th centuries): Bacchus, death, dancing dogs, hunting scenes, royal coats of arms, players cheating, much more. 96pp. 9¼ x 12¼. 29265-7

MAKING FURNITURE MASTERPIECES: 30 Projects with Measured Drawings, Franklin H. Gottshall. Step-by-step instructions, illustrations for constructing handsome, useful pieces, among them a Sheraton desk, Chippendale chair, Spanish desk, Queen Anne table and a William and Mary dressing mirror. 224pp. 8⅛ x 11¼. 29338-6

THE FOSSIL BOOK: A Record of Prehistoric Life, Patricia V. Rich et al. Profusely illustrated definitive guide covers everything from single-celled organisms and dinosaurs to birds and mammals and the interplay between climate and man. Over 1,500 illustrations. 760pp. 7½ x 10⅛. 29371-8

Paperbound unless otherwise indicated. Available at your book dealer, online at **www.doverpublications.com**, or by writing to Dept. GI, Dover Publications, Inc., 31 East 2nd Street, Mineola, NY 11501. For current price information or for free catalogues (please indicate field of interest), write to Dover Publications or log on to **www.doverpublications.com** and see every Dover book in print. Dover publishes more than 500 books each year on science, elementary and advanced mathematics, biology, music, art, literary history, social sciences, and other areas.